Seventh Edition

Ronald J. Tocci
Monroe Community College

Neal S. Widmer
Purdue University

DIGITAL SYSTEMS
Principles and Applications

Prentice Hall
Upper Saddle River, New Jersey   Columbus, Ohio

Library of Congress Cataloging-in-Publication Data

Tocci, Ronald J.
   Digital systems: principles and applications / Ronald J. Tocci,
Neal S. Widmer.—7th ed.
       p.   cm.
   Includes index.
   ISBN 0-13-700510-5 (case)
   1. Digital electronics.   I. Widmer, Neal S.   II. Title.
TK7868.D5T62   1998
621.39′5—dc21   97-15448
                                                          CIP

Editor: Linda Ludewig
Developmental Editor: Carol Hinklin Robison
Production Editor: Mary Harlan
Design Coordinator: Karrie M. Converse
Text Designer: Anne D. Flanagan
Cover Designer: Brian Deep
Production Manager: Patricia A. Tonneman
Copy Editor: Maggie Shaffer
Illustrations: Steve Botts
Marketing Manager: Debbie Yarnell

This book was set in Garamond by The Clarinda Company and was printed and bound by
Von Hoffmann Press, Inc. The cover was printed by Von Hoffmann Press, Inc.

 © 1998, 1995, 1991, 1988, 1985, 1980, 1977 by Prentice-Hall, Inc.
Simon & Schuster/A Viacom Company
Upper Saddle River, New Jersey 07458

Printed in the United States of America

10 9 8 7 6 5 4 3

ISBN: 0-13-700510-5

Prentice-Hall International (UK) Limited, *London*
Prentice-Hall of Australia Pty. Limited, *Sydney*
Prentice-Hall of Canada, Inc., *Toronto*
Prentice-Hall Hispanoamericana, S. A., *Mexico*
Prentice-Hall of India Private Limited, *New Delhi*
Prentice-Hall of Japan, Inc., *Tokyo*
Simon & Schuster Asia Pte. Ltd., *Singapore*
Editora Prentice-Hall do Brasil, Ltda., *Rio de Janeiro*

FLIP-FLOPS

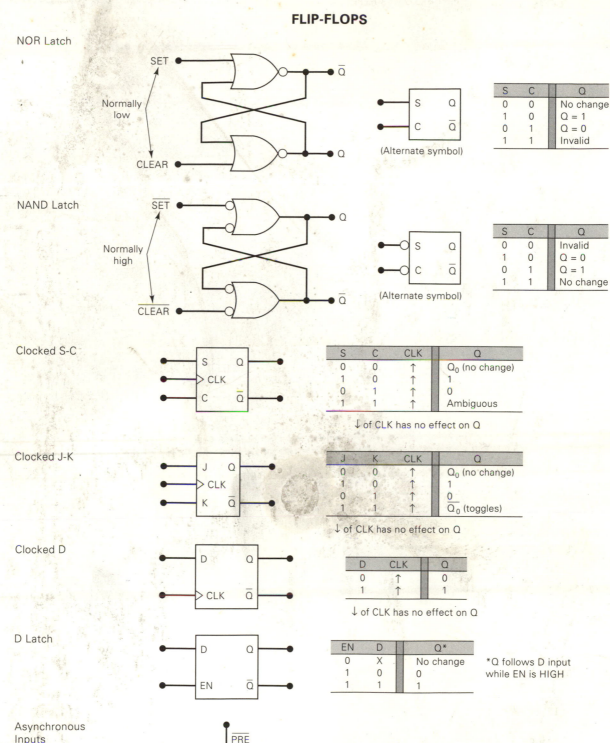

NOR Latch

S	C	Q
0	0	No change
1	0	Q = 1
0	1	Q = 0
1	1	Invalid

(Alternate symbol)

Normally low

SET / CLEAR

NAND Latch

S	C	Q
0	0	Invalid
1	0	Q = 0
0	1	Q = 1
1	1	No change

(Alternate symbol)

Normally high

$\overline{\text{SET}}$ / $\overline{\text{CLEAR}}$

Clocked S-C

S	C	CLK	Q
0	0	↑	Q_0 (no change)
1	0	↑	1
0	1	↑	0
1	1	↑	Ambiguous

↓ of CLK has no effect on Q

Clocked J-K

J	K	CLK	Q
0	0	↑	Q_0 (no change)
1	0	↑	1
0	1	↑	0
1	1	↑	$\overline{Q_0}$ (toggles)

↓ of CLK has no effect on Q

Clocked D

D	CLK	Q
0	↑	0
1	↑	1

↓ of CLK has no effect on Q

D Latch

EN	D	Q*
0	X	No change
1	0	0
1	1	1

*Q follows D input while EN is HIGH

Asynchronous Inputs

$\overline{\text{PRE}}$

$\overline{\text{CLR}}$

$\overline{\text{PRE}}$	$\overline{\text{CLR}}$	Q*
1	1	No effect; FF can respond to J, K and CLK
1	0	Q = 0 independent of synchronous inputs
0	1	Q = 1 independent of synchronous inputs
0	0	Ambiguous (not used)

*CLK can be in any state

Preface

This book is a comprehensive study of the principles and techniques of modern digital systems. It is intended for use in two- and four-year programs in technology, engineering, and computer science. Although a background in basic electronics is helpful, the majority of the material requires no electronics training. Those portions of the text that utilize electronic concepts can be skipped without adversely affecting the comprehension of the logic principles.

General Improvements

This seventh edition contains several general improvements to the sixth edition. All of the material has been checked for currency and updated wherever necessary. Some of the material has been rewritten for greater clarity and completeness. Several new examples, section review questions, and end-of-chapter problems have been added, both to reinforce the new text material and to better support the retained material.

IC TECHNOLOGY   This new edition continues the practice begun with the last edition of giving more prominence to CMOS as the principal IC technology in the small- and medium-scale integration applications. This has been accomplished while still retaining the substantial coverage of TTL logic.

CHAPTER REVIEW   To help students review what has been covered in each chapter, we have added a chapter summary and a list of important terms to the end of each chapter.

PROBLEM SETS   The questions and problems at the end of each chapter are now categorized according to type. Those problems that require the student to use the basic material of the chapter to obtain a solution are given no special designation. In addition to these basic problems, there are four specially designated types:

- **C (Challenging).** Problems that require more thought and effort than the basic problems, and which very often call on the student to combine what has been learned previously with material from the current chapter.

FIGURE P-1   Control sequencer from Figure 9-28.

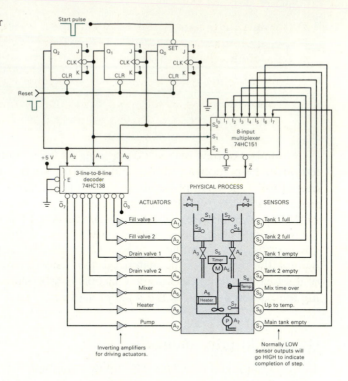

FIGURE P-2   Copy-machine jam-detection circuit from Figure 4-10.

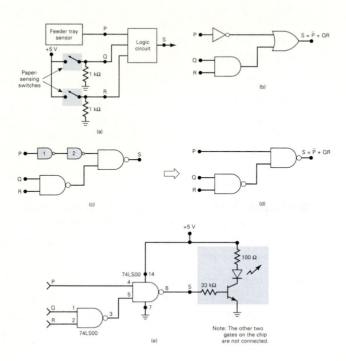

- **D (Design).** Problems that involve either the *design* of a logic circuit for a particular application not presented in the chapter or the *modification* of a circuit covered in the chapter to produce a different operation.

- **N (New).** Problems that introduce new concepts, techniques, or applications.

- **T (Troubleshooting).** Problems that require the student to use the kinds of analytical thought processes that are part of effective troubleshooting.

A number of new real-world applications have been distributed throughout this edition to help motivate those students who keep asking, "Why do we need to know this?" One example of these new applications is the control sequencer for a process that mixes two liquid ingredients and then cooks the mixture. The diagram for this application (Figure 9-28) is reproduced as Figure P-1. Another example of the real-world applications added to this edition is the copy-machine jam-detection circuit (Figure 4-10) which is reproduced as Figure P-2. Some other new applications are spaceship battery-voltage monitor, synchronous counter control of a stepper motor, digital thermometer, digital thermostat, ROM-based function generator, and microprocessor control of a microwave oven.

Specific Changes

The major changes in the topical coverage are as follows:

- **Chapter 4.** More on PLDs, especially used to implement logic circuits previously implemented using standard ICs. More real-world applications.

- **Chapter 5.** Added crystal-controlled clock generator.

- **Chapter 6.** Deleted multiplier circuit and added ALU integrated circuits. Also added hexadecimal representation of signed numbers.

- **Chapter 7.** This long chapter has been divided into two parts. PART I (Sections 1 through 15) covers asynchronous counters through shift-register counters. PART II (Sections 16 through 24) includes applications, registers, and troubleshooting. Also, more adherence to left-to-right signal flow convention. Expanded material on synchronous counters.

- **Chapter 8.** Deleted obsolete unit load method. Expanded and updated IC packaging conventions. Added 74AHC and 74AHCT series of CMOS logic. Increased emphasis on rapidly advancing low-voltage technologies. Introduction of LM339 analog comparator.

- **Chapter 9.** Improved coverage of liquid-crystal displays and more sophisticated display modules. Introduction of "divide-and-conquer" troubleshooting technique and troubleshooting tree diagrams.

- **Chapter 10.** New material on serial DACs, reconstruction of digitized signals, sigma/delta method of analog-to-digital conversion. New section on rapidly growing area of digital signal processing.

- **Chapter 11.** Increased emphasis on dominance of MOS technology. Expanded EEPROMs to include serial data interface. New material on CD-ROM storage,

JEDEC standard for packaging, DRAM refreshing, and incomplete address decoding. Added new section on user-upgradable memory modules used in PCs.

- **Chapter 12.** Introduced hardware description languages such as VHDL and new in-circuit programmable parts.
- **Chapter 13.** Added historical perspective on microprocessor evolution. Replaced 8085 with the 8051 family of microcontrollers to describe basic microprocessor concepts and operation.

Retained Features

This edition retains all of the features that made the previous editions so widely accepted. It utilizes a block diagram approach to teach the basic logic operations without confusing the reader with the details of internal operation. All but the most basic electrical characteristics of the logic ICs are withheld until the reader has a firm understanding of logic principles. In Chapter 8 the reader is introduced to the internal IC circuitry. At that point, the reader can interpret a logic block's input and output characteristics and "fit" it properly into a complete system.

The treatment of each new topic or device typically follows these steps: the principle of operation is introduced; thoroughly explained examples and applications are presented often using actual ICs; short review questions are posed at the end of the section; and finally, in-depth problems are available at the end of the chapter. Ranging from simple to complex, these problems provide instructors with a wide choice of student assignments. These problems are often intended to reinforce the material without simple repetition of the principles. They require the student to demonstrate comprehension of the principles by applying them to different situations. This also helps the student develop confidence and expand his or her knowledge of the material.

The IEEE/ANSI standard for logic symbols is introduced and discussed with minimum disruption of the topic flow, and, if desired, can be omitted completely or in part. The extensive troubleshooting coverage is spread over Chapters 4 through 11 and includes presentation of troubleshooting principles and techniques, case studies, 25 troubleshooting examples, and 60 *real* troubleshooting problems. When supplemented with hands-on lab exercises, this material can help foster the development of good troubleshooting skills.

The seventh edition offers over 200 worked-out examples, more than 400 review questions, and over 450 chapter problems/exercises. Some of these problems are applications that show how the logic devices presented in the chapter are used in a typical microcomputer system.

An IC index is provided to help the reader easily locate material on any IC cited or used in the text. The inside front cover contains tables of the most often used Boolean algebra theorems, logic gate summaries, and flip-flop truth tables for quick reference when doing problems or working in the lab.

A comprehensive glossary provides concise definitions of all terms in the text that have been highlighted in boldface type.

Sequencing

It is a rare instructor who uses the chapters of a textbook in the sequence in which they are presented. This book was written so that, for the most part, each chapter builds on previous material, but it is possible to alter the chapter sequence somewhat. The first part of Chapter 6 (arithmetic operations) can be covered right after Chapter 2 (number systems), although this would produce a long interval before the arithmetic circuits of Chapter 6 are encountered. Much of the material in Chapter 8 (IC characteristics) can be covered earlier (e.g., after Chapter 4 or 5) without causing any serious problems.

This book can be used either in a one-term course or in a two-term sequence. When used in one term, it may be necessary, depending on available class hours, to omit some topics. Here is a list of sections and chapters that can be deleted with minimum disruption. Obviously, the choice of deletions will depend on factors such as program or course objectives and student background:

Chapter 1:	All	Chapter 8:	Sections 9, 16, 18–23
Chapter 2:	Section 6	Chapter 9:	Sections 6, 10, 11
Chapter 4:	Sections 7, 10–14	Chapter 10:	Sections 7, 14–18
Chapter 5:	Sections 3, 24, 25	Chapter 11:	Sections 10, 19–21
Chapter 6:	Sections 5, 7, 11, 13, 16–20	Chapters 12 and 13:	All
Chapter 7:	Sections 10, 14, 23, 24		

Supplements

An extensive complement of teaching and learning tools has been developed to accompany this textbook. Each component of this package provides a unique function, and each can be used independently or in conjunction with the others. This package includes the following:

- **Instructor's Resource Manual** presents worked-out, step-by-step solutions to all text problems.
- **Lab Manual: A Design Approach,** by Gregory Moss, contains topical units with lab projects that emphasize simulation and design. It utilizes the CUPL software in its programmable logic exercises.
- **Lab Manual: A Troubleshooting Approach,** by Jim DeLoach and Frank Ambrosio, offers over 40 experiments with an analysis and troubleshooting approach.
- **Lab Manual Results** includes worked-out lab results for both Lab Manuals.
- **Transparency Masters** contains enlarged illustrations from the text—as well as some additional class examples (ACEs) not in the text—for making acetates or hand-outs.
- **Student Study Guide** provides reinforcement of all of the topics presented in the text with over 200 new questions and problems with solutions.
- **Test Item File** is a hardcopy set of hundreds of questions that can be used for tests and quizzes.
- **PH Custom Test** (Windows) (computerized test item file), for on-screen manipulation and editing of all test items, includes graphics capabilities and a sophisticated function plotter. It is a powerful tool.
- **CUPL,** by Logical Devices, is the software tool used in Chapter 12 in the PLD development process.

- **EWB (Electronics Workbench)** data disk provides 100 circuits from the text displayed using this popular software tool. The circuits can be manipulated and tested by the student.

- **Electronics Testbench** is a new on-line testing program brought to you by the makers of Electronics Workbench, Interactive Image Technologies, Ltd. It contains questions keyed directly to the book, and includes several customization options. An EWB button allows students to switch over to EWB if they need further explanation.

- **Tocci Website** at http://www.prenhall.com/tocci provides information about all Prentice Hall titles written by Ron Tocci, including the features, supplements packages, ordering information, and feedback for all titles. It also includes an on-line study guide where students can take quizzes, geared specifically to each title. The results can be e-mailed back to the instructor.

ACKNOWLEDGMENTS

We are grateful to all those who evaluated the sixth edition and provided answers to an extensive questionnaire: John Clark, NEC–Thompson Institute; Mike Clemmer, ITT Tech Inst.; Steve Duginski, NE Wisconsin Technical College; Tom Green, Ranken Technical College; Nasser Hedayat, Valencia Community College; Larry McDermott, DeVry Institute of Technology; and Tom Paine, Coleman College. Their comments, critiques, and suggestions were given serious consideration and were invaluable in determining the final form of the seventh edition.

We also are greatly indebted to several of our colleagues: Professor Frank Ambrosio, Monroe Community College, for his usual high quality work on the indexes, the Instructor's Resource Manual, and the Student Study Guide; Professor Greg Moss, Purdue University, for his many suggestions concerning topics and new directions for this edition; and Professor Anthony Oxtoby, Purdue University, for sharing his technical expertise on the new developments in digital technology.

A writing project of this magnitude requires conscientious and professional editorial support, and Prentice Hall came through again in typical fashion. We thank Mary Harlan, production editor, Carol Robison, senior development editor, and Maggie Shaffer, copy editor, for helping to make the publication process bearable.

And finally, we want to let our wives and our children (especially Neal's daughter and four sons) know how much we appreciate their support and their understanding. We hope that we can eventually make up for all of the hours we spent away from them while we worked on this revision.

Ronald J. Tocci
Neal S. Widmer

Contents

CHAPTER 8   Integrated-Circuit Logic Families   414

CHAPTER 9   MSI Logic Circuits   510

Introductory Concepts

■ OBJECTIVES

Upon completion of this chapter, you will be able to:

- Distinguish between analog and digital representations.
- Cite the advantages and drawbacks of digital techniques compared with analog.
- Understand the need for analog-to-digital converters (ADCs) and digital-to-analog converters (DACs).
- Convert between decimal and binary numbers.
- Identify typical digital signals.
- Cite several integrated-circuit fabrication technologies.
- Identify a timing diagram.
- State the differences between parallel and serial transmission.
- Describe the property of memory.
- Describe the major parts of a digital computer and understand their functions.
- Distinguish among microcomputers, microprocessors, and microcontrollers.

■ INTRODUCTION

In today's world, the term *digital* has become part of our everyday vocabulary because of the dramatic way that digital circuits and digital techniques have become so widely used in almost all areas of life: computers, automation, robots, medical science and technology, transportation, entertainment, space exploration, and on and on. You are about to begin an exciting educational journey in which you will discover the fundamental principles, concepts, and operations that are common to all digital systems from the simplest on/off switch to the most complex computer. If this book is successful, you should gain a deep understanding of how all digital systems work, and you should be able to apply this understanding to the analysis and troubleshooting of any digital system.

3

We start by introducing some underlying concepts that are a vital part of digital technology; these concepts will be expanded on as they are needed later in the book. We also introduce some of the terminology that is necessary when embarking on a new field of study, and add to it in every chapter.

1-1 NUMERICAL REPRESENTATIONS

In science, technology, business, and, in fact, most other fields of endeavor, we are constantly dealing with *quantities*. Quantities are measured, monitored, recorded, manipulated arithmetically, observed, or in some other way utilized in most physical systems. It is important when dealing with various quantities that we be able to represent their values efficiently and accurately. There are basically two ways of representing the numerical value of quantities: **analog** and **digital.**

Analog Representations

In **analog representation** a quantity is represented by a voltage, current, or meter movement that is proportional to the value of that quantity. An example is an automobile speedometer, in which the deflection of the needle is proportional to the speed of the auto. The angular position of the needle represents the value of the auto's speed, and the needle follows any changes that occur as the auto speeds up or slows down.

Another example is the common room thermostat, in which the bending of the bimetallic strip is proportional to the room temperature. As the temperature changes gradually, the curvature of the strip changes proportionally.

Still another example of an analog quantity is found in the familiar audio microphone. In this device an output voltage is generated in proportion to the amplitude of the sound waves that impinge on the microphone. The variations in the output voltage follow the same variations as the input sound.

Analog quantities such as those cited above have an important characteristic: *they can vary over a continuous range of values*. The automobile speed can have any value between zero and, say, 100 mph. Similarly, the microphone output might be anywhere within a range of zero to 10 mV (e.g., 1 mV, 2.3724 mV, 9.9999 mV).

Digital Representations

In **digital representation** the quantities are represented not by proportional quantities but by symbols called *digits*. As an example, consider the digital watch, which provides the time of day in the form of decimal digits which represent hours and minutes (and sometimes seconds). As we know, the time of day changes continuously, but the digital watch reading does not change continuously; rather, it changes in steps of one per minute (or per second). In other words, this digital representation of the time of day changes in *discrete* steps, as compared with the representation of time provided by an analog watch, where the dial reading changes continuously.

The major difference between analog and digital quantities, then, can be simply stated as follows:

$$\text{analog} \equiv \text{continuous}$$
$$\text{digital} \equiv \text{discrete (step by step)}$$

Because of the discrete nature of digital representations, there is no ambiguity when reading the value of a digital quantity, whereas the value of an analog quantity is often open to interpretation.

EXAMPLE 1-1

Which of the following involve analog quantities and which involve digital quantities?

(a) Ten-position switch
(b) Current flowing out of an electrical outlet
(c) Temperature of a room
(d) Sand grains on the beach
(e) Automobile speedometer

Solution

(a) Digital
(b) Analog
(c) Analog
(d) Digital, since the number of grains can be only certain discrete (integer) values and not every possible value over a continuous range
(e) Analog, if needle type; digital, if numerical readout type

---

Review Questions*   1. Concisely describe the major difference between analog and digital quantities.

1-2 DIGITAL AND ANALOG SYSTEMS

A **digital system** is a combination of devices designed to manipulate logical information or physical quantities that are represented in digital form; that is, the quantities can take on only discrete values. These devices are most often electronic, but they can also be mechanical, magnetic, or pneumatic. Some of the more familiar

---

*   Answers to review questions are found at the end of the chapter in which they occur.

digital systems include digital computers and calculators, digital audio and video equipment, and the telephone system—the world's largest digital system.

An **analog system** contains devices that manipulate physical quantities that are represented in analog form. In an analog system, the quantities can vary over a continuous range of values. For example, the amplitude of the output signal to the speaker in a radio receiver can have any value between zero and its maximum limit. Other common analog systems are audio amplifiers, magnetic tape recording and playback equipment, and a simple light dimmer switch.

Advantages of Digital Techniques

An increasing majority of applications in electronics, as well as in most other technologies, use digital techniques to perform operations that were once performed using analog methods. The chief reasons for the shift to digital technology are:

1. *Digital systems are generally easier to design*. This is because the circuits that are used are *switching circuits,* where *exact* values of voltage or current are not important, only the range (HIGH or LOW) in which they fall.

2. *Information storage is easy*. This is accomplished by special switching circuits that can latch onto information and hold it for as long as necessary.

3. *Accuracy and precision are greater*. Digital systems can handle as many digits of precision as you need simply by adding more switching circuits. In analog systems, precision is usually limited to three or four digits because the values of voltage and current are directly dependent on the circuit component values and are affected by random fluctuations (noise).

4. *Operation can be programmed*. It is fairly easy to design digital systems whose operation is controlled by a set of stored instructions called a *program*. As technology progresses, this is becoming even easier. Analog systems can also be *programmed,* but the variety and the complexity of the available operations are severely limited.

5. *Digital circuits are less affected by noise*. Spurious fluctuations in voltage (noise) are not as critical in digital systems because the exact value of a voltage is not important, as long as the noise is not large enough to prevent us from distinguishing a HIGH from a LOW.

6. *More digital circuitry can be fabricated on IC chips*. It is true that analog circuitry has also benefited from the tremendous development of IC technology, but its relative complexity and its use of devices that cannot be economically integrated (high-value capacitors, precision resistors, inductors, transformers) have prevented analog systems from achieving the same high degree of integration.

Limitations of Digital Techniques

There is really only one major drawback when using digital techniques:

The real world is mainly analog.

Most physical quantities are analog in nature, and it is these quantities that are often the inputs and outputs that are being monitored, operated on, and controlled by a system. Some examples are temperature, pressure, position, velocity, liquid level, flow rate, and so on. We are in the habit of expressing these quantities *digitally,* such as when we say that the temperature is 64° (63.8° when we want to be more precise); but we are really making a digital approximation to an inherently analog quantity.

To take advantage of digital techniques when dealing with analog inputs and outputs, three steps must be followed:

1. Convert the real-world analog inputs to digital form.
2. Process *(operate on)* the digital information.
3. Convert the digital outputs back to real-world analog form.

Figure 1-1 shows a block diagram of this for a typical temperature control system. As the diagram shows, the analog temperature is measured and the measured value is then converted to a digital quantity by an **analog-to-digital converter (ADC).** The digital quantity is then processed by the digital circuitry, which may or may not include a digital computer. Its digital output is converted back to an analog quantity by a **digital-to-analog converter (DAC).** This analog output is fed to a controller which takes some kind of action to adjust the temperature.

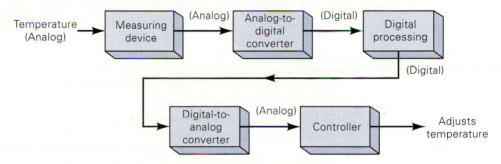

FIGURE 1-1   Block diagram of a temperature control system that requires analog/digital conversions in order to allow the use of digital processing techniques.

Another good example where conversion between analog and digital takes place is in the recording of audio. Compact disks (CDs) have taken the recording industry by storm because they provide a much better means for recording and playing back music. The process works something like this: (1) sounds from instruments and human voices produce an analog voltage signal in a microphone; (2) this analog signal is converted to a digital format using an analog-to-digital conversion process; (3) the digital information is stored on the CD's surface; (4) during playback, the CD player takes the digital information from the CD surface and converts it into an analog signal which is then amplified and fed to a speaker where it can be picked up by the human ear.

The need for conversion between analog and digital forms of information can be considered a drawback because of the added complexity and expense. Another factor that is often important is the extra time required to perform these conversions. In many applications, these factors are outweighed by the numerous advantages of using digital techniques, and so the conversion between analog and digital quantities has become quite commonplace in the current technology.

There are situations, however, where using only analog techniques is simpler and more economical. For example, the process of signal amplification is most easily accomplished using analog circuitry.

It is common to see both digital and analog techniques employed within the same system in order to profit from the advantages of each. In these *hybrid* systems, one of the most important parts of the design phase involves determining what parts of the system are to be analog and what parts are to be digital.

The Future Is Digital

It is pretty safe to predict that most of the future advances in many (if not all) areas of technology will take place in the digital realm. The rapid pace of those advances may even exceed the phenomenal growth we have been experiencing in the past few years—a period in which we have seen: 35 percent of American families and 50 percent of teenagers with personal computers at home; 30 million people estimated to be on the Internet; 90 percent of all home computers sold in 1995 with modems and CD-ROM drives; automobiles with 50 microprocessor chips; microprocessors in everyday things from toasters, thermostats, and greeting cards to answering machines, VCRs, and washing machines. And the future promises much more of the same. Early in the twenty-first century, your right and left cuff links or earrings may communicate with each other by low-orbiting satellites and have more computer power than your present home or office computer. Telephones will be able to receive, sort, and maybe respond to incoming calls like a well-trained secretary. Children in school will be able to gather ideas and information and socialize with other children all over the world. When you watch television for an hour, what you see will have been delivered to your home in less than a second and stored in your TV's (computer's) memory for viewing at your convenience. Reading about a place 5,000 miles away may include the sensory experience of being there. And that's only the tip of the iceberg.*

In other words, digital technology will continue its high-speed incursion into current areas of our lives as well as breaking new ground in ways we may not even have thought about. All we can do is try to learn as much as we can about this technology and hang on and enjoy the ride.

Review Questions

1. What are the advantages of digital techniques over analog?
2. What is the chief limitation to the use of digital techniques?

1-3 DIGITAL NUMBER SYSTEMS

Many number systems are in use in digital technology. The most common are the decimal, binary, octal, and hexadecimal systems. The decimal system is clearly the most familiar to us because it is a tool that we use every day. Examining some of its characteristics will help us to better understand the other systems.

---

* All of the figures cited here and all of the futuristic predictions are from *Being Digital* by Nicholas Negroponte, Vintage Books, 1995, pp. 5–7.

Decimal System

The **decimal system** is composed of *10* numerals or symbols. These 10 symbols are 0, 1, 2, 3, 4, 5, 6, 7, 8, 9; using these symbols as *digits* of a number, we can express any quantity. The decimal system, also called the *base-10* system because it has 10 digits, has evolved naturally as a result of the fact that people have 10 fingers. In fact, the word "digit" is derived from the Latin word for "finger."

The decimal system is a *positional-value system* in which the value of a digit depends on its position. For example, consider the decimal number 453. We know that the digit 4 actually represents 4 *hundreds,* the 5 represents 5 *tens,* and the 3 represents 3 *units.* In essence, the 4 carries the most weight of the three digits; it is referred to as the *most significant digit (MSD).* The 3 carries the least weight and is called the *least significant digit (LSD).*

Consider another example, 27.35. This number is actually equal to 2 tens plus 7 units plus 3 tenths plus 5 hundredths, or $2 \times 10 + 7 \times 1 + 3 \times 0.1 + 5 \times 0.01$. The decimal point is used to separate the integer and fractional parts of the number.

More rigorously, the various positions relative to the decimal point carry weights that can be expressed as powers of 10. This is illustrated in Figure 1-2, where the number 2745.214 is represented. The decimal point separates the positive powers of 10 from the negative powers. The number 2745.214 is thus equal to

$$(2 \times 10^{+3}) + (7 \times 10^{+2}) + (4 \times 10^{1}) + (5 \times 10^{0})$$
$$+ (2 \times 10^{-1}) + (1 \times 10^{-2}) + (4 \times 10^{-3})$$

In general, any number is simply the sum of the products of each digit value and its positional value.

FIGURE 1-2   Decimal position values as powers of 10.

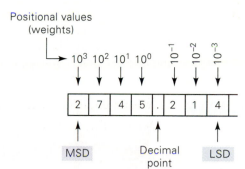

Decimal Counting

When counting in the decimal system, we start with 0 in the units position and take each symbol (digit) in progression until we reach 9. Then we add a 1 to the next higher position and start over with 0 in the first position (see Figure 1-3). This process continues until the count of 99 is reached. Then we add a 1 to the third position and start over with 0s in the first two positions. The same pattern is followed continuously as high as we wish to count.

FIGURE 1-3   Decimal counting.

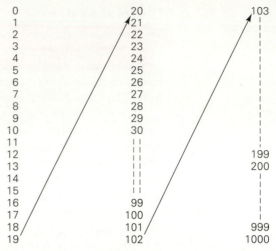

It is important to note that in decimal counting the units position (LSD) changes upward with each step in the count, the tens position changes upward every 10 steps in the count, the hundreds position changes upward every 100 steps in the count, and so on.

Another characteristic of the decimal system is that using only two decimal places, we can count through $10^2 = 100$ different numbers (0 to 99).* With three places we can count through 1000 numbers (0 to 999); and so on. In general, with N places or digits we can count through 10^N different numbers, starting with and including zero. The largest number will always be $10^N - 1$.

Binary System

Unfortunately, the decimal number system does not lend itself to convenient implementation in digital systems. For example, it is very difficult to design electronic equipment so that it can work with 10 different voltage levels (each one representing one decimal character, 0 through 9). On the other hand, it is very easy to design simple, accurate electronic circuits that operate with only two voltage levels. For this reason, almost every digital system uses the binary (base-2) number system as the basic number system of its operations, although other systems are often used in conjunction with binary.

In the **binary system** there are only two symbols or possible digit values, 0 and 1. Even so, this base-2 system can be used to represent any quantity that can be represented in decimal or other number systems. In general though, it will take a greater number of binary digits to express a given quantity.

All of the statements made earlier concerning the decimal system are equally applicable to the binary system. The binary system is also a positional-value system, wherein each binary digit has its own value or weight expressed as a power of 2. This is illustrated in Figure 1-4. Here, places to the left of the *binary point* (counter-

---

*   Zero is counted as a number.

FIGURE 1-4 Binary position values as powers of 2.

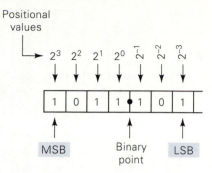

part of the decimal point) are positive powers of 2, and places to the right are negative powers of 2. The number 1011.101 is shown represented in the figure. To find its equivalent in the decimal system we simply take the sum of the products of each digit value (0 or 1) and its positional value:

$$1011.101_2 = (1 \times 2^3) + (0 \times 2^2) + (1 \times 2^1) + (1 \times 2^0)$$
$$+ (1 \times 2^{-1}) + (0 \times 2^{-2}) + (1 \times 2^{-3})$$
$$= 8 + 0 + 2 + 1 + 0.5 + 0 + 0.125$$
$$= 11.625_{10}$$

Notice in the preceding operation that subscripts (2 and 10) were used to indicate the base in which the particular number is expressed. This convention is used to avoid confusion whenever more than one number system is being employed. In the binary system, the term *binary digit* is often abbreviated to the term **bit,** which we will use henceforth. Thus, in the number expressed in Figure 1-4 there are four bits to the left of the binary point, representing the integer part of the number, and three bits to the right of the binary point, representing the fractional part. The most significant bit (MSB) is the leftmost bit (largest weight). The least significant bit (LSB) is the rightmost bit (smallest weight). These are indicated in Figure 1-4.

Binary Counting

When we deal with binary numbers, we will usually be restricted to a specific number of bits. This restriction is based on the circuitry that is used to represent these binary numbers. Let's use four-bit binary numbers to illustrate the method for counting in binary.

The sequence (shown in Figure 1-5) begins with all bits at 0; this is called the *zero count.* For each successive count, the units (2^0) position *toggles;* that is, it changes from one binary value to the other. Each time the units bit changes from a 1 to a 0, the twos (2^1) position will toggle (change states). Each time the twos position changes from 1 to 0, the fours (2^2) position will toggle (change states). Likewise, each time the fours position goes from 1 to 0, the eights (2^3) position toggles. This same process would be continued for the higher-order bit positions if the binary number had more than four bits.

FIGURE 1-5 Binary counting sequence.

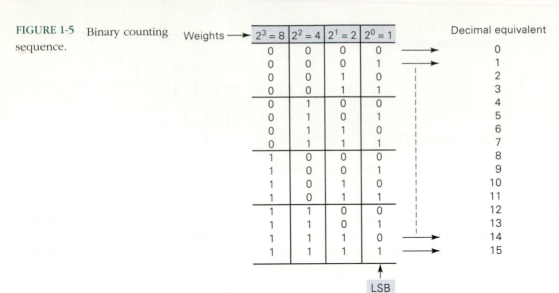

The binary counting sequence has an important characteristic, as shown in Figure 1-5. The units bit (LSB) changes either from 0 to 1 or 1 to 0 with *each* count. The second bit (twos position) stays at 0 for two counts, then at 1 for two counts, then at 0 for two counts, and so on. The third bit (fours position) stays at 0 for four counts, then at 1 for four counts, and so on. The fourth bit (eights position) stays at 0 for eight counts, then at 1 for eight counts. If we wanted to count further, we would add more places, and this pattern would continue with 0s and 1s alternating in groups of 2^{N-1}. For example, using a fifth binary place, the fifth bit would alternate sixteen 0s, then sixteen 1s, and so on.

As we saw for the decimal system, it is also true for the binary system that by using N bits or places, we can go through 2^N counts. For example, with two bits we can go through $2^2 = 4$ counts (00_2 through 11_2); with four bits we can go through $2^4 = 16$ counts (0000_2 through 1111_2); and so on. The last count will always be all 1s and is equal to $2^N - 1$ in the decimal system. For example, using four bits, the last count is $1111_2 = 2^4 - 1 = 15_{10}$.

EXAMPLE 1-2

What is the largest number that can be represented using eight bits?

Solution

$2^N - 1 = 2^8 - 1 = 255_{10} = 11111111_2$.

This has been a brief introduction of the binary number system and its relation to the decimal system. We will spend much more time on these two systems and several others in the next chapter.

1. What is the decimal equivalent of 1101011_2?
2. What is the next binary number following 10111_2 in the counting sequence?
3. What is the largest decimal value that can be represented using 12 bits?

1-4   REPRESENTING BINARY QUANTITIES

In digital systems the information that is being processed is usually present in binary form. Binary quantities can be represented by any device that has only two operating states or possible conditions. For example, a switch has only two states: open or closed. We can arbitrarily let an open switch represent binary 0 and a closed switch represent binary 1. With this assignment we can now represent any binary number as illustrated in Figure 1-6(a), where the states of the various switches represent 10010_2.

Another example is shown in Figure 1-6(b), where holes punched in paper are used to represent binary numbers. A punched hole is a binary 1, and absence of a hole is a binary 0.

FIGURE 1-6   Using (a) switches and (b) punched paper tape to represent binary numbers.

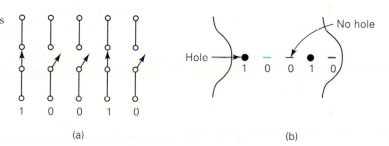

```
1   0   0   1   0
        (a)
```

```
Hole    1   0   0   1   0    No hole
                (b)
```

There are numerous other devices that have only two operating states or can be operated in two extreme conditions. Among these are: light bulb (bright or dark), diode (conducting or nonconducting), relay (energized or deenergized), transistor (cut off or saturated), photocell (illuminated or dark), thermostat (open or closed), mechanical clutch (engaged or disengaged), and spot on a magnetic disk (magnetized or demagnetized).

In electronic digital systems, binary information is represented by voltages (or currents) that are present at the inputs and outputs of the various circuits. Typically, the binary 0 and 1 are represented by two nominal voltage levels. For example, zero volts (0 V) might represent binary 0, and +5 V might represent binary 1. In actuality, because of circuit variations, the 0 and 1 would be represented by voltage ranges. This is illustrated in Figure 1-7(a), where any voltage between 0 and 0.8 V represents a 0 and any voltage between 2 and 5 V represents a 1. All input and output signals will normally fall within one of these ranges except during transitions from one level to another.

We can now see another significant difference between digital and analog systems. In digital systems, the exact value of a voltage *is not* important; for example, for the voltage assignments of Figure 1-7(a), a voltage of 3.6 V means the same as a

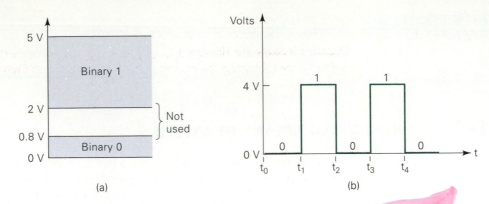

FIGURE 1-7   (a) Typical voltage assignments in digital system; (b) typical digital signal timing diagram.

voltage of 4.3 V. In analog systems, the exact value of a voltage *is* important. For instance, if the analog voltage is proportional to the temperature measured by a transducer, the 3.6 V would represent a different temperature than would 4.3 V. In other words, the voltage value carries significant information. This characteristic means that the design of accurate analog circuitry is generally more difficult than that of digital circuitry because of the way in which exact voltage values are affected by variations in component values, temperature, and noise (random voltage fluctuations).

Digital Signals and Timing Diagrams

Figure 1-7(b) shows a typical digital signal and how it varies over time. It is actually a graph of voltage versus time (t) and is called a **timing diagram.** The horizontal time scale is marked off at regular intervals beginning at t_0 and proceeding to t_1, t_2, and so on. For the example timing diagram shown here, the signal starts at 0 V (a binary 0) at time t_0 and remains there until time t_1. At t_1, the signal makes a rapid transition (jump) up to 4 V (a binary 1). At t_2, it jumps back down to 0 V. Similar transitions occur at t_3 and t_4.

The transitions on this timing diagram are drawn as vertical lines, and so they appear to be instantaneous, when in reality they are not. In many situations, however, the transition times are so short compared to the times between transitions that we can show them on the diagram as vertical lines. We will encounter situations later where it will be necessary to show the transitions more accurately on an expanded time scale.

Timing diagrams are used extensively to show how digital signals change with time, and especially to show the relationship between two or more digital signals in the same circuit or system. By displaying one or more digital signals on an *oscilloscope* or *logic analyzer,* we can compare the signals to their expected timing diagrams. This is a very important part of the testing and troubleshooting procedures used in digital systems.

1-5 DIGITAL CIRCUITS/LOGIC CIRCUITS

Digital circuits are designed to produce output voltages that fall within the prescribed 0 and 1 voltage ranges such as those defined in Figure 1-7. Likewise, digital circuits are designed to respond predictably to input voltages that are within the defined 0 and 1 ranges. What this means is that a digital circuit will respond in the same way to all input voltages that fall within the allowed 0 range; similarly, it will not distinguish between input voltages that lie within the allowed 1 range.

To illustrate, Figure 1-8 represents a typical digital circuit with input v_i and output v_o. The output is shown for two different input signal waveforms. Note that v_o is the same for both cases because the two input waveforms, while differing in their exact voltage levels, are at the same binary levels.

FIGURE 1-8 A digital circuit responds to an input's binary level (0 or 1) and not to its actual voltage.

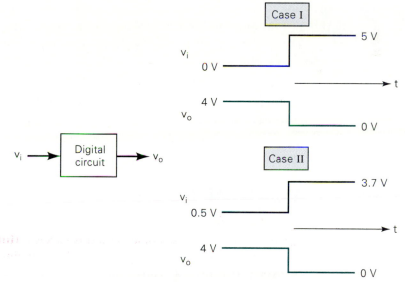

Logic Circuits

The manner in which a digital circuit responds to an input is referred to as the circuit's *logic*. Each type of digital circuit obeys a certain set of logic rules. For this reason, digital circuits are also called **logic circuits.** We will use both terms interchangeably throughout the text. In Chapter 3 we will see more clearly what is meant by a circuit's "logic."

We will be studying all the types of logic circuits that are currently used in digital systems. Initially, our attention will be focused only on the logical operation that these circuits perform—that is, the relationship between the circuit inputs and outputs. We will defer any discussion of the internal circuit operation of these logic circuits until after we have developed an understanding of their logical operation.

Digital Integrated Circuits

Almost all of the digital circuits used in modern digital systems are integrated circuits (ICs). The wide variety of available logic ICs has made it possible to construct complex digital systems that are smaller and more reliable than their discrete-component counterparts.

Several integrated-circuit fabrication technologies are used to produce digital ICs, the most common being TTL, CMOS, NMOS, and ECL. Each differs in the type of circuitry used to provide the desired logic operation. For example, TTL (transistor-transistor logic) uses the bipolar transistor as its main circuit element, while CMOS (complementary metal-oxide-semiconductor) uses the enhancement-mode MOSFET as its principal circuit element. We will learn about the various IC technologies, their characteristics, and their relative advantages and disadvantages after we master the basic logic circuit types.

Review Questions

1. *True or false:* The exact value of an input voltage is critical for a digital circuit.
2. Can a digital circuit produce the same output voltage for different input voltage values?
3. A digital circuit is also referred to as a _____ circuit.
4. A graph that shows how one or more digital signals change with time is called a _____ .

1-6 PARALLEL AND SERIAL TRANSMISSION

One of the most common operations that occur in any digital system is the transmission of information from one place to another. The information can be transmitted over a distance as small as a fraction of an inch on the same circuit board, or over a distance of many miles when an operator at a computer terminal is communicating with a computer in another city. The information that is transmitted is in binary form and is generally represented as voltages at the outputs of a sending circuit that are connected to the inputs of a receiving circuit. Figure 1-9 illustrates the two basic methods for digital information transmission: **parallel** and **serial.**

Figure 1-9(a) shows how the binary number 10110 is transmitted from circuit A to circuit B using parallel transmission. Each bit of the binary number is represented by one of the circuit A outputs, where output A_4 is the MSB and A_0 is the LSB. Each of the circuit A outputs is connected to a corresponding input of circuit B so that all five bits of information are transmitted simultaneously (in parallel).

In Figure 1-9(b) there is only one connection from circuit A to circuit B when serial transmission is used. Here the output of circuit A will produce a digital signal whose voltage level will change at regular intervals in accordance with the binary number being transmitted. In this way the information is being transmitted a bit at a time (serially) over the one signal line. The timing diagram in Fig-

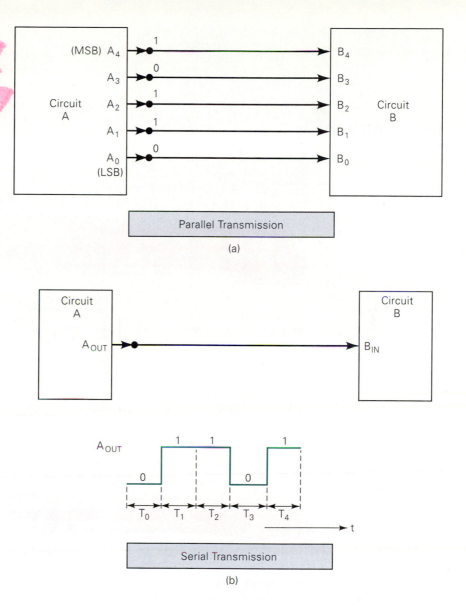

ure 1-9(b) shows how the signal level varies with time. During the first time interval, T_0, the signal is at the 0 level; during interval T_1 the signal is at the 1 level; and so on.

The principal trade-off between parallel and serial representations is one of speed versus circuit simplicity. The transmission of binary data from one part of a digital system to another can be done more quickly using parallel representation because all the bits are transmitted simultaneously, while serial representation transmits one bit at a time. On the other hand, parallel requires more signal lines connected between the sender and the receiver of the binary data than does serial. In other words, parallel is faster, and serial requires fewer signal lines. This comparison between parallel and serial methods for representing binary information will be encountered many times in discussions throughout the text.

1. Describe the relative advantages of parallel and serial transmission of binary data.

1-7   MEMORY

When an input signal is applied to most devices or circuits, the output somehow changes in response to the input, and when the input signal is removed, the output returns to its original state. These circuits do not exhibit the property of *memory,* since their outputs revert back to normal. In digital circuitry certain types of devices and circuits do have memory. When an input is applied to such a circuit, the output will change its state, but it will remain in the new state even after the input is removed. This property of retaining its response to a momentary input is called **memory.** Figure 1-10 illustrates nonmemory and memory operations.

FIGURE 1-10   Comparison of nonmemory and memory operation.

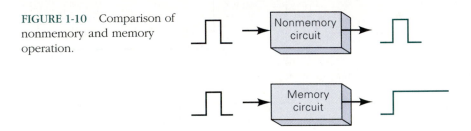

Memory devices and circuits play an important role in digital systems because they provide a means for storing binary numbers either temporarily or permanently, with the ability to change the stored information at any time. As we shall see, the various memory elements include magnetic types and those which utilize electronic latching circuits (called *latches* and *flip-flops*).

1-8   DIGITAL COMPUTERS

Digital techniques have found their way into innumerable areas of technology, but the area of automatic **digital computers** is by far the most notable and most extensive. Although digital computers affect some part of all of our lives, it is doubtful that many of us know exactly what a computer does. In simplest terms, *a computer is a system of hardware that performs arithmetic operations, manipulates data (usually in binary form), and makes decisions.*

For the most part, human beings can do whatever computers can do, but computers can do it with much greater speed and accuracy. This is in spite of the fact that computers perform all their calculations and operations one step at a time. For example, a human being can take a list of 10 numbers and find their sum all in one operation by listing the numbers one over the other and adding them column by column. A computer, on the other hand, can add numbers only two at a time, so that adding this same list of numbers will take nine actual addition steps. Of course, the fact that the computer requires only a microsecond or less per step makes up for this apparent inefficiency.

A computer is faster and more accurate than people are, but unlike most people it must be given a complete set of instructions that tell it *exactly* what to do at each step of its operation. This set of instructions, called a **program,** is prepared by one or more persons for each job the computer is to do. Programs are placed in the computer's memory unit in binary-coded form, with each instruction having a unique code. The computer takes these instruction codes from memory *one at a time* and performs the operation called for by the code. Much more will be said about this later.

Major Parts of a Computer

There are several types of computer systems, but each can be broken down into the same functional units. Each unit performs specific functions, and all units function together to carry out the instructions given in the program. Figure 1-11 shows the five major functional parts of a digital computer and their interaction. The solid lines with arrows represent the flow of data and information. The dashed lines with arrows represent the flow of timing and control signals.

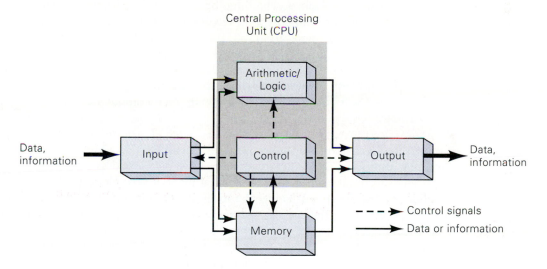

FIGURE 1-11   Functional diagram of a digital computer.

The major functions of each unit are:

1. **Input unit.** Through this unit a complete set of instructions and data is fed into the computer system and into the memory unit, to be stored until needed. The information typically enters the input unit from a keyboard or a disk.

2. **Memory unit.** The memory stores the instructions and data received from the input unit. It stores the results of arithmetic operations received from the arithmetic unit. It also supplies information to the output unit.

3. **Control unit.** This unit takes instructions from the memory unit one at a time and interprets them. It then sends appropriate signals to all the other units to cause the specific instruction to be executed.

4. **Arithmetic/logic unit.** All arithmetic calculations and logical decisions are performed in this unit, which can then send results to the memory unit to be stored.

5. **Output unit.** This unit takes data from the memory unit and prints out, displays, or otherwise presents the information to the operator (or process, in the case of a process control computer).

Central Processing Unit (CPU)

As the diagram in Figure 1-11 shows, the control and arithmetic/logic units are often considered as one unit called the **central processing unit (CPU).** The CPU contains all of the circuitry for fetching and interpreting instructions and for controlling and performing the various operations called for by the instructions.

TYPES OF COMPUTERS   All computers are made up of the basic units described above, but they can differ as to physical size, operating speed, memory capacity, and computational power, as well as other characteristics. Computers are often classified according to physical size which often, although not always, is an indication of their relative capabilities. The three basic classifications, from smallest to largest, are: *microcomputer, minicomputer (workstation),* and *mainframe.* As microcomputers have become more and more powerful, the distinction between microcomputers and minicomputers has become rather blurred, and we have begun to distinguish only between small computers—those that can fit in an office or on a desktop or a lap—and large computers—those that are too big for any of those places. In this book we will be concerned mainly with microcomputers.

A **microcomputer** is the smallest type of computer. It generally consists of several IC chips including a **microprocessor** chip, memory chips, and input/output interface chips along with input/output devices such as a keyboard, video display, printer, and disk drives. Microcomputers were developed as a result of tremendous advances in IC fabrication technology that made it possible to pack more and more digital circuits onto a small chip. For example, the microprocessor chip contains—at a minimum—all of the circuits that make up the CPU portion of the computer, that is, the control unit and the arithmetic/logic unit. The microprocessor, in other words, is a "CPU on a chip."

Most of us are familiar with general-purpose microcomputers such as the IBM PC and its clones and the Apple Macintosh, which are used in more than half of our homes and in almost all of our businesses. These microcomputers can perform a wide variety of tasks in a wide range of applications depending on the software (programs) they are running. There is a more specialized type of microcomputer called a **microcontroller** which is not a general-purpose computer. Rather, it is designed to be used as a *dedicated* or *embedded controller* which helps monitor and control the operation of a machine, a piece of equipment, or a process. Microcontrollers are microcomputers because they use a microprocessor chip as the CPU, but they are much smaller than general-purpose microcomputers because the input/output devices they normally use are much smaller. In fact, the input/output devices—as well as memory—are usually right on the same chip as the microprocessor. These single-chip microcontrollers are employed in a wide variety of control applications such as: appliance control, metal-working machines, VCRs, automated teller machines, photocopiers, automobile ignition systems, antilock brakes, medical instrumentation, and much more.

Review Questions	1. Explain how a digital circuit that has memory differs from one that does not.
	2. Name the five major functional units of a computer.
	3. Which two units make up the CPU?
	4. An IC chip that contains a CPU is called a _____ .

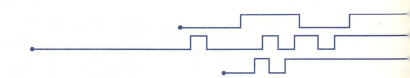

SUMMARY

1. The two basic ways of representing the numerical value of physical quantities are analog (continuous) and digital (discrete).

2. Most quantities in the real world are analog, but digital techniques are generally superior to analog techniques, and most of the predicted advances will be in the digital realm.

3. The binary number system (0 and 1) is the basic system used in digital technology.

4. Digital or logic circuits operate on voltages that fall in prescribed ranges that represent either a binary 0 or a binary 1.

5. The two basic ways to transfer digital information are parallel—all bits simultaneously—and serial—one bit at a time.

6. The main parts of all computers are the input, control, memory, arithmetic/logic, and output units.

7. The combination of the arithmetic/logic unit and the control unit makes up the CPU (central processing unit).

8. A microcomputer usually has a CPU that is on a single chip called a *microprocessor*.

9. A microcontroller is a microcomputer especially designed for dedicated (not general-purpose) control applications.

IMPORTANT TERMS*

analog representation	bit	memory unit
digital representation	timing diagram	control unit
digital system	digital/logic circuits	arithmetic/logic unit
analog system	parallel	output unit
analog-to-digital converter (ADC)	serial	central processing unit (CPU)
digital-to-analog converter (DAC)	memory	microcomputer
decimal system	digital computer	microprocessor
binary system	program	microcontroller
	input unit	

---

* These terms can be found in **boldface** type in the chapter and are defined in the Glossary at the end of the book.

PROBLEMS

SECTION 1-2

1-1. Which of the following are analog quantities, and which are digital?
   (a) Number of atoms in a sample of material
   (b) Altitude of an aircraft
   (c) Pressure in a bicycle tire
   (d) Current through a speaker
   (e) Timer setting on a microwave oven

SECTION 1-3

1-2. Convert the following binary numbers to their equivalent decimal values.
   (a) 11001_2
   (b) 1001.1001_2
   (c) 10011011001.10110_2
1-3. Using six bits, show the binary counting sequence from 000000 to 111111.
1-4. What is the maximum number that we can count up to using 10 bits?
1-5. How many bits are needed to count up to a maximum of 511?

SECTION 1-4

1-6. Draw the timing diagram for a digital signal that continuously alternates between 0.2 V (binary 0) for 2 ms and 4.4 V (binary 1) for 4 ms.

SECTION 1-6

1-7. Suppose that the decimal integer values from 0 to 15 are to be transmitted.
   (a) How many lines will be needed if parallel representation is used?
   (b) How many will be needed if serial representation is used?

SECTIONS 1-7 AND 1-8

1-8. How is a microprocessor different from a microcomputer?
1-9. How is a microcontroller different from a microcomputer?

ANSWERS TO SECTION REVIEW QUESTIONS

SECTION 1-1

1. Analog quantities can take on *any* value over a continuous range; digital quantities can take on only *discrete* values.

SECTION 1-2

1. Easier to design; easier to store information; greater accuracy and precision; programmability; less affected by noise; higher degree of integration   2. Real-world physical quantities are analog.

SECTION 1-3

1. 107_{10} 2. 11000_2 3. 4095_{10}

SECTION 1-5

1. False   2. Yes, provided that the two input voltages are within the same logic level range   3. Logic 4. Timing diagram

SECTION 1-6

1. Parallel is faster; serial requires only one signal line.

SECTION 1-8

1. One that has memory will have its output changed and *remain* changed in response to a momentary change in the input signal.   2. Input, output, memory, arithmetic/logic, control   3. Control and arithmetic/logic   4. Microprocessor

CHAPTER 2

Number Systems and Codes

■ OUTLINE

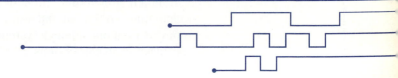

■ OBJECTIVES

Upon completion of this chapter, you will be able to:

- Use two different methods to perform decimal-to-binary conversions.
- Cite several advantages of the octal and hexadecimal number systems.
- Convert from the hexadecimal or octal number system to either the decimal or the binary number system.
- Express decimal numbers using the BCD code.
- Understand the difference between the BCD code and the straight binary code.
- Understand the need for alphanumeric codes, especially the ASCII code.
- Describe the parity method for error detection.
- Determine parity (odd or even) of digital data.

■ INTRODUCTION

The binary number system is the most important one in digital systems, but several others are also important. The decimal system is important because it is universally used to represent quantities outside a digital system. This means that there will be situations where decimal values must be converted to binary values before they are entered into the digital system. For example, when you punch a decimal number into your hand calculator (or computer), the circuitry inside the device converts the decimal number to a binary value.

Likewise, there will be situations where the binary values at the outputs of a digital system must be converted to decimal values for presentation to the outside world. For example, your calculator (or computer) uses binary numbers to calculate answers to a problem and then converts the answers to a decimal value before displaying them.

In addition to binary and decimal, two other number systems find widespread applications in digital systems. The *octal* (base-8) and *hexadecimal* (base-16) number systems are both used for the same purpose—to provide an efficient means for representing large binary numbers. As we shall see, both of these number systems have the advantage that they can be easily converted to and from binary.

In a digital system, three or four of these number systems may be in use at the same time, so that an understanding of the system operation requires the ability to convert from one number system to another. This chapter will show you how to perform these conversions. Although some of them will not be of immediate use in our study of digital systems, you will need them when you begin to study microprocessors.

This chapter will also introduce some of the *binary codes* that are used to represent various kinds of information. These binary codes will use 1s and 0s, but in a way that differs somewhat from that of the binary number system.

2-1   BINARY-TO-DECIMAL CONVERSIONS

As explained in Chapter 1, the binary number system is a positional system where each binary digit (bit) carries a certain weight based on its position relative to the LSB. Any binary number can be converted to its decimal equivalent simply by summing together the weights of the various positions in the binary number which contain a 1. To illustrate:

$$1 \quad 1 \quad 0 \quad 1 \quad 1_2 \qquad (binary)$$
$$2^4 + 2^3 + 0 + 2^1 + 2^0 = 16 + 8 + 2 + 1$$
$$= 27_{10} \quad (decimal)$$

Let's try another example with a greater number of bits:

$$1 \quad 0 \quad 1 \quad 1 \quad 0 \quad 1 \quad 0 \quad 1_2 =$$
$$2^7 + 0 + 2^5 + 2^4 + 0 + 2^2 + 0 + 2^0 = 181_{10}$$

Note that the procedure is to find the weights (i.e., powers of 2) for each bit position that contains a 1, and then to add them up. Also note that the MSB has a weight of 2^7 even though it is the eighth bit; this is because the LSB is the first bit and has a weight of 2^0.

| Review Questions | 1. Convert 100011011011_2 to its decimal equivalent. |
| | 2. What is the weight of the MSB of a 16-bit number? |

2-2 DECIMAL-TO-BINARY CONVERSIONS

There are two ways to convert a decimal *whole* number to its equivalent binary-system representation. The first method is the reverse of the process described in Section 2-1. The decimal number is simply expressed as a sum of powers of 2, and then 1s and 0s are written in the appropriate bit positions. To illustrate:

$$45_{10} = 32 + 8 + 4 + 1 = 2^5 + 0 + 2^3 + 2^2 + 0 + 2^0$$
$$= 1 \quad 0 \quad 1 \quad 1 \quad 0 \quad 1_2$$

Note that a 0 is placed in the 2^1 and 2^4 positions, since all positions must be accounted for. Another example is the following:

$$76_{10} = 64 + 8 + 4 = 2^6 + 0 + 0 + 2^3 + 2^2 + 0 + 0$$
$$= 1 \quad 0 \quad 0 \quad 1 \quad 1 \quad 0 \quad 0_2$$

Repeated Division

Another method for converting decimal integers uses repeated division by 2. The conversion, illustrated below for 25_{10}, requires repeatedly dividing the decimal number by 2 and writing down the remainder after each division until a quotient of 0 is obtained. Note that the binary result is obtained by writing the first remainder as the LSB and the last remainder as the MSB.

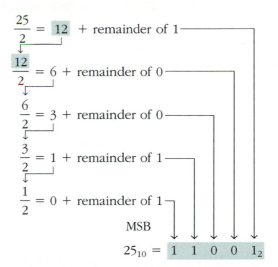

This process, diagrammed in the flowchart of Figure 2-1, can also be used to convert from decimal to any other number system.

If a calculator is being used to perform the divisions by 2, the remainders can be determined by noting whether or not the quotient has a fractional part. For example, the calculator would produce 25/2 = 12.5. The .5 indicates that there is a remainder of 1. The calculator would also produce 12/2 = 6.0, which indicates a remainder of 0. The following example is shown as it would occur using a calculator.

FIGURE 2-1 Flowchart for repeated-division method of decimal-to-binary conversion of integers. The same process can be used to convert a decimal integer to any other number system.

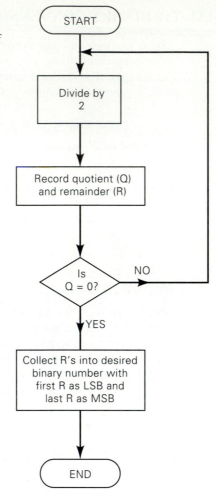

$$\frac{37}{2} = \boxed{18}.5 \longrightarrow \text{remainder of 1 (LSB)}$$

$$\frac{\boxed{18}}{2} = 9.0 \longrightarrow \qquad\qquad 0$$

$$\frac{9}{2} = 4.5 \longrightarrow \qquad\qquad 1$$

$$\frac{4}{2} = 2.0 \longrightarrow \qquad\qquad 0$$

$$\frac{2}{2} = 1.0 \longrightarrow \qquad\qquad 0$$

$$\frac{1}{2} = 0.5 \longrightarrow \qquad\qquad 1 \text{ (MSB)}$$

Thus, $37_{10} = 100101_2$.

Counting Range

Recall that using N bits, we can count through 2^N different decimal values ranging from 0 to $2^N - 1$. For example, for $N = 4$, we can count from 0000_2 to 1111_2, which is 0_{10} to 15_{10}, for a total of 16 different numbers. Here, the largest decimal value is $2^4 - 1 = 15$, and there are 2^4 different numbers.

In general, then, we can state:

Using N bits, we can represent decimal values ranging from 0 to $2^N - 1$, a total of 2^N values.

EXAMPLE 2-1

(a) What is the total range of decimal values that can be represented in eight bits?

(b) How many bits are needed to represent decimal values ranging from 0 to 12,500?

Solution

(a) Here we have $N = 8$. Thus, we can represent decimal numbers from 0 to $2^8 - 1 = 255$. We can verify this by checking to see that 11111111_2 converts to 255_{10}.

(b) With 13 bits, we can count from decimal 0 to $2^{13} - 1 = 8191$. With 14 bits, we can count from 0 to $2^{14} - 1 = 16,383$. Clearly, 13 bits aren't enough, but 14 bits will get us up beyond 12,500. Thus, the required number of bits is **14**.

Review Questions

1. Convert 83_{10} to binary using both methods.

2. Convert 729_{10} to binary using both methods. Check your answer by converting back to decimal.

3. How many bits are required to count up to decimal 1 million?

2-3 OCTAL NUMBER SYSTEM

The octal number system is very important in digital computer work. The **octal number system** has a base of *eight,* meaning that it has eight possible digits: 0, 1, 2, 3, 4, 5, 6, and 7. Thus, each digit of an octal number can have any value from 0 to 7. The digit positions in an octal number have weights as follows:

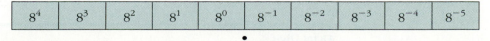

8^4	8^3	8^2	8^1	8^0	8^{-1}	8^{-2}	8^{-3}	8^{-4}	8^{-5}

●
octal point

Octal-to-Decimal Conversion

An octal number, then, can easily be converted to its decimal equivalent by multiplying each octal digit by its positional weight. For example:

$$372_8 = 3 \times (8^2) + 7 \times (8^1) + 2 \times (8^0)$$
$$= 3 \times 64 + 7 \times 8 + 2 \times 1$$
$$= 250_{10}$$

Another example follows:

$$24.6_8 = 2 \times (8^1) + 4 \times (8^0) + 6 \times (8^{-1})$$
$$= 20.75_{10}$$

Decimal-to-Octal Conversion

A decimal integer can be converted to octal by using the same repeated-division method that we used in the decimal-to-binary conversion (Figure 2-1), but with a division factor of 8 instead of 2. An example is shown below.

$$\frac{266}{8} = \boxed{33} + \text{remainder of } 2$$
$$\frac{\boxed{33}}{8} = 4 + \text{remainder of } 1$$
$$\frac{4}{8} = 0 + \text{remainder of } 4$$
$$266_{10} = \boxed{412}_8$$

Note that the first remainder becomes the least significant digit (LSD) of the octal number, and the last remainder becomes the most significant digit (MSD).

If a calculator is used to perform the divisions in the process above, the result will include a decimal fraction instead of a remainder. The remainder can be obtained, however, by multiplying the decimal fraction by 8. For example, 266/8 produces 33.25. The remainder becomes $0.25 \times 8 = 2$. Similarly, 33/8 will be 4.125, and the remainder becomes $0.125 \times 8 = 1$.

Octal-to-Binary Conversion

The primary advantage of the octal number system is the ease with which conversion can be made between binary and octal numbers. The conversion from octal to binary is performed by converting *each* octal digit to its three-bit binary equivalent. The eight possible digits are converted as indicated in Table 2-1.

TABLE 2-1

Octal Digit	0	1	2	3	4	5	6	7
Binary Equivalent	000	001	010	011	100	101	110	111

Using these conversions, we can convert any octal number to binary by individually converting each digit. For example, we can convert 472_8 to binary as follows:

$$
\begin{array}{ccc}
4 & 7 & 2 \\
\downarrow & \downarrow & \downarrow \\
100 & 111 & 010
\end{array}
$$

Hence, octal 472 is equivalent to binary 100111010. As another example, consider converting 5431_8 to binary:

$$
\begin{array}{cccc}
5 & 4 & 3 & 1 \\
\downarrow & \downarrow & \downarrow & \downarrow \\
101 & 100 & 011 & 001
\end{array}
$$

Thus, $5431_8 = 101100011001_2$.

Binary-to-Octal Conversion

Converting from binary integers to octal integers is simply the reverse of the foregoing process. The bits of the binary number are grouped into groups of *three* bits starting at the LSB. Then each group is converted to its octal equivalent (Table 2-1). To illustrate, consider the conversion of 100111010_2 to octal.

$$
\begin{array}{ccc}
\underline{1\ \ 0\ \ 0} & \underline{1\ \ 1\ \ 1} & \underline{0\ \ 1\ \ 0} \\
\downarrow & \downarrow & \downarrow \\
4 & 7 & 2_8
\end{array}
$$

Sometimes the binary number will not have even groups of three bits. For those cases, we can add one or two 0s to the left of the MSB of the binary number to fill out the last group. This is illustrated below for the binary number 11010110.

$$
\begin{array}{ccc}
\underline{0\ \ 1\ \ 1} & \underline{0\ \ 1\ \ 0} & \underline{1\ \ 1\ \ 0} \\
\downarrow & \downarrow & \downarrow \\
3 & 2 & 6_8
\end{array}
$$

Note that a 0 was placed to the left of the MSB to produce even groups of three bits.

Counting in Octal

The largest octal digit is 7, so that in counting in octal, a digit position is incremented upward from 0 to 7. Once it reaches 7, it recycles to 0 on the next count and causes the next higher digit position to be incremented. This is illustrated in the following sequences of octal counting: **(1)** 65, 66, 67, 70, 71 and **(2)** 275, 276, 277, 300.

With N octal digit positions, we can count from 0 up to $8^N - 1$, for a total of 8^N different counts. For example, with three octal digit positions we can count from 000_8 to 777_8, which is 0_{10} to 511_{10} for a total of $8^3 = 512_{10}$ different octal numbers.

Usefulness of Octal System

The ease with which conversions can be made between octal and binary makes the octal system attractive as a "shorthand" means of expressing large binary numbers. In computer work, binary numbers with up to 64 bits are not uncommon. These binary numbers, as we shall see, do not always represent a numerical quantity but are often some type of code that conveys nonnumerical information. In computers, binary numbers might represent (1) actual numerical data, (2) numbers corresponding to a location (address) in memory, (3) an instruction code, (4) a code representing alphabetic and other nonnumerical characters, or (5) a group of bits representing the status of devices internal or external to the computer.

When dealing with a large quantity of binary numbers of many bits, it is convenient and more efficient for us to write the numbers in octal rather than binary. Keep in mind, however, that the digital circuits and systems work strictly in binary; we are using octal only as a convenience for the operators of the system.

EXAMPLE 2-2

Convert 177_{10} to its eight-bit binary equivalent by first converting to octal.

Solution

$$\frac{177}{8} = 22 + \text{remainder of } 1$$

$$\frac{22}{8} = 2 + \text{remainder of } 6$$

$$\frac{2}{8} = 0 + \text{remainder of } 2$$

Thus, $177_{10} = 261_8$. Now we can convert this octal number to its binary equivalent 010110001_2, so that we finally have

$$177_{10} = 10110001_2$$

Note that we chop off the leading 0 to express the result as eight bits.

This method of decimal-to-octal-to-binary conversion is often quicker than going directly from decimal to binary, especially for large numbers. Similarly, it is often quicker to convert binary to decimal by first converting to octal.

---

1. Convert 614_8 to decimal.
2. Convert 146_{10} to octal, then from octal to binary.
3. Convert 10011101_2 to octal.
4. Write the next three numbers in this octal counting sequence: 624, 625, 626, ___ , ___ , ___ .
5. Convert 975_{10} to binary by first converting to octal.
6. Convert binary 1010111011 to decimal by first converting to octal.
7. What range of decimal values can be represented by a four-digit octal number?

2-4 HEXADECIMAL NUMBER SYSTEM

The **hexadecimal number system** uses base 16. Thus, it has 16 possible digit symbols. It uses the digits 0 through 9 plus the letters A, B, C, D, E, and F as the 16 digit symbols. Table 2-2 shows the relationships among hexadecimal, decimal, and binary. Note that each hexadecimal digit represents a group of four binary digits. It is important to remember that hex (abbreviation for "hexadecimal") digits A through F are equivalent to the decimal values 10 through 15.

TABLE 2-2

Hexadecimal	Decimal	Binary
0	0	0000
1	1	0001
2	2	0010
3	3	0011
4	4	0100
5	5	0101
6	6	0110
7	7	0111
8	8	1000
9	9	1001
A	10	1010
B	11	1011
C	12	1100
D	13	1101
E	14	1110
F	15	1111

Hex-to-Decimal Conversion

A hex number can be converted to its decimal equivalent by using the fact that each hex digit position has a weight that is a power of 16. The LSD has a weight of $16^0 = 1$; the next higher digit position has a weight of $16^1 = 16$; the next has a weight of $16^2 = 256$; and so on. The conversion process is demonstrated in the examples below:

$$356_{16} = 3 \times 16^2 + 5 \times 16^1 + 6 \times 16^0$$
$$= 768 + 80 + 6$$
$$= 854_{10}$$

$$2AF_{16} = 2 \times 16^2 + 10 \times 16^1 + 15 \times 16^0$$
$$= 512 + 160 + 15$$
$$= 687_{10}$$

Note that in the second example the value 10 was substituted for A and the value 15 for F in the conversion to decimal.

For practice, verify that $1BC2_{16}$ is equal to 7106_{10}.

Decimal-to-Hex Conversion

Recall that we did decimal-to-binary conversion using repeated division by 2, and decimal-to-octal using repeated division by 8. Likewise, decimal-to-hex conversion can be done using repeated division by 16 (Figure 2-1). The following two examples will illustrate.

EXAMPLE 2-3

Convert 423_{10} to hex.

Solution

$$\frac{423}{16} = \boxed{26} + \text{remainder of } 7$$

$$\frac{\boxed{26}}{16} = 1 + \text{remainder of } 10$$

$$\frac{1}{16} = 0 + \text{remainder of } 1$$

$$423_{10} = \boxed{1A7}_{16}$$

Convert 214_{10} to hex.

Solution

$$\frac{214}{16} = 13 + \text{remainder of } 6$$

$$\frac{13}{16} = 0 + \text{remainder of } 13$$

$$214_{10} = \boxed{D6_{16}}$$

Again note that the remainders of the division processes form the digits of the hex number. Also note that any remainders that are greater than 9 are represented by the letters A through F.

If a calculator is being used to perform the divisions in the conversion process, the results will include a decimal fraction instead of a remainder. The remainder can be obtained by multiplying the fraction by 16. To illustrate, in Example 2-4 the calculator would have produced

$$\frac{214}{16} = 13.375$$

The remainder becomes $(0.375) \times 16 = 6$.

Hex-to-Binary Conversion

Like the octal number system, the hexadecimal number system is used primarily as a "shorthand" method for representing binary numbers. It is a relatively simple matter to convert a hex number to binary. *Each* hex digit is converted to its four-bit binary equivalent (Table 2-2). This is illustrated below for $9F2_{16}$.

$$9F2_{16} = \quad 9 \qquad\qquad F \qquad\qquad 2$$
$$\qquad\qquad \downarrow \qquad\qquad \downarrow \qquad\qquad \downarrow$$
$$= 1\ 0\ 0\ 1 \quad 1\ 1\ 1\ 1 \quad 0\ 0\ 1\ 0$$
$$= 100111110010_2$$

For practice, verify that $BA6_{16} = 101110100110_2$.

Binary-to-Hex Conversion

Conversion from binary to hex is just the reverse of the process above. The binary number is grouped into groups of *four* bits, and each group is converted to its equivalent hex digit. Zeros are added, as needed, to complete a four-bit group (shown shaded).

$$1\ 1\ 1\ 0\ 1\ 0\ 0\ 1\ 1\ 0_2 = \underbrace{0\ 0\ 1\ 1}_{3}\ \underbrace{1\ 0\ 1\ 0}_{A}\ \underbrace{0\ 1\ 1\ 0}_{6}$$

$$= 3A6_{16}$$

In order to perform these conversions between hex and binary, it is necessary to know the four-bit binary numbers (0000 through 1111) and their equivalent hex digits. Once these are mastered, the conversions can be performed quickly without the need for any calculations. This is why hex (and octal) are so useful in representing large binary numbers.

For practice, verify that $101011111_2 = 15F_{16}$.

Counting in Hexadecimal

When counting in hex, each digit position can be incremented (increased by 1) from 0 to F. Once a digit position reaches the value F, it is reset to 0, and the next digit position is incremented. This is illustrated in the following hex counting sequences:

(a) 38, 39, 3A, 3B, 3C, 3D, 3E, 3F, 40, 41, 42

(b) 6F8, 6F9, 6FA, 6FB, 6FC, 6FD, 6FE, 6FF, 700

Note that when there is a 9 in a digit position, it becomes an A when it is incremented.

With N hex digit positions we can count from decimal 0 to $16^N - 1$, for a total of 16^N different values. For example, with three hex digits we can count from 000_{16} to FFF_{16}, which is 0_{10} to 4095_{10}, for a total of $4096 = 16^3$ different values.

EXAMPLE 2-5

Convert decimal 378 to a 16-bit binary number by first converting to hexadecimal.

Solution

$$\frac{378}{16} = 23 + \text{remainder of } 10$$

$$\frac{23}{16} = 1 + \text{remainder of } 7$$

$$\frac{1}{16} = 0 + \text{remainder of } 1$$

Thus, $378_{10} = 17A_{16}$. This hex value can easily be converted to binary 000101111010. Finally, we can express 378_{10} as a 16-bit number by adding four leading 0s:

$$378_{10} = 0000\ \ 0001\ \ 0111\ \ 1010_2$$

EXAMPLE 2-6

Convert $B2F_{16}$ to octal.

Solution

It's easiest to first convert hex to binary, then to octal.

$$
\begin{aligned}
B2F_{16} &= 1011 \quad 0010 \quad 1111 \qquad \{\text{convert to binary}\} \\
&= \ 101 \quad 100 \quad 101 \quad 111 \quad \{\text{group into three-bit groupings}\} \\
&= \ \ 5 \qquad 4 \qquad 5 \qquad 7_8 \quad \{\text{convert to octal}\}
\end{aligned}
$$

Summary of Conversions

At this point, your head is probably spinning as you try to keep all of these number systems straight—binary, decimal, octal, hex—and all the different conversions from one to another. You may not believe it, but eventually as you use these various systems more and more, you will know them very well. For now, the following summary should help you in doing the different conversions:

1. When converting from binary [or octal or hex] to decimal, use the method of taking the weighted sum of each digit position.

2. When converting from decimal to binary [or octal or hex], use the method of repeatedly dividing by 2 [or 8 or 16] and collecting remainders (Figure 2-1).

3. When converting from binary to octal [or hex], group the bits in groups of three [or four], and convert each group into the correct octal [or hex] digit.

4. When converting from octal [or hex] to binary, convert each digit into its three-bit [or four-bit] equivalent.

5. When converting from octal to hex [or vice versa], first convert to binary; then convert the binary into the desired number system.

Review Questions

1. Convert $24CE_{16}$ to decimal.

2. Convert 3117_{10} to hex, then from hex to binary.

3. Convert 1001011110110101_2 to hex.

4. Write the next four numbers in this hex counting sequence: E9A, E9B, E9C, E9D, ___ , ___ , ___ , ___ .

5. Convert 3527_8 to hex.

6. What range of decimal values can be represented by a four-digit hex number?

2-5 BCD CODE

When numbers, letters, or words are represented by a special group of symbols, we say that they are being encoded, and the group of symbols is called a *code*. Probably one of the most familiar codes is the Morse code, where series of dots and dashes represent letters of the alphabet.

We have seen that any decimal number can be represented by an equivalent binary number. The group of 0s and 1s in the binary number can be thought of as a code representing the decimal number. When a decimal number is represented by its equivalent binary number, we call it **straight binary coding.**

Digital systems all use some form of binary numbers for their internal operation, but the external world is decimal in nature. This means that conversions between the decimal and binary systems are being performed often. We have seen that the conversions between decimal and binary can become long and complicated for large numbers. For this reason, a means of encoding decimal numbers that combines some features of both the decimal and the binary systems is used in certain situations.

Binary-Coded-Decimal Code

If *each* digit of a decimal number is represented by its binary equivalent, the result is a code called **binary-coded-decimal** (hereafter abbreviated BCD). Since a decimal digit can be as large as 9, four bits are required to code each digit (the binary code for 9 is 1001).

To illustrate the BCD code, take a decimal number such as 874. Each *digit* is changed to its binary equivalent as follows:

$$
\begin{array}{cccl}
8 & 7 & 4 & \text{(decimal)} \\
\downarrow & \downarrow & \downarrow & \\
1000 & 0111 & 0100 & \text{(BCD)}
\end{array}
$$

As another example, let us change 943 to its BCD-code representation:

$$
\begin{array}{cccl}
9 & 4 & 3 & \text{(decimal)} \\
\downarrow & \downarrow & \downarrow & \\
1001 & 0100 & 0011 & \text{(BCD)}
\end{array}
$$

Once again, each decimal digit is changed to its straight binary equivalent. Note that four bits are *always* used for each digit.

The BCD code, then, represents each digit of the decimal number by a four-bit binary number. Clearly only the four-bit binary numbers from 0000 through 1001 are used. The BCD code does not use the numbers 1010, 1011, 1100, 1101, 1110, and 1111. In other words, only 10 of the 16 possible four-bit binary code groups are used. If any of the "forbidden" four-bit numbers ever occurs in a machine using the BCD code, it is usually an indication that an error has occurred.

EXAMPLE 2-7

Convert 0110100000111001 (BCD) to its decimal equivalent.

Solution

Divide the BCD number into four-bit groups and convert each to decimal.

$$
\underbrace{0110}_{6} \ \underbrace{1000}_{8} \ \underbrace{0011}_{3} \ \underbrace{1001}_{9}
$$

| EXAMPLE 2-8 | Convert the BCD number 011111000001 to its decimal equivalent. |

Solution

$$\underbrace{0111}_{7} \;\; 1100 \;\; \underbrace{0001}_{1}$$

$$7 \qquad \downarrow \qquad 1$$

The forbidden code group indicates an error in the BCD number.

Comparison of BCD and Binary

It is important to realize that BCD is not another number system like binary, octal, decimal, and hexadecimal. It is, in fact, the decimal system with each digit encoded in its binary equivalent. It is also important to understand that a BCD number is *not* the same as a straight binary number. A straight binary code takes the *complete* decimal number and represents it in binary; the BCD code converts *each* decimal *digit* to binary individually. To illustrate, take the number 137 and compare its straight binary and BCD codes:

$$137_{10} = 10001001_2 \qquad \text{(binary)}$$
$$137_{10} = 0001\ 0011\ 0111 \qquad \text{(BCD)}$$

The BCD code requires 12 bits while the straight binary code requires only eight bits to represent 137. BCD requires more bits than straight binary to represent decimal numbers of more than one digit. This is because BCD does not use all possible four-bit groups, as pointed out earlier, and is therefore somewhat inefficient.

The main advantage of the BCD code is the relative ease of converting to and from decimal. Only the four-bit code groups for the decimal digits 0 through 9 need to be remembered. This ease of conversion is especially important from a hardware standpoint because in a digital system it is the logic circuits that perform the conversions to and from decimal.

| Review Questions | 1. Represent the decimal value 178 by its straight binary equivalent. Then encode the same decimal number using BCD.
2. How many bits are required to represent an eight-digit decimal number in BCD?
3. What is an advantage of encoding a decimal number in BCD as compared with straight binary? What is a disadvantage? |

2-6 PUTTING IT ALL TOGETHER

Table 2-3 gives the representation of the decimal numbers 1 through 15 in the binary, octal, hex number systems, and in BCD code. Examine it carefully and make sure you understand how it was obtained. Especially note how the BCD representation always uses four bits for each decimal digit.

TABLE 2-3

Decimal	Binary	Octal	Hexadecimal	BCD
0	0	0	0	0000
1	1	1	1	0001
2	10	2	2	0010
3	11	3	3	0011
4	100	4	4	0100
5	101	5	5	0101
6	110	6	6	0110
7	111	7	7	0111
8	1000	10	8	1000
9	1001	11	9	1001
10	1010	12	A	0001 0000
11	1011	13	B	0001 0001
12	1100	14	C	0001 0010
13	1101	15	D	0001 0011
14	1110	16	E	0001 0100
15	1111	17	F	0001 0101

2-7 THE BYTE

Most microcomputers handle and store binary data and information in groups of eight bits, so a special name is given to a string of eight bits: it is called a **byte.** A byte always consists of eight bits, and it can represent any of numerous types of data or information. The following examples will illustrate.

EXAMPLE 2-9

How many bytes are in a 32-bit string (a string of 32 bits)?

Solution

32/8 = 4, so there are **four** bytes in a 32-bit string.

EXAMPLE 2-10

What is the largest decimal value that can be represented in binary using two bytes?

Solution

Two bytes is 16 bits, so the largest binary value will be equivalent to decimal $2^{16} - 1 = \mathbf{65,535}$.

| EXAMPLE 2-11 | How many bytes are needed to represent the decimal value 846,569 in BCD? |

Solution

Each decimal digit converts to a four-bit BCD code. Thus, a six-digit decimal number requires 24 bits. These 24 bits are equal to **three** bytes. This is diagrammed below.

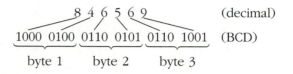

$$\underbrace{8 \quad 4}_{} \quad \underbrace{6 \quad 5}_{} \quad \underbrace{6 \quad 9}_{} \qquad \text{(decimal)}$$
$$\underbrace{1000 \quad 0100}_{\text{byte 1}} \quad \underbrace{0110 \quad 0101}_{\text{byte 2}} \quad \underbrace{0110 \quad 1001}_{\text{byte 3}} \quad \text{(BCD)}$$

| Review Questions | 1. How many bytes are needed to represent 235_{10} in binary? |
| | 2. What is the largest decimal value that can be represented in BCD using two bytes? |

2-8 ALPHANUMERIC CODES

In addition to numerical data, a computer must be able to handle nonnumerical information. In other words, a computer should recognize codes that represent letters of the alphabet, punctuation marks, and other special characters as well as numbers. These codes are called **alphanumeric codes.** A complete alphanumeric code would include the 26 lowercase letters, 26 uppercase letters, 10 numeric digits, 7 punctuation marks, and anywhere from 20 to 40 other characters, such as +, /, #, %, *, and so on. We can say that an alphanumeric code represents all of the various characters and functions that are found on a computer keyboard.

ASCII Code

The most widely used alphanumeric code is the **American Standard Code for Information Interchange (ASCII).** The ASCII code (pronounced "askee") is a seven-bit code, and so it has $2^7 = 128$ possible code groups. This is more than enough to represent all of the standard keyboard characters as well as control functions such as the ⟨RETURN⟩ and ⟨LINEFEED⟩ functions. Table 2-4 shows a partial listing of the ASCII code. In addition to the binary code group for each character, the table gives the octal and hexadecimal equivalents.

TABLE 2-4   Partial listing of ASCII code.

Character	Seven-Bit ASCII	Octal	Hex	Character	Seven-Bit ASCII	Octal	Hex
A	100 0001	101	41	Y	101 1001	131	59
B	100 0010	102	42	Z	101 1010	132	5A
C	100 0011	103	43	0	011 0000	060	30
D	100 0100	104	44	1	011 0001	061	31
E	100 0101	105	45	2	011 0010	062	32
F	100 0110	106	46	3	011 0011	063	33
G	100 0111	107	47	4	011 0100	064	34
H	100 1000	110	48	5	011 0101	065	35
I	100 1001	111	49	6	011 0110	066	36
J	100 1010	112	4A	7	011 0111	067	37
K	100 1011	113	4B	8	011 1000	070	38
L	100 1100	114	4C	9	011 1001	071	39
M	100 1101	115	4D	blank	010 0000	040	20
N	100 1110	116	4E	.	010 1110	056	2E
O	100 1111	117	4F	(	010 1000	050	28
P	101 0000	120	50	+	010 1011	053	2B
Q	101 0001	121	51	$	010 0100	044	24
R	101 0010	122	52	*	010 1010	052	2A
S	101 0011	123	53	)	010 1001	051	29
T	101 0100	124	54	—	010 1101	055	2D
U	101 0101	125	55	/	010 1111	057	2F
V	101 0110	126	56	,	010 1100	054	2C
W	101 0111	127	57	=	011 1101	075	3D
X	101 1000	130	58	⟨RETURN⟩	000 1101	015	0D
				⟨LINEFEED⟩	000 1010	012	0A

EXAMPLE 2-12

The following is a message encoded in ASCII code. What is the message?

1001000 1000101 1001100 1010000

Solution

Convert each seven-bit code to its hex equivalent. The results are

48 45 4C 50

Now locate these hex values in Table 2-4 and determine the character represented by each. The results are

H E L P

The ASCII code is used for the transfer of alphanumeric information between a computer and input/output devices such as video terminals or printers. A computer also uses it internally to store the information that an operator types in at the computer's keyboard. The following example illustrates this.

EXAMPLE 2-13

An operator is typing in a BASIC program at the keyboard of a certain microcomputer. The computer converts each keystroke into its ASCII code and stores the code as a byte in memory. Determine the binary strings that will be entered into memory when the operator types in the following BASIC statement:

GOTO 25

Solution

Locate each character (including the space) in Table 2-4 and record its ASCII code.

G	01000111
O	01001111
T	01010100
O	01001111
(space)	00100000
2	00110010
5	00110101

Note that a 0 was added to the leftmost bit of each ASCII code because the codes must be stored as bytes (eight bits). This adding of an extra bit is called *padding with 0s*.

Review Questions

1. Encode the following message in ASCII code using the hex representation: "COST = $72."

2. The following padded ASCII-coded message is stored in successive memory locations in a computer:

01010011 01010100 01001111 01010000

What is the message?

2-9 PARITY METHOD FOR ERROR DETECTION

The movement of binary data and codes from one location to another is the most frequent operation performed in digital systems. Here are some examples:

■ The transmission of digitized voice over a microwave link
■ The storage of data in and retrieval of data from external memory devices such as magnetic tape and disk

■ The transmission of information from a computer to a remote user terminal or another computer over telephone lines (i.e., using a modem)

Whenever information is transmitted from one device (the transmitter) to another device (the receiver), there is a possibility that errors can occur such that the receiver does not receive the identical information that was sent by the transmitter. The major cause of any transmission errors is *electrical noise,* which consists of spurious fluctuations in voltage or current that are present in all electronic systems to varying degrees. Figure 2-2 is a simple illustration of a type of transmission error.

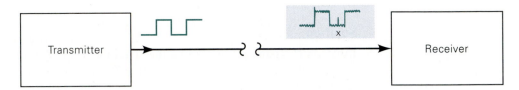

FIGURE 2-2   Example of noise causing an error in the transmission of digital data.

The transmitter sends a relatively noise-free serial digital signal over a signal line to a receiver. However, by the time the signal reaches the receiver, it contains a certain degree of noise superimposed on the original signal. Occasionally, the noise is large enough in amplitude that it will alter the logic level of the signal as it does at point *x.* When this occurs, the receiver may incorrectly interpret that bit as a logic 1, which is not what the transmitter has sent.

Most modern digital equipment is designed to be relatively error-free, and the probability of errors such as shown in Figure 2-2 is very low. However, we must realize that digital systems often transmit thousands, even millions, of bits per second, so that even a very low rate of occurrence of errors can produce an occasional error that might prove to be bothersome, if not disastrous. For this reason, many digital systems employ some method for detection (and sometimes correction) of errors. One of the simplest and most widely used schemes for error detection is the **parity method.**

Parity Bit

A **parity bit** is an extra bit that is attached to a code group that is being transferred from one location to another. The parity bit is made either 0 or 1, depending on the number of 1s that are contained in the code group. Two different methods are used.

In the *even-parity* method, the value of the parity bit is chosen so that the total number of 1s in the code group (including the parity bit) is an *even* number. For example, suppose that the group is 1000011. This is the ASCII character "C." The code group has *three* 1s. Therefore, we will add a parity bit of 1 to make the total number of 1s an even number. The *new* code group, including the parity bit, thus becomes

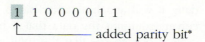

added parity bit*

If the code group contains an even number of 1s to begin with, the parity bit is given a value of 0. For example, if the code group were 1000001 (the ASCII code for "A"), the assigned parity bit would be 0, so that the new code, including the parity bit, would be 01000001.

The *odd-parity* method is used in exactly the same way except that the parity bit is chosen so the total number of 1s (including the parity bit) is an *odd* number. For example, for the code group 1000001, the assigned parity bit would be a 1. For the code group 1000011, the parity bit would be a 0.

Regardless of whether even parity or odd parity is used, the parity bit becomes an actual part of the code word. For example, adding a parity bit to the seven-bit ASCII code produces an eight-bit code. Thus, the parity bit is treated just like any other bit in the code.

The parity bit is issued to detect any *single-bit* errors that occur during the transmission of a code from one location to another (e.g., from a computer to a video terminal). For example, suppose that the character "A" is being transmitted and *odd* parity is being used. The transmitted code would be

1 1 0 0 0 0 0 1

When the receiver circuit receives this code, it will check that the code contains an odd number of 1s (including the parity bit). If so, the receiver will assume that the code has been correctly received. Now, suppose that because of some noise or malfunction the receiver actually receives the following code:

1 1 0 0 0 0 0 0

The receiver will find that this code has an *even* number of 1s. This tells the receiver that there must be an error in the code, since presumably the transmitter and receiver have agreed to use odd parity. There is no way, however, that the receiver can tell which bit is in error, since it does not know what the code is supposed to be.

It should be apparent that this parity method would not work if *two* bits were in error, because two errors would not change the "oddness" or "evenness" of the number of 1s in the code. In practice, the parity method is used only in situations where the probability of a single error is very low and the probability of double errors is essentially zero.

When the parity method is being used, the transmitter and the receiver must have agreement, in advance, as to whether odd or even parity is being used. There is no advantage of one over the other, although even parity seems to be used more often. The transmitter must attach an appropriate parity bit to each unit of information that it transmits. For example, if the transmitter is sending ASCII-coded

---

* The parity bit can be placed at either end of the code group but is usually placed to the left of the MSB.

data, it will attach a parity bit to each seven-bit ASCII code group. When the receiver examines the data that it has received from the transmitter, it checks each code group to see that the total number of 1s (including the parity bit) is consistent with the agreed-upon type of parity. This is often called *checking the parity* of the data. In the event that it detects an error, the receiver may send a message back to the transmitter asking it to retransmit the last set of data. The exact procedure that is followed when an error is detected will depend on the particular system design.

EXAMPLE 2-14

Computers often communicate with other remote computers over the telephone lines. For example, this is how communication over the Internet takes place. When one computer is transmitting a message to another, the information is usually encoded in ASCII. What actual bit strings would a computer transmit to send the message HELLO, using ASCII with even parity?

Solution

First look up the ASCII codes for each character in the message. Then for each code, count the number of 1s. If it is an even number, attach a 0 as the MSB. If it is an odd number, attach a 1. Thus, the resulting eight-bit codes (bytes) will all have an even number of 1s (including parity).

	attached even-parity bits
H-	0 1 0 0 1 0 0 0
E-	1 1 0 0 0 1 0 1
L-	1 1 0 0 1 1 0 0
L-	1 1 0 0 1 1 0 0
O-	1 1 0 0 1 1 1 1

Review Questions

1. Attach an odd-parity bit to the ASCII code for the $ symbol, and express the result in hexadecimal.
2. Attach an even-parity bit to the BCD code for decimal 69.
3. Why can't the parity method detect a double error in transmitted data?

2-10 REVIEW

By way of review, here are some more examples illustrating the operations covered in this chapter.

**EXAMPLE
2-15**

(a) Convert decimal 135 to binary.

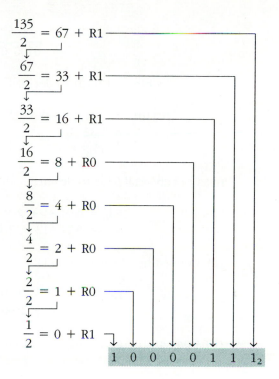

$$\frac{135}{2} = 67 + R1$$

$$\frac{67}{2} = 33 + R1$$

$$\frac{33}{2} = 16 + R1$$

$$\frac{16}{2} = 8 + R0$$

$$\frac{8}{2} = 4 + R0$$

$$\frac{4}{2} = 2 + R0$$

$$\frac{2}{2} = 1 + R0$$

$$\frac{1}{2} = 0 + R1$$

$$1\ 0\ 0\ 0\ 0\ 1\ 1\ 1_2$$

(b) Convert decimal 76 to octal.

$$\frac{76}{8} = 9 + R4$$

$$\frac{9}{8} = 1 + R1$$

$$\frac{1}{8} = 0 + R1$$

$$1\ 1\ 4_8$$

(c) Convert decimal 541 to hexadecimal.

$$\frac{541}{16} = 33 + R13$$

$$\frac{33}{16} = 2 + R1$$

$$\frac{2}{16} = 0 + R2$$

$$2\ 1\ D_{16}$$

(d) Convert decimal 479 to BCD.

$$
\begin{array}{ccc}
4 & 7 & 9 \\
\downarrow & \downarrow & \downarrow \\
\overline{0100} & \overline{0111} & \overline{1001} \quad \text{BCD}
\end{array}
$$

(e) Convert binary 101101 to decimal.

$$
\begin{aligned}
101101_2 &= 1 \times 2^5 + 0 \times 2^4 + 1 \times 2^3 + 1 \times 2^2 + 0 \times 2^1 + 1 \times 2^0 \\
&= 32 + 8 + 4 + 1 \\
&= 45_{10}
\end{aligned}
$$

(f) Convert octal 6254 to decimal.

$$
\begin{aligned}
6254_8 &= 6 \times 8^3 + 2 \times 8^2 + 5 \times 8^1 + 4 \times 8^0 \\
&= 6 \times 512 + 2 \times 64 + 5 \times 8 + 4 \times 1 = 3244_{10}
\end{aligned}
$$

(g) Convert hex 1A3F to decimal.

$$
\begin{aligned}
1A3F &= 1 \times 16^3 + 10 \times 16^2 + 3 \times 16^1 + 15 \times 16^0 \\
&= 4096 + 2560 + 48 + 15 = 6719_{10}
\end{aligned}
$$

(h) Convert 010010010110 (BCD) to decimal.

$$
\begin{array}{ccc}
\underline{0100} & \underline{1001} & \underline{0110} \quad \text{(BCD)} \\
4 & 9 & 6_{10}
\end{array}
$$

(i) Convert binary 10110111 to octal and hex.

$$
\begin{array}{ccc}
\underline{010} & \underline{110} & \underline{111} \\
2 & 6 & 7_8 \\
\underline{1011} & \underline{0111} & \\
B & 7_{16} &
\end{array}
$$

(j) Convert hexadecimal E61 to binary.

$$
\begin{array}{ccc}
E & 6 & 1 \\
\downarrow & \downarrow & \downarrow \\
\overline{1110} & \overline{0110} & \overline{0001}_2
\end{array}
$$

(k) Convert octal 724 to binary.

$$
\begin{array}{ccc}
7 & 2 & 4 \\
\downarrow & \downarrow & \downarrow \\
\overline{111} & \overline{010} & \overline{100}_2
\end{array}
$$

(l) Add an odd parity bit to the ASCII code for "Z."

From Table 2-4, the code for "Z" is 1011010. The number of 1s in this code group is four, an even number. Therefore, to achieve odd parity, we have to attach a 1 as a parity bit (MSB) as follows:

1 1011010

Note that the complete code group—including the parity bit—now has an odd number of 1s.

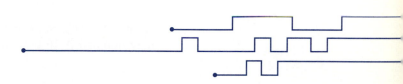

SUMMARY

1. The octal and hexadecimal number systems are used in digital systems and computers as efficient ways of representing binary quantities.

2. In conversions between octal and binary, one octal digit corresponds to three bits. In conversions between hex and binary, each hex digit corresponds to four bits.

3. The repeated-division method is used to convert decimal numbers to binary, octal, or hexadecimal.

4. Using an N-bit binary number, we can represent decimal values from 0 to $2^N - 1$.

5. The BCD code for a decimal number is formed by converting each digit of the decimal number to its four-bit binary equivalent.

6. A byte is a string of eight bits.

7. An alphanumeric code is one that uses groups of bits to represent all of the various characters and functions that are part of a typical computer's keyboard. The ASCII code is the most widely used alphanumeric code.

8. The parity method for error detection attaches a special parity bit to each transmitted group of bits.

IMPORTANT TERMS*

octal number system
hexadecimal number
   system
straight binary coding
binary-coded-decimal
   (BCD) code

byte
alphanumeric code
American Standard Code
   for Information
   Interchange (ASCII)

parity method
parity bit

---

* These terms can be found in **boldface** type in the chapter and are defined in the Glossary at the end of the book.

PROBLEMS

SECTIONS 2-1 AND 2-2

2-1. Convert these binary numbers to decimal.
 (a) 10110
 (b) 10001101
 (c) 100100001001
 (d) 1111010111
 (e) 10111111

2-2. Convert the following decimal values to binary.
 (a) 37
 (b) 14
 (c) 189
 (d) 205
 (e) 2313
 (f) 511

2-3. What is the largest decimal value that can be represented by an eight-bit binary number? A 16-bit number?

SECTION 2-3

2-4. Convert each octal number to its decimal equivalent.
 (a) 743
 (b) 36
 (c) 3777
 (d) 257
 (e) 1204

2-5. Convert each of the following decimal numbers to octal.
 (a) 59
 (b) 372
 (c) 919
 (d) 65,536
 (e) 255

2-6. Convert each of the octal values from Problem 2-4 to binary.

2-7. Convert the binary numbers in Problem 2-1 to octal.

2-8. List the octal numbers in sequence from 165_8 to 200_8.

2-9. When a large decimal number is to be converted to binary, it is sometimes easier to convert it first to octal, and then from octal to binary. Try this procedure for 2313_{10} and compare it with the procedure used in Problem 2-2(e).

2-10. How many octal digits are required to represent decimal numbers up to 20,000?

SECTION 2-4

2-11. Convert these hex values to decimal.
 (a) 92
 (b) 1A6
 (c) 37FD
 (d) 2C0
 (e) 7FF

2-12. Convert these decimal values to hex.
 (a) 75
 (b) 314
 (c) 2048
 (d) 25,619
 (e) 4095

2-13. Convert the binary numbers in Problem 2-1 to hexadecimal.

2-14. Convert the hex values in Problem 2-11 to binary.

2-15. List the hex numbers in sequence from 280 to 2A0.

2-16. How many hex digits are required to represent decimal numbers up to 1 million?

SECTION 2-5

2-17. Encode these decimal numbers in BCD.

(a) 47

(b) 962

(c) 187

(d) 42,689,627

(e) 1204

2-18. How many bits are required to represent the decimal numbers in the range from 0 to 999 using straight binary code? Using BCD code?

2-19. The following numbers are in BCD. Convert them to decimal.

(a) 1001011101010010

(b) 000110000100

(c) 0111011101110101

(d) 010010010010

SECTION 2-7

2-20. (a) How many bits are contained in eight bytes?

(b) What is the largest hex number that can be represented in four bytes?

(c) What is the largest BCD-encoded decimal value that can be represented in three bytes?

SECTIONS 2-8 AND 2-9

2-21. Represent the statement "X = 25/Y" in ASCII code (excluding quotes). Attach an odd-parity bit.

2-22. Attach an *even*-parity bit to each of the ASCII codes for Problem 2-21, and give the results in hex.

2-23. The following bytes (shown in hex) represent a person's name as it would be stored in a computer's memory. Each byte is a padded ASCII code. Determine the name of the person.

42   45   4E   20   53   4D   49   54   48

2-24. Convert the following decimal numbers to BCD code and then attach an *odd*-parity bit.

(a) 74

(b) 38

(c) 165

(d) 9201

2-25. In a certain digital system, the decimal numbers from 000 through 999 are represented in BCD code. An *odd*-parity bit is also included at the end of each code group. Examine each of the code groups below, and assume that each one has just been transferred from one location to another. Some of the groups contain errors. Assume that *no more than* two errors have occurred for each group. Determine which of the code groups have a single error and which of them *definitely* have a double error. (*Hint:* Remember that this is a BCD code.)

(a) 1001010110000

           ↑_____ parity bit

(b) 0100011101100

(c) 0111110000011

(d) 1000011000101

2-26. Suppose that the receiver received the following data from the transmitter of Example 2-14:

$$
\begin{array}{cccccccc}
0 & 1 & 0 & 0 & 1 & 0 & 0 & 0 \\
1 & 1 & 0 & 0 & 0 & 1 & 0 & 1 \\
1 & 1 & 0 & 0 & 1 & 1 & 0 & 0 \\
1 & 1 & 0 & 0 & 1 & 0 & 0 & 0 \\
1 & 1 & 0 & 0 & 1 & 1 & 0 & 0 \\
\end{array}
$$

What errors can the receiver determine in these received data?

DRILL QUESTIONS

2-27. Perform each of the following conversions. For some of them, you may want to try several methods to see which one works best for you. For example, a binary-to-decimal conversion may be done directly, or it may be done as a binary-to-octal conversion followed by an octal-to-decimal conversion.

(a) $1417_{10} = $ _____ $_2$

(b) $255_{10} = $ _____ $_2$

(c) 11010001_2 _____ $_{10}$

(d) $1110101000100111_2 = $ _____ $_{10}$

(e) $2497_{10} = $ _____ $_8$

(f) $511_{10} = $ _____ $_8$

(g) $235_8 = $ _____ $_{10}$

(h) $4316_8 = $ _____ $_{10}$

(i) $7A9_{16} = $ _____ $_{10}$

(j) $3E1C_{16} = $ _____ $_{10}$

(k) $1600_{10} = $ _____ $_{16}$

(l) $38,187_{10} = $ _____ $_{16}$

(m) $865_{10} = $ _____ (BCD)

(n) 100101000111 (BCD) $= $ _____ $_{10}$

(o) $465_8 = $ _____ $_{16}$

(p) $B34_{16} = $ _____ $_8$

(q) 01110100(BCD) $= $ _____ $_2$

(r) $111010_2 = $ _____ (BCD)

2-28. Represent the decimal value 37 in each of the following ways.

(a) straight binary   (c) hex   (e) octal

(b) BCD   (d) ASCII (i.e., treat each digit as a character)

2-29. Fill in the blanks with the correct word or words.

(a) Conversion from decimal to _____ requires repeated division by 8.

(b) Conversion from decimal to hex requires repeated division by _____ .

(c) In the BCD code, each _____ is converted to its four-bit binary equivalent.

(d) The _____ code has the characteristic that only one bit changes in going from one step to the next.

(e) A transmitter attaches a _____ to a code group to allow the receiver to detect _____ .

(f) The _____ code is the most common alphanumeric code used in computer systems.

(g) _____ and _____ are often used as a convenient way to represent large binary numbers.

(h) A string of eight bits is called a _____ .

2-30. Write the binary number that results when each of the following numbers is incremented by one.

(a) 0111　　(b) 010000　　(c) 1110

2-31. Repeat Problem 2-30 for the decrement operation.

2-32. Write the number that results when each of the following is incremented.

(a) 7777_8　　(c) 2000_8　　(e) $9FF_{16}$

(b) 7777_{16}　　(d) 2000_{16}　　(f) 1000_{16}

2-33. Repeat Problem 2-32 for the decrement operation.

CHALLENGING EXERCISES

2-34. In a microcomputer the *addresses* of memory locations are binary numbers that identify each memory circuit where a byte is stored. The number of bits that make up an address will depend on how many memory locations there are. Since the number of bits can be very large, the addresses are often specified in hex instead of binary.

(a) If a microcomputer uses a 20-bit address, how many different memory locations are there?

(b) How many hex digits are needed to represent the address of a memory location?

(c) What is the hex address of the 256th memory location? (*Note:* the first address is always 0.)

2-35. In an audio CD, the audio voltage signal is typically sampled about 44,000 times per second, and the value of each sample is recorded on the CD surface as a binary number. In other words, each recorded binary number represents a single voltage point on the audio signal waveform.

(a) If the binary numbers are six bits in length, how many different voltage values can be represented by a single binary number? Repeat for eight bits and ten bits.

(b) If ten-bit numbers are used, how many bits will be recorded on the CD in 1 second?

(c) If a CD can typically store 5 billion bits, how many seconds of audio can be recorded when ten-bit numbers are used?

2-36. A black-and-white electronic camera lays a fine grid over an image and then measures and records a binary number representing the level of gray it sees in each cell of the grid. For example, if four-bit numbers are used, the value of black is set to 0000 and the value of white to 1111, and any level of gray is somewhere between 0000 and 1111. If six-bit numbers are used, black is 000000, white is 111111, and all grays are in between.

Suppose we wanted to distinguish between 254 different levels of gray within each cell of the grid. How many bits would we need to use to represent these levels?

2-37. Construct a table showing the binary, octal, hex, and BCD representations of all decimal numbers from 0 to 15. Compare your table with Table 2-3.

ANSWERS TO SECTION REVIEW QUESTIONS

SECTION 2-1
1. 2267   2. 32768

SECTION 2-2
1. 1010011   2. 1011011001   3. 20 bits

SECTION 2-3
1. 396   2. 222; 010010010   3. 235   4. 627, 630, 631   5. 1111001111   6. 699   7. 0 to 4095

SECTION 2-4
1. 9422   2. C2D; 110000101101   3. 97B5
4. E9E, E9F, EA0, EA1   5. 757   6. 0 to 65,535

SECTION 2-5
1. 10110010_2; 000101111000 (BCD)   2. 32
3. Advantage: ease of conversion. Disadvantage: BCD requires more bits.

SECTION 2-7
1. Two   2. 99

SECTION 2-8
1. 43, 4F, 53, 54, 20, 3D, 20, 24, 37, 32   2. STOP

SECTION 2-9
1. A4   2. 001101001   3. Two errors in the data would not change the oddness or evenness of the number of 1s in the data.

Logic Gates and Boolean Algebra

■ OUTLINE

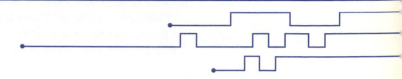

◼ OBJECTIVES

Upon completion of this chapter, you will be able to:

- ◼ Perform the three basic logic operations.
- ◼ Describe the operation of and construct the truth tables for the AND, NAND, OR, and NOR gates, and the NOT (INVERTER) circuit.
- ◼ Draw timing diagrams for the various logic-circuit gates.
- ◼ Write the Boolean expression for the logic gates and combinations of logic gates.
- ◼ Implement logic circuits using basic AND, OR, and NOT gates.
- ◼ Appreciate the potential of Boolean algebra to simplify complex logic circuits.
- ◼ Use DeMorgan's theorems to simplify logic expressions.
- ◼ Use either of the universal gates (NAND or NOR) to implement a circuit represented by a Boolean expression.
- ◼ Explain the advantages of constructing a logic-circuit diagram using the alternate gate symbols versus the standard logic-gate symbols.
- ◼ Describe the concept of active-LOW and active-HIGH logic signals.
- ◼ Draw and interpret logic circuits that use the IEEE/ANSI standard logic-gate symbols.

◼ INTRODUCTION

As pointed out in Chapter 1, digital (logic) circuits operate in the binary mode where each input and output voltage is either a 0 or a 1; the 0 and 1 designations represent predefined voltage ranges. This characteristic of logic circuits allows us to use **Boolean algebra** as a tool for the analysis and design of digital systems. Boolean algebra is a relatively simple mathematical tool that allows us to describe the relationship between a logic circuit's output(s) and its inputs as an algebraic equation (a Boolean expression). In this chapter we will study the most basic logic circuits—*logic gates*—which are the fundamental building blocks from which all other logic circuits and digital systems are constructed. We will see how the operation of the different logic gates and the more complex circuits formed from combinations of logic gates can be described and analyzed using Boolean algebra. We will also get a glimpse of how Boolean algebra can be used to simplify a circuit's Boolean expression so that the circuit can be rebuilt using fewer logic gates and/or fewer connections. Much more will be done with circuit simplification in Chapter 4.

Boolean algebra is also a valuable tool for coming up with a logic circuit that will produce a desired input/output relationship. We will introduce the basic idea in this chapter and will cover it more thoroughly under logic circuit design in Chapter 4.

Since Boolean algebra expresses a circuit's operation in the form of an algebraic equation, it is ideal for inputting the operation of a logic circuit into a computer that is running software that needs to know what the circuit looks like. The software may be a circuit simplification routine that takes the input Boolean algebra equation, simplifies it, and comes up with a simplified version of the original logic circuit. Another application would be the software that is used to generate the fuse maps needed to program a PLD (programmable logic device). The operator punches in the Boolean equations for the desired circuit operation, and the software converts it to a fuse map. We will study this process in detail in Chapter 12.

Clearly, Boolean algebra is an invaluable tool in describing, analyzing, designing, and implementing digital circuits. The student who expects to work in the digital realm is encouraged to work hard at understanding and becoming comfortable with Boolean algebra (believe us, it's much, much easier than conventional algebra). Do *all* of the examples, exercises, and problems, even the ones your instructor doesn't assign. When those run out, make up your own. The time you spend will be well worth it as you see your skills improve and your confidence grow.

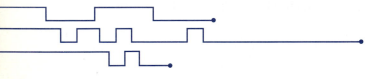

3-1 BOOLEAN CONSTANTS AND VARIABLES

Boolean algebra differs in a major way from ordinary algebra in that Boolean constants and variables are allowed to have only two possible values, 0 or 1. A Boolean variable is a quantity that may, at different times, be equal to either 0 or 1. Boolean variables are often used to represent the voltage level present on a wire or at the input/output terminals of a circuit. For example, in a certain digital system the Boolean value of 0 might be assigned to any voltage in the range from 0 to 0.8 V while the Boolean value of 1 might be assigned to any voltage in the range 2 to 5 V.*

---

* Voltages between 0.8 and 2 V are undefined (neither 0 nor 1) and under normal circumstances should not occur.

Thus, Boolean 0 and 1 do not present actual numbers but instead represent the state of a voltage variable, or what is called its **logic level.** A voltage in a digital circuit is said to be at the logic level 0 or the logic level 1, depending on its actual numerical value. In digital logic several other terms are used synonymously with 0 and 1. Some of the more common ones are shown in Table 3-1. We will use the 0/1 and LOW/HIGH designations most of the time.

TABLE 3-1

Logic 0	Logic 1
False	True
Off	On
Low	High
No	Yes
Open switch	Closed switch

As we said in the introduction, Boolean algebra is a means for expressing the relationship between a logic circuit's inputs and outputs. The inputs are considered logic variables whose logic levels at any time determine the output levels. In all our work to follow, we shall use letter symbols to represent logic variables. For example, A might represent a certain digital circuit input or output, and at any time we must have either $A = 0$ or $A = 1$: if not one, then the other.

Because only two values are possible, Boolean algebra is relatively easy to work with as compared with ordinary algebra. In Boolean algebra there are no fractions, decimals, negative numbers, square roots, cube roots, logarithms, imaginary numbers, and so on. In fact, in Boolean algebra there are only *three* basic operations: *OR, AND,* and *NOT.*

These basic operations are called *logic operations.* Digital circuits called *logic gates* can be constructed from diodes, transistors, and resistors connected in such a way that the circuit output is the result of a basic logic operation *(OR, AND, NOT)* performed on the inputs. We will be using Boolean algebra first to describe and analyze these basic logic gates, then later to analyze and design combinations of logic gates connected as logic circuits.

3-2 TRUTH TABLES

A **truth table** is a means for describing how a logic circuit's output depends on the logic levels present at the circuit's inputs. Figure 3-1(a) illustrates a truth table for one type of two-input logic circuit. The table lists all possible combinations of logic levels present at inputs A and B along with the corresponding output level x. The first entry in the table shows that when A and B are both at the 0 level, the output x is at the 1 level or, equivalently, in the 1 state. The second entry shows that when input B is changed to the 1 state, so that $A = 0$ and $B = 1$, the output x becomes a 0. In a similar way, the table shows what happens to the output state for any set of input conditions.

Figures 3-1(b) and (c) show samples of truth tables for three- and four-input logic circuits. Again, each table lists all possible combinations of input logic levels on the left, with the resultant logic level for output x on the right. Of course, the actual values for x will depend on the type of logic circuit.

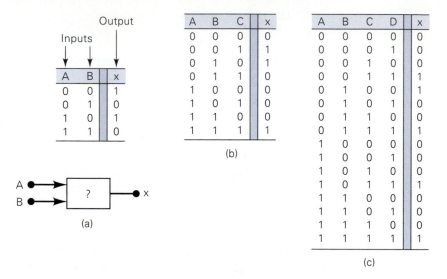

FIGURE 3-1 Example truth tables for (a) two-input, (b) three-input, and (c) four-input circuits.

Note that there are 4 table entries for the two-input truth table, 8 entries for a three-input truth table, and 16 entries for the four-input truth table. The number of input combinations will equal 2^N for an N-input truth table. Also note that the list of all possible input combinations follows the binary counting sequence, and so it is an easy matter to write down all of the combinations without missing any.

Review Questions

1. What is the output state of the four-input circuit represented in Figure 3-1(c) when all inputs are 1?
2. Repeat question 1 for the following input conditions: $A = 1, B = 0, C = 1, D = 0$.
3. How many table entries are needed for a five-input circuit?

3-3 OR OPERATION WITH OR GATES

The **OR operation** is the first of the three basic Boolean operations to be learned. The truth table in Figure 3-2(a) shows what happens when two logic inputs, A and B, are combined using the OR operation to produce the output x. The table shows that x is a logic 1 for every combination of input levels where one *or* more inputs are 1. The only case where x is a 0 is when both inputs are 0.

The Boolean expression for the OR operation is

$$x = A + B$$

In this expression, the + sign does not stand for ordinary addition; it stands for the OR operation. The OR operation is similar to ordinary addition except for the case

FIGURE 3-2 (a) Truth table
defining the OR operation; (b)
circuit symbol for a two-input OR
gate.

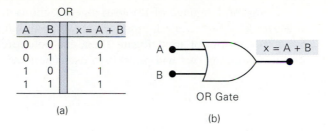

OR

A	B	x = A + B
0	0	0
0	1	1
1	0	1
1	1	1

(a)

OR Gate

(b)

where A and B are both 1; the OR operation produces $1 + 1 = 1$, not $1 + 1 = 2$. In Boolean algebra, 1 is as high as we go, so we can never have a result greater than 1. The same holds true for combining three inputs using the OR operation. Here we have $x = A + B + C$. If we consider the case where all three inputs are 1, we have

$$x = 1 + 1 + 1 = 1$$

Again, the result of performing the OR operation (ORing) when more than one input is a 1 is *always* a 1.

The expression $x = A + B$ is read as "x equals A OR B." The key thing to remember is that the + sign stands for the OR operation as defined by the truth table in Figure 3-2(a), and not for ordinary addition.

OR Gate

In digital circuitry an **OR gate*** is a circuit that has two or more inputs and whose output is equal to the OR combination of the inputs. Figure 3-2(b) is the logic symbol for a two-input OR gate. The inputs A and B are logic voltage levels, and the output x is a logic voltage level whose value is the result of the OR operation on A and B; that is, $x = A + B$. In other words, the OR gate operates in such a way that its output is HIGH (logic 1) if either input A *or B or both* are at a logic 1 level. The OR gate output will be LOW (logic 0) only if all its inputs are at logic 0.

This same idea can be extended to more than two inputs. Figure 3-3 shows a three-input OR gate and its truth table. Examination of this truth table shows again that the output will be 1 for every case where one or more inputs are 1. This general principle is the same for OR gates with any number of inputs.

FIGURE 3-3 Symbol and truth
table for a three-input OR gate.

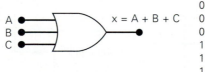

A	B	C	x = A + B + C
0	0	0	0
0	0	1	1
0	1	0	1
0	1	1	1
1	0	0	1
1	0	1	1
1	1	0	1
1	1	1	1

---

* The term *gate* derives from the inhibit/enable operation discussed in Chapter 4.

Using the language of Boolean algebra, the output x can be expressed as $x = A + B + C$, where again it must be emphasized that the + represents the OR operation. The output of any OR gate, then, can be expressed as the OR combination of its various inputs. We will put this to use when we subsequently analyze logic circuits.

Summary of the OR Operation

The important points to remember concerning the OR operation and OR gates are:

1. The OR operation produces a result of 1 when *any* of the input variables is 1.
2. The OR operation produces a result of 0 *only* when all the input variables are 0.
3. With the OR operation, $1 + 1 = 1$, $1 + 1 + 1 = 1$, and so on.
4. The OR gate is a logic circuit that performs the OR operation on the circuit's logic inputs.

EXAMPLE 3-1

In many industrial control systems it is required to activate an output function whenever any one of several inputs is activated. For example, in a chemical process it may be desired that an alarm be activated whenever the process temperature exceeds a maximum value *or* whenever the pressure goes above a certain limit. Figure 3-4 is a block diagram of this situation. The temperature transducer circuit produces an output voltage proportional to the process temperature. This voltage, V_T, is compared with a temperature reference voltage, V_{TR}, in a voltage comparator circuit. The comparator output is normally a low voltage (logic 0), but it switches to a high voltage (logic 1) when V_T exceeds V_{TR}, indicating that the process temperature is excessive. A similar arrangement is used for the pressure measurement, so that its associated comparator output goes from low to high when the pressure is excessive.

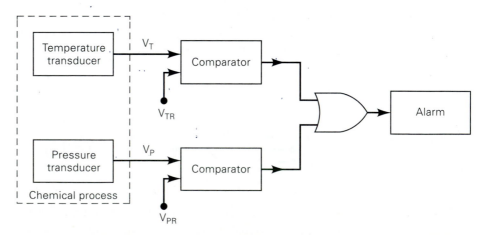

FIGURE 3-4   Example of the use of an OR gate in an alarm system.

Since we want the alarm to be activated when either temperature *or* pressure is too high, it should be apparent that the two comparator outputs can be fed to a two-input OR gate. The OR gate output thus goes HIGH (1) for either alarm condition and will activate the alarm. This same idea can obviously be extended to situations with more than two process variables.

EXAMPLE 3-2	Determine the OR gate output in Figure 3-5. The OR gate inputs *A* and *B* are varying according to the timing diagrams shown. For example, *A* starts out LOW at time t_0, goes HIGH at t_1, back LOW at t_3, and so on.

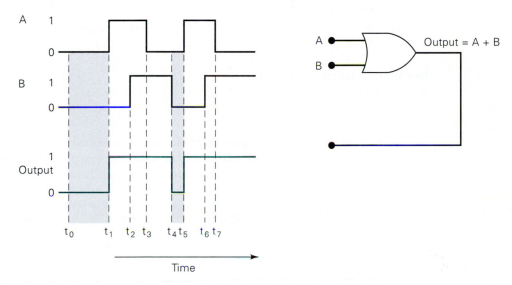

FIGURE 3-5 Example 3-2.

Solution

The OR gate output is determined by realizing that it will be HIGH whenever *any* input is at the high level. When *A* goes HIGH at t_1, OUTPUT will go HIGH. OUTPUT will stay HIGH until t_4, when both inputs are LOW. Note that the changes in the input levels that occur at t_2 and t_3 have no effect on OUTPUT, since one of the inputs remains at the HIGH level while the other is changing. As long as one input to an OR gate is HIGH, the output will stay HIGH regardless of what is happening at the other inputs. The same reasoning is used to determine the rest of the timing diagram for OUTPUT.

EXAMPLE 3-3A	For the situation depicted in Figure 3-6, determine the waveform at the OR gate output.

Solution

The three OR gate inputs *A, B,* and *C* are varying, as shown by their waveform diagrams. The OR gate output is determined by realizing that it will be high whenever *any* of the three inputs is at a high level. Using this reasoning, the OR output

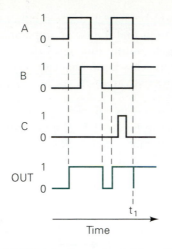

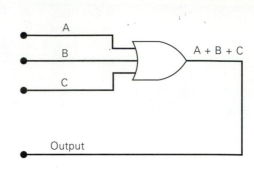

FIGURE 3-6 Examples 3-3A and B.

waveform is as shown in the figure. Particular attention should be paid to what occurs at time t_1. The diagram shows that at that instant of time, input A is going from high to low while input B is going from low to high. Since these inputs are making their transitions at approximately the same time, and since these transitions take a certain amount of time, there is a short interval when these OR gate inputs are both in the undefined range between 0 and 1. When this occurs, the OR gate output also becomes a value in this range, as evidenced by the glitch or spike on the output waveform at t_1. The occurrence of this glitch and its size (amplitude and width) depend on the speed with which the input transitions occur.

EXAMPLE 3-3B

What would happen to the glitch in the output in Figure 3-6 if input C sat in the HIGH state while A and B were changing at time t_1?

Solution

With the C input HIGH at t_1, the OR gate output will remain HIGH regardless of what is occurring at the other inputs, because any HIGH input will keep an OR gate output HIGH. Therefore, the glitch will not appear in the output.

Review Questions

1. What is the only set of input conditions that will produce a LOW output for any OR gate?

2. Write the Boolean expression for a six-input OR gate.

3. If the A input in Figure 3-6 is permanently kept at the 1 level, what will the resultant output waveform be?

3-4 AND OPERATION WITH AND GATES

The **AND operation** is the second basic Boolean operation. The truth table in Figure 3-7(a) shows what happens when two logic inputs, A and B, are combined using the AND operation to produce output x. The table shows that x is a logic 1 only when both A and B are at the logic 1 level. For any case where one of the inputs is 0, the output is 0.

FIGURE 3-7 (a) Truth table for the AND operation; (b) AND gate symbol.

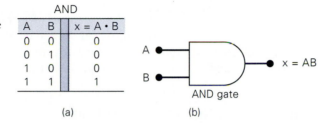

AND		
A	B	$x = A \cdot B$
0	0	0
0	1	0
1	0	0
1	1	1

(a)

(b)

The Boolean expression for the AND operation is

$$x = A \cdot B$$

In this expression the · sign stands for the Boolean AND operation and not the multiplication operation. However, the AND operation on Boolean variables operates the same as ordinary multiplication, as examination of the truth table shows, so we can think of them as being the same. This characteristic can be helpful when evaluating logic expressions that contain AND operations.

The expression $x = A \cdot B$ is read as "$x = A$ AND B." The · sign is usually omitted so that the expression simply becomes $x = AB$. The key thing to remember is that the AND operation will produce a result of 1 *only when* all inputs (variables) are 1, just like ordinary multiplication. This, of course, holds true for more than two inputs. For example, when three inputs are ANDed, we have $x = A \cdot B \cdot C = ABC$. The only time x can be a 1 is when $A = B = C = 1$.

AND Gate

The logic symbol for a two-input **AND gate** is shown in Figure 3-7(b). The AND gate output is equal to the AND product of the logic inputs; that is, $x = AB$. In other words, the AND gate is a circuit that operates in such a way that its output is HIGH only when all its inputs are HIGH. For all other cases the AND gate output is LOW.

This same operation is characteristic of AND gates with more than two inputs. For example, a three-input AND gate and its accompanying truth table are shown in Figure 3-8. Once again, note that the gate output is 1 only for the case where $A = B = C = 1$. The expression for the output is $x = ABC$. For a four-input AND gate, the output is $x = ABCD,$ and so on.

FIGURE 3-8 Truth table and symbol for a three-input AND gate.

A	B	C	x = ABC
0	0	0	0
0	0	1	0
0	1	0	0
0	1	1	0
1	0	0	0
1	0	1	0
1	1	0	0
1	1	1	1

Note the difference between the symbols for the AND gate and the OR gate. Whenever you see the AND symbol on a logic-circuit diagram, it tells you that the output will go HIGH *only* when *all* inputs are HIGH. Whenever you see the OR symbol, it means that the output will go HIGH when *any* input is HIGH.

Summary of the AND Operation

1. The AND operation is performed exactly like ordinary multiplication of 1s and 0s.
2. An output equal to 1 occurs only for the single case where all inputs are 1.
3. The output is 0 for any case where one or more inputs are 0.
4. An AND gate is a logic circuit that performs the AND operation on the circuit's inputs.

EXAMPLE 3-4

Determine the output x from the AND gate in Figure 3-9 for the given input waveforms.

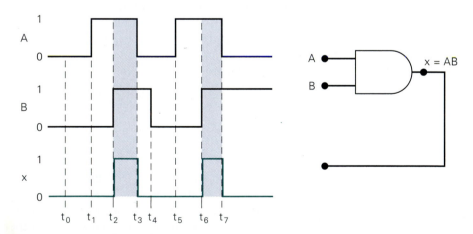

FIGURE 3-9 Example 3-4.

Solution

The output of an AND gate is determined by realizing that it will be HIGH only when all inputs are HIGH at the same time. For the input waveforms given, this condition is met only during intervals t_2–t_3 and t_6–t_7. At all other times, one or more of the inputs are 0, thereby producing a LOW output. Note that input level changes that occur while the other input is LOW have no effect on the output.

Determine the output waveform for the AND gate shown in Figure 3-10.

FIGURE 3-10 Examples 3-5A and B.

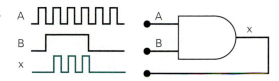

Solution

The output x will be at 1 only when A and B are both HIGH at the same time. Using this fact, we can determine the x waveform as shown in the figure.

Notice that the x waveform is 0 whenever B is 0, regardless of the signal at A. Also notice that whenever B is 1, the x waveform is the same as A. Thus, we can think of the B input as a *control* input whose logic level determines whether or not the A waveform gets through to the x output. In this situation, the AND gate is used as an *inhibit circuit*. We can say that $B = 0$ is the inhibit condition producing a 0 output. Conversely, $B = 1$ is the *enable* condition, which enables A to reach the output. This inhibit operation is an important application of AND gates which will be encountered later.

What will happen to the x output waveform in Figure 3-10 if the B input is kept at the 0 level?

Solution

With B kept LOW, the x output will also stay LOW. This can be reasoned in two different ways. First, with $B = 0$ we have $x = A \cdot B = A \cdot 0 = 0$, since anything multiplied (ANDed) by 0 will be 0. Another way to look at it is that an AND gate requires that all inputs be HIGH in order for the output to be HIGH, and this cannot happen if B is kept LOW.

Review Questions

1. What is the only input combination that will produce a HIGH at the output of a five-input AND gate?

2. What logic level should be applied to the second input of a two-input AND gate if the logic signal at the first input is to be inhibited (prevented) from reaching the output?

3. *True or false:* An AND gate output will always differ from an OR gate output for the same input conditions.

3-5 NOT OPERATION

The **NOT operation** is unlike the OR and AND operations in that it can be performed on a single input variable. For example, if the variable A is subjected to the NOT operation, the result x can be expressed as

$$x = \overline{A}$$

where the overbar represents the NOT operation. This expression is read as "x equals NOT A" or "x equals the *inverse* of A" or "x equals the *complement* of A." Each of these is in common usage, and all indicate that the logic value of $x = \overline{A}$ *is opposite to* the logic value of A. The truth table in Figure 3-11(a) clarifies this for the two cases $A = 0$ and $A = 1$. That is,

$$\overline{1} = 0 \qquad \text{because NOT 1 is 0}$$

and

$$\overline{0} = 1 \qquad \text{because NOT 0 is 1}$$

The NOT operation is also referred to as **inversion** or **complementation,** and these terms will be used interchangeably throughout the book. Although we will always use the overbar indicator to represent inversion, it is important to mention that another indicator for inversion is the prime symbol ('). That is,

$$A' = \overline{A}$$

Both should be recognized as indicating the inversion operation.

FIGURE 3-11 (a) Truth table; (b) symbol for the INVERTER (NOT circuit); (c) sample waveforms.

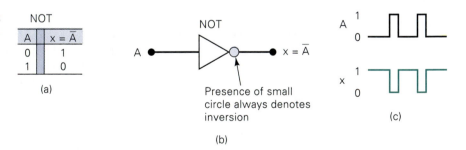

NOT Circuit (INVERTER)

Figure 3-11(b) shows the symbol for a **NOT circuit,** which is more commonly called an **INVERTER.** This circuit *always* has only a single input, and its output logic level is always opposite to the logic level of this input. Figure 3-11(c) shows how the INVERTER affects an input signal. It inverts (complements) the input signal at all points on the waveform.

Summary of Boolean Operations

The rules for the OR, AND, and NOT operations may be summarized as follows:

OR	*AND*	*NOT*
$0 + 0 = 0$	$0 \cdot 0 = 0$	$\bar{0} = 1$
$0 + 1 = 1$	$0 \cdot 1 = 0$	$\bar{1} = 0$
$1 + 0 = 1$	$1 \cdot 0 = 0$	
$1 + 1 = 1$	$1 \cdot 1 = 1$	

Review Questions

1. The output of the INVERTER of Figure 3-11 is connected to the input of a second INVERTER. Determine the output level of the second INVERTER for each level of input A.

2. The output of the AND gate in Figure 3-7 is connected to the input of an INVERTER. Write the truth table showing the INVERTER output, y, for each combination of inputs A and B.

3-6   DESCRIBING LOGIC CIRCUITS ALGEBRAICALLY

Any logic circuit, no matter how complex, may be completely described using the Boolean operations previously defined, because the OR gate, AND gate, and NOT circuit are the basic building blocks of digital systems. For example, consider the circuit in Figure 3-12. This circuit has three inputs, A, B, and C, and a single output, x. Utilizing the Boolean expression for each gate, we can easily determine the expression for the output.

FIGURE 3-12   Logic circuit with its Boolean expression.

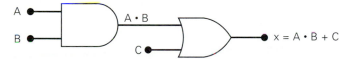

The expression for the AND gate output is written $A \cdot B$. This AND output is connected as an input to the OR gate along with C, another input. The OR gate operates on its inputs so that its output is the OR sum of the inputs. Thus, we can express the OR output as $x = A \cdot B + C$. (This final expression could also be written as $x = C + A \cdot B$, since it does not matter which term of the OR sum is written first.)

Occasionally, there may be confusion as to which operation in an expression is performed first. The expression $A \cdot B + C$ can be interpreted in two different ways: (1) $A \cdot B$ is ORed with C, or (2) A is ANDed with the term $B + C$. To avoid this confusion, it will be understood that if an expression contains both AND and OR operations, the AND operations are performed first, unless there are *parentheses* in the expression, in which case the operation inside the parentheses is to be performed first. This is the same rule that is used in ordinary algebra to determine the order of operations.

To illustrate further, consider the circuit in Figure 3-13. The expression for the OR gate output is simply $A + B$. This output serves as an input to the AND gate along with another input, C. Thus, we express the output of the AND gate as $x = (A + B) \cdot C$. Note the use of parentheses here to indicate that A and B are ORed *first*, before their OR sum is ANDed with C. Without the parentheses it would be interpreted *incorrectly*, since $A + B \cdot C$ means that A is ORed with the product $B \cdot C$.

FIGURE 3-13 Logic circuit whose expression requires parentheses.

Circuits Containing INVERTERs

Whenever an INVERTER is present in a logic-circuit diagram, its output expression is simply equal to the input expression with a bar over it. Figure 3-14 shows two examples using INVERTERs. In Figure 3-14(a), input A is fed through an INVERTER, whose output is therefore $\overline{A}$. The INVERTER output is fed to an OR gate together with B, so that the *OR* output is equal to $\overline{A} + B$. Note that the bar is over the A alone, indicating that A is first inverted and then ORed with B.

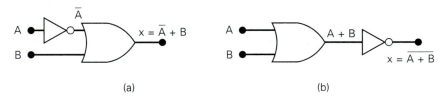

FIGURE 3-14 Circuits using INVERTERs.

(a)   (b)

In Figure 3-14(b) the output of the OR gate is equal to $A + B$ and is fed through an INVERTER. The INVERTER output is therefore equal to $\overline{(A + B)}$, since it inverts the *complete* input expression. Note that the bar covers the entire expression $(A + B)$. This is important because, as will be shown later, the expressions $\overline{(A + B)}$ and $(\overline{A} + \overline{B})$ are *not* equivalent. The expression $\overline{(A + B)}$ means that A is ORed with B and then their OR sum is inverted, whereas the expression $(\overline{A} + \overline{B})$ indicates that A is inverted and B is inverted and the results are then ORed together.

Figure 3-15 shows two more examples, which should be studied carefully. Note especially the use of *two* separate sets of parentheses in Figure 3-15(b). Also notice in Figure 3-15(a) that the input variable A is connected as an input to two different gates.

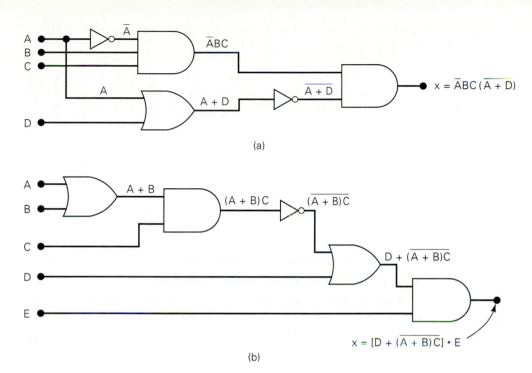

FIGURE 3-15 More examples.

Review Questions

1. In Figure 3-15(a) change each AND gate to an OR gate, and change the OR gate to an AND gate. Then write the expression for output x.

3-7 EVALUATING LOGIC-CIRCUIT OUTPUTS

Once the Boolean expression for a circuit output has been obtained, the output logic level can be determined for any set of input levels. For example, suppose that we want to know the logic level of the output x for the circuit in Figure 3-15(a) for the case where $A = 0$, $B = 1$, $C = 1$, and $D = 1$. As in ordinary algebra, the value of x can be found by "plugging" the values of the variables into the expression and performing the indicated operations as follows:

$$x = \overline{A}BC(\overline{A + D})$$
$$= \overline{0} \cdot 1 \cdot 1 \cdot (\overline{0 + 1})$$
$$= 1 \cdot 1 \cdot 1 \cdot (\overline{0 + 1})$$
$$= 1 \cdot 1 \cdot 1 \cdot (\overline{1})$$
$$= 1 \cdot 1 \cdot 1 \cdot 0$$
$$= 0$$

As another illustration, let us evaluate the output of the circuit in Figure 3-15(b) for $A = 0$, $B = 0$, $C = 1$, $D = 1$, and $E = 1$.

$$
\begin{aligned}
x &= [D + \overline{(A + B)C}] \cdot E \\
&= [1 + \overline{(0 + 0) \cdot 1}] \cdot 1 \\
&= [1 + \overline{0 \cdot 1}] \cdot 1 \\
&= [1 + \overline{0}] \cdot 1 \\
&= [1 + 1] \cdot 1 \\
&= 1 \cdot 1 \\
&= 1
\end{aligned}
$$

In general, the following rules must always be followed when evaluating a Boolean expression:

1. First, perform all inversions of single terms; that is, $\overline{0} = 1$ or $\overline{1} = 0$.
2. Then perform all operations within parentheses.
3. Perform an AND operation before an OR operation unless parentheses indicate otherwise.
4. If an expression has a bar over it, perform the operations of the expression first and then invert the result.

For practice, determine the outputs of both circuits in Figure 3-15 for the case where all inputs are 1. The answers are $x = 0$ and $x = 1$, respectively.

Determining Output Level from a Diagram

The output logic level for given input levels can also be determined directly from the circuit diagram *without* using the Boolean expression. This technique is often used by technicians during the troubleshooting or testing of a logic system since it also tells them what each gate output is supposed to be as well as the final output. To illustrate, the circuit of Figure 3-15(a) is redrawn in Figure 3-16 with the input levels $A = 0$, $B = 1$, $C = 1$, and $D = 1$. The procedure is to start from the inputs and to proceed through each INVERTER and gate, writing down each of their outputs in the process until the final output is reached.

FIGURE 3-16 Determining the output level from a circuit diagram.

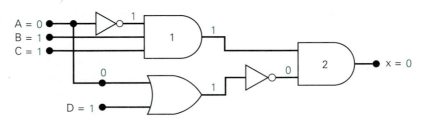

In Figure 3-16, AND gate 1 has *all* three inputs at the 1 level because the INVERTER changes the $A = 0$ to a 1. This condition produces a 1 at the AND output since $1 \cdot 1 \cdot 1 = 1$. The OR gate has inputs of 1 and 0, which produces a 1 output since $1 + 0 = 1$. This 1 is inverted to 0 and applied to AND gate 2 along with the 1 from the first AND output. The 0 and 1 inputs to AND gate 2 produce an output of 0 because $0 \cdot 1 = 0$.

EXAMPLE 3-6

Determine the output in Figure 3-16 for the condition where all inputs are LOW.

Solution

With $A = B = C = D = 0$, the output of AND gate 1 will be LOW. This LOW places a LOW at the input of AND gate 2, which automatically produces $x = 0$, regardless of the levels at other points in the circuit. This example shows that it is not always necessary to determine the logic level at every point in order to determine the output level.

Review Questions

1. Use the expression for x to determine the output of the circuit in Figure 3-15(a) for the conditions $A = 0$, $B = 1$, $C = 1$, and $D = 0$.

2. Use the expression for x to determine the output of the circuit in Figure 3-15(b) for the conditions $A = B = E = 1$, $C = D = 0$.

3. Determine the answers to questions 1 and 2 by finding the logic levels present at each gate input and output as was done in Figure 3-16.

3-8   IMPLEMENTING CIRCUITS FROM BOOLEAN EXPRESSIONS

If the operation of a circuit is defined by a Boolean expression, a logic-circuit diagram can be implemented directly from that expression. For example, if we needed a circuit that was defined by $x = A \cdot B \cdot C$, we would immediately know that all that was needed was a three-input AND gate. If we needed a circuit that was defined by $x = A + \overline{B}$, we would use a two-input OR gate with an INVERTER on one of the inputs. The same reasoning used for these simple cases can be extended to more complex circuits.

Suppose that we wanted to construct a circuit whose output is $y = AC + B\overline{C} + \overline{A}BC$. This Boolean expression contains three terms (AC, $B\overline{C}$, $\overline{A}BC$), which are ORed together. This tells us that a three-input OR gate is required with inputs that are equal to AC, $B\overline{C}$, and $\overline{A}BC$, respectively. This is illustrated in Figure 3-17(a), where a three-input OR gate is drawn with inputs labeled as AC, $B\overline{C}$, and $\overline{A}BC$.

Each OR gate input is an AND product term, which means that an AND gate with appropriate inputs can be used to generate each of these terms. This is shown in Figure 3-17(b), which is the final circuit diagram. Note the use of INVERTERs to produce the $\overline{A}$ and $\overline{C}$ terms required in the expression.

This same general approach can always be followed, although we shall find that there are some clever, more efficient techniques that can be employed. For now, however, this straightforward method will be used to minimize the number of new things that are to be learned.

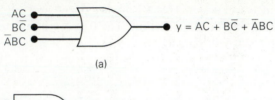

(a)

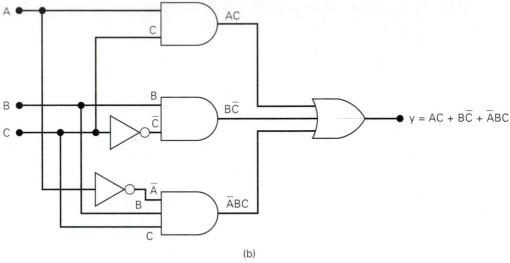

(b)

FIGURE 3-17 Constructing a logic circuit from a Boolean expression.

EXAMPLE 3-7

Draw the circuit diagram that implements the expression $x = AB + \overline{B}C$.

Solution

This expression indicates that the terms AB and $\overline{B}C$ are inputs to an OR gate, and each of these two terms is generated from a separate AND gate. The result is shown in Figure 3-18.

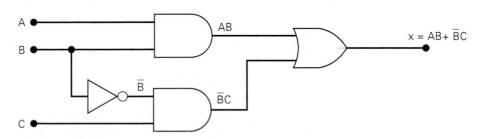

FIGURE 3-18 Example 3-7.

Review Questions

1. Draw the circuit diagram that implements the expression $x = \overline{A}BC(\overline{A + D})$ using gates with no more than three inputs.
2. Draw the circuit diagram for the expression $y = AC + B\overline{C} + \overline{A}BC$.
3. Draw the circuit diagram for $x = [D + (\overline{A + B})C] \cdot E$.

3-9 NOR GATES AND NAND GATES

Two other types of logic gates, NOR gates and NAND gates, are used extensively in digital circuitry. These gates actually combine the basic operations AND, OR, and NOT, which make it relatively easy to describe them using the Boolean algebra operations learned previously.

NOR Gate

The symbol for a two-input **NOR gate** is shown in Figure 3-19(a). It is the same as the OR gate symbol except that it has a small circle on the output. The small circle represents the inversion operation. Thus, the NOR gate operates like an OR gate followed by an INVERTER, so that the circuits in Figure 3-19(a) and (b) are equivalent, and the output expression for the NOR gate is $x = \overline{A + B}$.

FIGURE 3-19   (a) NOR symbol; (b) equivalent circuit; (c) truth table.

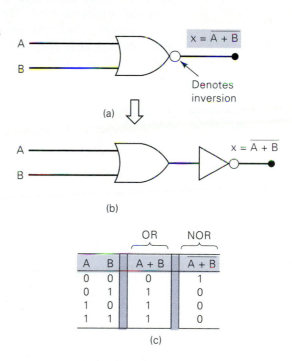

The truth table in Figure 3-19(c) shows that the NOR gate output is the exact inverse of the OR gate output for all possible input conditions. Whereas an OR gate output goes HIGH when any input is HIGH, the NOR gate output goes LOW when any input is HIGH. This same operation can be extended to NOR gates with more than two inputs.

EXAMPLE 3-8

Determine the waveform at the output of a NOR gate for the input waveforms shown in Figure 3-20.

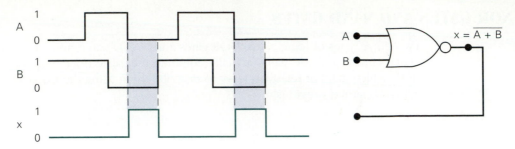

FIGURE 3-20   Example 3-8.

Solution

There are several ways to determine the NOR output waveform. One way is to first find the OR output waveform and then invert it (change all 1s to 0s, and vice versa). Another way utilizes the fact that a NOR gate output will be HIGH *only* when all inputs are LOW. Thus, you can examine the input waveforms, find those time intervals where they are all LOW, and make the NOR output HIGH for those intervals. The NOR output will be LOW for all other time intervals. The resultant output waveform is shown in the figure.

EXAMPLE 3-9

Determine the Boolean expression for a three-input NOR gate followed by an IN-VERTER.

FIGURE 3-21   Example 3-9.

$$A \quad B \quad C \qquad \overline{A + B + C} \qquad x = \overline{\overline{A + B + C}} = A + B + C$$

Solution

Refer to Figure 3-21, where the circuit diagram is shown. The expression at the NOR output is $(\overline{A + B + C})$, which is then fed through an INVERTER to produce

$$x = \overline{(\overline{A + B + C})}$$

The presence of the double inversion signs indicates that the quantity $(A + B + C)$ has been inverted and then inverted again. It should be clear that this simply results in the expression $(A + B + C)$ being unchanged. That is,

$$x = \overline{(\overline{A + B + C})} = A + B + C$$

Whenever two inversion bars are over the same variable or quantity, they cancel each other out, as in the example above. However, in cases such as $\overline{A} + \overline{B}$ the inversion bars do not cancel. This is because the smaller inversion bars invert the single variables A and B, respectively, while the wide bar inverts the quantity $(\overline{A} + \overline{B})$. Thus, $\overline{\overline{A} + \overline{B}} \neq A + B$. Similarly, $\overline{\overline{A}\,\overline{B}} \neq AB$.

NAND Gate

The symbol for a two-input **NAND gate** is shown in Figure 3-22(a). It is the same as the AND gate symbol except for the small circle on its output. Once again this small circle denotes the inversion operation. Thus, the NAND operates like an AND gate followed by an INVERTER, so that the circuits of Figures 3-22(a) and (b) are equivalent, and the output expression for the NAND gate is $x = \overline{AB}$.

FIGURE 3-22   (a) NAND symbol; (b) equivalent circuit; (c) truth table.

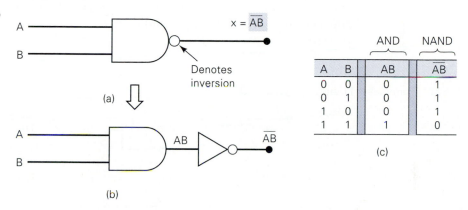

The truth table in Figure 3-22(c) shows that the NAND gate output is the exact inverse of the AND gate for all possible input conditions. The AND output goes HIGH only when all inputs are HIGH, while the NAND output goes LOW only when all inputs are HIGH. This same characteristic is true of NAND gates having more than two inputs.

EXAMPLE 3-10

Determine the output waveform of a NAND gate having the inputs shown in Figure 3-23.

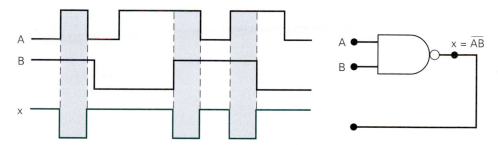

FIGURE 3-23   Example 3-10.

Solution

The output can be determined in several ways. One way is to first draw the output waveform for an AND gate and then invert it. Another way utilizes the fact that a NAND output will be LOW only when all inputs are HIGH. Thus, you can find those time intervals during which the inputs are all HIGH, and make the NAND output LOW for those intervals. The output will be HIGH at all other times.

EXAMPLE 3-11

Implement the logic circuit that has the expression $x = \overline{AB \cdot (\overline{C + D})}$ using only NOR and NAND gates.

Solution

The $(\overline{C + D})$ term is the expression for the output of a NOR gate. This term is ANDed with A and B, and the result is inverted; this, of course, is the NAND operation. Thus, the circuit is implemented as shown in Figure 3-24. Note that the NAND gate first ANDs the A, B, and $(\overline{C + D})$ terms, and then it inverts the *complete* result.

FIGURE 3-24   Examples 3-11 and 3-12.

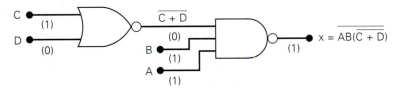

EXAMPLE 3-12

Determine the output level in Figure 3-24 for $A = B = C = 1$ and $D = 0$.

Solution

In the first method we use the expression for x.

$$
\begin{aligned}
x &= \overline{AB(\overline{C + D})} \\
  &= \overline{1 \cdot 1 \cdot (\overline{1 + 0})} \\
  &= \overline{1 \cdot 1 \cdot (\overline{1})} \\
  &= \overline{1 \cdot 1 \cdot 0} \\
  &= \overline{0} = 1
\end{aligned}
$$

In the second method we write down the input logic levels on the circuit diagram (shown in parentheses in Figure 3-24) and follow these levels through each gate to the final output. The NOR gate has inputs of 1 and 0 to produce an output of 0 (an OR would have produced an output of 1). The NAND gate thus has input levels of 0, 1, and 1 to produce an output of 1 (an AND would have produced an output of 0).

Review Questions

1. What is the only set of input conditions that will produce a HIGH output from a three-input NOR gate?

2. Determine the output level in Figure 3-24 for $A = B = 1$, $C = D = 0$.

3. Change the NOR gate of Figure 3-24 to a NAND gate, and change the NAND to a NOR. What is the new expression for x?

3-10 BOOLEAN THEOREMS

We have seen how Boolean algebra can be used to help analyze a logic circuit and express its operation mathematically. We will continue our study of Boolean algebra by investigating the various **Boolean theorems** (rules) that can help us to simplify logic expressions and logic circuits. The first group of theorems is given in Figure 3-25. In each theorem, x is a logic variable that can be either a 0 or a 1. Each theorem is accompanied by a logic-circuit diagram that demonstrates its validity.

FIGURE 3-25 Single-variable theorems.

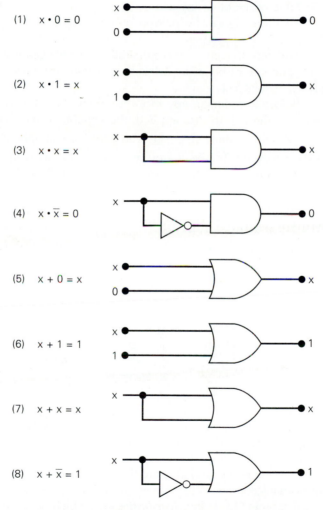

(1) $x \cdot 0 = 0$

(2) $x \cdot 1 = x$

(3) $x \cdot x = x$

(4) $x \cdot \bar{x} = 0$

(5) $x + 0 = x$

(6) $x + 1 = 1$

(7) $x + x = x$

(8) $x + \bar{x} = 1$

Theorem (1) states that if any variable is ANDed with 0, the result must be 0. This is easy to remember because the AND operation is just like ordinary multiplication, where we know that anything multiplied by 0 is 0. We also know that the output of an AND gate will be 0 whenever any input is 0, regardless of the level on the other input.

Theorem (2) is also obvious by comparison with ordinary multiplication.

Theorem (3) can be proved by trying each case. If $x = 0$, then $0 \cdot 0 = 0$; if $x = 1$, then $1 \cdot 1 = 1$. Thus, $x \cdot x = x$.

Theorem (4) can be proved in the same manner. However, it can also be reasoned that at any time either x or its inverse $\bar{x}$ must be at the 0 level, and so their AND product always must be 0.

Theorem (5) is straightforward, since 0 *added* to anything does not affect its value, either in regular addition or in OR addition.

Theorem (6) states that if any variable is ORed with 1, the result will always be 1. We check this for both values of x: $0 + 1 = 1$ and $1 + 1 = 1$. Equivalently, we can remember that an OR gate output will be 1 when *any* input is 1, regardless of the value of the other input.

Theorem (7) can be proved by checking for both values of x: $0 + 0 = 0$ and $1 + 1 = 1$.

Theorem (8) can be proved similarly, or we can just reason that at any time either x or $\bar{x}$ must be at the 1 level so that we are always ORing a 0 and a 1, which always results in 1.

Before introducing any more theorems, we should point out that when theorems (1) through (8) are applied, the variable x may actually represent an expression containing more than one variable. For example, if we have $A\bar{B}(\overline{A\bar{B}})$, we can invoke theorem (4) by letting $x = A\bar{B}$. Thus, we can say that $A\bar{B}(\overline{A\bar{B}}) = 0$. The same idea can be applied to the use of any of these theorems.

Multivariable Theorems

The theorems presented below involve more than one variable:

$$(9) \qquad x + y = y + x$$
$$(10) \qquad x \cdot y = y \cdot x$$
$$(11) \qquad x + (y + z) = (x + y) + z = x + y + z$$
$$(12) \qquad x(yz) = (xy)z = xyz$$
$$(13a) \qquad x(y + z) = xy + xz$$
$$(13b) \qquad (w + x)(y + z) = wy + xy + wz + xz$$
$$(14) \qquad x + xy = x$$
$$(15) \qquad x + \bar{x}y = x + y$$

Theorems (9) and (10) are called the *commutative laws*. These laws indicate that the order in which we OR or AND two variables is unimportant; the result is the same.

Theorems (11) and (12) are the *associative laws*, which state that we can group the variables in an AND expression or OR expression any way we want.

Theorem (13) is the *distributive law*, which states that an expression can be expanded by multiplying term by term just the same as in ordinary algebra. This theorem also indicates that we can factor an expression. That is, if we have a sum of two (or more) terms, each of which contains a common variable, the common variable can be factored out just as in ordinary algebra. For example, if we have the expression $A\bar{B}C + \bar{A}\bar{B}\bar{C}$, we can factor out the $\bar{B}$ variable:

$$A\bar{B}C + \bar{A}\bar{B}\bar{C} = \bar{B}(AC + \bar{A}\bar{C})$$

As another example, consider the expression $ABC + ABD$. Here the two terms have the variables A and B in common, and so $A \cdot B$ can be factored out of both terms. That is,

$$ABC + ABD = AB(C + D)$$

Theorems (9) to (13) are easy to remember and use since they are identical to those of ordinary algebra. Theorems (14) and (15), on the other hand, do not have any counterparts in ordinary algebra. Each can be proved by trying all possible cases for x and y. This is illustrated for theorem (14) as follows:

Case 1. For $x = 0$, $y = 0$,

$$x + xy = x$$
$$0 + 0 \cdot 0 = 0$$
$$0 = 0$$

Case 2. For $x = 0$, $y = 1$,

$$x + xy = x$$
$$0 + 0 \cdot 1 = 0$$
$$0 + 0 = 0$$
$$0 = 0$$

Case 3. For $x = 1$, $y = 0$,

$$x + xy = x$$
$$1 + 1 \cdot 0 = 1$$
$$1 + 0 = 1$$
$$1 = 1$$

Case 4. For $x = 1$, $y = 1$,

$$x + xy = x$$
$$1 + 1 \cdot 1 = 1$$
$$1 + 1 = 1$$
$$1 = 1$$

Theorem (14) can also be proved by factoring and using theorems (6) and (2) as follows:

$$x + xy = x(1 + y)$$
$$= x \cdot 1 \quad \text{[using theorem (6)]}$$
$$= x \quad \text{[using theorem (2)]}$$

All of these Boolean theorems can be useful in simplifying a logic expression—that is, in reducing the number of terms in the expression. When this is done, the reduced expression will produce a circuit that is less complex than the one that the original expression would have produced. A good portion of the next chapter will be devoted to the process of circuit simplification. For now, the following examples will serve to illustrate how the Boolean theorems can be applied.

EXAMPLE 3-13

Simplify the expression $y = A\bar{B}D + A\bar{B}\bar{D}$.

Solution

Factor out the common variables $A\bar{B}$ using theorem (13):

$$y = A\bar{B}(D + \bar{D})$$

Using theorem (8), the term in parentheses is equivalent to 1. Thus,

$$y = A\bar{B} \cdot 1$$
$$= A\bar{B} \quad \text{[using theorem (2)]}$$

EXAMPLE 3-14

Simplify $z = (\bar{A} + B)(A + B)$.

Solution

The expression can be expanded by multiplying out the terms [theorem (13)]:

$$z = \bar{A} \cdot A + \bar{A} \cdot B + B \cdot A + B \cdot B$$

Invoking theorem (4), the term $\bar{A} \cdot A = 0$. Also, $B \cdot B = B$ [theorem (3)]:

$$z = 0 + \bar{A} \cdot B + B \cdot A + B = \bar{A}B + AB + B$$

Factoring out the variable B [theorem (13)], we have

$$z = B(\bar{A} + A + 1)$$

Finally, using theorems (2) and (6),

$$z = B$$

EXAMPLE 3-15

Simplify $x = ACD + \bar{A}BCD$.

Solution

Factoring out the common variables CD, we have

$$x = CD(A + \bar{A}B)$$

Utilizing theorem (15), we can replace $A + \bar{A}B$ by $A + B$, so

$$x = CD(A + B)$$
$$= ACD + BCD$$

---

1. Use theorems (13) and (14) to simplify $y = A\overline{C} + AB\overline{C}$.
2. Use theorems (13) and (8) to simplify $y = \overline{A}\overline{B}CD + \overline{A}B\overline{C}D$.

3-11 DEMORGAN'S THEOREMS

Two of the most important theorems of Boolean algebra were contributed by a great mathematician named DeMorgan. **DeMorgan's theorems** are extremely useful in simplifying expressions in which a product or sum of variables is inverted. The two theorems are:

$$(16) \qquad \overline{(x + y)} = \overline{x} \cdot \overline{y}$$
$$(17) \qquad \overline{(x \cdot y)} = \overline{x} + \overline{y}$$

Theorem (16) says that when the OR sum of two variables is inverted, this is the same as inverting each variable individually and then ANDing these inverted variables. Theorem (17) says that when the AND product of two variables is inverted, this is the same as inverting each variable individually and then ORing them. Each of DeMorgan's theorems can readily be proven by checking for all possible combinations of x and y. This will be left as an end-of-chapter exercise.

Although these theorems have been stated in terms of single variables x and y, they are equally valid for situations where x and/or y are expressions that contain more than one variable. For example, let's apply them to the expression $\overline{(A\overline{B} + C)}$ as shown below:

$$\overline{(A\overline{B} + C)} = \overline{(A\overline{B})} \cdot \overline{C}$$

Note that here we treated $A\overline{B}$ as x and C as y. The result can be further simplified since we have a product $A\overline{B}$ that is inverted. Using theorem (17), the expression becomes

$$\overline{A\overline{B}} \cdot \overline{C} = (\overline{A} + \overline{\overline{B}}) \cdot \overline{C}$$

Notice that we can replace $\overline{\overline{B}}$ by B, so that we finally have

$$(\overline{A} + B) \cdot \overline{C} = \overline{A}\overline{C} + B\overline{C}$$

This final result contains only inverter signs that invert a single variable.

EXAMPLE 3-16

Simplify the expression $z = \overline{(A + C) \cdot (B + \overline{D})}$ to one having only single variables inverted.

Solution

Using theorem (17), we can rewrite this as

$$z = \overline{(A + C)} + \overline{(B + \overline{D})}$$

We can think of this as breaking the large inverter sign down the middle and changing the AND sign ($\cdot$) to an OR sign ($+$). Now the term $(\overline{\overline{A} + C})$ can be simplified by applying theorem (16). Likewise, $(\overline{B + \overline{D}})$ can be simplified:

$$z = (\overline{\overline{A} + C}) + (\overline{B + \overline{D}})$$
$$= (\overline{\overline{A}} \cdot \overline{C}) + \overline{B} \cdot \overline{\overline{D}}$$

Here we have broken the larger inverter signs down the middle and replaced the ($+$) with a ($\cdot$). Canceling out the double inversions, we have finally

$$z = A\overline{C} + \overline{B}D$$

Example 3-16 points out that when using DeMorgan's theorems to reduce an expression, we may break an inverter sign at any point in the expression and change the operator sign at that point in the expression to its opposite ($+$ is changed to $\cdot$, and vice versa). This procedure is continued until the expression is reduced to one in which one single variables are inverted. Two more examples are given below.

Example 1

$$z = \overline{A + \overline{B} \cdot C}$$
$$= \overline{A} \cdot (\overline{\overline{B} \cdot C})$$
$$= \overline{A} \cdot (\overline{\overline{B}} + \overline{C})$$
$$= \overline{A} \cdot (B + \overline{C})$$

Example 2

$$\omega = \overline{(A + BC) \cdot (D + EF)}$$
$$= \overline{(A + BC)} + \overline{(D + EF)}$$
$$= (\overline{A} \cdot \overline{BC}) + (\overline{D} \cdot \overline{EF})$$
$$= [\overline{A} \cdot (\overline{B} + \overline{C})] + [\overline{D} \cdot (\overline{E} + \overline{F})]$$
$$= \overline{A}\overline{B} + \overline{A}\overline{C} + \overline{D}\overline{E} + \overline{D}\overline{F}$$

DeMorgan's theorems are easily extended to more than two variables. For example, it can be proved that

$$\overline{x + y + z} = \overline{x} \cdot \overline{y} \cdot \overline{z}$$
$$\overline{x \cdot y \cdot z} = \overline{x} + \overline{y} + \overline{z}$$

Here we see that the large inverter sign is broken at *two* points in the expression and the operator sign changed to its opposite. This can be extended to any number of variables. Again, realize that the variables can themselves be expressions rather than single variables. Here is another example.

$$x = \overline{\overline{AB} \cdot \overline{CD} \cdot \overline{EF}}$$
$$= \overline{\overline{AB}} + \overline{\overline{CD}} + \overline{\overline{EF}}$$
$$= AB + CD + EF$$

Implications of DeMorgan's Theorems

Let us examine theorems (16) and (17) from the standpoint of logic circuits. First, consider theorem (16),

$$\overline{x + y} = \overline{x} \cdot \overline{y}$$

The left-hand side of the equation can be viewed as the output of a NOR gate whose inputs are x and y. The right-hand side of the equation, on the other hand, is the result of first inverting both x and y and then putting them through an AND gate. These two representations are equivalent and are illustrated in Figure 3-26(a). What this means is that an AND gate with INVERTERs on each of its inputs is equivalent to a NOR gate. In fact, both representations are used to represent the NOR function. When the AND gate with inverted inputs is used to represent the NOR function, it is usually drawn as shown in Figure 3-26(b), where the small circles on the inputs represent the inversion operation.

FIGURE 3-26 (a) Equivalent circuits implied by theorem (16); (b) alternative symbol for the NOR function.

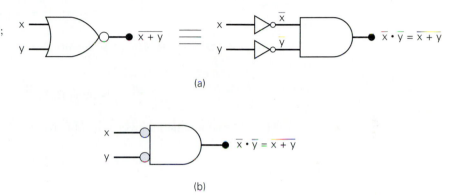

(a)

(b)

Now consider theorem (17),

$$\overline{x \cdot y} = \overline{x} + \overline{y}$$

The left side of the equation can be implemented by a NAND gate with inputs x and y. The right side can be implemented by first inverting inputs x and y and then putting them through an OR gate. These two equivalent representations are shown in Figure 3-27(a). The OR gate with INVERTERs on each of its inputs is equivalent to the NAND gate. In fact, both representations are used to represent the NAND function. When the OR gate with inverted inputs is used to represent the NAND function, it is usually drawn as shown in Figure 3-27(b), where the circles again represent inversion.

FIGURE 3-27 (a) Equivalent circuits implied by theorem (17); (b) alternative symbol for the NAND function.

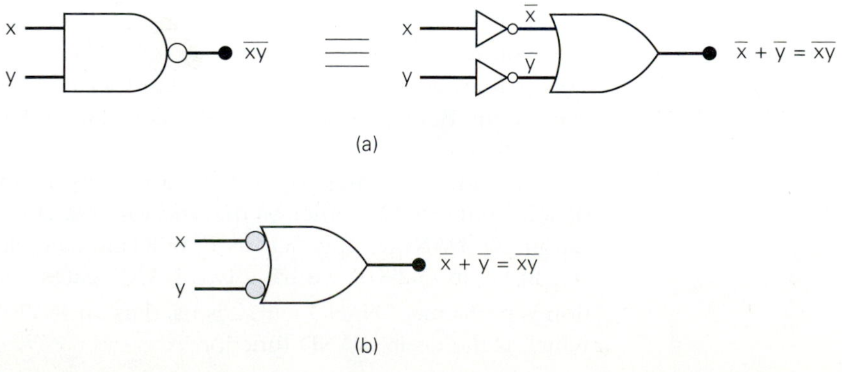

(a)

(b)

<table>
<tr><td>EXAMPLE
3-17</td><td>Determine the output expression for the circuit of Figure 3-28 and simplify it using DeMorgan's theorems.</td></tr>
</table>

FIGURE 3-28 Example 3-17.

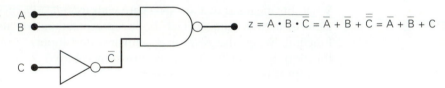

$$z = \overline{A \cdot B \cdot \overline{C}} = \overline{A} + \overline{B} + \overline{\overline{C}} = \overline{A} + \overline{B} + C$$

Solution

The expression for z is $z = \overline{AB\overline{C}}$. Use DeMorgan's theorem to break the large inversion sign:

$$z = \overline{A} + \overline{B} + \overline{\overline{C}}$$

Cancel the double inversions over C to obtain

$$z = \overline{A} + \overline{B} + C$$

Review Questions

1. Use DeMorgan's theorems to convert the expression $z = \overline{(A + B) \cdot \overline{C}}$ to one that has only single-variable inversions.
2. Repeat question 1 for the expression $y = \overline{\overline{RS}T + \overline{Q}}$.
3. Implement a circuit having output expression $z = \overline{A}\overline{B}C$ using only a NOR gate and an INVERTER.
4. Use DeMorgan's theorems to convert $y = \overline{\overline{A} + \overline{B} + \overline{C}D}$ to an expression containing only single-variable inversions.

3-12 UNIVERSALITY OF NAND GATES AND NOR GATES

All Boolean expressions consist of various combinations of the basic operations of OR, AND, and INVERT. Therefore, any expression can be implemented using combinations of OR gates, AND gates, and INVERTERs. It is possible, however, to implement any logic expression using *only* NAND gates and no other type of gate. This is because NAND gates, in the proper combination, can be used to perform each of the Boolean operations OR, AND, and INVERT. This is demonstrated in Figure 3-29.

First, in Figure 3-29(a) we have a two-input NAND gate whose inputs are purposely connected together so that the variable A is applied to both. In this configuration, the NAND simply acts as INVERTER, since its output is $x = \overline{A \cdot A} = \overline{A}$.

In Figure 3-29(b) we have two NAND gates connected so that the AND operation is performed. NAND gate 2 is used as an INVERTER to change $\overline{AB}$ to $\overline{\overline{AB}} = AB$, which is the desired AND function.

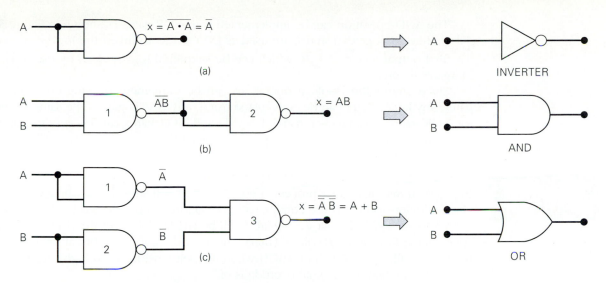

FIGURE 3-29   NAND gates can be used to implement any Boolean function.

The OR operation can be implemented using NAND gates connected as shown in Figure 3-29(c). Here NAND gates 1 and 2 are used as INVERTERs to invert the inputs, so that the final output is $x = \overline{\overline{A} \cdot \overline{B}}$, which can be simplified to $x = A + B$ using DeMorgan's theorem.

In a similar manner, it can be shown that NOR gates can be arranged to implement any of the Boolean operations. This is illustrated in Figure 3-30. Part (a) shows that a NOR gate with its inputs connected together behaves as an INVERTER, since the output is $x = \overline{A + A} = \overline{A}$.

In Figure 3-30(b) two NOR gates are arranged so that the OR operation is performed. NOR gate 2 is used as an INVERTER to change $\overline{A + B}$ to $\overline{\overline{A + B}} = A + B$, which is the desired OR function.

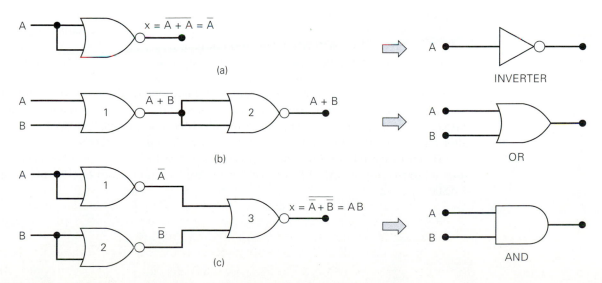

FIGURE 3-30   NOR gates can be used to implement any Boolean operation.

The AND operation can be implemented with NOR gates as shown in Figure 3-30(c). Here NOR gates 1 and 2 are used as INVERTERs to invert the inputs, so that the final output is $x = \overline{\overline{A} + \overline{B}}$, which can be simplified to $x = A \cdot B$ by use of De-Morgan's theorem.

Since any of the Boolean operations can be implemented using only NAND gates, any logic circuit can be constructed using only NAND gates. The same is true for NOR gates. This characteristic of NAND and NOR gates can be very useful in logic-circuit design, as the following example illustrates.

EXAMPLE 3-18

In a certain manufacturing process, a conveyor belt will shut down whenever specific conditions occur. These conditions are monitored and reflected by the states of four logic signals as follows: signal A will be HIGH whenever the conveyor belt speed is too fast; signal B will be HIGH whenever the collection bin at the end of the belt is full; signal C will be HIGH when the belt tension is too high; signal D will be high when the manual override is off.

A logic circuit is needed to generate a signal x that will go HIGH whenever conditions A and B exist simultaneously or whenever conditions C and D exist simultaneously. Clearly, the logic expression for x will be $x = AB + CD$. The circuit is to be implemented with a minimum number of ICs. The TTL integrated circuits shown in Figure 3-31 are available. Each IC is a *quad,* which means that it contains *four* identical gates on one chip.

Solution

The straightforward method for implementing the given expression uses two AND gates and an OR gate as shown in Figure 3-32(a). This implementation uses two gates from the 74LS08 IC and a single gate from the 74LS32 IC. The numbers in parentheses at each input and output are the pin numbers of the respective IC. These are always shown on any logic-circuit wiring diagram. For our purposes, most logic diagrams will not show pin numbers unless they are needed in the description of circuit operation.

Another implementation can be accomplished by taking the circuit of Figure 3-32(a) and replacing each AND gate and OR gate by its equivalent NAND gate implementation from Figure 3-29. The result is shown in Figure 3-32(b).

At first glance this new circuit looks as if it requires seven NAND gates. However, NAND gates 3 and 5 are connected as INVERTERs in series and can be eliminated from the circuit since they perform a double inversion of the signal out of NAND gate 1. Similarly, NAND gates 4 and 6 can be eliminated. The final circuit, after eliminating the double INVERTERs, is drawn in Figure 3-32(c).

This final circuit is more efficient than the one in Figure 3-32(a) because it uses three two-input NAND gates that can be implemented from one IC, the 74LS00.

FIGURE 3-31   ICs available for Example 3-18.

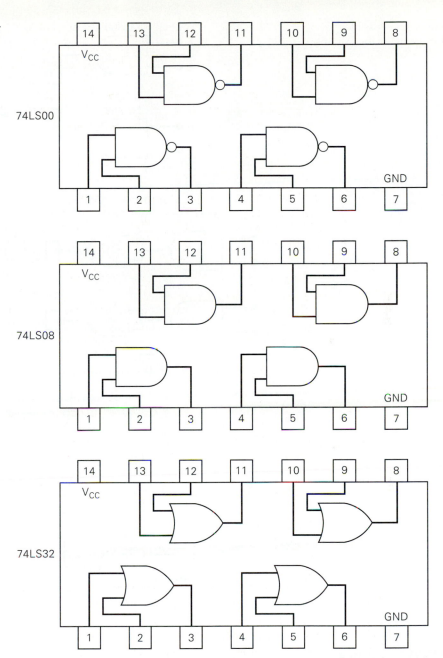

FIGURE 3-32 Possible implementations for Example 3-18.

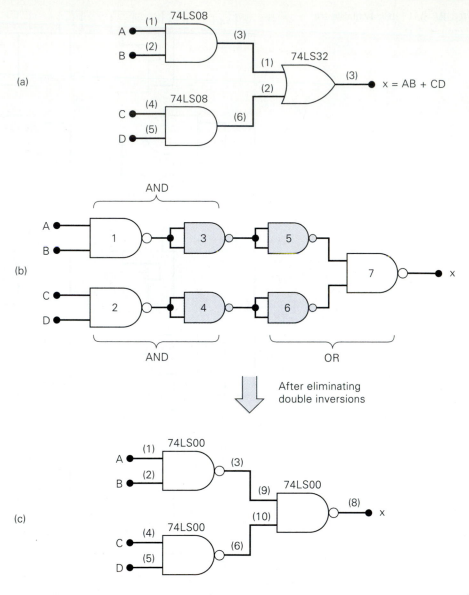

(a)

(b)

After eliminating double inversions

(c)

1. How many different ways do we now have to implement the inversion operation in a logic circuit?

2. Implement the expression $x = (A + B)(C + D)$ using OR and AND gates. Then implement the expression using only NOR gates by converting each OR and AND gate to its NOR implementation from Figure 3-30. Which circuit is more efficient?

3. Write the output expression for the circuit of Figure 3-32(c), and use DeMorgan's theorems to show that it is equivalent to the expression for the circuit of Figure 3-32(a).

3-13 ALTERNATE LOGIC-GATE REPRESENTATIONS

We have introduced the five basic logic gates (AND, OR, INVERTER, NAND, and NOR) and the standard symbols used to represent them on logic-circuit diagrams. Although you may find that some circuit diagrams still use these standard symbols exclusively, it has become increasingly more common to find circuit diagrams that utilize **alternate logic symbols** *in addition* to the standard symbols.

Before discussing the reasons for using an alternate symbol for a logic gate, we will present the alternate symbols for each gate and show that they are equivalent to the standard symbols. Refer to Figure 3-33; the left side of the illustration shows the standard symbol for each logic gate, and the right side shows the alternate symbol. The alternate symbol for each gate is obtained from the standard symbol by doing the following:

1. Invert each input and output of the standard symbol. This is done by adding bubbles (small circles) on input and output lines that do not have bubbles, and by removing bubbles that are already there.

2. Change the operation symbol from AND to OR, or from OR to AND. (In the special case of the INVERTER, the operation symbol is not changed.)

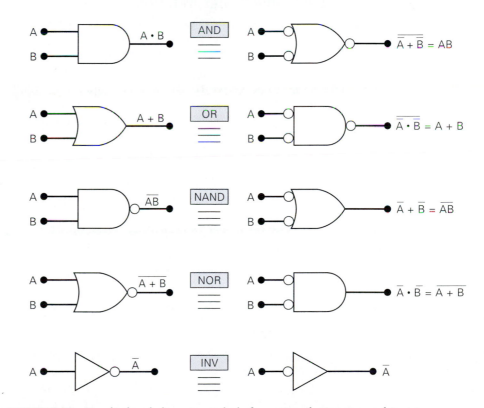

FIGURE 3-33 Standard and alternate symbols for various logic gates and inverter.

For example, the standard NAND symbol is an AND symbol with a bubble on its output. Following the steps outlined above, remove the bubble from the output, and add a bubble to each input. Then change the AND symbol to an OR symbol. The result is an OR symbol with bubbles on its inputs.

We can easily prove that this alternate symbol is equivalent to the standard symbol by using DeMorgan's theorems and recalling that the bubble represents an inversion operation. The output expression from the standard NAND symbol is $\overline{AB} = \overline{A} + \overline{B}$, which is the same as the output expression for the alternate symbol. This same procedure can be followed for each pair of symbols in Figure 3-33.

Several points should be stressed regarding the logic symbol equivalences:

1. The equivalences can be extended to gates with *any* number of inputs.
2. None of the standard symbols have bubbles on their inputs, and all the alternate symbols do.
3. The standard and alternate symbols for each gate represent the same physical circuit; *there is no difference in the circuits represented by the two symbols.*
4. NAND and NOR gates are inverting gates, and so both the standard and the alternate symbols for each will have a bubble on *either* the input or the output. AND and OR gates are *noninverting* gates, and so the alternate symbols for each will have bubbles on *both* inputs and output.

Logic-Symbol Interpretation

Each of the logic-gate symbols of Figure 3-33 provides a unique interpretation of how the gate operates. Before we can demonstrate these interpretations, we must first establish the concept of **active logic levels**.

When an input or output line on a logic circuit symbol has *no bubble* on it, that line is said to be **active-HIGH.** When an input or output line *does* have a *bubble* on it, that line is said to be **active-LOW.** The presence or absence of a bubble, then, determines the active-HIGH/active-LOW status of a circuit's inputs and output, and is used to interpret the circuit operation.

To illustrate, Figure 3-34(a) shows the standard symbol for a NAND gate. The standard symbol has a bubble on its output and no bubbles on its inputs. Thus, it has an active-LOW output and active-HIGH inputs. The logic operation represented by this symbol can therefore be interpreted as follows:

The output goes LOW only when *all* of the inputs are HIGH.

Note that this says that the output will go to its active state only when *all* of the inputs are in their active states. The word "all" is used because of the AND symbol.

FIGURE 3-34   Interpretation of the two NAND gate symbols.

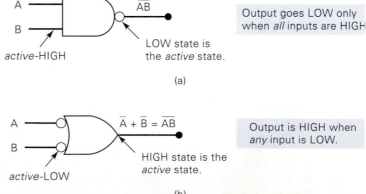

The alternate symbol for a NAND gate shown in Figure 3-34(b) has an active-HIGH output and active-LOW inputs, and so its operation can be stated as follows:

The output goes HIGH when *any input* is LOW.

This says that the output will be in its active state whenever *any* of the inputs is in its active state. The word "any" is used because of the OR symbol.

With a little thought, it can be seen that the two interpretations for the NAND symbols in Figure 3-34 are different ways of saying the same thing.

Summary

At this point you are probably wondering why there is a need to have two different symbols and interpretations for each logic gate. Hopefully, the reasons will become clear after reading the next section. For now, let us summarize the important points concerning the logic-gate representations.

1. To obtain the alternate symbol for a logic gate, take the standard symbol and change its operation symbol (OR to AND, or AND to OR), and change the bubbles on both inputs and output (i.e., delete bubbles that are present, and add bubbles where there are none).

2. To interpret the logic-gate operation, first note which logic state, 0 or 1, is the active state for the inputs and which is the active state for the output. Then realize that the output's active state is produced by having *all* of the inputs in their active state (if an AND symbol is used) or by having *any* of the inputs in its active state (if an OR symbol is used).

EXAMPLE 3-19

Give the interpretation of the two OR gate symbols.

Solution

The results are shown in Figure 3-35. Note that the word "any" is used when the operation symbol is an OR symbol and the word "all" is used when it includes an AND symbol.

FIGURE 3-35 Interpretation of the two OR gate symbols.

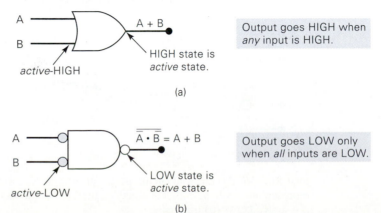

Output goes HIGH when *any* input is HIGH.

Output goes LOW only when *all* inputs are LOW.

Review Questions

1. Write the interpretation of the operation performed by the standard NOR gate symbol in Figure 3-33.
2. Repeat question 1 for the alternate NOR gate symbol.
3. Repeat question 1 for the alternate AND gate symbol.
4. Repeat question 1 for the standard AND gate symbol.

3-14 WHICH GATE REPRESENTATION TO USE

Some logic-circuit designers and some textbooks use only the standard logic-gate symbols in their circuit schematics. While this practice is not incorrect, it does nothing to make the circuit operation easier to follow. Proper use of the alternate gate symbols in the circuit diagram can make the circuit operation much clearer. This can be illustrated by considering the example shown in Figure 3-36.

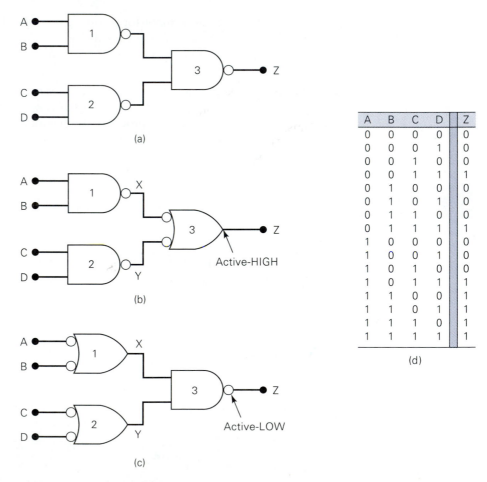

A	B	C	D	Z
0	0	0	0	0
0	0	0	1	0
0	0	1	0	0
0	0	1	1	1
0	1	0	0	0
0	1	0	1	0
0	1	1	0	0
0	1	1	1	1
1	0	0	0	0
1	0	0	1	0
1	0	1	0	0
1	0	1	1	1
1	1	0	0	1
1	1	0	1	1
1	1	1	0	1
1	1	1	1	1

(d)

FIGURE 3-36 (a) Original circuit using standard NAND symbols; (b) equivalent representation where output Z is active-HIGH; (c) equivalent representation where output Z is active-LOW; (d) truth table.

The circuit in Figure 3-36(a) contains three NAND gates connected to produce an output Z that depends on inputs A, B, C, and D. The circuit diagram uses the standard symbol for each of the NAND gates. While this diagram is logically correct, it does not facilitate any understanding of how the circuit functions. The improved circuit representations given in Figures 3-36(b) and (c), however, can be analyzed more easily to determine the circuit operation.

The representation of Figure 3-36(b) is obtained from the original circuit diagram by replacing NAND gate 3 with its alternate symbol. In this diagram, output Z is taken from a NAND gate symbol that has an active-HIGH output. Thus, we can say that Z will go HIGH when either X or Y is LOW. Now, since X and Y each appear at the output of NAND symbols having active-LOW outputs, we can say that X will go LOW only if $A = B = 1$, and Y will go LOW only if $C = D = 1$. Putting this all together, we can describe the circuit operation as follows:

Output Z will go HIGH whenever either $A = B = 1$ or $C = D = 1$ (or both).

This description can be translated to truth-table form by setting $Z = 1$ for those cases where $A = B = 1$ and for those cases where $C = D = 1$. For all other cases, Z is made a 0. The resultant truth table is shown in Figure 3-36(d).

The representation of Figure 3-36(c) is obtained from the original circuit diagram by replacing NAND gates 1 and 2 by their alternate symbols. In this equivalent representation the Z output is taken from a NAND gate that has an active-LOW output. Thus, we can say that Z will go LOW only when $X = Y = 1$. Since X and Y are active-HIGH outputs, we can say that X will be HIGH when either A or B is LOW, and Y will be HIGH when either C or D is LOW. Putting this all together, we can describe the circuit operation as follows:

Output Z will go LOW only when A or B is LOW and C or D is LOW.

This description can be translated to truth-table form by making $Z = 0$ for all cases where at least one of the A or B inputs is LOW at the same time that at least one of the C or D inputs is LOW. For all other cases, Z is made a 1. The resultant truth table is the same as that obtained for the circuit diagram of Figure 3-36(b).

Which Circuit Diagram Should Be Used?

The answer to this question depends on the particular function being performed by the circuit output. If the circuit is being used to cause some action (e.g., turn on an LED or activate another logic circuit) when output Z goes to the 1 state, then we say that Z is to be active-HIGH, and the circuit diagram of Figure 3-36(b) should be used. On the other hand, if the circuit is being used to cause some action when Z goes to the 0 state, then Z is to be active-LOW, and the diagram of Figure 3-36(c) should be used.

Of course, there will be situations where *both* output states are used to produce different actions and either one can be considered to be the active state. For these cases, either circuit representation can be used.

Bubble Placement

Refer to the circuit representation of Figure 3-36(b) and note that the symbols for NAND gates 1 and 2 were chosen to have active-LOW outputs to match the active-LOW inputs of NAND gate 3. Refer to the circuit representation of Figure 3-36(c) and note that the symbols for NAND gates 1 and 2 were chosen to have active-HIGH outputs to match the active-HIGH inputs of NAND gate 3. This leads to the following general rule for preparing logic-circuit schematics:

> **Whenever possible, choose gate symbols so that bubble outputs are connected to bubble inputs, and nonbubble outputs to nonbubble inputs.**

The following examples will show how this rule can be applied.

EXAMPLE 3-20

The logic circuit in Figure 3-37(a) is being used to activate an alarm when its output Z goes HIGH. Modify the circuit diagram so that it more effectively represents the circuit operation.

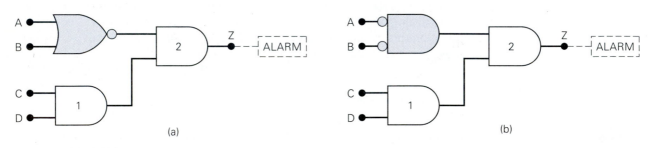

FIGURE 3-37 Example 3-20.

Solution

Since $Z = 1$ will activate the alarm, Z is to be active-HIGH. Thus, the AND gate 2 symbol does not have to be changed. The NOR gate symbol should be changed to the alternate symbol with a nonbubble (active-HIGH) output to match the nonbubble input of AND gate 2 as shown in Figure 3-37(b). Note that the circuit now has nonbubble outputs connected to the nonbubble inputs of gate 2.

EXAMPLE 3-21

When the output of the logic circuit in Figure 3-38(a) goes LOW, it activates another logic circuit. Modify the circuit diagram to more effectively represent the circuit operation.

Solution

Since Z is to be active-LOW, the symbol for OR gate 2 must be changed to its alternate symbol as shown in Figure 3-38(b). The new OR gate 2 symbol has bubble inputs, and so the AND gate and OR gate 1 symbols must be changed to bubbled

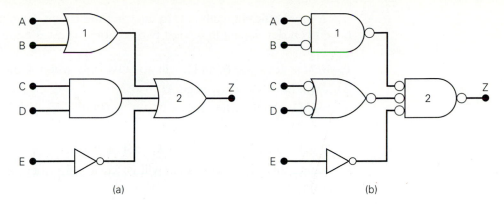

FIGURE 3-38   Example 3-21.

outputs as shown in Figure 3-38(b). The INVERTER already has a bubble output. Now the circuit has all bubble outputs connected to bubble inputs of gate 2.

Analyzing Circuits

When a logic-circuit schematic is drawn using the rules we followed in these examples, it is much easier for an engineer or technician (or student) to follow the signal flow through the circuit and to determine the input conditions that are needed to activate the output. This will be illustrated in the following examples—which, incidentally, use circuit diagrams taken from the logic schematics of an actual microcomputer.

EXAMPLE 3-22

The logic circuit in Figure 3-39 generates an output, *MEM,* that is used to activate the memory ICs in a particular microcomputer. Determine the input conditions necessary to activate *MEM*.

FIGURE 3-39   Example 3-22.

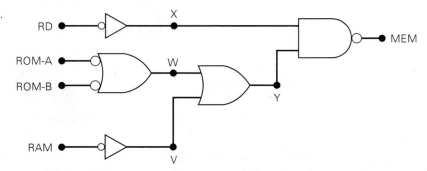

Solution

One way to do this would be to write the expression for *MEM* in terms of the inputs *RD, ROM-A, ROM-B,* and *RAM,* and to evaluate it for the 16 possible combinations of these inputs. While this method would work, it would require a lot more work than is necessary.

A more efficient method is to interpret the circuit diagram using the ideas we have been developing in the last two sections. These are the steps:

1. *MEM* is active-LOW, and it will go LOW only when *X* and *Y* are HIGH.
2. *X* will be HIGH only when *RD* = 0.
3. *Y* will be HIGH when either *W* or *V* is HIGH.
4. *V* will be HIGH when *RAM* = 0.
5. *W* will be HIGH when either *ROM-A* or *ROM-B* = 0.
6. Putting this all together, *MEM* will go LOW only when *RD* = 0 *and* at least one of the three inputs *ROM-A*, *ROM-B*, or *RAM* is LOW.

EXAMPLE 3-23

The logic circuit in Figure 3-40 is used to control the drive spindle motor for a floppy disk drive when the microcomputer is sending data to or receiving data from the disk. The circuit will turn on the motor when *DRIVE* = 1. Determine the input conditions necessary to turn on the motor.

FIGURE 3-40   Example 3-23.

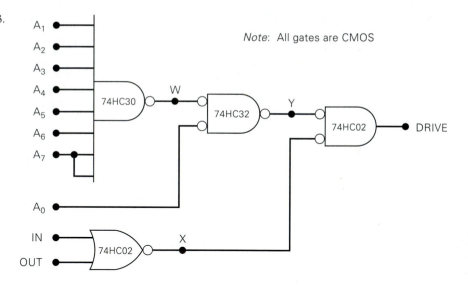

Solution

Once again we will interpret the diagram in a step-by-step fashion:

1. *DRIVE* is active-HIGH, and it will go HIGH only when *X* = *Y* = 0.
2. *X* will be LOW when either *IN* or *OUT* is HIGH.
3. *Y* will be LOW only when *W* = 0 and A_0 = 0.
4. *W* will be LOW only when A_1 through A_7 are all HIGH.
5. Putting this all together, *DRIVE* will be HIGH when $A_1 = A_2 = A_3 = A_4 = A_5 = A_6 = A_7 = 1$ and $A_0 = 0$, and either *IN* or *OUT* or both are 1.

Note the strange symbol for the eight-input CMOS NAND gate (74HC30); also note that signal A_7 is connected to two of the NAND inputs.

Asserted Levels

We have been describing logic signals as being active-LOW or active-HIGH. For example, the output *MEM* in Figure 3-39 is active-LOW, and the output *DRIVE* in Figure 3-40 is active-HIGH, since these are the output states that cause something to happen. Similarly, Figure 3-40 has active-HIGH inputs A_1 to A_7, and active-LOW input A_0.

When a logic signal is in its active state, it can be said to be **asserted.** For example, when we say that input A_0 is asserted, we are saying that it is in its active-LOW state. When a logic signal is not in its active state, it is said to be **unasserted.** Thus, when we say that *DRIVE* is unasserted, we mean that it is in its inactive state (LOW).

Clearly, the terms "asserted" and "unasserted" are synonymous with "active" and "inactive," respectively:

asserted = active
unasserted = inactive

Both sets of terms are in common use in the digital field, so you should recognize both ways of describing a logic signal's active state.

Labeling Active-LOW Logic Signals

It has become common practice to use an overbar to label active-LOW signals. The overbar serves as another indication that the signal is active-LOW; of course, the absence of an overbar means that the signal is active-HIGH.

To illustrate, all of the signals in Figure 3-39 are active-LOW, and so they can be labeled as follows:

$$\overline{RD}, \quad \overline{ROM\text{-}A}, \quad \overline{ROM\text{-}B}, \quad \overline{RAM}, \quad \overline{MEM}$$

Remember, the overbar is simply a way to emphasize that these are active-LOW signals. We will employ this convention for labeling logic signals whenever appropriate.

Labeling Bistate Signals

Very often, an output signal will have two active states; that is, it will have one important function in the HIGH state and another in the LOW state. It is customary to label such signals so that both active states are apparent. A common example is the read/write signal, $RD/\overline{WR}$, which is interpreted as follows: when this signal is HIGH, the read operation (*RD*) is performed; when it is LOW, the write operation (*WR*) is performed.

1. Use the method of Examples 3-22 and 3-23 to determine the input conditions needed to activate the output of the circuit in Figure 3-37(b).
2. Repeat question 1 for the circuit of Figure 3-38(b).
3. How many NAND gates are in Figure 3-39?
4. How many NOR gates are in Figure 3-40?
5. What will be the output level in Figure 3-38(b) when all of the inputs are asserted?
6. What inputs are required to assert the alarm output in Figure 3-37(b)?
7. Which of the following signals is active-LOW: RD, $\overline{W}$, $R/\overline{W}$?

3-15   IEEE/ANSI STANDARD LOGIC SYMBOLS

The logic symbols that we have used throughout this chapter are well-known standard symbols that have been widely used in the digital industry for many years. These symbols work well for the basic logic gates because each gate symbol has a distinctive shape, and each gate input has the same function. They do not provide enough useful information, however, for the more complex logic devices such as flip-flops, counters, decoders, multiplexers, memories, and microprocessor interface ICs. These complex ICs often have several inputs and outputs with different functions and modes of operation.

In order to provide more useful information about these complex logic devices, a new set of standard symbols was introduced in 1984 until IEEE/ANSI Standard 91-1984. These newer **IEEE/ANSI symbols** are gradually being accepted by more and more electronics companies and IC manufacturers, and they have begun to appear in their published literature. In addition, military contracts in the United States now require the use of these new symbols. It is therefore important to become familiar with these newer standard symbols.

The principal difference in the IEEE/ANSI standard is that it uses rectangular symbols for all devices instead of different symbol shapes for each device. A special *dependency notation* system is used to indicate how the outputs *depend* on the inputs. Figure 3-41 shows the newer rectangular symbols alongside the traditional symbols for the basic gates. Study them carefully and note the following points:

1. The rectangular symbols use a small right triangle in place of the small bubble of the traditional symbols to indicate the inversion of the logic level. The presence or absence of the triangle also signifies whether an input or output is active-LOW or active-HIGH.
2. A special notation inside each rectangular symbol describes the logic relation between inputs and output. The "1" inside the INVERTER symbol denotes a device with only *one* input; the triangle on the output indicates that the output will go to its active-LOW state when that one input is in its active-HIGH state. The "&" inside the AND symbol means that the output will go to its active-HIGH state when all of the inputs are in their active-HIGH state. The "≥" inside the OR gate means that the output will go to its active state (HIGH) whenever *one or more* inputs are in their active state (HIGH).

FIGURE 3-41 Standard logic symbols: (a) traditional; (b) rectangular.

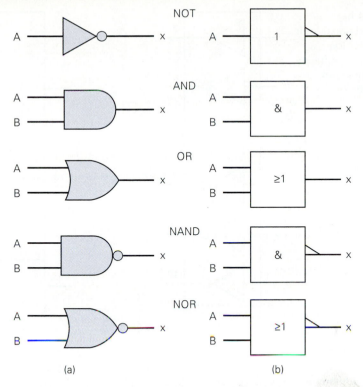

3. The rectangular symbols for the NAND and the NOR are the same as those for the AND and the OR, respectively, with the addition of the small inversion triangle on the output.

IEEE/ANSI Symbols for Logic-Gate ICs

The rectangular symbols can also be used to represent the complete logic of an IC package that contains a number of independent gates. This is illustrated in Figure 3-42 for the 74LS04 TTL hex* INVERTER IC, and in Figure 3-43 for the 74HC20 CMOS dual four-input NAND IC. Each logic gate is represented as a separate rectangular block. Note that the rectangular symbols indicate the logic operation notation only in the top block; it is understood to apply to all the other blocks representing the other gates on the chip.

It is important to understand the difference between the two alternate ways to represent a logic gate in a circuit and the difference between the two different standards for logic-gate symbols. You choose which set of standard logic symbols to use—either the traditional symbols (distinctive shapes for each type of gate) or the new standard rectangular symbols. Regardless of which symbols you choose to use, there are two possible ways to represent a gate in a circuit diagram depending on its active output state. This is illustrated in Example 3-24.

---

* Indicates six INVERTERS.

FIGURE 3-42 74LS04 hex
INVERTER IC: (a) traditional logic
symbol; (b) rectangular logic
symbol. The notation "1" appears
only in the top rectangle but
applies to all blocks below.

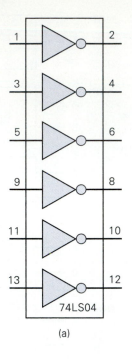
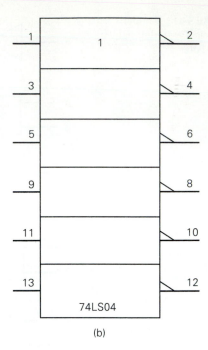

FIGURE 3-43 74HC20 dual four-
input NAND IC: (a) traditional
symbol; (b) rectangular symbol.

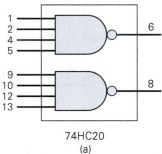
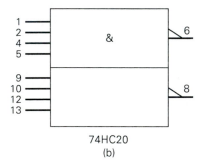

<table>
<tr><td>

EXAMPLE 3-24

</td><td>

Figure 3-44(a) shows the two representations for a NOR gate using the traditional
logic symbols. Remember, the choice of which representation to use in a circuit di-

</td></tr>
</table>

FIGURE 3-44 Both
representations of a NOR gate
using the two types of symbols:
(a) traditional; (b) rectangular.

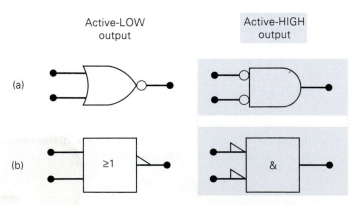

agram is determined by the desired active state of the output. Redraw the two representations using the new IEEE/ANSI symbols.

Solution

Figure 3-44(b) shows the results.

IEEE/ANSI Symbols for Complex ICs

There would be no real advantage to the new symbols if all we had to deal with were the basic logic gates. For the more complex logic devices, however, the new standard symbols with their *dependency notation* will specify the complete logic operation of the device. This makes it virtually unnecessary to refer to the manufacturer's data manual to find out how a particular logic IC is functioning in a circuit. We will see examples of this when we encounter the more complex logic circuits in subsequent chapters.

The traditional logic symbols are employed in most of the circuit diagrams throughout this book, and the IEEE/ANSI symbols will be used only occasionally. Some of the end-of-chapter problems require analysis or construction of circuits utilizing the newer notation. Additionally, whenever a new type of logic device or circuit is introduced, both types of symbols are presented. In this way, you will become familiar with the dependency notation that is the main benefit of the new standard.

Review Questions

1. What is the major advantage of the new IEEE/ANSI symbols?
2. Draw all of the basic logic gates using both the traditional symbols and the IEEE standard symbols.
3. Repeat question 2 for the alternate representation of each gate.

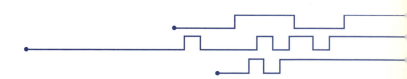

SUMMARY

1. Boolean algebra is a mathematical tool used in the analysis and design of digital circuits.
2. The basic Boolean operations are the OR, AND, and NOT operations.
3. An OR gate produces a HIGH output when any input is HIGH. An AND gate produces a HIGH output only when all inputs are HIGH. A NOT circuit (INVERTER) produces an output that is the opposite logic level as the input.

4. A NOR gate is the same as an OR gate with its output connected to an IN-VERTER. A NAND gate is the same as an AND gate with its output connected to an INVERTER.

5. Boolean theorems and rules can be used to simplify the expression of a logic circuit and can lead to a simpler way of implementing the circuit.

6. NAND gates can be used to implement any of the basic Boolean operations. NOR gates can be used likewise.

7. Either standard or alternate symbols can be used for each logic gate depending on whether the output is to be active-HIGH or active-LOW.

8. The IEEE/ANSI standard for logic symbols uses rectangular symbols for each logic device with special notations inside the rectangles to show how the outputs depend on the inputs.

IMPORTANT TERMS*

Boolean algebra	NOT operation	alternate logic symbols
logic level	inversion-complementation	active logic levels
truth table	NOT circuit (INVERTER)	active-HIGH
OR operation	NOR gate	active-LOW
OR gate	NAND gate	asserted
AND operation	Boolean theorems	unasserted
AND gate	DeMorgan's theorems	IEEE/ANSI symbols

PROBLEMS

The **blue** letters preceding some of the problems are used to indicate the nature or type of problem as follows:

    C   challenging problem

    T   troubleshooting problem

    D   design or circuit-modification problem

    N   new concept or technique not covered in text

SECTION 3-3

3-1. Draw the output waveform for the circuit of Figure 3-45.

3-2. Suppose that the A input in Figure 3-45 is unintentionally shorted to ground (i.e., $A = 0$). Draw the resulting output waveform.

3-3. Suppose that the A input in Figure 3-45 is unintentionally shorted to the +5 V supply line (i.e., $A = 1$). Draw the resulting output waveform.

3-4. Read the statements below concerning an OR gate. At first they may appear to be valid, but after some thought you should realize that neither one is *always* true. Prove this by showing a specific example to refute each statement.

---

* These terms can be found in **boldface** type in the chapter and are defined in the Glossary at the end of the book.

FIGURE 3-45

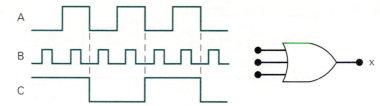

(a) If the output waveform from an OR gate is the same as the waveform at one of its inputs, the other input is being held permanently LOW.

(b) If the output waveform from an OR gate is always HIGH, one of its inputs is being held permanently HIGH.

3-5. How many different sets of input conditions will produce a HIGH output from a five-input OR gate?

SECTION 3-4

3-6. Change the OR gate in Figure 3-45 to an AND gate.
(a) Draw the output waveform.
(b) Draw the output waveform if the *A* input is permanently shorted to ground.
(c) Draw the output waveform if *A* is permanently shorted to +5 V.

D   3-7. Refer to Figure 3-4. Modify the circuit so that the alarm is to be activated only when the pressure and the temperature exceed their maximum limits at the same time.

3-8. Change the OR gate in Figure 3-6 to an AND gate and draw the output waveform.

3-9. Suppose that you have an unknown two-input gate that is either an OR gate or an AND gate. What combination of input levels should you apply to the gate's inputs to determine which type of gate it is?

3-10. *True or false:* No matter how many inputs it has, an AND gate will produce a HIGH output for only one combination of input levels.

SECTIONS 3-5 TO 3-7

3-11. Add an INVERTER to the output of the OR gate from Figure 3-45. Draw the waveform at the INVERTER output.

3-12. (a) Write the Boolean expression for output *x* in Figure 3-46(a). Determine the value of *x* for all possible input conditions, and list the values in a truth table.
(b) Repeat for the circuit in Figure 3-46(b).

3-13. Determine the complete truth table for the circuit of Figure 3-15(b) by finding the logic levels present at each gate output for each of the 32 possible input combinations.

3-14. Change each OR to an AND, and each AND to an OR, in Figure 3-15(b). Then write the expression for the output.

3-15. Determine the complete truth table for the circuit of Figure 3-16 by finding the logic levels present at each gate output for each of the 16 possible combinations of input levels.

FIGURE 3-46

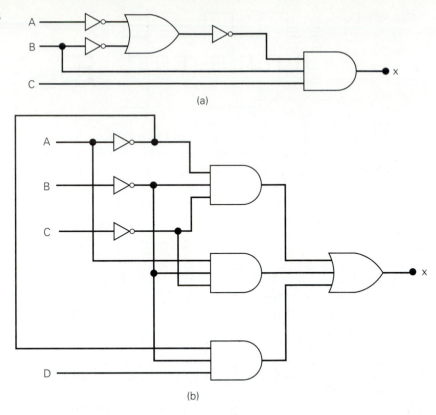

(a)

(b)

SECTION 3-8

3-16. For each of the following expressions, construct the corresponding logic circuit, using AND and OR gates and INVERTERs.

(a) $x = \overline{AB(C + D)}$

(b) $z = \overline{(A + B + \overline{C}D\overline{E})} + \overline{B}C\overline{D}$

(c) $y = \overline{(M + N + \overline{P}Q)}$

(d) $x = \overline{W + P\overline{Q}}$

(e) $z = MN(P + \overline{N})$

SECTION 3-9

3-17. (a) Apply the input waveforms of Figure 3-47 to a NOR gate, and draw the output waveform.

(b) Repeat with C held permanently LOW.

(c) Repeat with C held HIGH.

FIGURE 3-47

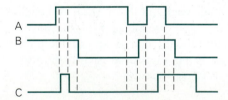

3-18. Repeat Problem 3-17 for a NAND gate.

3-19. Write the output expression for the circuit of Figure 3-48. Then determine the complete truth table.

FIGURE 3-48

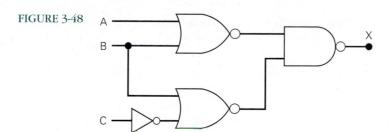

3-20. Determine the truth table for the circuit of Figure 3-24.

3-21. Modify the circuits that were constructed in Problem 3-16 so that NAND gates and NOR gates are used wherever appropriate.

SECTION 3-10

3-22. DRILL QUESTION

Complete each expression.

(a) $A + 1 =$ _____

(b) $A \cdot A =$ _____

(c) $B \cdot \overline{B} =$ _____

(d) $C + C =$ _____

(e) $x \cdot 0 =$ _____

(f) $D \cdot 1 =$ _____

(g) $D + 0 =$ _____

(h) $C + \overline{C} =$ _____

(i) $G + GF =$ _____

(j) $y + \overline{w}y =$ _____

3-23. (a) Prove theorem (15) by trying all possible cases.

(b) Prove it by using theorem (14) to substitute for x.

C **3-24.** (a) Simplify the following expression using theorems (13b), (3), and (4):

$$x = (M + N)(\overline{M} + P)(\overline{N} + \overline{P})$$

(b) Simplify the following expression using theorems (13a), (8), and (6):

$$z = \overline{A}B\overline{C} + AB\overline{C} + B\overline{C}D$$

SECTIONS 3-11 AND 3-12

3-25. Prove DeMorgan's theorems by trying all possible cases.

3-26. Simplify each of the following expressions using DeMorgan's theorems.

(a) $\overline{\overline{ABC}}$

(b) $\overline{\overline{A} + \overline{BC}}$

(c) $\overline{\overline{AB}\overline{CD}}$

(d) $\overline{A(B + \overline{C})D}$

(e) $\overline{(M + \overline{N})(\overline{M} + N)}$

(f) $\overline{\overline{ABCD}}$

3-27. Use DeMorgan's theorems to simplify the expression for the output of Figure 3-48.

C **3-28.** Convert the circuit of Figure 3-46(b) to one using only NAND gates. Then write the output expression for the new circuit, simplify it using DeMorgan's theorems, and compare it with the expression for the original circuit.

3-29. Convert the circuit of Figure 3-46(a) to one using only NOR gates. Then write the expression for the new circuit, simplify it using DeMorgan's theorems, and compare it with the expression for the original circuit.

3-30. Show how a two-input NAND gate can be constructed from two-input NOR gates.

3-31. Show how a two-input NOR gate can be constructed from two-input NAND gates.

3-32. A jet aircraft employs a system for monitoring the rpm, pressure, and temperature values of its engines using sensors that operate as follows:

RPM sensor output = 0 only when speed < 4800 rpm
P sensor output = 0 only when pressure < 220 psi
T sensor output = 0 only when temperature < 200°F

Figure 3-49 shows the logic circuit that controls a cockpit warning light for certain combinations of engine conditions. Assume that a HIGH at output *W* activates the warning light.

(a) Determine what engine conditions will give a warning to the pilot.

(b) Change this circuit to one using all NAND gates.

FIGURE 3-49

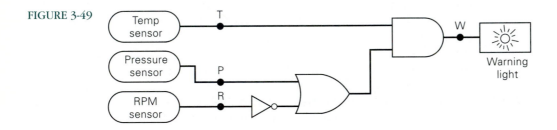

SECTIONS 3-13 AND 3-14

3-33. Draw the standard representations for each of the basic logic gates. Then draw the alternate representations.

3-34. For each statement below, draw the appropriate logic-gate representation, and indicate the type of gate.

(a) A HIGH output occurs only when all three inputs are LOW.

(b) A LOW output occurs when any of the four inputs is LOW.

(c) A LOW output occurs only when all eight inputs are HIGH.

3-35. The circuit of Figure 3-48 is supposed to be a simple digital combination lock whose output will generate an active-LOW $\overline{UNLOCK}$ signal for only one combination of inputs.

(a) Modify the circuit diagram so that it more effectively represents the circuit operation.

(b) Use the new circuit diagram to determine the input combination that will activate the output. Do this by working back from the output using the information given by the gate symbols as was done in Examples 3-22 and 3-23. Compare the results with the truth table obtained in Problem 3-19.

3-36. **(a)** Determine the input conditions needed to activate output Z in Figure 3-37(b). Do this by working back from the output as was done in Examples 3-22 and 3-23.

(b) Assume that it is the LOW state of Z that is to activate the alarm. Change the circuit diagram to reflect this, and then use the revised diagram to determine the input conditions needed to activate the alarm.

D **3-37.** Modify the circuit of Figure 3-40 so that $A_1 = 0$ is needed to produce $DRIVE = 1$ instead of $A_1 = 1$.

3-38. Determine the input conditions needed to cause the output in Figure 3-50 to go to its active state.

FIGURE 3-50

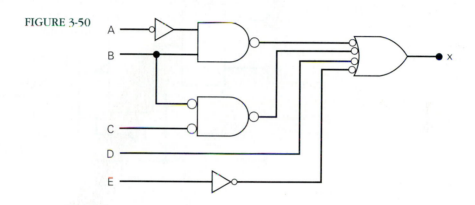

3-39. Use the results of Problem 3-38 to obtain the complete truth table for the circuit of Figure 3-50.

3-40. What is the asserted state for the output of Figure 3-50? For the output of Figure 3-36(c)?

3-41. Figure 3-51 shows an application of logic gates that simulates a two-way switch like the ones used in our homes to turn a light on or off from two different switches. Here the light is an LED which will be ON (conducting) when the NOR gate output is LOW. Note that this output is labeled $\overline{LIGHT}$ to indi-

FIGURE 3-51

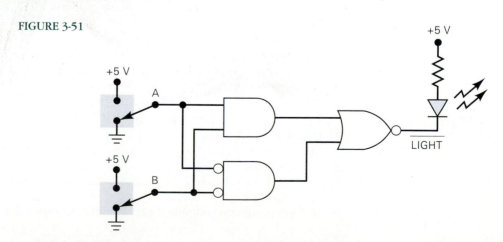

cate that it is active-LOW. Determine the input conditions needed to turn on the LED. Then verify that the circuit operates as a two-way switch using switches *A* and *B*. In Chapter 4 you will learn how to design circuits like this one to produce a given relationship between inputs and outputs.

SECTION 3-15

3-42. Redraw the circuits of **(a)** Figure 3-50 and **(b)** Figure 3-51 using the IEEE/ANSI symbols.

3-43. Determine the Boolean expression for output *Z* in Figure 3-52.

FIGURE 3-52

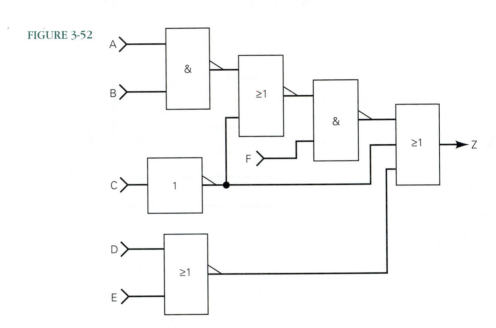

C 3-44. The output of the circuit of Figure 3-52 is supposed to be active-LOW. Redraw it to more effectively represent the circuit operation.

C 3-45. Use the redrawn version of the circuit of Figure 3-52, and do each of the following.
(a) Determine the various input conditions that will produce the active-LOW output state. Do this using only the circuit diagram without writing the expression for *Z* and without generating the complete truth table. The results should be:

A	B	C	D	E	F
1	1	1	1	1	1
1	1	1	1	0	1
1	1	1	0	1	1

(b) Verify that the simplified expression for output *Z* is given by

$$Z = \overline{ABCF(D + E)}$$

(c) Plug each of the sets of conditions from (a) into the expression you determined in (b), and verify that each one produces $Z = 0$.

MICROCOMPUTER APPLICATION

C **3-46.** Refer to Figure 3-40 in Example 3-23. Inputs A_7 through A_0 are *address* inputs that are supplied to this circuit from outputs of the microprocessor chip in a microcomputer. The eight-bit address code A_7 to A_0 selects which device the microprocessor wants to activate. In Example 3-23, the required address code to activate the disk drive was A_7 through $A_0 = 11111110_2 = FE_{16}$.

Modify the circuit so that the microprocessor must supply an address code of $4A_{16}$ to activate the disk drive.

CHALLENGING EXERCISES

C **3-47.** Show how $x = AB\overline{C}$ can be implemented with one two-input NOR and one two-input NAND gate.

C **3-48.** Implement $y = ABCD$ using two-input NAND gates.

ANSWERS TO SECTION REVIEW QUESTIONS

SECTION 3-2
1. $x = 1$ 2. $x = 0$ 3. 32

SECTION 3-3
1. All inputs LOW   2. $x = A + B + C + D + E + F$
3. Constant HIGH

SECTION 3-4
1. All five inputs $= 1$ 2. A LOW input will keep the output LOW.   3. False; see truth table of each gate.

SECTION 3-5
1. Output of second INVERTER will be same as input A.
2. y will be LOW only for $A = B = 1$.

SECTION 3-6
1. $x = \overline{A} + B + C + \overline{AD}$

SECTION 3-7
1. $x = 1$ 2. $x = 1$

SECTION 3-8
1. See Figure 3-15(a).   2. See Figure 3-17(b).
3. See Figure 3-15(b).

SECTION 3-9
1. All inputs LOW   2. $x = 0$
3. $x = A + B + \overline{CD}$

SECTION 3-10
1. $y = A\overline{C}$ 2. $y = \overline{A}\,\overline{B}\,\overline{D}$

SECTION 3-11
1. $z = \overline{A}\overline{B} + C$ 2. $y = (\overline{R} + S + \overline{T})Q$ 3. Same as Figure 3-28 except NAND is replaced by NOR.
4. $y = A\overline{B}(C + \overline{D})$

SECTION 3-12
1. Three   2. NOR circuit is more efficient because it can be implemented with one 74LS02 IC.
3. $x = \overline{(\overline{AB})(\overline{CD})} = \overline{(\overline{AB})} + \overline{(\overline{CD})} = AB + CD$

SECTION 3-13
1. Output goes LOW when any input is HIGH.
2. Output goes HIGH only when all inputs are LOW.
3. Output goes LOW when any input is LOW.
4. Output goes HIGH only when all inputs are HIGH.

SECTION 3-14
1. Z will go HIGH when $A = B = 0$ and $C = D = 1$.
2. Z will go LOW when $A = B = 0$, $E = 1$, and either C or D or both are 0.   3. Two   4. Two   5. LOW
6. $A = B = 0$, $C = D = 1$ 7. $\overline{W}$

SECTION 3-15
1. The IEEE symbols with their dependency notation specify the complete operation of the logic device.
2. See Figure 3-41.   3. See Figure 3-44.

Combinational Logic Circuits

■ OUTLINE

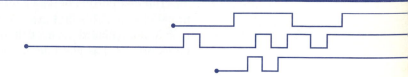

■ OBJECTIVES

Upon completion of this chapter, you will be able to:

- Convert a logic expression into a sum-of-products expression.
- Perform the necessary steps to derive a sum-of-products expression in order to design a combinational logic circuit in its simplest form.
- Use Boolean algebra and the Karnaugh map as tools to simplify and design logic circuits.
- Explain the operation of both exclusive-OR and exclusive-NOR circuits.
- Design simple logic circuits without the help of a truth table.
- Implement enable circuits.
- Cite the basic characteristics of digital ICs.
- Understand the inherent operative differences between TTL and CMOS.
- Use the basic troubleshooting rules of digital systems.
- Deduce from measured results the faults of malfunctioning combinational logic circuits.
- Describe the fundamental idea of programmable logic.

■ INTRODUCTION

In Chapter 3 we studied the operation of all of the basic logic gates, and we used Boolean algebra to describe and analyze circuits that were made up of combinations of logic gates. These circuits can be classified as *combinational* logic circuits because, at any time, the logic level at the output depends on the combination of logic levels present at the inputs. A combinational circuit has no *memory* characteristic, so its output depends *only* on the current value of its inputs.

In this chapter we will continue our study of combinational circuits. To start, we will go further into the simplification of logic circuits. Two methods will be used; one will use Boolean algebra theorems, the other a *mapping* technique. In addition, we will study simple techniques for designing logic circuits to satisfy a given set of requirements. A complete study of logic-circuit design is not one of our objectives, but the methods we introduce will provide a good introduction to logic design.

The last portion of the chapter is devoted to the troubleshooting of combinational circuits. This first exposure to troubleshooting should begin to develop the type of analytical skills needed for successful troubleshooting. To make this material as practical as possible, we will first present some of the basic characteristics of logic-gate ICs in the TTL and CMOS logic families along with a description of the most common types of faults encountered in digital IC circuits.

4-1 SUM-OF-PRODUCTS FORM

The methods of logic-circuit simplification and design that we will study require the logic expression to be in a **sum-of-products** form. Some examples of this form are:

1. $ABC + \overline{A}B\overline{C}$
2. $AB + \overline{A}B\overline{C} + \overline{C}D + D$
3. $\overline{A}B + C\overline{D} + EF + GK + H\overline{L}$

Each of these sum-of-products expressions consists of two or more AND terms (products) that are ORed together. Each AND term consists of one or more variables *individually* appearing in either complemented or uncomplemented form. For example, in the sum-of-products expression $ABC + \overline{A}B\overline{C}$, the first AND product contains the variables A, B, and C in their uncomplemented (not inverted) form. The second AND term contains A and C in their complemented (inverted) form. Note that in a sum-of-products expression, one inversion sign *cannot* cover more than one variable in a term (e.g., we cannot have $\overline{ABC}$ or $\overline{RST}$).

Product-of-Sums

Another general form for logic expressions is sometimes used in logic-circuit design. Called the **product-of-sums** form, it consists of two or more OR terms (sums) that are ANDed together. Each OR term contains one or more variables in complemented or uncomplemented form. Here are some product-of-sum expressions:

1. $(A + \overline{B} + C)(A + C)$
2. $(A + \overline{B})(\overline{C} + D)F$
3. $(A + C)(B + \overline{D})(\overline{B} + C)(A + \overline{D} + \overline{E})$

The methods of circuit simplification and design that we will be using are based on the sum-of-products form, so we will not be doing much with the product-of-sums form. It will, however, occur from time to time in some logic circuits that have a particular structure.

1. Which of the following expressions is a sum-of-products form?
   (a) $AB + CD + E$
   (b) $AB(C + D)$
   (c) $(A + B)(C + D + F)$
   (d) $\overline{MN} + PQ$
2. Repeat question 1 for the product-of-sums form.

4-2 SIMPLIFYING LOGIC CIRCUITS

Once the expression for a logic circuit has been obtained, we may be able to reduce it to a simpler form containing fewer terms or fewer variables in one or more terms. The new expression can then be used to implement a circuit that is equivalent to the original circuit but that contains fewer gates and connections.

To illustrate, the circuit of Figure 4-1(a) can be simplified to produce the circuit of Figure 4-1(b). Since both circuits perform the same logic, it should be obvious that the simpler circuit is more desirable because it contains fewer gates and will therefore be smaller and cheaper than the original. Furthermore, the circuit reliability will improve because there are fewer interconnections that can be potential circuit faults.

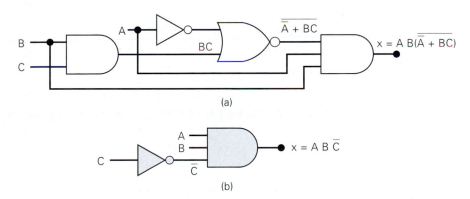

(a)

(b)

FIGURE 4-1 It is often possible to simplify a logic circuit such as that in part (a) to produce a more efficient implementation, shown in (b).

In subsequent sections we will study two methods for simplifying logic circuits. One method will utilize the Boolean algebra theorems and, as we shall see, is greatly dependent on inspiration and experience. The other method (Karnaugh mapping) is a systematic, step-by-step approach. Some instructors may wish to skip over this latter method because it is somewhat mechanical and probably does not contribute to a better understanding of Boolean algebra. This can be done without affecting the continuity or clarity of the rest of the text.

4-3 ALGEBRAIC SIMPLIFICATION

We can use the Boolean algebra theorems that we studied in Chapter 3 to help us simplify the expression for a logic circuit. Unfortunately, it is not always obvious which theorems should be applied in order to produce the simplest result. Furthermore, there is no easy way to tell whether the simplified expression is in its simplest form or whether it could have been simplified further. Thus, algebraic simplification often becomes a process of trial and error. With experience, however, one can become adept at obtaining reasonably good results.

The examples that follow will illustrate many of the ways in which the Boolean theorems can be applied in trying to simplify an expression. You should notice that these examples contain two essential steps:

1. The original expression is put into the sum-of-products form by repeated application of DeMorgan's theorems and multiplication of terms.

2. Once the original expression is in this form, the product terms are checked for common factors, and factoring is performed wherever possible. Hopefully, the factoring results in the elimination of one or more terms.

EXAMPLE 4-1

Simplify the logic circuit shown in Figure 4-2(a).

Solution

The first step is to determine the expression for the output using the method presented in Section 3-6. The result is

$$z = ABC + A\bar{B} \cdot (\overline{\overline{AC}})$$

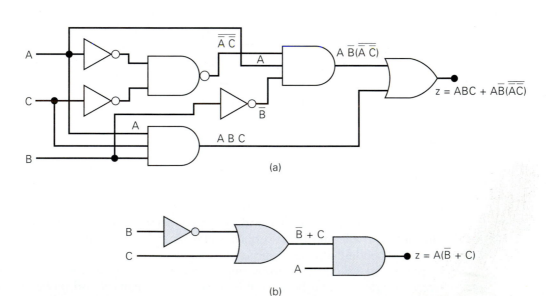

(a)

(b)

FIGURE 4-2   Example 4-1.

Once the expression is determined, it is usually a good idea to break down all large inverter signs using DeMorgan's theorems and then multiply out all terms.

$$
\begin{aligned}
z &= ABC + A\overline{B}(\overline{\overline{A} + \overline{C}}) &&\text{[theorem (17)]} \\
&= ABC + A\overline{B}(A + C) &&\text{[cancel double inversions]} \\
&= ABC + A\overline{B}A + A\overline{B}C &&\text{[multiply out]} \\
&= ABC + A\overline{B} + A\overline{B}C &&[A \cdot A = A]
\end{aligned}
$$

With the expression now in sum-of-products form, we should look for common variables among the various terms with the intention of factoring. The first and third terms above have AC in common, which can be factored out:

$$z = AC(B + \overline{B}) + A\overline{B}$$

Since $B + \overline{B} = 1$, then

$$
\begin{aligned}
z &= AC(1) + A\overline{B} \\
&= AC + A\overline{B}
\end{aligned}
$$

We can now factor out A, which results in

$$z = A(C + \overline{B})$$

This result can be simplified no further. Its circuit implementation is shown in Figure 4-2(b). It is obvious that the circuit in (b) is a great deal simpler than the original circuit in (a).

EXAMPLE 4-2

Simplify the expression $z = ABC + AB\overline{C} + A\overline{B}C$.

Solution

We will look at two different ways to arrive at the same result.

Method 1: The first two terms in the expression have the product AB in common. Thus,

$$
\begin{aligned}
z &= AB(C + \overline{C}) + A\overline{B}C \\
&= AB(1) + A\overline{B}C \\
&= AB + A\overline{B}C
\end{aligned}
$$

We can factor the variable A from both terms:

$$z = A(B + \overline{B}C)$$

Invoking theorem (15),

$$z = A(B + C)$$

Method 2: The original expression is $z = ABC + AB\overline{C} + A\overline{B}C$. The first two terms have AB in common. The first and last terms have AC in common. How do we know whether to factor AB from the first two terms or AC from the two end terms? Actually, we can do both by using the ABC term *twice*. In other words, we can rewrite the expression as

$$z = ABC + AB\overline{C} + A\overline{B}C + ABC$$

where we have added an extra term ABC. This is valid and will not change the value of the expression, since $ABC + ABC = ABC$ [theorem (7)]. Now we can factor AB from the first two terms and AC from the last two terms:

$$z = AB(C + \overline{C}) + AC(\overline{B} + B)$$
$$= AB \cdot 1 + AC \cdot 1$$
$$= AB + AC = A(B + C)$$

This is, of course, the same result as obtained with method 1. This trick of using the same term twice can always be used. In fact, the same term can be used more than twice if necessary.

<table>
<tr><td>EXAMPLE
4-3</td><td>

Simplify $z = \overline{AC}(\overline{ABD}) + \overline{A}B\overline{C}\,\overline{D} + A\overline{B}C$.

Solution

First, use DeMorgan's theorem on the first term:

$$z = \overline{AC}(A + \overline{B} + \overline{D}) + \overline{A}B\overline{C}\overline{D} + A\overline{B}C \qquad \text{(step 1)}$$

Multiplying out yields

$$z = \overline{AC}A + \overline{AC}\overline{B} + \overline{AC}\overline{D} + \overline{A}B\overline{C}\overline{D} + A\overline{B}C \qquad (2)$$

Since $\overline{A} \cdot A = 0$, the first term is eliminated:

$$z = \overline{A}\overline{B}C + \overline{A}C\overline{D} + \overline{A}B\overline{C}\overline{D} + A\overline{B}C \qquad (3)$$

This is the desired sum-of-products form. Now we must look for common factors among the various product terms. The idea is to check for the largest common factor between any two or more product terms. For example, the first and last terms have the common factor $\overline{B}C$, and the second and third terms share the common factor $\overline{A}\overline{D}$. We can factor these out as follows:

$$z = \overline{B}C(\overline{A} + A) + \overline{A}\overline{D}(C + B\overline{C}) \qquad (4)$$

Now, since $\overline{A} + A = 1$, and $C + B\overline{C} = C + B$ [theorem (15)], we have

$$z = \overline{B}C + \overline{A}\overline{D}(B + C) \qquad (5)$$

This same result could have been reached with other choices for the factoring. For example, we could have factored C from the first, second, and fourth product terms in step 3 to obtain

</td></tr>
</table>

$$z = C(\overline{AB} + \overline{AD} + A\overline{B}) + \overline{ABC}\,\overline{D}$$

The expression inside the parentheses can be factored further:

$$z = C(\overline{B}[\overline{A} + A] + \overline{AD}) + \overline{ABC}\,\overline{D}$$

Since $\overline{A} + A = 1$, this becomes

$$z = C(\overline{B} + \overline{AD}) + \overline{ABC}\,\overline{D}$$

Multiplying out yields

$$z = \overline{B}C + \overline{ACD} + \overline{ABC}\,\overline{D}$$

Now we can factor $\overline{A}\overline{D}$ from the second and third terms to get

$$z = \overline{B}C + \overline{AD}(C + B\overline{C})$$

Using theorem (15) the expression in parentheses becomes $B + C$. Thus, we finally have

$$z = \overline{B}C + \overline{AD}(B + C)$$

This is the same result that we obtained earlier, but it took us many more steps. This illustrates why you should look for the largest common factors: it will generally lead to the final expression in the fewest steps.

EXAMPLE 4-4

Simplify the expression $x = (\overline{A} + B)(A + B + D)\overline{D}$.

Solution

The expression can be put into sum-of-products form by multiplying out all the terms. The result is

$$x = \overline{A}A\overline{D} + \overline{A}B\overline{D} + \overline{A}D\overline{D} + BA\overline{D} + BB\overline{D} + BD\overline{D}$$

The first term can be eliminated, since $\overline{A}A = 0$. Likewise, the third and sixth terms can be eliminated, since $D\overline{D} = 0$. The fifth term can be simplified to $B\overline{D}$, since $BB = B$. This gives us

$$x = \overline{A}B\overline{D} + AB\overline{D} + B\overline{D}$$

We can factor $B\overline{D}$ from each term to obtain

$$x = B\overline{D}(\overline{A} + A + 1)$$

Clearly, the term inside the parentheses is always 1, so we finally have

$$x = B\overline{D}$$

EXAMPLE 4-5

Simplify the circuit of Figure 4-3(a).

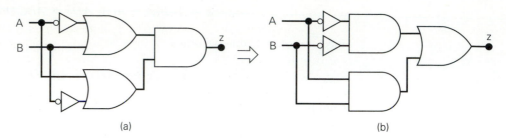

FIGURE 4-3   Example 4-5.

Solution

The expression for output z is

$$z = (\overline{A} + B)(A + \overline{B})$$

Multiplying out to get the sum-of-products form, we obtain

$$z = \overline{A}A + \overline{A}\,\overline{B} + BA + B\overline{B}$$

We can eliminate $\overline{A}A = 0$ and $B\overline{B} = 0$ to end up with

$$z = \overline{A}\,\overline{B} + AB$$

This expression is implemented in Figure 4-3(b), and if we compare it with the original circuit, we see that both circuits contain the same number of gates and connections. In this case the simplification process produced an equivalent, but not simpler, circuit.

EXAMPLE 4-6

Simplify $x = A\overline{B}C + \overline{A}BD + \overline{C}D$.

Solution

You can try, but you will not be able to simplify this expression any further.

1. State which of the following expressions are *not* in the sum-of-products form:
   (a) $RS\overline{T} + \overline{R}S\overline{T} + \overline{T}$
   (b) $AD\overline{C} + \overline{A}DC$
   (c) $MN\overline{P} + (M + \overline{N})P$
   (d) $AB + \overline{A}B\overline{C} + A\overline{B}\,\overline{C}D$
2. Simplify the circuit in Figure 4-1(a) to arrive at the circuit of Figure 4-1(b).
3. Change each AND gate in Figure 4-1(a) to a NAND gate. Determine the new expression for x and simplify it.

4-4 DESIGNING COMBINATIONAL LOGIC CIRCUITS

When the desired output level of a logic circuit is given for all possible input conditions, the results can be conveniently displayed in a truth table. The Boolean expression for the required circuit can then be derived from the truth table. For example, consider Figure 4-4(a), where a truth table is shown for a circuit that has two inputs, A and B, and output x. The table shows that output x is to be at the 1 level *only* for the case where $A = 0$ and $B = 1$. It now remains to determine what logic circuit will produce this desired operation. It should be apparent that one possible solution is that shown in Figure 4-4(b). Here an AND gate is used with inputs $\overline{A}$ and B, so that $x = \overline{A} \cdot B$. Obviously x will be 1 *only if* both inputs to the AND gate are 1, namely, $\overline{A} = 1$ (which means that $A = 0$) and $B = 1$. For all other values of A and B, the output x will be 0.

FIGURE 4-4 Circuit that produces a 1 output only for the $A = 0$, $B = 1$ condition.

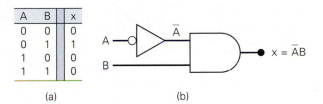

A	B	x
0	0	0
0	1	1
1	0	0
1	1	0

(a)

$x = \overline{A}B$

(b)

A similar approach can be used for the other input conditions. For instance, if x were to be high only for the $A = 1$, $B = 0$ condition, the resulting circuit would be an AND gate with inputs A and $\overline{B}$. In other words, for any of the four possible input conditions we can generate a high x output by using an AND gate with appropriate inputs to generate the required AND product. The four different cases are shown in Figure 4-5. Each of the AND gates shown generates an output that is 1 *only* for one given input condition and the output is 0 for all other conditions. It should be noted that the AND inputs are inverted or not inverted depending on the values that the variables have for the given condition. If the variable is 0 for the given condition, it is inverted before entering the AND gate.

FIGURE 4-5 An AND gate with appropriate inputs can be used to produce a 1 output for a specific set of input levels.

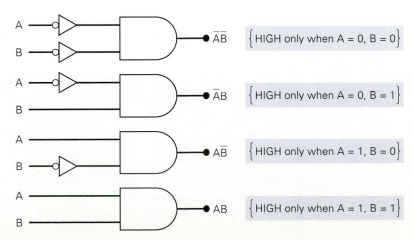

Let us now consider the case shown in Figure 4-6(a), where we have a truth table that indicates that the output x is to be 1 for two different cases: $A = 0$, $B = 1$ and $A = 1$, $B = 0$. How can this be implemented? We know that the AND term $\overline{A} \cdot B$ will generate a 1 only for the $A = 0$, $B = 1$ condition, and the AND term $A \cdot \overline{B}$ will generate a 1 for the $A = 1$, $B = 0$ condition. Since x must be HIGH for *either* condition, it should be clear that these terms should be ORed together to produce the desired output, x. This implementation is shown in Figure 4-6(b), where the resulting expression for the output is $x = \overline{A}B + A\overline{B}$.

FIGURE 4-6 Each set of input conditions that is to produce a HIGH output is implemented by a separate AND gate. The AND outputs are ORed to produce final output.

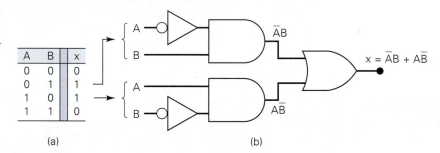

A	B	x
0	0	0
0	1	1
1	0	1
1	1	0

(a)

(b)

In this example, an AND term is generated for each case in the table where the output x is to be a 1. The AND gate outputs are then ORed together to produce the total output x, which will be 1 when either AND term is 1. This same procedure can be extended to examples with more than two inputs. Consider the truth table for a three-input circuit (Table 4-1). Here there are three cases where the output x is to be 1. The required AND term for each of these cases is shown. Again, note that for

TABLE 4-1

A	B	C	x	
0	0	0	0	
0	0	1	0	
0	1	0	1	$\rightarrow \overline{A}B\overline{C}$
0	1	1	1	$\rightarrow \overline{A}BC$
1	0	0	0	
1	0	1	0	
1	1	0	0	
1	1	1	1	$\rightarrow ABC$

each case where a variable is 0, it appears complemented in the AND term. The sum-of-products expression for x is obtained by ORing the three AND terms.

$$x = \overline{A}B\overline{C} + \overline{A}BC + ABC$$

Complete Design Procedure

Once the output expression has been determined from the truth table in sum-of-products form, it can easily be implemented using AND and OR gates and INVERTERs. Usually, however, the expression can be simplified, thereby resulting in a more efficient circuit. The following example illustrates the complete design procedure.

| EXAMPLE 4-7 | Design a logic circuit that has three inputs, A, B, and C, and whose output will be HIGH only when a majority of the inputs are HIGH. |

Solution

Step 1. Set up the truth table.

On the basis of the problem statement, the output x should be 1 whenever two or more inputs are 1; for all other cases, the output should be 0 (Table 4-2).

TABLE 4-2

A	B	C	x	
0	0	0	0	
0	0	1	0	
0	1	0	0	
0	1	1	1	$\rightarrow \overline{A}BC$
1	0	0	0	
1	0	1	1	$\rightarrow A\overline{B}C$
1	1	0	1	$\rightarrow AB\overline{C}$
1	1	1	1	$\rightarrow ABC$

Step 2. Write the AND term for each case where the output is a 1.

There are four such cases. The AND terms are shown next to the truth table (Table 4-2). Again note that each AND term contains each input variable in either inverted or noninverted form.

Step 3. Write the sum-of-products expression for the output.

$$x = \overline{A}BC + A\overline{B}C + AB\overline{C} + ABC$$

Step 4. Simplify the output expression.

This expression can be simplified in several ways. Perhaps the quickest way is to realize that the last term ABC has two variables in common with each of the other terms. Thus, we can use the ABC term to factor with each of the other terms. The expression is rewritten with the ABC term occurring three times (recall from Example 4-2 that this is legal in Boolean algebra):

$$x = \overline{A}BC + ABC + A\overline{B}C + ABC + AB\overline{C} + ABC$$

Factoring the appropriate pairs of terms, we have

$$x = BC(\overline{A} + A) + AC(\overline{B} + B) + AB(\overline{C} + C)$$

Since each term in parentheses is equal to 1, we have

$$x = BC + AC + AB$$

Step 5. Implement the circuit for the final expression.

This expression is implemented in Figure 4-7. Since the expression is in sum-of-products form, the circuit consists of a group of AND gates working into a single OR gate.

FIGURE 4-7   Example 4-7.

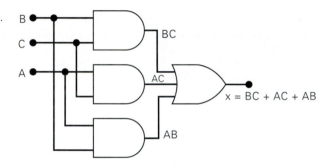

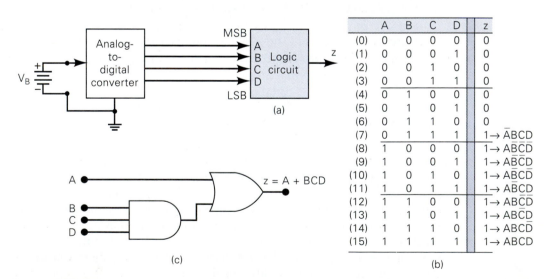

EXAMPLE 4-8   Refer to Figure 4-8(a) where an analog-to-digital converter is monitoring the dc voltage of a 12-V storage battery on an orbiting spaceship. The converter's output is a four-bit binary number, *ABCD*, corresponding to the battery voltage in steps of 1 V, with *A* as the MSB. The converter's binary outputs are fed to a logic circuit

	A	B	C	D	z
(0)	0	0	0	0	0
(1)	0	0	0	1	0
(2)	0	0	1	0	0
(3)	0	0	1	1	0
(4)	0	1	0	0	0
(5)	0	1	0	1	0
(6)	0	1	1	0	0
(7)	0	1	1	1	$1 \rightarrow \overline{A}BCD$
(8)	1	0	0	0	$1 \rightarrow A\overline{B}\,\overline{C}\,\overline{D}$
(9)	1	0	0	1	$1 \rightarrow A\overline{B}\,\overline{C}D$
(10)	1	0	1	0	$1 \rightarrow A\overline{B}C\overline{D}$
(11)	1	0	1	1	$1 \rightarrow A\overline{B}CD$
(12)	1	1	0	0	$1 \rightarrow AB\overline{C}\,\overline{D}$
(13)	1	1	0	1	$1 \rightarrow AB\overline{C}D$
(14)	1	1	1	0	$1 \rightarrow ABC\overline{D}$
(15)	1	1	1	1	$1 \rightarrow ABCD$

(a)

(b)

(c)

FIGURE 4-8   Example 4-8.

that is to produce a HIGH output as long as the binary value is greater than $0110_2 = 6_{10}$; that is, the battery voltage is greater than 6 V. Design this logic circuit.

Solution

The truth table is shown in Figure 4-8(b). For each case in the truth table we have indicated the decimal equivalent of the binary number represented by the $ABCD$ combination.

The output z is set equal to 1 for all those cases where the binary number is greater than 0110. For all other cases, z is set equal to 0. This truth table gives us the following sum-of-products expression:

$$z = \overline{A}BCD + A\overline{B}\,\overline{C}\,\overline{D} + A\overline{B}\,\overline{C}D + A\overline{B}C\overline{D} + A\overline{B}CD + AB\overline{C}\,\overline{D} + AB\overline{C}D + ABC\overline{D} + ABCD$$

Simplification of this expression will be a formidable task, but with a little care it can be accomplished. The step-by-step process involves factoring and eliminating terms of the form $A + \overline{A}$:

$$z = \overline{A}BCD + A\overline{B}\,\overline{C}(\overline{D} + D) + A\overline{B}C(\overline{D} + D) + AB\overline{C}(\overline{D} + D) + ABC(\overline{D} + D)$$
$$= \overline{A}BCD + A\overline{B}\,\overline{C} + A\overline{B}C + AB\overline{C} + ABC$$
$$= \overline{A}BCD + A\overline{B}(\overline{C} + C) + AB(\overline{C} + C)$$
$$= \overline{A}BCD + A\overline{B} + AB$$
$$= \overline{A}BCD + A(\overline{B} + B)$$
$$= \overline{A}BCD + A$$

This can be reduced further by invoking theorem (15), which says that $x + \overline{x}y = x + y$. In this case $x = A$ and $y = BCD$. Thus,

$$z = \overline{A}BCD + A = BCD + A$$

This final expression is implemented in Figure 4-8(c).

As this example demonstrates, the algebraic simplification method can be quite lengthy when the original expression contains a large number of terms. This is a limitation that is not shared by the Karnaugh mapping method, as we will see later.

Implementing the Final Design

In the design examples we have shown, the final circuit was implemented using AND and OR gates. In fact, the sum-of-products form always yields a circuit containing one or more AND gates driving a single OR gate. One of the reasons for using the sum-of-products form is that it can be implemented using all NAND gates with little, if any, increase in circuit complexity over the AND/OR implementation. Since NAND gates are the most readily available logic gates in the TTL logic family, this is an important characteristic.

To illustrate, Figure 4-9 shows the equivalent NAND implementation for the circuits of Figures 4-7 and 4-8(c). You may wish to work out these conversions yourself as a review of the procedure covered in Chapter 3.

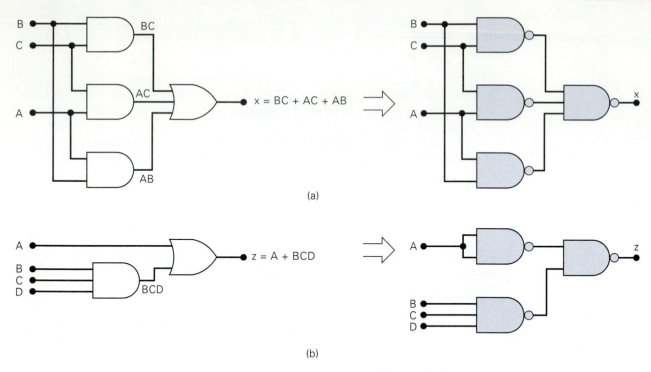

(a)

(b)

FIGURE 4-9 (a) Converting the circuit of Figure 4-7 to NAND; (b) converting the circuit of Figure 4-8(c) to NANDs.

Comparing the NAND implementation with its original circuit in Figure 4-9(a), we see that they are identical in structure; that is, *each* gate of the original circuit has been replaced by a single NAND gate. This characteristic is true only if the original circuit is in sum-of-products form. The only exception to this is when the sum-of-products form contains a single-variable term such as $z = A + BCD$ in Figure 4-9(b). Here the NAND implementation requires an extra NAND gate used as an INVERTER on the A input.

We can streamline the process of converting a *sum-of-products* circuit from AND/OR to NAND gates as follows:

1. Replace each AND gate, OR gate, and INVERTER by a *single* NAND gate.
2. Use a NAND gate to invert any single variable that is feeding the final OR gate.

Check out this process for the circuits in Figure 4-9.

EXAMPLE 4-9

Refer to Figure 4-10(a). In a simple copy machine, a stop signal, S, is to be generated to stop the machine operation and energize an indicator light whenever either of the following conditions exists: (1) there is no paper in the paper feeder tray; or (2) the two microswitches in the paper path are activated, indicating a jam in the paper path. The presence of paper in the feeder tray is indicated by a HIGH at logic signal P. Each of the microswitches produces a logic signal (Q and R) that

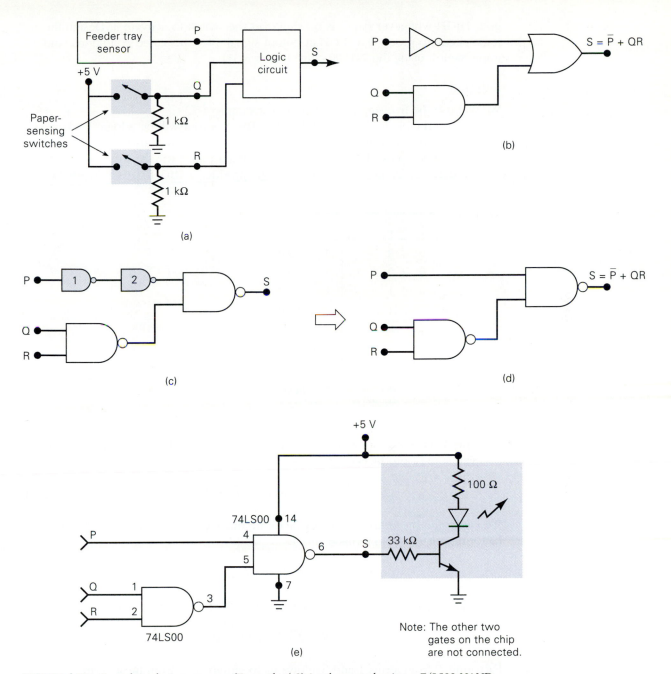

FIGURE 4-10   Complete design process (Example 4-9) implemented using a 74LS00 NAND chip.

goes HIGH whenever paper is passing over the switch to activate it. Design the logic circuit to produce a HIGH at output signal S for the stated conditions, and implement it using the 74LS00 chip (Figure 3-31).

Solution

We will use the five-step process used in Example 4-7.

The truth table is shown in Table 4-3. The S output will be a logic 1 whenever $P = 0$, since this indicates no paper in the feeder tray. S will also be a 1 for the two cases where Q and R are both 1, indicating a paper jam. As the table shows, there are five different input conditions that produce a HIGH output. (Step 1)

TABLE 4-3

P	Q	R	S	
0	0	0	1	$\overline{P}\,\overline{Q}\,\overline{R}$
0	0	1	1	$\overline{P}\,\overline{Q}\,R$
0	1	0	1	$\overline{P}\,Q\,\overline{R}$
0	1	1	1	$\overline{P}\,Q\,R$
1	0	0	0	
1	0	1	0	
1	1	0	0	
1	1	1	1	PQR

The AND terms for each of these cases are shown. (Step 2)
The sum-of-products expression becomes

$$S = \overline{P}\,\overline{Q}\,\overline{R} + \overline{P}\,\overline{Q}\,R + \overline{P}\,Q\,\overline{R} + \overline{P}\,Q\,R + PQR \qquad \text{(Step 3)}$$

We can begin the simplification by factoring out $\overline{P}\,\overline{Q}$ from terms 1 and 2 and by factoring out $\overline{P}Q$ from terms 3 and 4:

$$S = \overline{P}\,\overline{Q}(\overline{R} + R) + \overline{P}Q(\overline{R} + R) + PQR \qquad \text{(Step 4)}$$

Now we can eliminate the $\overline{R} + R$ terms, since they equal 1:

$$S = \overline{P}\,\overline{Q} + \overline{P}Q + PQR$$

Factoring $\overline{P}$ from terms 1 and 2 allows us to eliminate Q from these terms:

$$S = \overline{P} + PQR$$

Here we can apply theorem (15) $(x + \overline{x}y = x + y)$ to obtain

$$S = \overline{P} + QR$$

The AND/OR implementation for this circuit is shown in Figure 4-10(b). (Step 5)

Since the circuit is to be implemented using the 74LS00 quad two-input NAND chip, the circuit of Figure 4-10(b) must be converted to all NAND gates. Replace each OR and AND gate with a NAND gate, and replace the INVERTER by a NAND gate INVERTER [labeled 1 in Figure 4-10(c)]. In addition, since the top input to the OR gate is a single variable (*P*), a NAND gate INVERTER (labeled 2) must be placed at that input. Clearly we can eliminate the two INVERTERs to produce the NAND result of Figure 4-10(d).

Figure 4-10(e) is the final wired-up version of the circuit showing IC pin numbers, including the power pins (+5 V and GROUND) and the output driver transistor and LED indicator for the *S* signal.

Review Questions

1. Write the sum-of-products expression for a circuit with four inputs and an output that is to be HIGH only when input *A* is LOW at the same time that exactly two other inputs are LOW.

2. Implement the expression of question 1 using all four-input NAND gates. How many are required?

4-5   KARNAUGH MAP METHOD

The **Karnaugh map** is a graphical device used to simplify a logic equation or to convert a truth table to its corresponding logic circuit in a simple, orderly process. Although a Karnaugh map (henceforth abbreviated **K map**) can be used for problems involving any number of input variables, its practical usefulness is limited to six variables. The following discussion will be limited to problems with up to four inputs, since even five- and six-input problems are too involved and are best done by a computer program.

Karnaugh Map Format

The K map, like a truth table, is a means for showing the relationship between logic inputs and the desired output. Figure 4-11 shows three examples of K maps for two, three, and four variables, together with the corresponding truth tables. These examples illustrate the following important points:

1. The truth table gives the value of output *X* for each combination of input values. The K map gives the same information in a different format. Each case in the truth table corresponds to a square in the K map. For example, in Figure 4-11(a), the $A = 0$, $B = 0$ condition in the truth table corresponds to the $\overline{A}\overline{B}$ square in the K map. Since the truth table shows $X = 1$ for this case, a 1 is placed in the $\overline{A}\overline{B}$ square in the K map. Similarly, the $A = 1$, $B = 1$ condition in the truth table corresponds to the AB square of the K map. Since $X = 1$ for this case, a 1 is placed in the AB square. All other squares are filled with 0s. This same idea is used in the three- and four-variable maps shown in the figure.

FIGURE 4-11 Karnaugh maps
and truth tables for (a) two, (b)
three, and (c) four variables.

A	B	X	
0	0	1	$\rightarrow \overline{A}\overline{B}$
0	1	0	
1	0	0	
1	1	1	$\rightarrow AB$

$$\left\{ x = \overline{A}\overline{B} + AB \right\}$$

	$\overline{B}$	B
$\overline{A}$	1	0
A	0	1

(a)

A	B	C	X	
0	0	0	1	$\rightarrow \overline{A}\overline{B}\overline{C}$
0	0	1	1	$\rightarrow \overline{A}\overline{B}C$
0	1	0	1	$\rightarrow \overline{A}B\overline{C}$
0	1	1	0	
1	0	0	0	
1	0	1	0	
1	1	0	1	$\rightarrow AB\overline{C}$
1	1	1	0	

$$\left\{ \begin{array}{l} X = \overline{A}\overline{B}\overline{C} + \overline{A}\overline{B}C \\ + \overline{A}B\overline{C} + AB\overline{C} \end{array} \right\}$$

	$\overline{C}$	C
$\overline{A}\overline{B}$	1	1
$\overline{A}B$	1	0
AB	1	0
$A\overline{B}$	0	0

(b)

A	B	C	D	X	
0	0	0	0	0	
0	0	0	1	1	$\rightarrow \overline{A}\overline{B}\overline{C}D$
0	0	1	0	0	
0	0	1	1	0	
0	1	0	0	0	
0	1	0	1	1	$\rightarrow \overline{A}B\overline{C}D$
0	1	1	0	0	
0	1	1	1	0	
1	0	0	0	0	
1	0	0	1	0	
1	0	1	0	0	
1	0	1	1	0	
1	1	0	0	0	
1	1	0	1	1	$\rightarrow AB\overline{C}D$
1	1	1	0	0	
1	1	1	1	1	$\rightarrow ABCD$

$$\left\{ \begin{array}{l} X = \overline{A}\overline{B}\overline{C}D + \overline{A}B\overline{C}D \\ + AB\overline{C}D + ABCD \end{array} \right\}$$

	$\overline{C}\overline{D}$	$\overline{C}D$	CD	$C\overline{D}$
$\overline{A}\overline{B}$	0	1	0	0
$\overline{A}B$	0	1	0	0
AB	0	1	1	0
$A\overline{B}$	0	0	0	0

(c)

2. The K-map squares are labeled so that horizontally adjacent squares differ only in one variable. For example, the upper left-hand square in the four-variable map is $\overline{A}\overline{B}\,\overline{C}\overline{D}$, while the square immediately to its right is $\overline{A}\overline{B}\,\overline{C}D$ (only the D variable is different). Similarly, vertically adjacent squares differ only in one variable. For example, the upper left-hand square is $\overline{A}\overline{B}\,\overline{C}\overline{D}$, while the square directly below it is $\overline{A}B\overline{C}\,\overline{D}$ (only the B variable is different).

   Note that each square in the top row is considered to be adjacent to a corresponding square in the bottom row. For example, the $\overline{A}\overline{B}CD$ square in the top row is adjacent to the $A\overline{B}CD$ square in the bottom row, since they differ only in the A variable. You can think of the top of the map as being wrapped around to touch the bottom of the map. Similarly, squares in the leftmost column are adjacent to corresponding squares in the rightmost column.

3. In order for vertically and horizontally adjacent squares to differ in only one variable, the top-to-bottom labeling must be done in the order shown: $\overline{A}\overline{B}$, $\overline{A}B$, AB, $A\overline{B}$. The same is true of the left-to-right labeling.

4. Once a K map has been filled with 0s and 1s, the sum-of-products expression for the output X can be obtained by ORing together those squares that contain a 1. In the three-variable map of Figure 4-11(b), the $\overline{A}\,\overline{B}\,\overline{C}$, $\overline{A}\overline{B}C$, $\overline{A}B\overline{C}$, and $AB\overline{C}$ squares contain a 1, so that $X = \overline{A}\,\overline{B}\,\overline{C} + \overline{A}\overline{B}C + \overline{A}B\overline{C} + AB\overline{C}$.

Looping

The expression for output X can be simplified by properly combining those squares in the K map which contain 1s. The process for combining these 1s is called **looping**.

Looping Groups of Two (Pairs)

Figure 4-12(a) is the K map for a particular three-variable truth table. This map contains a pair of 1s that are vertically adjacent to each other; the first represents $\overline{A}B\overline{C}$, and the second represents $AB\overline{C}$. Note that in these two terms only the A variable appears in both normal and complemented form (B and $\overline{C}$ remain unchanged). These two terms can be looped (combined) to give a resultant that eliminates the A variable since it appears in both uncomplemented and complemented forms. This is easily proved as follows:

$$X = \overline{A}B\overline{C} + AB\overline{C}$$
$$= B\overline{C}(\overline{A} + A)$$
$$= B\overline{C}(1) = B\overline{C}$$

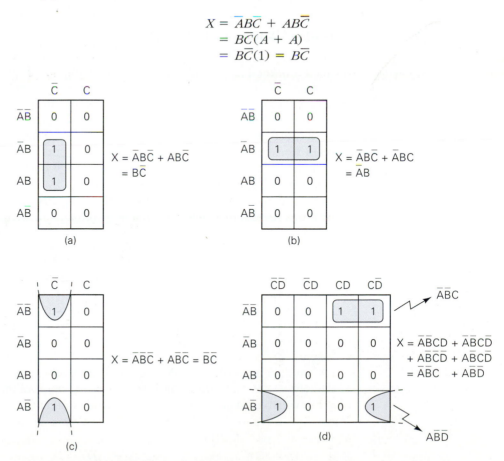

FIGURE 4-12   Examples of looping pairs of adjacent 1s.

This same principle holds true for any pair of vertically or horizontally adjacent 1s. Figure 4-12(b) shows an example of two horizontally adjacent 1s. These two can be looped and the C variable eliminated since it appears in both its uncomplemented and complemented forms to give a resultant of $X = \overline{A}B$.

Another example is shown in Figure 4-12(c). In a K map the top row and bottom row of squares are considered to be adjacent. Thus, the two 1s in this map can be looped to provide a resultant of $\overline{A}\,\overline{B}\,\overline{C} + A\overline{B}\,\overline{C} = \overline{B}\,\overline{C}$.

Figure 4-12(d) shows a K map that has two pairs of 1s that can be looped. The two 1s in the top row are horizontally adjacent. The two 1s in the bottom row are also adjacent, since in a K map the leftmost column and the rightmost column of squares are considered to be adjacent. When the top pair of 1s is looped, the D variable is eliminated (since it appears as both D and $\overline{D}$) to give the term $\overline{A}\,\overline{B}C$. Looping the bottom pair eliminates the C variable to give the term $A\overline{B}\,\overline{D}$. These two terms are ORed to give the final result for X.

To summarize:

Looping a pair of adjacent 1s in a K map eliminates the variable that appears in complemented and uncomplemented form.

Looping Groups of Four (Quads)

A K map may contain a group of four 1s that are adjacent to each other. This group is called a *quad*. Figure 4-13 shows several examples of quads. In part (a) the four 1s are vertically adjacent, and in part (b) they are horizontally adjacent. The K map in Figure 4-13(c) contains four 1s in a square, and they are considered adjacent to each other. The four 1s in Figure 4-13(d) are also adjacent, as are those in Figure 4-13(e) because, as pointed out earlier, the top and bottom rows are considered to be adjacent to each other, as are the leftmost and rightmost columns.

When a quad is looped, the resultant term will contain only the variables that do not change form for all the squares in the quad. For example, in Figure 4-13(a) the four squares that contain a 1 are $\overline{A}\,\overline{B}C$, $\overline{A}BC$, ABC, and $A\overline{B}C$. Examination of these terms reveals that only the variable C remains unchanged (both A and B appear in complemented and uncomplemented form). Thus, the resultant expression for X is simply $X = C$. This can be proved as follows:

$$X = \overline{A}\,\overline{B}C + \overline{A}BC + ABC + A\overline{B}C$$
$$= \overline{A}C(\overline{B} + B) + AC(B + \overline{B})$$
$$= \overline{A}C + AC$$
$$= C(\overline{A} + A) = C$$

As another example, consider Figure 4-13(d), where the four squares containing 1s are $AB\overline{C}\,\overline{D}$, $A\overline{B}\,\overline{C}D$, $ABC\overline{D}$, and $A\overline{B}C\overline{D}$. Examination of these terms indicates that only the variables A and $\overline{D}$ remain unchanged, so that the simplified expression for X is

$$X = A\overline{D}$$

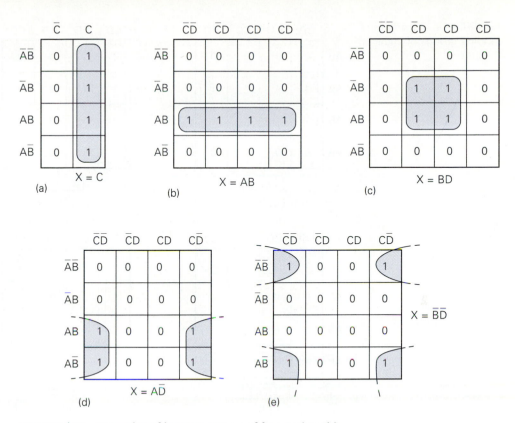

FIGURE 4-13 Examples of looping groups of four 1s (quads).

This can be proved in the same manner that was used above. The reader should check each of the other cases in Figure 4-13 to verify the indicated expressions for X.

To summarize:

Looping a quad of 1s eliminates the two variables that appear in both complemented and uncomplemented form.

Looping Groups of Eight (Octets)

A group of eight 1s that are adjacent to one another is called an *octet*. Several examples of octets are shown in Figure 4-14. When an octet is looped in a four-variable map, three of the four variables are eliminated because only one variable remains unchanged. For example, examination of the eight looped squares in Figure 4-14(a) shows that only the variable B is in the same form for all eight squares: the other variables appear in complemented and uncomplemented form. Thus, for this map, $X = B$. The reader can verify the results for the other examples in Figure 4-14.

To summarize:

Looping an octet of 1s eliminates the three variables that appear in both complemented and uncomplemented form.

FIGURE 4-14 Examples of looping groups of eight 1s (octets).

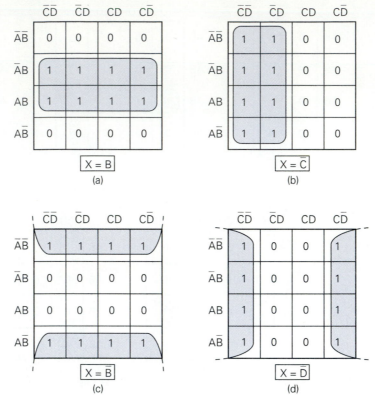

Complete Simplification Process

We have seen how looping of pairs, quads, and octets on a K map can be used to obtain a simplified expression. We can summarize the rule for loops of *any* size:

> **When a variable appears in both complemented and uncomplemented form within a loop, that variable is eliminated from the expression. Variables that are the same for all squares of the loop must appear in the final expression.**

It should be clear that a larger loop of 1s eliminates more variables. To be exact, a loop of two eliminates one variable, a loop of four eliminates two, and a loop of eight eliminates three. This principle will now be used to obtain a simplified logic expression from a K map that contains any combination of 1s and 0s.

The procedure will first be outlined and then applied to several examples. The steps below are followed in using the K-map method for simplifying a Boolean expression:

Step 1 Construct the K map and place 1s in those squares corresponding to the 1s in the truth table. Place 0s in the other squares.

Step 2 Examine the map for adjacent 1s and loop those 1s which are *not* adjacent to any other 1s. These are called *isolated* 1s.

Step 3 Next, look for those 1s which are adjacent to only one other 1. Loop *any* pair containing such a 1.

Step 4 Loop any octet even it contains some 1s that have already been looped.

Step 5 Loop any quad that contains one or more 1s that have not already been looped, *making sure to use the minimum number of loops.*

Step 6 Loop any pairs necessary to include any 1s that have not yet been looped, *making sure to use the minimum number of loops.*

Step 7 Form the OR sum of all the terms generated by each loop.

These steps will be followed exactly and referred to in the following examples. In each case, the resulting logic expression will be in its simplest sum-of-products form.

EXAMPLE 4-10

Figure 4-15(a) shows the K map for a four-variable problem. We will assume that the map was obtained from the problem truth table **(step 1)**. The squares are numbered for convenience in identifying each loop.

FIGURE 4-15 Examples 4-10 to 4-12.

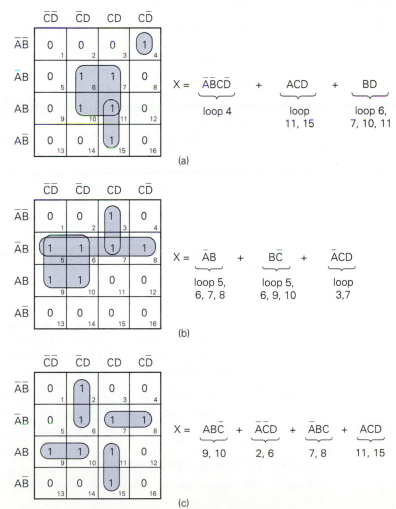

(a)

$$X = \overline{A}\overline{B}C\overline{D} \quad + \quad ACD \quad + \quad BD$$

loop 4   loop 11, 15   loop 6, 7, 10, 11

(b)

$$X = \overline{A}B \quad + \quad B\overline{C} \quad + \quad \overline{A}CD$$

loop 5, 6, 7, 8   loop 5, 6, 9, 10   loop 3, 7

(c)

$$X = AB\overline{C} \quad + \quad \overline{A}\overline{C}D \quad + \quad \overline{A}BC \quad + \quad ACD$$

9, 10   2, 6   7, 8   11, 15

Step 2   Square 4 is the only square containing a 1 that is not adjacent to any other 1. It is looped and is referred to as loop 4.

Step 3   Square 15 is adjacent *only* to square 11. This pair is looped and referred to as loop 11, 15.

Step 4   There are no octets.

Step 5   Squares 6, 7, 10, and 11 form a quad. This quad is looped (loop 6, 7, 10, 11). Note that square 11 is used again, even though it was part of loop 11, 15.

Step 6   All 1s have already been looped.

Step 7   Each loop generates a term in the expression for *X*. Loop 4 is simply $\overline{A}\overline{B}C\overline{D}$. Loop 11, 15 is ACD (the *B* variable is eliminated). Loop 6, 7, 10, 11 is BD (*A* and *C* are eliminated).

EXAMPLE 4-11

Consider the K map in Figure 4-15(b). Once again we can assume that step 1 has already been performed.

Step 2   There are no isolated 1s.

Step 3   The 1 in square 3 is adjacent *only* to the 1 in square 7. Looping this pair (loop 3, 7) produces the term $\overline{A}CD$.

Step 4   There are no octets.

Step 5   There are two quads. Squares 5, 6, 7, and 8 form one quad. Looping this quad produces the term $\overline{A}B$. The second quad is made up of squares 5, 6, 9, and 10. This quad is looped because it contains two squares that have not been looped previously. Looping this quad produces $B\overline{C}$.

Step 6   All 1s have already been looped.

Step 7   The terms generated by the three loops are ORed together to obtain the expression for *X*.

EXAMPLE 4-12

Consider the K map in Figure 4-15(c).

Step 2   There are no isolated 1s.

Step 3   The 1 in square 2 is adjacent only to the 1 in square 6. This pair is looped to produce $\overline{A}\,\overline{C}D$. Similarly, square 9 is adjacent only to square 10. Looping this pair produces $AB\overline{C}$. Likewise, loop 7, 8 and loop 11, 15 produce the terms $\overline{A}BC$ and ACD, respectively.

Step 4   There are no octets.

Step 5   There is one quad formed by squares 6, 7, 10, and 11. This quad, however, is *not* looped, because all the 1s in the quad have been included in other loops.

Step 6   All 1s have already been looped.

Step 7   The expression for *X* is shown in the figure.

	EXAMPLE	Consider the K map in Figure 4-16(a).
	4-13	

FIGURE 4-16   The same K map with two equally good solutions.

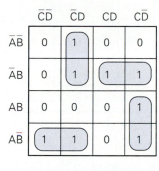

$$X = \overline{A}\overline{C}D + \overline{A}BC + A\overline{B}\overline{C} + AC\overline{D}$$

(a)

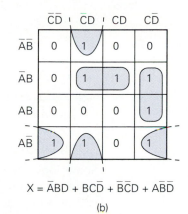

$$X = \overline{A}BD + BC\overline{D} + \overline{B}C\overline{D} + A\overline{B}D$$

(b)

Step 2   There are no isolated 1s.

Step 3   There are no 1s that are adjacent to only one other 1.

Step 4   There are no octets.

Step 5   There are no quads.

Steps 6 and 7   There are many possible pairs. The looping must use the minimum number of loops to account for all the 1s. For this map there are *two* possible loopings, which require only four looped pairs. Figure 4-16(a) shows one solution and its resultant expression. Figure 4-16(b) shows the other. Note that both expressions are of the same complexity, and so neither is better than the other.

	EXAMPLE	Use the K map to simplify the expression $y = \overline{A}\overline{B}\overline{C} + \overline{B}C + \overline{A}B$.
	4-14	

Solution

In this problem we are not given the truth table from which to fill in the K map. Instead, we must fill in the K map by taking each of the product terms in the expression and placing 1s in the corresponding squares.

The first term, $\overline{A}\overline{B}\overline{C}$, tells us to enter a 1 in the $\overline{A}\overline{B}\overline{C}$ square of the map (see Figure 4-17). The second term, $\overline{B}C$, tell us to enter a 1 in each square that contains a $\overline{B}C$ in its label. In Figure 4-17 this would be the $A\overline{B}C$ and $\overline{A}\overline{B}C$ squares. Likewise, the $\overline{A}B$ term tells us to place a 1 in the $\overline{A}BC$ and $\overline{A}B\overline{C}$ squares. All other squares will be filled with 0s.

Now the K map can be looped for simplification. The result is $y = \overline{A} + \overline{B}C$, as shown in the figure.

FIGURE 4-17   Example 4-14.

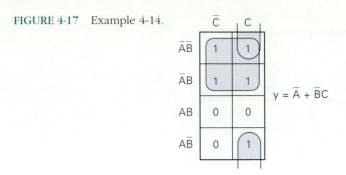

$$y = \bar{A} + \bar{B}C$$

"Don't-Care" Conditions

Some logic circuits can be designed so that there are certain input conditions for which there are no specified output levels, usually because these input conditions will never occur. In other words, there will be certain combinations of input levels where we "don't care" whether the output is HIGH or LOW. This is illustrated in the truth table of Figure 4-18(a).

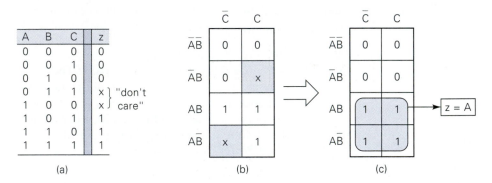

(a)   (b)   (c)

FIGURE 4-18   "Don't-care" conditions should be changed to 0 or 1 to produce K-map looping that yields the simplest expression.

Here the output z is not specified as either 0 or 1 for the conditions A, B, $C =$ 1, 0, 0 and A, B, $C = 0$, 1, 1. Instead, an x is shown for these conditions. The x represents the **don't-care condition**. A don't-care condition can come about for several reasons, the most common being that in some situations certain input combinations can never occur, and so there is no specified output for these conditions.

A circuit designer is free to make the output for any don't-care condition either a 0 or a 1 in order to produce the simplest output expression. For example, the K map for this truth table is shown in Figure 4-18(b) with an x placed in the $\overline{AB}\,\overline{C}$ and $\overline{A}BC$ squares. The designer here would be wise to change the x in the $A\overline{B}\,\overline{C}$ square to a 1 and the x in the $\overline{A}BC$ square to a 0, since this would produce a quad that can be looped to produce $z = A$, as shown in Figure 4-18(c).

Whenever don't-care conditions occur, we must decide which x to change to 0 and which to 1 to produce the best K-map looping (i.e., the simplest expression). This decision is not always an easy one. Several end-of-chapter problems will provide practice in dealing with don't-care cases.

Summary

The K-map process has several advantages over the algebraic method. K mapping is a more orderly process with well-defined steps as compared with the trial-and-error process sometimes used in algebraic simplification. K mapping usually requires fewer steps, especially for expressions containing many terms, and it always produces a minimum expression.

Nevertheless, some instructors prefer the algebraic method because it requires a thorough knowledge of Boolean algebra and is not simply a mechanical procedure. Each method has its advantages, and although most logic designers are adept at both, being proficient in one method is all that is necessary to produce acceptable results.

There are other, more complex, techniques that designers use to minimize logic circuits. These techniques are especially suited for circuits with large numbers of inputs where algebraic and K-mapping methods are not feasible. Most of these techniques can be translated into a computer program that will perform the minimization from input data that supply the truth table or the unsimplified expression.

Review Questions

1. Use K mapping to simplify the expression of Example 4-7.
2. Use K mapping to simplify the expression of Example 4-8. This should emphasize the advantage of K mapping for expressions containing many terms.
3. Simplify the expression of Example 4-9 using a K map.
4. What is a don't-care condition?

4-6 EXCLUSIVE-OR AND EXCLUSIVE-NOR CIRCUITS

Two special logic circuits that occur quite often in digital systems are the *exclusive-OR* and *exclusive-NOR* circuits.

Exclusive-OR

Consider the logic circuit of Figure 4-19(a). The output expression of this circuit is

$$x = \overline{A}B + A\overline{B}$$

The accompanying truth table shows that $x = 1$ for two cases: $A = 0$, $B = 1$ (the $\overline{A}B$ term) and $A = 1$, $B = 0$ (the $A\overline{B}$ term). In other words:

> **This circuit produces a HIGH output whenever the two inputs are at opposite levels.**

This is the **exclusive-OR** circuit, which will hereafter be abbreviated **EX-OR**.

This particular combination of logic gates occurs quite often and is very useful in certain applications. In fact, the EX-OR circuit has been given a symbol of its own, shown in Figure 4-19(b). This symbol is assumed to contain all of the logic

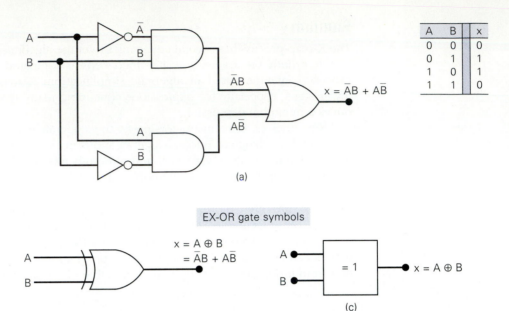

FIGURE 4-19 (a) Exclusive-OR circuit and truth table; (b) traditional EX-OR gate symbol; (c) IEEE/ANSI symbol for EX-OR gate.

contained in the EX-OR circuit and therefore has the same logic expression and truth table. This EX-OR circuit is commonly referred to as an EX-OR *gate,* and we consider it as another type of logic gate. The IEEE/ANSI symbol for an EX-OR gate is shown in Figure 4-19(c). The dependency notation (= 1) inside the block indicates that the output will be active-HIGH *only* when a single input is HIGH.

An EX-OR gate has only *two* inputs; there are no three-input or four-input EX-OR gates. The two inputs are combined so that $x = \overline{A}B + A\overline{B}$. A shorthand way that is sometimes used to indicate the EX-OR output expression is

$$x = A \oplus B$$

where the symbol $\oplus$ represents the EX-OR gate operation.

The characteristics of an EX-OR gate are summarized as follows:

1. It has only two inputs and its output is

$$x = \overline{A}B + A\overline{B} = A \oplus B$$

2. Its output is *HIGH* only when the two inputs are at *different* levels.

Several ICs are available that contain EX-OR gates. Those listed below are *quad* EX-OR chips containing four EX-OR gates.

■ **74LS86** Quad EX-OR (TTL family)

■ **74C86** Quad EX-OR (CMOS family)

■ **74HC86** Quad EX-OR (high-speed CMOS)

Exclusive-NOR

The **exclusive-NOR** circuit (abbreviated **EX-NOR**) operates completely opposite to the EX-OR circuit. Figure 4-20(a) shows an EX-NOR circuit and its accompanying truth table. The output expression is

$$x = AB + \overline{A}\overline{B}$$

which indicates along with the truth table that x will be 1 for two cases: $A = B = 1$ (the AB term) and $A = B = 0$ (the $\overline{A}\overline{B}$ term). In other words:

This circuit produces a HIGH output whenever the two inputs are at the same level.

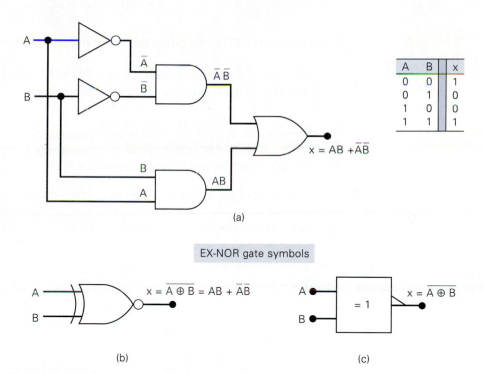

(a)

EX-NOR gate symbols

(b)   (c)

FIGURE 4-20 (a) Exclusive-NOR circuit; (b) traditional symbol for EX-NOR gate; (c) IEEE/ANSI symbol.

It should be apparent that the output of the EX-NOR circuit is the exact inverse of the output of the EX-OR circuit. The traditional symbol for an EX-NOR gate is obtained by simply adding a small circle at the output of the EX-OR symbol [Figure 4-20(b)]. The IEEE/ANSI symbol adds the small triangle on the output of the EX-OR symbol. Both symbols indicate an output that goes to its active-LOW state when *only* one input is HIGH.

The EX-NOR gate also has only *two* inputs, and it combines them so that its output is

$$x = AB + \overline{A}\overline{B}$$

A shorthand way to indicate the output expression of the EX-NOR is

$$x = \overline{A \oplus B}$$

which is simply the inverse of the EX-OR operation. The EX-NOR gate is summarized as follows:

1. It has only two inputs and its output is

$$x = AB + \overline{A}\overline{B} = \overline{A \oplus B}$$

2. Its output is HIGH only when the two inputs are at the *same* level.

Several ICs are available that contain EX-NOR gates. Those listed below are quad EX-NOR chips containing four EX-NOR gates.

■ **74LS266**   Quad EX-NOR (TTL family)
■ **74C266**   Quad EX-NOR (CMOS)
■ **74HC266**   Quad EX-NOR (high-speed CMOS)

Each of these EX-NOR chips, however, has special output circuitry that limits its use to special types of applications. Very often, a logic designer will obtain the EX-NOR function simply by connecting the output of an EX-OR to an INVERTER.

EXAMPLE 4-15

Determine the output waveform for the input waveforms given in Figure 4-21.

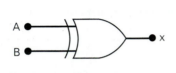
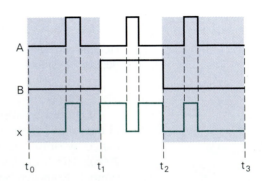

FIGURE 4-21   Example 4-15.

Solution

The output waveform is obtained using the fact that the EX-OR output will go HIGH only when its inputs are at different levels. The resulting output waveform reveals several interesting points:

1. The x waveform matches the A input waveform during those time intervals when $B = 0$. This occurs during the time intervals t_0 to t_1 and t_2 to t_3.

2. The x waveform is the *inverse* of the A input waveform during those time intervals when $B = 1$. This occurs during the interval t_1 to t_2.

3. These observations show that an EX-OR gate can be used as a *controlled INVERTER;* that is, one of its inputs can be used to control whether or not the signal at the other input will be inverted. This property will be useful in certain applications.

EXAMPLE 4-16

x_1x_0 represents a two-bit binary number that can have any value (00, 01, 10, or 11); for example, when $x_1 = 1$ and $x_0 = 0$, the binary number is 10, and so on. Similarly, y_1y_0 represents another two-bit binary number. Design a logic circuit, using x_1, x_0, y_1, and y_0 inputs, whose output will be HIGH only when the two binary numbers x_1x_0 and y_1y_0 are *equal.*

Solution

The first step is to construct a truth table for the 16 input conditions (Table 4-4). The output z must be HIGH whenever the x_1x_0 values match the y_1y_0 values, that is, whenever $x_1 = y_1$ and $x_0 = y_0$. The table shows that there are four such

TABLE 4-4

x_1	x_0	y_1	y_0	z (Output)
0	0	0	0	1
0	0	0	1	0
0	0	1	0	0
0	0	1	1	0
0	1	0	0	0
0	1	0	1	1
0	1	1	0	0
0	1	1	1	0
1	0	0	0	0
1	0	0	1	0
1	0	1	0	1
1	0	1	1	0
1	1	0	0	0
1	1	0	1	0
1	1	1	0	0
1	1	1	1	1

cases. We could now continue with the normal procedure, which would be to obtain a sum-of-products expression for z, attempt to simplify it, and then implement the result. However, the nature of this problem makes it ideally suited for implementation using EX-NOR gates, and a little thought will produce a simple solution with minimum work. Refer to Figure 4-22; in this logic diagram x_1 and y_1 are fed to one EX-NOR gate, and x_0 and y_0 are fed to another EX-NOR gate. The output of each EX-NOR will be HIGH only when its inputs are equal. Thus, for $x_0 = y_0$ and $x_1 = y_1$ both EX-NOR outputs will be HIGH. This is the condition we are looking for, because it means that the two two-bit numbers are equal. The AND gate output will be HIGH only for this case, thereby producing the desired output.

FIGURE 4-22   Circuit for detecting equality of two two-bit binary numbers.

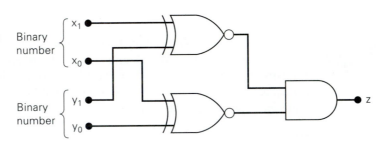

EXAMPLE 4-17

When simplifying the expression for the output of a combinational logic circuit, you may encounter the EX-OR or EX-NOR operations as you are factoring. This will often lead to the use of EX-OR or EX-NOR gates in the implementation of the final circuit. To illustrate, simplify the circuit of Figure 4-23(a).

Solution

The unsimplified expression for the circuit is obtained as

$$z = ABCD + A\overline{B}\,\overline{C}D + \overline{A}\overline{D}$$

We can factor AD from the first two terms:

$$z = AD(BC + \overline{B}\,\overline{C}) + \overline{A}\overline{D}$$

At first glance you might think that the expression in parentheses can be replaced by 1. But that would be true only if it were $BC + \overline{BC}$. You should recognize the expression in parentheses as the EX-NOR combination of B and C. This fact can be used to reimplement the circuit as shown in Figure 4-23(b). This circuit is much simpler than the original, since it uses gates with fewer inputs, and two INVERTERs have been eliminated.

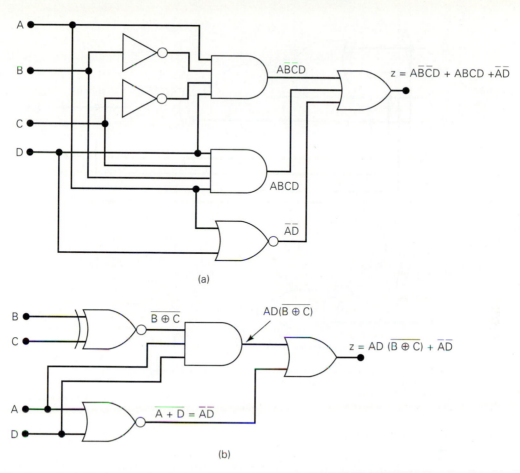

FIGURE 4-23 Example 4-17, showing how an EX-NOR gate may be used to simplify circuit implementation.

Review Questions

1. Use Boolean algebra to prove that the EX-NOR output expression is the exact inverse of the EX-OR output expression.

2. What is the output of an EX-NOR gate when a logic signal and its exact inverse are connected to its inputs?

3. A logic designer needs an INVERTER, and all that is available is one EX-OR gate from a 74HC86 chip. Does he need another chip?

4-7 PARITY GENERATOR AND CHECKER

In Chapter 2 we saw that a transmitter can attach a parity bit to a set of data bits before transmitting the data bits to a receiver. We also saw how this allows the receiver to detect any single-bit errors that may have occurred during the transmission. Figure 4-24 shows an example of one type of logic circuitry that is used for **parity gen-**

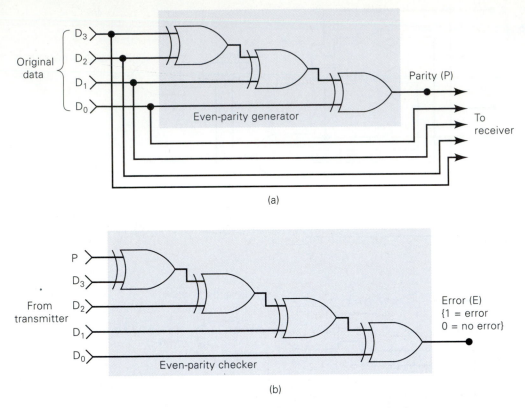

(a)

(b)

FIGURE 4-24 EX-OR gates used to implement the parity generator and the parity checker for an even-parity system.

eration and **parity checking**. This particular example uses a group of four bits as the data to be transmitted, and it uses an even-parity bit. It can readily be adapted to use odd parity and any number of bits.

In Figure 4-24(a), the set of data to be transmitted is applied to the parity-generator circuit, which produces the even-parity bit, P, at its output. This parity bit is transmitted to the receiver along with the original data bits, making a total of five bits. In Figure 4-24(b), these five bits (data + parity) enter the receiver's parity-checker circuit, which produces an error output, E, that indicates whether or not a single-bit error has occurred.

It should not be too surprising that both of these circuits employ EX-OR gates, when we consider that a single EX-OR gate operates in such a way that it produces a 1 output if an odd number of its inputs are 1, and a 0 output if an even number of its inputs are 1.

EXAMPLE 4-18

Determine the parity generator's output for each of the following sets of input data, $D_3D_2D_1D_0$: **(a)** 0111; **(b)** 1001; **(c)** 0000; **(d)** 0100. Refer to Figure 4-24(a).

Solution

For each case, apply the data levels to the parity-generator inputs and trace them through each gate to the P output. The results are: **(a)** 1; **(b)** 0; **(c)** 0; and **(d)** 1. Note that P is a 1 only when the original data contain an odd number of 1s. Thus, the total number of 1s sent to the receiver (data + parity) will be even.

EXAMPLE 4-19

Determine the parity checker's output (see Figure 4-24(b)) for each of the following sets of data from the transmitter:

	P	D_3	D_2	D_1	D_0
(a)	0	1	0	1	0
(b)	1	1	1	1	0
(c)	1	1	1	1	1
(d)	1	0	0	0	0

Solution

For each case, apply these levels to the parity-checker inputs and trace them through to the E output. The results are: **(a)** 0; **(b)** 0; **(c)** 1; **(d)** 1. Note that a 1 is produced at E only when an odd number of 1s appear in the inputs to the parity checker. This indicates that an error has occurred, since even parity is being used.

EXAMPLE 4-20

Does the parity-checker circuit have any way of "knowing" which input bit is in error?

Solution

No. The parity checker doesn't know what the state of each input bit should be; it knows only that an even number of 1s should be present. Regardless of which bit is wrong, a single-bit error will change the total number of 1s from even to odd (either by removing a 1 or by adding an extra 1) and cause E to go HIGH.

4-8 ENABLE/DISABLE CIRCUITS

Each of the basic logic gates can be used to control the passage of an input logic signal through to the output. This is depicted in Figure 4-25, where a logic signal, A, is applied to one input of each of the basic logic gates. The other input of each gate is the control input, B. The logic level at this control input will determine whether the input signal is **enabled** to reach the output or **disabled** from reaching the output. This controlling action is why these circuits came to be called *gates*.

Examine Figure 4-25 and you should notice that when the noninverting gates (AND, OR) are enabled, the output will follow the A signal exactly. Conversely, when the inverting gates (NAND, NOR) are enabled, the output will be the exact inverse of the A signal.

Also notice that AND and NOR gates produce a constant LOW output when they are in the disabled condition. Conversely, the NAND and OR gates produce a constant HIGH output in the disabled condition.

There will be many situations in digital-circuit design where the passage of a logic signal is to be enabled or disabled, depending on conditions present at one or more control inputs. Several are shown in the following examples.

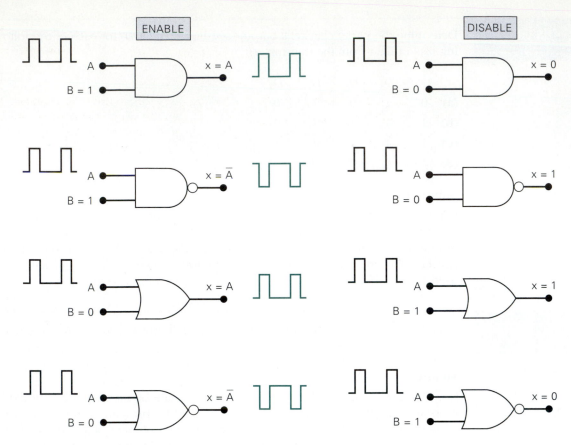

FIGURE 4-25 Four basic gates can either enable or disable the passage of an input signal, *A*, under control of the logic level at control input *B*.

EXAMPLE 4-21

Design a logic circuit that will allow a signal to pass to the output only when control inputs *B* and *C* are both HIGH; otherwise, the output will stay LOW.

Solution

An AND gate should be used because the signal is to be passed without inversion, and the disable output condition is a LOW. Since the enable condition must occur only when $B = C = 1$, a three-input AND gate is used, as shown in Figure 4-26(a).

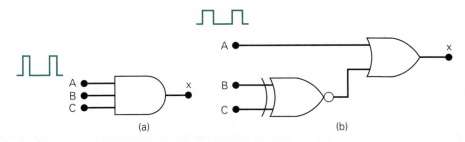

(a)   (b)

FIGURE 4-26 Examples 4-21 and 4-22.

EXAMPLE 4-22

Design a logic circuit that allows a signal to pass to the output only when one, but not both, of the control inputs are HIGH; otherwise, the output will stay HIGH.

Solution

The result is drawn in Figure 4-26(b). An OR gate is used because we want the output disable condition to be a HIGH, and we do not want to invert the signal. Control inputs B and C are combined in an EX-NOR gate. When B and C are different, the EX-NOR sends a LOW to enable the OR gate. When B and C are the same, the EX-NOR sends a HIGH to disable the OR gate.

EXAMPLE 4-23

Design a logic circuit with input signal A, control input B, and outputs X and Y to operate as follows:

1. When $B = 1$, output X will follow input A, and output Y will be 0.
2. When $B = 0$, output X will be 0, and output Y will follow input A.

Solution

The two outputs will be 0 when disabled and will follow the input signal when enabled. Thus, an AND gate should be used for each output. Since X is to be enabled when $B = 1$, its AND gate must be controlled by B, as shown in Figure 4-27. Since Y is to be enabled when $B = 0$, its AND gate is controlled by $\overline{B}$.

FIGURE 4-27 Example 4-23.

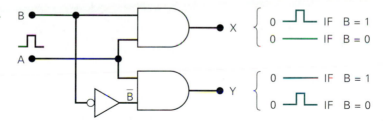

This circuit is called a *pulse-steering circuit* because it steers the input pulse to one output or the other, depending on B.

Review Questions

1. Design a logic circuit with three inputs A, B, C and an output that goes LOW only when A is HIGH while B and C are different.
2. Which logic gates produce a 1 output in the disabled state?
3. Which logic gates pass the inverse of the input signal when they are enabled?

4-9 BASIC CHARACTERISTICS OF DIGITAL ICS

Digital ICs are a collection of resistors, diodes, and transistors fabricated on a single piece of semiconductor material (usually silicon) called a *substrate,* which is commonly referred to as a *chip.* The chip is enclosed in a protective plastic or ceramic package from which pins extend for connecting the IC to other devices. One of the more common types of package is the **dual-in-line package (DIP),** shown in Figure 4-28(a), so called because it contains two parallel rows of pins. The pins are numbered counterclockwise when viewed from the top of the package with respect to an identifying notch or dot at one end of the package [see Figure 4-28(b)]. The DIP shown here is a 14-pin package that measures 0.75 in. by 0.25 in.; 16-, 20-, 24-, 28-, 40-, and 64-pin packages are also used.

FIGURE 4-28 (a) Dual-in-line package (DIP); (b) top view; (c) actual silicon chip is much smaller than the protective package.

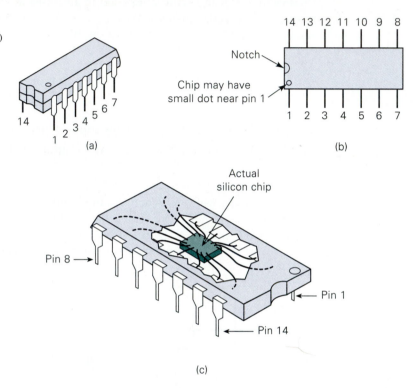

Figure 4-28(c) shows that the actual silicon chip is much smaller than the DIP; typically, it might be a 0.05-in. square. The silicon chip is connected to the pins of the DIP by very fine wires (1-mil diameter).

The DIP is probably the most common digital IC package found in digital equipment, but other types are becoming more and more popular. We will take a look at some of these other types of IC packages in Chapter 8.

Digital ICs are often categorized according to their circuit complexity as measured by the number of equivalent logic gates on the substrate. There are currently six levels of complexity that are commonly defined as shown in Table 4-5.

All of the specific ICs referred to in Chapter 3 and this chapter are **SSI** chips having a small number of gates. In modern digital systems, medium-scale integration **(MSI)** and large-scale integration devices **(LSI, VLSI, ULSI, GSI)** perform most of the functions that once required several circuit boards full of SSI devices. However, SSI chips are still used as the "interface," or "glue," between these more complex chips. Typically, small combinations of discrete gates are used to connect the larger ICs to each other or to external devices. Thus, it is necessary to know how to analyze, design, test, and troubleshoot simple combinational circuits.

TABLE 4-5

Complexity	Number of Gates
Small-scale integration (**SSI**)	Fewer than 12
Medium-scale integration (**MSI**)	12 to 99
Large-scale integration (**LSI**)	100 to 9999
Very large-scale integration (**VLSI**)	10,000 to 99,999
Ultra large-scale integration (**ULSI**)	100,000 to 999,999
Giga-scale integration (**GSI**)	1,000,000 or more

Bipolar and Unipolar Digital ICs

Digital ICs can also be categorized according to the principal type of electronic component used in their circuitry. *Bipolar ICs* are those that are made using the bipolar junction transistor (NPN and PNP) as their main circuit element. *Unipolar ICs* are those that use the unipolar field-effect transistors (P-channel and N-channel MOSFETs) as their main element.

The **TTL (transistor/transistor logic)** family has been the major family of bipolar digital ICs for the last 25 years. Figure 4-29(a) shows a TTL INVERTER circuit from the standard 74 series. The standard 74 series was the first series of TTL ICs. It is no longer used in new designs, but it is still the standard against which all other digital IC families are measured. Note that the TTL INVERTER circuit contains several bipolar transistors as the main circuit element. TTL had been the leading IC family in the small-scale and medium-scale integration (SSI and MSI) categories un-

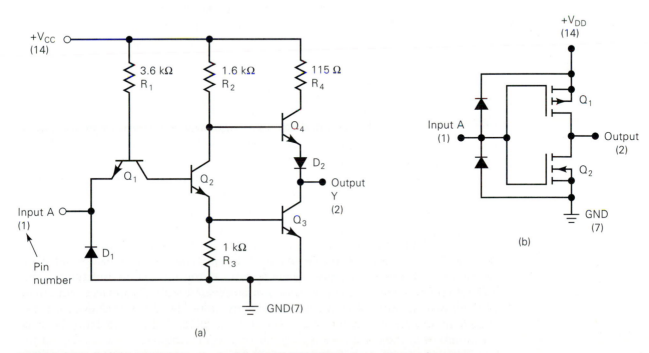

FIGURE 4-29   (a) TTL INVERTER circuit; (b) CMOS INVERTER circuit. Pin numbers are given in parentheses.

til its leading position was challenged by the CMOS family. The **CMOS (complementary metal-oxide-semiconductor)** family belongs to the category of unipolar digital ICs because it uses P- and N-channel MOSFETs as the main circuit element. Figure 4-29(b) shows a standard CMOS INVERTER circuit.

CMOS and TTL ICs dominate the field of SSI and MSI devices, and so we will concentrate on these two logic families throughout the text. Chapter 8 will provide a comprehensive study of the circuitry and characteristics of TTL and CMOS. For now we need to look at only a few of their basic characteristics so that we can talk about troubleshooting simple combinational circuits.

TTL Family

The TTL logic family actually consists of several subfamilies or series. Table 4-6 lists the name of each TTL series together with the prefix designation used to identify different ICs as being part of that series. For example, ICs that are part of the standard TTL series have an identification number that starts with 74. The 7402, 7438, and 74123 are all ICs in this series. Likewise, ICs that are part of the low-power Schottky TTL series have an identification number that starts with 74LS. The 74LS02, 74LS38, and 74LS123 are examples of devices in the 74LS series.

TABLE 4-6 Various series within the TTL logic family.

TTL Series	Prefix	Example IC
Standard TTL	74	7404 (hex INVERTER)
Schottky TTL	74S	74S04 (hex INVERTER)
Low-power Schottky TTL	74LS	74LS04 (hex INVERTER)
Advanced Schottky TTL	74AS	74AS04 (hex INVERTER)
Advanced low-power Schottky TTL	74ALS	74ALS04 (hex INVERTER)

The differences between the various TTL series are in their electrical characteristics, such as power dissipation, delay times, and switching speed. They do not differ in the pin layout or logic operations performed by the internal circuitry. For example, the 7402, 74S02, 74LS02, 74ALS02, and 74AS02 are all quad two-input NOR gates. We will compare the electrical characteristics of the different TTL series in Chapter 8.

CMOS Family

Several CMOS series are available and are listed in Table 4-7. The 4000 series is the oldest CMOS series. This series contains many of the same logic functions as the TTL family but was not designed to be *pin-compatible* with TTL devices. For example, the 4001 quad NOR chip contains four two-input NOR gates, as does the TTL 7402 chip, but the gate inputs and outputs on the CMOS chip will not have the same pin numbers as the corresponding signals on the TTL chip.

The 74C, 74HC, 74HCT, 74AC, and 74ACT series are newer CMOS series. The first three are pin-compatible with correspondingly numbered TTL devices. For example, the 74C02, 74HC02, and 74HCT02 have the same pin layout as the 7402, 74LS02, and so on. The 74HC and 74HCT series operate at a higher speed than 74C devices. The 74HCT series is designed to be *electrically compatible* with TTL devices; that is, a 74HCT integrated circuit can be connected directly to TTL devices without any interfacing circuitry. The 74AC and 74ACT series are advanced-performance ICs. Neither is pin-compatible with TTL. 74ACT devices are electrically compatible with TTL. We explore the various TTL and CMOS series in greater detail in Chapter 8.

TABLE 4-7 Various series within the CMOS logic family.

CMOS Series	Prefix	Example IC
Metal-gate CMOS	40	4001 (quad NOR gates)
Metal-gate, pin-compatible with TTL	74C	74C02 (quad NOR gates)
Silicon-gate, pin-compatible with TTL, high-speed	74HC	74HC02 (quad NOR gates)
Silicon-gate, high-speed, pin-compatible and electrically compatible with TTL	74HCT	74HCT02 (quad NOR gates)
Advanced-performance CMOS, not pin-compatible or electrically compatible with TTL	74AC	74AC02 (quad NOR)
Advanced-performance CMOS, not pin-compatible with TTL, but electrically compatible with TTL	74ACT	74ACT02 (quad NOR)

Power and Ground

To use digital ICs, it is necessary to make the proper connections to the IC pins. The most important connections are *dc power* and *ground*. These are required for the circuits on the chip to operate correctly. Referring to Figure 4-29, you can see that both the TTL and the CMOS circuits have a dc power supply voltage connected to one of their pins, and ground to another. The power supply pin is labeled V_{CC} for the TTL circuit, and V_{DD} for the CMOS circuit. Many of the newer CMOS integrated circuits that are designed to be compatible with TTL integrated circuits also use the V_{CC} designation as their power pin.

If either the power or the ground connection is not made to the IC, the logic gates on the chip will not respond properly to the logic inputs, and it will not produce the expected output logic levels.

Logic-Level Voltage Ranges

For TTL devices, V_{CC} is nominally +5 V. For CMOS integrated circuits, V_{DD} can range from +3 to +18 V, although +5 V is most often used when CMOS integrated circuits are used in the same circuit with TTL integrated circuits.

For standard TTL devices the acceptable input voltage ranges for the logic 0 and logic 1 levels are defined as shown in Figure 4-30(a). A logic 0 is any voltage in the range from 0 to 0.8 V; a logic 1 is any voltage from 2 to 5 V. Voltages that are not

FIGURE 4-30 Logic-level input voltage ranges for TTL and CMOS digital ICs.

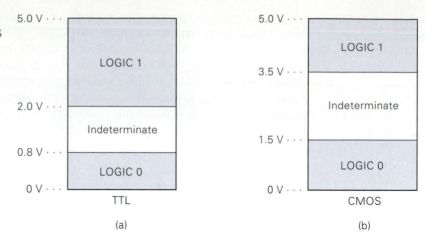

in either of these ranges are said to be **indeterminate** and should not be used as inputs to any TTL device. The IC manufacturers cannot guarantee how a TTL circuit will respond to input levels that are in the indeterminate range (between 0.8 and 2.0 V).

The logic input voltage ranges for CMOS integrated circuits operating with V_{DD} = +5 V are shown in Figure 4-30(b). Voltages between 0 and 1.5 V are defined as a logic 0, and voltages from 3.5 to 5 V as a logic 1. The indeterminate range includes voltages between 1.5 and 3.5 V.

Unconnected (Floating) Inputs

What happens when the input to a digital IC is left unconnected? An unconnected input is often called a **floating** input. The answer to this question will be different for TTL and CMOS.

A floating TTL input acts just like a logic 1. In other words, the IC will respond as if the input had a logic HIGH level applied to it. This characteristic is often used when testing a TTL circuit. A lazy technician might leave certain inputs unconnected instead of connecting them to a logic HIGH. Although this is logically correct, it is not a recommended practice, especially in final circuit designs, since the floating TTL input is extremely susceptible to picking up noise signals that will probably adversely affect the device's operation.

A floating TTL input will measure a dc level of between 1.4 and 1.8 V when checked with a VOM or an oscilloscope. Even though this is in the indeterminate range for TTL, it will produce the same response as a logic 1. Being aware of this characteristic of a floating TTL input can be valuable when troubleshooting TTL circuits.

If a CMOS input is left floating, it may have disastrous results. The IC may become overheated and eventually destroy itself. For this reason all inputs to a CMOS integrated circuit must be connected to a LOW or a HIGH level or to the output of another IC. A floating CMOS input will not measure as a specific dc voltage but will fluctuate randomly as it picks up noise. Thus, it does not act as logic 1 or logic 0, and so its effect on the output is unpredictable. Sometimes the output will oscillate as a result of the noise picked up by the floating input.

Logic-Circuit Connection Diagrams

A connection diagram shows *all* electrical connections, pin numbers, IC numbers, component values, signal names, and power supply voltages. Figure 4-31 shows a typical connection diagram for a simple logic circuit. Examine it carefully and note the following important points:

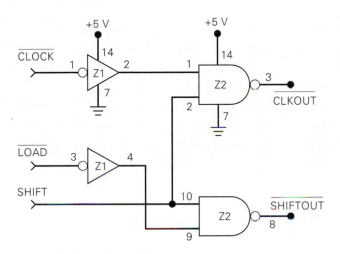

IC	Type
Z1	74HC04 hex inverter
Z2	74HC00 quad nand

FIGURE 4-31 Typical logic-circuit connection diagram.

1. The circuit uses logic gates from two different ICs. The two INVERTERs are part of a 74HC04 chip which has been given the designation Z1. The 74HC04 contains six INVERTERs; two of them are used in this circuit, and each is labeled as being part of chip Z1. Similarly, the two NAND gates are part of a 74HC00 chip that contains four NAND gates. All of the gates on this chip are designated with the label Z2. By numbering each gate as Z1, Z2, Z3, and so on, we can keep track of which gate is part of which chip. This is especially valuable in more complex circuits containing many ICs with several gates per chip.

2. Each gate input and output pin number is indicated on the diagram. These pin numbers and the IC labels are used to easily reference any point in the circuit. For example, Z1 pin 2 refers to the output pin of the top INVERTER. Similarly, we can say that Z1 pin 4 is connected to Z2 pin 9.

3. The power and ground connections to each IC are shown on the diagram. For example, Z1 pin 14 is connected to +5 V, and Z1 pin 7 is connected to ground. These connections provide power to *all* of the six INVERTERs that are part of Z1.

Manufacturers of electronic equipment generally supply detailed schematics that use a format similar to that in Figure 4-31. These connection diagrams are a virtual necessity when troubleshooting a faulty circuit. We have chosen to identify individual ICs as Z1, Z2, Z3, and so on. Other designations that are commonly used are IC1, IC2, IC3, and so on, and U1, U2, U3, and so on.

1. What is the most common type of digital IC package?
2. Name the six common categories of digital ICs according to complexity.
3. *True or false:* A 74S74 chip will contain the same logic and pin layout as the 74LS74.
4. *True or false:* A 74HC74 chip will contain the same logic and pin layout as the 74AS74.
5. Which CMOS series are not pin-compatible with TTL?
6. What is the acceptable input voltage range of a logic 0 for TTL? What is it for a logic 1?
7. Repeat question 6 for CMOS operating at $V_{DD} = 5$ V.
8. How does a TTL integrated circuit respond to a floating input?
9. How does a CMOS integrated circuit respond to a floating input?
10. Which CMOS series can be connected directly to TTL with no interfacing circuitry?

4-10 TROUBLESHOOTING DIGITAL SYSTEMS

There are three basic steps in fixing a digital circuit or system that has a fault (failure):

1. **Fault detection**. Observe the circuit/system operation and compare it with the expected correct operation.
2. **Fault isolation**. Perform tests and make measurements to isolate the fault.
3. **Fault correction**. Replace the faulty component, repair the faulty connection, remove the short, and so on.

Although these steps may seem relatively apparent and straightforward, the actual troubleshooting procedure that is followed is highly dependent on the type and complexity of the circuitry, and on the kinds of troubleshooting tools and documentation that are available.

Good troubleshooting techniques can be learned only in a laboratory environment through experimentation and actual troubleshooting of faulty circuits and systems. There is absolutely no better way to become an effective troubleshooter than to do as much troubleshooting as possible, and no amount of textbook reading can provide that kind of experience. We can, however, help you to develop the analytical skills that are the most essential part of effective troubleshooting. We will describe the types of faults that are common to systems that are made primarily from digital ICs and will tell you how to recognize them. We will then present typical case studies to illustrate the analytical processes involved in troubleshooting. In addition, there will be end-of-chapter problems to provide you with the opportunity to go through these analytical processes to reach conclusions about faulty digital circuits.

For the troubleshooting discussions and exercises we will be doing in this book, it will be assumed that the troubleshooting technician has the basic troubleshooting tools available: *logic probe, oscilloscope, logic pulser, current tracer.* Of course, the most important and effective troubleshooting tool is the technician's brain, and that's the tool we are hoping to develop by presenting troubleshooting principles and techniques, examples and problems, here and in the following chapters.

In the next three sections on troubleshooting, we will use only our brain and a **logic probe** such as the one illustrated in Figure 4-32. The other tools will be used in subsequent chapters. The logic probe has a pointy metal tip that is touched to the specific point you want to test. Here it is shown probing (touching) pin 3 of an IC. It can also be touched to a printed circuit board trace, an uninsulated wire, a connector pin, a lead on a discrete component such as a transistor, or any other conducting point in a circuit. The logic level that is present at the probe tip will be indicated by the status of an indicator light or LED in the probe. The four possibilities are given in the table of Figure 4-32. Note that an *indeterminate* logic level produces a dim indicator light. This includes the condition where the probe tip is touched to a point in a circuit that is open or floating—that is, not connected to any source of voltage.

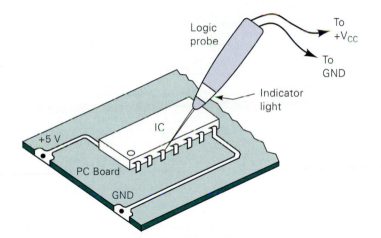

Indicator Light	Logic Level
OFF	LOW
ON (bright)	HIGH
DIM	INDETERMINATE*
FLASHING	PULSING

* Includes open or floating condition

FIGURE 4-32   A logic probe is used to monitor the logic level activity at an IC pin or any other accessible point in a logic circuit.

4-11   INTERNAL DIGITAL IC FAULTS

The most common internal failures of digital ICs are:

1. Malfunction in the internal circuitry
2. Inputs or outputs shorted to ground or V_{CC}
3. Inputs or outputs open-circuited
4. Short between two pins (other than ground or V_{CC})

We will now describe each of these types of failure.

Malfunction in Internal Circuitry

This is usually caused by one of the internal components failing completely or operating outside its specifications. When this happens, the IC outputs do not respond properly to the IC inputs. There is no way to predict what the outputs will do, because it depends on what internal component has failed. Examples of this type of failure would be a base–emitter short in transistor Q_4 or an extremely large resistance value for R_2 in the TTL INVERTER of Figure 4-29(a). This type of internal IC failure is not as common as the other three.

Input Internally Shorted to Ground or Supply

This type of internal failure will cause an IC input to be stuck in the LOW or HIGH state. Figure 4-33(a) shows input pin 2 of a NAND gate shorted to ground within the IC. This will cause pin 2 always to be in the LOW state. If this input pin is being driven by a logic signal B, it will effectively short B to ground. Thus, this type of fault will affect the output of the device that is generating the B signal.

FIGURE 4-33 (a) IC input internally shorted to ground; (b) IC input internally shorted to supply voltage. These two types of failures force the input signal at the shorted pin to stay in the same state. (c) IC output internally shorted to ground; (d) output internally shorted to supply voltage. These two failures do not affect signals at the IC inputs.

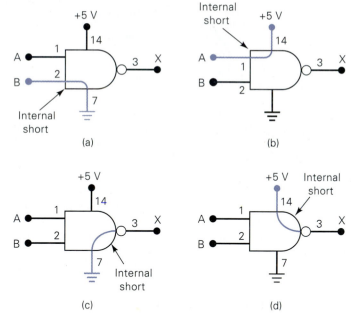

Similarly, an IC input pin could be internally shorted to +5 V as in Figure 4-33(b). This would keep that pin stuck in the HIGH state. If this input pin is being driven by a logic signal A, it will effectively short A to +5 V.

Output Internally Shorted to Ground or Supply

This type of internal failure will cause the output pin to be stuck in the LOW or HIGH state. Figure 4-33(c) shows pin 3 of the NAND gate shorted to ground within the IC. This output is stuck LOW, and it will not respond to the conditions applied to input pins 1 and 2; in other words, logic inputs *A* and *B* will have no effect on output *X.*

An IC output pin can also be shorted to +5 V within the IC as shown in Figure 4-33(d). This forces the output pin 3 to be stuck HIGH regardless of the state of the signals at the input pins. Note that this type of failure has no effect on the logic signals at the IC inputs.

EXAMPLE 4-24	Refer to the circuit of Figure 4-34. A technician uses a logic probe to determine the conditions at the various IC pins. The results are recorded in the figure. Examine these results and determine if the circuit is working properly. If not, suggest some of the possible faults.

FIGURE 4-34   Example 4-24.

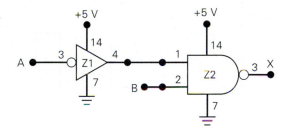

Pin	Condition
Z1-3	Pulsing
Z1-4	LOW
Z2-1	LOW
Z2-2	HIGH
Z2-3	HIGH

Solution

Output pin 4 of the INVERTER should be pulsing, since its input is pulsing. The recorded results, however, show that pin 4 is stuck LOW. Since this is connected to Z2 pin 1, this keeps the NAND output HIGH. From our preceding discussion, we can list three possible faults that could produce this operation

First, there could be an internal component failure in the INVERTER that prevents it from responding properly to its input. Second, pin 4 of the INVERTER could be shorted to ground internal to Z1, thereby keeping it stuck LOW. Third, pin 1 of Z2 could be shorted to ground internal to Z2. This would prevent the INVERTER output pin from changing.

In addition to these possible faults, there can be external shorts to ground anywhere in the conducting path between Z1 pin 4 and Z2 pin 1. We will see how to go about isolating the actual fault in a subsequent example.

Open-Circuited Input or Output

Sometimes the very fine conducting wire that connects an IC pin to the IC's internal circuitry will break, producing an open circuit. Figure 4-35 shows this for an input (pin 13) and an output (pin 6). If a signal is applied to pin 13, it will not reach the NAND-1 gate input and so will not have an effect on the NAND-1 output. The open gate input will be in the floating state. As stated earlier, TTL devices will respond as if this floating input is a logic 1, and CMOS devices will respond erratically and may even become damaged from overheating.

The open at the NAND-4 output prevents the signal from reaching IC pin 6, so there will be no stable voltage present at that pin. If this pin is connected to the input of another IC, it will produce a floating condition at that input.

<table>
<tr><td>**EXAMPLE 4-25**</td><td>What would a logic probe indicate at pin 13 and at pin 6 of Figure 4-35?</td></tr>
</table>

FIGURE 4-35   An IC with an internally open input will not respond to signals applied to that input pin. An internally open output will produce an unpredictable voltage at that output pin.

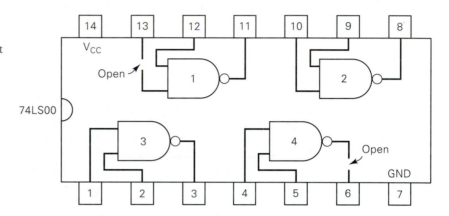

Solution

At pin 13, the logic probe will indicate the logic level of the external signal that is connected to pin 13 (which is not shown in the diagram). At pin 6, the logic probe will show a dim light for an indeterminate logic level since the NAND output level never makes it to pin 6.

<table>
<tr><td>**EXAMPLE 4-26**</td><td>Refer to the circuit of Figure 4-36 and the recorded logic probe indications. What are some of the possible faults that could produce the recorded results? Assume that the ICs are TTL.</td></tr>
</table>

FIGURE 4-36   Example 4-26.

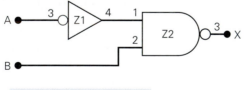

Note: V_{CC} and ground connections to each IC are not shown

Pin	Condition
Z1-3	HIGH
Z1-4	LOW
Z2-1	LOW
Z2-2	Pulsing
Z2-3	Pulsing

Solution

Examination of the recorded results indicates that the INVERTER appears to be working properly, but the NAND output is inconsistent with its inputs. The NAND output should be HIGH, since its input pin 1 is LOW. This LOW should prevent the NAND gate from responding to the pulses at pin 2. It is probable that this LOW is not reaching the internal NAND gate circuitry because of an internal open. Because the IC is TTL, this open circuit would produce the same effect as a logic HIGH at pin 1. If the IC had been CMOS, the internal open circuit at pin 1 might have produced an indeterminate output and possible overheating and destruction of the chip.

From our earlier statement regarding open TTL inputs, you might have expected that the voltage of pin 1 of Z2 would be 1.4 to 1.8 V and should have been registered as indeterminate by the logic probe. This would have been true if the open circuit had been *external* to the NAND chip. There is no open circuit between Z1 pin 4 and Z2 pin 1, and so the voltage at Z1 pin 4 is reaching Z2 pin 1, but it becomes disconnected *inside* the NAND chip.

Short Between Two Pins

An internal short between two pins of an IC will force the logic signals at those pins always to be identical. Whenever two signals that are supposed to be different show the same logic-level variations, there is a good possibility that the signals are shorted together.

Consider the circuit in Figure 4-37, where pins 5 and 6 of the NOR gate are internally shorted together. The short causes the two INVERTER output pins to be connected together so that the signals at Z1 pin 2 and Z1 pin 4 must be identical even when the two INVERTER input signals are trying to produce different outputs. To illustrate, consider the input waveforms shown in the diagram. Even though these input waveforms are different, the waveforms at outputs Z1-2 and Z1-4 are the same.

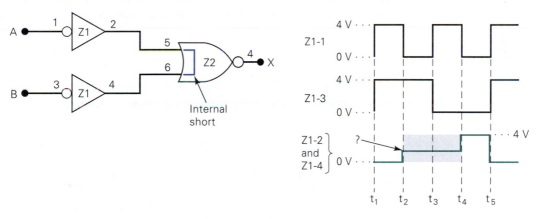

FIGURE 4-37   When two input pins are internally shorted, the signals driving these pins are forced to be identical, and usually a signal with three distinct levels results.

During the interval t_1 to t_2, both INVERTERs have a HIGH input and both are trying to produce a LOW output, so that their being shorted together makes no difference. During the interval t_4 to t_5, both INVERTERs have a LOW input and are trying to produce a HIGH output, so that again their being shorted has no effect. However, during the intervals t_2 to t_3 and t_3 to t_4, one INVERTER is trying to produce a HIGH output while the other is trying to produce a LOW output. For this situation the actual voltage level that appears at the shorted outputs will depend on the internal IC circuitry. For TTL devices it will usually be a voltage in the high end of the logic 0 range (i.e., close to 0.8 V), although it may also be in the indeterminate range. For CMOS devices it will often be a voltage in the indeterminate range.

Whenever you see a waveform like the Z1-2, Z1-4 signal in Figure 4-37 with three different levels, you should suspect that two output signals may be shorted together.

Review Questions

1. List the different internal digital IC faults.
2. Which internal IC fault can produce signals that show three different voltage levels?
3. What would a logic probe indicate at Z1-2 and Z1-4 of Figure 4-37 if $A = 0$ and $B = 1$?

4-12 EXTERNAL FAULTS

We have seen how to recognize the effects of various faults internal to digital ICs. Many more things can go wrong external to the ICs; we will describe the most common ones in this section.

Open Signal Lines

This category includes any fault that produces a break or discontinuity in the conducting path such that a voltage level or signal is prevented from going from one point to another. Some of the causes of open signal lines are:

1. Broken wire
2. Poor solder connection; loose wire-wrap connection
3. Crack or cut trace on a printed circuit board (some of these are hairline cracks that are difficult to see without a magnifying glass)
4. Bent or broken pin on an IC
5. Faulty IC socket such that the IC pin does not make good contact with the socket

This type of circuit fault can often be detected by a careful visual inspection and then verified by disconnecting power from the circuit and checking for continuity (i.e., a low-resistance path) with an ohmmeter between the two points in question.

EXAMPLE 4-27

Consider the CMOS circuit of Figure 4-38 and the accompanying logic probe indications. What is the most probable circuit fault?

Solution

The indeterminate level at the NOR gate output is probably due to the indeterminate input at pin 2. Since there is a LOW at Z1-6, this LOW should also be at Z2-2. Clearly, the LOW from Z1-6 is not reaching Z2-2, and there must be an open cir-

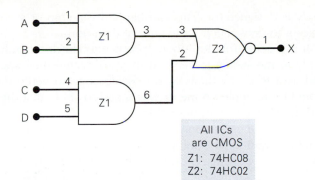

Pin	Condition
Z1-1	Pulsing
Z1-2	HIGH
Z1-3	Pulsing
Z1-4	LOW
Z1-5	Pulsing
Z1-6	LOW
Z2-3	Pulsing
Z2-2	Indeterminate
Z2-1	Indeterminate

All ICs
are CMOS
Z1: 74HC08
Z2: 74HC02

FIGURE 4-38 Example 4-27.

cuit in the signal path between these two points. The location of this open circuit
can be determined by starting at Z1-6 with the logic probe and tracing the LOW
level along the signal path toward Z2-2 until it changes into an indeterminate
level.

Shorted Signal Lines

This type of fault has the same effect as an internal short between IC pins. It causes
two signals to be exactly the same. A signal line may be shorted to ground or V_{CC}
rather than to another signal line. In those cases the signal will be forced to the
LOW or the HIGH state. The main causes for unexpected shorts between two points
in a circuit are as follows:

1. **Sloppy wiring.** An example of this is stripping too much insulation from ends of
   wires that are in close proximity.
2. **Solder bridges.** These are splashes of solder that short two or more points together. They commonly occur between points that are very close together, such
   as adjacent pins on a chip.
3. **Incomplete etching.** The copper between adjacent conducting paths on a printed
   circuit board is not completely etched away.

Again, a careful visual inspection can very often uncover this type of fault, and an
ohmmeter check can verify that the two points in the circuit are shorted together.

Faulty Power Supply

All digital systems have one or more dc power supplies that supply the V_{CC} and V_{DD}
voltages required by the chips. A faulty power supply or one that is overloaded
(supplying more than its rated amount of current) will provide poorly regulated
supply voltages to the ICs, and the ICs either will not operate or will operate erratically.

A power supply may go out of regulation because of a fault in its internal circuitry, or because the circuits that it is powering are drawing more current than the

supply is designed for. This can happen if a chip or a component has a fault that causes it to draw much more current than normal.

It is a good troubleshooting practice to check the voltage levels at each power supply in the system to see that they are within their specified ranges. It is also a good idea to check them on an oscilloscope to verify that there is no significant amount of ac ripple on the dc levels and to verify that the voltage levels stay regulated during the system operation.

One of the most common signs of a faulty power supply is one or more chips operating erratically or not at all. Some ICs are more tolerant of power supply variations and may operate properly, while others do not. You should always check the power and ground levels at each IC that appears to be operating incorrectly.

Output Loading

When a digital IC has its output connected to too many IC inputs, its output current rating will be exceeded, and the output voltage can fall into the indeterminate range. This effect is called *loading* the output signal (actually it's overloading the output signal) and is usually the result of poor design or an incorrect connection.

Review Questions
1. What are the most common types of external faults?
2. List some of the causes of signal-path open circuits.
3. What symptoms are caused by a faulty power supply?
4. How might loading affect an IC output voltage level?

4-13 TROUBLESHOOTING CASE STUDY

The following example will illustrate the analytical processes involved in troubleshooting digital circuits. Although the example is a fairly simple combinational logic circuit, the reasoning and the troubleshooting procedures used can be applied to the more complex digital circuits that we encounter in subsequent chapters.

EXAMPLE 4-28

Consider the circuit of Figure 4-39. Output Y is supposed to go HIGH for either of the following conditions:

1. $A = 1$, $B = 0$ regardless of the level on C
2. $A = 0$, $B = 1$, $C = 1$

You may wish to verify this for yourself.

When the circuit is tested, the technician observes that output Y goes HIGH whenever A is HIGH or C is HIGH regardless of the level at B. She takes logic probe measurements for the condition where $A = B = 0$, $C = 1$ and comes up with the indications recorded in Figure 4-39.

Examine the recorded levels and list the possible causes for the malfunction. Then develop a step-by-step procedure to determine the exact fault.

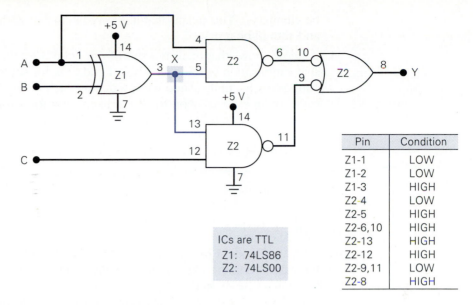

Pin	Condition
Z1-1	LOW
Z1-2	LOW
Z1-3	HIGH
Z2-4	LOW
Z2-5	HIGH
Z2-6,10	HIGH
Z2-13	HIGH
Z2-12	HIGH
Z2-9,11	LOW
Z2-8	HIGH

ICs are TTL

Z1: 74LS86
Z2: 74LS00

FIGURE 4-39   Example 4-28.

Solution

All of the NAND gate outputs are correct for the levels present at their inputs. The EX-OR gate, however, should be producing a LOW at output pin 3, since both of its inputs are at the same LOW level. It appears that Z1-3 is stuck HIGH even though its inputs should produce a LOW. There are several possible causes for this:

1. An internal component failure in Z1 that prevents its output from going LOW
2. An external short to V_{CC} from any point along the conductors connected to node X (shaded in diagram)
3. Pin 3 of Z1 internally shorted to V_{CC}
4. Pin 5 of Z2 internally shorted to V_{CC}
5. Pin 13 of Z2 internally shorted to V_{CC}

   All of these possibilities except for the first one will short node X (and every IC pin connected to it) directly to V_{CC}.
   The following procedure can be used to isolate the fault. This procedure is not the only approach that can be used, and as we stated earlier, the actual troubleshooting procedure that a technician uses is very dependent on what test equipment is available.

1. Check the V_{CC} and ground levels at the appropriate pins of Z1. Although it is unlikely that the absence of either of these might cause Z1-3 to stay HIGH, it is a good idea to make this check on any IC that is producing an incorrect output.
2. Turn off power to the circuit and use an ohmmeter to check for a short (resistance less than 1 Ω) between node X and any point connected to V_{CC} (such as Z1-14 or Z2-14). If no short is indicated, the last four possibilities in our list can

be eliminated. This means that it is very likely that Z1 has an internal failure and should be replaced.

3. If step 2 shows that there is a short from node X to V_{CC}, perform a thorough visual examination of the circuit board and look for solder bridges, unetched copper slivers, uninsulated wires touching each other, and any other possible cause of an external short to V_{CC}. A likely spot for a solder bridge would be between adjacent pins 13 and 14 of Z2. Pin 14 is connected to V_{CC}, and pin 13 to node X. If an external short is found, remove it and perform an ohmmeter check to verify that node X is no longer shorted to V_{CC}.

4. If step 3 does not reveal an external short, the three possibilities that remain are internal shorts to V_{CC} at Z1-3, Z2-13, or Z2-5. One of these is shorting node X to V_{CC}.

    To determine which of these IC pins is the culprit, we should disconnect each of them from node X *one at a time* and recheck for a short to V_{CC} after each disconnection. When the pin that is internally shorted to V_{CC} is disconnected, node X will no longer be shorted to V_{CC}.

    The process of disconnecting each suspected pin from node X can be easy or difficult depending on how the circuit is constructed. If the ICs are in sockets, all you need to do is to pull the IC from its socket, bend out the suspected pin, and reinsert the IC into its socket. If the ICs are soldered into a printed circuit board, you will have to cut the trace that is connected to the pin (or cut the pin) and repair the cut trace (or pin) when you are finished.

    There is a troubleshooting technique that makes it unnecessary to bend pins or cut traces when trying to isolate a short. It involves using a tool called a *current tracer* to trace the flow of current through the short circuit as the node is being pulsed. The current tracer senses the changing magnetic field around the conductor through which the current is being shorted. We will examine this in Chapter 8.

    Example 4-28, although fairly simple, shows you the kinds of thinking that a troubleshooter must employ in order to isolate a fault. You will have the opportunity to begin developing your own troubleshooting skills by working on Problems 4-34 to 4-44.

4-14   PROGRAMMABLE LOGIC*

As we have seen, the last step in the design of a logic circuit is to gather the appropriate ICs and make the proper connections so that the circuit's outputs are the desired logic functions of the circuit's inputs. Once this is done, the circuit can be tested. You have probably followed this procedure many times in the lab.

    Later in this book we will spend a great deal of time learning about another approach to implementing logic functions that differs markedly from this common one. It utilizes something called *programmable logic* and is especially useful in im-

---

*   This section may be skipped without any loss of continuity.

plementing more complex circuits containing tens or hundreds of logic gates. We will discuss the details of programmable logic later, but the basic concept will be introduced here with the help of Figure 4-40. The rectangular block represents a conceptual example of a **programmable logic device (PLD),** which is an integrated circuit that contains a particular arrangement of logic gates. There are many kinds of PLDs, all of which contain many more than the few gates in this example, but we will use this simple example to show the fundamental idea of all programmable logic.

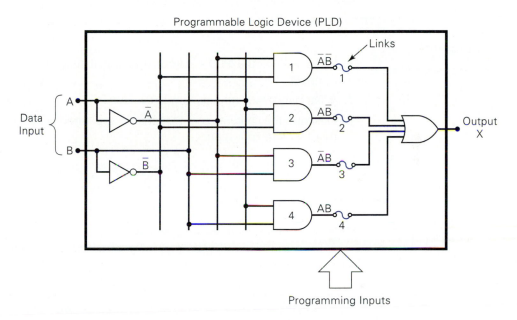

FIGURE 4-40   Simplified example of a programmable logic device.

The logic in this simplified PLD should be recognized as the sum-of-products structure with AND gates feeding a final OR gate. The output X will be a sum-of-products function of the data inputs A and B. The actual output function will depend upon which of the AND gate outputs are connected to the OR gate inputs. Right now, all of the AND outputs are shown connected to the OR gate through connecting links 1, 2, 3, and 4. Each of these links can be left intact, as shown, or they can be selectively opened up to disconnect the corresponding AND output from the OR gate. For example, if links 1, 2, and 3 are opened, only AND gate 4 will be connected, and the OR output will be $X = AB$; if links 1 and 4 are opened, the output will be $X = A\overline{B} + \overline{A}B$. The actual circuitry is such that an open link produces a LOW at its OR input.

In this way, we can implement any two-variable sum-of-products expression by opening up the appropriate links. The PLD chip comes with all of the links intact, and they are all inside the IC. How, then, do we accomplish this? Well, that's the trick we'll have to find out about later. For now let's just say that the PLD has programming inputs (represented as a large arrow in the diagram) that we can use to somehow selectively open up the links that will implement the particular logic function we want. This is called *programming* the PLD. The programming inputs are used only during the programming process to configure the chip's internal connections. Once this has been done, the PLD has been *programmed* to perform the desired logic operation on the data inputs *A* and *B*, and it is ready to be used for that purpose.

The structure in Figure 4-40 is just one of several types of PLD structures that we will study in detail in Chapters 11 and 12. It should be relatively easy to see how this simple AND-OR structure can be expanded to accommodate a larger number of data inputs. For example, for three data inputs, the PLD would contain three IN-VERTERs, eight AND gates (one for each possible AND product of three variables), eight links, and an eight-input OR gate.

Review Questions

1. What will be the PLD's output function if links 1 and 2 in Figure 4-40 are opened?
2. What will it be if all links are left intact?
3. Describe the contents of a PLD that is structured as shown in Figure 4-40 and that has *four* data inputs.

SUMMARY

1. The two general forms for logic expressions are the sum-of-products form and the product-of-sums form.

2. One approach to the design of a combinatorial logic circuit is to (1) construct its truth table, (2) convert the truth table to a sum-of-products expression, (3) simplify the expression using Boolean algebra or K mapping, (4) implement the final expression.

3. The K map is a graphical method for representing a circuit's truth table and generating a simplified expression for the circuit output.

4. An exclusive-OR circuit has the expression $x = A\overline{B} + \overline{A}B$. Its output x will be HIGH only when inputs A and B are at opposite logic levels.

5. An exclusive-NOR circuit has the expression $x = \overline{A}\,\overline{B} + AB$. Its output x will be HIGH only when inputs A and B are at the same logic level.

6. Each of the basic gates (AND, OR, NAND, NOR) can be used to enable or disable the passage of an input signal to its output.

7. The main digital IC families are the TTL and CMOS families. Digital ICs are available in a wide range of complexities (gates per chip), from the basic to the high-complexity logic functions.

8. To perform basic troubleshooting requires—at minimum—an understanding of circuit operation, a knowledge of the types of possible faults, a complete logic-circuit connection diagram, and a logic probe.

9. A programmable logic device (PLD) is an IC that contains a large number of logic gates whose interconnections can be programmed by the user to generate the desired logic relationship between inputs and outputs.

IMPORTANT TERMS

sum-of-products
product-of-sums
Karnaugh map (K map)
looping
"don't-care" condition
exclusive-OR (EX-OR)
exclusive-NOR (EX-NOR)
parity generator and
 checker

enable/disable
dual-in-line package (DIP)
SSI, MSI, LSI, VLSI, ULSI,
 GSI
transistor/transistor logic
 (TTL)
complementary metal-
 oxide-semiconductor
 (CMOS)

indeterminate
floating
logic probe
programmable logic device
 (PLD)

PROBLEMS

SECTION 4-2 AND 4-3

4-1. Simplify the following expressions using Boolean algebra.
 (a) $x = ABC + \overline{A}C$
 (b) $y = (Q + R)(\overline{Q} + \overline{R})$
 (c) $w = ABC + A\overline{B}C + \overline{A}$
 (d) $q = \overline{RST}\,(R + S + T)$
 (e) $x = \overline{A}\overline{B}\overline{C} + \overline{A}BC + ABC + A\overline{B}\overline{C} + A\overline{B}C$
 (f) $z = (B + \overline{C})(\overline{B} + C) + \overline{A} + B + \overline{C}$
 (g) $y = \overline{(C + D)} + \overline{A}C\overline{D} + A\overline{B}\overline{C} + \overline{A}BCD + AC\overline{D}$

4-2. Simplify the circuit of Figure 4-41 using Boolean algebra.

FIGURE 4-41 Problems 4-2 and 4-3.

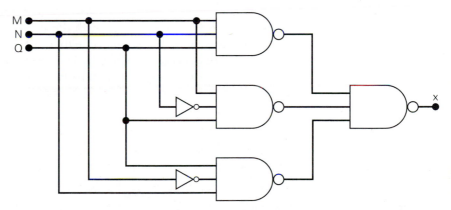

4-3. Change each gate in Problem 4-2 to a NOR gate, and simplify the circuit using Boolean algebra.

SECTION 4-4

D **4-4.** Design the logic circuit corresponding to the truth table shown in Table 4-8.

D **4-5.** Design a logic circuit whose output is HIGH *only* when a majority of inputs A, B, and C are LOW.

TABLE 4-8

A	B	C	x
0	0	0	1
0	0	1	0
0	1	0	1
0	1	1	1
1	0	0	1
1	0	1	0
1	1	0	0
1	1	1	1

D   4-6. A manufacturing plant needs to have a horn sound to signal quitting time. The horn should be activated when either of the following conditions is met:
1. It's after 5 o'clock and all machines are shut down.
2. It's Friday, the production run for the day is complete, and all machines are shut down.

Design a logic circuit that will control the horn. (*Hint:* Use four logic input variables to represent the various conditions; for example, input *A* will be HIGH only when the time of day is 5 o'clock or later.)

D   4-7. A four-bit binary number is represented as $A_3A_2A_1A_0$, where A_3, A_2, A_1, and A_0 represent the individual bits with A_0 equal to the LSB. Design a logic circuit that will produce a HIGH output whenever the binary number is greater than 0010 and less than 1000.

D   4-8. Figure 4-42 shows a diagram for an automobile alarm circuit used to detect certain undesirable conditions. The three switches are used to indicate the status of the door by the driver's seat, the ignition, and the headlights, respectively. Design the logic circuit with these three switches as inputs so that the alarm will be activated whenever either of the following conditions exists:
- The headlights are on while the ignition is off.
- The door is open while the ignition is on.

FIGURE 4-42   Problem 4-8.

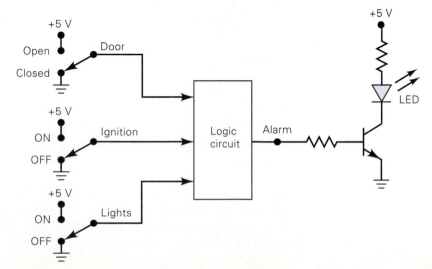

4-9. Implement the circuit of Problem 4-4 using all NAND gates.

4-10. Implement the circuit of Problem 4-5 using all NAND gates.

4-11. Implement the expression $z = \overline{D} + ABC + \overline{A}\,\overline{C}$ using ANDs, ORs, and INVERTERs; then convert to all NAND gates.

SECTION 4-5

4-12. Simplify the expression of Problem 4-1(e) using a K map.

4-13. Simplify the expression of Problem 4-1(g) using a K map.

4-14. Simplify the expression from Problem 4-7 using a K map.

4-15. Determine the minimum expression for each K map in Figure 4-43. For the map in (a), pay particular attention to step 5.

(a)

	$\overline{C}\overline{D}$	$\overline{C}D$	CD	$C\overline{D}$
$\overline{A}\overline{B}$	1	1	1	1
$\overline{A}B$	1	1	0	0
AB	0	0	0	1
$A\overline{B}$	0	0	1	1

(b)

	$\overline{C}\overline{D}$	$\overline{C}D$	CD	$C\overline{D}$
$\overline{A}\overline{B}$	1	0	1	1
$\overline{A}B$	1	0	0	1
AB	0	0	0	0
$A\overline{B}$	1	0	1	1

(c)

	$\overline{C}$	C
$\overline{A}\overline{B}$	1	1
$\overline{A}B$	0	0
AB	1	0
$A\overline{B}$	1	X

FIGURE 4-43 Problem 4-15.

D 4-16. Figure 4-44 shows a *BCD counter* that produces a four-bit output representing the BCD code for the number of pulses that have been applied to the counter input. For example, after four pulses have occurred, the counter outputs are $DCBA = 0100_2 = 4_{10}$. The counter resets to 0000 on the tenth pulse and starts counting over again. In other words, the *DCBA* outputs will never represent a number greater than $1001_2 = 9_{10}$. Design the logic circuit that produces a HIGH output whenever the count is 2, 3, or 9. Use K mapping and take advantage of the don't-care conditions.

FIGURE 4-44 Problem 4-16.

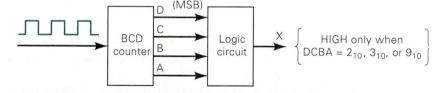

D 4-17. Figure 4-45 shows four switches that are part of the control circuitry in a copy machine. The switches are at various points along the path of the copy paper as the paper passes through the machine. Each switch is normally open, and as the paper passes over a switch, the switch closes. It is impossible for switches SW1 and SW4 to be closed at the same time. Design the logic circuit to produce a HIGH output whenever *two or more* switches are closed at the same time. Use K mapping and take advantage of the don't-care conditions.

FIGURE 4-45 Problem 4-17.

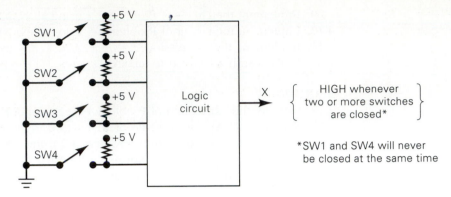

X { HIGH whenever
two or more switches
are closed* }

*SW1 and SW4 will never
be closed at the same time

SECTION 4-6

4-18. (a) Determine the output waveform for the circuit of Figure 4-46.
    (b) Repeat with the *B* input held LOW.
    (c) Repeat with *B* held HIGH.

FIGURE 4-46 Problem 4-18.

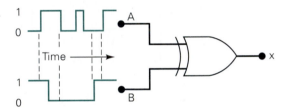

4-19. Determine the input conditions needed to produce $x = 1$ in Figure 4-47.

FIGURE 4-47 Problem 4-19.

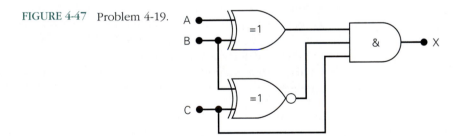

C, D 4-20. Design a logic circuit with three inputs to produce a HIGH output only when all three inputs are at the same logic level. Use only EX-NOR gates and one other gate.

C 4-21. Figure 4-48 represents a *relative-magnitude detector* that takes two three-bit binary numbers $x_2x_1x_0$ and $y_2y_1y_0$ and determines whether they are equal and, if not, which one is larger. There are three outputs, defined as follows:
1. $M = 1$ only if the two input numbers are equal
2. $N = 1$ only if $x_2x_1x_0$ is greater than $y_2y_1y_0$
3. $P = 1$ only if $y_2y_1y_0$ is greater than $x_2x_1x_0$
Design the logic circuitry for this detector. The circuit has *six* inputs and *three* outputs and is therefore much too complex to handle using the truth-table ap-

FIGURE 4-48   Problem 4-21.

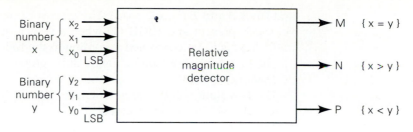

proach. Refer to Example 4-16 as a hint to how you might start to solve this problem.

MORE DESIGN PROBLEMS

C, D   **4-22.** Figure 4-49 represents a multiplier circuit that takes two-bit binary numbers $x_1 x_0$ and $y_1 y_0$ and produces an output binary number $z_3 z_2 z_1 z_0$ that is equal to the arithmetic product of the two input numbers. Design the logic circuit for the multiplier. (*Hint:* The logic circuit will have four inputs and four outputs.)

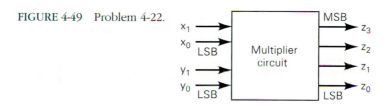

FIGURE 4-49   Problem 4-22.

D   **4-23.** A BCD code is being transmitted to a remote receiver. The bits are A_3, A_2, A_1, A_0 with A_3 as the MSB. The receiver circuitry includes a *BCD error detector* circuit that examines the received code to see if it is a legal BCD code (i.e., ≤ 1001). Design this circuit to produce a HIGH for any error condition.

D   **4-24.** Design a logic circuit whose output is HIGH whenever *A* and *B* are both HIGH as long as *C* and *D* are either both LOW or both HIGH. Try to do this without using a truth table. Then check your result by constructing a truth table for your circuit to see if it agrees with the problem statement.

D   **4-25.** Four large tanks at a chemical plant contain different liquids being heated. Liquid-level sensors are being used to detect whenever the level in tank *A* or tank *B* rises above a predetermined level. Temperature sensors in tanks *C* and *D* detect when the temperature in either of these tanks drops below a prescribed temperature limit. Assume that the liquid-level sensor outputs *A* and *B* are LOW when the level is satisfactory and HIGH when the level is too high. Also, the temperature-sensor outputs *C* and *D* are LOW when the temperature is satisfactory and HIGH when the temperature is too low. Design a logic circuit that will detect whenever the level in tank *A* or tank *B* is too high at the same time that the temperature in either tank *C* or tank *D* is too low.

C, D   **4-26.** Figure 4-50 shows the intersection of a main highway with a secondary access road. Vehicle-detection sensors are placed along lanes *C* and *D* (main road) and lanes *A* and *B* (access road). These sensor outputs are LOW (0) when no vehicle is present and HIGH (1) when a vehicle is present. The intersection traffic light is to be controlled according to the following logic:

1. The east-west (E-W) traffic light will be green whenever *both* lanes *C* and *D* are occupied.
2. The E-W light will be green whenever *either C* or *D* is occupied but lanes *A* and *B* are not *both* occupied.
3. The north-south (N-S) light will be green whenever *both* lanes *A* and *B* are occupied but *C* and *D* are not *both* occupied.
4. The N-S light will also be green when *either A* or *B* is occupied while *C* and *D* are *both* vacant.
5. The E-W light will be green when *no* vehicles are present.

Using the sensor outputs *A*, *B*, *C*, and *D* as inputs, design a logic circuit to control the traffic light. There should be two outputs, N-S and E-W, that go HIGH when the corresponding light is to be *green*. Simplify the circuit as much as possible and show *all* steps.

FIGURE 4-50   Problem 4-26.

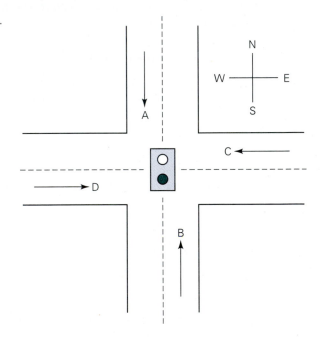

SECTION 4-7

D 4-27. Redesign the parity generator and checker of Figure 4-24 to operate using odd parity. (*Hint:* What is the relationship between an odd-parity bit and an even-parity bit for the same set of data bits?)

D 4-28. Redesign the parity generator and checker of Figure 4-24 to operate on eight data bits.

SECTION 4-8

D 4-29. Design a logic circuit that will allow input signal *A* to pass through to the output only when control input *B* is LOW while control input *C* is HIGH; otherwise, the output is LOW.

D **4-30.** Design a circuit that will *disable* the passage of an input signal only when control inputs B, C, and D are all HIGH; the output is to be HIGH in the disabled condition.

D **4-31.** Design a logic circuit that controls the passage of a signal A according to the following requirements:

1. Output X will equal A when control inputs B and C are the same.
2. X will remain HIGH when B and C are different.

D **4-32.** Design a logic circuit that has two signal inputs A_1 and A_0 and a control input S so that it functions according to the requirements given in Figure 4-51. This type of circuit is called a *multiplexer* (covered in Chapter 9).

FIGURE 4-51 Problem 4-32.

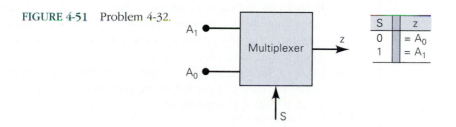

S	z
0	$= A_0$
1	$= A_1$

D **4-33.** Use K mapping to design a circuit to meet the requirements of Example 4-16. Compare this circuit with the solution in Figure 4-22. This points out that the K-map method cannot take advantage of the EX-OR and EX-NOR gate logic. The designer must be able to determine when these gates are applicable.

SECTIONS 4-9 TO 4-13

T* **4-34.** (a) A technician testing a logic circuit sees that the output of a particular INVERTER is stuck LOW while its input is pulsing. List as many possible reasons as you can for this faulty operation.

(b) Repeat part (a) for the case where the INVERTER output is stuck at an indeterminate logic level.

T **4-35.** The signals shown in Figure 4-52 are applied to the inputs of the circuit of Figure 4-31. Suppose that there is an internal open circuit at Z1-4.

(a) What will a logic probe indicate at Z1-4?

(b) What dc voltage reading would you expect a VOM to register at Z1-4? (Remember that the ICs are TTL.)

(c) Sketch what you think the $\overline{CLKOUT}$ and $\overline{SHIFTOUT}$ signals will look like.

(d) Instead of the open at Z1-4, suppose that pins 9 and 10 of Z2 are internally shorted. Sketch the probable signals at Z2-10, $\overline{CLOCKOUT}$, and $\overline{SHIFTOUT}$.

T **4-36.** Assume that the ICs in Figure 4-31 are CMOS. Describe how the circuit operation would be affected by an open circuit in the conductor connecting Z2-2 and Z2-10.

T **4-37.** In Example 4-24 we listed three possible faults for the situation of Figure 4-34. What procedure would you follow to determine which of the faults is the actual one?

---

* Recall that **T** indicates a troubleshooting exercise.

FIGURE 4-52 Problem 4-35.

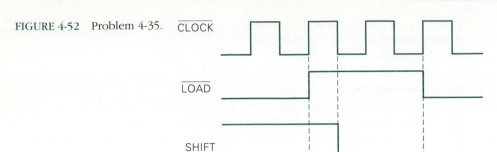

T **4-38.** Refer to the circuit of Figure 4-36. Assume that the devices are CMOS. Also assume that the logic probe indication at Z2-3 is "indeterminate" rather than "pulsing." List the possible faults, and write a procedure to follow to determine the actual fault.

T **4-39.** Refer to the logic circuit of Figure 4-39. Recall that output Y is supposed to be HIGH for either of the following conditions:
1. $A = 1$, $B = 0$, regardless of C
2. $A = 0$, $B = 1$, $C = 1$
When testing the circuit, the technician observes that Y goes HIGH only for the first condition but stays LOW for all other input conditions. Consider the following list of possible faults. For each one indicate "yes" or "no" as to whether or not it could be the actual fault. Explain your reasoning for each "no" response.
   (a) An internal short to ground at Z2-13
   (b) An open circuit in the connection to Z2-13
   (c) An internal short to V_{CC} at Z2-11
   (d) An open circuit in the V_{CC} connection to Z2
   (e) An internal open circuit at Z2-9
   (f) An open in the connection from Z2-11 to Z2-9
   (g) A solder bridge between pins 6 and 7 of Z2

T **4-40.** Develop a procedure for isolating the fault that is causing the malfunction described in Problem 4-39.

T **4-41.** Assume that the gates in Figure 4-39 are all CMOS. When the technician tests the circuit, he finds that it operates correctly except for the following conditions:
1. $A = 1$, $B = 0$, $C = 0$
2. $A = 0$, $B = 1$, $C = 1$
For these conditions, the logic probe indicates indeterminate levels at Z2-6, Z2-11, and Z2-8. What do you think is the probable fault in the circuit? Explain your reasoning.

T **4-42.** Figure 4-53 is a combinational logic circuit that operates an alarm in a car whenever the driver and/or passenger seats are occupied and the seat belts are not fastened when the car is started. The active-HIGH signals *DRIV* and *PASS* indicate the presence of the driver and passenger, respectively, and are taken from pressure-actuated switches in the seats. The signal *IGN* is active-HIGH when the ignition switch is on. The signal $\overline{BELTD}$ is active-LOW and indicates that the driver's seat belt is *unfastened*; $\overline{BELTP}$ is the corresponding signal for the passenger seat belt. The alarm will be activated (LOW) when-

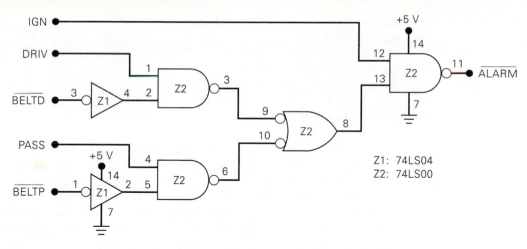

FIGURE 4-53   Problems 4-42, 4-43, and 4-44.

ever the car is started and either of the front seats is occupied and its seat belt is not fastened.

(a) Verify that the circuit will function as described.

(b) Describe how this alarm system would operate if Z1-2 were internally shorted to ground.

(c) Describe how it would operate if there were an open connection from Z2-6 to Z2-10.

T   4-43. Suppose that the system of Figure 4-53 is functioning in such a way that the alarm is activated as soon as the driver and/or passenger are seated and the car is started, regardless of the status of the seat belts. What are the possible faults? What procedure would you follow to find the actual fault?

T   4-44. Suppose that the alarm system of Figure 4-53 is operating in such a way that the alarm goes on continuously as soon as the car is started regardless of the state of the other inputs. List the possible faults and write a procedure to isolate the fault.

SECTION 4-14

C   4-45. (a) Modify the PLD diagram of Figure 4-40 so that it can handle three data inputs.

(b) Using this three-input PLD, show how to implement the circuit for Example 4-7. Note that it is not necessary to simplify the output expression in order to do this.

(c) The circuit of Example 4-7 was implemented using a quad NAND IC [Figure 4-9(a)]. Compare the number of *external* IC connections for that implementation with the one that uses the PLD.

DRILL QUESTION

4-46. Define each of the following terms.

(a) Karnaugh map

(b) Sum-of-products form

(c) Parity generator

(d) Octet

(e) Enable circuit

(f) Don't-care state

(g) Floating input

(h) Indeterminate voltage level

MICROCOMPUTER APPLICATIONS

C   4-47. In a microcomputer, the microprocessor unit (MPU) is always communicating with one of the following: (1) random-access memory (RAM), which stores programs and data that can be readily changed; (2) read-only memory (ROM), which stores programs and data that never change; (3) external input/output devices (I/O) such as keyboard, video displays, printers, and disk drives. As it is executing a program, the MPU will generate an address code that selects which type of device (RAM, ROM, or I/O) it wants to communicate with. Figure 4-54 shows a typical arrangement where the MPU outputs an eight-bit address code A_{15} through A_8. Actually, the MPU outputs a 16-bit address code, but the low-order bits A_7 through A_0 are not used in the device selection process. The address code is applied to a logic circuit which uses it to generate the device select signals: $\overline{RAM}$, $\overline{ROM}$, and $\overline{I/O}$.

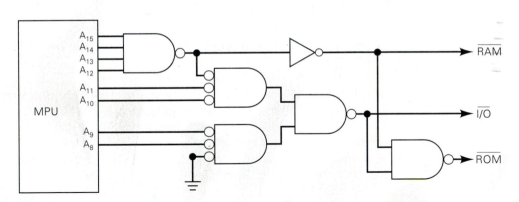

FIGURE 4-54

Analyze this circuit and determine the following.

(a) The range of addresses A_{15} through A_8 that will activate $\overline{RAM}$

(b) The range of addresses that activate $\overline{I/O}$

(c) The range of addresses that activate $\overline{ROM}$

Express the addresses in binary and hexadecimal. For example, the answer to (a) is A_{15} to $A_8 = 00000000_2$ to $11101111_2 = 00_{16}$ to EF_{16}.

C, D   4-48. In some microcomputers the MPU can be *disabled* for short periods of time while another device controls the RAM, ROM, and I/O. During these intervals a special control signal ($\overline{DMA}$) is activated by the MPU and is used to disable (deactivate) the device select logic so that the $\overline{RAM}$, $\overline{ROM}$, and $\overline{I/O}$ are all in their inactive state. Modify the circuit of Figure 4-54 so that $\overline{RAM}$, $\overline{ROM}$, and $\overline{I/O}$ will be deactivated whenever the signal $\overline{DMA}$ is active, regardless of the state of the address code.

ANSWERS TO SECTION REVIEW QUESTIONS

SECTION 4-1

1. Only (a)   2. Only (c)

SECTION 4-3

1. Expression (b) is not in sum-of-products form, because of the inversion sign over both the C and D variables (i.e., the $A\overline{CD}$ term). Expression (c) is not in sum-of-products form, because of the $(M + \overline{N})P$ term.
3. $x = \overline{A} + \overline{B} + \overline{C}$

SECTION 4-4

1. $x = \overline{A}\,\overline{B}\,\overline{C}D + \overline{A}\,\overline{B}C\overline{D} + \overline{A}B\overline{C}\,\overline{D}$ 2. Eight

SECTION 4-5

1. $x = AB + AC + BC$ 2. $x = A + BCD$ 4. An input condition for which there is no specific required output condition

SECTION 4-6

2. A constant LOW   3. No; the available EX-OR gate can be used as an INVERTER by connecting one of its inputs to a constant HIGH (see Example 4-15).

SECTION 4-8

1. $x = \overline{A(B \oplus C)}$ 2. OR, NAND   3. NAND, NOR

SECTION 4-9

1. DIP   2. SSI, MSI, LSI, VLSI, ULSI, GSI   3. True
4. True   5. 40, 74AC, 74ACT series   6. 0 to 0.8 V;
2.0 to 5.0 V   7. 0 to 1.5 V; 3.5 to 5.0 V   8. As if the input were HIGH   9. Unpredictably; it may overheat and be destroyed.   10. 74HCT and 74ACT

SECTION 4-11

1. Open inputs or outputs; inputs or outputs shorted to V_{CC}; inputs or outputs shorted to ground; pins shorted together; internal circuit failures   2. Pins shorted together   3. For TTL, a LOW; for CMOS, indeterminate

SECTION 4-12

1. Open signal lines; shorted signal lines; faulty power supply; output loading   2. Broken wires; poor solder connections; cracks or cuts in PC board; bent or broken IC pins; faulty IC sockets   3. ICs operating erratically or not at all   4. Logic level indeterminate

SECTION 4-14

1. $x = B$ 2. $x = 1$ 3. Four INVERTERs, 16 AND gates, 16 links, and a 16-input OR

CHAPTER 5

Flip-Flops and Related Devices

■ OUTLINE

■ OBJECTIVES

Upon completion of this chapter, you will be able to:

- Construct and analyze the operation of a latch flip-flop made from NAND or NOR gates.
- Debounce a mechanical switch by using a latch circuit.
- Describe the difference between synchronous and asynchronous systems.
- Understand several types of edge-triggered flip-flops, such as the J-K, D-type, and S-C.
- Analyze and apply the various flip-flop timing parameters specified by the manufacturers.
- Describe a pulse-steering and an edge-detector circuit.
- Understand the major differences between parallel and serial data transfers.
- Draw the output timing waveforms of several types of flip-flops in response to a set of input signals.
- Explain the various IEEE/ANSI flip-flop symbols.
- Use state transition diagrams to describe counter operation.
- Cite various flip-flop applications.
- Use flip-flops in synchronization circuits.
- Connect shift registers as data transfer circuits.
- Employ flip-flops as frequency-division and counting circuits.
- Understand the typical characteristics of Schmitt triggers.
- Apply two different types of one-shots in circuit design.
- Design a free-running oscillator using a 555 timer.
- Recognize and predict the effects of clock skew on synchronous circuits.
- Troubleshoot various types of flip-flop circuits.

■ INTRODUCTION

The logic circuits considered thus far have been combinational circuits whose output levels at any instant of time are dependent on the levels present at the inputs at that time. Any prior input-level conditions have no effect on the present outputs because combinational logic circuits have no memory. Most digital systems are made up of both combinational circuits and memory elements.

Figure 5-1 shows a block diagram of a general digital system that combines combinational logic gates with memory devices. The combinational portion accepts logic signals from external inputs and from the outputs of the memory elements. The combinational circuit operates on these inputs to produce various outputs, some of which are used to determine the binary values to be stored in the memory elements. The outputs of some of the memory elements, in turn, go to the inputs of logic gates in the combinational circuits. This process indicates that the external outputs of a digital system are a function of both its external inputs and the information stored in its memory elements.

FIGURE 5-1   General digital system diagram.

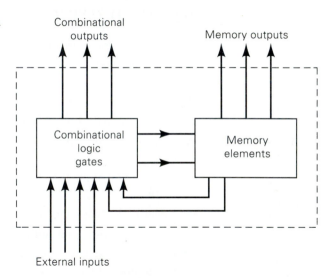

The most important memory element is the **flip-flop,** which is made up of an assembly of logic gates. Even though a logic gate, by itself, has no storage capability, several can be connected together in ways that permit information to be stored. Several different gate arrangements are used to produce these flip-flops (abbreviated FF).

Figure 5-2(a) is the general type of symbol used for a flip-flop. It shows two outputs, labeled Q and $\overline{Q}$, that are the inverse of each other. $Q/\overline{Q}$ are the most common designations used for a FF's outputs. From time to time, we will use other designations such as $X/\overline{X}$ and $A/\overline{A}$ for convenience in identifying different FFs in a logic circuit.

The Q output is called the *normal* FF output, and $\overline{Q}$ is the *inverted* FF output. Whenever we refer to the state of a FF, we are referring to the state of its normal (Q) output; it is understood that its inverted output ($\overline{Q}$) is in the opposite state. For example, if we say that a FF is in the HIGH (1) state, we mean that $Q = 1$; if we say that a FF is in the LOW (0) state, we mean that $Q = 0$. Of course, the $\overline{Q}$ state will always be the inverse of Q.

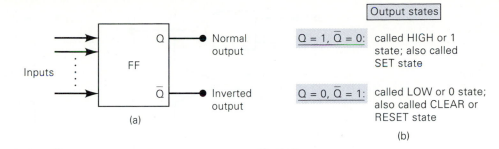

FIGURE 5-2   General flip-flop symbol and definition of its two possible output states.

The two possible operating states for a FF are summarized in Figure 5-2(b). Note that the HIGH or 1 state ($Q = 1/\overline{Q} = 0$) is also referred to as the **SET** state. Whenever the inputs to a FF cause it to go to the $Q = 1$ state, we call this *setting* the FF; the FF has been set. In a similar way, the LOW or 0 state ($Q = 0/\overline{Q} = 1$) is also referred to as the **CLEAR** or **RESET** state. Whenever the inputs to a FF cause it to go to the $Q = 0$ state, we call this *clearing* or *resetting* the FF; the FF has been cleared (reset). As we shall see, many FFs will have a **SET** input and/or a **CLEAR (RESET)** input that are used to drive the FF into a specific output state.

As the symbol in Figure 5-2(a) implies, a FF can have one or more inputs. These inputs are used to cause the FF to switch back and forth ("flip-flop") between its possible output states. We will find out that most FF inputs need only to be momentarily activated (pulsed) in order to cause a change in the FF output state, and the output will remain in that new state even after the input pulse is over. This is the FF's *memory* characteristic.

The flip-flop is known by other names, including *latch* and *bistable multivibrator*. The term *latch* is used for certain types of flip-flops that we will describe. The term *bistable multivibrator* is the more technical name for a flip-flop, but it is too much of a mouthful to be used regularly.

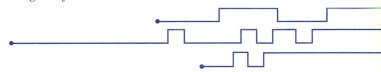

5-1   NAND GATE LATCH

The most basic FF circuit can be constructed from either two NAND gates or two NOR gates. The NAND gate version, called a **NAND gate latch** or simply a **latch,** is shown in Figure 5-3(a). The two NAND gates are cross-coupled so that the output of NAND-1 is connected to one of the inputs of NAND-2, and vice versa. The gate outputs, labeled Q and $\overline{Q}$, respectively, are the latch outputs. Under normal conditions, these outputs will always be the inverse of each other. There are two latch inputs: the SET input is the input that *sets* Q to the 1 state; the CLEAR input is the input that *clears* Q to the 0 state.

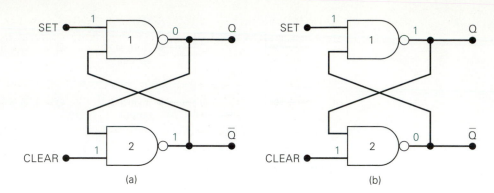

FIGURE 5-3   A NAND latch has two possible resting states when SET = CLEAR = 1.

The SET and CLEAR inputs are both normally resting in the HIGH state, and one of them will be pulsed LOW whenever we want to change the latch outputs. We begin our analysis by showing that there are two equally likely output states when SET = CLEAR = 1. One possibility is shown in Figure 5-3(a), where we have $Q = 0$ and $\overline{Q} = 1$. With $Q = 0$, the inputs to NAND-2 are 0 and 1, which produce $\overline{Q} = 1$. The 1 from $\overline{Q}$ causes NAND-1 to have a 1 at both inputs to produce a 0 output at Q. In effect, what we have is the LOW at the NAND-1 output producing a HIGH at the NAND-2 output, which, in turn, keeps the NAND-1 output LOW.

The second possibility is shown in Figure 5-3(b), where $Q = 1$ and $\overline{Q} = 0$. The HIGH from NAND-1 produces a LOW at the NAND-2 output, which, in turn, keeps the NAND-1 output HIGH. Thus, there are two possible output states when SET = CLEAR = 1; as we shall soon see, the one that actually exists will depend on what has occurred previously at the inputs.

Setting the Latch (FF)

Now let's investigate what happens when the SET input is momentarily pulsed LOW while CLEAR is kept HIGH. Figure 5-4(a) shows what happens when $Q = 0$ prior to the occurrence of the pulse. As SET is pulsed LOW at time t_0, Q will go HIGH, and

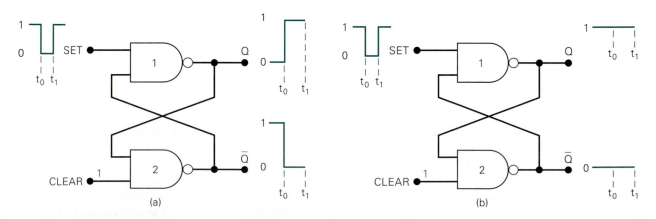

FIGURE 5-4   Pulsing the SET input to the 0 state when (a) $Q = 0$ prior to SET pulse; (b) $Q = 1$ prior to SET pulse. Note that in both cases Q ends up HIGH.

this HIGH will force $\overline{Q}$ to go LOW so that NAND-1 now has two LOW inputs. Thus, when SET returns to the 1 state at t_1, the NAND-1 output *remains* HIGH, which, in turn, keeps the NAND-2 output LOW.

Figure 5-4(b) shows what happens when $Q = 1$ and $\overline{Q} = 0$ prior to the application of the SET pulse. Since $\overline{Q} = 0$ is already keeping the NAND-1 output HIGH, the LOW pulse at SET will not change anything. Thus, when SET returns HIGH, the latch outputs are still in the $Q = 1$, $\overline{Q} = 0$ state.

We can summarize Figure 5-4 by stating that a LOW pulse on the SET input will always cause the latch to end up in the $Q = 1$ state. This operation is called *setting* the latch or FF.

Clearing the Latch (FF)

Now let's consider what occurs when the CLEAR input is pulsed LOW while SET is kept HIGH. Figure 5-5(a) shows what happens when $Q = 0$ and $\overline{Q} = 1$ prior to the application of the pulse. Since $Q = 0$ is already keeping the NAND-2 output HIGH, the LOW pulse at CLEAR will not have any effect. When CLEAR returns HIGH, the latch outputs are still $Q = 0$ and $\overline{Q} = 1$.

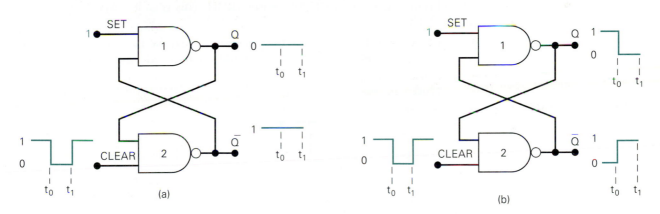

FIGURE 5-5 Pulsing the CLEAR input to the LOW state when (a) $Q = 0$ prior to CLEAR pulse; (b) $Q = 1$ prior to CLEAR pulse. In each case, Q ends up LOW.

Figure 5-5(b) shows the situation where $Q = 1$ prior to the occurrence of the CLEAR pulse. As CLEAR is pulsed LOW at t_0, $\overline{Q}$ will go HIGH, and this HIGH forces Q to go LOW so that NAND-2 now has two LOW inputs. Thus, when CLEAR returns HIGH at t_1, the NAND-2 output *remains* HIGH, which, in turn, keeps the NAND-1 output LOW.

Figure 5-5 can be summarized by stating that a LOW pulse on the CLEAR input will always cause the latch to end up in the $Q = 0$ state. This operation is called *clearing* or *resetting* the latch.

Simultaneous Setting and Clearing

The last case to consider is the case where the SET and CLEAR inputs are simultaneously pulsed LOW. This will produce HIGH levels at both NAND outputs so that $Q = \overline{Q} = 1$. Clearly, this is an undesired condition, since the two outputs are supposed to be inverses of each other. Furthermore, when the SET and CLEAR inputs return HIGH, the resulting output state will depend on which input returns HIGH first. Simultaneous transitions back to the 1 state will produce unpredictable results. For these reasons the SET = CLEAR = 0 condition is normally not used for the NAND latch.

Summary of NAND Latch

The operation described above can be conveniently placed in a truth table (Figure 5-6) and is summarized as follows:

1. **SET = CLEAR = 1.** This condition is the normal resting state, and it has no effect on the output state. The Q and $\overline{Q}$ outputs will remain in whatever state they were prior to this input condition.
2. **SET = 0, CLEAR = 1.** This will always cause the output to go to the $Q = 1$ state, where it will remain even after SET returns HIGH. This is called *setting* the latch.
3. **SET = 1, CLEAR = 0.** This will always produce the $Q = 0$ state, where the output will remain even after CLEAR returns HIGH. This is called *clearing* or *resetting* the latch.
4. **SET = CLEAR = 0.** This condition tries to set and clear the latch at the same time and can produce ambiguous results. It should not be used.

FIGURE 5-6 (a) NAND latch; (b) truth table.

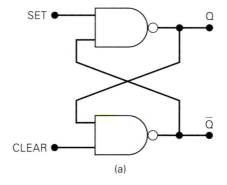

Set	Clear	Output
1	1	No change
0	1	Q = 1
1	0	Q = 0
0	0	Invalid*

*produces $Q = \overline{Q} = 1$

(b)

(a)

Alternate Representations

From the description of the NAND latch operation, it should be clear that the SET and CLEAR inputs are active-LOW. The SET input will set $Q = 1$ when SET goes LOW; the CLEAR input will clear $Q = 0$ when CLEAR goes LOW. For this reason, the NAND latch is often drawn using the alternate representation for each NAND gate, as shown in Figure 5-7(a). The bubbles on the inputs as well as the labeling of the signals as $\overline{SET}$ and $\overline{CLEAR}$ indicate the active-LOW status of these inputs.

Figure 5-7(b) shows a simplified block representation that we will sometimes use. The S and C labels represent the SET and CLEAR inputs, and the bubbles indicate the active-LOW nature of these inputs. Whenever we use this block symbol, it represents a NAND latch.

FIGURE 5-7 (a) NAND latch equivalent representation; (b) simplified block symbol.

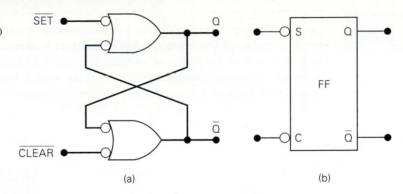

(a)   (b)

Terminology

The action of *clearing* a FF or a latch is also called *resetting,* and both terms are used interchangeably in the digital field. In fact, a CLEAR input can also be called a RESET input, and a SET-CLEAR latch can be called a SET-RESET latch.

EXAMPLE 5-1

The waveforms of Figure 5-8 are applied to the inputs of the latch of Figure 5-7. Assume that initially $Q = 0$, and determine the Q waveform.

FIGURE 5-8 Example 5-1.

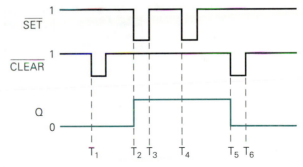

Solution

Initially, $\overline{SET} = \overline{CLEAR} = 1$ so that Q will remain in the 0 state. The LOW pulse that occurs on the $\overline{CLEAR}$ input at time T_1 will have no effect, since Q is already in the cleared (0) state.

The only way that Q can go to the 1 state is by a LOW pulse on the $\overline{SET}$ input. This occurs at time T_2 when $\overline{SET}$ first goes LOW. When $\overline{SET}$ returns HIGH at T_3, Q will remain in its new HIGH state.

At time T_4 when $\overline{SET}$ goes LOW again, there will be no effect on Q because Q is already set to the 1 state.

The only way to bring Q back to the 0 state is by a LOW pulse on the $\overline{CLEAR}$ input. This occurs at time T_5. When $\overline{CLEAR}$ returns to 1 at time T_6, Q remains in the LOW state.

This example shows that the latch output "remembers" the last input that was activated and will not change states until the opposite input is activated.

EXAMPLE
5-2

It is virtually impossible to obtain a "clean" voltage transition from a mechanical switch, because of the phenomenon of **contact bounce.** This is illustrated in Figure 5-9(a), where the action of moving the switch from contact position 1 to 2 produces several output voltage transitions as the switch bounces (makes and breaks contact with contact 2 several times) before coming to rest on contact 2.

FIGURE 5-9   (a) Mechanical contact bounce will produce multiple transitions; (b) NAND latch used to debounce a mechanical switch.

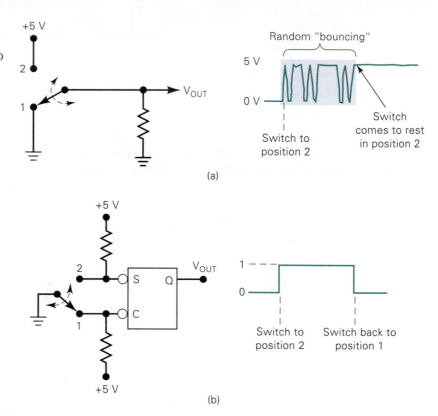

(a)

(b)

The multiple transitions on the output signal generally last no longer than a few milliseconds, but they would be unacceptable in many applications. A NAND latch can be used to prevent the presence of switch bounce from affecting the output. Describe the operation of the "switch debouncing" circuit in Figure 5-9(b).

Solution

Assume that the switch is resting in position 1 so that the $\overline{\text{CLEAR}}$ input is LOW and $Q = 0$. When the switch is moved to position 2, $\overline{\text{CLEAR}}$ will go HIGH, and a LOW will appear on the $\overline{\text{SET}}$ input as the switch first makes contact. This will set $Q = 1$ within a matter of a few nanoseconds (the response time of the NAND gate). Now if the switch bounces off contact 2, $\overline{\text{SET}}$ and $\overline{\text{CLEAR}}$ will both be HIGH, and Q will not be affected; it will stay HIGH. Thus, nothing will happen at Q as the switch bounces on and off contact 2 before finally coming to rest in position 2.

Likewise, when the switch is moved from position 2 back to position 1, it will place a LOW on the $\overline{\text{CLEAR}}$ input as it first makes contact. This clears Q to the LOW state, where it will remain even if the switch bounces on and off contact 1 several times before coming to rest.

Thus, the output at Q will consist of a single transition each time the switch is moved from one position to the other.

5-2 NOR GATE LATCH

Two cross-coupled NOR gates can be used as a **NOR gate latch.** The arrangement, shown in Figure 5-10(a), is similar to the NAND latch except that the Q and $\overline{Q}$ outputs have reversed positions.

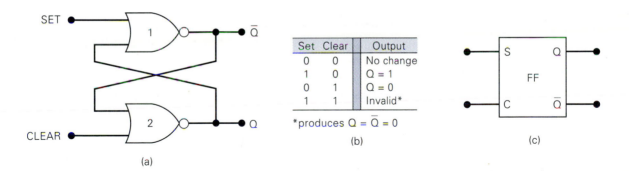

Set	Clear	Output
0	0	No change
1	0	Q = 1
0	1	Q = 0
1	1	Invalid*

*produces $Q = \overline{Q} = 0$

(a)   (b)   (c)

FIGURE 5-10   (a) NOR gate latch; (b) truth table; (c) simplified block symbol.

The analysis of the operation of the NOR latch can be performed in exactly the same manner as for the NAND latch. The results are given in the truth table in Figure 5-10(b) and are summarized as follows:

1. **SET = CLEAR = 0.** This is the normal resting state for the NOR latch, and it has no effect on the output state. Q and $\overline{Q}$ will remain in whatever state they were prior to the occurrence of this input condition.

2. **SET = 1, CLEAR = 0.** This will always set $Q = 1$, where it will remain even after SET returns to 0.

3. **SET = 0, CLEAR = 1.** This will always clear $Q = 0$, where it will remain even after CLEAR returns to 0.

4. **SET = 1, CLEAR = 1.** This condition tries to set and clear the latch at the same time, and it produces $Q = \overline{Q} = 0$. If the inputs are returned to 0 simultaneously, the resulting output state is unpredictable. This input condition should not be used.

The NOR gate latch operates exactly like the NAND latch except that the SET and CLEAR inputs are active-HIGH rather than active-LOW, and the normal resting state is SET = CLEAR = 0. Q will be set HIGH by a HIGH pulse on the SET input, and it will be cleared LOW by a HIGH pulse on the CLEAR input. The simplified block symbol for the NOR latch in Figure 5-10(c) is shown with no bubbles on the S and C inputs; this indicates that these inputs are active-HIGH.

EXAMPLE 5-3

Assume that $Q = 0$ initially, and determine the Q waveform for the NOR latch inputs of Figure 5-11.

FIGURE 5-11   Example 5-3.

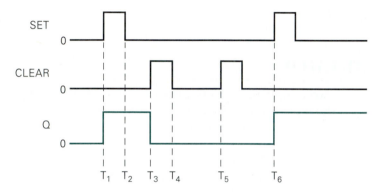

Solution

Initially, SET = CLEAR = 0, which has no effect on Q, and Q stays LOW. When SET goes HIGH at time T_1, Q will be set to 1 and will remain there even after SET returns to 0 at T_2.

At T_3 the CLEAR input goes HIGH and clears Q to the 0 state, where it remains even after CLEAR returns LOW at T_4.

The CLEAR pulse at T_5 has no effect on Q, since Q is already LOW. The SET pulse at T_6 again sets Q back to 1, where it will stay.

This example shows that the FF "remembers" the last input that was activated, and it will not change states until the opposite input is activated.

EXAMPLE 5-4

Figure 5-12 shows a simple circuit that can be used to detect the interruption of a light beam. The light is focused on a phototransistor that is connected in the common-emitter configuration to operate as a switch. Assume that the latch has previously been cleared to the 0 state by momentarily opening switch SW1, and describe what happens if the light beam is momentarily interrupted.

Solution

With light on the phototransistor, we can assume that it is fully conducting so that the resistance between the collector and the emitter is very small. Thus, v_0 will be close to 0 V. This places a LOW on the SET input of the latch so that SET = CLEAR = 0.

FIGURE 5-12 Example 5-4.

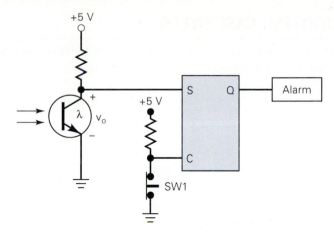

When the light beam is interrupted, the phototransistor turns off, and its collector-emitter resistance becomes very high (i.e., essentially an open circuit). This causes v_0 to rise to approximately 5 V; this activates the SET input which sets Q HIGH and turns on the alarm.

Q will remain HIGH and the alarm will remain on even if v_0 returns to 0 V (i.e., the light beam was interrupted only momentarily); this is because SET and CLEAR will both be LOW which will produce no change in Q.

In this application, the latch's memory characteristic is used to convert a momentary occurrence (beam interruption) into a constant output.

Flip-Flop State on Power-Up

When power is applied to a circuit, it is not possible to predict the starting state of a flip-flop's output if its SET and CLEAR inputs are in their inactive state (e.g., $S = C = 1$ for a NAND latch, $S = C = 0$ for a NOR latch). There is just as much chance that the starting state will be $Q = 0$ as $Q = 1$. It will depend on factors such as internal propagation delays, parasitic capacitance, and external loading. If a latch or FF must start off in a particular state to ensure the proper operation of a circuit, then it must be placed in that state by momentarily activating the SET or CLEAR input at the start of the circuit's operation. This is often achieved by application of a pulse to the appropriate input.

Review Questions

1. What is the normal resting state of the NOR latch inputs? What is the active state?

2. When a FF is set, what are the states of Q and $\overline{Q}$?

3. What is the only way to cause the Q output of a NOR latch to change from 1 to 0?

4. If the NOR latch in Figure 5-12 were replaced by a NAND latch, why wouldn't the circuit work properly?

5-3 TROUBLESHOOTING CASE STUDY

The following two examples will present an illustration of the kinds of reasoning used in troubleshooting a circuit containing a latch.

EXAMPLE 5-5

Analyze and describe the operation of the circuit in Figure 5-13.

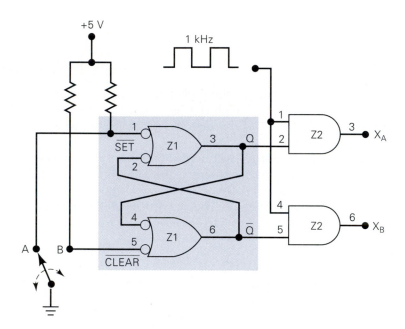

Switch position	X_A	X_B
A	Pulses	LOW
B	LOW	Pulses

FIGURE 5-13   Examples 5-5 and 5-6.

Solution

The switch is used to set or clear the NAND latch to produce clean, bounce-free signals at Q and $\overline{Q}$. These latch outputs control the passage of the 1-kHz pulse signal through to the AND outputs X_A and X_B.

When the switch moves to position A, the latch is set to $Q = 1$. This enables the 1-kHz pulses to pass through to X_A, while the LOW at $\overline{Q}$ keeps $X_B = 0$. When the switch moves to position B, the latch is cleared to $Q = 0$, which keeps $X_A = 0$, while the HIGH at $\overline{Q}$ enables the pulses to pass through to X_B.

EXAMPLE 5-6

A technician tests the circuit of Figure 5-13 and records the observations shown in Table 5-1. He notices that when the switch is in position B, the circuit functions correctly, but in position A the latch does not set to the $Q = 1$ state. What are the possible faults that could produce this malfunction?

TABLE 5-1

Switch Position	$\overline{SET}$ (Z1-1)	$\overline{CLEAR}$ (Z1-5)	Q (Z1-3)	$\overline{Q}$ (Z1-6)	X_A (Z2-3)	X_B (Z2-6)
A	LOW	HIGH	LOW	HIGH	LOW	Pulses
B	HIGH	LOW	LOW	HIGH	LOW	Pulses

Solution

There are several possibilities:

1. An internal open connection at Z1-1. This would prevent Q from responding to the $\overline{SET}$ input.

2. An internal component failure in NAND gate Z1 that prevents it from responding properly.

3. The Q output stuck LOW. This could be caused by:

   (a) Z1-3 internally shorted to ground

   (b) Z1-4 internally shorted to ground

   (c) Z2-2 internally shorted to ground

   (d) The Q node externally shorted to ground

   An ohmmeter check from Q to ground will determine if any of these conditions are present. A visual check should reveal any external short.

   What about $\overline{Q}$ internally or externally shorted to V_{CC}? A little thought will lead to the conclusion that this could not be the fault. If $\overline{Q}$ were shorted to V_{CC}, this would not prevent the Q output from going HIGH when $\overline{SET}$ goes LOW. Since Q *does not* go HIGH, this cannot be the fault. The reason that $\overline{Q}$ looks as if it is stuck HIGH is that Q is stuck LOW, and that keeps $\overline{Q}$ HIGH.

5-4 CLOCK SIGNALS AND CLOCKED FLIP-FLOPS

Digital systems can operate either *asynchronously* or *synchronously*. In asynchronous systems, the outputs of logic circuits can change state any time one or more of the inputs change. An asynchronous system is generally more difficult to design and troubleshoot than a synchronous system.

In synchronous systems, the exact times at which any output can change states are determined by a signal commonly called the **clock.** This clock signal is generally a rectangular pulse train or a square wave as shown in Figure 5-14. The clock signal is distributed to all parts of the system, and most (if not all) of the system outputs can change state only when the clock makes a transition. The transitions (also called *edges*) are pointed out in Figure 5-14. When the clock changes from a 0 to a 1, this is called the **positive-going transition (PGT);** when the clock goes from 1 to 0, this is the **negative-going transition (NGT).** We will use the abbreviations PGT and NGT, since these terms appear so often throughout the text.

FIGURE 5-14 Clock signals.

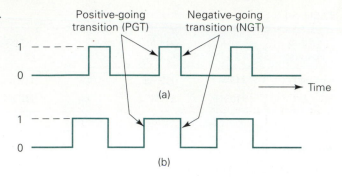

Most digital systems are principally synchronous (although there are always some asynchronous parts), since synchronous circuits are easier to design and troubleshoot. They are easier to troubleshoot because the circuit outputs can change only at specific instants of time. In other words, almost everything is synchronized to the clock-signal transitions.

The synchronizing action of the clock signals is accomplished through the use of **clocked flip-flops** that are designed to change states on one or the other of the clock's transitions.

Clocked Flip-Flops

Several types of clocked FFs are used in a wide range of applications. Before we begin our study of the different clocked FFs, we will describe the principal ideas that are common to all of them.

1. Clocked FFs have a **clock** input that is typically labeled *CLK*, *CK*, or *CP*. We will normally use *CLK*, as shown in Figure 5-15. In most clocked FFs the *CLK* input is **edge-triggered**, which means that it is activated by a signal transition; this is indicated by the presence of a small triangle on the *CLK* input. This contrasts with the latches, which are level-triggered.

FIGURE 5-15 Clocked FFs have a clock input (*CLK*) that is active on either (a) the PGT or (b) the NGT. The control inputs determine the effect of the active clock transition.

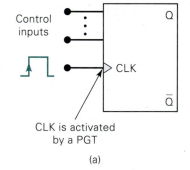

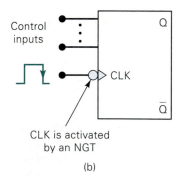

In Figure 5-15(a) the *CLK* input is activated only when a positive-going transition (PGT) occurs; it is not affected at any other time. In Figure 5-15(b) the *CLK* input is activated only by a negative-going transition (NGT), as symbolized by the presence of the small bubble.

2. Clocked FFs also have one or more **control inputs** that can have various names, depending on their operation. The control inputs will have no effect on Q until the active clock transition occurs. In other words, their effect is synchronized with the signal applied to *CLK*. For this reason they are called **synchronous control inputs.**

   For example, the control inputs of the FF in Figure 5-15(a) will have no effect on Q until the PGT of the clock signal occurs. Likewise, the control inputs in Figure 5-15(b) will have no effect until the NGT of the clock signal occurs.

3. In summary, we can say that the control inputs get the FF outputs ready to change, while the active transition at the *CLK* input actually *triggers* the change. The control inputs control the WHAT (i.e., what state the output will go to); the *CLK* input determines the WHEN.

Setup and Hold Times

Two timing requirements must be met if a clocked FF is to respond reliably to its control inputs when the active *CLK* transition occurs. These requirements are illustrated in Figure 5-16 for a FF that triggers on a PGT.

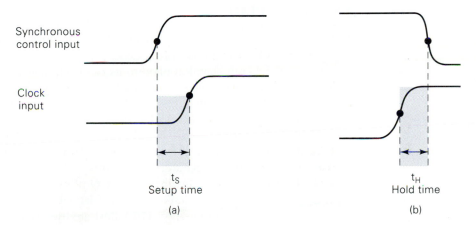

FIGURE 5-16 Control inputs must be held stable for (a) a time t_S prior to active clock transition and for (b) a time t_H after the active block transition.

The **setup time, t_S,** is the time interval immediately preceding the active transition of the *CLK* signal during which the control input must be maintained at the proper level. IC manufacturers usually specify the minimum allowable setup time $t_S(\text{min})$. If this time requirement is not met, the FF may not respond reliably when the clock edge occurs.

The **hold time, t_H,** is the time interval immediately following the active transition of the *CLK* signal during which the synchronous control input must be maintained at the proper level. IC manufacturers usually specify the minimum acceptable value of hold time $t_H(\text{min})$. If this requirement is not met, the FF will not trigger reliably.

Thus, to ensure that a clocked FF will respond properly when the active clock transition occurs, the control inputs must be stable (unchanging) for at least a time interval equal to t_S(min) *prior* to the clock transition, and for at least a time interval equal to t_H(min) *after* the clock transition.

IC flip-flops will have minimum allowable t_S and t_H values in the nanosecond range. Setup times are usually in the range 5 to 50 ns whereas hold times are generally from 0 to 10 ns. Notice that these times are measured between the 50 percent points on the transitions.

These timing requirements are very important in synchronous systems, because, as we shall see, there will be many situations where the synchronous control inputs to a FF are changing at approximately the same time as the *CLK* input.

Review Questions

1. What two types of inputs does a clocked FF have?
2. What is meant by the term *edge-triggered?*
3. *True or false:* The *CLK* input will affect the FF output only when the active transition of the control input occurs.
4. Define the setup time and hold time requirements of a clocked FF.

5-5 CLOCKED S-C FLIP-FLOP

Figure 5-17(a) shows the logic symbol for a **clocked S-C flip-flop** that is triggered by the positive-going edge of the clock signal. This means that the FF can change states *only* when a signal applied to its clock input makes a transition from 0 to 1. The *S* and *C* inputs control the state of the FF in the same manner as described earlier for the NOR gate latch, but the FF does not respond to these inputs until the occurrence of the PGT of the clock signal.

The truth table in Figure 5-17(b) shows how the FF output will respond to the PGT at the *CLK* input for the various combinations of *S* and *C* inputs. This truth table uses some new nomenclature. The up arrow ($\uparrow$) indicates that a PGT is required at *CLK*; the label Q_0 indicates the level at Q prior to the PGT. This nomenclature is widely used by IC manufacturers on their IC data sheets.

The waveforms in Figure 5-17(c) illustrate the operation of the clocked S-C flip-flop. If we assume that the setup and hold time requirements are being met in all cases, we can analyze these waveforms as follows:

1. Initially all inputs are 0 and the Q output is assumed to be 0; that is, $Q_0 = 0$.
2. When the PGT of the first clock pulse occurs (point *a*), the *S* and *C* inputs are both 0, so the FF is not affected and remains in the $Q = 0$ state (i.e., $Q = Q_0$).
3. At the occurrence of the PGT of the second clock pulse (point *c*), the *S* input is now high, with *C* still low. Thus, the FF sets to the 1 state at the rising edge of this clock pulse.
4. When the third clock pulse makes its positive transition (point *e*), it finds that $S = 0$ and $C = 1$, which causes the FF to clear to the 0 state.
5. The fourth pulse sets the FF once again to the $Q = 1$ state (point *g*) because $S = 1$ and $C = 0$ when the positive edge occurs.
6. The fifth pulse also finds that $S = 1$ and $C = 0$ when it makes its positive-going transition. However, Q is already high, so it remains in that state.

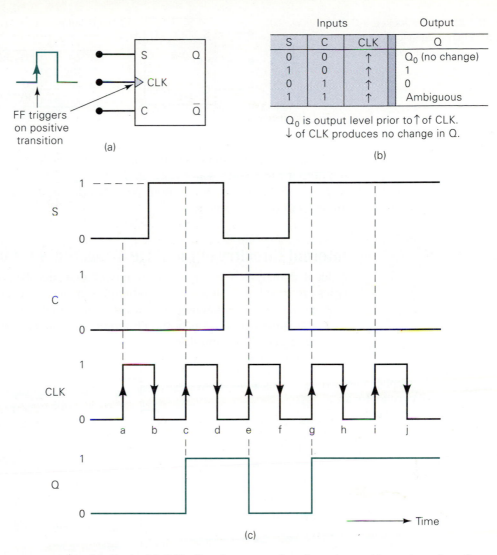

Inputs			Output
S	C	CLK	Q
0	0	↑	Q_0 (no change)
1	0	↑	1
0	1	↑	0
1	1	↑	Ambiguous

Q_0 is output level prior to ↑ of CLK.
↓ of CLK produces no change in Q.

FF triggers on positive transition

(a)

(b)

(c)

FIGURE 5-17   (a) Clocked S-C flip-flop that responds only to the positive-going edge of a clock pulse; (b) truth table; (c) typical waveforms.

7. The $S = C = 1$ condition should not be used, because it results in an ambiguous condition.

It should be noted from these waveforms that the FF is not affected by the negative-going transitions of the clock pulses. Also, note that the S and C levels have no effect on the FF, except upon the occurrence of a positive-going transition of the clock signal. The S and C inputs are synchronous *control* inputs; they control which state the FF will go to when the clock pulse occurs; the *CLK* input is the **trigger** input that causes the FF to change states according to what the S and C inputs are when the active clock transition occurs.

Figure 5-18 shows the symbol and the truth table for a clocked S-C flip-flop that triggers on the *negative*-going transition at its *CLK* input. The small circle and triangle on the *CLK* input indicates that this FF will trigger only when the *CLK* input goes

FIGURE 5-18 Clocked S-C flip-flop that triggers only on negative-going transitions.

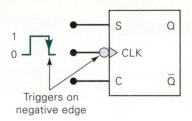

Triggers on
negative edge

Inputs			Output
S	C	CLK	Q
0	0	↓	Q_0 (no change)
1	0	↓	1
0	1	↓	0
1	1	↓	Ambiguous

from 1 to 0. This FF operates in the same manner as the positive-edge FF except that the output can change states only on the falling edge of the clock pulses (points *b*, *d*, *f*, *h*, and *j* in Figure 5-17). Both positive-edge and negative-edge triggering FFs are used in digital systems.

Internal Circuitry of the Edge-Triggered S-C Flip-Flop

A detailed analysis of the internal circuitry of a clocked FF is not necessary, since all types are readily available as ICs. Although our main interest is in the FF's external operation, our understanding of this external operation can be aided by taking a look at a simplified version of the FF's internal circuitry. Figure 5-19 shows this for an edge-triggered S-C flip-flop.

FIGURE 5-19 Simplified version of the internal circuitry for an edge-triggered S-C flip-flop.

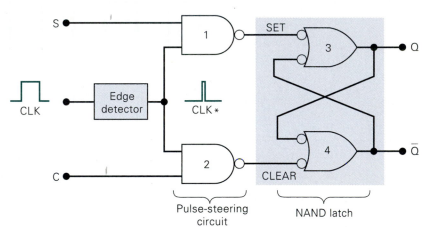

The circuit contains three sections:

1. A basic **NAND latch** formed by NAND-3 and NAND-4
2. A **pulse-steering** circuit formed by NAND-1 and NAND-2
3. An **edge-detector circuit**

As shown in Figure 5-19, the edge detector produces a narrow positive-going spike (*CLK**) that occurs coincident with the active transition of the *CLK* input pulse. The pulse-steering circuit "steers" the spike through to the SET or the CLEAR input of the latch in accordance with the levels present at *S* and *C*. For example, with *S* = 1 and *C* = 0, the *CLK** signal is inverted and passed through NAND-1 to produce a

LOW pulse at the SET input of the latch that sets $Q = 1$. With $S = 0$, $C = 1$, the CLK^* signal is inverted and passed through NAND-2 to produce a low pulse at the CLEAR input of the latch that resets $Q = 0$.

Figure 5-20(a) shows how the CLK^* signal is generated for edge-triggered FFs that trigger on a PGT. The INVERTER produces a delay of a few nanoseconds so that the transitions of $\overline{CLK}$ occur a little bit after those of CLK. The AND gate produces an output spike that is HIGH only for the few nanoseconds when CLK and $\overline{CLK}$ are both HIGH. The result is a narrow pulse at CLK^*, which occurs on the PGT of CLK. The arrangement of Figure 5-20(b) likewise produces CLK^* on the NGT of CLK for FFs that are to trigger on a NGT.

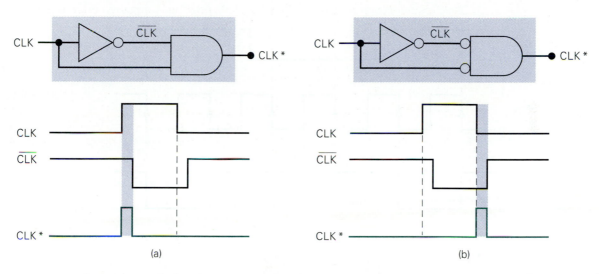

FIGURE 5-20 Implementation of edge-detector circuits used in edge-triggered flip-flops: (a) PGT; (b) NGT. The duration of the CLK^* pulses is typically 2–5 nanoseconds.

Since the CLK^* signal is HIGH for only a few nanoseconds, Q is affected by the levels at S and C only for a short time during and after the occurrence of the active edge of CLK. This is what gives the FF its edge-triggered property.

Review Questions

1. Suppose that the waveforms of Figure 5-17(c) are applied to the inputs of the FF of Figure 5-18. What will happen to Q at point b?

2. Explain why the S and C inputs affect Q only during the active transition of CLK.

5-6 CLOCKED J-K FLIP-FLOP

Figure 5-21(a) shows a **clocked J-K flip-flop** that is triggered by the positive-going edge of the clock signal. The J and K inputs control the state of the FF in the same ways as the S and C inputs do for the clocked S-C flip-flop except for one major difference: *the J = K = 1 condition does not result in an ambiguous output*. For this 1,

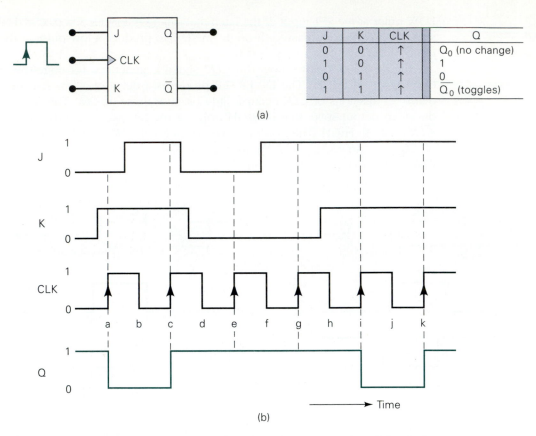

J	K	CLK	Q
0	0	↑	Q_0 (no change)
1	0	↑	1
0	1	↑	0
1	1	↑	$\overline{Q_0}$ (toggles)

(a)

(b)

FIGURE 5-21 (a) Clocked J-K flip-flop that responds only to the positive edge of the clock; (b) waveforms.

1 condition, the FF will always go to its *opposite* state upon the positive transition of the clock signal. This is called the **toggle mode** of operation. In this mode, if both *J* and *K* are left HIGH, the FF will change states (toggle) for each PGT of the clock.

The truth table in Figure 5-21(a) summarizes how the J-K flip-flop responds to the PGT for each combination of *J* and *K*. Notice that the truth table is the same as for the clocked S-C flip-flop (Figure 5-17) except for the $J = K = 1$ condition. This condition results in $Q = \overline{Q_0}$, which means that the new value of *Q* will be the inverse of the value it had prior to the PGT; this is the toggle operation.

The operation of this FF is illustrated by the waveforms in Figure 5-21(b). Once again we assume that the setup and hold time requirements are being met.

1. Initially all inputs are 0, and the *Q* output is assumed to be 1; that is, $Q_0 = 1$.

2. When the positive-going edge of the first clock pulse occurs (point *a*), the $J = 0$, $K = 1$ condition exists. Thus, the FF will be cleared to the $Q = 0$ state.

3. The second clock pulse finds $J = K = 1$ when it makes its positive transition (point *c*). This causes the FF to *toggle* to its opposite state, $Q = 1$.

4. At point *e* on the clock waveform, *J* and *K* are both 0, so that the FF does not change states on this transition.

5. At point g, $J = 1$ and $K = 0$. This is the condition that sets Q to the 1 state. However, it is already 1, and so it will remain there.

6. At point i, $J = K = 1$, and so the FF toggles to its opposite state. The same thing occurs at point k.

Note from these waveforms that the FF is not affected by the negative-going edge of the clock pulses. Also, the J and K input levels have no effect except upon the occurrence of the PGT of the clock signal. The J and K inputs by themselves cannot cause the FF to change states.

Figure 5-22 shows the symbol for a clocked J-K flip-flop that triggers on the negative-going clock-signal transitions. The small circle on the CLK input indicates that this FF will trigger when the CLK input goes from 1 to 0. This FF operates in the same manner as the positive-edge FF of Figure 5-21 except that the output can change states only on negative-going clock-signal transitions (points b, d, f, h, and j). Both polarities of edge-triggered J-K flip-flops are in common usage.

FIGURE 5-22 J-K flip-flop that triggers only on negative-going transitions.

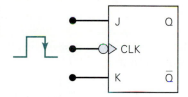

J	K	CLK	Q
0	0	↓	Q_0 (no change)
1	0	↓	1
0	1	↓	0
1	1	↓	$\overline{Q_0}$ (toggles)

The J-K flip-flop is much more versatile than the S-C flip-flop because it has no ambiguous states. The $J = K = 1$ condition, which produces the toggling operation, finds extensive use in all types of binary counters. In essence, the J-K flip-flop can do anything the S-C flip-flop can do *plus* operate in the toggle mode.

Internal Circuitry of the Edge-Triggered J-K Flip-Flop

A simplified version of the internal circuitry of an edge-triggered J-K flip-flop is shown in Figure 5-23. It contains the same three sections as the edge-triggered S-C flip-flop (Figure 5-19). In fact, the only difference between the two circuits is that the Q and $\overline{Q}$ outputs are fed back to the pulse-steering NAND gates. This feedback connection is what gives the J-K flip-flop its toggle operation for the $J = K = 1$ condition.

Let's examine this toggle condition more closely by assuming that $J = K = 1$ and that Q is sitting in the LOW state when a CLK pulse occurs. With $Q = 0$ and $\overline{Q} = 1$, NAND gate 1 will steer $CLK*$ (inverted) to the $\overline{SET}$ input of the NAND latch to produce $Q = 1$. If we assume that Q is HIGH when a CLK pulse occurs, NAND gate 2 will steer $CLK*$ (inverted) to the $\overline{CLEAR}$ input of the latch to produce $Q = 0$. Thus, Q always ends up in the opposite state.

In order for the toggle operation to work as described above, the $CLK*$ pulse must be very narrow. It must return to 0 before the Q and $\overline{Q}$ outputs toggle to their new values; otherwise the new values of Q and $\overline{Q}$ will cause the $CLK*$ pulse to toggle the latch outputs again.

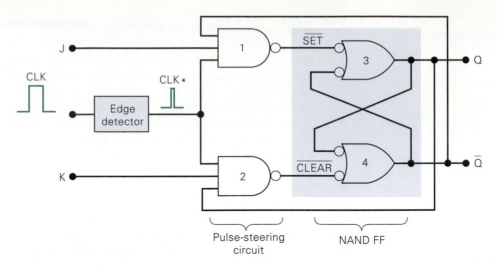

FIGURE 5-23   Internal circuit of the edge-triggered J-K flip-flop.

Review Questions

1. *True or false:* A J-K flip-flop can be used as an S-C flip-flop, but an S-C flip-flop cannot be used as a J-K flip-flop.

2. Does a J-K flip-flop have any ambiguous input conditions?

3. What *J-K* input condition will always set *Q* upon the occurrence of the active *CLK* transition?

5-7   CLOCKED D FLIP-FLOP

Figure 5-24(a) shows the symbol and the truth table for a **clocked D flip-flop** that triggers on a PGT. Unlike the S-C and J-K flip-flops, this flip-flop has only one synchronous control input, *D*, which stands for *data*. The operation of the D flip-flop is very simple: *Q* will go to the same state that is present on the *D* input when a PGT occurs at *CLK*. In other words, the level present at *D* will be *stored* in the flip-flop at the instant the PGT occurs. The waveforms in Figure 5-24(b) illustrate this operation.

Assume that *Q* is initially HIGH. When the first PGT occurs at point *a*, the *D* input is LOW; thus, *Q* will go to the 0 state. Even though the *D* input level changes between points *a* and *b*, it has no effect on *Q*; *Q* is storing the LOW that was on *D* at point *a*. When the PGT at *b* occurs, *Q* goes HIGH since *D* is HIGH at that time. *Q* stores this HIGH until the PGT at point *c* causes *Q* to go LOW, since *D* is LOW at that time. In a similar manner, the *Q* output takes on the levels present at *D* when the PGTs occur at points *d*, *e*, *f*, and *g*. Note that *Q* stays HIGH at point *e* because *D* is still HIGH.

Again, it is important to remember that *Q* can change only when a PGT occurs. The *D* input has no effect between PGTs.

A negative-edge-triggered D flip-flop operates in the same way just described except that *Q* will take on the value of *D* when a NGT occurs at *CLK*. The symbol for the D flip-flop that triggers on NGTs will have a bubble on the *CLK* input.

FIGURE 5-24   (a) D flip-flop that triggers only on positive-going transitions; (b) waveforms.

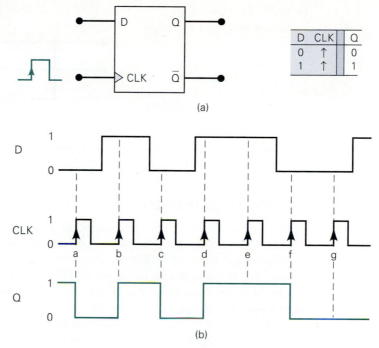

D	CLK	Q
0	↑	0
1	↑	1

(a)

(b)

Implementation of the D Flip-Flop

An edge-triggered D flip-flop is easily implemented by adding a single INVERTER to the edge-triggered S-C flip-flop as shown in Figure 5-25. If you try both values of D, you should see that Q takes on the level present at D when a PGT occurs.

FIGURE 5-25   Edge-triggered D flip-flop implementation from an S-C flip-flop.

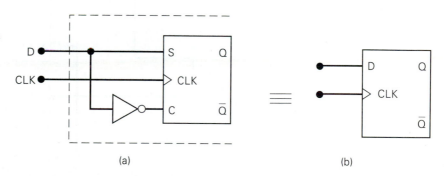

(a)   (b)

EXAMPLE 5-7

How can a J-K flip-flop be modified to operate as a D flip-flop?

Solution

The modification, shown in Figure 5-26, is the same as was done for the S-C flip-flop in Figure 5-25.

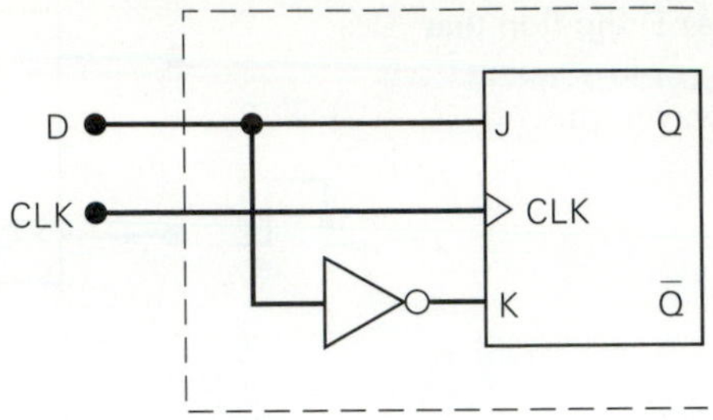

FIGURE 5-26 D flip-flop implementation from a J-K flip-flop.

Parallel Data Transfer

At this point you may well be wondering about the usefulness of the D flip-flop, since it appears that the Q output is the same as the D input. Not quite; remember, Q takes on the value of D only at certain time instances, and so it is not identical to D (e.g., see the waveforms in Figure 5-24).

In most applications of the D flip-flop, the Q output must take on the value at its D input only at precisely defined times. One example of this is illustrated in Figure 5-27. Outputs X, Y, Z from a logic circuit are to be transferred to FFs Q_1, Q_2, and Q_3 for storage. Using the D flip-flops, the levels present at X, Y, and Z will be transferred to Q_1, Q_2, and Q_3, respectively, upon application of a TRANSFER pulse to the common CLK inputs. The FFs can store these values for subsequent processing. This is an example of **parallel transfer** of binary data; the three bits X, Y, and Z are all transferred *simultaneously*.

FIGURE 5-27 Parallel transfer of binary data using D flip-flops.

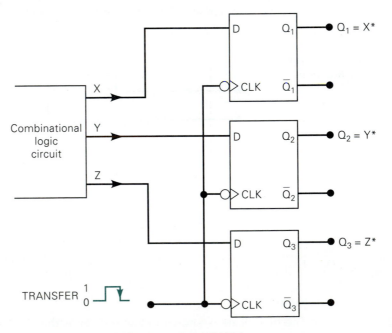

*After occurrence of NGT

Review Questions   1. What will happen to the *Q* waveform in Figure 5-24(b) if the *D* input is held permanently LOW?

2. *True or false:* The *Q* output will equal the level at the *D* input at all times.

3. Can J-K FFs be used for parallel data transfer?

5-8   *D* LATCH (TRANSPARENT LATCH)

The edge-triggered D flip-flop uses an edge-detector circuit to ensure that the output will respond to the *D* input *only* when the active transition of the clock occurs. If this edge detector is not used, the resultant circuit operates somewhat differently. It is called a ***D* latch** and has the arrangement shown in Figure 5-28(a).

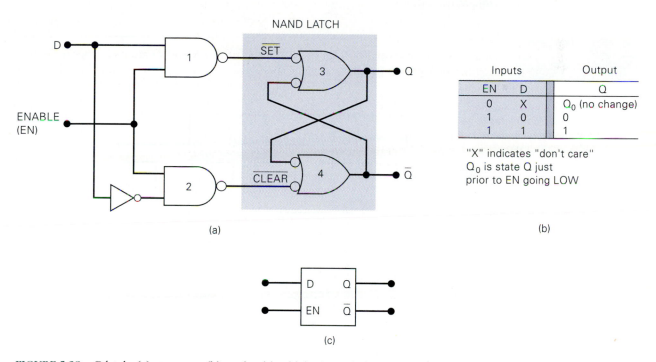

(a)

Inputs		Output
EN	D	Q
0	X	Q_0 (no change)
1	0	0
1	1	1

"X" indicates "don't care"
Q_0 is state Q just
prior to EN going LOW

(b)

(c)

FIGURE 5-28   *D* latch: (a) structure; (b) truth table; (c) logic symbol.

The circuit contains the NAND latch and the steering NAND gates 1 and 2 *without* the edge-detector circuit. The common input to the steering gates is called an *enable* input (abbreviated *EN*) rather than a clock input because its effect on the *Q* and $\overline{Q}$ outputs is not restricted to occurring only on its transitions. The operation of the *D* latch is described as follows:

1. When *EN* is HIGH, the *D* input will produce a LOW at either the $\overline{\text{SET}}$ or the $\overline{\text{CLEAR}}$ inputs of the NAND latch to cause *Q* to become the same level as *D*. If *D*

changes while *EN* is HIGH, *Q* will follow the changes exactly. In other words, while *EN* = 1, the *Q* output will look exactly like *D*; in this mode, the *D* latch is said to be "transparent."

2. When *EN* goes LOW, the *D* input is inhibited from affecting the NAND latch since the outputs of both steering gates will be held HIGH. Thus, the *Q* and $\overline{Q}$ outputs will stay at whatever level they had just before *EN* went LOW. In other words, the outputs are "latched" to their current level and cannot change while *EN* is LOW even if *D* changes.

This operation is summarized in the truth table in Figure 5-28(b). The logic symbol for the *D* latch is given in Figure 5-28(c). Note that even though the *EN* input operates much like the *CLK* input of an edge-triggered FF, there is no small triangle on the *EN* input. This is because the small triangle symbol is used strictly for inputs that can cause an output change only when a transition occurs. *The D latch is not edge-triggered.*

| EXAMPLE 5-8 | Determine the *Q* waveform for a *D* latch with the *EN* and *D* inputs of Figure 5-29. Assume that *Q* = 0 initially. |

FIGURE 5-29 Waveforms for Example 5-8 showing the two modes of operation of the transparent *D* latch.

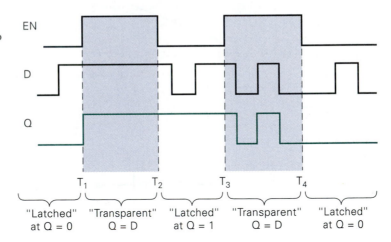

Solution

Prior to time T_1, *EN* is LOW, so that *Q* is "latched" at its current 0 level and cannot change even though *D* is changing. During the interval T_1 to T_2, *EN* is HIGH so that *Q* will follow the signal present at *D*. Thus, *Q* goes HIGH at T_1 and stays there since *D* is not changing. When *EN* returns LOW at T_2, *Q* will latch at the HIGH level that it has at T_2 and will remain there while *EN* is LOW.

At T_3 when *EN* goes HIGH again, *Q* will follow the changes in the *D* input until T_4 when *EN* returns LOW. During the interval T_3 to T_4, the *D* latch is "transparent" since the variations in *D* go through to the output *Q*. At T_4 when *EN* goes LOW, *Q* will latch at the 0 level since that is its level at T_4. After T_4 the variations in *D* will have no effect on *Q* since it is latched (i.e., *EN* = 0).

1. Describe how a *D* latch operates differently from an edge-triggered D flip-flop.
2. *True or false:* A *D* latch is in its transparent mode when *EN* = 0.
3. *True or false:* In a *D* latch, the *D* input can affect *Q* only when *EN* = 1.

5-9 ASYNCHRONOUS INPUTS

For the clocked flip-flops that we have been studying, the *S*, *C*, *J*, *K*, and *D* inputs have been referred to as *control* inputs. These inputs are also called **synchronous inputs**, because their effect on the FF output is synchronized with the *CLK* input. As we have seen, the synchronous control inputs must be used in conjunction with a clock signal to trigger the FF.

Most clocked FFs also have one or more **asynchronous inputs** which operate independently of the synchronous inputs and clock input. These asynchronous inputs can be used to set the FF to the 1 state or clear the FF to the 0 state *at any time, regardless of the conditions at the other inputs.* Stated in another way, the asynchronous inputs are **override inputs,** which can be used to override all the other inputs in order to place the FF in one state or the other.

Figure 5-30 shows a J-K flip-flop with two asynchronous inputs designated as $\overline{\text{PRESET}}$ and $\overline{\text{CLEAR}}$. These are active-LOW inputs, as indicated by the bubbles on the FF symbol. The accompanying truth table summarizes how they affect the FF output. Let's examine the various cases.

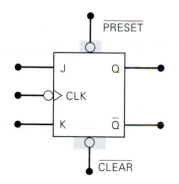

$\overline{\text{PRESET}}$	$\overline{\text{CLEAR}}$	FF response
1	1	Clocked operation*
0	1	Q = 1
1	0	Q = 0
0	0	Not used

*Q will respond to J, K, and CLK

FIGURE 5-30 Clocked J-K flip-flop with asynchronous inputs.

■ $\overline{\text{PRESET}} = \overline{\text{CLEAR}} = 1$. The asynchronous inputs are inactive and the FF is free to respond to the *J*, *K*, and *CLK* inputs; in other words, the clocked operation can take place.

■ $\overline{\text{PRESET}} = 0$; $\overline{\text{CLEAR}} = 1$. The $\overline{\text{PRESET}}$ is activated and *Q* is *immediately* set to 1 no matter what conditions are present at the *J*, *K*, and *CLK* inputs. The *CLK* input cannot affect the FF while $\overline{\text{PRESET}} = 0$.

■ $\overline{\text{PRESET}} = 1$; $\overline{\text{CLEAR}} = 0$. The $\overline{\text{CLEAR}}$ is activated and *Q* is *immediately* cleared to 0 independent of the conditions on the *J*, *K*, or *CLK* inputs. The *CLK* input has no effect while $\overline{\text{CLEAR}} = 0$.

■ $\overline{\text{PRESET}} = \overline{\text{CLEAR}} = 0$. This condition should not be used, since it can result in an ambiguous response.

It is important to realize that these asynchronous inputs respond to dc levels. This means that if a constant 0 is held on the $\overline{\text{PRESET}}$ input, the FF will remain in the $Q = 1$ state regardless of what is occurring at the other inputs. Similarly, a constant LOW on the $\overline{\text{CLEAR}}$ input holds the FF in the $Q = 0$ state. Thus, the asynchronous inputs can be used to hold the FF in a particular state for any desired interval. Most often, however, the asynchronous inputs are used to set or clear the FF to the desired state by application of a momentary pulse.

Many clocked FFs that are available as ICs will have both of these asynchronous inputs; some will have only the $\overline{\text{CLEAR}}$ input. Some FFs will have asynchronous inputs that are active-HIGH rather than active-LOW. For these FFs the FF symbol would not have a bubble on the asynchronous inputs.

Designations for Asynchronous Inputs

IC manufacturers have not agreed on what nomenclature is used for these asynchronous inputs. The most common designations are *PRE* (short for PRESET) and *CLR* (short for CLEAR). The designations S_D (direct SET) and R_D (direct RESET) are also used. From now on, we will use the labels *PRE* and *CLR* to represent the asynchronous inputs, since these seem to be the most commonly used labels. When these asynchronous inputs are active-LOW, as they generally are, we will use the overbar to indicate their active-LOW status, that is, $\overline{PRE}$ and $\overline{CLR}$.

Although most IC flip-flops have at least one or more asynchronous inputs, there are some circuit applications where they are not used. In such cases they are held permanently at their inactive level. Often, in our use of FFs throughout the remainder of the text, we will not show a FF's unused asynchronous inputs; it will be assumed that they are permanently connected to their inactive logic level.

EXAMPLE 5-9

Figure 5-31(a) shows the symbol for a J-K FF that responds to a NGT on its clock input and has active-LOW asynchronous inputs. Before proceeding with the example, take note of the way the inputs are labeled. First, note that the clock signal applied to the FF is labeled $\overline{CLK}$ (the overbar indicates that this signal is active on the NGT) whereas on the other side of the bubble (inside the block) it is labeled *CLK*. Likewise, the external active-LOW asynchronous inputs are labeled $\overline{PRE}$ and $\overline{CLR}$, whereas inside the block on the other side of the bubble, they are labeled *PRE* and *CLR*. The important thing to remember is that the presence of the bubble on an input means that the input responds to a logic LOW signal.

The *J* and *K* inputs are shown tied HIGH for this example. Determine the *Q* output in response to the input wave forms shown in Figure 5-31(a). Assume that *Q* is initially HIGH.

Solution

Initially, $\overline{PRE}$ and $\overline{CLR}$ are in their inactive HIGH state, so that they will have no effect on *Q*. Thus, when the first NGT of the $\overline{CLK}$ signal occurs at point *a*, *Q* will toggle to its opposite state; remember, $J = K = 1$ produces the toggle operation.

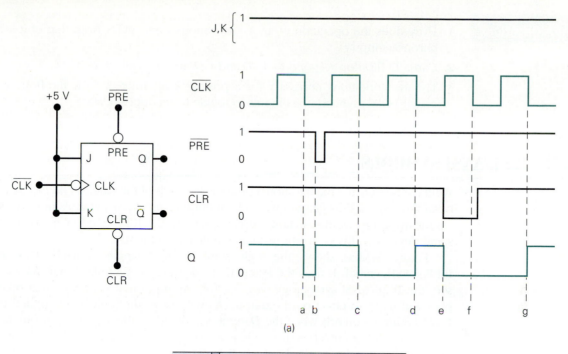

Point	Operation
a	Synchronous toggle on NGT of $\overline{CLK}$
b	Asynchronous set on PRE = 0
c	Synchronous toggle
d	Synchronous toggle
e	Asynchronous clear on $\overline{CLR}$ = 0
f	CLR over-rides the NGT of CLK
g	Synchronous toggle

(b)

FIGURE 5-31 Waveforms for Example 5-9 showing how a clocked flip-flop responds to asynchronous inputs.

At point *b*, the $\overline{PRE}$ input is pulsed to its active-LOW state. This will *immediately* set $Q = 1$. Note that $\overline{PRE}$ produces $Q = 1$ without waiting for a NGT at $\overline{CLK}$. The asynchronous inputs operate independent of $\overline{CLK}$.

At point *c*, the NGT of $\overline{CLK}$ will again cause Q to toggle to its opposite state. Note that $\overline{PRE}$ has returned to its inactive state prior to point *c*. Likewise, the NGT of $\overline{CLK}$ at point *d* will toggle Q back HIGH.

At point *e*, the $\overline{CLR}$ input is pulsed to its active-LOW state and will *immediately* clear $Q = 0$. Again, it does this independent of $\overline{CLK}$.

The NGT of $\overline{CLK}$ at point *f will not toggle* Q, because the $\overline{CLR}$ input is still active. The LOW at $\overline{CLR}$ overrides the $\overline{CLK}$ input and holds $Q = 0$.

When the NGT of $\overline{CLK}$ occurs at point *g*, it will toggle Q to the HIGH state since neither asynchronous input is active at that point.

These steps are summarized in Figure 5-31(b).

1. How does the operation of an asynchronous input differ from that of a synchronous input?
2. Can a D flip-flop respond to its D and CLK inputs while $\overline{PRE} = 1$?
3. List the conditions necessary for a positive-edge-triggered J-K flip-flop with active-LOW asynchronous inputs to toggle to its opposite state.

5-10   IEEE/ANSI SYMBOLS

We have been using the traditional symbols for each of the latches and FFs that have been introduced thus far, and we will continue to use these symbols in most of our circuit diagrams. In this section we will examine the IEEE/ANSI symbols for these same devices so that you can become familiar with them.

Figure 5-32(a) shows the logic symbol for a single D latch. This is the IEEE/ANSI symbol. It uses the letter "C" to denote the ENABLE input. As we shall see, the IEEE/ANSI symbology uses "C" for any input that *controls* when other inputs will have an effect on the output. As we know, the logic level applied to the ENABLE input controls when the D input is allowed to affect Q and $\overline{Q}$. Note that the outputs Q and $\overline{Q}$ are labeled outside the block, and note the right triangle on $\overline{Q}$ to indicate that it is the inverted output. This is standard for IEEE/ANSI. Recall that this right triangle is like the small bubble used in the older symbols.

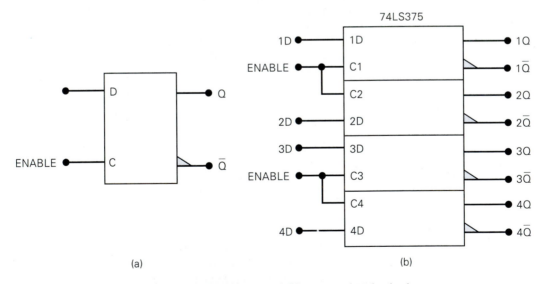

(a)   (b)

FIGURE 5-32   IEEE/ANSI symbols for (a) a single D latch and (b) an actual IC latch, the 74LS375 quad latch.

Figure 5-32(b) shows the IEEE/ANSI symbol for a specific IC: the 74LS375 TTL quad latch. This IC contains four D latches that operate individually in the manner described earlier. This symbol also applies to the corresponding ICs in the other TTL and CMOS series, for example, the 74HC375.

If we examine the logic symbol for this IC, several points should be noted. First, we can see that the overall symbol outline contains four smaller rectangles that represent the individual latches. Note how the inputs and outputs to each latch are labeled. For example, the D input to the top latch is labeled "$1D$," its enable input is labeled "$C1$," and its outputs are $1Q$ and $1\overline{Q}$. Finally, note that the top two latches have a common enable input; that is, $C1$ and $C2$ are connected together internally and brought out to a single pin on the IC package. Similarly, the bottom two latches share a common enable input.

Figure 5-33(a) shows the IEEE/ANSI logic symbol for a negative-edge-triggered J-K flip-flop with asynchronous inputs. The clock input is labeled "C" inside the symbol's rectangular outline. Note that there are two triangles on the clock input. The one inside the rectangle indicates that this input is edge-triggered; the one outside the rectangle indicates that it triggers on NGTs. The PRE and $\overline{CLR}$ inputs are active-LOW as symbolized by the right triangles. Interestingly, the IEEE/ANSI standard uses the labels "S" and "R" inside the rectangle to indicate asynchronous SET and RESET, which are equivalent to PRESET and CLEAR, respectively.

Figure 5-33(b) shows the IEEE/ANSI logic symbol for an IC that is part of the 74LS series of TTL devices. The 74LS112 is a dual negative-edge-triggered J-K flip-flop with preset and clear capabilities. It contains two J-K flip-flops, like the one symbolized in Figure 5-33(a). Note how the inputs and outputs are numbered. Also note that the input labels inside the rectangles are shown only for the top FF. It is understood that the inputs to the bottom FF are in the same arrangement as the top one. This same IC symbol applies to the CMOS 74HC112.

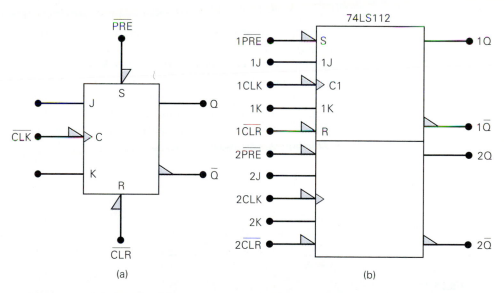

(a) (b)

FIGURE 5-33 IEEE/ANSI symbols for (a) a single edge-triggered J-K flip-flop and (b) an actual IC (74LS112 dual negative-edge-triggered J-K flip-flop).

Figure 5-34(a) is the IEEE/ANSI symbol for a positive-edge-triggered D flip-flop with asynchronous inputs. There is no right triangle on the clock input, since this FF is clocked by PGTs.

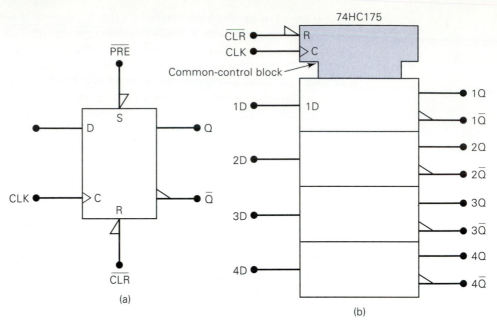

FIGURE 5-34 IEEE/ANSI symbols for (a) a single edge-triggered D flip-flop and (b) an actual IC (74HC175 quad flip-flop with common clock and clear).

Figure 5-34(b) is the IEEE/ANSI symbol for a 74HC175 IC, which contains four D flip-flops that share a common *CLK* input and a common $\overline{CLR}$ input. The FFs do not have a $\overline{PRE}$ input. This symbol contains a separate rectangle to represent each FF, and a special **common-control block,** which is the notched rectangle on top. The common-control block is used whenever an IC has one or more inputs that are common to more than one of the circuits on the chip. For the 74HC175, the *CLK* and $\overline{CLR}$ inputs are common to all four of the D flip-flops on the IC. This means that a PGT on *CLK* will cause each *Q* output to take on the level present at its *D* input; it also means that a LOW on $\overline{CLR}$ will clear all *Q* outputs to the LOW state.

Review Questions
1. Explain the meaning of the two different triangles that can be part of the IEEE/ANSI symbology at a clock input.
2. Describe the meaning of the common-control block.

5-11 FLIP-FLOP TIMING CONSIDERATIONS

Manufacturers of IC flip-flops will specify several important timing parameters and characteristics that must be considered before a FF is used in any circuit application. We will describe the most important of these and then give some actual examples of specific IC flip-flops from the TTL and CMOS logic families.

Setup and Hold Times

The setup and hold times have already been discussed, and you may recall from Section 5-4 that they represent requirements that must be met for reliable FF triggering. The manufacturer's IC data sheet will always specify the *minimum* values of t_S and t_H.

Propagation Delays

Whenever a signal is to change the state of a FF's output, there is a delay from the time the signal is applied to the time when the output makes its change. Figure 5-35 illustrates the **propagation delays** that occur in response to a positive transition on the *CLK* input. Note that these delays are measured between the 50 percent points on the input and output waveforms. The same types of delays occur in response to signals on a FF's asynchronous inputs (PRESET and CLEAR). The manufacturers' data sheets usually specify propagation delays in response to all inputs, and they usually specify the *maximum* values for t_{PLH} and t_{PHL}.

FIGURE 5-35 FF propagation delays.

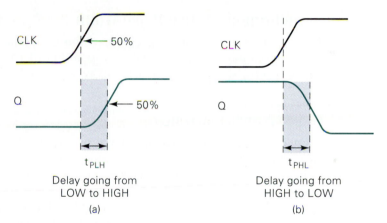

Delay going from LOW to HIGH

(a)

Delay going from HIGH to LOW

(b)

Modern IC flip-flops have propagation delays that range from a few nanoseconds to around 100 ns. The values of t_{PLH} and t_{PHL} are generally not the same, and they increase in direct proportion to the number of loads being driven by the Q output. FF propagation delays play an important part in certain situations that we will encounter later.

Maximum Clocking Frequency, f_{MAX}

This is the highest frequency that may be applied to the *CLK* input of a FF and still have it trigger reliably. The f_{MAX} limit will vary from FF to FF even with FFs having the same device number. For example, the manufacturer of the 7470 J-K flip-flop IC tests many of these FFs and may find that the f_{MAX} values fall in the range 20 to 35 MHz. He will then specify the *minimum* f_{MAX} as 20 MHz. This may seem confusing, but a little thought should make it clear that what the manufacturer is saying is that he cannot guarantee that the 7470 FF that you put in your circuit will work above 20 MHz; most of them will, but some of them will not. If you stay below 20 MHz, however, he guarantees that they will all work.

Clock Pulse HIGH and LOW Times

The manufacturer will also specify the *minimum* time duration that the *CLK* signal must remain LOW before it goes HIGH, sometimes called $t_W(L)$, and the *minimum* time that *CLK* must be kept HIGH before it returns LOW, sometimes called $t_W(H)$. These times are defined in Figure 5-36(a). Failure to meet these minimum time requirements can result in unreliable triggering. Note that these time values are measured between the halfway points on the signal transitions.

FIGURE 5-36   (a) Clock LOW and HIGH times; (b) asynchronous pulse width.

Asynchronous Active Pulse Width

The manufacturer will also specify the *minimum* time duration that a PRESET or CLEAR input must be kept in its active state in order to reliably set or clear the FF. Figure 5-36(b) shows $t_W(L)$ for active-LOW asynchronous inputs.

Clock Transition Times

For reliable triggering, the clock waveform transition times (rise and fall times) should be kept very short. If the clock signal takes too long to make the transitions from one level to the other, the FF may trigger erratically or not at all. Manufacturers usually do not list a maximum transition time requirement for each FF integrated circuit. Instead, it is usually given as a general requirement for all ICs within a given logic family. For example, the transition times should generally be ≤50 ns for TTL devices and ≤200 ns for CMOS. These requirements will vary among the different manufacturers and among the various subfamilies within the broad TTL and CMOS logic families.

Actual ICs

As practical examples of these timing parameters, let's take a look at several actual integrated-circuit FFs. In particular, we will look at the following ICs:

- **7474**   Dual edge-triggered D flip-flop (standard TTL)
- **74LS112**   Dual edge-triggered J-K flip-flop (low-power Schottky TTL)
- **74C74**   Dual edge-triggered D flip-flop (metal-gate CMOS)
- **74HC112**   Dual edge-triggered J-K flip-flop (high-speed CMOS)

Table 5-2 lists the various timing values for each of these FFs as they appear in the manufacturers' data books. All of the listed values are *minimum* values except for the propagation delays, which are *maximum* values. Examination of Table 5-2 reveals two interesting points.

TABLE 5-2   Flip-flop timing values (in nanoseconds).

		TTL		CMOS	
		7474	74LS112	74C74	74HC112
t_S		20	20	60	25
t_H		5	0	0	0
t_{PHL}	from CLK to Q	40	24	200	31
t_{PLH}	from CLK to Q	25	16	200	31
t_{PHL}	from $\overline{CLR}$ to Q	40	24	225	41
t_{PLH}	from $\overline{PRE}$ to Q	25	16	225	41
$t_W(L)$	CLK LOW time	37	15	100	25
$t_W(H)$	CLK HIGH time	30	20	100	25
$t_W(L)$	at $\overline{PRE}$ or $\overline{CLR}$	30	15	60	25
f_{MAX}	in MHz	15	30	5	20

1. All of the FFs have very low t_H requirements; this is typical of most modern edge-triggered FFs.

2. The 74HC series of CMOS devices has timing values that are comparable to those of the TTL devices. The 74C series is much slower than the 74HC series.

EXAMPLE 5-10

From Table 5-2 determine the following.

(a) Assume that $Q = 0$. How long can it take for Q to go HIGH when a PGT occurs at the CLK input of a 7474?

(b) Assume that $Q = 1$. How long can it take for Q to go LOW in response to the $\overline{CLR}$ input of a 74HC112?

(c) What is the narrowest pulse that should be applied to the $\overline{CLR}$ input of the 74LS112 FF to clear Q reliably?

(d) Which FF in Table 5-2 requires that the control inputs remain stable *after* the occurrence of the active clock transition?

(e) For which FFs must the control inputs be held stable for a minimum time prior to the active clock transition?

Solution

(a) The PGT will cause Q to go from LOW to HIGH. The delay from CLK to Q is listed as $t_{PLH} = 25$ ns for the 7474.

(b) For the 74HC112 the time required for Q to go from HIGH to LOW in response to the $\overline{CLR}$ input is listed as $t_{PHL} = 41$ ns.

(c) For the 74LS112 the narrowest pulse at the $\overline{CLR}$ input is listed as $t_W(L) = 15$ ns.

(d) The 7474 is the only FF in Table 5-2 that has a nonzero hold time requirement.

(e) All of the FFs have a nonzero setup time requirement.

1. Which FF timing parameters indicate the time it takes the Q output to respond to an input?

2. *True or false:* A FF that has an f_{MAX} rating of 25 MHz can be reliably triggered by any *CLK* pulse waveform with a frequency below 25 MHz.

5-12 POTENTIAL TIMING PROBLEM IN FF CIRCUITS

In many digital circuits, the output of one FF is connected either directly or through logic gates to the input of another FF, and both FFs are triggered by the same clock signal. This presents a potential timing problem. A typical situation is illustrated in Figure 5-37, where the output of Q_1 is connected to the J input of Q_2 and both FFs are clocked by the same signal at their *CLK* inputs.

FIGURE 5-37 Q_2 will properly respond to the level present at Q_1 prior to the NGT of *CLK*, provided that Q_2's hold time requirement, t_H, is less than Q_1's propagation delay.

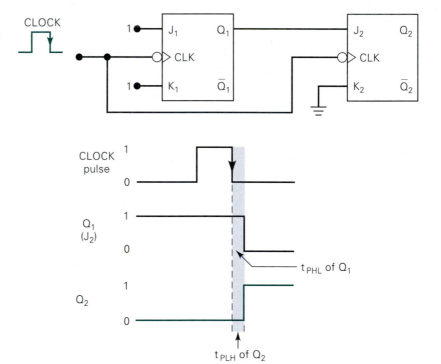

The potential timing problem is this: since Q_1 will change on the NGT of the clock pulse, the J_2 input of Q_2 will be changing as it receives the same NGT. This could lead to an unpredictable response at Q_2.

Let's assume that initially $Q_1 = 1$ and $Q_2 = 0$. Thus, the Q_1 FF has $J_1 = K_1 = 1$, and Q_2 has $J_2 = Q_1 = 1$, $K_2 = 0$ prior to the NGT of the clock pulse. When the NGT occurs, Q_1 will toggle to the LOW state, but it will not actually go LOW until after its propagation delay, t_{PHL}. The same NGT will reliably clock Q_2 to the HIGH state provided that t_{PHL} is greater than Q_2's hold time requirement, t_H. If this condition is not met, the response of Q_2 will be unpredictable.

Fortunately, all modern edge-triggered FFs have hold time requirements that are 5 ns or less; most have $t_H = 0$, which means that they have no hold time requirement. For these FFs, situations like that in Figure 5-37 will not be a problem.

Unless stated otherwise, in all of the FF circuits that we encounter throughout the text, we will assume that the FF's hold time requirement is short enough to respond reliably according to the following rule:

The FF output will go to a state determined by the logic levels present at its synchronous control inputs just prior to the active clock transition.

If we apply this rule to Figure 5-37, it says that Q_2 will go to a state determined by the $J_2 = 1$, $K_2 = 0$ condition that is present just prior to the NGT of the clock pulse. The fact that J_2 is changing in response to the same NGT has no effect.

| EXAMPLE 5-11 | Determine the Q output for a negative-edge-triggered J-K flip-flop for the input waveforms shown in Figure 5-38. Assume that $t_H = 0$ and that $Q = 0$ initially. |

FIGURE 5-38   Example 5-11.

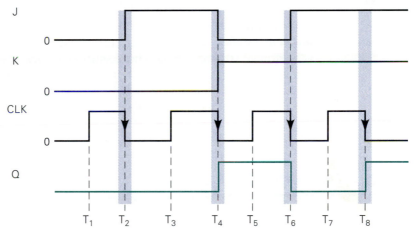

Solution

The FF will respond only at times T_2, T_4, T_6, and T_8. At T_2, Q will respond to the $J = K = 0$ condition present just prior to T_2. At T_4, Q will respond to the $J = 1$, $K = 0$ condition present just prior to T_4. At T_6, Q will respond to the $J = 0$, $K = 1$ condition present just prior to T_6. At T_8, Q responds to $J = K = 1$.

5-13   MASTER/SLAVE FLIP-FLOPS

Before the development of edge-triggered FFs with little or no hold-time requirements, timing problems such as that in Figure 5-37 were often handled by using a class of FFs called **master/slave FFs.** A master/slave FF actually contains two

FFs—a master and a slave. On the rising edge of the *CLK* signal, the levels on the control inputs (*D, J, K*) are used to determine the output of the master. When the *CLK* signal goes LOW, the state of the master is transferred to the slave, whose outputs are *Q* and $\overline{Q}$. Thus, *Q* and $\overline{Q}$ change just after the NGT of the clock. These master/slave FFs function very much like the negative-edge-triggered FFs except for one major disadvantage: the control inputs must be held stable while *CLK* is HIGH, or unpredictable operation may occur. This problem with master/slave FFs has been overcome with an improved master/slave version called a *master/slave with data lockout*.

The master/slave FF has become obsolete, although you may encounter it in older equipment. Examples of this type are the standard TTL 7473, 7476, and 74107, and the data lockout versions, 74110 and 74111. The newer IC technologies (74LS, 74AS, 74ALS, 74HC, 74HCT) do not include any master/slave FFs in their series. In fact, the 74LS76 and 74LS107 have been manufactured as edge-triggered FFs even though their standard 74 series counterparts are master/slave.

For most purposes, if you encounter a master/slave FF in a piece of equipment, you can analyze it like a negative-edge-triggered FF.

5-14 FLIP-FLOP APPLICATIONS

Earlier in this chapter we saw some examples of how the simple NAND flip-flop and NOR flip-flop were used to perform switch debouncing (Example 5-2) and event storage (Example 5-4). These simple unclocked FFs are somewhat limited in their applications. Clocked FFs offer the logic designer a group of versatile devices that have numerous applications. We will briefly introduce the more common applications in the following sections and will expand on them in subsequent chapters.

5-15 FLIP-FLOP SYNCHRONIZATION

Most digital systems are principally synchronous in their operation in that most of the signals will change states in synchronism with the clock transitions. In many cases, however, there will be an external signal that is not synchronized to the clock; in other words, it is asynchronous. Asynchronous signals often occur as a result of a human operator's actuating an input switch at some random time relative to the clock signal. This randomness can produce unpredictable and undesirable results. The following example illustrates how a FF can be used to synchronize the effect of an asynchronous input.

EXAMPLE 5-12

Figure 5-39(a) shows a situation where input signal *A* is generated from a debounced switch that is actuated by an operator (a debounced switch was first introduced in Example 5-2). *A* goes HIGH when the operator actuates the switch and goes LOW when the operator releases the switch. This *A* input is used to control the passage of the clock signal through the AND gate so that clock pulses appear at output *X* only as long as *A* is HIGH.

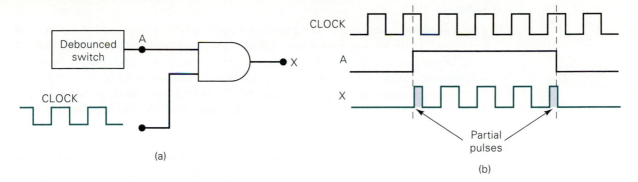

FIGURE 5-39   Asynchronous signal *A* can produce partial pulses at *X*.

The problem with this circuit is that *A* is asynchronous; it can change states at any time relative to the clock signal because the exact times when the operator actuates or releases the switch are essentially random. This can produce *partial* clock pulses at output *X* if either transition of *A* occurs while the clock signal is HIGH, as shown in the waveforms of Figure 5-39(b).

This type of output is often not acceptable, so a method for preventing the appearance of partial pulses at *X* must be developed. One solution is shown in Figure 5-40(a). Describe how this circuit solves the problem, and draw the *X* waveform for the same situation as in Figure 5-39(b).

FIGURE 5-40   An edge-triggered D flip-flop is used to synchronize the enabling of the AND gate to the NGTs of the clock.

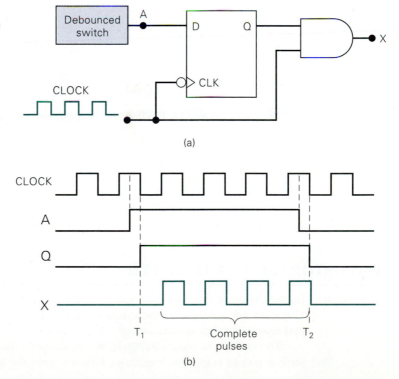

Solution

The *A* signal is connected to the *D* input of FF *Q*, which is clocked by the NGT of the clock signal. Thus, when *A* goes HIGH, *Q* will not go HIGH until the next NGT of the clock at time T_1. This HIGH at *Q* will enable the AND gate to pass subsequent *complete* clock pulses to *X*, as shown in Figure 5-40(b).

When *A* returns LOW, *Q* will not go LOW until the next NGT of the clock at T_2. Thus, the AND gate will not inhibit clock pulses until the clock pulse that ends at T_2 has been passed through to *X*. Therefore, output *X* contains only complete pulses.

5-16   DETECTING AN INPUT SEQUENCE

In many situations an output is to be activated only when the inputs are activated in a certain sequence. This cannot be accomplished using pure combinational logic but requires the storage characteristic of FFs.

For example, an AND gate can be used to determine when two inputs *A* and *B* are both HIGH, but its output will respond the same regardless of which input goes HIGH first. But suppose that we want to generate a HIGH output *only* if *A* goes HIGH and then *B* goes HIGH some time later. One way to accomplish this is shown in Figure 5-41(a).

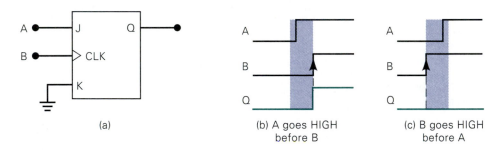

(a)   (b) A goes HIGH   (c) B goes HIGH
                      before B   before A

FIGURE 5-41   Clocked J-K flip-flop used to respond to a particular sequence of inputs.

The waveforms in Figure 5-41(b) and (c) show that *Q* will go HIGH only if *A* goes HIGH before *B* goes HIGH. This is because *A* must be HIGH in order for *Q* to go HIGH on the PGT of *B*.

In order for this circuit to work properly, *A* must go HIGH prior to *B* by at least an amount of time equal to the setup time requirement of the FF.

5-17   DATA STORAGE AND TRANSFER

By far the most common use of flip-flops is for the storage of data or information. The data may represent numerical values (e.g., binary numbers, BCD-coded decimal numbers). These data are generally stored in groups of FFs called **registers.**

The operation most often performed on data that are stored in a FF or a register is the **data transfer** operation. This involves the transfer of data from one FF or register to another. Figure 5-42 illustrates how data transfer can be accomplished between two FFs using clocked S-C, J-K, and D flip-flops. In each case, the logic value that is currently stored in FF *A* is transferred to FF *B* upon the NGT of the TRANSFER pulse. Thus, after this NGT, the *B* output will be the same as the *A* output.

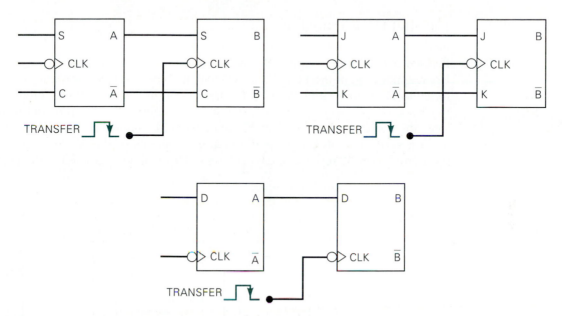

FIGURE 5-42 Synchronous data transfer operation performed by various types of FFs.

The transfer operations in Figure 5-42 are examples of **synchronous transfer,** since the synchronous control and *CLK* inputs are used to perform the transfer. A transfer operation can also be obtained using the asynchronous inputs of a FF. Figure 5-43 shows how an **asynchronous transfer** can be accomplished using the PRESET and CLEAR inputs of any type of FF. Here, the asynchronous inputs respond to LOW levels. When the TRANSFER ENABLE line is held LOW, the two NAND outputs are kept HIGH, with no effect on the FF outputs. When the TRANSFER ENABLE line is made HIGH, one of the NAND outputs will go LOW, depending on the state of the *A* and $\overline{A}$ outputs. This LOW will either set or clear FF *B* to the

FIGURE 5-43 Asynchronous data transfer operation.

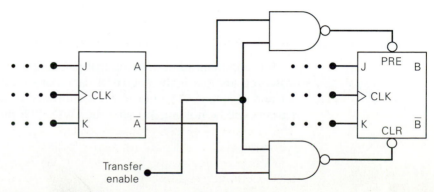

same state as FF *A*. This asynchronous transfer is done independently of the synchronous and *CLK* inputs of the FF. Asynchronous transfer is also called **jam transfer,** because the data can be "jammed" into FF *B* even if its synchronous inputs are active.

Parallel Data Transfer

Figure 5-44 illustrates data transfer from one register to another using D-type FFs. Register *X* consists of FFs X_1, X_2, and X_3; register *Y* consists of FFs Y_1, Y_2, and Y_3. Upon application of the PGT of the TRANSFER pulse, the level stored in X_1 is transferred to Y_1, X_2 to Y_2, and X_3 to Y_3. The transfer of the contents of the *X* register into the *Y* register is a synchronous transfer. It is also referred to as a **parallel transfer,** since the contents of X_1, X_2, and X_3 are transferred *simultaneously* into Y_1, Y_2, and Y_3. If a **serial transfer** were performed, the contents of the *X* register would be transferred to the *Y* register one bit at a time. This will be examined in the next section.

FIGURE 5-44 Parallel transfer of contents of register *X* into register *Y*.

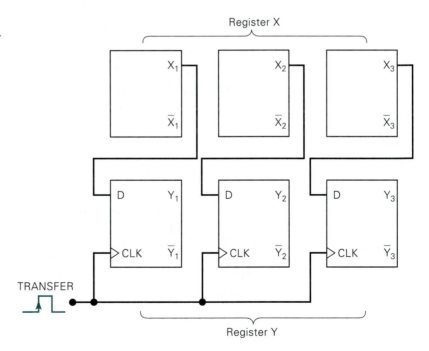

It is important to understand that parallel transfer does not change the contents of the register that is the source of data. For example, in Figure 5-44, if $X_1 X_2 X_3 =$ 101 and $Y_1 Y_2 Y_3 = 011$ prior to the occurrence of the TRANSFER pulse, then both registers will be holding 101 after the TRANSFER pulse.

Review Questions

1. *True or false:* Asynchronous data transfer uses the *CLK* input.

2. Which type of FF is best suited for synchronous transfer because it requires the fewest interconnections from one FF to the other?

3. If J-K flip-flops were used in the registers of Figure 5-44, how many total interconnections would be required from register *X* to register *Y*?

4. *True or false:* Synchronous data transfer requires less circuitry than asynchronous transfer.

5-18 SERIAL DATA TRANSFER: SHIFT REGISTERS

Before we describe the serial data transfer operation, we must first examine the basic *shift-register* arrangement. A **shift register** is a group of FFs arranged so that the binary numbers stored in the FFs are shifted from one FF to the next for every clock pulse. You have undoubtedly seen shift registers in action in devices such as an electronic calculator, where the digits shown on the display shift over each time you key in a new digit. This is the same action taking place in a shift register.

Figure 5-45(a) shows one way to arrange J-K flip-flops to operate as a four-bit shift register. Note that the FFs are connected so that the output of X_3 transfers into X_2, X_2 into X_1, and X_1 into X_0. What this means is that upon the occurrence of the NGT of a shift pulse, each FF takes on the value stored previously in the FF on its left. Flip-flop X_3 takes on a value determined by the conditions present on its J and K inputs when the NGT occurs. For now, we will assume that X_3's J and K inputs are fed by the DATA IN waveform shown in Figure 5-45(b). We will also assume that all FFs are in the 0 state before shift pulses are applied.

The waveforms in Figure 5-45(b) show how the input data are shifted from left to right from FF to FF as shift pulses are applied. When the first NGT occurs at T_1, each of the FFs X_2, X_1, and X_0 will have the $J = 0$, $K = 1$ condition present at its inputs because of the state of the FF on its left. Flip-flop X_3 will have $J = 1$, $K = 0$ because of DATA IN. Thus, at T_1 only X_3 will go HIGH, while all the other FFs remain LOW. When the second NGT occurs at T_2, flip-flop X_3 will have $J = 0$, $K = 1$ because of DATA IN. Flip-flop X_2 will have $J = 1$, $K = 0$ because of the current HIGH at X_3. Flip-flops X_1 and X_0 will still have $J = 0$, $K = 1$. Thus, at T_2 only FF X_2 will go HIGH, FF X_3 will go LOW, and FFs X_1 and X_0 will remain LOW.

Similar reasoning can be used to determine how the waveforms change at T_3 and T_4. Note that on each NGT of the shift pulses, each FF output takes on the level that was present at the output of the FF on its left just *prior* to the NGT. Of course, X_3 takes on the level that was present at DATA IN just prior to the NGT.

Hold Time Requirement

In this shift-register arrangement it is necessary that the FFs have a very small hold time requirement, because there are times when the J, K inputs are changing at about the same time as the *CLK* transition. For example, the X_3 output switches from 1 to 0 in response to the NGT at T_2, causing the J, K inputs of X_2 to change while its

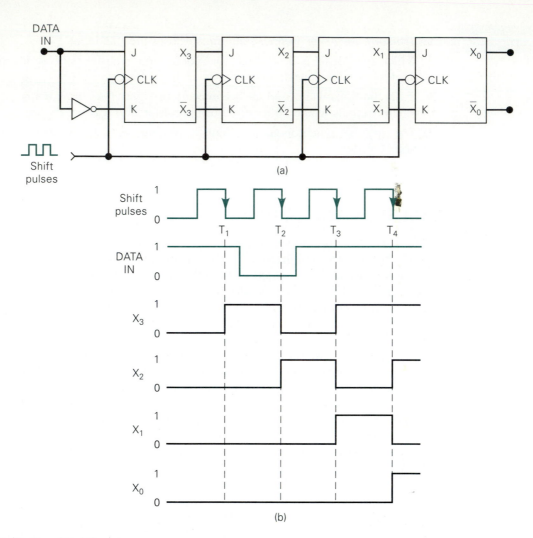

FIGURE 5-45   Four-bit shift register.

CLK input is changing. Actually, because of the propagation delay of X_3, the J, K inputs of X_2 won't change for a short time after the NGT. For this reason, a shift register should be implemented using edge-triggered FFs that have a t_H value less than one FF propagation delay (*CLK*-to-output). This latter requirement is easily satisfied by most modern edge-triggered FFs.

Serial Transfer between Registers

Figure 5-46(a) shows two three-bit shift registers connected so that the contents of the X register will be serially transferred (shifted) into register Y. We are using D flip-flops for each shift register, since this requires fewer connections than J-K flip-flops. Notice how X_0, the last FF of register X, is connected to the D input of Y_2, the first FF of register Y. Thus, as the shift pulses are applied, the information transfer takes place as follows: $X_2 \rightarrow X_1 \rightarrow X_0 \rightarrow Y_2 \rightarrow Y_1 \rightarrow Y_0$. The X_2 FF will go to a state

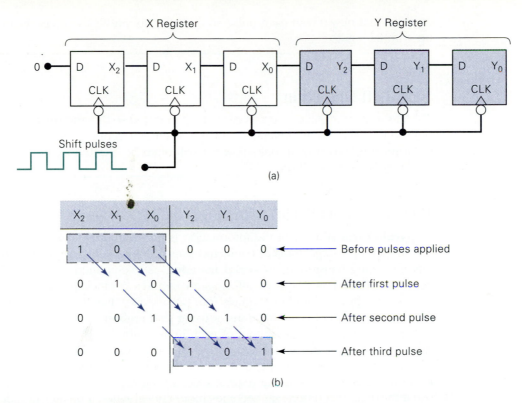

(a)

(b)

FIGURE 5-46 Serial transfer of information from X register into Y register.

determined by its D input. For now, D will be held LOW, so that X_2 will go LOW on the first pulse and will remain there.

To illustrate, let us assume that before any shift pulses are applied, the contents of the X register are 101 (i.e., $X_2 = 1$, $X_1 = 0$, $X_0 = 1$) and the Y register is at 000. Refer to the table in Figure 5-46(b), which shows how the states of each FF change as shift pulses are applied. The following points should be noted:

1. On the NGT of each pulse, each FF takes on the value that was stored in the FF on its left prior to the occurrence of the pulse.

2. After *three* pulses, the 1 that was initially in X_2 is in Y_2, the 0 initially in X_1 is in Y_1, and the 1 initially in X_0 is in Y_0. In other words, the 101 stored in the X register has now been shifted into the Y register. The X register is at 000; it has lost its original data.

3. The complete transfer of the *three* bits of data requires *three* shift pulses.

EXAMPLE 5-13

Assume the same initial contents of the X and Y registers in Figure 5-46. What will be the contents of each FF after the occurrence of the sixth shift pulse?

Solution

If we continue the process shown in Figure 5-46(b) for three more shift pulses, we will find that all of the FFs will be in the 0 state after the sixth pulse. Another way to arrive at this result is to reason as follows: the constant 0 level at the D input of

X_2 shifts in a new 0 with each pulse so that after six pulses the registers are filled up with 0s.

Shift-Left Operation

The FFs in Figure 5-46 can just as easily be connected so that information shifts from right to left. There is no general advantage of shifting in one direction over another; the direction chosen by a logic designer will often be dictated by the nature of the application, as we shall see.

Parallel versus Serial Transfer

In **parallel transfer,** all of the information is transferred simultaneously upon the occurrence of a *single* transfer command pulse (Figure 5-44), no matter how many bits are being transferred. In **serial transfer,** as exemplified by Figure 5-46, the complete transfer of N bits of information requires N clock pulses (three bits requires three pulses, four bits requires four pulses, etc.). Parallel transfer, then, is obviously much faster than serial transfer using shift registers.

In parallel transfer, the output of each FF in register X is connected to a corresponding FF input in register Y. In serial transfer, only the last FF in register X is connected to register Y. In general, then, parallel transfer requires more interconnections between the sending register (X) and the receiving register (Y) than does serial transfer. This difference becomes more critical when a greater number of bits of information are being transferred. This is an important consideration when the sending and receiving registers are remote from each other, since it determines how many lines (wires) are needed for the transmission of the information.

The choice of either parallel or serial transmission depends on the particular system application and specifications. Often, a combination of the two types is used to take advantage of the *speed* of parallel transfer and the *economy and simplicity* of serial transfer. More will be said later about information transfer.

Review Questions

1. *True or false:* The fastest method for transferring data from one register to another is parallel transfer.

2. What is the major advantage of serial transfer over parallel transfer?

3. Refer to Figure 5-46. Assume that the initial contents of the registers are $X_2 = 0$, $X_1 = 1$, $X_0 = 0$, $Y_2 = 1$, $Y_1 = 1$, $Y_0 = 0$. Also assume that the D input of X_2 is held HIGH. Determine the value of each FF output after the occurrence of the fourth shift pulse.

4. In which form of data transfer does the source of the data not lose its data?

5-19 FREQUENCY DIVISION AND COUNTING

Refer to Figure 5-47(a). Each FF has its *J* and *K* inputs at the 1 level, so that it will change states (toggle) whenever the signal on its *CLK* input goes from HIGH to LOW. The clock pulses are applied only to the *CLK* input of FF Q_0. Output Q_0 is connected to the *CLK* input of FF Q_1, and output Q_1 is connected to the *CLK* input of FF Q_2. The waveforms in Figure 5-47(b) show how the FFs change states as the pulses are applied. The following important points should be noted:

1. Flip-flop Q_0 toggles on the negative-going transition of each input clock pulse. Thus, the Q_0 output waveform has a frequency that is exactly one-half of the clock pulse frequency.

2. Flip-flop Q_1 toggles each time the Q_0 output goes from HIGH to LOW. The Q_1 waveform has a frequency equal to exactly one-half the frequency of the Q_0 output and therefore one-fourth of the clock frequency.

3. Flip-flop Q_2 toggles each time the Q_1 output goes from HIGH to LOW. Thus, the Q_2 waveform has one-half the frequency of Q_1 and therefore one-eighth of the clock frequency.

4. Each FF output is a square wave (50 percent duty cycle).

As described above, each FF divides the frequency of its input by 2. Thus, if we were to add a fourth FF to the chain, it would have a frequency equal to one-sixteenth

FIGURE 5-47 J-K flip-flops wired as a three-bit binary counter (MOD-8).

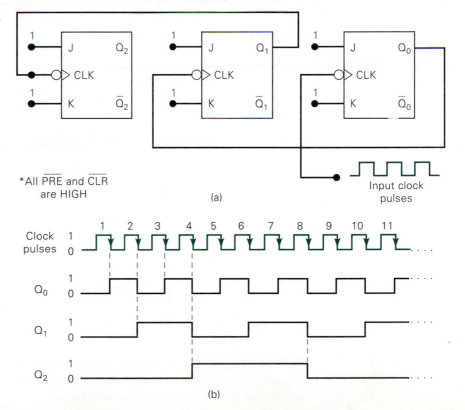

of the clock frequency, and so on. Using the appropriate number of FFs, this circuit could divide a frequency by any power of 2. Specifically, using *N* flip-flops would produce an output frequency from the last FF which is equal to $1/2^N$ of the input frequency.

This application of flip-flops is referred to as **frequency division.** Many applications require a frequency division. For example, your wristwatch is no doubt a "quartz" watch. We will explore crystal oscillators later in this chapter, but the term *quartz watch* means that a quartz crystal is used to generate a very stable oscillator frequency. The natural resonant frequency of the quartz crystal in your watch is likely 1 MHz or more. In order to advance the second hand once every second, the oscillator frequency is *divided* by a value that will produce a very stable and accurate 1 Hz output frequency.

Counting Operation

In addition to functioning as a frequency divider, the circuit of Figure 5-47 also operates as a **binary counter.** This can be demonstrated by examining the sequence of states of the FFs after the occurrence of each clock pulse. Figure 5-48 presents the results in a **state table.** Let the $Q_2Q_1Q_0$ values represent a binary number where Q_2 is in the 2^2 position, Q_1 is in the 2^1 position, and Q_0 is in the 2^0 position. The first eight $Q_2Q_1Q_0$ states in the table should be recognized as the binary counting sequence from 000 to 111. After the first NGT, the FFs are in the 001 state ($Q_2 = 0$, $Q_1 = 0$, $Q_0 = 1$), which represents 001_2 (equivalent to decimal 1); after the second NGT, the FFs represent 010_2, which is equivalent to 2_{10}; after three pulses, $011_2 = 3_{10}$; after four pulses, $100_2 = 4_{10}$; and so on, until after seven pulses, $111_2 = 7_{10}$. On the eighth NGT, the FFs return to the 000 state, and the binary sequence repeats itself for succeeding pulses.

FIGURE 5-48 Table of flip-flop states shows binary counting sequence.

2^2 Q_2	2^1 Q_1	2^0 Q_0	
0	0	0	Before applying clock pulses
0	0	1	After pulse #1
0	1	0	After pulse #2
0	1	1	After pulse #3
1	0	0	After pulse #4
1	0	1	After pulse #5
1	1	0	After pulse #6
1	1	1	After pulse #7
0	0	0	After pulse #8 recycles to 000
0	0	1	After pulse #9
0	1	0	After pulse #10
0	1	1	After pulse #11
.	.	.	. . .
.	.	.	. . .
.	.	.	. . .

Thus, for the first seven input pulses, the circuit functions as a binary counter in which the states of the FFs represent a binary number equivalent to the number of pulses that have occurred. This counter can count as high as $111_2 = 7_{10}$ before it returns to 000.

State Transition Diagram

Another way to show how the states of the FFs change with each applied clock pulse is to use a **state transition diagram** as illustrated in Figure 5-49. Each circle represents one possible state as indicated by the binary number inside the circle. For example, the circle containing the number 100 represents the 100 state (i.e., $Q_2 = 1$, $Q_1 = Q_0 = 0$).

FIGURE 5-49 State transition diagram shows how the states of the counter flip-flops change with each applied clock pulse.

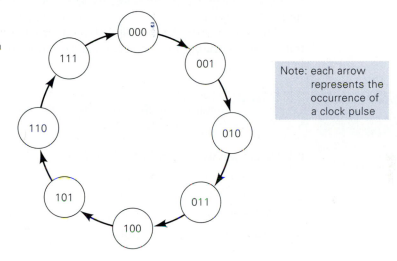

Note: each arrow represents the occurrence of a clock pulse

The arrows connecting one circle to another show how one state changes to another as a clock pulse is applied. By looking at a particular state circle, we can see which state precedes it and which state follows it. For example, looking at the 000 state, we see that this state is reached whenever the counter is in the 111 state and a clock pulse is applied. Likewise, we see that the 000 state is always followed by the 001 state.

We will use state transition diagrams to help describe, analyze, and design counters and other sequential FF circuits.

MOD Number

The counter of Figure 5-47 has $2^3 = 8$ different states (000 through 111). It would be referred to as a *MOD-8 counter*, where the **MOD number** indicates the number of states in the counting sequence. If a fourth FF were added, the sequence of states would count in binary from 0000 to 1111, a total of 16 states. This would be called a *MOD-16 counter*. In general, if N flip-flops are connected in the arrangement of Figure 5-47, the counter will have 2^N different states, and so it is a MOD-2^N counter. It would be capable of counting up to $2^N - 1$ before returning to its 0 state.

The MOD number of a counter also indicates the frequency division obtained from the last FF. For instance, a four-bit counter has four FFs, each representing one binary digit (bit), and so it is a MOD-2^4 = MOD-16 counter. It can therefore count up to 15 (= $2^4 - 1$). It can also be used to divide the input pulse frequency by a factor of 16 (the MOD number).

We have looked only at the basic FF binary counter. We examine counters in much more detail in Chapter 7.

EXAMPLE 5-14

Assume that the MOD-8 counter in Figure 5-47 is in the 101 state. What will be the state (count) after 13 pulses have been applied?

Solution

Locate the 101 state on the state transition diagram. Proceed around the state diagram through eight state changes, and you should be back in the 101 state. Now continue through five more state changes (for a total of 13), and you should end up in the 010 state.

Notice that since this is a MOD-8 counter with eight states, it takes eight state transitions to make one complete excursion around the diagram back to the starting state.

EXAMPLE 5-15

Consider a counter circuit that contains six FFs wired in the arrangement of Figure 5-47 (i.e., Q_5, Q_4, Q_3, Q_2, Q_1, Q_0).

(a) Determine the counter's MOD number.

(b) Determine the frequency at the output of the last FF (Q_5) when the input clock frequency is 1 MHz.

(c) What is the range of counting states for this counter?

(d) Assume a starting state (count) of 000000. What will be the counter's state after 129 pulses?

Solution

(a) MOD number $= 2^6 = 64$.

(b) The frequency at the last FF will equal the input clock frequency divided by the MOD number. That is,

$$f\,(\text{at }Q_5) = \frac{1\text{ MHz}}{64} = 15.625\text{ kHz}$$

(c) The counter will count from 000000_2 to 111111_2 (0 to 63_{10}) for a total of 64 states. Note that the number of states is the same as the MOD number.

(d) Since this is a MOD-64 counter, every 64 clock pulses will bring the counter back to its starting state. Therefore, after 128 pulses the count is back to 000000. The 129th pulse brings the counter to the 000001 counter.

Review Questions

1. A 20-kHz clock signal is applied to a J-K flip-flop with $J = K = 1$. What is the frequency of the FF output waveform?

2. How many FFs are required for a counter that will count 0 to 255_{10}?

3. What is the MOD number of this counter?

4. What is the frequency of the output of the eighth FF when the input clock frequency is 512 kHz?

5. If this counter starts at 00000000, what will be its state after 520 pulses?

5-20 MICROCOMPUTER APPLICATION

Your study of digital systems is still in a relatively early stage, and you have not learned very much about microprocessors and microcomputers. However, you can get a basic idea of how FFs are employed in a typical microprocessor-controlled application without being concerned with all of the details you will need to know later.

Figure 5-50 shows a microprocessor unit (MPU) with its outputs used to transfer binary data to register X, which consists of four D flip-flops X_3, X_2, X_1, X_0. One set of MPU outputs is the *address code* made up of the eight outputs A_{15}, A_{14}, A_{13}, A_{12}, A_{11}, A_{10}, A_9, A_8. Most MPUs have at least 16 available address outputs, but they are not always all used. A second set of MPU outputs consists of the four *data lines* D_3, D_2, D_1, D_0. Most MPUs have at least eight available data lines. The other MPU output is the clock signal CP.

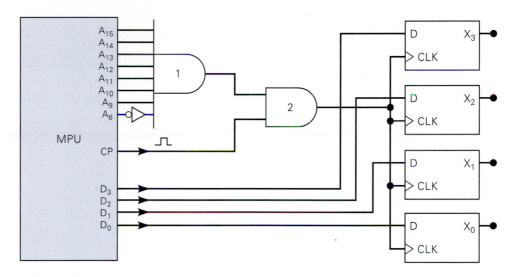

FIGURE 5-50   Example of a microprocessor transferring binary data to an external register.

Recall that the MPU is the central processing unit of a microcomputer, and its main function is to execute a program of instructions stored in the computer's memory. One of the instructions it might execute could be one that tells the MPU to transfer a binary number from a storage resister within the MPU to the external register X. In executing this instruction, the MPU would perform the following steps:

1. Place the binary number onto its data output lines D_3 through D_0.
2. Place the proper address code on its output lines A_{15} through A_8 to select register X as the recipient of the data.
3. Once the data and address outputs are stabilized, the MPU generates the clock pulse CP to clock the register and complete the parallel transfer of data into X.

There are many situations where an MPU, under the control of a program, will send data to an external register in order to control external events. For example, the individual FFs in the register can control the ON/OFF status of electromechanical devices such as solenoids, relays, motors, and so on (through appropriate interface circuits, of course). The data sent from the MPU to the register will determine which devices are ON and which are OFF. Another common example is where the register is used to hold a binary number for input to a digital-to-analog converter (DAC). The MPU sends the binary number to the register, and the DAC converts it to an analog voltage which may be used to control something such as the position of an electron beam on a CRT screen or the speed of a motor.

EXAMPLE 5-16

(a) What address code must the MPU generate in order for the data to be transferred into X?

(b) Assume that $X_3-X_0 = 0110$, $A_{15}-A_8 = 11111111$, and $D_3-D_0 = 1011$. What will be in X after a CP pulse occurs?

Solution

(a) In order for the data to be transferred into X, the clock pulse must pass through AND gate 2 into the CLK inputs of the FFs. This will happen only if the top input of AND gate 2 is HIGH. This means that all of the inputs to AND gate 1 must be HIGH; that is, A_{15} through A_9 must be 1, and A_8 must be 0. Thus, the presence of address code 11111110 is needed to allow data to be transferred into X.

(b) With $A_8 = 1$, the LOW from AND gate 1 will inhibit CP from getting through AND gate 2, and the FFs will not be clocked. Therefore, the contents of register X will not change from 0110.

Review Questions

1. Show how the 74HC175 IC of Figure 5-34 can be used for the X register of Figure 5-50.

5-21 SCHMITT-TRIGGER DEVICES

A **Schmitt-trigger circuit** is not classified as a flip-flop, but it does exhibit a type of memory characteristic that makes it useful in certain special situations. One of those situations is shown in Figure 5-51(a). Here a standard INVERTER is being driven by a logic input that has relatively slow transition times. When these transition times exceed the maximum allowed values (this depends on the particular logic family), the outputs of logic gates and INVERTERs may produce oscillations as the input signal passes through the indeterminate range. The same input conditions can also produce erratic triggering of FFs.

A device that has a Schmitt-trigger type of input is designed to accept slow-changing signals and produce an output that has oscillation-free transitions. The output will generally have very rapid transition times (typically 10 ns) that are independent of the input signal characteristics. Figure 5-51(b) shows a Schmitt-trigger INVERTER and its response to a slow-changing input.

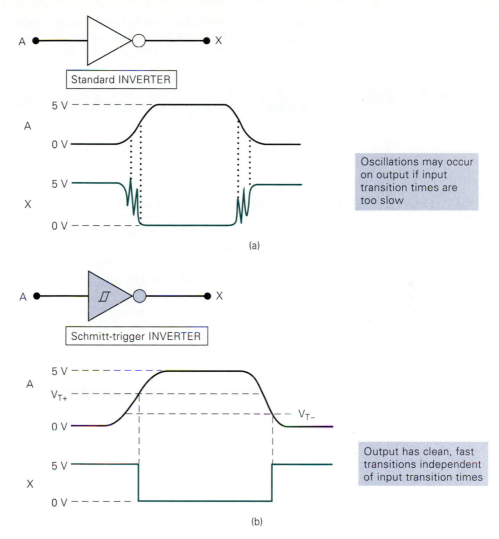

FIGURE 5-51 (a) If input transition times are too long, a standard logic device-output might oscillate or change erratically; (b) a logic device with a Schmitt-trigger type of input will produce clean, fast output transitions.

If you examine the waveforms in Figure 5-51(b), you should note that the output does not change from HIGH to LOW until the input exceeds the *positive-going threshold* voltage, V_{T+}. Once the output goes LOW, it will remain there even when the input drops back below V_{T+} (this is its memory characteristic) until it drops all the way down below the *negative-going threshold* voltage, V_{T-}. The values of the two threshold voltages will vary from logic family to logic family, but V_{T-} will always be less than V_{T+}.

The Schmitt-trigger INVERTER, and all other devices with Schmitt-trigger inputs, use the distinctive symbol shown in Figure 5-51(b) to indicate that they can reliably respond to slow-changing input signals. Logic designers use ICs with Schmitt-trigger inputs to convert slow-changing signals to clean, fast-changing signals that can drive standard IC inputs.

Several ICs are available with Schmitt-trigger inputs. The 7414, 74LS14, and 74HC14 are hex INVERTER ICs with Schmitt-trigger inputs. The 7413, 74LS13, and 74HC13 are dual four-input NANDs with Schmitt-trigger inputs.

1. What could occur when a slow-changing signal is applied to a standard logic IC?
2. How does a Schmitt-trigger logic device operate differently from a standard logic device?

5-22 ONE-SHOT (MONOSTABLE MULTIVIBRATOR)

A digital circuit that is somewhat related to the FF is the **one-shot** (abbreviated OS). Like the FF, the OS has two inputs, Q and $\overline{Q}$, which are the inverse of each other. Unlike the FF, the OS has only one *stable* output state (normally $Q = 0$, $\overline{Q} = 1$), where it remains until it is triggered by an input signal. Once triggered, the OS outputs switch to the opposite state ($Q = 1$, $\overline{Q} = 0$). It remains in this **quasi-stable state** for a fixed period of time, t_p, which is usually determined by an RC time constant which results from the values of external components connected to the OS. After a time t_p, the OS outputs return to their resting state until triggered again.

Figure 5-52(a) shows the logic symbol for a OS. The value of t_p is often indicated somewhere on the OS symbol. In practice, t_p can vary from several nanoseconds to several tens of seconds. The exact value of t_p is variable and is determined by the values of external components R_T and C_T.

Two types of one-shots are available in IC form: the **nonretriggerable OS** and the **retriggerable OS.**

Nonretriggerable One-Shot

The waveforms in Figure 5-52(b) illustrate the operation of a nonretriggerable OS that triggers on positive-going transitions at its trigger (T) input. The important points to note are:

1. The PGTs at points *a*, *b*, *c*, and *e* will trigger the OS to its quasi-stable state for a time t_p, after which it automatically returns to the stable state.
2. The PGTs at points *d* and *f* have no effect on the OS because it has already been triggered to the quasi-stable state. The OS must return to the stable state before it can be triggered.
3. The OS output-pulse duration is always the same regardless of the duration of the input pulses. As stated above, t_p depends only on R_T and C_T and the internal OS circuitry. A typical OS may have a t_p given by $t_p = 0.7\ R_T C_T$.

Retriggerable One-Shot

The retriggerable OS operates much like the nonretriggerable OS except for one major difference: *it can be retriggered while it is in the quasi-stable state, and it will begin a new t_p interval.* Figure 5-53(a) compares the response of both types of OS using a t_p of 2 ms. Let's examine these waveforms.

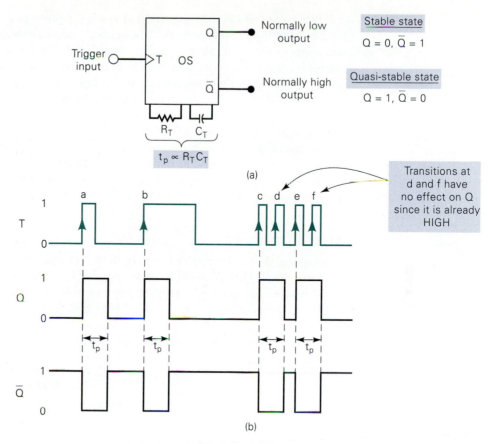

(a)

(b)

FIGURE 5-52   OS symbol and typical waveforms for nonretriggerable operation.

FIGURE 5-53   (a) Comparison of nonretriggerable and retriggerable OS responses for t_p = 2 ms. (b) Retriggerable OS begins a new t_p interval each time it receives a trigger pulse.

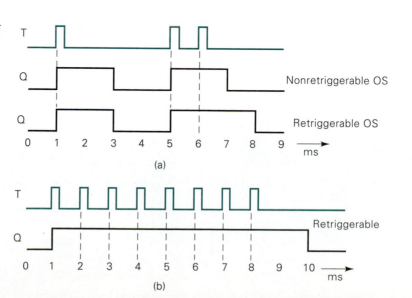

(a)

(b)

Both types of OS respond to the first trigger pulse at $t = 1$ ms by going HIGH for 2 ms and then returning LOW. The second trigger pulse at $t = 5$ ms triggers both one-shots to the HIGH state. The third trigger pulse at $t = 6$ ms has no effect on the nonretriggerable OS, since it is already in its quasi-stable state. However, this trigger pulse will *retrigger* the retriggerable OS to begin a new $t_p = 2$ ms interval. Thus, it will stay HIGH for 2 ms *after* this third trigger pulse.

In effect, then, a retriggerable OS begins a new t_p interval each time a trigger pulse is applied, regardless of the current state of its Q output. In fact, trigger pulses can be applied at a rate fast enough that the OS will always be retriggered before the end of the t_p interval and Q will remain HIGH. This is shown in Figure 5-53(b), where eight pulses are applied every 1 ms. Q does not return LOW until 2 ms after the last trigger pulse.

Actual Devices

Several one-shot ICs are available in both the retriggerable and the nonretriggerable versions. The 74121 is a single nonretriggerable one-shot IC; the 74221, 74LS221, and 74HC221 are dual nonretriggerable one-shot ICs; the 74122 and 74LS122 are single retriggerable one-shot ICs; the 74123, 74LS123, and 74HC123 are dual retriggerable one-shot ICs.

Figure 5-54(a) shows the traditional symbol for the 74121 nonretriggerable one-shot IC. Note that it contains internal logic gates to allow inputs A_1, A_2, and B to trigger the OS in a variety of ways. The B input is a Schmitt-trigger type of input that is allowed to have slow transition times and still reliably trigger the OS. The pins labeled R_{INT}, R_{EXT}/C_{EXT}, and C_{EXT} are used to connect an external resistor and capacitor to achieve the desired output pulse duration. Figure 5-54(b) is the IEEE/ANSI symbol for the 74121 nonretriggerable OS. Note how this symbol represents the logic gates. Also notice the presence of a small pulse with 1 in front of it. This indicates that the device is a nonretriggerable OS. The IEEE/ANSI symbol for a retriggerable OS would not have the 1 in front of the pulse.

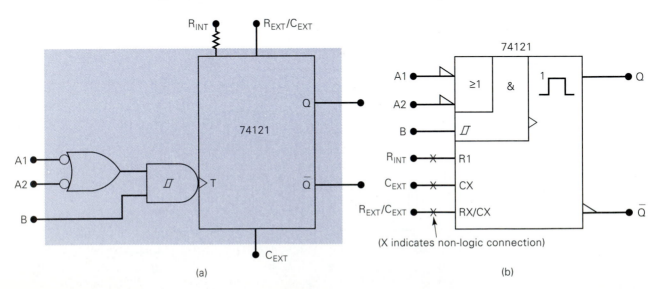

FIGURE 5-54 Logic symbols for the 74121 nonretriggerable one-shot; (a) traditional; (b) IEEE/ANSI.

Monostable Multivibrator

Another name for the one-shot is *monostable multivibrator* because it has only one stable state. One-shots find limited application in most synchronous clock-controlled systems, and experienced designers generally avoid using them because they are prone to false triggering by spurious noise. When they are used, it is usually in simple timing applications that utilize the predetermined t_p interval. Several of the end-of-chapter problems will illustrate how a OS is used.

Review Questions

1. In the absence of a trigger pulse, what will be the state of a OS output?
2. *True or false:* When a nonretriggerable OS is pulsed while it is in its quasi-stable state, the output is not affected.
3. What determines the t_p value for a OS?
4. Describe how a retriggerable OS operates differently from a nonretriggerable OS.

5-23 ANALYZING SEQUENTIAL CIRCUITS

Many logic circuits contain FFs, one-shots, and logic gates that are connected to perform a specific operation. Very often, a master clock signal is used to cause the logic levels in the circuit to go through a particular sequence of states. We can generally analyze these sequential circuits by following the procedure demonstrated in the following example.

EXAMPLE 5-17

Consider the circuit of Figure 5-55. Initially, all of the FF outputs are in the 0 state before the clock pulses are applied. These pulses have a repetition rate of 1 kHz. Determine the waveforms at X, Y, Z, and W for eight cycles of the clock input.

Solution

Step 1. Examine the circuit. Look for circuit arrangements that are familiar, such as counters, shift registers, and so on.

FFs X, Y, and Z are connected as a three-bit counter that will count the clock pulses provided that the J and K inputs of FF Z, which are driven by the NAND gate output W, are in the HIGH state. The NAND gate inputs are driven by the X, $\overline{Y}$, and $\overline{Z}$ outputs.

Step 2. On the circuit diagram, write down the logic levels present at each input and output prior to the occurrence of the first clock pulse.

The FFs are all initially in the 0 state. The NAND inputs are 0, 1, and 1, respectively, so that W is a HIGH. All J, K inputs are 1. These states are shown on the circuit diagram in color.

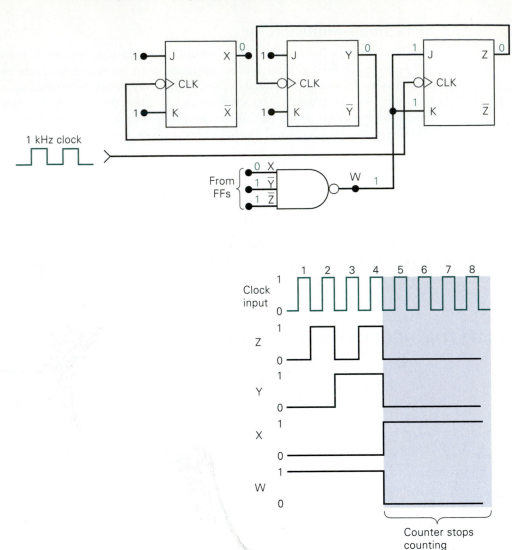

FIGURE 5-55   Example 5-17.

Step 3. Using these conditions, determine the new states of each FF in response to the first clock pulse.

The NGT of the first clock pulse will toggle Z to the 1 state, and X and Y remain LOW. See the waveforms of Figure 5-55.

Step 4. Go back and repeat steps 2 and 3 for the second clock pulse, the third pulse, and so on.

With Z now at 1, the NAND inputs are 0, 1, and 0, respectively, so that prior to the second clock pulse, W is still HIGH, all J, K inputs are HIGH, and each FF is ready to toggle (you may want to update these logic levels on the circuit diagram). The second NGT of the clock toggles Z from 1 to 0; the NGT at Z then toggles Y from 0 to 1. X remains at 0. See the waveforms.

Prior to the third clock pulse, the NAND inputs are 0, 0, and 1, respectively, so W is still HIGH and all J, K inputs are HIGH. The third NGT of the clock toggles Z from 0 to 1 while X and Y remain unchanged. See the waveforms.

Prior to the fourth clock pulse, the NAND inputs are all 0, so that output W and all J, K inputs are still HIGH. The fourth NGT toggles Z from 1 to 0, which in turn toggles Y from 1 to 0, which in turn toggles X from 0 to 1. See the waveforms.

Prior to the fifth clock pulse, the NAND inputs are all 1, so that output W is LOW. This places a LOW at the J and K inputs of FF Z so that it is in the *no-change* mode. The fifth NGT will have no effect on Z, and none of the logic levels in the circuit will change. In fact, none of the succeeding NGTs will cause any changes; the counter is prevented from counting any further. See the waveforms.

5-24 CLOCK GENERATOR CIRCUITS

Flip-flops have two stable states; therefore, we can say that they are *bistable multivibrators*. One-shots have one stable state, and so we call them *monostable multivibrators*. A third type of multivibrator has no stable states; it is called an **astable** or **free-running multivibrator.** This type of logic circuit switches back and forth (oscillates) between two unstable output states. It is useful for generating clock signals for synchronous digital circuits.

Several types of astable multivibrators are in common use. We will present three of them without any attempt to analyze their operation. They are presented here so that you can construct a clock generator circuit if needed for a project or for testing digital circuits in the lab.

Schmitt-Trigger Oscillator

Figure 5-56 shows how a Schmitt-trigger INVERTER can be connected as an oscillator. The signal at V_{OUT} is an approximate square wave with a frequency that depends on the R and C values. The relationship between the frequency and RC val-

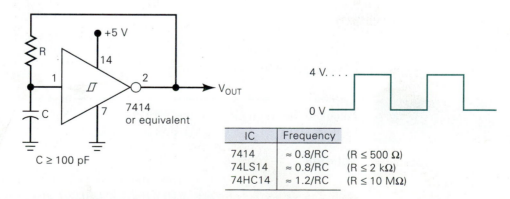

IC	Frequency	
7414	≈ 0.8/RC	(R ≤ 500 Ω)
74LS14	≈ 0.8/RC	(R ≤ 2 kΩ)
74HC14	≈ 1.2/RC	(R ≤ 10 MΩ)

FIGURE 5-56   Schmitt-trigger oscillator using a 7414 INVERTER. A 7413 Schmitt-trigger NAND may also be used.

ues is shown in Figure 5-56 for three different Schmitt-trigger INVERTERs. Note the maximum limits on the resistance value for each device. The circuit will fail to oscillate if R is not kept below these limits.

555 Timer Used as an Astable Multivibrator

The **555 timer** IC is a TTL-compatible device that can operate in several different modes. Figure 5-57 shows how external components can be connected to a 555 so that it operates as a free-running oscillator. Its output is a repetitive rectangular waveform that switches between two logic levels with the time intervals at each logic level determined by the R and C values. The formulas for these time intervals, t_1 and t_2, and the overall period of the oscillations, T, are given in the figure. The frequency of the oscillations is, of course, the reciprocal of T. As the formulas in the diagram indicate, the t_1 and t_2 intervals cannot be equal unless R_A is made zero. This cannot be done without producing excess current through the device. This means that it is impossible to produce a perfect 50 percent duty-cycle square wave output. It is possible, however, to get very close to a 50 percent duty cycle by making $R_B >> R_A$ (while keeping R_A greater than 1 kΩ), so that $t_1 \approx t_2$.

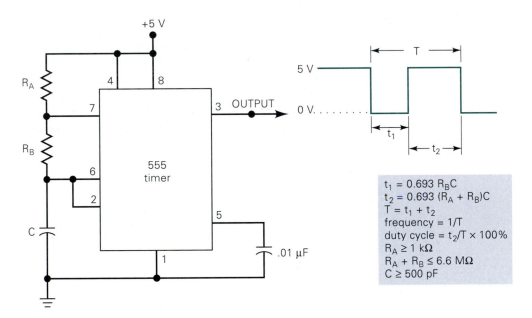

FIGURE 5-57   555 timer IC used as an astable multivibrator.

EXAMPLE 5-18

Calculate the frequency and the duty cycle of the 555 astable multivibrator output for $C = 0.001 \ \mu\text{F}$, $R_A = 2.2$ kΩ, and $R_B = 100$ kΩ.

Solution

$$t_1 = 0.693(100 \text{ k}\Omega)(0.001 \ \mu\text{F}) = 69.3 \ \mu\text{s}$$
$$t_2 = 0.693(102.2 \text{ k}\Omega)(0.001 \ \mu\text{F}) = 70.7 \ \mu\text{s}$$
$$T = 69.3 + 70.7 = 140 \ \mu\text{s}$$
$$f = 1/140 \ \mu\text{s} = 7.29 \text{ kHz}$$
$$\text{duty cycle} = 70.7/140 = 50.5\%$$

Note that the duty cycle is close to 50 percent (square wave) because R_B is much greater than R_A. It can be made even closer to 50 percent by making R_B even larger compared with R_A. For instance, you should verify that if we change R_A to 1 kΩ (its minimum allowed value), the results are f = 7.18 kHz and duty cycle = 50.3 percent.

Crystal-Controlled Clock Generators

The output frequencies of the signals from the clock-generating circuits described above depend on the values of resistors and capacitors, and thus they are not extremely accurate or stable. Even if variable resistors are used so that the desired frequency can be adjusted by "tweaking" the resistance values, changes in the R and C values will occur with changes in ambient temperature and with aging, thereby causing the adjusted frequency to drift. If frequency accuracy and stability are critical, another method of generating clock signals can be used: a **crystal-controlled clock generator.** It employs a highly stable and accurate component called a *quartz crystal.* A piece of quartz crystal can be cut to a specific size and shape to vibrate (resonate) at a precise frequency that is extremely stable with temperature and aging; frequencies from 10 kHz to 80 MHz are readily achievable. When a crystal is placed in certain circuit configurations, it can produce oscillations at an accurate and stable frequency equal to the crystal's resonant frequency. Two such circuits are shown in Figure 5-58.

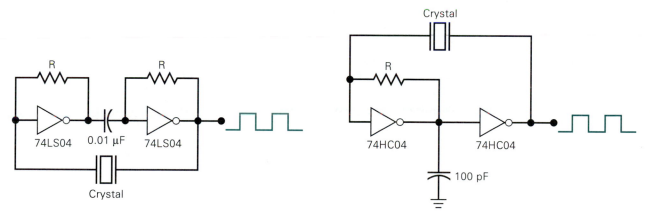

FIGURE 5-58 Crystal-controlled clock generator circuits: (a) using TTL inverters; (b) using CMOS inverters.

The circuit in Figure 5-58(a) is constructed using 74LS04 TTL inverters. It could also use the 74LS14 Schmitt-trigger inverters. The value of R is usually between 300 and 1500 Ω, and it depends on the type of crystal used and its frequency. This circuit is capable of producing clock frequencies up to 20 MHz. The circuit in Figure 5-58(b) uses CMOS inverters from the 74HC04 IC. A typical value for R is 100 kΩ. This circuit will oscillate at crystal frequencies up to about 10 MHz.

Crystal-controlled clock generator circuits such as those in Figure 5-58 are used in all microprocessor-based systems and microcomputers, and in any application in which a clock signal is used to generate accurate timing intervals. We will see this in some of the applications we encounter in the following chapters.

Review Questions
1. Determine the approximate frequency of a Schmitt-trigger oscillator that uses a 74HC14 with $R = 10$ kΩ and $C = 0.005$ μF.
2. Determine the approximate frequency and duty cycle of the 555 oscillator for $R_A = R_B = 2.2$ kΩ and $C = 2000$ pF.
3. What is the advantage of crystal-controlled clock generator circuits over *RC*-controlled circuits?

5-25   TROUBLESHOOTING FLIP-FLOP CIRCUITS

Flip-flop ICs are susceptible to the same kinds of internal and external faults that occur in combinational logic circuits. All of the troubleshooting ideas that were discussed in Chapter 4 can readily be applied to circuits that contain FFs as well as logic gates.

Because of their memory characteristic, FF circuits with one or more faults will often exhibit symptoms that would not occur in combinational circuits. Some of these are described below.

Open Inputs

Unconnected or floating inputs of any logic circuit are particularly susceptible to picking up spurious voltage fluctuations called *noise*. If the noise is large enough in amplitude and long enough in duration, the logic circuit's output may change states in response to the noise. In a logic gate, the output will return to its original state when the noise signal subsides. In a FF, however, the output will remain in its new state because of its memory characteristic. Thus, the effect of noise pickup at any open input is usually more critical for a FF or latch than it is for a logic gate.

The most susceptible FF inputs are those that can trigger the FF to a different state—such as the *CLK*, PRESET, and CLEAR. Whenever you see a FF output that is changing states erratically, you should consider the possibility of an open connection at one of these inputs.

EXAMPLE 5-19   Figure 5-59 shows a three-bit shift register made up of TTL flip-flops. Initially, all of the FFs are in the LOW state before clock pulses are applied. As clock pulses are applied, each PGT will cause the information to shift from each FF to the one on its right. The diagram shows the "expected" sequence of FF states after each clock pulse. Since $J_2 = 1$ and $K_2 = 0$, flip-flop X_2 will go HIGH on clock pulse 1 and will stay there for all subsequent pulses. This HIGH will shift into X_1, and then X_0 on clock pulses 2 and 3, respectively. Thus, after the third pulse, all FFs will be HIGH and should remain there as pulses are continually applied.

Now let's suppose that the "actual" response of the FF states is as shown in the diagram. Here the FFs change as expected for the first three clock pulses.

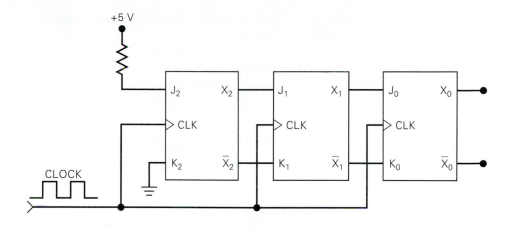

Clock pulse number	"Expected" X_2 X_1 X_0	"Actual" X_2 X_1 X_0
0	0 0 0	0 0 0
1	1 0 0	1 0 0
2	1 1 0	1 1 0
3	1 1 1	1 1 1
4	1 1 1	1 1 0
5	1 1 1	1 1 1
6	1 1 1	1 1 0
7	1 1 1	1 1 1
8	1 1 1	1 1 0

FIGURE 5-59   Example 5-19.

From then on, flip-flop X_0, instead of staying HIGH, alternates between HIGH and LOW. What possible circuit fault can produce this operation?

Solution

On the second pulse, X_1 goes HIGH. This should make $J_0 = 1$, $K_0 = 0$ so that all subsequent clock pulses should set $X_0 = 1$. Instead, we see X_0 changing states (toggling) on all pulses after the second one. This toggle operation would occur if J_0 and K_0 were both HIGH. The most probable fault is a break in the connection between $\overline{X}_1$ and K_0. Recall that a TTL device responds to an open input as if it were a logic HIGH, so that an open at K_0 is the same as a HIGH.

Shorted Outputs

The following example will illustrate how a fault in a FF circuit can cause a misleading symptom that may result in a longer time to isolate the fault.

EXAMPLE 5-20

Consider the circuit in Figure 5-60 and examine the logic probe indications shown in the accompanying table. There is a LOW at the D input of the FF when pulses are applied to its CLK input, but the Q output fails to go to the

LOW state. The technician testing this circuit considers each of the following possible circuit faults:

1. Z2-5 is internally shorted to V_{CC}.
2. Z1-4 is internally shorted to V_{CC}.
3. Z2-5 or Z1-4 is externally shorted to V_{CC}.
4. Z2-4 is internally or externally shorted to GROUND. This would keep $\overline{PRE}$ activated and would override the *CLK* input.
5. There is an internal failure in Z2 that prevents *Q* from responding properly to its inputs.

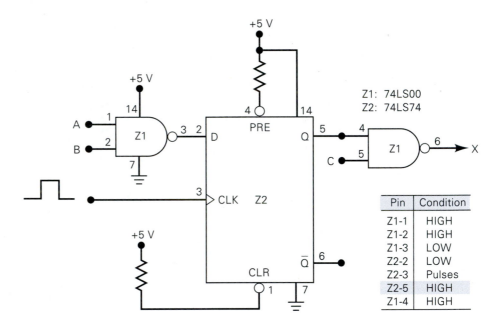

FIGURE 5-60   Example 5-20.

The technician after making the necessary ohmmeter checks, rules out the first four possibilities. He also checks Z2's V_{CC} and GROUND pins and finds that they are at the proper voltages. He is reluctant to unsolder Z2 from the circuit until he is certain that it is faulty, and so he decides to look at the clock signal. He uses an oscilloscope to check its amplitude, frequency, pulse width, and transition times. He finds that they are all within the specifications for the 74LS74. Finally, he concludes that Z2 is faulty.

He removes the 74LS74 chip and replaces it with another one. To his dismay, the circuit with the new chip behaves in exactly the same way. After scratching his head, he decides to change the NAND gate chip, although he doesn't know why. As expected, he sees no change in the circuit operation.

Becoming more puzzled, he recalls that his electronics lab instructor emphasized the value of performing a thorough visual check on the circuit board, and so he begins to examine it carefully. While he is doing that, he detects a solder bridge between pins 6 and 7 of Z2. He removes it and tests the circuit, and it functions correctly. Explain how this fault produced the operation observed.

Solution

The solder bridge was shorting the $\overline{Q}$ output to GROUND. This means that $\overline{Q}$ is permanently stuck LOW. Recall that in all latches and FFs, the $\overline{Q}$ and Q outputs are internally cross-coupled so that the level on one will affect the other. For example, take another look at the internal circuitry for a J-K flip-flop in Figure 5-23. Note that a constant LOW at $\overline{Q}$ would keep a LOW at one input of NAND gate 3 so that Q would have to stay HIGH regardless of the conditions at J, K, and CLK.

The technician learned a valuable lesson about troubleshooting FF circuits. He learned that both outputs should be checked for faults, even those that are not connected to other devices.

Clock Skew

One of the most common timing problems in synchronous circuits is **clock skew.** One type of clock skew occurs when a clock signal, because of propagation delays, arrives at the CLK inputs of different FFs at different times. In many situations the skew can cause a FF to go to a wrong state. This is best illustrated with an example.

Refer to Figure 5-61(a), where the signal $CLOCK1$ is connected directly to FF Q_1, and indirectly to Q_2 through a NAND gate and INVERTER. Both FFs are supposed to be clocked by the occurrence of a NGT of $CLOCK1$ provided that X is HIGH. If we assume that initially $Q_1 = Q_2 = 0$ and $X = 1$, the NGT of $CLOCK1$ should set $Q_1 = 1$ and have no effect on Q_2. The waveforms in Figure 5-61(b) show how clock skew can produce incorrect triggering of Q_2.

Because of the combined propagation delays of the NAND gate and INVERTER, the transitions of the $CLOCK2$ signal are delayed with respect to $CLOCK1$ by an amount of time t_1. The NGT of $CLOCK2$ arrives at Q_2's CLK input t_1 later than the NGT of $CLOCK1$ appears at Q_1's CLK input. This t_1 is the clock skew. The NGT of $CLOCK1$ will cause Q_1 to go HIGH after a time t_2 which is equal to Q_1's t_{PLH} propagation delay. If t_2 is less than the skew t_1, Q_1 will be HIGH when the NGT of $CLOCK2$ occurs, and this may incorrectly set $Q_2 = 1$ if its setup time requirement, t_S, is met.

For example, assume that the clock skew is 40 ns and the t_{PLH} of Q_1 is 25 ns. Thus, Q_1 will go HIGH 15 ns before the NGT of $CLOCK2$. If Q_2's setup time requirement is smaller than 15 ns, Q_2 will respond to the HIGH at its D input when the NGT of $CLOCK2$ occurs, and Q_2 will go HIGH. This, of course, is not the expected response of Q_2. It is supposed to remain LOW.

The effects of clock skew are not always easy to detect, because the response of the affected FF may be intermittent (sometimes it works correctly, sometimes it doesn't). This is because the situation is dependent on circuit propagation delays and FF timing parameters, which vary with temperature, length of connections, power supply voltage, and loading. Sometimes just connecting an oscilloscope probe to a FF or gate output will add enough load capacitance to increase the device's propagation delay so that the circuit functions correctly; then when the probe is removed, the incorrect operation reappears. This is the kind of situation that explains why some technicians are prematurely gray.

Problems caused by clock skew can be eliminated by equalizing the delays in the various paths of the clock signal so that the active transition arrives at each FF at approximately the same time. This is examined in Problem 5-49.

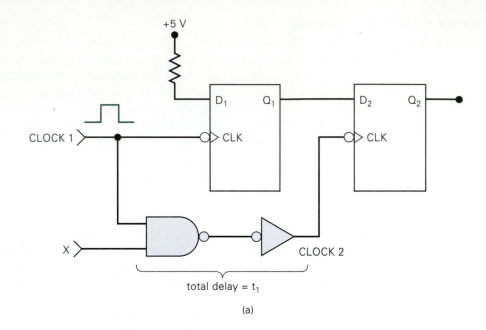

total delay = t_1

(a)

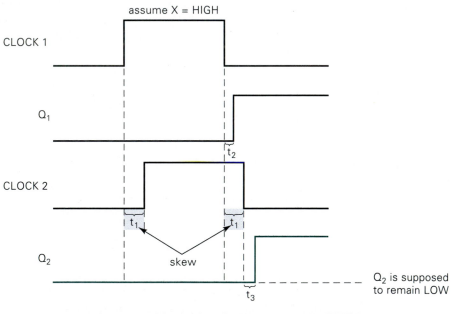

t_1 = skew = combined delay of NAND gate and INVERTER
t_2 = t_{PLH} of Q_1
t_3 = t_{PLH} of Q_2

(b)

FIGURE 5-61 Clock skew occurs when two flip-flops that are supposed to be clocked simultaneously are clocked at slightly different times due to a delay in the arrival of the clock signal at the second flip-flop.

Review Questions	1. What is clock skew? How can it cause a problem?

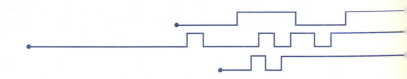

SUMMARY

1. A flip-flop is a logic circuit with a memory characteristic such that its Q and $\overline{Q}$ outputs will go to a new state in response to an input pulse and will remain in that new state after the input pulse is terminated.

2. A NAND latch and a NOR latch are simple FFs that respond to logic levels on their SET and CLEAR inputs.

3. Clearing (resetting) a FF means that its output ends up in the $Q = 0/\overline{Q} = 1$ state. Setting a FF means that it ends up in the $Q = 1/\overline{Q} = 0$ state.

4. Clocked FFs have a clock input (*CLK, CP, CK*) that is edge-triggered, meaning that it triggers the FF on a positive-going transition (PGT) or a negative-going transition (NGT).

5. Edge-triggered (clocked) FFs can be triggered to a new state by the active edge of the clock input according to the state of the FF's synchronous control inputs (*S, C* or *J, K* or *D*).

6. Most clocked FFs also have asynchronous inputs that can set or clear the FF independent of the clock input.

7. The *D* latch is a modified NAND latch that operates like a D flip-flop except that it is not edge-triggered.

8. Some of the principal uses of FFs include data storage and transfer, data shifting, counting, and frequency division.

9. A one-shot is a logic circuit that can be triggered from its normal resting state ($Q = 0$) to its triggered state ($Q = 1$) where it remains for a time interval proportional to an *RC* time constant.

10. Circuits that have a Schmitt-trigger type of input will respond reliably to slow-changing signals and will produce outputs with clean, sharp edges.

11. A variety of circuits can be used to generate clock signals at a desired frequency including Schmitt-trigger oscillators, a 555 timer, and a crystal-controlled oscillator.

12. A complete summary of the various types of FFs can be found on the inside front cover.

IMPORTANT TERMS

flip-flop	pulse-steering circuit	serial data transfer
SET, CLEAR, RESET states/ inputs	edge-detector circuit	shift register
	clocked J-K flip-flop	frequency division
NAND gate latch	toggle mode	binary counter
contact bounce	clocked D flip-flop	state table
NOR gate latch	parallel data transfer	state transition diagram
clock	D latch	MOD number
positive-going transition (PGT)	asynchronous inputs	Schmitt trigger
	override inputs	one-shot (OS)
negative-going transition (NGT)	common-control block	quasi-stable state
	propagation delay	nonretriggerable OS
clocked flip-flop	master/slave flip-flop	retriggerable OS
edge-triggered	registers	astable multivibrator
synchronous control inputs	data transfer	555 timer
setup time/hold time	synchronous transfer	crystal-controlled clock
clocked S-C flip-flop	asynchronous (jam)	generator
trigger	transfer	clock skew
NAND latch	parallel transfer	

PROBLEMS

SECTIONS 5-1 TO 5-3

5-1. Assuming that $Q = 0$ initially, apply the x and y waveforms of Figure 5-62 to the SET and CLEAR inputs of a NAND latch, and determine the Q and $\overline{Q}$ waveforms.

5-2. Invert the x and y waveforms of Figure 5-62, apply them to the SET and CLEAR inputs of a NOR latch, and determine the Q and $\overline{Q}$ waveforms. Assume that $Q = 0$ initially.

5-3. The waveforms of Figure 5-62 are connected to the circuit of Figure 5-63. Assume that $Q = 0$ initially, and determine the Q waveform.

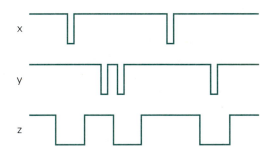

FIGURE 5-62   Problems 5-1 to 5-3.

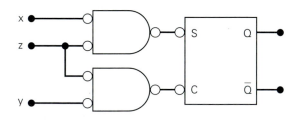

FIGURE 5-63   Problem 5-3.

D   **5-4.** Modify the circuit of Figure 5-9 to use a NOR gate latch.

D   **5-5.** Modify the circuit of Figure 5-12 to use a NAND gate latch.

T   **5-6.** Refer to the circuit of Figure 5-13. A technician tests the circuit operation by observing the outputs with a storage oscilloscope while the switch is moved from A to B. When the switch is moved from A to B, the scope display of X_B appears as shown in Figure 5-64. What circuit fault could produce this result? (*Hint:* What is the function of the NAND latch?)

FIGURE 5-64   Problem 5-6. X_B

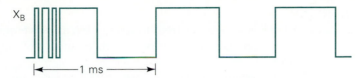

|← ———— 1 ms ————— →|

SECTIONS 5-4 AND 5-5

5-7. A certain clocked FF has minimum $t_S = 20$ ns and $t_H = 5$ ns. How long must the control inputs be stable prior to the active clock transition?

5-8. Apply the S, C, and CLK waveforms of Figure 5-17 to the FF of Figure 5-18, and determine the Q waveform.

N   **5-9.** A *toggle* FF is one that has a single input and operates in such a way that the FF output changes state for each pulse applied to its input. The clocked S-C flip-flop can be wired to operate in the toggle mode, as shown in Figure 5-65. The waveform applied to the CLK input is a 1-kHz square wave. Verify that this arrangement operates in the toggle mode; then determine the Q output waveform. Assume that $Q = 0$ initially.

FIGURE 5-65   Problem 5-9.

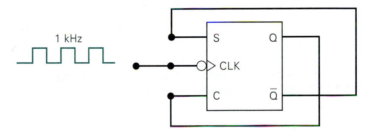

1 kHz

SECTION 5-6

5-10. Apply the J, K, and CLK waveforms of Figure 5-21 to the FF of Figure 5-22. Assume that $Q = 1$ initially, and determine the Q waveform.

5-11. **(a)** Show how the J-K flip-flop can be operated as a toggle FF. Apply a 10-kHz square wave to its input, and determine its output waveform.

(b) Connect the Q output of the FF from Problem 5-11(a) to the CLK input of a second J-K flip-flop that also has $J = K = 1$. Determine the frequency of the waveform at the second FF output.

5-12. The waveforms shown in Figure 5-66 are to be applied to two different FFs:

(a) positive-edge-triggered J-K

(b) negative-edge-triggered J-K

Draw the Q waveform response for each of these FFs, assuming that $Q = 0$ initially. Assume that each FF has $t_H = 0$.

FIGURE 5-66   Problem 5-12.

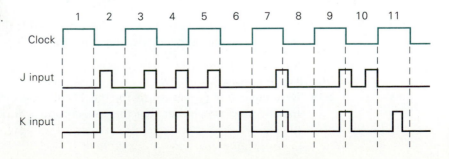

SECTION 5-7

5-13. A D FF is sometimes used to *delay* a binary waveform so that the binary information appears at the output a certain amount of time after it appears at the *D* input.

(a) Determine the *Q* waveform in Figure 5-67, and compare it with the input waveform. Note that it is delayed from the input by one clock period.

(b) How can a delay of two clock periods be obtained?

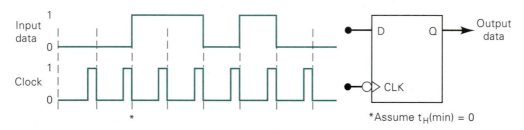

FIGURE 5-67   Problem 5-13.

5-14. An edge-triggered D flip-flop can be made to operate in the toggle mode by connecting it as shown in Figure 5-68. Assume that $Q = 0$ initially, and determine the *Q* waveform.

5-15. Change the circuit in Figure 5-68 so that *Q* is connected back to *D*. Then determine the *Q* waveform.

SECTION 5-8

5-16. Compare the operation of the *D* latch with a negative-edge-triggered D flip-flop by applying the waveforms of Figure 5-69 to each and determining the *Q* waveforms.

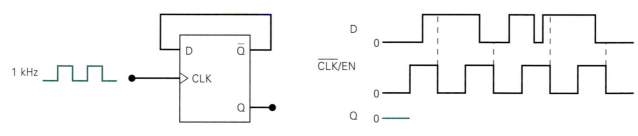

FIGURE 5-68   D flip-flop connected to toggle (Problems 5-14 and 5-15).

FIGURE 5-69   Problem 5-16.

5-17. In Problem 5-14 we saw how an edge-triggered D flip-flop can be operated in the toggle mode. Explain why this same idea will not work for a *D* latch.

SECTION 5-9

5-18. Determine the *Q* waveform for the FF in Figure 5-70. Assume that $Q = 0$ initially, and remember that the asynchronous inputs override all other inputs.

FIGURE 5-70   Problem 5-18.

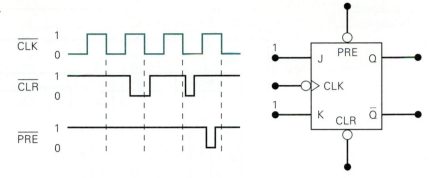

5-19. Apply the $\overline{CLK}$, $\overline{PRE}$, and $\overline{CLR}$ waveforms of Figure 5-31 to a positive-edge-triggered D flip-flop with active-LOW asynchronous inputs. Assume that D is kept HIGH and Q is initially LOW. Determine the Q waveform.

5-20. Examine the IEEE/ANSI symbol for the 74276 flip-flop IC in Figure 5-71.
   (a) Is it possible to set or clear individual flip-flops asynchronously without affecting the others?
   (b) What input conditions are necessary to cause output $1Q$ to toggle? (Note the overbar on the $\overline{K}$ inputs.)

FIGURE 5-71   Problem 5-20.

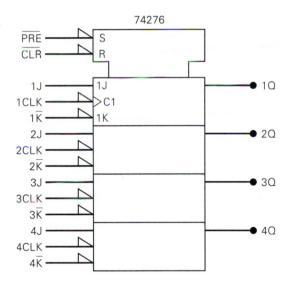

SECTION 5-11

5-21. Use Table 5-2 in Section 5-11 to determine the following.
   (a) How long can it take for the Q output of a 74C74 to switch from 0 to 1 in response to an active CLK transition?
   (b) Which FF in Table 5-2 requires its control inputs to remain stable for the longest time *after* the active CLK transition? *Before* the transition?
   (c) What is the narrowest pulse that can be applied to the $\overline{PRE}$ of a 7474 FF?

5-22. Refer to the circuit of Figure 5-72. It shows a 74LS112 IC with its two J-K flip-flops connected in a certain way. Assume that initially $Q_1 = Q_2 = 1$, and, using Table 5-2, determine the *total* propagation delay between the NGT of the clock pulse and the NGT of Q_2.

FIGURE 5-72 Connection diagram for Problem 5-22.

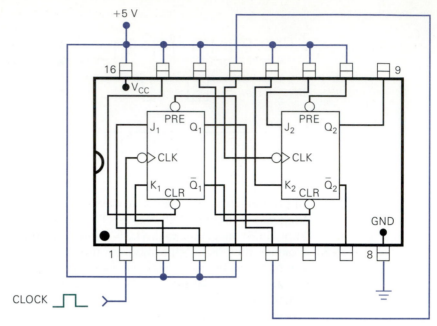

SECTIONS 5-15 AND 5-16

D   **5-23.** Modify the circuit of Figure 5-40 to use a J-K flip-flop.

D   **5-24.** In the circuit of Figure 5-73, inputs A, B, and C are all initially LOW. Output Y is supposed to go HIGH only when A, B, and C go HIGH in a certain sequence.

    (a) Determine the sequence that will make Y go HIGH.

    (b) Explain why the START pulse is needed.

    (c) Modify this circuit to use D FFs.

FIGURE 5-73 Problem 5-24.

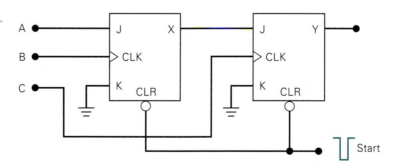

SECTIONS 5-17 AND 5-18

D   **5-25.** **(a)** Draw a circuit diagram for the synchronous parallel transfer of data from one three-bit register to another using J-K flip-flops.

    (b) Repeat for asynchronous parallel transfer.

   5-26. A *recirculating* shift register is a shift register that keeps the binary information circulating through the register as clock pulses are applied. The shift register of Figure 5-45 can be made into a circulating register by connecting X_0 to the DATA IN line. No external inputs are used. Assume that this circulating register starts out with 1011 stored in it (i.e., $X_3 = 1$, $X_2 = 0$, $X_1 = 1$, and $X_0 = 1$). List the sequence of states that the register FFs go through as eight shift pulses are applied.

D **5-27.** Refer to Figure 5-46, where a three-bit number stored in register X is serially shifted into register Y. How could the circuit be modified so that at the end of the transfer operation, the original number stored in X is present in both registers? (*Hint:* See Problem 5-26.)

SECTION 5-19

5-28. Refer to the binary counter of Figure 5-47. Change it by connecting $\overline{X}_0$ to the *CLK* of flip-flop X_1, and $\overline{X}_1$ to the *CLK* of flip-flop X_2. Start out with all FFs in the 1 state, and draw the various FF output waveforms (X_0, X_1, X_2) for 16 input pulses. Then list the sequence of FF states as was done in Figure 5-48. This counter is called a *down counter*. Why?

5-29. Draw the state transition diagram for this down counter, and compare it with the diagram of Figure 5-49. How are they different?

D **5-30.** Show how clocked D flip-flops can be used in a counter such as that in Figure 5-47. (*Hint:* See Problem 5-14.)

5-31. (a) How many FFs are required to build a binary counter that counts from 0 to 1023?

(b) Determine the frequency at the output of the last FF of this counter for an input clock frequency of 2 MHz.

(c) What is the counter's MOD number?

(d) If the counter is initially at zero, what count will it hold after 2060 pulses?

5-32. A binary counter is being pulsed by a 256-kHz clock signal. The output frequency from the last FF is 2 kHz.

(a) Determine the MOD number.

(b) Determine the counting range.

5-33. A photodetector circuit is being used to generate a pulse each time a customer walks into a certain establishment. The pulses are fed to an eight-bit counter. The counter is used to count these pulses as a means for determining how many customers have entered the store. After closing the store, the proprietor checks the counter and finds that it shows a count of $00001001_2 = 9_{10}$. He knows that this is incorrect, because there were many more than nine people in his store. Assuming that the counter circuit is working properly, what could be the reason for the discrepancy?

SECTION 5-20

D **5-34.** Modify the circuit of Figure 5-50 so that only the presence of address code 10110110 will allow data to be transferred to register X.

T **5-35.** Suppose that the circuit of Figure 5-50 is malfunctioning so that data are being transferred to X for either of the address codes 11111110 or 11111111. What are some circuit faults that could be causing this?

D **5-36.** Modify the circuit of Figure 5-50 so that the MPU has eight data output lines connected to transfer eight bits of data to an eight-bit register made up of two 74HC75 ICs [Figure 5-34(b)]. Show all circuit connections.

SECTION 5-22

N **5-37.** Figure 5-74 shows three nonretriggerable one-shots connected in a timing chain that produces three sequential output pulses. Note the "1" in front of the pulse on each OS symbol to indicate nonretriggerable operation. Draw a tim-

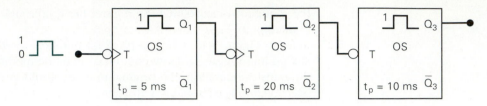

FIGURE 5-74 Problem 5-37.

ing diagram showing the relationship between the input pulse and the three OS outputs. Assume an input pulse duration of 10 ms.

5-38. A *retriggerable* OS can be used as a pulse-frequency detector that detects when the frequency of a pulse input is below a predetermined value. A simple example of this application is shown in Figure 5-75. The operation begins by momentarily closing switch SW1.

(a) Describe how the circuit responds to input frequencies above 1 kHz.

(b) Describe how the circuit responds to input frequencies below 1 kHz.

(c) How would you modify the circuit to detect when the input frequency drops below 50 kHz?

FIGURE 5-75 Problem 5-38.

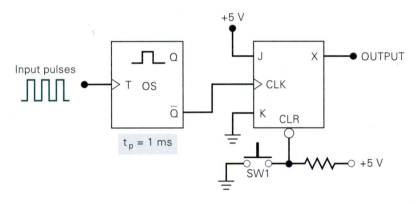

5-39. Refer to the logic symbol for a 74121 nonretriggerable one-shot in Figure 5-54(a).

(a) What input conditions are necessary for the OS to be triggered by a signal at the B input?

(b) What input conditions are necessary for the OS to be triggered by a signal at the A_1 input?

D, C 5-40. The output pulse width from a 74121 OS is given by the approximate formula

$$t_p \approx 0.7 \ R_T C_T$$

where R_T is the resistance connected between the R_{EXT}/C_{EXT} pin and V_{CC}, and C_T is the capacitance connected between the C_{EXT} pin and the R_{EXT}/C_{EXT} pin. The value for R_T can be varied between 2 and 40 kΩ, and C_T can be as large as 1000 μF.

(a) Show how a 74121 can be connected to produce a negative-going pulse with a 5-ms duration whenever either of two logic signals (E or F) makes a NGT. Both E and F are normally in the HIGH state.

(b) Modify the circuit so that a control input signal, *G*, can disable the OS output pulse regardless of what occurs at *E* or *F.*

SECTION 5-23

C   **5-41.** Consider the circuit of Figure 5-76. Initially all FFs are in the 0 state. The circuit operation begins with a momentary start pulse applied to the $\overline{\text{PRESET}}$ inputs of FFs *X* and *Y.* Determine the waveforms at *A, B, C, X, Y, Z,* and *W* for 20 cycles of the clock pulses after the start pulse. State all assumptions.

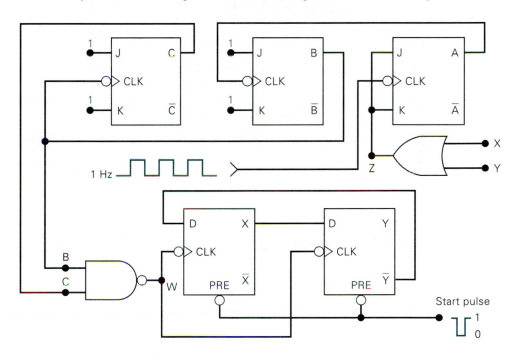

FIGURE 5-76   Problem 5-41.

SECTION 5-24

5-42. Show how to use a 74LS14 Schmitt-trigger INVERTER to produce an approximate square wave with a frequency of 10 kHz.

5-43. Design a 555 free-running oscillator to produce an approximate square wave at 40 kHz. *C* should be kept at 500 pF or greater.

5-44. A 555 oscillator can be combined with a J-K flip-flop to produce a perfect (50 percent duty cycle) square wave. Modify the circuit of Problem 5-43 to include a J-K flip-flop. The final output is still to be a 40-kHz square wave.

C, N   **5-45.** The circuit in Figure 5-77 can be used to generate two nonoverlapping clock signals at the same frequency. These clock signals are used in some microprocessor systems that require four different clock transitions to synchronize their operations.

(a) Draw the CP1 and CP2 timing waveforms if *CLOCK* is a 1-MHz square wave. Assume that t_{PLH} and t_{PHL} are 20 ns for the FF and 10 ns for the AND gates.

(b) This circuit would have a problem if the FF were changed to one that responds to a PGT at *CLK.* Draw the CP1 and CP2 waveforms for that situation. Pay particular attention to conditions that can produce glitches.

FIGURE 5-77   Problem 5-45.

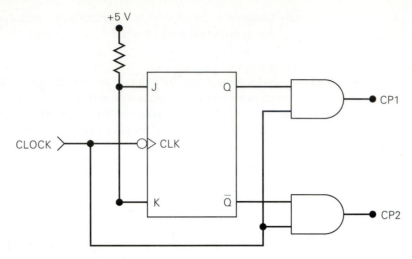

SECTION 5-25

T   **5-46.** Refer to the counter circuit in Figure 5-47. Assume that all asynchronous inputs are connected to V_{CC}. When tested, the circuit waveforms appear as shown in Figure 5-78. Consider the following list of possible faults. For each one indicate "yes" or "no" as to whether it could cause the observed results. Explain each response.

(a) *CLR* input of X_2 is open.

(b) X_1 output's transition times are too long, possibly due to loading.

(c) X_2 output is shorted to ground.

(d) X_2's hold time requirement is not being met.

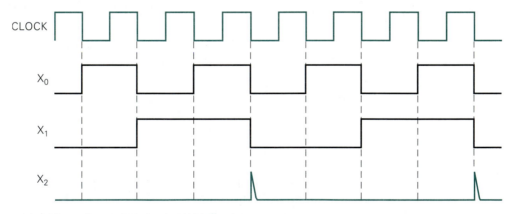

FIGURE 5-78   Problem 5-46.

T   **5-47.** Refer to the circuit of Figure 5-46. All FFs are TTL ICs. Assume the following initial conditions: $X_2X_1X_0 = 100$ and $Y_2Y_1Y_0 = 011$. After four shift pulses, the conditions are $X_2X_1X_0 = 001$ and $Y_2Y_1Y_0 = 111$. Subsequent shift pulses produce no change in any of the FFs. What are some of the possible causes of this faulty operation?

C, T   **5-48.** Consider the situation of Figure 5-61 for each of the following sets of timing values. For each indicate whether or not flip-flop Q_2 will respond correctly.

    (a) Each FF: t_{PLH} = 12 ns; t_{PHL} = 8 ns; t_S = 5 ns; t_H = 0 ns
        NAND gate: t_{PLH} = 8 ns; t_{PHL} = 6 ns
        INVERTER: t_{PLH} = 7 ns; t_{PHL} = 5 ns
    (b) Each FF: t_{PLH} = 10 ns; t_{PHL} = 8 ns; t_S = 5 ns; t_H = 0 ns
        NAND gate: t_{PLH} = 12 ns; t_{PHL} = 10 ns
        INVERTER: t_{PLH} = 8 ns; t_{PHL} = 6 ns

D   **5-49.** Show and explain how the clock skew problem in Figure 5-61 can be eliminated by the appropriate insertion of two INVERTERs.

T   **5-50.** Refer to the circuit of Figure 5-55. Describe how the circuit operation will change for each of the following faults.
    (a) An internal short to ground at the NAND gate's top input
    (b) An open connection to the *J* input of FF *Z*
    (c) An open connection to the bottom input of the NAND gate

T   **5-51.** Refer to the circuit of Figure 5-79. Assume that the ICs are of the TTL logic family. The *Q* waveform was obtained when the circuit was tested with the input signals shown and with the switch in the "up" position; it is not correct.

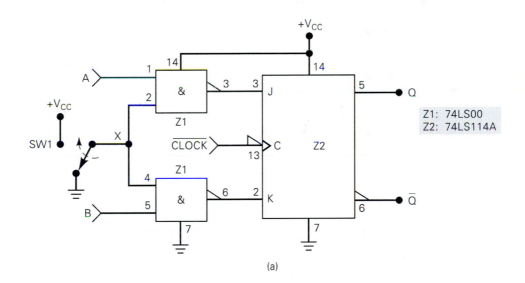

(a)

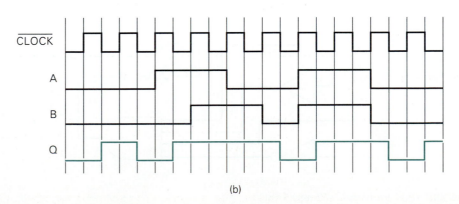

(b)

FIGURE 5-79   Problem 5-51.

Consider the following list of faults, and for each indicate "yes" or "no" as to whether it could be the actual fault. Explain each response.

(a) Point X is always LOW due to a faulty switch.

(b) Z1 pin 1 is internally shorted to V_{CC}.

(c) The connection from Z1-3 to Z2-3 is broken.

(d) There is a solder bridge between pins 6 and 7 of Z1.

C 5-52. The circuit of Figure 5-80 functions as a sequential combination lock. To operate the lock, proceed as follows:

1. Momentarily activate the RESET switch.

2. Set the switches SWA, SWB, and SWC to the first part of the combination. Then momentarily toggle the ENTER switch back and forth.

3. Set the switches to the second part of the combination, and toggle ENTER again. This should produce a HIGH at Q_2 to open the lock.

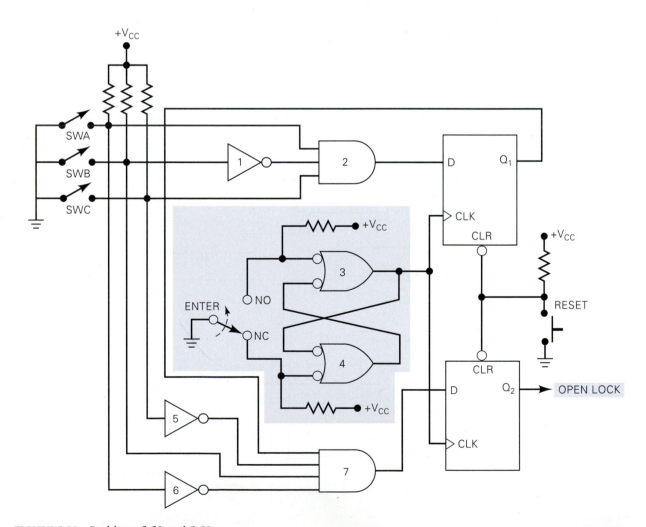

FIGURE 5-80 Problems 5-52 and 5-53.

If the incorrect combination is entered in either step, the operator must start the sequence over. Analyze the circuit and determine the correct sequence of combinations that will open the lock.

C, T   5-53. When the combination lock of Figure 5-80 is tested, it is found that entering the correct combination does not open the lock. A logic probe check shows that entering the correct first combination sets Q_1 HIGH, but entering the correct second combination produces only a momentary pulse at Q_2. Consider each of the following faults and indicate which one(s) could produce the observed operation. Explain each choice.
(a) Switch bounce at SWA, SWB, or SWC.
(b) *CLR* input of Q_2 is open.
(c) Connection from NAND gate 4 output to NAND gate 3 input is open.

DRILL QUESTIONS
5-54. For each statement indicate what type of FF is being described.
(a) Has a SET and a CLEAR input but does not have a *CLK* input
(b) Will toggle on each *CLK* pulse when its control inputs are both HIGH
(c) Has an ENABLE input instead of a *CLK* input
(d) Is used to easily transfer data from one FF register to another
(e) Has only one control input
(f) Has two outputs that are complements of each other
(g) Can change states only on the active transition of *CLK*
(h) Is used in binary counters
5-55. Define the following terms.
(a) Asynchronous inputs
(b) Edge-triggered
(c) Shift register
(d) Frequency division
(e) Asynchronous (jam) transfer
(f) State transition diagram
(g) Parallel data transfer
(h) Serial data transfer
(i) Retriggerable one-shot
(j) Schmitt-trigger inputs

ANSWERS TO SECTION REVIEW QUESTIONS

SECTION 5-1
1. HIGH; LOW   2. $Q = 0$, $\overline{Q} = 1$ 3. True
4. Apply a momentary LOW to $\overline{SET}$ input.

SECTION 5-2
1. LOW, HIGH   2. $Q = 1$ and $\overline{Q} = 0$ 3. Make $\overline{CLEAR} = 1$ 4. $\overline{SET}$ and $\overline{CLEAR}$ would both be normally in their active-LOW state.

SECTION 5-4
1. Synchronous control inputs and clock input
2. The FF output can change only when the appropriate

clock transition occurs.   3. False   4. Setup time is the required interval immediately prior to the active edge of the *CLK* signal during which the control inputs must be held stable. Hold time is the required interval immediately following the active edge of *CLK* during which the control inputs must be held stable.

SECTION 5-5
1. It will go HIGH.   2. Because *CLK** is HIGH only for a few nanoseconds

SECTION 5-6
1. True   2. No   3. $J = 1$, $K = 0$

SECTION 5-7

1. Q will go LOW at point a and remain LOW.
2. False. The D input can change without affecting Q because Q can change only on the active CLK edge.
3. Yes

SECTION 5-8

1. In a D latch the Q output can change while EN is HIGH. In a D flip-flop the output can change only on the active edge of CLK.   2. False   3. True

SECTION 5-9

1. Asynchronous inputs work independently of the CLK input.   2. Yes, since $\overline{PRE}$ is active-LOW
3. $J = K = 1$, $\overline{PRE} = \overline{CLR} = 1$, and a PGT at CLK

SECTION 5-10

1. The triangle inside the rectangle indicates edge-triggered operation; the right triangle outside the rectangle indicates triggering on a NGT.   2. It is used to indicate the function of those inputs that are common to more than one circuit on the chip.

SECTION 5-11

1. t_{PLH} and t_{PHL} 2. False; the waveform must also satisfy $t_W(L)$ and $t_W(H)$ requirements.

SECTION 5-17

1. False   2. D flip-flop   3. Six   4. True

SECTION 5-18

1. True   2. Fewer interconnections between registers
3. $X_2X_1X_0 = 111$; $Y_2Y_1Y_0 = 101$ 4. Parallel

SECTION 5-19

1. 10 kHz   2. Eight   3. 256   4. 2 kHz
5. $00001000_2 = 8_{10}$

SECTION 5-21

1. The output may contain oscillations.   2. It will produce clean, fast output signals even for slow-changing input signals.

SECTION 5-22

1. $Q = 0$, $\overline{Q} = 1$ 2. True   3. External R and C values   4. For a retriggerable OS, each new trigger pulse begins a new t_p interval regardless of the state of the Q output.

SECTION 5-24

1. 24 kHz   2. 109.3 kHz; 66.7 percent
3. Frequency stability

SECTION 5-25

1. Clock skew is the arrival of a clock signal at the CLK inputs of different FFs at different times. It can cause a FF to go to an incorrect state.

CHAPTER 6

Digital Arithmetic: Operations and Circuits

■ OUTLINE

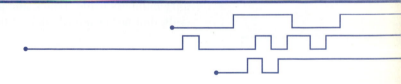

■ OBJECTIVES

Upon completion of this chapter, you will be able to:

- Perform binary addition, subtraction, multiplication, and division on two binary numbers.
- Add and subtract hexadecimal numbers.
- Know the difference between binary addition and OR addition.
- Compare the advantages and disadvantages among three different systems of representing signed binary numbers.
- Manipulate signed binary numbers using the 2's-complement system.
- Understand the BCD adder circuit and the BCD addition process.
- Describe the basic operation of an arithmetic/logic unit.
- Employ full adders in the design of parallel binary adders.
- Cite the advantages of parallel adders with the look-ahead carry feature.
- Explain the operation of a parallel adder/subtractor circuit.
- Use an ALU integrated circuit to perform various logic and arithmetic operations on input data.
- Read and understand the IEEE/ANSI symbol for a parallel adder.
- Analyze troubleshooting case studies of adder/subtractor circuits.

■ INTRODUCTION

Digital computers and calculators perform the various arithmetic operations on numbers that are represented in binary form. The subject of digital arithmetic can be a very complex one if we want to understand all of the various methods of computation and the theory behind them. Fortunately, this level of knowledge is not required by most technicians, at least not until they become experienced computer programmers. Our approach in this chapter will be to concentrate on those basic principles that are needed to understand how digital machines (i.e., computers) perform the basic arithmetic operations.

First we will see how the various arithmetic operations are performed on binary numbers using "pencil and paper," and then we will study the actual logic circuits that perform these operations in a digital system.

6-1 BINARY ADDITION

The addition of two binary numbers is performed in exactly the same manner as the addition of decimal numbers. In fact, binary addition is simpler, since there are fewer cases to learn. Let us first review decimal addition:

$$
\begin{array}{cccc}
 & 3 & 7 & 6 \quad \text{LSD} \\
+ & 4 & 6 & 1 \\
\hline
 & 8 & 3 & 7
\end{array}
$$

The least-significant-digit (LSD) position is operated on first, producing a sum of 7. The digits in the second position are then added to produce a sum of 13, which produces a **carry** of 1 into the third position. This produces a sum of 8 in the third position.

The same general steps are followed in binary addition. However, only four cases can occur in adding the two binary digits (bits) in any position. They are:

$$0 + 0 = 0$$
$$1 + 0 = 1$$
$$1 + 1 = 10 = 0 + \text{carry of 1 into next position}$$
$$1 + 1 + 1 = 11 = 1 + \text{carry of 1 into next position}$$

The last case occurs when the two bits in a certain position are 1 and there is a carry from the previous position. Here are several examples of the addition of two binary numbers (decimal equivalents are in parentheses):

$$
\begin{array}{ccc}
011 \ (3) & 1001 \ (9) & 11.011 \ (3.375) \\
+ \ \ 110 \ (6) & + \ \ 1111 \ (15) & + \ \ 10.110 \ (2.750) \\
\hline
1001 \ (9) & 11000 \ (24) & 110.001 \ (6.125)
\end{array}
$$

It is not necessary to consider the addition of more than two binary numbers at a time, because in all digital systems the circuitry that actually performs the addition can handle only two numbers at a time. When more than two numbers are to be added, the first two are added together and then their sum is added to the third number; and so on. This is not a serious drawback, since modern digital computers can typically perform an addition operation in several nanoseconds.

Addition is the most important arithmetic operation in digital systems. As we shall see, the operations of subtraction, multiplication, and division as they are performed in most modern digital computers and calculators actually use only addition as their basic operation.

Review Questions   1. Add the following pairs of binary numbers.

(a) $10110 + 00111$ (b) $011.101 + 010.010$ (c) $10001111 + 00000001$

6-2 REPRESENTING SIGNED NUMBERS

In digital computers, the binary numbers are represented by a set of binary storage devices (usually flip-flops). Each device represents one bit. For example, a six bit FF register could store binary numbers ranging from 000000 to 111111 (0 to 63 in decimal). This represents the *magnitude* of the number. Since most digital computers and calculators handle negative as well as positive numbers, some means is required for representing the *sign* of the number (+ or −). This is usually done by adding to the number another bit called the **sign bit.** In general, the common convention which has been adopted is that a 0 in the sign bit represents a positive number and a 1 in the sign bit represents a negative number. This is illustrated in Figure 6-1. Register A contains the bits 0110100. The 0 in the leftmost bit (A_6) is the sign bit that represents +. The other six bits are the magnitude of the number 110100_2, which is equal to 52 in decimal. Thus, the number stored in the A register is +52. Similarly, the number stored in the B register is −52, since the sign bit is 1, representing −.

FIGURE 6-1   Representation of signed numbers in sign-magnitude form.

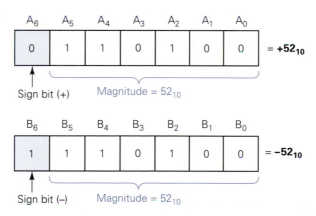

The sign bit is used to indicate the positive or negative nature of the stored binary number. The numbers in Figure 6-1 consist of a sign bit and six magnitude bits. The magnitude bits are the true binary equivalent of the decimal value being represented. This is called the **sign-magnitude system** for representing signed binary numbers.

Although the sign-magnitude system is straightforward, calculators and computers do not normally use it, because the circuit implementation is more complex than in other systems. The most commonly used system for representing signed binary numbers is the **2's-complement system.** Before we see how this is done, we must first see how to form the 1's complement and 2's complement of a binary number.

1's-Complement Form

The 1's complement of a binary number is obtained by changing each 0 to a 1 and each 1 to a 0. In other words, change each bit in the number to its complement. The process is shown below.

```
1  0  1  1  0  1     original binary number
↓  ↓  ↓  ↓  ↓  ↓
0  1  0  0  1  0     complement each bit to form 1's complement
```

Thus, we say that the 1's complement of 101101 is 010010.

2's Complement Form

The 2's complement of a binary number is formed by taking the 1's complement of the number and adding 1 to the least-significant-bit position. The process is illustrated below for $101101_2 = 45_{10}$.

```
  1 0 1 1 0 1     binary equivalent of 45
  0 1 0 0 1 0     complement each bit to form 1's complement
+         1       add 1 to form 2's complement
  0 1 0 0 1 1     2's complement of original binary number
```

Thus, we say that 010011 is the 2's complement representation of 101101.

Here's another example of converting a binary number to its 2's-complement representation:

```
  1 0 1 1 0 0     original binary number
  0 1 0 0 1 1     1's complement
+         1       add 1
  0 1 0 1 0 0     2's complement of original number
```

Representing Signed Numbers Using 2's Complement

The 2's-complement system for representing signed numbers works like this:

■ If the number is positive, the magnitude is represented in its true binary form, and a sign bit of 0 is placed in front of the MSB. This is shown in Figure 6-2 for $+45_{10}$.

■ If the number is negative, the magnitude is represented in its 2's-complement form, and a sign bit of 1 is placed in front of the MSB. This is shown in Figure 6-2 for -45_{10}.

FIGURE 6-2 Representation of signed numbers in the 2's-complement system.

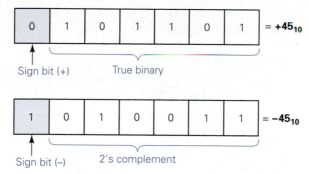

The 2's-complement system is used to represent signed numbers because, as we shall see, it allows us to perform the operation of subtraction by actually performing addition. This is significant because it means that a digital computer can use the same circuitry to both add and subtract, thereby realizing a saving in hardware.

EXAMPLE 6-1

Represent each of the following signed decimal numbers as a signed binary number in the 2's-complement system. Use a total of five bits including the sign bit.
(a) +13 (b) −9 (c) +3 (d) −2 (e) −8

Solution

(a) Since the number is positive, the magnitude (13) will be represented in its true-magnitude form, that is, $13 = 1101_2$. Attaching the sign bit of 0, we have

$$+13 = 01101$$
sign bit ⬏

(b) Since the number is negative, the magnitude (9) must be represented in 2's-complement form:

$$9_{10} = 1001_2$$

$$\begin{array}{ll} 0110 & \text{(1's complement)} \\ +\underline{1} & \text{(add 1 to LSB)} \\ 0111 & \text{(2's complement)} \end{array}$$

When we attach the sign bit of 1, the complete signed number becomes

$$-9 = 10111$$
sign bit ⬏

The procedure we have just followed required two steps. First we determined the 2's complement of the magnitude, and then we attached the sign bit. This can be accomplished in one step if we include the sign bit in the 2's-complement process. For example, to find the representation for −9, we start with the representation for $+9$, *including the sign bit,* and we take the 2's complement of it in order to obtain the representation for -9.

$$+9 = 01001$$
$$10110 \qquad \text{(1's complement of each bit including sign bit)}$$
$$+\underline{1} \qquad \text{(add 1 to LSB)}$$
$$10111 \qquad \text{(2's-complement representation of } -9)$$

The result is, of course, the same as before.

(c) The decimal value 3 can be represented in binary using only two bits. However, the problem statement requires a four-bit magnitude preceded by a sign bit. Thus, we have

$$+3_{10} = 00011$$

In many situations the number of bits is fixed by the size of the registers that will be holding the binary numbers, so that 0s may have to be added in order to fill the required number of bit positions.

(d) Start by writing $+2$ using five bits:

$$+2 = 00010$$
$$11101 \qquad \text{(1's complement)}$$
$$+\underline{1} \qquad \text{(add 1)}$$
$$\mathbf{11110} \qquad \text{(2's-complement representation of } -2)$$

(e) Start with $+8$:

$$+8 = 01000$$
$$10111 \qquad \text{(complement each bit)}$$
$$+\underline{1} \qquad \text{(add 1)}$$
$$\mathbf{11000} \qquad \text{(2's-complement representation of } -8)$$

Negation

Negation is the operation of converting a positive number to its negative equivalent or a negative number to its positive equivalent. When signed binary numbers are represented in the 2's-complement system, negation is performed simply by performing the 2's-complement operation. To illustrate, let's start with $+9$. Its signed representation is 01001. If we 2's-complement this, we get 10111. Clearly, this is a negative number since the sign bit is a 1. Actually, 10111 represents -9, which is the negative equivalent of the number we started with. Likewise, we can start with the representation for -9, which is 10111. If we 2's-complement this, we get 01001, which we recognize as $+9$. These steps are diagrammed below.

$$\text{start with} \rightarrow 01001 = +9$$
$$\text{2's-complement (negate)} \rightarrow 10111 = -9$$
$$\text{negate again} \rightarrow 01001 = +9$$

Thus, we negate a signed binary number by 2's-complementing it.

This negation changes the number to its equivalent of opposite sign. We used negation in steps (d) and (e) of Example 6-1 to convert positive numbers to their negative equivalents.

EXAMPLE 6-2

Each of the following numbers is a signed binary number in the 2's-complement system. Determine the decimal value in each case:
(a) 01100   (b) 11010   (c) 10001

Solution

(a) The sign bit is 0, so the number is *positive* and the other four bits represent the true magnitude of the number. That is, $1100_2 = 12_{10}$. Thus, the decimal number is **+12**.

(b) The sign bit of 11010 is a 1, so we know that the number is negative, but we can't tell what the magnitude is. We can find the magnitude by negating (2's-complementing) the number to convert it to its positive equivalent.

$$
\begin{array}{ll}
11010 & \text{(original negative number)} \\
00101 & \text{(1's complement)} \\
+\underline{\quad\quad 1} & \text{(add 1)} \\
00110 & \text{(+6)}
\end{array}
$$

Since the result of the negation is 00110 = +6, the original number 11010 must be equivalent to **−6**.

(c) Follow the same procedure as in (b):

$$
\begin{array}{ll}
10001 & \text{(original negative number)} \\
01110 & \text{(1's complement)} \\
+\underline{\quad\quad 1} & \text{(add 1)} \\
01111 & \text{(+15)}
\end{array}
$$

Thus, 10001 = **−15**.

Special Case in 2's-Complement Representation

Whenever a signed number has a 1 in the sign bit and all 0s for the magnitude bits, its decimal equivalent is -2^N, where N is the number of bits in the *magnitude*. For example,

$$
\begin{array}{l}
1000 = -2^3 = -8 \\
10000 = -2^4 = -16 \\
100000 = -2^5 = -32
\end{array}
$$

and so on.

Thus, we can state that the complete range of values that can be represented in the 2's-complement system having N magnitude bits is

$$-2^N \text{ to } +(2^N - 1)$$

There are a total of 2^{N+1} different values, *including* zero.

For example, Table 6-1 lists all signed numbers that can be represented in four bits using the 2's-complement system (note there are three magnitude bits, so $N = 3$). Note that the sequence starts at $-2^N = -2^3 = -8_{10} = 1000_2$ and proceeds upwards to $+(2^N - 1) = +2^3 - 1 = +7_{10} = 0111_2$ by adding 0001 at each step as in an up counter.

TABLE 6-1

Decimal Value	Signed Binary Using 2's Complement
$+7 = 2^3 - 1$	0111
$+6$	0110
$+5$	0101
$+4$	0100
$+3$	0011
$+2$	0010
$+1$	0001
0	0000
-1	1111
-2	1110
-3	1101
-4	1100
-5	1011
-6	1010
-7	1001
$-8 = -2^3$	1000

EXAMPLE 6-3

What is the range of *unsigned* decimal values that can be represented in a byte?

Solution

Recall that a byte is eight bits. Since we are interested in unsigned numbers here, there is no sign bit, so all of the eight bits are used for the magnitude. Therefore, the values will range from

$$00000000_2 = 0_{10}$$

to

$$11111111_2 = 255_{10}$$

This is a total of 256 different values, which we could have predicted since $2^8 = 256$.

EXAMPLE
6-4

What is the range of *signed* decimal values that can be represented in a byte?

Solution

Since the MSB is to be used as the sign bit, there are seven bits for the magnitude. The largest negative value is

$$10000000_2 = -2^7 = -128_{10}$$

The largest positive value is

$$01111111_2 = +2^7 - 1 = +127_{10}$$

Thus, the range is -128 to $+127$; this is a total of 256 different values, including zero. Alternatively, since there are seven magnitude bits ($N = 7$), then there are $2^{N+1} = 2^8 = 256$ different values.

EXAMPLE
6-5

A certain computer is storing the following two signed numbers in its memory using the 2's-complement system:

$$00011111_2 = +31_{10}$$
$$11110100_2 = -12_{10}$$

While executing a program, the computer is instructed to convert each number to its opposite sign; that is, change the $+31$ to -31 and change the -12 to $+12$. How will it do this?

Solution

This is simply the negation operation whereby a signed number can have its polarity changed simply by performing the 2's-complement operation on the *complete* number, including the sign bit. The computer circuitry will take the signed number from memory, find its 2's complement, and put the result back in memory.

1. Represent each of the following values as an eight-bit signed number in the 2's-complement system.

   (a) +13   (b) −7   (c) −128

2. Each of the following is a signed binary number in the 2's-complement system. Determine the decimal equivalent for each.

   (a) 100011   (b) 1000000   (c) 01111110

3. What range of signed decimal values can be represented in 12 bits (including the sign bit)?

4. How many bits are required to represent decimal values ranging from −50 to +50?

5. What is the largest negative decimal value that can be represented by a two-byte number?

6. Perform the 2's-complement operation on each of the following.

   (a) 10000   (b) 10000000   (c) 1000

7. Define the negation operation.

6-3   ADDITION IN THE 2's-COMPLEMENT SYSTEM

We will now investigate how the operations of addition and subtraction are performed in digital machines that use the 2's-complement representation for negative numbers. In the various cases to be considered, it is important to note that the sign bit of each number is operated on in the same manner as the magnitude bits.

Case I: Two Positive Numbers.   The addition of two positive numbers is straightforward. Consider the addition of +9 and +4:

$$
\begin{array}{rccl}
+9 \rightarrow & 0 & 1001 & \text{(augend)} \\
+4 \rightarrow & 0 & 0100 & \text{(addend)} \\
\hline
 & 0 & 1101 & \text{(sum} = +13) \\
\end{array}
$$

sign bits

Note that the sign bits of the **augend** and the **addend** are both 0 and the sign bit of the sum is 0, indicating that the sum is positive. Also note that the augend and the addend are made to have the same number of bits. This must *always* be done in the 2's-complement system.

Case II: Positive Number and Smaller Negative Number.   Consider the addition of +9 and −4. Remember that the −4 will be in its 2's-complement form. Thus, +4 (00100) must be converted to −4 (11100).

sign bits

$$
\begin{array}{rccl}
+9 \rightarrow & 0 & 1001 & \text{(augend)} \\
-4 \rightarrow & 1 & 1100 & \text{(addend)} \\
\hline
1 & 0 & 0101 & \\
\end{array}
$$

This carry is disregarded; the result is 00101 (sum = +5).

In this case, the sign bit of the addend is 1. Note that the sign bits also participate in the addition process. In fact, a carry is generated in the last position of addition. *This carry is always disregarded,* so that the final sum is 00101, which is equivalent to +5.

Case III: Positive Number and Larger Negative Number.   Consider the addition of −9 and +4:

$$
\begin{array}{r}
-9 \rightarrow \quad 10111 \\
+4 \rightarrow \quad 00100 \\
\hline
11011 \quad (\text{sum} = -5)
\end{array}
$$

↑ negative sign bit

The sum here has a sign bit of 1, indicating a negative number. Since the sum is negative, it is in 2's-complement form, so that the last four bits, 1011, actually represent the 2's complement of the sum. To find the true magnitude of the sum, we must negate (2's-complement) 11011; the result is 00101 = +5. Thus, 11011 represents −5.

Case IV: Two Negative Numbers

$$
\begin{array}{r}
-9 \rightarrow \quad 10111 \\
-4 \rightarrow \quad 11100 \\
\hline
1 \; 10011
\end{array}
$$

↑ ↑ sign bit
This carry is disregarded; the result is 10011 (sum = −13).

This final result is again negative and in 2's-complement form with a sign bit of 1. Negating (2's-complementing) this result produces 01101 = +13.

Case V: Equal and Opposite Numbers

$$
\begin{array}{r}
-9 \rightarrow \quad 10111 \\
+9 \rightarrow \quad 01001 \\
\hline
0 \quad 1 \; 00000
\end{array}
$$

↑ Disregard; the result is 00000 (sum = +0).

The result is obviously +0, as expected.

Review Questions

Assume the 2's-complement system for both questions.

1. *True or false:* Whenever the sum of two signed binary numbers has a sign bit of 1, the magnitude of the sum is in 2's-complement form.

2. Add the following pairs of signed numbers. Express the sum as a signed binary number and as a decimal number.

   (a) 100111 + 111011   (b) 100111 + 011001

6-4 SUBTRACTION IN THE 2's-COMPLEMENT SYSTEM

The subtraction operation using the 2's-complement system actually involves the operation of addition and is really no different from the various cases for addition considered in Section 6-3. When subtracting one binary number (the **subtrahend**) from another binary number (the **minuend**), use the following procedure:

1. **Negate the subtrahend.** This will change the subtrahend to its equivalent value of opposite sign.

2. **Add this to the minuend.** The result of this addition will represent the *difference* between the subtrahend and the minuend.

Once again, as in all 2's-complement arithmetic operations, it is necessary that both numbers have the same number of bits in their representations.

Let us consider the case where +4 is to be subtracted from +9.

$$\text{minuend } (+9) \rightarrow \quad 01001$$
$$\text{subtrahend } (+4) \rightarrow \quad 00100$$

Negate the subtrahend to produce 11100, which represents −4. Now add this to the minuend.

$$
\begin{array}{ll}
01001 & (+9) \\
+\ 11100 & (-4) \\
\hline
1\ 00101 & (+5)
\end{array}
$$

⌐ Disregard, so the result is 00101 = +5.

When the subtrahend is changed to its 2's complement, it actually becomes −4, so that we are *adding* −4 and +9, which is the same as subtracting +4 from +9. This is the same as case II of Section 6-3. Any subtraction operation, then, actually becomes one of addition when the 2's-complement system is used. This feature of the 2's-complement system has made it the most widely used of the methods available, since it allows addition and subtraction to be performed by the same circuitry.

The reader should verify the results of using the above procedure for the following subtractions: (a) +9 − (−4); (b) −9 − (+4); (c) −9 − (−4); (d) +4 − (−4). Remember that when the result has a sign bit of 1, it is negative and in 2's-complement form.

Arithmetic Overflow

In each of the previous addition and subtraction examples, the numbers that were added consisted of a sign bit and four magnitude bits. The answers also consisted of a sign bit and four magnitude bits. Any carry into the sixth bit position was disregarded. In all of the cases considered, the magnitude of the answer was small enough to fit into four bits. Let's look at the addition of +9 and +8.

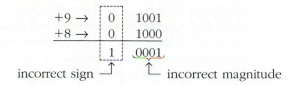

incorrect sign ⤴   ⤴ incorrect magnitude

The answer has a negative sign bit, which is obviously incorrect since we are adding two positive numbers. The answer should be +17, but the magnitude 17 requires more than four bits and therefore *overflows* into the sign-bit position. This **overflow** condition can occur only when two positive or two negative numbers are being added, and it always produces an incorrect result. Its occurrence is detected by examining the sign bit of the result and comparing it with the sign bits of the numbers being added. In a computer, a special circuit is used to detect any overflow condition and to signal that the answer is erroneous. We will encounter such a circuit in one of the end-of-chapter problems.

Review Questions

1. Perform the subtraction on the following pairs of signed numbers using the 2's-complement system. Express the results as signed binary numbers and as decimal values.

    (a) $01001 - 11010$ **(b)** $10010 - 10011$

2. How can arithmetic overflow be detected when signed numbers are being added?

6-5   MULTIPLICATION OF BINARY NUMBERS

The multiplication of binary numbers is done in the same manner as the multiplication of decimal numbers. The process is actually simpler, since the multiplier digits are either 0 or 1 and so we are always multiplying by 0 or 1 and no other digits. The following example illustrates for unsigned binary numbers:

1001	← multiplicand = 9_{10}
1011	← multiplier = 11_{10}
1001	
1001	
0000	partial products
1001	
1100011	final product = 99_{10}

In this example the multiplicand and the multiplier are in true binary form and no sign bits are used. The steps followed in the process are exactly the same as in decimal multiplication. First, the LSB of the multiplier is examined; in our example it is a 1. This 1 multiplies the multiplicand to produce 1001, which is written down as the first partial product. Next, the second bit of the multiplier is examined. It is a 1, and so 1001 is written for the second partial product. Note that this second partial product is *shifted* one place to the left relative to the first one. The third bit of the multiplier is 0, and 0000 is written as the third partial product; again, it is shifted one place to the left relative to the previous partial product. The fourth multiplier bit is 1, and so the last partial product is 1001 shifted again one position to the left. The four partial products are then summed to produce the final product.

Most digital machines can add only two binary numbers at a time. For this reason, the partial products formed during multiplication cannot all be added together at the same time. Instead, they are added together two at a time; that is, the first is added to the second, their sum is added to the third, and so on. This process is now illustrated for the example above:

$$
\text{Add} \begin{cases} \quad 1001 & \leftarrow \text{first partial product} \\ \underline{\quad 1001} & \leftarrow \text{second partial product shifted left} \end{cases}
$$

$$
\text{Add} \begin{cases} \quad 11011 & \leftarrow \text{sum of first two partial products} \\ \underline{\quad 0000} & \leftarrow \text{third partial product shifted left} \end{cases}
$$

$$
\text{Add} \begin{cases} \quad 011011 & \leftarrow \text{sum of first three partial products} \\ \underline{1001} & \leftarrow \text{fourth partial product shifted left} \end{cases}
$$

$$
1100011 \quad \leftarrow \text{sum of four partial products which equals final total product}
$$

Multiplication in the 2's-Complement System

In computers that use the 2's-complement representation, multiplication is carried on in the manner described above provided that both the multiplicand and the multiplier are put in true binary form. If the two numbers to be multiplied are positive, they are already in true binary form and are multiplied as they are. The resulting product is, of course, positive and is given a sign bit of 0. When the two numbers are negative, they will be in 2's-complement form. The 2's complement of each is taken to convert it to a positive number, and then the two numbers are multiplied. The product is kept as a positive number and is given a sign bit of 0.

When one of the numbers is positive and the other is negative, the negative number is first converted to a positive magnitude by taking its 2's complement. The product will be in true-magnitude form. However, the product must be negative, since the original numbers are of opposite sign. Thus, the product is then changed to 2's-complement form and is given a sign bit of 1.

Review Questions   1. Multiply the unsigned numbers 0111 and 1110.

6-6   BINARY DIVISION

The process for dividing one binary number (the *dividend*) by another (the *divisor*) is the same as that which is followed for decimal numbers, that which we usually refer to as "long division." The actual process is simpler in binary because when we are checking to see how many times the divisor "goes into" the dividend, there are only two possibilities, 0 or 1. To illustrate, consider the following simple division examples:

$$
\begin{array}{r}
0011 \\
11{\overline{\smash{\big)}\,1001}} \\
\underline{011} \\
0011 \\
\underline{11} \\
0
\end{array}
\qquad
\begin{array}{r}
0010.1 \\
100{\overline{\smash{\big)}\,1010.0}} \\
\underline{100} \\
100 \\
\underline{100} \\
0
\end{array}
$$

In the first example, we have 1001_2 divided by 11_2 which is equivalent to $9 \div 3$ in decimal. The resulting quotient is $0011_2 = 3_{10}$. In the second example, 1010_2 is divided by 100_2, or $10 \div 4$ in decimal. The result is $0010.1_2 = 2.5_{10}$.

In most modern digital machines the subtractions that are part of the division operation are usually carried out using 2's-complement subtraction, that is, taking the 2's complement of the subtrahend and then adding.

The division of signed numbers is handled in the same way as multiplication. Negative numbers are made positive by complementing, and the division is then carried out. If the dividend and the divisor are of opposite sign, the resulting quotient is changed to a negative number by taking its 2's-complement and is given a sign bit of 1. If the dividend and the divisor are of the same sign, the quotient is left as a positive number and is given a sign bit of 0.

6-7 BCD ADDITION

In Chapter 2 we stated that many computers and calculators use the BCD code to represent decimal numbers. Recall that this code takes *each* decimal digit and represents it by a four-bit code ranging from 0000 to 1001. The addition of decimal numbers that are in BCD form can be best understood by considering the two cases that can occur when two decimal digits are added.

Sum Equals 9 or Less

Consider adding 5 and 4 using BCD to represent each digit:

$$
\begin{array}{rll}
5 & 0101 & \leftarrow \text{BCD for } 5 \\
+4 & +\ 0100 & \leftarrow \text{BCD for } 4 \\
\hline
9 & 1001 & \leftarrow \text{BCD for } 9
\end{array}
$$

The addition is carried out as in normal binary addition, and the sum is 1001, which is the BCD code for 9. As another example, take 45 added to 33:

$$
\begin{array}{rlll}
45 & 0100 & 0101 & \leftarrow \text{BCD for } 45 \\
+33 & +\ 0011 & 0011 & \leftarrow \text{BCD for } 33 \\
\hline
78 & 0111 & 1000 & \leftarrow \text{BCD for } 78
\end{array}
$$

In this example the four-bit codes for 5 and 3 are added in binary to produce 1000, which is BCD for 8. Similarly, adding the second-decimal-digit positions produces 0111, which is BCD for 7. The total is 01111000, which is the BCD code for 78.

In the examples above, none of the sums of the pairs of decimal digits exceeded 9; therefore, *no decimal carries were produced*. For these cases the BCD addition process is straightforward and is actually the same as binary addition.

Sum Greater Than 9

Consider the addition of 6 and 7 in BCD:

$$
\begin{array}{rl}
6 & 0110 \quad \leftarrow \text{BCD for 6} \\
+7 & +\ \underline{0111} \quad \leftarrow \text{BCD for 7} \\
\hline
+13 & 1101 \quad \leftarrow \text{invalid code group for BCD}
\end{array}
$$

The sum 1101 does not exist in the BCD code; it is one of the six forbidden or invalid four-bit code groups. This has occurred because the sum of the two digits exceeds 9. Whenever this occurs, the sum must be corrected by the addition of six (0110) to take into account the skipping of the six invalid code groups:

$$
\begin{array}{cc}
 & 0110 \quad \leftarrow \text{BCD for 6} \\
+ & \underline{0111} \quad \leftarrow \text{BCD for 7} \\
 & 1101 \quad \leftarrow \text{invalid sum} \\
 & \underline{0110} \quad \leftarrow \text{add 6 for correction} \\
\underline{0001} & 0011 \quad \leftarrow \text{BCD for 13} \\
\underbrace{}_{1} & \underbrace{}_{3}
\end{array}
$$

As shown above, 0110 is added to the invalid sum and produces the correct BCD result. Note that a carry is produced into the second decimal position. This addition of 0110 must be performed whenever the sum of the two decimal digits is greater than 9.

As another example, take 47 plus 35 in BCD:

$$
\begin{array}{rll}
47 & 0100 & 0111 \quad \leftarrow \text{BCD for 47} \\
+35 & +\ \underline{0011} & 0101 \quad \leftarrow \text{BCD for 35} \\
\hline
82 & 0111 & 1100 \quad \leftarrow \text{invalid sum in first digit} \\
 & 1\leftarrow & \underline{0110} \quad \leftarrow \text{add 6 to correct} \\
 & \underline{1000} & \underline{}\ 0010 \quad \leftarrow \text{correct BCD sum} \\
 & \underbrace{}_{8} & \underbrace{}_{2}
\end{array}
$$

The addition of the four-bit codes for the 7 and 5 digits results in an invalid sum and is corrected by adding 0110. Note that this generates a carry of 1, which is carried over to be added to the BCD sum of the second-position digits.

Consider the addition of 59 and 38 in BCD:

```
                    1
    59     0101  │ 1001    ← BCD for 59
   +38   + 0011  │ 1000    ← BCD for 38
    97     1001    0001    ← perform addition
                   0110    ← add 6 to correct
           1001    0111      BCD for 97
            9        7
```

Here, the addition of the least significant digits (LSDs) produces a sum of $17 = 10001$. This generates a carry into the next digit position to be added to the codes for 5 and 3. Since $17 > 9$, a correction factor of 6 must be added to the LSD sum. Addition of this correction does not generate a carry; the carry was already generated in the original addition.

To summarize the BCD addition procedure:

1. Using ordinary binary addition, add the BCD code groups for each digit position.
2. For those positions where the sum is 9 or less, no correction is needed. The sum is in proper BCD form.
3. When the sum of two digits is greater than 9, a correction of 0110 should be added to that sum to get the proper BCD result. This case always produces a carry into the next digit position, either from the original addition (step 1) or from the correction addition.

The procedure for BCD addition is clearly more complicated than straight binary addition. This is also true of the other BCD arithmetic operations. Readers should perform the addition of $275 + 641$. Then check the correct procedure below.

```
    275      0010    0111    0101    ← BCD for 275
   +641    + 0110    0100    0001    ← BCD for 641
    916      1000    1011    0110    ← perform addition
         +           0110            ← add 6 to correct 2nd digit
             1001    0001    0110    ← BCD for 916
```

1. How can you tell when a correction is needed in BCD addition?
2. Represent 135_{10} and 265_{10} in BCD and then perform BCD addition. Check your work by converting the result back to decimal.

6-8 HEXADECIMAL ARITHMETIC

Hex numbers are used extensively in machine-language computer programming and in conjunction with computer memories (i.e., addresses). When working in these areas, you will encounter situations where hex numbers must be added or subtracted.

Hex Addition

Addition of hexadecimal numbers is done in much the same way as decimal addition as long as you remember that the largest hex digit is F instead of 9. The following procedure is suggested:

1. Add the two hex digits in decimal, mentally inserting the decimal equivalent for those digits larger than 9.
2. If the sum is 15 or less, it can be directly expressed as a hex digit.
3. If the sum is greater than or equal to 16, subtract 16 and carry a 1 to the next digit position.

The following examples will illustrate the procedure.

EXAMPLE 6-6

Add the hex numbers 58 and 24.

Solution

$$
\begin{array}{r}
58 \\
+24 \\
\hline
7C
\end{array}
$$

Adding the LSDs (8 and 4) produces 12, which is C in hex. There is no carry into the next digit position. Adding 5 and 2 produces 7.

EXAMPLE 6-7

Add the hex numbers 58 and 4B.

Solution

$$
\begin{array}{r}
58 \\
+4B \\
\hline
A3
\end{array}
$$

Start by adding 8 and B, mentally substituting decimal 11 for B. This produces a sum of 19. Since 19 is greater than 16, subtract 16 to get 3; write down the 3 and carry a 1 into the next position. This carry is added to the 5 and 4 to produce a sum of 10_{10}, which is then converted to hexadecimal A.

EXAMPLE 6-8

Add 3AF to 23C.

Solution

$$
\begin{array}{r}
3AF \\
+23C \\
\hline
5EB
\end{array}
$$

The sum of F and C is considered as $15 + 12 = 27_{10}$. Since this is greater than 16, subtract 16 to get 11_{10}, which is hexadecimal B, and carry a 1 into the second position. Add this carry to A and 3 to obtain E. There is no carry into the MSD position.

Hex Subtraction

Remember that hex numbers are just an efficient way to represent binary numbers. Thus, we can subtract hex numbers using the same method we used for binary numbers. The 2's complement of the hex subtrahend will be taken and then *added* to the minuend, and any carry out of the MSD position will be disregarded.

How do we find the 2's complement of a hex number? One way is to convert it to binary, take the 2's complement of the binary equivalent, and then convert it back to hex. This process is illustrated below.

$$
\begin{array}{ccc}
& 73A & \leftarrow \text{ hex number} \\
0111 \quad 0011 \quad 1010 & & \leftarrow \text{ convert to binary} \\
1000 \quad 1100 \quad 0110 & & \leftarrow \text{ take 2's complement} \\
& 8C6 & \leftarrow \text{ convert back to hex}
\end{array}
$$

There is a quicker procedure: subtract *each* hex digit from F; then add 1. Let's try this for the same hex number from the example above.

$$
\begin{array}{ccc}
F & F & F \\
-7 & -3 & -A \\
\hline
8 & C & 5
\end{array} \Bigg\} \leftarrow \text{ subtract each digit from F}
$$

$$
\begin{array}{ccc}
& & +1 \quad \leftarrow \text{ add 1} \\
\hline
8 & C & 6 \quad \leftarrow \text{ hex equivalent of 2's complement}
\end{array}
$$

Try either of the procedures above on the hex number E63. The correct result for the 2's complement is 19D.

EXAMPLE 6-9	Subtract $3A5_{16}$ from 592_{16}.

Solution

First, convert the subtrahend (3A5) to its 2's-complement form by using either method presented above. The result is C5B. Then add this to the minuend (592):

$$
\begin{array}{r}
592 \\
+\ \underline{C5B} \\
\underset{\uparrow}{1}1ED \\
\end{array}
$$

Disregard carry.

Ignoring the carry out of the MSD addition, the result is 1ED. We can prove that this is correct by adding 1ED to 3A5 and checking to see that it equals 592_{16}.

Hex Representation of Signed Numbers

The data stored in a microcomputer's internal working memory or on a hard disk or CD ROM are typically stored in bytes (groups of eight bits). The data byte stored in a particular memory location is often expressed in hexadecimal because it is more efficient and less error-prone than expressing it in binary. When the data consist of *signed* numbers, it is helpful to be able to recognize whether a hex value represents a positive or a negative number. For example, Table 6-2 lists the data stored in a small segment of memory starting at address 4000.

TABLE 6-2

Hex Address	Stored Binary Data	Hex Value	Decimal Value
4000	00111010	3A	+58
4001	11100101	E5	−29
4002	01010111	57	+87
4003	10000000	80	−128

In each memory location, the data value (which actually represents a signed decimal number) is stored as a binary byte. The hex equivalent of this binary value is a two-digit hex number. Whenever the binary data value is negative, there will be a 1 in the sign bit (MSB); this will always make the MSD of the hex number 8 or greater (i.e., 8, 9, A, B, C, D, E, or F). When the binary data value is positive (0 in sign bit), the MSD of the hex number will be 7 or less (i.e., 7, 6, 5, 4, 3, 2, 1, or 0). This characteristic should make it easy to recognize whether a hex number is representing a positive or a negative value.

Review Questions

1. Add 67F + 2A4.
2. Subtract 67F − 2A4.
3. Which of the following hex numbers represent positive values: 2F, 77EC, C000, 6D, FFFF?

6-9 ARITHMETIC CIRCUITS

One essential function of most computers and calculators is the performance of arithmetic operations. These operations are all performed in the arithmetic/logic unit of a computer, where logic gates and flip-flops are combined so that they can add, subtract, multiply, and divide binary numbers. These circuits perform arithmetic operations at speeds that are not humanly possibly. Typically, an addition operation will take less than 100 ns.

We will now study some of the basic arithmetic circuits that are used to perform the arithmetic operations discussed earlier. In some cases we will go through the actual design process, even though the circuits may be commercially available in integrated-circuit form, to provide more practice in the use of the techniques learned in Chapter 4.

Arithmetic/Logic Unit

All arithmetic operations take place in the **arithmetic/logic unit (ALU)** of a computer. Figure 6-3 is a block diagram showing the major elements included in a typical ALU. The main purpose of the ALU is to accept binary data that are stored in the memory and to execute arithmetic and logic operations on these data according to instructions from the control unit.

FIGURE 6-3 Functional parts of an ALU.

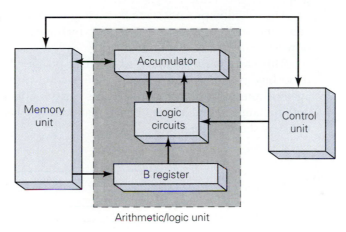

Arithmetic/logic unit

The arithmetic/logic unit contains at least two flip-flop registers: the *B register* and the **accumulator register.** It also contains combinational logic, which performs the arithmetic and logic operations on the binary numbers that are stored in the *B* register and the accumulator. A typical sequence of operations may occur as follows:

1. The control unit receives an instruction (from the memory unit) specifying that a number stored in a particular memory location (address) is to be added to the number presently stored in the accumulator register.

2. The number to be added is transferred from memory to the *B* register.

3. The number in the *B* register and the number in the accumulator register are added together in the logic circuits (upon command from the control unit). The resulting sum is then sent to the accumulator to be stored.

4. The new number in the accumulator can remain there so that another number can be added to it, or, if the particular arithmetic process is finished, it can be transferred to memory for storage.

These steps should make it apparent how the accumulator register derives its name. This register "accumulates" the sums that occur when performing successive additions between new numbers acquired from memory and the previously accumulated sum. In fact, for any arithmetic problem containing several steps, the accumulator usually contains the results of the intermediate steps as they are completed as well as the final result when the problem is finished.

6-10 PARALLEL BINARY ADDER

Computers and calculators perform the addition operation on two binary numbers at a time, where each binary number can have several binary digits. Figure 6-4 illustrates the addition of two five-bit numbers. The **augend** is stored in the accumulator register; that is, the accumulator contains five FFs, storing the values 10101 in successive FFs. Similarly, the **addend,** the number that is to be added to the augend, is stored in the *B* register (in this case, 00111).

The addition process starts by adding the least significant bits (LSBs) of the augend and addend. Thus, $1 + 1 = 10$, which means that the *sum* for that position is 0, with a *carry* of 1.

This carry must be added to the next position along with the augend and addend bits in that position. Thus, in the second position, $1 + 0 + 1 = 10$, which is again a sum of 0 and a carry of 1. This carry is added to the next position together with the augend and addend bits in that position, and so on for the remaining positions, as shown in Figure 6-4.

FIGURE 6-4 Typical binary addition process.

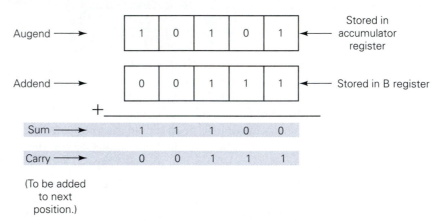

At each step in this addition process we are performing the addition of three bits: the augend bit, the addend bit, and a carry bit from the previous position. The result of the addition of these three bits produces two bits: a *sum* bit, and a *carry* bit which is to be added to the next position. It should be clear that the same process is followed for each bit position. Thus, if we can design a logic circuit that can duplicate this process, then all we have to do is to use the identical circuit for each of the bit positions. This is illustrated in Figure 6-5.

In this diagram, variables A_4, A_3, A_2, A_1, and A_0 represent the bits of the augend that are stored in the accumulator (which is also called the *A* register). Variables B_4, B_3, B_2, B_1, and B_0 represent the bits of the addend stored in the *B* register. Variables C_4, C_3, C_2, C_1, and C_0 represent the carry bits into the corresponding positions. Variables S_4, S_3, S_2, S_1, S_0 are the sum output bits for each position. Corresponding bits of the augend and addend are fed to a logic circuit called a **full adder,** along with a carry bit from the previous position. For example, bits A_1 and B_1 are fed into full adder 1 along with C_1, which is the carry bit produced by the addition of the A_0 and B_0 bits. Bits A_0 and B_0 are fed into full adder 0 along with C_0. Since A_0 and B_0 are the LSBs of the augend and addend, it appears that C_0 would always have to be 0,

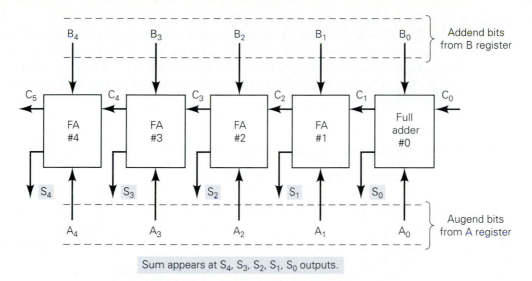

FIGURE 6-5   Block diagram of five-bit parallel adder circuit using full adders.

since there can be no carry into that position. However, we shall see that there will be situations when C_0 can also be 1.

The full-adder circuit used in each position has three inputs: an A bit, a B bit, and a C bit. It also produces two outputs: a sum bit and a carry bit. For example, full adder 0 has inputs A_0, B_0, and C_0, and it produces outputs S_0 and C_1. Full adder 1 had A_1, B_1, and C_1 as inputs and S_1 and C_2 as outputs; and so on. This arrangement is repeated for as many positions as there are in the augend and addend. Although this illustration is for five-bit numbers, in modern computers the numbers usually range from 8 to 64 bits.

The arrangement in Figure 6-5 is called a **parallel adder** because all of the bits of the augend and addend are present and are fed into the adder circuits *simultaneously*. This means that the additions in each position are taking place at the same time. This is different from how we add on paper, taking each position one at a time starting with the LSB. Clearly, parallel addition is extremely fast. More will be said about this later.

Review Questions

1. How many inputs does a full adder have? How many outputs?
2. Assume the following input levels in Figure 6-5: $A_4A_3A_2A_1A_0 = 01001$; $B_4B_3B_2B_1B_0 = 00111$; $C_0 = 0$.

    (a) What are the logic levels at the outputs of FA #2?

    (b) What is the logic level at the C_5 output?

6-11   DESIGN OF A FULL ADDER

Now that we know the function of the full adder, we can proceed to design a logic circuit that will perform this function. First, we must construct a truth table showing the various input and output values for all possible cases. Figure 6-6 shows the truth table having three inputs, A, B, and C_{IN}, and two outputs, S and C_{OUT}. There are eight possible cases for the three inputs, and for each case the desired output values are listed. For example, consider the case $A = 1$, $B = 0$, and $C_{IN} = 1$. The full adder (hereafter abbreviated **FA**) must add these bits to produce a sum (S) of 0 and a carry (C_{OUT}) of 1. The reader should check the other cases to be sure they are understood.

FIGURE 6-6   Truth table for a full-adder circuit.

Augend bit input	Addend bit input	Carry bit input	Sum bit output	Carry bit output
A	B	C_{IN}	S	C_{OUT}
0	0	0	0	0
0	0	1	1	0
0	1	0	1	0
0	1	1	0	1
1	0	0	1	0
1	0	1	0	1
1	1	0	0	1
1	1	1	1	1

Since there are two outputs, we will design the circuitry for each output individually, starting with the S output. The truth table shows that there are four cases where S is to be a 1. Using the sum-of-products method, we can write the expression for S as

$$S = \overline{A}\,\overline{B}C_{IN} + \overline{A}B\overline{C}_{IN} + A\overline{B}\,\overline{C}_{IN} + ABC_{IN} \qquad (6\text{-}1)$$

We can now try to simplify this expression by factoring. Unfortunately, none of the terms in the expression has two variables in common with any of the other terms. However, $\overline{A}$ can be factored from the first two terms, and A can be factored from the last two terms:

$$S = \overline{A}(\overline{B}C_{IN} + B\overline{C}_{IN}) + A(\overline{B}\,\overline{C}_{IN} + BC_{IN})$$

The first term in parentheses should be recognized as the exclusive-OR combination of B and C_{IN}, which can be written as $B \oplus C_{IN}$. The second term in parentheses should be recognized as the exclusive-NOR of B and C_{IN}, which can be written as $\overline{B \oplus C_{IN}}$. Thus, the expression for S becomes

$$S = \overline{A}(B \oplus C_{IN}) + A(\overline{B \oplus C_{IN}})$$

If we let $X = B \oplus C_{IN}$, this can be written as

$$S = \overline{A} \cdot X + A \cdot \overline{X} = A \oplus X$$

which is simply the EX-OR of A and X. Replacing the expression for X, we have

$$S = A \oplus [B \oplus C_{IN}] \tag{6-2}$$

Consider now the output C_{OUT} in the truth table of Figure 6-6. We can write the sum-of-products expression for C_{OUT} as follows:

$$C_{OUT} = \overline{A}BC_{IN} + A\overline{B}C_{IN} + AB\overline{C}_{IN} + ABC_{IN}$$

This expression can be simplified by factoring. We will employ the trick introduced in Chapter 4, whereby we will use the ABC_{IN} term *three* times since it has common factors with each of the other terms. Hence,

$$
\begin{aligned}
C_{OUT} &= BC_{IN}(\overline{A} + A) + AC_{IN}(\overline{B} + B) + AB(\overline{C}_{IN} + C_{IN}) \\
&= BC_{IN} + AC_{IN} + AB
\end{aligned}
\tag{6-3}
$$

This expression cannot be simplified further.

Expressions (6-2) and (6-3) can be implemented as shown in Figure 6-7. Several other implementations can be used to produce the same expressions for S and C_{OUT}, none of which has any particular advantage over those shown. The complete circuit with inputs A, B, and C_{IN} and outputs S and C_{OUT} represents the full adder. Each of the FAs in Figure 6-5 contains this same circuitry (or its equivalent).

FIGURE 6-7 Complete circuitry for a full adder.

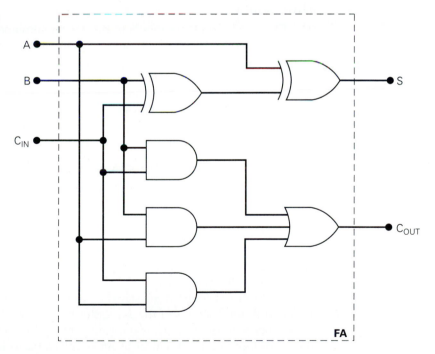

K-Map Simplification

We simplified the expressions for S and C_{OUT} using algebraic methods. The K-map method can also be used. Figure 6-8(a) shows the K map for the S output. This map has no adjacent 1s, and so there are no pairs or quads to loop. Thus, the expression for S cannot be simplified using the K map. This points out a limitation of the K-map method as compared with the algebraic method. We were able to simplify the expression for S through factoring and the use of EX-OR and EX-NOR operations.

The K map for the C_{OUT} output is shown in Figure 6-8(b). The three pairs that are looped will produce the same expression obtained from the algebraic method.

FIGURE 6-8 K mappings for the full-adder outputs.

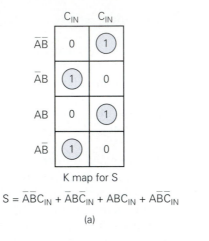

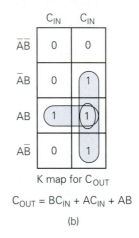

$$S = \overline{A}\,\overline{B}C_{IN} + \overline{A}B\overline{C}_{IN} + ABC_{IN} + A\overline{B}\overline{C}_{IN}$$

$$C_{OUT} = BC_{IN} + AC_{IN} + AB$$

(a)

(b)

Half Adder

The FA operates on three inputs to produce a sum and carry output. In some cases a circuit is needed that will add only two input bits, to produce a sum and carry output. An example would be the addition of the LSB position of two binary numbers where there is no carry input to be added. A special logic circuit can be designed to take *two* input bits, A and B, and to produce sum (S) and carry (C_{OUT}) outputs. This circuit is called a **half adder (HA).** Its operation is similar to that of a FA except that it operates on only two bits. We shall leave the design of the HA as an exercise at the end of the chapter (see Problem 6-19).

6-12 COMPLETE PARALLEL ADDER WITH REGISTERS

In a computer, the numbers that are to be added are stored in FF registers. Figure 6-9 shows the diagram of a four-bit parallel adder including the storage registers. The augend bits A_3 through A_0 are stored in the accumulator (A register); the addend bits B_3 through B_0 are stored in the B register. Each of these registers is made up of D flip-flops for easy transfer of data.

The contents of the A register (i.e., the binary number stored in A_3 through A_0) is added to the contents of the B register by the four FAs, and the sum is produced at outputs S_3 through S_0. C_4 is the carry out of the fourth FA, and it can be used as the carry input to a fifth FA, or as an *overflow* bit to indicate that the sum exceeds 1111.

Note that the sum outputs are connected to the D inputs of the A register. This will allow the sum to be parallel-transferred into the A register on the PGT (positive-going transition) of the TRANSFER pulse. In this way, the sum can be stored in the A register.

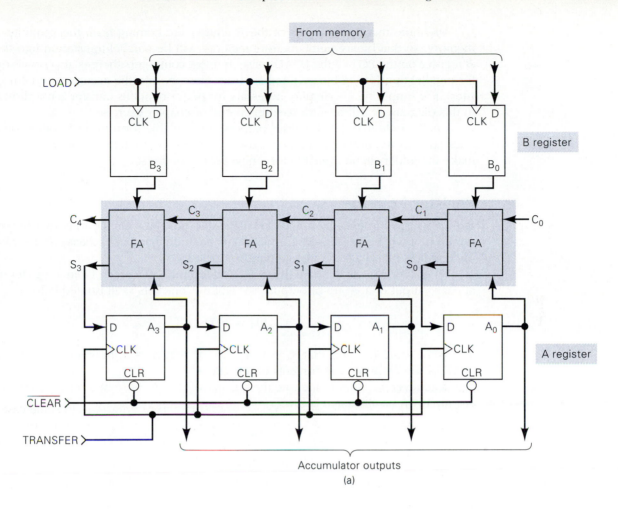

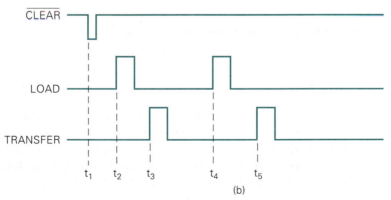

FIGURE 6-9 (a) Complete four-bit parallel adder with registers; (b) signals used to add binary numbers from memory and store their sum in the accumulator.

Also note that the *D* inputs of the *B* register are coming from the computer's memory, so that binary numbers from memory will be parallel-transferred into the *B* register on the PGT of the LOAD pulse. In most computers there is also provision for parallel-transferring binary numbers from memory into the accumulator (*A* register). For simplicity, the circuitry necessary for performing this transfer is not shown in this diagram; it will be addressed in an end-of-chapter exercise.

Finally, note that the *A* register outputs are available for transfer to other locations such as to another computer register or to the computer's memory. This will make the adder circuit available for a new set of numbers.

Register Notation

Before we go through the complete process of how this circuit adds two binary numbers, it will be helpful to introduce some notation that makes it easy to describe the contents of a register and data transfer operations.

Whenever we want to give the levels that are present at each FF in a register or at each output of a group of outputs, we will use brackets as illustrated below:

$$[A] = 1011$$

This is the same as saying that $A_3 = 1$, $A_2 = 0$, $A_1 = 1$, $A_0 = 1$. In other words, think of [*A*] as representing "the contents of register *A*."

Whenever we want to indicate the transfer of data to or from a register, we will use an arrow as illustrated below:

$$[B] \rightarrow [A]$$

This means that the contents of the *B* register have been transferred to the *A* register. The old contents of the *A* register will be lost as a result of this operation, and the *B* register will be unchanged.

Sequence of Operations

We will now describe the process by which the circuit of Figure 6-9 will add the binary numbers 1001 and 0101. Assume that $C_0 = 0$; that is, there is no carry into the LSB position.

1. **[*A*] = 0000.** A CLEAR pulse is applied to the asynchronous inputs (*CLR*) of each FF in register *A*. This occurs at time t_1.
2. **[*M*] → [*B*].** This first binary number is transferred from memory (*M*) to the *B* register. In this case, the binary number 1001 is loaded into register *B* on the PGT of the LOAD pulse at t_2.
3. **[*S*]* → [*A*].** With [*B*] = 1001 and [*A*] = 0000, the full adders produce a sum of 1001; that is, [*S*] = 1001. These sum outputs are transferred into the *A* register on the PGT of the TRANSFER pulse at t_3. This makes [*A*] = 1001.

---

*   Even though *S* is not a register, we will use [*S*] to represent the group of *S* outputs.

4. $[M] \rightarrow [B]$. The second binary number, 0101, is transferred from memory into the B register on the PGT of the second LOAD pulse at t_4. This makes $[B] = 0101$.

5. $[S] \rightarrow [A]$. With $[B] = 0101$ and $[A] = 1001$, the FAs produce $[S] = 1110$. These sum outputs are transferred into the A register when the second TRANSFER pulse occurs at t_5. Thus, $[A] = 1110$.

6. At this point, the sum of the two binary numbers is present in the accumulator. In most computers the contents of the accumulator, $[A]$, will usually be transferred to the computer's memory so that the adder circuit can be used for a new set of numbers. The circuitry that performs this $[A] \rightarrow [M]$ transfer is not shown in Figure 6-9.

Review Questions

1. Suppose that four different four-bit numbers are to be taken from memory and added by the circuit of Figure 6-9. How many CLEAR pulses will be needed? How many TRANSFER pulses? How many LOAD pulses?

2. Determine the contents of the A register after the following sequence of operations: $[A] = 0000$, $[0110] \rightarrow [B]$, $[S] \rightarrow [A]$, $[1110] \rightarrow [B]$, $[S] \rightarrow [A]$.

6-13   CARRY PROPAGATION

The parallel adder of Figure 6-9 performs additions at a relatively high speed, since it adds the bits from each position simultaneously. However, its speed is limited by an effect called **carry propagation** or **carry ripple,** which can best be explained by considering the following addition:

$$
\begin{array}{r}
0111 \\
+\ 0001 \\
\hline
1000
\end{array}
$$

Addition of the LSB position produces a carry into the second position. This carry, when added to the bits of the second position, produces a carry into the third position. The latter carry, when added to the bits of the third position, produces a carry into the last position. The key thing to notice in this example is that the sum bit generated in the *last* position (MSB) depended on the carry that was generated by the addition in the *first* position (LSB).

Looking at this from the viewpoint of the circuit of Figure 6-9, S_3 out of the last full adder depends on C_1 out of the first full adder. But the C_1 signal must pass through three FAs before it produces S_3. What this means is that the S_3 output will not reach its correct value until C_1 has propagated through the intermediate FAs. This represents a time delay that depends on the propagation delay produced in a FA. For example, if each FA has a propagation delay of 40 ns, then S_3 will not reach its correct level until 120 ns after C_1 is generated. This means that the add command pulse cannot be applied until 160 ns after the augend and addend numbers are present in the FF registers (the extra 40 ns is due to the delay of the LSB full adder, which generates C_1).

Obviously, the situation becomes much worse if we extend the adder circuitry to add a greater number of bits. If the adder were handling 32-bit numbers, the carry propagation delay could be 1280 ns = 1.28 μs. The add pulse could not be applied until at least 1.28 μs after the numbers were present in the registers.

This magnitude of delay is prohibitive for high-speed computers. Fortunately, logic designers have come up with several ingenious schemes for reducing this delay. One of the schemes, called **look-ahead carry,** utilizes logic gates to look at the lower-order bits of the augend and addend to see if a higher-order carry is to be generated. For example, it is possible to build a logic circuit with B_2, B_1, B_0, A_2, A_1, and A_0 as inputs and C_3 as an output. This logic circuit would have a shorter delay than is obtained by the carry propagation through the FAs. This scheme requires a large amount of extra circuitry but is necessary to produce high-speed adders. The extra circuitry is not a significant consideration with the present use of integrated circuits. Many high-speed adders available in integrated-circuit form utilize the look-ahead carry or a similar technique for reducing overall propagation delays.

6-14 INTEGRATED-CIRCUIT PARALLEL ADDER

Several parallel adders are available as ICs. The most common is a four-bit parallel adder IC that contains four interconnected FAs and the look-ahead carry circuitry needed for high-speed operation. The 7483A, 74LS83A, 74283, and 74LS283 are all TTL four-bit parallel-adder chips. The 283s are identical to the 83s except that they have V_{CC} and ground on pins 16 and 8, respectively; it has become standard on all new chips to have the power and ground pins at the corners of the chip. The 74HC283 is the high-speed CMOS version of the same four-bit parallel adder.

Figure 6-10(a) shows the functional symbol for the 74HC283 four-bit parallel adder (and its equivalents). The inputs to this IC are two four-bit numbers, $A_3A_2A_1A_0$ and $B_3B_2B_1B_0$, and the carry, C_0, into the LSB position. The outputs are the sum bits and the carry, C_4, out of the MSB position. The sum bits are labeled $\Sigma_3\Sigma_2\Sigma_1\Sigma_0$, where Σ is the Greek capital letter *sigma*. The Σ label is just a common alternative to the S label for a sum bit.

Cascading Parallel Adders

Two or more parallel-adder blocks can be connected (cascaded) to accommodate the addition of larger binary numbers. To illustrate, Figure 6-10(b) shows how two 7HC283 adders can be connected to add two eight-bit numbers. The adder on the right adds the four least significant bits of the numbers. The C_4 output of this adder is connected as the input carry to the first position of the second adder, which adds the four most significant bits of the numbers. The eight sum outputs represent the resultant sum of the two eight-bit numbers. C_8 is the carry out of the last position (MSB) of the second adder. C_8 can be used as an overflow bit or as a carry into another adder stage if larger binary numbers are to be handled.

FIGURE 6-10 (a) Block symbol for the 74HC283 four-bit parallel adder; (b) cascading two 74HC283s.

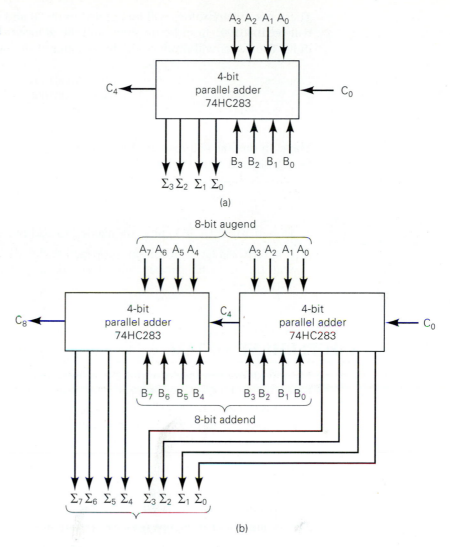

| EXAMPLE |
| 6-10 |

EXAMPLE 6-10

Determine the logic levels at the inputs and outputs of the eight-bit adder in Figure 6-10(b) when 72_{10} is added to 137_{10}.

Solution

First convert each number to an eight-bit binary number:

$$137 = 10001001$$
$$72 = 01001000$$

These two binary values will be applied to the A and B inputs; that is, the A inputs will be 10001001 from left to right, and the B inputs will be 01001000 from left to right. The adder will produce the binary sum of the two numbers:

$$[A] = 10001001$$
$$[B] = \underline{01001000}$$
$$[\Sigma] = 11010001$$

The sum outputs will read 11010001 from left to right. There is no overflow into the C_8 bit, and so it will be a 0.

Review Questions

1. How many 74HC283 chips are needed to add two 20-bit numbers?
2. If a 74HC283 has a maximum propagation delay of 30 ns from C_0 to C_4, what will be the total propagation delay of a 32-bit adder constructed from 74HC283s?

6-15 2's-COMPLEMENT SYSTEM

Most modern computers use the 2's-complement system to represent negative numbers and to perform subtraction. The operations of addition and subtraction of signed numbers can be performed using only the addition operation if we use the 2's-complement form to represent negative numbers.

Addition

Positive and negative numbers, including the sign bits, can be added together in the basic parallel-adder circuit when the negative numbers are in 2's-complement form. This is illustrated in Figure 6-11 for the addition of −3 and +6. The −3 is represented in its 2's-complement form as 1101, where the first 1 is the sign bit; the +6 is represented as 0110, with the first zero as the sign bit. These numbers are stored in their corresponding registers. The four-bit parallel adder produces sum outputs of 0011, which represents +3. The C_4 output is 1, but remember that it is disregarded in the 2's-complement method.

Subtraction

When the 2's-complement system is used, the number to be subtracted (the subtrahend) is changed to its 2's complement and then *added* to the minuend (the number the subtrahend is being subtracted from). For example, we can assume that the minuend is already stored in the accumulator (A register). The subtrahend is then placed in the B register (in a computer it would be transferred here from memory) and is changed to its 2's-complement form before it is added to the number in the A register. The sum outputs of the adder circuit now represent the *difference* between the minuend and the subtrahend.

011
1 1 01

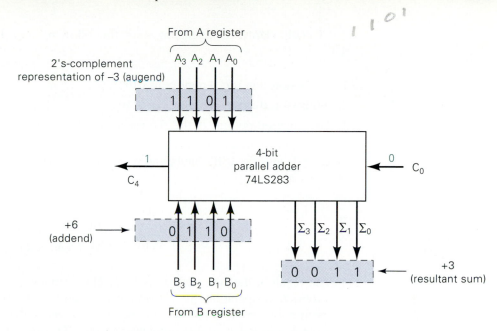

FIGURE 6-11   Parallel adder used to add + and − numbers in 2's-complement system.

The parallel-adder circuit that we have been discussing can be adapted to perform the subtraction described above if we provide a means for taking the 2's complement of the *B* register number. The 2's complement of a binary number is obtained by complementing (inverting) each bit and then adding 1 to the LSB. Figure 6-12 shows how this can be accomplished. The *inverted* outputs of the *B* register are used rather than the normal outputs; that is, $\overline{B}_0$, $\overline{B}_1$, $\overline{B}_2$, and $\overline{B}_3$ are fed to the adder inputs (remember, B_3 is the sign bit). This takes care of complementing each bit of the *B* number. Also, C_0 is made a logical 1, so that it adds an extra 1 into the LSB of the adder; this accomplishes the same effect as adding 1 to the LSB of the *B* register for forming the 2's complement.

FIGURE 6-12   Parallel adder used to perform subtraction ($A − B$) using the 2's-complement system. The bits of the subtrahend (B) are inverted, and $C_0 = 1$ to produce the 2's complement.

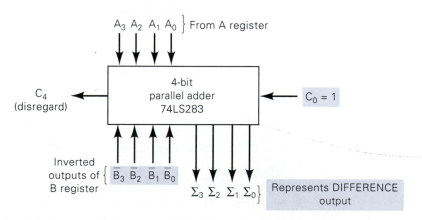

The outputs Σ_3 to Σ_0 represent the results of the subtraction operation. Of course, Σ_3 is the sign bit of the result and indicates whether the result is + or −. The carry output C_4 is again disregarded.

To help clarify this operation, study the following steps for subtracting $+6$ from $+4$:

1. $+4$ is stored in the A register as 0100.
2. $+6$ is stored in the B register as 0110.
3. The inverted outputs of the B-register FFs (1001) are fed to the adder.
4. The parallel-adder circuitry adds $[A] = 0100$ to $[\overline{B}] = 1001$ along with a carry, $C_0 = 1$, into the LSB. The operation is shown below.

$$
\begin{array}{rl}
1 & \leftarrow C_0 \\
0100 & \leftarrow [A] \\
+\ \underline{1001} & \leftarrow [\overline{B}] \\
1110 & \leftarrow [\Sigma] = [A] - [B]
\end{array}
$$

The result at the sum outputs is 1110. This actually represents the result of the *subtraction* operation, the *difference* between the number in the A register and the number in the B register, that is, $[A] - [B]$. Since the sign bit $= 1$, it is a negative result and is in 2's-complement form. We can verify that 1110 represents -2_{10} by taking its 2's-complement and obtaining $+2_{10}$:

$$
\begin{array}{r}
1110 \\
0001 \\
+\ \underline{1} \\
0010 = +2_{10}
\end{array}
$$

Combined Addition and Subtraction

It should now be clear that the basic parallel-adder circuit can be used to perform addition or subtraction depending on whether the B number is left unchanged or is converted to its 2's complement. A complete circuit that can perform *both* addition and subtraction in the 2's-complement system is shown in Figure 6-13.

This adder/subtractor circuit is controlled by the two control signals ADD and SUB. When the ADD level is HIGH, the circuit performs addition of the numbers stored in the A and B registers. When the SUB level is HIGH, the circuit subtracts the B-register number from the A-register number. The operation is described as follows:

1. Assume that ADD $= 1$ and SUB $= 0$. The SUB $= 0$ *disables* (inhibits) AND gates 2, 4, 6, and 8, holding their outputs at 0. The ADD $= 1$ *enables* AND gates 1, 3, 5, and 7, allowing their outputs to pass the B_0, B_1, B_2 and B_3 levels, respectively.
2. The levels B_0 to B_3 pass through the OR gates into the four-bit parallel adder to be added to the bits A_0 to A_3. The *sum* appears at the outputs Σ_0 to Σ_3.
3. Note that SUB $= 0$ causes a carry $C_0 = 0$ into the adder.
4. How assume that ADD $= 0$ and SUB $= 1$. The ADD $= 0$ inhibits AND gates 1, 3, 5, and 7. The SUB $= 1$ enables AND gates 2, 4, 6, and 8, so that their outputs pass the $\overline{B}_0$, $\overline{B}_1$, $\overline{B}_2$, and $\overline{B}_3$ levels, respectively.

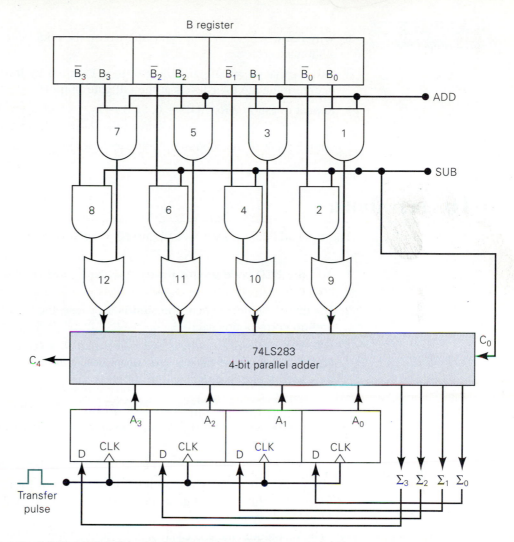

FIGURE 6-13   Parallel adder/subtractor using the 2's-complement system.

5. The levels $\overline{B}_0$ to $\overline{B}_3$ pass through the OR gates into the adder to be added to the bits A_0 to A_3. Note also that C_0 is now 1. Thus, the B-register number has essentially been converted to its 2's complement.

6. The *difference* appears at the *outputs* Σ_0 to Σ_3.

Circuits like the adder/subtractor of Figure 6-13 are used in computers because they provide a relatively simple means for adding and subtracting signed binary numbers. In most computers the outputs present at the Σ output lines are usually transferred into the A register (accumulator), so that the results of the addition or subtraction always end up stored in the A register. This is accomplished by applying a TRANSFER pulse to the *CLK* inputs of register A.

Review Questions

1. Why does C_0 have to be a 1 in order to use the adder circuit in Figure 6-12 as a subtractor?
2. Assume that $[A]$ = 0011 and $[B]$ = 0010 in Figure 6-13. If ADD = 1 and SUB = 0, determine the logic levels at the OR gate outputs.
3. Repeat question 2 for ADD = 0, SUB = 1.
4. *True or false:* When the adder/subtractor circuit is used for subtraction, the 2's complement of the subtrahend appears at the input of the adder.

6-16 BCD ADDER

The BCD addition process was discussed in Section 6-7 and is reviewed below:

1. Add the BCD code groups for each decimal digit position; use ordinary binary addition.
2. For those positions where the sum is 9 or less, the sum is in proper BCD form and no correction is needed.
3. When the sum of two digits is greater than 9, a correction of 0110 should be added to that sum to produce the proper BCD result. This will produce a carry to be added to the next decimal position.

A BCD adder circuit must be able to operate in accordance with the above steps. In other words, the circuit must be able to do the following:

1. Add two four-bit BCD code groups, using straight binary addition.
2. Determine if the sum of this addition is greater than 1001 (decimal 9); if it is, add 0110 (6) to this sum and generate a carry to the next decimal position.

The first requirement is easily met by using a four-bit binary parallel adder such as the 74HC283 and its equivalents. For example, if the two BCD code groups represented by $A_3A_2A_1A_0$ and $B_3B_2B_1B_0$, respectively, are applied to a four-bit parallel adder, the adder will perform the following operation:

$$
\begin{array}{rl}
A_3A_2A_1A_0 & \leftarrow \text{BCD code group} \\
+ \ \underline{B_3B_2B_1B_0} & \leftarrow \text{BCD code group} \\
S_4S_3S_2S_1S_0 & \leftarrow \text{straight binary sum}
\end{array}
$$

S_4 is actually C_4, the carry out of the MSB.

The sum outputs $S_4S_3S_2S_1S_0$ can range anywhere from 00000 to 10010 (when both BCD code groups are 1001 = 9). The circuitry for a BCD adder must include the logic needed to detect whenever the sum is greater than 01001, so that the correction can be added in. These cases where the sum is greater than 01001 are listed in Table 6-3. Let's define X as a logic output that will go HIGH only when the sum is greater than 01001 (i.e., for the cases listed in Table 6-3). If we examine these

TABLE 6-3

S_4	S_3	S_2	S_1	S_0	
0	1	0	1	0	(10)
0	1	0	1	1	(11)
0	1	1	0	0	(12)
0	1	1	0	1	(13)
0	1	1	1	0	(14)
0	1	1	1	1	(15)
1	0	0	0	0	(16)
1	0	0	0	1	(17)
1	0	0	1	0	(18)

cases, it can be reasoned that X will be HIGH for either of the following conditions:

1. Whenever $S_4 = 1$ (sums greater than 15)
2. Whenever $S_3 = 1$ and either S_2 or S_1 or both are 1 (sums 10 to 15)

This can be expressed as

$$X = S_4 + S_3(S_2 + S_1)$$

Whenever $X = 1$, it is necessary to add the correction 0110 to the sum bits and to generate a carry. Figure 6-14 shows the complete circuitry for a BCD adder, including the logic-circuit implementation for X.

The circuit consists of three basic parts. The two code groups $A_3A_2A_1A_0$ and $B_3B_2B_1B_0$ are added together in the upper four-bit adder to produce the sum $S_4S_3S_2S_1S_0$. The logic gates implement the expression for X. The lower four-bit adder will add the correction 0110 to the sum bits *only* when $X = 1$, producing the final BCD sum output represented by $\Sigma_3\Sigma_2\Sigma_1\Sigma_0$. X is also the carry output that is produced when the sum is greater than 01001. Of course, when $X = 0$, there is no carry and no addition of 0110. In such cases, $\Sigma_3\Sigma_2\Sigma_1\Sigma_0 = S_3S_2S_1S_0$.

To help in the understanding of the BCD adder, the reader should try several cases by following them through the circuit. The following cases would be particularly instructive:

Inputs

(a) $[A] = 0101$, $[B] = 0011$, $C_0 = 0$
(b) $[A] = 0111$, $[B] = 0110$, $C_0 = 0$

Outputs

(a) $[S] = 01000$, $X = 0$, $[\Sigma] = 1000$, CARRY = 0
(b) $[S] = 01101$, $X = 1$, $[\Sigma] = 0011$, CARRY = 1

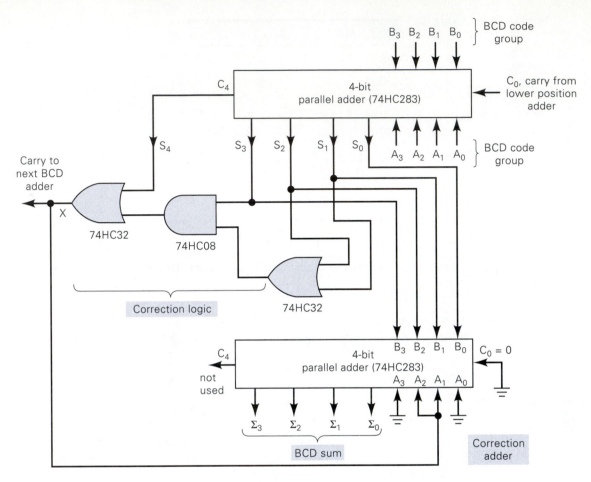

FIGURE 6-14 A BCD adder contains two four-bit adders and a correction-detector circuit.

Cascading BCD Adders

The circuit of Figure 6-14 is used for adding two decimal digits that have been encoded in BCD code. When decimal numbers with several digits are to be added together, it is necessary to use a separate BCD adder for each digit position. Figure 6-15 is a block diagram of a circuit for the addition of two three-digit decimal numbers. The *A* register contains 12 bits, which are the three BCD code groups for one of the three-digit decimal numbers; similarly, the *B* register contains the BCD representation of the other three-digit decimal number. The code groups A_3–A_0 and B_3–B_0 representing the least significant digits are fed to the first BCD adder. Each BCD adder block is assumed to contain the circuitry of Figure 6-14. This first BCD adder produces sum outputs $\Sigma_3\Sigma_2\Sigma_1\Sigma_0$, which is the BCD code for the least significant digit of the sum. It also produces a carry output that is sent to the second BCD adder, which is adding A_7 through A_4 and B_7 through B_4, the BCD code groups for the second-decimal-digit position. The second BCD adder produces $\Sigma_7\Sigma_6\Sigma_5\Sigma_4$, the BCD code for the second digit of the sum, and so on. This arrangement can, of course, be extended to decimal numbers of any size by simply adding more FFs to the registers and including a BCD adder for each digit position.

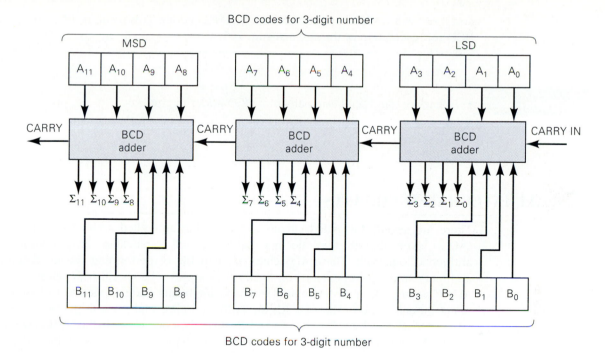

BCD codes for 3-digit number

FIGURE 6-15   Cascading BCD adders to add two three-digit decimal numbers.

EXAMPLE 6-11

Determine the inputs and outputs when the circuit of Figure 6-15 is used to add 538_{10} to 247_{10}.

Solution

First, the decimal numbers are represented in BCD.

$$247 = 0010\quad 0100\quad 0111\quad \text{(BCD)}$$
$$538 = 0101\quad 0011\quad 1000\quad \text{(BCD)}$$

These BCD numbers will be placed in the A and B registers, respectively, so that

$$[A] = 0010\quad 0100\quad 0111$$
$$[B] = 0101\quad 0011\quad 1000$$

The CARRY IN to the LSD adder will be a 0.

Once the data are in the registers, the BCD adders will begin to produce the correct BCD sums at their outputs. The LSD adder will add the 0111 (7) and 1000 (8) to produce a sum of 0101 (5) and a CARRY of 1 into the middle adder. The middle adder will add the 0100 (4) and 0011 (3) and the CARRY of 1 to produce a sum of 1000 (8) and a CARRY of 0 into the MSD adder. The MSD adder will add 0010 (2) and 0101 (5) for a sum of 0111 (7) and no CARRY OUT. Thus, at the sum outputs we have

$$[\Sigma] = 0111\quad 1000\quad 0101$$

and there is a CARRY output of 0 from the MSD adder. This result is, of course, the BCD representation of the decimal sum 785_{10}.

Review Questions

1. What are the three basic parts of a BCD adder circuit?
2. Describe how the BCD adder circuit detects the need for a correction and executes it.

6-17   ALU INTEGRATED CIRCUITS

There are several integrated circuits available that are called arithmetic/logic units (ALUs) even though they do not have the full capabilities of a computer's arithmetic/logic unit. These ALU chips are capable of performing several different arithmetic and logic operations on binary data inputs. The specific operation that an ALU IC is to perform is determined by a specific binary code applied to its function-select inputs. Some of the ALU ICs are fairly complex, and it would require a great amount of time and space to explain and illustrate their operation. In this section we will use a relatively simple, yet useful, ALU chip to show the basic concepts behind all ALU chips. The ideas presented here can then be extended to the more complex devices.

The 74LS382/HC382 ALU

Figure 6-16(a) shows the block symbol for an ALU that is available as a 74LS382 (TTL) and as a 74HC382 (CMOS). This 20-pin IC operates on two four-bit input numbers, $A_3A_2A_1A_0$ and $B_3B_2B_1B_0$, to produce a four-bit output result $F_3F_2F_1F_0$. This ALU can perform *eight* different operations. At any given time, the operation that it is performing depends on the input code applied to the function-select inputs $S_2S_1S_0$. The table in Figure 6-16(b) shows the eight available operations. We will now describe each of these operations.

CLEAR OPERATION   With $S_2S_1S_0 = 000$, the ALU will *clear* all of the bits of the F output so that $F_3F_2F_1F_0 = 0000$.

ADD OPERATION   With $S_2S_1S_0 = 011$, the ALU will add $A_3A_2A_1A_0$ to $B_3B_2B_1B_0$ to produce their sum at $F_3F_2F_1F_0$. For this operation, C_N is the carry into the LSB position, and it must be made a 0. C_{N+4} is the carry output from the MSB position. *OVR* is the overflow indicator output; it detects overflow when signed numbers are being used. *OVR* will be a 1 when an add or a subtract operation produces a result that is too large to fit into four bits (including the sign bit).

SUBTRACT OPERATIONS   With $S_2S_1S_0 = 001$, the ALU will subtract the A input number from the B input number. With $S_2S_1S_0 = 010$, the ALU will subtract B from A. In either case the difference appears at $F_3F_2F_1F_0$. Note that the subtract operations require that the C_N input be a 1.

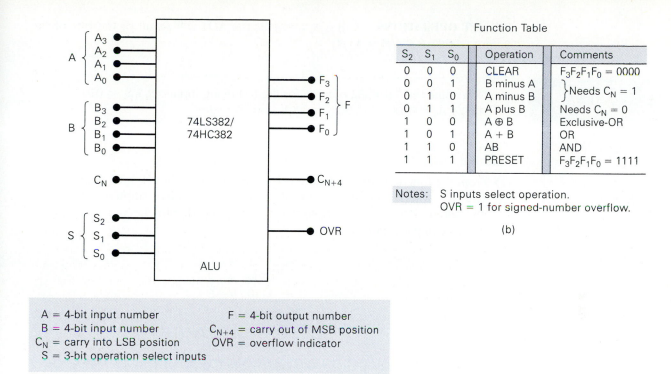

Function Table

S_2	S_1	S_0	Operation	Comments
0	0	0	CLEAR	$F_3F_2F_1F_0 = 0000$
0	0	1	B minus A	}Needs $C_N = 1$
0	1	0	A minus B	
0	1	1	A plus B	Needs $C_N = 0$
1	0	0	A ⊕ B	Exclusive-OR
1	0	1	A + B	OR
1	1	0	AB	AND
1	1	1	PRESET	$F_3F_2F_1F_0 = 1111$

Notes: S inputs select operation.
OVR = 1 for signed-number overflow.

(b)

A = 4-bit input number
B = 4-bit input number
C_N = carry into LSB position
S = 3-bit operation select inputs

F = 4-bit output number
C_{N+4} = carry out of MSB position
OVR = overflow indicator

(a)

FIGURE 6-16 (a) Block symbol for 74LS382/HC382 ALU chip; (b) function table showing how select inputs (S) determine what operation is to be performed on A and B inputs.

EX-OR OPERATION With $S_2S_1S_0 = 100$, the ALU will perform a bit-by-bit EX-OR operation on the A and B inputs. This is illustrated below for $A_3A_2A_1A_0 = 0110$ and $B_3B_2B_1B_0 = 1100$.

$$A_3 \oplus B_3 = 0 \oplus 1 = 1 = F_3$$
$$A_2 \oplus B_2 = 1 \oplus 1 = 0 = F_2$$
$$A_1 \oplus B_1 = 1 \oplus 0 = 1 = F_1$$
$$A_0 \oplus B_0 = 0 \oplus 0 = 0 = F_0$$

The result is $F_3F_2F_1F_0 = 1010$.

OR OPERATION With $S_2S_1S_0 = 101$, the ALU will perform a bit-by-bit OR operation on the A and B inputs. For example, with $A_3A_2A_1A_0 = 0110$ and $B_3B_2B_1B_0 = 1100$, the ALU will generate a result of $F_3F_2F_1F_0 = 1110$.

AND OPERATION With $S_2S_1S_0 = 110$, the ALU will perform a bit-by-bit AND operation on the A and B inputs. For example, with $A_3A_2A_1A_0 = 0110$ and $B_3B_2B_1B_0 = 1100$, the ALU will generate a result of $F_3F_2F_1F_0 = 0100$.

PRESET OPERATIONS With $S_2 S_1 S_0 = 111$, the ALU will *set* all of the bits of the output so that $F_3 F_2 F_1 F_0 = 1111$.

EXAMPLE 6-12

(a) Determine the 74HC382 outputs for the following inputs: $S_2 S_1 S_0 = 010$, $A_3 A_2 A_1 A_0 = 0100$, $B_3 B_2 B_1 B_0 = 0001$, and $C_N = 1$.

(b) Change the select code to 011 and repeat.

Solution

(a) From the function table in Figure 6-16(b), 010 selects the $(A - B)$ operation. The ALU will perform the 2's-complement subtraction by complementing B and adding it to A and C_N. Note that $C_N = 1$ is needed to effectively complete the 2's complement of B.

$$
\begin{array}{r}
1 \quad \leftarrow C_N \\
0100 \quad \leftarrow A \\
+ \quad 1110 \quad \leftarrow \overline{B} \\
\hline
10011
\end{array}
$$

$$C_{N+4} \quad\uparrow\quad\uparrow\quad F_3 F_2 F_1 F_0$$

As always in 2's-complement subtraction, the CARRY OUT of the MSB is discarded. The correct result of the $(A - B)$ operation appears at the F outputs.

The *OVR* output is determined by considering the input numbers to be signed numbers. Thus, we have $A_3 A_2 A_1 A_0 = 0100 = +4_{10}$ and $B_3 B_2 B_1 B_0 = 0001 = +1_{10}$. The result of the subtract operation is $F_3 F_2 F_1 F_0 = 0011 = +3_{10}$, which is correct. Therefore, no overflow has occurred, and $OVR = 0$. If the result had been negative, it would have been in 2's-complement form.

(b) A select code of 011 will produce the sum of the A and B inputs. However, since $C_N = 1$, there will be a carry of 1 added into the LSB position. This will produce a result of $F_3 F_2 F_1 F_0 = 0110$, which is 1 greater than $(A + B)$. The C_{N+4} and *OVR* outputs will both be 0. For the correct sum to appear at F, the C_N input must be at 0.

Expanding the ALU

A single 74LS382 or 74HC382 operates on four-bit numbers. Two or more of these chips can be connected together to operate on larger numbers. Figure 6-17 shows how two four-bit ALUs can be combined to add two eight-bit numbers, $B_7 B_6 B_5 B_4 B_3 B_2 B_1 B_0$ and $A_7 A_6 A_5 A_4 A_3 A_2 A_1 A_0$, to produce the output sum $\Sigma_7 \Sigma_6 \Sigma_5 \Sigma_4 \Sigma_3 \Sigma_2 \Sigma_1 \Sigma_0$. Study the circuit diagram and note the following points:

1. Chip Z1 operates on the four lower-order bits of the two input numbers. Chip Z2 operates on the four higher-order bits.

2. The sum appears at the F outputs of Z1 and Z2. The lower-order bits appear at Z1, and the higher-order bits at Z2.

3. The C_N input of Z1 is the carry into the LSB position. For addition, it is made a 0.

4. The carry output $[C_{N+4}]$ of Z1 is connected to the carry input $[C_N]$ of Z2.

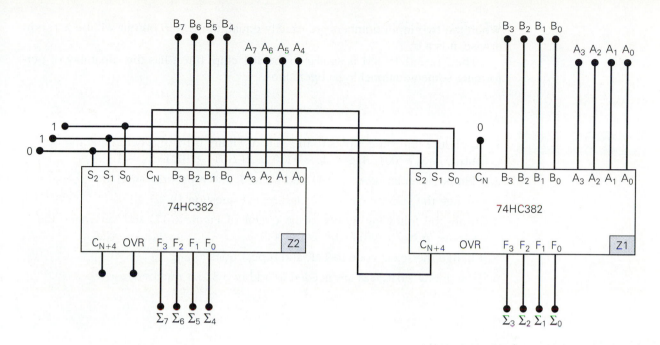

Notes: Z1 adds lower-order bits.
         Z2 adds higher-order bits.
         $\Sigma_7 - \Sigma_0$ = 8-bit sum.
         OVR of Z2 is 8-bit overflow indicator.

FIGURE 6-17   Two 74HC382 ALU chips connected as an eight-bit adder.

5. The *OVR* output of Z2 is the overflow indicator when signed eight-bit numbers are being used.

6. The corresponding select inputs of the two chips are connected together so that Z1 and Z2 are always performing the same operation. For addition, the select inputs are shown as 011.

EXAMPLE 6-13

How would the arrangement of Figure 6-17 have to be changed in order to perform the subtraction $(B - A)$?

Solution

The select input code [see table in Figure 6-16(b)] must be changed to 001, and the C_N input of Z1 must be made a 1.

Other ALUs

The 74LS181/HC181 is another four-bit ALU. It has four select inputs which can select any of 16 different operations. It also has a mode input bit that can switch between logic operations and arithmetic operations (add and subtract). This ALU has an $A = B$ output that is used to compare the magnitudes of the A and B inputs.

When the two input numbers are exactly equal, the $A = B$ output will be a 1; otherwise, it is a 0.

The 74LS881/HC881 is similar to the 181 chip, but it has the capability of performing some additional logic operations.

Review Questions

1. Apply the following inputs to the ALU of Figure 6-16, and determine the outputs: $S_2S_1S_0 = 001$, $A_3A_2A_1A_0 = 1110$, $B_3B_2B_1B_0 = 1001$, $C_N = 1$.

2. Change the select code to 011 and C_N to 0, and repeat question 1.

3. Change the select code to 110, and repeat question 1.

4. Apply the following inputs to the circuit of Figure 6-17, and determine the outputs: $B = 01010011$, $A = 00011000$.

5. Change the select code to 111, and repeat question 4.

6. How many 74HC382s are needed to add two 32-bit numbers?

6-18 IEEE/ANSI SYMBOLS

Figure 6-18(a) shows the IEEE/ANSI symbol for a one-bit adder (full adder). Note that the symbol Σ is used to indicate the addition operation. Figure 6-18(b) is the IEEE/ANSI symbol for the 7483/74283 four-bit parallel adder. Note that the letters P and Q are used to represent the two four-bit inputs, and Σ is used for the four-bit output sum. The P, Q, and Σ are specified by the IEEE/ANSI standard and must be used inside the symbol outline. The letters used for the inputs and outputs external to the symbol outline are not specified by the standard.

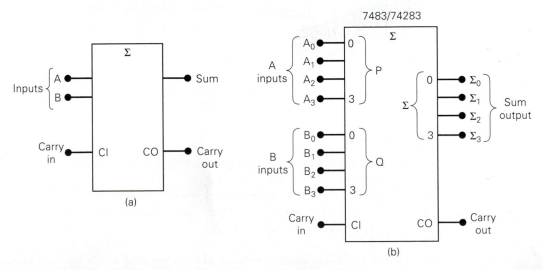

FIGURE 6-18   IEEE/ANSI symbols for (a) a full adder and (b) a four-bit parallel adder IC (7483/74283).

6-19 TROUBLESHOOTING CASE STUDY

A technician is testing the adder/subtractor redrawn in Figure 6-19 and records the following test results for the various operating modes:

- **Mode 1: ADD = 0, SUB = 0.** The sum outputs are always equal to the number in the *A* register *plus one*. For example, when [*A*] = 0110, the sum is [Σ] = 0111. This is incorrect, since the OR outputs and C_0 should all be 0 in this mode to produce [Σ] = [*A*].

- **Mode 2: Add = 1, SUB = 0.** The sum is always 1 more than it should be. For example, with [*A*] = 0010 and [*B*] = 0100, the sum output is 0111 instead of 0110.

- **Mode 3: Add = 0, SUB = 1.** The Σ outputs are always equal to [*A*] − [*B*], as expected.

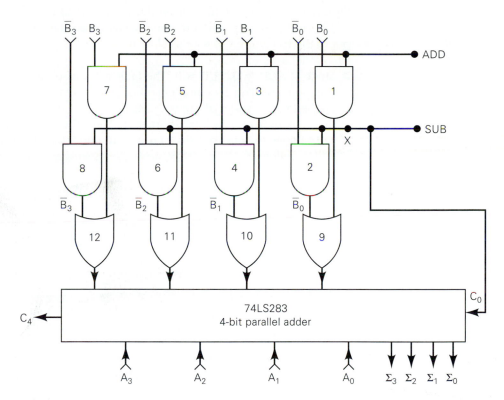

FIGURE 6-19   Parallel adder/subtractor circuit.

When she examines these test results, the technician sees that the sum outputs exceed the expected results by 1 for the first two modes of operation. At first she suspects a possible fault in one of the LSB inputs to the adder, but she dismisses this because such a fault would also affect the subtraction operation, which is working correctly. Eventually, she realizes that there is another fault that could add an extra 1 to the results for the first two modes without causing an error in the subtraction mode.

Recall that C_0 is made a 1 in the subtraction mode as part of the 2's-complement operation on $[B]$. For the other modes, C_0 is to be a 0. The technician checks the connection between the *SUB* signal and the C_0 input to the adder and finds that it is open due to a bad solder connection. This open connection explains the observed results, since the TTL adder responds as if C_0 were a constant logic 1, causing an extra 1 to be added to the result in modes 1 and 2. The open connection would have no effect on mode 3, because C_0 is supposed to be a 1 anyway.

EXAMPLE 6-14

Consider again the adder/subtractor circuit. Suppose that there is a break in the connection path between the SUB input and the AND gates at point *X* in Figure 6-19. Describe the effects of this open on the circuit operation for each mode.

Solution

First, realize that this fault will produce a logic 1 at the affected input of AND gates 2, 4, 6, and 8, which will permanently enable each of these gates to pass its $\overline{B}$ input to the following OR gate as shown.

- **Mode 1: ADD = 0, SUB = 0.** The fault will cause the circuit to perform subtraction—almost. The 1's complement of $[B]$ will reach the OR gate outputs and be applied to the adder along with $[A]$. With $C_0 = 0$, the 2's complement of $[B]$ will not be complete; it will be short by 1. Thus, the adder will produce $[A] - [B] - 1$. To illustrate, let's try $[A] = +6 = 0110$ and $[B] = +3 = 0011$. The adder will add as follows:

$$
\begin{array}{r}
\text{1's complement of } [B] = 1100 \\
[A] = 0110 \\
\hline
\text{result} = \cancel{1}0010
\end{array}
$$

$\longleftarrow$ Disregard carry.

The result is $0010 = +2$ instead of $0011 = +3$, as it would be for normal subtraction.

- **Mode 2: ADD = 1, SUB = 0.** With ADD = 1, AND gates 1, 3, 5, and 7 will pass the B inputs to the following OR gate. Thus, each OR gate will have a $\overline{B}$ and a B at its inputs, thereby producing a 1 output. For example, the inputs to OR gate 9 will be $\overline{B}_0$ coming from AND gate 2 (because of the fault), and B_0 coming from AND gate 1 (because ADD = 1). Thus, OR gate 9 will produce an output of $\overline{B}_0 + B_0$ which will always be a logic 1.

  The adder will add the 1111 from the OR gates to the $[A]$ to produce a sum that is 1 less than $[A]$. Why? Because $1111_2 = -1_{10}$.

- **Mode 3: ADD = 0, SUB = 1.** This mode will work correctly since SUB = 1 is supposed to enable AND gates 2, 4, 6, and 8 anyway.

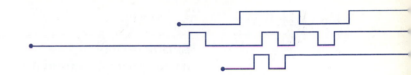

SUMMARY

1. To represent signed numbers in binary, a sign bit is attached as the MSB. A + sign is a 0, and a − sign is a 1.

2. The 2's complement of a binary number is obtained by complementing each bit and then adding 1 to the result.

3. In the 2's-complement method of representing signed binary numbers, positive numbers are represented by a sign bit of 0 followed by the magnitude in its true binary form. Negative numbers are represented by a sign bit of 1 followed by the magnitude in 2's-complement form.

4. A signed binary number is negated (changed to a number of equal value but opposite sign) by taking the 2's complement of the number, including the sign bit.

5. Subtraction can be performed on signed binary numbers by negating (2's-complementing) the subtrahend and adding it to the minuend.

6. In BCD addition, a special correction step is needed whenever the sum of a digit position exceeds 9 (1001).

7. When signed binary numbers are represented in hexadecimal, the MSD of the hex number will be 8 or greater when the number is negative; it will be 7 or less when the number is positive.

8. The arithmetic/logic unit (ALU) of a computer contains the circuitry needed to perform arithmetic and logic operations on binary numbers stored in memory.

9. The accumulator is a register in the ALU. It holds one of the numbers being operated upon, and it also is where the result of the operation is stored in the ALU.

10. A full adder performs the addition on two bits plus a carry input. A parallel binary adder is made up of cascaded full adders.

11. The problem of excessive delays caused by carry propagation can be reduced by a look-ahead carry logic circuit.

12. IC adders such as the 74LS83/HC83 and the 74LS283/HC283 can be used to construct high-speed parallel adders and subtractors.

13. A BCD adder circuit requires special correction circuitry.

14. Integrated-circuit ALUs are available that can be commanded to perform a wide range of arithmetic and logic operations on two input numbers.

IMPORTANT TERMS

carry	addend	full adder (FA)
sign bit	subtrahend	parallel adder/subtractor
sign-magnitude system	minuend	half adder (HA)
2's-complement system	overflow	carry propagation (carry
negation	arithmetic/logic unit (ALU)	ripple)
augend	accumulator register	look-ahead carry

PROBLEMS

SECTION 6-1

6-1. Add the following in binary. Check your results by doing the addition in decimal.

(a) 1010 + 1011   (d) 0.1011 + 0.1111
(b) 1111 + 0011   (e) 10011011 + 10011101
(c) 1011.1101 + 11.1

SECTION 6-2

6-2. Represent each of the following signed decimal numbers in the 2's-complement system. Use a total of eight bits including the sign bit.

(a) +32   (e) +127   (i) −1
(b) −14   (f) −127   (j) −128
(c) +63   (g) +89   (k) +169
(d) −104   (h) −55   (l) 0

6-3. Each of the following numbers represents a signed decimal number in the 2's-complement system. Determine the decimal value in each case. (*Hint:* Use negation to convert negative numbers to positive.)

(a) 01101   (f) 10000000
(b) 11101   (g) 11111111
(c) 01111011   (h) 10000001
(d) 10011001   (i) 01100011
(e) 01111111   (j) 11011001

6-4. (a) What range of signed decimal values can be represented using 12 bits including the sign bit?

(b) How many bits would be required to represent decimal numbers from −32,768 to +32,767?

6-5. List, in order, all of the signed numbers that can be represented in five bits using the 2's-complement system.

6-6. Represent each of the following decimal values as five-bit signed binary values. Then negate each one.

(a) +7   (b) −12   (c) +15   (d) −1

6-7. What is the range of unsigned decimal values that can be represented in 10 bits? What is the range of signed decimal values using the same number of bits?

SECTIONS 6-3 AND 6-4

6-8. The reason why the sign-magnitude method for representing signed numbers is not used in most computers can readily be illustrated by performing the following.

(a) Represent +12 in five bits using the sign-magnitude form.
(b) Represent −12 in five bits using the sign-magnitude form.
(c) Add the two binary numbers and note that the sum does not look anything like zero.

6-9. Perform the following operations in the 2's-complement system. Use eight bits (including the sign bit) for each number. Check your results by converting the binary result back to decimal.

(a) Add $+9$ to $+6$.

(f) Subtract $+21$ from -13.

(b) Add $+14$ to -17.

(g) Subtract $+47$ from $+47$.

(c) Add $+19$ to -24.

(h) Subtract -36 from -15.

(d) Add -48 to -80.

(i) Add $+17$ to -17.

(e) Subtract $+16$ from $+17$.

(j) Subtract -17 from -17.

6-10. Repeat Problem 6-9 for the following cases, and show that overflow occurs in each case.

(a) Add $+37$ to $+95$.

(b) Subtract $+37$ from -95.

SECTIONS 6-5 AND 6-6

6-11. Multiply the following pairs of binary numbers, and check your results by doing the multiplication in decimal.

(a) 111×101

(c) 101.101×110.010

(b) 1011×1011

(d) $.1101 \times .1011$

6-12. Perform the following divisions. Check your results by doing the division in decimal.

(a) $1100 \div 100$

(c) $10111 \div 100$

(b) $111111 \div 1001$

(d) $10110.1101 \div 1.1$

SECTIONS 6-7 AND 6-8

6-13. Add the following decimal numbers after converting each to its BCD code.

(a) $74 + 23$

(d) $385 + 118$

(b) $58 + 37$

(e) $998 + 003$

(c) $147 + 380$

(f) $623 + 599$

6-14. Find the sum of each of the following pairs of hex numbers.

(a) $3E91 + 2F93$

(d) $2FFE + 0002$

(b) $91B + 6F2$

(e) $FFF + 0FF$

(c) $ABC + DEF$

(f) $D191 + AAAB$

6-15. Perform the following subtractions on the pairs of hex numbers.

(a) $3E91 - 2F93$

(d) $0200 - 0003$

(b) $91B - 6F2$

(e) $F000 - EFFF$

(c) $0300 - 005A$

(f) $2F00 - 4000$

6-16. The owner's manual for a small microcomputer states that the computer has usable memory locations at the following hex addresses: 0200 through 03FF, and 4000 through 7FD0. What is the total number of available memory locations?

6-17. (a) A certain memory location holds the hex data 77. If this represents an *unsigned* number, what is its decimal value?

(b) If this represents a *signed* number, what is its decimal value?

(c) Repeat (a) and (b) if the data value is E5.

SECTION 6-11

6-18. Convert the FA circuit of Figure 6-7 to all NAND gates.

6-19. Write the truth table for a half adder (inputs A and B; outputs SUM and CARRY). From the truth table, design a logic circuit that will act as a half adder.

6-20. A full adder can be implemented in many different ways. Figure 6-20 shows how one may be constructed from two half adders. Construct a truth table for this arrangement, and verify that it operates as a FA.

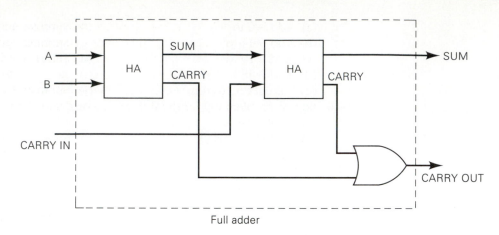

Full adder

FIGURE 6-20   Problem 6-20.

SECTION 6-12

6-21. Refer to Figure 6-9. Determine the contents of the A register after the following sequence of operations: $[A] = 0000$, $[0100] \rightarrow [B]$, $[S] \rightarrow [A]$, $[1011] \rightarrow [B]$, $[S] \rightarrow [A]$.

6-22. Refer to Figure 6-9. Assume that each FF has $t_{PLH} = t_{PHL} = 30$ ns and a setup time of 10 ns, and that each FA has a propagation delay of 40 ns. What is the minimum time allowed between the PGT of the LOAD pulse and the PGT of the TRANSFER pulse for proper operation?

D   6-23. In the adder and subtractor circuits discussed in this chapter, we gave no consideration to the possibility of *overflow*. Overflow occurs when the two numbers being added or subtracted produce a result that contains more bits than the capacity of the accumulator. For example, using four-bit registers, including a sign bit, numbers ranging from $+7$ to -8 (in 2's complement) can be stored. Therefore, if the result of an addition or subtraction exceeds $+7$ or -8, we would say that an overflow has occurred. When an overflow occurs, the results are useless since they cannot be stored correctly in the accumulator register. To illustrate, add $+5$ (0101) and $+4$ (0100), which results in 1001. This 1001 would be interpreted incorrectly as a negative number since there is a 1 in the sign-bit position.

In computers and calculators there are usually circuits that are used to detect an overflow condition. There are several ways to do this. One method that can be used for the adder that operates in the 2's-complement system works as follows:

1. Examine the sign bits of the two numbers being added.

2. Examine the sign bit of the result.

3. Overflow occurs whenever the numbers being added are *both positive* and the sign bit of the result is 1 *or* when the numbers are *both negative* and the sign bit of the result is 0.

This method can be verified by trying several examples. Readers should try the following cases for their own clarification: **(1)** 5 + 4: **(2)** $-4 + (-6)$;

(3) 3 + 2. Cases 1 and 2 will produce an overflow, and case 3 will not. Thus, by examining the sign bits, one can design a logic circuit that will produce a 1 output whenever the overflow condition occurs. Design this overflow circuit for the adder of Figure 6-9.

C, D 6-24. Add the necessary logic circuitry to Figure 6-9 to accommodate the transfer of data from memory into the A register. The data values from memory are to enter the A register through its D inputs on the PGT of the *first* TRANSFER pulse; the data from the sum outputs of the FAs will be loaded into A on the PGT of the *second* TRANSFER. In other words, a LOAD pulse followed by two TRANSFER pulses is required to perform the complete sequence of loading the B register from memory, loading the A register from memory, and then transferring their sum into the A register. (*Hint:* Use a flip-flop X to control which source of data gets loaded into the D inputs of the accumulator.)

SECTION 6-13

C, D 6-25. Design a look-ahead carry circuit for the adder of Figure 6-9 which generates the carry C_3 to be fed to the FA of the MSB position based on the values of A_0, B_0, C_0, A_1, B_1, A_2, and B_2. In other words, derive an expression for C_3 in terms of A_0, B_0, C_0, A_1, B_1, A_2, and B_2. (*Hint:* Begin by writing the expression for C_1 in terms of A_0, B_0, and C_0. Then write the expression for C_2 in terms of A_1, B_1, and C_1. Substitute the expression for C_1 into the expression for C_2. Then write the expression for C_3 in terms of A_2, B_2, and C_2. Substitute the expression for C_2 into the expression for C_3. Simplify the final expression for C_3 and put it in sum-of-products form. Implement the circuit.)

SECTION 6-14

6-26. Show the logic levels at each input and output of Figure 6-10(a) when 354_8 is added to 103_8.

SECTION 6-15

6-27. For the circuit of Figure 6-13, determine the sum outputs for the following cases.
(a) A register = 0101 (+5), B register = 1110 (−2); SUB = 1, ADD = 0
(b) A register = 1100 (−4), B register = 1110 (−2); SUB = 0, ADD = 1
(c) Repeat (b) with ADD = SUB = 0.

D 6-28. Show how the gates of Figure 6-13 can be implemented using three 74LS00 chips.

D 6-29. Modify the circuit of Figure 6-13 so that a single control input, X, is used in place of ADD and SUB. The circuit is to function as an adder when $X = 0$, and as a subtractor when $X = 1$. Then simplify each set of gates. (*Hint:* Note that now each set of gates is functioning as a controlled inverter.)

SECTION 6-16

6-30. Assume the following inputs in Figure 6-14: $[A]$ = 0101, $[B]$ = 1001, C_0 = 0. Determine the logic levels at $[S]$, X, $[\Sigma]$, and CARRY.

C 6-31. Would it make any difference in the BCD adder of Figure 6-14 if the C_0 of the upper adder was held LOW while the C_0 of the lower adder was used as the carry input? Explain.

6-32. Assume that the *A* register in Figure 6-15 holds the BCD code for 376 and that the *B* register holds the BCD code for 469. Determine the outputs.

SECTION 6-17

6-33. Determine the *F*, C_{N+4}, and *OVR* outputs for each of the following sets of inputs applied to a 74LS382.
   (a) $[S] = 011$, $[A] = 0110$, $[B] = 0011$, $C_N = 0$
   (b) $[S] = 001$, $[A] = 0110$, $[B] = 0011$, $C_N = 1$
   (c) $[S] = 010$, $[A] = 0110$, $[B] = 0011$, $C_N = 1$

D 6-34. Show how the 74HC382 can be used to produce $[F] = [\overline{A}]$. (*Hint:* Recall that special property of an EX-OR gate.)

6-35. Determine the Σ outputs in Figure 6-17 for the following sets of inputs.
   (a) $[S] = 110$, $[A] = 10101100$, $[B] = 00001111$
   (b) $[S] = 100$, $[A] = 11101110$, $[B] = 00110010$

C, D 6-36. Add the necessary logic to Figure 6-17 to produce a single HIGH output whenever the binary number at *A* is exactly the same as the binary number at *B*. Apply the appropriate select input code (three codes can be used).

SECTION 6-19

T 6-37. Consider the circuit of Figure 6-9. Assume that the A_2 output is stuck LOW. Follow the sequence of operations for adding two numbers, and determine the results that will appear in the *A* register after the second TRANSFER pulse for each of the following cases. Note that the numbers are given in decimal, and the first number is the one loaded into *B* by the first LOAD pulse.
   (a) 2 + 3   (d) 8 + 3
   (b) 3 + 7   (e) 9 + 3
   (c) 7 + 3

T 6-38. A technician breadboards the adder/subtractor of Figure 6-13. During testing, she finds that whenever an addition is performed, the result is 1 more than expected, and when a subtraction is performed, the result is 1 less than expected. What is the likely error that the technician made in connecting this circuit?

T 6-39. The BCD adder of Figure 6-14 is tested, and the results are recorded in Table 6-4. Consider each of the following possible faults, and indicate whether or not it could be the actual fault. Explain each answer.
   (a) The A_1 and A_0 inputs of the correction adder are internally shorted together.
   (b) There is an open path from *X* to the correction adder.
   (c) The upper OR gate inputs are internally shorted together.
   (d) The AND gate output is stuck LOW.

TABLE 6-4

	$B_3B_2B_1B_0$	$A_3A_2A_1A_0$	$\Sigma_3\Sigma_2\Sigma_1\Sigma_0$	CARRY (*X*)
(1)	0011	0110	1001	0
(2)	0111	1000	1111	0
(3)	1001	1001	0010	0

DRILL QUESTION

6-40. Define each of the following terms.

(a) Full adder   (f) Accumulator

(b) 2's-complement   (g) Parallel adder

(c) Arithmetic/logic unit   (h) Look-ahead carry

(d) Sign bit   (i) Negation

(e) Overflow   (j) *B* register

MICROCOMPUTER APPLICATIONS

C, D   6-41. In a typical microprocessor ALU, the results of every arithmetic operation are usually (but not always) transferred to the accumulator register as in Figures 6-9, 6-13, and 6-16. In most microprocessor ALUs, the result of each arithmetic operation is also used to control the states of several special flip-flops called *flags*. These flags are used by the microprocessor when it is making decisions during the execution of certain types of instructions. The three most common flags are:

S (sign flag). This FF is always in the same state as the sign of the last result from the ALU.

Z (zero flag). This flag is set to 1 whenever the result from an ALU operation is exactly 0. Otherwise, it is cleared to 0.

C (carry flag). This FF is always in the same state as the carry from the MSB of the ALU.

Using the adder/subtractor of Figure 6-13 as the ALU, design the logic circuit that will implement these flags. The sum outputs and C_4 output are to be used to control what state each flag will go to upon the occurrence of the TRANS-FER pulse. For example, if the sum is exactly 0 (i.e., 0000), the Z flag should be set by the PGT of TRANSFER; otherwise, it should be cleared.

6-42. In working with microcomputers it is often necessary to move binary numbers from an 8-bit register to a 16-bit register. Consider the numbers 01001001 and 10101110, which represent +73 and −82, respectively, in the 2's-complement system. Determine the 16-bit representations for these decimal numbers.

6-43. Compare the 8- and 16-bit representations for +73 from Problem 6-42. Then compare the two representations for −82. There is a general rule that can be used to convert easily from 8-bit to 16-bit representations. Can you see what it is? It has something to do with the sign bit of the 8-bit number.

ANSWERS TO SECTION REVIEW QUESTIONS

SECTION 6-1

1. (a) 11101   (b) 101.111   (c) 10010000

SECTION 6-2

1. (a) 00001101   (b) 11111001   (c) 10000000
2. (a) −29   (b) −64   (c) +126
3. −2048 to +2047   4. Seven   5. −32768
6. (a) 10000   (b) 10000000   (c) 1000
7. Refer to text.

SECTION 6-3

1. True   2. (a) $100010_2 = -30_{10}$
(b) $000000_2 = 0_{10}$

SECTION 6-4

1. (a) $01111_2 = +15_{10}$ (b) $11111_2 = -1_{10}$ 2. By comparing the sign bit of the sum with the sign bits of the numbers being added

SECTION 6-5
1. 1100010

SECTION 6-7
1. The sum of at least one decimal digit position is greater than 1001 (9).   2. The correction factor is added to both the units and the tens digit positions.

SECTION 6-8
1. 923   2. 3DB   3. 2F, 77EC, 6D

SECTION 6-10
1. Three; two   2. (a) $S_2 = 0$, $C_3 = 1$ (b) $C_5 = 0$

SECTION 6-12
1. One; four; four   2. 0100

SECTION 6-14
1. Five chips   2. 240 ns

SECTION 6-15
1. To add the 1 needed to complete the 2's-complement representation of the number in the B register
2. 0010   3. 1101   4. False; the 1's complement appears there.

SECTION 6-16
1. Two four-bit adders and correction logic   2. The correction logic detects a sum greater than 9 and then causes a 0110 to be added to the sum.

SECTION 6-17
1. $F = 1011$; $OVR = 0$; $C_{N+4} = 0$ 2. $F = 0111$; $OVR = 1$; $C_{N+4} = 1$ 3. $F = 1000$
4. $\Sigma = 01101011$; $C_{N+4} = OVR = 0$
5. $\Sigma = 11111111$ 6. Eight

CHAPTER 7

Counters and Registers

■ OUTLINE

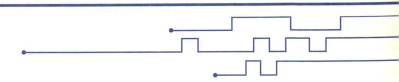

■ OBJECTIVES

Upon completion of this chapter, you will be able to:

- Understand the operation and characteristics of synchronous and asynchronous counters.
- Construct counters with MOD numbers less than 2^N.
- Identify IEEE/ANSI symbols used in IC counters and registers.
- Construct both up and down counters.
- Connect up multistage counters.
- Analyze and evaluate various types of presettable counters.
- Design arbitrary-sequence synchronous counters.
- Understand several types of schemes used to decode different types of counters.
- Anticipate and eliminate the effects of decoding glitches.
- Compare the major differences between ring and Johnson counters.
- Analyze the operation of a frequency counter and of a digital clock.
- Recognize and understand the operation of various types of IC registers.
- Apply existing troubleshooting techniques used for combinational logic systems to troubleshoot sequential logic systems.

■ INTRODUCTION

In Chapter 5 we saw how flip-flops could be connected to function as counters and registers. At that time we studied only the basic counter and register circuits. Digital systems employ many variations of these basic circuits, mostly in integrated-circuit form. In this chapter we will look at how FFs and logic gates can be combined to produce different types of counters and registers.

Because there are a great number of topics in this chapter, it has been divided into two parts. In **PART I** we will cover the principles of counter operation, the various counter circuit arrangements, and representative IC counters. **PART II** will present counter applications, types of IC registers, and troubleshooting.

An understanding of the material in this chapter is a good indication that the material of the preceding chapters has been mastered.

PART I

7-1 ASYNCHRONOUS (RIPPLE) COUNTERS

Figure 7-1 shows a four-bit binary counter circuit such as the one discussed in Chapter 5. Recall the following points concerning its operation:

1. The clock pulses are applied only to the *CLK* input of flip-flop *A*. Thus, flip-flop *A* will toggle (change to its opposite state) each time the clock pulses make a negative (HIGH-to-LOW) transition. Note that $J = K = 1$ for all FFs.

2. The normal output of flip-flop *A* acts as the *CLK* input for flip-flop *B*, and so flip-flop *B* will toggle each time the *A* output goes from 1 to 0. Similarly, flip-flop *C* will toggle when *B* goes from 1 to 0, and flip-flop *D* will toggle when *C* goes from 1 to 0.

3. FF outputs *D*, *C*, *B*, and *A* represent a four-bit binary number with *D* as the MSB. Let's assume that all FFs have been cleared to the 0 state (CLEAR inputs are not shown). The waveforms in Figure 7-1 show that a binary counting sequence from 0000 to 1111 is followed as clock pulses are continuously applied.

4. After the NGT of the fifteenth clock pulse has occurred, the counter FFs are in the 1111 condition. On the sixteenth NGT, flip-flop *A* goes from 1 to 0, which causes flip-flop *B* to go from 1 to 0, and so on until the counter is in the 0000 state. In other words, the counter has gone through one complete cycle (0000 through 1111) and has *recycled* back to 0000, from where it will begin a new counting cycle as subsequent clock pulses are applied.

In this counter, each FF output drives the *CLK* input of the next FF. This type of counter arrangement is called an **asynchronous counter** because the FFs do not change states in exact synchronism with the applied clock pulses; only flip-flop *A* responds to the clock pulses. FF *B* must wait for FF *A* to change states before it can toggle; FF *C* must wait for FF *B*, and so on. Thus, there is a delay between the responses of successive FFs. This delay is typically 5–20 ns per FF. In some cases, as we shall see, this delay can be troublesome. This type of counter is also often referred to as a **ripple counter** due to the way the FFs respond one after another in a kind of rippling effect. We will use the terms *asynchronous counter* and *ripple counter* interchangeably.

320

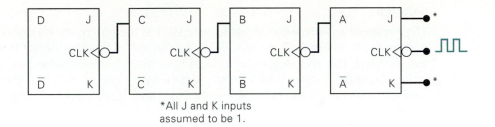

*All J and K inputs
assumed to be 1.

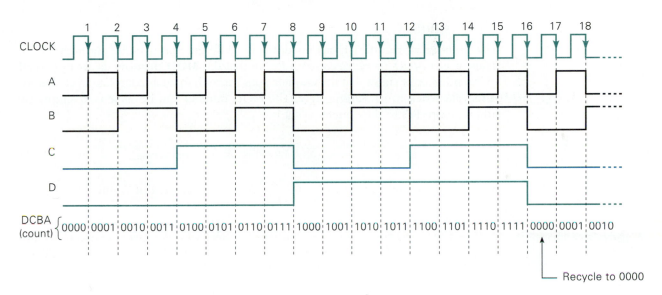

FIGURE 7-1 Four-bit asynchronous (ripple) counter.

Signal Flow

It is conventional in circuit schematics to draw the circuits (wherever possible) such that the signal flow is from left to right, with inputs on the left and outputs on the right. In this chapter we will often break with this convention, especially in diagrams showing counters. For example, in Figure 7-1, the *CLK* inputs of each FF are on the right, the outputs are on the left, and the input clock signal is shown coming in from the right. We will use this arrangement because it makes the counter operation easier to understand and follow, since the order of the FFs is the same as the order of the bits in the binary number that the counter represents. In other words, FF *A* which is the LSB is the rightmost FF, and FF *D* which is the MSB is the leftmost FF. If we adhered to the conventional left-to-right signal flow, we would have to put FF *A* on the left and FF *D* on the right, which is opposite to their positions in the binary number that the counter represents. In some of the counter diagrams later in the chapter, we will employ the conventional left-to-right signal flow so that you will get used to seeing it.

**EXAMPLE
7-1**

The counter in Figure 7-1 starts off in the 0000 state, and then clock pulses are applied. Some time later the clock pulses are removed, and the counter FFs read 0011. How many clock pulses have occurred?

Solution

The apparent answer seems to be 3, since 0011 is the binary equivalent of 3. However, with the information given there is no way to tell whether or not the counter has recycled. This means that there could have been 19 clock pulses; the first 16 pulses bring the counter back to 0000, and the last 3 bring it to 0011. There could have been 35 pulses (two complete cycles and then three more), or 51 pulses, and so on.

MOD Number

The counter in Figure 7-1 has 16 distinctly different states (0000 through 1111). Thus, it is a *MOD-16 ripple counter.* Recall that the **MOD number** is always equal to the number of states that the counter goes through in each complete cycle before it recycles back to its starting state. The MOD number can be increased simply by adding more FFs to the counter. That is,

$$MOD \text{ number} = 2^N \tag{7-1}$$

where N is the number of FFs connected in the arrangement of Figure 7-1.

EXAMPLE 7-2

A counter is needed that will count the number of items passing on a conveyor belt. A photocell and light source combination is used to generate a single pulse each time an item crosses its path. The counter must be able to count as many as one thousand items. How many FFs are required?

Solution

It is a simple matter to determine what value of N is needed so that $2^N \geq 1000$. Since $2^9 = 512$, 9 FFs will not be enough. $2^{10} = 1024$, so 10 FFs would produce a counter that could count as high as $1111111111_2 = 1023_{10}$. Therefore, we should use 10 FFs. We could use more than 10, but it would be a waste of FFs, since any FF past the tenth one will not be needed.

Frequency Division

In Chapter 5 we saw that in the basic counter each FF provides an output waveform that is exactly *half* the frequency of the waveform at its *CLK* input. To illustrate, suppose that the clock signal in Figure 7-1 is 16 kHz. Figure 7-2 shows the FF output waveforms. The waveform at output A is an 8-kHz *square wave,* at output B it is 4 kHz, at output C it is 2 kHz, and at output D it is 1 kHz. Notice that the output of flip-flop D has a frequency equal to the original clock frequency divided by 16. In general, *for any counter, the output from the last FF (i.e., the MSB) divides the input clock frequency by the MOD number of the counter.* For example, a MOD-16 counter could also be called a *divide-by-16 counter.*

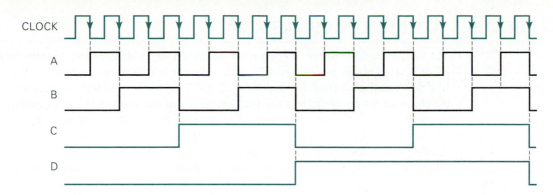

FIGURE 7-2   Counter-waveforms showing frequency division by 2 for each FF.

<table>
<tr><td>**EXAMPLE 7-3**</td><td>The first step involved in building a digital clock is to take the 60-Hz signal and feed it into a Schmitt-trigger, pulse-shaping circuit* to produce a square wave as illustrated in Figure 7-3. The 60-Hz square wave is then put into a MOD-60 counter, which is used to divide the 60-Hz frequency by exactly 60 to produce a 1-Hz waveform. This 1-Hz waveform is fed to a series of counters, which then count seconds, minutes, hours, and so on. How many FFs are required for the MOD-60 counter?</td></tr>
</table>

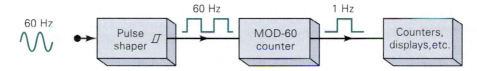

FIGURE 7-3   Example 7-3.

Solution

There is no integer power of 2 that will equal 60. The closest is $2^6 = 64$. Thus, a counter using six FFs would act as a MOD-64 counter. Obviously, this will not satisfy the requirement. It seems that there is no solution using a counter of the type shown in Figure 7-1. This is partly true; in the next section we will see how to modify this basic binary counter so that virtually *any* MOD number can be obtained and we will not be limited to values of 2^N.

Review Questions

1. *True or false:* In an asynchronous counter, all FFs change states at the same time.

2. Assume that the counter in Figure 7-1 is holding the count 0101. What will be the count after 27 clock pulses?

3. What would the MOD number of the counter be if three more FFs were added?

---

*   See Section 5-21.

7-2 COUNTERS WITH MOD NUMBERS < 2^N

The basic ripple counter of Figure 7-1 is limited to MOD numbers that are equal to 2^N, where N is the number of FFs. This value is actually the maximum MOD number that can be obtained using N flip-flops. The basic counter can be modified to produce MOD numbers less than 2^N by allowing the counter to *skip states* that are normally part of the counting sequence. One of the most common methods for doing this is illustrated in Figure 7-4, where a three-bit ripple counter is shown. Disregarding the NAND gate for a moment, we can see that the counter is a MOD-8 binary counter which will count in sequence from 000 to 111. However, the presence of the NAND gate will alter this sequence as follows:

1. The NAND output is connected to the asynchronous CLEAR inputs of each FF. As long as the NAND output is HIGH, it will have no effect on the counter. When it goes LOW, however, it will clear all of the FFs so that the counter immediately goes to the 000 state.

2. The inputs to the NAND gate are the outputs of the B and C flip-flops, and so the NAND output will go LOW whenever $B = C = 1$. This condition will occur when the counter goes from the 101 state to the 110 state on the NGT of input pulse 6. The LOW at the NAND output will immediately (generally within a few nanoseconds) clear the counter to the 000 state. Once the FFs have been cleared, the NAND output goes back HIGH, since the $B = C = 1$ condition no longer exists.

3. The counting sequence is, therefore,

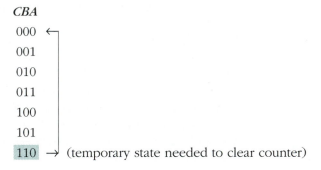

Although the counter does go to the 110 state, it remains there for only a few nanoseconds before it recycles to 000. Thus, we can essentially say that this counter counts from 000 (zero) to 101 (five) and then recycles to 000. It essentially skips 110 and 111 so that it goes through only six different states; thus, it is a MOD-6 counter.

Notice that the waveform at the B output contains a *spike* or *glitch* caused by the momentary occurrence of the 110 state before clearing. This glitch is very narrow and so would not produce any visible indication on indicator LEDs or numerical displays. It could, however, cause a problem if the B output were being used to drive other circuitry outside the counter. It should also be noted that the C output has a frequency equal to one-sixth of the input frequency; in other words, this MOD-6 counter has divided the input frequency by *six*. The waveform at C is *not* a

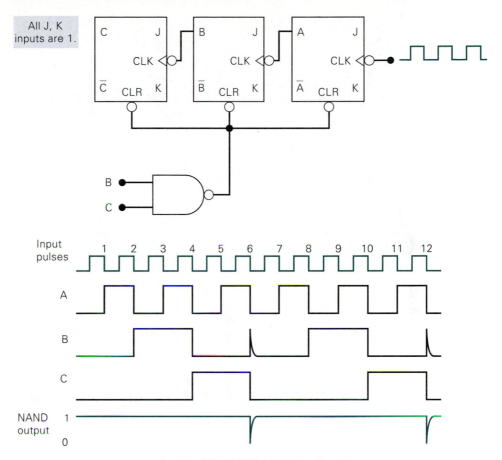

FIGURE 7-4 MOD-6 counter produced by clearing a MOD-8 counter when a count of six (110) occurs.

symmetrical square wave (50 percent duty cycle), because it is HIGH for only two clock cycles, whereas it is LOW for four cycles.

State Transition Diagram

Figure 7-5(a) is the state transition diagram for the MOD-6 counter of Figure 7-4, showing how FFs C, B, and A change states as pulses are applied to the *CLK* input of flip-flop A. Recall that each circle represents one of the possible counter states and that the arrows indicate how one state changes to another in response to an input clock pulse.

If we assume a starting count of 000, the diagram shows that the states of the counter change normally up until the count of 101. When the next clock pulse occurs, the counter temporarily goes to the 110 count before going to the stable 000 count. The dotted lines indicate the temporary nature of the 110 state. As stated earlier, the duration of this temporary state is so short that for most purposes we can consider that the counter goes directly from 101 to 000 (solid arrow).

Note that the 111 state is never reached, not even temporarily.

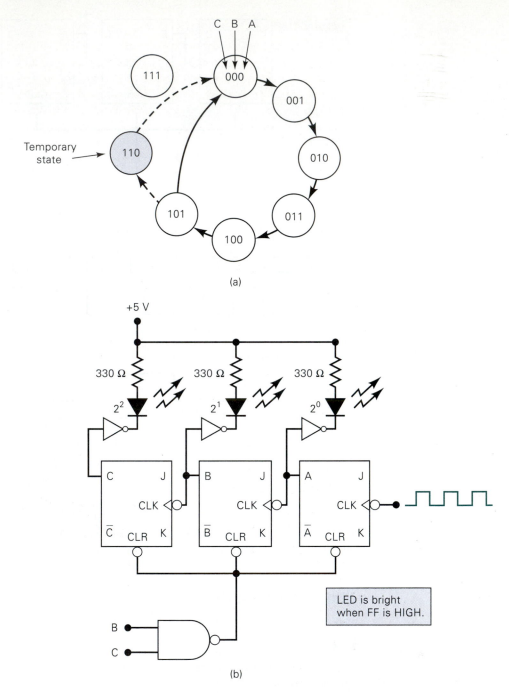

(a)

(b)

FIGURE 7-5 (a) State transition diagram for the MOD-6 counter of Figure 7-4. (b) LEDs are often used to display the states of a counter.

Displaying Counter States

Sometimes during normal operation, and very often during testing, it is necessary to have a visible display of how a counter is changing states in response to the input pulses. We will take a detailed look at several ways of doing this later in the text. For now, Figure 7-5(b) shows one of the simplest methods using individual indicator LEDs for each FF output. Each FF output is connected to an INVERTER whose output provides the current path for the LED. For example, when output A is HIGH, the INVERTER output goes LOW and the LED turns ON. The bright LED indicates $A = 1$. When output A is LOW, the INVERTER output is HIGH and the LED turns OFF. The dark LED indicates $A = 0$.

EXAMPLE 7-4

(a) What will be the status of the LEDs when the counter is holding the count of five?

(b) What will the LEDs display as the counter is clocked by a 1-kHz input?

(c) Will the 110 state be visible on the LEDs?

Solution

(a) Since $5_{10} = 101_2$, the 2^0 and 2^2 LEDs will be ON, and the 2^1 LED will be OFF.

(b) At 1 kHz, the LEDs will be switching ON and OFF so rapidly that they will appear to the human eye to be ON all the time at about half the normal brightness.

(c) No; the 110 state will persist for only a few nanoseconds as the counter recycles to 000.

Changing the MOD Number

The counter of Figures 7-4 and 7-5 is a MOD-6 counter because of the choice of inputs to the NAND gate. Any desired MOD number can be obtained by changing these inputs. For example, using a three-input NAND gate with inputs A, B, and C, the counter would function normally until the 111 condition was reached, at which point it would immediately reset to the 000 state. Ignoring the very temporary excursion into the 111 state, the counter would go from 000 through 110 and then recycle back to 000, resulting in a MOD-7 counter (seven states).

EXAMPLE 7-5

Determine the MOD number of the counter in Figure 7-6(a). Also determine the frequency at the D output.

Solution

This is a four-bit counter, which would normally count from 0000 through 1111. The NAND inputs are D, C, and B, which means that the counter will immediately recycle to 0000 when the 1110 (decimal 14) count is reached. Thus, the counter

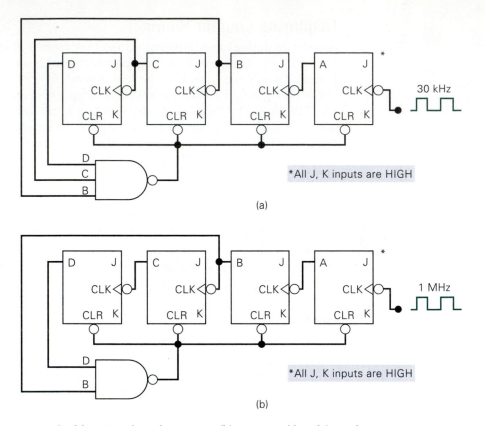

FIGURE 7-6   (a) MOD-14 ripple counter; (b) MOD-10 (decade) ripple counter.

actually has 14 stable states 0000 through 1101 and is therefore a *MOD-14* counter. Since the input frequency is 30 kHz, the frequency at output D will be

$$\frac{30 \text{ kHz}}{14} = 2.14 \text{ kHz}$$

General Procedure

To construct a counter that starts counting from all 0s and has a MOD number of X:

1. Find the smallest number of FFs such that $2^N \geq X$, and connect them as a counter. If $2^N = X$, do not do steps 2 and 3.
2. Connect a NAND gate to the asynchronous CLEAR inputs of all the FFs.
3. Determine which FFs will be in the HIGH state at a count $= X$; then connect the normal outputs of these FFs to the NAND gate inputs.

EXAMPLE 7-6

Construct a MOD-10 counter that will count from 0000 (zero) through 1001 (decimal 9).

Solution

$2^3 = 8$ and $2^4 = 16$; thus, four FFs are required. Since the counter is to have stable operation up to the count of 1001, it must be reset to zero when the count of 1010 is reached. Therefore, FF outputs D and B must be connected as the NAND gate inputs. Figure 7-6(b) shows the arrangement.

Decade Counters/BCD Counters

The MOD-10 counter of Example 7-6 is also referred to as a **decade counter.** In fact, a decade counter is any counter that has 10 distinct states, no matter what the sequence. A decade counter such as the one in Figure 7-6(b), which counts in sequence from 0000 (zero) through 1001 (decimal 9), is also commonly called a **BCD counter,** because it uses only the 10 BCD code groups 0000, 0001, . . ., 1000, and 1001. To reiterate, any MOD-10 counter is a decade counter; and any decade counter that counts in binary from 0000 to 1001 is a BCD counter.

Decade counters, especially the BCD type, find widespread use in applications where pulses or events are to be counted and the results displayed on some type of decimal numerical readout. We shall examine this later in more detail. A decade counter is also often used for dividing a pulse frequency *exactly* by 10. The input pulses are applied to flip-flop A, and the output pulses are taken from the output of flip-flop D, which has one-tenth the frequency of the input.

EXAMPLE 7-7

In Example 7-3, a MOD-60 counter was needed to divide the 60-Hz line frequency down to 1 Hz. Construct an appropriate MOD-60 counter.

Solution

$2^5 = 32$ and $2^6 = 64$, and so we need six FFs, as shown in Figure 7-7. The counter is to be cleared when it reaches the count of 60 (111100). Thus, the outputs of flip-flops Q_2 Q_3, Q_4, and Q_5 must be connected to the NAND gate. The output of flip-flop Q_5 will have a frequency of 1 Hz.

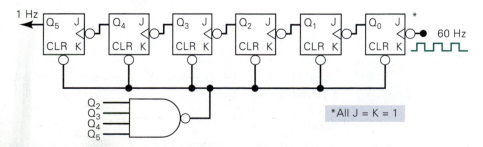

FIGURE 7-7 MOD-60 counter.

1. What FF outputs should be connected to the clearing NAND gate to form a MOD-13 counter?

2. *True or false:* All BCD counters are decade counters.

3. What is the output frequency of a decade counter that is clocked from a 50-kHz signal?

7-3 IC ASYNCHRONOUS COUNTERS

There are several TTL and CMOS asynchronous counter ICs. One of them is the TTL 74LS293. Figure 7-8(a) shows the logic diagram for the 74LS293 as it would appear in the manufacturer's TTL data book. Some of the nomenclature is different from what we have been using, but it should be easy to figure out. Note the following points:

1. The 74LS293 has four J-K flip-flops with outputs Q_0, Q_1, Q_2, Q_3, where Q_0 is the LSB and Q_3 is the MSB. The FFs are shown arranged with the LSB on the left. This is done to satisfy the convention that the circuit input signals appear on the left. We have been drawing our counters with the LSB on the right so that the order of the FFs is the same as the order of the bits in the binary count.

2. Each FF has a *CP* (clock pulse) input, which is just another name for the *CLK* input. The clock inputs to Q_0 and Q_1, labeled $\overline{CP}_0$ and $\overline{CP}_1$, respectively, are externally accessible. The inversion bars over these inputs indicate that they are activated by a NGT.

3. Each FF has an asynchronous CLEAR input, C_D. These are connected together to the output of a two-input NAND gate with inputs MR_1 and MR_2, where *MR* stands for *master reset*. Both *MR* inputs must be HIGH to clear the counter to 0000.

4. Flip-flops Q_1, Q_2, and Q_3 are already connected as a three-bit ripple counter. Flip-flop Q_0 is not connected to anything internally. This allows the user the option of either connecting Q_0 to Q_1 to form a four-bit counter or using Q_0 separately if desired.

The following examples will illustrate some of the ways the 74LS293 can be wired to produce different counters. In these examples we will use the simplified logic symbol shown in Figure 7-8(b).

EXAMPLE 7-8

Show how the 74LS293 should be connected to operate as a MOD-16 counter with a 10-kHz clock input.

Solution

A MOD-16 counter requires four FFs, and so we must connect the Q_0 output to $\overline{CP}_1$, the clock input of flip-flop Q_1 (see Figure 7-9). The 10-kHz pulses are applied to $\overline{CP}_0$, the clock input of Q_0. The output is taken at Q_3.

74LS293

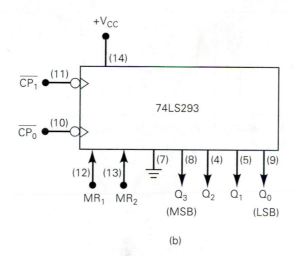

(a)

*All J, K inputs are internally connected HIGH.

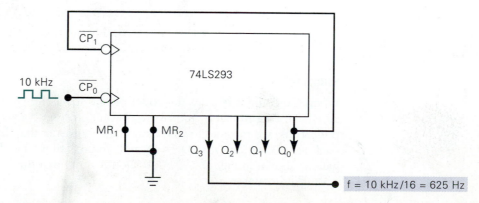

(b)

FIGURE 7-8 (a) Logic diagram for 74LS293 asynchronous counter IC; (b) block symbol with pin numbers in parentheses. (Courtesy of Fairchild, a Schlumberger company)

FIGURE 7-9 74LS293 wired as a MOD-16 counter.

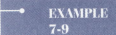

EXAMPLE 7-9

Show how to wire the 74LS293 as a MOD-10 counter.

Solution

A MOD-10 counter requires four FFs, and so again we need to connect Q_0 to $\overline{CP_1}$. This time, however, we want the counter to recycle back to 0000 when it tries to go to the count of 1010 (10). Thus, the Q_3 and Q_1 outputs must be connected to the master reset inputs; when they both go HIGH at the count of 1010, the NAND output will immediately reset the counter to 0000.

The circuit wiring is shown in Figure 7-10. The state transition diagram is also shown. Note that the temporary 1010 state is not shown.

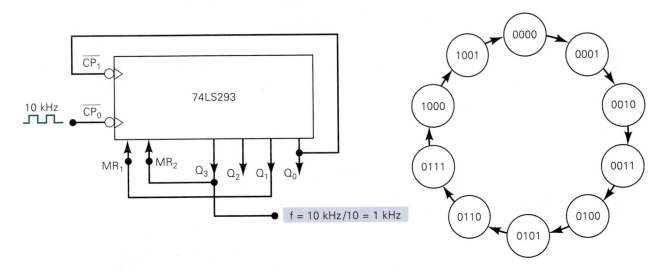

FIGURE 7-10 74LS293 wired as a MOD-10 counter.

EXAMPLE 7-10

Show how to wire a 74LS293 as a MOD-14 counter.

Solution

When the counter reaches the count of 1110 (14), the Q_3, Q_2, and Q_1 outputs are all HIGH. Unfortunately, the 74LS293's built-in reset NAND gate has only two inputs. Thus, we must add some extra logic to ensure that the counter will reset back to 0000 when $Q_3 = Q_2 = Q_1 = 1$. In fact, all we need is a two-input AND gate as shown in Figure 7-11. You should verify that this arrangement operates as a MOD-14 counter.

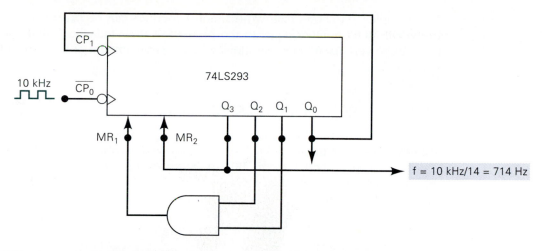

FIGURE 7-11   An external AND gate is needed to wire the 74LS293 as a MOD-14 counter.

EXAMPLE 7-11   In Example 7-7 we divided the input frequency by 60 with a MOD-60 counter using six J-K flip-flops and a NAND gate. Another way to get a MOD-60 counter is shown in Figure 7-12. Explain how this circuit works.

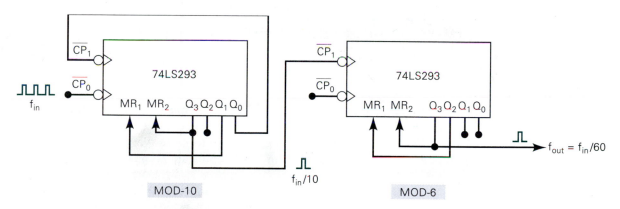

FIGURE 7-12   Two 74LS293s combined to provide a frequency division of 60 by successive divisions by 10 (MOD-10) and 6 (MOD-6). Note that the MOD-6 does not use $\overline{CP}_0$ or Q_0; it uses only Q_3, Q_2, and Q_1.

Solution

This circuit divides the input frequency by 60 in two steps. The 74LS293 counter on the left is wired as a MOD-10 counter so that its output Q_3 has a frequency of $f_{in}/10$. This signal is connected to the $\overline{CP}_1$ input of the second 74LS293 counter, which is wired as a MOD-6 counter (note that Q_0 is not being used). Thus, the Q_3 output of the second counter will have the following frequency:

$$f_{out} = \frac{f_{in}/10}{6} = \frac{f_{in}}{60}$$

Example 7-11 shows that two (or more) counters can be cascaded to produce an overall MOD number equal to the *product* of their individual MOD numbers. This can be very useful in applications where a large amount of frequency division is required.

IEEE/ANSI Symbol for 74LS293 Counter

Figure 7-13 shows the IEEE/ANSI symbol for the 74LS293. This symbol contains several new aspects of the IEEE/ANSI standard. As we describe these, you should continue to appreciate how the new IEEE/ANSI symbology is designed to tell us a lot about the IC's operation.

FIGURE 7-13 IEEE/ANSI symbol for the 74LS293 IC.

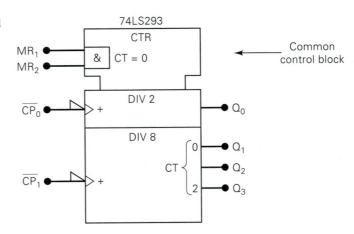

The symbol contains three distinct blocks. The top block (with the notches) is the common-control block. The notation "CTR" defines this IC as a counter. Recall from our discussion in Chapter 5 that the common-control block is used whenever an IC has one or more inputs that are common to more than one of the circuits on the chip. For the 74LS293, the MR_1 and MR_2 inputs are common to all the FFs in the counter.

MR_1 and MR_2 are shown as active-HIGH inputs that are internally combined using the AND operation as indicated by the "&" notation. This indicates that *both* MR_1 and MR_2 must be in their active states in order to clear the counter. The notation "CT = 0" tells us that the action of the *MR* inputs is to make the count equal zero.

The middle block is labeled "DIV2" to indicate that it is a MOD-2 counter, which, of course, is a single FF. DIV2 means that the counter will divide its clock input frequency by 2. The bottom block is labeled "DIV8" to indicate that it is a MOD-8 counter. The clock inputs to each of these blocks are shown as activated by negative-going transitions. The "+" notation on each clock input indicates that the NGT of the clock will cause the count to be *incremented by 1*. In other words, this is an **up counter**, meaning that it *counts up* on each NGT. A "−" notation would be used for a **down counter** (see Section 7-4).

While we will continue to use the traditional symbol for the 74LS293 and other counters, we will use some of the notation from the IEEE/ANSI symbology. For example, we will indicate a counter's MOD number using the DIV*n* notation, where *n* is the MOD number.

CMOS Asynchronous Counters

There are several asynchronous counters in the CMOS family. Most of them are equivalents to the TTL versions. However, some CMOS asynchronous counter ICs do not have a TTL counterpart. One of these is the 74HC4024; its logic symbol is shown in Figure 7-14. It is a seven-bit counter with one asynchronous master reset input. The seven FFs are internally connected as a MOD-128 ripple counter. The *MR* input is active-HIGH and can be used to reset all of the FFs to the 0 state. Note that we have used the notation "CTR DIV128" to signify that this is a MOD-128 counter.

FIGURE 7-14 Logic symbol for the CMOS 74HC4024 ripple counter. The + sign indicates count-up operation.

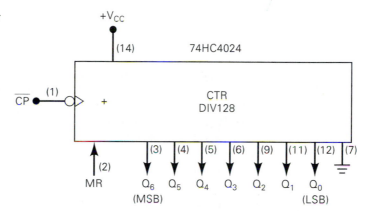

Another CMOS ripple counter that has no TTL counterpart is the 74HC4040, which is a 12-bit counter with a single active-HIGH master reset input. The clock input to this counter is a Schmitt-trigger type of input that permits the use of slow-changing signals without producing erratic counting.

Review Questions

1. A 2-kHz clock signal is applied to $\overline{CP}_1$ of a 74LS293. What is the frequency at Q_3?

2. What would be the final output frequency if the order of the counters were reversed in Figure 7-12?

3. What is the MOD number of a 74HC4040 counter?

4. What would the notation "DIV64" mean on a counter symbol?

5. Connect Q_6 and Q_5 as inputs to an AND gate in Figure 7-14, and connect the AND output to *MR*. What will be the new MOD number?

7-4 ASYNCHRONOUS DOWN COUNTER

All of the counters we have looked at thus far have counted *upward* from zero; that is, they were **up counters.** It is a relatively simple matter to construct asynchronous (ripple) **down counters,** which will count downward from a maximum count to zero. Before looking at the circuit for a ripple down counter, let us examine the count-down sequence for a three-bit down counter:

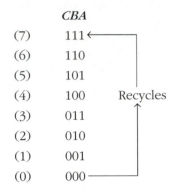

CBA

(7)	111←	
(6)	110	
(5)	101	
(4)	100	Recycles
(3)	011	
(2)	010	
(1)	001	
(0)	000	

A, *B*, and *C* represent the FF output states as the counter goes through its sequence. It can be seen that the *A* flip-flop (LSB) changes states (toggles) at each step in the sequence just as it does in the up counter. The *B* flip-flop changes states each time *A* goes from LOW to HIGH; *C* changes states each time *B* goes from LOW to HIGH. Thus, in a down counter each FF, except the first, must toggle when the preceding FF goes from LOW to HIGH. If the FFs have *CLK* inputs that respond to negative transitions (HIGH to LOW), then an inverter can be placed in front of each *CLK* input; however, the same effect can be accomplished by driving each FF *CLK* input from the *inverted* output of the preceding FF. This is illustrated in Figure 7-15 for a MOD-8 down counter.

The input pulses are applied to the *A* flip-flop. The $\overline{A}$ output serves as the *CLK* input for the *B* flip-flop; the $\overline{B}$ output serves as the *CLK* input for the *C* flip-flop. The waveforms at *A*, *B*, and *C* show that *B* toggles whenever *A* goes LOW to HIGH (so that $\overline{A}$ goes HIGH to LOW) and *C* toggles whenever *B* goes LOW to HIGH. This results in the desired down-counting sequence at the *C*, *B*, and *A* outputs. The state transition diagram shows the sequence. Compare it with the diagram for the MOD-8 up counter in Figure 5-49.

Down counters are not as widely used as up counters. Their major application is in situations where it must be known when a desired number of input pulses have occurred. In these situations the down counter is *preset* to the desired number and then allowed to count down as the pulses are applied. When the counter reaches the *zero* state, it is detected by a logic gate whose output then indicates that the preset number of pulses has occurred. We shall discuss presettable counters in Section 7-8.

Review Questions

1. What is the difference between the counting sequence of an up counter and a down counter?
2. Describe how an asynchronous down-counter circuit differs from an up-counter circuit.

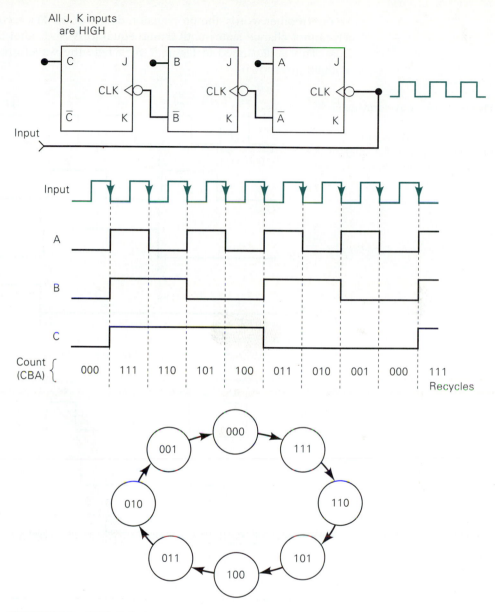

FIGURE 7-15 MOD-8 down counter.

7-5 PROPAGATION DELAY IN RIPPLE COUNTERS

Ripple counters are the simplest type of binary counters, since they require the fewest components to produce a given counting operation. They do, however, have one major drawback, which is caused by their basic principle of operation: each FF is triggered by the transition at the output of the preceding FF. Because of the inherent propagation delay time (t_{pd}) of each FF, this means that the second FF will not respond until a time t_{pd} after the first FF receives an active clock transition; the third FF will not respond until a time equal to $2 \times t_{pd}$ after that clock transition; and so on. In other words, the propagation delays of the FFs accumulate so that the Nth FF cannot change states until a time equal to $N \times t_{pd}$ after the clock transition occurs. This is illustrated in Figure 7-16, where the waveforms for a three-bit ripple counter are shown.

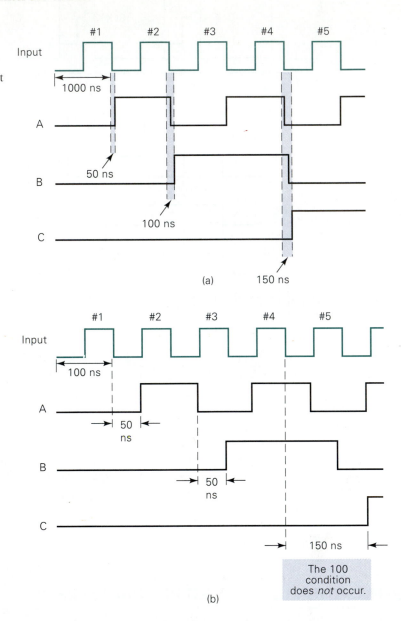

FIGURE 7-16 Waveforms of a three-bit ripple counter illustrating the effects of FF propagation delays for different input pulse frequencies.

The first set of waveforms in Figure 7-16(a) shows a situation where an input pulse occurs every 1000 ns (the clock period $T = 1000$ ns) and it is assumed that each FF has a propagation delay of 50 ns ($t_{pd} = 50$ ns). Notice that the A flip-flop output toggles 50 ns after the NGT of each input pulse. Similarly, B toggles 50 ns after A goes from 1 to 0, and C toggles 50 ns after B goes from 1 to 0. As a result, when the fourth input NGT occurs, the C output goes HIGH after a delay of 150 ns. In this situation the counter does operate properly in the sense that the FFs do eventually get to their correct states, representing the binary count. However, the situation worsens if the input pulses are applied at a much higher frequency.

The waveforms in Figure 7-16(b) show what happens if the input pulses occur once every 100 ns. Again, each FF output responds 50 ns after the 1-to-0 transition at its *CLK* input (note the change in the relative time scale). Of particular interest is the situation after the falling edge of the *fourth* input pulse, where the *C* output does not go HIGH until 150 ns later, which is the same time that the *A* output goes HIGH in response to the *fifth* input pulse. In other words, the condition $C = 1$, $B = A = 0$ (count of 100) never appears, because the input frequency is too high. This could cause a serious problem if this condition were supposed to be used to control some other operation in a digital system. Problems such as this can be avoided if the period between input pulses is made longer than the total propagation delay of the counter. That is, for proper counter operation we need

$$T_{clock} \geq N \times t_{pd} \tag{7-2}$$

where $N =$ number of FFs. Stated in terms of input-clock frequency, the maximum frequency that can be used is given by

$$f_{max} = \frac{1}{N \times t_{pd}} \tag{7-3}$$

For example, suppose that a four-bit ripple counter is constructed using the 74LS112 J-K flip-flop. Table 5-2 shows that the 74LS112 has $t_{PLH} = 16$ ns and $t_{PHL} = 24$ ns as the propagation delays from *CLK* to *Q*. To calculate f_{max}, we will assume the "worst case"; that is, we will use $t_{pd} = t_{PHL} = 24$ ns, so that

$$f_{max} = \frac{1}{4 \times 24 \text{ ns}} = 10.4 \text{ MHz}$$

Clearly, as the number of FFs in the counter increases, the total propagation delay increases and f_{max} decreases. For example, a ripple counter that uses six 74LS112 FFs will have

$$f_{max} = \frac{1}{6 \times 24 \text{ ns}} = 6.9 \text{ MHz}$$

Thus, asynchronous counters are not useful at very high frequencies, especially for large numbers of bits. Another problem caused by propagation delays in asynchronous counters occurs when the counter outputs are *decoded*. This problem is discussed in Section 7-12. Despite these problems, the simplicity of asynchronous counters makes them useful for applications where their frequency limitation is not critical.

Review Questions

1. Explain why a ripple counter's maximum frequency limitation decreases as more FFs are added to the counter.
2. A certain J-K flip-flop has $t_{pd} = 12$ ns. What is the largest MOD counter that can be constructed from these FFs and still operate up to 10 MHz?

7-6 SYNCHRONOUS (PARALLEL) COUNTERS

The problems encountered with ripple counters are caused by the accumulated FF propagation delays; stated another way, the FFs do not all change states simultaneously in synchronism with the input pulses. These limitations can be overcome with the use of **synchronous** or **parallel counters** in which all of the FFs are triggered simultaneously (in parallel) by the clock input pulses. Since the input pulses are applied to all the FFs, some means must be used to control when a FF is to toggle and when it is to remain unaffected by a clock pulse. This is accomplished by using the *J* and *K* inputs and is illustrated in Figure 7-17 for a four-bit, MOD-16 synchronous counter.

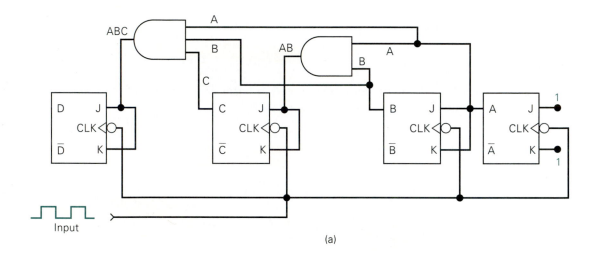

(a)

Count	D	C	B	A
0	0	0	0	0
1	0	0	0	1
2	0	0	1	0
3	0	0	1	1
4	0	1	0	0
5	0	1	0	1
6	0	1	1	0
7	0	1	1	1
8	1	0	0	0
9	1	0	0	1
10	1	0	1	0
11	1	0	1	1
12	1	1	0	0
13	1	1	0	1
14	1	1	1	0
15	1	1	1	1
0	0	0	0	0
.	.	.	.	.
.	.	.	.	.
.	.	etc.	.	.

(b)

FIGURE 7-17 Synchronous MOD-16 counter. Each FF is clocked by the NGT of the clock input signal so that all FF transitions occur at the same time.

If we compare the circuit arrangement for this synchronous counter with its asynchronous counterpart in Figure 7-1, we can see the following notable differences:

- The *CLK* inputs of all of the FFs are connected together so that the input clock signal is applied to each FF simultaneously.
- Only flip-flop *A*, the LSB, has its *J* and *K* inputs permanently at the HIGH level. The *J*, *K* inputs of the other FFs are driven by some combination of FF outputs.
- The synchronous counter requires more circuitry than does the asynchronous counter.

Circuit Operation

For this circuit to count properly, on a given NGT of the clock, only those FFs that are supposed to toggle on that NGT should have $J = K = 1$ when that NGT occurs. Let's look at the counting sequence in Figure 7-17(b) to see what this means for each FF.

The counting sequence shows that the *A* flip-flop must change states at each NGT. For this reason, its *J* and *K* inputs are permanently HIGH so that it will toggle on each NGT of the clock input.

The counting sequence shows that flip-flop *B* must change states on each NGT that occurs while $A = 1$. For example, when the count is 0001, the next NGT must toggle *B* to the 1 state; when the count is 0011, the next NGT must toggle *B* to the 0 state; and so on. This operation is accomplished by connecting output *A* to the *J* and *K* inputs of flip-flop *B* so that $J = K = 1$ only when $A = 1$.

The counting sequence shows that flip-flop *C* must change states on each NGT that occurs while $A = B = 1$. For example, when the count is 0011, the next NGT must toggle *C* to the 1 state; when the count is 0111, the next NGT must toggle *C* to the 0 state; and so on. By connecting the logic signal *AB* to FF *C*'s *J* and *K* inputs, this FF will toggle only when $A = B = 1$.

In a like manner, we can see that flip-flop *D* must toggle on each NGT that occurs while $A = B = C = 1$. When the count is 0111, the next NGT must toggle *D* to the 1 state; when the count is 1111, the next NGT must toggle *D* to the 0 state. By connecting the logic signal *ABC* to FF *D*'s *J* and *K* inputs, this FF will toggle only when $A = B = C = 1$.

The basic principle for constructing a synchronous counter can therefore be stated as follows:

> **Each FF should have its *J* and *K* inputs connected such that they are HIGH only when the outputs of all lower-order FFs are in the HIGH state.**

Advantage of Synchronous Counters over Asynchronous

In a parallel counter all of the FFs will change states simultaneously; that is, they are all synchronized to the NGTs of the input clock pulses. Thus, unlike the asynchronous counters, the propagation delays of the FFs do not add together to produce the overall delay. Instead, the total response time of a synchronous counter like the one in Figure 7-17 is the time it takes *one* FF to toggle plus the time for the new logic levels to propagate through a *single* AND gate to reach the *J, K* inputs. That is, for a synchronous counter,

$$\text{total delay} = \text{FF } t_{pd} + \text{AND gate } t_{pd}$$

This total delay is the same no matter how many FFs are in the counter, and it will generally be much lower than with an asynchronous counter with the same number of FFs. Thus, a synchronous counter can operate at a much higher input frequency. Of course, the circuitry of the synchronous counter is more complex than that of the asynchronous counter.

Actual ICs

There are many synchronous ICs in both the TTL and the CMOS logic families. Some of the most commonly used devices are:

- 74LS160/162, 74HC160/162: synchronous decade counters
- 74LS161/163, 74HC161/163: synchronous MOD-16 counters

EXAMPLE 7-12

(a) Determine f_{max} for the counter of Figure 7-17(a) if t_{pd} for each FF is 50 ns and t_{pd} for each AND gate is 20 ns. Compare this value with f_{max} for a MOD-16 ripple counter.

(b) What must be done to convert this counter to MOD-32?

(c) Determine f_{max} for the MOD-32 parallel counter.

Solution

(a) The total delay that must be allowed between input clock pulses is equal to FF t_{pd} + AND gate t_{pd}. Thus, $T_{clock} \geq 50 + 20 = 70$ ns, and so the parallel counter has

$$f_{max} = \frac{1}{70 \text{ ns}} = 14.3 \text{ MHz (parallel counter)}$$

A MOD-16 ripple counter uses four FFs with $t_{pd} = 50$ ns. Thus, f_{max} for the ripple counter is

$$f_{max} = \frac{1}{4 \times 50 \text{ ns}} = 5 \text{ MHz (ripple counter)}$$

(b) A fifth FF must be added, since $2^5 = 32$. The *CLK* input of this FF is also tied to the input pulses. Its *J* and *K* inputs are fed by the output of a four-input AND gate whose inputs are *A, B, C,* and *D.*

(c) f_{max} is still determined as in (a) regardless of the number of FFs in the parallel counter. Thus, f_{max} is still 14.3 MHz.

Review Questions
1. What is the advantage of a synchronous counter over an asynchronous counter? What is the disadvantage?
2. How many logic devices are required for a MOD-64 parallel counter?
3. What logic signal drives the J, K inputs of the MSB flip-flop for the counter of question 2?

7-7 SYNCHRONOUS DOWN AND UP/DOWN COUNTERS

In Section 7-4 we saw that a ripple counter could be made to count down by using the inverted output of each FF to drive the next FF in the counter. A parallel down counter can be constructed in a similar manner—that is, by using the inverted FF outputs to drive the following J, K inputs. For example, the parallel up counter of Figure 7-17 can be converted to a down counter by connecting the $\overline{A}$, $\overline{B}$, and $\overline{C}$ outputs in place of A, B, and C, respectively. The counter will then proceed to count 15, 14, 13, 12, . . ., 3, 2, 1, 0, 15, 14, 13, and so on.

Figure 7-18(a) shows how to form a parallel **up/down counter.** The control input Up/$\overline{\text{Down}}$ controls whether the normal FF outputs or the inverted FF outputs are fed to the J and K inputs of the successive FFs. When Up/$\overline{\text{Down}}$ is held HIGH, AND gates 1 and 2 are enabled while AND gates 3 and 4 are disabled (note the inverter). This allows the A and B outputs through gates 1 and 2 to the J and K inputs of FFs B and C. When Up/$\overline{\text{Down}}$ is held LOW, AND gates 1 and 2 are disabled while AND gates 3 and 4 are enabled. This allows the A and B outputs through gates 3 and 4 into the J and K inputs of FFs B and C. The waveforms in Figure 7-18(b) illustrate the operation. Notice that for the first five clock pulses, Up/$\overline{\text{Down}}$ = 1 and the counter counts up; for the last five pulses, Up/$\overline{\text{Down}}$ = 0, and the counter counts down.

The nomenclature used for the control signal (Up/$\overline{\text{Down}}$) was chosen to make it clear how it affects the counter. The count-up operation is active-HIGH; the count-down operation is active-LOW.

EXAMPLE 7-13

What problems might be caused if the Up/$\overline{\text{Down}}$ signal changes levels on the NGT of the clock?

Solution

The FFs might operate unpredictably since some of them would have their J and K inputs changing at about the same time that a NGT occurs at their *CLK* input. However, the effects of the change in the control signal must propagate through two gates before reaching the J, K inputs, so it is more likely that the FFs will respond predictably to the levels that are at J, K prior to the NGT of *CLK*.

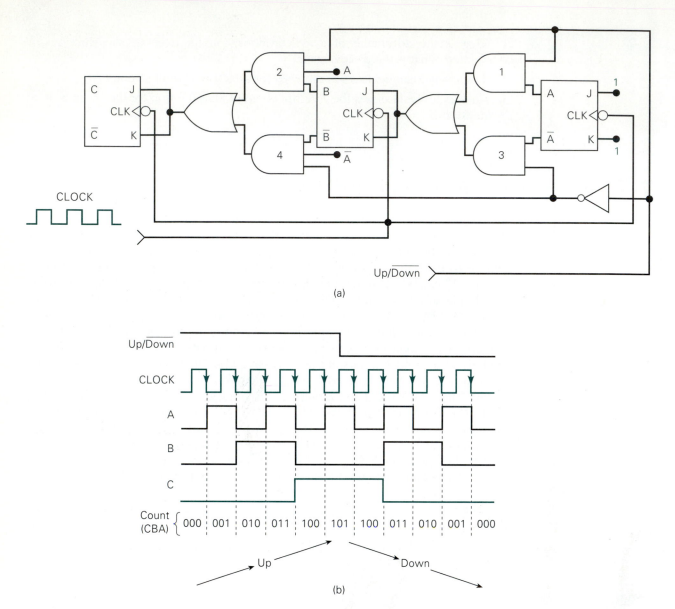

FIGURE 7-18 (a) MOD-8 synchronous up/down counter. (b) The counter counts up when the control input Up/$\overline{\text{Down}}$ = 1; it counts down when the control input = 0.

7-8 PRESETTABLE COUNTERS

Many synchronous (parallel) counters that are available as ICs are designed to be **presettable;** in other words, they can be preset to any desired starting count either asynchronously (independent of the clock signal) or synchronously (on the active transition of the clock signal). This presetting operation is also referred to as **parallel loading** the counter.

Figure 7-19 shows the logic circuit for a three-bit presettable parallel up counter. The *J, K,* and *CLK* inputs are wired for operation as a parallel up counter. The asynchronous PRESET and CLEAR inputs are wired to perform asynchronous presetting. The counter is loaded with any desired count at any time by doing the following:

1. Apply the desired count to the parallel data inputs, P_2, P_1, and P_0.
2. Apply a LOW pulse to the PARALLEL LOAD input, $\overline{PL}$.

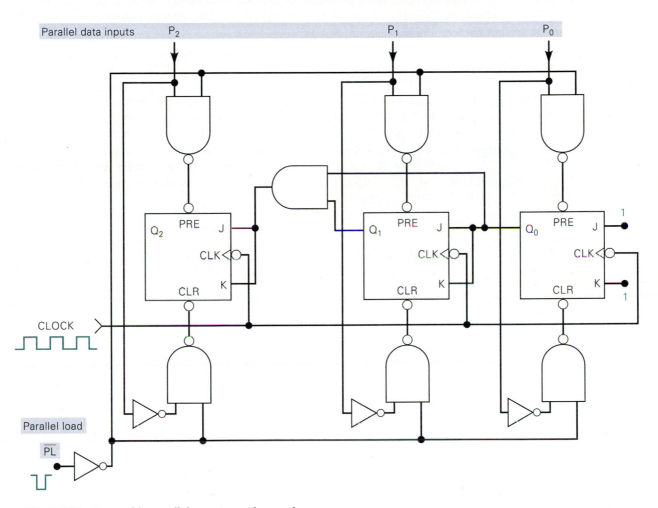

FIGURE 7-19   Presettable parallel counter with asynchronous preset.

This procedure will perform an asynchronous transfer of the P_2, P_1, and P_0 levels into flip-flops Q_2, Q_1, and Q_0, respectively (Section 5-17). This *jam transfer* occurs independently of the *J*, *K*, and *CLK* inputs. The effect of the *CLK* input will be disabled as long as $\overline{PL}$ is in its active-LOW state, since each FF will have one of its asynchronous inputs activated while $\overline{PL} = 0$. Once $\overline{PL}$ returns HIGH, the FFs can respond to their *CLK* inputs and can resume the counting-up operation starting from the count that was loaded into the counter.

For example, let's say that $P_2 = 1$, $P_1 = 0$, and $P_0 = 1$. While $\overline{PL}$ is HIGH, these parallel data inputs have no effect. If clock pulses are present, the counter will perform the normal count-up operation. Now let's say that $\overline{PL}$ is pulsed LOW when the counter is at the 010 count (i.e., $Q_2 = 0$, $Q_1 = 1$, and $Q_0 = 0$). This LOW at $\overline{PL}$ will produce LOWs at the *CLR* input of Q_1 and at the *PRE* inputs of Q_2 and Q_0 so that the counter will go to the 101 count *regardless of what is occurring at the CLK input.* The count will hold at 101 until $\overline{PL}$ is deactivated (returned HIGH); at that time the counter will resume counting up clock pulses from the count of 101.

This asynchronous presetting is used by several IC counters, such as the TTL 74LS190, 74LS191, 74LS192, and 74LS193 and the CMOS equivalents, 74HC190, 74HC191, 74HC192, and 74HC193.

Synchronous Presetting

Many IC parallel counters use *synchronous presetting* whereby the counter is preset on the active transition of the same clock signal that is used for counting. The logic level applied to the $\overline{PL}$ input determines whether the active clock transition will pre-set the counter or whether it will be counted as in the normal counting operation.

Examples of IC counters that use synchronous presetting include the TTL 74LS160, 74LS161, 74LS162, and 74LS163 and their CMOS equivalents, 74HC160, 74HC161, 74HC162, and 74HC163.

Review Questions

1. What is meant when we say that a counter is presettable?
2. Describe the difference between asynchronous and synchronous presetting.

7-9   THE 74LS193/HC193

Figure 7-20 shows the logic symbol and the input/output description for the 74LS193 counter. This counter can be described as a MOD-16, presettable up/down counter with synchronous counting, asynchronous preset, and asynchronous master reset. Let us look at the function of each input and output.

Clock Inputs CP_U and CP_D

The counter will respond to the positive-going transitions at one of to clock inputs. CP_U is the *count-up clock* input. When pulses are applied to this input, the counter will increment (count up) on each PGT to a maximum count of 1111; then it recy-cles to 0000 and starts over. CP_D is the *count-down clock* input. When pulses are applied to this input, the counter will decrement (count down) on each PGT to a min-imum count of 0000; then it recycles to 1111 and starts over. Thus, one clock input or the other will be used for counting while the other clock input is inactive (kept HIGH).

Master Reset (*MR*)

The master reset is an active-HIGH asynchronous input that resets the counter to the 0000 state. *MR* is a dc reset, and so it will hold the counter at 0000 as long as *MR* = 1. It also overrides *all* other inputs.

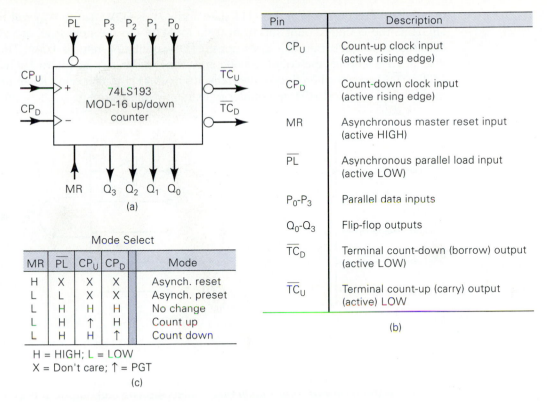

Pin	Description
CP_U	Count-up clock input (active rising edge)
CP_D	Count-down clock input (active rising edge)
MR	Asynchronous master reset input (active HIGH)
$\overline{PL}$	Asynchronous parallel load input (active LOW)
P_0-P_3	Parallel data inputs
Q_0-Q_3	Flip-flop outputs
$\overline{TC_D}$	Terminal count-down (borrow) output (active LOW)
$\overline{TC_U}$	Terminal count-up (carry) output (active) LOW

(b)

Mode Select

MR	$\overline{PL}$	CP_U	CP_D	Mode
H	X	X	X	Asynch. reset
L	L	X	X	Asynch. preset
L	H	H	H	No change
L	H	↑	H	Count up
L	H	H	↑	Count down

H = HIGH; L = LOW
X = Don't care; ↑ = PGT

(c)

FIGURE 7-20 74LS193 presettable up/down counter: (a) logic symbol; (b) input/output description; (c) mode-select table. (Courtesy of Fairchild, a Schlumberger company)

Preset Inputs

The counter FFs can be preset to the logic levels present on the parallel data inputs P_3 through P_0 by momentarily pulsing the parallel load input $\overline{PL}$ from HIGH to LOW. This is an asynchronous preset that overrides the counting operation. $\overline{PL}$ will have no effect, however, if the *MR* input is in its active-HIGH state.

Count Outputs

The current count is always present at the FF outputs Q_3 through Q_0, where Q_0 is the LSB and Q_3 is the MSB.

Terminal Count Outputs

The terminal count outputs are used when two or more 74LS193s are connected as a multistage counter to produce a larger MOD number. In the count-up mode, the $\overline{TC_U}$ output of the lower-order counter is connected to the CP_U input of the next higher-order counter. In the count-down mode, the $\overline{TC_D}$ output of the lower-order counter is connected to the CP_D input of the next higher-order counter.

$\overline{TC_U}$ is the *terminal count-up* (also called the *carry*) output. It is generated on the 74LS193 chip using the logic shown in Figure 7-21(a). Clearly, $\overline{TC_U}$ will be LOW only when the counter is in the 1111 state and CP_U is LOW. Thus, $\overline{TC}_U$ will remain HIGH as the counter counts up from 0000 to 1110. On the next PGT of CP_U, the count goes to 1111, but $\overline{TC}_U$ does not go LOW until CP_U returns LOW. The next PGT at CP_U recycles the count to 0000 and also causes $\overline{TC}_U$ to return HIGH. This PGT at $\overline{TC}_U$ occurs when the counter recycles from 1111 to 0000, and it can be used to clock a second 74LS193 up counter to its next higher count.

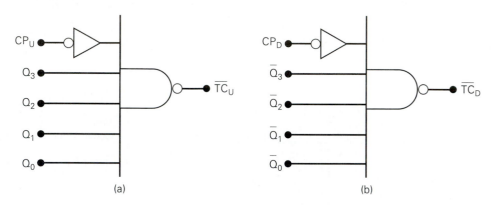

FIGURE 7-21 (a) Logic on the 74LS193 for generating $\overline{TC}_U$; (b) logic for generating $\overline{TC}_D$.

$\overline{TC}_D$ is the *terminal count-down* (also called the *borrow*) output. It is generated as shown in Figure 7-21(b). It is normally HIGH and does not go LOW until the counter has counted down to the 0000 state and CP_D is LOW. When the next PGT at CP_D recycles the counter to 1111, it causes $\overline{TC}_D$ to return HIGH. This PGT at $\overline{TC}_D$ can be used to clock a second 74LS193 down counter to its next lower count.

EXAMPLE 7-14

Refer to Figure 7-22(a), where a 74LS193 is wired as an *up counter*. The parallel data inputs are permanently connected as 1011, and the CP_U, $\overline{PL}$, and MR input waveforms are shown in Figure 7-22(b). Assume that the counter is initially in the 0000 state, and determine the counter output waveforms.

Solution

Initially (at t_0) the counter FFs are all LOW. This causes $\overline{TC}_U$ to be HIGH. Just prior to time t_1 the $\overline{PL}$ input is pulsed LOW. This immediately loads the counter with 1011 to produce $Q_3 = 1$, $Q_2 = 0$, $Q_1 = 1$, and $Q_0 = 1$. At t_1 the CP_U input makes a PGT, but the counter cannot respond to this because $\overline{PL}$ is still active at that time. At times t_2, t_3, t_4, and t_5 the counter counts up on each PGT at CP_U. After the PGT at t_5 the counter is in the 1111 state, but $\overline{TC}_U$ does not go LOW until CP_U goes LOW at t_6. When the next PGT occurs at t_7, the counter recycles to 0000, and $\overline{TC}_U$ returns HIGH.

The counter will count up in response to the PGTs at t_8 and t_9. The PGT at t_{10} will have no effect, because the MR goes HIGH prior to t_{10} and remains active at t_{10}. This will reset all FFs to 0 and overrides the CP_U signal.

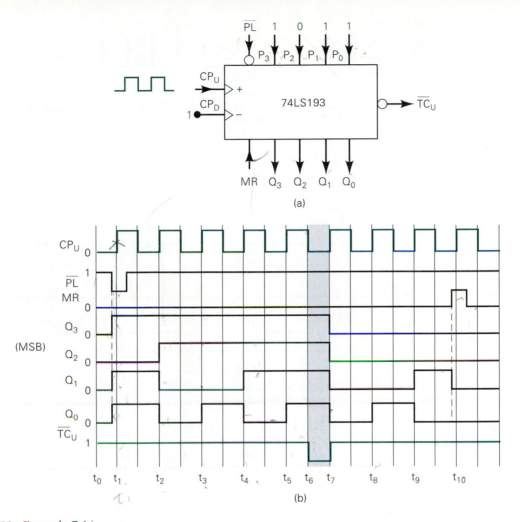

FIGURE 7-22 Example 7-14.

EXAMPLE 7-15

Figure 7-23(a) shows the 74LS193 wired as a *down counter*. The parallel data inputs are permanently wired as 0111, and the CP_D and $\overline{PL}$ waveforms are shown in Figure 7-23(b). Assume that the counter is initially in the 0000 state, and determine the output waveforms.

Solution

At t_0 all of the FF outputs are LOW and CP_D is LOW. These are the conditions that produce $\overline{TC_D} = 0$. Prior to t_1 the $\overline{PL}$ input is pulsed LOW. This immediately presets the counter to 0111 and therefore causes $\overline{TC_D}$ to go HIGH. The PGT of CP_D at t_1 will have no effect, since $\overline{PL}$ is still active. The counter will respond to the PGTs at t_2 to t_8 and counts down to 0000 at t_8. $\overline{TC_D}$ does not go LOW until t_9, when CP_D goes LOW. At t_{10} the PGT of CP_D causes the counter to recycle to 1111 and also drives $\overline{TC_D}$ back HIGH.

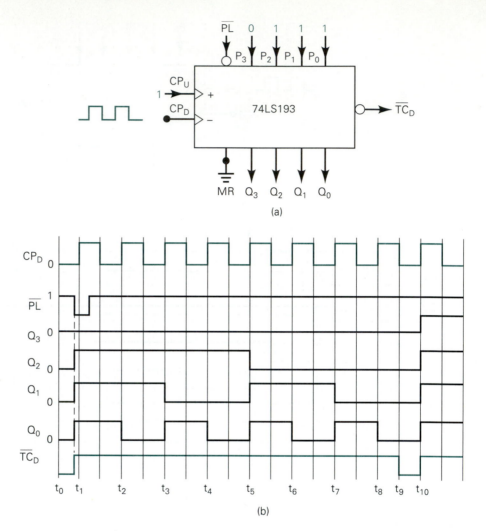

FIGURE 7-23   Example 7-15.

Variable MOD Number Using the 74LS193

Presettable counters can be easily wired for different MOD numbers without the need for additional logic circuitry. We will demonstrate this for the 74LS193 using the circuit of Figure 7-24(a). Here, the 74LS193 is used as a down counter with its parallel load inputs permanently connected at 0101 (5_{10}). Note that the $\overline{TC}_D$ output is connected back to the $\overline{PL}$ input.

We will begin our analysis by assuming that the counter is in the 0101 state at time t_0. Refer to Figure 7-24(b) for the counter waveforms.

The counter will decrement (count down) on the PGTs of CP_D at times t_1 to t_5. At t_5 the counter is in the 0000 state. When CP_D goes LOW at t_6, it drives $\overline{TC}_D$ LOW. This immediately activates the $\overline{PL}$ input and presets the counter back to the 0101 state. Note that $\overline{TC}_D$ stays LOW for only a short interval because once the counter

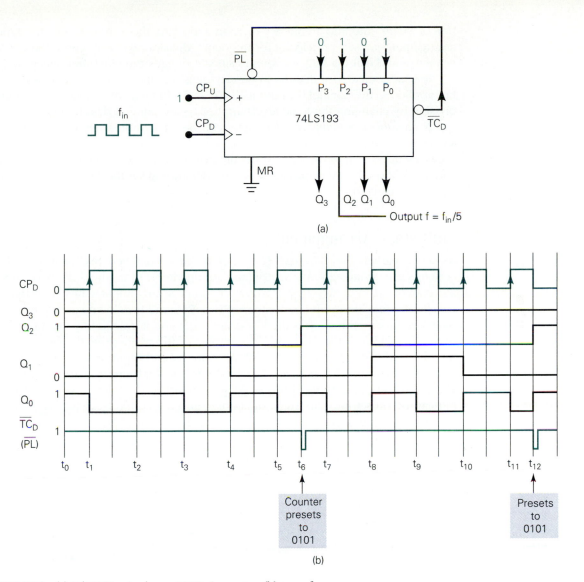

FIGURE 7-24   (a) 74LS193 wired as a MOD-5 counter; (b) waveforms.

outputs go to 0101 in response to $\overline{PL} = 0$, the condition needed to keep $\overline{TC}_D = 0$ is removed. Thus, there is only a narrow glitch at $\overline{TC}_D$.

   This same sequence is repeated at times t_7 to t_{12} and at equal intervals thereafter. If we examine the Q_2 waveform, we can see that it goes through one complete cycle for every *five* cycles of CP_D. For example, there are *five* clock cycles between the PGT of Q_2 at t_6 and the PGT of Q_2 at t_{11}. Thus, the frequency of the Q_2 waveform is one-fifth of the clock frequency.

   This arrangement does have a peculiarity which you may have noticed: it counts through *six* different states (5, 4, 3, 2, 1, 0), yet it divides the frequency by *five*. This is due to the unusual way the count gets preset back to 5 in the middle of a clock cycle. Thus, this counter's operation violates our general rule that the number of states and the frequency-division ratio are the same. Since this type of arrangement is used principally for frequency division, we will ignore the counting sequence and call it a MOD-5 counter since it divides the clock frequency by 5.

It is no coincidence that the frequency-division ratio (5) is the same as the number applied to the parallel data inputs (0101 = 5). In fact, we can vary the frequency division by changing the logic levels applied to the parallel data inputs.

A *variable frequency-divider* circuit can be easily implemented by connecting switches to the parallel data inputs of the circuit in Figure 7-24. The switches can be set to a value equal to the desired frequency-division ratio. Notice that care must be taken to choose the appropriate Q output, depending on the frequency-division ratio that is selected.

Multistage Arrangement

As stated earlier, the $\overline{TC}_D$ and $\overline{TC}_U$ outputs are used when two or more 74LS193 counters are connected in a **multistage** arrangement. In Figure 7-25, two 74LS193s are connected in a two-stage up/down counter arrangement which effectively increases the maximum up-count range to $0 \rightarrow 255$ and the down-count range to $255 \rightarrow 0$. The block on the left is the low-order stage and is clocked by one or the other of the clock inputs; the $\overline{TC}_U$ and $\overline{TC}_D$ outputs of this stage drive the clock inputs of the high-order stage. Note the use of a common $\overline{\text{Load}}$ input and common Reset input. Also note that the parallel data inputs to the high-order stage are labeled as $P_4P_5P_6P_7$, and the outputs of this stage are labeled as $Q_4Q_5Q_6Q_7$. An eight-bit number can be preset into this eight-bit counter, and the counter can be made to count up or count down from that starting count. The count at any time appears at the Q_0–Q_7 outputs.

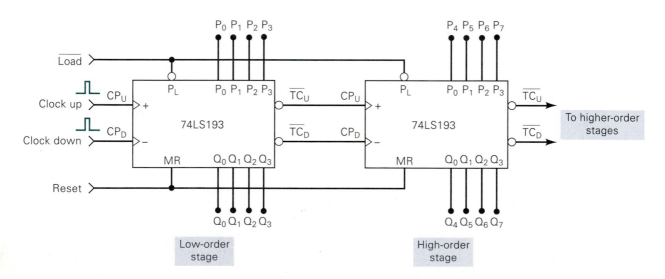

Note: $\overline{\text{Reset}}$ input has priority over $\overline{\text{Load}}$ and clock inputs.
Load input has priority over clock inputs.

FIGURE 7-25 Two 74LS193s connected in a two-stage arrangement to extend maximum counting range.

Review Questions   1. Describe the function of the inputs $\overline{PL}$ and P_0 to P_3.

2. Describe the function of the MR input.

3. *True or false:* The 74LS193 cannot be preset while MR is active.

4. What logic levels must be present at CP_D, $\overline{PL}$, and MR in order for the 74LS193 to count pulses that appear at CP_U?

5. What would be the maximum counting range for a four-stage counter made up of 74LS193 ICs?

7-10   MORE ON THE IEEE/ANSI DEPENDENCY NOTATION*

We can learn more about the dependency notation that is such an important part of the new IEEE/ANSI symbology by examining the IEEE/ANSI symbol for the 74LS193 IC shown in Figure 7-26. Each type of IC that we examine in this way will add to your understanding of the new symbology and will help to prepare you for the more extensive use of these symbols in the future.

FIGURE 7-26   IEEE/ANSI symbol for the 74LS193 IC.

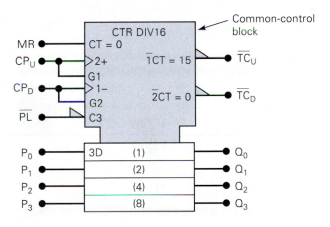

Once again, it should be stated that only the labels inside the rectangular outlines are specified by the IEEE/ANSI standard. The names or labels shown outside the outlines are not standard, and in fact they will vary from one IC manufacturer to another.

Some of the notation used in Figure 7-26 should be familiar. The symbol outline is divided into the common-control block that affects all of the counter FFs, and the four narrow rectangles representing the individual FFs. The bracketed number inside each FF rectangle denotes its relative weight in the counter. The label CTR DIV16 signifies that this device, when operated normally, is a counter (CTR) with 16 states (i.e., a divide-by-16 counter). The MR input to the common-control block has the notation "CT = 0" to indicate that the counter will reset to zero when MR is HIGH.

---

* This section may be skipped without loss of continuity.

Control Dependency (C)

The letter C in the label for an input denotes that that input *controls* the entry of data into a storage element (i.e., a FF). Usually, C is used for block inputs that clock data into a FF on its active transition. We saw this when we looked at the IEEE/ANSI symbols for FFs in Chapter 5. In Figure 7-26, C is used for the parallel load input $\overline{PL}$, since this input controls the entry of data into the four counter FFs. Specifically, the label C3 indicates that this input will control any other input that has the digit 3 as a prefix in its label. In this case that includes inputs P_0, P_1, P_2, and P_3, since they all have the label 3D (it is shown only on the top FF block, but it is assumed to be the same for the other FF blocks). The "D" part of the label denotes "data."

What this all means is that when $\overline{PL}$ is in its active-LOW state, data from P_0 through P_3 will be entered into flip-flops Q_0 to Q_3. Since there is no edge-triggered symbol at $\overline{PL}$, it is understood that $\overline{PL}$ is in effect as long as it stays at its active-LOW level.

Counting Direction (+ or −)

The CP_U and CP_D inputs are shown in Figure 7-26 as having two separate labels because they have several distinct internal effects. Let's first consider the upper label. This label for the CP_U input is 2+. The plus sign (+) indicates that a PGT at this input will increment the count by 1; in other words, it will cause the counter to count up. Likewise, the upper label for the CP_D input has a minus sign (−) to show that this input will decrement the count by 1; in other words, it will cause it to count down. The significance of the digits in front of the plus and minus signs will be explained in the following paragraphs.

AND Dependency (G)

The letter G in the label for an input denotes AND dependency. This means that an input designated by a G followed by a digit is internally ANDed with any other input or output that has the same digit as a prefix in its label. In Figure 7-26 we see that the lower label for the CP_U input is G1. This means that CP_U is internally ANDed with any input or output that has a 1 in its label. The upper label for CP_D is 1−, and so there must be an AND dependency between CP_D and CP_U. Specifically, this AND dependency tells us that CP_U must be HIGH in order for CP_D to perform its count-down function.

The lower label for CP_D is G2, which indicates that there is an AND dependency between CP_D and any input or output that has a 2 in its label. For example, the upper label for CP_U is 2+, which tells us that CP_D must be HIGH in order for CP_U to perform its count-up function.

Now let's look at the $\overline{TC}_D$ output label. It is $\overline{2}CT = 0$. It includes a 2 in its label, indicating that it has an AND dependency with CP_D. Actually, since it is a $\overline{2}$, the AND dependency is with $\overline{CP}_D$. Thus, the label for $\overline{TC}_D$ tells us that $\overline{TC}_D$ will go to its active-LOW state when $\overline{CP}_D$ is LOW *and* the count is zero ($CT = 0$). In a like manner, the label for $\overline{TC}_U$ tells us that $\overline{TC}_U$ will go to its active-LOW state when $\overline{CP}_U$ is LOW *and* the count is 15 ($CT = 15$).

1. Explain the meaning of control dependency and AND dependency.
2. Give the meaning of the following input labels:

    (a) + (b) G4 (c) C5 (d) 5D

7-11 DECODING A COUNTER

Digital counters are often used in applications where the count represented by the states of the FFs must somehow be determined or displayed. One of the simplest means for displaying the contents of a counter involves just connecting the output of each FF to a small indicator LED [see Figure 7-5(b)]. In this way the states of the FFs are visibly represented by the LEDs (bright = 1, dark = 0), and the count can be mentally determined by **decoding** the binary states of the LEDs. For instance, suppose that this method is used for a BCD counter and the states of the LEDs are dark–bright–bright–dark, respectively. This would represent 0110, which we would mentally decode as decimal 6. Other combinations of LED states would represent the other possible counts.

The indicator LED method becomes inconvenient as the size (number of bits) of the counter increases, because it is much harder to mentally decode the displayed results. For this reason it would be preferable to develop a means for *electronically* decoding the contents of a counter and displaying the results in a form that would be immediately recognizable and would require no mental operations.

An even more important reason for electronic decoding of a counter occurs because of the many applications in which counters are used to control the timing or sequencing of operations *automatically* without human intervention. For example, a certain system operation might have to be initiated when a counter reaches the 101100 state (count of 44_{10}). A logic circuit can be used to decode for or detect when this particular count is present and then initiate the operation. Many operations may have to be controlled in this manner in a digital system. Clearly, human intervention in this process would be undesirable except in extremely slow systems.

Active-HIGH Decoding

A MOD-X counter has X different states; each state is a particular pattern of 0s and 1s stored in the counter FFs. A decoding network is a logic circuit that generates X different outputs, each of which detects (decodes) the presence of one particular state of the counter. The decoder outputs can be designed to produce either a HIGH or a LOW level when the detection occurs. An active-HIGH decoder produces HIGH outputs to indicate detection. Figure 7-27 shows the complete active-HIGH decoding logic for a MOD-8 counter. The decoder consists of eight three-input AND gates. Each AND gate produces a HIGH output for one particular state of the counter.

For example, AND gate 0 has at its inputs the FF outputs $\overline{C}$, $\overline{B}$, and $\overline{A}$. Thus, its output will be LOW at all times *except* when $A = B = C = 0$, that is, on the count of 000 (zero). Similarly, AND gate 5 has as its inputs the FF outputs C, $\overline{B}$, and A, so that its output will go HIGH only when $C = 1$, $B = 0$, and $A = 1$, that is, on the count of 101 (decimal 5). The rest of the AND gates perform in the same manner for

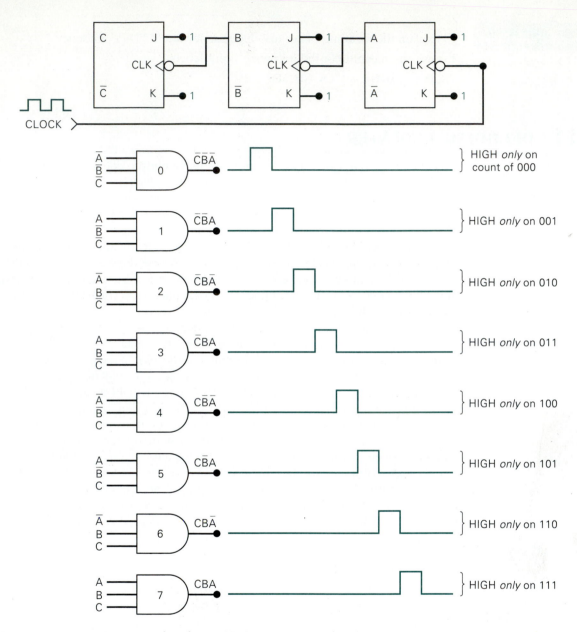

FIGURE 7-27   Using AND gates to decode a MOD-8 counter.

the other possible counts. At any one time only one AND gate output is HIGH, the one which is decoding for the particular count that is present in the counter. The waveforms in Figure 7-27 show this clearly.

The eight AND outputs can be used to control eight separate indicator LEDs, which represent the decimal numbers 0 through 7. Only one LED will be on at a given time, indicating the proper count.

The AND gate decoder can be extended to counters with any number of states. The following example illustrates.

| EXAMPLE 7-16 | How many AND gates are required to completely decode all of the states of a MOD-32 binary counter? What are the inputs to the gate that decodes for the count of 21? |

Solution

A MOD-32 counter has 32 possible states. One AND gate is needed to decode for each state; therefore, the decoder requires 32 AND gates. Since $32 = 2^5$, the counter contains five FFs. Thus, each gate will have five inputs, one from each FF. To decode for the count of 21 (that is, 10101_2) requires AND gate inputs of E, $\overline{D}$, C, $\overline{B}$, and A, where E is the MSB flip-flop.

Active-LOW Decoding

If NAND gates are used in place of AND gates, the decoder outputs will produce a normally HIGH signal, which goes LOW only when the number being decoded occurs. Both types of decoders are used, depending on the type of circuits being driven by the decoder outputs.

| EXAMPLE 7-17 | Figure 7-28 shows a common situation in which a counter is used to generate a control waveform which could be used to control devices such as a motor, solenoid valve, or heater. The MOD-16 counter cycles and recycles through its counting sequence. Each time it goes to the count of 8 (1000), the upper NAND gate |

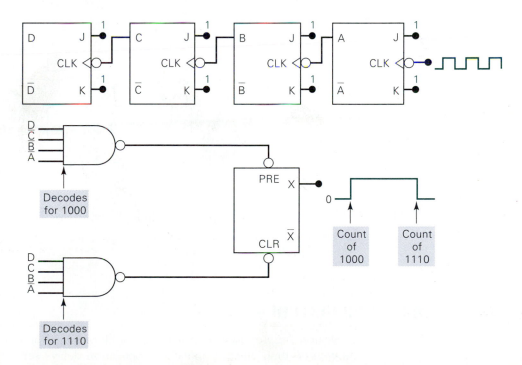

FIGURE 7-28 Example 7-17.

will produce a LOW output, which sets flip-flop X to the 1 state. Flip-flop X stays HIGH until the counter reaches the count of 14 (1110), at which time the lower NAND gate decodes it and produces a LOW output to clear X to the 0 state. Thus, the X output is HIGH between the counts of 8 and 14 for each cycle of the counter.

BCD Counter Decoding

A BCD counter has 10 states, which can be decoded using the techniques described previously. BCD decoders provide 10 outputs corresponding to the decimal digits 0 through 9 represented by the states of the counter FFs. These 10 outputs can be used to control 10 indicator LEDs for a visual display. More often, instead of using 10 separate LEDs, a signal display device is used to display the decimal numbers 0 through 9. One such device, called a *nixie tube,* contains 10 very thin, numerically shaped filaments stacked on top of each other. The BCD decoder outputs control which filament is illuminated. A newer class of decimal displays contains seven small segments made of a material (usually LEDs or liquid-crystal displays) which either emits light or reflects ambient light. The BCD decoder outputs control which segments are illuminated in order to produce a pattern representing one of the decimal digits.

We will go into more detail concerning these types of decoders and displays in Chapter 9. However, since BCD counters and their associated decoders and displays are very commonplace, we will use the decoder/display unit (see Figure 7-29) to represent the complete circuitry used to visually display the contents of a BCD counter as a decimal digit.

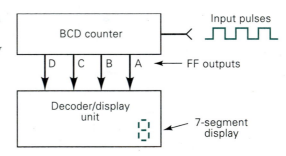

FIGURE 7-29 BCD counters usually have their count displayed on a single display device.

Review Questions

1. How many gates are needed to fully decode a six-bit counter?
2. Describe the decoding gate needed to produce a LOW output when a MOD-64 counter is at the count of 23.

7-12 DECODING GLITCHES

In Section 7-5 we discussed the effects of FF propagation delays in ripple counters. As we saw then, the accumulated propagation delays serve to essentially limit the frequency response of ripple counters. The delays between FF transitions can also cause problems when decoding a ripple counter. The problem occurs in the form of **decoding glitches** or spikes at the outputs of some of the decoding gates. This is illustrated in Figure 7-30 for a MOD-4 ripple counter.

FIGURE 7-30   FF and decoding waveforms for a MOD-4 ripple counter showing glitches at the X_0 and X_2 outputs.

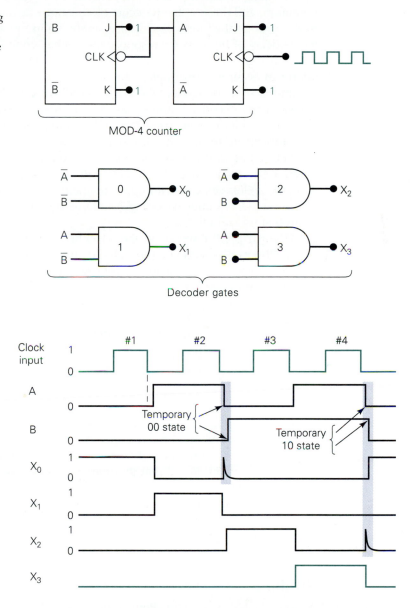

The waveforms at the outputs of each FF and decoding gate are shown in the figure. Notice the propagation delay between the clock waveform and the A output waveform and between the A waveform and the B waveform. The glitches in the X_0 and X_2 decoding waveforms are caused by the delay between the A and B waveforms. X_0 is the output of the AND gate decoding for the normal 00 count. The 00 condition also occurs momentarily as the counter goes from the 01 to the 10 count, as shown by the waveforms. This is because B cannot change states until A goes

LOW. This momentary 00 state lasts only for several nanoseconds (depending on t_{pd} of flip-flop B) but can be detected by the decoding gate if the gate's response is fast enough. Hence, the spike at the X_0 output.

A similar situation produces a glitch at the X_2 output. X_2 is decoding for the 10 condition, and this condition occurs momentarily as the counter goes from 11 to 00 in response to the fourth clock pulse, as shown in the waveforms. Again, this is due to the delay of flip-flop B's response after A has gone LOW.

Although the situation is illustrated for a MOD-4 counter, the same type of situation can occur for *any* ripple counter. This is because ripple counters work on the "chain-reaction" principle, whereby each FF triggers the next one and so on. The spikes at the decoder outputs may or may not present a problem, depending on how the counter is being used. When the counter is being used only to count pulses and display the results, the decoding spikes are of no consequence because they are very short in duration and will not even show up on the display. However, when the counter is used to control other logic circuits, such as was done in Figure 7-28, the spikes can cause improper operation. For example, in Figure 7-28, a spike at the output of either decoding NAND gate would cause flip-flop X to be set or cleared at the wrong time.

We can predict where in the asynchronous counter's sequence a temporary state will occur by stepping through a counter state transition one FF at a time. For example, let's look at the actual step-by-step process by which a ripple counter goes from 011 (3) to 100 (4):

$$
\begin{array}{ccc}
C & B & A \\
0 & 1 & 1 \quad (3)
\end{array}
$$

$$
\text{temporary states}
\begin{cases}
0 & 1 & 0 \quad (2) < \qquad \text{FF } A \text{ toggles first} \\
0 & 0 & 0 \quad (0) < \qquad \text{and causes } B \text{ to toggle}
\end{cases}
$$

$$
\begin{array}{ccc}
1 & 0 & 0 \quad (4) < \qquad \text{which causes } C \text{ to toggle.}
\end{array}
$$

Note the occurrence of two temporary states, 010 and 000.

In situations where the decoding spikes cannot be tolerated, there are two basic solutions to the problem. The first possibility is to use a parallel counter instead of a ripple counter. Recall that in a parallel counter the FFs are all triggered at the same time by the clock pulses so that it appears that the conditions that produced the decoder spikes cannot occur. However, even in a parallel counter the spikes may occur because the FFs will not all necessarily have the same t_{pd}, especially when some FFs may be loaded more heavily than others.

Strobing

A more reliable method for eliminating the decoder spikes is to use a technique called **strobing.** This technique uses a signal called a *strobe signal* to keep the decoding AND gates disabled (outputs at 0) until all of the FFs have reached a stable state in response to the negative clock transition. This is illustrated in Figure 7-31, where the strobe signal is connected as an input to each decoding gate. The accompanying waveforms show that the strobe signal goes LOW when the clock pulse goes HIGH. During the time that the strobe is LOW, the decoding gates are kept LOW. The strobe signal goes HIGH to enable the decoding gates some time t_D *after* the clock pulse goes LOW. t_D is chosen to be greater than the total time it takes the counter to reach a stable count, and it depends, of course, on the FF delays and the number of FFs in the counter. In this way the decoding gate outputs will not contain any spikes, because they are disabled during the time the FFs are in transition.

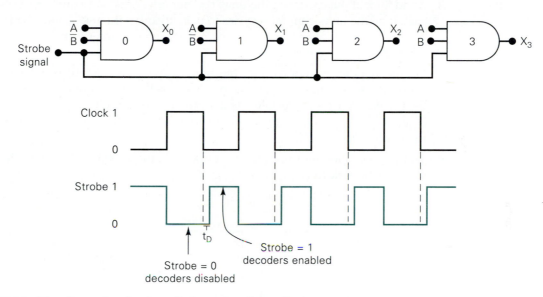

FIGURE 7-31 Use of a strobe signal to eliminate decoding spikes.

The strobe method is not used if a counter is used only for display purposes, since the decoding spikes are too narrow to affect the display. The strobe signal is used when the counter is used in control applications like that of Figure 7-28, where the spikes could cause erroneous operation.

Review Questions

1. Explain why the decoding gates for an asynchronous counter may have glitches on their outputs.
2. How does strobing eliminate decoding glitches?

7-13 CASCADING BCD COUNTERS

BCD counters are often used whenever pulses are to be counted and the results displayed in decimal. A single BCD counter counts from 0 through 9 and then recycles to 0. To count to larger decimal values, we can **cascade** BCD counter stages as shown in Figure 7-32. This multistage arrangement operates as follows:

1. Initially, all counters are cleared to the 0 state. Thus, the decimal display is 000.
2. As input pulses arrive, the units BCD counter advances one count per pulse. After nine pulses have occurred, the hundreds and tens BCD counters are still at 0, and the units counter is at 9 (binary 1001). Thus, the decimal display reads 009.

3. On the tenth input pulse the units counter recycles to 0, causing its flip-flop D output to go from 1 to 0. This 1-to-0 transition acts as the clock input for the tens counter and causes it to advance one count. Thus, after 10 input pulses, the decimal readout is 010.

4. As additional pulses occur, the units counter advances one count per pulse, and each time the units counter recycles to 0, it advances the tens counter one count. Thus, after 99 input pulses have occurred, the tens counter is at 9, as is the units counter. The decimal readout is thus 099.

5. On the hundredth input pulse, the units counter recycles to 0, which in turn causes the tens counter to recycle to 0. The flip-flop D output of the tens counter thus makes a 1-to-0 transition which acts as the clock input for the hundreds counter and causes it to advance one count. Thus, after 100 pulses the decimal readout is 100.

6. This process continues up until 999 pulses. On the 1000th pulse, all of the counters recycle back to 0.

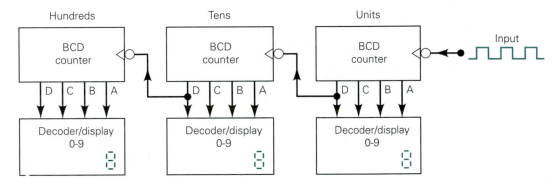

FIGURE 7-32   Cascading BCD counters to count and display numbers from 000 to 999.

It should be obvious that this arrangement can be expanded to any desired number of decimal digits simply by adding on more stages. For example, to count up to 999,999 will require six BCD counters and associated decoders and displays. In general, then, we need one BCD counter per decimal digit.

Each BCD counter in a cascaded arrangement such as in Figure 7-32 could be a variable-MOD counter such as the 74LS293 wired as a MOD-10 counter; or it could be an IC that is internally wired as a BCD counter such as the 74LS90 and 74LS192/HC192 ICs.

7-14   SYNCHRONOUS COUNTER DESIGN*

Many different counter arrangements are available as ICs—asynchronous, synchronous, and combined asynchronous/synchronous. Most of these count in a normal binary sequence although their counting sequences can be somewhat altered using

---

* This topic may be omitted without affecting the continuity of the remainder of the book.

the methods we demonstrated for the 74293 and 74193 ICs. There are situations, however, where a counter is required that follows a sequence that is not counting in normal binary, for example 000, 010, 101, 001, 110, 000, . . .

Several methods exist for designing counters that follow arbitrary sequences. We will present the details for one common method that uses J-K flip-flops in a synchronous counter configuration. The same method can be used in designs with D flip-flops. The technique is one of several design procedures that are part of an area of digital circuit design called **sequential circuit design,** which is normally part of an advanced course.

Basic Idea

In synchronous counters all of the FFs are clocked at the same time. Before each clock pulse, the J and K input of each FF in the counter must be at the correct level to ensure that the FF goes to the correct state. For example, consider the situation shown in Table 7-1. When the next clock pulse occurs, the J and K inputs of the FFs must be at the correct levels that will cause flip-flop C to change from 1 to 0, flip-flop B from 0 to 1, and flip-flop A from 1 to 1 (i.e., no change).

The process of designing a synchronous counter, then, becomes one of designing the logic circuits that *decode* the various states of the counter to supply the logic levels to each J and K input. The inputs to these decoder circuits will come from the outputs of one or more of the FFs. To illustrate, for the synchronous counter of Figure 7-17, the AND gate that feeds the J and K inputs of flip-flop C decodes the states of flip-flops A and B. Likewise, the AND gate that feeds the J and K inputs of flip-flop D decodes the states of A, B, and C.

J-K Excitation Table

Before we begin the process of designing the decoder circuits for each J and K input, we must first review the operation of the J-K flip-flop using a different approach called an *excitation table* (Table 7-2). The leftmost column of this table lists each possible FF output transition. The second and third columns list the FF's present state, symbolized as $Q(N)$, and the next state, symbolized as $Q(N + 1)$, for each transition. The last two columns list the J and K levels required to produce each transition. Let's examine each case.

TABLE 7-1

Present State			Next State		
C	B	A	C	B	A
1	0	1	0	1	1

TABLE 7-2   J-K flip-flop excitation table.

Transition at Output	PRESENT State $Q(N)$	NEXT State $Q(N + 1)$	J	K
$0 \rightarrow 0$	0	0	0	x
$0 \rightarrow 1$	0	1	1	x
$1 \rightarrow 0$	1	0	x	1
$1 \rightarrow 1$	1	1	x	0

0 → 0 TRANSITION   The FF present state is at 0 and is to remain at 0 when a clock pulse is applied. From our understanding of how a J-K flip-flop works, this can happen when either $J = K = 0$ (no-change condition) or $J = 0$ and $K = 1$ (clear condition). Thus, J must be at 0, but K can be at either level. The table indicates this with a "0" under J and an "x" under K. Recall that "x" means the "don't-care" condition.

0 → 1 TRANSITION   The present state is 0 and is to change to a 1. This can happen when either $J = 1$ and $K = 0$ (set condition) or $J = K = 1$ (toggle condition). Thus, J must be a 1, but K can be at either level for this transition to occur.

1 → 0 TRANSITION   The present state is 1 and is to change to a 0. This can happen when either $J = 0$ and $K = 1$ or $J = K = 1$. Thus, K must be a 1, but J can be at either level.

1 → 1 TRANSITION   The present state is a 1 and is to remain a 1. This can happen when either $J = K = 0$ or $J = 1$ and $K = 0$. Thus, K must be a 0 while J can be at either level.
     The use of this **J-K excitation table** (Table 7-2) is a principal part of the synchronous counter design procedure.

Design Procedure

We will now go through a complete synchronous counter design procedure. Although we will do it for a specific counting sequence, the same steps can be followed for any desired sequence.

> **Step 1.**   Determine the desired number of bits (FFs) and the desired counting sequence.

TABLE 7-3

C	B	A
0	0	0
0	0	1
0	1	0
0	1	1
1	0	0
0	0	0
0	0	1
etc.		

For our example, we will design a three-bit counter that goes through the sequence shown in Table 7-3. Notice that this sequence does not include the 101, 110, and 111 states. We will refer to these states as *undesired states*.

> **Step 2.**   Draw the state transition diagram showing **all** possible states, including those that are not part of the desired counting sequence.

For our example, the state transition diagram appears as shown in Figure 7-33. The 000 through 100 states are connected in the expected sequence. The new idea used in this diagram is the inclusion of the undesired states. They must be included in our design in case the counter accidentally gets into one of these states upon power-up or due to noise. The circuit designer can choose to have each of these undesired states go to any state upon the application of the next clock pulse. We choose to have them all go to the 000 state from which the correct sequence will be generated.

FIGURE 7-33 State transition diagram for the synchronous counter design example.

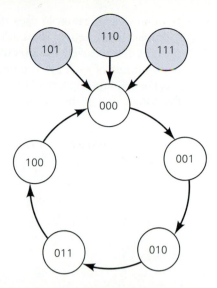

Step 3. Use the state transition diagram to set up a table that lists **all** PRESENT states and their NEXT states.

For our example, the information is shown in Table 7-4. The left-hand portion of the table lists *every* possible state, even those that are not part of the sequence. We label these as the PRESENT states. The right-hand portion lists the NEXT state for each PRESENT state. These are obtained from the state transition diagram in Figure 7-33. For instance, line 1 shows that the PRESENT state of 000 has the NEXT state of 001, and line 5 shows that the PRESENT state of 100 has the NEXT state of 000. Lines 6, 7, and 8 show that the undesired PRESENT states 101, 110, and 111 all have the NEXT state of 000.

TABLE 7-4

	PRESENT State			NEXT State		
	C	B	A	C	B	A
line 1	0	0	0	0	0	1
2	0	0	1	0	1	0
3	0	1	0	0	1	1
4	0	1	1	1	0	0
5	1	0	0	0	0	0
6	1	0	1	0	0	0
7	1	1	0	0	0	0
8	1	1	1	0	0	0

Step 4. Add a column to this table for each J and K input. For each PRESENT state, indicate the levels required at each J and K input in order to produce the transition to the NEXT state.

Our design example uses three FFs—C, B, and A—and each one has a J and a K input. Therefore, we must add six new columns as shown in Table 7-5. This completed table is called the **circuit excitation table.** The six new columns are the J and K inputs of each FF. The entries under each J and K are obtained by using Table 7-2, the J-K flip-flop excitation table that we developed earlier. We will demonstrate this for several of the cases, and you can verify the rest.

TABLE 7-5 Circuit excitation table.

	PRESENT State			NEXT State								
	C	B	A	C	B	A	J_C	K_C	J_B	K_B	J_A	K_A
line 1	0	0	0	0	0	1	0	x	0	x	1	x
2	0	0	1	0	1	0	0	x	1	x	x	1
3	0	1	0	0	1	1	0	x	x	0	1	x
4	0	1	1	1	0	0	1	x	x	1	x	1
5	1	0	0	0	0	0	x	1	0	x	0	x
6	1	0	1	0	0	0	x	1	0	x	x	1
7	1	1	0	0	0	0	x	1	x	1	0	x
8	1	1	1	0	0	0	x	1	x	1	x	1

Let's look at line 1 in Table 7-5. The PRESENT state of 000 is to go to the NEXT state of 001 on the occurrence of a clock pulse. For this state transition, the C flip-flop goes from 0 to 0. From the J-K excitation table, we see that J_C must be at 0 and K_C at "x" for this transition to occur. The B flip-flop also goes from 0 to 0, and so $J_B = 0$ and $K_B = x$. The A flip-flop goes from 0 to 1. Also from Table 7-2, we see that $J_A = 1$ and $K_A = x$ for this transition.

In line 4 in Table 7-5, the PRESENT state of 011 has a NEXT state of 100. For this state transition, flip-flop C goes from 0 to 1, which requires $J_C = 1$ and $K_C = x$. Flip-flops B and A are both going from 1 to 0. The J-K excitation table indicates that these two FFs need $J = x$ and $K = 1$ for this to occur.

The required J and K levels for all other lines in Table 7-5 can be determined in the same manner.

Step 5. Design the logic circuits to generate the levels required at each J and K input.

Table 7-5, the circuit excitation table, lists six J, K inputs—J_C, K_C, J_B, K_B, J_A, and K_A. We must consider each of these as an output from its own logic circuit with inputs from flip-flops C, B, and A. Then we must design the circuit for each one. Let's design the circuit for J_A.

To do this we need to look at the PRESENT states of C, B, and A and the desired levels at J_A for each case. This information has been extracted from Table 7-5 and presented in Figure 7-34(a). This truth table shows the desired levels at J_A for each PRESENT state. Of course, for some of the cases J_A is a "don't care." To develop the logic circuit for J_A, we must first determine its expression in terms of C, B, and A. We will do this by transferring the truth-table information to a three-variable Karnaugh map and performing the K-map simplification as in Figure 7-34(b).

FIGURE 7-34 (a) Portion of circuit excitation table showing J_A for each PRESENT state; (b) K map used to obtain the simplified expression for J_A.

PRESENT			
C	B	A	J_A
0	0	0	1
0	0	1	x
0	1	0	1
0	1	1	x
1	0	0	0
1	0	1	x
1	1	0	0
1	1	1	x

(a)

	$\overline{A}$	A
$\overline{BC}$	1	x
$\overline{B}C$	0	x
BC	0	x
$B\overline{C}$	1	x

$J_A = \overline{C}$

(b)

There are only two 1s in this K map, and they can be looped to obtain the term $\overline{A}\,\overline{C}$, but if we use the don't-care conditions at $\overline{A}\overline{B}\,\overline{C}$ and $AB\overline{C}$ as 1s, we can loop a quad to obtain the simpler term $\overline{C}$. Thus, the final expression is

$$J_A = \overline{C}$$

Now let's consider K_A. We can follow the same steps as we did for J_A. However, a look at the entries under K_A in the circuit excitation table shows only 1s and don't cares. If we change all the don't cares to 1s, then K_A is always a 1. Thus, the final expression is

$$K_A = 1$$

In a similar manner, we can derive the expressions for J_C, K_C, J_B, and K_B. The K maps for these expressions are given in Figure 7-35. You might want to confirm their correctness by checking them against the circuit excitation table.

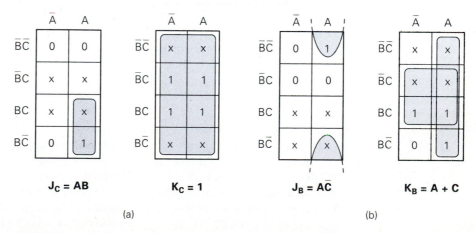

$J_C = AB$ $K_C = 1$ $J_B = A\overline{C}$ $K_B = A + C$

(a)   (b)

FIGURE 7-35 (a) K mappings for the J_C and K_C logic circuits; (b) K mappings for the J_B and K_B logic circuits.

Step 6. Implement the final expressions.

The logic circuits for each *J* and *K* input are implemented from the expressions obtained from the K mapping. The complete synchronous counter design is implemented in Figure 7-36. Note that all FFs are clocked in parallel. You might want to verify that the logic for the *J* and *K* inputs agrees with Figures 7-34 and 7-35.

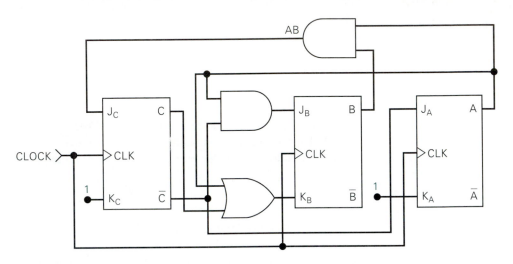

FIGURE 7-36   Final implementation of the synchronous counter design example.

Stepper Motor Control

We will now apply this design procedure to a practical situation—driving a *stepper motor*. A stepper motor is a motor that rotates in steps rather than in a continuous motion, typically 15° per step. Magnetic coils or windings within the motor must be energized and deenergized in a specific sequence in order to produce this stepping action. Digital signals are normally used to control the current in each of the motor's coils. Stepper motors are used extensively in situations where precise position control is needed, such as in positioning of read/write heads on magnetic disks, in controlling print heads in printers, and in robots.

Figure 7-37(a) is a diagram of a typical stepper motor with four coils. For the motor to rotate properly, coils 1 and 2 must always be in opposite states; that is, when coil 1 is energized, coil 2 is not, and vice versa. Likewise, coil 3 and coil 4 must always be in opposite states. The outputs of a two-bit synchronous counter are used to control the current in the four coils; *A* and $\overline{A}$ control coils 1 and 2, and *B* and $\overline{B}$ control coils 3 and 4. The current amplifiers are needed because the FF outputs cannot supply the amount of current that the coils require.

Since this stepper motor can rotate either clockwise (CW) or counterclockwise (CCW), we have a Direction input, *D*, which is used to control the direction of rotation. The state diagrams in Figure 7-37(b) show the two cases. For CW rotation to occur, we must have *D* = 0, and the state of the counter, *BA*, must follow the sequence 11, 10, 00, 01, 11, 10, . . ., and so on, as it is clocked by the Step input signal. For CCW rotation, *D* = 1, and the counter must follow the sequence 11, 01, 00, 10, 11, 01, . . ., and so on.

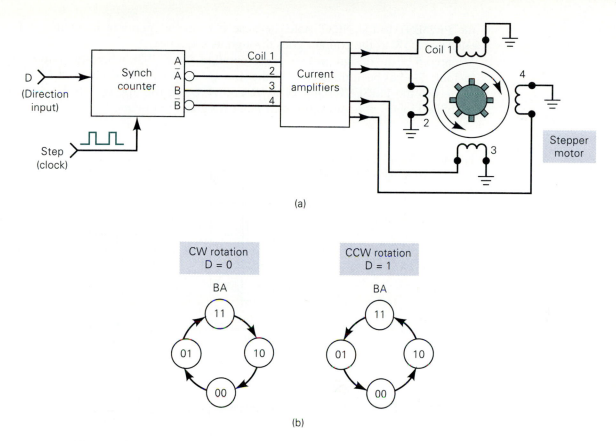

FIGURE 7-37 (a) A synchronous counter supplies the appropriate sequential outputs to drive a stepper motor; (b) state transition diagrams for both states of Direction input, D.

We are now ready to follow the six steps of the synchronous counter design procedure. Steps 1 and 2 have already been done, so we can proceed with steps 3 and 4. Table 7-6 shows each possible PRESENT state of *D*, *B*, and *A* and the desired NEXT state, along with the levels at each *J* and *K* input needed to achieve the transitions. Note that in all cases, the Direction input, *D*, does not change in going from

TABLE 7-6 Circuit excitation table for Figure 7-37(b).

PRESENT State			NEXT State						
D	*B*	*A*	*D*	*B*	*A*	J_B	K_B	J_A	K_A
0	0	0	0	0	1	0	x	1	x
0	0	1	0	1	1	1	x	x	0
0	1	0	0	0	0	x	1	0	x
0	1	1	0	1	0	x	0	x	1
1	0	0	1	1	0	1	x	0	x
1	0	1	1	0	0	0	x	x	1
1	1	0	1	1	1	x	0	1	x
1	1	1	1	0	1	x	1	x	0

the PRESENT to the NEXT state, because it is an independent input that is held HIGH or LOW as the counter goes through its sequence.

Step 5 of the design process is presented in Figure 7-38 where the information in Table 7-6 has been transferred to the K maps showing how each J and K signal is related to the PRESENT states of D, B, and A. Using the appropriate looping, the simplified logic expressions for each J and K signal are obtained.

FIGURE 7-38 (a) K maps for J_B and K_B; (b) K maps for J_A and K_A.

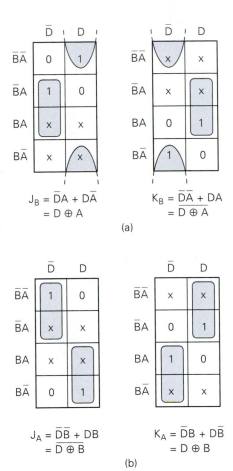

$$J_B = \overline{D}A + D\overline{A}$$
$$= D \oplus A$$

$$K_B = \overline{D}\,\overline{A} + DA$$
$$= \overline{D \oplus A}$$

(a)

$$J_A = \overline{D}\,\overline{B} + DB$$
$$= \overline{D \oplus B}$$

$$K_A = \overline{D}B + D\overline{B}$$
$$= D \oplus B$$

(b)

The final step is shown in Figure 7-39, where the two-bit synchronous counter is implemented using the J, K expressions obtained from the K maps.

Review Questions

1. List the six steps in the procedure for designing a synchronous counter.
2. What information is contained in a J-K excitation table?
3. What information is contained in the circuit excitation table?
4. *True or false:* The synchronous counter design procedure can be used for the following sequence: 0010, 0011, 0100, 0111, 1010, 1110, 1111, and repeat.

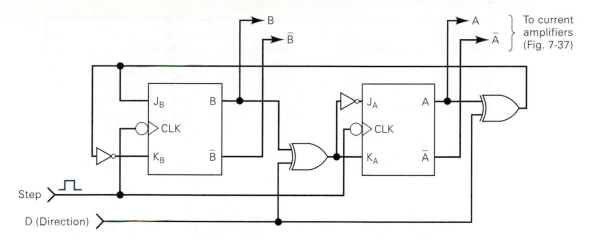

FIGURE 7-39 Synchronous counter implemented from the *J, K* equations.

7-15 SHIFT-REGISTER COUNTERS

In Section 5-18 we saw how to connect FFs in a shift-register arrangement to transfer data left to right, or vice versa, one bit at a time (serially). Shift-register counters use *feedback*, which means that the output of the last FF in the register is connected back to the first FF in some way.

Ring Counter

The simplest shift-register counter is essentially a **circulating shift register** connected so that the last FF shifts its value into the first FF. This arrangement is shown in Figure 7-40 using D-type FFs (J-K flip-flops can also be used). The FFs are connected so that information shifts from left to right and back around from Q_0 to Q_3. In most instances only a single 1 is in the register, and it is made to circulate around the register as long as clock pulses are applied. For this reason it is called a **ring counter.**

The waveforms, sequence table, and state diagram in Figure 7-40 show the various states of the FFs as pulses are applied, assuming a starting state of $Q_3 = 1$ and $Q_2 = Q_1 = Q_0 = 0$. After the first pulse, the 1 has shifted from Q_3 to Q_2 so that the counter is in the 0100 state. The second pulse produces the 0010 state, and the third pulse produces the 0001 state. On the *fourth* clock pulse, the 1 from Q_0 is transferred to Q_3, resulting in the 1000 state, which is, of course, the initial state. Subsequent pulses cause the sequence to repeat.

This counter functions as a MOD-4 counter, since it has *four* distinct states before the sequence repeats. Although this circuit does not progress through the normal binary counting sequence, it is still a counter because each count corresponds to a unique set of FF states. Note that each FF output waveform has a frequency equal to one-fourth of the clock frequency, since this is a MOD-4 ring counter.

Ring counters can be constructed for any desired MOD number; a MOD-N ring counter uses N flip-flops connected in the arrangement of Figure 7-40. In general, a ring counter will require more FFs than a binary counter for the same MOD num-

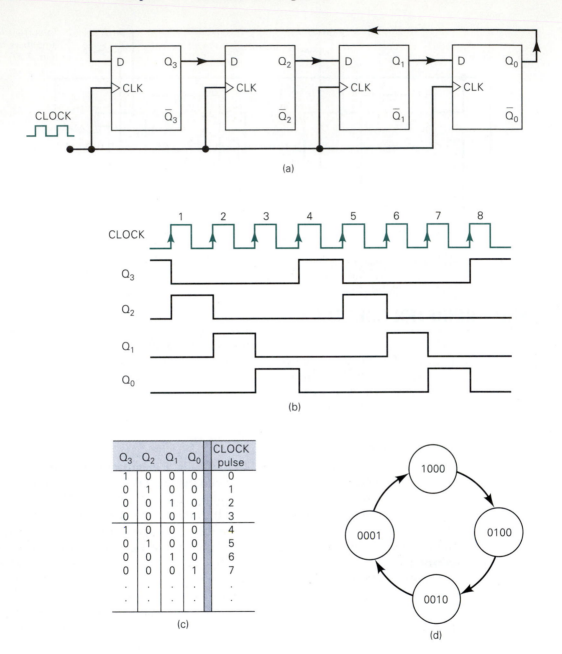

FIGURE 7-40 (a) Four-bit ring counter; (b) waveforms; (c) sequence table; (d) state diagram.

ber; for example, a MOD-8 ring counter requires eight FFs, while a MOD-8 binary counter requires only three.

Despite the fact that it is less efficient in the use of FFs, a ring counter is still useful because it can be decoded without the use of decoding gates. The decoding signal for each state is obtained at the output of its corresponding FF. Compare the FF waveforms of the ring counter with the decoding waveforms in Figure 7-27. In some cases a ring counter might be a better choice than a binary counter with its associated decoding gates. This is especially true in applications where the counter is being used to control the sequencing of operations in a system.

Starting a Ring Counter

To operate properly, a ring counter must start off with only one FF in the 1 state and all the others in the 0 state. Since the starting states of the FFs will be unpredictable on power-up, the counter must be preset to the required starting state before clock pulses are applied. One way to do this is to apply a momentary pulse to the asynchronous $\overline{PRE}$ input of one of the FFs (e.g., Q_3 in Figure 7-40) and to the $\overline{CLR}$ input of all other FFs. Another method is shown in Figure 7-41. On power-up, the capacitor will charge up relatively slowly toward $+V_{CC}$. The output of Schmitt-trigger IN-VERTER 1 will stay HIGH, and the output of INVERTER 2 will remain LOW until the capacitor voltage exceeds the positive-going threshold voltage (V_{T+}) of the IN-VERTER 1 input (about 1.7 V). This will hold the $\overline{PRE}$ input of Q_3 and the $\overline{CLR}$ inputs of Q_2, Q_1, and Q_0 in the LOW state long enough during power-up to ensure that the counter starts at 1000.

FIGURE 7-41 Circuit for ensuring that the ring counter of Figure 7-40 starts in the 1000 state on power-up.

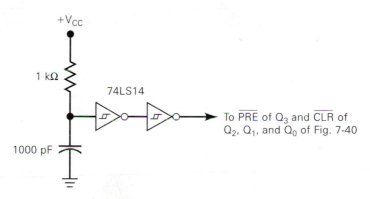

Johnson Counter

The basic ring counter can be modified slightly to produce another type of shift-register counter, which will have somewhat different properties. The **Johnson** or **twisted-ring counter** is constructed exactly like a normal ring counter except that the *inverted* output of the last FF is connected to the input of the first FF. A three-bit Johnson counter is shown in Figure 7-42. Note that the $\overline{Q_0}$ output is connected back to the D input of Q_2. This means that the *inverse* of the level stored in Q_0 will be transferred to Q_2 on the clock pulse.

The Johnson-counter operation is easy to analyze if we realize that on each positive clock-pulse transition, the level at Q_2 shifts into Q_1, the level at Q_1 shifts into Q_0, and the *inverse* of the level at Q_0 shifts into Q_2. Using these ideas and assuming that all FFs are initially 0, the waveforms, sequence table, and state diagram of Figure 7-42 can be generated.

Examination of the waveforms and sequence table reveals the following important points:

1. This counter has six distinct states: 000, 100, 110, 111, 011, and 001 before it repeats the sequence. Thus, it is a MOD-6 Johnson counter. Note that it does not count in a normal binary sequence.

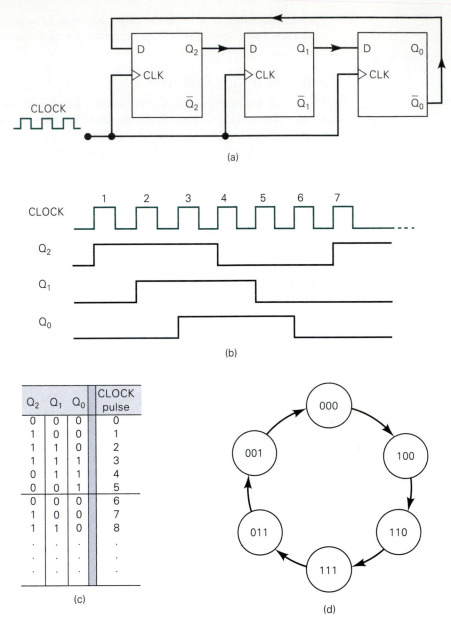

FIGURE 7-42 (a) MOD-6 Johnson counter; (b) waveform; (c) sequence table; (d) state diagram.

2. The waveform of each FF is a square wave (50 percent duty cycle) at one-sixth the frequency of the clock. In addition, the FF waveforms are shifted by one clock period with respect to each other.

The MOD number of a Johnson counter will always be equal to *twice* the number of FFs. For example, if we connect five FFs in the arrangement of Figure 7-42, the result is a MOD-10 Johnson counter, where each FF output waveform is a square wave at one-tenth the clock frequency. Thus, it is possible to construct a MOD-N counter (where N is an even number) by connecting $N/2$ flip-flops in a Johnson-counter arrangement.

Decoding a Johnson Counter

For a given MOD number, a Johnson counter requires only half the number of FFs that a ring counter requires. However, a Johnson counter requires decoding gates, whereas a ring counter does not. As in the binary counter, the Johnson counter uses one logic gate to decode for each count, but each gate requires only two inputs, regardless of the number of FFs in the counter. Figure 7-43 shows the decoding gates for the six states of the Johnson counter of Figure 7-42.

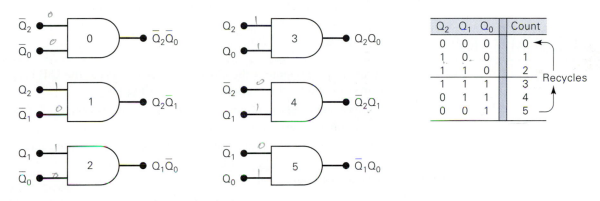

Q_2	Q_1	Q_0	Count
0	0	0	0
1	0	0	1
1	1	0	2
1	1	1	3
0	1	1	4
0	0	1	5

Recycles

FIGURE 7-43   Decoding logic for a MOD-6 Johnson counter.

Notice that each decoding gate has only two inputs, even though there are three FFs in the counter. This is because for each count, two of the three FFs are in a unique combination of states. For example, the combination $Q_2 = Q_0 = 0$ occurs only once in the counting sequence, at the count of 0. Thus, AND gate 0 with inputs $\overline{Q}_2$ and $\overline{Q}_0$ can be used to decode for this count. This same characteristic is shared by all of the other states in the sequence, as the reader can verify. In fact, for *any size* Johnson counter, the decoding gates will have only two inputs.

Johnson counters represent a middle ground between ring counters and binary counters. A Johnson counter requires fewer FFs than a ring counter but generally more than a binary counter; it has more decoding circuitry than a ring counter but less than a binary counter. Thus, it sometimes represents a logical choice for certain applications.

IC Shift-Register Counters

Very few ring counters or Johnson counters are available as ICs. The reason is that it is relatively simple to take a shift-register IC and to wire it as either a ring counter or a Johnson counter (see Example 7-20). Some of the CMOS Johnson-counter ICs (74HC4017, 74HC4022) include the complete decoding circuitry on the same chip as the counter.

1. Which shift-register counter requires the most FFs for a given MOD number?
2. Which shift-register counter requires the most decoding circuitry?
3. How can a ring counter be converted to a Johnson counter?
4. *True or false:*
   (a) The outputs of a ring counter are always square waves.
   (b) The decoding circuitry for a Johnson counter is simpler than for a binary counter.
   (c) Ring and Johnson counters are synchronous counters.

PART I SUMMARY

1. In asynchronous (ripple) counters, the clock signal is applied to the LSB FF, and all other FFs are clocked by the output of the preceding FF.
2. A counter's MOD number is the number of stable states in its counting cycle; it is also the maximum frequency-division ratio.
3. The normal (maximum) MOD number of a counter is 2^N. One way to modify a counter's MOD number is to add circuitry that will cause it to recycle before it reaches its normal last count.
4. Counters can be cascaded (chained together) to produce greater counting ranges and frequency-division ratios.
5. In a synchronous (parallel) counter all of the FFs are simultaneously clocked from the input clock signal.
6. The maximum clock frequency for an asynchronous counter, f_{max}, decreases as the number of bits increases. For a synchronous counter, f_{max} remains the same regardless of the number of bits.
7. A decade counter is any MOD-10 counter. A BCD counter is a decade counter that sequences through the 10 BCD codes (0–9).
8. A presettable counter can be loaded with any desired starting count.
9. An up/down counter can be commanded to count up or count down.
10. Logic gates can be used to decode (detect) any or all states of a counter.
11. Asynchronous counters can produce glitches in decoding gates due to the counter propagation delays. Synchronous counters are less likely to cause decoding glitches. Strobing is a technique for eliminating the effects of decoding glitches.
12. Synchronous counters with arbitrary counting sequences can be implemented by following a standard design procedure.
13. A ring counter is actually an N-bit shift register that continuously recirculates a single 1, thereby acting as a MOD-N counter. A Johnson counter is a modified ring counter that operates as a MOD-$2N$ counter.

PART I IMPORTANT TERMS

asynchronous (ripple) counter	up/down counters	sequential circuit design
MOD number	presettable counters	J-K excitation table
decade counter	parallel load	circuit excitation table
BCD counter	multistage counters	circulating shift register
up counter	decoding	ring counter
down counter	decoding glitches	Johnson counter
synchronous (parallel) counters	strobing	
	cascading	

PART II

7-16 COUNTER APPLICATIONS: FREQUENCY COUNTER

There are numerous applications for the many types of counters we have been discussing. In this section and the next we will look at two representative applications that illustrate the uses of counters in digital systems.

A **frequency counter** is a circuit that can measure and display the frequency of a signal. One of the most straightforward methods for constructing a frequency counter is shown in Figure 7-44(a) in simplified form. It contains a counter with its associated decoder/display circuitry and an AND gate. The AND gate inputs include the pulses with unknown frequency, f_x, and a SAMPLE pulse that controls how long these pulses are allowed to pass through the AND gate into the counter. The counter is usually made up of cascaded BCD counters (Figure 7-32), and the decoder/display unit converts the BCD outputs into a decimal display for easy monitoring.

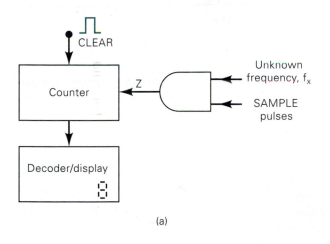

(a)

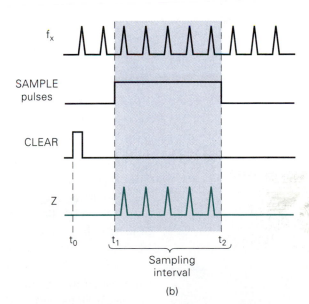

(b)

FIGURE 7-44   Basic frequency-counter method.

The waveforms in Figure 7-44(b) show that a CLEAR pulse is applied to the counter at t_0 to start the counter at 0. Prior to t_1 the SAMPLE pulse waveform is LOW, and so the AND output, Z, will be LOW and the counter will not be counting. The SAMPLE pulse goes HIGH from t_1 to t_2; this is called the **sampling interval.** During this sampling interval the unknown frequency pulses will pass through the AND gate and will be counted by the counter. After t_2 the AND output returns LOW and the counter stops counting. Thus, the counter will have counted the number of pulses that occurred during the sampling interval, and the resulting contents of the counter are a direct measure of the frequency of the pulse waveform.

EXAMPLE 7-18

The unknown frequency is 3792 pulses per second (pps). The counter is cleared to the 0 state prior to t_1. Determine the counter reading after a sampling interval of (a) 1 s, (b) 0.1 s, and (c) 10 ms.

Solution

(a) Within a sampling interval of 1 s there will be 3792 pulses entering the counter, and so after t_2 the contents of the counter will read 3792.

(b) With a 0.1-s sampling interval the number of pulses passing through the AND gate into the counter will be 3792 pulses/s $\times$ 0.1 s = 379.2. This means that either 379 or 380 pulses will be counted, depending on what part of a pulse cycle t_1 occurs in.

(c) With a sampling interval of 10 ms = 0.01 s, the counter will read either 37 or 38.

The accuracy of this method depends almost entirely on the duration of the sampling interval, which must be very accurately controlled. A commonly used method for obtaining very accurate sample pulses is shown in Figure 7-45. A crystal-controlled oscillator is used to generate a very accurate 100-kHz waveform, which is shaped into square pulses and fed to a series of decade counters that are being used to successively divide this 100-kHz frequency by 10. The frequencies at the outputs of each decade counter are as accurate (percentagewise) as the crystal frequency. These decade counters are usually binary or Johnson counters.

The rotary switch is used to select one of the decade-counter output frequencies to be fed to a single FF to be divided by 2. For example, in switch position 1 the 1-Hz pulses are fed to flip-flop Q, which is acting as a toggle FF so that its output will be a square wave with a period of $T = 2$ s and a pulse duration of $t_p = T/2 = 1$ s. This pulse duration is the desired 1-s sampling interval. In position 2 the sampling interval would be 0.1 s, and so on for the other positions.

EXAMPLE 7-19

Assume that the counter in Figure 7-44 is made up of three cascaded BCD counters and their associated displays. If the unknown input frequency is between 1 kpps and 9.99 kpps, what is the best setting for the switch position in Figure 7-45?

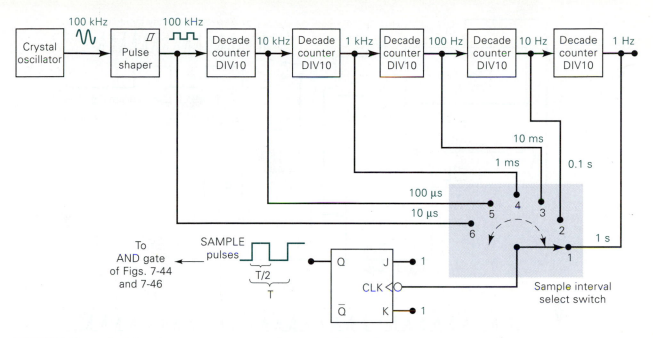

FIGURE 7-45 Method for obtaining accurate sampling intervals for a frequency counter.

Solution

With three BCD counters the total capacity of the counter is 999. A 9.99-kpps frequency would produce a count of 999 if a 0.1-s sample interval were used. Thus, in order to use the full capacity of the counter, the switch should be set to position 2. If a 1-s sampling interval were used, the counter capacity would always be exceeded for frequencies in the specified range. If a shorter sample interval were used, the counter would count only between 1 and 99; this would give a reading to only two significant figures and would be a waste of the counter's capacity.

Complete Frequency Counter

We will now look at a more complete frequency-counter circuit in Figure 7-46(a). The circuit now contains a one-shot and a J-K flip-flop operating in the toggle mode, and the AND gate has three inputs, one of which is the FF output X. The SAMPLE pulses are connected to the AND gate and also to the *CLK* input of the FF. These SAMPLE pulses would be generated from a circuit such as that in Figure 7-45. The following step-by-step description refers to the waveforms in Figure 7-46(b).

1. Assume that flip-flop X is in the 0 state (it has toggled to 0 on the falling edge of the previous sample pulse).

2. This LOW from X is fed to the AND gate, disabling its output, so that no pulses are fed to the counter even when the first SAMPLE pulse occurs between t_1 and t_2.

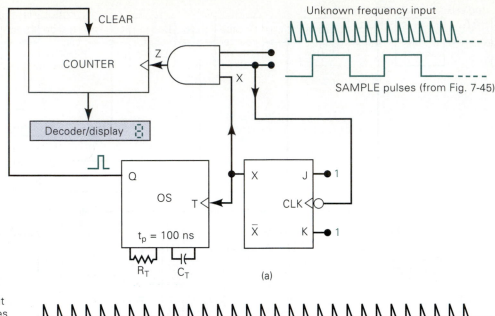

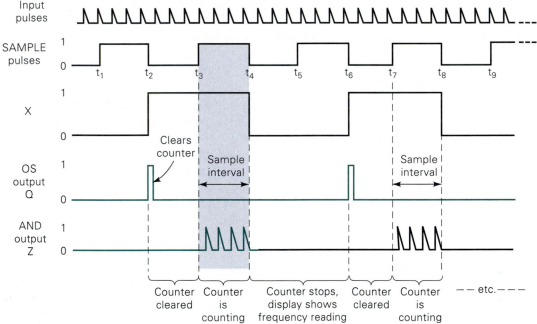

FIGURE 7-46 Frequency counter.

3. At t_2 the NGT of the first SAMPLE pulse toggles flip-flop X to the 1 state (note that $J = K = 1$). This positive transition at X triggers the OS, which generates a 100-ns pulse to *clear* the counter. The counter now displays *zero*.

4. At t_3 the second SAMPLE pulse enables the AND gate (since X is now 1) and allows the unknown frequency into the counter to be counted until t_4.

5. At t_4 the SAMPLE pulse returns LOW and toggles X LOW, disabling the AND gate. The counter stops counting.

6. Between t_4 and t_6 the counter holds and displays the count that it had reached at t_4. Note that the third SAMPLE pulse does not enable the AND gate, because flip-flop X is LOW.

7. At t_6 the NGT of the SAMPLE pulse toggles X HIGH, and the operation follows the same sequence that began at t_2.

This frequency counter, then, goes through a repetitive sequence of clearing to 0, counting, holding for display, clearing to 0, counting, and so on. For example, let's assume that the counter has three BCD stages and a three-digit display. If we use a sample interval of 1 s and the unknown frequency is 237 pps, the counter and the display will go through the following sequence over and over:

■ Clear to 0 and display 0 for 1 s [t_2 to t_3 in Figure 7-46(b)].

■ Starting at 0, count unknown frequency pulses during the 1-s sample interval (t_3 to t_4); the count will stop at 237.

■ Hold and display the count of 237 for 2 s (t_4 to t_6).

Since the display is connected directly to the counter outputs, the display will show the clearing and counting action of the counter. This makes it very difficult to read the display to determine the unknown frequency except at very slow sample intervals. This problem can be solved by inserting a *buffer register* between the counter and the decoder/display unit. We will consider this feature in Problem 7-43.

1. What is the best sample interval setting to use if the pulse counter has four BCD stages and the input frequency is between 2 and 8 Mpps?

2. Describe the sequence of operations of the complete frequency counter of Figure 7-46.

3. Why would it be unwise to use ring counters instead of Johnson counters for the decade counters in Figure 7-45?

7-17 COUNTER APPLICATIONS: DIGITAL CLOCK

One of the most common applications of counters is the digital clock—a time clock that displays the time of day in hours, minutes, and sometimes seconds. In order to construct an accurate digital clock, a very closely controlled basic clock frequency is required. For battery-operated digital clocks (or watches) the basic frequency is normally obtained from a quartz-crystal oscillator. Digital clocks operated from the ac power line can use the 60-Hz power frequency as the basic clock frequency. In either case, the basic frequency must be divided down to a frequency of 1 Hz or 1 pulse per second (pps). Figure 7-47 shows the basic block diagram for a digital clock operating from 60 Hz.

The 60-Hz signal is sent through a Schmitt-trigger circuit to produce square pulses at the rate of 60 pps. This 60-pps waveform is fed into a MOD-60 counter which is used to divide the 60 pps down to 1 pps. The 1-pps signal is fed into the SECONDS section, which is used to count and display seconds from 0 through 59.

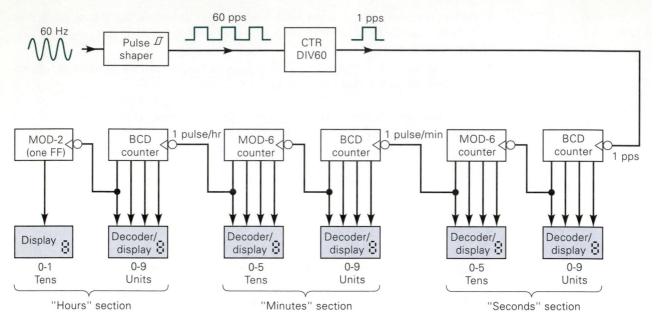

FIGURE 7-47 Block diagram for a digital clock.

The BCD counter advances one count per second. After 9 seconds the BCD counter recycles to 0, which triggers the MOD-6 counter and causes it to advance one count. This continues for 59 s, at which point the MOD-6 counter is at the 101 (5) count and the BCD counter is at 1001 (9), so that the display reads 59 s. The next pulse recycles the BCD counter to 0, which in turn recycles the MOD-6 counter to 0 (remember, the MOD-6 counts from 0 through 5).

The output of the MOD-6 counter in the SECONDS section has a frequency of 1 pulse per minute (the MOD-6 recycles every 60 s). This signal is fed to the MINUTES section, which counts and displays minutes from 0 through 59. The MINUTES section is identical to the seconds section and operates in exactly the same manner.

The output of the MOD-6 counter in the MINUTES section has a frequency of 1 pulse per hour (the MOD-6 recycles every 60 min). This signal is fed to the HOURS section, which counts and displays hours from 1 through 12. This HOURS section is different from the SECONDS and MINUTES sections in that it never goes to the 0 state. The circuitry in this section is sufficiently unusual to warrant a closer investigation.

Figure 7-48 shows the detailed circuitry contained in the HOURS section. It includes a BCD counter to count units of hours, and a single FF (MOD-2) to count tens of hours. The BCD counter is a 74LS192, which operates exactly like the 74LS193 that we studied earlier except that it counts only between 0000 and 1001. In other words, the 74LS192 can either count up in BCD fashion (i.e., 0 to 9, recycling to 0) or count down in BCD fashion (i.e., 9 to 0, recycling to 9). Here it is used to count up in response to the 1-pulse/hour signal coming from the MINUTES section. The INVERTER on the CP_U input is needed because the 74LS192 responds to PGTs, and we want it to respond to the NGT that occurs when the MINUTES section recycles back to 0.

The incoming pulses advance the BCD counter once per hour. For example, at 7 o'clock this counter will be at 0111, and its decoder/display circuitry will display

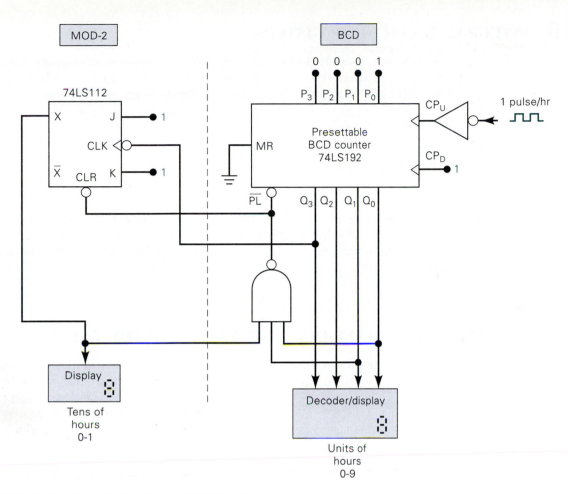

FIGURE 7-48 Detailed circuitry for the HOURS section.

the numeral 7. At the same time, X will be LOW and its display will show a 0. Thus, the two displays will show "07." When the BCD counter is in the 1001 (9) state and the next input pulse occurs, it will recycle back to 0000. The NGT at Q_3 will toggle flip-flop X from 0 to 1. This produces a numeral 1 on the X display and a numeral 0 on the BCD display so that the combined displays show "10" for 10 o'clock.

The next two pulses advance the BCD counter so that "11" and "12" are displayed at 11 o'clock and 12 o'clock, respectively. The next pulse advances the BCD counter to 0011 (3). In this state, the counter's Q_1 and Q_0 outputs are both HIGH, and X is still HIGH. Thus, the NAND gate output goes LOW and activates the $\overline{CLR}$ of flip-flop X and the $\overline{PL}$ input of the 74LS192. This clears X to 0 and presets the BCD counter to 0001. The result is a display of "01" for 1 o'clock. Several of the end-of-chapter problems will provide more details on the digital clock circuit.

Review Questions

1. Name the basic blocks that make up a digital clock circuit.
2. Why is an INVERTER needed in Figure 7-48?

7-18   INTEGRATED-CIRCUIT REGISTERS

The various types of registers can be classified according to the manner in which data can be entered into the register for storage and the manner in which data are outputted from the register. The various classifications are listed below.

1. Parallel in/parallel out
2. Serial in/serial out
3. Parallel in/serial out
4. Serial in/parallel out

Each of these types and several variations are available in IC form so that a logic designer can usually find exactly what is required for a given application. In the following sections we will examine a representative IC from each of the above categories.

7-19   PARALLEL IN/PARALLEL OUT—THE 74174 AND THE 74178

There are actually two types of registers in the **parallel in/parallel out** category. One is strictly parallel, and the other is actually a shift register that can be loaded with parallel data and has parallel outputs available.

The 74174

Figure 7-49(a) shows the logic diagram for the 74174 (also 74LS174 and 74HC174), a six-bit register that has parallel inputs D_5 through D_0 and parallel outputs Q_5 through Q_0. Parallel data are loaded into the register on the PGT of the clock input CP. A master reset input $\overline{MR}$ can be used to asynchronously reset all of the register FFs to 0.

The logic symbol for the 74174 is shown in Figure 7-49(b). This symbol is used in circuit diagrams to represent the circuitry of Figure 7-49(a).

The 74178

Figure 7-50(a) shows the logic diagram for the 74178 (also 74HC178), a four-bit shift register that has parallel data entry (P_0 through P_3) and parallel outputs (Q_0 through Q_3). It has a serial data input, D_S, and two enable inputs: PE (parallel enable) and SE (serial enable).

Figure 7-50(b) is the mode-select table that describes the various modes of operation for this IC. The first entry gives the input conditions necessary for the shift-right operation. With $SE = 1$, the data will shift from left to right on the NGT of clock input $\overline{CP}$ regardless of the logic level at the PE input (recall that X rep-

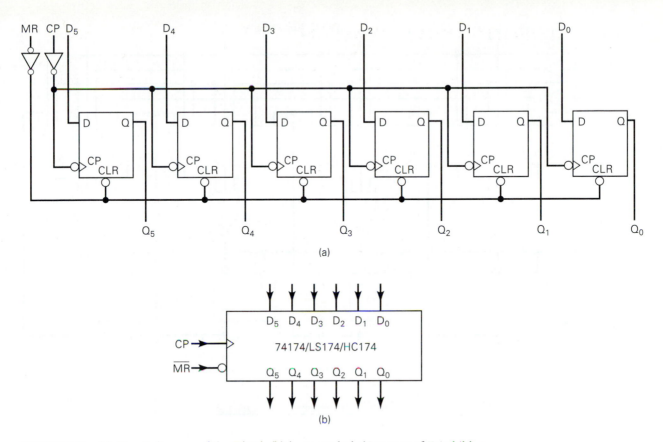

(a)

(b)

FIGURE 7-49 (a) Circuit diagram of the 74174; (b) logic symbol. (Courtesy of Fairchild, a Schlumberger company)

resents the don't-care condition). You can verify this by tracing through the logic diagram and noting that when $SE = 1$, the D_S input passes through the logic gates and appears at the D input of the Q_0 flip-flop. Likewise, Q_0 will appear at the D input of Q_1; Q_1 will appear at the D input of Q_2; and Q_2 will appear at the D input of Q_3.

The second entry in the table gives the conditions needed to produce parallel transfer from the parallel data inputs (P_0 through P_3) to the outputs (Q_0 through Q_3). When $SE = 0$ and $PE = 1$, this parallel transfer occurs on the NGT of $\overline{CP}$. Note that this is a *synchronous* transfer. Again, by tracing through the logic diagram, you can see that when $SE = 0$ and $PE = 1$, the parallel data inputs will get through the logic gates and will appear at the D inputs of their respective FFs.

The final entry in the table indicates that the $SE = 0$, $PE = 0$ condition will cause the register FFs to hold their current levels regardless of what happens at the clock input. For this input condition, each FF output is allowed to pass through its respective logic gates and appear at the D input of the same FF. Thus, a NGT on $\overline{CP}$ will not change the state of the FF.

Figure 7-51 shows the logic symbol for the 74178/74HC178.

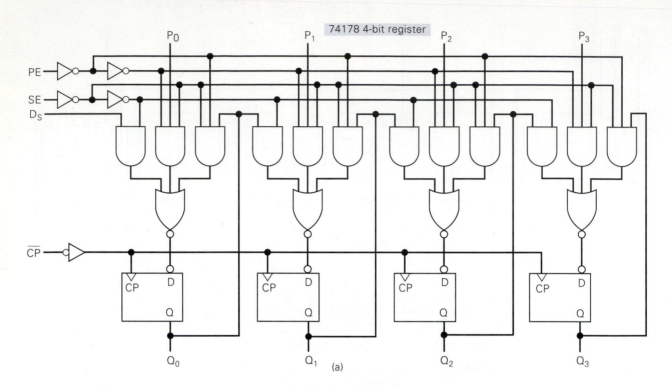

74178 4-bit register

(a)

Mode-select table

Inputs			Response
SE	PE	$\overline{CP}$	
H	X	⌐L	Right shift $D_S \rightarrow Q_0$; $Q_0 \rightarrow Q_1$, etc.
L	H	⌐L	Parallel load $P_0 \rightarrow Q_0$; $P_1 \rightarrow Q_1$, etc.
L	L	X	Hold (Q's do not change)

H = HIGH voltage level
L = LOW voltage level
X = immaterial

(b)

FIGURE 7-50 (a) Logic diagram for the 74178; (b) mode-select table. (Courtesy of Fairchild, a Schlumberger company)

FIGURE 7-51 Logic symbol for the 74178/HC178.

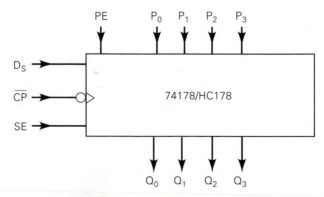

| EXAMPLE 7-20 | Describe how the 74178 can be connected as a ring counter and as a Johnson counter. |

Solution

The ring-counter connections are shown in Figure 7-52. The Q_3 output is connected back around to the D_S input. The parallel data inputs are permanently set at 0001, and the PE input is connected permanently HIGH. The SE input is initially connected LOW. This allows each NGT at $\overline{CP}$ to parallel-load the shift register with 0001. Then SE is switched to the HIGH state (shift mode), where it remains as the NGTs at $\overline{CP}$ cause the single 1 to shift and recirculate through the register.

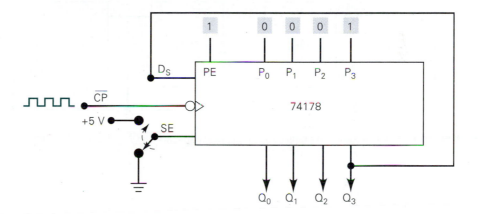

FIGURE 7-52   The 74178 wired as a ring counter.

To form a Johnson counter, add an INVERTER between the Q_3 output and D_S, and change the parallel data inputs to 0000 to preset the counter to 0000.

7-20 SERIAL IN/SERIAL OUT—THE 4731B

The 4731B is a CMOS *quad* 64-bit **serial in/serial out** shift register. It contains four identical 64-bit shift registers on one chip. Figure 7-53 shows the logic diagram for one of the 64-bit registers. It has a serial input, D_S, a clock input $\overline{CP}$ that responds to NGTs, and a serial output from the last FF, Q_{63}. This is the only output that is externally accessible. Note that this output goes through a *buffer* circuit (triangle symbol with no inversion bubble). A buffer does not change the signal's logic level; it is used to provide a greater output-current capability than normal. Also note that there is no means for parallel data entry into the register FFs.

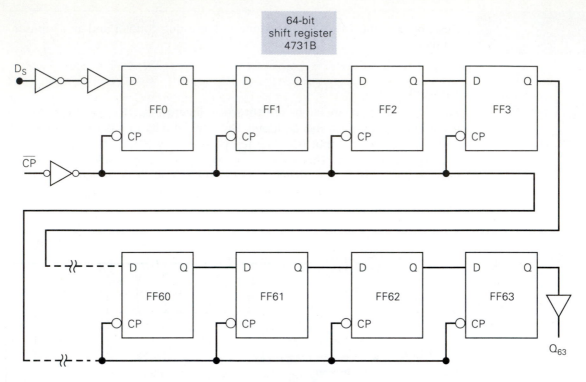

FIGURE 7-53 Logic diagram for one of four 64-bit shift registers on a 4731B. (Courtesy of Fairchild, a Schlumberger company)

EXAMPLE 7-21 A shift register is often used as a way to delay a digital signal by an integral number of clock cycles. The digital signal is applied to the shift register's serial input and is shifted through the shift register by successive clock pulses until it reaches

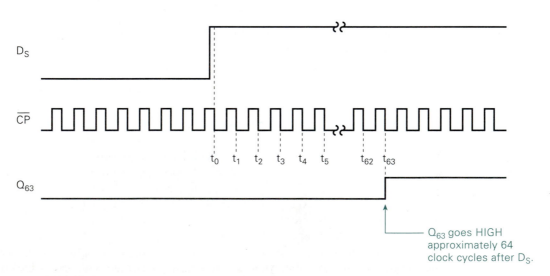

FIGURE 7-54 Waveforms showing how one of the 4731B shift registers can be used to delay a digital signal.

the end of the shift register, where it appears as the output signal. This is illustrated in Figure 7-54 using one of the 64-bit registers on the 4731B chip.

Let's assume that the serial input D_S has been LOW for a long time as clock pulses have been applied, so that the register is filled with all 0s and Q_{63} starts out LOW as shown. Then D_S goes HIGH just prior to t_0. The NGTs at $\overline{CP}$ will cause this HIGH to shift into and through the shift register, making each FF go HIGH in succession until finally at t_{63} the Q_{63} output goes HIGH. The net effect, then, is that the change in the D_S signal is not felt at the Q_{63} output until approximately 64 clock cycles later.

This method for delaying the effect of a digital signal is common in the digital communications field. For instance, the digital signal might be the *digitized* version of an audio signal that is to be delayed before it is transmitted.

7-21 PARALLEL IN/SERIAL OUT—THE 74165/74LS165/74HC165

The logic symbol for the 74165, an eight-bit **parallel in/serial out** register, is shown in Figure 7-55(a). It actually has both serial data entry via D_S and asynchronous parallel data entry via P_0 through P_7. The only accessible FF outputs are Q_7 and $\overline{Q_7}$. *CP* is the clock input used for the shift operation. The clock inhibit input, *CP INH*, can be used to inhibit the effect of pulses at *CP*. The shift/load input, *SH/$\overline{LD}$*, determines which operation is being performed.

FIGURE 7-55 Logic symbol for the 74LS165 parallel in/serial out register.

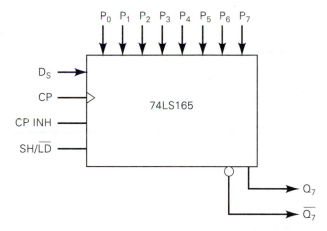

EXAMPLE 7-22 Examine the 74LS165 logic symbol and determine the conditions necessary to load the register with parallel data.

Solution

Since there is an inversion bar over the $\overline{LD}$ in the *SH/$\overline{LD}$* input symbol, the parallel load operation takes place when *SH/$\overline{LD}$* is LOW. The load operation is asynchronous, which means that it takes place independent of the clock input. Data present at the P_0–P_7 inputs will be loaded into the eight register FFs as soon as

$SH/\overline{LD}$ goes LOW. Of course, only the output of the rightmost bit, FF Q_7, will be externally available.

EXAMPLE 7-23

What conditions are needed for the 74LS165 to perform a shift-right operation?

Solution

The $SH/\overline{LD}$ input must be HIGH for the shift operation. The *CP INH* input must be LOW; otherwise, the clock pulses at *CP* will be inhibited (prevented) from clocking the register FFs. When these conditions are met, data will shift right on the PGT of each clock pulse, with D_S supplying the data for FF Q_0.

7-22 SERIAL IN/PARALLEL OUT—THE 74164/74LS164/74HC164

The logic diagram for the 74164 is shown in Figure 7-56(a). It is an eight-bit **serial in/parallel out** shift register with each FF output externally accessible. Instead of a single serial input, an AND gate combines inputs *A* and *B* to produce the serial input to flip-flop Q_0.

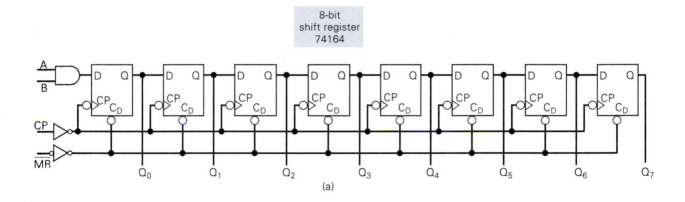

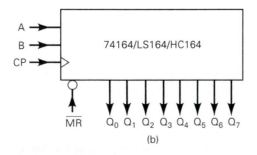

FIGURE 7-56 (a) Logic diagram for the 74164; (b) logic symbol. (Courtesy of Fairchild, a Schlumberger company)

The shift operation occurs on the PGTs of the clock input CP. The $\overline{MR}$ input provides asynchronous resetting of all FFs on a LOW level.

EXAMPLE 7-24	Assume that the initial contents of the 74164 register in Figure 7-57(a) are 00000000. Determine the sequence of states as clock pulses are applied.

FIGURE 7-57 Example 7-24.

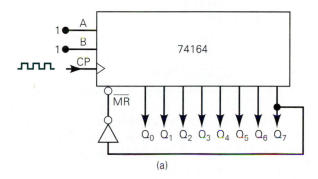

(a)

Input pulse number	Q_0	Q_1	Q_2	Q_3	Q_4	Q_5	Q_6	Q_7	
0	0	0	0	0	0	0	0	0	
1	1	0	0	0	0	0	0	0	
2	1	1	0	0	0	0	0	0	
3	1	1	1	0	0	0	0	0	
4	1	1	1	1	0	0	0	0	Recycles
5	1	1	1	1	1	0	0	0	
6	1	1	1	1	1	1	0	0	
7	1	1	1	1	1	1	1	0	
8	1	1	1	1	1	1	1	1	

Temporary state

(b)

Solution

The correct sequence is given in Figure 7-57(b). With $A = B = 1$, the serial input is 1, so that 1s will shift into the register on each PGT of CP. Since Q_7 is initially at 0, the $\overline{MR}$ input is inactive.

On the eighth pulse, the register tries to go to the 11111111 state as the 1 from Q_6 shifts into Q_7. This state occurs only momentarily because $Q_7 = 1$ produces a LOW at $\overline{MR}$ that immediately resets the register back to 00000000. The sequence is then repeated on the next eight clock pulses.

The following is a list of some other register ICs that are variations on those already presented:

■ **74194/LS194/HC194.** This is a four-bit *bidirectional universal shift-register* IC which can perform shift-left, shift-right, parallel in, and parallel out operations. These operations are selected by a two-bit mode-select code applied as inputs to the device. Problem 7-56 will provide you with a chance to find out more about this versatile chip.

■ **74373/LS373/HC373/HCT373.** This is an eight-bit (octal) parallel in/parallel out register containing eight *D* latches with *tristate* outputs. A tristate output is a special type of logic circuit output that allows device outputs to be safely tied together. We will cover the characteristics of tristate devices such as the 74373 in the next chapter.

■ **74374/LS374/HC374/HCT374.** This is an eight-bit (octal) parallel in/parallel out register containing eight edge-triggered D flip-flops with tristate outputs.

The IC registers that have been presented here are representative of the various types that are commercially available. Although there are many variations on these basic registers, most of them should now be relatively easy to understand from the manufacturers' data sheets.

We will present several register applications in the end-of-chapter problems and in the material covered in subsequent chapters.

Review Questions

1. What kind of register can have a complete binary number loaded into it in one operation, and then have it shifted out one bit at a time?

2. *True or false:* A serial in/parallel out register can have all of its bits displayed at one time.

3. What type of register can have data entered into it only one bit at a time, but has all data bits available as outputs?

4. In what type of register do we have access only to the leftmost or the rightmost FFs?

5. How does the parallel data entry differ for the 74165 and the 74178?

6. How does the *CP INH* input of the 74LS165 work?

7-23 IEEE/ANSI REGISTER SYMBOLS

We will present two examples of the IEEE/ANSI symbols for register ICs. First, let's consider the 74174 parallel in/parallel out IC whose internal logic and traditional logic symbol was shown in Figure 7-49. The IEEE/ANSI symbol for the 74174 is given in Figure 7-58(a). Its outline consists of the notched common-control block and the six narrow rectangles representing the six FFs.

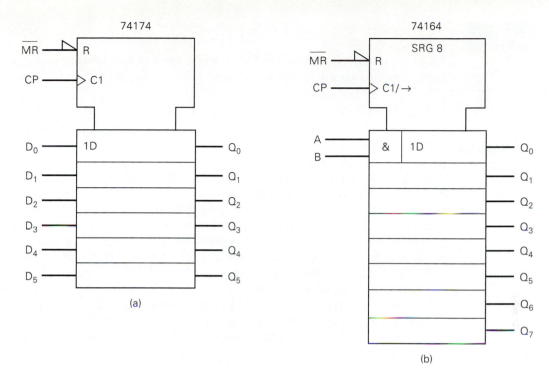

FIGURE 7-58 IEEE/ANSI symbols for (a) the 74174 parallel in/parallel out register and (b) the 74164 serial in/parallel out shift register.

The common-control block has the inputs that are common to all of the elements in the IC; in this case, the $\overline{MR}$ and CP inputs are common to the six FFs Q_0 through Q_5 that make up the register. The internal label for the $\overline{MR}$ input is shown as an R to indicate that its function is to *reset* each FF. The internal label for the CP input is C1, which tells us that this input controls the entry of data into any storage element that has a prefix of 1 in its input label. Each FF's D input has an internal label of 1D (shown only for Q_0, but assumed the same for each FF). The "1" in C1 and 1D establishes the dependency of the flip-flop D inputs on the common clock input CP.

The IEEE/ANSI symbol for the 74164 serial in/parallel out shift register is presented in Figure 7-58(b). Its outline consists of the common-control block and the eight FFs that make up the register. The notation SRG 8 identifies this IC as being an eight-bit shift register.

The CP input has the internal label C1/→. The slash (/) is used to separate the two functions C1 and → performed by this input. The C1 indicates that CP controls the data entry into flip-flop Q_0 since Q_0 has the input label 1D. Note that the data bit entered into Q_0 is indicated as the AND combination of inputs A and B. Also note that since there are no external data inputs to Q_1 through Q_7, CP does not control data entry into these FFs. The → denotes that the active transition of CP will produce the shift-right operation (from Q_0 toward Q_7).

1. What does the slash (/) mean when it appears in an input label?
2. What notation would be used to describe the function performed by one of the registers on the 4731B IC of Figure 7-53?

7-24 TROUBLESHOOTING

Flip-flops, counters, and registers are the major components in **sequential logic systems.** A sequential logic system, because of its storage devices, has the characteristic that its outputs and sequence of operations depend on both the present inputs and the inputs that occurred earlier. Even though sequential logic systems are generally more complex than combinational logic systems, the essential procedures for troubleshooting apply equally well to both types of systems. Sequential systems suffer from the same types of failures (open circuits, shorts, internal IC faults, and the like) as do combinational systems.

Many of the same steps used to isolate faults in a combinational system can be applied to sequential systems. One of the most effective troubleshooting techniques begins with the troubleshooter observing the system operation and, by analytical reasoning, determining the possible causes of the system malfunction. Then he or she uses available test instruments to isolate the exact fault. The following examples will show the kinds of analytical reasoning that should be the initial step in troubleshooting sequential systems. After studying these examples, you should be ready to tackle the troubleshooting problems at the end of the chapter.

EXAMPLE 7-25

Figure 7-59(a) shows a 74LS293 wired as a MOD-10 counter. A technician tests the counter operation by applying a 1-kHz clock signal and observing the Q outputs with an oscilloscope. The displayed waveforms are shown in Figure 7-59(b). Determine the possible causes for the incorrect circuit behavior.

Solution

The waveforms show that Q_0 is toggling in response to the NGTs of the clock, but all other FFs are stuck in the LOW state. Several possible faults could produce this operation.

1. The Q_1 output is internally or externally shorted to ground. Referring to the 74LS293 diagram in Figure 7-8(a), we can see that this would prevent Q_2 and Q_3 from toggling, since Q_1 is the clock signal for Q_2 and Q_2 is the clock signal for Q_3.
2. The connection from Q_0 to $\overline{CP}_1$ is open, so that Q_1 receives no clock signal.
3. There is an internal fault in the IC that prevents Q_1 from toggling.
4. The MR_1 input is internally shorted to ground, forcing $Q_1 = 0$.

FIGURE 7-59   Example 7-25.

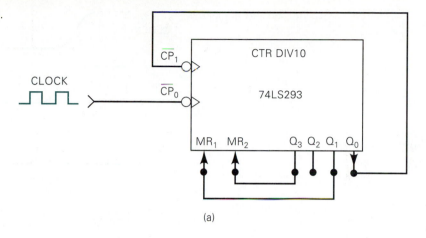

(a)

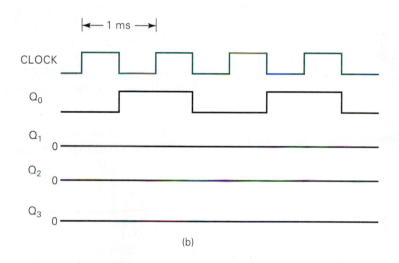

(b)

EXAMPLE 7-26

After analyzing the situation described in Example 7-25, the technician proceeds to isolate the fault. He performs ohmmeter checks and verifies that Q_1 is not shorted to ground and that Q_0 is connected to $\overline{CP}_1$. This eliminates the first two possible faults. Concluding that the IC is bad, he replaces it. To his surprise, the circuit operation exhibits the same symptoms. Scratching his head, he decides to take a closer look at the FF waveforms by displaying them using a 10-ns/cm time scale. On this scale he can see a very narrow glitch occurring on the Q_1 signal at the time when Q_0 makes a NGT (see Figure 7-60). What is the probable fault?

Solution

When the counter is operating correctly, there should be a glitch at Q_1 when the counter goes to the 1010 (10) state, at which point the HIGHs at Q_3 and Q_1 cause the MR inputs to clear the count back to 0000. The waveforms in Figure 7-60, however, do not show Q_3 HIGH when the glitch at Q_1 occurs. The most probable fault is an open connection at MR_2, since this would be interpreted as a constant

FIGURE 7-60   Example 7-26.

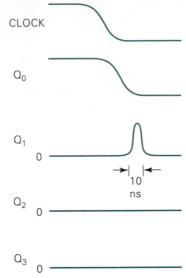

logic HIGH by the TTL integrated circuit. Thus, as soon as Q_1 goes HIGH, the *MR* inputs are both HIGH and the counter resets to 0000.

EXAMPLE 7-27

A technician tests the frequency counter of Figure 7-46 for various settings of the sample interval and for different unknown input frequencies. In all cases she finds that the displayed frequency is exactly *twice* what it should be. What is the probable cause of the malfunction?

Solution

Referring to Figure 7-46, we see that the unknown frequency is allowed through the AND gate into the counter during the interval t_3 to t_4 while SAMPLE and X are both HIGH. If the middle input to the AND gate were open, it would act like a permanent HIGH (assuming TTL devices). This would allow the unknown frequency pulses through the gate while X is HIGH during the interval t_2 to t_4. This is twice the normal interval, and so the counter will count to twice the normal value.

EXAMPLE 7-28

A technician wires up the digital clock of Figures 7-47 and 7-48. He observes that the SECONDS section is counting properly. In order to quickly test the operation of the MINUTES and HOURS sections, he bypasses the MOD-60 counter so that the counters will be pulsed at a rate that is 60 times faster than normal. He observes that the MINUTES section is working correctly, but the HOURS section counts and displays in the manner shown in Table 7-7. What is the probable cause of this incorrect sequence?

Solution

Since the problem is in the HOURS section, we need to refer to Figure 7-48. The sequence above is correct except that the tens digit is incremented from 0 to 1 when the units digit goes from 7 to 8 instead of when it goes from 9 to 0. This op-

TABLE 7-7

Tens of HOURS	Units of HOURS
0	1
0	2
0	3
0	4
0	5
0	6
0	7
1	8
1	9
1	0
1	1
1	2

recycle and repeat

eration would occur if the *CLK* input of flip-flop *X* were mistakenly connected to Q_2 rather than Q_3 of the BCD counter. If this is the case, then when the BCD counter increments from 7 to 8, its Q_2 flip-flop makes a NGT that will toggle flip-flop *X* earlier than expected.

PART II SUMMARY

1. A frequency counter is a circuit that uses binary counters to measure and display the frequency of an incoming signal.

2. A digital clock circuit uses binary counters to keep track of and display the time of day.

3. Numerous IC registers are available which can be classified according to whether their inputs are parallel (all bits entered simultaneously), serial (one bit at a time), or both. Likewise, registers can have outputs that are parallel (all bits available simultaneously) or serial (one bit at a time).

4. A sequential logic system uses FFs, counters, and registers, along with logic gates. Its outputs and sequence of operations depend on present and past inputs.

5. Troubleshooting a sequential logic system begins with observation of the system operation, followed by analytical reasoning to determine the possible causes of any malfunction, and finally test measurements to isolate the actual fault.

PART II IMPORTANT TERMS

frequency counter
sampling interval
parallel in/parallel out

serial in/serial out
parallel in/serial out

serial in/parallel out
sequential logic system

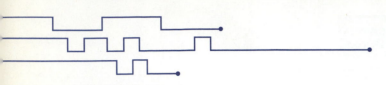

PROBLEMS

PART I

SECTIONS 7-1 AND 7-2

7-1. An 8-MHz square wave clocks a five-bit ripple counter. What is the frequency of the last FF (MSB)? What is the duty cycle of this output waveform?

7-2. Repeat Problem 7-1 if the input has a 20 percent duty cycle.

7-3. Assume that the five-bit binary counter starts in the 00000 state. What will be the count after 144 input pulses?

D   **7-4.** Use J-K flip-flops and any other necessary logic to construct a MOD-24 asynchronous counter.

7-5. Draw the waveforms for all the FFs in the decade counter of Figure 7-6(b) in response to a 1-kHz clock frequency. Show any glitches that might appear on any of the FF outputs. Determine the frequency at the *D* output.

7-6. Repeat Problem 7-5 for the counter of Figure 7-6(a).

7-7. Change the inputs to the NAND gate of Figure 7-7 so that the counter divides the frequency by 50. Repeat for a frequency division of 100.

7-8. A counter or a group of counters is often used to divide a high-frequency clock signal down to a lower-frequency output. When these counters are binary counters (i.e., they count in the binary sequence), the output will not be a symmetrical square wave if the binary sequence has been shortened in order to produce the desired MOD number. For example, refer to the *C* waveform of the MOD-6 counter in Figure 7-4.

When a counter is being used only for frequency division, it is not necessary that it count in a binary sequence as long as it has the desired MOD number. A symmetrical square-wave output can be obtained for any *even* MOD number by breaking the MOD number into the product of two MOD numbers, one of which is a power of 2. For example, a MOD-6 counter can be formed from a MOD-3 counter and MOD-2 counter as shown in Figure 7-61.

Here flip-flops *A* and *B* and the NAND gate make up the MOD-3 counter, whose *B* output has one-third the frequency of the input pulses. This *B* output is connected to the input of flip-flop *C*, which is acting as a MOD-2 counter to divide the frequency down to one-sixth the frequency of the input pulses.

(a) Assume that all FFs are initially LOW, and sketch the waveforms at each FF output for 12 cycles of the input.

(b) Construct the state transition diagram, and show that it is not a normal binary sequence.

SECTION 7-3

D   **7-9.** Show how a 74LS293 counter can be used to produce a 1.2-kpps output from an 18-kpps input.

D   **7-10.** Show how two 74LS293s can be connected to divide an input frequency by 60 while producing a symmetrical square-wave output.

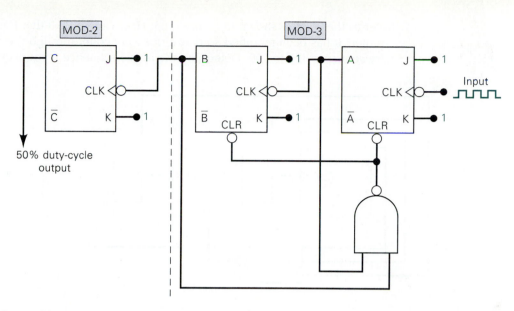

FIGURE 7-61   Problem 7-8.

C   **7-11.** Determine the frequency at output X in Figure 7-62.

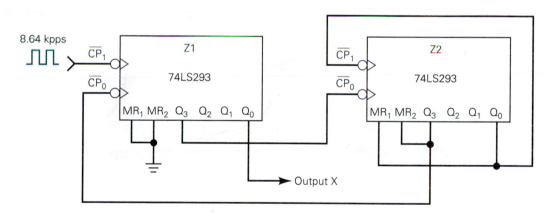

FIGURE 7-62   Problems 7-11 and 7-64.

D   **7-12. (a)** Add the necessary logic to a 74HC4024 so that it operates as a MOD-100 counter.

(b) Use 74HC4024s and any necessary logic to convert a 10-kpps signal to 1 pps.

SECTION 7-4

7-13. (a) Draw the diagram for a MOD-16 *down* counter.

(b) Construct the state transition diagram.

(c) If the counter is initially in the 0110 state, what state will it be in after 37 clock pulses?

7-14. Refer to the counter shown in Figure 7-63. How can you tell that it is a down counter? It has been modified so that it does *not* count through the entire binary sequence 111 to 000. Determine the actual sequence it counts through.

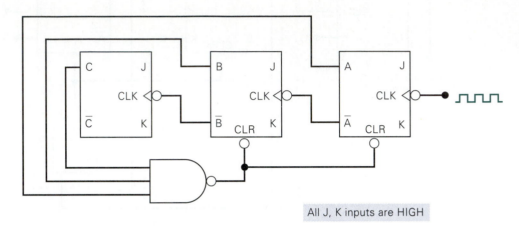

All J, K inputs are HIGH

FIGURE 7-63 Problem 7-14.

SECTION 7-5

7-15. A four-bit ripple counter is driven by a 20-MHz clock signal. Draw the waveforms at the output of each FF if each FF has $t_{pd} = 20$ ns. Determine which counter states, if any, will not occur because of the propagation delays.

7-16. (a) What is the maximum clock frequency that can be used with the counter of Problem 7-15?
   (b) What could f_{max} be if the counter were expanded to six bits?

SECTIONS 7-6 AND 7-7

7-17. (a) Draw the circuit diagram for a MOD-64 parallel counter.
   (b) Determine f_{max} for this counter if each FF has $t_{pd} = 20$ ns and each gate has $t_{pd} = 10$ ns.

C 7-18. Figure 7-64 shows a four-bit parallel counter which is designed so that it does not sequence through the entire 16 binary states. Analyze its operation by determining its counting sequence, and then draw the waveforms at each FF output. (See Section 5-23 to review the analysis procedure.) Assume that all FFs are initially in the 0 state.

7-19. Draw the diagram for a MOD-8 synchronous down counter.

T 7-20. Describe how the up/down counter of Figure 7-18 would operate if the INVERTER output were stuck HIGH.

SECTIONS 7-8 AND 7-9

C 7-21. Show how to connect two 74LS193s to form an eight-bit counter that divides the clock frequency by 100. Use the $\overline{TC}_D$ output of one stage as the clock for the second stage. (*Hint:* The counter is to be preset when both stages are simultaneously at their end counts.)

N, C 7-22. Figure 7-65 shows how a presettable down counter can be used in a *programmable timer* circuit. The input clock frequency is an accurate 1 Hz derived from the 60-Hz line frequency after division by 60. Switches S1 to S4 are

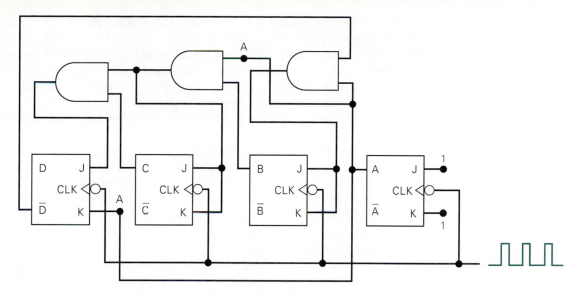

FIGURE 7-64   Problem 7-18.

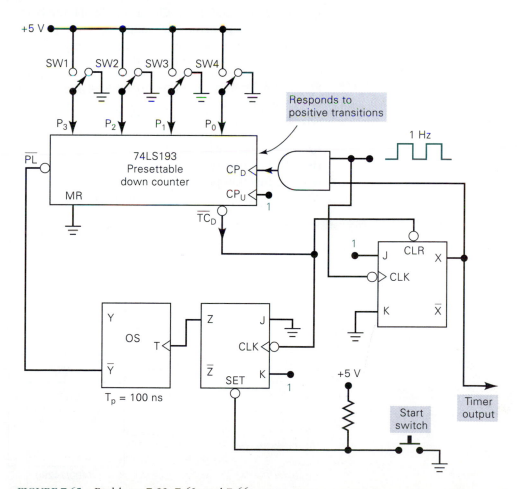

FIGURE 7-65   Problems 7-22, 7-63, and 7-66.

used to preset the counter to a desired starting count when a momentary pulse is applied to $\overline{PL}$. The timer operation is initiated by depressing the START pushbutton switch. Flip-flop Z is used to eliminate effects of bounce in the START switch. The OS is used to provide a very narrow pulse to the $\overline{PL}$ input. The output of flip-flop X will be a waveform that goes HIGH for a number of seconds equal to the number set on the switches.

(a) Assume that all FFs and the counter are in the 0 state, and analyze and explain the circuit operation, showing waveforms when necessary, for the case where S1 and S4 are LOW and S2 and S3 are HIGH. Be sure to explain the function of flip-flop X.

(b) Why can't the timer output be taken at the $\overline{TC}_D$ output?

(c) Why can't the START switch be used to trigger the OS directly?

(d) What will happen if the START switch is held down too long? Add the necessary logic needed to ensure that holding the START switch down will not affect the timer operation.

7-23. Modify the circuit of Figure 7-24 so that it functions as a MOD-10 counter. The frequency at the Q_3 output should be one-tenth the frequency of the CP_D input. Draw the waveforms at Q_3, Q_2, Q_1, Q_0, and $\overline{TC}_D$.

7-24. Change the parallel data inputs in Figure 7-24 to 1001. Draw the waveforms at Q_3, Q_2, Q_1, Q_0, and $\overline{TC}_D$. What is the MOD number?

7-25. Draw the waveforms for the input signals required to perform the following sequence of operations in the circuit of Figure 7-25: (1) clear the count to 0; (2) count up to 24_{10}; (3) preset the count to 76_{10}; (4) count down to 0.

SECTION 7-10

7-26. Figure 7-66 shows the IEEE/ANSI symbol for a 7490 or 74290 counter IC. Examine the symbol and determine the following.

(a) The overall MOD number

(b) The function performed by the MR inputs

(c) The function performed by the MS inputs

(d) Is this an up counter or a down counter?

FIGURE 7-66 Problem 7-26.

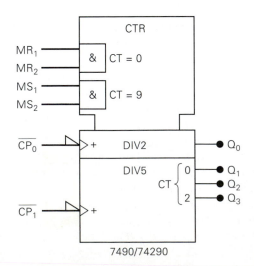

(e) How would you connect it to function as a BCD counter? (Refer to the data sheet in the Appendix.)

(f) How would you connect it to divide the clock frequency by 10 and produce a symmetrical square wave?

7-27. The 74192 counter IC operates exactly like the 74193 except for the following differences:

- The 74192 is a BCD counter that either counts up from 0 to 9 or counts down from 9 to 0.
- The $\overline{TC}_U$ output is activated when the count is 9 and the CP_U input is LOW.

Modify the IEEE/ANSI symbol of Figure 7-26 so that it represents the 74192.

SECTION 7-11 AND 7-12

7-28. Draw the gates necessary to decode all of the states of a MOD-16 counter using active-LOW outputs.

7-29. Draw the AND gates necessary to decode the 10 states of the BCD counter of Figure 7-6(b).

7-30. Figure 7-67 shows a ripple counter being used to help generate control waveforms. Control waveforms 1 and 2 could be used for many purposes, including control of motors, solenoids, valves, and heaters. Determine the control waveforms, assuming that all FFs are initially LOW. Ignore decoding glitches. Assume that clock frequency = 1 kpps.

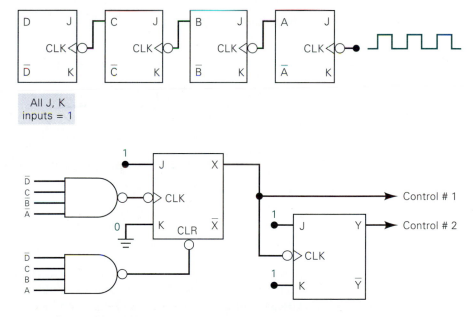

FIGURE 7-67   Problem 7-30.

7-31. Draw the complete waveforms at the output of the decoding gates of a MOD-16 *ripple* counter, including any glitches or spikes that can occur due to the FF delays. Why are the gates that are decoding for *even* numbers the only ones that have glitches?

7-32. The circuit of Figure 7-67 might malfunction because of glitches at the outputs of the decoding NAND gates.
(a) Determine at what point(s) the glitches can cause erroneous operation.
(b) What are two ways that can be used to eliminate the possibility of erroneous operation?

SECTION 7-13

7-33. How many FFs are used in Figure 7-32? Indicate the states of each of these FFs after 795 pulses have occurred.

7-34. How many cascaded BCD counters are needed to be able to count up to 8000? How many FFs does this require? Compare this with the number of FFs required for a normal binary counter to count up to 8000. Since it uses more FFs, why is the cascaded BCD method used?

SECTION 7-14

D 7-35. (a) Design a synchronous counter that has the following sequence: 000, 010, 101, 110, and repeat. The undesired (unused) states 001, 011, 100, and 111 must always go to 000 on the NEXT clock pulse.
(b) Redesign the counter of part (a) without any requirement on the unused states; that is, their NEXT states can be don't cares. Compare with the design from (a).

C, D 7-36. Use the synchronous counter design procedure to design a four-bit synchronous down counter that counts through all states from 1111 down to 0000. Compare your result with the synchronous down counter described in Section 7-7.

C, D 7-37. Using a procedure similar to the one followed in the design of the counter to drive the stepper motor (Figure 7-39), design a three-bit synchronous counter that will count up or count down under the control of Direction input, D. It should count up when $D = 1$ and count down when $D = 0$. (*Hint:* This is a *four*-variable problem.)
Compare your final circuit to the synchronous up/down counter of Figure 7-18.

SECTION 7-15

7-38. Draw the diagram for a five-bit ring counter using J-K flip-flops.

7-39. Combine the ring counter of Problem 7-38 with a *single* J-K flip-flop to produce a MOD-10 counter. Determine the sequence of states for this counter. This is an example of a decade counter that is not a BCD counter.

7-40. Draw the diagram for a MOD-10 Johnson counter using J-K flip-flops, and determine its counting sequence. Draw the decoding circuit needed to decode each of the 10 states. This is another example of a decade counter that is not a BCD counter.

7-41. Determine the frequency of the pulses at points w, x, y, and z in the circuit of Figure 7-68.

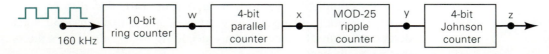

FIGURE 7-68 Problem 7-41.

7-42. **(a)** A group of eight display lights on a pinball machine are controlled by the FFs of an eight-bit ring counter that is being clocked by a 2-pps signal. Describe the visual effect that is produced.

(b) Repeat for an eight-bit Johnson counter.

PART II

SECTION 7-16

7-43. As pointed out in the text, the frequency counter of Figure 7-46 has the disadvantage that the display shows all of the counter operations (resetting, counting, holding) and would therefore be confusing, if not unreadable. This can be overcome by the addition of buffer registers to store the contents of the counter at the end of each counting interval (t_3 to t_4 in Figure 7-46) and hold it for display until the end of the next counting interval (t_7 to t_8). Figure 7-69 shows this modification. A register consisting of

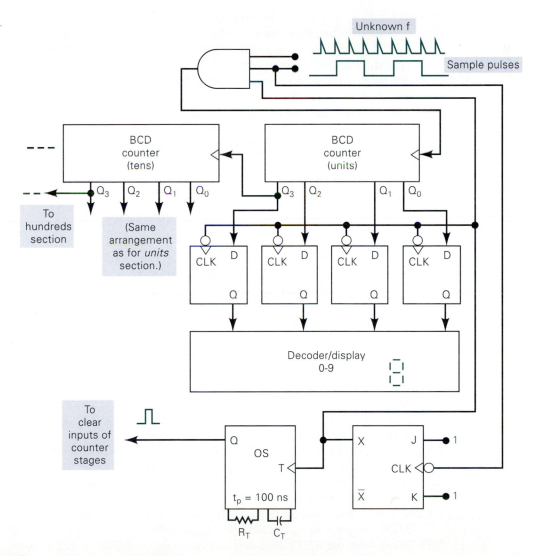

FIGURE 7-69 Problems 7-43 and 7-48.

four D flip-flops has been inserted between each BCD counter and its decoder/display unit.

(a) Analyze this circuit and describe its operation, particularly the transferring of data from the counters to the display.

(b) What would you see on a three-digit display if the unknown frequency were constant at 2570 pps and the sample interval were 0.1 s?

(c) What would you see on this display if the unknown frequency were suddenly changed to 3230 pps?

7-44. The frequency counter of Figure 7-69 uses three BCD counters and a sampling interval of 100 μs. Determine the readings on the three frequency-counter displays for each of the following input frequencies.

(a) 220 kpps

(b) 4.5 Mpps

(c) 750 pps

SECTION 7-17

7-45. Design the complete circuit for the SECONDS section of the digital clock circuit of Figure 7-47. Use a 74LS293 for the MOD-6 and a 74LS290 for the BCD (see the data sheet in the Appendix).

D   7-46. The digital clock of Figure 7-47 must have some means for manually setting the HOURS and MINUTES sections to the correct starting time. For example, this can be done by switching the 1-pps signal into the input of the MINUTES section when a SET MINUTES pushbutton is activated. A similar operation can be done with a SET HOURS pushbutton. Design the necessary logic to provide this capability using two pushbutton switches.

D   7-47. Modify the HOURS section of the digital clock (Figure 7-48) so that it counts and displays military time (i.e., 00 to 23 hours).

SECTIONS 7-19 AND 7-20

D   7-48. Modify the frequency counter of Figure 7-69 so that it uses 74147 ICs. Assume that the counter contains three BCD counters and a three-digit display.

D   7-49. Show how to connect two 74178s as an eight-bit ring counter.

N, C   7-50. Figure 7-70 shows how a 74178 can be used as a *parallel-to-serial converter*. The parallel data that are entered at P_0 through P_3 are shifted out serially so that a serial waveform appears at Q_3. The shifting out of the parallel data is controlled by the occurrence of the START pulse. This START pulse occurs asynchronously to the clock pulses, and so the D flip-flops are used to synchronize the parallel loading and shifting of the 74178.

Assume that the START pulse has been LOW and that clock pulses have been continually applied to the circuit for a long time before time t_0 (see the waveforms). Draw the waveforms that appear at Q_X, $\overline{Q}_X$, Q_Y, and Q_3 in response to the START pulse shown in the figure.

D   7-51. The 74LS174 is a parallel in/parallel out register. However, it can be connected so that it functions as a shift register (serial in/serial out). Show how this can be done. Then show how, with the addition of the necessary logic, it can function as a Johnson counter.

7-52. Consider the situation depicted by the waveforms in Figure 7-54. If D_S goes LOW just prior to t_{247}, when will Q_{63} go LOW?

7-53. Show how the 4731B chip can be connected as a 256-bit shift register.

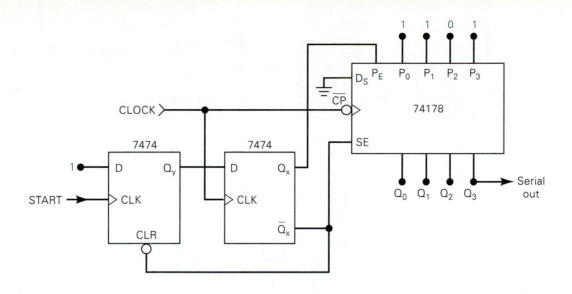

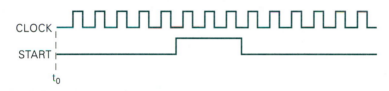

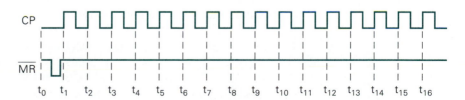

FIGURE 7-70   Problem 7-50.

SECTIONS 7-21 AND 7-22

C, D   **7-54.** Modify the circuit of Figure 7-57 so that the INVERTER output is connected to the A input instead of to $\overline{MR}$.

(a) Draw the waveforms at each FF output in response to the input waveforms shown in Figure 7-71.

(b) Add the necessary logic to produce a timing-signal output that goes HIGH only during time intervals t_1 to t_2 and t_8 to t_9.

(c) Add the necessary logic to produce a timing signal that goes LOW only during the interval t_4 to t_7.

FIGURE 7-71   Problem 7-54.

7-55. A 74HC165 is connected as shown in Figure 7-72. Assume that prior to t_0, pulses have been applied to CP, and the $SH/\overline{LD}$ input has been held HIGH

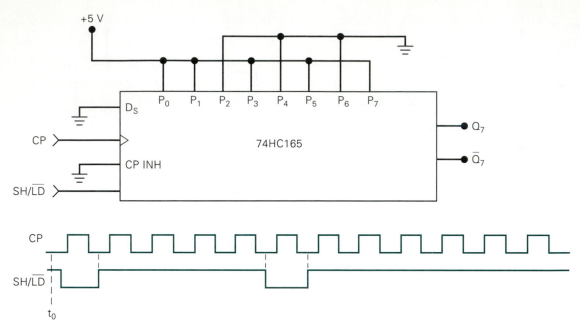

+5 V

D_S

CP

CP INH

SH/$\overline{LD}$

P_0 P_1 P_2 P_3 P_4 P_5 P_6 P_7

74HC165

Q_7

$\overline{Q}_7$

CP

SH/$\overline{LD}$

t_0

FIGURE 7-72   Problem 7-55.

for a long time. Draw the Q_7 waveform in response to the *CP* and *SH/$\overline{LD}$* waveforms beginning at t_0.

N   **7-56.** While examining the schematic for a piece of equipment, a technician or an engineer will often come across an IC that is unfamiliar. In such cases, it is often necessary to consult the manufacturer's IC data book for specifications on the device. The information on the IC data sheets is always complete, but it is sometimes difficult to understand, especially by someone with very little experience. This problem will give you practice in obtaining information about a fairly complex IC—the 74194 bidirectional universal shift register. Consult a TTL or CMOS data book to answer the following questions. Support your answers.

(a) Is the *CLR* input asynchronous or synchronous?

(b) *True or false:* When *CLK* is LOW, the S_0 and S_1 levels have no effect on the register.

(c) Assume the following conditions:

$$Q_A Q_B Q_C Q_D = 1\ 0\ 1\ 1$$
$$ABCD = 0\ 1\ 1\ 0$$
$$\overline{CLR} = 1$$
$$SR\ SER = 0$$
$$SL\ SER = 1$$

If $S_0 = 0$ and $S_1 = 1$, what will the register outputs be after one *CLK* pulse? After two *CLK* pulses? After three? After four?

(d) Use the same conditions except $S_0 = 1$, $S_1 = 0$ and repeat part (c).

(e) Repeat part (c) with $S_0 = S_1 = 1$.

(f) Repeat part (c) with $S_0 = S_1 = 0$.

(g) Use the same conditions as in part (c) except assume that output Q_A is connected to SL SER. What will be the register outputs after four *CLK* pulses?

(h) Show how to connect this IC to function as a ring counter that counts through the following Q_A Q_B Q_C Q_D sequence: 0001, 0010, 0100, 1000, and repeat.

SECTION 7-24

T **7-57.** A technician tests the counter of Figure 7-59(a) by applying a low-frequency clock signal and monitoring the FF outputs on indicator LEDs. He observes a repetitive sequence indicated by the LEDs (Table 7-8). What are the possible reasons why the counter is not counting properly?

TABLE 7-8

Q_3	Q_2	Q_1	Q_0
0	0	0	0
0	0	0	1
0	0	1	0
0	0	1	1
0	1	0	0
0	1	0	1
0	1	1	0
0	1	1	1

recycle and repeat

T **7-58.** Refer to the digital clock circuit of Figures 7-47 and 7-48. A technician testing the circuit observes that the SECONDS and MINUTES sections count properly, but the HOURS section counts as follows: 01, 02, 03, 04, 05, 06, 07, 08, 09, 10, 11, 12, 11, 12, 11, 12, ... What is the probable cause of the malfunction?

T **7-59.** A technician tests the digital clock circuit (Figures 7-47 and 7-48) and observes that the HOURS section does not count and the MINUTES section counts from 00 to 39, and then recycles to 00 and repeats. What are the possible causes of this incorrect behavior?

T **7-60.** Refer to the modified frequency counter of Figure 7-69. Assume that there are three BCD counter stages with associated buffer registers. The sample interval is set at 1 s, and the unknown frequency is 125 pps. Describe what will appear on the display for each of the following circuit faults.

(a) An open connection at the top input of the AND gate

(b) A burned-out resistor R_T

T **7-61.** A technician tests the frequency counter of Figure 7-69 using a sample interval of 1 s and an unknown frequency of 125 pps. She expects to see a display of 125 but instead sees the display changing every few seconds as follows: 125, 250, 375, 500, 625, 750, 875, 000, 125, 250, ... What can be the cause of this malfunction?

T   7-62. Refer to the up/down counter of Figure 7-18. Describe how each of the following circuit faults will affect the count-up and count-down operations.
(a) The AND gate 4 output is internally shorted to V_{CC}.
(b) A solder bridge is shorting the AND gate 1 output to the AND gate 3 output.

T   7-63. A technician runs a test on the timer circuit of Figure 7-65 and records the results shown in Table 7-9. Examine the recorded data and determine the possible causes of the faulty operation.

TABLE 7-9

S1	S2	S3	S4	Timer Output(s)
5 V	0 V	0 V	0 V	10
0 V	0 V	5 V	5 V	3
5 V	0 V	5 V	5 V	11
5 V	5 V	5 V	0 V	14
0 V	5 V	0 V	5 V	7
5 V	5 V	0 V	0 V	14

T   7-64. A technician wires up the counter circuit of Figure 7-62. He applies an accurate 8.64-kpps signal to the input and measures a frequency of 54 pps at X instead of the expected 60 pps. What is the most probable wiring error that he made?

DRILL QUESTION

7-65. For each of the following statements, indicate the type(s) of counter being described.
(a) Each FF is clocked at the same time.
(b) Each FF divides the frequency at its *CLK* input by 2.
(c) The counting sequence is 111, 110, 101, 100, 011, 010, 001, 000.
(d) The counter has 10 distinct states.
(e) The total switching delay is the sum of the individual FFs' delays.
(f) This counter requires no decoding logic.
(g) The MOD number is always twice the number of FFs.
(h) This counter divides the input frequency by its MOD number.
(i) This counter can begin its counting sequence at any desired starting state.
(j) This counter can count in either direction.
(k) Can suffer from decoding glitches.
(l) Counts from 0 to 99.
(m) Can be designed to count through arbitrary sequences by determining logic needed at each flip-flop's *J* and *K* input.

MICROCOMPUTER APPLICATION

C, D   7-66. A microprocessor that is used in a control application must often control the timing of external events such as the turning on and off of devices such as solenoids, motors, and relays. Such actions can be timed using software by repetitively executing a program loop a specific number of times. This, however, places a heavy burden on the MPU, since it can't do anything else while it is executing the loop over and over. For this reason, most timed intervals are usually generated by hardware that is *under control of the MPU*. In other words, the MPU will send data to the hardware to tell it how long a time interval to generate.

In Problem 7-22 we saw how the 74LS193 IC could be used in a timer circuit (Figure 7-65) to generate accurate time intervals corresponding to the binary data from four switches. This circuit can be modified so that the binary data come from an MPU instead of the switches. In Section 5-20 we saw how an MPU could transfer data to an external device using its address, data, and clock outputs (Figure 5-50).

Show how to combine these two circuits so that the timer output X will generate a HIGH level for a time interval (in seconds) equal to the binary number that the MPU presets into the 74LS193 counter. You can eliminate any circuitry that is not needed. Assume that the MPU's *CP* signal is a 1-MHz square wave. Remember that $\overline{PL}$ is an asynchronous input.

ANSWERS TO SECTION REVIEW QUESTIONS

PART I

SECTION 7-1
1. False   2. 0000   3. 128

SECTION 7-2
1. *D, C,* and *A*   2. True, since a BCD counter has 10 distinct states   3. 5 kHz

SECTION 7-3
1. 250 Hz   2. $f_{in}/60$ 3. 4096   4. The counter is MOD-64 and divides the frequency by 64.   5. 96

SECTION 7-4
1. In an up counter, the count is increased by 1 with each clock pulse; in a down counter, the count is decreased by 1 with each pulse.   2. The inverted output of each FF is connected to the *CLK* input of the following FF.

SECTION 7-5
1. Each FF adds its propagation delay to the total counter delay in response to a clock pulse.
2. MOD-256

SECTION 7-6
1. Can operate at higher clock frequencies and has more complex circuitry   2. Six FFs and four AND gates   3. *ABCDE*

SECTION 7-8
1. It can be preset to any desired starting count.
2. Asynchronous presetting is independent of the clock

input, while synchronous presetting occurs on the active edge of the clock signal.

SECTION 7-9
1. When $\overline{PL}$ is pulsed LOW, the counter is preset to the binary number present at inputs P_0 to P_3.   2. A HIGH at *MR* overrides all other inputs to reset the counter to 0000.
3. True   4. 1, 1, 0, respectively   5. 0 to 65,535

SECTION 7-10
1. See appropriate text.   2. (a) Up-counter operation.   (b) This input is ANDed with any other input or output that has a "4" in its label.   (c) This input controls the effect of any inputs that have "5" in their label.   (d) Data input that is controlled by input labeled C5.

SECTION 7-11
1. Sixty-four   2. A six-input NAND gate with inputs *A, B, C,* $\overline{D}$, *E,* and $\overline{F}$

SECTION 7-12
1. The glitches would be caused by the FFs' changing states one at a time during counter state transitions.
2. The strobe signal inhibits the decoding gates until all FFs have completed their transitions.

SECTION 7-14
1. See text.   2. It shows the necessary levels at *J* and *K* to produce every possible FF state transition.   3. It shows the necessary levels at each flip-flop's *J* and *K* input to produce the counter's state transitions.
4. True

SECTION 7-15

1. Ring counter **2.** Johnson counter **3.** The inverted output of the last FF is connected to the input of the first FF. **4. (a)** False **(b)** True **(c)** True

PART II

SECTION 7-16

1. 1 ms **2.** Counter cleared; counter counts pulses during sample interval; counter stops and holds count for display. **3.** A ring counter uses more FFs than a Johnson counter.

SECTION 7-17

1. Pulse shaper, frequency divider, seconds counter and display, minutes counter and display, hours counter and display **2.** To change the NGT from the MINUTES section to a PGT needed by the 74192

SECTION 7-18 TO SECTION 7-22

1. Parallel in/serial out **2.** True **3.** Serial in/parallel out **4.** Serial in/serial out **5.** The 74165 uses asynchronous parallel data transfer; the 74178 uses synchronous. **6.** A HIGH prevents shifting on *CP*.

SECTION 7-23

1. It separates the two indicated functions performed by that input. **2.** SRG 64

CHAPTER 8

Integrated-Circuit Logic Families

■ OUTLINE

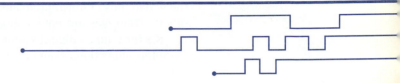

■ OBJECTIVES

Upon completion of this chapter, you will be able to:

- Read and understand digital IC terminology as specified in manufacturers' data sheets.
- Compare the characteristics of standard TTL and the various TTL series.
- Determine the fan-out for a particular logic device.
- Use logic devices with open-collector outputs.
- Analyze circuits containing tristate devices.
- Compare the characteristics of the various CMOS series.
- Analyze circuits that use a CMOS bilateral switch to allow a digital system to control analog signals.
- Describe the major characteristics of and differences among TTL, ECL, MOS, and CMOS logic families.
- Cite and implement the various considerations that are required when interfacing digital circuits from different logic families.
- Use voltage comparators to allow a digital system to be controlled by analog signals.
- Use a logic pulser and a current tracer as digital circuit troubleshooting tools.

■ INTRODUCTION

As we described in Chapter 4, digital IC technology has advanced rapidly from small-scale integration (SSI), with fewer than 12 gates per chip; through medium-scale integration (MSI, with 12 to 99 equivalent gates per chip; on to large-scale and very large-scale integration (LSI and VLSI), which can have tens of thousands of gates per chip; and, most recently, to ULSI with over 100,000 gates per chip, and GSI with one million or more gates.

Most of the reasons that modern digital systems use integrated circuits are obvious. ICs pack a lot more circuitry in a small package, so that the overall size of almost any digital system is reduced. The cost is dramatically reduced because of the economies of mass-producing large volumes of similar devices. Some of the other advantages are not so apparent.

ICs have made digital systems more reliable by reducing the number of external interconnections from one device to another. Before we had ICs, every circuit connection was from one discrete component (transistor, diode, resistor, etc.) to another. Now most of the connections are internal to the ICs, where they are protected from poor soldering, breaks or shorts in connecting paths on a circuit board, and other physical problems. ICs have also drastically reduced the amount of electrical power needed to perform a given function, since their miniature circuitry typically requires less power than their discrete counterparts. In addition to the savings in power-supply costs, this reduction in power has also meant that a system does not require as much cooling.

There are some things that ICs cannot do. They cannot handle very large currents or voltages because the heat generated in such small spaces would cause temperatures to rise beyond acceptable limits. In addition, ICs cannot easily implement certain electrical devices such as inductors, transformers, and large capacitors. For these reasons, ICs are principally used to perform low-power circuit operations that are commonly called *information processing*. The operations that require high power levels or devices that cannot be integrated are still handled by discrete components.

With the widespread use of ICs comes the necessity to know and understand the electrical characteristics of the most common IC logic families. Remember that the various logic families differ in the major components that they use in their circuitry. TTL and ECL use *bipolar* transistors as their major circuit element; PMOS, NMOS, and CMOS use unipolar *MOS*FET transistors as their principal component. In this chapter we will present the important characteristics of each of these IC families and their subfamilies. Once these are understood, you will be much better prepared to do analysis, troubleshooting, and some design of digital circuits that contain any combination of IC families.

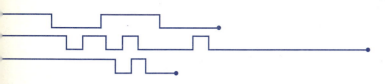

8-1 DIGITAL IC TERMINOLOGY

Although there are many digital IC manufacturers, much of the nomenclature and terminology is fairly standardized. The most useful terms are defined and discussed below.

Current and Voltage Parameters (see Figure 8-1)

■ V_{IH}(min)—**High-Level Input Voltage.** The minimum voltage level required for a logical 1 at an *input*. Any voltage below this level will not be accepted as a HIGH by the logic circuit.

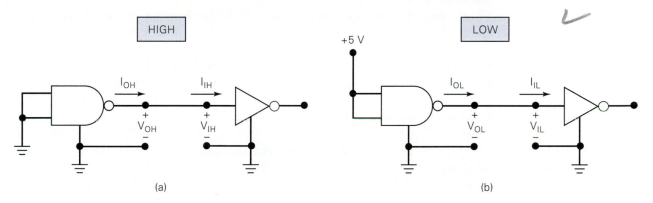

FIGURE 8-1   Currents and voltages in the two logic states.

■ V_{IL}(max)—**Low-Level Input Voltage.** The maximum voltage level required for a logic 0 at an *input*. Any voltage above this level will not be accepted as a LOW by the logic circuit.

■ V_{OH}(min)—**High-Level Output Voltage.** The minimum voltage level at a logic circuit *output* in the logical 1 state under defined load conditions.

■ V_{OL}(max)—**Low-Level Output Voltage.** The maximum voltage level at a logic circuit *output* in the logical 0 state under defined load conditions.

■ I_{IH}—**High-Level Input Current.** The current that flows into an input when a specified high-level voltage is applied to that input.

■ I_{IL}—**Low-Level Input Current.** The current that flows into an input when a specified low-level voltage is applied to that input.

■ I_{OH}—**High-Level Output Current.** The current that flows from an output in the logical 1 state under specified load conditions.

■ I_{OL}—**Low-Level Output Current.** The current that flows from an output in the logical 0 state under specified load conditions.

Note: The actual current directions may be opposite to those shown, depending on the logic family. All descriptions of current flow in this text refer to conventional current flow (from higher potential to lower potential). In keeping with the conventions of most data books, current flowing into a node or device is considered positive, and current flowing out of a node or device is considered negative.

Fan-Out

In general, a logic-circuit output is required to drive several logic inputs. The **fanout** (also called *loading factor*) is defined as the *maximum* number of standard logic inputs that an output can drive reliably. For example, a logic gate that is specified to have a fan-out of 10 can drive 10 standard logic inputs. If this number is exceeded, the output logic-level voltages cannot be guaranteed.

Propagation Delays

A logic signal always experiences a delay in going through a circuit. The two propagation delay times are defined as follows:

- t_{PLH}. Delay time in going from logical 0 to logical 1 state (LOW to HIGH)
- t_{PHL}. Delay time in going from logical 1 to logical 0 state (HIGH to LOW)

Figure 8-2 illustrates these propagation delays for an INVERTER. Note that t_{PHL} is the delay in the output's response as it goes from HIGH to LOW. It is measured between the 50 percent points on the input and output transitions. The t_{PLH} value is the delay in the output's response as it goes from LOW to HIGH.

FIGURE 8-2 Propagation delays.

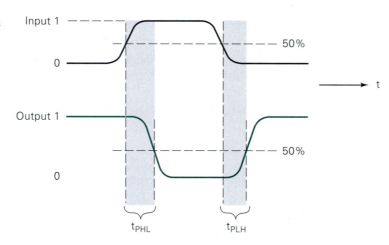

In general, t_{PHL} and t_{PLH} are not the same value, and both will vary depending on capacitive loading conditions. The values of propagation times are used as a measure of the relative speed of logic circuits. For example, a logic circuit with values of 10 ns is a faster logic circuit than one with values of 20 ns under specified load conditions.

Power Requirements

Every IC requires a certain amount of electrical power to operate. This power is supplied by one or more power-supply voltages connected to the power pin(s) on the chip. Usually there is only one power-supply terminal on the chip, and it is labeled V_{CC} (for TTL) or V_{DD} (for MOS devices).

The amount of power that an IC requires is determined by the current, I_{CC}, that it draws from the V_{CC} supply, and the actual power is the product $I_{CC} \times V_{CC}$. For many ICs the current drain on the supply will vary depending on the logic states of the circuits on the chip. For example, Figure 8-3(a) shows a NAND chip where *all* of the gate *outputs* are HIGH. The current drain on the V_{CC} supply for this case is called I_{CCH}. Likewise, Figure 8-3(b) shows the current drain when *all* of the gate *outputs* are LOW. This current is called I_{CCL}. The values are always measured with the outputs open circuit (no load), since the size of the load would also have an effect on I_{CCH}.

FIGURE 8-3 I_{CCH} and I_{CCL}.

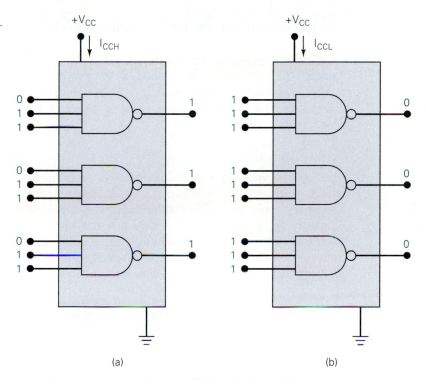

(a)   (b)

In general, I_{CCH} and I_{CCL} will be different values. The average current is computed based on assuming that gate outputs will be LOW half the time and HIGH half the time.

$$I_{CC}(\text{avg}) = \frac{I_{CCH} + I_{CCL}}{2}$$

This can be used to calculate average power drain as

$$P_D(\text{avg}) = I_{CC}(\text{avg}) \times V_{CC}$$

Speed–Power Product

Digital IC families have historically been characterized for both speed and power. It is generally more desirable to have shorter gate propagation delays (higher speed) and lower values of power dissipation. As we shall soon see, the various logic families and subfamilies provide a wide spectrum of speed and power ratings. A common means for measuring and comparing the overall performance of an IC family is the **speed–power product,** which is obtained by multiplying the gate propagation delay by the gate power dissipation. For example, suppose that an IC family has an average propagation delay of 10 ns and an average power dissipation of 5 mW. The speed–power product is

$$10 \text{ ns} \times 5 \text{ mW} = 50 \times 10^{-12} \text{ watt-second}$$
$$= 50 \text{ picojoules (pJ)}$$

Note that when propagation delay is in nanoseconds and power is in milliwatts, the speed–power product is in picojoules.

Clearly, a low value of speed–power product is desirable. IC designers are continually striving to reduce the speed–power product by increasing the speed of an IC (i.e., reducing propagation delay) or by decreasing its power dissipation. Because of the nature of transistor switching circuits, it is difficult to do both.

Noise Immunity

Stray electric and magnetic fields can induce voltages on the connecting wires between logic circuits. These unwanted, spurious signals are called *noise* and can sometimes cause the voltage at the input to a logic circuit to drop below $V_{IH}(\text{min})$ or rise above $V_{IL}(\text{max})$, which could produce unpredictable operation. The **noise immunity** of a logic circuit refers to the circuit's ability to tolerate noise without causing spurious changes in the output voltage. A quantitative measure of noise immunity is called **noise margin,** illustrated in Figure 8-4.

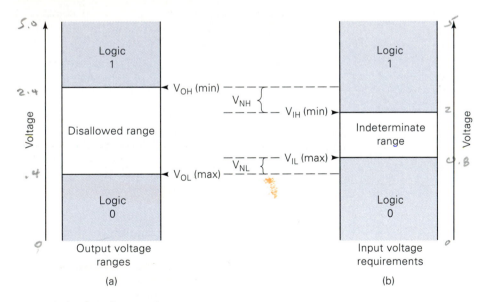

FIGURE 8-4   dc noise margins.

Figure 8-4(a) is a diagram showing the range of voltages that can occur at a logic-circuit output. Any voltages greater than $V_{OH}(\text{min})$ are considered a logic 1, and any voltages lower than $V_{OL}(\text{max})$ are considered a logic 0. Voltages in the indeterminate range should not appear at a logic circuit output under normal conditions. Figure 8-4(b) shows the voltage requirements at a logic circuit input. The logic circuit will respond to any input greater than $V_{IH}(\text{min})$ as a logic 1, and it will respond to voltages lower than $V_{IL}(\text{max})$ as a logic 0. Voltages in the indeterminate range will produce an unpredictable response and should not be used.

The *high-state noise margin* V_{NH} is defined as

$$V_{NH} = V_{OH}(\text{min}) - V_{IH}(\text{min}) \tag{8-1}$$

as illustrated in Figure 8-4. V_{NH} is the difference between the lowest possible HIGH output and the minimum input voltage required for a HIGH. When a HIGH logic output is driving a logic-circuit input, any negative noise spikes greater than V_{NH} appearing on the signal line can cause the voltage to drop into the indeterminate range, where unpredictable operation can occur.

The *low-state noise margin* V_{NL} is defined as

$$V_{NL} = V_{IL}(\text{max}) - V_{OL}(\text{max}) \tag{8-2}$$

and it is the difference between the largest possible LOW output and the maximum input voltage required for a LOW. When a LOW logic output is driving a logic input, any positive noise spikes greater than V_{NL} can cause the voltage to rise into the indeterminate range.

| EXAMPLE 8-1 | The input/output voltage specifications for the standard TTL family are listed in Table 8-1. Use these values to determine the following. |

(a) The maximum-amplitude noise spike that can be tolerated when a HIGH output is driving an input.

(b) The maximum-amplitude noise spike that can be tolerated when a LOW output is driving an input.

TABLE 8-1

Parameter	Min (V)	Typical (V)	Max (V)
V_{OH}	2.4	3.4	
V_{OL}		0.2	0.4
V_{IH}	2.0*		
V_{IL}			0.8*

* Normally only the minimum V_{IH} and maximum V_{IL} values are given.

Solution

(a) When an output is HIGH, it may be as low as $V_{OH}(\text{min}) = 2.4$ V. The minimum voltage that an input will respond to as a HIGH is $V_{IH}(\text{min}) = 2.0$ V. A negative noise spike can drive the actual voltage below 2.0 V if its amplitude is greater than

$$V_{NH} = V_{OH}(\text{min}) - V_{IH}(\text{min})$$
$$= 2.4 \text{ V} - 2.0 \text{ V} = 0.4 \text{ V}$$

(b) When an output is LOW, it may be as high as $V_{OL}(max) = 0.4$ V. The maximum voltage that an input will respond to as a LOW is $V_{IL}(max) = 0.8$ V. A positive noise spike can drive the actual voltage above the 0.8-V level if its amplitude is greater than

$$V_{NL} = V_{IL}(max) - V_{OL}(max)$$
$$= 0.8 \text{ V} - 0.4 \text{ V} = 0.4 \text{ V}$$

Invalid Voltage Levels

For proper operation the input voltage levels to a logic circuit must be kept outside the indeterminate range shown in Figure 8-4(b); that is, they must be either lower than $V_{IL}(max)$ or higher than $V_{IH}(min)$. For the standard TTL specifications given in Example 8-1, this means that the input voltage must be less than 0.8 V or greater than 2.0 V. An input voltage between 0.8 and 2.0 V is considered an *invalid* voltage that will produce an unpredictable output response, and so must be avoided. In normal operation a logic input voltage will not fall into the invalid region because it comes from a logic output that is within the stated specifications. However, when this logic output is malfunctioning or is being overloaded (i.e., its fan-out is being exceeded), then its voltage may be in the invalid region. Invalid voltage levels in a digital circuit can also be caused by power-supply voltages that are outside the acceptable range. It is important to know the valid voltage ranges for the logic family being used so that invalid conditions can be recognized when testing or troubleshooting.

Current-Sourcing and Current-Sinking Action

Logic families can be described according to how current flows between the output of one logic circuit and the input of another. Figure 8-5(a) illustrates **current-sourcing action.** When the output of gate 1 is in the HIGH state, it supplies a current

FIGURE 8-5

Comparison of current-sourcing and current-sinking actions.

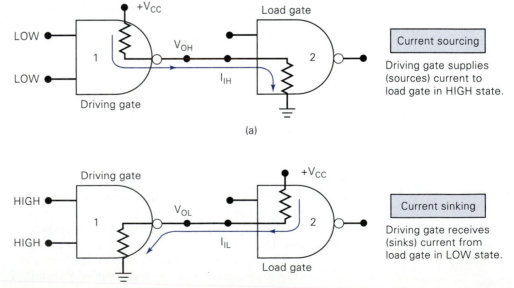

I_{IH} to the input of gate 2, which acts essentially as a resistance to ground. Thus, the output of gate 1 is acting as a *source* of current for the gate 2 input. We can think of it as being like a faucet that acts as a *source* of water.

Current-sinking action is illustrated in Figure 8-5(b). Here the input circuitry of gate 2 is represented as a resistance tied to $+V_{CC}$, the positive terminal of a power supply. When the gate 1 output goes to its LOW state, current will flow in the direction shown from the input circuit of gate 2 back through the output resistance of gate 1 to ground. In other words, in the LOW state the circuit output that drives the input of gate 2 must be able to *sink* a current, I_{IL}, coming from that input. We can think of this as acting like a *sink* into which water is flowing.

The distinction between current sourcing and current sinking is an important one which will become more apparent as we examine the various logic families.

IC Packages

Developments and advancements in integrated circuits continue at a rapid pace. The same is true of IC packaging. There are a variety of types of packages, which differ as to physical size, the environmental and power-consumption conditions under which the device can be operated reliably, and the way in which the IC package is mounted to the circuit board. Figure 8-6 shows three representative IC packages.

The package in Figure 8-6(a) is the **DIP** (dual-in-line package), which has been around for a long time. Its pins (or leads) run down the two long sides of the rectangular package. The device shown is a 24-pin DIP. Note the presence of the notch on one end which is used to locate pin 1. Some DIPs use a small dot on the top surface of the package to locate pin 1. The leads extend straight out of the DIP package so that the IC can be plugged into an IC socket or inserted into holes drilled through a printed circuit board. The spacing between pins **(lead pitch)** is typically 100 mils (a mil is a thousandth of an inch). DIP packages are still the most popular package for prototyping, breadboarding, and educational experimentation.

Nearly all new circuit boards that are produced using automated manufacturing equipment have moved away from using DIP packages whose leads are inserted through holes in the board. New manufacturing methods use **surface-mount technology** which places an IC onto conductive pads on the surface of the board. They are held in place by a solder paste, and the entire board is heated to create a soldered connection. The precision of the placement machine allows for very tight lead spacing. The leads on these surface-mount packages are bent out from the plastic case, providing adequate surface area for the solder joint. The shape of these leads has resulted in the nickname of "gull's-wing" package. Many different packages are available for surface-mount devices. Some of the most common packages used for logic ICs are shown in Figure 8-6. Table 8-2 gives the definition of each acronym along with its dimensions.

The need for more and more connections to a complex IC has resulted in another very popular package which has pins on= all four sides of the chip. The PLCC has J-shaped leads that curl under the IC as shown in Figure 8-6(c). These devices can be surface-mounted to a circuit board but can also be placed in a special PLCC socket. This is commonly used for components that are likely to need to be re-

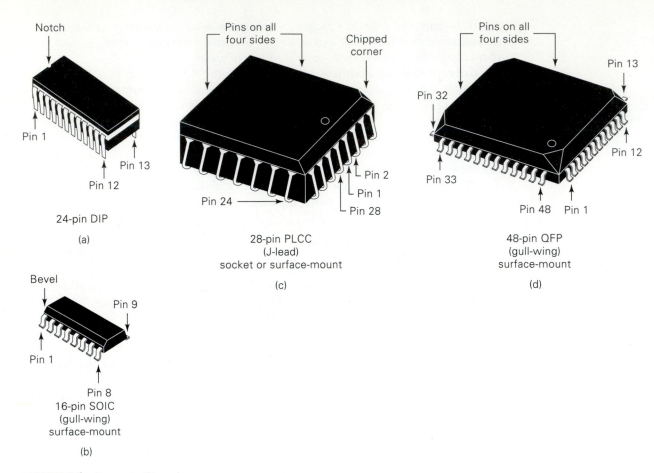

FIGURE 8-6 Common IC packages.

TABLE 8-2 IC packages.

Acronym	Package Name	Height	Lead Pitch
DIP	Dual-In-line Package	200 mils (5.1 mm)	100 mils (2.54 mm)
SOIC	Small Outline Integrated Circuit	2.65 mm	50 mils (1.27 mm)
SSOP	Shrink Small Outline Package	2.0 mm	0.65 mm
TSSOP	Thin Shrink Small Outline Package	1.1 mm	0.65 mm
TVSOP	Thin Very Small Outline Package	1.2 mm	0.4 mm
PLCC	Plastic Leaded Chip Carrier	4.5 mm	1.27 mm
QFP	Quad Flat Pack	4.5 mm	0.635 mm
TQFP	Thin Quad Flat Pack	1.6 mm	0.5 mm

placed for repair or upgrade, such as programmable logic devices or central processing units in computers. The QFP and TQFP packages have pins on all four sides in a gull-wing surface-mount package as shown in Figure 8-6(d).

1. Define each of the following: V_{OH}, V_{IL}, I_{OL}, I_{IH}, t_{PLH}, t_{PHL}, I_{CCL}, I_{CCH}.

2. *True or false:* If a logic circuit has a fan-out of 5, the circuit has five outputs.

3. *True or false:* The HIGH-stage noise margin is the difference between $V_{IH}(min)$ and V_{CC}.

4. *True or false:* A logic family with $t_{pd}(avg) = 12$ ns and $P_D(avg) = 15$ mW has a greater speed–power product than one with 8 ns and 30 mW.

5. Describe the difference between current sinking and current sourcing.

6. Which IC package can be plugged into sockets?

7. Which package has leads bent under the IC?

8. How do surface-mount packages differ from DIPs?

9. Will a standard TTL device work with an input level of 1.7 V?

8-2 THE TTL LOGIC FAMILY

At this writing, small- to medium-scale ICs (SSI and MSI) are still available in the standard **TTL** technology series that has been available for over 30 years. This original series of devices and their descendants in the TTL family have had a tremendous influence on the characteristics of all logic devices today. TTL devices are still used as "glue" logic that connects the more complex devices in digital systems. They are also used as interface circuits to devices that require high current drive. Even though the bipolar TTL family as a whole is on the decline, we will begin our discussion of logic ICs with the devices that shaped digital technology.

The basic TTL logic circuit is the NAND gate. Its detailed circuit diagram, shown in Figure 8-7(a), has several distinctive characteristics. First, note that transistor Q_1 has two emitters; thus, it has two emitter–base (E–B) junctions that can be used to turn Q_1 on. This *multiple-emitter* input transistor can have up to eight emitters for an eight-input NAND gate.

Also note that on the output side of the circuit, transistors Q_3 and Q_4 are in a **totem-pole** arrangement. As we will see shortly, in normal operation either Q_3 or Q_4 will be conducting, depending on the logic state of the output.

Circuit Operation—LOW State

Although this circuit looks extremely complex, we can simplify its analysis somewhat by using the diode equivalent of the multiple-emitter transistor Q_1 as shown in Figure 8-7(b). Diodes D_2 and D_3 represent the two E–B junctions of Q_1, and D_4 is the collector–base (C–B) junction. In the following analysis we will use this representation for Q_1.

First, let's consider the case where the output is LOW. Figure 8-8(a) shows this situation with inputs A and B both at +5 V. The +5 V at the cathodes of D_2 and D_3

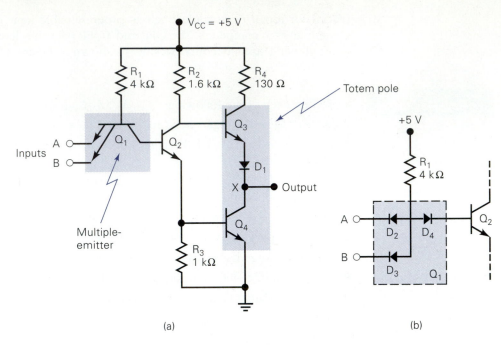

FIGURE 8-7 (a) Basic TTL NAND gate; (b) diode equivalent for Q_1.

will turn these diodes off, and they will conduct almost no current. The +5 V supply will push current through R_1 and D_4 into the base of Q_2, which turns on. Current from Q_2's emitter will flow into the base of Q_4 and turn Q_4 on. At the same time, the flow of Q_2 collector current produces a voltage drop across R_2 that reduces Q_2's collector voltage to a low value that is insufficient to turn Q_3 on.

The voltage at Q_2's collector is shown as approximately 0.8 V. This is because Q_2's emitter is at 0.7 V relative to ground due to Q_4's E–B forward voltage, and Q_2's collector is at 0.1 V relative to its emitter due to $V_{CE}(\text{sat})$. This 0.8 V at Q_3's base is not enough to forward-bias both Q_3's E–B junction and diode D_1. In fact, D_1 is needed to keep Q_3 off in this situation.

With Q_4 on, the output terminal, X, will be at a very low voltage, since Q_4's ON-state resistance will be low (1 to 25 Ω). Actually, the output voltage, V_{OL}, will depend on how much collector current Q_4 conducts. With Q_3 off, there is no current coming from the +5 V terminal through R_4. As we shall see, Q_4's collector current will come from the TTL inputs that terminal X is connected to.

It is important to note that the HIGH inputs at A and B will have to supply only a very small diode leakage current. Typically, this current I_{IH} is only around 10 μA at room temperature.

Circuit Operation—HIGH State

Figure 8-8(b) shows the situation where the circuit output is HIGH. This situation can be produced by connecting either or both inputs LOW. Here, input B is connected to ground. This will forward-bias D_3 so that current will flow from the +5 V source terminal, through R_1 and D_3, and through terminal B to ground. The forward voltage across D_3 will hold point Y at approximately 0.7 V. This voltage

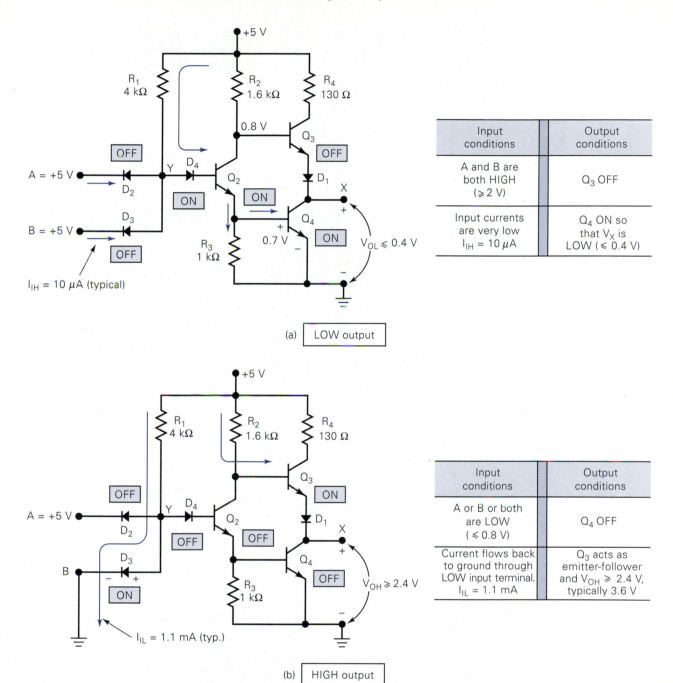

Input conditions		Output conditions
A and B are both HIGH (≥ 2 V)		Q_3 OFF
Input currents are very low $I_{IH} = 10\,\mu A$		Q_4 ON so that V_X is LOW (≤ 0.4 V)

(a) | LOW output

Input conditions		Output conditions
A or B or both are LOW (≤ 0.8 V)		Q_4 OFF
Current flows back to ground through LOW input terminal. $I_{IL} = 1.1$ mA		Q_3 acts as emitter-follower and $V_{OH} \geq 2.4$ V, typically 3.6 V

(b) | HIGH output

FIGURE 8-8   TTL NAND gate in its two output states.

is not enough to forward-bias D_4 and the E–B junction of Q_2 sufficiently for conduction.

    With Q_2 off, there is no base current for Q_4, and it turns off. Since there is no Q_2 collector current, the voltage at Q_3's base will be large enough to forward-bias Q_3 and D_1, so that Q_3 will conduct. Actually, Q_3 acts as an emitter follower, because output terminal X is essentially at its emitter. With no load connected from point X

to ground, V_{OH} will be around 3.4 to 3.8 V, because two 0.7-V diode drops (E–B of Q_3, and D_1) subtract from the 5 V applied to Q_3's base. This voltage will decrease under load because the load will draw emitter current from Q_3, which draws base current through R_2, thereby increasing the voltage drop across R_2.

It's important to note that there is a substantial current flowing back through input terminal B to ground. This current, I_{IL}, is typically around 1.1 mA. The LOW B input acts as a *sink* to ground for this current.

Current-Sinking Action

A TTL output acts as a current sink in the LOW state in that it *receives* current from the input of the gate that it is driving. Figure 8-9 shows one TTL gate driving the input of another gate (the load) for both output voltage states. In the output LOW state situation depicted in Figure 8-9(a), transistor Q_4 of the driving gate is on and essentially "shorts" point X to ground. This LOW voltage at X forward-biases the emitter–base junction of Q_1, and current flows, as shown, back through Q_4. Thus, Q_4 is performing a current-sinking action that derives its current from the input current (I_{IL}) of the load gate. We will often refer to Q_4 as the **current-sinking transistor** or as the **pull-down transistor** because it brings the output voltage down to its LOW state.

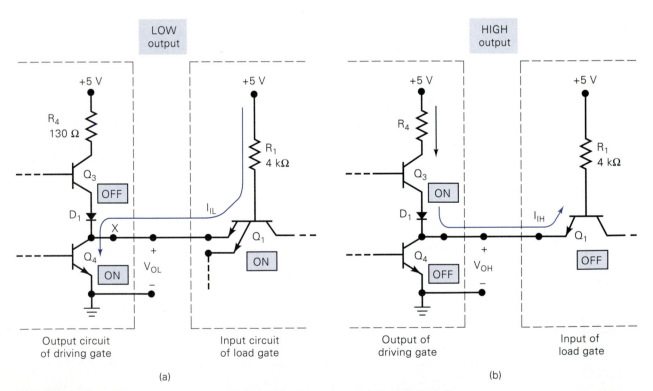

FIGURE 8-9 (a) When the TTL output is in the LOW state, Q_4 acts as a current sink, deriving its current from the load. (b) In the output HIGH state, Q_3 acts as a current source, providing current to the load gate.

Current-Sourcing Action

A TTL output acts as a current source in the HIGH state. This is shown in Figure 8-9(b), where transistor Q_3 is supplying the input current, I_{IH}, required by the Q_1 transistor of the load gate. As stated above, this current is a small reverse-bias leakage current (typically 10 μA). We will often refer to Q_3 as the **current-sourcing transistor** or **pull-up transistor.**

Totem-Pole Output Circuit

Several points should be mentioned concerning the totem-pole arrangement of the TTL output circuit, as shown in Figure 8-9, since it is not readily apparent why it is used. The same logic could be accomplished by eliminating Q_3 and D_1 and connecting the bottom of R_4 to the collector of Q_4. But this would mean that Q_4 would conduct a fairly heavy current in its saturation state (5 V/130 $\Omega \approx$ 40 mA). With Q_3 in the circuit, there will be no current through R_4 in the output LOW state. This is important because it keeps the circuit power dissipation down.

   Another advantage of this arrangement occurs in the output HIGH state. Here Q_3 is acting as an emitter follower with its associated low output impedance (typically 10 Ω). This low output impedance provides a short time constant for charging up any capacitive load on the output. This action (commonly called *active pull-up*) provides very fast rise-time waveforms at TTL outputs.

   A disadvantage of the totem-pole output arrangement occurs during the transition from LOW to HIGH. Unfortunately, Q_4 turns off more slowly than Q_3 turns on, and so there is a period of a few nanoseconds during which both transistors are conducting and a relatively large current (30 to 40 mA) will be drawn from the 5-V supply. This can present a problem that will be examined later.

TTL NOR Gate

Figure 8-10 shows the internal circuit for a TTL NOR gate. We will not go through a detailed analysis of this circuit, but it is important to note how it compares to the NAND circuit of Figure 8-8. On the input side, we can see that the NOR circuit *does*

FIGURE 8-10   TTL NOR gate circuit.

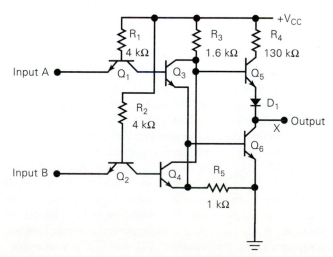

not use a multiple-emitter transistor; instead, each input is applied to the emitter of a separate transistor. On the output side, the NOR circuit uses the same totem-pole arrangement as the NAND circuit.

Summary

All TTL circuits have a similar structure. NAND and AND gates use multiple-emitter transistor inputs; NOR and OR gates use separate input transistors. In either case, the input will be the cathode (N-region) of a P–N junction, so that a HIGH input voltage will turn off the junction and only a small leakage current (I_{IH}) will flow. Conversely, a LOW input voltage turns on the junction, and a relatively large current (I_{IL}) will flow back through the signal source. Most, but not all, TTL circuits will have some type of totem-pole output configuration. There are some exceptions that will be discussed later.

Review Questions	1. *True or false:* A TTL output acts as a current sink in the LOW state.
	2. In which TTL input state does the largest amount of input current flow?
	3. State the advantages and disadvantages of a totem-pole output.
	4. Which TTL transistor is the pull-up transistor in the NAND circuit?
	5. Which TTL transistor is the pull-down transistor in the NOR circuit?
	6. How does the TTL NOR circuit differ from the NAND circuit?

8-3   STANDARD TTL SERIES CHARACTERISTICS

In 1964 Texas Instruments Corporation introduced the first line of standard TTL ICs. The 54/74 series, as it is called, has been one of the most widely used IC logic families. We will simply refer to it as the 74 series, since the major difference between the 54 and 74 versions is that devices in the 54 series can operate over a wider range of temperatures and power-supply voltages. Many semiconductor manufacturers now produce TTL ICs. Fortunately, they all use the same numbering system, so that the basic IC number is the same from one manufacturer to another. Each manufacturer, however, usually attaches its own special prefix to the IC number. For example, Texas Instruments uses the prefix SN, National Semiconductor uses DM, and Signetics uses S. Thus, depending on the manufacturer, you may see a quad NOR gate chip labeled as a DM7402, SN7402, S7402, or some other similar designation. The important part is the number 7402, which is the same for all manufacturers.

As we learned in Chapter 4, there are several series in the TTL family of logic devices (74, 74LS, 74S, etc.). The original standard series and its immediate descendants (74, 74LS, 74S) are no longer recommended by the manufacturers for use in new designs. In spite of this there is still enough demand in the market to keep them in production. An understanding of the characteristics that define the capabilities and limitations of any logic device is vital. This section will define those characteristics using the standard TTL series as an example since it is the "Granddaddy of them all." Later we introduce the other TTL series and compare their characteristics with those of the standard series.

Manufacturers' Data Sheets

To illustrate the characteristics of the standard TTL series, we use the 7400 quad NAND gate IC. We can find all of the information we need on any IC by consulting the manufacturer's data manual for that particular IC family. Figure 8-11 is the manufacturer's data sheet for the 5400/7400 NAND gate IC showing the recommended operating conditions, electrical characteristics, and switching characteristics. Most of the quantities discussed in the following paragraphs in this section can be found on this data sheet. As we discuss each quantity, you should refer to this data sheet to see where the information came from.

Recommended operating conditions

		SN5400			SN7400			UNIT
		MIN	NOM	MAX	MIN	NOM	MAX	
V_{CC}	Supply voltage	4.5	5	5.5	4.75	5	5.25	V
V_{IH}	High-level input voltage	2			2			V
V_{IL}	Low-level input voltage			0.8			0.8	V
I_{OH}	High-level output current			−0.4			−0.4	mA
I_{OL}	Low-level output current			16			16	mA
T_A	Operating free-air temperature	−55		125	0		70	°C

Electrical characteristics over recommended operating free-air temperature range (unless otherwise noted)

PARAMETER	TEST CONDITIONS†			SN5400			SN7400			UNIT
				MIN	TYP‡	MAX	MIN	TYP‡	MAX	
V_{IK}	V_{CC} = MIN,	I_I = −12 mA				−1.5			−1.5	V
V_{OH}	V_{CC} = MIN,	V_{IL} = 0.8 V,	I_{OH} = −0.4 mA	2.4	3.4		2.4	3.4		V
V_{OL}	V_{CC} = MIN,	V_{IH} = 2 V,	I_{OL} = 16 mA		0.2	0.4		0.2	0.4	V
I_I	V_{CC} = MAX,	V_I = 5.5 V				1			1	mA
I_{IH}	V_{CC} = MAX,	V_I = 2.4 V				40			40	μA
I_{IL}	V_{CC} = MAX,	V_I = 0.4 V				−1.6			−1.6	mA
I_{OS}§	V_{CC} = MAX			−20		−55	−18		−55	mA
I_{CCH}	V_{CC} = MAX,	V_I = 0 V			4	8		4	8	mA
I_{CCL}	V_{CC} = MAX,	V_I = 4.5 V			12	22		12	22	mA

† For conditions shown as MIN or MAX, use the appropriate value specified under recommended operating conditions.
‡ All typical values are at V_{CC} = 5 V, T_A = 25°C.
§ Not more than one output should be shorted at a time.

Switching characteristics, V_{CC} = 5 V, TA = 25°C (see note 2)

PARAMETER	FROM (INPUT)	TO (OUTPUT)	TEST CONDITIONS		MIN	TYP	MAX	UNIT
t_{PLH}	A or B	Y	R_L = 400 Ω	C_L = 15 pF		11	22	ns
t_{PHL}						7	15	ns

NOTE 2: See General Information Section for load circuits and voltage waveforms.

FIGURE 8-11   Data sheet for the 7400 NAND gate IC. (Courtesy of Texas Instruments)

Supply Voltage and Temperature Range

Both the 74 series and the 54 series use a nominal supply voltage (V_{CC}) of 5 V. The 74 series will operate reliably over the range 4.75 to 5.25 V, while the 54 series can tolerate a supply variation of 4.5 to 5.5 V. The 74 series is designed to operate properly in ambient temperatures ranging from 0 to 70°C, while the 54 series can handle −55 to +125°C. Because of its greater tolerance of voltage and temperature variations, the 54 series is more expensive. It is employed only in applications where reliable operation must be maintained over an extreme range of conditions. Examples are military and space applications.

Voltage Levels

The input and output logic voltage levels for the standard 74 series can be found on the data sheet of Figure 8-11. Table 8-3 presents them in summary form. The minimum and maximum values shown are for worst-case conditions of power supply, temperature, and loading conditions. Inspection of the table reveals a guaranteed maximum logical 0 output $V_{OL} = 0.4$ V, which is 400 mV less than the logical 0 voltage needed at the input $V_{IL} = 0.8$ V. This means that the guaranteed LOW-state dc noise margin is 400 mV. That is,

$$V_{NL} = V_{IL}(\text{max}) - V_{OL}(\text{max}) = 0.8 \text{ V} - 0.4 \text{ V} = 0.4 \text{ V} = 400 \text{ mV}$$

Similarly, the logical 1 output V_{OH} is a guaranteed minimum of 2.4 V, which is 400 mV greater than the logical 1 voltage needed at the input, $V_{IH} = 2.0$ V. Thus, the HIGH-state dc noise margin is 400 mV.

$$V_{NH} = V_{OH}(\text{min}) - V_{IH}(\text{min}) = 2.4 \text{ V} - 2.0 \text{ V} = 0.4 \text{ V} = 400 \text{ mV}$$

Thus, the *guaranteed worst-case* dc noise margins for the 74 series are both 400 mV.

TABLE 8-3 Standard 74 series voltage levels.

	Minimum	Typical	Maximum
V_{OL}	—	0.2	0.4
V_{OH}	2.4	3.4	—
V_{IL}	—	—	0.8
V_{IH}	2.0	—	—

Maximum Voltage Ratings

The voltage values in Table 8-3 *do not include* the absolute maximum ratings beyond which the useful life of the IC may be impaired. The voltages applied to any input of a standard 74 series IC must never exceed +5.5 V. A voltage greater than +5.5 V applied to an input emitter can cause reverse breakdown of the E–B junction of Q_1.

There is also a limit on the maximum *negative* voltage that can be applied to a TTL input. This limit, −0.5 V, is caused by the fact that most TTL circuits employ protective shunt diodes on each input. These diodes were purposely left out of our earlier analysis, since they do not enter into the normal circuit operation. They are connected from each input to ground to limit the negative input voltage excursions that often occur when logic signals have excessive ringing. With these diodes, we should not apply more than -0.5 V to an input, because the protective diodes would begin to conduct and draw substantial current, probably causing the diode to short out, resulting in a permanently faulty input.

Power Dissipation

A standard TTL NAND gate draws an average power of 10 mW. This is a result of $I_{CCH} = 4$ mA and $I_{CCL} = 12$ mA, which produces $I_{CC}(\text{avg}) = 8$ mA and $P_D(\text{avg}) = 8$ mA $\times$ 5 V $= 40$ mW. This 40 mW is the total power required by all four gates on the chip. Thus, one NAND gate requires an average power of 10 mW.

Propagation Delays

The standard TTL AND gate has typical propagation delays of $t_{PLH} = 11$ ns and $t_{PHL} = 7$ ns, which is an *average* propagation delay $t_{pd}(\text{avg})$ of 9 ns.

Fan-Out

A standard TTL output can typically drive 10 standard TTL inputs. Some IC data sheets give the device's fan-out explicitly, but this is not the case for the data sheet in Figure 8-11. Later we will see how the fan-out can be determined from the input and output current values given in Figure 8-11.

EXAMPLE 8-2

Refer to the data sheet for the 7400 quad two-input NAND IC in Figure 8-11. Determine the *maximum* average power dissipation and the *maximum* average propagation delay of a *single* gate.

Solution

Look under the electrical characteristics for the *maximum* I_{CCH} and I_{CCL} values. The values are 8 mA and 22 mA, respectively. The average I_{CC} is therefore $(8 + 22)/2 = 15$ mA. The average power is obtained by multiplying by V_{CC}. The data sheet indicates that these I_{CC} values were obtained when V_{CC} was at its maximum value (5.25 V for the 74 series). Thus, we have

$$P_D(\text{avg}) = 15 \text{ mA} \times 5.25 \text{ V} = 78.75 \text{ mW}$$

as the power drawn by the *complete* IC. We can determine the power drain of one NAND gate by dividing this by 4:

$$P_D(\text{avg}) = 19.7 \text{ mW per gate}$$

Since this average power drain was calculated using the maximum current and voltage values, it is the maximum average power that a 7400 NAND gate will draw under worst-case conditions. Designers often use worst-case values to ensure that their circuits will work under all conditions.

The maximum propagation delays for a 7400 NAND gate are listed as

$$t_{PLH} = 22 \text{ ns} \qquad t_{PHL} = 15 \text{ ns}$$

so that the average propagation delay is

$$t_{pd}(\text{avg}) = \frac{22 + 15}{2} = 18.5 \text{ ns}$$

Again, this is a worst-case maximum possible average propagation delay.

8-4   IMPROVED TTL SERIES

The standard TTL series of ICs offers a wide variety of gates, FFs, and one-shots in the small-scale integration (SSI) line, and counters, registers, decoders/encoders, arithmetic circuits, and many other logic functions in its medium-scale integration (MSI) line. The basic circuitry of the standard TTL series forms the central part of several other TTL series; but standard TTL (74 series) devices are rarely used in new system designs because of the improved performance of the newer TTL series that have been developed over the years. These other TTL series—often called "subfamilies"—provide a wide range of speed and power capabilities.

74L and 74H Series

The 74L and 74H series were developed to provide low-power and high-speed versions of TTL, respectively. Both had the same basic circuit as the standard 74 series, but differences in circuit component values gave these two series their different characteristics. Compared to the 74 series, the 74L series was a low-power version that consumed less power (1 mW) but at the expense of a much longer propagation delay (33 ns); the 74H series was a high-speed version that had a reduced propagation delay (6 ns) at the cost of higher power consumption (23 mW). Neither of these series is in current production since their performance has been surpassed by newer series.

Schottky TTL, 74S Series

The 74, 74H, and 74L series all operate using saturated switching in which many of the transistors, when conducting, will be in the saturated condition. This operation causes a storage-time delay, t_S, when the transistors switch from ON to OFF, and it limits the circuit's switching speed.

The 74S series reduces this storage-time delay by not allowing the transistor to go as deeply into saturation. It accomplishes this by using a Schottky barrier diode (SBD) connected between the base and the collector of each transistor as shown in Figure 8-12(a). The SBD has a forward voltage of only 0.25 V. Thus, when the C–B

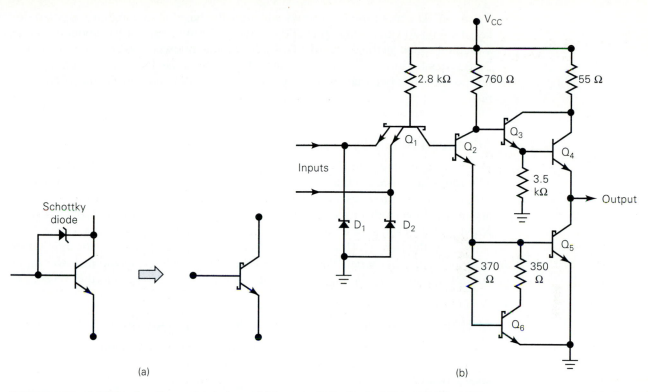

FIGURE 8-12   (a) Schottky-clamped transistor; (b) basic NAND gate in S-TTL series. (Courtesy of Fairchild, a Schlumberger company)

junction becomes forward-biased at the onset of saturation, the SBD will conduct and divert some of the input current away from the base. This reduces the excess base current and decreases the storage-time delay at turn-off.

As shown in Figure 8-12(a), the transistor/SBD combination is given a special symbol. This symbol is used for all of the transistors in the circuit diagram for the 74S00 NAND gate shown in Figure 8-12(b). This 74S00 NAND gate has an average propagation delay of only 3 ns, which is twice as fast as the 74H00. Note the presence of shunt diodes D_1 and D_2 to limit negative input voltages.

Circuits in the 74S series also use smaller resistor values to help improve switching times. This increases the circuit average power dissipation to about 20 mW, about the same as for 74H. The 74S circuits also use a Darlington pair (Q_3 and Q_4) to provide a shorter output rise time when switching from ON to OFF.

Low-Power Schottky TTL, 74LS Series (LS-TTL)

The 74LS series is a lower-powered, slower-speed version of the 74S series. It uses the Schottky-clamped transistor, but with larger resistor values than the 74S series. The larger resistor values reduce the circuit power requirement, but at the expense of an increase in switching times.

A NAND gate in the 74LS series will typically have an average propagation delay of 9.5 ns and an average power dissipation of 2 mW. Since it has about the same switching speed as the standard TTL series at a much lower power requirement, the 74LS series became the mainstay of the TTL family in the 1980s. However, its leading position has been taken over by CMOS, particularly the 74HC and 74 HCT series.

Advanced Schottky TTL, 74AS Series (AS-TTL)

Innovations in integrated-circuit design led to the development of two improved TTL series: advanced Schottky (74AS) and advanced low-power Schottky (74ALS). The 74AS series provides a considerable improvement in speed over the 74S series at a much lower power requirement. The comparison is shown in Table 8-4 for a NAND gate in each series. This comparison clearly shows the advantage of the 74AS series. It is the fastest TTL series, and its speed–power product is significantly lower than that of the 74S series. The 74AS has other improvements, including lower input current requirements (I_{IL}, I_{IH}), that result in a greater fan-out than in the 74S series.

Advanced Low-Power Schottky TTL, 74ALS Series

This series offers an improvement over the 74LS series in both speed and power dissipation, as the numbers in Table 8-5 illustrate. The 74ALS series has the lowest speed–power product and the lowest gate power dissipation of all the TTL series. Its slightly higher cost has kept it from displacing 74LS except in high-speed applications.

TABLE 8-4

	74S	74AS
Propagation delay	3 ns	1.7 ns
Power dissipation	20 mW	8 mW
Speed–power product	60 pJ	13.6 pJ

TABLE 8-5

	74LS	74ALS
Propagation delay	9.5 ns	4 ns
Power dissipation	2 mW	1.2 mW
Speed–power product	19 pJ	4.8 pJ

74F-Fast TTL

This is the newest TTL series. It uses a new integrated-circuit fabrication technique to reduce interdevice capacitances to achieve reduced propagation delays. A typical NAND gate has an average propagation delay of 3 ns and a power consumption of 6 mW. ICs in this series are designated with the letter F in their part number. For instance, the 74F04 is a hex-inverter chip. These high-performance TTL series (74AS, 74ALS, 74F) serve rather small niches in the digital industry.

Comparison of TTL Series Characteristics

Table 8-6 gives the typical values for some of the more important characteristics of each of the TTL series. All of the performance ratings, except for the maximum clock rate, are for a NAND gate in each series. The maximum clock rate is speci-

TABLE 8-6 Typical TTL series characteristics.

	74	74S	74LS	74AS	74ALS	74F
Performance ratings						
Propagation delay (ns)	9	3	9.5	1.7	4	3
Power dissipation (mW)	10	20	2	8	1.2	6
Speed–power product (pJ)	90	60	19	13.6	4.8	18
Max. clock rate (MHz)	35	125	45	200	70	100
Fan-out (same series)	10	20	20	40	20	33
Voltage parameters						
V_{OH}(min)	2.4	2.7	2.7	2.5	2.5	2.5
V_{OL}(max)	0.4	0.5	0.5	0.5	0.4	0.5
V_{IH}(min)	2.0	2.0	2.0	2.0	2.0	2.0
V_{IL}(max)	0.8	0.8	0.8	0.8	0.8	0.8

fied as the maximum frequency that can be used to toggle a J-K flip-flop. This gives a useful measure of the frequency range over which each IC series can be operated.

EXAMPLE 8-3

Use Table 8-6 to calculate the dc noise margins for a typical 74LS IC. How does this compare with the standard TTL noise margins obtained in Section 8-3?

Solution

$$V_{NH} = V_{OH}(\text{min}) - V_{IH}(\text{min})$$
$$= 2.7 \text{ V} - 2.0 \text{ V}$$
$$= 0.7 \text{ V}$$

as compared with $V_{NH} = 0.4$ V for standard TTL.

$$V_{NL} = V_{IL}(\text{max}) - V_{OL}(\text{max})$$
$$= 0.8 \text{ V} - 0.5 \text{ V}$$
$$= 0.3 \text{ V}$$

as compared with $V_{NL} = 0.4$ V for TTL.

EXAMPLE 8-4

Which TTL series can drive the most device inputs of the same series?

Solution

The 74AS series has the highest fan-out (40). This means that a 74AS00 NAND gate can drive 40 standard inputs of other 74AS devices. If we want to determine the number of inputs of a *different* TTL series that an output can drive, we will need to know the input and output currents of the two series. This will be dealt with in the next section.

Review Questions

1. (a) Which TTL series is the best at high frequencies?

   (b) Which TTL series has the largest HIGH-state noise margin?

   (c) Which series have essentially become obsolete?

   (d) Which series use a special diode to reduce switching time?

   (e) Which series would be best for a battery-powered circuit operating at 10 MHz?

2. Assuming the same cost for each, why should you choose to use a 74ALS193 counter over a 74LS193 or a 74AS193 in a circuit operating from a 40-MHz clock?

3. Identify the pull-up and pull-down transistors for the 74S circuit in Figure 8-12.

8-5   TTL LOADING AND FAN-OUT

It is important to understand what determines the fan-out or load drive capability of an IC output. Figure 8-13(a) shows a standard TTL output in the LOW state connected to drive several standard TTL inputs. Transistor Q_4 is on and is acting as a current sink for an amount of current I_{OL} that is the sum of the I_{IL} currents from each input. In its ON state, Q_4's collector–emitter resistance is very small, but it is not zero, and so the current I_{OL} will produce a voltage drop V_{OL}. This voltage must not exceed the $V_{OL}(\text{max})$ limit of the IC. This limits the maximum value of I_{OL} and thus the number of loads that can be driven.

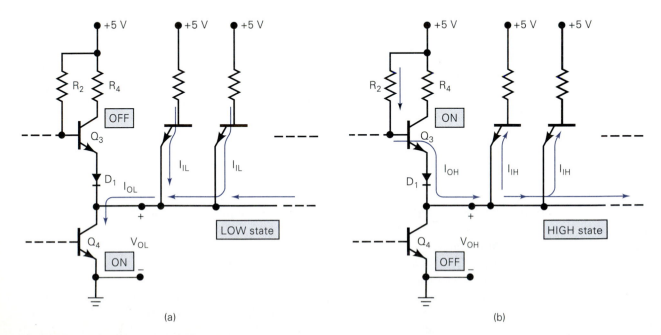

(a)   (b)

FIGURE 8-13   Currents when a TTL output is driving several inputs.

To illustrate, suppose that the ICs are in the 74 series and each I_{IL} is 1.6 mA. From Table 8-6 we see that the 74 series has $V_{OL}(\text{max}) = 0.4$ V and $V_{IL}(\text{max}) = 0.8$ V. Let's suppose further that Q_4 can sink up to 16 mA before its output voltage reaches $V_{OL}(\text{max}) = 0.4$ V. This means that it can sink the current from up to 16 mA/1.6 mA = 10 loads. If it is connected to more than 10 loads, its I_{OL} will increase and cause V_{OL} to increase above 0.4 V. This is usually undesirable because it reduces the noise margin at the IC inputs [remember, $V_{NL} = V_{IL}(\text{max}) - V_{OL}(\text{max})$]. In fact, if V_{OL} rises above $V_{IL}(\text{max}) = 0.8$ V, it will be in the indeterminate range.

A similar situation occurs in the HIGH state depicted in Figure 8-13(b). Here Q_3 is acting as an emitter follower that is sourcing (supplying) a total current I_{OH} that is the sum of the I_{IH} currents of the different TTL inputs. If too many loads are being driven, this current I_{OH} will become large enough to cause the voltage drops across R_2, Q_3's emitter–base junction, and D_1 to bring V_{OH} below $V_{OH}(\text{min})$. This too is undesirable since it reduces the HIGH-state noise margin and could even cause V_{OH} to go into the indeterminate range.

What this all means is that a TTL output has a limit, $I_{OL}(\text{max})$, on how much current it can sink in the LOW state. It also has a limit, $I_{OH}(\text{max})$, on how much current it can source in the HIGH state. These output current limits must not be exceeded if the output voltage levels are to be maintained within their specified ranges.

Determining the Fan-Out

To determine how many different inputs an IC output can drive, you need to know the current drive capability of the output [i.e., $I_{OL}(\text{max})$ and $I_{OH}(\text{max})$] and the current requirements of each input (i.e., I_{IL} and I_{IH}). This information is always presented in some form on the manufacturer's IC data sheet. The following examples will illustrate one type of situation.

EXAMPLE 8-5

How many 7400 NAND gate inputs can be driven by a 7400 NAND gate output?

Solution

We will consider the LOW state first as depicted in Figure 8-14. Refer to the 7400 data sheet in Figure 8-11 and find

$$I_{OL}(\text{max}) = 16 \text{ mA}$$
$$I_{IL}(\text{max}) = 1.6 \text{ mA}$$

This says that a 7400 output can sink a maximum of 16 mA and that each 7400 input will source a maximum of 1.6 mA back through the driving gate's output. Thus, the number of inputs that can be driven in the LOW state is obtained as

$$\text{fan-out (LOW)} = \frac{I_{OL}(\text{max})}{I_{IL}(\text{max})}$$

$$= \frac{16 \text{ mA}}{1.6 \text{ mA}}$$

$$= 10$$

FIGURE 8-14   Example 8-5.

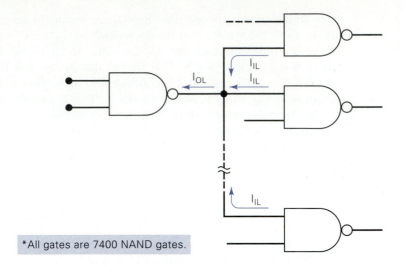

*All gates are 7400 NAND gates.

(*Note:* The entry for I_{IL} is actually -1.6 mA. The negative sign is used to indicate that this current flows *out of* the input terminal; we can ignore this sign for our purposes here.) The HIGH state is analyzed in the same manner. Refer to the data sheet to find values for I_{OH} and I_{IH}, ignoring any negative signs.

$$I_{OH}(\text{max}) = 0.4 \text{ mA} = 400 \text{ }\mu\text{A}$$
$$I_{IH}(\text{max}) = 40 \text{ }\mu\text{A}$$

Thus, the number of inputs that can be driven in the HIGH state is

$$\text{fan-out (HIGH)} = \frac{I_{OH}(\text{max})}{I_{IH}(\text{max})}$$

$$= \frac{400 \text{ }\mu\text{A}}{40 \text{ }\mu\text{A}}$$

$$= 10$$

These results indicate that the fan-out is 10 in both voltage states. Thus, the 7400 NAND gate can drive up to 10 other 7400 NAND gates. If fan-out (LOW) and fan-out (HIGH) are not the same, as will sometimes occur, the fan-out is chosen as the smaller of the two.

EXAMPLE 8-6

Refer to the data sheet in the Appendix and determine how many 74ALS20 NAND gates can be driven by the output of another 74ALS20.

Solution

The 74ALS20 data sheet gives the following values:

$$I_{OH}(\text{max}) = 0.4 \text{ mA} = 400 \text{ }\mu\text{A}$$
$$I_{OL}(\text{max}) = 8 \text{ mA}$$
$$I_{IH}(\text{max}) = 20 \text{ }\mu\text{A}$$
$$I_{IL}(\text{max}) = 0.1 \text{ mA}$$

Considering the HIGH state first, we have

$$\text{fan-out (HIGH)} = \frac{400 \ \mu A}{20 \ \mu A} = 20$$

For the LOW state we have

$$\text{fan-out (LOW)} = \frac{8 \ mA}{0.1 \ mA} = 80$$

In this case, the overall fan-out is chosen to be 20 since it is the lower of the two values. Thus, one 74ALS20 can drive 20 other 74ALS20 inputs.

In older equipment, you will notice that most of the logic ICs were often chosen from the same logic family. In today's digital systems there is much more likely to be a combination of various logic families. Consequently, loading and fan-out calculations are not as straightforward as they once were. A good method for determining the loading of any digital output is as follows:

Step 1. Add up the I_{IH} for all inputs connected to an output. This sum must be less than the output's I_{OH} specification.

Step 2. Add up the I_{IL} for all inputs connected to an output. This sum must be less than the output's I_{OL} specification.

Table 8-7 shows the limiting specifications for input and output currents in simple logic gates of the various TTL families. Notice that some of the current values are given as negative numbers. This convention is used to show the direction of current flow. Positive values indicate current flowing into the specified node whether it is an input or an output. Negative values indicate current flowing out of the specified node. Consequently, all I_{OH} values are negative as current flows out of the output (sourcing current), and all I_{OL} values are positive as load current flows into the out-

TABLE 8-7 Current ratings of TTL series logic gates.*

TTL Series	Outputs		Inputs	
	I_{OH}	I_{OL}	I_{IH}	I_{IL}
74	−0.4 mA	16 mA	40 μA	−1.6 mA
74S	−1 mA	20 mA	50 μA	−2 mA
74LS	−0.4 mA	8 mA	20 μA	−0.4 mA
74AS	−2 mA	20 mA	20 μA	−0.5 mA
74ALS	−0.4 mA	8 mA	20 μA	−0.1 mA
74F	−1 mA	20 mA	20 μA	−0.6 mA

* Some devices may have different input or output current ratings. Always consult the data sheet.

put pin on its way to ground (sinking current). Likewise, I_{IH} is positive, while I_{IL} is negative. When calculating loading and fan-out as described above, you should ignore these signs.

EXAMPLE
8-7

A 74ALS00 NAND gate output is driving three 74S gate inputs and one 7406 input. Determine if there is a loading problem.

Solution

1. Add all of the I_{IH} values:

$$3 \cdot (I_{IH} \text{ for 74S}) + 1 \cdot (I_{IH} \text{ for 74})$$
$$\text{Total} = 3 \cdot (50 \ \mu A) + 1 \cdot (40 \ \mu A) = 190 \ \mu A$$

The I_{OH} for the 74ALS output is 400 μA (max) which is greater than the sum of the loads (190 μA). This poses no problem when the output is HIGH.

2. Add all of the I_{IL} values:

$$3 \cdot (I_{IL} \text{ for 74S}) + 1 \cdot (I_{IL} \text{ for 74})$$
$$\text{Total} = 3 \cdot (2 \text{ mA}) + 1 \cdot (1.6 \text{ mA}) = 7.6 \text{ mA}$$

The I_{OH} for the 74ALS output is 8 mA (max) which is greater than the sum of the loads (7.6 mA). This poses no problem when the output is LOW.

EXAMPLE
8-8

The 74ALS00 NAND gate output in Example 8-7 needs to be used to drive some 74ALS inputs in addition to the load inputs described in Example 8-7. How many additional 74ALS inputs could the output drive without being overloaded?

Solution

From the calculations of Example 8-7, only in the LOW state are we close to being overloaded. A 74ALS input has an I_{IL} of 0.1 mA. The maximum sink current (I_{OL}) is 8 mA, and the load current is 7.6 mA (as calculated in Example 8-7). The additional current that the output can sink is found by

$$\text{additional current} = I_{OLmax} - \text{sum of loads } (I_{IL})$$
$$= 8 \text{ mA} - 7.6 \text{ mA} = 0.4 \text{ mA}$$

This output can drive up to four more 74ALS inputs which have an I_{IL} of 0.1 mA.

EXAMPLE
8-9

The output of a 74AS04 inverter is providing the CLEAR signal to a parallel register made up of 74AS74 D flip-flops. What is the maximum number of FF *CLR* inputs that this gate can drive?

Solution

The input specifications for flip-flop inputs are not always the same as those for a logic gate input in the same family. Refer to the 74AS74 data sheet in the Appendix. The clock and *D* inputs are similar to the gate inputs in Table 8-7. However, the *PRE* and *CLR* inputs have specifications of $I_{IH} = 40\ \mu A$ and $I_{IL} = 1.8$ mA. The 74AS04 has specifications of $I_{OH} = 2$ mA and $I_{OL} = 20$ mA.

$$\text{Maximum number of inputs (HIGH)} = 2\ \text{mA}/40\ \mu A = 50$$
$$\text{Maximum number of inputs (LOW)} = 20\ \text{mA}/1.8\ \text{mA} = 11.11$$

We must limit the fan-out to 11 *CLR* inputs.

Review Questions

1. What factors determine a device's $I_{OL}(\text{max})$ rating?
2. How many 7407 inputs can a 74AS chip drive?
3. What can happen if a TTL output is connected to more gate inputs than it is rated to handle?
4. How many 74S112 $\overline{CP}$ inputs can be driven by a 74LS04 output? By a 74F00 output?

8-6 OTHER TTL CHARACTERISTICS

Several other characteristics of TTL logic must be understood if one is to intelligently use TTL in a digital-system application.

Unconnected Inputs (Floating)

Any input to a TTL circuit that is left disconnected (open) acts exactly like a logical 1 applied to that input, because in either case the emitter–base junction or diode at the input will not be forward-biased. This means that on *any* TTL IC, *all* of the inputs are 1s if they are not connected to some logic signal or to ground. When an input is left unconnected, it is said to be **floating.**

Unused Inputs

Frequently, not all of the inputs on a TTL IC are being used in a particular application. A common example is when not all the inputs to a logic gate are needed for the required logic function. For example, suppose that we needed the logic operation $\overline{AB}$ and we were using a chip that had a three-input NAND gate. The possible ways of accomplishing this are shown in Figure 8-15.

FIGURE 8-15 Three ways to handle unused logic inputs.

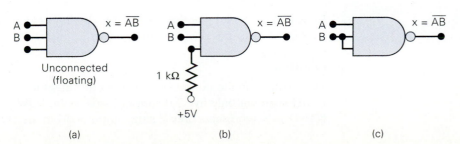

(a)   (b)   (c)

In Figure 8-15(a) the unused input is left disconnected, which means that it acts as a logical 1. The NAND gate output is therefore $x = \overline{A \cdot B \cdot 1} = \overline{A \cdot B}$, which is the desired result. Although the logic is correct, it is highly undesirable to leave an input disconnected, because it will act like an antenna, which is liable to pick up stray radiated signals that could cause the gate to operate improperly. A better technique is shown in Figure 8-15(b). Here the unused input is connected to +5 V through a 1-kΩ resistor, so that the logic level is a 1. The 1-kΩ resistor is simply for current protection of the emitter–base junctions of the gate inputs in case of spikes on the power-supply line. This same technique can be used for AND gates, since a 1 on an unused input will not affect the output. As many as 30 unused inputs can share the same 1-kΩ resistor tied to V_{CC}.

A third possibility is shown in Figure 8-15(c), where the unused input is tied to a used input. This is satisfactory provided that the circuit driving input B is not going to have its fan-out exceeded. This technique can be used for *any* type of gate. For OR gates and NOR gates, the unused inputs cannot be left disconnected or tied to +5 V since this would produce a constant-output logic level (1 for OR, 0 for NOR) regardless of the other inputs. Instead, for these gates the unused inputs must either be connected to ground (0 V) for a logic 0 or be tied to a used input as in Figure 8-15(c).

Tied-Together Inputs

When two (or more) TTL inputs on the same gate are connected together to form a common input as in Figure 8-15(c), the common input will generally represent a load that is the sum of the load current rating of each individual input. The only exception is for NAND and AND gates. For these gates, the LOW-state input load *will be the same as a single input* no matter how many inputs are tied together.

To illustrate, assume that each input of the three-input NAND gate in Figure 8-15(c) is rated at 0.5 mA for I_{IL} and 20 μA for I_{IH}. The common input B will therefore represent an input load of 40 μA in the HIGH state but only 0.5 mA in the LOW state. The same would be true if this were an AND gate. If it were an OR or a NOR gate, the common B input would present an input load 40 μA in the HIGH state and 1 mA in the LOW state.

The reason for this characteristic can be found by looking back at the circuit diagram of the TTL NAND gate in Figure 8-8(b). The current I_{IL} is limited by the resistance R_1. Even if inputs A and B were tied together and grounded, this current would not change; it would merely divide up and flow through the parallel paths provided by diodes D_2 and D_3. The situation is different for OR and NOR gates, since they do not use multiple-emitter transistors, but rather have a separate input transistor for each input, as we saw in Figure 8-10.

EXAMPLE 8-10	Determine the load that the X output is driving in Figure 8-16. Assume that each gate is a 74LS series device with $I_{IH} = 20$ μA and $I_{IL} = 0.4$ mA.

Solution

The loading on the output of gate 1 is equivalent to six 74LS input loads in the HIGH state but only five 74LS input loads in the LOW state. This is because the NAND gate represents only a single input load in the LOW state.

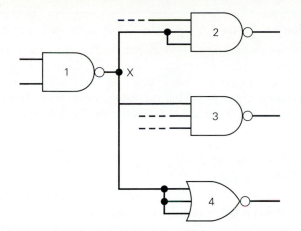

Loading on gate 1 output			
HIGH		LOW	
Load Current	Gate	Load Current	Gate
40 µA	2	0.4 mA	2
20 µA	3	0.4 mA	3
60 µA	4	1.2 mA	4
120 µA	Total	2.0 mA	Total

FIGURE 8-16 Example 8-10.

Biasing TTL Inputs Low

Occasionally, the situation arises where a TTL input must be held normally LOW and then caused to go HIGH by the actuation of a mechanical switch. This is illustrated in Figure 8-17 for the input to a one-shot. This OS triggers on a positive transition that occurs when the switch is momentarily closed. The resistor R serves to keep the T input LOW while the switch is open. Care must be taken to keep the value of R low enough so that the voltage developed across it by the current I_{IL} that flows out of the OS input to ground will not exceed $V_{IL}(\text{max})$. Thus, the largest value of R is given by

$$I_{IL} \times R_{\text{max}} = V_{IL}(\text{max})$$

$$R_{\text{max}} = \frac{V_{IL}(\text{max})}{I_{IL}} \qquad (8\text{-}3)$$

R must be kept below this value to ensure that the OS input will be at an acceptable LOW level while the switch is open. The minimum value of R is determined by the current drain on the 5-V supply when the switch is closed. In practice, this current drain should be minimized by keeping R just slightly below R_{max}.

FIGURE 8-17

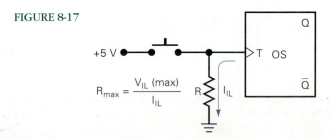

Determine an acceptable value for R if the OS is a 74LS TTL IC with an I_{IL} input rating of 0.4 mA.

Solution

The value of I_{IL} will be a maximum of 0.4 mA. This maximum value should be used to calculate R_{max}. From Table 8-6, $V_{IL}(\text{max}) = 0.8$ V for the 74LS series. Thus, we have

$$R_{max} = \frac{0.8 \text{ V}}{0.4 \text{ mA}} = 2000 \ \Omega$$

A good choice here would be $R = 1.8$ kΩ, a standard resistor value.

Current Transients

TTL logic circuits suffer from internally generated current transients or spikes because of the totem-pole output structure. When the output is switching from the LOW state to the HIGH state (see Figure 8-18), the two output transistors are changing states: Q_3 OFF to ON, and Q_4 ON to OFF. Since Q_4 is changing from the saturated condition, it will take longer than Q_3 to switch states. Thus, there is a short interval of time (about 2 ns) during the switching transition when both transistors are conducting and a relatively large surge of current (30 to 50 mA) is drawn from the +5 V supply. The duration of this current transient is extended by the effects of any load capacitance on the

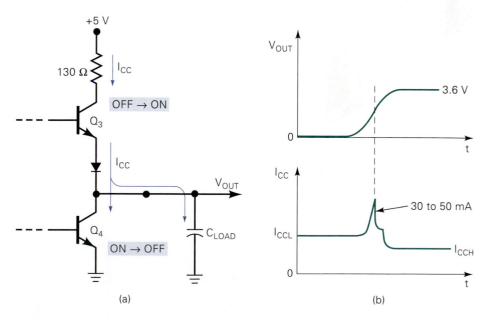

FIGURE 8-18   A large current spike is drawn from V_{CC} when a totem-pole output switches from LOW to HIGH.

circuit output. This capacitance consists of stray wiring capacitance and the input capacitance of any load circuits and must be charged up to the HIGH-state output voltage. This overall effect can be summarized as follows:

> **Whenever a totem-pole TTL output goes from LOW to HIGH, a high-amplitude current spike is drawn from the V_{CC} supply.**

In a complex digital circuit or system, there may be many TTL outputs switching states at the same time, each one drawing a narrow spike of current from the power supply. The accumulative effect of all of these current spikes will be to produce a voltage spike on the common V_{CC} line, mostly due to the distributed inductance on the supply line [remember: $V = L(di/dt)$ for inductance, and di/dt is very large for a 2-ns current spike]. This voltage spike can cause serious malfunctions during switching transitions unless some type of filtering is used. The most common technique uses small radio-frequency capacitors connected from V_{CC} to GROUND to essentially "short out" these high-frequency spikes. This is called **power-supply decoupling.**

It is standard practice to connect a 0.01-μF or 0.1-μF low-inductance, ceramic disk capacitor between V_{CC} and ground near each TTL IC on a circuit board. The capacitor leads are kept very short to minimize series inductance.

In addition, it is standard practice to connect a single large capacitor (2 to 20 μF) between V_{CC} and ground on each board to filter out relatively low-frequency variations in V_{CC} caused by the large changes in I_{CC} levels as outputs switch states.

Review Questions

1. What will be the logic output of a TTL NAND gate that has all of its inputs unconnected?
2. What are two acceptable ways to handle unused inputs to an AND gate?
3. Repeat question 2 for a NOR gate.
4. *True or false:* When NAND gate inputs are tied together, they are always treated as a single load on the signal source.
5. What is power-supply decoupling? Why is it used?

8-7 CONNECTING TTL OUTPUTS TOGETHER

As strange as it may seem, there are situations in which it is advantageous to connect the *outputs* of two or more logic gates (or other devices). Whenever this is done, we must be concerned about the situation where one gate output is trying to go LOW while another gate output is trying to go HIGH; since they are tied together, we have a HIGH/LOW conflict. As we will soon see, with TTL devices the LOW always wins. Up to now, we have become familiar only with the totem-pole output structure for TTL devices. Two other kinds of output structures will be presented shortly. Let's first consider tying totem-pole outputs together.

Totem-pole outputs should not be tied together.

The reason for this absolute rule can be seen if we look at Figure 8-19, where the totem-pole outputs of two separate gates are connected together at point X. Suppose that the gate A output is in the HIGH state (Q_{3A} on, Q_{4A} off) and the gate B output is in the LOW state (Q_{3B} off, Q_{4B} on). In this situation Q_{4B} is a very low-resistance load on Q_{3A} and will draw a current that can go as high as 55 mA. This current might not damage Q_{3B} or Q_{4A} immediately, but over a period of time it can cause overheating and deterioration in performance and eventual device failure. The situation worsens when more than two totem-pole outputs are tied together.

FIGURE 8-19 Totem-pole outputs tied together can produce harmful current through Q_4.

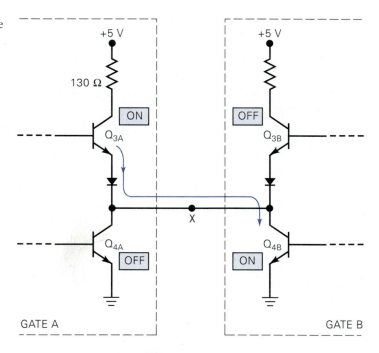

Another problem caused by this relatively high current flowing through Q_{4A} is that it will produce a larger voltage drop across the transistor collector–emitter, making V_{OL} greater than the allowable V_{OL}(max).

Sometimes totem-pole outputs are unintentionally tied together because of wiring errors or accidental shorting together on a printed circuit board. When this happens, the signal at the common point will usually be the logical AND of the outputs; that is, it will be LOW when any one of the tied-together output signals tries to go LOW. This is true only of TTL circuits; MOS and CMOS behave less predictably when outputs are tied together.

Open-Collector Outputs

Some TTL circuits are designed with **open-collector outputs.** As shown in Figure 8-20(a), the open-collector structure eliminates the pull-up transistor Q_3, D_1, and R_4. The output is taken at Q_4's collector, which is open (unconnected). In the output LOW state, Q_4 is ON (has base current and is essentially a short between collector and emitter); in the output HIGH state, Q_4 is OFF (has no base current and is essentially an open between collector and emitter). For proper operation an external pull-up resistor R_P should be connected as shown in Figure 8-20(b). This resistor is not part of the TTL device's internal circuitry; it is a separate resistor that you must connect to the device output.

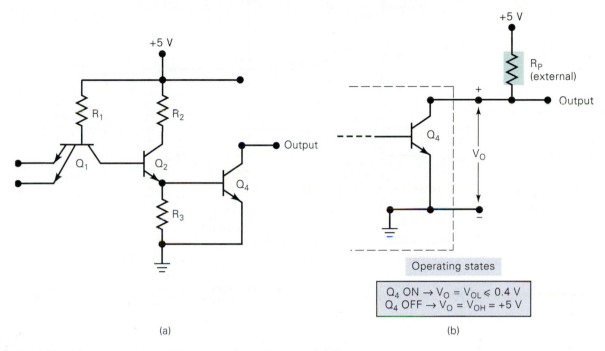

FIGURE 8-20   (a) Open-collector TTL circuit; (b) with external pull-up resistor.

When Q_4 is ON, it pulls the output voltage down to a LOW. When Q_4 is OFF, R_P pulls the output voltage to a HIGH. Note that without the pull-up resistor, the output voltage would be indeterminate (floating). That's why the pull-up resistor is used. The value of this resistor is usually chosen to be 10 kΩ. This value is small enough so that in the HIGH state the voltage dropped across it due to load current will not lower the output voltage below the TTL minimum. It is large enough so that in the LOW state it will limit the current through Q_4 to a value below I_{OL}(max).

Wired-AND Connection

Devices with open-collector (OC) outputs can have their outputs connected together safely. Figure 8-21 shows three two-input OC NAND gates (74LS01s) whose outputs are tied together. This connection is called a **wired-AND** connection because it is equivalent to the logical AND operation. The logic expression of the output is the same as if the three gate outputs had been fed into an AND gate. This is shown symbolically by the dotted AND gate symbol. There is no actual AND gate there.

FIGURE 8-21 Wired-AND operation using open-collector gates.

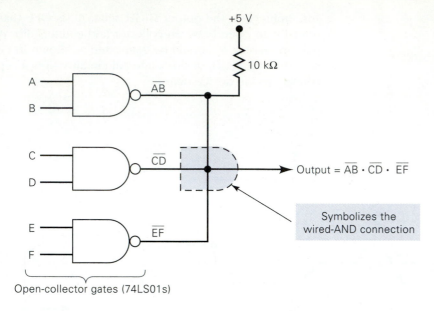

Output = $\overline{AB} \cdot \overline{CD} \cdot \overline{EF}$

Symbolizes the wired-AND connection

Open-collector gates (74LS01s)

This wired-AND configuration eliminates the need for an actual AND gate, but OC devices suffer from a much slower switching speed than totem-pole outputs, which have a pull-up transistor (Q_3) to change up load capacitance rapidly. For this reason, OC circuits should not be used where speed is a principal consideration.

Open-Collector Buffer/Drivers

Any logic circuit that is called a *buffer,* a *driver,* or a **buffer/driver** is designed to have a greater output current and/or voltage capability than an ordinary logic circuit. Buffer/driver ICs are available with totem-pole outputs and with open-collector outputs.

Due to their high output current and voltage specifications, the 7406 and 7407 are the only standard TTL devices that are still recommended for new designs. The 7406 is an open-collector buffer/driver IC that contains six INVERTERs with open-

FIGURE 8-22 An open-collector buffer/driver drives a high-current, high-voltage load.

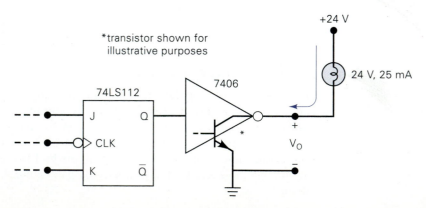

collector outputs that can sink up to 40 mA in the LOW state. In addition, the 7406 can handle output voltages up to 30 V. This means that the output transistor can be connected to a voltage greater than 5 V.

This is illustrated in Figure 8-22, where a 7406 is used as a buffer between a 74LS112 flip-flop and an incandescent indicator lamp that is rated at 24 V, 25 mA. The 7406 controls the lamp's ON/OFF status to indicate the state of FF output Q. Note that the lamp is powered from +24 V, and it acts as the pull-up resistor for the open-collector output.

When $Q = 1$, the 7406 output goes LOW, its output transistor sinks the 25 mA of lamp current supplied by the 24-V source, and the lamp is on. When $Q = 0$, the 7406 output transistor turns off; there is no path for current, and the lamp turns off. In this state, the full 24 V will appear across the OFF output transistor so that $V_{OH} = 24$ V, which is lower than the 7406 maximum V_{OH} rating.

Open-collector outputs are often used to drive indicator LEDs as shown in Figure 8-23. The resistor is used to limit the current to a safe value. When the IN-VERTER output is LOW, its output transistor will provide a low-resistance path to ground for the LED current, so that the LED will be on. When the INVERTER output is HIGH, its output transistor will be off, and there will be no path for LED current; in this state the LED will be off.

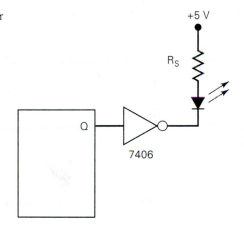

FIGURE 8-23 An open-collector output can be used to drive an LED indicator.

The 7407 is an open-collector, noninverting buffer with the same voltage and current ratings as a 7406.

IEEE/ANSI Symbol for Open-Collector Outputs

The traditional symbols for logic circuits with open-collector outputs are the same as for totem-pole outputs. The new IEEE/ANSI symbology, however, does use a distinctive notation to identify open-collector outputs. Figure 8-24 shows the standard IEEE/ANSI designation for an open-collector output. It is an underlined diamond. Although we will not normally use the complete IEEE/ANSI symbology in this book, we will use this underlined diamond to indicate open-collector outputs.

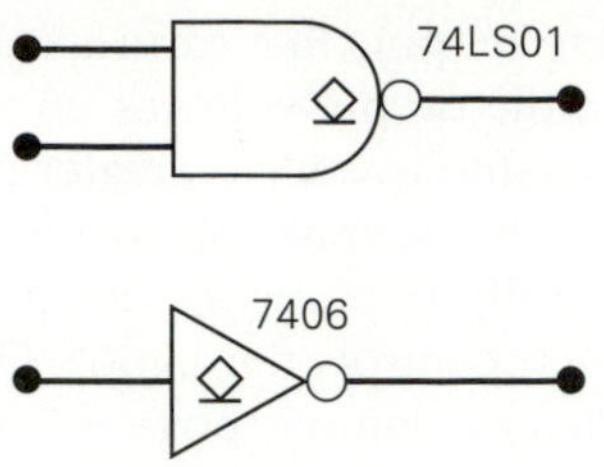

FIGURE 8-24 IEEE/ANSI notation for open-collector outputs.

Review Questions

1. When does a HIGH/LOW conflict occur?
2. Why shouldn't totem-pole outputs be tied together?
3. How do open-collector outputs differ from totem-pole outputs?
4. Why do open-collector outputs need a pull-up resistor?
5. What is the logic expression for the wired-AND connection of six 7406 outputs?
6. Why are open-collector outputs generally slower than totem-pole?
7. What is the IEEE/ANSI symbol for open-collector outputs?

8-8 TRISTATE (THREE-STATE) TTL

The **tristate** configuration is a third type of TTL output configuration. It utilizes the high-speed operation of the totem-pole arrangement while permitting outputs to be connected together. It is called *tristate* TTL because it allows *three* possible output states: HIGH, LOW, and high-impedance (Hi-Z). The Hi-Z state is a condition in which both transistors in the totem-pole arrangement are turned off so that the output terminal is a high impedance to ground and to V_{CC}. In other words, the output is an open or floating terminal that is neither a LOW nor a HIGH. In practice, the output terminal is not an exact open circuit, but it has a resistance of several megohms or more relative to ground and V_{CC}.

The tristate operation is obtained by modifying the basic totem-pole circuit. Figure 8-25(a) shows the circuit for a tristate INVERTER where the portion enclosed in dotted lines has been added to the basic circuit. The circuit has two inputs: A is the normal logic input, and E is an ENABLE input that can produce the Hi-Z state. We will examine the operation for both states of E.

The Enabled State

With $E = 1$, the circuit operates as a normal INVERTER because the HIGH voltage at E has no effect on Q_1 or D_2. In this enabled condition, the output is simply the inverse of logic input A.

The Disabled State (Hi-Z)

When $E = 0$, the circuit goes into its Hi-Z state regardless of the state of logic input A. The LOW at E forward-biases the emitter–base junction of Q_1 and shunts the R_1 current away from Q_2 so that Q_2 turns off, which turns Q_4 off. The LOW at E also

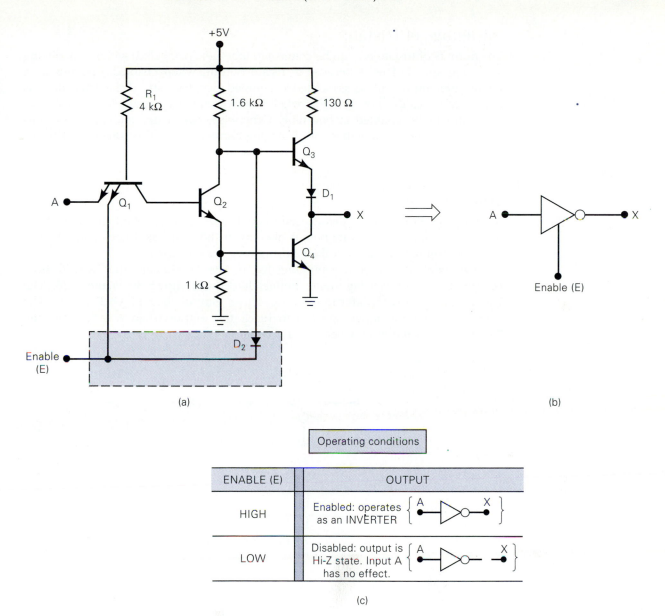

FIGURE 8-25   Tristate TTL INVERTER.

forward-biases diode D_2 to shunt current away from the base of Q_3, so that Q_3 also turns off.

With both totem-pole transistors in the nonconducting state, the output terminal is essentially an open circuit. This is shown symbolically in the table of Figure 8-25(c).

The logic symbol for the tristate INVERTER is shown in Figure 8-25(b). Note where the ENABLE input is placed on the INVERTER symbol. Also note that E is active-HIGH; that is, the INVERTER is enabled when $E = 1$.

Advantage of Tristate

The outputs of tristate ICs can be connected together (paralleled) without sacrificing switching speed. This is because a tristate output, when enabled, operates as a totem-pole output with its associated low-impedance, high-speed characteristic. It is important to realize, however, that when tristate outputs are paralleled, only one of them should be enabled at one time. Otherwise, two active totem-pole outputs would be connected together and damaging currents could flow (Figure 8-19). We will elaborate on this in our discussion of tristate buffers.

Tristate Buffers

A *tristate buffer* is a circuit that is used to control the passage of a logic signal from input to output. Some tristate buffers also invert the signal as it goes through. The circuit in Figure 8-25 can be called an *inverting tristate buffer*.

Two commonly used tristate buffer ICs are the 74LS125 and the 74LS126. Both contain four *noninverting* tristate buffers like those shown in Figure 8-26. The 74LS125 and 74LS126 differ only in the active state of their ENABLE inputs. The 74LS125 allows the input signal A to reach the output when $\bar{E} = 0$, while the 74LS126 passes the input when $E = 1$.

FIGURE 8-26 Tristate noninverting buffers.

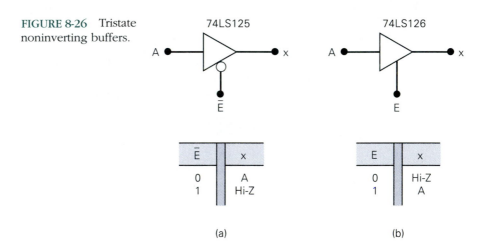

$\bar{E}$	x
0	A
1	Hi-Z

(a)

E	x
0	Hi-Z
1	A

(b)

Tristate buffers have many applications in circuits where several signals are connected to common lines (buses). We will examine some of these applications in Chapter 9, but we can get the basic idea from Figure 8-27(a). Here we have three logic signals A, B, and C connected to a common bus line through 74LS126 tristate buffers. This arrangement permits us to transmit any one of these signals over the bus line to other circuits by enabling the appropriate buffer.

For example, consider the situation in Figure 8-27(b) where $E_B = 1$ and $E_A = E_C = 0$. This disables the upper and lower buffers so that their outputs are in the Hi-Z state and are essentially disconnected from the bus. This is symbolized by the **X**'s on the diagram. The middle buffer is enabled so that its input, B, is passed through to its output and onto the bus, from where it is routed to other circuits connected to the bus. When tristate outputs are connected together as in Figure 8-27, it is impor-

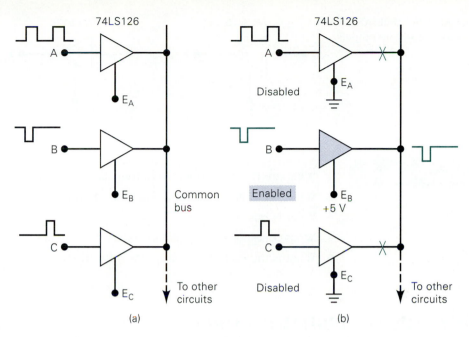

FIGURE 8-27 (a) Tristate buffers used to connect several signals to a common bus; (b) conditions for transmitting *B* to the bus.

tant to remember that no more than one output should be enabled at one time. Otherwise, two or more active totem-pole outputs would be connected, which could produce damaging currents. Even if damage did not occur, this situation would produce a signal on the bus that is a combination of more than one signal. This is commonly referred to as **bus contention.** In tristate bus systems the designer must make sure that the enable signals do not allow bus contention to occur.

Tristate ICs

In addition to tristate buffers, many ICs are designed with tristate outputs. For example, the 74LS374 is an octal D-type FF register IC with tristate outputs. This means that it is an eight-bit register made up of D-type FFs whose outputs are connected to tristate buffers. This type of register can be connected to common bus lines along with the outputs from other, similar devices to allow efficient transfer of data over the bus. We examine this *tristate data bus* arrangement in Chapter 9. Other types of logic devices that are available with tristate outputs include decoders, multiplexers, analog-to-digital converters, memory chips, and microprocessors.

IEEE/ANSI Symbol for Tristate Outputs

The traditional logic symbology has no special notation for tristate outputs. Figure 8-28 shows the notation used in the IEEE/ANSI symbology to indicate a tristate output. It is a triangle that points downward. Although it is not part of the traditional symbology, we will use this triangle to designate tristate outputs throughout the remainder of the book.

FIGURE 8-28 IEEE/ANSI notation for tristate outputs.

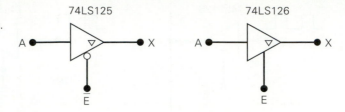

1. What are the three possible output states of a tristate IC?
2. What is the state of a tristate output when it is disabled?
3. What is bus contention?
4. What conditions are necessary to transmit signal *C* onto the bus in Figure 8-27?
5. What is the IEEE/ANSI designation for tristate outputs?

8-9 THE ECL DIGITAL IC FAMILY

The TTL family uses transistors operating in the saturated mode. As a result, their switching speed is limited by the storage delay time associated with a transistor that is driven into saturation. Another *bipolar* logic family has been developed that prevents transistor saturation, thereby increasing overall switching speed. This logic family is called **emitter-coupled logic** (ECL), and it operates on the principle of current switching whereby a fixed bias current less than I_C(sat) is switched from one transistor's collector to another. Because of this current-mode operation, this logic form is also referred to as *current-mode logic* (CML).

Basic ECL Circuit

The basic circuit for emitter-coupled logic is essentially the differential amplifier configuration of Figure 8-29(a). The V_{EE} supply produces an essentially fixed current I_E which remains around 3 mA during normal operation. This current is allowed to flow through either Q_1 or Q_2, depending on the voltage level at V_{IN}. In other words, this current will switch between Q_1's collector and Q_2's collector as V_{IN} switches between its two logic levels of -1.7 V (logical 0 for ECL) and -0.8 V (logical 1 for ECL). The table in Figure 8-29(a) shows the resulting output voltages for these two conditions at V_{IN}. Two important points should be noted: (1) V_{C1} and V_{C2} are the *complements* of each other, and (2) the output voltage levels are not the same as the input logic levels.

The second point noted above is easily taken care of by connecting V_{C1} and V_{C2} to emitter-follower stages (Q_3 and Q_4), as shown in Figure 8-29(b). The emitter followers perform two functions: (1) they subtract approximately 0.8 V from V_{C1} and V_{C2} to shift the output levels to the correct ECL logic levels; and (2) they provide a very low output impedance (typically 7 Ω), which provides for large fan-out and fast charging of load capacitance. This circuit produces two complementary outputs: V_{OUT1}, which equals $\overline{V_{IN}}$, and V_{OUT2}, which is equal to V_{IN}.

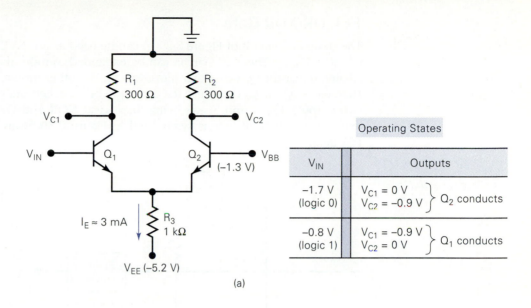

	Operating States		
V_IN	**Outputs**		
−1.7 V (logic 0)	V_{C1} = 0 V V_{C2} = −0.9 V	}	Q_2 conducts
−0.8 V (logic 1)	V_{C1} = −0.9 V V_{C2} = 0 V	}	Q_1 conducts

(a)

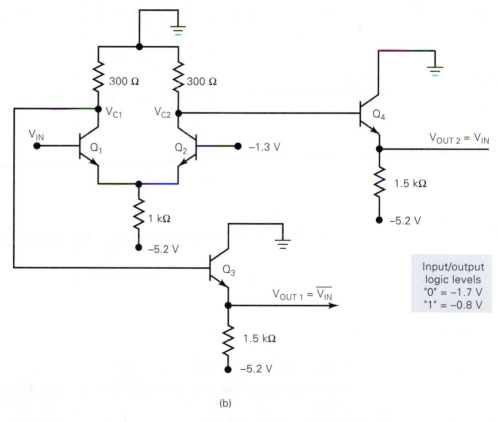

Input/output
logic levels
"0" = −1.7 V
"1" = −0.8 V

(b)

FIGURE 8-29 (a) Basic ECL circuit; (b) with addition of emitter followers.

ECL OR/NOR Gate

The basic ECL circuit of Figure 8-29(b) can be used as an INVERTER if the output is taken at V_{OUT1}. This basic circuit can be expanded to more than one input by paralleling transistor Q_1 with other transistors for the other inputs, as in Figure 8-30(a). Here either Q_1 or Q_3 can cause the current to be switched out of Q_2, resulting in the two outputs V_{OUT1} and V_{OUT2} being the logical NOR and OR operations, respectively. This OR/NOR gate is symbolized in Figure 8-30(b) and is the fundamental ECL gate.

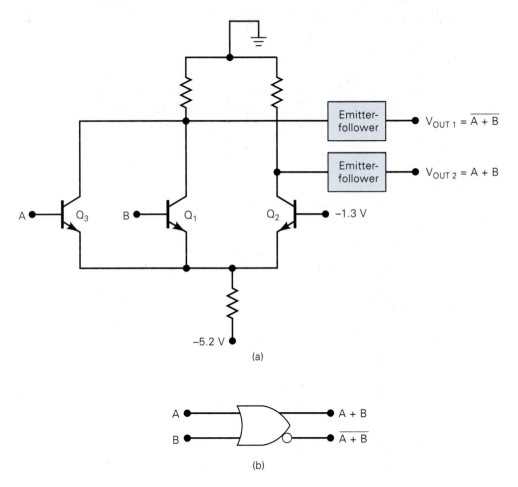

FIGURE 8-30 (a) ECL NOR/OR circuit; (b) logic symbol.

ECL Characteristics

The following are the most important characteristics of the ECL family of logic circuits:

1. The transistors never saturate, and so switching speed is very high. Typical propagation delay time is 1 ns, which makes ECL somewhat faster than advanced Schottky TTL (74AS series).

2. The logic levels are nominally -0.8 V and -1.70 V for the logical 1 and 0, respectively.

3. Worst-case ECL noise margins are approximately 250 mV. These low noise margins make ECL somewhat unreliable for use in heavy industrial environments.

4. An ECL logic block usually produces an output and its complement. This eliminates the need for inverters.

5. Fan-outs are typically around 25, owing to the low-impedance emitter-follower outputs.

6. Typical power dissipation for a basic ECL gate is 25 mW, somewhat higher than with the 74AS series.

7. The total current flow in an ECL circuit remains relatively constant regardless of its logic state. This helps to maintain an unvarying current drain on the circuit power supply even during switching transitions. Thus, no noise spikes will be internally generated like those produced by TTL totem-pole circuits.

Table 8-8 shows how ECL compares with the important TTL logic families. The ECL family of ICs does not include a wide range of general-purpose logic devices as do the TTL and CMOS families. ECL does include complex, special-purpose ICs used in applications such as high-speed data transmission, high-speed memories, and high-speed arithmetic units. The relatively low noise margins and high power drain of ECL are disadvantages compared with TTL and CMOS. Another drawback is its negative power-supply voltage and logic levels, which are not compatible with those of the other logic families. This makes it difficult to use ECL devices in conjunction with TTL and/or CMOS ICs; special level-shifting circuits must be connected between ECL devices and the TTL (or CMOS) devices on both input and output.

TABLE 8-8

Logic Family	t_{pd} (ns)	P_D (mW)	Worst-Case Noise Margin (mV)	Maximum Clock Rate (MHz)
74	9	10	400	35
74AS	1.7	8	300	200
74ALS	4	1.2	400	70
74S	3	20	300	125
74LS	9.5	2	300	45
74F	3	6	300	100
ECL	1	25	250	600

Review Questions

1. *True or false:*

   (a) ECL obtains high-speed operation by preventing transistor saturation.

   (b) ECL circuits usually have complementary outputs.

   (c) The noise margins for ECL circuits are larger than TTL noise margins.

   (d) ECL circuits do not generate noise spikes during state transitions.

   (e) ECL devices require less power than standard TTL.

   (f) ECL can easily be used with TTL.

8-10 MOS DIGITAL INTEGRATED CIRCUITS

MOS (metal-oxide-semiconductor) technology derives its name from the basic MOS structure of a metal electrode over an oxide insulator over a semiconductor substrate. The transistors of MOS technology are field-effect transistors called **MOSFETs.** This means that the electric *field* on the *metal* electrode side of the *oxide* insulator has an *effect* on the resistance of the substrate. Most of the MOS digital ICs are constructed entirely of MOSFETs and no other components.

The chief advantages of the MOSFET are that it is relatively simple and inexpensive to fabricate, it is small, and it consumes very little power. The fabrication of MOS ICs is approximately one-third as complex as the fabrication of bipolar ICs (TTL, ECL, etc.). In addition, MOS devices occupy much less space on a chip than bipolar transistors; typically, a MOSFET requires 1 square mil of chip area while a bipolar transistor requires about 50 square mils. More important, MOS digital ICs normally do not use the IC resistor elements that take up so much of the chip area of bipolar ICs.

All of this means that MOS ICs can accommodate a much larger number of circuit elements on a single chip than bipolar ICs. This advantage is evidenced by the fact that MOS ICs have dominated bipolar ICs in the area of large-scale integration (LSI, VLSI). The high packing density of MOS ICs makes them especially well suited for complex ICs such as microprocessor and memory chips. Improvements in MOS IC technology have led to devices that are faster than 74, 74LS, and 74ALS TTL with comparable current drive characteristics. Consequently, MOS devices (specifically CMOS) have also become dominant in the SSI and MSI market. The 74AS TTL family is still faster than the best MOS devices, but at the price of much greater power dissipation.

The principal disadvantage of MOS devices is their susceptibility to static-electricity damage. Although this can be minimized by proper handling procedures, TTL is still more durable for laboratory experimentation. Consequently, you are likely to see TTL devices used in education as long as they are available.

8-11 THE MOSFET

There are presently two general types of MOSFETs: *depletion* and *enhancement*. MOS digital ICs use enhancement MOSFETs exclusively, and so only this type will be considered in the following discussion. Furthermore, we will concern ourselves only with the operation of these MOSFETs as on/off switches.

Figure 8-31 shows the schematic symbols for the N-channel and P-channel enhancement MOSFETs, where the direction of the arrow indicates either P- or N-channel. The symbols show a broken line between the *source* and the *drain* to indicate that there is *normally* no conducting channel between these electrodes. The symbol also shows a separation between the *gate* and the other terminals to indicate the very high resistance (typically around 10^{12} Ω) of the oxide layer between the gate and the channel, which is formed in the substrate.

FIGURE 8-31 Schematic symbols for enhancement MOSFETs.

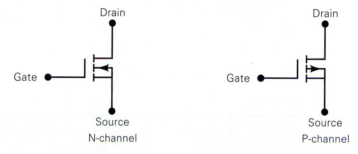

Basic MOSFET Switch

Figure 8-32 shows the switching operation of an N-channel *MOSFET.* For the N-channel device the drain is always biased positive relative to the source. The gate-to-source voltage V_{GS} is the input voltage, which is used to control the resistance between drain and source (i.e., the channel resistance) and therefore determines whether the device is on or off.

FIGURE 8-32 N-channel MOSFET switching states.

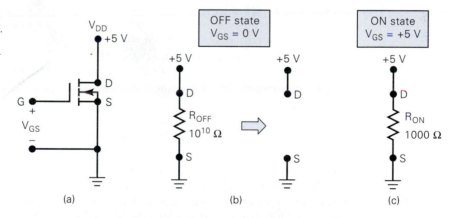

When $V_{GS} = 0$ V, there is no conductive channel between source and drain, and the device is off. Typically the channel resistance in this OFF state is 10^{10} Ω, which for most purposes is an *open circuit.* The MOSFET will remain off as long as V_{GS} is zero or negative. As V_{GS} is made positive (gate positive relative to source), a threshold voltage (V_T) is reached, at which point a conductive channel begins to form between source and drain. Typically $V_T = +1.5$ V for N-MOSFET, and so any $V_{GS} \geq 1.5$ V will cause the MOSFET to conduct. Generally, a value of V_{GS} much larger than V_T is used to turn on the MOSFET more completely. As shown in Figure 8-32(b), when $V_{GS} = +5$ V, the channel resistance between source and drain has dropped to a value of $R_{ON} = 1000 \; \Omega$.

In essence, then, the N-MOSFET will switch from a very high resistance to a low resistance as the gate voltage switches from a LOW voltage to a HIGH voltage. It is helpful simply to think of the MOSFET as a switch that is either opened or closed between source and drain.

The P-channel MOSFET operates in exactly the same manner as the N-channel except that it uses voltages of the opposite polarity. For P-MOSFETs the drain is connected to $-V_{DD}$ so that it is biased negative relative to the source. To turn the P-MOSFET on, a negative voltage that exceeds V_T must be applied to the gate.

Table 8-9 summarizes the P- and N-channel switching characteristics.

TABLE 8-9

	Drain-to-Source Bias	Gate-to-Source Voltage (V_{GS}) Needed for Conduction	R_{ON} (Ω)	R_{OFF} (Ω)
P-channel	Negative	Typically more negative than -1.5 V	1000 (typical)	10^{10}
N-channel	Positive	Typically more positive than $+1.5$ V	1000 (typical)	10^{10}

8-12 DIGITAL MOSFET CIRCUITS

Digital circuits employing MOSFETs are broken down into three categories: (1) **P-MOS,** which uses *only* P-channel enhancement MOSFETs; (2) **N-MOS,** which uses *only* N-channel enhancement MOSFETs; and (3) **CMOS** (complementary MOS), which uses both P- and N-channel devices.

P-MOS and N-MOS digital ICs have a greater packing density (more transistors per chip) and are therefore more economical than CMOS. N-MOS has about twice the packing density of P-MOS. In addition, N-MOS is also about twice as fast as P-MOS, owing to the fact that free electrons are the current carrier in N-MOS whereas holes (slower-moving positive charges) are the current carriers for P-MOS. CMOS has the greatest complexity and lowest packing density of the MOS families, but it possesses the important advantages of higher speed and much lower power dissipation. N-MOS and CMOS ICs are widely used in the digital field, but P-MOS ICs are no longer part of new designs. However, P-MOSFETs are still important because they are used as part of CMOS circuits.

In this section we look at some of the basic N-MOS logic circuits. It is understood that the corresponding P-MOS circuits would be the same except for the voltage polarities. Since N-MOS finds its widest applications in LSI and VLSI (microprocessors, memories, etc.), we will defer any applications of N-MOS devices until later. CMOS, which, like TTL, is used in MSI applications, is covered in detail beginning in Section 8-14.

N-MOS INVERTER

Figure 8-33 shows the basic N-MOS INVERTER circuit. It contains two N-channel MOSFETs: Q_1 is called the *load* MOSFET, and Q_2 the *switching* MOSFET. Q_1 has its gate *permanently* connected to +5 V, and so it is *always* in the ON state and essentially acts as a load resistor of value R_{ON}. Q_2 will switch from ON to OFF in response to V_{IN}. The Q_1 MOSFET is designed to have a narrower channel than Q_2, and so Q_1's R_{ON} is much greater than Q_2's. Typically, R_{ON} for Q_1 is 100 kΩ, and R_{ON} for Q_2 is 1 kΩ. R_{OFF} for Q_2 is usually around 10^{10} Ω.

FIGURE 8-33   N-MOS INVERTER.

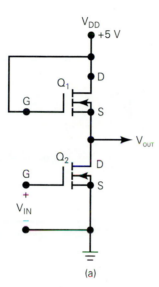

V_{IN}	Q_1	Q_2	$V_{OUT} = \overline{V_{IN}}$
0 V (logic 0)	$R_{ON} =$ 100 kΩ	$R_{OFF} =$ 10^{10} Ω	+5 V (logic 1)
+5 V (logic 1)	$R_{ON} =$ 100 kΩ	$R_{ON} =$ 1 kΩ	+0.05 V (logic 0)

(a)   (b)

The two states of the INVERTER are summarized in Figure 8-33(b). The best way to analyze this circuit is to consider each MOSFET channel as a resistance so that the output voltage is taken from a voltage divider formed by the two resistances. With $V_{IN} = 0$ V, transistor Q_2 is off, with a very large resistance of 10^{10} Ω. Since Q_1 has $R_{ON} = 100$ Ω, the voltage-divider output will be essentially +5 V. With $V_{IN} = +5$ V, Q_2 is on, with $R_{ON} = 1$ kΩ. The voltage divider is now 100 kΩ and 1 kΩ, so that $V_{OUT} = 1/101 \times (+5$ V$) \approx 0.05$ V.

The circuit functions as an INVERTER since a LOW input produces a HIGH output, and vice versa. This basic INVERTER can be modified to form NAND and NOR logic gates.

N-MOS NAND Gate

The NAND operation is performed by the circuit of Figure 8-34(a), where Q_1 is again acting as a load resistance while Q_2 and Q_3 are switches controlled by input levels A and B. If either A or B is at 0 V (logical 0), the corresponding FET is off, thereby presenting a high resistance from the output terminal to ground so that output X is HIGH (+5 V). When both A and B are +5 V (logical 1), both Q_2 and Q_3 are on, so that output X is LOW. Clearly, the output equals the NAND of the inputs ($X = \overline{AB}$).

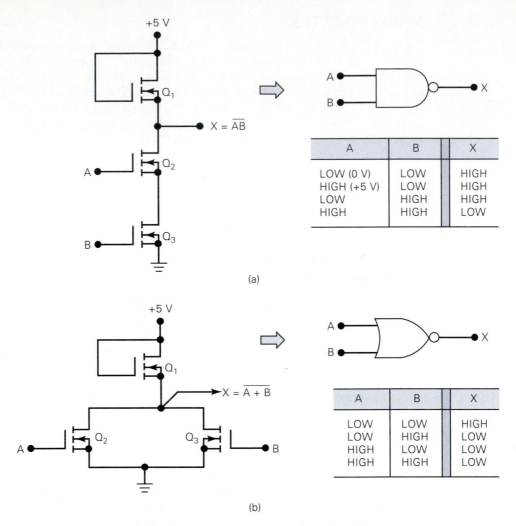

FIGURE 8-34 (a) N-MOS NAND gate; (b) NOR gate.

N-MOS NOR Gate

The NOR gate of Figure 8-34(b) uses Q_2 and Q_3 as parallel switches with Q_1 again acting as a load resistance. When either input A or input B is at +5 V, the corresponding MOSFET is on, forcing the output to be LOW. When both inputs are at 0 V, both Q_2 and Q_3 are off, so that the output goes HIGH. Clearly, this is the NOR operation with $X = \overline{A + B}$.

N-MOS OR gates and AND gates are easily formed by combining the NOR or NAND with INVERTERs.

N-MOS Flip-Flops

Two N-MOS NOR gates or NAND gates can be cross-coupled to form simple latches (see Figures 5-3 and 5-10). Additional gating circuitry can be added to convert the basic latch to a clocked J-K or clocked D flip-flop (see Figure 5-23). N-MOS flip-flops are important in some types of computer memory circuits.

8-13 CHARACTERISTICS OF MOS LOGIC

Compared with the bipolar logic families, the N-MOS and P-MOS logic families are slower in operating speed; require much less power; have a better noise margin, a greater supply voltage range, and a higher fan-out; and, as was mentioned earlier, require much less "real estate" (chip area).

Operating Speed

A typical N-MOS NAND gate has a propagation delay time of 50 ns. This is due to *two* factors: (1) the relatively high output resistance (100 kΩ) in the HIGH state and (2) the capacitive loading presented by the inputs of the logic circuits being driven. MOS logic inputs have very high input resistance ($>10^{12}$ Ω), and they have a reasonably high input capacitance (MOS capacitor), typically 2 to 5 picofarads. This combination of large R_{OUT} and large C_{LOAD} serves to increase switching time.

Noise Margin

Typically, N-MOS noise margins are around 1.5 V when operated from $V_{DD} = 5$ V and will be proportionally higher for larger values of V_{DD}.

Fan-Out

Because of the extremely high input resistance at each MOSFET input, one would expect that the fan-out capabilities of MOS logic would be virtually unlimited. This is essentially true for dc or low-frequency operation. However, for frequencies greater than around 100 kHz, the gate input capacitances cause a deterioration in switching time which increases in proportion to the number of loads being driven. Even so, MOS logic can easily operate at a fan-out of 50, which is much better than most of the bipolar families.

Power Drain

MOS logic circuits draw small amounts of power because of the relatively large resistances being used. To illustrate, we can calculate the power dissipation of the IN-VERTER of Figure 8-33 for its two operating states.

1. $V_{IN} = 0$ V: $R_{ON(Q1)} = 100$ kΩ; $R_{OFF(Q2)} = 10^{10}$ Ω. Therefore, I_D (current from V_{DD} supply) ≈ 0.5 nA, and $P_D = 5$ V × 0.5 nA = 2.5 nW.

2. $V_{IN} = +5$ V: $R_{ON(Q1)} = 100$ kΩ; $R_{ON(Q2)} = 1$ kΩ. Therefore, $I_D = 5$ V/101 kΩ ≈ 50 μA, and $P_D = 5$ V × 50 μA = 0.25 mW.

This gives an *average* P_D of a little over 0.1 mW for the INVERTER. The low power drain of MOS logic makes it suitable for LSI and VLSI, where many gates, FFs, and other circuits can be on one chip without causing overheating that can damage the chip.

Process Complexity

MOS logic is the simplest logic family to fabricate since it uses only one basic element, an N-MOS (or a P-MOS) transistor. It requires no other elements, such as resistors or diodes. This characteristic, together with its lower P_D, makes it ideally suited for LSI (large memories, calculator chips, microprocessors), and this is where MOS logic has made its greatest impact in the digital field. The operating speed of P-MOS and N-MOS is not comparable with that of TTL, and so very little has been done with them in SSI and MSI applications. In fact, there are very few MOS logic circuits in the SSI or MSI categories (gates, FFs, and counters, for instance). CMOS, however, is competitive in the MSI area, which was until recently dominated by TTL.

Static Sensitivity

All electronic devices, to varying degrees, are sensitive to damage by static electricity. The human body is a great storehouse of electrostatic charges. For example, when you walk across a carpet, a static charge of over 30,000 V can be built up on your body. If you then touch an electronic device, some of this sizable charge can be transferred to the device. The MOS logic families (and all MOSFETs) are especially susceptible to static-charge damage. All of this potential difference (static charge) applied across the thin oxide film overcomes the film's dielectric insulation capability. When it breaks down, the resulting flow of current (discharge) is like a lightning strike, blowing a hole in the oxide layer and permanently damaging the device.

Electrostatic discharge (ESD) is responsible for billions of dollars of damage to electronic equipment annually, and equipment manufacturers have devoted considerable attention to developing special handling procedures for all electronic devices and circuits. Even though most modern ICs have on-chip resistor–diode networks to protect inputs and outputs from the effects of ESD, the following precautions are used by most engineering labs, production facilities, and field service departments:

1. Connect the chassis of all test instruments, soldering-iron tips, and your workbench (if metal) to earth ground (i.e., the round prong in the 120 VAC plug). This prevents the buildup of static charge on these devices that could be transferred to any circuit board or IC that they come in contact with.

2. Connect yourself to earth ground with a special wrist strap. This will allow potentially dangerous charges from your body to be discharged to ground. The wrist strap contains a 1-MΩ resistor that limits current to a nonlethal value should you accidentally touch a "live" voltage while working with the equipment.

3. Keep ICs (especially MOS) in conductive foam or aluminum foil. This will keep all IC pins shorted together so that no dangerous voltages can be developed between any two pins.

4. Avoid touching IC pins, and insert the IC into the circuit immediately after removing it from the protective carrier.

5. Place shorting straps across the edge connectors of PC boards when the boards are being carried or transported. Avoid touching the edge connectors. Store PC boards in conductive plastic or metallic envelopes.

6. Do not leave any unused IC inputs unconnected, because open inputs tend to pick up stray static charges.

Review Questions

1. Describe the relative advantages and disadvantages of N-MOS circuits as compared with TTL.
2. What determines the fan-out limitations of MOS logic?
3. What factors limit the switching speed of N-MOS circuits?
4. What makes MOS circuitry so well suited for LSI?
5. Why are MOS ICs especially sensitive to static charges?
6. List five precautions for handling ICs and circuit boards to minimize static charge damage.

8-14 COMPLEMENTARY MOS LOGIC

The *complementary MOS* (**CMOS**) logic family uses *both* P- and N-channel MOS-FETs in the same circuit to realize several advantages over the P-MOS and N-MOS families. Generally speaking, CMOS is faster and consumes even less power than the other MOS families. These advantages are offset somewhat by the increased complexity of the IC fabrication process and a lower packing density.

CMOS INVERTER

The circuitry for the basic CMOS INVERTER is shown in Figure 8-35. For this diagram and those that follow, the standard symbols for the MOSFETs have been replaced by blocks labeled P and N to denote a P-MOSFET and an N-MOSFET, respectively. This is done simply for convenience in analyzing the circuits. The CMOS INVERTER has two MOSFETs in series in such a way that the P-channel device has its source connected to $+V_{DD}$ (a positive voltage), and the N-channel device has its source connected to ground.* The gates of the two devices are connected together as a common input. The drains of the two devices are connected together as the common output.

The logic levels for CMOS are essentially $+V_{DD}$ for logical 1 and 0 V for logical 0. Consider, first, the case where $V_{IN} = +V_{DD}$. In this situation the gate of Q_1 (P-channel) is at 0 V relative to the source of Q_1. Thus, Q_1 will be in the OFF state with $R_{OFF} \approx 10^{10}$ Ω. The gate of Q_2 (N-channel) will be at $+V_{DD}$ relative to its source. Thus, Q_2 will be on with typically $R_{ON} = 1$ kΩ. The voltage divider between Q_1's R_{OFF} and Q_2's R_{ON} will produce $V_{OUT} \approx 0$ V.

Next, consider the case where $V_{IN} = 0$ V. Q_1 now has its gate at a negative potential relative to its source while Q_2 has $V_{GS} = 0$ V. Thus, Q_1 will be on with $R_{ON} = 1$ kΩ and Q_2 off with $R_{OFF} = 10^{10}$ Ω, producing a V_{OUT} of approximately $+V_{DD}$. These two operating states are summarized in Figure 8-35(b), showing that the circuit does act as a logic INVERTER.

CMOS NAND Gate

Other logic functions can be constructed by modifying the basic INVERTER. Figure 8-36 shows a NAND gate formed by adding a parallel P-channel MOSFET and a series N-channel MOSFET to the basic INVERTER. To analyze this circuit, it helps

---

* Most manufacturers label this terminal V_{SS}.

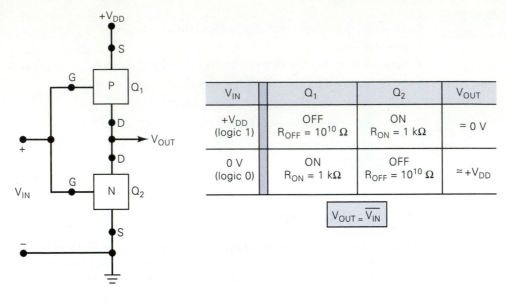

V_{IN}		Q_1	Q_2	V_{OUT}
$+V_{DD}$ (logic 1)		OFF $R_{OFF} = 10^{10}\ \Omega$	ON $R_{ON} = 1\ k\Omega$	$\approx 0\ V$
$0\ V$ (logic 0)		ON $R_{ON} = 1\ k\Omega$	OFF $R_{OFF} = 10^{10}\ \Omega$	$\approx +V_{DD}$

$$V_{OUT} = \overline{V_{IN}}$$

FIGURE 8-35   Basic CMOS INVERTER.

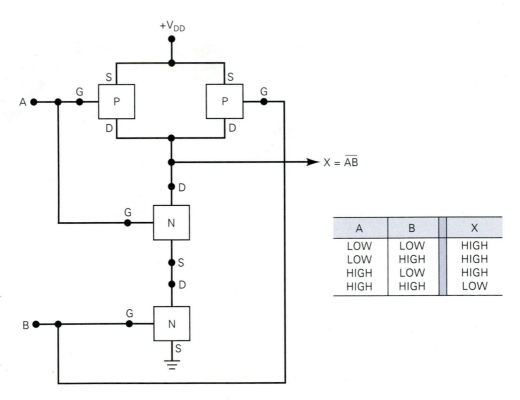

A	B		X
LOW	LOW		HIGH
LOW	HIGH		HIGH
HIGH	LOW		HIGH
HIGH	HIGH		LOW

FIGURE 8-36   CMOS NAND gate.

to realize that a 0-V input turns on its corresponding P-MOSFET and turns off its corresponding N-MOSFET, and vice versa for a $+V_{DD}$ input. Thus, it can be seen that the only time a LOW output will occur is when inputs A and B are both HIGH ($+V_{DD}$) to turn on both N-MOSFETs, thereby providing a low resistance from the output terminal to ground. For all other input conditions, at least one P-MOSFET will be on while at least one N-MOSFET will be off. This produces a HIGH output.

CMOS NOR Gate

A CMOS NOR gate is formed by adding a series P-MOSFET and a parallel N-MOS-FET to the basic INVERTER as shown in Figure 8-37. Once again this circuit can be analyzed by realizing that a LOW at any input turns on its corresponding P-MOSFET and turns off its corresponding N-MOSFET, and vice versa for a HIGH input. It is left to the reader to verify that this circuit operates as a NOR gate.

CMOS AND and OR gates can be formed by combining NANDs and NORs with INVERTERs.

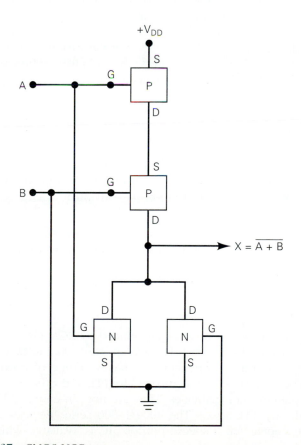

A	B	X
LOW	LOW	HIGH
LOW	HIGH	LOW
HIGH	LOW	LOW
HIGH	HIGH	LOW

$X = \overline{A + B}$

FIGURE 8-37   CMOS NOR gate.

CMOS SET-CLEAR FF

Two CMOS NOR gates or NAND gates can be cross-coupled to form a simple SET-CLEAR latch. Additional gating circuitry is used to convert the basic SET-CLEAR latch to clocked D and J-K flip-flops.

Review Questions

1. How does CMOS internal circuitry differ from N-MOS?
2. How many P-channel MOSFETs are in a CMOS INVERTER?
3. How many MOSFETS are in a three-input NAND gate?

8-15   CMOS SERIES CHARACTERISTICS

The CMOS family of integrated circuits competes directly with TTL in the small- and medium-scale integration (SSI, MSI) areas. As CMOS technology has produced better and better performance characteristics, CMOS has gradually taken over the field that has been dominated by TTL for so long. TTL devices will be around for a long time, but more and more new equipment is using primarily CMOS logic circuits.

CMOS ICs provide not only all of the same logic functions that are available in TTL, but also several special-purpose functions not provided by TTL. Several different CMOS series have been developed over time as manufacturers have sought to improve performance characteristics. Before we look at the various CMOS series, it will be helpful to define a few terms that are used when ICs from different families or series are to be used together or as replacements for one another.

- **Pin-compatible.** Two ICs are pin-compatible when their pin configurations are the same. For example, pin 7 on both ICs is GROUND, pin 1 on both is an input to the first INVERTER, and so on.
- **Functionally equivalent.** Two ICs are functionally equivalent when the logic functions they perform are exactly the same. For example, both contain four two-input NAND gates, or both contain six D flip-flops with positive-edge clock triggering.
- **Electrically compatible.** Two ICs are electrically compatible when they can be connected directly to each other without taking any special measures to ensure proper operation.

4000/14000 Series

The oldest CMOS series is the 4000 series first introduced by RCA, and its functionally equivalent 14000 series from Motorola. Devices in the 4000/14000 series have very low power dissipation and can operate over a wide range of power-supply voltages (3 to 15 V). They are very slow compared to TTL and other CMOS series and have very low output current capabilities. They are not pin-compatible or electrically compatible with any TTL series. The 4000/14000 series devices are rarely used in new designs except when a special-purpose IC is available which is not available in other series.

74C Series

This CMOS series is pin-compatible with and functionally equivalent to TTL devices having the same number. For example, a 74C74 is a dual edge-triggered D flip-flop that has the same pin configuration as the TTL 7474 dual edge-triggered D flip-flop IC. Many but not all functions that are available in TTL are also available in this CMOS series. This makes it possible to replace some TTL circuits by an equivalent CMOS design. The performance characteristics of the 74C series are about the same as those of the 4000 series.

74HC/HCT (High-Speed CMOS)

This is an improved version of the 74C series, which has a tenfold increase in switching speed, comparable to that of the 74LS devices, and a much higher output current capability than that of the 74C. 74HC/HCT ICs are pin-compatible with and functionally equivalent to TTL ICs with the same device number. 74HCT devices are electrically compatible with TTL, but 74HC devices are not. This means, for example, that a 74HCT04 hex-INVERTER chip can replace a 74LS04 chip, and vice versa. It also means that a 74HCT IC can be connected directly to any TTL IC. The 74HC/HCT series has become the most widely used CMOS series.

74AC/ACT (Advanced CMOS)

This series is often referred to as ACL for advanced CMOS logic. The series is functionally equivalent to the various TTL series but is *not* pin-compatible with TTL. The reason for this is that the pin placements on 74AC or 74ACT chips have been chosen to improve noise immunity so that the device inputs are less sensitive to signal changes occurring on other IC pins. 74AC devices are not electrically compatible with TTL; 74ACT devices can be connected directly to TTL. ACL offers advantages over the HC series in noise immunity, propagation delay, and maximum clock speed.

Device numbering for this series differs slightly from TTL, 74C, and 74HC/HCT numbering. It uses a five-digit device number beginning with the digits 11. The following examples illustrate:

$$74\text{AC}11\ \boxed{004} \equiv 74\text{HC}\ \boxed{04}$$
$$74\text{ACT}11\ \boxed{293} \equiv 74\text{HCT}\ \boxed{293}$$

74AHC (Advanced High-Speed CMOS)

This newest series of CMOS devices offers a natural migration path from the HC series to faster, lower-power, low drive applications. The devices in this series are three times faster and can be used as direct replacements for HC series devices. They offer similar noise immunity to HC without the overshoot/undershoot problems often associated with higher drive characteristics required for comparable speed.

BiCMOS Logic

Several IC manufacturers have developed a logic series that combines the best features of bipolar and CMOS logic—called BiCMOS logic. The low-power characteristics of CMOS and the high-speed characteristics of bipolar circuits are integrated to produce an extremely low-power, high-speed logic family. BiCMOS ICs are not available in most SSI and MSI functions, but are limited to functions that are used in microprocessor interfacing and memory applications such as latches, buffers, drivers, and transceivers. The 74BCT (BiCMOS Bus-Interface Technology) series offers 75 percent reduction in power consumption over the 74F family while maintaining similar speed and drive characteristics. Parts in this series are pin-compatible with industry standard TTL parts and operate on standard 5-V logic levels. The 74ABT (Advanced BiCMOS Technology) series is the second generation of BiCMOS bus-interface devices. As computer system speeds increase, this series offers the system designer parts that will appear transparent to (i.e., that will not adversely affect) signals while connecting the high-speed components of a computer. Some parts in this series are designed for 3.3-V low-voltage systems which will be described in a later section.

Power-Supply Voltage

The 4000/14000 series and 74C series devices will operate with V_{DD} values ranging from 3 to 15 V, which makes them very versatile. They can be used in low-voltage battery-operated circuits, in standard 5-V circuits, and in circuits where a higher supply voltage is used to attain the noise margins required for operation in a high-noise environment. The 74HC/HCT and 74AC/ACT series operate over a much narrower range of supply voltages, typically between 2 and 6 V.

Whenever CMOS and TTL are used together, the supply voltage is usually made 5 V, so that a single 5-V power supply can serve as both V_{DD} for CMOS and V_{CC} for TTL. In those situations where the CMOS devices are being operated from a supply voltage other than 5 V, special measures must be taken if the CMOS and TTL devices are to be connected together. We examine these measures later.

Logic Voltage Levels

The input and output voltage levels will be different for the different CMOS series. Table 8-10 lists these voltage values for the various CMOS series as well as those for the TTL series. The values listed in the table assume that all devices are operating from a supply voltage of 5 V and that all device outputs are driving inputs of the same logic family.

Examination of this table discloses some important points. First, note that V_{OL} for the CMOS devices is very close to 0 V, and V_{OH} is very close to 5 V. The reason for this is that the CMOS outputs do not have to source or sink any significant amount of current when they are driving CMOS inputs with their extremely high input resistance (10^{12} Ω). Also note that except for 74HCT and 74ACT, the required input voltage levels are greater for CMOS than for TTL. Recall that 74HCT and 74ACT are designed to be electrically compatible with TTL, so they must be able to accept the same input voltage levels as TTL.

TABLE 8-10 Input/output voltage levels (in volts) with $V_{DD} = V_{CC} = +5$ V.

Parameter	CMOS							TTL			
	4000B	74HC	74HCT	74AC	74ACT	74AHC	74AHCT	74	74LS	74AS	74ALS
$V_{IH}(min)$	3.5	3.5	2.0	3.5	2.0	3.85	2.0	2.0	2.0	2.0	2.0
$V_{IL}(max)$	1.5	1.0	0.8	1.5	0.8	1.65	0.8	0.8	0.8	0.8	0.8
$V_{OH}(min)$	4.95	4.9	4.9	4.9	4.9	4.4	3.15	2.4	2.7	2.7	2.7
$V_{OL}(max)$	0.05	0.1	0.1	0.1	0.1	0.44	0.1	0.4	0.5	0.5	0.4
V_{NH}	1.45	1.4	2.9	1.4	2.9	0.55	1.15	0.4	0.7	0.7	0.7
V_{NL}	1.45	0.9	0.7	1.4	0.7	1.21	0.7	0.4	0.3	0.3	0.4

Noise Margins

The noise margins for each series are also given in Table 8-10. They are calculated using

$$V_{NH} = V_{OH}(min) - V_{IH}(min)$$
$$V_{NL} = V_{IL}(max) - V_{OL}(max)$$

Note that, in general, the CMOS devices have greater noise margins than TTL. The difference would be even greater if the CMOS devices were operated at a supply voltage greater than 5 V.

Power Dissipation

When a CMOS logic circuit is in a static state (not changing), its power dissipation is extremely low. We can see the reason by examining each of the circuits shown in Figures 8-35 to 8-37. Note that regardless of the state of the output, there is always a very high resistance between the V_{DD} terminal and ground because there is always an off MOSFET in the current path. This results in a typical CMOS dc power dissipation of only 2.5 nW per gate when $V_{DD} = 5$ V; even at $V_{DD} = 10$ V this power increases to only 10 nW. With these values for P_D, it is easy to see why CMOS is ideally suited for applications using battery power or battery backup power.

P_D Increases with Frequency

The power dissipation of a CMOS IC will be very low as long as it is in a dc condition. Unfortunately, P_D will increase in proportion to the frequency at which the circuits are switching states. For example, a CMOS NAND gate that has $P_D = 10$ nW under dc conditions will have $P_D = 0.1$ mW at a frequency of 100 kpps, and 1 mW at 1 MHz. The reason for this dependence on frequency is illustrated in Figure 8-38.

Each time a CMOS output switches from LOW to HIGH, a transient charging current must be supplied to the load capacitance. This capacitance consists of the combined input capacitances of any loads being driven and the device's own out-

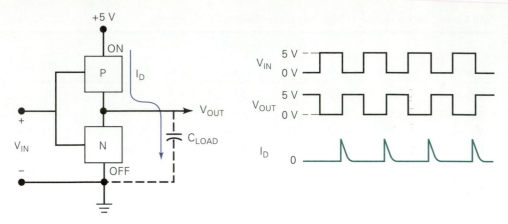

FIGURE 8-38 Current spikes are drawn from the V_{DD} supply each time the output switches from LOW to HIGH. This is due mainly to the charging current of the load capacitance.

put capacitance. These narrow spikes of current are supplied by V_{DD} and can have a typical amplitude of 5 mA and a duration of 20 to 30 ns. Clearly, as the switching frequency increases, there will be more of these current spikes occurring per second, and the average current drawn from V_{DD} will increase. Even with very low capacitive loads, there is a brief point in the transition from LOW to HIGH or HIGH to LOW when the two output transistors are partially turned on. This effectively lowers the resistance from the supply to ground, causing a current spike as well.

Thus, at higher frequencies, CMOS begins to lose some of its advantage over other logic families. As a general rule, a CMOS gate will have the same average P_D as a 74LS gate at frequencies near 2 to 3 MHz. For MSI chips, the situation is somewhat more complex than stated here, and a logic designer must do a detailed analysis to determine whether or not CMOS has a power-dissipation advantage at a particular frequency of operation.

Fan-Out

Like N-MOS and P-MOS, CMOS inputs have an extremely large resistance (10^{12} Ω) that draws essentially no current from the signal source. Each CMOS input, however, typically presents a 5-pF load to ground. This input capacitance limits the number of CMOS inputs that one CMOS output can drive (see Figure 8-39). The CMOS output must charge and discharge the parallel combination of all of the input capacitances, so that the output switching time will be increased in proportion to the number of loads being driven. Typically, each CMOS load increases the driving circuit's propagation delay by 3 ns. For example, NAND gate 1 in Figure 8-39 might have a t_{PLH} of 25 ns if it were driving no loads; this would increase to 25 ns + 20(3 ns) = 85 ns if it were driving *twenty* loads.

Thus, CMOS fan-out depends on the permissible maximum propagation delay. Typically, CMOS outputs are limited to a fan-out of 50 for low-frequency operation ($\leq$1 MHz). Of course, for higher-frequency operation the fan-out would have to be less.

FIGURE 8-39 Each CMOS input adds to the total load capacitance seen by the driving gate's output.

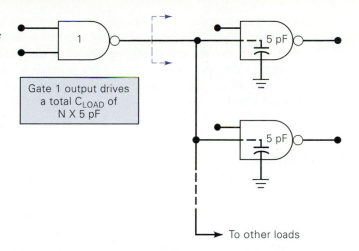

Gate 1 output drives a total C_{LOAD} of N X 5 pF

To other loads

Switching Speed

Although CMOS, like N-MOS and P-MOS, must drive relatively large load capacitances, its switching speed is somewhat faster because of its low output resistance in each state. Recall that an N-MOS output must charge the load capacitance through a relatively large (100-kΩ) resistance. In the CMOS circuit, the output resistance in the HIGH state is the R_{ON} of the P-MOSFET, which is typically 1 kΩ or less. This allows more rapid charging of load capacitance.

A 4000 series NAND gate will typically have an average t_{pd} of 50 ns at $V_{DD} = 5$ V, and 25 ns at $V_{DD} = 10$ V. The reason for the improvement in t_{pd} as V_{DD} is increased is that the R_{ON} on the MOSFETs decreases significantly at higher supply voltages. Thus, it appears that V_{DD} should be made as large as possible for operation at higher frequencies. However, the larger V_{DD} will result in increased power dissipation.

A typical NAND gate in the 74HC or 74HCT series has an average t_{pd} of around 8 ns when operated at $V_{DD} = 5$ V. A 74AC/ACT NAND gate has an average t_{pd} of around 4.7 ns. A 74AHC NAND gate has an average t_{pd} of around 4.3 ns.

Unused Inputs

CMOS inputs should never be left disconnected. All CMOS inputs must be tied either to a fixed voltage level (0 V or V_{DD}) or to another input.

This rule applies even to the inputs of extra unused logic gates on a chip. An unconnected CMOS input is susceptible to noise and static charges that could easily bias both the P-channel and the N-channel MOSFETs in the conductive state, resulting in increased power dissipation and possible overheating.

Static-Charge Susceptibility

The high input resistance of CMOS inputs makes them especially prone to static-charge buildup that can produce voltages large enough to break down the dielectric insulation between the MOSFET gate and channel. Most of the newer CMOS devices are protected against static charge damage by on-chip diode–resistor networks at each input. These diodes are designed to turn on and limit the size of the input voltage to well below any damaging value. While these diodes usually do the job, sometimes they do not turn on quickly enough to prevent the IC from being damaged, and so it is still a good idea to observe the special handling precautions presented in Section 8-13.

Latch-Up

Because of the unavoidable existence of *parasitic* (unwanted) PNP and NPN transistors embedded in the substrate of CMOS ICs, a condition known as **latch-up** can occur under certain circumstances. If these parasitic transistors on a CMOS chip are triggered into conduction, they will latch-up (stay ON permanently), and a large current may flow and destroy the IC. Most modern CMOS ICs are designed with protection circuitry that helps prevent latch-up, but it can still occur when the device's maximum voltage ratings are exceeded. Latch-up can be triggered by high-voltage spikes or ringing at the device inputs and outputs. Clamping diodes can be connected externally to protect against such transients, especially when the ICs are used in industrial environments where high-voltage and/or high-current load switching takes place (motor controllers, relays, etc.). A well-regulated power supply will minimize spikes on the V_{DD} line; if the supply also has current limiting, it will limit current should latch-up occur. Additionally, all unused CMOS inputs must be connected to GROUND or V_{DD} to reduce the chance that stray voltage transients appear at those inputs and trigger the device into the latch-up condition.

Comparison of CMOS and TTL Series

Table 8-11 compares the typical characteristics of the principal series of digital ICs.

TABLE 8-11   Digital IC series comparison*

	4000B	74HC/HCT	74AC/ACT	74AHC/T	74	74LS	74AS	74ALS	ECL
Power dissipation per gate (mW)									
Static	1.0×10^{-3}	2.5×10^{-3}	5.0×10^{-3}	9.0×10^{-5}	10	2	8	1.2	25
At 100 kHz	0.1	0.17	0.08	0.006	10	2	8	1.2	25
Propagation delay (ns)	50	8	4.7	3.7	9	9.5	1.7	4	1
Speed–power (at 100 kHz) (pJ)	5	1.4	0.37	0.02	90	19	13.6	4.8	25
Maximum clock rate (MHz)	12	40	100	130	35	45	200	70	300
Worst-case noise margin (V)	1.5	0.9	0.7	0.55	0.4	0.3	0.3	0.4	0.25

* All CMOS values are for $V_{DD} = 5$ V. Parameters for specific devices may vary.

1. Which CMOS series are pin-compatible with TTL?
2. Which CMOS series are electrically compatible with TTL?
3. Which CMOS series are functionally equivalent to TTL?
4. What logic family combines the best features of CMOS and bipolar logic?
5. What factors determine CMOS fan-out?
6. What precautions should be taken when handling CMOS ICs?
7. Which IC family (CMOS, TTL, ECL) is best suited for battery-powered applications?
8. *True or false:*
   (a) CMOS power drain increases with operating frequency.
   (b) Unused CMOS inputs can be left unconnected.
   (c) TTL is better suited than CMOS for operation in high-noise environments.
   (d) CMOS switching speed increases with operating frequency.
   (e) CMOS switching speed increases with supply voltage.
   (f) The latch-up condition is an advantage of CMOS over TTL.

8-16 LOW-VOLTAGE TECHNOLOGY

IC manufacturers are continually looking for ways to put semiconductor devices (diodes, resistors, transistors, etc.) closer together on a chip, that is, to increase the chip density. This higher density has at least two major benefits. First, it allows more circuits to be packed onto the chip; second, with the circuits closer together, the time for signals to propagate from one circuit to another will decrease, thereby improving overall circuit operating speed. There are also drawbacks to higher chip density. When circuits are placed closer together, the insulating material that isolates one circuit from another is narrower. This decreases the amount of voltage that the device can withstand before dielectric breakdown occurs. Increasing the chip density will increase the overall chip power dissipation, which can raise the chip temperature above the maximum level allowed for reliable operation.

These drawbacks can be neutralized by operating the chip at lower voltage levels. IC manufacturers are doing just that by developing a new line of logic devices that operate from a nominal power-supply voltage of 3.3 V instead of the current 5-V standard. Some standards were adopted as far back as 1984 to define the voltage and current characteristics of low-voltage devices. However, as the applications have evolved, the requirements have also changed, and new standards are currently under development. This low-voltage technology may very well signal the beginning of a gradual transition in the digital equipment field that will eventually find all digital ICs operating from a new 3.3-V standard.

Low-voltage devices are currently designed for applications ranging from electronic games to engineering workstations. The newer microprocessors are 3.3-V devices, and 3.3-V, 64-Mbit, dynamic RAM chips are available in memory modules for computers. The low-voltage operation is particularly valuable in battery-operated equipment, where the number of required battery cells is reduced.

Several 3.3-V logic series are currently available. It is not possible to cover all of the families and series from all manufacturers, so we will describe those currently offered by Texas Instruments.

■ The *74LVC (Low-Voltage CMOS)* series contains the widest assortment of the familiar SSI gates and MSI functions of the 5-V families, along with many bus-interface devices such as buffers, latches, drivers, and so on. This series can handle 5-V logic levels on its inputs, so it is able to convert from 5-V systems to 3-V systems. As long as the current drive is kept low enough to keep the output voltage within acceptable limits, the 74LVC can also drive 5-V TTL inputs. The V_{IH} input requirements of 5-V CMOS parts such as the 74HC/AHC do not allow LVC devices to drive them.

■ The *74ALVC (Advanced Low-Voltage CMOS)* series currently offers the highest performance. The devices in this series are intended primarily for bus-interface applications that use 3.3-V logic only.

■ The *74LV (Low-Voltage)* series offers CMOS technology and many of the common SSI gates and MSI logic functions, along with some popular octal buffers, latches, and flip-flops. It is intended to operate only with other 3.3-V devices.

■ The *74LVT (Low-Voltage BiCMOS Technology)* contains BiCMOS parts that are intended for 8- and 16-bit bus-interface applications. As with the LVC series, the inputs can handle 5-V logic levels and serve as a 5-V to 3-V translator. Since the output levels [V_{OH}(min) and V_{OL}(max)] are equivalent to TTL levels, they are fully electrically compatible with TTL. Table 8-12 compares the various features.

TABLE 8-12   Low-voltage series characteristics.

	LVC	ALVC	LV	LVT
V_{CC} (recommended)	2.0 to 3.6	2.3 to 3.6	2.7 to 3.6	2.7 to 3.6
t_{pd} (ns)	6.5 ns	3 ns	18 ns	4 ns
V_{IH} range (V)	2.0 to 6.5	2.0 to 4.6	2.0 to V_{CC} + 0.5	2.0 to 7
V_{IL}(max) (V)	0.8	0.8	0.8	0.8
I_{OH} (mA)	24	12	6	32 mA
I_{OL} (mA)	24	12	6	64 mA

Other families will no doubt be introduced during this phase of transition. Digital technicians and engineers can no longer assume that every IC in a digital circuit, system, or piece of equipment is operating at 5 V, and they must be prepared to deal with the necessary interfacing considerations in mixed-voltage systems. The interfacing skills you have learned in this chapter will allow you to accomplish this regardless of what develops as we approach the year 2000.

The continued development of LVT promises to bring about a complete revolution from the present 5-V systems, to mixed-voltage systems, and, finally, to pure 3.3-V designs. Although 5-V logic will be with us for quite awhile yet, its days appear to be numbered. To put all of this in perspective, Figure 8-40 shows Texas Instruments' perception of the life cycle of the various logic families.

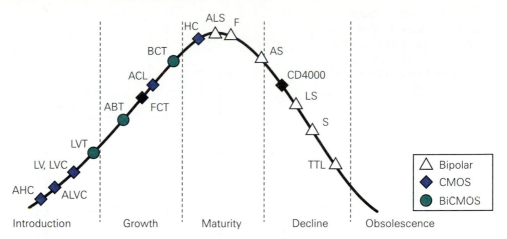

TI remains committed to be the last supplier in the older families.

FIGURE 8-40 Logic family life cycle. (Courtesy of Texas Instruments)

1. What are the two advantages of higher-density ICs?
2. What are the drawbacks?
3. What is the minimum HIGH voltage at a 74LVT input?
4. Which low-voltage series can work only with other low-voltage series ICs?
5. Which low-voltage series is fully electrically compatible with TTL?

8-17 CMOS OPEN-DRAIN AND TRISTATE OUTPUTS

Conventional CMOS outputs should never be connected together.

Figure 8-41 illustrates what can happen when two CMOS INVERTER outputs are shorted together. The output on the left is trying to go to the HIGH state, and its P-channel MOSFET is conducting with $R_{ON} = 1$ kΩ. The other output is trying to go to the LOW state, and its N-channel MOSFET is conducting with $R_{ON} = 1$ kΩ. The common output terminal X will be at a voltage of approximately $V_{DD}/2$ because of the voltage-divider action between the two 1-kΩ resistances.

This voltage is in the indeterminate range for most CMOS series (see Table 8-10) and is therefore unacceptable for driving other devices. Furthermore, the current through the two conducting MOSFETs will be much greater than normal, especially at higher values of V_{DD}, and it can damage the ICs.

It is relatively easy to recognize when two CMOS outputs have been unintentionally wired or shorted together because the signals at the outputs will have three different levels: (1) HIGH when both outputs are trying to be HIGH, (2) LOW when both are trying to be LOW, and (3) approximately $V_{DD}/2$ when the outputs are trying to be at different levels. This is illustrated in Figure 8-42.

FIGURE 8-41 When CMOS outputs are shorted together, the common output terminal will be approximately $V_{DD}/2$ if the outputs are trying to be at different levels.

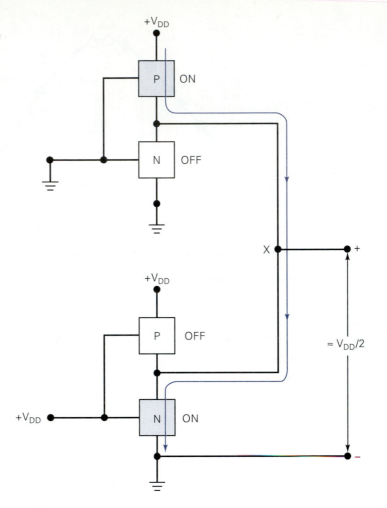

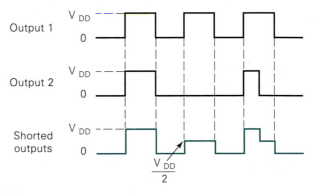

FIGURE 8-42 If two ordinary CMOS outputs are shorted together, the shorted outputs will be at approximately $V_{DD}/2$ when the outputs are trying to be different.

Open-Drain Outputs

Some CMOS devices are available with open-drain outputs that are the counterpart to TTL open-collector outputs. In these devices, the output stage consists only of an N-channel MOSFET whose drain is unconnected since the upper P-channel MOS-FET has been eliminated. An external pull-up resistor is needed to produce a HIGH-state voltage level. Like open-collector outputs, open-drain outputs can be wired-

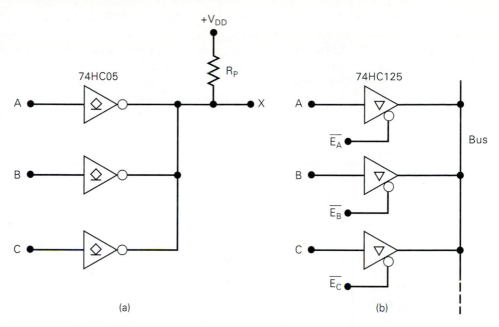

FIGURE 8-43 (a) CMOS open-drain devices in wired-AND connection; (b) CMOS tristate outputs in bus arrangement.

ANDed. Figure 8-43(a) shows three 74HC05 open-drain INVERTERs connected in a wired-AND arrangement.

Tristate Outputs

Several CMOS ICs have tristate outputs whose operation is similar to TTL tristate outputs. Everything we said about tristate TTL can be applied to CMOS tristate. CMOS tristate outputs can be connected together in a bus arrangement provided that only one output is enabled at one time. Figure 8-43(b) shows three 74HC125 tristate buffers connected in a bus arrangement.

Review Questions

1. What is the clue that two conventional CMOS outputs are shorted together?
2. What is an open-drain output?

8-18 CMOS TRANSMISSION GATE (BILATERAL SWITCH)

A special CMOS circuit that has no TTL or ECL counterpart is the **transmission gate** or **bilateral switch,** which acts essentially as a single-pole, single-throw switch controlled by an input logic level. This transmission gate will pass signals in both directions and is useful for digital and analog applications.

Figure 8-44(a) is the basic arrangement for the bilateral switch. It consists of a P-MOSFET and an N-MOSFET in parallel so that both polarities of input voltage can be switched. The CONTROL input and its inverse are used to turn the switch on (closed) and off (open). When the CONTROL is HIGH, both MOSFETs are turned on and the switch is closed. When CONTROL is LOW, both MOSFETs are turned off and the switch is open. Ideally, this circuit operates like an electromechanical relay. In practice, however, it is not a perfect short circuit when the switch is closed; the switch resistance R_{ON} is typically 200 Ω. In the open state, the switch resistance is very large, typically 10^{12} Ω, which for most purposes is an open circuit. The symbol in Figure 8-44(b) is used to represent the bilateral switch.

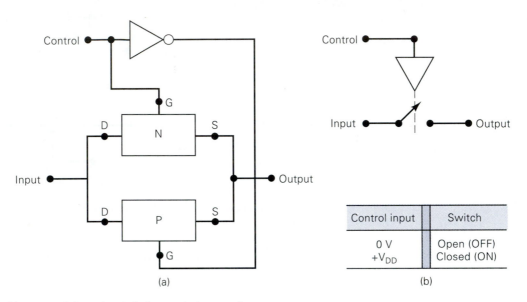

Control input	Switch
0 V	Open (OFF)
+V_{DD}	Closed (ON)

(a)   (b)

FIGURE 8-44   CMOS bilateral switch (transmission gate).

This circuit is called a *bilateral* switch because the input and output terminals can be interchanged. The signals applied to the switch input can be either digital or analog signals, provided that they stay within the limits of 0 to V_{DD} volts.

Figure 8-45(a) shows the traditional logic diagram for a 4016 quad bilateral switch IC, which is also available in the 74HC series as a 74HC4016. The IC contains four bilateral switches that operate as described above. Each switch is independently controlled by its own control input. For example, the ON/OFF status of the top switch is controlled by input CONT$_A$. Since the switches are bidirectional, either switch terminal can serve as input or output, as the labeling indicates.

The IEEE/ANSI symbol for this IC is shown in Figure 8-45(b). Each small rectangle contains one bilateral switch, but, as is customary, only the top rectangle is labeled with the internal IEEE dependency notation. In the top rectangle, the control input is labeled as X1. The "X" is the symbol used to denote a control input that controls the bidirectional transmission between like-numbered input/output terminals. The "1" in the label X1 indicates that this control input controls the transmission between the terminals with the internal label 1. Outside the rectangle, a double-ended arrow is shown on the switch terminals to denote their bidirectional operation. The "horseshoe" is used to indicate that these terminals can handle analog signals and are not restricted to digital levels.

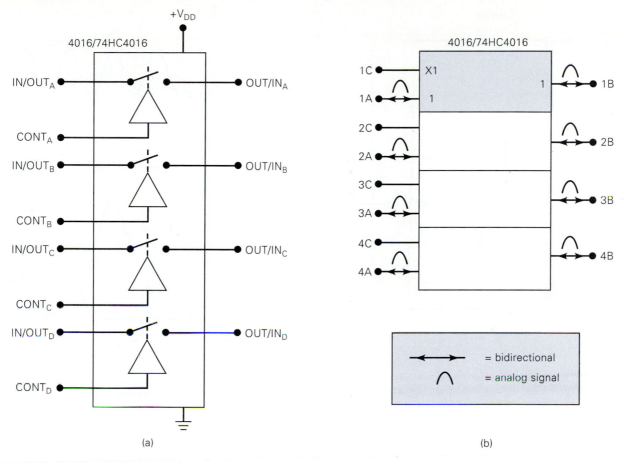

FIGURE 8-45 The 4016/74HC4016 quad bilateral switch: (a) traditional logic symbol; (b) IEEE/ANSI symbol.

EXAMPLE 8-12

Describe the operation of the circuit of Figure 8-46.

Solution

Here two of the bilateral switches are connected so that a common analog input signal can be switched to either output X or output Y, depending on the logic state of the OUTPUT SELECT input. When OUTPUT SELECT is LOW, the upper switch is closed and the lower one is open so that V_{IN} is connected to output X. When OUTPUT SELECT is HIGH, the upper switch is open and the lower one is closed so that V_{IN} is connected to output Y. Figure 8-46(b) shows some typical waveforms. Note that for proper operation, V_{IN} must be within the range 0 V to $+V_{DD}$.

The 4016/74HC4016 bilateral switch can switch only input voltages that lie between 0 V and V_{DD}, and so it could not be used for signals that were both positive and negative relative to ground. The 4316 and 74HC4316 ICs are quad bilateral switches that can switch *bipolar* analog signals. These devices have a second power-supply terminal called V_{EE}, which can be made negative with respect to ground. This permits input signals that can range from V_{EE} to V_{DD}. For example,

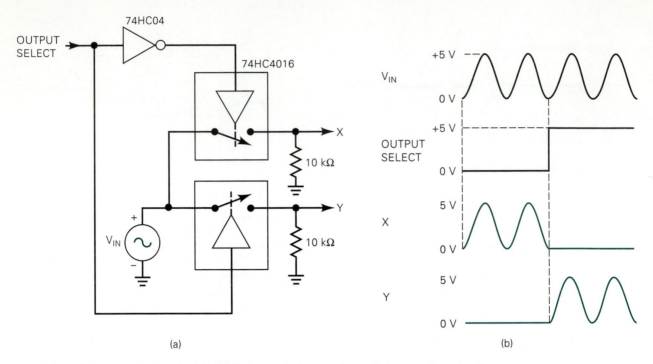

(a)

(b)

FIGURE 8-46   Example 8-12: 74HC4016 bilateral switches used to switch an analog signal to two different outputs.

with $V_{EE} = -5$ V and $V_{DD} = +5$ V, the analog input signal can be anywhere from -5 V to $+5$ V.

Review Questions

1. Describe the operation of a CMOS bilateral switch.
2. *True or false:* There is no TTL bilateral switch.

8-19   IC INTERFACING

Interfacing means connecting the output(s) of one circuit or system to the input(s) of another circuit or system that has different electrical characteristics. Often a direct connection cannot be made because of the difference in the electrical characteristics of the *driver* circuit that is providing the output signal and the *load* circuit that is receiving the signal.

An *interface circuit* is a circuit connected between the driver and the load; its function is to take the driver output signal and condition it so that it is compatible with requirements of the load.

In the following sections we will address the problems involved in interfacing devices from one logic family to those of a different logic family. This type of interfacing occurs quite often in the more complex digital systems, where designers utilize different logic families for different parts of the system in order to take advantage of the strong points of each family. For example, high-speed TTL (74AS, 74S) might be used in those parts of the system that are operating at the highest frequency, 74HCT in the slower parts of the system, and N-MOS for the LSI and VLSI parts of the system.

ICs from the same logic series are designed to be connected together without any special considerations, provided that the fan-out limitation of each output is not exceeded. When you connect the output of an IC to the input of an IC from a different logic family or a different series within the same logic family, you generally must be concerned with the voltage and current parameters of the two devices. This usually involves checking the device data sheets for values of input and output current/voltage parameters. Table 8-10, which we have been using, has the input/output voltage parameters for the various IC series. These values will generally be valid for most devices in the series indicated. Table 8-13 lists the input/output current values for *standard* devices in the various CMOS and TTL series, that is, for ICs with no special input or output circuitry. These values are not valid for devices such as buffers which have greater output current capability, or for ICs whose external inputs are internally connected to more than one gate on the chip. We use these two tables in the following sections to demonstrate the ideas and procedures for IC interfacing, but it should be understood that, in practice, it is best to consult individual IC data sheets to get the actual voltage and current values.

TABLE 8-13 Input/output currents for standard devices with a supply voltage of 5 V.

Parameter	CMOS				TTL				
	4000B	74HC/HCT	74AC/ACT	74AHC/AHCT	74	74LS	74AS	74ALS	74F
I_{IH}(max)	1 μA	1 μA	1 μA	1 μA	40 μA	20 μA	200 μA	20 μA	20 μA
I_{IL}(max)	1 μA	1 μA	1 μA	1 μA	1.6 mA	0.4 mA	2 mA	100 mA	0.6 mA
I_{OH}(max)	0.4 mA	4 mA	24 mA	8 mA	0.4 mA	0.4 mA	2 mA	400 mA	1.0 mA
I_{OL}(max)	0.4 mA	4 mA	24 mA	8 mA	16 mA	8 mA	20 mA	8 mA	20 mA

8-20 TTL DRIVING CMOS

When interfacing different types of ICs, we must check that the driving device can meet the current and voltage requirements of the load device. Examination of Table 8-13 indicates that the input current values for CMOS are extremely low compared with the output current capabilities of any TTL series. Thus, TTL has no problem meeting the CMOS input current requirements.

There is a problem, however, when we compare the TTL output voltages with the CMOS input voltage requirements. Table 8-10 shows that V_{OH}(min) of every TTL series is too low when compared with the V_{IH}(min) requirement of the 4000B, 74HC, and 74AC series. For these situations, something must be done to raise the TTL output voltage to an acceptable level for CMOS.

The most common solution to this interface problem is shown in Figure 8-47, where the TTL output is connected to +5 V with a pull-up resistor. The presence of the pull-up resistor will cause the TTL output to rise to approximately 5 V in the

FIGURE 8-47 External pull-up resistor is used when TTL drives CMOS.

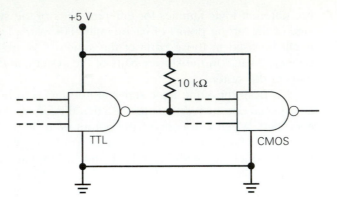

HIGH state, thereby providing an adequate CMOS input voltage level. This pull-up resistor is not required if the CMOS device is a 74HCT or a 74ACT because these series are designed to accept TTL outputs directly as Table 8-10 shows.

TTL Driving High-Voltage CMOS

If the CMOS IC is operating with V_{DD} greater than 5 V, the situation becomes somewhat more difficult. For example, with $V_{DD} = 10$ V, the CMOS input requires $V_{IH}(\text{min}) = 7$ V. The outputs of many TTL devices cannot be operated at more than 5 V, and so a pull-up resistor connected to +10 V is prohibited. The LS-TTL series from certain manufacturers (e.g., Fairchild) can operate with an output pull-up to 10 V. In general, the device's data sheet should be checked before using a pull-up to more than 5 V.

When the TTL output cannot be pulled up to V_{DD}, there are some alternatives. One common solution is shown in Figure 8-48, where a 7407 open-collector buffer is used as the interface between a TTL totem-pole output and CMOS operating at $V_{DD} > 5$ V. The 7407 is the noninverting counterpart of the 7406 and has an output voltage rating of 30 V.

FIGURE 8-48 A 7407 open-collector buffer can be used to interface TTL to high-voltage CMOS.

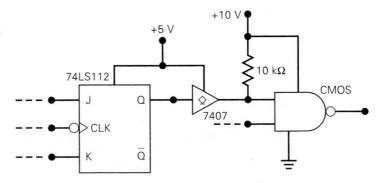

Another solution is to utilize a **voltage level-translator** circuit such as the 40104. This is a CMOS chip that is designed to take a low-voltage input (e.g., from TTL) and translate it to a high-voltage output for CMOS.

1. What must be done to interface a standard TTL output to a 74AC or a 74HC input? Assume that $V_{DD} = +5$ V.
2. What are the various ways to interface TTL to high-voltage CMOS?

8-21 CMOS DRIVING TTL

Before we consider the problem of interfacing CMOS outputs to TTL inputs, it will be helpful to review the CMOS output characteristics for the two logic states.

Figure 8-49(a) shows the equivalent output circuit in the HIGH state. The R_{ON} of the P-MOSFET connects the output terminal to V_{DD} (remember, the N-MOSFET is off). Thus, the CMOS output circuit acts like a V_{DD} source with a source resistance of R_{ON}. The value of R_{ON} typically ranges from 100 to 1000 Ω.

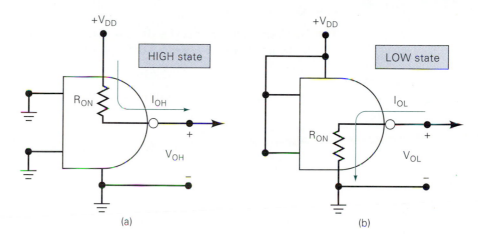

FIGURE 8-49 Equivalent CMOS output circuits for both logic states.

Figure 8-49(b) shows the equivalent output circuit in the LOW state. The R_{ON} of the N-MOSFET connects the output terminal to ground (remember, the P-MOSFET is off). Thus, the CMOS output acts as a low resistance to ground; that is, it acts as a current sink.

CMOS Driving TTL in the HIGH State

Table 8-10 shows that CMOS outputs can easily supply enough voltage (V_{OH}) to satisfy the TTL input requirement in the HIGH state (V_{IH}). Table 8-13 shows that CMOS outputs can supply more than enough current (I_{OH}) to meet the TTL input current requirements (I_{IH}). Thus, no special consideration is needed for the HIGH state.

CMOS Driving TTL in the LOW State

Table 8-13 shows that TTL inputs have a relatively high input current in the LOW state, ranging from 100 μA to 2 mA. The 74HC and 74HCT series can sink up to 4 mA, and so they would have no trouble driving a *single* TTL load of any series. The

4000B series, however, is much more limited. Its low I_{OL} capability is not sufficient to drive even one input of the 74 or 74AS series. The 74AHC series has output drive comparable to that of the 74LS series.

EXAMPLE 8-13

How many 74LS inputs can be driven by a 74HC output? Repeat for a 4000B output.

Solution

The 74LS series has $I_{IL}(\text{max}) = 0.4$ mA. The 74HC can sink up to $I_{OL}(\text{max}) = 4$ mA. Thus, the 74HC can drive *ten* 74LS loads (4 mA/0.4 mA = 10).

The 4000B can sink only 0.4 mA, and so it can drive only *one* 74LS input.

EXAMPLE 8-14

How many 74ALS inputs can be driven by a 74HC output? Repeat for 74AS inputs.

Solution

The 74ALS series has $I_{IL}(\text{max}) = 100$ μA. Thus, the 74HC can drive *forty* 74ALS inputs (4 mA/100 μA = 40). A 74HC can drive only two 74AS inputs (4 mA/2 mA = 2).

EXAMPLE 8-15

What's wrong with the circuit in Figure 8-50(a)?

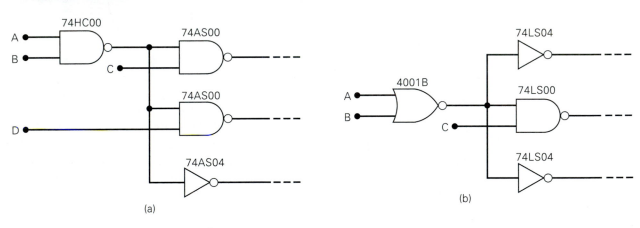

(a)

(b)

FIGURE 8-50   Examples 8-15 and 8-16.

Solution

The 74HC00 can sink 4 mA, but the three 74AS inputs require 3 × 2 mA = 6 mA.

EXAMPLE 8-16

What's wrong with the circuit in Figure 8-50(b)?

Solution

The 4001B NOR gate can sink 0.4 mA, but the three 74LS inputs require 3 × 0.4 mA = 1.2 mA.

Situations like those in Figure 8-50 can occur when older equipment is being interfaced to newer equipment or when several digital modules are being combined to implement a system. The simplest solution to the case of Figure 8-50(a) is to replace the 74HC00 gate with a 74AHC00. If the device is already soldered to a board or if a higher drive device is not available in a pin-compatible package as in Figure 8-50(b), then some type of interface circuit is necessary. The interface circuit should have a low input current requirement and a sufficiently high output current rating to drive the loads. Figure 8-51 shows a possible interface for the case of Figure 8-50(b). In Figure 8-51 the 74LS125 is a permanently enabled, noninverting, tristate buffer which can be driven by the 4001B. Its output can easily drive the 74LS loads. In this circuit, the interface buffer simply passes the 4001B output signal to the 74LS loads with the assurance that a logic "0" will pull LS inputs to their LOW state.

FIGURE 8-51   A buffer used to interface low-current CMOS to 74LS inputs.

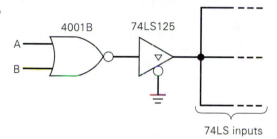

High-Voltage CMOS Driving TTL

Some IC manufacturers have produced several 74LS TTL devices that can withstand input voltages as high as 15 V. These devices can be driven directly from CMOS outputs operating at V_{DD} = 15 V. Most TTL inputs cannot handle more than 7 V before becoming damaged, and so an interface is necessary if they are to be driven from high-voltage CMOS. The interface functions as a voltage-level translator that converts the high-voltage input to a 5-V output that can be connected to TTL. Figure 8-52 shows how the 4050B performs this level translation between 15 and 5 V.

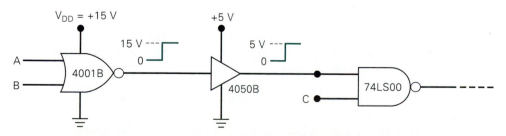

FIGURE 8-52   A 4050B buffer can also serve as a level translator between high-voltage CMOS and TTL.

1. What is the function of an *interface* circuit?
2. *True or false:* All CMOS outputs can drive TTL in the HIGH state.
3. *True or false:* Any CMOS output can drive any single TTL input.
4. Which CMOS series can TTL drive without a pull-up resistor?
5. How many 7400 inputs can be driven from a 74HCT00 output?
6. How is high-voltage CMOS interfaced to TTL?

8-22 ANALOG VOLTAGE COMPARATORS

Another very useful device for interfacing to digital systems is the **analog voltage comparator.** It is especially useful in systems that contain both analog voltages as well as digital components. An analog voltage comparator compares two voltages. If the voltage on the (+) input is greater than the voltage on the (−) input, the output is HIGH. If the voltage on the (−) input is greater than the voltage on the (+) input, the output is LOW. The inputs to a comparator can be thought of as analog inputs, but the output is digital since it will always be either HIGH or LOW. For this reason, the comparator is often referred to as a one-bit analog-to-digital (A/D) converter. We will examine A/D converters in detail in Chapter 10.

An LM339 is an analog linear IC that contains four voltage comparators. The output of each comparator is an open-collector transistor just like an open-collector TTL output. V_{CC} can range from 2 to 36 V but is usually set slightly greater than the analog input voltages that are being compared. A pull-up resistor must be connected from the output to the same supply that the digital circuits use (normally 5 V).

EXAMPLE 8-17

Suppose that an incubator must have an emergency alarm to warn if the temperature exceeds a dangerous level. The temperature-measuring device may be an LM34 that puts out a voltage that is directly proportional to the temperature. The output voltage goes up 10 mV per degree F. The digital system alarm must sound when the temperature exceeds 100°F. Design a circuit to interface the temperature sensor to the digital circuit.

Solution

We need to compare the voltage from the sensor with a fixed threshold voltage. First we must calculate the proper threshold voltage. We want the comparator output to go HIGH when the temperature exceeds 100°F. The voltage out of the LM34 at 100°F will be

$$100°F \cdot 10 \text{ mV/°F} = 1.0 \text{ V}$$

This means that we must set the (−) input pin of the comparator to 1.0 V and connect the LM34 to the (+) input. In order to create a 1.0-V reference voltage, we can use a voltage-divider circuit and choose a bias current of 100 μA. The LM339 input

FIGURE 8-53 A temperature-limit detector using an LM339 analog voltage comparator.

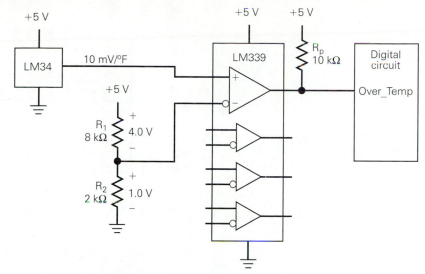

current will be relatively negligible since it will draw less than 1 μA. This means that $R_1 + R_2$ must total 10 kΩ. In this example we can operate everything from a +5 V power supply. Figure 8-53 shows the complete circuit. The calculations are as follows:

$$V_{R2} = V_{CC} \cdot \frac{R_2}{R_1 + R_2}$$

$$R_2 = V_{R2} \cdot (R_1 + R_2)/V_{CC}$$
$$= 1.0 \text{ V}(10 \text{ k}\Omega)/5 \text{ V} = 2 \text{ k}\Omega$$
$$R_1 = 10 \text{ k}\Omega - R_2 = 10 \text{ k}\Omega - 2 \text{ k}\Omega = 8 \text{ k}\Omega$$

Review Questions

1. What causes the output of a comparator to go to the HIGH logic state?
2. What causes the output of a comparator to go to the LOW logic state?
3. Is an LM339 output more similar to a TTL totem-pole or an open-collector output?

8-23 TROUBLESHOOTING

A **logic pulser** is a testing and troubleshooting tool that generates a short-duration pulse when manually actuated, usually by pressing a pushbutton. The logic pulser shown in Figure 8-54 has a needle-shaped tip that is touched to the circuit node that is to be pulsed. The logic pulser is designed so that it senses the existing voltage level at the node and produces a voltage pulse in the opposite direction. In other words, if the node is LOW, the logic pulser produces a narrow positive-going pulse; if the node is HIGH, it produces a narrow negative-going pulse.

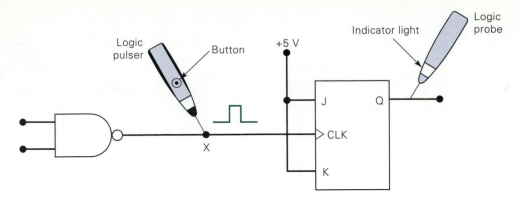

FIGURE 8-54 A logic pulser can inject a pulse at any node that is not shorted directly to ground or V_{CC}.

The logic pulser is used to momentarily change the logic level at a circuit node even though the output of another device may be connected to that same node. In Figure 8-54 the logic pulser is contacting node X, which is also connected to the output of the NAND gate. The logic pulser has a very low output impedance (typically 2 Ω or less), so that it can overcome the NAND gate's output and can change the voltage at the node. The logic pulser, however, cannot produce a voltage pulse at a node that is shorted directly to ground or V_{CC} (e.g., through a solder bridge).

Using Logic Pulser and Probe to Test a Circuit

A logic pulser can be used to manually inject a pulse or a series of pulses into a circuit in order to test the circuit's response. A logic probe is almost always used to monitor the circuit's response to the logic pulser. In Figure 8-54, the J-K flip-flop's toggle operation is being tested by applying pulses from the logic pulser and monitoring Q with the logic probe. This logic pulser/logic probe combination is very useful for checking the operation of a logic device while it is wired into a circuit. Note that the logic pulser is applied to the circuit node *without* disconnecting the output of the NAND gate that is driving that node.

Finding Shorted Nodes

The logic pulser and logic probe can be used to check for nodes that are shorted directly to ground or V_{CC}. When you touch a logic pulser and a logic probe to the same node and press the logic pulser button, the logic probe should indicate the occurrence of a pulse at the node. If the probe indicates a constant LOW, the node is shorted to ground; if the probe indicates a constant HIGH, the node is shorted to V_{CC}.

The Current Tracer

A current tracer is a troubleshooting tool that can detect a *changing* current in a wire or printed-circuit-board trace without breaking the circuit. The current tracer has an insulated tip that contains a magnetic pickup coil. When the tip is placed at a point in the circuit, it senses a changing magnetic field produced by a changing current and causes a small indicator LED to flash. The current tracer does not respond to static current levels, no matter how great the current may be. It responds only to a change in current level.

A current tracer is used with a logic pulser to trace the exact location of shorts to ground or V_{CC}. This is illustrated in Figure 8-55, where node X is shorted to ground through the internal short at gate 2's input. If the logic pulser is touched to X and its button is pressed, no voltage pulse will be detected, because of the short to ground. However, there will be a pulse of current flowing from the pulser's output to ground through the short (I_{sc}). This current pulse can be detected by a current tracer.

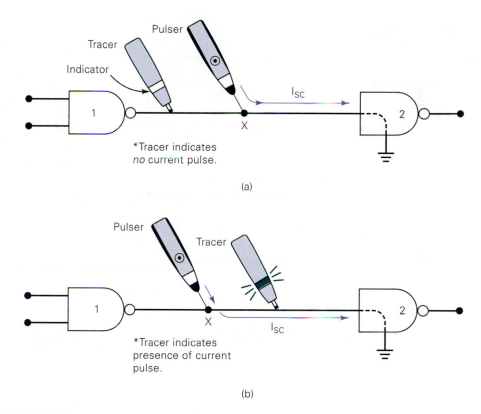

FIGURE 8-55   A logic pulser and a current tracer can be used to trace shorted nodes.

In Figure 8-55(a), the current tracer is placed to the left of X, and the logic pulser is pulsed. The tracer will indicate no current pulse through the path that it is monitoring. In Figure 8-55(b), the tracer is moved to the other side of X. This time when the logic pulser is pulsed, the current tracer will indicate the occurrence of a current pulse through the path that it is monitoring. This proves that the short to ground is inside gate 2's input rather than gate 1's output.

The current tracer/logic pulser combination is very useful in troubleshooting circuits where many open-collector, open-drain, or tristate outputs are connected to a common point that is stuck LOW or HIGH. Any one of the outputs can be producing the fault, and the current tracer/logic pulser technique used above can be employed to track down the faulty output.

1. What is the function of a logic pulser?
2. *True or false:* A logic pulser will produce a voltage pulse at any node.
3. What is the function of a current tracer?
4. *True or false:* A current tracer detects only a changing current.

SUMMARY

1. All digital logic devices are similar in nature but very much different regarding the details of their characteristics. An understanding of the terms that are used to describe these characteristics is important and allows us to compare and contrast the performance of devices. By understanding the capabilities and limitations of each type of device, we can intelligently combine devices to take advantage of each device's strengths in building reliable digital systems.

2. The TTL family of logic devices has been in use for over 30 years. The circuitry uses bipolar transistors. This family offers many SSI logic gates, and MSI devices. Numerous series of similarly numbered devices have been developed as advances in technology have offered improved characteristics.

3. When one is connecting devices together, it is vital to know how many inputs a given output can drive without compromising reliability. This is referred to as *fan-out.*

4. Open-collector outputs can be wired together to implement a "wired-AND" function. Tristate outputs can be wired together to allow numerous devices to share a common data path known as a *bus.* In such a case only one device is allowed to assert a logic level on the bus (i.e., drive the bus) at any one time.

5. The *fastest* logic devices are from a family that uses emitter-coupled logic (ECL). This technology also uses bipolar transistors but is not as widely used as TTL due to inconvenient input/output characteristics.

6. MOSFET transistors can also be used to implement logic functions. The main advantage of MOS logic is lower power and greater packing density.

7. The use of complementary MOSFETs has produced CMOS logic families. CMOS technology has captured the market due to its very low power and competitive speed.

8. The ongoing need to reduce power and size has led to a new line of devices that operate on 3.3 V instead of 5 V.

9. Logic devices that use various technologies cannot always be directly connected together and operate reliably. The voltage and current characteristics of inputs and outputs must be considered and precautions taken to ensure proper operation.

10. CMOS technology allows a digital system to control analog switches called *transmission gates*. These devices can pass or block an analog signal, depending on the digital logic level that controls it.

11. Analog voltage comparators offer another bridge between analog signals and digital systems. These devices compare analog voltages and output a digital logic level based on which voltage is greater. They allow an analog system to control a digital system.

IMPORTANT TERMS

fan-out	pull-up transistor	N-MOS
speed–power product	floating inputs	CMOS
noise immunity	power-supply decoupling	electrostatic discharge
noise margin	open-collector output	(ESD)
current sourcing	wired-AND	latch-up
current sinking	buffer/driver	transmission gate
DIP	tristate	bilateral switch
lead pitch	bus contention	interfacing
surface mount	emitter-coupled logic	voltage-level translator
TTL	MOSFETs	analog voltage comparator
totem pole	P-MOS	logic pulser
pull-down transistor		

PROBLEMS

(Data sheets for the ICs referred to in these problems can be found in the Appendix.)

SECTIONS 8-1 TO 8-3

8-1. Two different logic circuits have the characteristics shown in Table 8-14.
   (a) Which circuit has the best LOW-state dc noise immunity? The best HIGH-state dc noise immunity?
   (b) Which circuit can operate at higher frequencies?
   (c) Which circuit draws the most supply current?

TABLE 8-14

	Circuit A	Circuit B
V_{supply} (V)	6	5
$V_{\text{IH}}(\text{min})$ (V)	1.6	1.8
$V_{\text{IL}}(\text{max})$ (V)	0.9	0.7
$V_{\text{OH}}(\text{min})$ (V)	2.2	2.5
$V_{\text{OL}}(\text{max})$ (V)	0.4	0.3
t_{PLH} (ns)	10	18
t_{PHL} (ns)	8	14
P_{D} (mW)	16	10

8-2. Refer to the Appendix for the IC data sheets, and use *maximum* values to determine $P_D(avg)$, $t_{pd}(avg)$, and the speed–power product for one gate on each of the following TTL ICs. (See Example 8-2 in Section 8-3.)

    (a) 7432   (b) 74S32   (c) 74LS20   (d) 74ALS20   (e) 74AS20

8-3. A certain logic family has the following voltage parameters:

$$V_{IH}(min) = 3.5\ V \qquad V_{IL}(max) = 1.0\ V$$
$$V_{OH}(min) = 4.9\ V \qquad V_{OL}(max) = 0.1\ V$$

    (a) What is the largest positive-going noise spike that can be tolerated?

    (b) What is the largest negative-going noise spike that can be tolerated?

DRILL QUESTION

8-4. For each statement, indicate the term or parameter being described.

    (a) Current at an input when a logic 1 is applied to that input

    (b) Current drawn from the V_{CC} source when all outputs are LOW

    (c) Time required for an output to switch from the 1 to the 0 state

    (d) A common measure used to compare overall performance of different IC families

    (e) The size of voltage spike that can be tolerated on a HIGH input without causing indeterminate operation

    (f) An IC package that does not require holes to be drilled in the printed circuit board

    (g) When a LOW output receives current from the input of the circuit it is driving

    (h) Number of different inputs that an output can safely drive

    (i) Arrangement of output transistors in a standard TTL circuit

    (j) Another term that describes pull-down transistor Q_4

    (k) Range of V_{CC} values allowed for 74 series TTL

    (l) $V_{OH}(min)$ and $V_{IH}(min)$ for 74 series

    (m) $V_{IL}(max)$ and $V_{OL}(max)$ for 74 series

    (n) When a HIGH output supplies current to a load

SECTION 8-4

8-5. (a) From Table 8-6 determine the noise margins when a 74LS device is driving a 74ALS input.

    (b) Repeat part (a) for a 74ALS driving a 74LS.

    (c) What will be the overall noise margin of a logic circuit that uses 74LS and 74ALS circuits in combination?

    (d) A certain logic circuit has $V_{IL}(max) = 450$ mV. Which TTL series can be used with this circuit?

SECTIONS 8-5 AND 8-6

8-6. DRILL QUESTION

    (a) Define *fan-out*.

    (b) In which type of gates do tied-together inputs always count as a single input load in the LOW state?

    (c) Define "floating" inputs.

(d) What causes current spikes in TTL? What undesirable effect can they produce? What can be done to reduce this effect?

(e) When a TTL output drives a TTL input, where does I_{OL} come from? Where does I_{OH} go?

8-7. Refer to the data sheet for the 74LS112 J-K flip-flop.

(a) Determine the HIGH and LOW load current at the J and K inputs.

(b) Determine the HIGH and LOW load current at the clock and clear inputs.

(c) How many 74LS112 clock inputs can the output of one 74LS112 drive?

8-8. Figure 8-56(a) shows a 74LS112 J-K flip-flop whose output is required to drive a total of 8 standard TTL inputs. Since this exceeds the fan-out of the 74LS112, a buffer of some type is needed. Figure 8-56(b) shows one possibility using one of the NAND gates from the 74LS37 quad NAND buffer, which has a much higher fan-out than the 74LS112. Note that $\overline{Q}$ is used since the NAND is acting as an INVERTER. Refer to the data sheet for the 74LS37.

(a) Determine its maximum fan-out to standard TTL.

(b) Determine its maximum sink current in the LOW state.

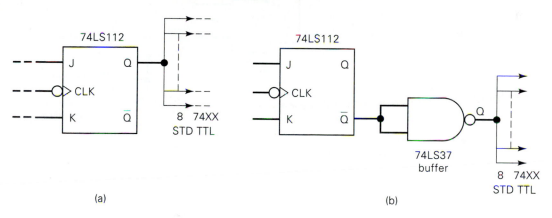

(a)   (b)

FIGURE 8-56   Problems 8-8 and 8-9.

D   **8-9.** Buffer gates are generally more expensive than ordinary gates, and sometimes there are unused ordinary gates available that can be used to solve a loading problem such as that in Figure 8-56(a). Show how 74LS00 NAND gates can be used to solve this problem.

8-10. Refer to the logic diagram of Figure 8-57, where the 74LS86 exclusive-OR output is driving several 74LS20 inputs. Determine whether the fan-out of the 74LS86 is being exceeded, and explain. Repeat using all 74AS devices.

8-11. How long does it take for the output of a typical 74LS04 to change states in response to a positive-going transition at its input?

8-12. For the circuit of Figure 8-57 determine the longest time it will take for a change in the A input to be felt at output W. Use all worst-case conditions and maximum values of gate propagation delays. (*Hint:* Remember that NAND gates are inverting gates.) Repeat using all 74ALS devices.

8-13. (a) Figure 8-58 shows a 74LS193 counter with its active-HIGH master reset input activated by a pushbutton switch. Resistor R is used to hold MR LOW

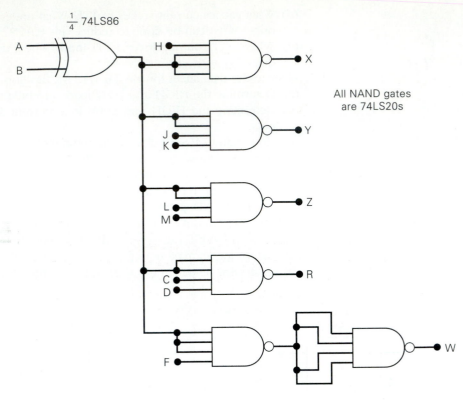

FIGURE 8-57 Problems 8-10 and 8-12.

FIGURE 8-58 Problem 8-13.

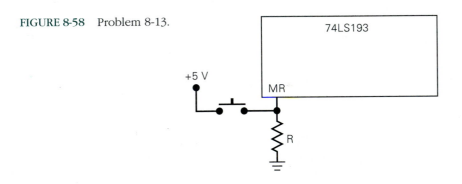

while the switch is open. What is the maximum value that can be used for *R*?

(b) Repeat part (a) for the 74ALS193.

C, T **8-14.** Figure 8-59(a) shows a circuit that is used to convert a 60-Hz since wave to a 60-pps signal that can reliably trigger FFs and counters. This type of circuit might be used in a digital clock.

(a) Explain the circuit operation.

(b) A technician is testing this circuit and observes that the 74LS14 output stays LOW. He checks the waveform at the INVERTER input, and it appears as shown in Figure 8-59(b). Thinking that the INVERTER is faulty, he replaces the chip and observes the same results. What do you think is causing the problem, and how can it be fixed? (*Hint:* Examine the v_x waveform carefully.)

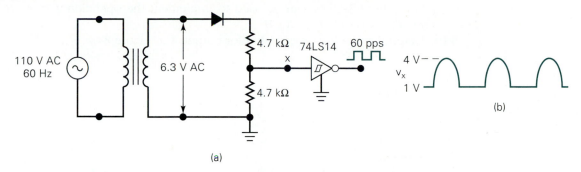

(a)

(b)

FIGURE 8-59   Problem 8-14.

T   **8-15.** For each waveform in Figure 8-60, determine *why* it will *not* reliably trigger a 74LS112 flip-flop at its *CLK* input.

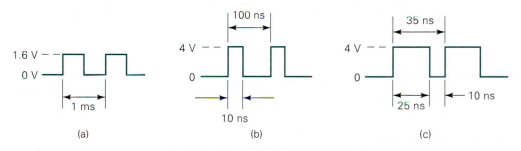

(a)   (b)   (c)

FIGURE 8-60   Problem 8-15.

T   **8-16.** A technician breadboards a logic circuit for testing. As she tests the circuit's operation, she finds that many of the FFs and counters are triggering errati- cally. Like any good technician, she checks the V_{CC} line with a dc meter and reads 4.97 V, which is acceptable for TTL. She then checks all circuit wiring and replaces each IC one by one; but the problem persists. Finally she decides to observe V_{CC} on the scope and sees the waveform shown in Figure 8-61. What is the probable cause of the noise on V_{CC}? What did the technician for- get to include when she breadboarded the circuit?

FIGURE 8-61   Problem 8-16. V_{CC} 4.97 V 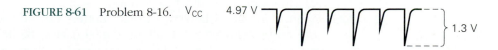 1.3 V

SECTIONS 8-7 AND 8-8

8-17. DRILL QUESTION
  (a) Define *wired-AND*.
  (b) What is a pull-up resistor? Why is it used?

(c) What types of TTL outputs can safely be tied together?

(d) What is bus contention?

D 8-18. The 74LS09 TTL IC is a quad two-input AND with open-collector outputs. Show how 74LS09s can be used to implement the operation $x = A \cdot B \cdot C \cdot D \cdot E \cdot F \cdot G \cdot H \cdot I \cdot J \cdot K \cdot M$.

8-19. Determine the logic expression for output X in Figure 8-62.

FIGURE 8-62 Problem 8-19.

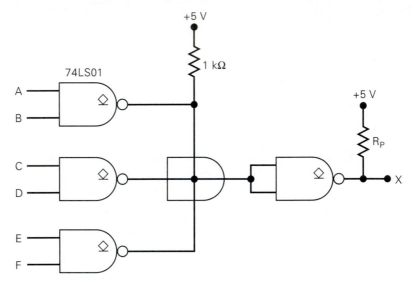

8-20. Which of the following would be most likely to destroy a TTL totem-pole output while it is trying to switch from HIGH to LOW?

(a) Tying the output to +5 V

(b) Tying the output to ground

(c) Applying an input of 7 V

(d) Tying the output to another TTL totem-pole output

8-21. Figure 8-63(a) shows a 7406 open-collector inverting buffer used to control the ON/OFF status of an LED to indicate the state of FF output Q. The LED's nominal specification is $V_F = 2.4$ V at $I_F = 20$ mA, and $I_F(\text{max}) = 30$ mA.

(a) What voltage will appear at the 7406 output when $Q = 0$?

(b) Choose an appropriate value for the series resistor for proper operation.

8-22. In Figure 8-63(b) the 7406 output is used to switch current to a relay.

(a) What voltage will be at the 7406 output when $Q = 0$?

(b) What is the largest current relay that can be used?

(c) How can we modify this circuit to use a 7407?

8-23. Figure 8-64 shows how two tristate buffers can be used to construct a *bi-directional transceiver* that allows digital data to be transmitted in either direction (A to B, or B to A). Describe the circuit operation for the two states of the DIRECTION input.

8-24. The circuit of Figure 8-65 is used to provide the enable inputs for the circuit of Figure 8-27.

(a) Determine which of the data inputs (A, B, or C) will appear on the bus for each combination of inputs x and y.

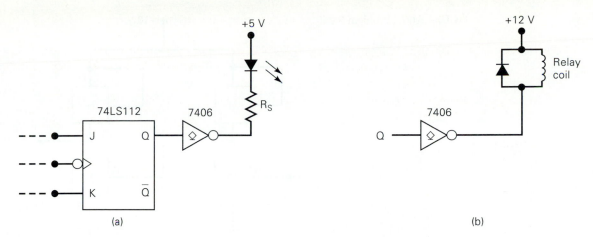

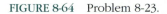

FIGURE 8-63   Problems 8-21 and 8-22.

FIGURE 8-64   Problem 8-23.

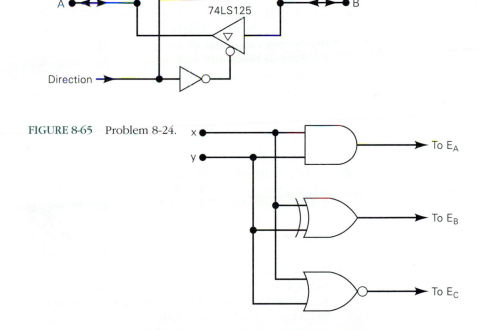

FIGURE 8-65   Problem 8-24.

(b) Explain why the circuit will not work if the NOR is changed to an EX-
NOR.

SECTIONS 8-10 TO 8-13

8-25. The circuit of Figure 8-66 is an N-MOS logic gate. Determine what type of gate
it is. Use $+16$ V $=$ logic 1 and 0 V $=$ logic 0.

8-26. Draw the circuitry for an NMOS OR gate.

FIGURE 8-66   Problem 8-25.

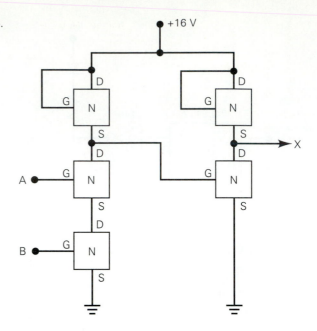

8-27. Which of the following are advantages that N-MOS logic has over TTL?
   (a) Greater packing density
   (b) Greater operating speed
   (c) Greater fan-out
   (d) More suitable for LSI
   (e) Lower P_D
   (f) Complementary outputs
   (g) Greater noise immunity
   (h) Simpler fabrication process
   (i) More SSI and MSI functions
   (j) Lower supply-voltage requirement

SECTIONS 8-14 AND 8-15

8-28. Which of the following are advantages that CMOS generally has over TTL?
   (a) Greater packing density
   (b) Higher speed
   (c) Greater fan-out
   (d) Lower output impedance
   (e) Simpler fabrication process
   (f) More suited for LSI
   (g) Lower P_D (below 1 MHz)
   (h) Transistors as only circuit element
   (i) Lower input capacitance
   (j) Less susceptible to ESD

8-29. Which of the following operating conditions will probably result in the lowest average P_D for a CMOS logic system? Explain.
   (a) $V_{DD} = 5$ V, switching frequency $f_{max} = 1$ MHz
   (b) $V_{DD} = 5$ V, $f_{max} = 10$ kHz
   (c) $V_{DD} = 10$ V, $f_{max} = 10$ kHz

8-30. The output of each INVERTER on a 74LS04 IC is driving two 74HCT08 inputs. The input to each INVERTER is LOW over 99 percent of the time. What is the maximum power that the 74LS04 chip is dissipating?

8-31. Use the values from Table 8-10 to calculate the HIGH-state noise margin when a 74HC gate drives a standard 74LS input.

8-32. What will cause latch-up in a CMOS IC? What might happen in this condition? What precautions should be taken to prevent latch-up?

8-33. Refer to the data sheet for the 74HC20 NAND gate IC in the Appendix. Use maximum values to calculate P_D(avg), t_{pd}(avg), and the speed–power product. Compare with the values calculated in Problem 8-2 for TTL.

SECTIONS 8-17 AND 8-18

8-34. Determine the approximate values of V_{OUT} for both states of the CONTROL input in Figure 8-67.

FIGURE 8-67 Problem 8-34.

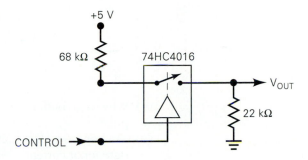

8-35. Determine the waveform at output X in Figure 8-68 for the given input waveforms. Assume that $R_{ON} \approx 200 \ \Omega$ for the bilateral switch.

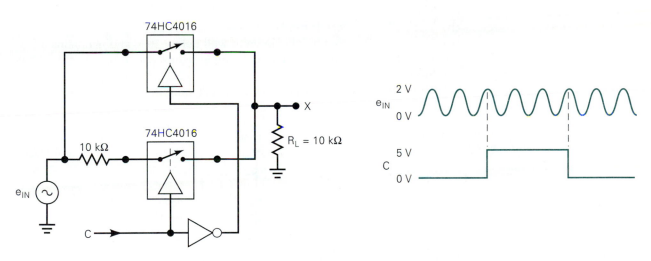

FIGURE 8-68 Problem 8-35.

N, D, C **8-36.** Determine the gain of the op-amp circuit of Figure 8-69 for the two states of the GAIN SELECT input. This circuit shows the basic principle of digitally controlled signal amplification.

SECTIONS 8-19 TO 8-21

8-37. DRILL QUESTION
  (a) Which CMOS series can have its inputs driven directly from a TTL output?
  (b) What is the function of a level translator? When is it used?

FIGURE 8-69   Problem 8-36.

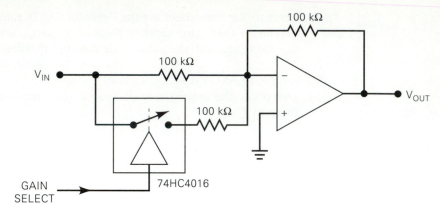

(c) Why is a buffer required between some CMOS outputs and TTL inputs?

(d) *True or false:* Most CMOS outputs have trouble supplying the TTL HIGH-state input current.

T   **8-38.** Refer to Figure 8-70(a), where a 74LS TTL output, Q, is driving a CMOS INVERTER operating at $V_{DD} = 10$ V. The waveforms at Q and X appear as shown in Figure 8-70(b). Which of the following is a possible reason why X stays HIGH?

(a) The 10-V supply is faulty.

(b) The pull-up resistor is too large.

(c) The 74LS112 output breaks down at well below 10 V and maintains a 5.5-V level in the HIGH state. This is in the indeterminate range for the CMOS input.

(d) The CMOS input is loading down the TTL output.

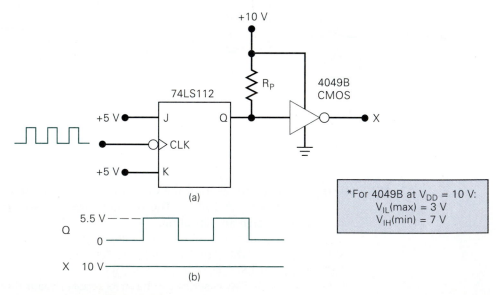

FIGURE 8-70   Problem 8-38.

8-39. (a) Use Table 8-13 to determine how many 74AS inputs can typically be driven by a 4000B output.

(b) Repeat part (a) for a 74HC output.

T 8-40. Figure 8-71 is a logic circuit that was poorly designed. It contains at least eight instances where the characteristics of the ICs have not been properly taken into account. Find as many of these as you can.

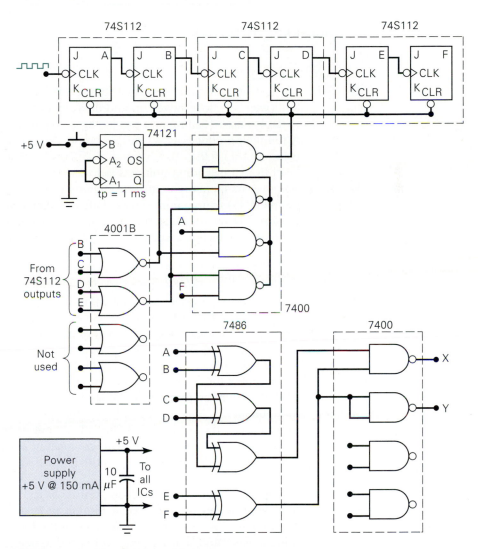

FIGURE 8-71   Problems 8-40 and 8-41.

T 8-41. Repeat Problem 8-40 with the following changes in the circuit:
  ■ Each TTL IC is replaced with its 74LS equivalent.
  ■ The 4001B is replaced with a 74HCT02.

8-42. Use Table 8-13 to explain why the circuit of Figure 8-72 will not work as it is. How can the problem be corrected?

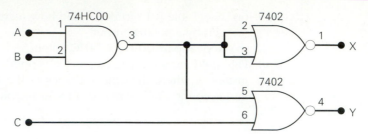

FIGURE 8-72   Problem 8-42.

SECTION 8-22

D   **8-43.** The gas tank on your car has a fuel-level sending unit that works like a potentiometer. A float moves up and down with the gasoline level, changing the variable resistor setting and producing a voltage proportional to the gas level. A full tank produces 12 V, and an empty tank produces 0 V. Design a circuit using an LM339 that turns on the "Fuel Low" indicator lamp when the voltage level from the sending unit gets below 0.5 V.

D   **8-44.** The over-temperature comparator circuit in Figure 8-53 is modified by replacing the LM34 temperature sensor with an LM35 that outputs 10 mV per degree Celsius. The alarm must still be activated (HIGH) when the temperature is over 100°F, which is equal to approximately 38°C. Recalculate the values of R_1 and R_2 to complete the modification.

SECTION 8-23

T   **8-45.** The circuit in Figure 8-73 uses a 74HC05 IC that contains six open-drain INVERTERs. The INVERTERs are connected in a wired-AND arrangement. Using a pulser and a logic probe, it is determined that node X is stuck in the HIGH state. Describe a procedure for using a current tracer to isolate the fault.

T   **8-46.** The circuit of Figure 8-54 has a solder bridge to ground somewhere between the output of the NAND gate and the input of the FF. Describe a procedure for tracking down the location of the solder bridge.

T   **8-47.** In Figure 8-47 a logic probe indicates that the lower end of the pull-up resistor is stuck in the LOW state. Using a logic pulser and a current tracer, a technician detects a current in the wire connecting the TTL output to the resistor. Which of the following is the possible fault?
    (a) R_P is open.
    (b) The TTL gate's current-sinking transistor has a collector–emitter short.
    (c) There is a break in the connection from R_P to the CMOS gate.

T   **8-48.** In Figure 8-47 a logic probe indicates that the lower end of R_P is stuck HIGH. A logic pulser and a current tracer are used to detect a current in the path connecting R_P to the CMOS gate. What is the probable fault?

MICROCOMPUTER APPLICATION

C, N   **8-49.** In Section 5-20, Figure 5-50, we saw how a microprocessor (MPU), under software control, transfers data to an external register. The diagram is repeated in Figure 8-74. Once the data are in the register, they are stored there and used for whatever purpose they are needed. Sometimes, each individual bit in the register has a unique function. For example, in automobile computers each bit could represent the status of a different physical variable being monitored by

FIGURE 8-73 Problem 8-45.

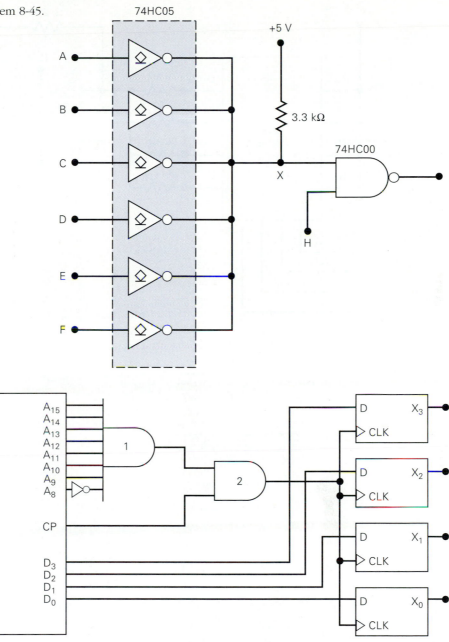

FIGURE 8-74 Problem 8-49.

the MPU. One bit might indicate when the engine temperature is too high. Another bit might signal when oil pressure is too low. In other applications, the bits in the register are used to produce an analog output that can be used to drive devices requiring analog inputs that have many different voltage levels.

Figure 8-75 shows how we can use the MPU to generate an analog voltage by taking the register data from Figure 8-74 and using them to control the inputs to a summing amplifier. Assume that the MPU is executing a program

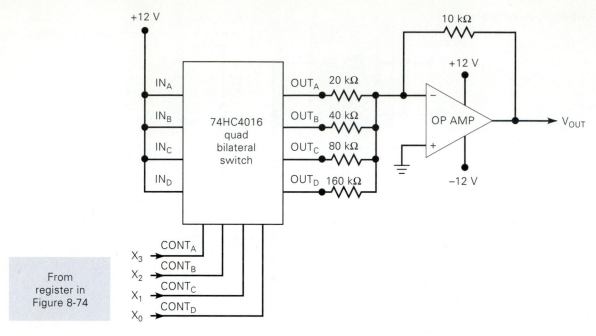

<figure>FIGURE 8-75 Problem 8-49.</figure>

that is transferring a new set of data to the register every 10 μs according to Table 8-15. Sketch the resulting waveform at V_{OUT}.

TABLE 8-15

Time (μs)	MPU Data
0	0000
10	0010
20	0100
30	0111
40	1010
50	1110
60	1111
70	1111
80	1110
90	1100
100	1000

ANSWERS TO SECTION REVIEW QUESTIONS

SECTION 8-1

1. See text. 2. False 3. False; V_{NH} is the difference between V_{OH}(min) and V_{IH}(min). 4. False 5. Current sinking: an output actually receives (sinks) current from the input of the circuit it is driving. Current sourcing: an output supplies (sources) current to the circuit it is driving. 6. DIP 7. J-lead 8. Its leads are bent 9. No

SECTION 8-2

1. True   2. LOW   3. Fast switching times, low power dissipation; large current spike during switching from LOW to HIGH   4. Q_3 5. Q_6 6. No multiple-emitter transistor

SECTION 8-4

1. (a) 74AS   (b) 74S, 74LS   (c) 74H, 74L   (d) 74S, 74LS, 74AS, 74ALS   (e) 74ALS   2. All three can operate at 40 MHz, but the 74ALS193 will use less power.   3. Q_4, Q_5, respectively

SECTION 8-5

1. Q_4's ON-state resistance and V_{OL}(max)   2. 12   3. Its output voltages may not remain in the allowed logic 0 and 1 ranges.   4. Two; five

SECTION 8-6

1. LOW   2. Connect to $+V_{CC}$ through a 1-kΩ resistor; connect to another used input   3. Connect to ground; connect to another used input   4. False; only in the LOW state   5. Connecting small RF capacitors between V_{CC} and ground near each TTL IC to filter out voltage spikes caused by rapid current changes during output transitions from LOW to HIGH

SECTION 8-7

1. When TTL outputs are connected together
2. Damaging current can flow; V_{OL} exceeds V_{OL}(max).
3. Current-sinking transistor Q_4's collector is unconnected (there is no Q_3).   4. To produce a V_{OH} level   5. $\overline{ABCDEF}$ 6. No active pull-up transistor   7. See Figure 8-24.

SECTION 8-8

1. HIGH, LOW, Hi-Z 2. Hi-Z 3. When two or more tristate outputs tied to a common bus are enabled at the same time   4. $E_A = E_B = 0$, $E_C = 1$ 5. See Figure 8-28.

SECTION 8-9

1. (a) True   (b) True   (c) False   (d) True   (e) False   (f) False

SECTION 8-13

1. Advantages: lower power; higher packing density; simple, inexpensive fabrication process. Disadvantages: slower speed; more sensitive to static electricity.
2. Gate input capacitances that cause an increase in load capacitance for each additional load. This total load capacitance increases switching times.   3. Large R_{OUT} and C_{LOAD} 4. High packing density due to its simple circuit structure   5. See text.   6. See text.

SECTION 8-14

1. CMOS uses both P- and N-channel MOSFETs.
2. One   3. Six

SECTION 8-15

1. 74C, HC, HCT, AHC, AHCT   2. 74ACT, HCT, AHCT   3. 74C, HC/HCT, AC/ACT, AHC/AHCT
4. BiCMOS   5. Maximum permissible propagation delay; input capacitance of each load   6. See Section 8-13.   7. CMOS   8. (a) True   (b) False   (c) False   (d) False   (e) True   (f) False

SECTION 8-16

1. More circuits on chip; higher operating speed
2. Can't handle higher voltages: increased power dissipation can overheat the chip.   3. Same as standard TTL: 2.0 V   4. 74ALVC, 74LV   5. 74LVT

SECTION 8-17

1. The common output voltage will be in the indeterminate range.   2. Output stage consists only of an N-channel MOSFET whose drain is unconnected.

SECTION 8-18

1. The logical level at the control input controls the open/closed status of a bidirectional switch that can pass analog signals in either direction.   2. True

SECTION 8-20

1. A pull-up resistor must be connected to +5 V at the TTL output.   2. A high-voltage buffer (7407) or a voltage-level translator (40104) should be connected between TTL output and CMOS input.

SECTION 8-21

1. It takes the output from a driver circuit and conditions it so that it is compatible with the input requirements of the load.   2. True   3. False; for example, the 4000B series cannot sink I_{IL} of a 74 or a 74AS device.   4. 74HCT and ACT   5. Two
6. Through a voltage-level translator such as the 4050B

SECTION 8-22

1. $V^{(+)} > V^{(-)}$ 2. $V^{(-)} > V^{(+)}$ 3. Open-collector

SECTION 8-23

1. It injects a voltage pulse of selected polarity at a node that is not shorted to V_{CC} or ground.   2. False
3. It indicates the occurrence of a current pulse.
4. True

CHAPTER 9

MSI Logic Circuits

■ OUTLINE

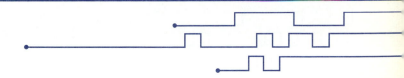

■ OBJECTIVES

Upon completion of this chapter, you will be able to:

- Analyze and use decoders and encoders in various types of circuit applications.
- Compare the advantages and disadvantages of LEDs and LCDs.
- Utilize the observation/analysis technique for troubleshooting digital circuits.
- Understand the operation of multiplexers and demultiplexers by analyzing several circuit applications.
- Compare two binary numbers by using the magnitude comparator circuit.
- Understand the function and operation of code converters.
- Cite the precautions that must be considered when connecting digital circuits using the data bus concept.
- Interpret the notation used on the IEEE/ANSI symbols for various MSI devices.

■ INTRODUCTION

Digital systems obtain binary-coded data and information that are continuously being operated on in some manner. Some of the operations include: (1) *decoding and encoding;* (2) *multiplexing;* (3) *demultiplexing;* (4) *comparison;* (5) *code conversion;* (6) *data busing.* All of these operations and others have been facilitated by the availability of numerous ICs in the MSI (medium-scale-integration) category.

In this chapter we study many of the common types of MSI devices. For each type, we start with a brief discussion of its basic operating principle and then introduce specific ICs. We then show how they can be used alone or in combination with other ICs in various applications.

511

9-1 DECODERS

A **decoder** is a logic circuit that accepts a set of inputs that represents a binary number and activates only the output that corresponds to that input number. In other words, a decoder circuit looks at its inputs, determines which binary number is present there, and activates the one output that corresponds to that number; all other outputs remain inactive. The diagram for a general decoder is shown in Figure 9-1 with N inputs and M outputs. Since each of the N inputs can be 0 or 1, there are 2^N possible input combinations or codes. For each of these input combinations only one of the M outputs will be active (HIGH); all the other outputs are LOW. Many decoders are designed to produce active-LOW outputs, where only the selected output is LOW while all others are HIGH. This would be indicated by the presence of small circles on the output lines in the decoder diagram.

FIGURE 9-1 General decoder diagram.

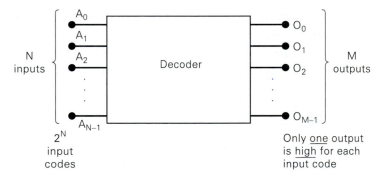

Some decoders do not utilize all of the 2^N possible input codes but only certain ones. For example, a BCD-to-decimal decoder has a four-bit input code and *ten* output lines that correspond to the *ten* BCD code groups 0000 through 1001. Decoders of this type are often designed so that if any of the unused codes are applied to the input, *none* of the outputs will be activated.

In Chapter 7 we saw how decoders are used in conjunction with counters to detect the various states of the counter. In that application it was the FFs in the counter that provided the binary code inputs for the decoder. The same basic decoder circuitry is used no matter where the inputs come from. Figure 9-2 shows the circuitry for a decoder with three inputs and $2^3 = 8$ outputs. It uses all AND gates, and so the

FIGURE 9-2 3-line-to-8-line (or 1-of-8) decoder.

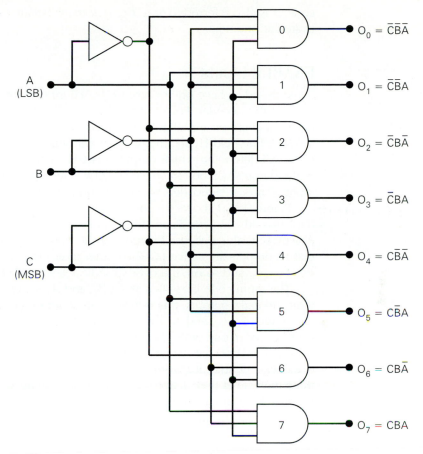

C	B	A	O_0	O_1	O_2	O_3	O_4	O_5	O_6	O_7
0	0	0	1	0	0	0	0	0	0	0
0	0	1	0	1	0	0	0	0	0	0
0	1	0	0	0	1	0	0	0	0	0
0	1	1	0	0	0	1	0	0	0	0
1	0	0	0	0	0	0	1	0	0	0
1	0	1	0	0	0	0	0	1	0	0
1	1	0	0	0	0	0	0	0	1	0
1	1	1	0	0	0	0	0	0	0	1

outputs are active-HIGH. Note that for a given input code, the only output that is active (HIGH) is the one corresponding to the decimal equivalent of the binary input code (e.g., output O_6 goes HIGH only when $CBA = 110_2 = 6_{10}$).

This decoder can be referred to in several ways. It can be called a *3-line-to-8-line decoder*, because it has three input lines and eight output lines. It could also be called a *binary-to-octal decoder* or *converter* because it takes a three-bit binary input code and activates the one of the eight (octal) outputs corresponding to that code. It is also referred to as a *1-of-8 decoder,* because only 1 of the 8 outputs is activated at one time.

ENABLE Inputs

Some decoders have one or more ENABLE inputs that are used to control the operation of the decoder. For example, refer to the decoder in Figure 9-2 and visualize having a common ENABLE line connected to a fourth input of each gate. With this ENABLE line held HIGH, the decoder will function normally, and the *A, B, C* input code will determine which output is HIGH. With ENABLE held LOW, however, *all* of the outputs will be forced to the LOW state regardless of the levels at the *A, B, C* inputs. Thus, the decoder is enabled only if ENABLE is HIGH.

Figure 9-3(a) shows the logic diagram for the 74LS138 decoder as it appears in the Fairchild *TTL Data Book.* By examining this diagram carefully, we can determine exactly how this decoder functions. First, notice that it has NAND gate outputs, so that its outputs are active-LOW. Another indication is the labeling of the outputs as $\overline{O}_7$, $\overline{O}_6$, $\overline{O}_5$, and so on; the overbar indicates active-LOW outputs.

The input code is applied at A_2, A_1, and A_0, where A_2 is the MSB. With three inputs and eight outputs, this is a 3-to-8 decoder or, equivalently, a 1-of-8 decoder.

Inputs $\overline{E}_1$, $\overline{E}_2$, and E_3 are separate enable inputs that are combined in the AND gate. In order to enable the output NAND gates to respond to the input code at $A_2A_1A_0$, this AND gate output must be HIGH. This will occur only when $\overline{E}_1 = \overline{E}_2 = 0$ and $E_3 = 1$. In other words, $\overline{E}_1$ and $\overline{E}_2$ are active-LOW, E_3 is active-HIGH, and all three must be in their active states to activate the decoder outputs. If one or more of the enable inputs is in its inactive state, the AND output will be LOW, which will force all NAND outputs to their inactive HIGH state regardless of the input code. This operation is summarized in the truth table in Figure 9-3(b). Recall that *x* represents the don't-care condition.

The logic symbol for the 74LS138 is shown in Figure 9-3(c). Note how the active-LOW outputs are represented and how the enable inputs are represented. Even though the enable AND gate is shown as external to the decoder block, it is part of the IC's internal circuitry. The 74HC138 is the high-speed CMOS version of this decoder.

EXAMPLE 9-1

Indicate the states of the 74LS138 outputs for each of the following sets of inputs.

(a) $E_3 = \overline{E}_2 = 1$, $\overline{E}_1 = 0$, $A_2 = A_1 = 1$, $A_0 = 0$
(b) $E_3 = 1$, $\overline{E}_2 = \overline{E}_1 = 0$, $A_2 = 0$, $A_1 = A_0 = 1$

Solution

(a) With $\overline{E}_2 = 1$, the decoder is disabled and all of its outputs will be in their inactive HIGH state. This can be determined from the truth table or by following the input levels through the circuit logic.

(b) All of the enable inputs are activated, so that the decoding portion is enabled. It will decode the input code $011_2 = 3_{10}$ to activate output $\overline{O}_3$. Thus, $\overline{O}_3$ will be LOW and all other outputs will be HIGH.

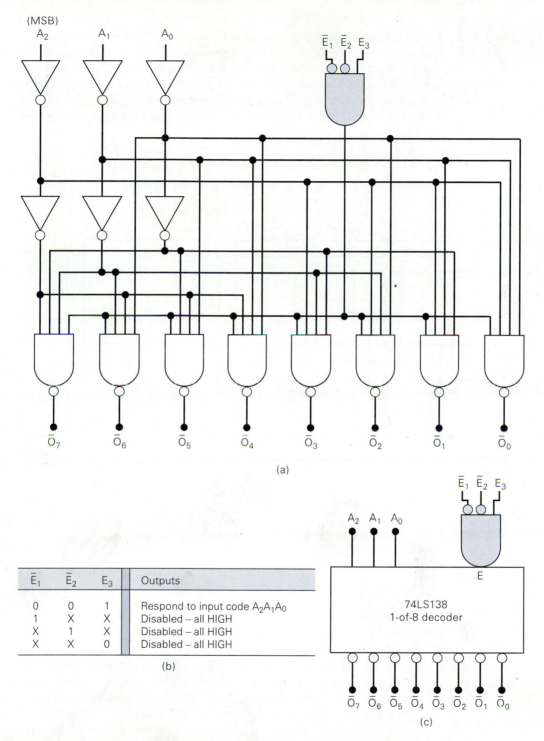

(a)

$\overline{E}_1$	$\overline{E}_2$	E_3	Outputs
0	0	1	Respond to input code $A_2A_1A_0$
1	X	X	Disabled – all HIGH
X	1	X	Disabled – all HIGH
X	X	0	Disabled – all HIGH

(b)

74LS138
1-of-8 decoder

(c)

FIGURE 9-3 (a) Logic diagram for the 74LS138 decoder; (b) truth table; (c) logic symbol. (Courtesy of Fairchild, a Schlumberger company)

Figure 9-4 shows how four 74LS138s and an INVERTER can be arranged to function as a 1-of-32 decoder. The decoders are labeled Z_1 to Z_4 for easy reference, and the eight outputs from each one are combined into 32 outputs. Z_1's outputs are $\overline{O}_0$ to $\overline{O}_7$; Z_2's outputs $\overline{O}_0$ to $\overline{O}_7$ are renamed $\overline{O}_8$ to $\overline{O}_{15}$, respectively; Z_3's outputs are renamed $\overline{O}_{16}$ to $\overline{O}_{23}$; and Z_4's are renamed $\overline{O}_{24}$ to $\overline{O}_{31}$. A five-bit input code $A_4A_3A_2A_1A_0$ will activate only one of these 32 outputs for each of the 32 possible input codes.

(a) Which output will be activated for $A_4A_3A_2A_1A_0$ = 01101?

(b) What range of input codes will activate the Z_4 chip?

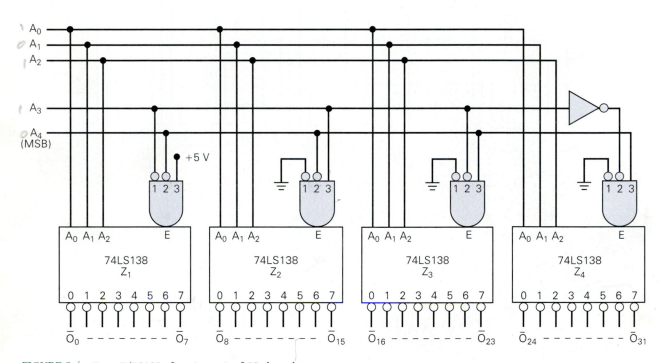

FIGURE 9-4   Four 74LS138s forming a 1-of-32 decoder.

Solution

(a) The five-bit code has two distinct portions. The A_4 and A_3 bits determine which one of the decoder chips Z_1 to Z_4 will be enabled, while $A_2A_1A_0$ determine which output of the enabled chip will be activated. With A_4A_3 = 01, only Z_2 has all of its enable inputs activated. Thus, Z_2 responds to the $A_2A_1A_0$ = 101 code and activates its $\overline{O}_5$ output, which has been renamed $\overline{O}_{13}$. Thus, the input code 01101, which is the binary equivalent of decimal 13, will cause output $\overline{O}_{13}$ to go LOW, while all others stay HIGH.

(b) To enable Z_4, both A_4 and A_3 must be HIGH. Thus, all input codes ranging from 11000 (24_{10}) to 11111 (31_{10}) will activate Z_4. This corresponds to outputs $\overline{O}_{24}$ to $\overline{O}_{31}$.

BCD-to-Decimal Decoders

Figure 9-5(a) shows the logic diagram for a 7442 **BCD-to-decimal decoder.** It is also available as a 74LS42 and a 74HC42. Each output goes LOW only when its corresponding BCD input is applied. For example, $\overline{O}_5$ will go LOW only when inputs $DCBA = 0101$; $\overline{O}_8$ will go LOW only when $DCBA = 1000$. For input combinations that are invalid for BCD, none of the outputs will be activated. This decoder can

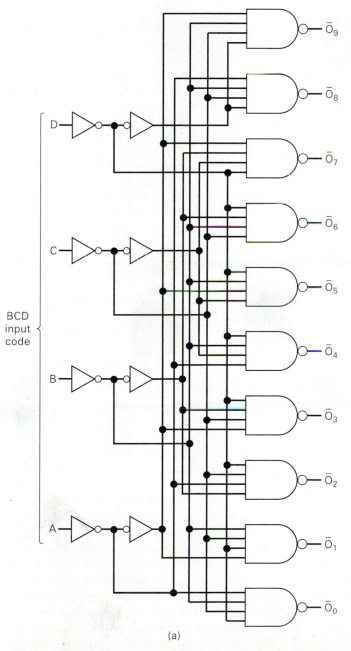

(a)

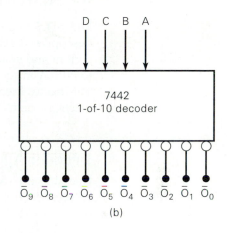

(b)

		Inputs		
D	C	B	A	Active Output
L	L	L	L	$\overline{O}_0$
L	L	L	H	$\overline{O}_1$
L	L	H	L	$\overline{O}_2$
L	L	H	H	$\overline{O}_3$
L	H	L	L	$\overline{O}_4$
L	H	L	H	$\overline{O}_5$
L	H	H	L	$\overline{O}_6$
L	H	H	H	$\overline{O}_7$
H	L	L	L	$\overline{O}_8$
H	L	L	H	$\overline{O}_9$
H	L	H	L	None
H	L	H	H	None
H	H	L	L	None
H	H	L	H	None
H	H	H	L	None
H	H	H	H	None

H = HIGH Voltage Level
L = LOW Voltage Level

(c)

FIGURE 9-5   (a) Logic diagram for the 7442 BCD-to-decimal decoder; (b) logic symbol; (c) truth table. (Courtesy of Fairchild, a Schlumberger company)

also be referred to as a *4-to-10 decoder* or a *1-of-10 decoder.* The logic symbol and the truth table for the 7442 are also shown in the figure. Note that this decoder does not have an enable input. In Problem 9-7 we will see how the 7442 can be used as a 3-to-8 decoder with the *D* input used as an enable input.

BCD-to-Decimal Decoder/Driver

The TTL 7445 is a BCD-to-decimal decoder/**driver.** The term *driver* is added to its description because this IC has open-collector outputs that can operate at higher current and voltage limits than a normal TTL output. The 7445's outputs can sink up to 80 mA in the LOW state, and they can be pulled up to 30 V in the HIGH state. This makes them suitable for directly driving loads such as indicator LEDs or lamps, relays, or dc motors.

Decoder Applications

Decoders are used whenever an output or a group of outputs is to be activated only on the occurrence of a specific combination of input levels. These input levels are often provided by the outputs of a counter or a register. When the decoder inputs come from a counter that is being continually pulsed, the decoder outputs will be activated sequentially, and they can be used as timing or sequencing signals to turn devices on or off at specific times. An example of this operation is shown in Figure 9-6 using the 74LS293 counter and the 7445 decoder/driver described above.

EXAMPLE 9-3	Describe the operation of the circuit in Figure 9-6(a).

Solution

The counter is being pulsed by a 1-pps signal so that it will sequence through the binary counts at the rate of 1 count/s. The counter FF outputs are connected as the inputs to the decoder. The 7445 open-collector outputs $\overline{O}_3$ and $\overline{O}_6$ are used to switch relays K_1 and K_2 on and off. For instance, when $\overline{O}_3$ is in its inactive HIGH state, its output transistor will be off (nonconducting) so that no current can flow through relay K_1 and it will be deenergized. When $\overline{O}_3$ is in its active-LOW state, its output transistor is on and acts as a current sink for current through K_1 so that K_1 is energized. Note that the relays operate from +24 V. Also note the presence of the diodes across the relay coils; these protect the decoder's output transistors from the large "inductive kick" voltage that would be produced when coil current is abruptly stopped.

The timing diagram in Figure 9-6(b) shows the sequence of events. If we assume that the counter is in the 0000 state at time 0, then both outputs $\overline{O}_3$ and $\overline{O}_6$ are initially in the inactive HIGH state, where their output transistors are off and both relays are deenergized. As clock pulses are applied, the counter will be incremented once per second. On the NGT of the third pulse (time 3), the counter will go to the 0011 (3) state. This will activate decoder output $\overline{O}_3$ and thereby energize K_1. On the NGT of the fourth pulse, the counter goes to the 0100 (4) state. This will deactivate $\overline{O}_3$ and deenergize relay K_1.

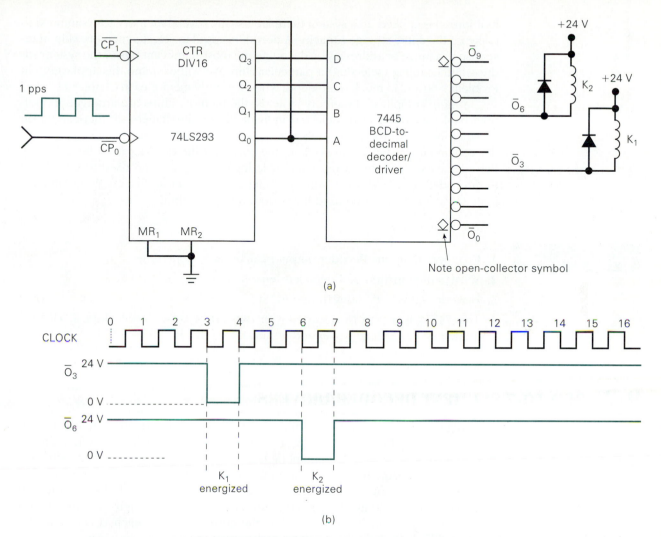

FIGURE 9-6 Example 9-3: counter/decoder combination used to provide timing and sequencing operations.

Similarly, at time 6 the counter will go to the 0110 (6) state; this will make $\overline{O}_6 = 0$ and energize K_2. At time 7 the counter goes to 0111 (7) and deactivates O_6 to deenergize K_2.

The counter will continue counting as pulses are applied. After 16 pulses, the sequence just described will start over.

Decoders are widely used in the memory system of a computer where they respond to the address code generated by the central processor to activate a particular memory location. Each memory IC contains many registers that can store binary numbers (data). Each register needs to have its own unique address to distinguish it from all the other registers. A decoder is built into the memory IC's circuitry and allows a particular storage register to be activated when a unique combination of inputs (i.e., its address) is applied. In a system there are usually several memory ICs combined to make up the entire storage capacity. A decoder is used to select a memory chip in response to a range of addresses by decoding the most significant bits of the system address and enabling (selecting) a particular chip. We will examine this application in Problem 9-60 and in much more depth when we study memories in Chapter 11.

In more complicated memory systems, the memory chips are arranged in multiple banks which must be selected individually or simultaneously, depending on whether the microprocessor wants one or more bytes at a time. This means that under certain circumstances, more than one output of the decoder must be activated. For systems such as this, a programmable logic device is often used to implement the decoder since a simple 1-of-8 decoder alone is not sufficient. Programmable logic devices can easily be used for custom decoding applications.

Review Questions

1. Can more than one decoder output be activated at one time?
2. What is the function of a decoder's enable input(s)?
3. How does the 7445 differ from the 7442?
4. The 74154 is a 4-to-16 decoder with two active-LOW enable inputs. How many pins (including power and ground) does this IC have?

9-2   BCD-TO-7-SEGMENT DECODER/DRIVERS

Most digital equipment has some means for displaying information in a form that can be understood readily by the user or operator. This information is often numerical data but can also be alphanumeric (numbers and letters). One of the simplest and most popular methods for displaying numerical digits uses a 7-segment configuration [Figure 9-7(a)] to form the decimal characters 0 through 9 and sometimes the hex characters A through F. One common arrangement uses light-emitting diodes (LEDs) for each segment. By controlling the current through each LED, some segments will be light and others will be dark so that the desired character pattern will be generated. Figure 9-7(b) shows the segment patterns that are used to display the various digits. For example, to display a "6," the segments a, c, d, e, f, and g are made bright while segment b is dark.

A **BCD-to-7-segment decoder/driver** is used to take a four-bit BCD input and provide the outputs that will pass current through the appropriate segments to display the decimal digit. The logic for this decoder is more complicated than the logic of decoders that we have looked at previously because each output is activated for more than one combination of inputs. For example, the e segment must be activated for any of the digits 0, 2, 6, and 8, which means whenever any of the codes 0000, 0010, 0110, or 1000 occurs.

Figure 9-8(a) shows a BCD-to-7-segment decoder/driver (TTL 7446 or 7447) being used to drive a 7-segment LED readout. Each segment consists of one or two LEDs. The anodes of the LEDs are all tied to V_{CC} (+5 V). The cathodes of the LEDs are connected through current-limiting resistors to the appropriate outputs of the decoder/driver. The decoder/driver has active-LOW outputs which are open-collector driver transistors that can sink a fairly large current. This is because LED readouts may require 10 to 40 mA per segment, depending on their type and size.

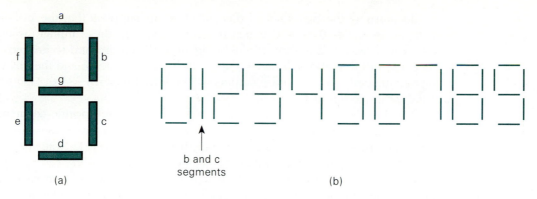

(a)

b and c
segments

(b)

FIGURE 9-7 (a) 7-segment arrangement; (b) active segments for each digit.

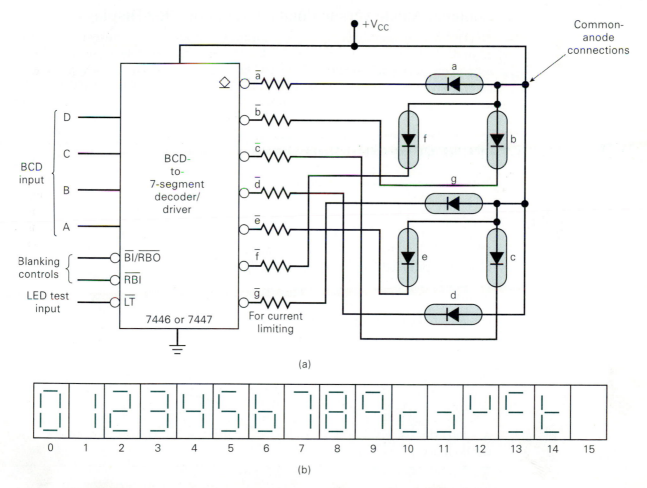

(a)

(b)

FIGURE 9-8 (a) BCD-to-7-segment decoder/driver driving a common-anode 7-segment LED display; (b) segment patterns for all possible input codes.

To illustrate the operation of this circuit, let us suppose that the BCD input is $D = 0$, $C = 1$, $B = 0$, $A = 1$, which is BCD for 5. With these inputs the decoder/driver outputs $\bar{a}$, $\bar{f}$, $\bar{g}$, $\bar{c}$, and $\bar{d}$ will be driven LOW (connected to ground), allowing current to flow through the a, f, g, c, and d LED segments and thereby displaying the numeral 5. The $\bar{b}$ and $\bar{e}$ outputs will be HIGH (open), so that LED segments b and e cannot conduct.

The 7446/47 decoder/drivers are designed to activate specific segments even for non-BCD input codes (greater than 1001). Figure 9-8(b) shows the activated segment patterns for all possible input codes from 0000 to 1111. Note that an input code of 1111 (15) will blank out all the segments.

Seven-segment decoder/drivers such as the 7446/47 are exceptions to the rule that decoder circuits activate only one output for each combination of inputs. Rather, they activate a unique pattern of outputs for each combination of inputs.

Common-Anode versus Common-Cathode LED Displays

The LED display used in Figure 9-8 is a **common-anode** type because the anodes of all of the segments are tied together to V_{CC}. Another type of 7-segment LED display uses a **common-cathode** arrangement where the cathodes of all of the segments are tied together and connected to ground. This type of display must be driven by a BCD-to-7-segment decoder/driver with active-HIGH outputs that apply a HIGH voltage to the anodes of those segments that are to be activated. Since each segment requires 10 to 20 mA of current to light it, TTL and CMOS devices are normally not used to directly drive the common-cathode display. Recall from Chapter 8 that TTL and CMOS outputs are not able to source large amounts of current. A transistor interface circuit is often used between decoder chips and the common-cathode display.

EXAMPLE 9-4

Each segment of a typical 7-segment LED display is rated to operate at 10 mA at 2.7 V for normal brightness. Calculate the value of the current-limiting resistor needed to produce approximately 10 mA per segment.

Solution

Referring to Figure 9-8(a), we can see that the series resistor must have a voltage drop equal to the difference between $V_{CC} = 5$ V and the segment voltage of 2.7 V. This 2.3 V across the resistor must produce a current of about 10 mA. Thus, we have

$$R_S = \frac{2.3 \text{ V}}{10 \text{ mA}} = 230 \ \Omega$$

A standard resistor value close to this can be used. A 220-Ω resistor would be a good choice.

Review Questions

1. Which LED segments will be on for a decoder/driver input of 1001?
2. *True or false:* More than one output of a BCD-to-7-segment decoder/driver can be active at one time.

9-3 LIQUID-CRYSTAL DISPLAYS

An LED display generates or emits light energy as current is passed through the individual segments. A liquid-crystal display **(LCD)** controls the reflection of available light. The available light may simply be ambient (surrounding) light such as sunlight or normal room lighting; *reflective* LCDs use ambient light. Or the available light might be provided by a small light source that is part of the display unit; *back-lit* LCDs use this method. In any case, LCDs have gained wide acceptance because of their very low power consumption compared to LEDs, especially in battery-operated equipment such as calculators, digital watches, and portable electronic measuring instruments. LEDs have the advantage of a much brighter display, which, unlike reflective LCDs, is easily visible in dark or poorly lit areas.

Basically, LCDs operate from a low-voltage (typically 3 to 15 V rms), low-frequency (25 to 60 Hz) ac signal and draw very little current. They are often arranged as 7-segment displays for numerical readouts as shown in Figure 9-9(a). The ac voltage needed to turn on a segment is applied between the segment and the **backplane,** which is common to all segments. The segment and the backplane form a capacitor that draws very little current as long as the ac frequency is kept low. It is generally not lower than 25 Hz, because this would produce visible flicker.

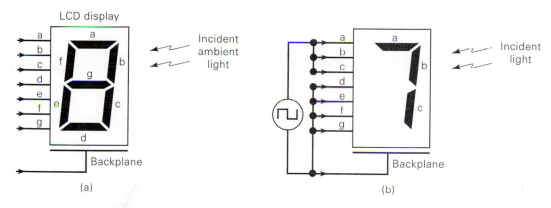

FIGURE 9-9   Liquid-crystal display: (a) basic arrangement; (b) applying a voltage between the segment and the backplane turns ON the segment. Zero voltage turns the segment OFF.

An admittedly simplified explanation of how an LCD operates goes something like this. When there is no difference in voltage between a segment and the backplane, the segment is said to be *nonactivated* (OFF). Segments *d*, *e*, *f*, and *g* in Figure 9-9(b) are OFF and will reflect incident light so that they appear invisible against their background. When an appropriate ac voltage is applied between a segment and the backplane, the segment is activated (ON). Segments *a*, *b*, and *c* in Figure 9-9(b) are ON and will not reflect the incident light, and thus they appear dark against their background.

Driving an LCD

An LCD segment will turn ON when an ac voltage is applied between the segment and the backplane, and will turn OFF when there is no voltage between the two. Rather than generating an ac signal, it is common practice to produce the required ac voltage by applying out-of-phase square waves to the segment and the backplane. This is illustrated in Figure 9-10 for one segment. A 40-Hz square wave is applied to the backplane and also to the input of a CMOS 74HC86 EX-OR. The other input to the EX-OR is a CONTROL input that will control whether the segment is ON or OFF.

FIGURE 9-10 Method for driving an LCD segment. When the CONTROL is LOW, the segment is off. When the CONTROl is HIGH, the segment is on.

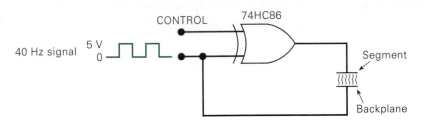

When the CONTROL input is LOW, the EX-OR output will be exactly the same as the 40-Hz square wave, so that the signals applied to the segment and the backplane are equal. Since there is no difference in voltage, the segment will be OFF. When the CONTROL input is HIGH, the EX-OR output will be the INVERSE of the 40-Hz square wave, so that the signal applied to the segment is out of phase with the signal applied to the backplane. As a result, the segment voltage will alternately be at +5 V and at −5 V relative to the backplane. This ac voltage will turn ON the segment.

This same idea can be extended to a complete 7-segment LCD display as shown in Figure 9-11. Here the CMOS 74HC4511 BCD-to-7-segment decoder/driver supplies the CONTROL signals to each of seven EX-ORs for the seven segments. The 74HC4511 has active-HIGH outputs, since a HIGH is required to turn on a segment. The decoder/driver and EX-OR gates of Figure 9-11 are available on a single chip. The CMOS 74HC4543 is one such device. It takes the BCD input code and provides the outputs to drive the LCD segments directly.

In general, CMOS devices are used to drive LCDs for two reasons: (1) they require much less power than TTL and are more suited to the battery-operated applications where LCDs are used; (2) the TTL LOW-state voltage is not exactly 0 V and can be as much as 0.4 V. This will produce a dc component of voltage between the segment and the backplane that considerably shortens the life of an LCD.

Types of LCDs

Liquid crystals are available as multidigit 7-segment decimal numeric displays. They come in many sizes and with many special characters such as colons (:) for clock displays; +/− indicators for digital voltmeters; decimal points for calculators; and battery-low indicators, since many LCD devices are battery-powered. These displays must be driven by a decoder/driver chip such as the 74HC4543 or the 74C945.

A more complicated but readily available LCD display is the alphanumeric LCD module. These are available from many companies in numerous formats such as 1-line-by-16-character up to 4-lines-by-40-characters. The interface to these modules has been standardized so that an LCD module from any manufacturer will use the same signals and data format. The module includes some VLSI chips that make this device simple to use. Eight data lines are used to send the ASCII code for whatever you wish to display. These data lines also carry special control codes to the LCD command regis-

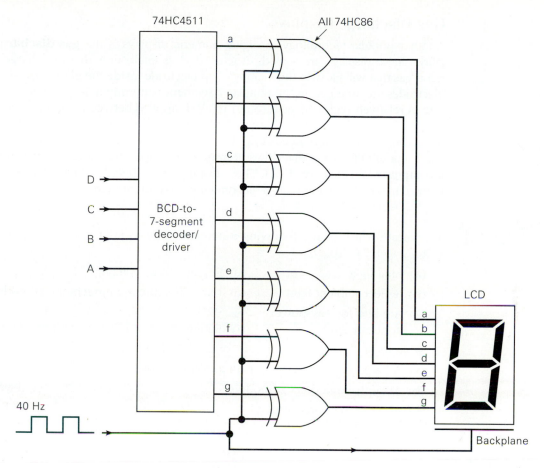

FIGURE 9-11   Method for driving a 7-segment LCD.

ter. Three other inputs (Register Select, Read/Write, and Enable) are used to control the location, direction, and timing of the data transfer. As characters are sent to the module, it stores them in its own memory and types them across the display screen.

Other LCD modules allow the user to create a graphical display by controlling individual dots on the screen called **pixels.** Larger LCD panels can be scanned at a high rate, producing high-quality video motion pictures. In these displays the control lines are arranged in a grid of rows and columns. At the intersection of each row and column is a pixel that acts like a "window" that can be electronically opened and closed to control the amount of light that is transmitted through the cell. The voltage from a row to a column determines the brightness of each pixel. In a laptop computer, a binary number for each pixel is stored in the "video" memory. These numbers are converted to voltages that are applied to the display.

Each pixel on a color display is actually made up of three subpixels. These subpixels control the light that passes through a red, green, or blue filter to produce the color of each pixel. On a 640-by-480 LCD screen there would be 640 × 3 connections for columns and 480 connections for rows for a total of 2400 connections to the LCD. Obviously, the driver circuitry for such a device is a very complicated VLSI circuit that is manufactured as part of the display.

Gas Discharge Displays

Another popular technology in digital numeric displays is the **gas discharge display.** These displays are sealed, evacuated glass enclosures that are charged with neon gas that will glow in the vicinity of an electrode inside the glass enclosure. The electrodes are arranged in the familiar 7-segment pattern in a 5-by-7 dot-matrix pattern. A relatively high voltage (around 100 V) is applied between a segment electrode and a reference electrode that is sealed inside the display but usually not visible to the user. The driver circuitry needs to pull a segment down to ground level and sink the small amount of current that flows. It must also be able to handle high potentials on its outputs when they are HIGH. These displays have the advantage of high visibility in the dark and large segments while drawing less current than LED displays.

Review Questions

1. Indicate which of the following statements refer to LCD displays and which refer to LED displays.

   (a) Emit light
   (b) Reflect ambient light
   (c) Are best for low-power applications
   (d) Require an ac voltage
   (e) Use a 7-segment arrangement to produce digits
   (f) Require current-limiting resistors

2. What form of data is sent to each of the following?

   (a) A 7-segment LCD display with a decoder/driver
   (b) An alphanumeric LCD module
   (c) An LCD computer display

9-4   ENCODERS

Most decoders accept an input code and produce a HIGH (or a LOW) at *one and only one* output line. In other words, we can say that a decoder identifies, recognizes, or detects a particular code. The opposite of this decoding process is called **encoding** and is performed by a logic circuit called an **encoder.** An encoder has a number of input lines, only one of which is activated at a given time, and produces an N-bit output code, depending on which input is activated. Figure 9-12 is the general diagram for an encoder with M inputs and N outputs. Here the inputs are active-HIGH, which means that they are normally LOW.

FIGURE 9-12   General encoder diagram.

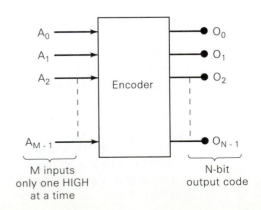

A_0 O_0
A_1 O_1
A_2 O_2

Encoder

A_{M-1} O_{N-1}

M inputs
only one HIGH
at a time

N-bit
output code

We saw that a *binary-to-octal decoder (3-line-to-8-line decoder)* accepts a three-bit input code and activates one of eight output lines corresponding to that code. An *octal-to-binary encoder (8-line-to-3-line encoder)* performs the opposite function: it accepts eight input lines and produces a three-bit output code corresponding to the activated input. Figure 9-13 shows the logic circuit and the truth table for an octal-to-binary encoder with active-LOW inputs.

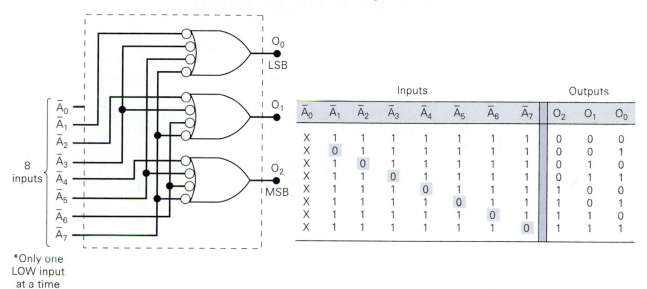

			Inputs						Outputs		
$\overline{A}_0$	$\overline{A}_1$	$\overline{A}_2$	$\overline{A}_3$	$\overline{A}_4$	$\overline{A}_5$	$\overline{A}_6$	$\overline{A}_7$		O_2	O_1	O_0
X	1	1	1	1	1	1	1		0	0	0
X	0	1	1	1	1	1	1		0	0	1
X	1	0	1	1	1	1	1		0	1	0
X	1	1	0	1	1	1	1		0	1	1
X	1	1	1	0	1	1	1		1	0	0
X	1	1	1	1	0	1	1		1	0	1
X	1	1	1	1	1	0	1		1	1	0
X	1	1	1	1	1	1	0		1	1	1

*Only one
LOW input
at a time

FIGURE 9-13   Logic circuit for an octal-to-binary (8-line-to-3-line) encoder. For proper operation, only one input should be active at one time.

By following through the logic, you can verify that a LOW at any single input will produce the output binary code corresponding to that input. For instance, a LOW at $\overline{A}_3$ (while all other inputs are HIGH) will produce $O_2 = 0$, $O_1 = 1$, and $O_0 = 1$, which is the binary code for 3. Notice that $\overline{A}_0$ is not connected to the logic gates because the encoder outputs will normally be at 000 when none of the inputs $\overline{A}_1$ to $\overline{A}_9$ is LOW.

<table>
<tr><td>

**EXAMPLE
9-5**

</td><td>

Determine the outputs of the encoder in Figure 9-13 when $\overline{A}_3$ and $\overline{A}_5$ are simultaneously LOW.

Solution

Following through the logic gates, we see that the LOWs at these two inputs will produce HIGHs at each output, in other words, the binary code 111. Clearly, this is not the code for either activated input.

</td></tr>
</table>

Priority Encoders

This last example identifies a drawback of the simple encoder circuit of Figure 9-13 when more than one input is activated at one time. A modified version of this circuit, called a **priority encoder,** includes the necessary logic to ensure that when two or more inputs are activated, the output code will correspond to the highest-numbered input. For example, when both $\overline{A}_3$ and $\overline{A}_5$ are LOW, the output code will be 101 (5). Similarly, when $\overline{A}_6$, $\overline{A}_2$, and $\overline{A}_0$ are all LOW, the output code is 110 (6). The 74148, 74LS148, and 74HC148 are all octal-to-binary priority encoders.

74147 Decimal-to-BCD Priority Encoder

Figure 9-14 shows the logic symbol and the truth table for the 74147 (74LS147, 74HC147), which functions as a decimal-to-BCD priority encoder. It has nine active-LOW inputs representing the decimal digits 1 through 9, and it produces the *inverted* BCD code corresponding to the highest-numbered activated input.

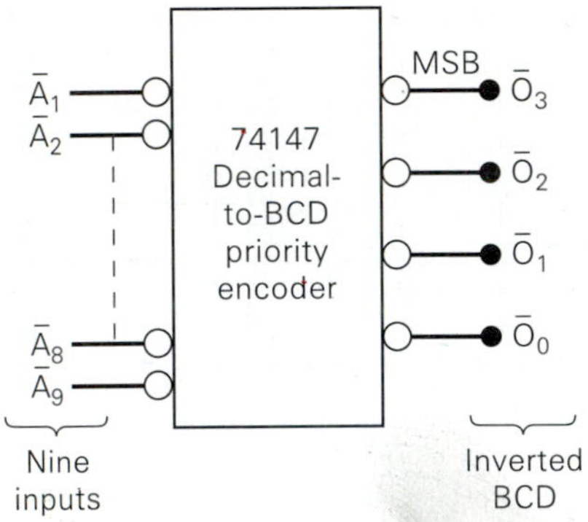

$\overline{A}_1$	$\overline{A}_2$	$\overline{A}_3$	$\overline{A}_4$	$\overline{A}_5$	$\overline{A}_6$	$\overline{A}_7$	$\overline{A}_8$	$\overline{A}_9$	$\overline{O}_3$	$\overline{O}_2$	$\overline{O}_1$	$\overline{O}_0$
1	1	1	1	1	1	1	1	1	1	1	1	1
X	X	X	X	X	X	X	X	0	0	1	1	0
X	X	X	X	X	X	X	0	1	0	1	1	1
X	X	X	X	X	X	0	1	1	1	0	0	0
X	X	X	X	X	0	1	1	1	1	0	0	1
X	X	X	X	0	1	1	1	1	1	0	1	0
X	X	X	0	1	1	1	1	1	1	0	1	1
X	X	0	1	1	1	1	1	1	1	1	0	0
X	0	1	1	1	1	1	1	1	1	1	0	1
0	1	1	1	1	1	1	1	1	1	1	1	0

X = either 0 or 1

FIGURE 9-14 74147 decimal-to-BCD priority encoder.

Let's examine the truth table to see how this IC works. The first line in the table shows all inputs in their inactive HIGH state. For this condition the outputs are 1111, which is the inverse of 0000, the BCD code for 0. The second line in the table indicates that a LOW at $\overline{A}_9$, regardless of the states of the other inputs, will produce an output code of 0110, which is the inverse of 1001, the BCD code for 9. The third line shows that a LOW at $\overline{A}_8$, provided that $\overline{A}_9$ is HIGH, will produce an output code of 0111, the inverse of 1000, the BCD code for 8. In a similar manner, the remaining lines in the table show that a LOW at any input, provided that all higher-numbered inputs are HIGH, will produce the inverse of the BCD code for that input.

The 74147 outputs will normally be HIGH when none of the inputs are activated. This corresponds to the decimal 0 input condition. There is no $\overline{A}_0$ input, since the encoder assumes the decimal 0 input state when all other inputs are HIGH. The 74147 inverted BCD outputs can be converted to normal BCD by putting each one through an INVERTER.

EXAMPLE 9-6

Determine the states of the outputs in Figure 9-14 when $\overline{A}_5$, $\overline{A}_7$, and $\overline{A}_3$ are LOW and all other inputs are HIGH.

Solution

The truth table shows that when $\overline{A}_7$ is LOW, the levels at $\overline{A}_5$ and $\overline{A}_3$ do not matter. Thus, the outputs will be 1000, respectively, the inverse of 0111 (7).

Switch Encoder

Figure 9-15 shows how a 74147 can be used as a *switch encoder*. The 10 switches might be the keyboard switches on a calculator representing digits 0 through 9. The switches are of the normally open type, so that the encoder inputs are all normally HIGH and the BCD output is 0000 (note the INVERTERs). When a digit key is depressed, the circuit will produce the BCD code for that digit. Since the 74LS147 is a priority encoder, simultaneous key depressions will produce the BCD code for the higher-numbered key.

FIGURE 9-15 Decimal-to-BCD switch encoder.

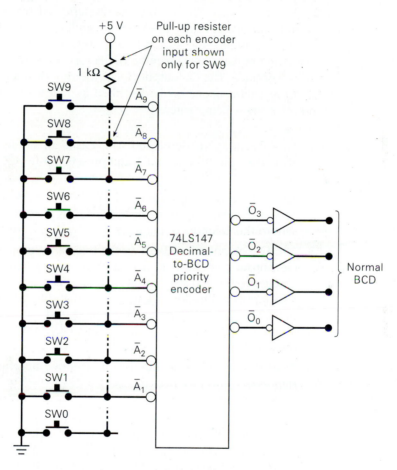

The switch encoder of Figure 9-15 can be used whenever BCD data must be manually entered into a digital system. A prime example would be in an electronic calculator, where the operator depresses several keyboard switches in succession to enter a decimal number. In a simple, basic calculator the BCD code for each decimal digit is entered into a four-bit storage register. In other words, when the first key is depressed, the BCD code for that digit is sent to a four-bit FF register; when the second switch is depressed, the BCD code for that digit is sent to *another* four-bit FF register, and so on. Thus, a calculator that can handle eight digits will have eight four-bit registers to store the BCD codes for these digits. Each four-bit register drives a decoder/driver and a numerical display so that the eight-digit number can be displayed.

The operation described above can be accomplished with the circuit in Figure 9-16. This circuit will take three decimal digits entered from the keyboard in sequence, encode them in BCD, and store the BCD in three FF output registers. The 12 D-type flip-flops Q_0 to Q_{11} are used to receive and store the BCD codes for the digits. Q_8 to Q_{11} store the BCD code for the most significant digit (MSD), which is the first one entered on the keyboard. Q_4 to Q_7 store the second entered digit, and Q_0 to Q_3 store the third entered digit. Flip-flops X, Y, and Z form a ring counter (Chapter 7) which controls the transfer of data from the encoder outputs to the appropriate output register. The OR gate produces a HIGH output any time one of the keys is depressed. This output may be affected by switch contact bounce, which would produce several pulses before settling down to the HIGH state. The OS is used to neutralize the switch bounce by triggering on the first positive transition from the OR gate and remaining HIGH for 20 ms, well past the time duration of the switch bounce. The OS output clocks the ring counter.

The circuit operation is described as follows for the case where the decimal number 309 is being entered:

1. The CLEAR key is depressed. This clears all storage flip-flops Q_0 to Q_{11} to 0. It also clears flip-flops X and Y and presets flip-flop Z to 1, so that the ring counter begins in the 001 state.

2. The CLEAR key is released and the "3" key is depressed. The encoder outputs 1100 are inverted to produce 0011, the BCD code for 3. These binary values are sent to the D inputs of the three four-bit output registers.

3. The OR output goes HIGH (since two of its inputs are HIGH) and triggers the OS output $Q = 1$ for 20 ms. After 20 ms, Q returns LOW and clocks the ring counter to the 100 state (X goes HIGH). The positive transition at X is fed to the CLK inputs of flip-flops Q_8 to Q_{11}, so that the encoder outputs are transferred to these FFs. That is, $Q_{11} = 0$, $Q_{10} = 0$, $Q_9 = 1$, and $Q_8 = 1$. Note that flip-flops Q_0 to Q_7 are not affected, because their CLK inputs have not received a positive transition.

4. The "3" key is released and the OR gate output returns LOW. The "0" key is then depressed. This produces the BCD code of 0000, which is fed to the inputs of the three registers.

5. The OR output goes HIGH in response to the "0" key (note the INVERTER) and triggers the OS for 20 ms. After 20 ms the ring counter shifts to the 010 state (Y goes HIGH). The positive transition at Y is fed to the CLK inputs of Q_4 to Q_7 and transfers the 0000 to these FFs. Note that flip-flops Q_0 to Q_3 and Q_8 to Q_{11} are not affected by the Y transition.

6. The "0" key is released and the OR output returns LOW. The "9" key is depressed, producing BCD outputs 1001, which are fed to the storage registers.

7. The OR output goes HIGH again, triggering the OS, which in turn clocks the ring counter to the 001 state (Z goes HIGH). The positive transition at Z is fed to the CLK inputs of Q_0 to Q_3 and transfers the 1001 into these FFs. The other storage FFs are unaffected.

8. At this point the storage register contains 001100001001, beginning with Q_{11}. This is the BCD code of 309. These register outputs feed decoder/drivers which drive appropriate displays for indicating the decimal digits 309.

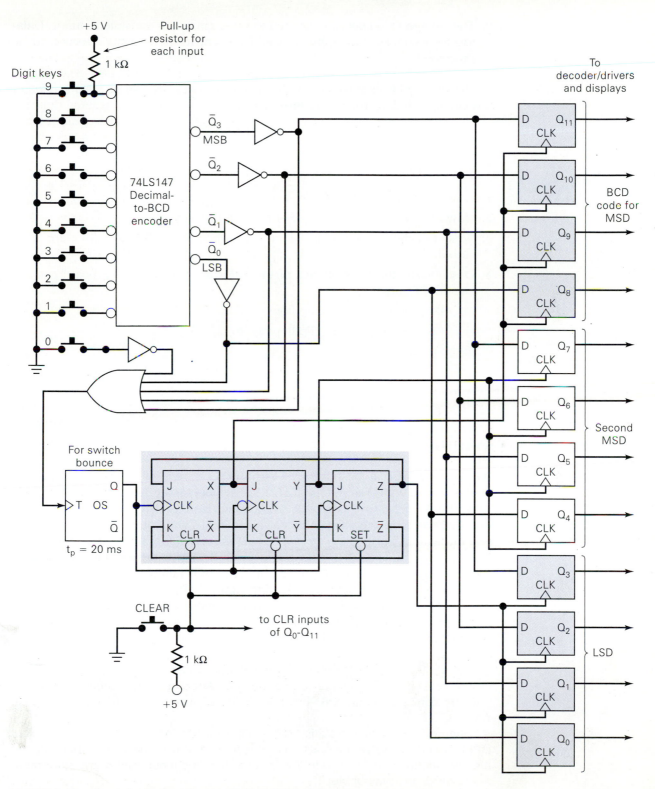

FIGURE 9-16 Circuit for keyboard entry of three-digit number into storage registers.

9. The storage FF outputs are also fed to other circuits in the system. In a calculator, for example, these outputs would be sent to the arithmetic section to be processed.

Several problems at the end of the chapter will deal with some other aspects of this circuit including troubleshooting exercises.

Review Questions

1. How does an encoder differ from a decoder?
2. How does a priority encoder differ from an ordinary encoder?
3. What will the outputs be in Figure 9-15 when SW6, SW5, and SW2 are all closed?
4. Describe the functions of each of the following parts of the keyboard entry circuit of Figure 9-16.
   (a) OR gate   (d) Flip-flops X, Y, Z
   (b) 74147 encoder   (e) Flip-flops Q_0 to Q_{11}
   (c) One-shot

9-5 IEEE/ANSI SYMBOLS

We will now look at the IEEE/ANSI symbols for several of the decoders and encoders. Figure 9-17(a) shows the IEEE/ANSI symbol for the 7442 decoder. It is fairly straightforward. Note the label BCD/DEC, which denotes that it is a BCD-to-decimal decoder. Also note the manner in which the inputs and outputs are numbered inside the symbol block. These are *not* IC pin numbers. For example, the inputs to the 7442 have the numbers 1, 2, 4, and 8, respectively, inside the rectangle. These indicate the respective weights of each input in the BCD number.

The IEEE/ANSI symbol for the 7445 in Figure 9-17(b) is similar to the 7442, with two differences. First, each output has the underlined diamond symbol to indicate its open-collector structure. Second, the triangle in the middle of the symbol denotes that this device is a buffer or a driver with greater-than-normal current and/or voltage capabilities.

Figure 9-17(c) is the symbol for the 74LS138 decoder. Note the BIN/OCT label to denote its binary-to-octal decoding function. Also note how the three enable inputs are combined in an AND block to produce an overall internal enable signal, *EN*.

Figure 9-18 shows the IEEE/ANSI symbol for the 74147 encoder IC. The label HPRI/BCD denotes that the function of this IC is to convert the active input with the highest priority to its BCD code. Again, note how the inputs and outputs are numbered inside the symbol block.

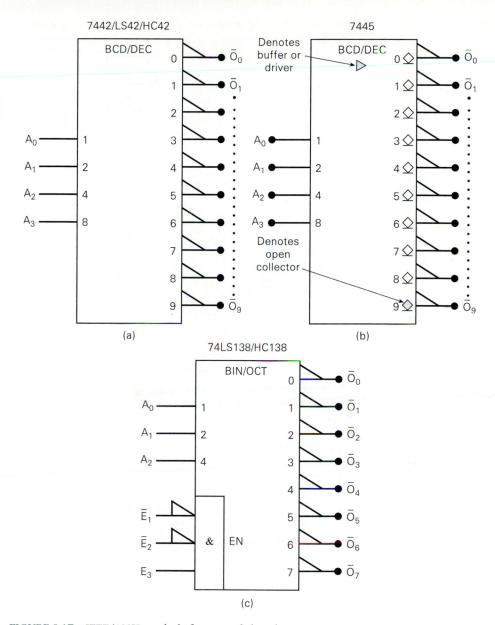

FIGURE 9-17 IEEE/ANSI symbols for several decoders.

FIGURE 9-18 IEEE/ANSI symbol for the 74147 encoder.

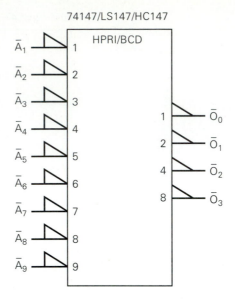

Review Questions

1. What does the label BCD/DEC mean?
2. What does the label HPRI mean?
3. What does the symbol ▷ mean inside a symbol block?

9-6 TROUBLESHOOTING

As circuits and systems become more complex, the number of possible causes of failure obviously increases. Whereas the procedure for fault isolation and correction remains essentially the same, the application of the **observation/analysis** process is more important for complex circuits because it helps the troubleshooter narrow the location of the fault to a small area of the circuit. This reduces to a reasonable amount the testing steps and resulting data that must be analyzed. By understanding the circuit operation, observing the symptoms of the failure, and reasoning through the operation, the troubleshooter can often predict the possible faults before ever picking up a logic probe or an oscilloscope. This observation/analysis process is one that inexperienced troubleshooters are hesitant to apply, probably because of the great variety and capabilities of modern test equipment available to them. It is easy to become overly reliant on these tools while not adequately utilizing the human brain's reasoning and analytical skills.

The following examples illustrate how the observation/analysis process can be applied. Many of the end-of-chapter troubleshooting problems will provide you with the opportunity to develop your skill at applying this process.

Another vital strategy in troubleshooting is known as **divide-and-conquer.** It is used to identify the location of the problem after observation/analysis has generated a number of possibilities. A less efficient method would be to investigate each possible cause, one by one. The divide-and-conquer method finds a point in the circuit that can be tested, thereby dividing the total possible number of causes in half. In simple systems this may seem unnecessary, but as complexity increases, the total number of possible causes also increases. If there are eight possible causes, then a test should be performed that eliminates four of them. The next test should eliminate two more, and the third test should identify the problem.

**EXAMPLE
9-7**

A technician tests the circuit of Figure 9-4 by using a set of switches to apply the input code at A_4 through A_0. She runs through each possible input code and checks the corresponding decoder output to see if it is activated. She observes that all of the odd-numbered outputs respond correctly, but all of the even-numbered outputs fail to respond when their code is applied. What are the most probable faults?

Solution

In a situation where so many outputs are failing, it is unreasonable to expect that each of these outputs has a fault. It is much more likely that some faulty input condition is causing the output failures. What do all of the even-numbered outputs have in common? The input codes for several of them are listed in Table 9-1.

TABLE 9-1

Output	Input Code
$\overline{O}_0$	00000
$\overline{O}_4$	00100
$\overline{O}_{14}$	01110
$\overline{O}_{18}$	10010

Clearly, each even-numbered output requires an input code with an $A_0 = 0$ in order to be activated. Thus, the most probable faults would be those that prevent A_0 from going LOW. These include:

1. A faulty switch connected to the A_0 input
2. A break in the path between the switch and the A_0 line
3. An external short from the A_0 line to V_{CC}
4. An internal short to V_{CC} at the A_0 inputs of any one of the decoder chips

Through observation and analysis the technician has identified several possible causes. Potential causes #1 and #2 are in the switches generating the address. Causes #3 and #4 are in the decoder circuit itself. The circuit can be divided by opening the connection between the least significant switch and the A_0 input as shown in Figure 9-19. A logic probe can be used to see if the switch can generate a LOW as well as a HIGH. Regardless of the outcome, two of the four possible causes have been eliminated.

Thus, the fault is narrowed to a specific area of the circuit. The exact fault can be traced with the testing and measurement techniques that we are already familiar with.

FIGURE 9-19 Troubleshooting circuitry in Example 9-7.

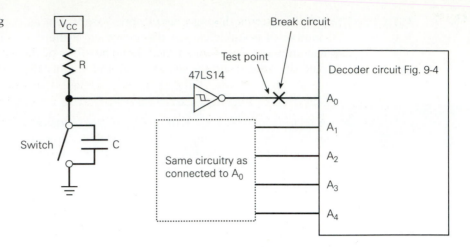

EXAMPLE 9-8

A technician wires the outputs from a BCD counter to the inputs of the decoder/driver of Figure 9-8. He applies pulses to the counter at a very slow rate and observes the LED display, which is shown below, as the counter counts up from 0000 to 1001. Examine this observed sequence carefully and try to predict the most probable fault.

COUNT	0	1	2	3	4	5	6	7	8	9
Observed display	0	1	2	3	4	5	6	7	8	9
Expected display	0	1	2	3	4	5	6	7	8	9

Solution

Comparing the observed display with the expected display for each count, we see several important points:

■ For those counts where the observed display is incorrect, the observed display is not one of the segment patterns that correspond to counts greater than 1001.

■ This rules out a faulty counter or faulty wiring from the counter to the decoder/driver.

■ The correct segment patterns (0, 1, 3, 6, 7, and 8) have the common property that segments *e* and *f* are either both on or both off.

■ The incorrect segment patterns have the common property that segments *e* and *f* are in opposite states, and if we interchange the states of these two segments, the correct pattern is obtained.

   Giving some thought to these points should lead us to conclude that the technician has probably "crossed" the connections to the *e* and *f* segments.

9-7 MULTIPLEXERS (DATA SELECTORS)

A modern home stereo system may have a switch that selects music from one of four sources: a cassette tape, a compact disc (CD), a turntable, or a radio. The switch selects one of the electronic signals from one of these four sources and sends it to the power amplifier and speakers. In simple terms, this is what a **multiplexer (MUX)** does: it selects one of several input signals and passes it on to the output.

A *digital multiplexer* or *data selector* is a logic circuit that accepts several digital data inputs and selects one of them at any given time to pass on to the output. The routing of the desired data input to the output is controlled by SELECT inputs (often referred to as ADDRESS inputs). Figure 9-20 shows the functional diagram of a general digital multiplexer. The inputs and outputs are drawn as wide arrows rather than lines; this indicates that they may actually be more than one signal line.

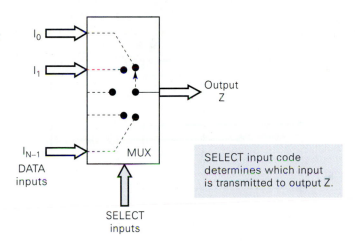

FIGURE 9-20 Functional diagram of a digital multiplexer (MUX).

SELECT input code determines which input is transmitted to output Z.

The multiplexer acts like a digitally controlled multiposition switch where the digital code applied to the SELECT inputs controls which data inputs will be switched to the output. For example, output Z will equal data input I_0 for some particular SELECT input code; Z will equal I_1 for another particular SELECT input code; and so on. Stated another way, a multiplexer selects 1 out of N input data sources and transmits the selected data to a single output channel. This is called **multiplexing.**

Basic Two-Input Multiplexer

Figure 9-21 shows the logic circuitry for a two-input multiplexer with data inputs I_0 and I_1 and SELECT input S. The logic level applied to the S input determines which AND gate is enabled so that its data input passes through the OR gate to output Z. Looking at it another way, the Boolean expression for the output is

$$Z = I_0\overline{S} + I_1 S$$

FIGURE 9-21   Two-input multiplexer.

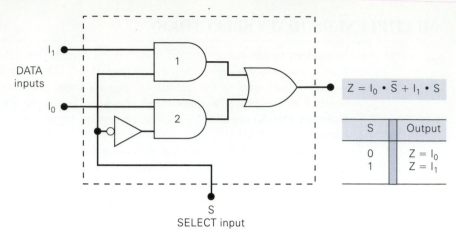

$$Z = I_0 \cdot \bar{S} + I_1 \cdot S$$

S	Output
0	$Z = I_0$
1	$Z = I_1$

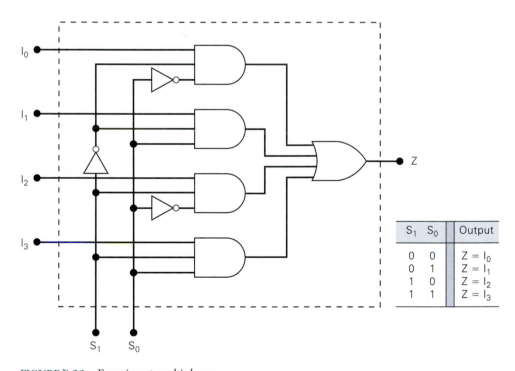

S_1	S_0	Output
0	0	$Z = I_0$
0	1	$Z = I_1$
1	0	$Z = I_2$
1	1	$Z = I_3$

FIGURE 9-22   Four-input multiplexer.

With $S = 0$, this expression becomes

$$Z = I_0 \cdot 1 + I_1 \cdot 0 \quad \text{\{gate 2 enabled\}}$$
$$= I_0$$

which indicates that Z will be identical to input signal I_0, which can be a fixed logic level or a time-varying logic signal. With $S = 1$, the expression becomes

$$Z = I_0 \cdot 0 + I_1 \cdot 1 = I_1 \quad \text{\{gate 1 enabled\}}$$

showing that output Z will be identical to input signal I_1.

An example of where a two-input MUX could be used is in a computer system that uses two different MASTER CLOCK signals: a high-speed clock (say, 10 MHz) for some programs, and a slow-speed clock (say, 4.77 MHz) for others. Using the circuit of Figure 9-20, the 10-MHz clock would be tied to I_0, and the 4.77-MHz clock to I_1. A signal from the computer's control logic section would drive the SELECT input to control which clock signal appears at output Z for routing to the other computer circuits.

Four-Input Multiplexer

The same basic idea can be used to form the four-input multiplexer shown in Figure 9-22. Here there are four inputs, which are selectively transmitted to the output according to the four possible combinations of the $S_1 S_0$ select inputs. Each data input is gated with a different combination of select input levels. I_0 is gated with $\overline{S_1}\overline{S_0}$ so that I_0 will pass through its AND gate to output Z only when $S_1 = 0$ and $S_0 = 0$. The table in the figure gives the outputs for the other three input-select codes.

Two, four-, eight-, and 16-input multiplexers are readily available in the TTL and CMOS logic families. These basic ICs can be combined for multiplexing a larger number of inputs.

Eight-Input Multiplexer

Figure 9-23(a) shows the logic diagram for the 74151 (74LS151, 74HC151) eight-input multiplexer. This multiplexer has an enable input $\overline{E}$ and provides both the normal and the inverted outputs. When $\overline{E} = 0$, the select inputs $S_2 S_1 S_0$ will select one data input (from I_0 through I_7) for passage to output Z. When $\overline{E} = 1$, the multiplexer is disabled so that $Z = 0$ regardless of the select input code. This operation is summarized in Figure 9-23(b), and the 74151 logic symbol is shown in Figure 9-23(c).

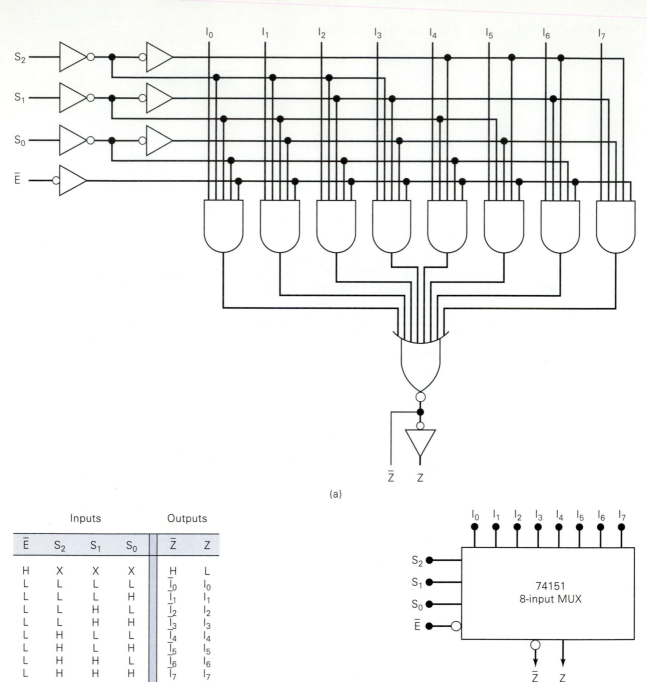

(a)

	Inputs			Outputs	
$\bar{E}$	S_2	S_1	S_0	$\bar{Z}$	Z
H	X	X	X	H	L
L	L	L	L	$\bar{I}_0$	I_0
L	L	L	H	$\bar{I}_1$	I_1
L	L	H	L	$\bar{I}_2$	I_2
L	L	H	H	$\bar{I}_3$	I_3
L	H	L	L	$\bar{I}_4$	I_4
L	H	L	H	$\bar{I}_5$	I_5
L	H	H	L	$\bar{I}_6$	I_6
L	H	H	H	$\bar{I}_7$	I_7

(b)

(c)

FIGURE 9-23 (a) Logic diagram for the 74151 multiplexer; (b) truth table; (c) logic symbol. (Courtesy of Fairchild, a Schlumberger company)

EXAMPLE
9-9
The circuit in Figure 9-24 uses two 74HC151s, an INVERTER, and an OR gate. Describe this circuit's operation.

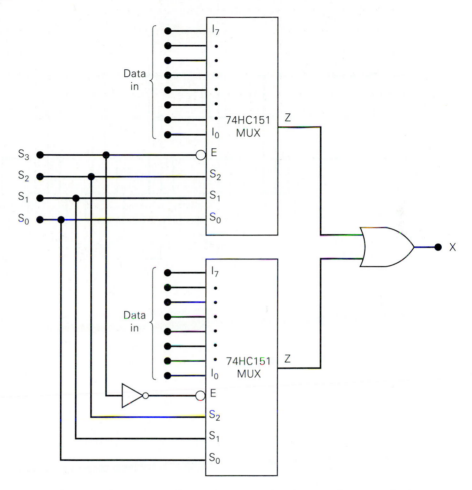

FIGURE 9-24   Example 9-9: two 74HC151s combined to form a 16-input multiplexer.

Solution

This circuit has a total of 16 data inputs, eight applied to each multiplexer. The two multiplexer outputs are combined in the OR gate to produce a single output X. The circuit functions as a 16-input multiplexer. The four select inputs $S_3 S_2 S_1 S_0$ will select one of the 16 inputs to pass through to X.

The S_3 input determines which multiplexer is enabled. When $S_3 = 0$, the top multiplexer is enabled, and the $S_2 S_1 S_0$ inputs determine which of its data inputs will appear at its output and pass through the OR gate to X. When $S_3 = 1$, the bottom multiplexer is enabled, and the $S_2 S_1 S_0$ inputs select one of its data inputs for passage to output X.

Quad Two-Input MUX (74157/LS157/HC157)

The 74157 is a very useful multiplexer IC that contains four two-input multiplexers like the one in Figure 9-21. The logic diagram for the 74157 is shown in Figure 9-25(a). Note the manner in which the data inputs and outputs are labeled.

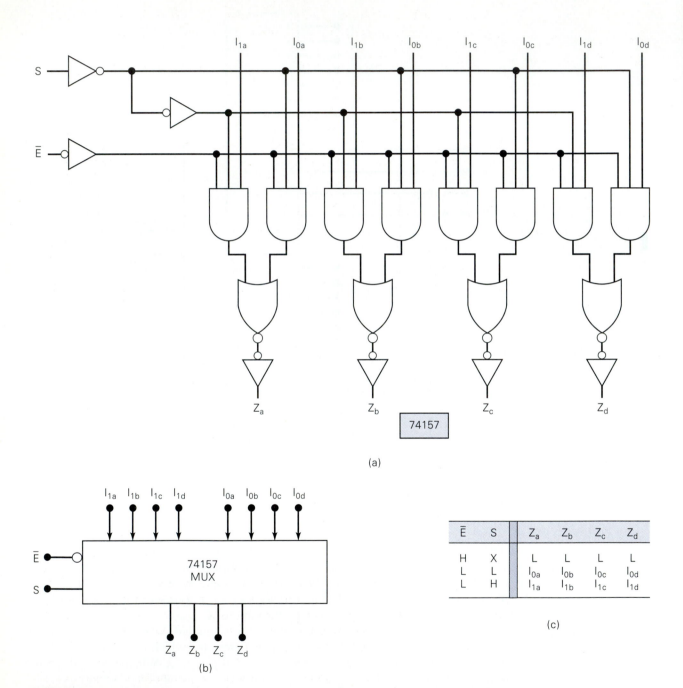

(a)

(b)

$\overline{E}$	S	Z_a	Z_b	Z_c	Z_d
H	X	L	L	L	L
L	L	I_{0a}	I_{0b}	I_{0c}	I_{0d}
L	H	I_{1a}	I_{1b}	I_{1c}	I_{1d}

(c)

FIGURE 9-25 (a) Logic diagram for the 74157 multiplexer; (b) logic symbol; (c) truth table. (Courtesy of Fairchild, a Schlumberger company)

| EXAMPLE 9-10 | Determine the input conditions required for each Z output to take on the logic level of its corresponding I_0 input. Repeat for I_1. |

Solution

First of all, the enable input must be active; that is, $\overline{E} = 0$. In order for Z_a to equal I_{0a}, the select input must be LOW. These same conditions will produce $Z_b = I_{0b}$, $Z_c = I_{0c}$, and $Z_d = I_{0d}$.

With $\overline{E} = 0$ and $S = 1$, the Z outputs will follow the set of I_1 inputs; that is, $Z_a = I_{1a}$, $Z_b = I_{1b}$, $Z_c = I_{1c}$, and $Z_d = I_{1d}$.

All of the outputs will be disabled (LOW) when $\overline{E} = 1$.

It is helpful to think of this multiplexer as being a simple two-input multiplexer, but one in which each input is four lines and the output is four lines. The four output lines switch back and forth between the two sets of four input lines under the control of the select input. This operation is represented by the 74157's logic symbol in Figure 9-25(b).

Review Questions

1. What is the function of a multiplexer's select inputs?
2. A certain multiplexer can switch one of 32 data inputs to its output. How many different inputs does this MUX have?

9-8 MULTIPLEXER APPLICATIONS

Multiplexer circuits find numerous and varied applications in digital systems of all types. These applications include data selection, data routing, operation sequencing, parallel-to-serial conversion, waveform generation, and logic-function generation. We shall look at some of these applications here and several more in the problems at the end of the chapter.

Data Routing

Multiplexers can route data from one of several sources to one destination. One typical application uses 74LS157 multiplexers to select and display the contents of either of two BCD counters using a *single* set of decoder/drivers and LED displays. The circuit arrangement is shown in Figure 9-26.

Each counter consists of two cascaded BCD stages, and each one is driven by its own clock signal. When the COUNTER SELECT line is HIGH, the outputs of counter 1 will be allowed to pass through the multiplexers to the decoder/drivers to be displayed on the LED readouts. When COUNTER SELECT = 0, the outputs of counter 2 will pass through the multiplexers to the displays. In this way the decimal contents of one counter or the other will be displayed under the control of the COUNTER SELECT input. A common situation where this might be used is in a digital watch. The digital watch circuitry contains many counters and registers that keep track of seconds, minutes, hours, days, months, alarm settings, and so on. A

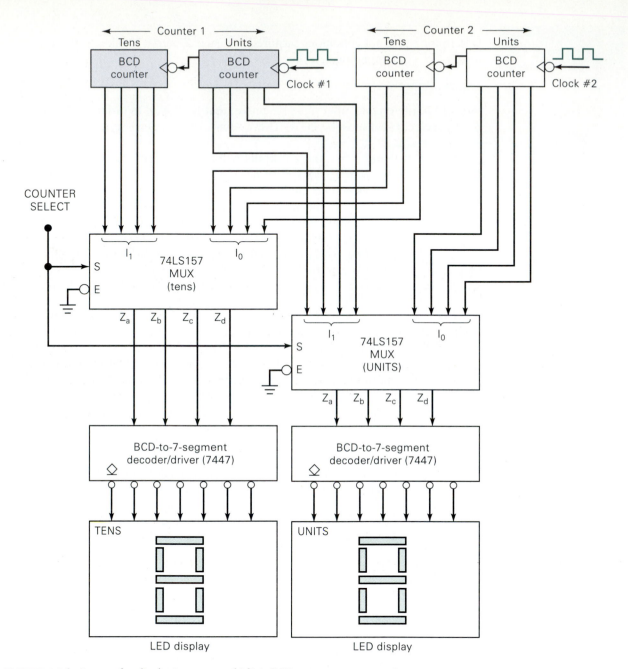

FIGURE 9-26   System for displaying two multidigit BCD counters one at a time.

multiplexing scheme such as this one allows different data to be displayed on the limited number of decimal readouts.

The purpose of the multiplexing technique, as it is used here, is to *time-share* the decoder/drivers and display circuits between the two counters rather than have a separate set of decoder/drivers and displays for each counter. This results in a significant saving in the number of wiring connections, especially when more BCD stages are added to each counter. Even more important, it represents a significant decrease in power consumption, because decoder/drivers and LED readouts typically draw relatively large amounts of current from the V_{CC} supply. Of course, this technique has the limitation that only one counter's contents can be displayed at a time. However, in many applications this is not a drawback. A mechanical switching arrangement could have been used to perform the function of switching first one counter and then the other to the decoder/drivers and displays, but the number of required switch contacts, the complexity of wiring, and the physical size could all be disadvantages over the completely logic method of Figure 9-26.

Parallel-to-Serial Conversion

Many digital systems process binary data in parallel form (all bits simultaneously) because it is faster. When data are to be transmitted over relatively long distances, however, the parallel arrangement is undesirable because it requires a large number of transmission lines. For this reason, binary data or information in parallel form is often converted to serial form before being transmitted to a remote destination. One method for performing this **parallel-to-serial conversion** uses a multiplexer, as illustrated in Figure 9-27.

The data are present in parallel form at the outputs of the X register and are fed to the eight-input multiplexer. A three-bit (MOD-8) counter is used to provide the select code bits $S_2 S_1 S_0$ so that they cycle through from 000 to 111 as clock pulses are applied. In this way, the output of the multiplexer will be X_0 during the first clock period, X_1 during the second clock period, and so on. The output Z is a waveform that is a serial representation of the parallel input data. The waveforms in the figure are for the case where $X_7 X_6 X_5 X_4 X_3 X_2 X_1 X_0 = 10110101$. This conversion process takes a total of eight clock cycles. Note that X_0 (the LSB) is transmitted first and the X_7 (MSB) is transmitted last.

Operation Sequencing

The circuit of Figure 9-28 uses an eight-input multiplexer as part of a control sequencer that steps through seven steps, each of which actuates some portion of the physical process being controlled. This could be, for example, a process that mixes two liquid ingredients and then cooks the mixture. The circuit also uses a 3-line-to-8-line decoder and a MOD-8 binary counter. The operation is described as follows:

1. Initially the counter is reset to the 000 state. The counter outputs are fed to the select inputs of the multiplexer and to the inputs of the decoder. Thus, the decoder output $\overline{O}_0 = 0$ and the others are all 1, so that all the ACTUATOR inputs of the process are LOW. The SENSOR outputs of the process all start out LOW. The multiplexer output $\overline{Z} = \overline{I}_0 = 1$, since the S inputs are 000.

2. The START pulse initiates the sequencing operation by setting flip-flop Q_0 HIGH, bringing the counter to the 001 state. This causes decoder output $\overline{O}_1$ to go LOW, thereby activating actuator 1, which is the first step in the process (opening fill valve #1).

3. Some time later, SENSOR output 1 goes HIGH, indicating the completion of the first step (the float switch indicates that the tank is full). This HIGH is now present at the I_1 input of the multiplexer. It is inverted and reaches the $\overline{Z}$ output since the select code from the counter is 001.

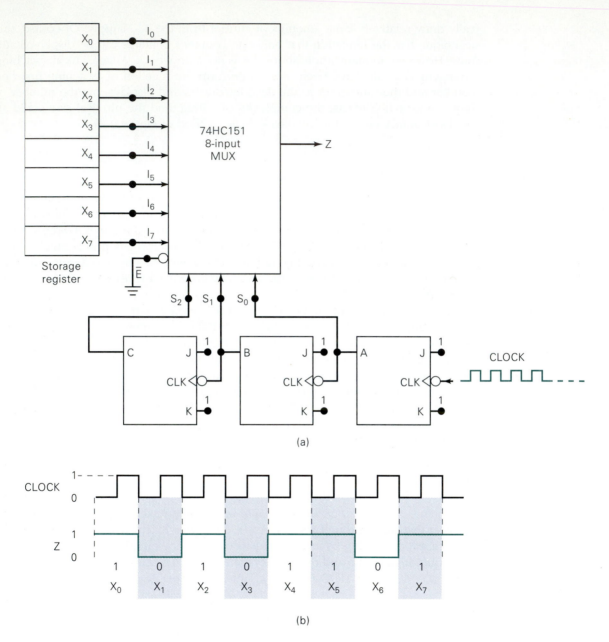

(a)

(b)

FIGURE 9-27 (a) Parallel-to-serial converter; (b) waveforms for $X_7X_6X_5X_4X_3X_2X_1X_0 =$ 10110101.

4. The LOW transition at $\overline{Z}$ is fed to the *CLK* of flip-flop Q_0. This negative transition advances the counter to the 010 state.

5. Decoder output $\overline{O}_2$ now goes LOW, activating actuator 2, which is the second step in the process (opening fill valve #2). $\overline{Z}$ now equals $\overline{I}_2$ (the select code is 010). Since SENSOR output 2 is still LOW, $\overline{Z}$ will go HIGH.

6. When the second process step is complete, SENSOR output 2 goes HIGH, producing a LOW at $\overline{Z}$ and advancing the counter to 011.

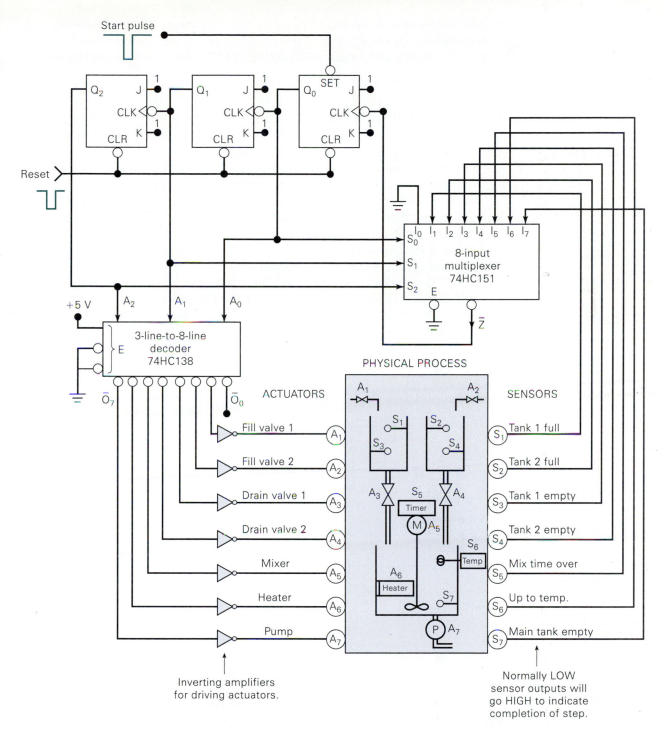

FIGURE 9-28 Seven-step control sequencer.

7. This same action is repeated for each of the other steps. When the seventh step is completed, SENSOR output 7 goes HIGH, causing the counter to go from 111 to 000, where it will remain until another START pulse reinitiates the sequence.

Logic Function Generation

Multiplexers can be used to implement logic functions directly from a truth table without the need for simplification. When a multiplexer is used for this purpose, the select inputs are used as the logic variables, and each data input is connected permanently HIGH or LOW as necessary to satisfy the truth table.

Figure 9-29 illustrates how an eight-input multiplexer can be used to implement the logic circuit that satisfies the given truth table. The input variables A, B, C are connected to S_0, S_1, S_2, respectively, so that the levels on these inputs determine which data input appears at output Z. According to the truth table, Z is supposed to be LOW when $CBA = 000$. Thus, multiplexer input I_0 should be connected LOW. Likewise, Z is supposed to be LOW for $CBA = 011$, 100, 101, and 110, so that inputs I_3, I_4, I_5, and I_6 should also be connected LOW. The other sets of CBA conditions must produce $Z = 1$, and so multiplexer inputs I_1, I_2, and I_7 are connected permanently HIGH.

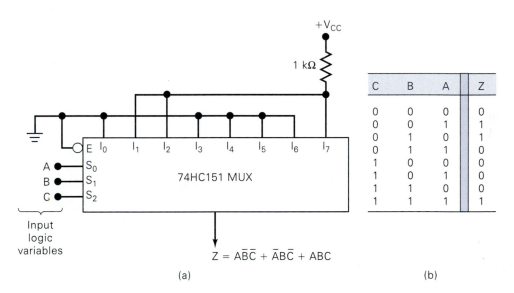

$$Z = A\overline{B}\overline{C} + \overline{A}B\overline{C} + ABC$$

(a)

C	B	A	Z
0	0	0	0
0	0	1	1
0	1	0	1
0	1	1	0
1	0	0	0
1	0	1	0
1	1	0	0
1	1	1	1

(b)

FIGURE 9-29 Multiplexer used to implement a logic function described by the truth table.

It is easy to see that any three-variable truth table can be implemented with this eight-input multiplexer. This method of implementation is often more efficient than using separate logic gates. For example, if we can write the sum-of-products expression for the truth table in Figure 9-29, we have

$$Z = A\overline{B}\overline{C} + \overline{A}B\overline{C} + ABC$$

This *cannot* be simplified either algebraically or by K mapping, and so its gate implementation would require three INVERTERs and four NAND gates, for a total of two ICs.

There is an even more efficient method for using multiplexers to implement logic functions. This method will allow the logic designer to use a multiplexer with three select inputs (e.g., a 74HC151) to implement a *four-variable* logic function. We will present this method in Problem 9-35.

1. What are some of the major applications of multiplexers?
2. *True or false:* When a multiplexer is used to implement a logic function, the logic variables are applied to the multiplexer's data inputs.
3. What type of circuit provides the select inputs when a MUX is used as a parallel-to-serial converter?

9-9   DEMULTIPLEXERS (DATA DISTRIBUTORS)

A multiplexer takes several inputs and transmits *one* of them to the output. A **demultiplexer (DEMUX)** performs the reverse operation: it takes a single input and distributes it over several outputs. Figure 9-30 shows the functional diagram for a digital demultiplexer. The large arrows for inputs and outputs can represent one or more lines. The select input code determines to which output the DATA input will be transmitted. In other words, the demultiplexer takes one input data source and selectively distributes it to 1 of N output channels just like a multiposition switch.

FIGURE 9-30   General demultiplexer.

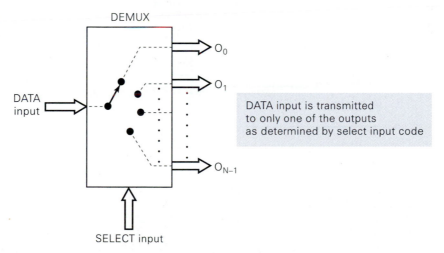

DATA input is transmitted to only one of the outputs as determined by select input code

1-Line-to-8-Line Demultiplexer

Figure 9-31 shows the logic diagram for a demultiplexer that distributes one input line to eight output lines. The single data input line I is connected to all eight AND gates, but only one of these gates will be enabled by the SELECT input lines. For ex-

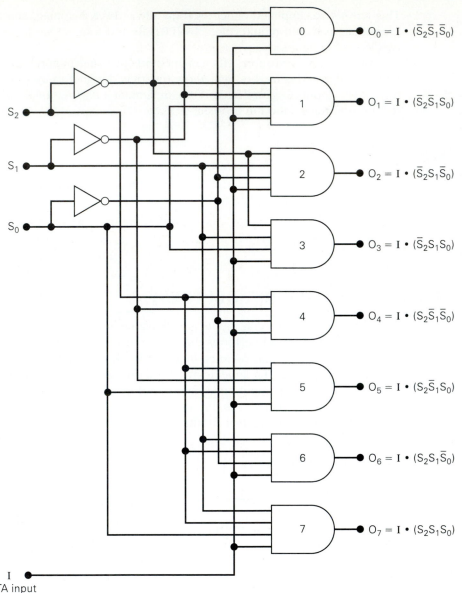

SELECT code			OUTPUTS							
S_2	S_1	S_0	O_7	O_6	O_5	O_4	O_3	O_2	O_1	O_0
0	0	0	0	0	0	0	0	0	0	I
0	0	1	0	0	0	0	0	0	I	0
0	1	0	0	0	0	0	0	I	0	0
0	1	1	0	0	0	0	I	0	0	0
1	0	0	0	0	0	I	0	0	0	0
1	0	1	0	0	I	0	0	0	0	0
1	1	0	0	I	0	0	0	0	0	0
1	1	1	I	0	0	0	0	0	0	0

Note: I is the
data input

FIGURE 9-31   1-line-to-8-line demultiplexer.

ample, with $S_2S_1S_0 = 000$, only AND gate 0 will be enabled, and data input I will appear at output O_0. Other SELECT codes cause input I to reach the other outputs. The truth table summarizes the operation.

The demultiplexer circuit of Figure 9-31 is very similar to the 3-line-to-8-line decoder circuit in Figure 9-2 except that a fourth input (I) has been added to each gate. It was pointed out earlier that many IC decoders have an ENABLE input, which is an extra input added to the decoder gates. This type of decoder chip can therefore be used as a demultiplexer, with the binary code inputs (e.g., A, B, C in Figure 9-2) serving as the SELECT inputs and the ENABLE input serving as the data input I. For this reason, IC manufacturers often call this type of device a *decoder/demultiplexer,* and it can be used for either function.

We saw earlier how the 74LS138 is used as a 1-of-8 decoder. Figure 9-32 shows how it can be used as a demultiplexer. The enable input $\overline{E}_1$ is used as the data input I, while the other two enable inputs are held in their active states. The $A_2A_1A_0$ inputs are used as the select code. To illustrate the operation, let's assume that the select inputs are 000. With this input code, the only output that can be activated is $\overline{O}_0$, while all other outputs are HIGH. $\overline{O}_0$ will go LOW only if $\overline{E}_1$ goes LOW and will be HIGH if $\overline{E}_1$ goes HIGH. In other words, $\overline{O}_0$ *will follow the signal on* $\overline{E}_1$ (i.e., the data input, I) while all other outputs stay HIGH. In a similar manner, a different select code applied to $A_2A_1A_0$ will cause the corresponding output to follow the data input, I.

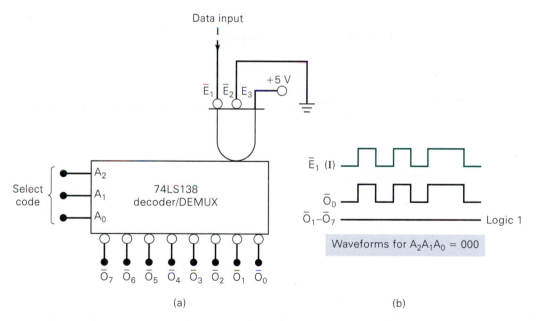

(a)   (b)

FIGURE 9-32   (a) The 74LS138 decoder can function as a demultiplexer with $\overline{E}_1$ used as the data input. (b) Typical waveforms for a select code of $A_2A_1A_0 = 000$ show that $\overline{O}_0$ is identical to the data input I on $\overline{E}_1$.

Figure 9-32(b) shows typical waveforms for the case where $A_2A_1A_0 = 000$ selects output $\overline{O}_0$. For this case, the data signal applied to $\overline{E}_1$ will be transmitted to $\overline{O}_0$, and all other outputs will remain in their inactive HIGH state.

Clock Demultiplexer

Many applications of the demultiplexing principle are possible. Figure 9-33 shows the 74LS138 demultiplexer being used as a *clock demultiplexer*. Under control of the SELECT lines, the clock signal is routed to the desired destination. For example, with $S_2 S_1 S_0 = 000$, the clock signal applied to I will appear at output $\overline{O}_0$. With $S_2 S_1 S_0 = 101$, the clock will appear at $\overline{O}_5$.

FIGURE 9-33 A clock demultiplexer transmits the clock signal to a destination determined by the select code inputs.

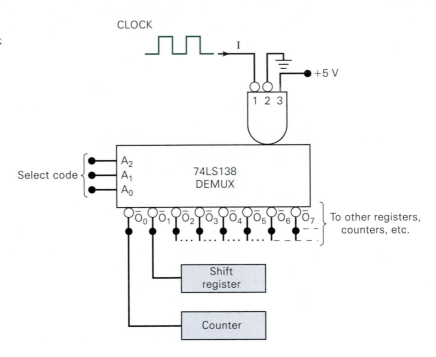

Security Monitoring System

Consider the case of a security monitoring system in an industrial plant where the open/closed status of many access doors is to be monitored. Each door controls the state of a switch, and it is necessary to display the state of each switch on LEDs that are mounted on a remote monitoring panel at the security guard's station. One way to do this would be to run a separate signal from each door switch to an LED on the monitoring panel. This would require running many wires over a long distance. A better approach that would reduce the amount of wiring to the monitoring panel uses a multiplexer/demultiplexer combination. Figure 9-34 shows a system that can handle eight doors, but the basic idea can be expanded to any number.

EXAMPLE 9-11

Examine Figure 9-34 carefully and describe the complete operation.

Solution

The eight door switches are the data inputs to the MUX; they produce a HIGH when a door is open and a LOW when it is closed. The MOD-8 counter provides the select inputs to the MUX and also to the DEMUX on the remote monitoring

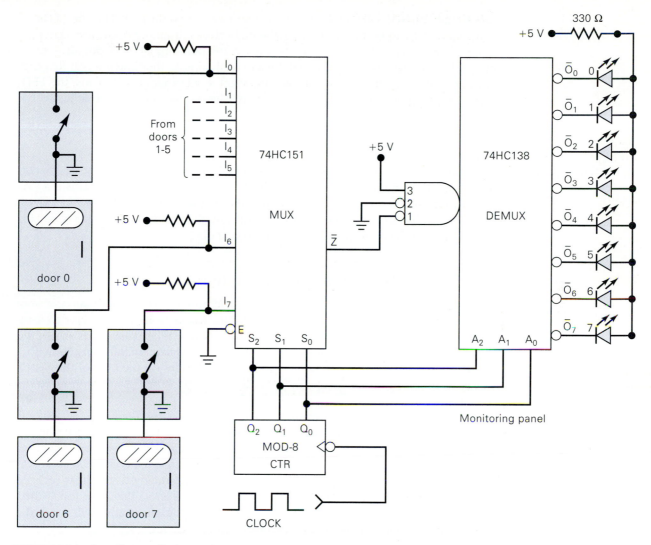

FIGURE 9-34   Security monitoring system.

panel. Each DEMUX output is connected to an indicator LED that will be on when the output is LOW. Clock pulses applied to the counter will cause the select inputs to sequence through all of the possible states 000 through 111. At each number of the counter, the switch status for the door of the same number will be inverted by the MUX and passed to output $\overline{Z}$. From there it is transmitted to the DEMUX input, which passes it through to the output corresponding to the same number.

For example, let's say that the counter is at the count of 110 (6). While the counter is in this state, let's say that door 6 is closed. The LOW at I_6 will pass through the MUX and be inverted to produce a HIGH at $\overline{Z}$. This HIGH will be passed through the DEMUX to output $\overline{O}_6$ so that LED 6 will be off, indicating that door 6 is closed. Now let's say that door 6 is open. A LOW will appear at $\overline{Z}$ and $\overline{O}_6$ so that LED 6 will be on to signal that door 6 is open. Of course, all other LEDs will be off during this time since $\overline{O}_6$ is the only active output.

As the counter is clocked through its eight states 000 through 111, the LEDs will sequentially indicate the status of the eight doors. If all the doors are closed, none of the LEDs will be on even when the corresponding DEMUX output is selected. If a door is open, its LED will turn on only during the time interval that the counter is at the appropriate count; it will be off at all other counts. Thus, the LED will be flashing on and off if its door is open. The flashing rate can be adjusted by changing the frequency of the clock.

Note that there are only four signal lines going from the "door-sensing" circuitry to the remote monitoring panel: the $\overline{Z}$ output and the three select lines. This is a saving of four lines when compared with the alternative of having one line per door. The MUX/DEMUX combination is used to transmit the status of each door to its LED one at a time (serially) instead of all at once (parallel).

Synchronous Data Transmission System

Figure 9-35 shows the logic diagram for a synchronous data transmission system that is used to serially transmit four four-bit data words from a transmitter to a remote receiver. Let's look at the transmitter circuitry first. The data words are stored in registers A, B, C, and D that are connected as recirculating shift registers with a common SHIFT (clock) input. Each register will shift right on the PGT of the SHIFT pulses from AND gate 2. The LSB of each register is connected as a data input to the four-input multiplexer.

The two MOD-4 counters control the transmission of the data register contents to the multiplexer output Z. The *word counter* selects the register data that will appear at Z. As this counter counts from 00 to 11, the data from each register will sequentially appear at Z. The *bit counter* makes sure that four data bits from each register are transmitted through the multiplexer before advancing to the next register. The bit counter advances one count for each SHIFT pulse, so that after four SHIFT pulses, it recycles to 00. The NGT at the Q_1 output of the bit counter will cause the word counter to be incremented to the next count to select the next data register for transmission. In this way the contents of each of the data registers will be transmitted to Z, one bit at a time, starting with register A (for $S_1 S_0 = 00$) and proceeding through each register as the word counter advances one count for every four SHIFT pulses. The Z signal will thus contain 16 bits of serial data, 4 bits from each register. These data are said to be *time-division-multiplexed* because four different sets of data are appearing on the same output line at different times.

The transmission process is controlled by the two D flip-flops, AND gates 1 and 2, and the one-shot. The operation of this control logic will be described in a later paragraph.

The Receiver

The receiver circuitry contains a 1-to-4 demultiplexer that receives the Z signal from the transmitter's multiplexer and *demultiplexes* it; that is, it separates the four different sets of data and distributes them to four different outputs so that the data that came from register A will appear serially at O_0, the data from register B at O_1, and

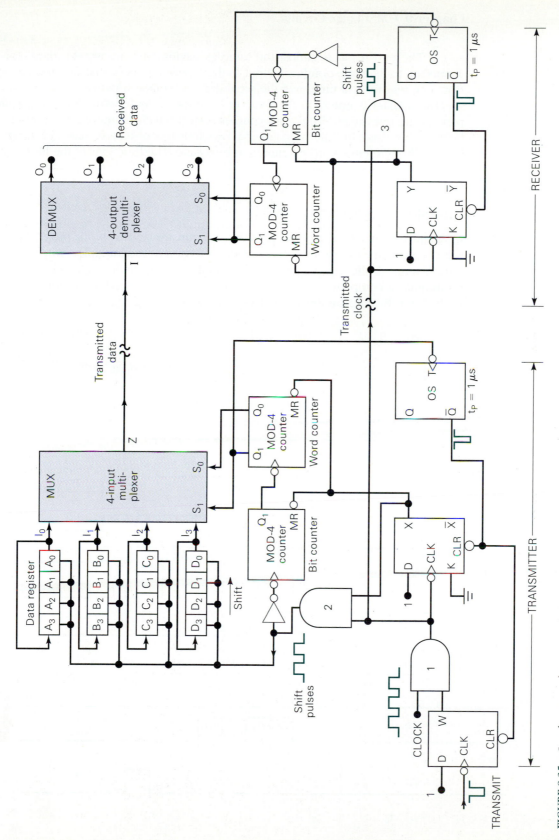

FIGURE 9-35 Synchronous data transmission system.

so on. The end result is almost the same as having each transmitter data register connected to its corresponding output in the receiver, except that the data are sent from one register at a time over the serial data transmission path.

The MOD-4 counters in the receiver have the same function as their counterparts in the transmitter. The word counter selects which demultiplexer output will be receiving data, and the bit counter allows four bits of data to reach each output before advancing the word counter to its next state. The functions of the FF, OS, and AND gate are described below.

Complete Operation

It should be clear that in order for this data transmission to work properly, there must be some means for synchronizing the selection of the multiplexer inputs in the transmitter with the selection of the demultiplexer outputs in the receiver. We will go through a complete operation cycle to see how this synchronization is accomplished. For this illustration we will assume the following register data:

$$[A] = 0110 \qquad [B] = 1001 \qquad [C] = 1011 \qquad [D] = 0100$$

As we go through the following steps, we will refer to the waveforms in Figure 9-36:

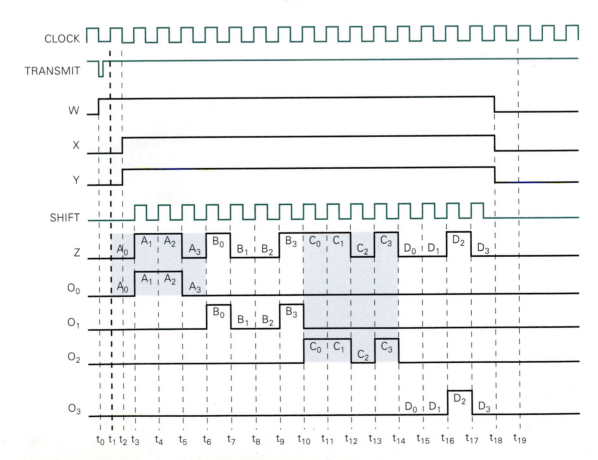

FIGURE 9-36 Waveforms during one complete transmission cycle.

1. Flip-flops W and X in the transmitter and flip-flop Y in the receiver are normally LOW. The LOWs from X and Y will keep both sets of counters in the 0 state. The LOW at W prevents CLOCK pulses from getting through AND gate 1.

2. With both word counters at 00, the LOW at A_0 passes through the multiplexer to Z into the demultiplexer to output O_0. All other demultiplexer outputs are LOW, since they are not selected.

3. This is the situation prior to time t_0. At t_0, the TRANSMIT pulse sets $W = 1$ to enable AND gate 1 to pass CLOCK pulses. These CLOCK pulses also become the TRANSMITTED CLOCK that is sent to the receiver along with the TRANS-MITTED DATA.

4. The NGT of the first CLOCK pulse out of AND gate 1 will set X and Y both HIGH at time t_2. This removes the resets from the counters and also enables AND gates 2 and 3 to pass CLOCK pulses starting at t_3. The pulses out of AND gate 2 are the SHIFT pulses. The pulses out of AND gate 3 are exactly the same as the SHIFT pulses out of AND gate 2.

5. The PGTs of the SHIFT pulses at t_3, t_4, and t_5 will shift A_1, A_2, and A_3 into the multiplexer, out of Z, into the demultiplexer, and out of output O_0. These three PGTs are also counted by both bit counters.

6. The PGT at t_6 will shift all of the registers back to their original data and will re-cycle the bit counters to 00. The NGT at Q_1 of the bit counters will increment the transmitter and receiver word counters to 01 to select I_1 and O_1, respec-tively. Thus, the HIGH at B_0 will pass through the multiplexer into the demulti-plexer and out of O_1.

7. The SHIFT pulses at t_7, t_8, and t_9 will shift B_1, B_2, and B_3 into the multiplexer and out of O_1. At t_{10} the bit counters will recycle and increment the word coun-ters to 10 to select I_2 and O_2. This places the HIGH from C_0 at Z and at O_2.

8. The SHIFT pulses at t_{11}, t_{12}, and t_{13} will shift C_1, C_2, and C_3 into the multiplexer and out of O_2. At t_{14} the bit counters recycle and increment the word counters to 11 to select I_3 and O_3. This places the LOW from D_0 at Z and at O_3.

9. The SHIFT pulses at t_{15}, t_{16}, and t_{17} will shift D_1, D_2, and D_3 into the multiplexer and out of O_3. At t_{18} the bit counters recycle and increment the word counters to 00. The NGT at Q_1 of the *word* counters will trigger their respective one-shots to produce narrow clearing pulses for FFs W, X, and Y. With these FFs all LOW, all CLOCK pulses and SHIFT pulses are inhibited, and all of the counters remain in the 0 state.

10. The circuit conditions are back to their original state. No more data will be transmitted until the next TRANSMIT pulse occurs.

The waveforms at Z and O_0 to O_3 show how the register data are multiplexed onto the Z signal and then demultiplexed so that each output receives the correct data.

Review Questions

1. Explain the difference between a DEMUX and a MUX.

2. *True or false:* The circuit for a DEMUX is basically the same as for a decoder.

3. For the system of Figure 9-34, what will the security guard see on the moni-toring panel when all of the doors are open?

9-10   MORE IEEE/ANSI SYMBOLOGY*

We will now look at the IEEE/ANSI symbols for the MUX and DEMUX integrated circuits that we have been using. First consider the symbol for the 74151 shown in Figure 9-37(a). The label $G\frac{0}{7}$ within the block denotes the AND dependency between the select inputs and each of the data inputs 0 through 7. In other words, each data input is ANDed with one specific combination of select inputs, and when that combination occurs, the data input is routed to the output.

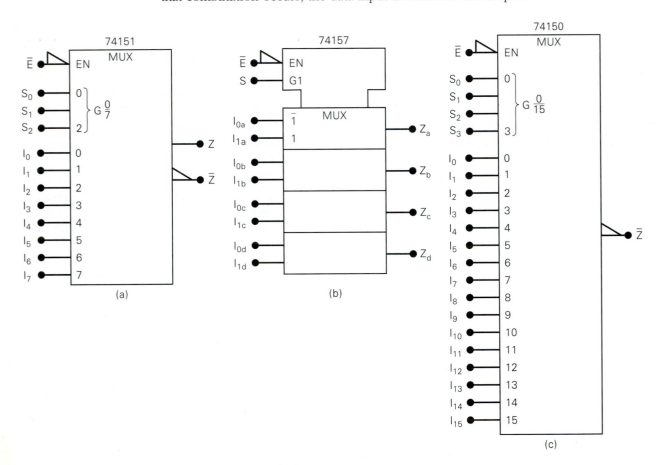

FIGURE 9-37   IEEE/ANSI symbols for various multiplexers.

Figure 9-37(b) is the IEEE/ANSI symbol for the 74157 multiplexer. Recall from Figure 9-25 that this IC contains four two-input MUXes that operate identically. The common-control block shows that the enable and select inputs are common to all of the MUXes. The notation G1 on the select input and the $\overline{1}$ and 1 labels on the data inputs indicate the AND dependency between the select input and the data inputs. The $\overline{1}$ label for I_{0a} means that this input will be routed to output Z_a only when the select input is a 0. Similarly, the 1 on the I_{1a} input indicates that this input will be

---

*   This section may be skipped without affecting the continuity of the rest of the book.

routed to Z_a only when the select input is a 1. The other three MUXes operate the same way.

EXAMPLE
9-12

The IEEE/ANSI symbol for the 74150 IC is shown in Figure 9-37(c). What is the function of this device?

Solution

The 74150 is a 16-input multiplexer. Note the four select inputs required to select one of the 16 data inputs for transmission to the output. Also note that the output is inverted, so that it will be the inverse of the selected data input.

Figure 9-38 is the IEEE/ANSI symbol for the 74LS138/HC138 DEMUX. Compare it to the symbol in Figure 9-17(c), where the same IC is used as a decoder.

FIGURE 9-38   IEEE/ANSI symbol for the 74LS138 DEMUX.

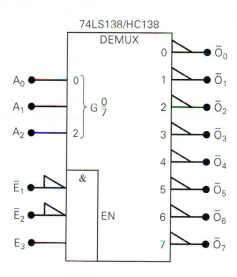

9-11   MORE TROUBLESHOOTING

Here are three more examples to illustrate the observation/reasoning process that is such an important initial step when troubleshooting. For each case, try to determine the circuit fault before looking at the solutions.

EXAMPLE
9-13

Consider the circuit of Figure 9-26. A test performed on this circuit yields the result shown in Table 9-2. What is the probable circuit fault?

Solution

In each of the test cases, the display of counter 1 matches the counter's actual count. This indicates that the I_1 inputs, all MUX outputs, and both displays are probably working correctly. On the other hand, each test case shows that counter

TABLE 9-2

		Actual Count	Displayed Count
Case 1	Counter 1	25	25
	Counter 2	37	35
Case 2	Counter 1	49	49
	Counter 2	72	79
Case 3	Counter 1	96	96
	Counter 2	14	16

2's *tens* digit is displayed correctly but its *units* digit is displayed incorrectly. This could mean that there is a fault somewhere between the output of the units section of counter 2 and the I_0 inputs of the units MUX. We should compare the bit patterns of the actual and displayed values of the units for counter 2 (Table 9-3). The idea is to look for things like a bit that does not change (stuck LOW or HIGH) or two bits that are reversed (crossed connections). The data in Table 9-3 reveal no obvious pattern.

TABLE 9-3

	Actual Units	Displayed Units
Case 1	0111 (7)	0101 (5)
Case 2	0010 (2)	1001 (9)
Case 3	0100 (4)	0110 (6)

If we take another look at the recorded test results, we see that the displayed units digit of counter 2 is always the same as the units digit of counter 1. This symptom is probably the result of a constant logic HIGH at the select input of the units MUX, since that would continually pass the units digit of counter 1 to the units MUX output. This constant HIGH at the select input is most likely caused by an open path somewhere between the select input of the tens MUX and the select input of the units MUX. It could not be caused by a short to V_{CC}, since that would also keep the select input of the tens MUX at a constant HIGH, and we know that the tens MUX is working.

EXAMPLE 9-14

The security monitoring system of Figure 9-34 is tested and the results are recorded in Table 9-4. What are the possible faults that could produce these results?

Solution

Again, the data should be reviewed to see if there is some pattern that could help to narrow down the search for the fault to a small area of the circuit. The data in Table 9-4 reveal that the correct LEDs flash for open doors 4 through 7. They also show that for open doors 0 through 3 the number of the flashing LED is *four* more than the number of the door, and LEDs 0 through 3 are always off. This is most probably caused by a constant logic HIGH at A_2, the MSB of the select input of the

TABLE 9-4

Condition	LEDs
All doors closed	All LEDs off
Door 0 open	LED 4 flashing
Door 1 open	LED 5 flashing
Door 2 open	LED 6 flashing
Door 3 open	LED 7 flashing
Door 4 open	LED 4 flashing
Door 5 open	LED 5 flashing
Door 6 open	LED 6 flashing
Door 7 open	LED 7 flashing

DEMUX, since this would always make the select code 4 or greater, and it would add 4 to the select codes 0 through 3.

Thus, we have two possibilities: A_2 is somehow shorted to V_{CC}, or there is an open connection at A_2. A little thought will eliminate the first choice as a possibility since this would also mean that S_2 of the MUX would also be stuck HIGH. If that were so, then the status of doors 0 through 3 would not get through the MUX and into the DEMUX. We know that this is not true because the data show that when any of these doors is open, it affects one of the DEMUX outputs.

EXAMPLE 9-15

Suppose that the synchronous data transmission system of Figure 9-35 is malfunctioning as follows: the Z waveform is correct, but the O_0 waveform is identical to the Z waveform at all times while the other outputs are constantly LOW. Assume that the receiver circuit is soldered on a PC board with no IC sockets.

Solution

Observation/analysis should be used to determine the possible causes. Divide-and-conquer should be used to isolate the problem. The most obvious cause appears to be that S_1 and S_0 of the DEMUX are always LOW as data are transmitted. If this is *not* the case, then the DEMUX *must* be faulty. Using a logic probe, we should eliminate this possibility first since it is a simple test that could isolate the problem from all other circuitry. Assuming that we find that S_1 and S_0 *are* always LOW, there are many possible causes for this symptom. Let's list them:

1. S_0 of the MUX or Q_0 of the word counter could be shorted to ground, preventing the counter from incrementing.
2. The word counter could be defective (shorted or open *CLK* line, *MR* shorted to ground, or internal faults).
3. The bit counter could be defective (shorted or open *CLK* or Q_1, *MR* shorted to ground, or internal faults).
4. The INVERTER or the AND gate could be defective (shorted or open outputs or inputs, or internal faults).
5. FF Y could be defective (*D*, *CLR*, or *Y* shorted to ground, or internal faults).

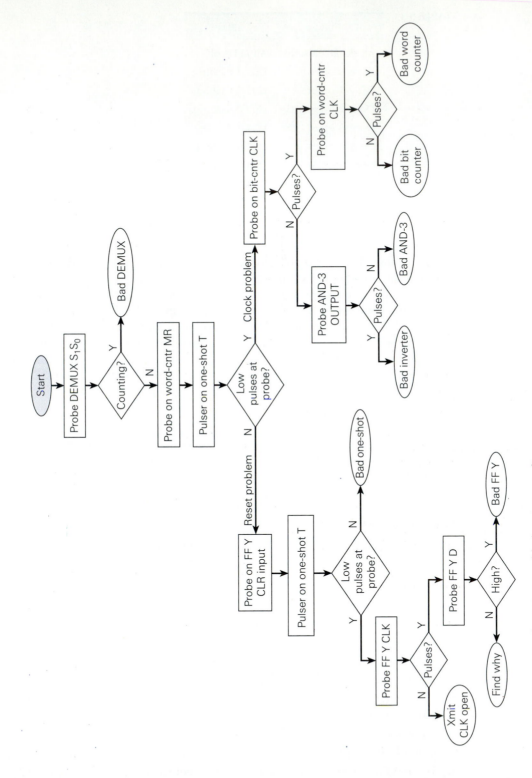

FIGURE 9-39 Example 9-15: a troubleshooting tree diagram.

6. The one-shot could be defective (trigger shorted or open, Q_0 shorted to ground, faulty RC circuit connected to the one-shot, or internal faults).

7. The transmitted clock line may be open between the transmitter and the receiver.

Since replacing all components means desoldering 14- and 16-pin IC chips, we do not want to employ the "shot-gun" approach to troubleshooting. We must find a way to eliminate possible faults by the divide-and-conquer approach. Starting at the word counter, we decide that either the clock is not getting pulsed or the MR pin is being held LOW. If either of these two assumptions can be proven false, we have removed half of the ICs from the suspect list! We place our probe on the MR of the word counter to see if it goes HIGH. If it is HIGH, it is likely that the transmit clock line is not open, FF Y works, and there is no reason to suspect the one-shot. This could all be verified by putting a logic probe on MR and injecting a pulse into the T input of the one-shot. If we detect a negative pulse on MR (about the width of one clock cycle), we have eliminated causes 5, 6, and 7. A troubleshooting tree diagram is shown in Figure 9-39. As you follow it through, notice that tests are always made at a point in the circuit that will eliminate as many possible faults as we can. This diagram does not cover every possible fault in this circuit; and when it concludes that a component is bad, it may require some local troubleshooting to confirm that the chip is bad before replacing it. However, it does show the logic that a good troubleshooter should utilize to isolate the problem. A good troubleshooter is like a good detective, always looking for clues and making wise deductions from the facts.

9-12 MAGNITUDE COMPARATOR

Another useful member of the MSI category of ICs is the *magnitude comparator*. It is a combinational logic circuit that compares two input binary quantities and generates outputs to indicate which one has the greater magnitude. Figure 9-40 shows the logic symbol and the truth table for the 74HC85 four-bit magnitude comparator, which is also available as the 7485 and the 74LS85.

Data Inputs

The 74HC85 compares two *unsigned* four-bit binary numbers. One of them is $A_3A_2A_1A_0$, which is called word A; the other is $B_3B_2B_1B_0$, which is called word B. The term *word* is used in the digital computer field to designate a group of bits that represents some specific type of information. Here word A and word B represent numerical quantities.

Outputs

The 74HC85 has three active-HIGH outputs. Output $O_{A>B}$ will be HIGH when the magnitude of word A is greater than the magnitude of word B. Output $O_{A<B}$ will be HIGH when the magnitude of word A is less than the magnitude of word B. Output $O_{A=B}$ will be HIGH when word A and word B are identical.

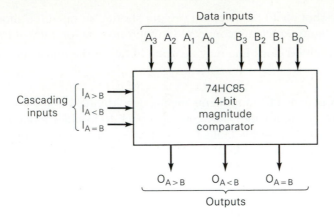

TRUTH TABLE

COMPARING INPUTS				CASCADING INPUTS			OUTPUTS		
A_3, B_3	A_2, B_2	A_1, B_1	A_0, B_0	$I_{A>B}$	$I_{A<B}$	$I_{A=B}$	$O_{A>B}$	$O_{A<B}$	$O_{A=B}$
$A_3 > B_3$	X	X	X	X	X	X	H	L	L
$A_3 < B_3$	X	X	X	X	X	X	L	H	L
$A_3 = B_3$	$A_2 > B_2$	X	X	X	X	X	H	L	L
$A_3 = B_3$	$A_2 < B_2$	X	X	X	X	X	L	H	L
$A_3 = B_3$	$A_2 = B_2$	$A_1 > B_1$	X	X	X	X	H	L	L
$A_3 = B_3$	$A_2 = B_2$	$A_1 < B_1$	X	X	X	X	L	H	L
$A_3 = B_3$	$A_2 = B_2$	$A_1 = B_1$	$A_0 > B_0$	X	X	X	H	L	L
$A_3 = B_3$	$A_2 = B_2$	$A_1 = B_1$	$A_0 < B_0$	X	X	X	L	H	L
$A_3 = B_3$	$A_2 = B_2$	$A_1 = B_1$	$A_0 = B_0$	H	L	L	H	L	L
$A_3 = B_3$	$A_2 = B_2$	$A_1 = B_1$	$A_0 = B_0$	L	H	L	L	H	L
$A_3 = B_3$	$A_2 = B_2$	$A_1 = B_1$	$A_0 = B_0$	X	X	H	L	L	H
$A_3 = B_3$	$A_2 = B_2$	$A_1 = B_1$	$A_0 = B_0$	L	L	L	H	H	L
$A_3 = B_3$	$A_2 = B_2$	$A_1 = B_1$	$A_0 = B_0$	H	H	L	L	L	L

H = HIGH Voltage Level
L = LOW Voltage Level
X = Immaterial

FIGURE 9-40 Logic symbol and truth table for a 74HC85 (7485, 74LS85) four-bit magnitude comparator.

Cascading Inputs

Cascading inputs provide a means for expanding the comparison operation to more than four bits by cascading two or more four-bit comparators. Note that the cascading inputs are labeled the same as the outputs. When a four-bit comparison is being made as in Figure 9-41(a), the cascading inputs should be connected as shown in order for the comparator to produce the correct outputs.

When two comparators are to be cascaded, the outputs of the lower-order comparator are connected to the corresponding inputs of the higher-order comparator. This is shown in Figure 9-41(b), where the comparator on the left is comparing the lower-order four bits of the two eight-bit words: $A_7A_6A_5A_4A_3A_2A_1A_0$ and $B_7B_6B_5B_4B_3B_2B_1B_0$. Its outputs are fed to the cascade inputs of the comparator on

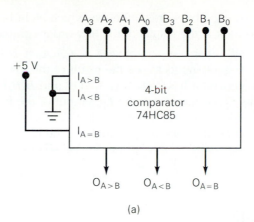

(a)

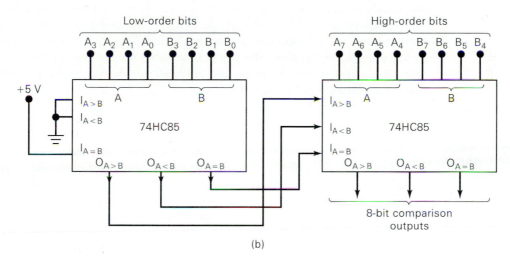

(b)

FIGURE 9-41   (a) 74HC85 wired as a four-bit comparator; (b) two 74HC85s cascaded to perform an eight-bit comparison.

the right, which is comparing the high-order bits. The outputs of the high-order comparator are the final outputs that indicate the result of the eight-bit comparison.

EXAMPLE 9-16

Describe the operation of the eight-bit comparison arrangement in Figure 9-41(b) for the following cases.

(a) $A_7A_6A_5A_4A_3A_2A_1A_0 = 10101111$; $B_7B_6B_5B_4B_3B_2B_1B_0 = 10110001$

(b) $A_7A_6A_5A_4A_3A_2A_1A_0 = 10101111$; $B_7B_6B_5B_4B_3B_2B_1B_0 = 10101001$

Solution

(a) The high-order comparator compares its inputs $A_7A_6A_5A_4 = 1010$ and $B_7B_6B_5B_4 = 1011$ and produces $O_{A<B} = 1$ regardless of what levels are applied to its cascade inputs from the low-order comparator. In other words, once the high-order comparator senses a difference in the high-order bits of

the two eight-bit words, it knows which eight-bit word is greater without having to look at the results of the low-order comparison.

(b) The high-order comparator sees $A_7A_6A_5A_4 = B_7B_6B_5B_4 = 1010$, so it must look at its cascade inputs to see the result of the low-order comparison. The low-order comparator has $A_3A_2A_1A_0 = 1111$ and $B_3B_2B_1B_0 = 1001$, which produces a 1 at its $O_{A>B}$ output and the $I_{A>B}$ input of the high-order comparator. The high-order comparator senses this 1, and since its data inputs are equal, it produces a HIGH at its $O_{A>B}$ to indicate the result of the eight-bit comparison.

Applications

Magnitude comparators are also useful in control applications where a binary number representing the physical variable being controlled (e.g., position, speed, or temperature) is compared with a reference value. The comparator outputs are used to actuate circuitry to drive the physical variable toward the reference value. The following example will illustrate one application. We will examine another comparator application in Problem 9-49.

EXAMPLE 9-17

Consider a digital thermostat in which the measured room temperature is converted to a digital number and applied to the A inputs of a comparator. The desired room temperature, entered from a keypad, is stored in a register that is connected to the B inputs. If $A < B$, the furnace should be activated to heat the room. The furnace should continue to heat while $A = B$ and shut off when $A > B$. As the room cools off, the furnace should stay off while $A = B$ and turn on again when $A < B$. What digital circuit could be used to interface a magnitude comparator to a furnace to perform the thermostat control application described above?

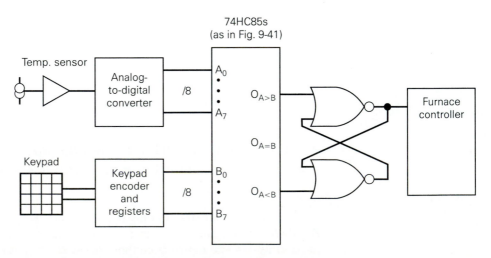

FIGURE 9-42 Magnitude comparator used in a digital thermostat.

Solution

Using the $O_{A<B}$ output to directly drive the furnace would cause it to turn off as soon as the values became equal. This can cause severe on/off cycling of the furnace when the actual temperature is very close to the boundary between $A < B$ and $A = B$. By using a NOR gate SET-CLEAR latch circuit (refer to Chapter 5) as shown in Figure 9-42, the system will operate as described. Notice that $O_{A<B}$ is connected to the SET input and $O_{A>B}$ is connected to the CLEAR input of the latch. When the temperature is hotter than desired, it clears the latch, shutting off the furnace. When the temperature is cooler than desired, it sets the latch, turning the furnace on.

IEEE/ANSI Symbol

Figure 9-43 shows the IEEE/ANSI symbol for the 74HC85 comparator. Note that the symbol uses P and Q to represent the input variables. This is the preferred designation used by the IEEE/ANSI standard.

FIGURE 9-43 IEEE/ANSI symbol for comparator.

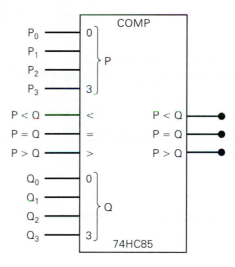

Review Questions

1. What is the purpose of the cascading inputs of the 74HC85?
2. What are the outputs of a 74HC85 with the following inputs: $A_3A_2A_1A_0 = B_3B_2B_1B_0 = 1001$, $I_{A>B} = I_{A<B} = 0$, and $I_{A=B} = 1$?

9-13 CODE CONVERTERS

A code converter is a logic circuit that changes data presented in one type of binary code to another type of binary code. The BCD-to-7-segment decoder/driver that we presented earlier is a code converter because it changes a BCD input code to the 7-

segment code needed by the LED display. A partial list of some of the more common code conversions is given in Table 9-5.

As an example of a code converter circuit, let's consider a BCD-to-binary converter. Before we get started on the circuit implementation, we should review the BCD representation.

Two-digit decimal values ranging from 00 to 99 can be represented in BCD by two four-bit code groups. For example, 57_{10} is represented as

$$\overbrace{\quad}^{5} \qquad \overbrace{\quad}^{7}$$
$$0101 \qquad\quad 0111 \qquad\quad \text{(BCD)}$$

The straight binary representation for decimal 57 is

$$57_{10} = 111001_2$$

The largest two-digit decimal value of 99 has the following representations:

$$99_{10} = 10011001 \text{ (BCD)} = 1100011_2$$

Note that the binary representation requires only seven bits.

Basic Idea

The diagram of Figure 9-44 shows the basic idea for a two-digit BCD-to-binary converter. The inputs to the converter are the two four-bit code groups $D_0C_0B_0A_0$, representing the 10^0 or units digit, and $D_1C_1B_1A_1$, representing the 10^1 or tens digit of the decimal value. The outputs from the converter are $b_6b_5b_4b_3b_2b_1b_0$, the seven bits of the binary equivalent of the same decimal value. Note the difference in the weights of the BCD bits and those of the binary bits.

FIGURE 9-44 Basic idea of a two-digit BCD-to-binary converter.

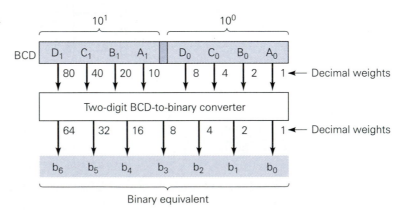

A typical use of a BCD-to-binary converter would be where BCD data from an instrument such as a DMM (digital multimeter) are being transferred to a computer for storage or processing. The data must be converted to binary so that they can be operated on in binary by the computer ALU, which may not have the capability of performing arithmetic operations on BCD data. The BCD-to-binary conversion can be accomplished with either hardware or software. The hardware method (which we will look at momentarily) is generally faster but requires extra circuitry. The software method uses no extra circuitry, but it takes more time, since the software does the conversion step by step. The method chosen in a particular application depends on whether or not conversion time is an important consideration.

Conversion Process

The bits in a BCD representation have decimal weights which are 8, 4, 2, 1 within each code group but which differ by a factor of 10 from one code group (decimal digit) to the next. Figure 9-44 shows the bit weights for the two-digit BCD representation.

The decimal weight of each bit in the BCD representation can be converted to its binary equivalent. The results are given in Table 9-6. Using these weights, we can perform the BCD-to-binary conversion by simply doing the following:

Compute the binary sum of the binary equivalents of all bits in the BCD representation that are 1s.

TABLE 9-6 Binary equivalents of decimal weights of each BCD bit.

BCD Bit	Decimal Weight	b_6	b_5	b_4	b_3	b_2	b_1	b_0
				Binary Equivalent				
A_0	1	0	0	0	0	0	0	1
B_0	2	0	0	0	0	0	1	0
C_0	4	0	0	0	0	1	0	0
D_0	8	0	0	0	1	0	0	0
A_1	10	0	0	0	1	0	1	0
B_1	20	0	0	1	0	1	0	0
C_1	40	0	1	0	1	0	0	0
D_1	80	1	0	1	0	0	0	0

The following example will illustrate.

EXAMPLE 9-18

Convert 01010010 (BCD for decimal 52) to binary. Repeat for 10010101 (decimal 95).

Solution

Write down the binary equivalents for all the 1s in the BCD representation. Then add them all together in binary.

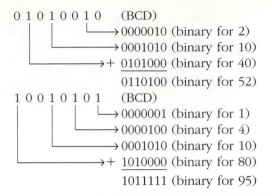

```
0 1 0 1 0 0 1 0   (BCD)
          └──────→ 0000010 (binary for 2)
        └────────→ 0001010 (binary for 10)
    └──────────→ + 0101000 (binary for 40)
                  0110100 (binary for 52)
1 0 0 1 0 1 0 1   (BCD)
          └──────→ 0000001 (binary for 1)
        └────────→ 0000100 (binary for 4)
      └──────────→ 0001010 (binary for 10)
    └──────────→ + 1010000 (binary for 80)
                  1011111 (binary for 95)
```

Circuit Implementation

Clearly, one way to implement the logic circuit that performs this conversion process is to use binary adder circuits. Figure 9-45 shows how two 74LS83 four-bit parallel adders can be wired to perform the conversion. This is one of several pos-

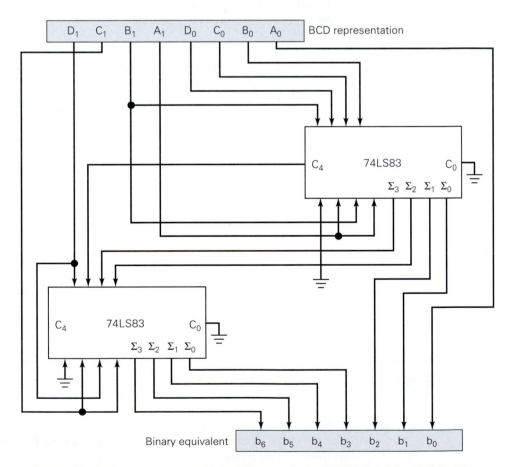

FIGURE 9-45 BCD-to-binary converter implemented with 74LS83 four-bit parallel adders.

sible adder arrangements that will work. You may want to review the operation of this IC in Section 6-14.

The two adder ICs perform the addition of the BCD bits in the proper combinations according to Table 9-6. For instance, Table 9-6 shows that A_0 is the only BCD bit that contributes to the LSB, b_0, of the binary equivalent. Since there is no carry into this bit position, A_0 is connected directly as output b_0. The table also shows that only BCD bits B_0 and A_1 contribute to bit b_1 of the binary output. These two bits are combined in the upper adder to produce output b_1. Likewise, only BCD bits D_0, A_1, and C_1 contribute to bit b_3. The upper adder combines D_0 and A_1 to generate Σ_2, which is connected to the lower adder, where C_1 is added to it to produce b_3.

EXAMPLE 9-19

The BCD representation for decimal 56 is applied to the converter of Figure 9-45. Determine the Σ outputs from each adder and the final binary output.

Solution

Write down the bits of the BCD representation 01010110 on the circuit diagram. Since $A_0 = 0$, the b_0 bit of the output is 0.

The top inputs to the upper adder are 0011. The bottom inputs are 0101. This adder adds these to produce

$$
\begin{array}{r}
0011 \\
+\ 0101 \\
\hline
1000
\end{array} = \Sigma_3\Sigma_2\Sigma_1\Sigma_0 \text{ outputs of upper adder}
$$

The Σ_1 and Σ_0 bits become binary outputs b_2 and b_1, respectively. The Σ_3 and Σ_2 bits are fed to the lower adder. The top inputs to the lower adder are therefore 0010. The bottom inputs are 0101. This adder adds these to produce

$$
\begin{array}{r}
0010 \\
+\ 0101 \\
\hline
0111
\end{array} = \Sigma_3\Sigma_2\Sigma_1\Sigma_0 \text{ outputs of lower adder}
$$

These bits become $b_6 b_5 b_4 b_3$, respectively.

Thus, we have $b_6 b_5 b_4 b_3 b_2 b_1 b_0 = 0111000$ as the correct binary equivalent for decimal 56.

Other Code Converter Implementations

Whereas all types of code converters can be made by combining logic gates, adder circuits, or other combinational logic, the circuitry can become quite complex, requiring many ICs. It is often more efficient to use a read-only memory (ROM) or programmable logic device (PLD) to function as a code converter. As we will see in Chapters 11 and 12, these devices contain the equivalent of hundreds of logic gates, and they can be programmed to provide a wide range of logic functions.

1. What is a code converter?
2. How many binary outputs would a three-digit BCD-to-binary converter have?

9-14 DATA BUSING

In most modern computers the transfer of data takes place over a common set of connecting lines called a **data bus.** In these bus-organized computers, many different devices can have their outputs and inputs tied to the common data bus lines. Because of this, the devices that are tied to the data bus will often have tristate outputs, or they will be tied to the data bus through tristate buffers.

Some of the devices that are commonly connected to a data bus are (1) microprocessors, discussed in Chapter 13; (2) semiconductor memory chips, covered in

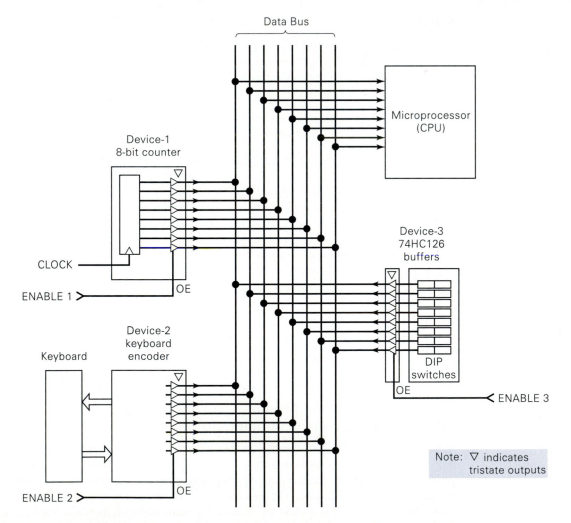

FIGURE 9-46 Three different devices can transmit eight-bit data over an eight-line data bus to a microprocessor; only one device at a time is enabled so that bus contention is avoided.

Chapter 11; and (3) digital-to-analog converters (DACs) and analog-to-digital converters (ADCs), described in Chapter 10.

Figure 9-46 illustrates a typical situation in which a microprocessor (the CPU chip in a microcomputer) is connected to several devices over an eight-line data bus. The data bus is simply a collection of conducting paths over which digital data are transmitted from one device to another. Each device provides an eight-bit output that is sent to the inputs of the microprocessor over the eight-line data bus. Clearly, since the outputs of each of the three devices are connected to the same microprocessor inputs over the data bus conducting paths, we must be aware of bus contention problems (Section 8-8) where two or more signals tied to the same bus line are active and are essentially fighting each other. Bus contention is avoided if the devices have tristate outputs or are connected to the bus through tristate buffers (Section 8-8). The output enable inputs (OE) to each device (or its buffer) are used to ensure that no more than one device's outputs are active at a given time.

EXAMPLE 9-20	(a) For Figure 9-46, describe the conditions necessary to transmit data from device 3 to the microprocessor.
	(b) What will the status of the data bus be when none of the devices is enabled?

Solution

(a) ENABLE 3 must be activated; ENABLE 1 and ENABLE 2 must be in their inactive state. This will put the outputs of device 1 and device 2 in the Hi-Z state and essentially disconnect them from the bus. The outputs of device 3 will be activated so that their logic levels will appear on the data bus lines and be transmitted to the inputs of the microprocessor. We can visualize this by covering up device 1 and device 2 as if they are not even part of the circuit; then we are left with device 3 alone connected to the microprocessor over the data bus.

(b) If none of the device enable inputs are activated, all of the device outputs are in the Hi-Z state. This disconnects all device outputs from the bus. Thus, there is no definite logic level on any of the data bus lines; they are in the indeterminate state. This condition is known as a **floating bus,** and each data bus line is said to be in a *floating* (indeterminate) state. An oscilloscope display of a floating bus line would be unpredictable. A logic probe would indicate an indeterminate logic level.

Review Questions	1. What is meant by the term *data bus?*
	2. What is *bus contention,* and what must be done to prevent it?
	3. What is a *floating bus?*

9-15 THE 74173/LS173/HC173 TRISTATE REGISTER

The devices connected to a data bus will contain registers (usually flip-flops) that hold the device data. The outputs of these registers are usually connected to tristate buffers that allow them to be tied to a data bus. We are going to demonstrate the de-

	Inputs				FF Outputs
MR	CP	$\overline{IE_1}$	$\overline{IE_2}$	D_n	Q
H	X	X	X	X	L
L	L	X	X	X	Q_0
L	⌐	H	X	X	Q_0
L	⌐	X	H	X	Q_0
L	⌐	L	L	L	L
L	⌐	L	L	H	H

When either $\overline{OE_1}$ or $\overline{OE_2}$ is HIGH the output is in the OFF state (high impedance); however, this does not affect the contents or sequential operating of the register

H = HIGH voltage level Q_0 = output prior to PGT
L = LOW voltage level
X = immaterial

Logic Diagram

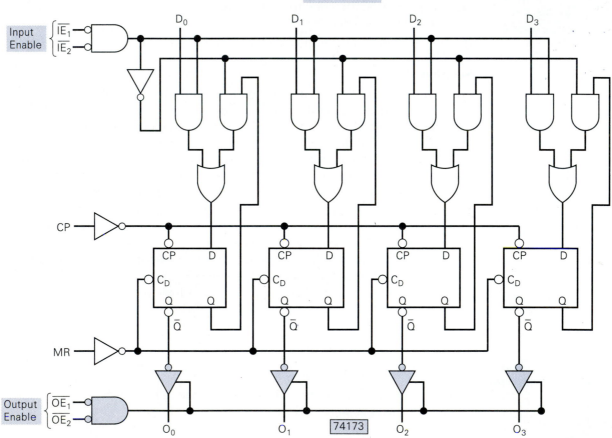

FIGURE 9-47 Truth table and logic diagram for the 74173 tristate register. (Courtesy of Fairchild, a Schlumberger company)

tails of data bus operation by using an IC register that includes the tristate buffers on the same chip: the TTL 74173 (also available in 74LS173 and CMOS 74HC173 versions). Its logic diagram and truth table are shown in Figure 9-47.

The 74173 is a four-bit register with parallel in/parallel out capability. Note that the FF outputs are connected to tristate buffers that provide outputs O_0 through O_3. Also note that the data inputs D_0 through D_3 are connected to the D inputs of the register FFs through logic circuitry. This logic allows two modes of operation: (1) *load,* where the data at inputs D_0 to D_3 are transferred into the FFs on the PGT of the clock pulse at *CP*; and (2) *hold,* where the data in the register do not change when the PGT of *CP* occurs.

EXAMPLE 9-21

(a) What input conditions will produce the load operation?

(b) What input conditions will produce the hold operation?

(c) What input conditions will allow the internal register outputs to appear at O_0 to O_3?

Solution

(a) The last two entries in the truth table show that each Q output takes on the value present at its D input when a PGT occurs at *CP* provided that *MR* is LOW and *both* input-enable inputs, $\overline{IE}_1$ and $\overline{IE}_2$, are LOW.

(b) The third and fourth lines of the truth table state that when either $\overline{IE}$ input is HIGH, the D inputs have no effect, and the Q outputs will retain their current values when the PGT occurs.

(c) The output buffers are enabled when *both* output-enable inputs, $\overline{OE}_1$ and $\overline{OE}_2$, are LOW. This will pass the register outputs through to the external outputs O_0 to O_3. If either output-enable input is HIGH, the buffers will be disabled, and the outputs will be in the Hi-Z state.

Note that the $\overline{OE}$ inputs have no effect on the data load operation. They are used only to control whether or not the register outputs are passed to the external outputs.

The logic symbol for the 74173/LS173/HC173 is given in Figure 9-48. We have included the IEEE/ANSI "&" notation to indicate the AND relationship of the two pairs of enable inputs.

Review Questions

1. Assume that both *IE* inputs are LOW and that $D_0D_1D_2D_3 = 1011$. What logic levels are present at the FF D inputs?

2. *True or false:* The register cannot be loaded when the master reset input (*MR*) is held HIGH.

3. What will the output levels be when *MR* = HIGH and both *OE* inputs are held low?

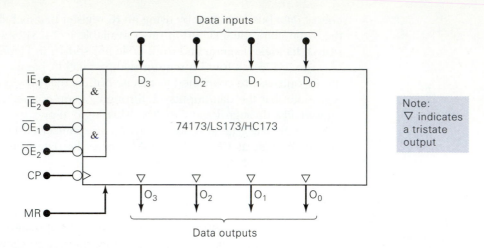

FIGURE 9-48   Logic symbol for the 74173/LS173/HC173 IC.

9-16   DATA BUS OPERATION

The data bus is very important in computer systems, and its significance will not be appreciated until our later studies of memories and microprocessors. For now, we will illustrate the data bus operation for register-to-register data transfer. Figure 9-49 shows a bus-organized system for three 74HC173 tristate registers. Note that each register has its pair of $\overline{OE}$ inputs tied together as one $\overline{OE}$ input, and likewise for the $\overline{IE}$ inputs. Also note that the registers will be referred to as registers A, B, and C from top to bottom. This is indicated by the subscripts on each input and output.

In this arrangement, the data bus consists of four lines labeled DB_0 to DB_3. Corresponding outputs of each register are connected to the same data bus line (e.g., O_{3A}, O_{3B}, and O_{3C} are connected to DB_3). Since the three registers have their outputs connected together, it is imperative that only one register have its outputs enabled and that the other two register outputs remain in the Hi-Z state. Otherwise, there will be bus contention (two or more sets of outputs fighting each other), producing uncertain levels on the bus and possible damage to the register output buffers.

Corresponding register inputs are also tied to the same bus line (e.g., D_{3A}, D_{3B}, and D_{3C} are tied to DB_3). Thus, the levels on the bus will always be ready to be transferred to one or more of the registers depending on the $\overline{IE}$ inputs.

Data Transfer Operation

The contents of any one of the three registers can be parallel-transferred over the data bus to one of the other registers through the proper application of logic levels to the register enable inputs. In a typical system, the control unit of a computer (i.e., the CPU) will generate the signals that select which register will put its data on the data bus and which one will take the data from the data bus. The following example will illustrate this.

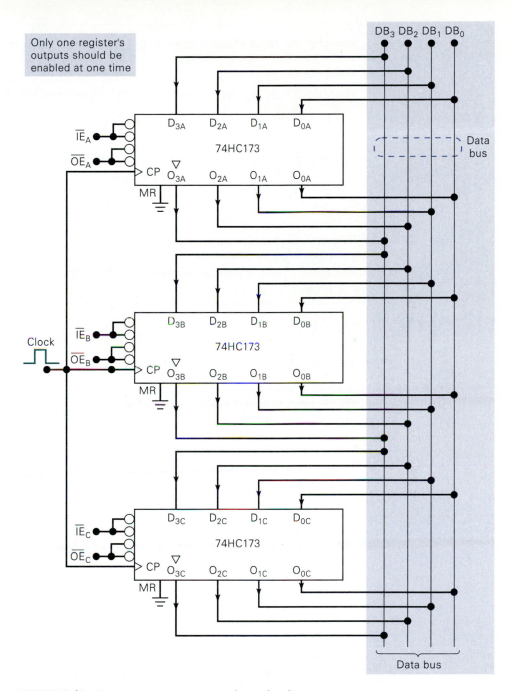

FIGURE 9-49 Tristate registers connected to a data bus.

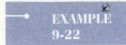

EXAMPLE
9-22
Describe the input signal requirements for transferring $[A] \rightarrow [C]$.

Solution

First of all, only register A should have its outputs enabled. That is, we need

$$\overline{OE}_A = 0 \qquad\qquad \overline{OE}_B = \overline{OE}_C = 1$$

This will place the contents of register A onto the data bus lines.

Next, only register C should have its inputs enabled. For this, we want

$$\overline{IE}_C = 0 \qquad\qquad \overline{IE}_A = \overline{IE}_B = 1$$

This will allow only register C to accept data from the data bus when the PGT of the clock signal occurs.

Finally, a clock pulse is required to actually transfer the data from the bus into the register C flip-flops.

Bus Signals

The timing diagram in Figure 9-50 shows the various signals involved in the transfer of the data 1011 from register A to register C. The $\overline{IE}$ and $\overline{OE}$ lines that are not shown are assumed to be in their inactive HIGH state. Prior to time t_1, the $\overline{IE}_C$ and $\overline{OE}_A$ lines are also HIGH, so that all of the register outputs are disabled, and none of the registers will be placing their data on the bus lines. In other words, the data bus lines are in the Hi-Z or "floating" state as represented by the hatched lines on the timing diagram. The Hi-Z state does not correspond to any particular voltage level.

At t_1 the $\overline{IE}_C$ and $\overline{OE}_A$ inputs are activated. The outputs of register A are enabled, and they start changing the data bus lines DB_3 through DB_0 from the Hi-Z state to the logic levels 1011. After allowing time for the logic levels to stabilize on the bus, the PGT of the clock is applied at t_2. This PGT will transfer these logic levels into register C, since $\overline{IE}_C$ is active. If the PGT occurs before the data bus has valid logic levels, unpredictable data will be transferred into C.

At t_3, the $\overline{IE}_C$ and $\overline{OE}_A$ lines return to the inactive state. As a result, register A's outputs go to the Hi-Z state. This removes the register A output data from the bus lines, and the bus lines return to the Hi-Z state.

Note that the data bus lines show valid logic levels only during the time interval when register A's outputs are enabled. At all other times, the data bus lines are floating, and there is no way to easily predict what they would look like if displayed on an oscilloscope. A logic probe would give an "indeterminate" indication if it were monitoring a floating bus line. Also note the relatively slow rate at which the signals on the data bus lines are changing. Although this effect has been somewhat exaggerated in the diagram, it is a characteristic common to bus systems and is caused by the capacitive load on each line. This load consists of a combination of parasitic capacitance and the capacitances contributed by each input and output connected to the line.

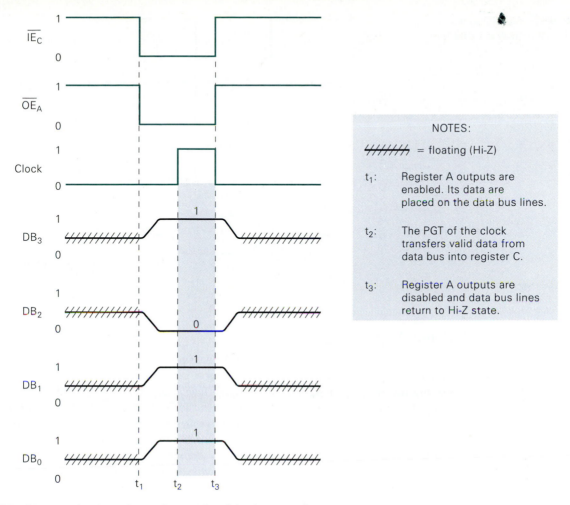

NOTES:

/////// = floating (Hi-Z)

t_1: Register A outputs are enabled. Its data are placed on the data bus lines.

t_2: The PGT of the clock transfers valid data from data bus into register C.

t_3: Register A outputs are disabled and data bus lines return to Hi-Z state.

FIGURE 9-50   Signal activity during the transfer of the data 1011 from register *A* to register *C*.

Simplified Bus Timing Diagram

The timing diagram in Figure 9-50 shows the signals on each of the four data bus lines. This same kind of signal activity occurs in digital systems that use the more common data buses of 8, 16, or 32 lines. For these larger buses, the timing diagrams like Figure 9-50 would get excessively large and cumbersome. There is a simplified method for showing the signal activity that occurs on a set of bus lines that uses only a single timing waveform to represent the complete set of bus lines. This is illustrated in Figure 9-51 for the same data transfer situation depicted in Figure 9-50. Notice how the data bus activity is represented. Especially note how the valid data 1011 are indicated on the diagram during the t_2–t_3 interval. We will generally use this simplified bus timing diagram from now on.

FIGURE 9-51 Simplified way to show signal activity on data bus lines.

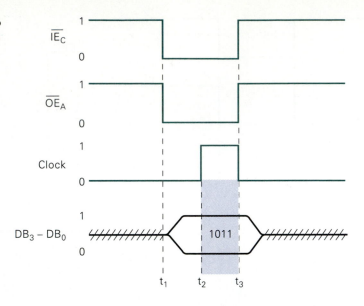

Expanding the Bus

The data transfer operation of the four-line data bus of Figure 9-49 is typical of the operation of larger data buses found in most computers and other digital systems, usually the 8-, 16-, or 32-line data buses. These larger buses generally have many more than three devices tied to the bus, but the basic data transfer operation is the same: *one device has its outputs enabled so that its data are placed on the data bus; another device has its inputs enabled so that it can take these data off the bus and latch them into its internal circuitry on the appropriate clock edge.*

The number of lines on the data bus will depend on the size of the data **word** (unit of data) that is to be transferred over the bus. A computer that has an 8-bit word size will have an 8-line data bus, a computer that has a 16-bit word size will have a 16-line data bus, and so on. The number of devices connected to a data bus will vary from one computer to another and depends on factors such as how much memory the computer has and the number of input and output devices that must communicate with the CPU over the data bus.

All device outputs must be tied to the bus through tristate buffers. Some devices, like the 74173 register, have these buffers on the same chip. Other devices will need to be connected to the bus through an IC called a **bus driver.** A bus driver IC has tristate outputs with a very low output impedance that can rapidly charge and discharge the bus capacitance. This bus capacitance represents the cumulative effect of all of the parasitic capacitances of the different inputs and outputs tied to the bus, and it can cause deterioration of the bus signal transition times if they are not driven from a low-impedance signal source. Figure 9-52 shows a 74HC541 octal bus driver IC connecting the outputs of an 8-bit analog-to-digital converter (ADC) to a data bus. The ADC has tristate outputs but lacks the drive capability to charge the bus capacitance (shown as capacitors to ground in the drawing). Notice that data bit 0 is driving the bus directly without the assistance of the bus driver. If the transition time is slow enough, the voltage may never reach a HIGH logic level in the allotted enable time. The bus driver's two enable inputs are tied together so that a LOW on

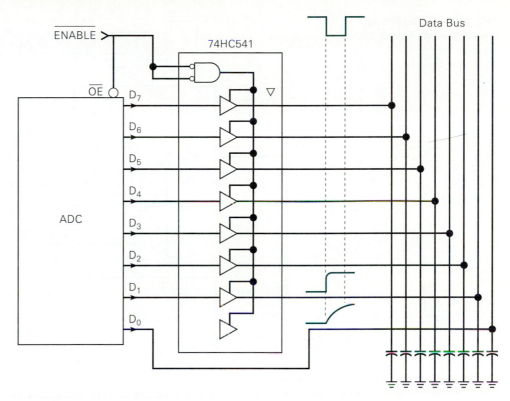

FIGURE 9-52 A 74HC541 octal bus driver connects the outputs of an analog-to-digital converter (ADC) to an eight-line data bus. The D_0 output connects directly to the bus showing the capacitive effects.

the common enable line will allow the ADC's outputs through the buffers and onto the data bus from where they can be transferred to another device.

Simplified Bus Representation

Usually, many devices are connected to the same data bus. On a circuit schematic this can produce a confusing array of lines and connections. For this reason, a more simplified representation of data bus connections is often used on block diagrams and in some circuit schematics. One type of simplified representation is shown in Figure 9-53 for an eight-line data bus.

The connections to and from the data bus are represented by wide arrows. The numbers in brackets indicate the number of bits that each register contains, as well as the number of lines connecting the register inputs and outputs to the bus.

Another common method for representing buses on a schematic is presented in Figure 9-54 for an eight-line data bus. It shows the eight individual output lines from a 74HC541 bus driver labeled D_7-D_0 bundled (not connected) together and shown as a single line. These bundled data output lines are then connected to the data bus, which is also shown as one line (i.e., the eight data bus lines are bundled together). The "/8" notation indicates the number of lines represented by each bundle. This bundle method is used to represent the connections from the data bus to the eight

FIGURE 9-53 Simplified representation of bus arrangement.

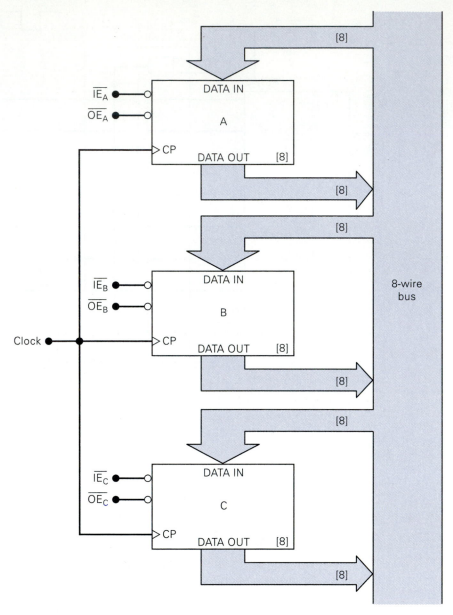

microprocessor data inputs. When the bundle method is used, it is very important to label both ends of every wire that is in the bundle, since the connection cannot be visually traced on the diagram.

Bidirectional Busing

Each register in Figure 9-49 has both its inputs and its outputs connected to the data bus, so that corresponding inputs and outputs are shorted together. For example, each register has output O_2 connected to input D_2 because of their common connection to DB_2. This, of course, would not be true if external bus drivers were connected between the register outputs and the data bus.

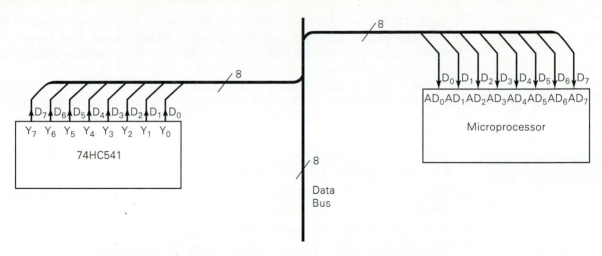

FIGURE 9-54 Bundle method for simplified representation of data bus connections. The "/8" denotes an eight-line data bus.

Because inputs and outputs are often connected together in bus systems, IC manufacturers have developed ICs that connect inputs and outputs together *internal* to the chip in order to reduce the number of IC pins and the number of connections to the bus. Figure 9-55 illustrates this for a four-bit register. The separate data input lines (D_0 to D_3) and output lines (O_0 to O_3) have been replaced by input/output lines (I/O$_0$ to I/O$_3$).

FIGURE 9-55 Bidirectional register connected to data bus.

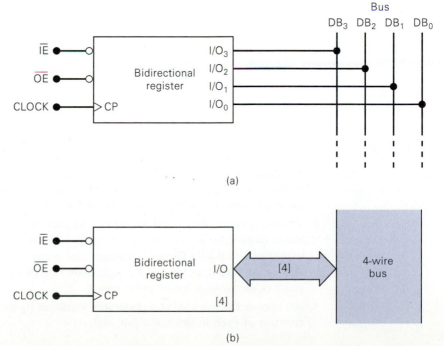

Each I/O line will function as either an input or an output depending on the states of the enable inputs. Thus, they are called **bidirectional data lines.** The 74LS299 is an eight-bit register with common I/O lines. Many memory ICs and microprocessors have bidirectional transfer of data.

We will return to the important topic of data busing in our comprehensive coverage of memory systems in Chapter 11 and in our introduction to microprocessors and microcomputers in Chapter 12.

Review Questions

1. What will happen if $\overline{OE_A} = \overline{OE_B} = $ LOW in Figure 9-49?
2. What logic level is on a data bus line when all devices tied to the bus are disabled?
3. What is the function of a bus driver?
4. What are the reasons for having registers with common I/O lines?
5. Redraw Figure 9-55(a) using the bundled line representation. (The answer is shown in Figure 9-56.)

FIGURE 9-56

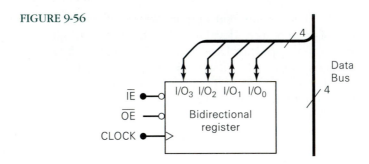

SUMMARY

1. A decoder is a device whose output is activated only when a unique binary combination (code) is presented on its inputs. Many MSI decoders have several outputs, each one corresponding to only one of the many possible input combinations.

2. Digital systems often need to display decimal numbers. This is done using 7-segment displays that are driven by special chips that decode the binary number and translate it into segment patterns that represent decimal numbers to people. The segment elements can be light-emitting diodes, liquid crystals, or glowing electrodes surrounded by neon gas.

3. An encoder is a device that generates a unique binary code in response to the activation of each individual input.

4. Troubleshooting a digital system involves *observation/analysis* to identify the possible causes, and a process of elimination called *divide-and-conquer* to isolate and identify the cause.

5. Multiplexers act like digitally controlled switches that select and connect one logic input at a time to the output pin. By taking turns, many different data signals can share the same data path using multiplexers. Demultiplexers are used at the other end of the data path to separate the signals that are sharing a data path and distribute them to their respective destinations.

6. Magnitude comparators serve as an indicator of the relationship between two binary numbers, with outputs that show $>$, $<$, and $=$.

7. It is often necessary to translate between and among various methods of representing quantities with binary numbers. Code converters are devices that take in one form of binary representation and convert it to another form.

8. In digital systems, many devices must often share the same data path. This data path is often called a *data bus*. Even though many devices can be "riding" on the bus, there can be only one bus "driver" at any one time. This means that devices must take turns applying logic signals to the data bus.

9. In order to take turns, the devices must have *tristate outputs* which can be disabled when another device is driving the bus. In the disabled state the device's output is essentially electrically disconnected from the bus by going into a state that offers a high-impedance path to both ground and the positive power supply. Devices that are designed to interface to a bus have outputs that can be HIGH, LOW, or disabled (high impedance).

IMPORTANT TERMS

decoder	backplane	multiplexing
BCD-to-decimal decoder	pixel	parallel-to-serial conversion
driver	gas discharge display	demultiplexer (DEMUX)
BCD-to-7-segment decoder/	encoder	data bus
driver	priority encoder	floating bus
common anode	observation/analysis	word
common cathode	divide-and-conquer	bus driver
LCD	multiplexer (MUX)	bidirectional data lines

PROBLEMS

SECTION 9-1

9-1. Refer to Figure 9-3. Determine the levels at each decoder output for the following sets of input conditions.
    (a) All inputs LOW
    (b) All inputs LOW except $E_3 =$ HIGH
    (c) All inputs HIGH except $\bar{E}_1 = \bar{E}_2 =$ LOW
    (d) All inputs HIGH

9-2. What is the number of inputs and outputs of a decoder that accepts 64 different input combinations?

9-3. What set of input conditions will produce a LOW at $\overline{O}_6$ of a 74LS138?

D   9-4. Show how to use 74LS138s to form a 1-of-16 decoder.

9-5. Figure 9-57 shows how a decoder can be used in the generation of control signals. Assume that a RESET pulse has occurred at time t_0, and determine the CONTROL waveform for 32 clock pulses.

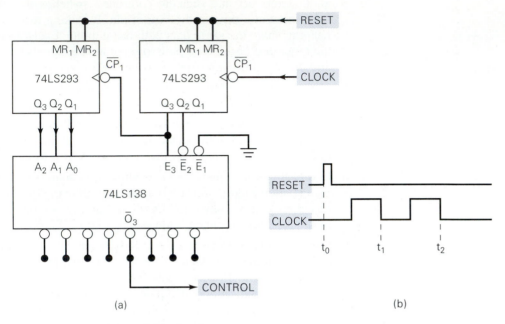

FIGURE 9-57 Problems 9-5 and 9-6.

D   9-6. Modify the circuit of Figure 9-57 to generate a CONTROL waveform that goes LOW from t_{20} to t_{24}. (*Hint:* The modification does not require additional logic.)

9-7. The 7442 decoder of Figure 9-5 does not have an ENABLE input. However, we can operate it as a 1-of-8 decoder by not using outputs $\overline{O}_8$ and $\overline{O}_9$ and by using the D input as an ENABLE. This is illustrated in Figure 9-58. Describe how this arrangement works as an enabled 1-of-8 decoder, and state how the level on D either enables or disables the outputs.

FIGURE 9-58   Problem 9-7.

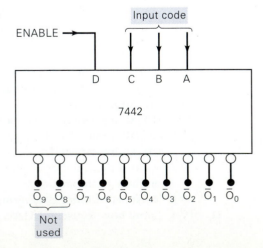

9-8. Consider the waveforms in Figure 9-59. Apply these signals to the 74LS138 as follows:

$$A \rightarrow A_0 \qquad B \rightarrow A_1 \qquad C \rightarrow A_2 \qquad D \rightarrow E_3$$

Assume that $\bar{E}_1$ and $\bar{E}_2$ are tied LOW, and draw the waveforms for outputs $\bar{O}_0$, $\bar{O}_3$, $\bar{O}_6$, and $\bar{O}_7$.

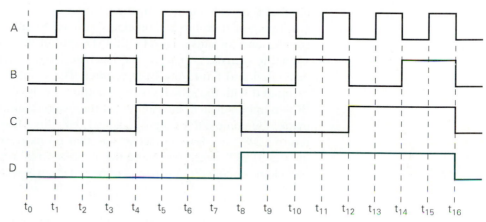

FIGURE 9-59   Problems 9-8 and 9-39.

D 9-9. Modify the circuit of Figure 9-6 so that relay K_1 stays energized from t_3 to t_5 and K_2 stays energized from t_6 to t_9. (*Hint:* This modification requires no additional circuitry.)

SECTIONS 9-2 AND 9-3

9-10. Show how to connect BCD-to-7 segment decoder/drivers and LED 7-segment displays to the clock circuit of Figure 7-45 to display minutes and hours. Assume that each segment is to operate at approximately 10 mA at 2.5 V.

9-11. (a) Refer to Figure 9-10 and draw the segment and backplane waveforms relative to ground for CONTROL = 0. Then draw the waveform of segment voltage relative to backplane voltage.

   (b) Repeat part (a) for CONTROL = 1.

C, D 9-12. The BCD-to-7-segment decoder/driver of Figure 9-8 contains the logic for activating each segment for the appropriate BCD inputs. Design the logic for activating the *g* segment.

SECTION 9-4

9-13. DRILL QUESTION

For each statement indicate whether it is referring to a decoder or an encoder.

   (a) Has more inputs than outputs.

   (b) Is used to convert key actuations to a binary code.

   (c) Only one output can be activated at one time.

   (d) Can be used to interface a BCD input to an LED display.

   (e) Often has driver-type outputs to handle large *I* and *V*.

9-14. Determine the output levels for the 74147 encoder when $\bar{A}_8 = \bar{A}_4 = 0$ and all other inputs are HIGH.

9-15. Apply the signals of Figure 9-59 to the inputs of a 74147 as follows:

$$A \rightarrow \overline{A}_7 \qquad B \rightarrow \overline{A}_4 \qquad C \rightarrow \overline{A}_2 \qquad D \rightarrow \overline{A}_1$$

Draw the waveforms for the encoder's outputs.

C, D **9-16.** Figure 9-60 shows the block diagram of a logic circuit used to control the number of copies made by a copy machine. The machine operator selects the number of desired copies by closing one of the selector switches S_1 to S_9. This number is encoded in BCD by the encoder and is sent to a comparator circuit. The operator then hits a momentary-contact START switch, which clears the counter and initiates a HIGH OPERATE output that is sent to the machine to signal it to make copies. As the machine makes each copy, a copy pulse is generated and fed to the BCD counter. The counter outputs are continually compared with the switch encoder outputs by the comparator. When the two BCD numbers match, indicating that the desired number of copies have been made, the comparator output $\overline{X}$ goes LOW; this causes the OPERATE level to return LOW and stop the machine so that no more copies are made. Activating the START switch will cause this process to be repeated. Design the complete logic circuitry for the comparator and control sections of this system.

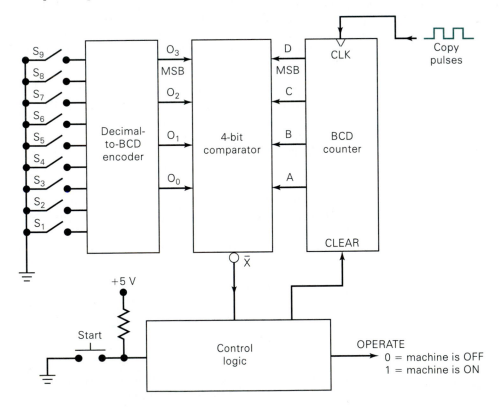

FIGURE 9-60 Problems 9-16 and 9-49.

C, D **9-17.** The keyboard circuit of Figure 9-16 is designed to accept a three-digit decimal number. What would happen if *four* digit keys were activated (e.g., 3095)? Design the necessary logic to be added to this circuit so that after three digits have been entered, any further digits will be ignored until the CLEAR key is depressed. In other words, if 3095 is entered on the keyboard, the output registers will display 309 and will ignore the 5 and any subsequent digits until the circuit is cleared.

SECTION 9-6

T **9-18.** A technician breadboards the keyboard entry circuit of Figure 9-16 and tests its operation by trying to enter a series of three-digit numbers. He finds that sometimes the digit "0" is entered instead of the digit he pressed. He also observes that it happens with all of the keys more or less randomly, although it is worse for some keys than others. He replaces all of the ICs, and the malfunction persists. Which of the following circuit faults would explain his observations? Explain each choice.

(a) The technician forgot to ground the unused inputs of the OR gate.

(b) He has mistakenly used $\overline{Q}$ instead of Q from the one-shot.

(c) The switch bounce from the digit keys lasts longer than 20 ms.

(d) The Y and Z outputs are shorted together.

T **9-19.** Repeat Problem 9-18 with the following symptom: the registers and displays stay at 0 no matter how many times a key is pressed.

T **9-20.** While testing the circuit of Figure 9-16, a technician finds that every odd-numbered key results in the correct digit being entered, but every even-numbered key results in the wrong digit being entered as follows: the "0" key causes a "1" to be entered, the "2" key causes a "3" to be entered, the "4" key causes a "5" to be entered, and so on. Consider each of the following faults as possible causes of the malfunction. For each one explain why it can or cannot be the actual cause.

(a) There is an open connection from the output of the LSB inverter to the D inputs of the FFs.

(b) The D input of flip-flop Q_8 is internally shorted to V_{CC}.

(c) A solder bridge is shorting $\overline{O}_0$ to ground.

T **9-21.** A technician tests the circuit of Figure 9-4 as described in Example 9-7, and she obtains the following results: all of the outputs work except $\overline{O}_{16}$ to $\overline{O}_{19}$ and $\overline{O}_{24}$ to $\overline{O}_{27}$, which are permanently HIGH. What is the most probable circuit fault?

T **9-22.** A technician tests the circuit of Figure 9-4 as described in Example 9-7 and finds that the correct output is activated for each possible input code except those listed in Table 9-7. Examine this table and determine the probable cause of the malfunction.

TABLE 9-7

Input Code $A_4A_3A_2A_1A_0$	Activated Outputs
1 0 0 0 0	$\overline{O}_{16}$ and $\overline{O}_{24}$
1 0 0 0 1	$\overline{O}_{17}$ and $\overline{O}_{25}$
1 0 0 1 0	$\overline{O}_{18}$ and $\overline{O}_{26}$
1 0 0 1 1	$\overline{O}_{19}$ and $\overline{O}_{27}$
1 0 1 0 0	$\overline{O}_{20}$ and $\overline{O}_{28}$
1 0 1 0 1	$\overline{O}_{21}$ and $\overline{O}_{29}$
1 0 1 1 0	$\overline{O}_{22}$ and $\overline{O}_{30}$
1 0 1 1 1	$\overline{O}_{23}$ and $\overline{O}_{31}$

T **9-23.** Suppose that a 22-Ω resistor was mistakenly used for the *g* segment in Figure 9-8. How would this affect the display? What possible problems could occur?

T **9-24.** Repeat Example 9-8 with the observed sequence shown below.

COUNT	0	1	2	3	4	5	6	7	8	9
Observed display	$\square$	$/$	2	3	8	9	c	$\exists$	4	5

T **9-25.** Repeat Example 9-8 with the observed sequence shown below.

COUNT	0	1	2	3	4	5	6	7	8	9
Observed display	$\square$	7	2	3	9	9	8	7	8	9

T **9-26.** To test the circuit of Figure 9-11, a technician connects a BCD counter to the 74HC4511 inputs and pulses the counter at a very slow rate. She notices that the *f* segment works erratically, and no particular pattern is evident. What are some of the possible causes of the malfunction? (*Hint:* Remember, the ICs are CMOS.)

SECTIONS 9-7 AND 9-8

9-27. The circuit in Figure 9-61 uses three two-input multiplexers (Figure 9-21). Determine the function performed by this circuit.

FIGURE 9-61 Problem 9-27.

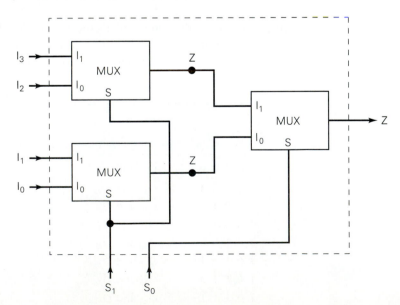

D 9-28. Use the idea from Problem 9-27 to arrange several 74151 1-of-8 multiplexers to form a 1-of-64 multiplexer.

C, D 9-29. Show how two 74157s and a 74151 can be arranged to form a 1-of-16 multiplexer with no other required logic. Label the inputs I_0 to I_{15} to show how they correspond to the select code.

D 9-30. (a) Expand the circuit of Figure 9-26 to display the contents of two three-stage BCD counters.

(b) Count the number of connections in this circuit, and compare it with the number required if a separate decoder/driver and display were used for each stage of each counter.

9-31. Figure 9-62 shows how a multiplexer can be used to generate logic waveforms with any desirable pattern. The pattern is programmed using eight SPDT switches, and the waveform is repetitively produced by pulsing the MOD-8 counter. Draw the waveform at Z for the given switch positions.

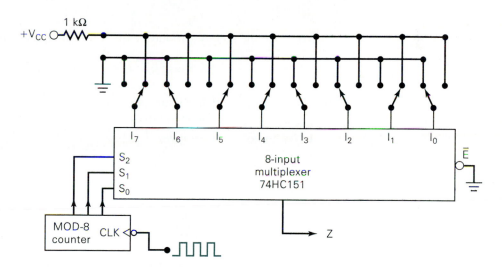

FIGURE 9-62   Problems 9-31 and 9-32.

9-32. Change the MOD-8 counter in Figure 9-62 to a MOD-16 counter, and connect the MSB to the multiplexer $\overline{E}$ input. Draw the Z waveform.

D 9-33. Show how a 74151 can be used to generate the logic function $Z = AB + BC + AC$.

D 9-34. Show how a 16-input multiplexer such as the 74150 (Figure 9-37) is used to generate the function $Z = \overline{A}\overline{B}\overline{C}D + BCD + A\overline{B}\overline{D} + AB\overline{C}D$.

N 9-35. The circuit of Figure 9-63 shows how an eight-input MUX can be used to generate a four-variable logic function even though the MUX has only three SE-LECT inputs. Three of the logic variables A, B, and C are connected to the SE-LECT inputs. The fourth variable D and its inverse $\overline{D}$ are connected to selected data inputs of the MUX as required by the desired logic function. The other MUX data inputs are tied to a LOW or a HIGH as required by the function.

(a) Set up a truth table showing the output Z for the 16 possible combinations of input variables.

FIGURE 9-63   Problems 9-35 and 9-36.

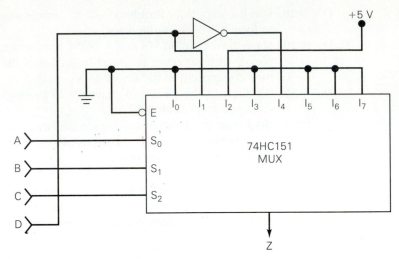

(b) Write the sum-of-products expression for Z and simplify it to verify that

$$Z = \overline{C}B\overline{A} + D\overline{C}\overline{B}A + \overline{D}C\overline{B}\,\overline{A}$$

C, D   9-36. The method used in Figure 9-63 can be used to generate any four-variable logic function by following these steps:

1. Set up the truth table for the desired function with Z as the output.
2. Write the sum-of-products expression for Z; do not simplify it. For example, $Z = DC\overline{B}A + \overline{D}CB\overline{A} + D\overline{C}B\overline{A} + D\overline{C}BA + \overline{D}\overline{C}BA + \overline{D}C\overline{B}A$.
3. Look for terms that have the same combination of C, B, and A, and factor:

$$Z = DC\overline{B}A + CB\overline{A}\,(\overline{D} + D) + \overline{C}BA(D + D) + \overline{D}\,\overline{C}\,\overline{B}A$$
$$= DC\overline{B}A + CB\overline{A} + \overline{C}BA + \overline{D}\,\overline{C}\,\overline{B}A$$

4. Consider those terms that contain only C, B, and A in normal or complemented form. For each of these, connect the corresponding MUX data input to a HIGH:

$$CB\overline{A} \rightarrow \text{connect HIGH to input } I_6$$
$$\overline{C}BA \rightarrow \text{connect HIGH to input } I_3$$

5. Consider the terms that contain the D variable. Connect the D or $\overline{D}$ variable to the MUX input that corresponds to the CBA variables:

$$DC\overline{B}A \rightarrow \text{connect } D \text{ to input } I_5$$
$$\overline{D}\,\overline{C}\,\overline{B}A \rightarrow \text{connect } \overline{D} \text{ to input } I_1$$

6. Connect the remaining MUX inputs to a LOW.
   (a) Verify the design of Figure 9-63 using this method.
   (b) Use this method to implement a function that will produce a HIGH only when the four input variables are at the same level or when the B and C variables are at different levels.

SECTION 9-9

9-37. DRILL QUESTION

For each statement indicate whether it is referring to a decoder, an encoder, a MUX, or a DEMUX.

(a) Has more inputs than outputs.

(b) Uses SELECT inputs.

(c) Can be used in parallel-to-serial conversion.

(d) Produces a binary code at its output.

(e) Only one of its outputs can be active at one time.

(f) Can be used to route an input signal to one of several possible outputs.

(g) Can be used to generate arbitrary logic functions.

9-38. Show how the 7442 decoder can be used as 1-to-8 demultiplexer. (*Hint:* See Problem 9-7.)

9-39. Apply the waveforms of Figure 9-59 to the inputs of the 74LS138 DEMUX of Figure 9-32(a) as follows:

$$D \rightarrow A_2 \qquad C \rightarrow A_1 \qquad B \rightarrow A_0 \qquad A \rightarrow \overline{E}_1$$

Draw the waveforms at the DEMUX outputs.

9-40. Consider the system of Figure 9-34. Assume that the clock frequency is 10 pps. Describe what the monitoring panel indications will be for each of the following cases.

(a) All doors closed

(b) All doors open

(c) Doors 2 and 6 open

C, D 9-41. Modify the system of Figure 9-34 to handle 16 doors. Use a 74150 16-input MUX and two 74LS138 DEMUXes. How many lines are going to the remote monitoring panel?

9-42. Draw the waveforms at Z, O_0, O_1, O_2, and O_3 in Figure 9-35 for the following register data: $[A] = 0011$, $[B] = 0110$, $[C] = 1001$, $[D] = 0111$.

SECTION 9-11

T 9-43. Consider the control sequencer of Figure 9-28. Describe how each of the following faults will affect the operation.

(a) The I_3 input of the MUX is shorted to ground.

(b) The connections from sensors 3 and 4 to the MUX are reversed.

T 9-44. Consider the circuit of Figure 9-26. A test of the circuit yields the results shown in Table 9-8. What are the possible causes of the malfunction?

TABLE 9-8

		Actual Count	Displayed Count
Case 1	Counter 1	33	33
	Counter 2	47	47
Case 2	Counter 1	82	02
	Counter 2	64	64
Case 3	Counter 1	63	63
	Counter 2	95	15

T   **9-45.** A test of the security monitoring system of Figure 9-34 produces the results recorded in Table 9-9. What are the possible faults that could cause this operation?

T   **9-46.** A test of the security monitoring system of Figure 9-34 produces the results recorded in Table 9-10. What are the possible faults that could cause this operation? How can this be verified or eliminated as a fault?

TABLE 9-9

Condition	LEDs
All doors closed	All LEDs off
Door 0 open	LED 0 flashing
Door 1 open	LED 2 flashing
Door 2 open	LED 1 flashing
Door 3 open	LED 3 flashing
Door 4 open	LED 4 flashing
Door 5 open	LED 6 flashing
Door 6 open	LED 5 flashing
Door 7 open	LED 7 flashing

TABLE 9-10

Condition	LEDs
All doors closed	All LEDs off
Door 0 open	LED 0 flashing
Door 1 open	LED 1 flashing
Door 2 open	LED 2 flashing
Door 3 open	LED 3 flashing
Door 4 open	LED 4 flashing
Door 5 open	LED 5 flashing
Door 6 open	No LED flashing
Door 7 open	No LED flashing
Doors 6 and 7 open	LEDs 6 and 7 flashing

T   **9-47.** The synchronous data transmission system of Figure 9-35 is malfunctioning. An oscilloscope is used to monitor the MUX and DEMUX outputs during the transmission cycle with the results shown in Figure 9-64. What are the possible causes of the malfunction?

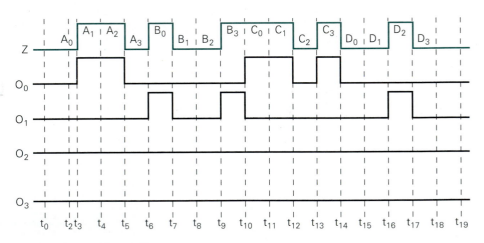

FIGURE 9-64   Problem 9-47.

T   **9-48.** The synchronous data transmission system of Figure 9-35 is malfunctioning, and the waveforms are displayed on a high-speed oscilloscope (Figure 9-65). Note the glitches on the O_1 signal. Consider the two possible faults given below. For each one, explain whether or not it can be the cause of the malfunction.

(a) The connections to the S_1 and S_0 pins of the DEMUX are reversed.

(b) The connections to the Q_1 and Q_0 pins of the receiver's word counter are reversed.

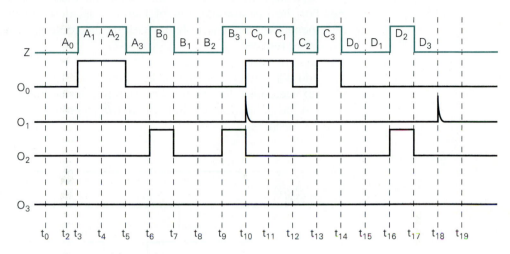

FIGURE 9-65 Problem 9-48.

SECTION 9-12

C, D 9-49. Redesign the circuit of Problem 9-16 using a 74HC85 magnitude comparator. Add a "copy overflow" feature that will activate an ALARM output if the OP-ERATE output fails to stop the machine when the requested number of copies are done.

D 9-50. Show how to connect 74HC85s to compare two 10-bit numbers.

SECTION 9-13

9-51. Assume a BCD input of 69 to the code converter of Figure 9-45. Determine the levels at each Σ output and at the final binary output.

T 9-52. A technician tests the code converter of Figure 9-45 and observes the following results:

BCD Input	Binary Output
52	0110011
95	1100000
27	0011011

What is the probable circuit fault?

SECTIONS 9-14 TO 9-16

9-53. DRILL QUESTION

True or false:

(a) A device connected to a data bus should have tristate outputs.

(b) Bus contention occurs when more than one device takes data from the bus.

(c) Larger units of data can be transferred over an eight-line data bus than over a four-line data bus.

(d) A bus driver IC generally has a high output impedance.

(e) Bidirectional registers and buffers have common I/O lines.

9-54. For the bus arrangement of Figure 9-49, describe the input signal requirements for simultaneously transferring the contents of register C to both of the other registers.

9-55. Assume that the registers in Figure 9-49 are initially $[A] = 1011$, $[B] = 1000$, and $[C] = 0111$. The signals in Figure 9-66 are applied to the register inputs.

(a) Determine the contents of each register at times t_1, t_2, t_3 and t_4.

(b) Describe what would happen if $\overline{IE}_A$ were LOW when the third clock pulse occurred.

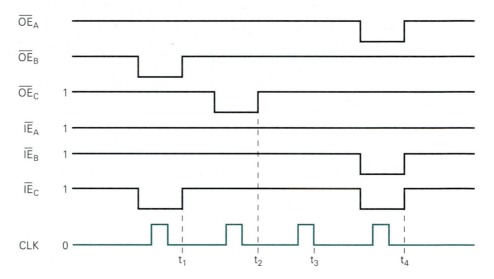

FIGURE 9-66 Problems 9-55 and 9-56.

9-56. Assume the same initial conditions of Problem 9-55, and sketch the signal on DB_3 for the waveforms of Figure 9-66.

9-57. Figure 9-67 shows two more devices that are to be added to the data bus of Figure 9-49. One is a set of buffered switches that can be used to manually enter data into any of the bus registers. The other device is an output register that is used to latch any data that are on the bus during a data transfer operation and display them on a set of LEDs.

(a) Assume that all registers contain 0000. Outline the sequence of operations needed to load the registers with the following data from the switches: $[A] = 1011$, $[B] = 0001$, $[C] = 1110$.

(b) What will the state of the LEDs be at the end of this sequence?

C 9-58. Now that the circuitry of Figure 9-67 has been added to Figure 9-49, a total of five devices are connected to the data bus. The circuit in Figure 9-68(a) will now be used to generate the enable signals needed to perform the different data transfers over the data bus. It uses a 74HC139 chip that contains two identical independent 1-of-4 decoders with an active-LOW enable. The top

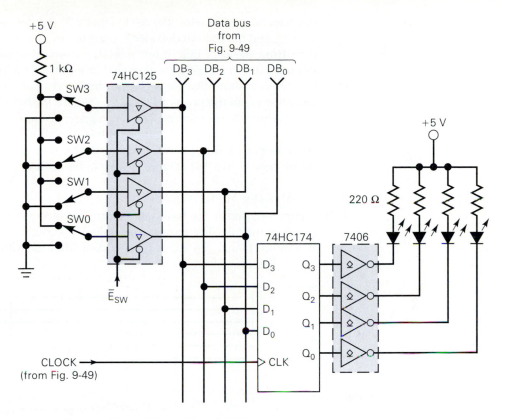

FIGURE 9-67   Problems 9-57, 9-58, and 9-59.

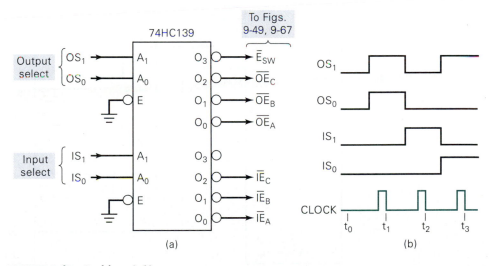

FIGURE 9-68   Problem 9-58.

decoder is used to select the device that will put data on the data bus (output select), and the bottom decoder is used to select the device that is to take the data from the data bus (input select). Assume that the decoder outputs are connected to the corresponding enable inputs of the devices tied to the data bus. Also assume that all registers initially contain 0000 at time t_0, and the switches are in the positions shown in Figure 9-67.

(a) Determine the contents of each register at times t_1, t_2, and t_3 in response to the waveforms in Figure 9-68(b).

(b) Can bus contention ever occur with this circuit? Explain.

9-59. Show how a 74HC541 (Figure 9-52) can be used in the circuit of Figure 9-67.

MICROCOMPUTER APPLICATIONS

C, N 9-60. Figure 9-69 shows the basic circuitry to interface a microprocessor (MPU) to a memory module. The memory module will contain one or more memory ICs (Chapter 11) that can either receive data from the MPU (a WRITE operation)

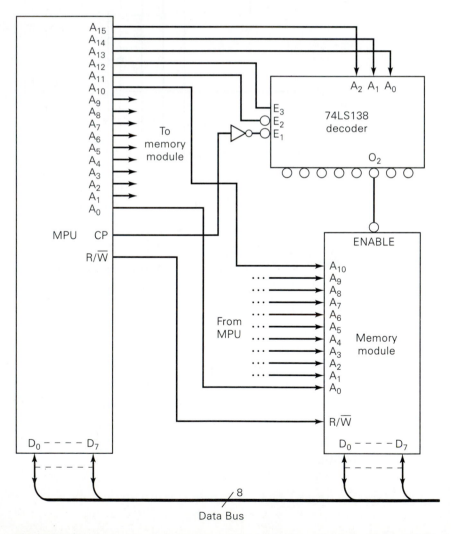

FIGURE 9-69 Basic microprocessor-to-memory interface circuit for Problem 9-60.

or send data to the MPU (a READ operation). The data are transferred over the eight-line data bus. The MPU's data lines and the memory's I/O data lines are connected to this common bus. For now we will be concerned with how the MPU controls the selection of the memory module for a READ or WRITE operation.

The steps involved are as follows:

1. The MPU places the memory address on its address output lines A_{15} to A_0.
2. The MPU generates the $R/\overline{W}$ signal to inform the memory module which operation is to be performed: $R/\overline{W} = 1$ for READ, $R/\overline{W} = 0$ for WRITE.
3. The upper five bits of the MPU address lines are decoded by the 74LS138, which controls the ENABLE input of the memory module. This ENABLE input must be active in order for the memory module to do a READ or WRITE operation.
4. The other 11 address bits are connected to the memory module, which uses them to select the specific *internal* memory location being accessed by the MPU, provided that ENABLE is active.

In order to read from or write into the memory module, the MPU must put the correct address on the address lines to enable the memory, and then pulse *CP* to the HIGH state.

(a) Determine which, if any, of these hexadecimal addresses will activate the memory module: 607F, 57FA, 5F00.
(b) Determine what range of hex addresses will activate the memory. (*Hint:* Inputs A_0 to A_{10} to memory can be any combination.)
(c) Assume that a second identical memory module is added to the circuit with its address, $R/\overline{W}$, and data I/O lines connected exactly the same as the first module *except* that its ENABLE input is tied to decoder output $\overline{O}_4$. What range of hex addresses will activate this second module?
(d) Is it possible for the MPU to read from or write to both modules at the same time? Explain.

DESIGN PROBLEM

C, D   **9-61.** The keyboard entry circuit of Figure 9-16 is to be used as part of an electronic digital lock that operates as follows: When activated, an UNLOCK output goes HIGH. This HIGH is used to energize a solenoid that retracts a bolt and allows a door to be opened. To activate UNLOCK, the operator must press the CLEAR key and then enter the correct three-key sequence.

(a) Show how 74HC85 comparators and any other needed logic can be added to the keyboard entry circuit to produce the digital lock operation described above for a key sequence of CLEAR–3–5–8.
(b) Modify the circuit to activate an ALARM output if the operator enters something other than the correct three-key sequence.

ANSWERS TO SECTION REVIEW QUESTIONS

SECTION 9-1

1. No   2. The enable input controls whether or not the decoder logic responds to the input binary code.   3. The 7445 has open-collector outputs that can handle up to 30 V and 80 mA.   4. 24 pins: 2 enables, 16 inputs, 4 outputs, V_{CC}, and ground

SECTION 9-2

1. *a, b, c, f, g*   2. True

SECTION 9-3

1. LEDs: (a), (e), (f). LCDs: (b), (c), (d), (e)
2. (a) four-bit BCD,   (b) seven- or eight-bit ASCII,
(c) binary value for pixel intensity

SECTION 9-4

1. An encoder produces an output code corresponding to the activated input. A decoder activates one output corresponding to an applied input code. 2. In a priority encoder, the output code corresponds to the *highest*-numbered input that is activated. 3. Normal BCD = 0110 4. (a) produces a PGT when a key is pressed, (b) converts key actuation to its BCD code, (c) Generates bounce-free pulse to trigger the ring counter, (d) form a ring counter that sequentially clocks output registers, (e) store BCD codes generated by key actuations

SECTION 9-5

1. BCD-to-decimal decoder 2. High priority 3. Buffer or driver

SECTION 9-7

1. The binary number at the select inputs determines which data input will pass through to the output. 2. Thirty-two data inputs and five select inputs

SECTION 9-8

1. Parallel-to-serial conversion, data routing, logic-function generation, operations sequencing 2. False; they are applied to the select inputs. 3. Counter

SECTION 9-9

1. A MUX selects one of many input signals to be passed to its output; a DEMUX selects one of many outputs to receive the input signal. 2. True, provided that the decoder has an ENABLE input 3. The LEDs will go on and off in sequence.

SECTION 9-12

1. To provide a means for expanding the compare operations to numbers with more than four bits. 2. $O_{A=B} = 1$; other outputs are 0.

SECTION 9-13

1. A code converter takes input data represented in one type of binary code and converts it to another type of binary code. 2. Three digits can represent decimal values up to 999. To represent 999 in straight binary requires 10 bits.

SECTION 9-14

1. A set of connecting lines to which the inputs and outputs of many different devices can be connected 2. Bus contention occurs when the outputs of more than one device connected to a bus are enabled at the same time. It is prevented by controlling the device enable inputs so that this cannot happen. 3. A condition in which all devices connected to a bus are in the Hi-Z state

SECTION 9-15

1. 1011 2. True 3. 0000

SECTION 9-16

1. Bus contention 2. Floating, Hi-Z 3. Provides tristate low-impedance outputs 4. Reduces number of IC pins and number of connections to data bus 5. See Figure 9-56.

Interfacing with the Analog World

■ OUTLINE

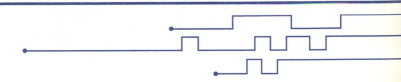

■ OBJECTIVES

Upon completion of this chapter, you will be able to:

- Understand the theory of operation and the circuit limitations of several types of digital-to-analog converters (DACs).
- Read and understand the various DAC manufacturer specifications.
- Use different test procedures to troubleshoot DAC circuits.
- Compare the advantages and disadvantages among the digital-ramp analog-to-digital converter (ADC), successive-approximation ADC, and flash ADC.
- Analyze the process by which a computer in conjunction with an ADC digitizes an analog signal and then reconstructs that analog signal from the digital data.
- Describe the basic operation of a digital voltmeter.
- Understand the need for using sample-and-hold circuits in conjunction with ADCs.
- Describe the operation of an analog multiplexing system.
- Understand the features and basic operation of a digital storage oscilloscope.
- Understand the basic concepts of digital signal processing.

10-1 INTERFACING WITH THE ANALOG WORLD

Review of Digital versus Analog

A **digital quantity** will have a value that is specified as one of two possibilities such as 0 or 1, LOW or HIGH, true or false, and so on. In practice, a digital quantity such as a voltage may actually have a value that is anywhere within specified ranges, and we define values within a given range to have the same digital value. For example, for TTL logic we know that

$$0 \text{ V to } 0.8 \text{ V} = \text{logic } 0$$
$$2 \text{ V to } 5 \text{ V} = \text{logic } 1$$

Any voltage falling in the range 0 to 0.8 V is given the digital value 0, and any voltage in the range 2 to 5 V is assigned the digital value 1. The exact voltage values are not significant, because the digital circuits respond in the same way to all voltage values within a given range.

By contrast, an **analog quantity** can take on any value over a continuous range of values, and, most important, its exact value is significant. For example, the output of an analog temperature-to-voltage converter might be measured as 2.76 V, which may represent a specific temperature of 27.6°C. If the voltage were measured as something different, such as 2.34 V or 3.78 V, this would represent a completely different temperature. In other words, each possible value of an analog quantity has a different meaning. Another example of this is the output voltage from an audio amplifier into a speaker. This voltage is an analog quantity because each of its possible values produces a different response in the speaker.

Most physical variables are analog in nature and can take on any value within a continuous range of values. Examples include temperature, pressure, light intensity, audio signals, position, rotational speed, and flow rate. Digital systems perform all of their internal operations using digital circuitry and digital operations. Any information that must be inputted to a digital system must first be put into digital form. Similarly, the outputs from a digital system are always in digital form. When a digital system such as a computer is to be used to monitor and/or control a physical process, we must deal with the difference between the digital nature of the computer and the analog nature of the process variables. Figure 10-1 illustrates the situation. This diagram shows the five elements that are involved when a computer is monitoring and controlling a physical variable that is assumed to be analog:

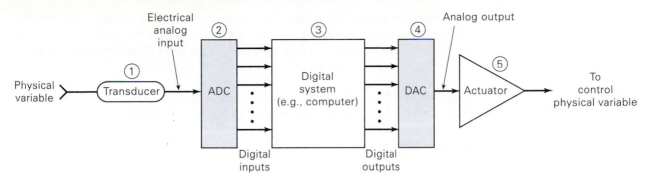

FIGURE 10-1 Analog-to-digital converter (ADC) and digital-to-analog converter (DAC) are used to interface a computer to the analog world so that the computer can monitor and control a physical variable.

1. **Transducer.** The physical variable is normally a nonelectrical quantity. A **transducer** is a device that converts the physical variable to an electrical variable. Some common transducers include thermistors, photocells, photodiodes, flow meters, pressure transducers, and tachometers. The electrical output of the transducer is an analog current or voltage that is proportional to the physical variable that it is monitoring. For example, the physical variable could be the temperature of water in a large tank that is being filled from cold and hot water pipes. Let's say that the water temperature varies from 80 to 150°F and that a thermistor and its associated circuitry convert this water temperature to a voltage ranging from 800 to 1500 mV. Note that the transducer's output is directly proportional to temperature such that each 1°F produces a 10-mV output. This proportionality factor was chosen for convenience.

2. **Analog-to-digital converter (ADC).** The transducer's electrical analog output serves as the analog input to the ADC. The ADC converts this analog input to a digital output. This digital output consists of a number of bits that represent the value of the analog input. For example, the ADC might convert the transducer's 800- to 1500-mV analog values to binary values ranging from 01010000 (80) to 10010110 (150). Note that the binary output from the ADC is proportional to the analog input voltage so that each unit of the digital output represents 10 mV.

3. **Computer.** The digital representation of the process variable is transmitted from the ADC to the digital computer, which stores the digital value and processes it according to a program of instructions that it is executing. The program might perform calculations or other operations on this digital representation of temperature to come up with a digital output that will eventually be used to control the temperature.

4. **Digital-to-analog converter (DAC).** This digital output from the computer is connected to a DAC, which converts it to a proportional analog voltage or current. For example, the computer might produce a digital output ranging from 00000000 to 11111111, which the DAC converts to a voltage ranging from 0 to 10 V.

5. **Actuator.** The analog signal from the DAC is often connected to some device or circuit that serves as an actuator to control the physical variable. For our water

temperature example, the actuator might be an electrically controlled valve that regulates the flow of hot water into the tank in accordance with the analog voltage from the DAC. The flow rate would vary in proportion to this analog voltage, with 0 V producing no flow and 10 V producing the maximum flow.

Thus, we see that ADCs and DACs function as *interfaces* between a completely digital system, such as a computer, and the analog world. This function has become increasingly more important as inexpensive microcomputers have moved into areas of process control where computer control was previously not feasible.

Review Questions

1. What is the function of a transducer?
2. What is the function of an ADC?
3. What does a computer often do with the data that it receives from an ADC?
4. What function does a DAC perform?
5. What is the function of an actuator?

10-2 DIGITAL-TO-ANALOG CONVERSION

We will now begin our study of digital-to-analog (D/A) and analog-to-digital (A/D) conversion. Since many A/D conversion methods utilize the D/A conversion process, we will examine D/A conversion first.

Basically, D/A *conversion* is the process of taking a value represented in *digital* code (such as straight binary or BCD) and converting it to a voltage or current that is proportional to the digital value. Figure 10-2(a) shows the symbol for a typical four-bit D/A converter. We will not concern ourselves with the internal circuitry until later. For now, we will examine the various input/output relationships.

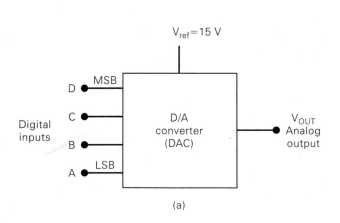

D	C	B	A	V_{OUT}	
0	0	0	0	0	volts
0	0	0	1	1	
0	0	1	0	2	
0	0	1	1	3	
0	1	0	0	4	
0	1	0	1	5	
0	1	1	0	6	
0	1	1	1	7	
1	0	0	0	8	
1	0	0	1	9	
1	0	1	0	10	
1	0	1	1	11	
1	1	0	0	12	
1	1	0	1	13	
1	1	1	0	14	
1	1	1	1	15	volts

(b)

FIGURE 10-2 Four-bit DAC with voltage output.

Notice that there is an input for a voltage reference, V_{ref}. This input is used to determine the **full-scale output** or maximum value that the D/A converter can produce. The digital inputs $D, C, B,$ and A are usually derived from the output register of a digital system. The $2^4 = 16$ different binary numbers represented by these four bits are listed in Figure 10-2(b). For each input number, the D/A converter output voltage is a unique value. In fact, for this case, the analog output voltage V_{OUT} is equal in volts to the binary number. It could also have been twice the binary number or some other proportionality factor. The same idea would hold true if the D/A output were a current I_{OUT}.

In general,

$$\text{analog output} = K \times \text{digital input} \tag{10-1}$$

where K is the proportionality factor and is a constant value for a given DAC connected to a fixed reference voltage. The analog output can, of course, be a voltage or a current. When it is a voltage, K will be in voltage units, and when the output is a current, K will be in current units. For the DAC of Figure 10-2, $K = 1$ V, so that

$$V_{\text{OUT}} = (1 \text{ V}) \times \text{digital input}$$

We can use this to calculate V_{OUT} for any value of digital input. For example, with a digital input of $1100_2 = 12_{10}$, we obtain

$$V_{\text{OUT}} = 1 \text{ V} \times 12 = 12 \text{ V}$$

EXAMPLE 10-1A

A five-bit DAC has a current output. For a digital input of 10100, an output current of 10 mA is produced. What will I_{OUT} be for a digital input of 11101?

Solution

The digital input 10100_2 is equal to decimal 20. Since $I_{\text{OUT}} = 10$ mA for this case, the proportionality factor must be 0.5 mA. Thus, we can find I_{OUT} for any digital input such as $11101_2 = 29_{10}$ as follows:

$$I_{\text{OUT}} = (0.5 \text{ mA}) \times 29$$
$$= 14.5 \text{ mA}$$

Remember, the proportionality factor, K, will vary from one DAC to another and depends on the reference voltage.

EXAMPLE 10-1B

What is the largest value of output voltage from an eight-bit DAC that produces 1.0 V for a digital input of 00110010?

Solution

$$00110010_2 = 50_{10}$$
$$1.0 \text{ V} = K \times 50$$

Therefore,

$$K = 20 \text{ mV}$$

The largest output will occur for an input of $11111111_2 = 255_{10}$.

$$V_{OUT}(\text{max}) = 20 \text{ mV} \times 255$$
$$= 5.10 \text{ V}$$

Analog Output

The output of a DAC is technically not an analog quantity because it can take on only specific values such as the 16 possible voltage levels for V_{OUT} in Figure 10-2 as long as V_{ref} is constant. Thus, in that sense, it is actually digital. However, as we will see, the number of different possible output values can be increased and the difference between successive values decreased by increasing the number of input bits. This will allow us to produce an output that is more and more like an analog quantity that varies continuously over a range of values. In other words, the DAC output is a "pseudo-analog" quantity. We will continue to refer to it as analog, keeping in mind that it is an approximation to a pure analog quantity.

Input Weights

For the DAC of Figure 10-2 it should be noted that each digital input contributes a different amount to the analog output. This is easily seen if we examine the cases where only one input is HIGH (Table 10-1). The contributions of each digital input are *weighted* according to their position in the binary number. Thus, A, which is the LSB, has a *weight* of 1 V, B has a weight of 2 V, C has a weight of 4 V, and D, the MSB, has the largest weight, 8 V. The weights are successively doubled for each bit, beginning with the LSB. Thus, we can consider V_{OUT} to be the weighted sum of the digital inputs. For instance, to find V_{OUT} for the digital input 0111, we can add the weights of the C, B, and A bits to obtain $4 \text{ V} + 2 \text{ V} + 1 \text{ V} = 7 \text{ V}$.

TABLE 10-1

D	C	B	A		V_{OUT} (V)
0	0	0	1	→	1
0	0	1	0	→	2
0	1	0	0	→	4
1	0	0	0	→	8

EXAMPLE 10-2

A five-bit D/A converter produces $V_{OUT} = 0.2$ V for a digital input of 00001. Find the value of V_{OUT} for an input of 11111.

Solution

Obviously, 0.2 V is the weight of the LSB. Thus, the weights of the other bits must be 0.4 V, 0.8 V, 1.6 V, and 3.2 V, respectively. For a digital input of 11111, then, the value of V_{OUT} will be $3.2 \text{ V} + 1.6 \text{ V} + 0.8 \text{ V} + 0.4 \text{ V} + 0.2 \text{ V} = 6.2 \text{ V}$.

Resolution (Step Size)

Resolution of a D/A converter is defined as the smallest change that can occur in the analog output as a result of a change in the digital input. Referring to the table in Figure 10-2, we can see that the resolution is 1 V, since V_{OUT} can change by no less than 1 V when the digital input value is changed. The resolution is always equal to the weight of the LSB and is also referred to as the **step size,** since it is the amount that V_{OUT} will change as the digital input value is changed from one step to the next. This is illustrated better in Figure 10-3, where the outputs from a four-bit binary counter provide the inputs to our DAC. As the counter is being continually cycled through its 16 states by the clock signal, the DAC output is a **staircase** waveform that goes up 1 V per step. When the counter is at 1111, the DAC output is at its maximum value of 15 V; this is its **full-scale output.** When the counter recycles to 0000, the DAC output returns to 0 V. The resolution or step size is the size of the jumps in the staircase waveform; in this case, each step is 1 V.

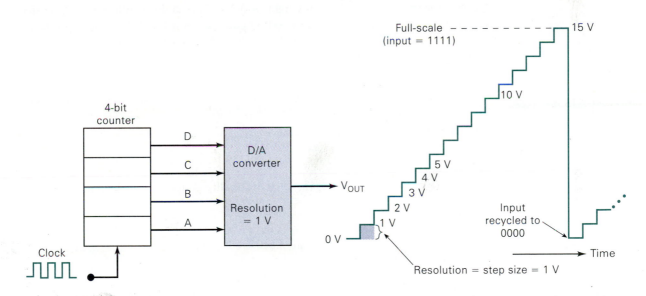

FIGURE 10-3   Output waveforms of a DAC as inputs are provided by a binary counter.

Note that the staircase has 16 levels corresponding to the 16 input states, but there are only 15 steps or jumps between the 0-V level and full-scale. In general, for an *N*-bit DAC the number of different levels will be 2^N, and the number of steps will be $2^N - 1$.

You may have already figured out that resolution (step size) is the same as the proportionality factor in the DAC input/output relationship:

$$\text{analog output} = K \times \text{digital input}$$

A new interpretation of this expression would be that the digital input is equal to the number of steps, *K* is the amount of voltage (or current) per step, and the analog output is the product of the two. We now have a convenient way of calculating the value of K for the D/A:

$$\text{resolution} = K = \frac{A_{\text{fs}}}{(2^n - 1)} \qquad\qquad (10\text{-}2)$$

where A_{fs} is the analog full-scale output and n is the number of bits.

EXAMPLE 10-3A

What is the resolution (step size) of the DAC of Example 10-2? Describe the staircase signal out of this DAC.

Solution

The LSB for this converter has a weight of 0.2 V. This is the resolution or step size. A staircase waveform can be generated by connecting a five-bit counter to the DAC inputs. The staircase will have 32 levels from 0 V up to a full-scale output of 6.2 V, and 31 steps of 0.2 V each.

EXAMPLE 10-3B

For the DAC of Example 10-2, determine V_{OUT} for a digital input of 10001.

Solution

The step size is 0.2 V, which is the proportionality factor K. The digital input is $10001 = 17_{10}$. Thus, we have

$$V_{\text{OUT}} = (0.2 \text{ V}) \times 17$$
$$= 3.4 \text{ V}$$

Percentage Resolution

Although resolution can be expressed as the amount of voltage or current per step, it is also useful to express it as a percentage of the *full-scale output*. To illustrate, the DAC of Figure 10-3 has a maximum full-scale output of 15 V (when the digital input is 1111). The step size is 1 V, which gives a percentage resolution of

$$\% \text{ resolution} = \frac{\text{step size}}{\text{full scale (F.S.)}} \times 100\% \qquad\qquad (10\text{-}3)$$

$$= \frac{1 \text{ V}}{15 \text{ V}} \times 100\% = 6.67\%$$

EXAMPLE 10-4

A 10-bit DAC has a step size of 10 mV. Determine the full-scale output voltage and the percentage resolution.

Solution

With 10 bits, there will be $2^{10} - 1 = 1023$ steps of 10 mV each. The full-scale output will therefore be 10 mV $\times$ 1023 = 10.23 V, and

$$\% \text{ resolution} = \frac{10 \text{ mV}}{10.23 \text{ V}} \times 100\% \approx 0.1\%$$

Example 10-4 helps to illustrate the fact that the percentage resolution becomes smaller as the number of input bits is increased. In fact, the percentage resolution can also be calculated from

$$\% \text{ resolution} = \frac{1}{\text{total number of steps}} \times 100\% \qquad (10\text{-}4)$$

For an N-bit binary input code the total number of steps is $2^N - 1$. Thus, for the previous example,

$$\% \text{ resolution} = \frac{1}{2^{10} - 1} \times 100\%$$

$$= \frac{1}{1023} \times 100\%$$

$$\approx 0.1\%$$

This means that it is *only the number of bits* that determines the *percentage* resolution. Increasing the number of bits increases the number of steps to reach full scale, so that each step is a smaller part of the full-scale voltage. Most DAC manufacturers specify resolution as the number of bits.

What Does Resolution Mean?

A DAC cannot produce a continuous range of output values, and so, strictly speaking, its output is not truly analog. A DAC produces a finite set of output values. In our water temperature example of Section 10-1, the computer generates a digital output to provide an analog voltage between 0 and 10 V to an electrically controlled valve. The DAC's resolution (number of bits) determines how many possible voltage values the computer can send to the valve. If a six-bit DAC is used, there will be 63 possible steps of 0.159 V between 0 and 10 V. When an eight-bit DAC is used, there will be 255 possible steps of 0.039 V between 0 and 10 V. The greater the number of bits, the finer the resolution (the smaller the step size).

The system designer must decide what resolution is needed on the basis of the required system performance. The resolution limits how close the DAC output can come to a given analog value. Generally, the cost of DACs increases with the number of bits, and so the designer will use only as many bits as necessary.

**EXAMPLE
10-5**

Figure 10-4 shows a computer controlling the speed of a motor. The 0 to 2-mA analog current from the DAC is amplified to produce motor speeds from 0 to 1000 rpm (revolutions per minute). How many bits should be used if the computer is to be able to produce a motor speed that is within 2 rpm of the desired speed?

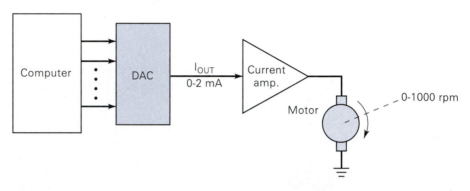

FIGURE 10-4   Example 10-5.

Solution

The motor speed will range from 0 to 1000 rpm as the DAC goes from zero to full scale. Each step in the DAC output will produce a step in the motor speed. We want the step size to be no greater than 2 rpm. Thus, we need at least 500 steps (1000/2). Now we must determine how many bits are required so that there are at least 500 steps from zero to full scale. We know that the number of steps is $2^N - 1$, and so we can say

$$2^N - 1 \geq 500$$

or

$$2^N \geq 501$$

Since $2^8 = 256$ and $2^9 = 512$, the smallest number of bits that will produce at least 500 steps is *nine*. We could use more than nine bits, but this might add to the cost of the DAC.

**EXAMPLE
10-6**

Using nine bits, how close to 326 rpm can the motor speed be adjusted?

Solution

With nine bits, there will be 511 steps ($2^9 - 1$). Thus, the motor speed will go up in steps of 1000 rpm/511 = 1.957 rpm. The number of steps needed to reach 326 rpm is 326/1.957 = 166.58. This is not a whole number of steps, and so we will round it to 167. The actual motor speed on the 167th step will be 167 × 1.957 =

326.8 rpm. Thus, the computer must output the nine-bit binary equivalent of 167_{10} to produce the desired motor speed within the resolution of the system.

In all of our examples, we have assumed that the DACs have been perfectly accurate in producing an analog output that is directly proportional to the binary input, and that the resolution is the only thing that limits how close we can come to a desired analog value. This, of course, is unrealistic, since all devices contain inaccuracies. We will examine the causes and effects of DAC inaccuracy in a later section.

BCD Input Code

The DACs we have considered thus far have used a binary input code. Many DACs use a BCD input code where four-bit code groups are used for each decimal digit. Figure 10-5 shows the diagram of an eight-bit (two-digit) converter of this type. Each four-bit code group can range from 0000 to 1001, and so the BCD inputs represent decimal numbers from 00 to 99. Within each code group the weights of the different bits are in the normal binary proportions (1, 2, 4, 8), but the relative weights of each code group are different by a factor of 10. Figure 10-5 shows the relative weights of the various bits. Note that the bits that make up the BCD code for the most significant digit (MSD) have a relative weight that is 10 times that of the corresponding bits of the LSD.

FIGURE 10-5 DAC using BCD input code. This converter accepts a two-digit input and generates 100 possible analog output values.

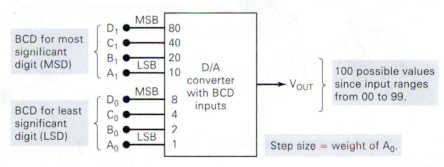

EXAMPLE 10-7A

If the weight of A_0 is 0.1 V in Figure 10-5, find the following values:

(a) Step size

(b) Full-scale output and percentage resolution

(c) V_{OUT} for $D_1C_1B_1A_1 = 0101$ and $D_0C_0B_0A_0 = 1000$

Solution

(a) Step size is the weight of the LSB of the LSD, 0.1 V.

(b) There are 99 steps since there are two BCD digits. Thus, full-scale output is $99 \times 0.1 = 9.9$ V. The resolution is [using equation (10-3)]

$$\frac{\text{step size}}{\text{F.S.}} \times 100\% = \frac{0.1}{9.9} \times 100\% \approx 1\%$$

We could also have used equation (10-4) to calculate percentage resolution, since the total number of steps is 99.

(c) The exact weights in volts are listed in Table 10-2. One way to find V_{OUT} for a given input is to add the weights of all bits that are 1s. Thus, for an input of 0101 1000, we have

$$V_{OUT} = \overset{C_1}{4\ V} + \overset{A_1}{1\ V} + \overset{D_0}{0.8\ V} = 5.8\ V$$

An easier way is to realize that the BCD input code represents 58_{10} and the step size is 0.1 V, so that

$$V_{OUT} = (0.1\ V) \times 58 = 5.8\ V$$

TABLE 10-2

MSD				LSD			
D_1	C_1	B_1	A_1	D_0	C_0	B_0	A_0
8.0	4.0	2.0	1.0	0.8	0.4	0.2	0.1

EXAMPLE 10-7B

A certain 12-bit BCD digital-to-analog converter has a full-scale output of 9.99 V.

(a) Determine the percent resolution.

(b) Determine the converter's step size.

Solution

(a) Twelve bits correspond to three decimal digits, that is, decimal numbers from 000 to 999. Therefore, the output of this DAC has 999 possible steps from 0 to 9.99 V. Thus, we have

$$\% \text{ resolution} = \frac{1}{\text{number of steps}} \times 100\%$$

$$= \frac{1}{999} \times 100\%$$

$$\approx 0.1\%$$

(b)

$$\text{step size} = \frac{\text{F.S.}}{\text{number of steps}}$$

$$= 9.99\ V/999$$

$$= 0.01\ V$$

Bipolar DACs

Up to this point we have assumed that the binary input to a DAC has been an unsigned number and that the DAC output has been a positive voltage or current. Some DACs are designed to produce both positive and negative values, such as -10 to $+10$ V. This is generally done by using the binary input as a signed number with the MSB as the sign bit (0 for $+$ and 1 for $-$). Negative input values are often represented in 2's-complement form, although the true-magnitude form is also used by some DACs. For example, suppose that we have a six-bit bipolar DAC that uses the 2's-complement system and has a resolution of 0.2 V. The binary input values range from 100000 (-32) to 011111 ($+31$) to produce analog outputs in the range from -6.4 to $+6.2$ V. There are 63 steps ($2^6 - 1$) of 0.2 V between these negative and positive limits.

1. An eight-bit DAC has an output of 3.92 mA for an input of 01100010. What are the DAC's resolution and full-scale output?

2. What is the weight of the MSB of the DAC of question 1?

3. What is the percentage resolution of an eight-bit DAC?

4. How many different output voltages can a 12-bit DAC produce?

5. For the system of Figure 10-4, how many bits should be used if the computer is to control the motor speed within 0.4 rpm?

6. Consider a 12-bit DAC with BCD inputs and a resolution of 10 mV. What will its output be for an input of 100001110011?

7. *True or false:* The percentage resolution of a DAC depends *only* on the number of bits.

8. What is the advantage of a smaller (finer) resolution?

10-3   D/A-CONVERTER CIRCUITRY

There are several methods and circuits for producing the D/A operation that has been described. We shall examine several of the basic schemes to gain an insight into the ideas used. It is not important to be familiar with all of the various circuit schemes because D/A converters are available as ICs or as encapsulated packages that do not require any circuit knowledge. Instead, it is important to know the significant performance characteristics of DACs, in general, so that they can be used intelligently. These will be covered in Section 10-4.

Figure 10-6(a) shows the basic circuit for one type of four-bit DAC. The inputs A, B, C, and D are binary inputs that are assumed to have values of either 0 or 5 V. The *operational amplifier* is employed as a summing amplifier, which produces the weighted sum of these input voltages. It may be recalled that the summing amplifier multiplies each input voltage by the ratio of the feedback resistor R_F to the corresponding input resistor R_{IN}. In this circuit $R_F = 1$ kΩ, and the input resistors range from 1 to 8 kΩ. The D input has $R_{IN} = 1$ kΩ, so the summing amplifier passes the voltage at D with no attenuation. The C input has $R_{IN} = 2$ kΩ, so that it will be attenuated by ½. Similarly, the *B* input will be attenuated by ¼, and the *A* input by ⅛. The amplifier output can thus be expressed as

$$V_{OUT} = -(V_D + \tfrac{1}{2}V_C + \tfrac{1}{4}V_B + \tfrac{1}{8}V_A) \tag{10-5}$$

The negative sign is present because the summing amplifier is a polarity-inverting amplifier, but it will not concern us here.

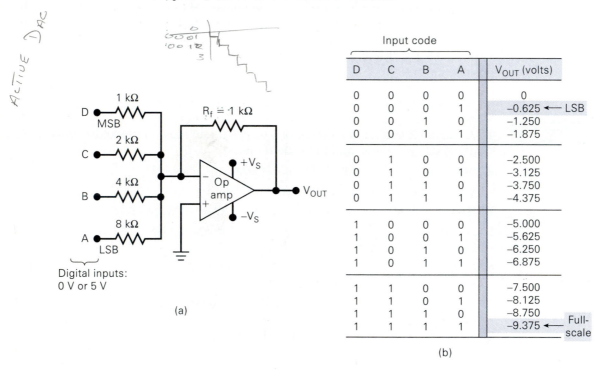

	Input code			
D	C	B	A	V_{OUT} (volts)
0	0	0	0	0
0	0	0	1	−0.625 ← LSB
0	0	1	0	−1.250
0	0	1	1	−1.875
0	1	0	0	−2.500
0	1	0	1	−3.125
0	1	1	0	−3.750
0	1	1	1	−4.375
1	0	0	0	−5.000
1	0	0	1	−5.625
1	0	1	0	−6.250
1	0	1	1	−6.875
1	1	0	0	−7.500
1	1	0	1	−8.125
1	1	1	0	−8.750
1	1	1	1	−9.375 ← Full-scale

(a)

(b)

FIGURE 10-6 Simple DAC using an op-amp summing amplifier with binary-weighted resistors.

Clearly, the summing amplifier output is an analog voltage which represents a weighted sum of the digital inputs, as shown by the table in Figure 10-6(b). This table lists all of the possible input conditions and the resultant amplifier output voltage. The output is evaluated for any input condition by setting the appropriate inputs to either 0 or 5 V. For example, if the digital input is 1010, then $V_D = V_B = 5$ V and $V_C = V_A = 0$ V. Thus, using equation (10-5),

$$V_{OUT} = -(5 \text{ V} + 0 \text{ V} + \tfrac{1}{4} \times 5 \text{ V} + 0 \text{ V})$$
$$= -6.25 \text{ V}$$

The resolution of this D/A converter is equal to the weighting of the LSB, which is $\tfrac{1}{8} \times 5$ V = 0.625 V. As shown in the table, the analog output increases by 0.625 V as the binary input number advances one step.

EXAMPLE 10-8	(a) Determine the weight of each input bit of Figure 10-6(a). (b) Change R_F to 250 Ω and determine the full-scale output.

Solution

(a) The MSB passes with gain = 1, so its weight in the output is 5 V. Thus,

$$\begin{aligned} \text{MSB} &\to 5\text{V} \\ \text{2nd MSB} &\to 2.5 \text{ V} \\ \text{3rd MSB} &\to 1.25 \text{ V} \\ \text{4th MSB} = \text{LSB} &\to 0.625 \text{ V} \end{aligned}$$

(b) If R_F is reduced by a factor of 4, to 250 Ω, each input weight will be four times *smaller* than the values above. Thus, the full-scale output will be reduced by this same factor and becomes $-9.375/4 = -2.344$ V.

If we look at the input resistor values in Figure 10-6, it should come as no surprise that they are *binarily weighted*. In other words, starting with the MSB resistor, the resistor values increase by a factor of 2. This, of course, produces the desired weighting in the voltage output.

Conversion Accuracy

The table in Figure 10-6(b) gives the *ideal* values of V_{OUT} for the various input cases. How close the circuit comes to producing these values depends primarily on two factors: (1) the precision of the input and feedback resistors and (2) the precision of the input voltage levels. The resistors can be made very accurate (within 0.01 percent of the desired values) by trimming, but the input voltage levels must be handled differently. It should be clear that the digital inputs cannot be taken directly from the outputs of FFs or logic gates because the output logic levels of these devices are not precise values like 0 V and 5 V but vary within given ranges. For this reason, it is necessary to add some more circuitry between each digital input and its input resistor to the summing amplifier as shown in Figure 10-7.

Each digital input controls a semiconductor switch such as the CMOS transmission gate we studied in Chapter 8. When the input is HIGH, the switch closes and connects a *precision reference supply* to the input resistor; when the input is LOW, the switch is open. The reference supply produces a very stable, precise voltage needed to generate an accurate analog output.

DAC with Current Output

Figure 10-8(a) shows one basic scheme for generating an analog output current proportional to a binary input. The circuit shown is a four-bit DAC using binarily weighted resistors. The circuit uses four parallel current paths, each controlled by a semiconductor switch such as the CMOS transmission gate. The state of each switch is controlled

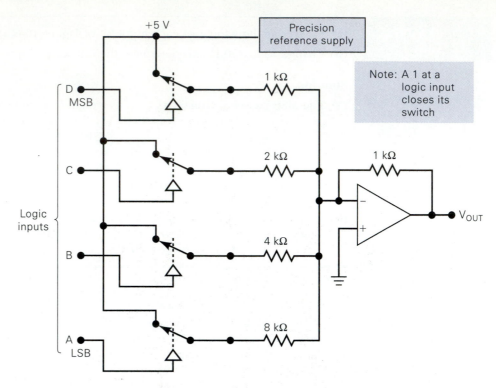

FIGURE 10-7 Complete four-bit DAC including a precision reference supply.

by logic levels at the binary inputs. The current through each path is determined by an accurate reference voltage, V_{REF}, and a precision resistor in the path. The resistors are binarily weighted so that the various currents will be binarily weighted, and the total current, I_{OUT}, will be the sum of the individual currents. The MSB path has the smallest resistor, R; the next path has a resistor of twice the value; and so on. The output current can be made to flow through a load R_L which is much smaller than R, so that it has no effect on the value of current. Ideally, R_L should be a short to ground.

EXAMPLE 10-9

Assume that $V_{REF} = 10$ V and $R = 10$ kΩ. Determine the resolution and the full-scale output for this DAC. Assume that R_L is much smaller than R.

Solution

$I_{OUT} = V_{REF}/R = 1$ mA. This is the weight of the MSB. The other three currents will be 0.5, 0.25, and 0.125 mA. The LSB is 0.125 mA, which is also the resolution.

The full-scale output will occur when the binary inputs are all HIGH so that each current switch is closed and

$$I_{OUT} = 1 + 0.5 + 0.25 + 0.125 = 1.875 \text{ mA}$$

Note that the output current is proportional to V_{REF}. If V_{REF} is increased or decreased, the resolution and the full-scale output will change proportionally.

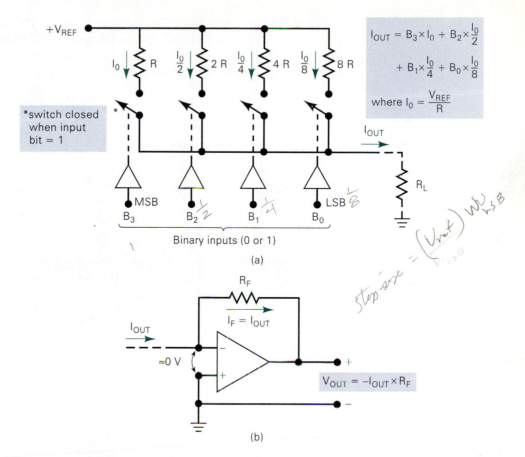

FIGURE 10-8   (a) Basic current-output DAC; (b) connected to an op-amp current-to-voltage converter.

For I_{OUT} to be accurate, R_L should be a short to ground. One common way to accomplish this is to use an op amp as a current-to-voltage converter, as shown in Figure 10-8(b). Here the I_{OUT} from the DAC is connected to the op-amp's "−" input, which is virtually at ground. The op-amp negative feedback forces a current equal to I_{OUT} to flow through R_F to produce $V_{OUT} = -I_{OUT} \times R_F$. Thus, V_{OUT} will be an analog voltage that is proportional to the binary input to the DAC. This analog output can drive a wide range of loads without being loaded down.

R/2R Ladder

The DAC circuits we have looked at thus far use binary-weighted resistors to produce the proper weighting of each bit. Whereas this method works in theory, it has some practical limitations. The biggest problem is the large difference in resistor values between the LSB and the MSB, especially in high-resolution DACs (i.e., many bits). For example, if the MSB resistor is 1 kΩ in a 12-bit DAC, the LSB resistor will be over 2 MΩ. With the current IC fabrication technology, it is very difficult to produce resistance values over a wide resistance range that maintain an accurate ratio especially with variations in temperature.

For this reason it is preferable to have a circuit that uses resistances that are fairly close in value. One of the most widely used DAC circuits that satisfies this requirement is the *R/2R ladder* network, where the resistance values span a range of only 2 to 1. One such DAC is shown in Figure 10-9.

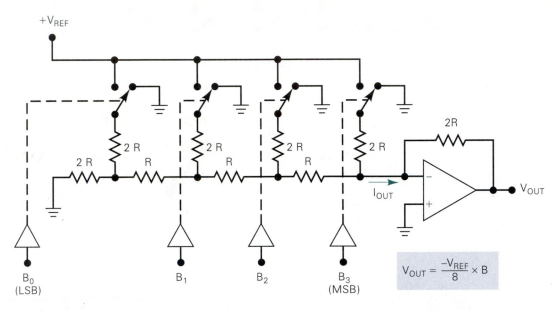

FIGURE 10-9   Basic *R/2R* ladder DAC.

Note how the resistors are arranged, and especially note that only two different values are used, *R* and *2R*. The current I_{OUT} depends on the positions of the four switches, and the binary inputs $B_3B_2B_1B_0$ control the states of the switches. This current is allowed to flow through an op-amp current-to-voltage converter to develop V_{OUT}. We will not perform a detailed analysis of this circuit here, but it can be shown that the value of V_{OUT} is given by the expression

$$V_{OUT} = \frac{-V_{REF}}{8} \times B \qquad\qquad (10\text{-}6)$$

where *B* is the value of the binary input, which can range from 0000 (0) to 1111 (15).

| EXAMPLE 10-10 | Assume that $V_{REF} = 5$ V for the DAC in Figure 10-9. What are the resolution and full-scale output of this converter? |

Solution

The resolution is equal to the weight of the LSB, which we can determine by setting $B = 0001 = 1$ in equation (10-6):

$$\text{resolution} = \frac{-5 \text{ V} \times 1}{8}$$

$$= -0.625 \text{ V}$$

The full-scale output occurs for $B = 1111 = 15_{10}$. Again using equation (10-6),

$$\text{full-scale} = \frac{-5 \text{ V} \times 15}{8}$$

$$= -9.375 \text{ V}$$

---

1. What is the advantage of $R/2R$ ladder DACs over those that use binary-weighted resistors?

2. A certain six-bit DAC uses binary-weighted resistors. If the MSB resistor is 20 kΩ, what is the LSB resistor?

3. What will the resolution be if the value of R_F in Figure 10-6 is changed to 800 Ω?

4. What will happen to both resolution and full-scale output when V_{REF} is increased by 20 percent?

10-4   DAC SPECIFICATIONS

A wide variety of DACs are currently available as ICs or as self-contained, encapsulated packages. One should be familiar with the more important manufacturers' specifications in order to evaluate a DAC for a particular application.

Resolution

As mentioned earlier, the percentage resolution of a DAC is dependent solely on the number of bits. For this reason, manufacturers usually specify a DAC resolution as the number of bits. A 10-bit DAC has a finer (smaller) resolution than an 8-bit DAC.

Accuracy

DAC manufacturers have several ways of specifying accuracy. The two most common are called **full-scale error** and **linearity error,** which are normally expressed as a percentage of the converter's full-scale output (% F.S.).

Full-scale error is the maximum deviation of the DAC's output from its expected (ideal) value, expressed as a percentage of full scale. For example, assume that the DAC of Figure 10-6 has an accuracy of $\pm 0.01\%$ F.S. Since this converter has a full-scale output of 9.375 V, this percentage converts to

$$\pm 0.01\% \times 9.375 \text{ V} = \pm 0.9375 \text{ mV}$$

This means that the output of this DAC can, at any time, be off by as much as 0.9375 mV from its expected value.

Linearity error is the maximum deviation in step size from the ideal step size. For example, the DAC of Figure 10-6 has an expected step size of 0.625 V. If this converter has a linearity error of ±0.01% F.S., this would mean that the actual *step size* could be off by as much as 0.9375 mV.

It is important to understand that accuracy and resolution of a DAC must be compatible. It is illogical to have a resolution of, say, 1 percent and an accuracy of 0.1 percent, or vice versa. To illustrate, a DAC with a resolution of 1 percent and an F.S. output of 10 V can produce an output analog voltage within 0.1 V of any desired value, assuming perfect accuracy. It makes no sense to have a costly accuracy of 0.01% F.S. (or 1 mV) if the resolution already limits the closeness of the desired value to 0.1 V. The same can be said for having a resolution that is very small (many bits) while the accuracy is poor; it is a waste of input bits.

EXAMPLE 10-11

A certain eight-bit DAC has a full-scale output of 2 mA and a full-scale error of ±0.5% F.S. What is the range of possible outputs for an input of 10000000?

Solution

The step size is 2 mA/255 = 7.84 μA. Since 10000000 = 128_{10}, the ideal output should be 128 × 7.84 μA = 1004 μA. The error can be as much as

$$\pm 0.5\% \times 2 \text{ mA} = \pm 10 \text{ } \mu A$$

Thus, the actual output can deviate by this amount from the ideal 1004 μA, so the actual output can be anywhere from 994 to 1014 μA.

Offset Error

Ideally, the output of a DAC will be zero volts when the binary input is all 0s. In practice, however, there will be a very small output voltage for this situation; this is called **offset error.** This offset error, if not corrected, will be added to the expected DAC output for *all* input cases. For example, let's say that a four-bit DAC has an offset error of +2 mV and a *perfect* step size of 100 mV. Table 10-3 shows the ideal and the actual DAC output for several input cases. Note that the actual output is 2 mV greater than expected; this is due to the offset error. Offset error can be negative as well as positive.

TABLE 10-3

Input Code	Ideal Output (mV)	Actual Output (mV)
0000	0	2
0001	100	102
1000	800	802
1111	1500	1502

Many DACs will have an external offset adjustment that allows you to zero the offset. This is usually accomplished by applying all 0s to the DAC input and monitoring the output while an *offset adjustment potentiometer* is adjusted until the output is as close to 0 V as required.

Settling Time

The operating speed of a DAC is usually specified by giving its **settling time,** which is the time required for the DAC output to go from zero to full scale as the binary input is changed from all 0s to all 1s. Actually, the settling time is measured as the time for the DAC output to settle within $\pm 1/2$ step size (resolution) of its final value. For example, if a DAC has a resolution of 10 mV, settling time is measured as the time it takes the output to settle within 5 mV of its full-scale value.

Typical values for settling time range from 50 ns to 10 μs. Generally speaking, DACs with a current output will have shorter settling times than those with voltage outputs. For instance, the DAC1280 can operate as either current output or voltage output. In the current output mode, its settling time is 300 ns; in the voltage output mode, its settling time is 2.5 μs. The main reason for this difference is the response time of the op amp that is used as the current-to-voltage converter.

Monotonicity

A DAC is **monotonic** if its output increases as the binary input is incremented from one value to the next. Another way to describe this is that the staircase output will have no downward steps as the binary input is incremented from zero to full scale.

Review Questions

1. Define *full-scale error.*
2. What is *settling time?*
3. Describe offset error and its effect on a DAC output.
4. Why are voltage DACs generally slower than current DACs?

10-5 AN INTEGRATED-CIRCUIT DAC

The AD7524, a CMOS IC available from several IC manufacturers, is an eight-bit D/A converter that uses an $R/2R$ ladder network. Its block symbol is given in Figure 10-10(a). This DAC has an eight-bit input that can be latched internally under the control of the Chip Select ($\overline{CS}$) and WRITE ($\overline{WR}$) inputs. When both of these control inputs are LOW, the digital data inputs D_7–D_0 produce the analog output current *OUT 1* (the *OUT 2* terminal is normally grounded). When either control input goes HIGH, the digital input data are latched, and the analog output remains at the level corresponding to that latched digital data. Subsequent changes in the digital inputs will have no effect on *OUT 1* in this latched state.

The maximum settling time for the AD7524 is typically 100 ns, and its full-range accuracy is rated at $\pm 0.2\%$ F.S. The V_{REF} can range over both negative and positive voltages from 0 to 25 V, so that analog output currents of both polarities can be produced. The output current can be converted to a voltage using an op-amp connected as in Figure 10-10(b). Note that the op-amp's feedback resistor is already on the DAC chip.

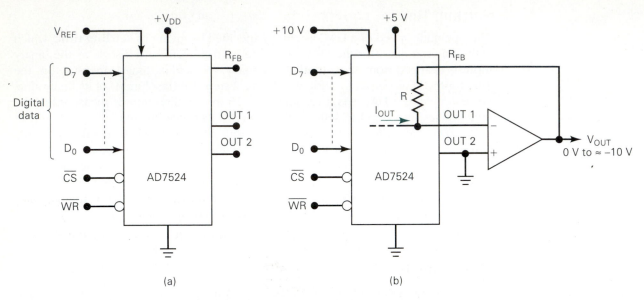

(a)   (b)

FIGURE 10-10   (a) AD7524 eight-bit DAC with latched inputs; (b) AD7524 connected to produce analog output voltage ranging from 0 V to approximately −10 V.

10-6   DAC APPLICATIONS

DACs are used whenever the output of a digital circuit must provide an analog voltage or current to drive an analog device. Some of the most common applications are described in the following paragraphs.

Control

The digital output from a computer can be converted to an analog control signal to adjust the speed of a motor or the temperature of a furnace, or to control almost any physical variable.

Automatic Testing

Computers can be programmed to generate the analog signals (through a DAC) needed to test analog circuitry. The test circuit's analog output response will normally be converted to a digital value by an ADC and fed into the computer to be stored, displayed, and sometimes analyzed.

Signal Reconstruction

In many applications, an analog signal is **digitized;** that is, successive points on the signal are converted to their digital equivalents and stored in memory. This conversion is performed by an analog-to-digital converter (ADC). A DAC can then be used to convert the stored digitized data back to analog—one point at a time—thereby reconstructing the original signal. This combination of digitizing and reconstruction is used in digital storage oscilloscopes, audio compact disk systems, and digital audio and video recording. We will look at this further after we learn about ADCs.

A/D Conversion

Several types of ADCs use DACs as part of their circuitry, as we shall see in Section 10-8.

Serial DACs

Many of these DAC applications involve a microprocessor. The main problem with using the parallel-data DACs that have been described thus far is that they occupy so many port bits of the microcomputer. In cases where speed of data transfer is of little concern, a microprocessor can output the digital value to a DAC over a serial interface. Serial DACs are now readily available with a built-in serial in/parallel out shift register. Many of these devices have more than one DAC on the same chip. The digital data, along with a code that specifies which DAC you want, are sent to the chip, one bit at a time. As each bit is presented on the DAC input, a pulse is applied to the serial clock input to shift the bit in. After the proper number of clock pulses, the data value is latched and converted to its analog value.

10-7 TROUBLESHOOTING DACs

DACs are both digital and analog. Logic probes and pulsers can be used on the digital inputs, but a meter or an oscilloscope must be used on the analog output. There are basically two ways to test a DAC's operation: a *static accuracy test* and a *staircase test*.

The static test involves setting the binary input to a fixed value and measuring the analog output with a high-accuracy meter. This test is used to check that the output value falls within the expected range consistent with the DAC's specified accuracy. If it does not, there can be several possible causes. Here are some of them:

■ Drift in the DAC's internal component values (e.g., resistor values) caused by temperature, aging, or some other factors. This can easily produce output values outside the expected accuracy range.

■ Open connections or shorts in any of the binary inputs. This could either prevent an input from adding its weight to the analog output or cause its weight to be permanently present in the output. This is especially hard to detect when the fault is in the less significant inputs.

■ A faulty voltage reference. Since the analog output is directly dependent on V_{REF}, this could produce results that are way off. For DACs that use external reference sources, the reference voltage can easily be checked with a digital voltmeter. Many DACs have internal reference voltages which cannot be checked, except on some DACs that bring the reference voltage out to a pin of the IC.

■ Excessive offset error caused by component aging or temperature. This would produce outputs that are off by a fixed amount. If the DAC has an external offset adjustment capability, this type of error can initially be zeroed out, but changes in operating temperature can cause the offset error to reappear.

The staircase test is used to check the monotonicity of the DAC; that is, it checks to see that the output increases step by step as the binary input is incremented as in Figure 10-3. The steps on the staircase must be of the same size, and there should be no missing steps or downward steps until full scale is reached. This test can help detect internal or external faults that cause an input to have either no contribution or a permanent contribution to the analog output. The following example will illustrate.

EXAMPLE 10-12

How would the staircase waveform appear if the C input to the DAC of Figure 10-3 is open? Assume that the DAC inputs are TTL-compatible.

FIGURE 10-11 Example 10-12.

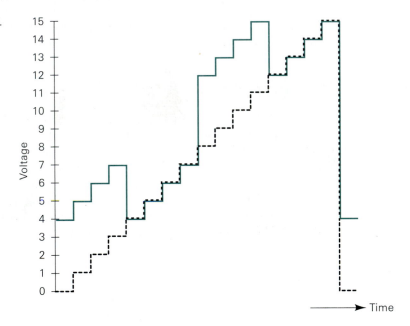

Solution

An open connection at C will be interpreted as a constant logic 1 by the DAC. Thus, this will contribute a constant 4 V to the DAC output so that the DAC output waveform will appear as shown in Figure 10-11. The dotted lines are the staircase as it would appear if the DAC were working correctly. Note that the faulty output waveform matches the correct one during those times when the bit C input would normally be HIGH.

10-8 ANALOG-TO-DIGITAL CONVERSION

An **analog-to-digital converter** takes an analog input voltage and after a certain amount of time produces a digital output code that represents the analog input. The A/D conversion process is generally more complex and time-consuming than the D/A process, and many different methods have been developed and used. We shall examine several of these methods in detail, even though it may never be necessary to design or construct ADCs (they are available as completely packaged units). However, the techniques that are used provide an insight into what factors determine an ADC's performance.

Several important types of ADCs utilize a DAC as part of their circuitry. Figure 10-12 is a general block diagram for this class of ADC. The timing for the operation is provided by the input clock signal. The control unit contains the logic circuitry for generating the proper sequence of operations in response to the START COMMAND, which initiates the conversion process. The op-amp comparator has two *analog* inputs and a *digital* output that switches states, depending on which analog input is greater.

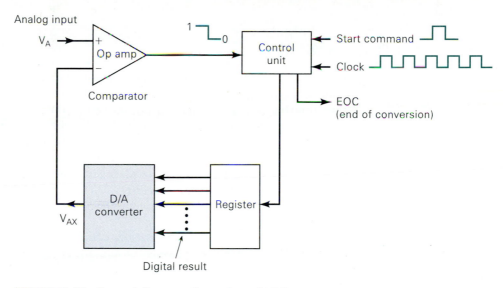

FIGURE 10-12 General diagram of one class of ADCs.

The basic operation of ADCs of this type consists of the following steps:

1. The START COMMAND pulse initiates the operation.

2. At a rate determined by the clock, the control unit continually modifies the binary number that is stored in the register.

3. The binary number in the register is converted to an analog voltage, V_{AX}, by the DAC.

4. The comparator compares V_{AX} with the analog input V_A. As long as $V_{AX} < V_A$, the comparator output stays HIGH. When V_{AX} exceeds V_A by at least an amount equal to V_T (threshold voltage), the comparator output goes LOW and stops the process of modifying the register number. At this point, V_{AX} is a close approxi-

mation to V_A. The digital number in the register, which is the digital equivalent of V_{AX}, is also the approximate digital equivalent of V_A, within the resolution and accuracy of the system.

5. The control logic activates the end-of-conversion signal, *EOC*, when the conversion is complete.

The several variations of this A/D conversion scheme differ mainly in the manner in which the control section continually modifies the numbers in the register. Otherwise, the basic idea is the same, with the register holding the required digital output when the conversion process is complete.

Review Questions

1. What is the function of the comparator in the ADC?
2. Where is the approximate digital equivalent of V_A when the conversion is complete?
3. What is the function of the *EOC* signal?

10-9 DIGITAL-RAMP ADC

One of the simplest versions of the general ADC of Figure 10-12 uses a binary counter as the register and allows the clock to increment the counter one step at a time until $V_{AX} \geq V_A$. It is called a **digital-ramp ADC** because the waveform at V_{AX} is a step-by-step ramp (actually a staircase) like the one shown in Figure 10-3. It is also referred to as a *counter-type* ADC.

Figure 10-13 is the diagram for a digital-ramp ADC. It contains a counter, a DAC, an analog comparator, and a control AND gate. The comparator output serves as the active-LOW end-of-conversion signal $\overline{EOC}$. If we assume that V_A, the analog voltage to be converted, is positive, the operation proceeds as follows:

1. A START pulse is applied to reset the counter to 0. The HIGH at START also inhibits clock pulses from passing through the AND gate into the counter.

2. With all 0s at its input, the DAC's output will be $V_{AX} = 0$ V.

3. Since $V_A > V_{AX}$, the comparator output, $\overline{EOC}$, will be HIGH.

4. When START returns LOW, the AND gate is enabled and clock pulses get through to the counter.

5. As the counter advances, the DAC output, V_{AX}, increases one step at a time as shown in Figure 10-13(b).

6. This continues until V_{AX} reaches a step that exceeds V_A by an amount equal to or greater than V_T (typically 10 to 100 μV). At this point, $\overline{EOC}$ will go LOW and inhibit the flow of pulses into the counter, and the counter will stop counting.

7. The conversion process is now complete as signaled by the HIGH-to-LOW transition at $\overline{EOC}$, and the contents of the counter are the digital representation of V_A.

8. The counter will hold the digital value until the next START pulse initiates a new conversion.

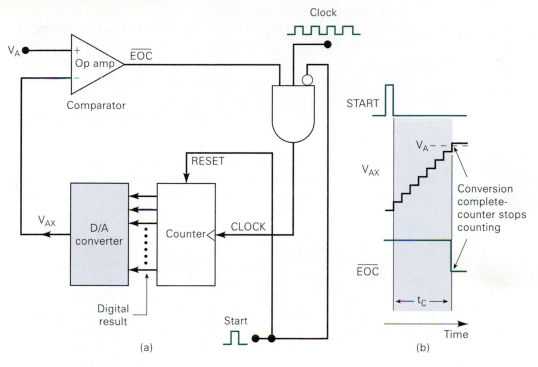

FIGURE 10-13   Digital-ramp ADC.

EXAMPLE 10-13A

Assume the following values for the ADC of Figure 10-13: clock frequency = 1MHz; $V_T = 0.1$ mV; DAC has F.S. output = 10.23 V and a 10-bit input. Determine the following values.

$V_T = $ THRESHOLD of VOLTAGE of COMPARATOR

(a) The digital equivalent obtained for $V_A = 3.728$ V

(b) The conversion time

(c) The resolution of this converter

Solution

(a) The DAC has a 10-bit input and a 10.23-V F.S. output. Thus, the number of total possible steps is $2^{10} - 1 = 1023$, and so the step size is

$$\frac{10.23 \text{ V}}{1023} = 10 \text{ mV}$$

This means that V_{AX} increases in steps of 10 mV as the counter counts up from 0. Since $V_A = 3.728$ V and $V_T = 0.1$ mV, V_{AX} must reach 3.7281 V or more before the comparator switches LOW. This will require

$$\frac{3.7281 \text{ V}}{10 \text{ mV}} = 372.81 = 373 \text{ steps}$$

At the end of the conversion, then, the counter will hold the binary equivalent of 373, which is 0101110101. This is the desired digital equivalent of $V_A = 3.728$ V, as produced by this ADC.

(b) Three hundred seventy-three steps were required to complete the conversion. Thus, 373 clock pulses occurred at the rate of one per microsecond. This gives a total conversion time of 373 μs.

(c) The resolution of this converter is equal to the step size of the DAC, which is 10 mV. In percent it is $1/1023 \times 100\% \approx 0.1\%$.

EXAMPLE 10-13B

For the same ADC of Example 10-13A determine the approximate range of analog input voltages that will produce the same digital result of $0101110101_2 = 373_{10}$.

Solution

TABLE 10-4

Step	V_{AX} (V)
371	3.71
372	3.72
373	3.73
374	3.74
375	3.75

Table 10-4 shows the ideal DAC output voltage, V_{AX}, for several of the steps on and around the 373rd. If V_A is slightly smaller than 3.72 V (by an amount $<V_T$), then $\overline{EOC}$ won't go LOW when V_{AX} reaches the 3.72-V step, but it will go LOW on the 3.73-V step. If V_A is slightly smaller than 3.73 V (by an amount $<V_T$), then $\overline{EOC}$ won't go LOW until V_{AX} reaches the 3.74-V step. Thus, as long as V_A is between approximately 3.72 and 3.73 V, $\overline{EOC}$ will go LOW when V_{AX} reaches the 3.73-V step. The exact range of V_A values is

$$3.72 \text{ V} - V_T \quad \text{to} \quad 3.73 \text{ V} - V_T$$

but since V_T is so small, we can simply say that the range is approximately 3.72 to 3.73 V—a range equal to 10 mV, the DAC's resolution. This is illustrated in Figure 10-14.

FIGURE 10-14   Example 10-13B.

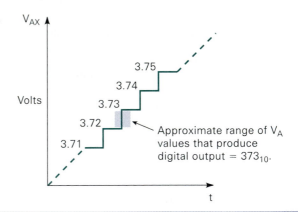

A/D Resolution and Accuracy

It is very important to understand the errors associated with making any kind of measurements. An unavoidable source of error in the digital-ramp method is that the step size or resolution of the internal DAC is the smallest unit of measure. Imagine trying to measure basketball players' heights by standing them next to a staircase with 12-inch steps and assigning them the height of the first step higher than their head. Anyone over 6 feet would be measured as 7 feet tall! Likewise, the output voltage V_{AX} is a staircase waveform that goes up in discrete steps until it exceeds the input voltage, V_A. By making the step size smaller, we can reduce the potential error, but there will always be a difference between the actual (analog) quantity and the digital value assigned to it. This is called **quantization error.** Thus, V_{AX} is an approximation to the value of V_A, and the best we can expect is that V_{AX} is within 10 mV of V_A if the resolution (step size) is 10 mV. This quantization error, which can be reduced by increasing the number of bits in the counter and the DAC, is sometimes specified as an error of $+1$ LSB, indicating that the result could be off by as much as the weight of the LSB. In Problem 10-28 we will see how this quantization error can be modified so that it is $\pm\frac{1}{2}$ LSB, which is a more common situation.

Looking at it from a different aspect, the input V_A can take on an *infinite* number of values from 0 V to F.S. The approximation V_{AX}, however, can take on only a finite number of discrete values. This means that a small range of V_A values will have the same digital representation. In Example 10-13B we saw that values of V_A from ≈ 3.72 V to ≈ 3.73 V will require 373 steps, thereby resulting in the same digital representation. In other words, V_A must change by 10 mV (the resolution) to produce a change in digital output.

As in the DAC, *accuracy* is not related to the resolution but is dependent on the accuracy of the circuit components, such as the comparator, the DAC's precision resistors and current switches, the reference supplies, and so on. An error specification of 0.01% F.S. indicates that the ADC result may be off by 0.01% F.S., owing to nonideal components. This error is *in addition* to the quantization error due to the resolution. These two sources of error are usually of the same order of magnitude for a given ADC.

EXAMPLE 10-14	A certain eight-bit ADC has a full-scale input of 2.55 V (i.e., $V_A = 2.55$ V produces a digital output of 11111111). It has a specified error of 0.1% F.S. Determine the maximum amount by which the V_{AX} output can differ from the analog input.

Solution

The step size is 2.55 V/$(2^8 - 1)$, which is exactly 10 mV. This means that even if the DAC has no inaccuracies, the V_{AX} output could be off by as much as 10 mV because V_{AX} can change only in 10-mV steps; this is the quantization error. The specified error of 0.1% F.S. is 0.1% $\times$ 2.55 V = 2.55 mV. This means that the V_{AX} value can be off by as much as 2.55 mV because of component inaccuracies. Thus, the total possible error could be as much as 10 mV + 2.55 mV = 12.55 mV.

For example, suppose that the analog input was 1.268 V. If the DAC output were perfectly accurate, the staircase would stop at the 127th step (1.27 V). But let's say V_{AX} was off by -2 mV, so it was 1.268 V at the 127th step. This would not be large enough to stop the conversion; it would stop at the 128th step. Thus, the digital output would be $10000000_2 = 128_{10}$ for an analog input of 1.268 V, an error of 12 mV.

Conversion Time, t_C

The conversion time is shown in Figure 10-13(b) as the time interval between the end of the START pulse and the activation of the $\overline{EOC}$ output. The counter starts counting from 0 and counts up until V_{AX} exceeds V_A, at which point $\overline{EOC}$ goes LOW to end the conversion process. It should be clear that the value of conversion time, t_C, depends on V_A. A larger value will require more steps before the staircase voltage exceeds V_A.

The maximum conversion time will occur when V_A is just below full scale so that V_{AX} must go to the last step to activate $\overline{EOC}$. For an N-bit converter this will be

$$t_C(\text{max}) = (2^N - 1) \text{ clock cycles}$$

For example, the ADC in Example 10-13A would have a maximum conversion time of

$$t_C(\text{max}) = (2^{10} - 1) \times 1 \ \mu s = 1023 \ \mu s$$

Sometimes, average conversion time is specified; it is half of the maximum conversion time. For the digital-ramp converter, this would be

$$t_C(\text{avg}) = \frac{t_C(\text{max})}{2} \approx 2^{N-1} \text{ clock cycles}$$

The major disadvantage of the digital-ramp method is that conversion time essentially doubles for each bit that is added to the counter, so that resolution can be improved only at the cost of a longer t_C. This makes this type of ADC unsuitable for applications where repetitive A/D conversions of a fast-changing analog signal must be made. For low-speed applications, however, the relative simplicity of the digital-ramp converter is an advantage over the more complex, higher-speed ADCs.

EXAMPLE 10-15

What will happen to the operation of a digital-ramp ADC if the analog input V_A is greater than the full-scale value?

Solution

Referring to Figure 10-13, it should be clear that the comparator output will never go LOW since the staircase voltage can never exceed V_A. Thus, pulses will be continually applied to the counter, so that the counter will repetitively count up from 0 to maximum, recycle back to 0, count up, and so on. This will produce repetitive staircase waveforms at V_{AX} going from 0 to full scale, and this will continue until V_A is decreased below full scale.

---

1. Describe the basic operation of the digital-ramp ADC.
2. Explain *quantization error.*
3. Why does conversion time increase with the value of the analog input voltage?
4. *True or false:* Everything else being equal, a 10-bit digital-ramp ADC will have a better resolution, but a longer conversion time, than an 8-bit ADC.
5. Give one advantage and one disadvantage of a digital-ramp ADC.
6. For the converter of Example 10-13, determine the digital output for $V_A = 1.345$ V. Repeat for $V_A = 1.342$ V.

10-10   DATA ACQUISITION

There are many applications in which analog data must be *digitized* (converted to digital) and transferred into a computer's memory. The process by which the computer acquires these digitized analog data is referred to as *data acquisition.* The computer can do several different things with the data, depending on the application. In a storage application, such as digital audio recording, video recording, or a digital oscilloscope, the internal microcomputer will store the data and then transfer them to a DAC at a later time to reproduce the original analog signal. In a process control application, the computer can examine the data or perform computations on them to determine what control outputs to generate.

Figure 10-15(a) shows how a microcomputer is connected to a digital-ramp ADC for the purpose of data acquisition. The computer generates the START pulses that initiate each new A/D conversion. The $\overline{EOC}$ (end-of-conversion) signal from the ADC is fed to the computer. The computer monitors $\overline{EOC}$ to find out when the current A/D conversion is complete; then it transfers the digital data from the ADC output into its memory.

The waveforms in Figure 10-15(b) illustrate how the computer acquires a digital version of the analog signal, V_A. The V_{AX} staircase waveform that is generated internal to the ADC is shown superimposed on the V_A waveform for purposes of illustration. The process begins at t_0, when the computer generates a START pulse to start an A/D conversion cycle. The conversion is completed at t_1, when the staircase first exceeds V_A, and $\overline{EOC}$ goes LOW. This NGT at $\overline{EOC}$ signals the computer that the ADC has a digital output that now represents the value of V_A at point *a,* and the computer will load these data into its memory.

The computer generates a new START pulse shortly after t_1 to initiate a second conversion cycle. Note that this resets the staircase to 0 and $\overline{EOC}$ back HIGH because the START pulse resets the counter in the ADC. The second conversion ends at t_2 when the staircase again exceeds V_A. The computer then loads the digital data corresponding to point *b* into its memory. These steps are repeated at t_3, t_4, and so on.

The process whereby the computer generates a START pulse, monitors $\overline{EOC}$, and loads ADC data into memory is done under the control of a program that the computer is executing. This data acquisition program will determine how many data points from the analog signal will be stored in the computer memory.

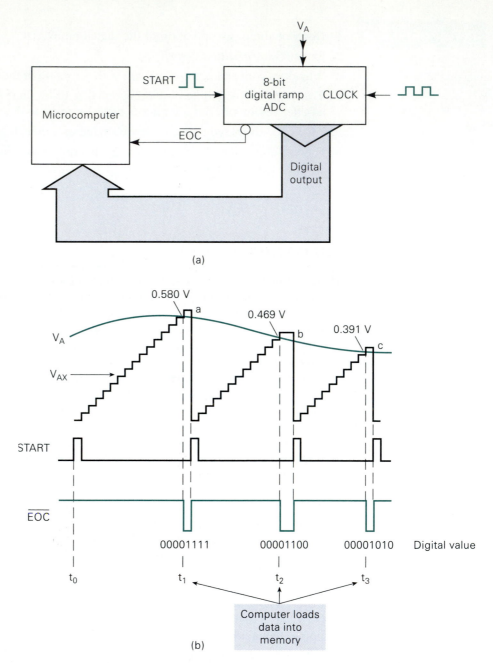

FIGURE 10-15 (a) Typical computer data acquisition system; (b) waveforms showing how the computer initiates each new conversion cycle and then loads the digital data into memory at end of conversion.

Reconstructing a Digitized Signal

In Figure 10-15(b) the ADC is operating at its maximum speed since a new START pulse is generated immediately after the computer acquires the ADC output data from the previous conversion. Note that the conversion times are not constant, because the analog input value is changing. The problem with this method of storing a waveform is that in order to reconstruct the waveform, we would need to know the point in time that each data value is to be plotted. Normally, when storing a digitized waveform the samples are taken at fixed intervals at a rate that is at least two times greater than the highest frequency in the analog signal. The digital system will store the waveform as a list of sample data values. Table 10-5 shows the list of data that would be stored if the signal in Figure 10-16(a) were digitized.

TABLE 10-5 Digitized data samples.

Point	Actual Voltage (V)	Digital Equivalent
a	1.22	01111010
b	1.47	10010011
c	1.74	10101110
d	1.70	10101010
e	1.35	10000111
f	1.12	01110000
g	0.91	01011011
h	0.82	01010010

FIGURE 10-16 (a) Digitizing an analog signal; (b) reconstructing the signal from the digital data.

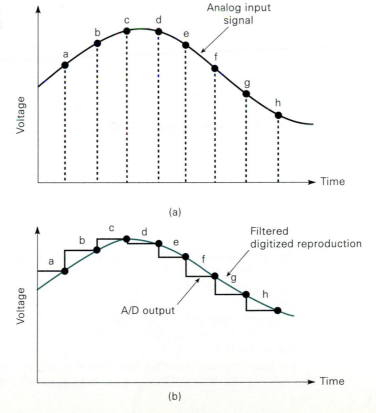

In Figure 10-16(a) we see how the ADC continually performs conversions to digitize the analog signal at points *a, b, c, d,* and so on. If these digital data are used to reconstruct the signal, the result will look like that in Figure 10-16(b). The black line represents the voltage waveform that would actually come out of the D/A converter. The green line would be the result of passing the signal through a simple low-pass RC filter. We can see that it is a fairly good reproduction of the original analog signal. This is because the analog signal does not make any rapid changes between digitized points. If the analog signal contained higher-frequency variations, the ADC would not be able to follow the variations, and the reproduced version would be much less accurate. For this reason it is important to keep the ADC conversion time short enough so that the analog signal does not change significantly between conversions. This emphasizes the need for ADCs with shorter conversion times than those of the simple digital-ramp converters. We will examine much faster ADC methods in the next sections.

Review Questions

1. What is *digitizing a signal?*
2. Describe the steps in a computer data acquisition process.

10-11   SUCCESSIVE-APPROXIMATION ADC

The **successive-approximation converter** is one of the most widely used types of ADC. It has more complex circuitry than the digital-ramp ADC but a much shorter conversion time. In addition, successive-approximation converters (SACs) have a fixed value of conversion time that is not dependent on the value of the analog input.

The basic arrangement, shown in Figure 10-17(a), is similar to that of the digital-ramp ADC. The SAC, however, does not use a counter to provide the input to the DAC block but uses a register instead. The control logic modifies the contents of the register bit by bit until the register data are the digital equivalent of the analog input V_A within the resolution of the converter. The basic sequence of operation is given by the flowchart in Figure 10-17(b). We will follow this flowchart as we go through the example illustrated in Figure 10-18.

For this example we have chosen a simple four-bit converter with a step size of 1 V. Even though most practical SACs would have more bits and smaller resolution than our example, the operation will be exactly the same. At this point you should be able to determine that the four register bits feeding the DAC have weights of 8, 4, 2, and 1 V, respectively.

Let's assume that the analog input is $V_A = 10.4$ V. The operation begins with the control logic clearing all of the register bits to 0 so that $Q_3 = Q_2 = Q_1 = Q_0 = 0$. We will express this as $[Q] = 0000$. This makes the DAC output $V_{AX} = 0$ V, as indicated at time t_0 on the timing diagram in Figure 10-18. With $V_{AX} < V_A$, the comparator output is HIGH.

At the next step (time t_1), the control logic sets the MSB of the register to 1 so that $[Q] = 1000$. This produces $V_{AX} = 8$ V. Since $V_{AX} < V_A$, the COMP output is still

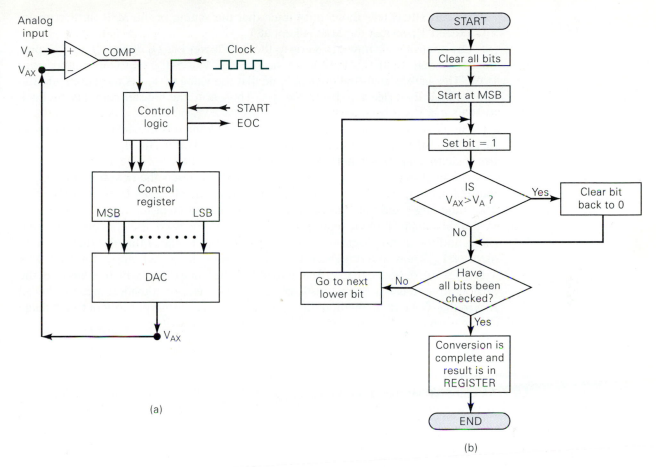

FIGURE 10-17 Successive-approximation ADC: (a) simplified block diagram; (b) flowchart of operation.

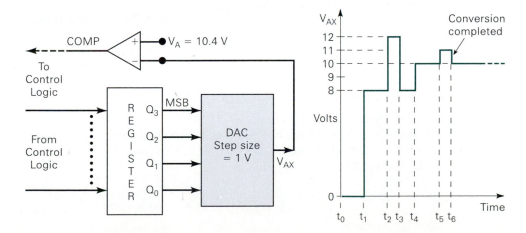

FIGURE 10-18 Illustration of four-bit SAC operation using DAC step size of 1 V and V_A = 10.4 V.

HIGH. This HIGH tells the control logic that the setting of the MSB did not make V_{AX} exceed V_A, so that the MSB is kept at 1.

The control logic now proceeds to the next lower bit, Q_2. It sets Q_2 to 1 to produce $[Q] = 1100$ and $V_{AX} = 12$ V at time t_2. Since $V_{AX} > V_A$, the COMP output goes LOW. This LOW signals the control logic that the value of V_{AX} is too large, and the control logic then clears Q_2 back to 0 at t_3. Thus, at t_3, the register contents are back to 1000 and V_{AX} is back to 8 V.

The next step occurs at t_4, where the control logic sets the next lower bit Q_1 so that $[Q] = 1010$ and $V_{AX} = 10$ V. With $V_{AX} < V_A$, COMP is HIGH and tells the control logic to keep Q_1 set at 1.

The final step occurs at t_5, where the control logic sets the next lower bit Q_0 so that $[Q] = 1011$ and $V_{AX} = 11$ V. Since $V_{AX} > V_A$, COMP goes LOW to signal that V_{AX} is too large, and the control logic clears Q_0 back to 0 at t_6.

At this point, all of the register bits have been processed, the conversion is complete, and the control logic activates its $\overline{EOC}$ output to signal that the digital equivalent of V_A is now in the register. For this example, the digital output for $V_A = 10.4$ V is $[Q] = 1010$. Notice that 1010 is actually equivalent to 10 V, which is *less than* the analog input; this is a characteristic of the successive-approximation method. Recall that in the digital-ramp method the digital output was always equivalent to a voltage that was on the step above V_A.

EXAMPLE 10-16	An eight-bit SAC has a resolution of 20 mV. What will its digital output be for an analog input of 2.17 V?

Solution

$$2.17 \text{ V}/20 \text{ mV} = 108.5$$

so that step 108 would produce $V_{AX} = 2.16$ V and step 109 would produce 2.18 V. The SAC always produces a final V_{AX} that is at the step *below* V_A. Therefore, for the case of $V_A = 2.17$ V, the digital result would be $108_{10} = 01101100_2$.

Conversion Time

In the operation just described, the control logic goes to each register bit, sets it to 1, decides whether or not to keep it at 1, and goes on to the next bit. The processing of each bit takes one clock cycle, so that the total conversion time for an N-bit SAC will be N clock cycles. That is,

$$t_C \text{ for SAC} = N \times 1 \text{ clock cycle}$$

This conversion time will be the same *regardless of the value of V_A*. This is because the control logic must process each bit to see whether or not a 1 is needed.

EXAMPLE
10-17
Compare the maximum conversion times of a 10-bit digital-ramp ADC and a 10-bit successive-approximation ADC if both utilize a 500-kHz clock frequency.

Solution

For the digital-ramp converter, the maximum conversion time is

$$(2^N - 1) \times (1 \text{ clock cycle}) = 1023 \times 2 \ \mu s = 2046 \ \mu s$$

For a 10-bit successive-approximation converter, the conversion time is always 10 clock periods or

$$10 \times 2 \ \mu s = 20 \ \mu s$$

Thus, it is about 100 times faster than the digital-ramp converter.

Since SACs have relatively fast conversion times, their use in data acquisition applications will permit more data values to be acquired in a given time interval. This can be very important when the analog data are changing at a relatively fast rate.

Because many SACs are available as ICs, it is rarely necessary to design the control logic circuitry, and so we will not cover it here. For those who are interested in the details of the control logic, many manufacturers' data books should provide sufficient detail.

An Actual IC: The ADC0804 Successive-Approximation ADC

ADCs are available from several IC manufacturers with a wide range of operating characteristics and features. We will take a look at one of the more popular devices to get an idea of what is actually used in system applications. Figure 10-19 is the pin layout for the ADC0804, which is a 20-pin CMOS IC that performs A/D conversion using the successive-approximation method. Some of its important characteristics are as follows:

- It has two analog inputs, $V_{IN}(+)$ and $V_{IN}(-)$, to allow **differential inputs.** In other words, the actual analog input, V_{IN}, is the difference in the voltages applied to these pins [analog $V_{IN} = V_{IN}(+) - V_{IN}(-)$]. In single-ended measurements, the analog input is applied to $V_{IN}(+)$, while $V_{IN}(-)$ is connected to analog ground. During normal operation, the converter uses $V_{CC} = +5$ V as its reference voltage, and the analog input can range from 0 to 5 V full scale.
- It converts the analog input voltage to an eight-bit digital output. The digital outputs are tristate buffered so that they can be easily connected in a data bus arrangement. With eight bits, the resolution is 5 V/255 = 19.6 mV.
- It has an internal clock generator circuit that produces a frequency of $f = 1/(1.1RC)$, where R and C are values of externally connected components. A typical clock frequency is 606 kHz using $R = 10 \ k\Omega$ and $C = 150$ pF. An external clock signal can be used, if desired, by connecting it to the CLK IN pin.

FIGURE 10-19 ADC0804 eight-bit successive-approximation ADC with tristate outputs. The numbers in parentheses are the IC's pin numbers.

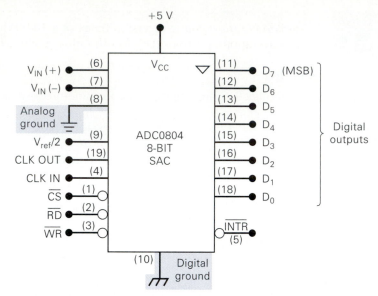

- Using a 606-kHz clock frequency, the conversion time is approximately 100 μs.

- It has separate ground connections for digital and analog voltages. Pin 8 is the analog ground that is connected to the common reference point of the analog circuit that is generating the analog voltage. Pin 10 is the digital ground that is the one used by all of the digital devices in the system. (Note the different symbols used for the different grounds.) The digital ground is inherently noisy because of the rapid current changes that occur as digital devices change states. Although it is not necessary to use a separate analog ground, doing so ensures that the noise from digital ground is prevented from causing premature switching of the analog comparator inside the ADC.

This IC is designed to be easily interfaced to a microprocessor data bus. For this reason, the names of some of the ADC0804 inputs and outputs are based on functions that are common to microprocessor-based systems. The functions of these inputs and outputs are defined as follows:

- $\overline{CS}$ **(Chip Select).** This input must be in its active-LOW state for $\overline{RD}$ or $\overline{WR}$ inputs to have any effect. With $\overline{CS}$ HIGH, the digital outputs are in the Hi-Z state, and no conversions can take place.

- $\overline{RD}$ **(READ).** This input is used to enable the digital output buffers. With $\overline{CS}$ = $\overline{RD}$ = LOW, the digital output pins will have logic levels representing the results of the *last* A/D conversion. The microcomputer can then *read* (fetch) this digital data value over the system data bus.

- $\overline{WR}$ **(WRITE).** A LOW pulse is applied to this input to signal the start of a new conversion. This is actually a start conversion input. It is called a **WRITE** input because in a typical application the microcomputer generates a WRITE pulse (similar to one used for writing to memory) that drives this input.

- $\overline{INTR}$ **(INTERRUPT).** This output signal will go HIGH at the start of a conversion and will return LOW to signal the end of conversion. This is actually an end-of-conversion output signal, but it is called INTERRUPT because in a typical situation it is sent to a microprocessor's interrupt input to get the microprocessor's attention and let it know that the ADC's data are ready to be read.

■ $V_{ref}/2$. This is an optional input that can be used to reduce the internal reference voltage and thereby change the analog input range that the converter can handle. When this input is unconnected, it sits at 2.5 V ($V_{CC}/2$), since V_{CC} is being used as the reference voltage. By connecting an external voltage to this pin, the internal reference is changed to twice that voltage, and the analog input range is changed accordingly. Table 10-6 shows this.

TABLE 10-6

$V_{ref}/2$	Analog Input Range (V)	Resolution (mV)
Open	0–5	19.6
2.25	0–4.5	17.6
2.0	0–4	15.7
1.5	0–3	11.8

■ **CLK OUT.** A resistor is connected to this pin to use the internal clock. The clock signal appears on this pin.

■ **CLK IN.** Used for external clock input, or for a capacitor connection when the internal clock is used.

Figure 10-20(a) shows a typical connection of the ADC0804 to a microcomputer in a data acquisition application. The microcomputer controls when a conversion is to take place by generating the and $\overline{WR}$ signals. It then acquires the ADC output data by generating the $\overline{CS}$ and $\overline{RD}$ signals after detecting an NGT at $\overline{INTR}$ indicating the end of conversion. The waveforms in Figure 10-20(b) show the signal activity during the data acquisition process. Note that $\overline{INTR}$ goes HIGH when $\overline{CS}$ and $\overline{WR}$ are LOW, but the conversion process does not begin until $\overline{WR}$ returns HIGH. Also note that the ADC output data lines are in their Hi-Z state until the microcomputer activates $\overline{CS}$ and $\overline{RD}$; at that point the ADC's data buffers are enabled so that the ADC data are sent to the microcomputer over the data bus. The data lines return to the Hi-Z state when either $\overline{CS}$ or $\overline{RD}$ is returned HIGH.

In this application of the ADC0804, the input signal is varying over a range of 0.5 to 3.5 V. In order to make full use of the eight-bit resolution, the A/D must be matched to the analog signal specifications. In this case the full-scale range is 3.0 V. However, it is offset from ground by 0.5 V. The offset of 0.5 V is applied to the negative input $V_{IN}(-)$, establishing this as the 0 value reference. The range of 3.0 V is set by applying 1.5 V to $V_{ref}/2$, which establishes V_{ref} as 3.0 V. An input of 0.5 V will produce a digital value of 00000000, and an input of 3.5 V will produce 11111111.

Another major concern when interfacing digital and analog signals is *noise*. Notice that the digital and analog ground paths are separated. The two grounds are tied together at a point that is very close to the A/D converter. A very low-resistance path ties this point directly to the negative terminal of the power supply. It is also wise to route the positive supply lines separately to digital and analog devices and

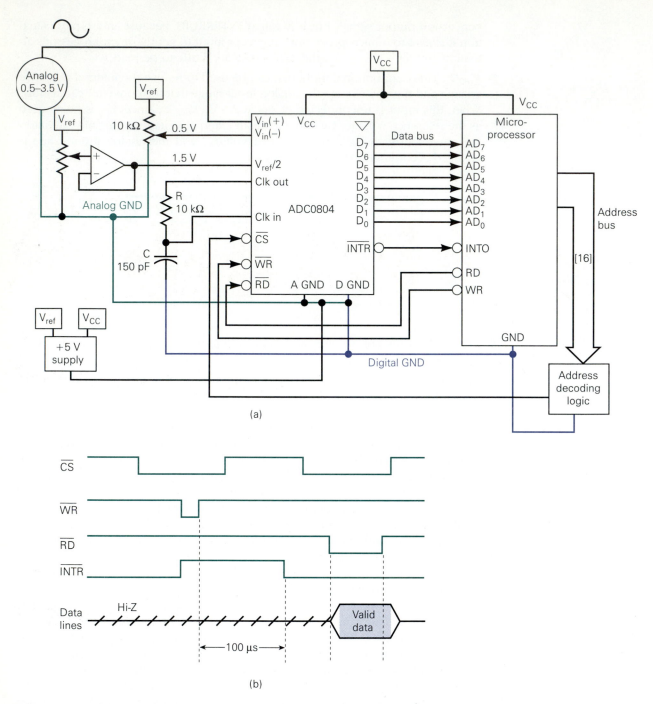

(a)

(b)

FIGURE 10-20   (a) An application of an ADC0804; (b) typical timing signals during data acquisition.

make extensive use of decoupling capacitors (0.01 μF) from very near each chip's supply connection to ground.

Review Questions

1. What is the main advantage of a SAC over a digital-ramp ADC?
2. What is its principal disadvantage compared with the digital-ramp converter?
3. *True or false:* The conversion time for a SAC increases as the analog voltage increases.
4. Answer the following concerning the ADC0804.
   (a) What is its resolution in bits?
   (b) What is the normal analog input voltage range?
   (c) Describe the functions of the $\overline{CS}$, $\overline{WR}$, and $\overline{RD}$ inputs.
   (d) What is the function of the $\overline{INTR}$ output?
   (e) Why does it have two separate grounds?
   (f) What is the purpose of $V_{IN}(-)$?

10-12 FLASH ADCs

The **flash converter** is the highest-speed ADC available, but it requires much more circuitry than the other types. For example, a six-bit flash ADC requires 63 analog comparators, while an eight-bit unit requires 255 comparators, and a ten-bit converter requires 1023 comparators. The large number of comparators has limited the size of flash converters. IC flash converters are commonly available in two- to eight-bit units, and most manufacturers offer nine- and ten-bit units as well.

The principle of operation will be described for a three-bit flash converter in order to keep the circuitry at a workable level. Once the three-bit converter is understood, it should be easy to extend the basic idea to higher-bit flash converters.

The flash converter in Figure 10-21(a) has a three-bit resolution and a step size of 1 V. The voltage divider sets up reference levels for each comparator so that there are seven levels corresponding to 1 V (weight of LSB), 2V, 3V, . . ., and 7 V (full scale). The analog input, V_A, is connected to the other input of each comparator.

With $V_A < 1$ V, all of the comparator outputs C_1 through C_7 will be HIGH. With $V_A > 1$ V, one or more of the comparator outputs will be LOW. The comparator outputs are fed into an active-LOW priority encoder that generates a binary output corresponding to the highest-numbered comparator output that is LOW. For example, when V_A is between 3 and 4 V, outputs C_1, C_2, and C_3 will be LOW and all others will be HIGH. The priority encoder will respond only to the LOW at C_3 and will produce a binary output $CBA = 011$, which represents the digital equivalent of V_A, within the resolution of 1 V. When V_A is greater than 7 V, C_1 to C_7 will all be LOW, and the encoder will produce $CBA = 111$ as the digital equivalent of V_A. The table in Figure 10-21(b) shows the responses for all possible values of analog input.

The flash ADC of Figure 10-21 has a resolution of 1 V because the analog input must change by 1 V in order to bring the digital output to its next step. To achieve finer resolutions, we would have to increase the number of input voltage levels (i.e.,

FIGURE 10-21 (a) Three-bit flash ADC; (b) truth table.

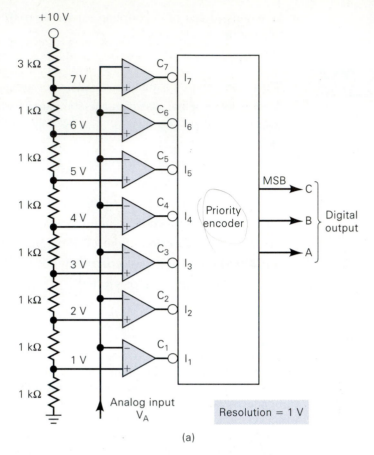

(a)

Analog in	Comparator outputs							Digital outputs		
V_A	C_1	C_2	C_3	C_4	C_5	C_6	C_7	C	B	A
0-1 V	1	1	1	1	1	1	1	0	0	0
1-2 V	0	1	1	1	1	1	1	0	0	1
2-3 V	0	0	1	1	1	1	1	0	1	0
3-4 V	0	0	0	1	1	1	1	0	1	1
4-5 V	0	0	0	0	1	1	1	1	0	0
5-6 V	0	0	0	0	0	1	1	1	0	1
6-7 V	0	0	0	0	0	0	1	1	1	0
> 7 V	0	0	0	0	0	0	0	1	1	1

(b)

use more voltage-divider resistors) and the number of comparators. For example, an eight-bit flash converter would require $2^8 = 256$ voltage levels, including 0 V. This would require 256 resistors and 255 comparators (there is no comparator for the 0-V level). The 255 comparator outputs would feed a priority encoder circuit that would produce an eight-bit code corresponding to the highest-order comparator output that is LOW. In general, an N-bit flash converter would require $2^N - 1$ comparators, 2^N resistors, and the necessary encoder logic.

Conversion Time

The flash converter uses no clock signal, because no timing or sequencing is required. The conversion takes place continuously. When the value of analog input changes, the comparator outputs will change, thereby causing the encoder outputs to change. The conversion time is the time it takes for a new digital output to appear in response to a change in V_A, and it depends only on the propagation delays of the comparators and encoder logic. For this reason, flash converters have extremely short conversion times. For example, the MC10319 from Motorola is an eight-bit ADC that uses high-speed ECL circuits internally but has TTL-compatible logic inputs and outputs. Its typical conversion time is less than 20 ns. The Analog Devices AD9010 is a 10-bit flash converter with a conversion time under 15 ns.

Review Questions

1. *True or false:* A flash ADC does not contain a DAC.
2. How many comparators would a 12-bit flash converter require? How many resistors?
3. State the major advantage and disadvantage of a flash converter.

10-13 OTHER A/D CONVERSION METHODS

Several other methods of A/D conversion have been in use for some time, each with its relative advantages and disadvantages. We will briefly describe some of them now.

Up/Down Digital-Ramp ADC (Tracking ADC)

As we have seen, the digital-ramp ADC is relatively slow because the counter is reset to 0 at the start of each new conversion. The staircase always begins at 0 V and steps its way up to the "switching point" where V_{AX} exceeds V_A and the comparator output switches LOW. The time it takes the staircase to reset to 0 and step back up to the new switching point is really wasted. The **up/down digital-ramp ADC** uses an up/down counter to reduce this wasted time.

The up/down counter replaces the up counter that feeds the DAC. It is designed to count up whenever the comparator output indicates that $V_{AX} < V_A$ and to count down whenever $V_{AX} > V_A$. Thus, the DAC output is always being stepped in the direction of the V_A value. Each time the comparator output switches states, it indicates that V_{AX} has "crossed" the V_A value, the digital equivalent of V_A is in the counter, and the conversion is complete.

When a new conversion is to begin, the counter is *not reset to 0* but begins counting either up or down from its last value, depending on the comparator output. It will count until the staircase crosses V_A again to end the conversion. The V_{AX} waveform, then, will contain both positive-going and negative-going staircase signals that "track" the V_A signal. For this reason, this ADC is often called a *tracking ADC*.

Clearly, the conversion times will generally be reduced because the counter does not start over from 0 each time but simply counts up or down from its previous value. Of course, the value of t_C will still depend on the value of V_A, and so it will not be constant.

Dual-Slope Integrating ADC

The **dual-slope converter** has one of the slowest conversion times (typically 10 to 100 ms) but has the advantage of relatively low cost because it does not require precision components such as a DAC or a VCO. The basic operation of this converter involves the *linear* charging and discharging of a capacitor using constant currents. First, the capacitor is charged up for a fixed time interval from a constant current derived from the analog input voltage, V_A. Thus, at the end of this fixed charging interval, the capacitor voltage will be proportional to V_A. At that point, the capacitor is linearly discharged from a constant current derived from a precise reference voltage, V_{ref}. When the capacitor voltage reaches 0, the linear discharging is terminated. During the discharge interval, a digital reference frequency is fed to a counter and counted. The duration of the discharge interval will be proportional to the initial capacitor voltage. Thus, at the end of the discharge interval, the counter will hold a count proportional to the initial capacitor voltage, which, as we said, is proportional to V_A.

In addition to its low cost, another advantage of the dual-slope ADC is its low sensitivity to noise and to variations in its component values caused by temperature changes. Because of its slow conversion times, the dual-slope ADC is not used in any data acquisition applications. The slow conversion times, however, are not a problem in applications such as digital voltmeters or multimeters, and this is where they find their major application.

Voltage-to-Frequency ADC

The **voltage-to-frequency ADC** is simpler than other ADCs because it does not use a DAC. Instead it uses a *linear voltage-controlled oscillator (VCO)* that produces an output frequency that is proportional to its input voltage. The analog voltage that is to be converted is applied to the VCO to generate an output frequency. This frequency is fed to a counter to be counted for a fixed time interval. The final count is proportional to the value of the analog voltage.

To illustrate, suppose that the VCO generates a frequency of 10 kHz for each volt of input (i.e., 1 V produces 10 kHz, 1.5 V produces 15 kHz, 2.73 V produces 27.3 kHz). If the analog input voltage is 4.54 V, then the VCO output will be a 45.4-kHz signal that clocks a counter for, say, 10 ms. After the 10-ms counting interval, the counter will hold the count of 454, which is the digital representation of 4.54 V.

Although this is a simple method of conversion, it is difficult to achieve a high degree of accuracy because of the difficulty in designing VCOs with accuracies of better than 0.1 percent.

One of the main applications of this type of converter is in noisy industrial environments where small analog signals must be transmitted from transducer circuits to a control computer. The small analog signals can be drastically affected by noise if they are directly transmitted to the control computer. A better approach is to feed the analog signal to a VCO, which generates a digital signal whose output frequency changes according to the analog input. This digital signal is transmitted to the computer and will be much less affected by noise. Circuitry in the control computer will count the digital pulses (i.e., perform a frequency-counting function) to produce a digital value equivalent to the original analog input.

Sigma/Delta Modulation

Another approach to representing analog information in digital form is called **sigma/delta modulation.** A sigma/delta A/D converter is an oversampling device, which means that it effectively samples the analog information more often than the minimum sample rate. The minimum sample rate is two times higher than the highest frequency in the analog wave coming in. Oversampling provides interpolated data points in between those that would be taken at the minimum sample rate. The sigma/delta approach, like voltage-to-frequency, does not produce a multibit number for each sample. Instead, it represents the analog voltage by varying the density of logic 1s in a single-bit stream of serial data. To represent the positive portions of a waveform, a stream of bits with a high density of 1s is generated by the ADC (e.g., 011111101111110111110111). To represent the negative portions, a lower density of 1s (i.e., a higher density of 0s) is generated (e.g., 000100010000100000010). Figure 10-22 shows the relationship between analog signals and their single-bit digital equivalent bit stream.

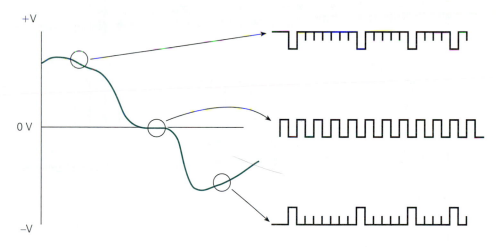

FIGURE 10-22 Sigma/delta modulation.

Review Questions

1. How does the up/down digital-ramp ADC improve on the digital-ramp ADC?
2. What is the main element of a voltage-to-frequency ADC?
3. Cite two advantages and one disadvantage of the dual-slope ADC.
4. Name three types of ADCs that do not use a DAC.
5. How many data bits does a sigma/delta modulator use?

10-14 DIGITAL VOLTMETER

A digital voltmeter (DVM) converts an analog voltage to its BCD-code representation, which is then decoded and displayed on some type of readout. Figure 10-23 shows a three-digit DVM circuit that uses a digital-ramp ADC (shown inside the dashed lines). Three cascaded BCD counters provide the inputs to a three-digit BCD-to-analog converter that has a step size of 10 mV and a full-scale output of 9.99 V. Each BCD counter stage also drives a four-bit register that feeds a decoder/driver and a display. The contents of the BCD counters are transferred to the registers at the end of each conversion cycle, so that the displays do not show the counters resetting and counting, but only the final count that represents the unknown voltage.

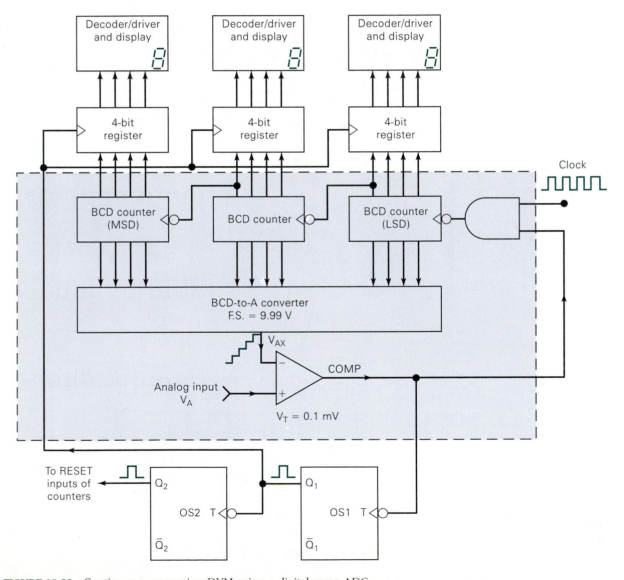

FIGURE 10-23 Continuous-conversion DVM using a digital-ramp ADC.

As long as $V_{AX} < V_A$, the COMP output stays HIGH, and clock pulses pass through the AND gate to the counter. As the counter increments, the V_{AX} signal increases at 10 mV per step until it exceeds V_A (see Figure 10-24). At that point COMP goes LOW to disable the AND gate and stop the counter, thereby ending the conversion. The NGT of COMP also triggers one-shot 1 (OS1) to produce a 1-μs pulse at Q_1. The PGT of Q_1 transfers the outputs of the BCD counter stages to their respective registers to be stored and displayed. The NGT of Q_1 triggers a second one-shot, OS2, to produce a pulse that resets all the counters to 0. This brings V_{AX} back to 0, and COMP returns HIGH, allowing pulses into the counter to begin a new conversion cycle.

FIGURE 10-24 Waveforms for a DVM.

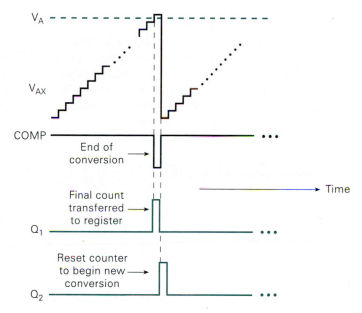

Thus, this DVM will perform one conversion right after another. Of course, the storage registers will keep the displays from showing the conversion process. The display readings will change only if V_A changes, so that different counter contents are transferred to the registers at the end of the conversion cycle.

A numerical example will help illustrate this circuit's operation. Assume that V_A is 6.372 V. In order for the COMP output to switch LOW, V_A must exceed 6.3721 V. Since the DAC output increases by 10 mV/step, this requires

$$\frac{6.3721 \text{ V}}{10 \text{ mV}} = 637.21 \rightarrow 638 \text{ steps}$$

Thus, the counters will count up to 638, which will be transferred to the registers and displayed. A small LED can be used to display a decimal point so that the operator sees 6.38 V.

EXAMPLE 10-18	What will happen if $V_A > 9.99$ V?

Solution

With $V_A > 9.99$ V, the comparator output will stay HIGH, allowing clock pulses into the counter continuously. The counter will repetitively count up to 999 and recycle to 000. One-shot Q_1 will *never* be triggered, and the register contents will not change from their previous value. A well-designed DVM would have some means of detecting this *over-range* condition and activating some type of over-range indicator. One possible method would simply add a thirteenth bit to the counter string. This bit would go HIGH only if the counter recycled from 999 to 000, and then it would indicate the over-range condition.

The DVM can be modified to read input voltages over several ranges by using a suitable amplifier or attenuator between V_A and the comparator. For example, if V_A were 63.72 V, it could be attenuated by a factor of 10, so that the comparator would receive 6.372 V at its + input and the counters would display 638 at the end of the conversion. The decimal-point indicator would be placed in front of the LSD, so that the display would read 63.8 V.

The DVM can be modified to operate as a DMM that can measure current and resistance as well as voltage. To measure current, the unknown current is made to flow through a fixed reference resistor to produce a voltage. To measure resistance, a fixed reference current is made to flow through the unknown resistance to develop a voltage. In each case, the resulting voltage is fed to a circuit like that of Figure 10-23 to be measured and displayed. The circuit may require an attenuation scaling factor so that the displayed value correctly represents the quantity (current or resistance) being measured.

AC voltages can be measured by this same DVM if they are first converted to a dc voltage. This can be done by using a circuit that converts the true rms value of a signal (pure ac or otherwise) to a dc value. The AD536A from Analog Devices is one such IC that performs this true rms-to-dc conversion.

Review Questions
1. What is the purpose of the registers in the DVM circuit?
2. What is the purpose of the two one-shots?
3. How would the performance of the DVM change if a SAC were used?

10-15 SAMPLE-AND-HOLD CIRCUITS

When an analog voltage is connected directly to the input of an ADC, the conversion process can be adversely affected if the analog voltage is changing during the conversion time. The stability of the conversion process can be improved by using a **sample-and-hold circuit** to hold the analog voltage constant while the A/D conversion is taking place. A simplified diagram of a sample-and-hold (S/H) circuit is shown in Figure 10-25.

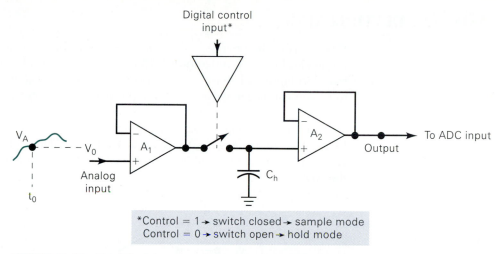

FIGURE 10-25   Simplified diagram of a sample-and-hold circuit.

The S/H circuit contains a unity-gain buffer amplifier A_1 that presents a high impedance to the analog signal and has a low output impedance that can rapidly charge the hold capacitor, C_h. The capacitor will be connected to the output of A_1 when the digitally controlled switch is closed. This is called the *sample* operation. The switch will be closed long enough for C_h to charge to the current value of the analog input. For example, if the switch is closed at time t_0, the A_1 output will quickly charge C_h up to a voltage V_0. When the switch opens, C_h will *hold* this voltage so that the output of A_2 will apply this voltage to the ADC. The unity-gain buffer amplifier A_2 presents a high input impedance that will not discharge the capacitor voltage appreciably during the conversion time of the ADC, and so the ADC will essentially receive a dc input voltage V_0.

In a computer-controlled data acquisition system such as the one discussed earlier, the sample-and-hold switch would be controlled by a digital signal from the computer. The computer signal would close the switch in order to charge C_h to a new sample of the analog voltage; the amount of time the switch would have to remain closed is called the **acquisition time,** and it depends on the value of C_h and the characteristics of the S/H circuit. The LF198 is an integrated S/H circuit that has a typical acquisition time of 4 μs for C_h = 1000 pF and 20 μs for C_h = 0.01 μF. The computer signal would then open the switch to allow C_h to hold its value and provide a relatively constant analog voltage at the A_2 output. For example, with the LF198, the capacitor voltage will typically discharge at the rate of only 30 mV per second for a 1000-pF capacitor.

Review Questions

1. Describe the function of a sample-and-hold circuit.

2. *True or false:* The amplifiers in an S/H circuit are used to provide voltage amplification.

10-16 MULTIPLEXING

When analog inputs from several sources are to be converted, a multiplexing technique can be used so that one ADC may be time-shared. The basic scheme is illustrated in Figure 10-26 for a four-channel acquisition system. Rotary switch S is used to switch each analog signal to the input of the ADC, one at a time in sequence. The control circuitry controls the switch position according to the *select address* bits, A_1, A_0, from the MOD-4 counter. For example, with $A_1A_0 = 00$, the switch connects V_{A0} to the ADC input; $A_1A_0 = 01$ connects V_{A1} to the ADC input; and so on. Each input channel has a specific address code which, when present, connects that channel to the ADC.

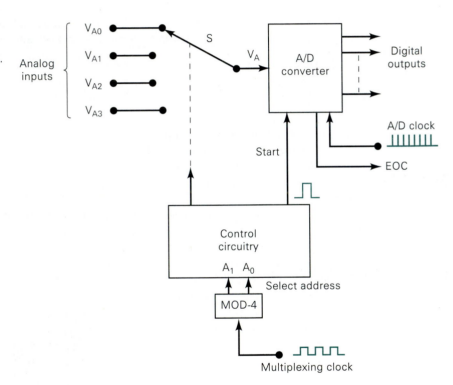

FIGURE 10-26 Conversion of four analog inputs by multiplexing through one ADC.

The operation proceeds as follows:

1. With select address = 00, V_{A0} is connected to the ADC input.
2. The control circuit generates a START pulse to initiate the conversion of V_{A0} to its digital equivalent.
3. When the conversion is complete, *EOC* signals that the ADC output data are ready. Typically, these data will be transferred to a computer over a data bus.
4. The multiplexing clock increments the select address to 01, which connects V_{A1} to the ADC.
5. Steps 2 and 3 are repeated with the digital equivalent of V_{A1} now present at the ADC outputs.

6. The multiplexing clock increments the select address to 10, and V_{A2} is connected to the ADC.

7. Steps 2 and 3 are repeated with the digital equivalent of V_{A2} now present at the ADC outputs.

8. The multiplexing clock increments the select address to 11, and V_{A3} is connected to the ADC.

9. Steps 2 and 3 are repeated with the digital equivalent of V_{A3} now present at the ADC outputs.

The multiplexing clock controls the rate at which the analog signals are sequentially switched into the ADC. The maximum rate is determined by the delay time of the switches and the conversion time of the ADC. The switch delay time can be minimized by using semiconductor switches such as the CMOS bilateral switch described in Chapter 8. It may be necessary to connect a sample-and-hold circuit at the input of the ADC if the analog inputs will change significantly during the ADC conversion time.

Many integrated ADCs contain the multiplexing circuitry on the same chip as the ADC. The ADC0808, for example, can multiplex eight different analog inputs into one ADC. It uses a three-bit select input code to determine which analog input is connected to the ADC.

Review Questions

1. What is the advantage of this multiplexing scheme?
2. How would the address counter be changed if there were eight analog inputs?

10-17 DIGITAL STORAGE OSCILLOSCOPE

As a final example of the application of D/A and A/D converters, we will take a brief look at the digital storage oscilloscope (DSO). The DSO uses both of these devices to digitize, store, and display analog waveforms. A DSO has many advantages over the conventional storage oscilloscope (CSO), which stores the waveform image as electrical charges on a mesh screen between the CRT's electron gun and the phosphor-coated screen. Here are some of them:

■ The DSO can store the waveforms for an indefinite time because the digital values are stored in digital memory (i.e., flip-flops). In a CSO, the image gradually fades as the charges on the mesh screen are slowly neutralized.

■ In many DSOs, the stored waveform can be positioned anywhere on the CRT screen, and its vertical and horizontal scales can be changed to suit the measurement situation. This is not possible with a CSO.

■ With a DSO, it is possible to store and display portions of the waveform that occur *before* the occurrence of the trigger point. Again, this cannot be done with a CSO.

■ Many DSOs can store several waveforms and print them out on a standard printer.

A block diagram of a DSO is shown in Figure 10-27. The overall operation is controlled and synchronized by the circuits in the CONTROL block, which usually contains a microprocessor executing a control program stored in ROM (read-only memory). The data acquisition portion of the system contains a sample-and-hold (S/H) and an ADC that repetitively samples and digitizes the input signal at a rate determined by the SAMPLE CLOCK and then sends the digitized data to memory for storage. The CONTROL block makes sure that successive data points are stored in successive memory locations by continually updating the memory's ADDRESS COUNTER.

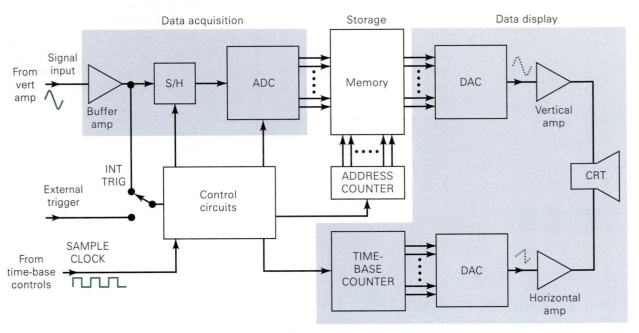

FIGURE 10-27   Block diagram of a digital storage oscilloscope.

When memory is full, the next data point from the ADC is stored in the first memory location, writing over the old data, and so on, for successive data points. This data acquisition and storage process continues until the CONTROL block receives a trigger signal from either the input waveform (INTERNAL trigger) or an EXTERNAL trigger source. When the trigger occurs, the system stops acquiring new data and enters the display mode of operation, in which all or part of the memory data is repetitively displayed on the CRT.

The display operation uses two DACs to provide the vertical and horizontal deflection voltages for the CRT. Data from memory produce the vertical deflection of the electron beam, while the TIME-BASE COUNTER provides the horizontal deflection in the form of a staircase sweep signal. The CONTROL block synchronizes the display operation by incrementing the memory ADDRESS COUNTER and the TIME-BASE COUNTER at the same time so that each horizontal step of the electron beam is accompanied by a new data value from memory to the vertical DAC. The counters are continuously recycled so that the stored data points are repetitively replotted on the CRT screen. The screen display consists of discrete dots representing the various data points, but the number of dots is usually so large (typically 1000 or more) that they tend to blend together and appear to be a smooth, continuous waveform. The display operation is terminated when the operator presses a front-panel button that commands the DSO to begin a new data acquisition cycle.

Related Applications

The same sequence of operations performed in a DSO—data acquisition/digitizing/storage/data outputting—is used in other applications of DACs and ADCs. For example, in digital audio recording, the analog audio signal produced by a microphone is digitized (using an ADC) and then stored on some medium such as magnetic tape, magnetic disk, or optical disk. Later the stored data are "played back" by sending them to a DAC to reconstruct the analog signal, which is fed to the amplifier and speaker system to produce the recorded sound.

Review Questions

1. What are some of the advantages of a DSO over a CSO?
2. Describe the functions of the ADC and DACs that are part of the DSO.

10-18 DIGITAL SIGNAL PROCESSING (DSP)

One of the most dynamic areas of digital systems today is in the field of **digital signal processing** or **DSP**. A DSP is a very specialized form of microprocessor that has been optimized to perform repetitive calculations on streams of digitized data. The digitized data are usually being fed to the DSP from an A/D converter. It is beyond the scope of this text to explain the mathematics that allow a DSP to process these data values, but suffice it to say that for each new data point that comes in, a calculation is performed (very quickly). This calculation involves the most recent data point as well as several of the preceding data samples. The result of the calculation produces a new output data point, which is usually sent to a D/A converter. A block diagram of such a system is shown in Figure 10-28(a).

A major application for DSP is in filtering and conditioning of analog signals. As a very simple example, a DSP can be programmed to take in an analog waveform, such as the output from an audio preamplifier, and pass to the output only those frequency components that are below a certain frequency. All higher frequencies are attenuated by the filter. Perhaps you recall from your study of analog circuits that the same thing can be accomplished by a simple low-pass filter made from a resistor and capacitor as shown in Figure 10-28(b). The advantage of DSP over resistors and capacitors is the flexibility of being able to change the critical frequency without switching any components. Instead, numbers are simply changed in the calculations to adapt the dynamic response of the filter. Have you ever been in an auditorium when the PA system started to squeal? This can be prevented if the degenerative feedback frequency can be filtered out. Unfortunately, the frequency that causes the squeal changes with the number of people in the room, the clothes they wear, and many other factors. With a DSP-based audio equalizer, the oscillation frequency can be detected and the filters dynamically adjusted to tune it out.

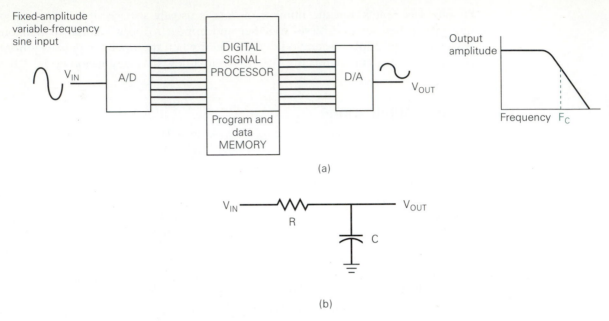

FIGURE 10-28   (a) A DSP performing low-pass filtering; (b) a simple RC low-pass filter.

DSP is being integrated into many common systems that you are familiar with. In CD players, for example, DSP is used to implement a digital noise-shaping filter. The data come off the CD in a serial data stream and are decoded into a standard inter-IC sound (I^2S) digital format. The I^2S data words are fed into a DSP circuit that performs oversampling interpolation filtering which translates the unwanted noise components to a higher frequency range that can be easily removed by analog filters. The output of the digital filter is sent to the D/A converter. The data may be either in parallel bytes for a current-steered D/A (Figure 10-9) or a sigma/delta-modulated digital waveform for a sigma/delta D/A converter. The D/A converter then translates this digital information into an analog waveform that goes through analog filtering to smooth out the rough edges, attenuate unwanted high frequencies, and produce an audio signal almost exactly like the original.

DSP applications are growing right now at the same rate that microprocessor applications grew in the early 1980s. They provide a digital solution to many traditionally analog problems. Some examples of applications include audio special effects, speech recognition, telecommunications data encryption, echo cancellation, Fast Fourier Transforms, image processing in digital television, beam forming in medical electronics, and noise cancellation in industrial controls. As this trend continues, you can expect to see nearly all electronic systems containing digital signal processing circuitry.

Review Questions

1. What is a major application of DSP?
2. What is the typical source of digital data for a DSP to process?
3. What advantage does a DSP filter have over an analog filter circuit?

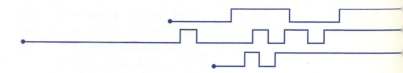

SUMMARY

1. Physical variables that we want to measure, such as temperature, pressure, humidity, distance velocity, and so on, are continuously variable quantities. A transducer can be used to translate these quantities into an electrical signal of voltage or current that fluctuates in proportion to the physical variable. These continuously variable voltage or current signals are called *analog* signals.

2. To measure a physical variable, a digital system must assign a binary number to the analog value that is present at that instant. This is accomplished by an A/D converter. To generate variable voltages or current values that can control physical processes, a digital system must translate binary numbers into a voltage or current magnitude. This is accomplished by a D/A converter.

3. A D/A converter with n bits divides a range of analog values (voltage or current) into $2^n - 1$ pieces. The size or magnitude of each piece is the analog equivalent weight of the least significant bit. This is called the *resolution* or *step size*.

4. Most D/A converters use resistor networks that can cause weighted amounts of current to flow when any of its binary inputs are activated. The amount of current that flows is proportional to the binary weight of each input bit. These weighted currents are summed to create the analog signal out.

5. An A/D converter must assign a binary number to an analog (continuously variable) quantity. The precision with which an A/D converter can perform this conversion is dependent on how many different numbers it can assign and how wide the analog range is. The smallest change in analog value that an A/D can measure is called its *resolution*, the weight of its least significant bit.

6. By repeatedly sampling the incoming analog signal, converting it to digital, and storing the digital values in a memory device, an analog waveform can be captured. To reconstruct the signal, the digital values are read from the memory device at the same rate at which they were stored, and then they are fed into a D/A converter. The output of the D/A is then filtered to smooth the stair steps and re-create the original waveform.

7. A digital-ramp A/D is the simplest to understand but not often used due to its variable conversion time. A successive-approximation converter has a constant conversion time and is probably the most common general-purpose converter.

8. Flash converters use analog comparators and a priority encoder to assign a digital value to the analog input. These are the fastest converters since the only delays involved are propagation delays.

9. Other popular methods of A/D include up/down tracking, integrating, voltage-to-frequency conversion, and sigma/delta conversion. Each type of converter has its own niche of applications.

10. Any D/A converter can be used with other circuitry such as analog multiplexers which select one of several analog signals to be converted, one at a time. Sample-and-hold circuits can be used to "freeze" a rapidly changing analog signal while the conversion is taking place.

11. Digital signal processing is an exciting new growth field in electronics. These devices allow calculations to be performed quickly in order to digitally emulate the operation of many analog filter circuits. DSP is responsible for many of the recent advances in high-fidelity audio, high-definition TV, and telecommunications by providing methods to eliminate random noise, crosstalk, and interference without adversely affecting the desired signal.

IMPORTANT TERMS

digital representation	linearity error	WRITE
analog representation	offset error	flash ADC
transducer	settling time	up/down digital-ramp ADC
analog-to-digital	monotonicity	dual-slope ADC
converter (ADC)	digitization	voltage-to-frequency ADC
digital-to-analog converter	digital-ramp ADC	sigma/delta modulation
(DAC)	quantization error	sample-and-hold circuit
full-scale output	successive-approximation	acquisition time
step size/resolution	ADC	digital signal processing
staircase	differential inputs	(DSP)
full-scale output		
full-scale error		

PROBLEMS

SECTIONS 10-1 AND 10-2

10-1. DRILL QUESTION
   (a) What is the expression relating the output and inputs of a DAC?
   (b) Define *step size* of a DAC.
   (c) Define *resolution* of a DAC.
   (d) Define *full scale*.
   (e) Define *percentage resolution*.
   (f) *True or false:* A 10-bit DAC will have a smaller resolution than a 12-bit DAC for the same full-scale output.
   (g) *True or false:* A 10-bit DAC with full-scale output of 10 V has a smaller percentage resolution than a 10-bit DAC with 12 V full scale.

10-2. An eight-bit DAC produces an output voltage of 2.0 V for an input code of 01100100. What will the value of V_{OUT} be for an input code of 10110011?

10-3. Determine the weight of each input bit for the DAC of Problem 10-2.

10-4. What is the resolution of the DAC of Problem 10-2? Express it in volts and in percent.

10-5. What is the resolution in volts of a 10-bit DAC whose F.S. output is 5 V?

10-6. How many bits are required for a DAC so that its F.S. output is 10 mA and its resolution is less than 40 μA?

10-7. What is the percentage resolution of the DAC of Figure 10-29? What is the step size if the top step is 2 V?

C   **10-8.** What is the cause of the negative-going spikes on the V_{OUT} waveform of Figure 10-29? (*Hint:* Note that the counter is a ripple counter and that the spikes occur on every other step.)

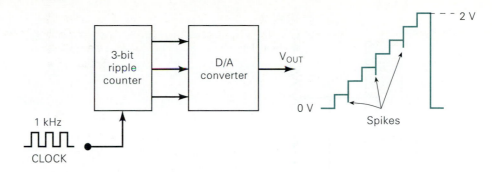

FIGURE 10-29   Problem 10-8.

10-9. Assuming a 12-bit DAC with perfect accuracy, how close to 250 rpm can the motor speed be adjusted in Figure 10-4?

10-10. A 12-bit (three-digit) DAC that uses the BCD input code has a full-scale output of 9.99 V. Determine the step size, the percentage resolution, and the value of V_{OUT} for an input code of 011010010101.

10-11. Compare the step size and the percentage resolution of a DAC with an eight-bit binary input with those of a DAC having an eight-bit BCD input. Assume 990 mV full scale for each DAC.

10-12. Determine the weight of each bit for the BCD DAC of Problem 10-10. What do you think the output would be if the input were 100000100011?

SECTION 10-3

D   10-13. The step size of the DAC of Figure 10-6 can be changed by changing the value of R_F. Determine the required value of R_F for a step size of 0.5 V. Will the new value of R_F change the percentage resolution?

D   10-14. Assume that the output of the DAC in Figure 10-8(a) is connected to the op amp of Figure 10-8(b).
(a) With $V_{REF} = 5$ V, $R = 20$ kΩ, and $R_F = 10$ kΩ, determine the step size and the full-scale voltage at V_{OUT}.
(b) Change the value of R_F so that the full-scale voltage at V_{OUT} is -2 V.
(c) Use this new value of R_F, and determine the proportionality factor, K, in the relationship $V_{OUT} = K(V_{REF} \times B)$.

10-15. What is the advantage of the DAC of Figure 10-9 over that of Figure 10-8, especially for a larger number of input bits?

SECTIONS 10-4 TO 10-6

10-16. An eight-bit DAC has a full-scale error of 0.2% F.S. If the DAC has a full-scale output of 10 mA, what is the most that it can be in error for any digital input? If the D/A output reads 50 μA for a digital input of 00000001, is this within the specified range of accuracy? (Assume no offset error.)

C, N   10-17. The control of a positioning device may be achieved using a *servomotor,* which is a motor designed to drive a mechanical device as long as an error signal exists. Figure 10-30 shows a simple servo-controlled system that is controlled by a digital input that could be coming directly from a computer or from an output medium such as magnetic tape. The lever arm is moved vertically by the servomotor. The motor rotates clockwise or counterclock-

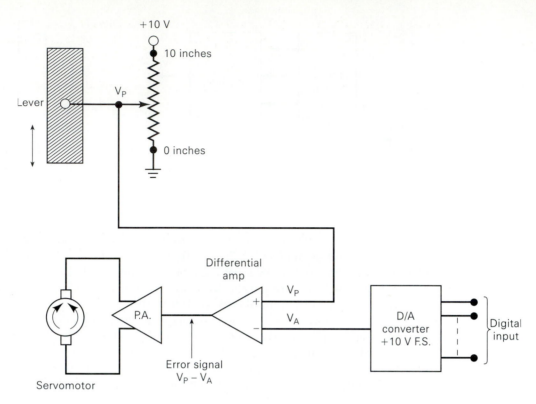

FIGURE 10-30   Problem 10-17.

wise, depending on whether the voltage from the power amplifier (P.A.) is positive or negative. The motor stops when the P.A. output is 0.

The mechanical position of the lever is converted to a dc voltage by the potentiometer arrangement shown. When the lever is at its 0 reference point, $V_P = 0$ V. The value of V_P increases at the rate of 1 V/inch until the lever is at its highest point (10 inches) and $V_P = 10$ V. The desired position of the lever is provided as a digital code from the computer and is then fed to a DAC, producing V_A. The *difference* between V_P and V_A (called *error*) is produced by the *differential* amplifier and is amplified by the P.A. to drive the motor in the direction that causes the error signal to decrease to 0—that is, moves the lever until $V_P = V_A$.

(a) If it is desired to position the lever within a resolution of 0.1 inch, what is the number of bits needed in the digital input code?

(b) In actual operation, the lever arm might oscillate slightly around the desired position, especially if a *wire-wound* potentiometer is used. Can you explain why?

10-18. DRILL QUESTION

(a) Define *binary-weighted resistor network*.

(b) Define *R/2R ladder network*.

(c) Define *DAC settling time*.

(d) Define *full-scale error*.

(e) Define *offset error*.

10-19. A particular six-bit DAC has a full-scale output rated at 1.260 V. Its accuracy is specified as ±0.1% F.S., and it has an offset error of ±1 mV. Assume that the offset error has not been zeroed out. Consider the measurements made on this DAC (Table 10-7), and determine which of them are not within the device's specifications. (*Hint:* The offset error is added to the error caused by component inaccuracies.)

SECTION 10-7

T   **10-20.** A certain DAC has the following specifications: eight-bit resolution, full scale = 2.55 V, offset ≤ 2 mV; accuracy = ±0.1% F.S. A static test on this DAC produces the results shown in Table 10-8. What is the probable cause of the malfunction?

TABLE 10-7

Input Code	Output
000010	41.5 mV
000111	140.2 mV
001100	242.5 mV
111111	1.258 V

TABLE 10-8

Input Code	Output
00000000	8 mV
00000001	18.2 mV
00000010	28.5 mV
00000100	48.3 mV
00001111	158.3 mV
10000000	1.289 V

T   **10-21.** Repeat Problem 10-20 using the measured data given in Table 10-9.

TABLE 10-9

Input Code	Output
00000000	20.5 mV
00000001	30.5 mV
00000010	20.5 mV
00000100	60.6 mV
00001111	150.6 mV
10000000	1.300 V

T   **10-22.** A technician connects a counter to the DAC of Figure 10-3 to perform a staircase test using a 1-kHz clock. The result is shown in Figure 10-31. What is the probable cause of the incorrect staircase signal?

SECTIONS 10-8 AND 10-9

10-23. DRILL QUESTION

Fill in the blanks in the following description of the ADC of Figure 10-13. Each blank may be one or more words.

A START pulse is applied to _____ the counter and to keep _____ from passing through the AND gate into the _____. At this point, the DAC output, V_{AX}, is _____ and $\overline{EOC}$ is _____ .

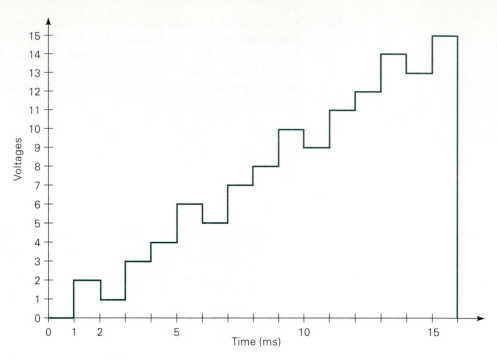

FIGURE 10-31 Problem 10-22.

When START returns _____, the AND gate is _____, and the counter is allowed to _____. The V_{AX} signal is increased one _____ at a time until it _____ V_A. At that point, _____ goes LOW to _____ further pulses from _____. This signals the end of conversion, and the digital equivalent of V_A is present at the _____ .

10-24. An eight-bit digital-ramp ADC with a 40-mV resolution uses a clock frequency of 2.5 MHz and a comparator with $V_T = 1$ mV. Determine the following values.

    (a) The digital output for $V_A = 6.000$ V

    (b) The digital output for 6.035 V

    (c) The maximum and average conversion times for this ADC

10-25. Why were the digital outputs the same for parts (a) and (b) of Problem 10-24?

D   10-26. What would happen in the ADC of Problem 10-24 if an analog voltage of $V_A = 10.853$ V were applied to the input? What waveform would appear at the D/A output? Incorporate the necessary logic in this ADC so that an "over-scale" indication will be generated whenever V_A is too large.

10-27. An ADC has the following characteristics: resolution, 12 bits; full-scale error, 0.03% F.S.; full scale output, +5 V.

    (a) What is the quantization error in volts?

    (b) What is the total possible error in volts?

C, N 10-28. The quantization error of an ADC such as the one in Figure 10-13 is always positive since the V_{AX} value must exceed V_A in order for the comparator output to switch states. This means that the value of V_{AX} could be as much as 1 LSB greater than V_A. This quantization error can be modified so that V_{AX} would be within $\pm\frac{1}{2}$ LSB of V_A. This can be done by adding a fixed voltage equal to $\frac{1}{2}$ LSB ($\frac{1}{2}$ step) to the value of V_A. Figure 10-32 shows this symbolically for a converter that has a resolution of 10 mV/step. A fixed voltage of +5 mV is added to the D/A output in the summing amplifier, and the result, V_{AY}, is fed to the comparator, which has $V_T = 1$ mV.

For this modified converter, determine the digital output for the following V_A values.

(a) $V_A = 5.022$ V

(b) $V_A = 50.28$ V

Determine the quantization error in each case by comparing V_{AX} and V_A. Note that the error is positive in one case and negative in the other.

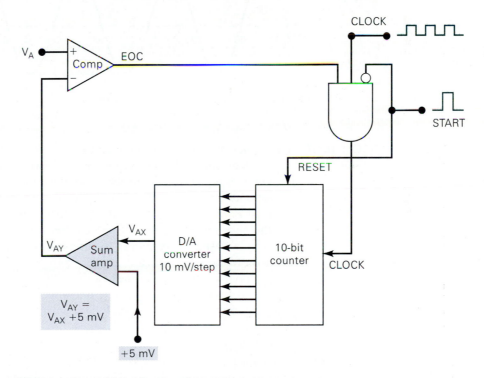

FIGURE 10-32 Problems 10-28 and 10-29.

C 10-29. For the ADC of Figure 10-32, determine the range of analog input values that will produce a digital output of 0100011100.

SECTION 10-10

N 10-30. Assume that the analog signal in Figure 10-33(a) is to be digitized by performing continuous A/D conversions using an eight-bit digital-ramp converter whose staircase rises at the rate of 1 V every 25 μs. Sketch the reconstructed signal using the data obtained during the digitizing process. Compare it with the original signal, and discuss what could be done to make it a more accurate representation.

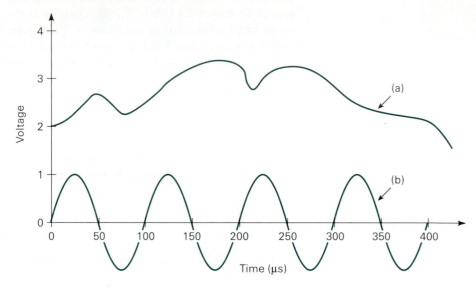

FIGURE 10-33 Problems 10-30, 10-31, and 10-40.

N, C 10-31. If a frequency higher than one-half the sample rate is applied to an A/D converter, an erroneous lower-frequency waveform will be reconstructed whose frequency is equal to the difference between the sample frequency (samples per second) and the input frequency (cycles per second). This phenomenon is called *aliasing* and is of great concern when sampling an analog signal. On the sine wave of Figure 10-33(b), mark the points where samples are taken by a flash A/D converter at intervals of 75 μs (starting at the origin). Then draw the reconstructed output from the D/A converter (connect the sample points with straight lines to show filtering). Calculate the sample frequency, the sine input frequency, and the difference between them. Then compare to the resulting reconstructed waveform frequency.

SECTION 10-11

10-32. DRILL QUESTION
Indicate whether each of the following statements refers to the digital-ramp ADC, the successive-approximation ADC, or both.
(a) Produces a staircase signal at its DAC output
(b) Has a constant conversion time independent of V_A
(c) Has a shorter average conversion time
(d) Uses an analog comparator
(e) Uses a DAC
(f) Uses a counter
(g) Has complex control logic
(h) Has an $\overline{EOC}$ output

10-33. Draw the waveform for V_{AX} as the SAC of Figure 10-18 converts $V_A = 6.7$ V.

10-34. Repeat Problem 10-33 for $V_A = 16$ V.

10-35. A certain eight-bit successive-approximation converter has 2.55 V full scale. The conversion time for $V_A = 1$ V is 80 μs. What will be the conversion time for $V_A = 1.5$ V?

10-36. Figure 10-34 shows the waveform at V_{AX} for a six-bit SAC with a step size of 40 mV during a complete conversion cycle. Examine this waveform and describe what is occurring at times t_0 to t_5. Then determine the resultant digital output.

FIGURE 10-34   Problem 10-36.

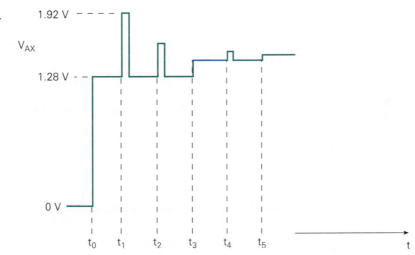

10-37. Refer to Figure 10-20. What is the approximate value of the analog input if the microcomputer's data bus is at 10010111 when $\overline{RD}$ is pulsed LOW?

D **10-38.** Connect a 2.0-V reference source to $V_{ref}/2$, and repeat Problem 10-37.

C, D **10-39.** Design the ADC interface to a digital thermostat using an LM34 temperature sensor and the ADC 0804. Your system must measure accurately ($\pm 0.2°$F) from 50 to 101°F. The LM34 puts out 0.01 V per degree F (0°F = 0 V).

(a) What should the digital value for 50°F be for the best resolution?

(b) What voltage must be applied to $V_{in}(-)$?

(c) What is the full-scale range of voltage that will come in?

(d) What voltage must be applied to $V_{ref}/2$?

(e) What binary value will represent 72°F?

(f) What is the resolution in °F? In volts?

SECTION 10-12

10-40. Discuss how a flash ADC with a conversion time of 1 μs would work for the situation of Problem 10-30.

D **10-41.** Draw the circuit diagram for a four-bit flash converter with BCD output and a resolution of 0.1 V. Assume that a +5 V precision supply voltage is available.

DRILL QUESTION

10-42. For each of the following statements, indicate which type of ADC is being described—digital-ramp, SAC, or flash.
(a) Fastest method of conversion
(b) Needs a START pulse
(c) Requires the most circuitry
(d) Does not use a DAC
(e) Generates a staircase signal
(f) Uses an analog comparator
(g) Has a relatively fixed conversion time independent of V_A

SECTION 10-13

10-43. DRILL QUESTION

For each statement indicate what type(s) of ADC is (are) being described.
(a) Uses a counter that is never reset to 0
(b) Uses a large number of comparators
(c) Uses a VCO
(d) Is used in noisy industrial environments
(e) Uses a capacitor
(f) Is relatively insensitive to temperature

SECTION 10-14

10-44. A voltage $V_A = 3.853$ V is applied to the DVM of Figure 10-23. Assume that the counters are initially reset to 0, and sketch the waveforms at V_{AX}, COMP, Q_1, Q_2, and the AND gate output for *two* complete cycles. Use a 100-kHz clock, and assume that both one-shots have $t_p = 1$ μs.

T 10-45. Refer to the DVM circuit in Figure 10-23. Assume that the circuit works correctly for V_A values up to about 7.99 V. However, when V_A is increased above 8 V, the displays do not change from their previous reading, the staircase waveform at V_{AX} steps up to only about 7.99 V before jumping back down to 0, and COMP remains HIGH. What are some possible causes for this malfunction?

D 10-46. Add the necessary logic to the DVM of Figure 10-23 to turn on an over-scale LED whenever the analog input voltage exceeds 9.99 V. The LED should be turned off at the start of each new conversion.

SECTIONS 10-15 AND 10-16

T 10-47. Refer to the sample-and-hold circuit of Figure 10-25. What circuit fault would result in V_{OUT} looking exactly like V_A? What fault would cause V_{OUT} to be stuck at 0?

C, D 10-48. Use the CMOS 4016 IC (Section 8-17) to implement the switching in Figure 10-26, and design the necessary control logic so that each analog input is converted to its digital equivalent in sequence. The ADC is a 10-bit, successive-approximation type using a 50-kHz clock signal, and it requires a 10-μs-duration start pulse to begin each conversion. The digital outputs are to remain stable for 100 μs after the conversion is complete before switching to the next analog input. Choose an appropriate multiplexing clock frequency.

MICROCOMPUTER APPLICATION

C, N, D   **10-49.** Figure 10-20 shows how the ADC 8004 is interfaced to a microcomputer. It shows three control signals, $\overline{CS}$, $\overline{RD}$, and $\overline{WR}$, that come from the microcomputer to the ADC. These signals are used to start each new A/D conversion and to read (transfer) the ADC data output into the microcomputer over the data bus.

Figure 10-35 shows one way the address decoding logic could be implemented. The $\overline{CS}$ signal that activates the ADC 0804 is developed from the eight high-order address lines of the MPU address bus. Whenever the MPU wants to communicate with the ADC 0804, it places the address of the ADC 0804 onto the address bus, and the decoding logic drives the $\overline{CS}$ signal LOW. Notice that in addition to the address lines, a timing and control signal (*ALE*) is connected to the $\overline{E_2}$ enable input. Whenever *ALE* is HIGH, it means that the address is potentially in transition so the decoder should be disabled until *ALE* goes LOW (at which time the address will be valid and stable). This serves a purpose for timing but has no effect on the address of the ADC.

(a) Determine the address of the ADC 0804.

(b) Modify the diagram of Figure 10-35 to place the ADC 0804 at address E8XX hex.

(c) Modify the diagram of Figure 10-35 to place the ADC 0804 at address FFXX hex

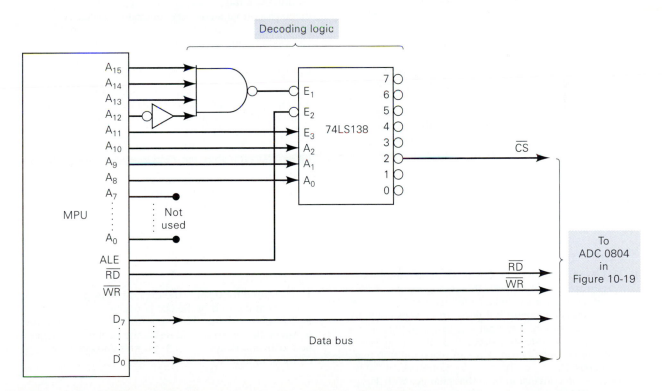

FIGURE 10-35   Problem 10-49: MPU interfaced to the ADC0804 of Figure 10-19.

D **10-50.** You have available a 10-bit SAC A/D converter (AD 573), but your system requires only eight bits of resolution and you only have eight port bits available on your microprocessor. Can you use this A/D converter, and, if so, which of the 10 data lines will you attach to the port?

ANSWERS TO SECTION REVIEW QUESTIONS

SECTION 10-1

1. Converts a nonelectrical physical quantity to an electrical quantity   2. Converts an analog voltage or current to a digital representation   3. Stores it; performs calculation or some other operation on it   4. Converts digital data to their analog representation   5. Controls a physical variable according to an electrical input signal

SECTION 10-2

1. 40 μA; 10.2 mA   2. 5.12 mA   3. 0.39 percent   4. 4096   5. 12   6. 8.73 V   7. True   8. It produces a greater number of possible analog outputs between 0 and full scale.

SECTION 10-3

1. It only uses two different sizes of resistors.   2. 640 kΩ 3. 0.5 V   4. Increases by 20 percent

SECTION 10-4

1. Maximum deviation of DAC output from its ideal value, expressed as percentage of full scale   2. Time it takes DAC output to settle to within $\frac{1}{2}$ step size of its full-scale value when the digital input changes from 0 to full scale   3. Offset error adds a small constant positive or negative value to the expected analog output for any digital input.   4. Because of the response time of the op-amp current-to-voltage converter

SECTION 10-8

1. Tells control logic when the DAC output exceeds the analog input   2. At outputs of register   3. Tells us when conversion is complete and digital equivalent of V_A is at register outputs

SECTION 10-9

1. The digital input to a DAC is incremented until the DAC staircase output exceeds the analog input.
2. The built-in error caused by the fact that V_{AX} does not continuously increase but goes up in steps equal to the DAC's resolution. The final V_{AX} can be different from V_A by as much as one step size.   3. If V_A increases, it will take more steps before V_{AX} can reach the step that first exceeds V_A.   4. True   5. Simple circuit; relatively long conversion time that changes with V_A
6. $0010000111_2 = 135_{10}$ for both cases

SECTION 10-10

1. Process of converting different points on an analog signal to digital and storing the digital data for later use   2. Computer generates START signal to begin an A/D conversion of the analog signal. When *EOC* goes LOW, it signals the computer that the conversion is complete. The computer then loads the ADC output into memory. The process is repeated for the next point on the analog signal.

SECTION 10-11

1. The SAC has a shorter conversion time which doesn't change with V_A.   2. It has more complex control logic.   3. False   4. **(a)** 8 **(b)** 0–5 V **(c)** $\overline{CS}$ controls the effect of the $\overline{RD}$ and $\overline{WR}$ signals; $\overline{WR}$ is used to start a new conversion; $\overline{RD}$ enables the output buffers. **(d)** When LOW, it signals the end of a conversion. **(e)** It separates the usually noisy digital ground from the analog ground so as not to contaminate the analog input signal. **(f)** All analog voltages on $V_{in}(+)$ are measured with reference to this pin. This allows the input range to be offset from ground.

SECTION 10-12

1. True   2. 4095 comparators and 4096 resistors
3. Major advantage is its conversion speed; disadvantage is the number of required circuit components for a practical resolution.

SECTION 10-13

1. It reduces conversion time by using an up/down counter that allows V_{AX} to track V_A without starting from 0 for each conversion.   2. A VCO   3. Advantages: low cost, temperature immunity. Disadvantage: slow conversion time   4. Flash ADC, voltage-to-frequency ADC, and dual-slope ADC   5. One

SECTION 10-14

1. They hold for display the digital values present in the counters at the end of the last conversion.   2. The PGT of OS1 transfers the result of the conversion to the registers; the pulse at OS2 resets the counters to begin a new conversion cycle.   3. Shorter and constant conversion time

SECTION 10-15

1. It takes a sample of an analog voltage signal and stores it on a capacitor.   2. False; they are unity-gain buffers with high input impedance and low output impedance.

SECTION 10-16

1. Uses a single ADC   2. It would become a MOD-8 counter.

SECTION 10-17

1. Displayed waveform can be moved and manipulated; can display portions of the waveform occurring prior to the trigger; indefinite storage time   2. The ADC digitizes the points on the input waveform for storage in memory; the vertical DAC converts the stored data points back to analog voltages to produce the vertical deflection of the electron beam; the horizontal DAC produces a staircase sweep voltage that provides the horizontal deflection of the electron beam.

SECTION 10-18

1. Filtering analog signals   2. An A/D converter
3. To change their dynamic response, you simply change the numbers in the software program, not the hardware components.

CHAPTER 11

Memory Devices

■ OUTLINE

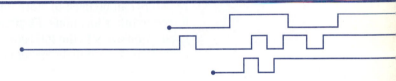

■ OBJECTIVES

Upon completion of this chapter, you will be able to:

- Understand and correctly use the terminology associated with memory systems.
- Describe the difference between read/write memory and read-only memory.
- Discuss the difference between volatile and nonvolatile memory.
- Determine the capacity of a memory device from its inputs and outputs.
- Outline the steps that occur when the CPU reads from or writes to memory.
- Distinguish among the various types of ROMs and cite some common applications.
- Understand and describe the organization and operation of static and dynamic RAMs.
- Describe the architecture of the basic types of programmable logic devices and determine the fuse pattern for a given set of logic functions.
- Compare the relative advantages and disadvantages of EPROM, EEPROM, and flash memory.
- Combine memory ICs to form memory modules with larger word size and/or capacity.
- Use the test results on a RAM or ROM system to determine possible faults in the memory system.

■ INTRODUCTION

A major advantage of digital over analog systems is the ability to easily store large quantities of digital information and data for short or long periods. This memory capability is what makes digital systems so versatile and adaptable to many situations. For example, in a digital computer the internal main memory stores instructions that tell the computer what to do under *all* possible circumstances so that the computer will do its job with a minimum amount of human intervention.

This chapter is devoted to a study of the most commonly used types of memory devices and systems. We have already become very familiar with the flip-flop, which is an electronic memory device. We have also seen how groups of FFs called *registers* can be used to store information and how this information can be transferred to other locations. FF registers are high-speed memory elements that are used extensively in the internal operations of a digital computer, where digital information is continually being moved from one location to another. Advances in LSI and VLSI technology have made it possible to obtain large numbers of FFs on a single chip arranged in various memory-array formats. These bipolar and MOS semiconductor memories are the fastest memory devices available, and their cost has been continuously decreasing as LSI technology improves.

Digital data can also be stored as charges on capacitors, and a very important type of semiconductor memory uses this principle to obtain high-density storage at low power-requirement levels.

Semiconductor memories are used as the **main memory** of a computer (Figure 11-1), where fast operation is important. A computer's main memory—also called its *working memory*—is in constant communication with the central processing unit (CPU) as a program of instructions is being executed. A program and any data used by the program reside in the main memory while the computer is working on that program. RAM and ROM (to be defined shortly) make up main memory.

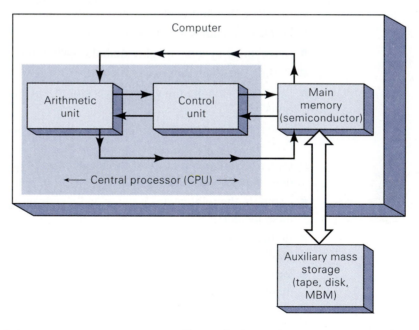

FIGURE 11-1   A computer system normally uses high-speed main memory and slower external auxiliary memory.

Another form of storage in a computer is performed by **auxiliary memory** (Figure 11-1), which is separate from the main working memory. Auxiliary memory—also called *mass storage*—has the capacity to store massive amounts of data without the need for electrical power. Auxiliary memory operates at a much slower speed than main memory, and it stores programs and data that are not currently being used by the CPU. This information is transferred to the main memory when the computer needs it. Common auxiliary memory devices are magnetic disk, magnetic tape, and compact disk (CD). Semiconductor *flash memory*—with its higher speed, lower power requirements, smaller size, and nonmechanical operation—shows promise as a major competitor to disk memories.

We will take a detailed look at the characteristics of the most common memory devices used as the internal memory of a computer. First we define some of the common terms used in memory systems.

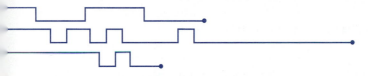

11-1 MEMORY TERMINOLOGY

The study of memory devices and systems is filled with terminology that can sometimes be overwhelming to a student. Before we get into any comprehensive discussion of memories, it would be helpful if you had the meaning of some of the more basic terms under your belt. Other new terms will be defined as they appear in the chapter.

- **Memory Cell.** A device or an electrical circuit used to store a single bit (0 or 1). Examples of memory cells include a flip-flop, a charged capacitor, and a single spot on magnetic tape or disk.

- **Memory Word.** A group of bits (cells) in a memory that represents instructions or data of some type. For example, a register consisting of eight FFs can be considered to be a memory that is storing an 8-bit word. Word sizes in modern computers typically range from 4 to 64 bits, depending on the size of the computer.

- **Byte.** A special term used for a group of 8 bits. A byte always consists of 8 bits. Word sizes can be expressed in bytes as well as in bits. For example, a word size of 8 bits is also a word size of one byte; a word size of 16 bits is two bytes, and so on.

- **Capacity.** A way of specifying how many bits can be stored in a particular memory device or complete memory system. To illustrate, suppose that we have a memory that can store 4096 20-bit words. This represents a total capacity of 81,920 bits. We could also express this memory's capacity as 4096×20. When expressed this way, the first number (4096) is the number of words, and the second number (20) is the number of bits per word (word size). The number of words in a memory is often a multiple of 1024. It is common to use the designation "1K" to represent $1024 = 2^{10}$ when referring to memory capacity. Thus, a memory that has a storage capacity of $4K \times 20$ is actually a 4096×20 memory. The development of larger memories has brought about the designation "1M" or "1 meg" to represent $2^{20} = 1,048,576$. Thus, a memory that has a capacity of $2M \times 8$ is actually one with a capacity of $2,097,152 \times 8$. The designation "giga" refers to $2^{30} = 1,073,741,824$.

EXAMPLE 11-1A

A certain semiconductor memory chip is specified as 2K × 8. How many words can be stored on this chip? What is the word size? How many total bits can this chip store?

Solution

$$2K = 2 \times 1024 = 2048 \text{ words}$$

Each word is 8 bits (one byte). The total number of bits is therefore

$$2048 \times 8 = 16{,}384 \text{ bits}$$

EXAMPLE 11-1B

Which memory stores the most bits: a 5M × 8 memory or a memory that stores 1M words at a word size of 16 bits?

Solution

$$5M \times 8 = 5 \times 1{,}048{,}576 \times 8 = 41{,}943{,}040 \text{ bits}$$
$$1M \times 16 = 1{,}048{,}576 \times 16 = 16{,}777{,}216 \text{ bits}$$

The 5M × 8 memory stores more bits.

■ **Density.** Another term for *capacity*. When we say that one memory device has a greater density than another, we mean that it can store more bits in the same amount of space. It is more dense.

■ **Address.** A number that identifies the location of a word in memory. Each word stored in a memory device or system has a unique address. Addresses always exist in a digital system as a binary number, although octal, hexadecimal, and decimal numbers are often used to represent the address for convenience. Figure 11-2 illustrates a small memory consisting of eight words. Each of these eight words has a specific address represented as a three-bit number ranging from 000 to 111. Whenever we refer to a specific word location in memory, we use its address code to identify it.

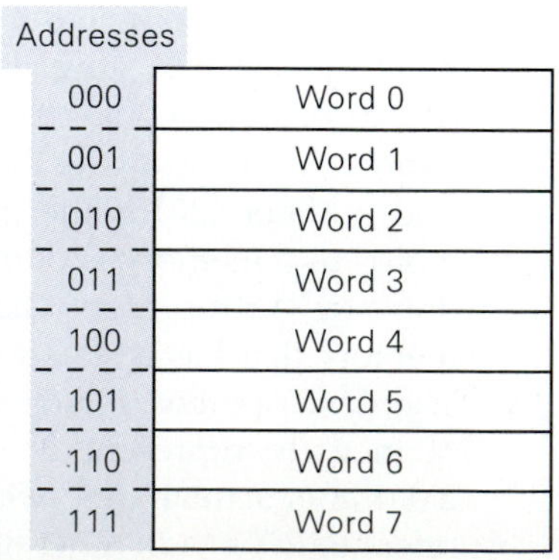

FIGURE 11-2   Each word location has a specific binary address.

Addresses	
000	Word 0
001	Word 1
010	Word 2
011	Word 3
100	Word 4
101	Word 5
110	Word 6
111	Word 7

- **Read Operation.** The operation whereby the binary word stored in a specific memory location (address) is sensed and then transferred to another device. For example, if we want to use word 4 of the memory of Figure 11-2 for some purpose, we must perform a read operation on address 100. The read operation is often called a *fetch* operation, since a word is being fetched from memory. We will use both terms interchangeably.

- **Write Operation.** The operation whereby a new word is placed into a particular memory location. It is also referred to as a *store* operation. Whenever a new word is written into a memory location, it replaces the word that was previously stored there.

- **Access Time.** A measure of a memory device's operating speed. It is the amount of time required to perform a read operation. More specifically, it is the time between the memory receiving a new address input and the data becoming available at the memory output. The symbol t_{ACC} is used for access time.

- **Volatile Memory.** Any type of memory that requires the application of electrical power in order to store information. If the electrical power is removed, all information stored in the memory will be lost. Many semiconductor memories are volatile, while all magnetic memories are *nonvolatile,* which means that they can store information without electrical power.

- **Random-Access Memory (RAM).** Memory in which the actual physical location of a memory word has no effect on how long it takes to read from or write into that location. In other words, the access time is the same for any address in memory. Most semiconductor memories are RAMs.

- **Sequential-Access Memory (SAM).** A type of memory in which the access time is not constant but varies depending on the address location. A particular stored word is found by sequencing through all address locations until the desired address is reached. This produces access times that are much longer than those of random-access memories. An example of a sequential-access memory device is a magnetic tape backup. To illustrate the difference between SAM and RAM, consider the situation where you have recorded 60 minutes of songs on an audio tape cassette. When you want to get to a particular song, you have to rewind or fast-forward the tape until you find it. The process is relatively slow, and the amount of time required depends on where on the tape the desired song is recorded. This is SAM, since you have to sequence through all intervening information until you find what you are looking for. The RAM counterpart to this would be an audio CD, where you can quickly select any song by punching in the appropriate code, and it takes approximately the same time no matter what song you select. Sequential-access memories are used where the data to be accessed will always come in a long sequence of successive words. Video memory, for example, must output its contents in the same order over and over again to keep the image refreshed on the CRT screen.

- **Read/Write Memory (RWM).** Any memory that can be read from or written into with equal ease.

- **Read-Only Memory (ROM).** A broad class of semiconductor memories designed for applications where the ratio of read operations to write operations is very high. Technically, a ROM can be written into (programmed) only once, and this operation is normally performed at the factory. Thereafter information can only be read from the memory. Other types of ROM are actually read-mostly memories (RMM), which can be written into more than once; but the write operation is more complicated than the read operation, and it is not performed very often. The various types of ROM will be discussed later. *All ROM is nonvolatile* and will store data when electrical power is removed.

■ **Static Memory Devices.** Semiconductor memory devices in which the stored data will remain permanently stored as long as power is applied, without the need for periodically rewriting the data into memory.

■ **Dynamic Memory Devices.** Semiconductor memory devices in which the stored data *will not* remain permanently stored, even with power applied, unless the data are periodically rewritten into memory. The latter operation is called a *refresh* operation.

■ **Main Memory.** Also referred to as the computer's *working memory*. It stores instructions and data the CPU is currently working on. It is the highest-speed memory in the computer and is always a semiconductor memory.

■ **Auxiliary Memory.** Also referred to as *mass storage* because it stores massive amounts of information external to the main memory. It is slower in speed than main memory and is always nonvolatile. Magnetic disks and CDs are common auxiliary memory devices.

Review Questions

1. Define the following terms.
   (a) *Memory cell*
   (b) *Memory word*
   (c) *Address*
   (d) *Byte*
   (e) *Access time*
2. A certain memory has a capacity of 8K × 16. How many bits are in each word? How many words are being stored? How many memory cells does this memory contain?
3. Explain the difference between the read (fetch) and write (store) operations.
4. *True or false:* A volatile memory will lose its stored data when electrical power is interrupted.
5. Explain the difference between SAM and RAM.
6. Explain the difference between RWM and ROM.
7. *True or false:* A dynamic memory will hold its data as long as electrical power is applied.

11-2 GENERAL MEMORY OPERATION

Although each type of memory is different in its internal operation, certain basic operating principles are the same for all memory systems. An understanding of these basic ideas will help in our study of individual memory devices.

Every memory system requires several different types of input and output lines to perform the following functions:

1. Select the address in memory that is being accessed for a read or write operation.
2. Select either a read or a write operation to be performed.
3. Supply the input data to be stored in memory during a write operation.
4. Hold the output data coming from memory during a read operation.
5. Enable (or disable) the memory so that it will (or will not) respond to the address inputs and read/write command.

Figure 11-3(a) illustrates these basic functions in a simplified diagram of a 32×4 memory that stores thirty-two four-bit words. Since the word size is four bits, there are four data input lines I_0 to I_3 and four data output lines O_0 to O_3. During a write operation the data to be stored into memory must be applied to the data input lines. During a read operation the word being read from memory appears at the data output lines.

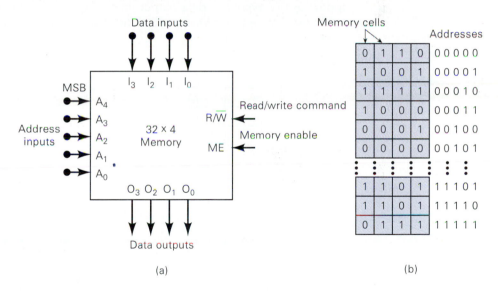

FIGURE 11-3   (a) Diagram of a 32×4 memory; (b) virtual arrangement of memory cells into 32 four-bit words.

Address Inputs

Since this memory stores 32 words, it has 32 different storage locations and there-fore 32 different binary addresses ranging from 00000 to 11111 (0 to 31 in decimal). Thus, there are five address inputs, A_0 to A_4. To access one of the memory locations for a read or a write operation, the five-bit address code for that particular location is applied to the address inputs. In general, N address inputs are required for a memory that has a capacity of 2^N words.

We can visualize the memory of Figure 11-3(a) as an arrangement of 32 regis-ters, with each register holding a four-bit word as illustrated in Figure 11-3(b). Each address location is shown containing four memory cells that hold 1s and 0s that make up the data word stored at that location. For example, the data word 0110 is stored at address 00000, the data word 1001 is stored at address 00001, and so on.

The $R/\overline{W}$ Input

This input controls which memory operation is to take place: read (R) or write (W). The input is labeled $R/\overline{W}$; since there is no bar over the R, this indicates that the read operation occurs when $R/\overline{W} = 1$. The bar over the W indicates that the write operation takes place when $R/\overline{W} = 0$. Other labels are often used for this input. Two of the more common ones are $\overline{W}$ (write) and $\overline{WE}$ (write enable). Again, the bar indicates that the write operation occurs when the input is LOW. It is understood that the read operation occurs for a HIGH.

A simplified illustration of the read and write operations is shown in Figure 11-4. Part (a) shows the data word 0100 being written into the memory register at address location 00011. This data word would have been applied to the memory's data input lines, and it replaces the data previously stored at address 00011. Part (b) shows the data word 1101 being read from address 11110. This data word would appear at the memory's data output lines. After the read operation, the data word 1101 is still stored in address 11110. In other words, the read operation does not change the stored data.

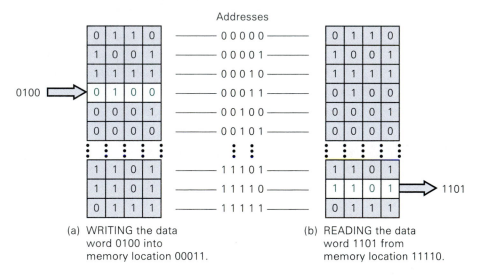

(a) WRITING the data word 0100 into memory location 00011.

(b) READING the data word 1101 from memory location 11110.

FIGURE 11-4   Simplified illustration of the read and write operations on the 32 × 4 memory: (a) writing the data word 0100 into memory location 00011; (b) reading the data word 1101 from memory location 11110.

Memory Enable

Many memory systems have some means for completely disabling all or part of the memory so that it will not respond to the other inputs. This is represented in Figure 11-3 as the MEMORY ENABLE input, although it can have different names in the various memory systems such as chip enable (*CE*) or chip select (*CS*). Here it is shown as an active-HIGH input that enables the memory to operate normally when it is kept HIGH. A LOW on this input disables the memory so that it will not respond to the address and $R/\overline{W}$ inputs. This type of input is useful when several memory modules are combined to form a larger memory. We will examine this idea later.

EXAMPLE 11-2

Describe the conditions at each input and output when the contents of address location 00100 are to be read.

Solution

Address inputs: 00100

Data inputs: xxxx (not used)

$R/\overline{W}$: HIGH

MEMORY ENABLE: HIGH

Data outputs: 0001

EXAMPLE 11-3

Describe the conditions at each input and output when the data word 1110 is to be written into address location 01101.

Solution

Address inputs: 01101

Data inputs: 1110

$R/\overline{W}$: LOW

MEMORY ENABLE: HIGH

Data outputs: xxxx (not used; usually Hi-Z)

EXAMPLE 11-4

A certain memory has a capacity of 4K × 8.

(a) How many data input and data output lines does it have?

(b) How many address lines does it have?

(c) What is its capacity in bytes?

Solution

(a) Eight of each, since the word size is eight.

(b) The memory stores 4K = 4 × 1024 = 4096 words. Thus, there are 4096 memory addresses. Since $4096 = 2^{12}$, it requires a 12-bit address code to specify one of 4096 addresses.

(c) A byte is 8 bits. This memory has a capacity of 4096 bytes.

The example memory in Figure 11-3 illustrates the important input and output functions common to most memory systems. Of course, each type of memory may have other input and output lines that are peculiar to that memory. These will be described as we discuss the individual memory types.

1. How many address inputs, data inputs, and data outputs are required for a 16K × 12 memory?
2. What is the function of the $R/\overline{W}$ input?
3. What is the function of the MEMORY ENABLE input?

11-3 CPU–MEMORY CONNECTIONS

A major part of this chapter is devoted to semiconductor memory, which, as pointed out earlier, makes up the main memory of most modern computers. Remember, this main memory is in constant communication with the CPU (central processing unit). It is not necessary to be familiar with the detailed operation of a CPU at this point, and so the following simplified treatment of the CPU–memory interface will provide the perspective needed to make our study of memory devices more meaningful.

A computer's main memory is made up of RAM and ROM ICs that are interfaced to the CPU over three groups of signal lines or buses. These are shown in Figure 11-5 as the address lines or address bus, the data lines or data bus, and the control lines or control bus. Each of these buses consists of several lines (note that they are represented by a single line with a slash), and the number of lines in each bus will vary from one computer to the next. The three buses play a necessary part in allowing the CPU to write data into memory and to read data from memory.

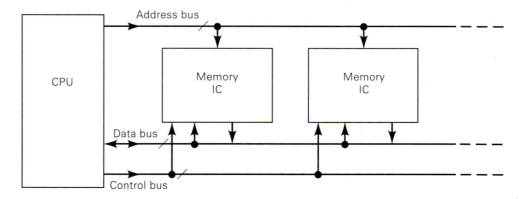

FIGURE 11-5 Three groups of lines (buses) connect the main memory ICs to the CPU.

When a computer is executing a program of instructions, the CPU continually fetches (reads) information from those locations in memory that contain (1) the program codes representing the operations to be performed and (2) the data to be operated upon. The CPU will also store (write) data into memory locations as dictated by the program instructions. Whenever the CPU wants to write data to a particular memory location, the following steps must occur:

Write Operation

1. The CPU supplies the binary address of the memory location where the data are to be stored. It places this address on the address bus lines.
2. The CPU places the data to be stored on the data bus lines.

3. The CPU activates the appropriate control signal lines for the memory write operation.

4. The memory ICs decode the binary address to determine which location is being selected for the store operation.

5. The data on the data bus are transferred to the selected memory location.

Whenever the CPU wants to read data from a specific memory location, the following steps must occur:

Read Operation

1. The CPU supplies the binary address of the memory location from which data are to be retrieved. It places this address on the address bus lines.

2. The CPU activates the appropriate control signal lines for the memory read operation.

3. The memory ICs decode the binary address to determine which location is being selected for the read operation.

4. The memory ICs place data from the selected memory location onto the data bus, from where they are transferred to the CPU.

The steps above should make clear the function of each of the system buses:

■ **Address Bus.** This is a *unidirectional* bus that carries the binary address outputs from the CPU to the memory ICs to select one memory location.

■ **Data Bus.** This is a *bidirectional* bus that carries data between the CPU and the memory ICs.

■ **Control Bus.** This bus carries control signals (such as the $R/\overline{W}$ signal) from the CPU to the memory ICs.

As we get into discussions of actual memory ICs, we will examine the signal activity that appears on these buses for the read and write operations.

Review Questions
1. Name the three groups of liens that connect the CPU and the internal memory.
2. Outline the steps that take place when the CPU reads from memory.
3. Outline the steps that occur when the CPU writes to memory.

11-4 READ-ONLY MEMORIES

The read-only memory is a type of semiconductor memory that is designed to hold data that either are permanent or will not change frequently. During normal operation, no new data can be written into a ROM, but data can be read from ROM. For some ROMs the data that are stored must be built-in during the manufacturing process; for other ROMs the data can be entered electrically. The process of entering data is called **programming** or *burning-in* the ROM. Some ROMs cannot have their data changed once they have been programmed; others can be *erased* and reprogrammed as often as desired. We will take a detailed look later at these various types of ROMs. For now, we will assume that the ROMs have been programmed and are holding data.

ROMs are used to store data and information that are not to change during the normal operation of a system. A major use for ROMs is in the storage of programs in microcomputers. Since all ROMs are *nonvolatile,* these programs are not lost when electrical power is turned off. When the microcomputer is turned on, it can immediately begin executing the program stored in ROM. ROMs are also used for program and data storage in microprocessor-controlled equipment such as electronic cash registers, appliances, and security systems.

ROM Block Diagram

A typical block diagram for a ROM is shown in Figure 11-6(a). It has three sets of signals: address inputs, control input(s), and data outputs. From our previous discussions we can determine that this ROM is storing 16 words, since it has $2^4 = 16$ possible addresses, and each word contains eight bits, since there are eight data outputs. Thus, this is a 16×8 ROM. Another way to describe this ROM's capacity is to say that it stores 16 bytes of data.

The data outputs of most ROM ICs are tristate outputs to permit the connection of many ROM chips to the same data bus for memory expansion. The most common numbers of data outputs for ROMs are 4, 8, and 16 bits, with 8-bit words being the most common.

The control input $\overline{CS}$ stands for **chip select.** This is essentially an enable input that enables or disables the ROM outputs. Some manufacturers use different labels for the control input, such as *CE* (chip enable) or *OE* (output enable). Many ROMs have two or more control inputs that must be active in order to enable the data outputs so that data can be read from the selected address. In some ROM ICs, one of the control inputs (usually the *CE*) is used to place the ROM in a low-power standby mode when it is not being used. This reduces the current drain from the system power supply.

The $\overline{CS}$ input shown in Figure 11-6(a) is active-LOW; therefore, it must be in the LOW state to enable the ROM data to appear at the data outputs. Notice that there is no $R/\overline{W}$ (read/write) input, because the ROM cannot be written into during normal operation.

The Read Operation

Let's assume that the ROM has been programmed with the data shown in the table of Figure 11-6(b). Sixteen different data words are stored at the 16 different address locations. For example, the data word stored at location 0011 is 10101111. Of course, the data are stored in binary inside the ROM, but very often we use hexadecimal notation to efficiently show the programmed data. This is done in Figure 11-6(c).

In order to read a data word from ROM, we need to do two things: (1) apply the appropriate address inputs and then (2) activate the control inputs. For example, if we want to read the data stored at location 0111 of the ROM in Figure 11-6, we must apply $A_3A_2A_1A_0 = 0111$ to the address inputs and then apply a LOW to $\overline{CS}$.

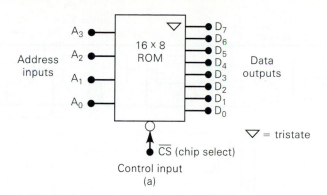

= tristate

Control input
(a)

	Address				Data							
Word	A_3	A_2	A_1	A_0	D_7	D_6	D_5	D_4	D_3	D_2	D_1	D_0
0	0	0	0	0	1	1	0	1	1	1	1	0
1	0	0	0	1	0	0	1	1	1	0	1	0
2	0	0	1	0	1	0	0	0	0	1	0	1
3	0	0	1	1	1	0	1	0	1	1	1	1
4	0	1	0	0	0	0	0	1	1	0	0	1
5	0	1	0	1	0	1	1	1	1	0	1	1
6	0	1	1	0	0	0	0	0	0	0	0	0
7	0	1	1	1	1	1	1	0	1	1	0	1
8	1	0	0	0	0	0	1	1	1	1	0	0
9	1	0	0	1	1	1	1	1	1	1	1	1
10	1	0	1	0	1	0	1	1	1	0	0	0
11	1	0	1	1	1	1	0	0	0	1	1	1
12	1	1	0	0	0	0	1	0	0	1	1	1
13	1	1	0	1	0	1	1	0	1	0	1	0
14	1	1	1	0	1	1	0	1	0	0	1	0
15	1	1	1	1	0	1	0	1	1	0	1	1

(b)

	Address	Data
Word	A_3 A_2 A_1 A_0	D_7–D_0
0	0	DE
1	1	3A
2	2	85
3	3	AF
4	4	19
5	5	7B
6	6	00
7	7	ED
8	8	3C
9	9	FF
10	A	B8
11	B	C7
12	C	27
13	D	6A
14	E	D2
15	F	5B

(c)

FIGURE 11-6 (a) Typical ROM block symbol; (b) table showing binary data at each address location; (c) the same table in hex.

The address inputs will be decoded inside the ROM to select the correct data word, 11101101, that will appear at outputs D_7 to D_0. If $\overline{CS}$ is kept HIGH, the ROM outputs will be disabled and will be in the Hi-Z state.

Review Questions

1. *True or false:* All ROMs are nonvolatile.
2. Describe the procedure for reading from ROM.
3. What is *programming* or *burning-in* a ROM?

11-5 ROM ARCHITECTURE

The internal architecture (structure) of a ROM IC is very complex, and we need not be familiar with all of its detail. It is instructive, however, to look at a simplified diagram of the internal architecture, such as that shown in Figure 11-7 for the 16 × 8

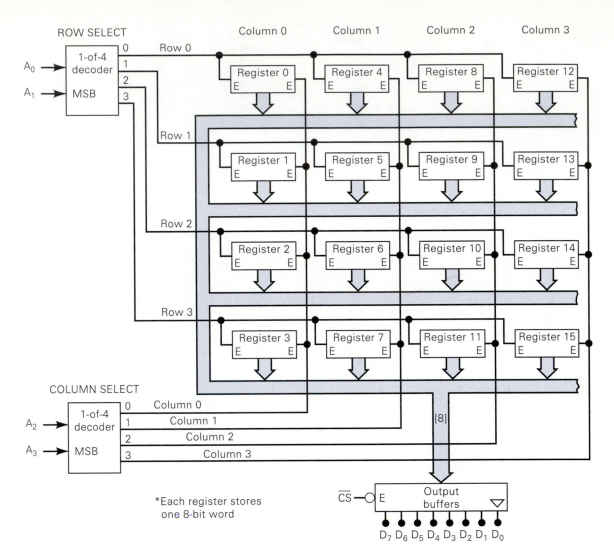

FIGURE 11-7 Architecture of a 16 × 8 ROM.

ROM. There are four basic parts: *register array, row decoder, column decoder, output buffers*.

Register Array

The register array stores the data that have been programmed into the ROM. Each register contains a number of memory cells equal to the word size. In this case, each register stores an eight-bit word. The registers are arranged in a square matrix array that is common to many semiconductor memory chips. We can specify the position of each register as being in a specific row and a specific column. For example, register 0 is in row 0, column 0, and register 9 is in row 1, column 2.

The eight data outputs of each register are connected to an internal data bus that runs through the entire circuit. Each register has two enable inputs (*E*); both must be HIGH in order for the register's data to be placed on the bus.

Address Decoders

The applied address code $A_3A_2A_1A_0$ determines which register in the array will be enabled to place its eight-bit data word onto the bus. Address bits A_1A_0 are fed to a 1-of-4 decoder which activates one row-select line, and address bits A_3A_2 are fed to a second 1-of-4 decoder which activates one column-select line. Only one register will be in both the row and the column selected by the address inputs, and this one will be enabled.

EXAMPLE 11-5

Which register will be enabled by input address 1101?

Solution

$A_3A_2 = 11$ will cause the column decoder to activate the column 3 select line, and $A_1A_0 = 01$ will cause the row decoder to activate the row 1 select line. This will place HIGHs at both enable inputs of register 13, thereby causing its data outputs to be placed on the bus. Note that the other registers in column 3 will have only one enable input activated; the same is true for the other row 1 registers.

EXAMPLE 11-6

What input address will enable register 7?

Solution

The enable inputs of this register are connected to the row 3 and column 1 select lines, respectively. To select row 3, the A_1A_0 inputs must be at 11, and to select column 1, the A_3A_2 inputs must be at 01. Thus, the required address will be $A_3A_2A_1A_0 = 0111$.

Output Buffers

The register that is enabled by the address inputs will place its data on the data bus. These data feed into the output buffers, which will pass the data to the external data outputs, provided that $\overline{CS}$ is LOW. If $\overline{CS}$ is HIGH, the output buffers are in the Hi-Z state, and D_7 through D_0 will be floating.

The architecture shown in Figure 11-7 is similar to that of many IC ROMs. Depending on the number of stored data words, the registers in some ROMs will not be arranged in a square array. For example, the Intel 2764 is a MOS ROM that stores 8192 eight-bit words. Its 8192 registers are arranged in an array of 256 rows × 32 registers. ROM capacities range from 256 × 4 to 8M × 8.

EXAMPLE 11-7

Describe the internal architecture of a ROM that stores 4K bytes and uses a square register array.

Solution

4K is actually $4 \times 1024 = 4096$, and so this ROM holds 4096 eight-bit words. Each word can be thought of as being stored in an eight-bit register, and there are 4096 registers connected to a common data bus internal to the chip. Since $4096 = 64^2$, the registers are arranged in a 64 × 64 array; that is, there are 64 rows and 64 columns. This requires a 1-of-64 decoder to decode six address inputs for the row select, and a second 1-of-64 decoder to decode six other address inputs for the column select. Thus, a total of 12 address inputs is required. This makes sense, since $2^{12} = 4096$, and there are 4096 different addresses.

Review Questions

1. What input address code is required if we want to read the data from register 9 in Figure 11-7?

2. Describe the function of the row-select decoder, the column-select decoder, and the output buffers in the ROM architecture.

11-6 ROM TIMING

There will be a propagation delay between the application of a ROM's inputs and the appearance of the data outputs during a read operation. This time delay, called **access time,** t_{ACC}, is a measure of the ROM's operating speed. Access time is described graphically by the waveforms in Figure 11-8.

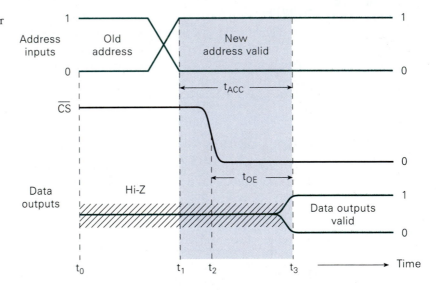

FIGURE 11-8 Typical timing for a ROM read operation.

The top waveform represents the address inputs; the middle waveform is an active-LOW chip select, $\overline{CS}$; and the bottom waveform represents the data outputs. At time t_0 the address inputs are all at some specific level, some HIGH and some LOW. $\overline{CS}$ is HIGH, so that the ROM data outputs are in their Hi-Z state (represented by the hatched line).

Just prior to t_1, the address inputs are changing to a new address for a new read operation. At t_1 the new address is valid; that is, each address input is at a valid logic level. At this point the internal ROM circuitry begins to decode the new address inputs to select the register that is to send its data to the output buffers. At t_2 the $\overline{CS}$

input is activated to enable the output buffers. Finally, at t_3, the outputs change from the Hi-Z state to the valid data that represent the data stored at the specified address.

The time delay between t_1, when the new address becomes valid, and t_3, when the data outputs become valid, is the access time t_{ACC}. Typical bipolar ROMs will have access times in the range 30 to 90 ns; access times of NMOS devices will range from 35 to 500 ns. Improvements to CMOS technology have brought access times into the 20-to-60-ns range. Consequently, bipolar and NMOS devices are rarely produced in newer (larger) ROMs.

Another important timing parameter is the *output enable time*, t_{OE}, which is the delay between the $\overline{CS}$ input and the valid data output. Typical values for t_{OE} are 10 to 20 ns for bipolar, 25 to 100 ns for NMOS, and 12 to 50 ns for CMOS ROMs. This timing parameter is important in situations where the address inputs are already set to their new values, but the ROM outputs have not yet been enabled. When $\overline{CS}$ goes LOW to enable the outputs, the delay will be t_{OE}.

11-7   TYPES OF ROMs

Now that we have a general understanding of the internal architecture and external operation of ROM devices, we will look at the various types of ROMs to see how they differ in the way they are programmed, erased, and reprogrammed.

Mask-Programmed ROM

The mask-programmed ROM has its storage locations written into (programmed) by the manufacturer according to the customer's specifications. A photographic negative called a *mask* is used to control the electrical interconnections on the chip. A special mask is required for each different set of information to be stored in the ROM. Since these masks are expensive, this type of ROM is economical only if you need a very large quantity of the same ROM. Some ROMs of this type are available as off-the-shelf devices preprogrammed with commonly used information or data such as certain mathematical tables and character generator codes for CRT displays. A major disadvantage of this type of ROM is that it cannot be reprogrammed in the event of a design change requiring a modification of the stored data. The ROM would have to be replaced by a new one with the desired data written into it. Several types of user-programmable ROMs have been developed to overcome this disadvantage. Mask-programmed ROMs, however, still represent the most economical approach when a large quantity of identically programmed ROMs are needed.

Mask-programmed ROMs are commonly referred to as just ROMs, but this can be confusing since the term ROM actually represents the broad category of devices that, during normal operation, are only read from. We will use the acronym MROM whenever we refer to mask-programmed ROMs.

Figure 11-9 shows the structure of a small MOS MROM. It consists of 16 memory cells arranged in four rows of four cells. Each cell is an N-channel MOSFET transistor connected in the common-drain configuration (input at gate, output at source). The top row of cells (ROW 0) constitutes a four-bit register. Note that some of the transistors in this row (Q_0 and Q_2) have their source connected to the output column line, while others (Q_1 and Q_3) do not. The same is true of the cells in each

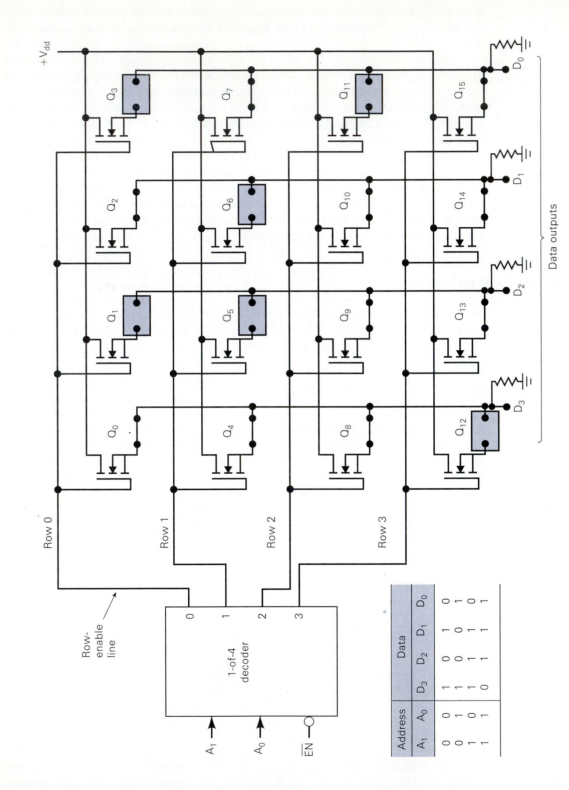

Address		Data			
A_1	A_0	D_3	D_2	D_1	D_0
0	0	1	0	1	0
0	1	1	0	0	1
1	0	1	1	1	0
1	1	0	1	1	1

FIGURE 11-9 Structure of a MOS MROM shows one MOSFET used for each memory cell. An open source connection stores a "0"; a closed source connection stores a "1."

of the other rows. The presence or absence of these source connections determines whether a cell is storing a 1 or a 0, respectively. The condition of each source connection is controlled during production by the photographic mask based on the customer-supplied data.

Notice that the data outputs are connected to column lines. Referring to output D_3, for instance, any transistor that has a connection from the source (such as Q_0, Q_4, and Q_8) to the output column can switch V_{dd} onto the column, making it a HIGH logic level. If V_{dd} is not connected to the column line, the output will be held at a LOW logic level by the pull-down resistor. At any given time, a maximum of one transistor in a column will ever be turned on due to the row decoder.

The 1-of-4 decoder is used to decode the address inputs $A_1 A_0$ to select which row (register) is to have its data read. The decoder's active-HIGH outputs provide the ROW enable lines that are the gate inputs for the various rows of cells. If the decoder's enable input, $\overline{EN}$, is held HIGH, all of the decoder outputs will be in their inactive LOW state, and all of the transistors in the array will be off because of the absence of any gate voltage. For this situation, the data outputs will all be in the LOW state.

When $\overline{EN}$ is in its active-LOW state, the conditions at the address inputs determine which row (register) will be enabled so that its data can be read at the data outputs. For example, to read ROW 0, the $A_1 A_0$ inputs are set to 00. This places HIGH at the ROW 0 line; all other row lines are at 0 V. This HIGH at ROW 0 turns on transistors Q_0, Q_1, Q_2, and Q_3. With all of the transistors in the row conducting, V_{dd} will be switched on to each transistor's source lead. Outputs D_3 and D_1 will go HIGH, since Q_0 and Q_2 are connected to their respective columns. D_2 and D_0 will remain LOW because there is no path from the Q_1 and Q_3 source leads to their columns. In a similar manner, application of the other address codes will produce data outputs from the corresponding register. The table in Figure 11-9 shows the data for each address. You should verify how this correlates with the source connections to the various cells.

EXAMPLE 11-8

MROMs can be used to store tables of mathematical functions. Show how the MROM in Figure 11-9 can be used to store the function $y = x^2 + 3$, where the input address supplies the value for x, and the value of the output data is y.

Solution

The first step is to set up a table showing the desired output for each set of inputs. The input binary number, x, is represented by the address $A_1 A_0$. The output binary number is the desired value of y. For example, when $x = A_1 A_0 = 10_2 = 2_{10}$, the output should be $2^2 + 3 = 7_{10} = 0111_2$. The complete table is shown in Table 11-1. This

TABLE 11-1

| \multicolumn{2}{c}{x} | \multicolumn{4}{c}{$y = x^2 + 3$} |
A_1	A_0	D_3	D_2	D_1	D_0
0	0	0	0	1	1
0	1	0	1	0	0
1	0	0	1	1	1
1	1	1	1	0	0

table is supplied to the MROM manufacturer for developing the mask that will make the appropriate connections within the memory cells during the fabrication process. For instance, the first row in the table indicates that the connections to the source of Q_0 and Q_1 will be left unconnected, while the connections to Q_2 and Q_3 will be made.

Bipolar MROMs have an internal structure similar to Figure 11-9 except that the cells are bipolar transistors rather than MOSFETs. The TMS47256 is an NMOS version that has a capacity of 32K × 8. Its symbol is shown in Figure 11-10. Note that it has tristate outputs to permit easy interfacing to a computer data bus. In addition to the 14 address inputs, it has two enable inputs, $\overline{E}$ and $\overline{S}$. Both of these must be LOW to enable the MROM outputs. The $\overline{E}$ input also performs a **power-down** function. When $\overline{E}$ is kept HIGH, the chip's internal circuitry is put into a low-power standby state where it draws about one-fourth of the normal supply current. The TMS47256 has an access time of 200 ns and a standby power of 82.5 mW. The CMOS version, the TMS47C256, has an access time of 100 ns and a standby power of only 2.8 mW.

FIGURE 11-10 Logic symbol for the TMS47256 MROM made using NMOS/CMOS technology.

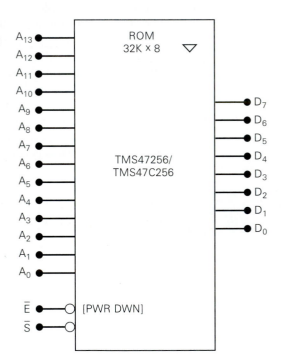

Programmable ROMs (PROMs)

A mask-programmable ROM is very expensive and would not be used except in high-volume applications, where the cost would be spread out over many units. For lower-volume applications, manufacturers have developed **fusible-link** PROMs that are user-programmable; that is, they are not programmed during the manufacturing process but are custom-programmed by the user. Once programmed, however, a PROM is like an MROM in that it cannot be erased and reprogrammed. Thus, if the program in the PROM is faulty or must be changed, the PROM must be thrown away. For this reason, these devices are often referred to as "one-time programmable" (OTP) ROMs.

The fusible-link PROM structure is very similar to the MROM structure in that certain connections either are left intact or are opened in order to program a memory cell as a 1 or a 0, respectively. In the MROM of Figure 11-9 these connections were from the MOSFET source lead to the output column. In a PROM each of these connections is made with a thin fuse link that comes intact from the manufacturer (see Figure 11-11).

FIGURE 11-11 PROMs use fusible links that can be selectively blown open by the user to program a logic 0 into a cell.

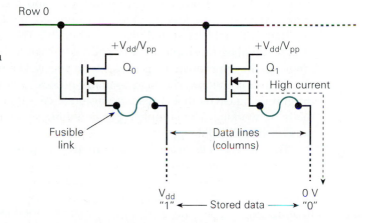

The user can selectively *blow* any of these fuse links to produce the desired stored memory data. Typically, a data value is programmed or "burned-into" an address location by: applying the address to the address inputs; placing the desired data at the data pins; and then applying V_{pp}, a high-voltage pulse (10–30 V), to a special programming pin on the IC. Figure 11-11 shows the programming operation. All of the transistors in the selected row (row 0) are turned on, and V_{pp} is applied to their drain leads. Those columns (data lines) that have a logic 0 on them (e.g., Q_1) will provide a high-current path through the fusible link, burning it open and permanently storing a logic 0. Those columns that have a logic 1 (e.g., Q_0) have V_{pp} on one side of the fuse and V_{dd} on the other side, drawing much less current and leaving the fuse intact. Once all address locations have been programmed in this manner, the data are permanently stored in the PROM and can be read over and over again by accessing the appropriate address. The data will not change when power is removed from the PROM chip, because nothing will cause an open fuse link to become closed again.

The process of programming a PROM and verifying that the stored data are correct is rarely done manually; rather, it is done automatically by a special apparatus called a PROM **programmer.** Typically, the PROM chip is plugged into a socket on the PROM programmer. The programmer circuitry selects each address of the PROM, burns in the correct data at that address, verifies the data, and sequences to the next address to repeat the process. The data to be burned into the PROM are input to the programmer from a keyboard or from a disk drive, or they are transferred from a computer. The latter operation, called *downloading,* allows the user to develop and test the program/data on a computer and then, when it is finished and working, transfer it from the computer's memory to the PROM programmer, which will "burn it" into the PROM.

Very few bipolar PROMs are still available today. Almost all use MOS technology, with CMOS becoming the most popular. The TMS27PC256 is a very popular CMOS PROM with a capacity of 32K × 8 and a standby power dissipation of only 1.4 mW. It is available with maximum access times ranging from 100 to 250 ns.

Erasable Programmable ROM (EPROM)

An EPROM can be programmed by the user, and it can also be *erased* and reprogrammed as often as desired. Once programmed, the EPROM is a *nonvolatile* memory that will hold its stored data indefinitely. The process for programming an EPROM involves the application of special voltage levels (typically in the 10-to-25-V range) to the appropriate chip inputs for a specified amount of time (typically 50 ms per address location). The programming process is usually performed by a special programming circuit that is separate from the circuit in which the EPROM will eventually be working. The complete programming process can take up to several minutes for one EPROM chip.

The storage cells in an EPROM are MOS transistors with a silicon gate that has no electrical connections (i.e., a *floating gate*). In its normal state, each transistor is off and each cell is storing a logic 1. A transistor can be turned on by the application of a high-voltage programming pulse that injects high-energy electrons into the floating-gate region. These electrons remain trapped in this region once the pulse is terminated, since there is no discharge path. This keeps the transistor on *permanently* even when power is removed from the device, and the cell is now storing a logic 0. During the programming process, the EPROM's address and data pins are used to select which memory cells will be programmed as 0s and which ones will be left as 1s.

Once an EPROM cell has been programmed, it can be erased by exposing it to ultraviolet (UV) light applied through a window on the chip package. The UV light produces a photocurrent from the floating gate back to the silicon substrate, thereby removing the stored charges, turning the transistor off, and restoring the cell to the logic 1 state. This erasing process typically requires 15 to 20 minutes of exposure to UV rays. Unfortunately, there is no way to erase only selected cells; *the UV light erases all cells at the same time* so that an erased EPROM stores all 1s. Once erased, the EPROM can be reprogrammed.

EPROMs are available in a wide range of capacities and access times; devices with a capacity of 512K × 8 and an access time of 45 ns are commonplace. The 2732 is an example of a small EPROM. The 2732 is a 4K × 8 NMOS EPROM that operates from a single +5 V power source during normal operation. Figure 11-12(a) is the logic symbol for the 2732. Note that it shows 12 address inputs, since $2^{12} = 4096$, and 8 data outputs. It has two control inputs. $\overline{CE}$ is the chip enable input that is used to place the device in a standby mode where its power consumption is reduced. $\overline{OE}/V_{PP}$ is a dual-purpose input whose function will depend on the device operating mode. $\overline{OE}$ is the output enable and is used to control the device's data output buffers so that the device can be connected to a microprocessor data bus without bus contention. V_{PP} is the special programming voltage required during the programming process.

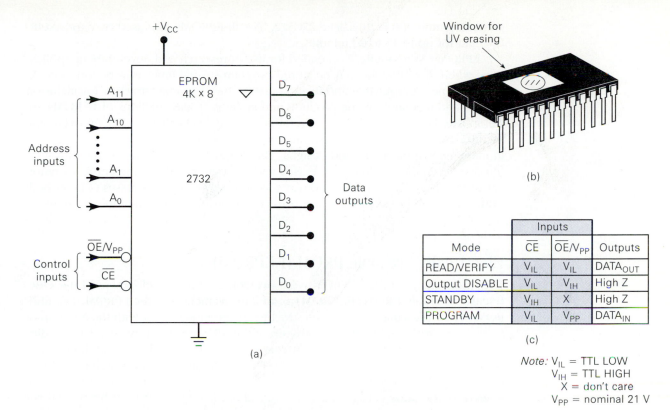

FIGURE 11-12 (a) Logic symbol for 2732 EPROM; (b) typical EPROM package showing ultraviolet window; (c) 2732 operating modes.

The 2732 package in Figure 11-12(b) shows the characteristic "window," which allows the internal circuitry to be exposed to UV light when the complete memory contents are to be erased. A sticker is placed over the window after erasure and re-programming to protect against accidental erasure from ambient light.

The 2732 has several operating modes that are controlled by the $\overline{CE}$ and $\overline{OE}/V_{PP}$ pins as presented in Figure 11-12(c). The program mode is used to write new data into the EPROM cells. This is most often done on a "clean" EPROM, one that has pre-viously been erased with UV light so that all cells are 1s. The programming process writes one eight-bit word into one address location at one time as follows: (1) the ad-dress is applied to the address pins; (2) the desired data are placed at the data pins, which function as inputs during the programming process; (3) a high voltage, nomi-nally 21 V, is applied to V_{PP}; and (4) $\overline{CE}$ is pulsed LOW, typically for 50 ms. This process is repeated for all memory locations. If done manually, this can take several hours. Usually, however, it is done automatically with a commercial EPROM program-mer much like the PROM programmers described above. A clean EPROM can be pro-grammed in a few minutes once the desired data have been entered, transferred, or downloaded into the EPROM programmer.

The Intel 27C512 is a 64K × 8 EPROM that can be programmed much more rapidly than the 2732. The 27C512 requires a $\overline{CE}$ pulse of only 100 μs to write a sin-gle byte, as compared to 50 ms for the 2732; this translates into a total chip programming time of 8 to 10 s. The 27C512, like all EPROMs, is erased by exposure to UV light for up to 15 to 20 minutes.

EPROMs were originally intended for use in research and development applications where the need to alter the stored program several times is very common. As they became more reliable and less expensive, they became attractive for inclusion in low- and medium-volume products and systems. Today, millions of EPROMs are still in use. However, they have several major drawbacks that have been overcome by the newer EEPROMs and flash memory devices, so EPROMs are not being used in many new applications and designs. These drawbacks include: (1) they must be removed from their circuit to be erased and reprogrammed; (2) the erase operation erases the entire chip—there is no way to select only certain addresses to be erased; (3) the erase and reprogramming process can typically take 20 minutes or more.

Electrically Erasable PROM (EEPROM)

The disadvantages of the EPROM were overcome by the development of the **electrically erasable PROM (EEPROM)** as an improvement over the EPROM. The EEPROM retains the same floating-gate structure as the EPROM, but with the addition of a very thin oxide region above the drain of the MOSFET memory cell. This modification produces the EEPROM's major characteristic—its electrical erasability. By applying a high voltage (21 V) between the MOSFET's gate and drain, a charge can be induced onto the floating gate, where it will remain even when power is removed; reversal of the same voltage causes a removal of the trapped charges from the floating gate and erases the cell. Since this charge-transport mechanism requires very low currents, the erasing and programming of an EEPROM can be done *in circuit* (i.e., without a UV light source and a special PROM programmer unit).

Another advantage of the EEPROM over the EPROM is the ability to electrically erase and rewrite *individual* bytes (eight-bit words) in the memory array. During a write operation, internal circuitry automatically erases all of the cells at an address location prior to writing in the new data. This byte erasability makes it much easier to make changes in the data stored in an EEPROM. Additionally, an EEPROM can be programmed more rapidly than many EPROMs; typically, it takes 5 ms to write into an EEPROM location, compared to 50 ms for an EPROM, although newer EPROMs are much faster (100 μs).

The early EEPROMs, such as Intel's 2816, required appropriate support circuitry external to the memory chips. This support circuitry included the 21-V programming voltage (V_{PP}), usually generated from a +5 V supply through a dc-to-dc converter, and it included circuitry to control the timing and sequencing of the erase and programming operations. The newer devices, such as the Intel 2864, have integrated this support circuitry onto the same chip with the memory array, so that it requires only a single 5-V power pin. This makes the EEPROM as easy to use as the read/write memory we will be discussing shortly.

The byte erasability of the EEPROM and its high level of integration come with two penalties: density and cost. The memory cell complexity and the on-chip support circuitry place EEPROMs far behind an EPROM in bit capacity per square millimeter of silicon; a 1-Mbit EEPROM requires about twice as much silicon as a 1-Mbit EPROM. So, despite its operational superiority, the EEPROM's shortcomings in density and cost-effectiveness have kept it from replacing the EPROM in applications where density and cost are paramount factors.

The logic symbol for the Intel 2864 is shown in Figure 11-13(a). It is organized as an 8K × 8 array with 13 address inputs (2^{13} = 8192) and eight data I/O pins. Three control inputs determine the operating mode according to the table given in Figure 11-13(b). With $\overline{CE}$ = HIGH the chip is in its low-power standby mode, in which no operations are being performed on any memory location and the data pins are in the Hi-Z state.

To read the contents of a memory location, the desired address is applied to the address pins; $\overline{CE}$ is driven LOW; and the output enable pin, $\overline{OE}$, is driven LOW to enable the chip's output data buffers. The write enable pin, $\overline{WE}$, is held HIGH during a read operation.

To write into (program) a memory location, the output buffers are disabled so that the data to be written can be applied as inputs to the I/O pins. The timing for the write operation is diagrammed in Figure 11-13(c). Prior to t_1 the device is in the standby mode. A new address is applied at that time. At t_2 the $\overline{CE}$ and $\overline{WE}$ inputs are driven LOW to begin the write operation; $\overline{OE}$ is HIGH so that the data pins will remain in the Hi-Z state. Data are applied to the I/O pins at t_3 and are written into the address location on the rising edge of $\overline{WE}$ at t_4. The data are removed at t_5. Actually, the data are first latched (on the rising edge of $\overline{WE}$) into a FF buffer memory that is part of the 2864 circuitry. The data are held there while other circuitry on the chip performs an erase operation on the selected address location in the EEPROM array, after which the data byte is transferred from the buffer to the EEPROM array and stored at that location. This erase and store operation typically takes 5 ms. With $\overline{CE}$ returned HIGH at t_4, the chip is back in the standby mode while the internal erase and store operations are completed.

The 2864 has an enhanced write mode that allows the user to write up to 16 bytes of data into the FF buffer memory, where it is held while the EEPROM circuitry erases the selected address locations. The 16 bytes of data are then transferred to the EEPROM array for storage at these locations. This process also takes about 5 ms.

Since the internal process of storing a data value in an EEPROM is quite slow, the speed of the data transfer operation can also be slower. Consequently, many manufacturers offer EEPROM devices in eight-pin packages that are interfaced to a two- or three-wire *serial* bus. This saves physical space on the system board as opposed to using a 2864 in a 28-pin, wide-DIP package. It also simplifies the hardware interface between the CPU and the EEPROM.

CD ROM

A very prominent type of read-only storage used today in computer systems is the compact disk (CD). The disk technology and the hardware necessary to retrieve the information are the same as those used in audio systems. Only the format of the data is different. The disks are manufactured with a highly reflective surface. To store data on the disks, a very intense laser beam is focused on a *very* small point on the disk. The heat from this beam burns a light-diffracting pit at that point on the disk surface. Digital data (1s and 0s) are stored on the disk one bit at a time by burning or not burning a pit into the reflective coating. The digital information is arranged on the disk as a continuous spiral of data points. The precision of the laser beam allows very large quantities of data (over 550 Mbytes) to be stored on a small, 120-mm disk.

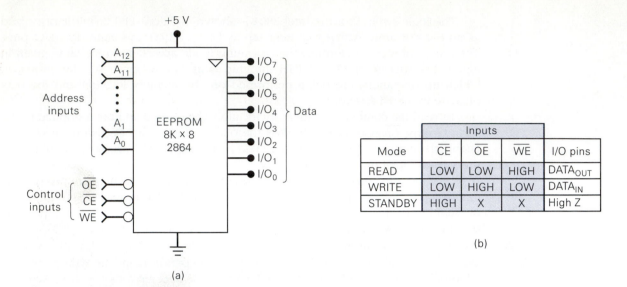

	Inputs			
Mode	$\overline{CE}$	$\overline{OE}$	$\overline{WE}$	I/O pins
READ	LOW	LOW	HIGH	DATA$_{OUT}$
WRITE	LOW	HIGH	LOW	DATA$_{IN}$
STANDBY	HIGH	X	X	High Z

(b)

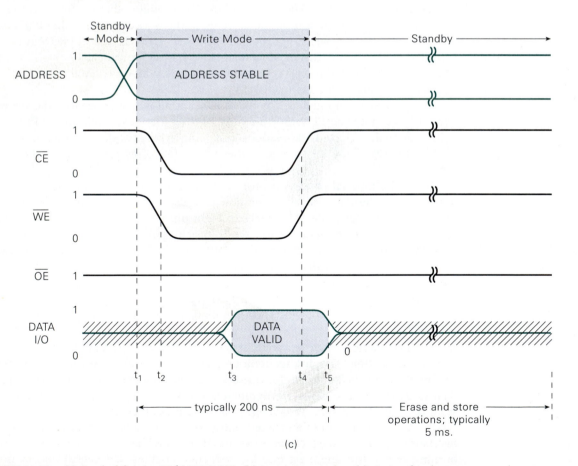

(c)

FIGURE 11-13 (a) Symbol for the 2864 EEPROM; (b) operating modes; (c) timing for the write operation.

In order to read the data, a much less powerful laser beam is focused onto the surface of the disk. At any point, the reflected light is sensed as either a 1 or a 0. This optical system is mounted on a mechanical carriage that moves back and forth along the radius of the disk, following the spiral of data as the disk rotates. The data retrieved from the optical system come one bit at a time in a serial data stream. The angular rotation of the disk is controlled to maintain a constant rate of incoming data points. If the disk is being used for audio recording, this stream of data is converted into an analog waveform. If the disk is being used as ROM, the data are decoded into parallel bytes that the computer can use. The CD player technology, although very sophisticated, is relatively inexpensive and is becoming a standard way of loading large amounts of data into a personal computer. The major improvements that are occurring now in CD-ROM technology involve quicker access time in retrieving data.

Review Questions

1. *True or false:* An MROM can be programmed by the user.
2. How does a PROM differ from an MROM? Can it be erased and reprogrammed?
3. *True or false:* A PROM stores a logic "1" when its fusible link is intact.
4. How is an EPROM erased?
5. *True or false:* There is no way to erase only a portion of an EPROM's memory.
6. What function is performed by PROM and EPROM programmers?
7. What EPROM shortcomings are overcome by EEPROMs?
8. What are the major drawbacks of EEPROM?
9. What type of ROM can erase one byte at a time?
10. How many bits are read from a CD-ROM disk at any point in time?

11-8 FLASH MEMORY

EPROMs are nonvolatile, offer fast read access times (typically 120 ns), and have high density and low cost per bit. They do, however, require removal from their circuit/system to be erased and reprogrammed. EEPROMs are nonvolatile, offer fast read access, and allow rapid in-circuit erasure and reprogramming of individual bytes. They suffer from lower density and much higher cost than EPROMs.

The challenge for semiconductor engineers was to fabricate a nonvolatile memory with the EEPROM's in-circuit electrical erasability, but with densities and costs much closer to those of EPROMs, while retaining the high-speed read access of both. The response to this challenge was the **flash memory.**

Structurally, a flash memory cell is like the simple single-transistor EPROM cell (and unlike the more complex two-transistor EEPROM cell), being only slightly larger. It has a thinner gate-oxide layer that allows electrical erasability but can be built with much higher densities than EEPROMs. The cost of flash memory is considerably less than for EEPROM, although not yet as close to EPROM as it will be as flash technology improves. Figure 11-14 illustrates the trade-offs for the various semiconductor nonvolatile memories. As erase/programming flexibility increases (from base to apex of the triangle), so do device complexity and cost. MROM and PROM are the simplest and cheapest devices, but they cannot be erased and reprogrammed. EEPROM is the most complex and expensive because it can be erased and reprogrammed in circuit on a byte-by-byte basis.

FIGURE 11-14 Trade-offs for semiconductor nonvolatile memories show that complexity and cost increase as erase and programming flexibility increases.

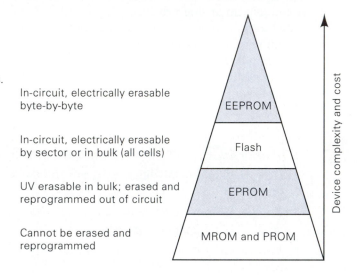

Flash memories are so-called because of their rapid erase and write times. Most flash chips use a *bulk erase* operation in which all cells on the chip are erased simultaneously; this bulk erase process typically requires hundreds of milliseconds compared to 20 minutes for UV EPROMs. Some newer flash memories offer a *sector erase* mode, where specific sectors of the memory array (e.g., 512 bytes) can be erased at one time. This prevents having to erase and reprogram all cells when only a portion of the memory needs to be updated. A typical flash memory has a write time of 10 μs per byte compared to 100 μs for the most advanced EPROM and 5 ms for EEPROM (which includes automatic byte erase time).

Memory manufacturers everywhere are working on developing and improving flash memory devices, and each has its own approach as to what features and performance characteristics are the most important. We will not attempt to survey the vast array of manufacturers and devices here. Instead, we present a representative flash memory IC from one of the leading memory manufacturers and use it as a vehicle for learning the main aspects of flash memory operation. By looking at this representative device, we will also be exposed to the use of *command codes* as a means by which we can control the internal operations of the more complex logic chips. This will serve as a good introduction to the many types of command-controlled ICs that are part of most microprocessor-based systems.

The 28F256A CMOS Flash Memory IC

Figure 11-15(a) shows the logic symbol for Intel Corporation's 28F256A CMOS flash memory chip, which has a capacity of 32K × 8. The diagram shows 15 address inputs (A_0–A_{14}) needed to select the different memory addresses; that is, $2^{15} = 32K =$

32,768. The eight data input/output pins (DQ_0–DQ_7) are used as inputs during memory write operations and as outputs during memory read operations. These data pins float to the Hi-Z state when the chip is deselected ($\overline{CE}$ = HIGH) or when the outputs are disabled ($\overline{OE}$ = HIGH). The write enable input ($\overline{WE}$) is used to control memory write operations. Note that the chip requires two power-supply voltages: V_{CC} is the standard +5 V used for the logic circuitry; V_{PP} is the erase/programming power-supply voltage, nominally +12 V, which is needed for the erase and programming (write) operations.

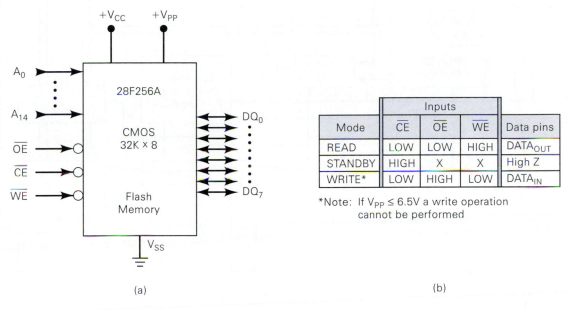

	Inputs			
Mode	$\overline{CE}$	$\overline{OE}$	$\overline{WE}$	Data pins
READ	LOW	LOW	HIGH	$DATA_{OUT}$
STANDBY	HIGH	X	X	High Z
WRITE*	LOW	HIGH	LOW	$DATA_{IN}$

*Note: If $V_{PP} \leq 6.5V$ a write operation cannot be performed

(a)

(b)

FIGURE 11-15 (a) Logic symbol for the 28F256A flash memory chip; (b) control inputs $\overline{CE}$, $\overline{WE}$, and $\overline{OE}$.

The control inputs ($\overline{CE}$, $\overline{OE}$, and $\overline{WE}$) control what happens at the data pins in much the same way as for the 2864 EEPROM, as the table in Figure 11-15(b) shows. These data pins are normally connected to a data bus. During a write operation, data are transferred over the bus—usually from the microprocessor—and into the chip. During a read operation, data from inside the chip are transferred over the data bus—usually to the microprocessor. It is important to note that if the V_{PP} pin is not held at a high voltage (over 6.5 V), write operations cannot be performed, and the chip can only be read from; so it acts as a read-only memory (ROM), and the memory contents cannot be altered.

The operation of this flash memory chip can be better understood by looking at its internal structure. Figure 11-16 is a diagram of the 28F256A showing its major functional blocks. You should refer to this diagram as needed during the following discussion. The unique feature of this structure is the *command register*, which is used to manage all of the chip functions. Command codes are written into this register to control which operations take place inside the chip (e.g., erase, erase-verify, program, program-verify). These command codes usually come over the data bus from the microprocessor. State control logic examines the contents of the command

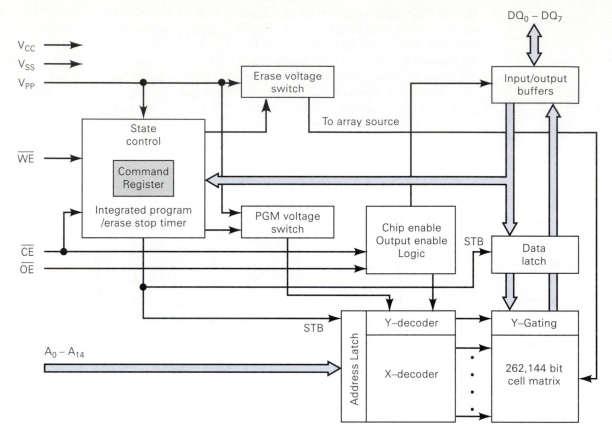

FIGURE 11-16 Functional diagram of the 28F256A flash memory chip. (Courtesy of Intel Corporation.)

register and generates logic and control signals to the rest of the chip's circuits to carry out the steps in the operation. Let's look at how this works for some of the commands.

Read Command

To set up the chip for read operations, it is necessary first to *write* all 0s ($00000000_2 = 00_{16}$) into the command register. This is done by applying 00_{16} to the data pins and pulsing $\overline{WE}$ LOW while $\overline{CE}$ = LOW and $\overline{OE}$ = HIGH [as shown in the table in Figure 11-15(b)]. The address inputs can be in any state for this step because the input data will automatically be routed to the command register. Once this is done, the device is set up to have data *read* from the 262,144-bit (32,768-byte) memory matrix (array). Memory data are read in the usual way: (1) apply the address to be read from; and (2) set $\overline{WE}$ = HIGH, $\overline{CE}$ = LOW, and pulse $\overline{OE}$ = LOW to enable the output buffers to pass data from the cell matrix to the data output pins. The read access time for the 28F256A is 120 ns, maximum. The device remains enabled for memory reads as long as the command register contents remain at 00_{16}.

Set-Up Erase/Erase Commands

To erase the entire contents of the memory array requires two steps: (1) writing the code 20_{16} to the command register to set up the chip for the erase operation and (2) again writing the code 20_{16} to the command register to begin the erase operation. This two-step sequence makes it less likely that the memory contents will be erased accidentally. After the second command code has been written, the 12 V from V_{PP} is used to erase all cells in the array. This process takes about 10 ms.

Erase-Verify Command

After the erase operation, it is necessary to verify that all memory cells have been erased; that is, all bytes = 11111111_2 = FF_{16}. The erase-verify operation must be done for each byte address. It is initiated by writing $A0_{16}$ to the command register. Then a read operation is done on the address to be verified, and the output data value is checked to see that it equals FF_{16}. These two steps are done for each address, and the total time to verify all addresses is about 1 s. If the data at an address do not show up as FF, the chip must be erased again using the erase command sequence above.

Set-Up Program/Program Commands

The device can be set up for byte programming by writing the code 40_{16} to the command register. This is followed by writing the data that are to be programmed to the desired address.

Program-Verify Command

After a byte has been programmed into an address, the content of that address must be verified to assure that it has been programmed successfully. This is done by first writing the code $C0_{16}$ to the command register to set up the verify operation. This is followed by a read operation, which will cause the chip to output the data from the address that was just programmed so that it can be compared to the desired data.

The complete process of programming and verifying each address location takes about 500 ms for the 28F256A.

Review Questions

1. What is the main advantage of flash memory over EPROMs?
2. What is the main advantage of flash memory over EEPROMs?
3. Where does the word *flash* come from?
4. What is V_{PP} needed for?
5. What is the function of the 28F256A's command register?
6. What is the purpose of an erase-verify command?
7. What is the purpose of the program-verify command?

11-9 ROM APPLICATIONS

With the exception of MROM and PROM, most ROM devices can be reprogrammed, so technically they are not *read-only* memories. However, the term *ROM* can still be used to include EPROMs, EEPROMs, and flash memory, because during normal operation the stored contents of these devices is not changed nearly as often as it is read. So ROMs are taken to include all semiconductor, nonvolatile memory devices, and they are used in applications where nonvolatile storage of information, data, or program codes is needed and where the stored data rarely or never change. Here are some of the most common application areas.

Firmware

The most widespread application of ROMs is in the storage of data and program codes that must be available on power-up in microprocessor-based systems. These data and program codes are called **firmware** because they are firmly stored in hardware (i.e., ROM chips) and are not subject to change during normal system operation. Some PCs, business computers, and laptop computers store their operating system programs and language interpreters (e.g., BASIC, Pascal) in ROM firmware so that the computer can be used immediately after power is turned on.

In addition to the familiar microcomputers, there are many other microprocessor-based systems that use ROM firmware. Consumer products such as automobiles, VCRs, CD players, and microwave ovens, as well as all kinds of production machinery, have embedded microcontrollers which consist of a microprocessor that controls and monitors the operation according to programs and data that are stored in ROM.

In all of these systems, system operation depends to a great degree on what is stored in the ROM, and changes in system operation are usually made by changing the contents of ROM. With EPROMs, this requires either removing the chips from the system for erasure and reprogramming, or replacing the chips with new ones. This necessitates suspension of system operation for anywhere from a few minutes to an hour. The use of EEPROMs, and better still, flash memory, cuts this down considerably since they can be rapidly erased and reprogrammed in system.

Bootstrap Memory

Many microcomputers and most larger computers do not have their operating system programs stored in ROM. Instead, these programs are stored in external mass memory, usually magnetic disk. How, then, do these computers know what to do when they are powered on? A relatively small program, called a **bootstrap program,** is stored in ROM. (The term *bootstrap* comes from the idea of pulling oneself up by one's own bootstraps.) When the computer is powered on, it will execute the instructions that are in this bootstrap program. These instructions typically cause the CPU to initialize the system hardware. The bootstrap program then loads the operating system programs from mass storage (disk) into its main internal memory. At that point the computer begins executing the operating system program and is ready to respond to the user commands. This startup process is often called "booting up the system."

Data Tables

ROMs are often used to store tables of data that do not change. Some examples are the trigonometric tables (i.e., sine, cosine, etc.) and code-conversion tables. The digital system can use these data tables to "look up" the correct value. For example, a ROM could be used to store the sine function for angles from 0° to 90°. It could be organized as a 128 × 8 with seven address inputs and eight data outputs. The address inputs represent the angle in increments of approximately 0.7°. For example, address 0000000 is 0°, address 0000001 is 0.7°, address 0000010 is 1.41°, and so on, up to address 1111111, which is 89.3°. When an address is applied to the ROM, the data outputs will represent the approximate sine of the angle. For example, with input address 1000000 (representing approximately 45°) the data outputs will be 10110101. Since the sine is less than or equal to 1, these data are interpreted as a fraction, that is, .10110101, which when converted to decimal equals .707 (the sine of 45°). It is vital that the user of this ROM understands the format in which the data are stored.

Standard look-up-table ROMs for functions such as these were at one time readily available TTL chips. Only a few are still in production. Today most systems that need to look up equivalent values involve a microprocessor, and the "look-up" table data are stored in the same ROM that holds the program instructions.

Data Converter

The data-converter circuit takes data expressed in one type of code and produces an output expressed in another type. Code conversion is needed, for example, when a computer is outputting data in straight binary code and we want to convert it to BCD in order to display it on 7-segment LED readouts.

One of the easiest methods of code conversion uses a ROM programmed so that the application of a particular address (the old code) produces a data output that represents the equivalent in the new code. The 74185 is a TTL ROM that stores the binary-to-BCD code conversion for a six-bit binary input. To illustrate, a binary address input of 100110 (decimal 38) will produce a data output of 00111000, which is the BCD code for decimal 38. Problem 11-20 will deal with this ROM.

Function Generator

The function generator is a circuit that produces waveforms such as sine waves, sawtooth waves, triangle waves, and square waves. Figure 11-17 shows how a ROM look-up table and a DAC are used to generate a sine-wave output signal.

The ROM stores 256 different eight-bit values, each one corresponding to a different waveform value (i.e., a different voltage point on the sine wave). The eight-bit counter is continuously pulsed by a clock signal to provide sequential address inputs to the ROM. As the counter cycles through the 256 different addresses, the ROM outputs the 256 data points to the DAC. The DAC output will be a waveform that steps through the 256 different analog voltage values corresponding to the data points. The low-pass filter smooths out the steps in the DAC output to produce a smooth waveform.

Circuits such as this are used in some commercial function generators. The same idea is employed in some speech synthesizers, where the digitized speech

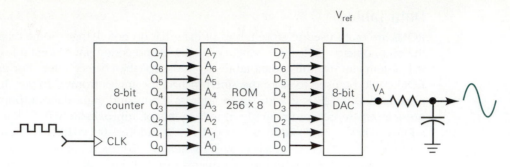

FIGURE 11-17   Function generator using a ROM and a DAC.

waveform values are stored in the ROM. The ML2035, illustrated in Figure 11-18, is a programmable sine-wave generator chip that incorporates this basic strategy to generate a sine wave of fixed amplitude and a frequency that can be selected from dc to 50 kHz. The number that is shifted into the 16-bit shift register is used to determine the clocking frequency for the counter that drives the address inputs on the ROM look-up table. The ML2035 is intended for telecommunications applications that require precise tones of various frequencies to be generated.

FIGURE 11-18   The ML2035 programmable sine-wave generator. (Courtesy of MicroLinear)

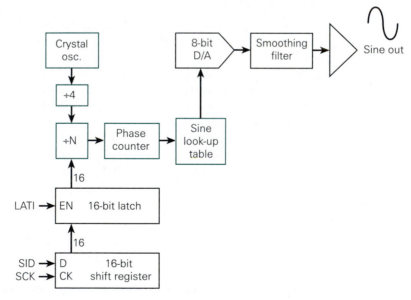

Auxiliary Storage

Because of their nonvolatility, high speed, low power requirements, and lack of moving parts, flash memory modules have become feasible alternatives to magnetic disk storage. This is especially true for lower capacities (5 Mbytes or less) where flash is cost-competitive with magnetic disk. The low power consumption of flash memory makes it particularly attractive for laptop and notebook computers which use battery power. We can expect to see more and more of these "semiconductor disk drives"—that is, flash memory cards made up of several flash ICs and control logic—being used in place of the slower, bulkier, less reliable, and more power-hungry disk drives.

Review Questions

1. What is firmware?
2. Describe how a computer uses a bootstrap program.
3. What is a code converter?
4. What are the main elements of a function generator?
5. Why are flash memory modules a feasible alternative to auxiliary disk storage?

11-10   PROGRAMMABLE LOGIC DEVICES (PLDs)

Logic designers have a wide range of standard ICs available to them with numerous logic functions and logic circuit arrangements on a chip. In addition, these ICs are available from many manufacturers and at a reasonably low cost. For these reasons, designers have been interconnecting standard ICs to form an almost endless variety of different circuits and systems and will continue to do so in the indefinite future.

However, there are some problems with circuit and system designs that use only standard ICs. Some system designs might require hundreds or thousands of these ICs. This large number of ICs requires a considerable amount of circuit board space and a great deal of time and cost in inserting, soldering, and testing of the ICs. The equipment manufacturer must keep a significant inventory of all of the different types of ICs used in the design. Reducing the number of ICs used in a design can have several advantages: less board space and therefore fewer printed circuit boards and smaller enclosures; lower power requirements (smaller power supplies); faster and less costly assembly processes; higher reliability, since there are fewer ICs and circuit connections that can fail; and easier troubleshooting.

In order to reduce the number of ICs to be used in a design, it is necessary to put more and more logic functions on a chip. This, of course, has been done with LSI and VLSI technologies for standard functions such as memory, microprocessors, voice synthesizers, calculator chips, and so on. These devices contain hundreds and thousands of logic gates internally interconnected to operate in a predefined way. There are many design situations, however, for which there is no LSI or VLSI solution. These situations have typically required designers to interconnect several SSI and MSI chips to achieve the necessary logic functions. The recent development of **programmable logic devices (PLDs)** has presented logic designers with a way to replace a large number of standard ICs with a single IC.

A PLD is an IC that contains large numbers of gates, FFs, and registers that are interconnected on the chip. Many of the connections, however, are fusible links that can be broken. The IC is said to be *programmable* because the specific function of the IC for a given application is determined by the selective breaking of some of the interconnections while leaving others intact. The "fuse-blowing" process can be done by the manufacturer in accordance with the customer's instructions, or it can be done by the customer. This process is called **programming** because it produces the desired circuit pattern interconnecting the gates, FFs, registers, and so on.

Basic Idea

Figure 11-19 demonstrates the basic idea used by programmable logic ICs. It shows an array of AND gates and an array of OR gates, the latter of which can be interconnected to generate four outputs, each of which can be any logic function of the two input variables A and B.

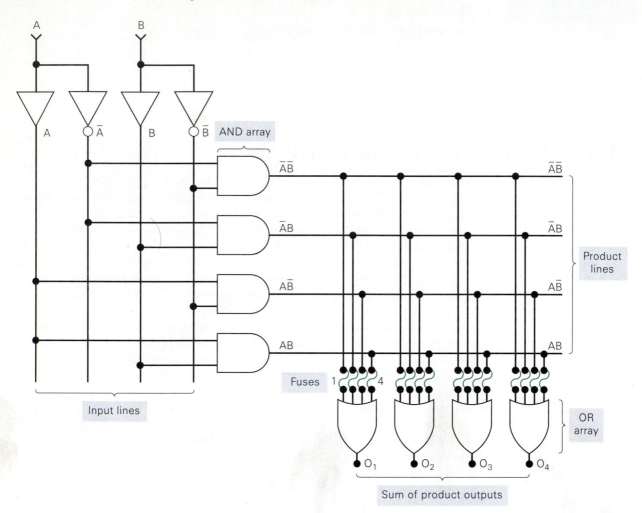

FIGURE 11-19 Example of a programmable logic device.

Each input feeds both a noninverting buffer and an inverting buffer to produce the true and inverted forms of each variable. These are the *input lines* to the AND gate array. Each AND gate is connected to two different input lines so as to generate a unique product of the input variables. The AND outputs are called the *product lines*.

Each of the product lines is connected to one of the four inputs of each OR gate through a fusible link. With all of the links initially intact, each OR output will be a constant 1. Here's the proof:

$$O_1 = \overline{A}\,\overline{B} + \overline{A}B + A\overline{B} + AB$$
$$= \overline{A}(\overline{B} + B) + A(\overline{B} + B)$$
$$= \overline{A} + A = 1$$

Each of the four outputs O_1, O_2, O_3, and O_4 can be *programmed* to be any function of A and B by selectively blowing the appropriate fuses. PLDs are designed so that a blown OR input acts as a logic 0. For example, if we blow fuses 1 and 4 at OR gate 1, the O_1 output becomes

$$O_1 = 0 + \overline{A}B + A\overline{B} + 0 = \overline{A}B + A\overline{B}$$

We can program each of the OR outputs to any desired function in a similar manner. Once all of the outputs have been programmed, the device will permanently generate the selected output functions.

PLD Symbology

The example in Figure 11-19 has only two input variables, and the circuit diagram is already quite cluttered. You can imagine how messy the diagram would be for PLDs with many more inputs. For this reason, PLD manufacturers have adopted a simplified symbology to represent the internal circuitry of these devices.

Figure 11-20 shows an example of the symbology for a four-input AND gate. First note that the input buffers are represented as a single buffer with two outputs. Next, note that a single line is shown going into the AND gate to represent the four inputs. The connections from the input variable lines to the AND gate are indicated as either an X or a dot. An X represents an intact fuse. A dot represents a hard-wired connection (i.e., one that cannot be changed). The absence of either of these indicates no connection. In this example, inputs A and $\overline{B}$ are connected to the AND gate to generate the product $A\overline{B}$. The $\overline{A}$ and B inputs are not connected to the AND gate (no X or dot), so they have no effect on its output. The important thing to understand about this symbology is that the AND gate has *four* different inputs even though only a single line is shown. The actual inputs that get connected to the AND gate are symbolized by the X's and/or the dots.

FIGURE 11-20   Simplified symbology for PLDs.

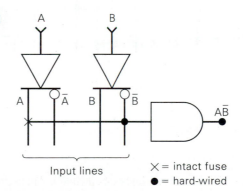

PLD Architectures—the PROM

Several common architectures are used for PLDs. The first one we will examine is the PROM. Figure 11-21(a) shows a 16 × 4 PROM which can also function as a type of PLD. It has four inputs that are completely decoded by the AND array; that is, each gate generates one of the 16 possible AND products. The connections from the input lines to the AND array are hard-wired, whereas the connections from the AND output product lines to the OR gate inputs are all programmable.

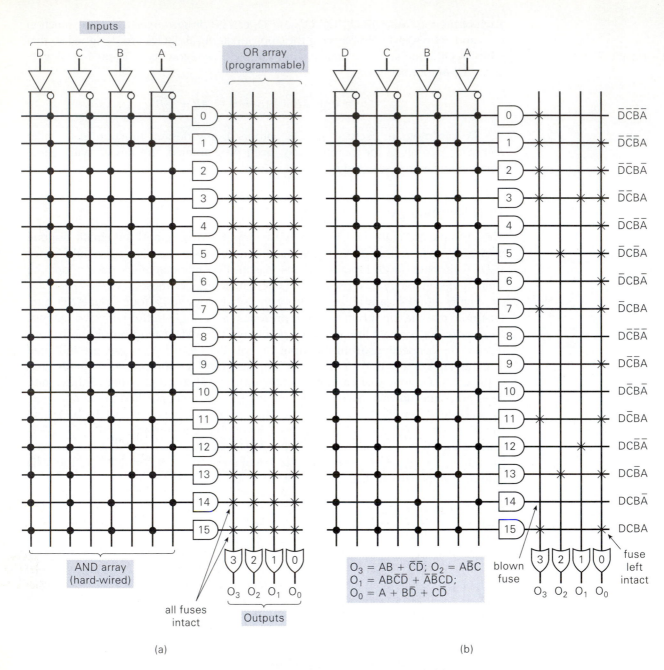

FIGURE 11-21 (a) PROM architecture makes it suitable for PLDs; (b) fuses are blown to program outputs for given functions.

Figure 11-21(b) shows how the PROM would be programmed to generate four specified logic functions. Let's follow the procedure for output $O_3 = AB + \overline{C}\,\overline{D}$. The first step is to draw a truth table showing the desired O_3 output level for all possible input combinations (Table 11-2).

Next, write down the AND products for those cases where the output is to be a 1. The O_3 output is to be the OR sum of these products. Thus, only the fuses that

TABLE 11-2

D	C	B	A	O_3		
0	0	0	0	1	→	$\overline{D}\,\overline{C}\,\overline{B}\,\overline{A}$
0	0	0	1	1	→	$\overline{D}\,\overline{C}\,\overline{B}A$
0	0	1	0	1	→	$\overline{D}\,\overline{C}B\overline{A}$
0	0	1	1	1	→	$\overline{D}\,\overline{C}BA$
0	1	0	0	0		
0	1	0	1	0		
0	1	1	0	0		
0	1	1	1	1	→	$\overline{D}CBA$
1	0	0	0	0		
1	0	0	1	0		
1	0	1	0	0		
1	0	1	1	1	→	$D\overline{C}BA$
1	1	0	0	0		
1	1	0	1	0		
1	1	1	0	0		
1	1	1	1	1	→	$DCBA$

connect these product terms to the inputs of OR gate 3 are to be left intact. All others are to be blown, as indicated in Figure 11-21(b). This same procedure is followed to determine the status of the fuses at the other OR gate inputs.

The PROM can generate any possible logic function of the input variables because it generates every possible AND product term. In general, any application that requires every input combination to be available is a good candidate for a PROM. However, PROMs become impractical when a large number of input variables must be accommodated, because the number of fuses doubles for each added input variable.

An example of an actual PROM that is used as a PLD is the AM27S13, which is a 512 × 4 PROM manufactured using high-speed Schottky TTL technology. Since $512 = 2^9$, this PROM has nine address inputs and four data outputs. Thus, the AM27S13 can be programmed to generate four outputs, each of which can be any logic function of the nine different inputs.

Programmable Array Logic (PAL)

The PROM architecture is well suited for those applications where every possible input combination is required to generate the output functions. Examples are code converters and data storage tables. Many applications, however, do not require that all input combinations be programmable. For example, not all of the logic functions shown in Figure 11-21(b) use all of the available AND product lines. This has led to the development of a class of PLDs called **programmable array logic (PAL).** The architecture of a PAL differs slightly from that of a PROM, as shown in Figure 11-22(a).

The PAL has the same AND and OR arrays as with PROMs, but in the PAL the inputs to the AND gates are programmable whereas the inputs to the OR gates are

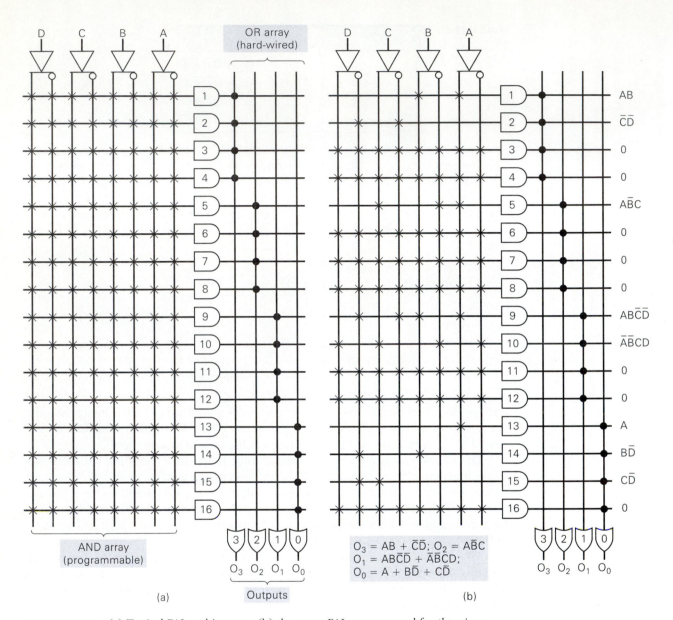

D C B A   OR array (hard-wired)   D C B A

1
2
3
4
5
6
7
8
9
10
11
12
13
14
15
16

AND array (programmable)

3 2 1 0

O_3 O_2 O_1 O_0

(a)

Outputs

1 — AB
2 — $\overline{C}\overline{D}$
3 — 0
4 — 0
5 — $A\overline{B}C$
6 — 0
7 — 0
8 — 0
9 — $AB\overline{C}\overline{D}$
10 — $\overline{A}BCD$
11 — 0
12 — 0
13 — A
14 — $B\overline{D}$
15 — $C\overline{D}$
16 — 0

$O_3 = AB + \overline{C}\overline{D}$; $O_2 = A\overline{B}C$
$O_1 = AB\overline{C}\overline{D} + \overline{A}BCD$;
$O_0 = A + B\overline{D} + C\overline{D}$

3 2 1 0

O_3 O_2 O_1 O_0

(b)

FIGURE 11-22 (a) Typical PAL architecture; (b) the same PAL programmed for the given functions.

hard-wired. This means that every AND gate can be programmed to generate any desired product of the four input variables and their complements. Each OR gate is hard-wired to only four AND outputs. This limits each output function to four product terms. If a function requires more than four product terms, it cannot be implemented with this PAL; one having more OR inputs would have to be used. If fewer than four product terms are required, the unneeded ones can be made 0.

Figure 11-22(b) shows how this PAL is programmed to generate four specified logic functions. Let's follow the procedure for output $O_3 = AB + \overline{C}\,\overline{D}$. First, we must express this output as the OR sum of four terms because the OR gates have four inputs. We do this by putting in 0s. Thus, we have

$$O_3 = AB + \overline{C}\,\overline{D} + 0 + 0$$

Next, we must determine how to program the inputs to AND gates 1, 2, 3, and 4 so that they provide the correct product terms to OR gate 3. We do this term by term. The first term, *AB,* is obtained by leaving intact the fuses that connect inputs *A* and *B* to AND gate 1 and by blowing all other fuses on that line. Likewise, the second term, $\overline{C}\,\overline{D}$, is obtained by leaving intact only the fuses that connect inputs $\overline{C}$ and $\overline{D}$ to AND gate 2. The third term is a 0. A constant 0 is produced at the output of AND gate 3 by leaving all of its input fuses intact. This would produce an output of $A\overline{A}B\overline{B}C\overline{C}D\overline{D}$, which, as we know, is 0. The fourth term is also 0, so the input fuses to AND gate 4 are also left intact.

The inputs to the other AND gates are programmed in a like manner to generate the other output functions. Note especially that many of the AND gates have all of their input fuses intact, since they need to generate 0s.

An example of an actual PAL integrated circuit is the PAL18L8A from Texas Instruments, Inc. It is manufactured using low-power Schottky technology and has ten logic inputs and eight output functions. Each output OR gate is hard-wired to seven AND gate outputs, and so it can generate functions that include up to seven terms. An added feature of this particular PAL is that six of the eight outputs are fed back into the AND array, where they can be connected as inputs to any AND gate. This makes it very useful in generating all sorts of combinational logic.

Polarity Fuse

Many PLDs include a **programmable output polarity** feature that gives the designer the option to invert any of the device outputs. This is illustrated in Figure 11-23, where an EX-OR gate and a *polarity fuse* have been added to the OR gate output. The EX-OR gate acts as a controlled inverter which will invert or not, depending on the state of the fuse. When the fuse is intact (logic 0), the EX-OR will pass the OR gate output with no inversion; when the fuse is open (logic 1), the EX-OR will invert the OR gate output.

This programmable output feature is available on many PAL devices, including the GAL16V8, which we will study in detail in Chapter 12.

Other PLD Features

Many PLDs include one or more of the following as part of their architecture: FFs, latches, input registers, and output registers. Very often the operating characteristics of these devices are programmable, as are the connections to the other devices on the chip. This gives the logic designer a great deal of flexibility in designing counters and other sequential logic circuits. This type of PLD is sometimes called a *programmable logic sequencer.*

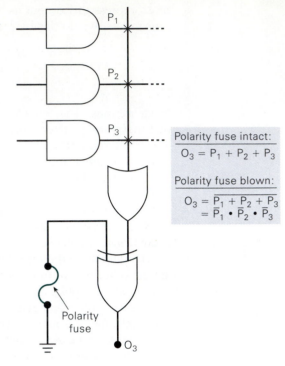

FIGURE 11-23   Many PLDs include a programmable polarity feature that provides the option of inverting any of the output functions.

Other PLDs

The **field programmable logic array (FPLA)** was developed in the mid-1970s as the first nonmemory programmable logic device. It used a programmable AND array as well as a programmable OR array. Although the FPLA is more flexible than the PAL architecture, it was not as widely accepted by engineers. FPLAs are used mostly in state-machine design where a large number of product terms are needed in each SOP expression.

Complex PLDs (CPLDs), also referred to as *multilevel arrays,* are devices that combine a number of PAL-type circuits on the same chip. The logic blocks themselves are programmable AND, fixed OR, with fewer product terms than most PAL devices. When more product terms are needed, an expander NAND array can be connected as an input term, or several logic blocks can be combined to implement the expression.

Field programmable gate arrays (FPGAs) offer a number of configurable logic blocks that contain programmable combinational logic and registers for sequential circuits. There is also a set of input/output blocks that can be configured as fixed input, fixed output, or bidirectional. The outputs have tristate capability, and registers can be used to latch incoming or outgoing data. All of the configurable logic blocks and input/output blocks can be programmably interconnected to implement virtually any logic circuit.

Obviously, any device that is programmed to implement a logic design is application-specific. The term **application-specific integrated circuit (ASIC)** is most commonly used to describe a user-defined IC that may contain analog as well as digital circuitry and that is generally mask-programmed or manufactured as a fully custom device. Many products today, such as personal computers, television sets, CD players, and a host of telecommunications products, use ASICs to achieve their high-tech results in a very small package.

Programming

When PLDs were first introduced, the logic designer would develop a *fuse map* which showed which fuses to blow and would send the map off to the PROM, PAL, or FPLA manufacturer. The manufacturer would then program the device according to the fuse map, test it, and ship it off to the designer. In recent years the availability of relatively inexpensive programming equipment has made it convenient for users to program their own PLDs. There are universal programmers on the market that can program most common PROMs, PALs, and FPLAs. The device to be programmed is plugged into a socket on the programmer, and the programmer will program and test the device according to data that have been supplied by the user.

The programming and test data are typically developed using commonly available software that will run on standard PCs. Using this software, the user enters data into the computer describing the logic functions he wants programmed into the PLD, as well as information on how the device is to be tested. The software then generates a fuse map and test data in a form that can be sent over a cable to the PLD programmer's memory. Once the programmer has the data, it can proceed to program and test the device. When finished, the programmer will indicate whether the device has passed or failed the testing procedure. If it passes, it can be removed from the programmer's socket and placed in the prototype circuit for further testing.

Figure 11-24 is a flowchart showing the various steps in the process of designing, programming, and testing a PLD. In Chapter 12 we will go through this complete process using the GAL16V8 chip and CUPL—one of the more popular PLD

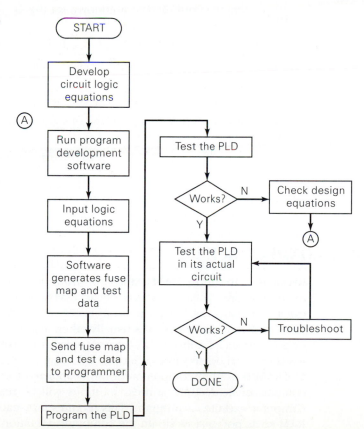

FIGURE 11-24   Flowchart of PLD designing, programming, and testing process.

program development software packages. A disk containing the CUPL software will be provided to instructors using this book so that you can try out the chapter examples and exercises and can develop your own design projects.

Erasable PLDs

The PLDs we have been talking about are programmed by zapping fuses. Once a fuse is zapped, it cannot be reconnected. Thus, if you make a mistake in programming, or if you want to change the design, the device will no longer be useful and you might as well drop it into the wastebasket. This drawback has been addressed by several companies that have developed PLDs that can be erased and reprogrammed over and over. Called *erasable programmable logic devices (EPLDs)*, these devices are programmed and erased just like EEPROMs. The GAL16V8 is such a device. In erasable PLDs, the fuses are electronic switches rather than fusible links, so their state (open or closed) can be electrically changed over and over just as an EEPROM memory cell can be electrically erased and reprogrammed.

Review Questions

1. What is a PLD?
2. What would output O_1 be in Figure 11-19 if fuses 1 and 2 were blown?
3. What does an X represent on a PLD diagram?
4. What does a dot represent on a PLD diagram?
5. Verify that the correct fuses are blown for the O_2, O_1, and O_0 functions in Figure 11-21(b).
6. How does the architecture of a PAL differ from that of a PROM?
7. Verify that the correct fuses are blown for the O_2, O_1, and O_0 functions in Figure 11-22(b).
8. How does the architecture of FLPAs differ from that of PROMs and PALs?
9. What are the steps involved in the designing, programming, and testing of a PLD?
10. What capability does a polarity fuse give a PLD designer?
11. What is the main advantage of an EPLD?
12. Which device offers greater functionality, an FPGA or a CPLD?

11-11 SEMICONDUCTOR RAM

Recall that the term **RAM** stands for *random-access memory,* meaning that any memory address location is as easily accessible as any other. Many types of memory can be classified as having random access, but when the term *RAM* is used with semiconductor memories, it is usually taken to mean read/write memory (RWM) as opposed to ROM. Since it is common practice to use RAM to mean semiconductor RWM, we will do so throughout the following discussions.

RAM is used in computers for the *temporary* storage of programs and data. The contents of many RAM address locations will be read from and written to as the computer executes a program. This requires fast read and write cycle times for the RAM so as not to slow down the computer operation.

A major disadvantage of RAM is that it is volatile and will lose all stored information if power is interrupted or turned off. Some CMOS RAMs, however, use such small amounts of power in the standby mode (no read or write operations taking place) that they can be powered from batteries whenever the main power is interrupted. Of course, the main advantage of RAM is that it can be written into and read from rapidly with equal ease.

The following discussion of RAM will draw on some of the material covered in our treatment of ROM, since many of the basic concepts are common to both types of memory.

11-12   RAM ARCHITECTURE

As with the ROM, it is helpful to think of the RAM as consisting of a number of registers, each storing a single data word, and each having a unique address. RAMs typically come with word capacities of 1K, 4K, 8K, 16K, 64K, 128K, 256K, and 1024K, and with word sizes of 1, 4, or 8 bits. As we will see later, the word capacity and the word size can be expanded by combining memory chips.

Figure 11-25 shows the simplified architecture of a RAM that stores 64 words of four bits each (i.e., a 64×4 memory). These words have addresses ranging from 0 to 63_{10}. In order to select one of the 64 address locations for reading or writing, a binary address code is applied to a decoder circuit. Since $64 = 2^6$, the decoder requires a six-bit input code. Each address code activates one particular decoder output, which, in turn, enables its corresponding register. For example, assume an applied address code of

$$A_5A_4A_3A_2A_1A_0 = 011010$$

Since $011010_2 = 26_{10}$, decoder output 26 will go high, selecting register 26 for either a read or a write operation.

Read Operation

The address code picks out one register in the memory chip for reading or writing. In order to *read* the contents of the selected register, the READ/WRITE ($R/\overline{W}$)* input must be a 1. In addition, the CHIP SELECT ($\overline{CS}$) input must be activated (a 0 in this case). The combination of $R/\overline{W} = 1$ and $\overline{CS} = 0$ enables the output buffers so that the contents of the selected register will appear at the four data outputs. $R/\overline{W} = 1$ also *disables* the input buffers so that the data inputs do not affect the memory during a read operation.

Write Operation

To write a new four-bit word into the selected register requires $R/\overline{W} = 0$ and $\overline{CS} = 0$. This combination *enables* the input buffers so that the four-bit word applied to the data inputs will be loaded into the selected register. The $R/\overline{W} = 0$ also *disables*

---

*   Some manufacturers use the symbol $\overline{WE}$ (write enable) or $\overline{W}$ instead of $R/\overline{W}$. In any case, the operation is the same.

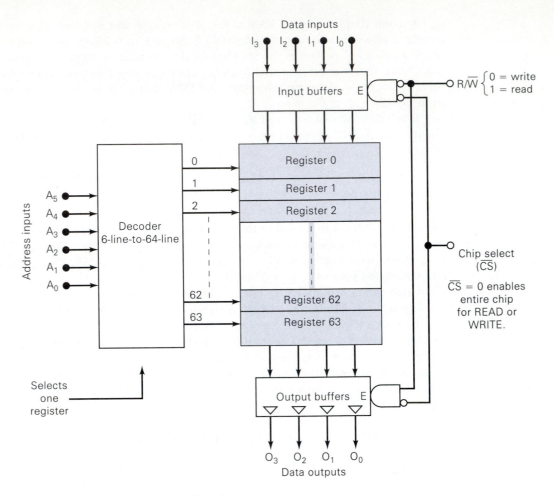

FIGURE 11-25 Internal organization of a 64×4 RAM.

the output buffers, which are tristate, so that the data outputs are in their Hi-Z state during a write operation. The write operation, of course, destroys the word that was previously stored at that address.

Chip Select

Most memory chips have one or more *CS* inputs which are used to enable the entire chip or disable it completely. In the disabled mode all data inputs and data outputs are disabled (Hi-Z) so that neither a read nor a write operation can take place. In this mode the contents of the memory are unaffected. The reason for having *CS* inputs will become clear when we combine memory chips to obtain larger memories. Note that many manufacturers call these inputs CHIP ENABLE (*CE*). When the *CS* or *CE* inputs are in their active state, the memory chip is said to be *selected*; otherwise it is said to be *deselected*. Many memory ICs are designed to consume much lower power when they are deselected. In large memory systems, for a given memory operation, one or more memory chips will be selected while all others are deselected. More will be said on this later.

Common Input/Output Pins

In order to conserve pins on an IC package, manufacturers often combine the data input and data output functions using common input/output pins. The $R/\overline{W}$ input controls the function of these I/O pins. During a read operation, the I/O pins act as data outputs which reproduce the contents of the selected address location. During a write operation, the I/O pins act as data inputs to which the data to be written are applied.

We can see why this is done by considering the chip in Figure 11-25. With separate input and output pins, a total of 18 pins is required (including ground and power supply). With four common I/O pins, only 14 pins are required. The pin saving becomes even more significant for chips with larger word size.

EXAMPLE 11-9

The 2147H is an NMOS RAM that is organized as a 4K × 1 with separate data input and output and a single active-LOW chip select input. Draw the logic symbol for this chip, showing all pin functions.

Solution

The logic symbol is shown in Figure 11-26(a).

FIGURE 11-26 Logic symbols for (a) the 2147H RAM chip; (b) the MCM6206C RAM.

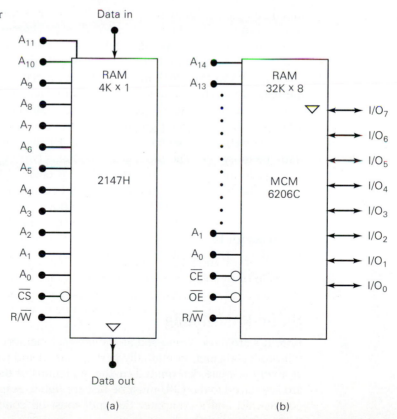

EXAMPLE
11-10

The MCM6206C is a CMOS RAM with 32K × 8 capacity, common I/O pins, an active-LOW chip enable, and an active-LOW output enable. Draw the logic symbol.

Solution

The logic symbol is shown in Figure 11-26(b).

Review Questions

1. Describe the input conditions needed to read a word from a specific RAM address location.
2. Why do some RAM chips have common input/output pins?
3. How many pins are required for the MCM6208C 64K × 4 RAM with one *CS* input and common I/O?

11-13 STATIC RAM (SRAM)

The RAM operation that we have been discussing up to this point applies to a **static RAM**—one that can store data as long as power is applied to the chip. Static-RAM memory cells are essentially flip-flops that will stay in a given state (store a bit) indefinitely, provided that power to the circuit is not interrupted. Later we will describe **dynamic RAMs,** which store data as charges on capacitors. With dynamic RAMs the stored data will gradually disappear because of capacitor discharge, so that it is necessary to periodically **refresh** the data (i.e., recharge the capacitors).

Static RAMs **(SRAMs)** are available in bipolar, MOS, and BiCMOS technologies; the majority of applications use NMOS or CMOS RAMs. As stated earlier, the bipolars have the advantage in speed (although CMOS is gradually closing the gap), and MOS devices have much greater capacities and lower power consumption. Figure 11-27 shows for comparison a typical bipolar static memory cell and a typical NMOS static memory cell. The bipolar cell contains two bipolar transistors and two resistors, while the NMOS cell contains four N-channel MOSFETs. The bipolar cell requires more chip area than the MOS cell because a bipolar transistor is more complex than a MOSFET, and because the bipolar cell requires separate resistors while the MOS cell uses MOSFETS as resistors (Q_3 and Q_4). A CMOS memory cell would be similar to the NMOS cell except that it would use P-channel MOSFETs in place of Q_3 and Q_4. This results in the lowest power consumption but increases the chip complexity.

Static-RAM Timing

RAM ICs are most often used as the internal memory of a computer. The CPU (central processing unit) continually performs read and write operations on this memory at a very fast rate determined by the limitations of the CPU. The memory chips that are interfaced to the CPU must be fast enough to respond to the CPU read and write commands, and a computer designer must be concerned with the RAM's various timing characteristics.

FIGURE 11-27 Typical bipolar and NMOS static-RAM cells.

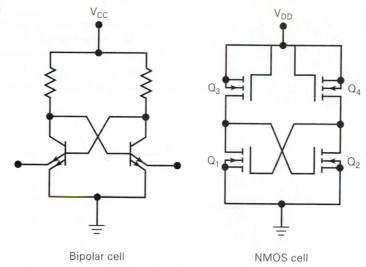

Bipolar cell   NMOS cell

Not all RAMs have the same timing characteristics, but most of them are similar, and so we will use a typical set of characteristics for illustrative purposes. The nomenclature for the different timing parameters will vary from one manufacturer to another, but the meaning of each parameter is usually easy to determine from the memory timing diagrams on the RAM data sheets. Figure 11-28 shows the timing diagrams for a complete read cycle and a complete write cycle for a typical RAM chip.

Read Cycle

The waveforms in Figure 11-28(a) show how the address, $R/\overline{W}$, and chip select inputs behave during a memory read cycle. As noted, the CPU supplies these input signals to the RAM when it wants to read data from a specific RAM address location. Although a RAM may have many address inputs coming from the CPU's address bus, for clarity the diagram shows only two. The RAM's data output is also shown; we will assume that this particular RAM has one data output. Recall that the RAM's data output is connected to the CPU data bus (Figure 11-5).

The read cycle begins at time t_0. Prior to that time, the address inputs will be whatever address is on the address bus from the preceding operation. Since the RAM's chip select is not active, it will not respond to his "old" address. Note that the $R/\overline{W}$ line is HIGH prior to t_0 and stays HIGH throughout the read cycle. In most memory systems, $R/\overline{W}$ is normally kept in the HIGH state except when it is driven LOW during a write cycle. The RAM's data output is in its Hi-Z state since $\overline{CS} = 1$.

At t_0, the CPU applies a new address to the RAM inputs; this is the address of the location to be read. After allowing time for the address signals to stabilize, the C $\overline{CS}$ line is activated. The RAM responds by placing the data from the addressed location onto the data output line at t_1. The time between t_0 and t_1 is the RAM's access time, t_{ACC}, and is the time between the application of the new address and the appearance of valid output data. The timing parameter, t_{CO}, is the time it takes for the RAM output to go from Hi-Z to a valid data level once $\overline{CS}$ is activated.

At time t_2, the $\overline{CS}$ is returned HIGH, and the RAM output returns to its Hi-Z state after a time interval, t_{OD}. Thus, the RAM data will be on the data bus between t_1 and

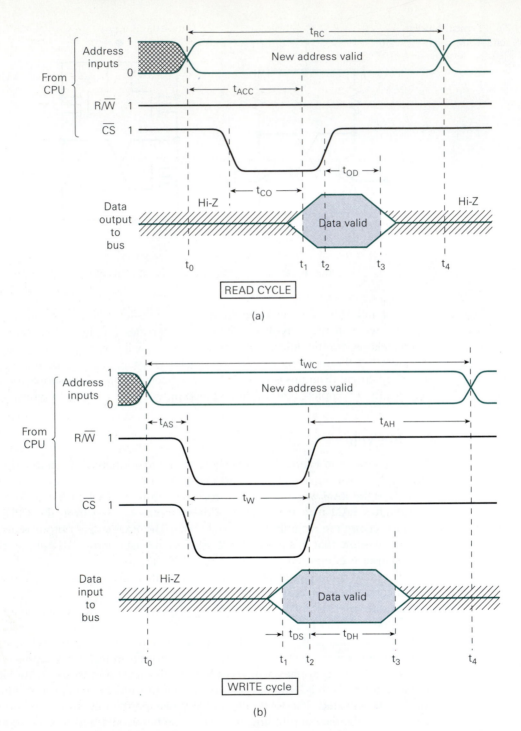

(a)

WRITE cycle

(b)

FIGURE 11-28   Typical timing for static RAM: (a) read cycle; (b) write cycle.

t_3. The CPU can take the data from the data bus at any point during this interval. In most computers, the CPU will use the PGT of the $\overline{CS}$ signal at t_2 to latch these data into one of its internal registers.

The complete read cycle time, t_{RC}, extends from t_0 to t_4, when the CPU changes the address inputs to a different address for the next read or write cycle.

Write Cycle

Figure 11-28(b) shows the signal activity for a write cycle that begins when the CPU supplies a new address to the RAM at a time t_0. The CPU drives the $R/\overline{W}$ and $\overline{CS}$ lines LOW after waiting for a time interval t_{AS}, called the *address setup time*. This gives the RAM's address decoders time to respond to the new address. $R/\overline{W}$ and $\overline{CS}$ are held LOW for a time interval t_W, called the *write time interval*.

During this write time interval, at time t_1 the CPU applies valid data to the data bus to be written into the RAM. These data must be held at the RAM input for at least a time interval t_{DS} prior to, and for at least a time interval t_{DH} after, the deactivation of $R/\overline{W}$ and $\overline{CS}$ at t_2. The t_{DS} interval is called the *data setup time*, and t_{DH} is called the *data hold time*. Similarly, the address inputs must remain stable for the address hold time interval, t_{AH}, after t_2. If any of these setup time or hold time requirements are not met, the write operation will not take place reliably.

The complete write-cycle time, t_{WC}, extends from t_0 to t_4, when the CPU changes the address lines to a new address for the next read or write cycle.

The read-cycle time, t_{RC}, and write-cycle time, t_{WC}, are what essentially determine how fast a memory chip can operate. For example, in an actual application, a CPU will often be reading successive data words from memory one right after the other. If the memory has a t_{RC} of 50 ns, the CPU can read one word every 50 ns, or 20 million words per second; with $t_{RC} = 10$ ns, the CPU can read 100 million words per second. Table 11-3 shows the minimum read-cycle and write-cycle times for some representative static-RAM chips.

TABLE 11-3

Device	t_{RC}(min) (ns)	t_{WC}(min) (ns)
CMOS MCM6206C, 32K × 8	15	15
NMOS 2147H, 4K × 1	35	35
BiCMOS MCM6708A, 64K × 4	8	8

Actual SRAM Chip

An example of an actual SRAM IC is the MCM6264C CMOS 8K × 8 RAM with read-cycle and write-cycle times of 12 ns and a standby power consumption of only 100 mW. The logic symbol for this IC is shown in Figure 11-29. Notice that it has 13 address inputs, since $2^{13} = 8192 = 8K$, and eight data I/O lines. The four control inputs determine the device's operating mode according to the accompanying mode table.

The $\overline{WE}$ input is the same as the $R/\overline{W}$ input that we have been using. A LOW at $\overline{WE}$ will write data into the RAM, provided that the device is selected—both chip select inputs are active. Note that the "&" symbol is used to denote that *both* must

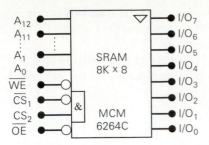

	Inputs				
Mode	$\overline{WE}$	$\overline{CS_1}$	CS_2	$\overline{OE}$	I/O pins
READ	1	0	1	0	DATA$_{OUT}$
WRITE	0	0	1	X	DATA$_{IN}$
Output disable	1	X	X	1	High Z
Not selected (power down)	X	1	X	X	High Z
	X	X	0	X	

X = don't care

FIGURE 11-29   Symbol and mode table for the CMOS MCM6264C.

be active. A HIGH at $\overline{WE}$ will produce the read operation, provided that the device is selected and the output buffers are enabled by $\overline{OE}$ = LOW. When deselected, the device is in its low-power mode, and none of the other inputs have any effect.

Most of the devices that have been discussed in this chapter are available from a number of different manufacturers. Each manufacturer may offer a number of different devices of the same dimension (e.g., 32K × 8) but with different specifications or features. There are also various types of packaging available such as DIP, PLCC, and various forms of gull-wing, surface-mount.

As you look at the various memory devices that have been described in this chapter, you will notice some similarities. For example, look at the chips in Figure 11-30 and take note of the pin assignments. The fact that the same function is assigned to the same pins on all of these diverse devices, manufactured by different companies, is no coincidence. Industry standards created by the Joint Electronic Device Engineering Council (**JEDEC**) have led to memory devices that are very interchangeable.

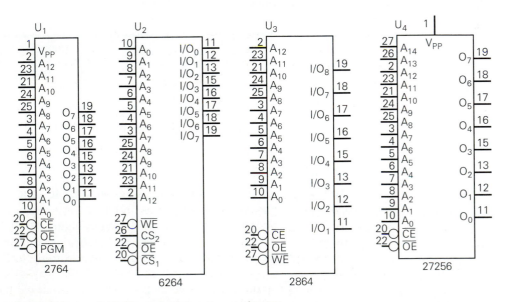

FIGURE 11-30   JEDEC standard memory packaging.

EXAMPLE 11-11

A system is wired for an 8K × 8 ROM chip (2764) and two 8K × 8 SRAM chips (6264). The entire 8K of ROM space is being used for storage of the microprocessor's instructions. You want to upgrade the system to have some nonvolatile read/write storage. Can the existing circuit be modified to accommodate the new revisions?

Solution

A 2864 EEPROM chip can simply be substituted into one of the RAM sockets. The only functional difference is the much longer write-cycle time requirements of the EEPROM. This can usually be handled by changing the program of the microcomputer that is using the memory device. Since there is no room left in the ROM for these changes, we need a larger ROM. A 32K × 8 ROM (27C256) has basically the same pin-out as a 2764. We simply need to connect two more address lines (A_{13} and A_{14}) to the ROM socket and replace the old chip with a 27C256 chip.

Many memory systems take advantage of the versatility that the JEDEC standards provide. The pins that are common for all of the devices are hard-wired to the system buses. The few pins that are different between the various devices are connected to circuitry that can easily be modified to configure the system for the proper size and type of memory device. This allows the user to reconfigure the hardware without needing to cut or solder on the board. The configuration circuitry can be as simple as movable jumpers or DIP switches that the user sets up and as complicated as an in-circuit programmable logic device that the computer can set up or modify to meet the system requirements.

Review Questions

1. How does a static-RAM cell differ from a dynamic-RAM cell?
2. Which memory technology generally uses the least power?
3. What device places data on the data bus during a read cycle?
4. What device places data on the data bus during a write cycle?
5. What RAM timing parameters determine its operating speed?
6. *True or false:* A LOW at $\overline{OE}$ will enable the output buffers of an MCM6264C provided that both chip select inputs are active.
7. What must be done with pin 26 and pin 27 if a 27256 is replaced with a 2764?

11-14   DYNAMIC RAM (DRAM)

Dynamic RAMs are fabricated using MOS technology and are noted for their high capacity, low power requirement, and moderate operating speed. As we stated earlier, unlike static RAMs, which store information in FFs, dynamic RAMs store 1s and 0s as charges on a small MOS capacitor (typically a few picofarads). Because of the tendency for these charges to leak off after a period of time, dynamic RAMs require periodic recharging of the memory cells; this is called **refreshing** the dynamic RAM. In modern DRAM chips, each memory cell must be refreshed typically every 2, 4, or 8 ms, or its data will be lost.

The need for refreshing is a drawback of dynamic RAM as compared to static RAM because it may require external support circuitry. Some DRAM chips have built-in refresh control circuitry that does not require extra external hardware but does require special timing of the chip's input control signals. Additionally, as we shall see, the address inputs to a DRAM must be handled in a less straightforward way than SRAM. So, all in all, designing with and using DRAM in a system is more complex than with SRAM. However, their much larger capacities and much lower power consumption make DRAMs the memory of choice in systems where the most important design considerations are keeping down size, cost, and power.

For applications where speed and reduced complexity are more critical than cost, space, and power considerations, static RAMs are still the best. They are generally faster than dynamic RAMs and require no refresh operation. They are simpler to design with, but they cannot compete with the higher capacity and lower power requirement of dynamic RAMs.

Because of their simple cell structure, DRAMs typically have four times the density of SRAMs. This increased density allows four times as much memory capacity to be placed on a single board, or alternatively it requires one-fourth as much board space for the same amount of memory. The cost per bit of dynamic RAM storage is typically one-fifth to one-fourth that of static RAMs. A further cost saving is realized because the lower power requirements of a dynamic RAM, typically one-sixth to one-half those of a static RAM, allow the use of smaller, less expensive power supplies.

The main applications of SRAMs are in areas where only small amounts of memory are needed (up to 64K) or where high speed is required. Many microprocessor-controlled instruments and appliances have very small memory capacity requirements. Some instruments, such as digital storage oscilloscopes and logic analyzers, require very high-speed memory. For applications such as these, SRAM is normally used.

The main internal memory of most personal microcomputers (e.g., Windows-based PCs or Macs) uses DRAM because of its high capacity and low power consumption. These computers, however, sometimes use some small amounts of SRAM for functions requiring maximum speed, such as video graphics, look-up tables, and cache memory.

Review Questions

1. What are the main drawbacks of dynamic RAM compared with static?
2. List the advantages of dynamic RAM compared with static RAM.
3. Which type of RAM would you expect to see in battery-operated equipment?

11-15 DYNAMIC RAM STRUCTURE AND OPERATION

The dynamic RAM's internal architecture can be visualized as an array of single-bit cells as illustrated in Figure 11-31. Here, 16,384 cells are arranged in a 128 × 128 array. Each cell occupies a unique row and column position within the array. Fourteen address inputs are needed to select one of the cells ($2^{14} = 16{,}384$); the lower address bits, A_0 to A_6, select the row, and the higher-order bits, A_7 to A_{13}, select the column. Each 14-bit address selects a unique cell to be written into or read from. The structure in Figure 11-31 is a 16K $\times$ 1 DRAM chip. DRAM chips are currently available in capacities of up to 64 Mbits in various configurations. DRAMs with a four-bit (or greater) word size have a cell arrangement similar to that of Figure 11-31 except that each position in the array contains four cells, and each applied address selects a group of four cells for a read or a write operation. As we will see later, larger word sizes can also be attained by combining several chips in the appropriate arrangement.

FIGURE 11-31 Cell arrangement in a 16K $\times$ 1 dynamic RAM.

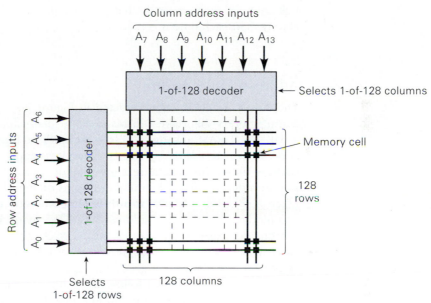

Figure 11-32 is a symbolic representation of a dynamic memory cell and its associated circuitry. Many of the circuit details are not shown, but this simplified diagram can be used to describe the essential ideas involved in writing to and reading from a DRAM. The switches SW1 through SW4 are actually MOSFETs that are controlled by various address decoder outputs and the $R/\overline{W}$ signal. The capacitor, of course, is the actual storage cell.

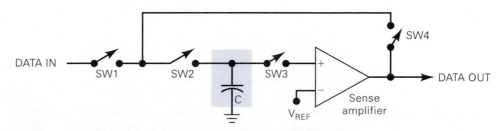

FIGURE 11-32 Symbolic representation of a dynamic memory cell. During a WRITE operation, semiconductor switches SW1 and SW2 are closed. During a read operation, all switches are closed except SW1.

To write data to the cell, signals from the address decoding and read/write logic will close switches SW1 and SW2, while keeping SW3 and SW4 open. This connects the input data to *C*. A logic 1 at the data input charges *C,* and a logic 0 discharges it. Then the switches are open so that *C* is disconnected from the rest of the circuit. Ideally, *C* would retain its charge indefinitely, but there is always some leakage path through the off switches, so that *C* will gradually lose its charge.

To read data from the cell, switches SW2, SW3, and SW4 are closed, and SW1 is kept open. This connects the stored capacitor voltage to the *sense amplifier*. The sense amplifier compares the voltage with some reference value to determine if it is a logic 0 or 1, and it produces a solid 0 V or 5 V for the data output. This data output is also connected to *C* (SW2 and SW4 are closed) and refreshes the capacitor voltage by recharging or discharging. In other words, the data bit in a memory cell is refreshed each time it is read.

Address Multiplexing

The 16K × 1 DRAM array depicted in Figure 11-31 is nearly obsolete. Only a few manufacturers still make DRAMs in such small capacities. It has 14 address inputs; a 64K × 1 DRAM array would have 16 address inputs. A 1M × 4 DRAM needs 20 address inputs; a 4M × 1 needs 22 address inputs. High-capacity memory chips such as these would require many pins if each address input required a separate pin. In order to reduce the number of pins on their high-capacity DRAM chips, manufacturers utilize **address multiplexing** whereby each address input pin can accommodate two different address bits. The saving in pin count translates to a significant decrease in the size of the IC packages. This is very important in large-capacity memory boards, where you want to maximize the amount of memory that can fit on one board.

In the discussions that follow we will be describing the order in which the address is multiplexed into the DRAM chips. It should be noted that in older, small-capacity DRAMs, the convention was to present the low-order address first specifying the row, followed by the high-order address specifying the column. The newer DRAMs and the controllers that perform the multiplexing use the opposite convention of applying the high-order bits as the row address and then the low-order bits as the column address. We will describe the more recent convention, but you should be aware of this change as you investigate older systems.

We will use the TMS44100 4M × 1 DRAM from Texas Instruments to illustrate the operation of DRAM chips today. The functional block diagram of this chip's internal architecture (shown in Figure 11-33) is typical of diagrams you will find in data books. The layout of the memory array in this diagram may appear complicated at first glance, but it can be thought of as just a bigger version of the 16K × 1 DRAM in Figure 11-31. Functionally, it is an array of cells arranged as 2048 rows by 2048 columns. A single row is selected by address decoder circuitry that can be thought of as a 1-of-2048 decoder. Likewise, a single column is selected by what is effectively a 1-of-2048 decoder. Since the address lines are multiplexed, the entire 22-bit address cannot be presented simultaneously. Notice that there are only 11 address lines and that they go to both the row and the column address registers. Each of the two address registers stores half of the 22-bit address. The row register stores the upper half, and the column register stores the lower half. Two very important **strobe** inputs control when the address information is latched. The **row address** strobe (**$\overline{RAS}$**) clocks the 11-bit row address register. The **column address strobe** (**$\overline{CAS}$**) clocks the 11-bit column address register.

A 22-bit address is applied to this DRAM in two steps using $\overline{RAS}$ and $\overline{CAS}$. The timing is shown in Figure 11-33(b). Initially, $\overline{RAS}$ and $\overline{CAS}$ are both HIGH. At time t_0, the 11-bit row address (A_{11} to A_{21}) is applied to the address inputs. After allowing time for the setup time requirement (t_{RS}) of the row address register, the $\overline{RAS}$ in-

FUNCTIONAL BLOCK DIAGRAM

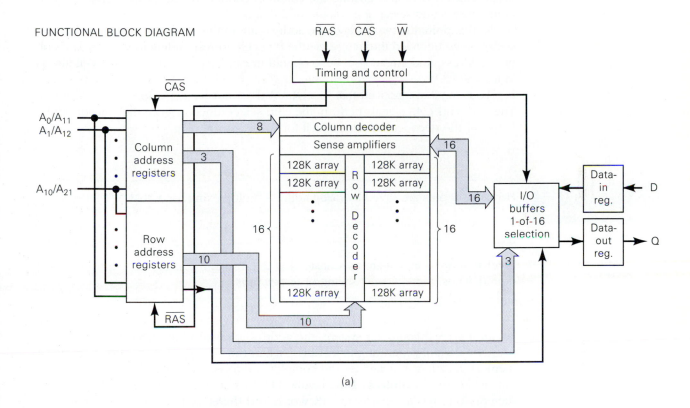

(a)

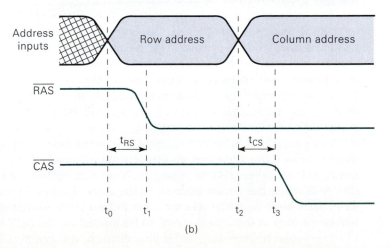

(b)

FIGURE 11-33   (a) Simplified architecture of the TMS44100 4M × 1 DRAM; (b) $\overline{RAS}/\overline{CAS}$ timing. (Courtesy of Texas Instruments.)

put is driven LOW at t_1. This NGT loads the row address into the row address register so that A_{11} to A_{21} now appear at the row decoder inputs. The LOW at $\overline{RAS}$ also enables this decoder so that it can decode the row address and select one row of the array.

At time t_2, the 11-bit column address (A_0 to A_{10}) is applied to the address inputs. At t_3, the $\overline{CAS}$ input is driven LOW to load the column address into the column address register. $\overline{CAS}$ also enables the column decoder so that it can decode the column address and select one column of the array.

At this point the two parts of the address are in their respective registers, the decoders have decoded them to select the one cell corresponding to the row and column address, and a read or a write operation can be performed on that cell just as in a static RAM.

You may have noticed that this DRAM does not have a chip select (CS) input. The $\overline{RAS}$ and $\overline{CAS}$ signals perform the chip select function since they must both be LOW for the decoders to select a cell for reading or writing.

EXAMPLE 11-12

How many pins are saved by using address multiplexing for a 16M × 1 DRAM?

Solution

Twelve address inputs are used instead of 24; $\overline{RAS}$ and $\overline{CAS}$ are added; no $\overline{CS}$ is required. Thus, there is a net saving of *eleven* pins.

In a typical computer system, the address inputs to the memory system come from the central processing unit (CPU). When the CPU wants to access a particular memory location, it generates the complete address and places it on address lines that make up an **address bus.** Figure 11-34(a) shows this for a small computer memory that has a capacity of 64K words and therefore requires a 16-line address bus going directly from the CPU to the memory.

This arrangement works for ROM or for static RAM, but it must be modified for DRAM that uses multiplexed addressing. If all 64K of the memory is DRAM, it will have only 8 address inputs. This means that the 16 address lines from the CPU address bus must be fed into a multiplexer circuit that will transmit 8 address bits at a time to the memory address inputs. This is shown symbolically in Figure 11-34(b). The multiplexer select input, labeled *MUX*, controls whether CPU address lines A_0 to A_7 or address lines A_8 to A_{15} will be present at the DRAM address inputs.

The timing of the *MUX* signal must be synchronized with the $\overline{RAS}$ and $\overline{CAS}$ signals that clock the addresses into the DRAM. This is shown in Figure 11-35. *MUX* must be LOW when $\overline{RAS}$ is pulsed LOW so that address lines A_8 to A_{15} from the CPU will reach the DRAM address inputs to be loaded on the NGT of $\overline{RAS}$. Likewise, *MUX* must be HIGH when $\overline{CAS}$ is pulsed LOW so that A_0 to A_7 from the CPU will be present at the DRAM inputs to be loaded on the NGT of $\overline{CAS}$.

The actual multiplexing and timing circuitry will not be shown here but will be left to the end-of-chapter problems (Problems 11-26 and 11-27).

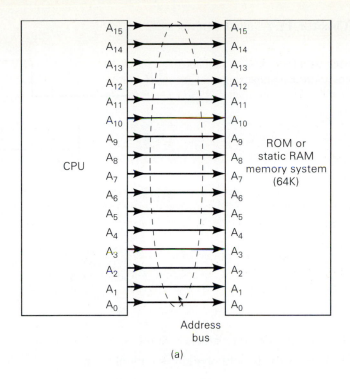

(a)

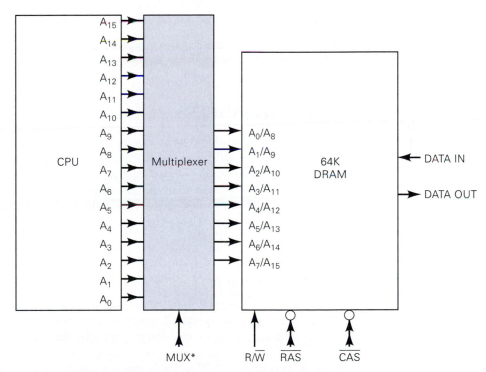

• MUX = 0 transmits CPU address $A_8 - A_{15}$ to DRAM. MUX = 1 transmits $A_0 - A_7$ to DRAM.

(b)

FIGURE 11-34 (a) CPU address bus driving ROM or static-RAM memory; (b) CPU addresses driving a multiplexer that is used to multiplex the CPU address lines into the DRAM.

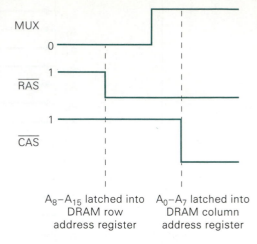

FIGURE 11-35 Timing required for address multiplexing.

A_8-A_{15} latched into DRAM row address register

A_0-A_7 latched into DRAM column address register

Review Questions

1. Describe the array structure of a 64K × 1 DRAM.
2. What is the benefit of address multiplexing?
3. How many address inputs would there be on a 1M × 1 DRAM chip?
4. What are the functions of the $\overline{RAS}$ and $\overline{CAS}$ signals?
5. What is the function of the *MUX* signal?

11-16 DRAM READ/WRITE CYCLES

The timing of the read and write operations of a DRAM is much more complex than for a static RAM, and there are many critical timing requirements that the DRAM memory designer must consider. At this point, a detailed discussion of these requirements would probably cause more confusion than enlightenment. We will concentrate on the basic timing sequence for the read and write operations for a small DRAM system like that of Figure 11-34(b).

DRAM Read Cycle

Figure 11-36 shows typical signal activity during the read operation. It is assumed that $R/\overline{W}$ is in its HIGH state throughout the operation. The following is a step-by-step description of the events that occur at the times indicated on the diagram.

- t_0: *MUX* is driven LOW to apply the row address bits (A_8 to A_{15}) to the DRAM address inputs.
- t_1: $\overline{RAS}$ is driven LOW to load the row address into the DRAM.
- t_2: *MUX* goes HIGH to place the column address (A_0 to A_7) at the DRAM address inputs.

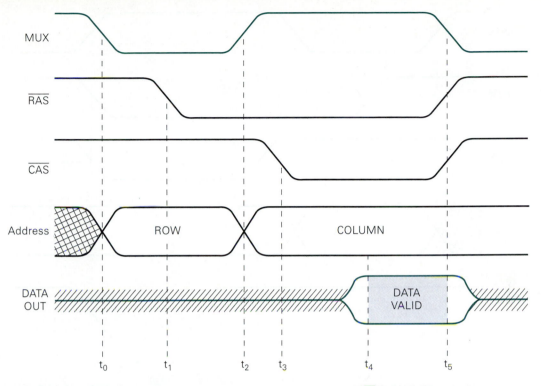

FIGURE 11-36 Signal activity for a read operation on a dynamic RAM. The $R/\overline{W}$ input (not shown) is assumed to be HIGH.

- t_3: $\overline{CAS}$ goes LOW to load the column address into the DRAM.
- t_4: The DRAM responds by placing valid data from the selected memory cell onto the DATA OUT line.
- t_5: MUX, $\overline{RAS}$, $\overline{CAS}$, and DATA OUT return to their initial states.

DRAM Write Cycle

Figure 11-37 shows typical signal activity during a DRAM write operation. Here is a description of the sequence of events.

- t_0: The LOW at MUX places the row address at the DRAM inputs.
- t_1: The NGT at $\overline{RAS}$ loads the row address into the DRAM.
- t_2: MUX goes HIGH to place the column address at the DRAM inputs.
- t_3: The NGT at $\overline{CAS}$ loads the column address into the DRAM.
- t_4: Data to be written are placed on the DATA IN line.
- t_5: $R/\overline{W}$ is pulsed LOW to write the data into the selected cell.
- t_6: Input data are removed from DATA IN.
- t_7: MUX, $\overline{RAS}$, $\overline{CAS}$, and $R/\overline{W}$ are returned to their initial states.

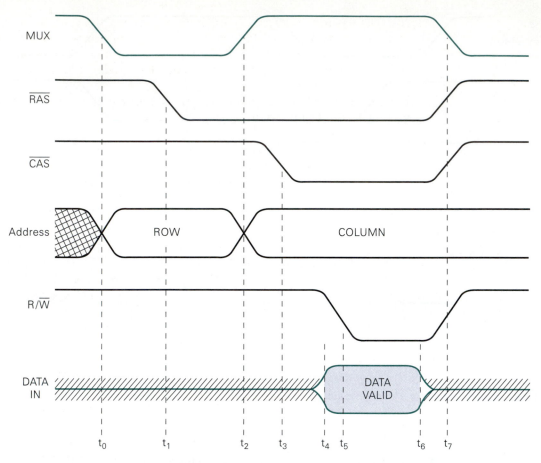

FIGURE 11-37   Signal activity for a write operation on a dynamic RAM.

Review Questions

1. *True or false:*

   (a) During a read cycle the $\overline{RAS}$ signal is activated before the $\overline{CAS}$ signal.

   (b) During a write operation $\overline{CAS}$ is activated before $\overline{RAS}$.

   (c) $R/\overline{W}$ is held LOW for the entire write operation.

   (d) The address inputs to a DRAM will change twice during a read or a write operation.

2. Which signal makes sure that the correct portion of the complete address appears at the DRAM inputs?

11-17   DRAM REFRESHING

A DRAM cell is refreshed each time a read operation is performed on that cell. Each memory cell must be refreshed periodically (typically, every 4 to 16 ms, depending on the device) or its data will be lost. This requirement would appear to be extremely difficult, if not impossible, to meet for large-capacity DRAMs. For example, a 1M × 1 DRAM has $10^{20} = 1,048,576$ cells. To ensure that each cell is refreshed within 4 ms, it would require that read operations be performed on successive addresses at the rate of one every 4 ns (4 ms/1,048,576 ≈ 4 ns). This is much too fast for any DRAM chip. Fortunately, manufacturers have designed DRAM chips so that

> **whenever a read operation is performed on a cell, all of the cells in that row will be refreshed.**

Thus, it is necessary to do a read operation only on each *row* of a DRAM array once every 4 ms to guarantee that each *cell* of the array is refreshed. Referring to the 4M × 1 DRAM of Figure 11-33(a), if any address is strobed into the row address register, all 2048 cells in that row are automatically refreshed.

Clearly, this row-refreshing feature makes it easier to keep all DRAM cells refreshed. However, during the normal operation of the system in which a DRAM is functioning, it is unlikely that a read operation will be performed on each row of the DRAM within the required refresh time limit. Therefore, some kind of refresh control logic is needed either external to the DRAM chip or as part of its internal circuitry. In either case, there are two refresh modes: a *burst* refresh and a *distributed* refresh.

In a burst refresh mode, the normal memory operation is suspended, and each row of the DRAM is refreshed in succession until all rows have been refreshed. In a distributed refresh mode, the row refreshing is interspersed with the normal operations of the memory.

The most universal method for refreshing a DRAM is the $\overline{RAS}$-**only refresh.** It is performed by strobing in a row address with $\overline{RAS}$ while $\overline{CAS}$ and $R/\overline{W}$ remain HIGH. Figure 11-38 illustrates how $\overline{RAS}$-only refresh is used for a burst refresh of the TMS44100. Some of the complexity of the memory array in this chip is there to make refresh operations simpler. Since two banks are lined up in the same row, both banks can be refreshed at the same time, effectively making it the same as if there were only 1024 rows. A **refresh counter** is used to supply 10-bit row addresses to the DRAM address inputs starting at 0000000000 (row 0). $\overline{RAS}$ is pulsed LOW to load this address into the DRAM, and this refreshes row 0 in both banks. The counter is incremented and the process is repeated up to address 1111111111 (row 1023). For the TMS44100 a burst refresh can be completed in just over 113 μs and must be repeated every 16 ms or less.

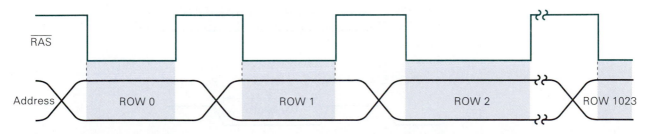

RAS

Address ROW 0 ROW 1 ROW 2 ROW 1023

*R/$\overline{W}$ and $\overline{CAS}$ lines held HIGH

FIGURE 11-38 The $\overline{RAS}$-only refresh method uses only the $\overline{RAS}$ signal to load the row address into the DRAM to refresh all cells in that row. The $\overline{RAS}$-only refresh can be used to perform a burst refresh as shown. A refresh counter supplies the sequential row addresses from row 0 to row 1023 (for a 4M × 1 DRAM).

While the refresh counter idea seems easy enough, we must realize that the row addresses from the refresh counter cannot interfere with the addresses coming from the CPU during normal read/write operations. For this reason, the refresh counter addresses must be multiplexed with the CPU addresses, so that the proper source of DRAM addresses is activated at the proper times.

In order to relieve the computer's CPU from some of these burdens, a special chip called a **dynamic RAM (DRAM) controller** is often used. As a minimum, this chip will perform address multiplexing and refresh count sequence generation, leaving the generation of the timing for $\overline{RAS}$, $\overline{CAS}$, and MUX signals up to some other logic circuitry and the person who programs the computer. Other DRAM controllers are fully automatic. Their inputs look very much like a static RAM or ROM. They automatically generate the refresh sequence often enough to maintain the memory, multiplex the address bus, generate the $\overline{RAS}$ and $\overline{CAS}$ signals, and arbitrate control of the DRAM between the CPU read/write cycles and local refresh operations. In current personal computers, the DRAM controller and other high-level controller circuits are integrated into an application-specific integrated circuit (ASIC).

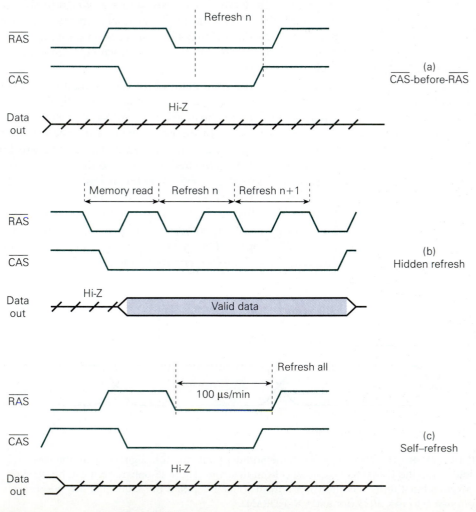

FIGURE 11-39 TMS44100 refresh modes.

Most of the DRAM chips in production today have on-chip refreshing capability that eliminates the need to supply external refresh addresses. One of these methods, shown in Figure 11-39(a), is called $\overline{CAS}$-before-$\overline{RAS}$ refresh. In this method the $\overline{CAS}$ signal is driven LOW first and is held LOW until after $\overline{RAS}$ goes LOW. This sequence will refresh one row of the memory array and increment an internal counter which generates the row addresses. To perform a burst refresh using this feature, $\overline{CAS}$ can be held LOW while $\overline{RAS}$ is pulsed once for each row until all are refreshed. During this refresh cycle, all external addresses are ignored. The TMS44100 also offers "hidden refresh" which allows a row to be refreshed while holding data on the output. This is done by holding $\overline{CAS}$ LOW after a read cycle and then pulsing $\overline{RAS}$ as in Figure 11-39(b).

The self-refresh mode of Figure 11-39(c) fully automates the process. By forcing $\overline{CAS}$ LOW before $\overline{RAS}$ and then holding them both LOW for at least 100 μs, an internal oscillator clocks the row address counter until all cells are refreshed. The mode that a system designer chooses depends on how busy the computer's CPU is. If it can spare 100 μs without access to its memory, and if it can do this every 16 ms, then the self-refresh is the way to go. However, if this will slow the program execution down too much, it may require some distributed refreshing using $\overline{CAS}$-before-$\overline{RAS}$ or hidden refresh cycles. In any case, all cells must be refreshed within the allotted time or data will be lost.

Review Questions

1. *True or false:*
   (a) In most DRAMs it is necessary to read only from one cell in each row in order to refresh all cells in that row.
   (b) In the burst refresh mode the entire array is refreshed by one $\overline{RAS}$ pulse.
2. What is the function of a refresh counter?
3. What functions does a DRAM controller perform?
4. *True or false:*
   (a) In the $\overline{RAS}$-only refresh method the $\overline{CAS}$ signal is held LOW.
   (b) $\overline{CAS}$-before-$\overline{RAS}$ refresh can be used only by DRAMs with on-chip refresh control circuitry.

11-18 DRAM TECHNOLOGY*

In selecting a particular type of RAM device for a system, a designer has some difficult decisions. The capacity (as large as possible), the speed (as fast as possible), the power needed (as little as possible), the cost (as low as possible), and the convenience (as easy to change as possible) must all be kept in a reasonable balance because no single type of RAM can maximize all of these desired features. The semiconductor RAM market is constantly trying to produce the ideal mix of these characteristics in its products for various applications. This section explains some of the current terms used regarding RAM technology. This is a very dynamic topic, and

---

* This topic may be omitted without affecting the continuity of the remainder of the book.

perhaps some of these terms will be history before this book is printed, but here is the state of the art today.

SIMMs and DIMMs

With many companies manufacturing motherboards for personal computer systems, standard memory interface connectors have been adopted. These connectors receive a small printed circuit card with contact points on both sides of the edge of the card. These modular cards allow for easy installation or replacement of memory components in a computer. The single-in-line memory module (SIMM) is a circuit card with 72 functionally equivalent contacts on both sides of the card. These modules use 5-V-only DRAM chips that vary in capacity from 1 to 16 Mbits in surface-mount gull-wing or J-lead packages. The memory modules vary in capacity from 1 to 32 Mbytes.

The newer, 168-pin, dual-in-line memory module (DIMM) has 84 functionally unique contacts on each side of the card. Both 3.3-V and 5-V versions are available. The capacity of the module depends on the DRAM chips that are mounted on it; and as DRAM capacity increases, the capacity of the DIMMs will increase. For compact applications, such as lap-top computers, a small-outline, dual-in-line memory module is available (SODIMM).

The primary problem in the personal computer industry is providing a memory system that is fast enough to keep up with the ever-increasing clock speeds of the microprocessors while keeping the cost at an affordable level. Special features are being added to the basic DRAM devices to enhance their total bandwidth. Although these methods of improving performance are constantly changing, the following terms are currently being used extensively in memory-related literature.

FPM DRAM

Fast page mode (FPM) allows quicker access to random memory locations within the current "page." A page is simply a range of memory addresses that have identical upper address bit values. In order to access data on the current page, only the lower address lines must be changed. The FPM DRAMs have been the primary workhorse of the DRAM industry for the past several years.

EDO DRAM

Extended data output (EDO) DRAMs offer a minor improvement to FPM DRAMs. For accesses on a given page, the data value at the current memory location is sensed and latched onto the output pins. In the FPM DRAMs the sense amplifier drives the output without a latch, requiring $\overline{CAS}$ to remain low until data values become valid. With EDO, while these data are present on the outputs, $\overline{CAS}$ can complete its cycle, a new address on the current page can be decoded, and the data path circuitry can be reset for the next access. This allows the memory controller to be outputting the next address at the same time the current word is being read.

BEDO DRAM

Burst EDO DRAMs take advantage of the fact that most data in memory are being accessed sequentially. The less random nature of this mode of access allows data to be delivered in a burst of one, two, four, or eight sequential memory locations, one right after the other. The first location to be accessed is the slowest due to the overhead of latching the row and column addresses. However, the next several data locations can be accessed very quickly by generating the lower (column) addresses inside the memory chip instead of latching it from the external bus. These devices require a clock to increment the address counter and strobe the data off chip. The clocking action is performed by pulsing the $\overline{CAS}$ line to read successive data bytes from the RAM. While the last byte of a burst is being clocked out by $\overline{CAS}$, a new column address can be strobed in without incurring any additional wait states. This allows a continuous stream of data to be read from the current page at the fastest rate possible.

SDRAM

Synchronous DRAM seems to hold great promise of being the next standard for high-speed systems. The data values are clocked out by the system clock (instead of the $\overline{CAS}$ control line) in bursts of memory locations within the same page. Internally, SDRAMs are organized in two banks. This allows data to be read out at a very fast rate by alternately accessing each of the two banks. In order to provide all of the features and the flexibility needed for this type of DRAM to work with a wide variety of system requirements, the circuitry within the SDRAM has become more complex. A command sequence is necessary to tell the SDRAM which options are needed, such as burst length, sequential or interleaved data, and $\overline{CAS}$-before-$\overline{RAS}$ or self-refresh modes. Self-refresh mode allows the memory device to perform all of the necessary functions to keep its cells refreshed. The SDRAMs are naturally more expensive, but they do reduce the need for support circuitry. This makes the overall system cost using SDRAM similar to that of previous systems.

Review Questions	1. Are SIMMs and DIMMs interchangeable?
	2. What is a "page" of memory?
	3. Why is "page mode" faster?
	4. What does *EDO* stand for?
	5. What is the term used for accessing several consecutive memory locations?
	6. What is an SDRAM synchronized to?

11-19 EXPANDING WORD SIZE AND CAPACITY

In many memory applications the required RAM or ROM memory capacity or word size cannot be satisfied by one memory chip. Instead, several memory chips must be combined to provide the capacity and/or the word size. We will see how this is done through several examples that illustrate the important ideas that are used when memory chips are interfaced to a microprocessor. The examples that follow are intended to be instructive, and the memory chip sizes that are used were chosen so as to conserve space. The same techniques as those that are presented can be extended to larger memory chips.

Expanding Word Size

Suppose that we need a memory that can store 16 eight-bit words and all we have are RAM chips that are arranged as 16×4 memories with common I/O lines. We can combine two of these 16×4 chips to produce the desired memory. The configuration for doing so is shown in Figure 11-40. Examine this diagram carefully and see what you can find out from it before reading on.

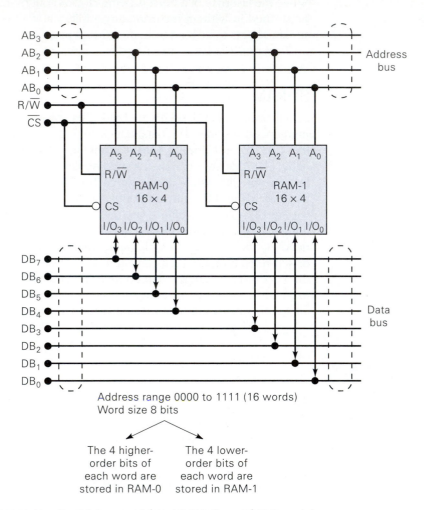

FIGURE 11-40 Combining two 16×4 RAMs for a 16×8 module.

Since each chip can store 16 four-bit words and we want to store 16 eight-bit words, we are using each chip to store *half* of each word. In other words, RAM-0 stores the four *higher*-order bits of each of the 16 words, and RAM-1 stores the four *lower*-order bits of each of the 16 words. A full eight-bit word is available at the RAM outputs connected to the data bus.

Any one of the 16 words is selected by applying the appropriate address code to the four-line *address bus* (AB_3, AB_2, AB_1, AB_0). The address lines typically originate at the CPU. Note that each address bus line is connected to the corresponding address input of each chip. This means that once an address code is placed on the address bus, this same address code is applied to both chips so that the same location in each chip is accessed at the same time.

Once the address is selected, we can read or write at this address under control of the common $R/\overline{W}$ and $\overline{CS}$ line. To read, $R/\overline{W}$ must be high and $\overline{CS}$ must be low. This causes the RAM I/O lines to act as *outputs*. RAM-0 places its selected four-bit word on the upper four data bus lines and RAM-1 places its selected four-bit word on the lower four data bus lines. The data bus then contains the full selected eight-bit word, which can now be transmitted to some other device (usually a register in the CPU).

To write, $R/\overline{W} = 0$ and $\overline{CS} = 0$ causes the RAM I/O lines to act as *inputs*. The eight-bit word to be written is placed on the data bus (usually by the CPU). The higher four bits will be written into the selected location of RAM-0, and the lower four bits will be written into RAM-1.

In essence, the combination of the two RAM chips acts like a single 16×8 memory chip. We would refer to this combination as a 16×8 *memory module*.

The same basic idea for expanding word size will work for many different situations. Read the following example and draw a rough diagram for what the system will look like before looking at the solution.

EXAMPLE 11-13	The 2125A is a static-RAM IC that has a capacity of $1K \times 1$, one active-LOW chip select input, and separate data input and output. Show how to combine several 2125A ICs to form a $1K \times 8$ module.

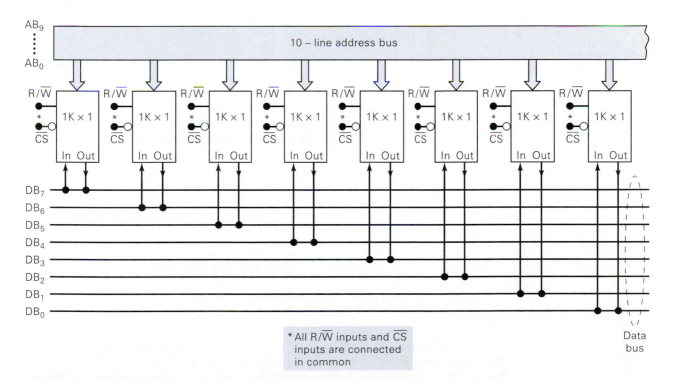

FIGURE 11-41   Eight 2125A $1K \times 1$ chips arranged as a $1K \times 8$ memory.

Solution

The arrangement is shown in Figure 11-41, where eight 2125A chips are used for a 1K × 8 module. Each chip stores one of the bits of each of the 1024 eight-bit words. Note that all of the $R/\overline{W}$ and $\overline{CS}$ inputs are wired together, and the 10-line address bus is connected to the address inputs of each chip. Also note that since the 2125A has separate data in and data out pins, both of these pins of each chip are tied to the same data bus line.

Expanding Capacity

Suppose that we need a memory that can store 32 four-bit words and all we have are the 16 × 4 chips. By combining two 16 × 4 chips as shown in Figure 11-42, we can produce the desired memory. Once again, examine this diagram and see what you can determine from it before reading on.

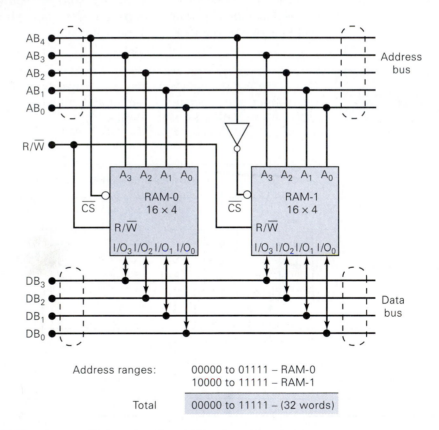

FIGURE 11-42 Combining two 16 × 4 chips for a 32 × 4 memory.

Each RAM is used to store 16 four-bit words. The four data I/O pins of each RAM are connected to a common four-line data bus. Only one of the RAM chips can be selected (enabled) at one time so that there will be no bus-contention problems. This is ensured by driving the respective $\overline{CS}$ inputs from different logic signals.

Since the total capacity of this memory module is 32 × 4, there must be 32 different addresses. This requires *five* address bus lines. The upper address line AB_4 is used to select one RAM or the other (via the $\overline{CS}$ inputs) as the one that will be read from or written into. The other four address lines AB_0 to AB_3 are used to select the one memory location out of 16 from the selected RAM chip.

To illustrate, when $AB_4 = 0$, the $\overline{CS}$ of RAM-0 enables this chip for read or write. Then any address location in RAM-0 can be accessed by AB_3 through AB_0. The latter four address lines can range from 0000 to 1111 to select the desired location. Thus, the range of addresses representing locations in RAM-0 is

$$AB_4 AB_3 AB_2 AB_1 AB_0 = 00000 \text{ to } 01111$$

Note that when $AB_4 = 0$, the $\overline{CS}$ of RAM-1 is high, so that its I/O lines are disabled (Hi-Z) and cannot communicate with (give data to or take data from) the data bus.

It should be clear that when $AB_4 = 1$, the roles of RAM-0 and RAM-1 are reversed. RAM-1 is now enabled, and the lines AB_3 to AB_0 select one of its locations. Thus, the range of addresses located in RAM-1 is

$$AB_4 AB_3 AB_2 AB_1 AB_0 = 10000 \text{ to } 11111$$

EXAMPLE 11-14

It is desired to combine several 2K × 8 PROMs to produce a total capacity of 8K × 8. How many PROM chips are needed? How many address bus lines are required?

Solution

Four PROM chips are required, with each one storing 2K of the 8K words. Since $8K = 8 \times 1024 = 8192 = 2^{13}$, *thirteen* address lines are needed.

The configuration for the memory of Example 11-14 is similar to the 32 × 4 memory of Figure 11-42. However, it is slightly more complex, because it requires a decoder circuit for generating the $\overline{CS}$ input signals. The complete diagram for this 8192 × 8 memory is shown in Figure 11-43.

Since the total capacity is 8192 words, 13 address bus lines are required. The two highest-order lines, AB_{11} and AB_{12}, are used to select *one* of the PROM chips; the other 11 address bus lines go to each PROM to select the desired location within the selected PROM. The PROM selection is accomplished by feeding AB_{11} and AB_{12} into the 74LS138 decoder. The four possible combinations are decoded to generate active-LOW signals, which are applied to the $\overline{CS}$ inputs. For example, when $AB_{11} = AB_{12} = 0$, the K0 output of the decoder goes LOW (all others are HIGH) and enables PROM-0. This causes the PROM-0 outputs to generate the data word internally stored at the address determined by AB_0 through AB_{10}. All other PROMs are disabled, so there is no bus contention.

While $AB_{12} = AB_{11} = 0$, the values of AB_{10} through AB_0 can range from all 0s to all 1s. Thus, PROM-0 will respond to the following range of 13-bit addresses:

$$AB_{12} - AB_0 = 0000000000000 \text{ to } 0011111111111$$

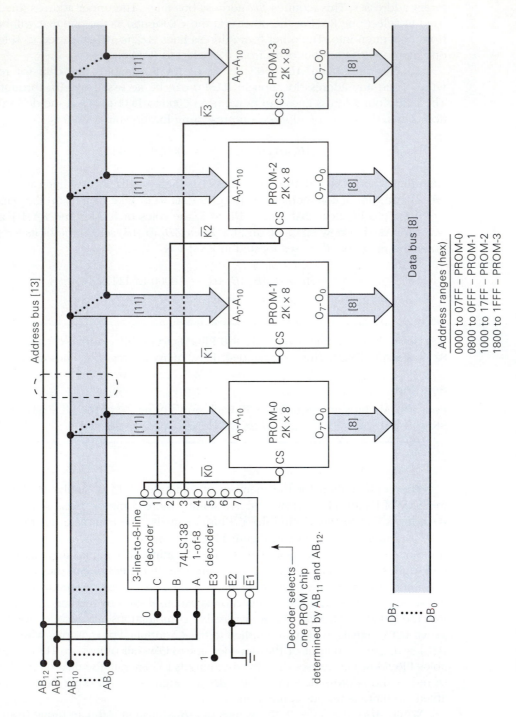

FIGURE 11-43 Four 2K × 8 PROMs arranged to form a total capacity of 8K × 8.

For convenience, these addresses can be expressed more easily in hexadecimal code to give a range of 0000 to 07FF.

Similarly, when $AB_{12} = 0$ and $AB_{11} = 1$, the decoder selects PROM-1, which then responds by outputting the data word that it has internally stored at the address AB_{10} through AB_0. Thus, PROM-1 responds to the following range of addresses:

$$0100000000000 \text{ to } 0111111111111 \text{ (binary)}$$

or

$$0800 \text{ to } 0FFF \text{ (hex)}$$

You should verify the PROM-2 and PROM-3 address ranges given in the figure.

Clearly, address lines AB_{12} and AB_{11} are used to select one of the four PROM chips, while AB_{10} through AB_0 select the word stored in the selected PROM.

EXAMPLE 11-15

What size decoder would be needed to expand the memory of Figure 11-43 to 32K × 8? Describe what address lines are used.

Solution

A 32K capacity will require 16 PROM chips. To select one of the 16 PROMs will require a 4-line-to-16-line decoder. Four address lines (AB_{14}, AB_{13}, AB_{12}, AB_{11}) will be connected as inputs to this decoder. The address lines AB_{10} to AB_0 are connected to the address inputs of each of the 16 PROMs. Thus, a total of 15 address lines are used. This agrees with the fact that $2^{15} = 32{,}768 = 32K$.

Incomplete Address Decoding

In many instances there is a need to use various memory devices in the same memory system. For example, consider the requirements of a digital dashboard system on an automobile. Such a system is typically implemented using a microprocessor. Consequently, we need some nonvolatile ROM to store the program instructions. We need some read/write memory to store the digits that represent the speed, RPM, gallons of fuel, and so on. Other digitized values must be stored to represent oil pressure, engine temperature, battery voltage, and so on. We also need some nonvolatile read/write storage (EEPROM) for the odometer readout since it would not be good to have this number reset to 0 or assume a random value whenever the car battery is disconnected.

Figure 11-44 shows a memory system that could be used in a microcomputer system. Notice that the ROM portion is made up of two 8K × 8 devices (PROM-0 and PROM-1). The RAM section requires a single 8K × 8 device. The EEPROM available is only a 2K × 8 device. The memory system requires a decoder to select only one device at a time. This decoder divides the entire memory space (assuming

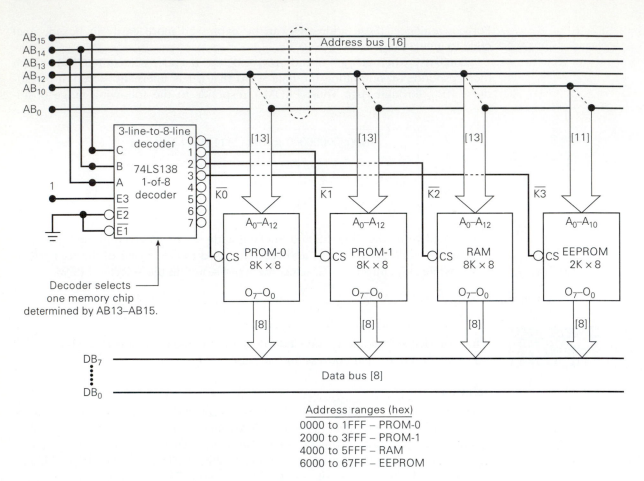

FIGURE 11-44 A system with incomplete address decoding.

16 address bits) into 8K address blocks. In other words, each decoder output is activated by 8192 (8K) different addresses. Notice that the upper three address lines control the decoder. The 13 lower-order address lines are tied directly to the address inputs on the memory chips. The only exception to this is the EEPROM which has only 11 address lines for its 2-Kbyte capacity. If the address (in hex) of this EEPROM is intended to range from 6000 to 67FF, it will respond to these addresses as intended. However, the two address lines, A_{11} and A_{12}, are not involved in the decoding scheme for this chip. The decoder output ($K3$) is active for 8K addresses, but the chip that it is connected to contains only 2K locations. As a result, the EEPROM will also respond to the other 6K of addresses in this decoded block of memory. The same contents of the EEPROM will also appear at addresses 6800–6FFF, 7000–77FF, and 7800–7FFF. These areas of memory that are redundantly occupied by a device due to incomplete address decoding are referred to as **memory foldback** areas. This occurs frequently in systems where there is an abundance of address space and a need to minimize decoding logic. A **memory map** of this system

FIGURE 11-45 A memory map of a digital dashboard system.

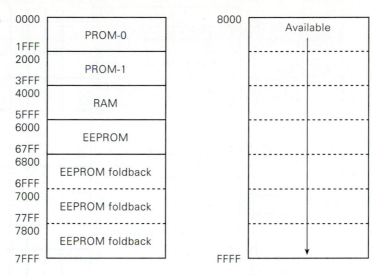

as shown in Figure 11-45 clearly shows the addresses that each device is assigned to as well as the memory space that is available for expansion.

Combining DRAM Chips

DRAM ICs often come with word sizes of one or four bits, so it is necessary to combine several of them to form larger word size modules. Figure 11-46 shows how to combine eight TMS44100 DRAM chips to form a 4M × 8 module. Each chip has a 4M × 1 capacity.

There are several important points to note. First, since 4M = 2^{22}, the TMS44100 chip has *eleven* address inputs; remember, DRAMs use multiplexed address inputs. The address multiplexer takes the 22-line CPU address bus and changes it to an 11-line address bus for the DRAM chips. Second, the $\overline{RAS}$, $\overline{CAS}$, and $\overline{WE}$ inputs of all eight chips are connected together so that all chips are activated simultaneously for each memory operation. Finally, recall that the TMS44100 has on-chip refresh control circuitry, so there is no need for an external DRAM controller.

Review Questions

1. The MCM6209C is a 64K × 4 static-RAM chip. How many of these are needed to form a 1M × 4 module?

2. How many are needed for a 64K × 16 module?

3. *True or false:* When memory chips are combined to form a module with a larger word size or capacity, the *CS* inputs of each chip are always connected together.

4. *True or false:* When memory chips are combined for a larger capacity, each chip is connected to the same data bus lines.

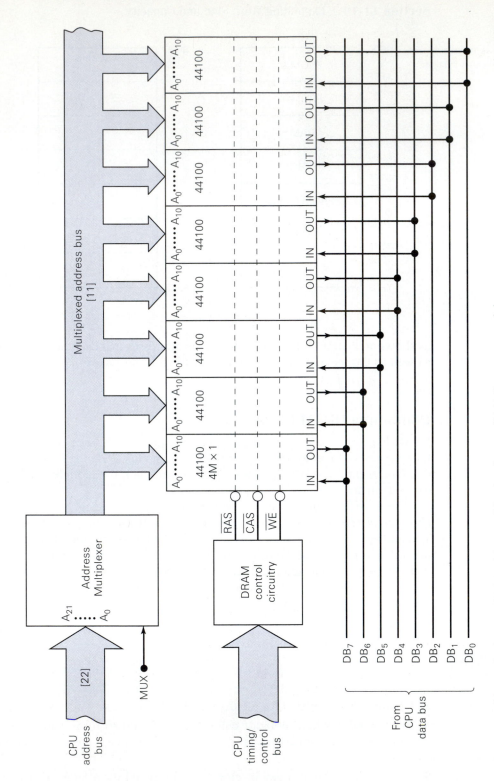

FIGURE 11-46 Eight 4M × 8 memory module.

11-20 SPECIAL MEMORY FUNCTIONS

We have seen that RAM and ROM devices are used as a computer's high-speed internal memory that communicates directly with the CPU (e.g., microprocessor). In this section we briefly describe some of the special functions that semiconductor memory devices perform in computers and other digital equipment and systems. The discussion is not intended to provide details of how these functions are implemented, but to introduce the basic ideas.

Power-Down Storage

In many applications, the volatility of semiconductor RAM can mean the loss of critical data when system power is shut down—either purposely or as the result of an unplanned power interruption. Just two of many examples of this are:

1. Critical operating parameters for graphics terminals, intelligent terminals, and printers. These changeable parameters determine the operating modes and attributes that will be in effect upon power-up.
2. Industrial process control systems which must never "lose their place" in the middle of a task when power unexpectedly fails.

There are several approaches to providing storage of critical data in power-down situations. In one method, all critical data during normal system operation are stored in RAM that can be powered from backup batteries whenever power is interrupted. Some CMOS RAM chips have very low standby power requirements (as low as 0.5 mW) and are particularly well suited for this task. Some CMOS SRAMs actually include a small lithium battery right on the chip. Of course, even with their low power consumption, these CMOS RAMs will eventually drain the batteries if power is out for prolonged periods, and data will be lost.

Another approach stores all critical system data in nonvolatile flash memory. This approach has the advantage of not requiring backup battery power, and so it presents no risk of data loss even for long power outages. Flash memory, however, cannot have its data changed as easily as static RAM. Recall that with a flash chip we cannot erase and write to one or two bytes; it must be done a sector at a time (usually 512 bytes). This requires the CPU to have to rewrite a large block of data even when only a few bytes need to be changed.

In a third approach, the CPU stores all data in high-speed, volatile RAM during normal system operation. On power-down, the CPU executes a short power-down program (from ROM) that transfers critical data from the system RAM into either battery-backup CMOS RAM or nonvolatile flash memory. This requires a special circuit that senses the onset of a power interruption and sends a signal to the CPU to tell it to begin executing the power-down sequence.

In any case, when power is turned back on, the CPU executes a power-up program (from ROM) that transfers the critical data from the backup storage memory to the system RAM so that the system can resume operation where it left off when power was interrupted.

Cache Memory

Computers and other digital systems may have thousands or millions of bytes of internal memory (RAM and ROM) that store programs and data that the CPU needs during normal operation. Normally, this would require that all of the internal memory have an operating speed comparable to that of the CPU in order to achieve maximum system operation. In many systems it is not economical to use high-speed memory devices for all of the internal memory. Instead, system designers use a small block of high-speed *cache* memory which might hold, say, 512 words. This cache memory block is the only block that communicates directly with the CPU at high speed; program instructions and data are transferred from the slower, cheaper internal memory to the cache memory when they are needed by the CPU. The success of cache memory depends on many complex factors, and some systems will not benefit from using cache memory.

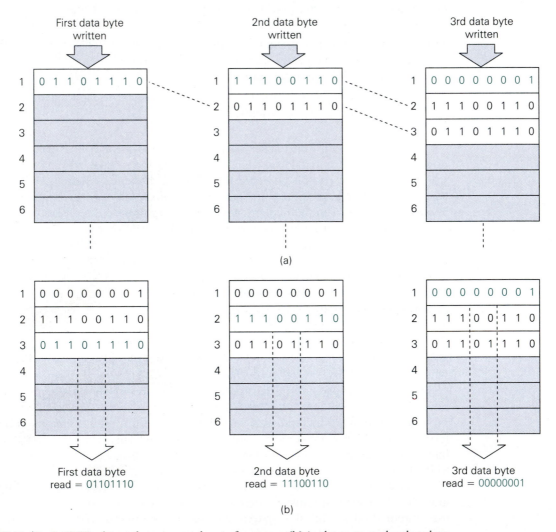

FIGURE 11-47 In FIFO, data values are read out of memory (b) in the same order that they were written into memory (a).

First-In, First-Out Memory (FIFO)

In **FIFO** memory systems, data that are written into the RAM storage area are read out in the same order that they were written in. In other words, the first word written into the memory block is the first word that is read out of the memory block: hence the name FIFO. This idea is illustrated in Figure 11-47.

Part (a) shows the sequence of writing three data bytes into the memory block. Note that as each new byte is written into location 1, the other bytes move to the next location. Part (b) shows the sequence of reading the data out of the FIFO block. The first byte read is the same as the first byte that was written, and so on. The FIFO operation is controlled by special *address pointer registers* that keep track of where data are to be written and from where they are to be read.

A FIFO is useful as a **data-rate buffer** between systems that transfer data at widely different rates. One example is the transfer of data from a computer to a printer. The computer sends character data to the printer at a very high rate, say, one byte every 10 μs. These data fill up a FIFO memory in the printer. The printer then reads out the data from the FIFO at a much slower rate, say, one byte every 5 ms, and prints out the corresponding characters in the same order as sent by the computer.

A FIFO can also be used as a data-rate buffer between a slow device, such as a keyboard, and a high-speed computer. Here the FIFO accepts keyboard data at a slow rate and stores them; the computer can then read the stored keyboard data at a fast rate. In this way, the computer can be performing other tasks while the FIFO is slowly being filled with data.

Review Questions

1. What are the various ways to handle the possible loss of critical data when power is interrupted?
2. What is the principal reason for using a cache memory?
3. What does *FIFO* mean?
4. What is a data-rate buffer?

11-21 TROUBLESHOOTING RAM SYSTEMS

All computers use RAM. Many general-purpose computers and most special-purpose computers (such as microprocessor-based controllers and process-control computers) also use some form of ROM. Each RAM and ROM IC that is part of a computer's internal memory typically contains thousands of memory cells. A single faulty memory cell can cause a complete system failure (commonly referred to as a "system crash") or, at the least, unreliable system operation. The testing and troubleshooting of memory systems involves the use of techniques that are not often used on other parts of the digital system. Because memory consists of thousands of identical circuits acting as storage locations, any tests of its operation must involve checking to see exactly which locations are working and which are not. Then, by looking at the pattern of good and bad locations along with the organization of the memory circuitry, one can determine the possible causes of the memory malfunction. The problem typically can be traced to a bad memory IC; a bad decoder IC, logic gate, or signal buffer; or a problem in the circuit connections (i.e., shorts or open connections).

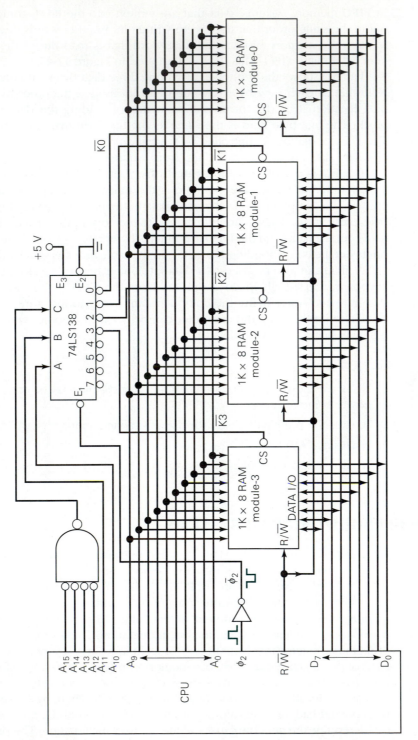

FIGURE 11-48 4K × 8 RAM memory connected to a CPU.

Because RAM must be written to and read from, testing RAM is generally more complex than testing ROM. In this section we will look at some common procedures for testing the RAM portion of memory and interpreting the test results. We will examine ROM testing in the next section.

Know the Operation

The RAM memory system shown in Figure 11-48 will be used in our examples. As we emphasized in earlier discussions, successful troubleshooting of a relatively complex circuit or system begins with a thorough knowledge of its operation. Before we can discuss the testing of this RAM system, we should first analyze it carefully so that we fully understand its operation.

The total capacity is $4K \times 8$ and is made up of four $1K \times 8$ RAM modules. A module may be just a single IC, or it may consist of several ICs (e.g., two $1K \times 4$ chips). Each module is connected to the CPU through the address and data buses and through the $R/\overline{W}$ control line. The modules have common I/O data lines. During a read operation these lines become data output lines through which the selected module places its data on the bus for the CPU to read. During a write operation, these lines act as input lines to accept CPU-generated data from the data bus for writing into the selected location.

The 74LS138 decoder and the four-input OR gate combine to decode the six high-order address lines to generate the chip select signals $\overline{K0}$, $\overline{K1}$, $\overline{K2}$, and $\overline{K3}$. These signals enable a specific RAM module for a read or a write operation. The INVERTER is used to invert the CPU output clock signal ϕ_2 so that the decoder is enabled only while ϕ_2 is HIGH. The ϕ_2 pulse occurs only after allowing enough time for the address lines to stabilize following the application of a new address on the address bus. ϕ_2 will be LOW while the address and $R/\overline{W}$ lines are changing; this prevents the occurrence of decoder output glitches that could erroneously activate a memory chip and possibly cause invalid data to be stored.

Each RAM module has its address inputs connected to the CPU address bus lines A_0 through A_9. The high-order address lines A_{10} through A_{15} select one of the RAM modules. The selected module decodes address lines A_0 through A_9 to find the word location that is being addressed. The following examples will show how to determine the addresses that correspond to each module.

EXAMPLE 11-16

Assume that the CPU is performing a read operation from address 06A3 (hex). Which RAM module, if any, is being read from?

Solution

First write out the address in binary.

A_{15}	A_{14}	A_{13}	A_{12}	A_{11}	A_{10}	A_9	A_8	A_7	A_6	A_5	A_4	A_3	A_2	A_1	A_0
0	0	0	0	0	1	1	0	1	0	1	0	0	0	1	1

You should be able to verify that levels A_{15} to A_{10} will activate decoder output $\overline{K1}$ to select RAM module-1. This module internally decodes the address lines A_9 to A_0 to select the location whose data are to be placed on the data bus.

EXAMPLE
11-17

Which RAM module will have data written into it when the CPU executes a write operation to address 1C65?

Solution

Writing out the address in binary, we can see that $A_{12} = 1$. This produces a HIGH out of the OR gate and at the C input of the decoder. With $A_{11} = A_{10} = 1$, the decoder inputs are 111, which activates output 7. Outputs $\overline{K0}$ to $\overline{K3}$ will be inactive, and so none of the RAM modules will be enabled. In other words, the data placed on the data bus by the CPU will not be accepted by any of the RAMs.

EXAMPLE
11-18

Determine the range of addresses for each module in Figure 11-48.

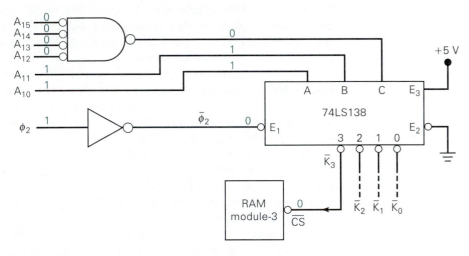

FIGURE 11-49   Example 11-18, showing address bus conditions needed to select RAM module-3.

Solution

Each module stores 1024 eight-bit words. To determine the addresses of the words stored in any module, we start by determining the address bus conditions that activate that module's chip select input. For example, module-3 will be selected when decoder input $\overline{K3}$ is LOW (Figure 11-49). $\overline{K3}$ will be LOW for $CBA = 011$. Working back to the CPU address lines A_{15} to A_{10}, we see that module-3 will be enabled when the following address is placed on the address bus:

A_{15}	A_{14}	A_{13}	A_{12}	A_{11}	A_{10}	A_9	A_8	A_7	A_6	A_5	A_4	A_3	A_2	A_1	A_0
0	0	0	0	1	1	x	x	x	x	x	x	x	x	x	x

The x's under A_9 through A_0 indicate "don't care" because these address lines are not used by the decoder to select module-3. A_9 to A_0 can be any combination ranging from 0000000000 to 1111111111, depending on which word in module-3 is being accessed. Thus, the complete range of addresses for module-3 is determined by using all 0s, and then all 1s for the x's.

A_{15}	A_{14}	A_{13}	A_{12}	A_{11}	A_{10}	A_9	A_8	A_7	A_6	A_5	A_4	A_3	A_2	A_1	A_0	
0	0	0	0	1	1	0	0	0	0	0	0	0	0	0	0	$\rightarrow$ 0C00$_{16}$
0	0	0	0	1	1	1	1	1	1	1	1	1	1	1	1	$\rightarrow$ 0FFF$_{16}$

Finally, this gives us 0C00 to 0FFF as the range of hex addresses stored in module-3. When the CPU places any address in this range onto the address bus, only module-3 will be enabled for either a read or a write, depending on the state of $R/\overline{W}$.

A similar analysis can be used to determine the address ranges for each of the other RAM modules. The results are as follows:

- Module-0: 0000–03FF
- Module-1: 0400–07FF
- Module-2: 0800–0BFF
- Module-3: 0C00–0FFF

Note that the four modules combine for a total address range of 0000 to 0FFF.

Testing the Decoding Logic

In some situations, the decoding logic portion of the RAM circuit (Figure 11-49) can be tested using the various techniques that we have applied to combinatorial circuits. It can be tested by applying signals to the six most significant address lines and ϕ_2 and by monitoring the decoder outputs. To do this, it must be possible to easily disconnect the CPU from these signal lines. If the CPU is a microprocessor chip in a socket, it can simply be removed from its socket.

Once the CPU is disconnected, you can supply the A_{10}–A_{15} and ϕ_2 signals from an external test circuit to perform a static test, using manually operated switches for each signal, or a dynamic test, using some type of counter to cycle through the various address codes. With these test signals applied, the decoder output lines can be checked for the proper response. Standard signal-tracing techniques can be used to isolate any faults in the decoding logic.

If you do not have access to the system address lines or do not have a convenient way of generating the static logic signals, it is often possible to force the system to generate a sequence of addresses. Most computer systems that are used for development have a program stored in a ROM that allows the user to display and change the contents of any memory location. Whenever the computer accesses a memory location, the proper address must be placed on the bus, which should cause the decoder output to go low, even if it is for a short time. Enter the following command to the computer:

```
Display    from  0400  to    07FF
```

Then place the logic probe on the $\overline{K1}$ output. The logic probe should show pulses during the time the data values are being displayed.

EXAMPLE
11-19

A dynamic test is performed on the decoding logic of Figure 11-49 by keeping $\phi_2 = 1$ and connecting the outputs of a six-bit counter to the address inputs A_{10} through A_{15}. The decoder outputs are monitored as the counter repetitively cycles through all six-bit codes. A logic probe check on the decoder outputs shows pulses at $\overline{K1}$ and $\overline{K3}$, but shows $\overline{K0}$ and $\overline{K2}$ remaining HIGH. What are the most probable faults?

Solution

It is possible, but highly unlikely, that $\overline{K0}$ and $\overline{K2}$ could both be stuck HIGH due to either an internal or an external short to V_{CC}. A more likely fault is an open between A_{10} and the A input of the decoder, since this would act as a logic HIGH and prevent any even-numbered decoder output from being activated. It is also possible that the decoder's A input is shorted to V_{CC}, but this is also unlikely because this short would have probably affected the operation of the counter that is supplying the address inputs.

Testing the Complete RAM System

Testing and troubleshooting the decoding logic will not reveal problems with the memory chips and their connections to the CPU buses. The most common methods for testing the operation of the *complete* RAM system involve writing known patterns of 1s and 0s to each memory location and reading them back to verify that the location has stored the pattern properly. While many different patterns can be used, one of the most widely used is the "checkerboard pattern." In this pattern, 1s and 0s are alternated as in 01010101. Once all locations have been tested using this pattern, the pattern is reversed (i.e., 10101010), and each location is tested again. Note that this sequence of tests will check each cell for the ability to store and read both a 1 and a 0. Because it alternates 1s and 0s, the checkerboard pattern will also detect any interactions or shorts between adjacent cells. Many other patterns can be used to detect various failure modes within RAM chips.

No memory test can catch all possible RAM faults with 100 percent accuracy, even though it may show that each cell can store and read a 0 or a 1. Some faulty RAMs can be pattern-sensitive. For instance, a RAM may be able to store and read 01010101 and 10101010, but it may fail when 11100011 is stored. Even for a small RAM system, it would take a prohibitively long time to try storing and reading every possible pattern in each location. For this reason, if a RAM system passes the checkerboard test, you can conclude that it is *probably* good; if it fails the test, then it *definitely* contains a fault.

Manually testing thousands of RAM locations by storing and reading checkerboard patterns would take hundreds of hours and is obviously not feasible. RAM pattern testing is usually done automatically either by having the CPU run a memory test program or by connecting a special test instrument to the RAM system buses in place of the CPU. In fact, in many computers and microprocessor-based equipment the CPU will automatically run a memory test program every time it is powered up; this is called a **power-up self-test.** The self-test routine (we will call it SELF-TEST) is stored in ROM, and it is executed whenever the system is turned on or when the operator requests it from the keyboard. As the CPU executes SELF-TEST, it will write test patterns to and read test patterns from each RAM location and

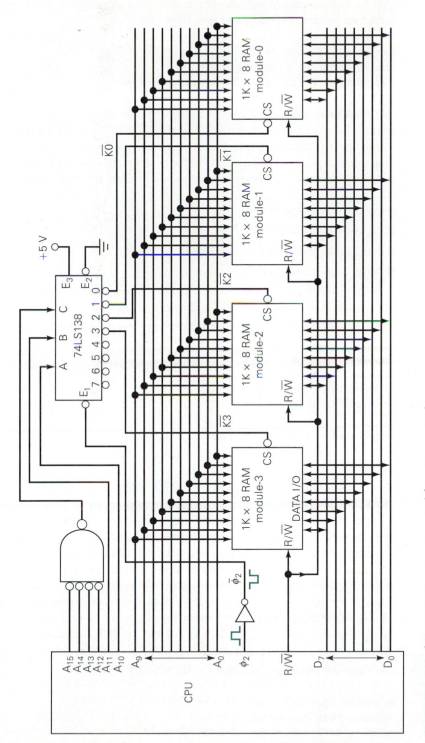

FIGURE 11-50 4K × 8 RAM system repeated from Figure 11-48.

will display some type of message to the user. It may be something as simple as an LED to indicate faulty memory, or it may be a descriptive message printed on the screen or printer. Typical messages might be:

```
RAM module-3 test OK
ALL RAM working properly
Location 027F faulty in bit positions 6 and 7
```

With messages like these and a knowledge of the RAM system operation, the troubleshooter can determine what further action is needed to isolate the fault. The following two examples will illustrate the procedure for the 4K × 8 RAM system; its diagram is repeated in Figure 11-50 for convenience. Remember from our previous examples that the addresses for each RAM module are as follows:

- Module-0: 0000–03FF
- Module-1: 0400–07FF
- Module-2: 0800–0BFF
- Module-3: 0C00–0FFF

EXAMPLE 11-20

The following messages are printed out after the SELF-TEST is run:

```
module-0 test OK
module-1 test OK
address 09A7 faulty at bit 6
module-3 test OK
```

Examine these messages and decide what to do next.

Solution

The faulty address location is in module-2. There is no circuit fault external to module-2 that could cause only that single address to be bad and no others. Thus, it appears that there is an internal fault in module-2. Before we reach this conclusion, however, the SELF-TEST program should be run several more times to see if the same messages appear. The original fault message may have been the result of noise rather than a bad memory cell; if so, further tests may produce no fault messages or different fault messages. This would point up the need to check for sources of noise in the system such as nonexistent or nonfunctioning power-supply decoupling capacitors, or crosstalk between closely spaced signal lines.

EXAMPLE 11-21

Consider the following messages from SELF-TEST:

```
module-0 test OK
address 0400 faulty at bits 0-7
address 0401 faulty at bits 0-7
address 0402 faulty at bits 0-7
      .     .     .     .     .
      .     .     .     .     .
```

```
    .    .    .    .    .
    .    .    .    .    .
address 07FE faulty at bits 0-7
address 07FF faulty at bits 0-7
module-2 test OK
module-3 test OK
```

Examine these messages, list the possible faults, and describe what to do next.

Solution

Clearly, every address in module-1 is listed as being faulty, and so module-1 is not working at all. Here are several possible faults that could cause this:

- An open connection at the $R/\overline{W}$ input to module-1
- An open path between $\overline{K1}$ and the module-1 chip select
- A faulty decoder output $\overline{K1}$ (stays HIGH)
- The $\overline{K1}/\overline{CS}$ node externally shorted to V_{CC}
- A faulty RAM module-1 (does not respond to $\overline{CS}$)
- An unconnected V_{CC} or ground on module-1

Standard troubleshooting techniques can now be used to isolate the fault.

As these examples have shown, the memory test program is useful in narrowing the problem to a specific area of the circuit. The troubleshooter uses the information provided from the memory test to determine possible faults and then proceeds to locate the actual fault.

It should be pointed out that there are some RAM circuit faults that will prevent the CPU from executing the SELF-TEST program on power-up. For example, any RAM circuit fault that causes a data line or an address line to be stuck LOW or HIGH will cause erroneous operation when the CPU tries to execute the SELF-TEST program in ROM (remember, the ROM shares the address and data buses with the RAM). When this happens, you should check for stuck bus lines and, if one is found, use the standard techniques for determining the exact cause of the stuck line.

Review Questions

1. What is ϕ_2's function in the RAM circuit of Figure 11-48?
2. What is the checkerboard test? Why is it used?
3. What is a power-up self-test?

11-22 TESTING ROM

The ROM circuitry in a computer is very similar to the RAM circuitry (compare Figures 11-45 and 11-48). The ROM decoding logic can be tested in the same manner described in the preceding section for the RAM system. The ROM chips, however, must be tested differently from RAM chips, because we cannot write patterns into

ROM and read them back as we can for RAM. Several methods are used to check the contents of a ROM IC.

In one approach the ROM is placed in a socket in a special test instrument which is typically microprocessor-controlled. The special test instrument can be programmed to read every location in the test ROM and print out a listing of the contents of each location. The listing can then be compared with what the ROM is supposed to contain. Except for low-capacity ROM chips, this process can be very time-consuming.

In a more efficient approach, the test instrument has the correct data stored in its own *reference ROM* chip. The test instrument is then programmed to read the contents of each location of the test ROM and compare it with the contents of the reference ROM. This approach, of course, requires the availability of a preprogrammed reference ROM.

A third approach uses a **checksum,** a special code placed in the last one or two locations of the ROM chip when it is programmed. This code is derived by adding up the data words to be stored in all of the ROM locations (excluding those containing the checksum). As the test instrument reads the data from each test ROM location, it will add them up and develop its own checksum. It then compares its calculated checksum with that stored in the last ROM locations, and they should agree. If so, there is a high probability that the ROM is good (there is a very small chance that a combination of errors in the test ROM data could still produce the same checksum value). If they do not agree, then there is a definite problem in the test ROM.

The checksum idea is illustrated in Figure 11-51(a) for a very small ROM. The data word stored in the last address is the eight-bit sum of the other seven data words (ignoring carries from the MSB). When this ROM is programmed, the checksum is placed in the last location. Figure 11-51(b) shows the data that might actually be read from a faulty ROM that was originally programmed with the data in (a). Note the error in the word at address 011. As the test instrument reads the data from each location of the faulty ROM, it calculates its own checksum from those data. Because of the error, the calculated checksum will be 10010011. When the test instrument compares this with the checksum value stored at ROM location 111, it sees that they disagree, and a ROM error is indicated. Of course, the exact location of the error cannot be determined.

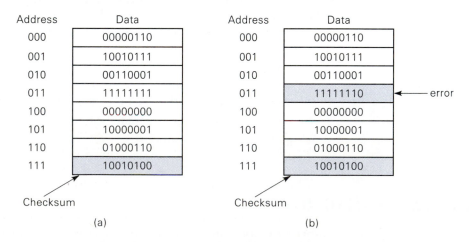

FIGURE 11-51 Checksum method for an 8 × 8 ROM: (a) ROM with correct data; (b) ROM with error in its data.

The checksum method can also be used by a computer or microprocessor-based equipment during an automatic power-up self-test to check out the contents of the system ROMs. Again, as in the self-test used for RAM, the CPU would execute a program on power-up that would do a checksum test on each ROM chip and would print out some type of status message. The self-test program itself will be located in a ROM, and so any error in that ROM could prevent the successful execution of the checksum tests.

1. What is a checksum? What is its purpose?

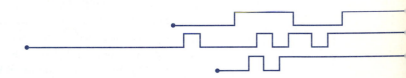

SUMMARY

1. All memory devices store binary logic levels (1s and 0s) in an array structure. The size of each binary word (number of bits) that is stored varies depending on the memory device. These binary values are referred to as *data*.

2. The place (location) in the memory device where any data value is stored is identified by another binary number referred to as an *address*. Each memory location has a unique address.

3. All memory devices operate in the same general way. To write data in memory, the address to be accessed is placed on the address input, the data value to be stored is applied to the data inputs, and the control signals are manipulated to store the data. To read data from memory, the address is applied, the control signals are manipulated, and the data value appears on the output pins.

4. Memory devices are often used along with a microprocessor CPU which generates the addresses and control signals and either provides the data to be stored or uses the data from the memory. Reading and writing are *always* done from the CPU's perspective. Writing puts data into the memory, and reading gets data out of the memory.

5. Most read-only memories (ROMs) have data entered one time, and from then on, their contents do not change. This storage process is called *programming*. They do not lose their data when power is removed from the device. MROMs are programmed during the manufacturing process. PROMs are programmed one time by the user. EPROMs are just like PROMs but can be erased using UV light. EEPROMs and flash memory devices are electrically erasable and can have their contents altered after programming. CD ROMs are used for mass storage of information that does not need to change.

6. Programmable logic devices (PLDs) are devices that contain an array of elements of basic logic circuits such as AND, OR, and NOT gates, as well as flip-flops and tristate buffers. A memory section is also contained in each PLD. The logic elements can be interconnected to form logic circuits. Each interconnection is controlled by a particular bit location in the memory. PLDs can imple-

ment any combinational logic function, limited only by the number of logic inputs and the number of potential outputs for a given programmable device. Sequential circuits are limited by the number of available flip-flops and the architectural restrictions of clocking them.

7. PLDs are programmed by using software on a PC and controlling a programmer that can be configured to accept the part you are using. With their versatility and ease of use, PLDs are gradually replacing conventional logic chips to implement digital systems.

8. Random access memory (RAM) is a generic term given to devices that can have data easily stored and retrieved. Data are retained in a RAM device only as long as power is applied.

9. Static RAM (SRAM) uses storage elements that are basically latch circuits. Once the data are stored, they will remain unchanged as long as power is applied to the chip. Static RAM is easier to use but more expensive per bit and consumes more power than dynamic RAM.

10. Dynamic RAM (DRAM) uses capacitors to store data by charging or discharging them. The simplicity of the storage cell allows DRAMs to store a great deal of data. Since the charge on the capacitors must be refreshed regularly, DRAMs are more complicated to use than SRAMs. Extra circuitry is often added to DRAM systems to control the reading, writing, and refreshing cycles. On many new devices these features are being integrated into the DRAM chip itself. The goal of DRAM technology is to put more bits on a smaller piece of silicon such that it consumes less power and responds faster.

11. Memory systems require a wide variety of different configurations. Memory chips can be combined to implement any desired configuration whether your system needs more bits per location or more total word capacity. All of the various types of ROM and RAM can be combined within the same memory system.

IMPORTANT TERMS

main memory	programmer-program-	application-specific
auxiliary memory	programming	integrated circuit (ASIC)
memory cell	chip select	refresh
memory word	power-down	JEDEC
byte	fusible link	address multiplexing
capacity	EEPROM	strobing
density	flash memory	row address strobe (RAS)
address	firmware	column address strobe
read operation	bootstrap program	(CAS)
write operation	programmable logic device	RAS-only refresh
access time	(PLD)	refresh counter
volatile memory	programmable array logic	DRAM controller
RAM	(PAL)	memory foldback
SAM	programmable output	memory map
RWM	polarity	FIFO
ROM	field programmable logic	data-rate buffer
static RAM (SRAM)	array (FPLA)	power-up self-test
dynamic RAM	complex PLDs	checksum
address bus	field programmable gate	
data bus	array (FPGA)	
control bus		

PROBLEMS

11-1. A certain memory has a capacity of 16K × 32. How many words does it store? What is the number of bits per word? How many memory cells does it contain?

11-2. How many different addresses are required by the memory of Problem 11-1?

11-3. What is the capacity of a memory that has 16 address inputs, four data inputs, and four data outputs?

11-4. A certain memory stores 8K 16-bit words. How many data input and data output lines does it have? How many address lines does it have? What is its capacity in bytes?

DRILL QUESTIONS

11-5. Define each of the following terms.

(a) RAM	(f) Capacity
(b) RWM	(g) Volatile
(c) ROM	(h) Density
(d) Internal memory	(i) Read
(e) Auxiliary memory	(j) Write

11-6. (a) What are the three buses in a computer memory system?

(b) Which bus is used by the CPU to select the memory location?

(c) Which bus is used to carry data from memory to the CPU during a read operation?

(d) What is the source of data on the data bus during a write operation?

11-7. Refer to Figure 11-6. Determine the data outputs for each of the following input conditions.

(a) $[A] = 1011$; $CS = 1$

(b) $[A] = 0111$; $CS = 0$

11-8. Refer to Figure 11-7.

(a) What register is enabled by input address 1011?

(b) What input address code selects register 4?

11-9. A certain ROM has a capacity of 16K × 4 and an internal structure like that shown in Figure 11-7.

(a) How many registers are in the array?

(b) How many bits are there per register?

(c) What size decoders does it require?

DRILL QUESTION

11-10. (a) *True or false:* ROMs cannot be erased.

(b) What is meant by *programming* or *burning* a ROM?

(c) Define a ROM's access time.

(d) How many data inputs, data outputs, and address inputs are needed for a 1024 × 4 ROM?

(e) What is the function of the decoders on a ROM chip?

SECTION 11-6

C, D **11-11.** Figure 11-52 shows how data from a ROM can be transferred to an external register. The ROM has the following timing parameters: $t_{ACC} = 250$ ns and $t_{OE} = 120$ ns. Assume that the new address inputs have been applied to the ROM 500 ns before the occurrence of the TRANSFER pulse. Determine the minimum duration of the TRANSFER pulse for reliable transfer of data.

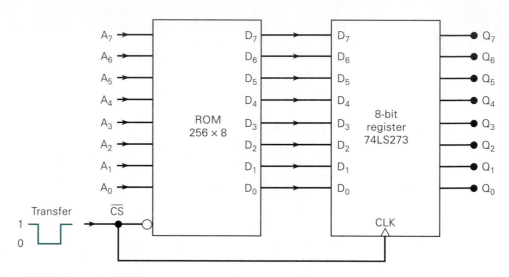

FIGURE 11-52 Problem 11-11.

C, D **11-12.** Repeat Problem 11-11 if the address inputs are changed 70 ns prior to the TRANSFER pulse.

SECTIONS 11-7 AND 11-8

11-13. DRILL QUESTION

For each statement below, indicate the type of memory being described: MROM, PROM, EPROM, EEPROM, flash. Some statements will correspond to more than one memory type.

(a) Can be programmed by the user, but cannot be erased.
(b) Is programmed by the manufacturer.
(c) Is volatile.
(d) Can be erased and reprogrammed over and over.
(e) Individual words can be erased and rewritten.
(f) Is erased with UV light.
(g) Is erased electrically.
(h) Uses fusible links.
(i) Can be erased in bulk or in sectors of 512 bytes.
(j) Does not have to be removed from system to be erased and reprogrammed.
(k) Requires a special supply voltage for reprogramming.
(l) Erase time is about 15 to 20 min.

11-14. Which transistors in Figure 11-9 will be conducting when $A_1 = A_0 = 1$ and $\overline{EN} = 0$?

11-15. Change the MROM connections in Figure 11-9 so that the MROM stores the function $y = 3x + 5$.

D **11-16.** Figure 11-53 shows a simple circuit for manually programming a 2732 EPROM. Each EPROM data pin is connected to a switch that can be set at a 1 or a 0 level. The address inputs are driven by a 12-bit counter. The 50-ms programming pulse comes from a one-shot each time the PROGRAM pushbutton is actuated.

(a) Explain how this circuit can be used to sequentially program the EPROM memory locations with the desired data.

(b) Show how 74293s and a 74121 can be used to implement this circuit.

(c) Should switch bounce have any effect on the circuit operation?

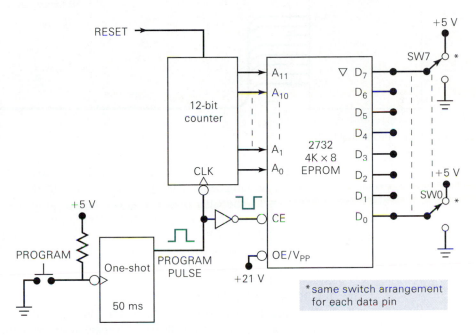

FIGURE 11-53 Problem 11-16.

N **11-17.** Figure 11-54 shows a 28F256A flash memory chip connected to a CPU over a data bus and an address bus. The CPU can write to or read from the flash memory array by sending the desired memory address and generating the appropriate control signals to the chip [Figure 11-15(b)]. The CPU can also write to the chip's command register (Figure 11-16) by generating the appropriate control signals and sending the desired command code over the data bus. For this latter operation, the CPU does not have to send a specific memory address to the chip; in other words, the address lines are "don't cares."

(a) Consider the following sequence of CPU operations. Determine what will have happened to the flash memory at the completion of the sequence. Assume that the command register is holding 00_{16}.

1. The CPU places 20_{16} on the data bus and pulses $\overline{CE}$ and $\overline{WE}$ LOW while holding $\overline{OE}$ HIGH. The address bus is at 0000_{16}.

2. The CPU repeats step 1.

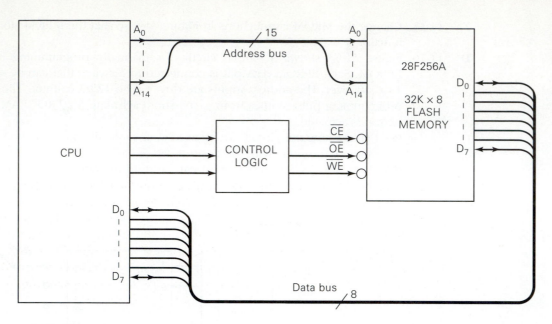

FIGURE 11-54 Problem 11-17.

(b) After the sequence above has been executed, the CPU executes the following sequence. Determine what this does to the flash memory chip.

1. The CPU places 40_{16} on the data bus and pulses $\overline{CE}$ and $\overline{WE}$ LOW while holding $\overline{OE}$ HIGH. The address bus is at 0000_{16}.

2. The CPU places $3C_{16}$ on the data bus and 2300_{16} onto the address bus, and it pulses $\overline{CE}$ and $\overline{WE}$ LOW while holding $\overline{OE}$ HIGH.

SECTION 11-9

N **11-18.** Another ROM application is the generation of timing and control signals. Figure 11-55 shows a 16 × 8 ROM with its address inputs driven by a MOD-16 counter so that the ROM addresses are incremented with each input pulse. Assume that the ROM is programmed as in Figure 11-6, and sketch the waveforms at each ROM output as the pulses are applied. Ignore ROM delay times. Assume that the counter starts at 0000.

FIGURE 11-55 Problem 11-18.

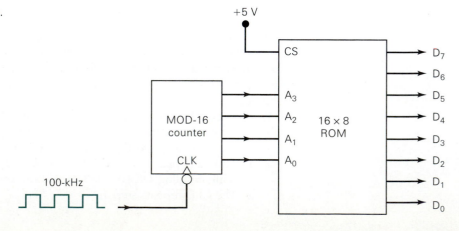

D   **11-19.** Change the program stored in the ROM of Problem 11-18 to generate the D_7 waveform of Figure 11-56.

FIGURE 11-56 Problem 11-19. D_7

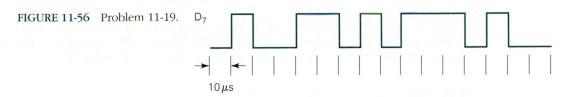

10 μs

C, N   **11-20.** Figure 11-57(a) shows the logic symbol for the 74185 IC, which is an "off-the-shelf" ROM that is programmed as a *binary-to-BCD converter*. It converts a six-bit binary input to a two-digit BCD output. Note that the LSB of the six-bit binary input is not connected to the ROM as an address input; instead, it is simply routed to the output and becomes the LSB of the LSD of the output. Figure 11-57(b) shows part of the truth table showing the contents of some of the locations in this ROM. Examine it to verify how the conversion from binary to BCD is taking place. Then fill in the missing entries in the table.

FIGURE 11-57 Problem 11-20.

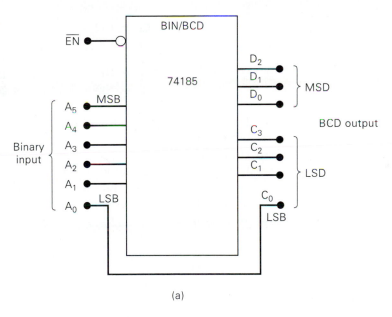

(a)

Binary						BCD						
A_5	A_4	A_3	A_2	A_1	A_0	D_2	D_1	D_0	C_3	C_2	C_1	C_0
1	0	0	1	0	1	0	1	1	0	1	1	1
0	0	1	1	1	0	0	0	1	0	1	0	0
1	1	1	1	1	0	1	1	0	0	0	1	0
0	1	1	1	0	0	0	1	0	1	0	0	0
1	1	0	1	0	1							
0	0	0	1	1	0							
						0	0	1	1	0	0	1
						1	0	0	1	0	0	0

(b)

D   **11-21.** Refer to the function generator of Figure 11-17.
      (a) What clock frequency will result in a 100-Hz sine wave at the output?
      (b) What method could be used to vary the peak-to-peak amplitude of the sine wave?

C   **11-22.** For the ML2035 of Figure 11-18, assume that a value of 038E (hex) in the latch will produce the desired frequency. Draw the timing diagram for the *LATI, SID,* and *SCK* inputs assuming that the LSB is shifted in first.

SECTION 11-12

11-23. **(a)** Draw the logic symbol for an MCM101514, a CMOS static RAM organized as a 256K × 4 with separate data in and data out, and an active-LOW chip enable.
      (b) Draw the logic symbol for an MCM6249, a CMOS static RAM organized as a 1M × 4 with common I/O, an active-LOW chip enable, and an active-LOW output enable.

SECTION 11-13

11-24. A certain static RAM has the following timing parameters (in nanoseconds):

$$t_{RC} = 100 \qquad t_{AS} = 20$$
$$t_{ACC} = 100 \qquad t_{AH} = \text{not given}$$
$$t_{CO} = 70 \qquad t_{W} = 40$$
$$t_{OD} = 30 \qquad t_{DS} = 10$$
$$t_{WC} = 100 \qquad t_{DH} = 20$$

  (a) How long after the address lines stabilize will valid data appear at the outputs during a read cycle?
  (b) How long will output data remain valid after $\overline{CS}$ returns HIGH?
  (c) How many read operations can be performed per second?
  (d) How long should $R/\overline{W}$ and $\overline{CS}$ be kept HIGH after the new address stabilizes during a write cycle?
  (e) What is the minimum time that input data must remain valid for a reliable write operation to occur?
  (f) How long must the address inputs remain stable after $R/\overline{W}$ and $\overline{CS}$ return HIGH?
  (g) How many write operations can be performed per second?

SECTIONS 11-14 TO 11-18

11-25. Draw the logic symbol for the TMS4256, which is a 256K × 1 DRAM. How many pins are saved by using address multiplexing for this DRAM?

D   **11-26.** Figure 11-58(a) shows a circuit that generates the $\overline{RAS}$, $\overline{CAS}$, and *MUX* signals needed for proper operation of the circuit of Figure 11-34(b). The 10-MHz master clock signal provides the basic timing for the computer. The memory request signal (*MEMR*) is generated by the CPU in synchronism with the master clock as shown in part (b) of the figure. *MEMR* is normally LOW and is driven HIGH whenever the CPU wants to access memory for a read or a write operation. Determine the waveforms at Q_0, $\overline{Q}_1$, and Q_2, and compare them with the desired waveforms of Figure 11-35.

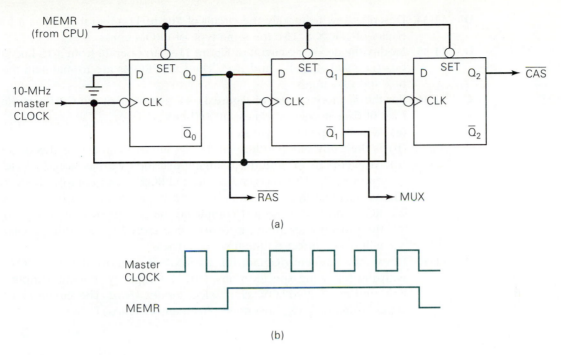

FIGURE 11-58   Problem 11-26.

D   **11-27.** Show how to connect two 74157 multiplexers (Section 9-7) to provide the multiplexing function required in Figure 11-34(b).

11-28. Refer to the signals in Figure 11-36. Describe what occurs at each of the labeled time points.

11-29. Repeat Problem 11-28 for Figure 11-37.

C   **11-30.** The 21256 is a 256K × 1 DRAM that consists of a 512 × 512 array of cells. The cells must be refreshed within 4 ms for data to be retained. Figure 11-39(a) shows the signals used to execute a $\overline{CAS}$-before-$\overline{RAS}$ refresh cycle. Each time a cycle such as this occurs, the on-chip refresh circuitry will refresh a row of the array at the row address specified by a refresh counter. The counter is incremented after each refresh. How often should $\overline{CAS}$-before-$\overline{RAS}$ cycles be applied in order for all of the data to be retained?

11-31. Study the functional block diagram of the TMS44100 DRAM in Figure 11-33.
   (a) What are the actual dimensions of the DRAM cell array?
   (b) If the cell array were actually square, how many rows would there be?
   (c) How would this affect the refresh time?

SECTION 11-19

D   **11-32.** Show how to combine two 6206 RAM chips (Figure 11-26) to produce a 32K × 16 module.

D   **11-33.** Show how to connect two of the 6264 RAM chips symbolized in Figure 11-29 to produce a 16K × 8 RAM module. The circuit should not require any additional logic. Draw a memory map showing the address range of each RAM chip.

D 11-34. Describe how to modify the circuit of Figure 11-43 so that it has a total capacity of 16K × 8. Use the same type of PROM chips.

D 11-35. Modify the decoding circuit of Figure 11-43 to operate from a 16-line address bus (i.e., add A_{13}, A_{14}, and A_{15}). The four PROMs are to maintain the same hex address ranges.

C 11-36. For the memory system of Figure 11-44, assume that the CPU is storing one byte of data at system address 4000 (hex).
(a) Which chip is the byte stored in?
(b) Is there any other address in this system that can access this data byte?
(c) Answer parts (a) and (b) assuming that the CPU has stored a byte at address 6007. (*Hint:* Remember, the EEPROM is not completely decoded.)
(d) Assume that the program is storing a sequence of data bytes in the EEPROM and that it has just completed the 2048th byte at address 67FF. If the programmer allows it to store one more byte at address 6800, what will be the effect on the first 2048 bytes?

D 11-37. Draw the complete diagram for a 256K × 8 memory that uses RAM chips with the following specifications: 64K × 4 capacity, common input/output line, and two active-LOW chip select inputs. [*Hint:* The circuit can be designed using only two inverters (plus memory chips).]

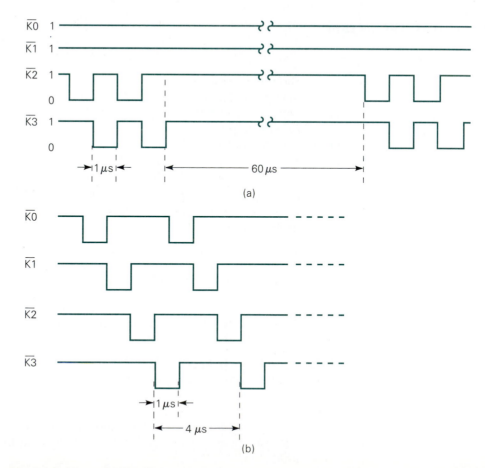

FIGURE 11-59 Problems 11-40 and 11-41.

SECTION 11-21

11-38. Modify the RAM circuit of Figure 11-48 as follows: change the OR gate to an AND gate and disconnect its output from C; connect the AND output to E_3; connect C to ground. Determine the address range for each RAM module.

C, D   **11-39.** Show how to expand the system of Figure 11-48 to an 8K × 8 with addresses ranging from 0000 to 1FFF. (*Hint:* This can be done by adding the necessary memory modules and modifying the existing decoding logic.)

T   **11-40.** A dynamic test is performed on the decoding logic of Figure 11-48 by keeping $\phi_2 = 1$ and connecting the outputs of a six-bit counter to address inputs A_{10} to A_{15}. The decoder outputs are monitored with an oscilloscope (or a logic analyzer) as the counter is continuously pulsed by a 1-MHz clock. Figure 11-59(a) shows the displayed signals. What are the most probable faults?

C, T   **11-41.** Repeat Problem 11-40 for the decoder outputs shown in Figure 11-59(b).

C, D   **11-42.** Consider the RAM system of Figure 11-48. The checkerboard pattern test will not be able to detect certain types of faults. For instance, assume that there is a break in the connection to the A input to the decoder. If a checkerboard pattern SELF-TEST is performed on this circuit, the displayed messages will state that the memory is OK.

(a) Explain why the circuit fault was not detected.

(b) How would you modify the SELF-TEST so that faults such as this will be detected?

T   **11-43.** Assume that the 1K × 8 modules used in Figure 11-48 are formed from two 1K × 4 RAM chips. The following messages are printed out when the power-up self-test is performed on this RAM system:

```
module-0 test OK
module-1 test OK
address 0800 faulty at bits 4-7
address 0801 faulty at bits 4-7
address 0802 faulty at bits 4-7
    .   .   .   .      .     .   .
    .   .   .   .      .     .   .
    .   .   .   .      .     .   .
address 0BFE faulty at bits 4-7
address 0BFF faulty at bits 4-7
module-3 test OK
```

Examine these messages and list the possible faults.

T   **11-44.** The following messages are printed out when the power-up self-test is performed on the RAM system of Figure 11-50.

```
module-0 test OK
module-1 test OK
module-2 test OK
address 0C00 faulty at bit 7
address 0C01 faulty at bit 7
address 0C02 faulty at bit 7
    .      .  .      .     .
    .      .  .      .     .
    .      .  .      .     .
address 0FFE faulty at bit 7
address 0FFF faulty at bit 7
```

Examine these messages and list the possible faults.

T **11-45.** What messages would be printed out when a power-up self-test is performed on the RAM system of Figure 11-50 if there is a short between the decoder's $\overline{K2}$ and $\overline{K3}$ outputs?

SECTION 11-22

T **11-46.** Consider the 16 × 8 ROM in Figure 11-6. Replace the data word stored at address location 1111 with a checksum calculated from the other 15 data words.

ANSWERS TO SECTION REVIEW QUESTIONS

SECTION 11-1

1. See text. 2. 16 bits per word; 8192 words; 131,072 bits or cells 3. In a read operation, a word is taken from a memory location and is transferred to another device. In a write operation, a new word is placed in a memory location, replacing the one previously stored there. 4. True 5. SAM: Access time is not constant but depends on the physical location of the word being accessed. RAM: Access time is the same for any address location. 6. RWM is memory that can be read from or written to with equal ease. ROM is memory that is mainly read from and is written into very infrequently. 7. False; its data must be periodically refreshed.

SECTION 11-2

1. 14, 12, 12 2. Commands the memory to perform either a read operation or a write operation 3. When in its active state, this input enables the memory to perform the read or the write operation selected by the $R/\overline{W}$ input. When in its inactive state, this input disables the memory so that it cannot perform the read or the write function.

SECTION 11-3

1. Address lines, data lines, control lines 2, 3. See text.

SECTION 11-4

1. True 2. Apply desired address inputs; activate control input(s); data appear at data outputs.
3. Process of entering data into ROM

SECTION 11-5

1. $A_3A_2A_1A_0 = 1001$ 2. The row-select decoder activates one of the enable inputs of all registers in the selected row. The column-select decoder activates one of the enable inputs of all registers in the selected column. The output buffers pass the data from the internal data bus to the ROM output pins when the CS input is activated.

SECTION 11-7

1. False; by the manufacturer 2. A PROM can be programmed once by the user. It cannot be erased and reprogrammed. 3. True 4. By exposure to UV light 5. True 6. Automatically programs data into memory cells one address at a time 7. An EEPROM can be electrically erased and reprogrammed without removal from its circuit, and in a much shorter time than EPROM. 8. Low density; high cost
9. EEPROM 10. One

SECTION 11-8

1. Electrically erasable and programmable in circuit
2. Higher density; lower cost 3. Short erase and programming times 4. For the erase and programming operations 5. Contents of this register control all internal chip functions. 6. To confirm that a memory address has been successfully erased (i.e., data = all 1s) 7. To confirm that a memory address has been programmed with the correct data

SECTION 11-9

1. Microcomputer programs stored in ROM 2. On power-up, the computer executes a small bootstrap program from ROM to initialize the system hardware and to load the operating system from mass storage (disk). 3. Circuit that takes data represented in one type of code and converts it to another type of code
4. Counter, ROM, DAC, low-pass filter 5. They are nonvolatile, fast, reliable, small, and low-power.

SECTION 11-10

1. An IC that contains large numbers of gates, FFs, and registers whose interconnections can be modified by the user to perform specific functions 2. $O_1 = A$
3. An intact fuse 4. A hard-wired connection
6. The PAL has a programmable AND array; the PROM has a programmable OR array. 8. An FLPA contains both programmable AND and OR arrays. 9. See Figure 11-24. 10. To invert or not invert the device outputs 11. Can be erased and reprogrammed
12. An FPGA

SECTION 11-12

1. Desired address applied to address inputs; $R/\overline{W} = 1$; CS or CE activated   2. To reduce pin count   3. 24, including V_{CC} and ground

SECTION 11-13

1. SRAM cells are flip-flops; DRAM cells use capacitors.
2. CMOS   3. RAM   4. CPU   5. Read- and write-cycle times   6. False; when $\overline{WE}$ is LOW, the I/O pins act as data inputs regardless of the state of $\overline{OE}$ (second entry in mode table).   7. A_{13} can remain connected to pin 26. A_{14} must be removed, and pin 27 must be connected to +5 V.

SECTION 11-14

1. Generally slower speed; need to be refreshed
2. Low power; high capacity; lower cost per bit
3. DRAM

SECTION 11-15

1. 256 rows $\times$ 256 columns   2. It saves pins on the chip.   3. 1M = 1024K = 1024 $\times$ 1024. Thus, there are 1024 rows by 1024 columns. Since $1024 = 2^{10}$, the chip needs 10 address inputs.   4. $\overline{RAS}$ is used to latch the row address into the DRAM's row address register. $\overline{CAS}$ is used to latch the column address into the column address register.   5. MUX multiplexes the full address into the row and column addresses for input to the DRAM.

SECTION 11-16

1. (a) True   (b) False   (c) False   (d) True
2. MUX

SECTION 11-17

1. (a) True   (b) False   2. It provides row addresses to the DRAM during refresh cycles.
3. Address multiplexing and the refresh operation
4. (a) False   (b) True

SECTION 11-18

1. No   2. Memory locations with same upper address (same row)   3. Only the column address must be latched.   4. Extended data output   5. *Burst*
6. The system clock

SECTION 11-19

1. Sixteen   2. Four   3. False; when expanding memory capacity, each chip is selected by a different decoder output (see Figure 11-43).   4. True

SECTION 11-20

1. Battery backup for CMOS RAM; flash memory
2. Economics   3. Data are read out of memory in the same order they were written in.   4. A FIFO used to transfer data between devices with widely different operating speeds

SECTION 11-21

1. Prevents decoding glitches by disabling the decoder while the address lines are changing   2. A way to test RAM by writing a checkerboard pattern (first 01010101, then 10101010) into each memory location and then reading it. It is used because it will detect any shorts or interactions between adjacent cells.   3. An automatic test of RAM performed by a computer on power-up

SECTION 11-22

1. A code placed in the last one or two ROM locations that represents the sum of the expected ROM data from all other locations. It is used as a means to test for errors in one or more ROM locations.

CHAPTER 12

Applications of a Programmable Logic Device

■ **OUTLINE**

Diagrams of the GAL 16V8A device presented in this chapter have been reproduced through the courtesy of Lattice Semiconductor Corporation, Hillsboro, Oregon.

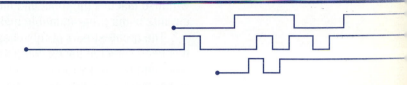

■ OBJECTIVES

Upon completion of this chapter, you will be able to:

- Identify applications of programmable logic devices.
- Understand the hardware architecture of a typical programmable logic device.
- Use software tools capable of programming a large variety of programmable devices.
- Implement a logic design completely using programmable logic devices.

■ INTRODUCTION

Throughout this book we have examined the various building blocks of digital systems. As each building block was described, an actual integrated circuit was cited that could be used to implement the logic function in a circuit. Many systems in use today are combinations of integrated circuits that meet the needs of the system. Imagine for a moment that you are the circuit designer and have developed a conceptual circuit made up of combinational logic, decoders, counters, registers, and so on. How will you actually implement your conceptual circuit? How will you prove that your design works? Once the actual parts have been specified and the final schematic diagram is drawn, you will probably build it on a breadboard.

This process is, by nature, prone to errors in wiring. Use of many different integrated circuits tends to create massive numbers of interconnecting wires. Even with very orderly breadboarding techniques, it is often very difficult to trace the path of a wire in a circuit visually. By using the troubleshooting techniques presented in this book, you can isolate the problem, but correcting a wiring error may still be difficult on the breadboard.

Imagine being able to consolidate all of the various devices into a single integrated circuit that has been "programmed" to behave as needed by your circuit design. The programmable logic devices introduced in Chapter 11 provide this capability. With these devices, the possibility of errors shifts from the wiring to the programming. Consequently, a device that is capable of being erased and reprogrammed is ideal in situations where it is likely that changes and revisions will be made repeatedly. The purpose of this chapter is to provide more detailed information on specific programmable logic devices (PLDs) that are reprogrammable. We will also discuss the tools and methods used to develop logic designs into working circuits using programmable logic.

The greatest part of this chapter covers a particular device, the GAL 16V8A. It has been selected for its compatibility with nearly all PAL devices, its reasonable cost, and its ability to be erased and reprogrammed. These features lend themselves well to the laboratory and prototyping environments. The concepts that apply to this device are equally applicable to other types of PLDs. CUPL, one of the many software packages used to program PLDs, will also be described to enable you to set up a development system. It was chosen because of its ease of use, its popularity in industry, and the company's willingness to allow it to be distributed with this book.

12-1 THE GAL 16V8A (GENERIC ARRAY LOGIC)

The GAL 16V8A was introduced by *Lattice Semiconductor*. Its architecture is very similar to that of the PAL devices described in Chapter 11 (Figure 11-22). Consequently, it can be used as a generic pin-compatible replacement for most PAL devices. Instead of using one-time programmable fuse links to select the input terms that produce the proper product terms, the GAL devices use an EEPROM array. Certain locations in the memory array are designated to control programmable connections for the **input term matrix.** Each bit in the input term matrix represents a programmable connection between a row and a column. This allows the device to be erased and reprogrammed. CMOS technology allows the device to operate at low power with speeds comparable to TTL speeds. Fortunately, it is not necessary to delve into the addresses of each bit location in the matrix. The programming software takes care of these details in a user-friendly manner.

The complete logic diagram of the GAL 16V8A is shown in Figure 12-1. This device has eight dedicated input pins (pins 2–9), two special function inputs (pins 1 and 11), and eight pins (12–19) that can be used as inputs or outputs. The major components of the GAL devices are the input term matrix; the AND gates, which generate the products of input terms; and the **output logic macro cells (OLMCs).** Notice that the eight inputs (pins 2–9) are each connected directly to a column of the input term matrix. The complement of each of these inputs is also connected to a column of the matrix. These pins must always be specified as inputs when programming the 16V8A. A logic level and its complement are also fed from each OLMC back to a column of the input matrix. The source of these logic levels is determined by the configuration of each OLMC, as will be discussed later. This accounts for the 32 input variables (columns in the input matrix) that can be programmed as connections to the 64 multiple-input AND gates.

GAL16V8 LOGIC DIAGRAM

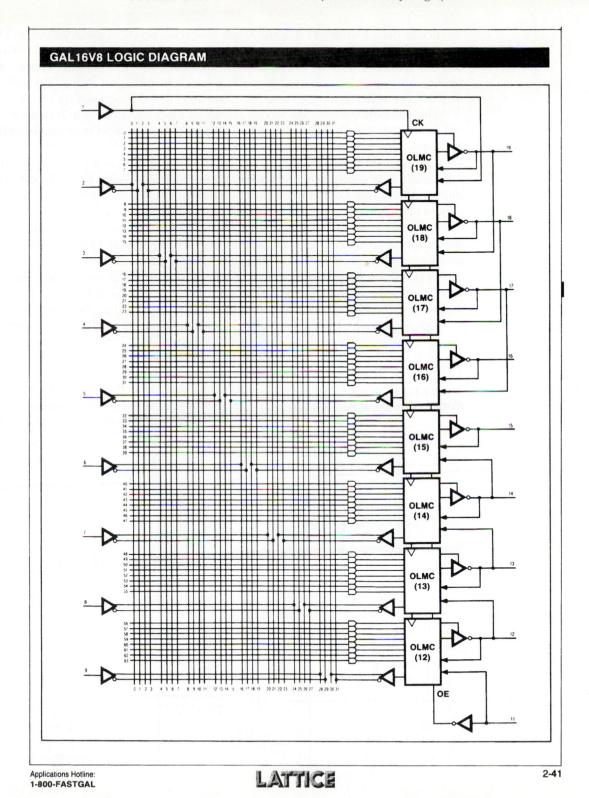

FIGURE 12-1   GAL 16V8A logic diagram.

Recall from Chapter 11 that the single row line shown as an input to the AND gates actually represents up to 32 inputs to the gate (see Figure 11-20). Any column that is shown as connected (designated by an X) to a row is being ANDed with any other column that is connected to the same row. In the input matrix, any column may be connected to an AND gate input row during the programming process.

The flexibility of the GAL 16V8A lies in its programmable output logic macro cell. Eight different products (outputs of AND gates) are applied as inputs to each of the eight output logic macro cells. Within each OLMC the products are ORed together to generate the sum of products (SOP). Recall from Chapter 4 that any logic function can be expressed in SOP form. Within the OLMC, the SOP output may be routed to the output pin to implement a combinational circuit, or it may be clocked into a D flip-flop to implement a registered output circuit.

To understand the detailed operation of the OLMC, refer to Figure 12-2, which shows the structure of OLMC(n), where n is a number from 12 to 19. Notice that seven of the products are unconditionally connected to the OR gate inputs. The eighth product term is connected to a two-input product term multiplexer (PTMUX) which drives the eighth input to the OR gate. The eighth product term also connects to one input of a four-input multiplexer (TSMUX) which enables the tristate inverter that drives the output pin [I/O(n)]. The output multiplexer (OMUX) is a two-input MUX that selects between the combinational output (OR gate) and the registered output (the D flip-flop). A fourth MUX selects the logic signal that is fed back to the input matrix. This is called the *feedback* multiplexer (FMUX).

Each of these multiplexers is controlled by programmable bits in the EEPROM matrix. This is the way that the OLMC configuration can be altered by the program-

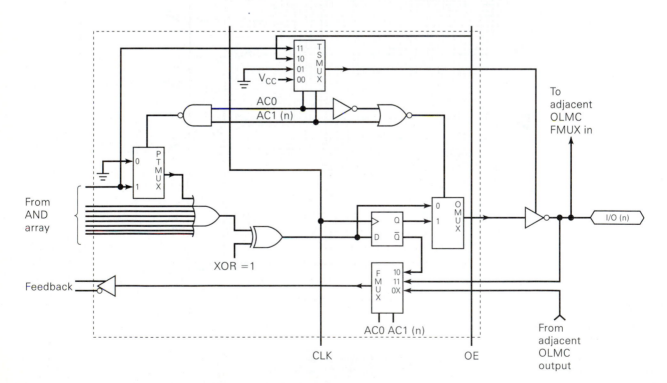

FIGURE 12-2 Output logic macro cell for the GAL 16V8A.

mer. Another programmable bit is the input to the XOR gate. This provides the programmable output polarity feature as described in Chapter 11 (see Figure 11-23). Recall that an EX-OR gate can be used to complement a logic signal selectively, as shown in Figure 12-3.

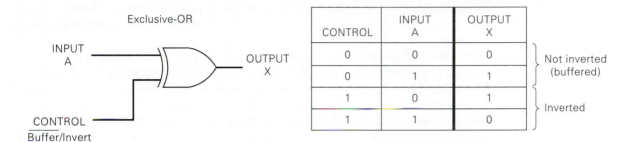

CONTROL	INPUT A	OUTPUT X	
0	0	0	Not inverted (buffered)
0	1	1	
1	0	1	Inverted
1	1	0	

FIGURE 12-3   Using EX-OR to selectively complement.

We can understand the various configuration options by studying the possible inputs to each multiplexer. The TSMUX controls the tristate buffer's enable input. If the V_{CC} input is selected, the output is always enabled, like a standard combinational logic gate. If the grounded input is selected, the tristate output of the inverter is always in its high-impedance state (allowing the I/O pin to be used as an input). Another input to the MUX that may be selected comes from the *OE* input, which is pin 11. This allows the output to be enabled or disabled by an external logic signal applied to pin 11. The last possible input selection is a product term from the eighth AND gate. This allows an AND combination of terms from the input matrix to enable or disable the output.

The FMUX selects the signal that is fed back into the input matrix. In this case there are three possible selections. Selecting the *MUX* input that is connected to an adjacent stage or the *MUX* input connected to its own OLMC I/O pin allows an existing output state to be fed back to the input matrix in some of the modes of operation. This feature gives the GAL 16V8A the ability to implement sequential circuits such as the cross-coupled NAND gate latch circuit described in Chapter 5. These feedback options also allow I/O pins to be used as a dedicated input as opposed to an output. One of these two feedback paths is chosen, depending on the MODE that the chip is programmed for. The third option, selecting the output from the D flip-flop, allows the present state of the flip-flop (which can be used to determine the next state) to be fed back to the input matrix. This allows synchronous sequential circuits to be implemented, such as counters and shift registers.

With all of these options it would seem that there must be a long list of possible configurations. In actual practice all of these configuration decisions are made by the software, as we will see later in this chapter. Actually, the GAL 16V8A has only three different modes, but it is very important to understand how the hardware is configured in each mode in order to understand the capabilities and limitations of the device. The three configuration modes are: (1) *simple mode* which is used to implement simple SOP combinational logic without tristate outputs; (2) *complex mode* which implements SOP combinational logic with tristate outputs that are enabled by an AND product expression; and (3) *registered mode* which allows individual OLMCs to operate in a combinational configuration with tristate outputs (similar to the complex mode) or in a synchronous mode with clocked D FFs synchronized to a common clock signal.

Row 60 of the EEPROM array stores the 82-bit *architecture control word*. Each of the bits plays a role in determining the hardware configuration of the OLMCs. Figure 12-4 shows how the bits are arranged. Unless you are manually programming the GAL 16V8A (which is almost never done), you will not have to be concerned about the bit pattern of this control word; it will be taken care of by the programming software. You should, however, understand the functions of each bit. The SYN and AC0 bits are used to specify one of the three configuration modes above for the entire chip. The AC1(*n*) bits (one per OLMC) determine the operation of each individual OLMC in that mode. The eight XOR(*n*) bits are used to selectively complement the respective OLMC outputs. The 64 product term disable (PTD) bits are used to disable those AND gates in the array that are not being used.

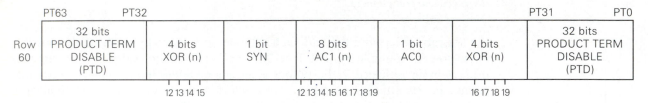

FIGURE 12-4 The architecture control word for the GAL 16V8A.

Simple Mode

The chip is programmed in the simple mode by setting SYN = 1 and AC0 = 0 in the control word. In this mode two configurations are possible for each macrocell (OLMC):

Dedicated input [when AC1(*n*) = 1]
Dedicated combinational output [when AC1(*n*) = 0]

Each OLMC is independently programmed in one of these two configurations. The dedicated input configuration connects an OLMC I/O pin to the input matrix by routing the signal through the adjacent OLMC, indicated by the colored line in Figure 12-5 for pin 18. The tristate inverter for pin 18 is unconditionally disabled (high impedance). Pin 11 and pin 1 serve as inputs that are routed through OLMCs 12 and 19, respectively. In this mode, pins 15 and 16 cannot be used as dedicated input since they do not have a connection to an adjacent cell.

The dedicated output configuration for an OLMC has the tristate inverter enabled at all times as shown in Figure 12-5 for OLMC 19. This is the only configuration capable of getting eight product terms into an SOP expression to generate a combinational output. OLMCs 15 and 16 are always in the dedicated output configuration with no feedback in the simple mode. The other six OLMCs are capable of having their outputs fed back into the input matrix by way of an adjacent cell. For example, note that the OLMC 19 output is fed back to the input matrix through OLMC 18.

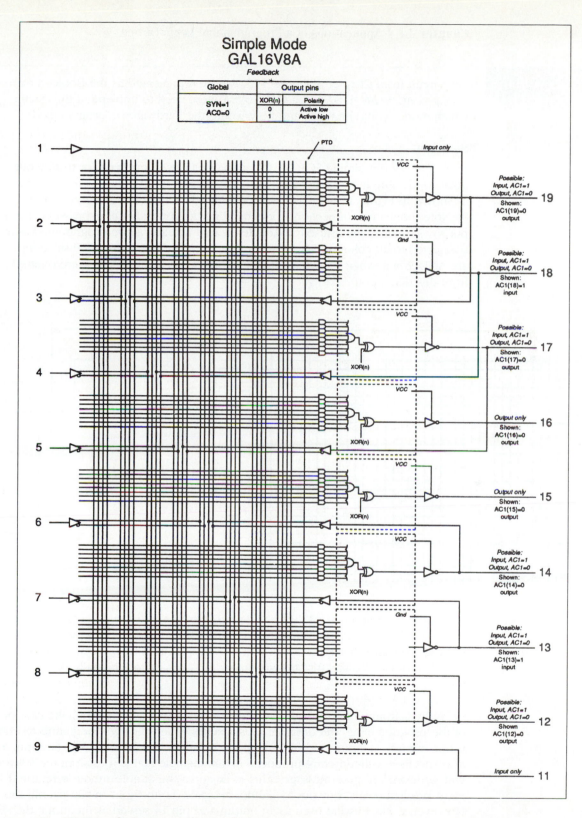

FIGURE 12-5   OLMC configurations in the simple mode.

EXAMPLE 12-1	The circuit from Chapter 3, Figure 3-17, can be represented as the Boolean expression $y = AC + B\overline{C} + \overline{A}BC$. If a GAL 16V8A were used to implement this circuit, which mode would be used, and how would the hardware be programmed?

Solution

The expression is simple SOP combinational logic with no need for tristate outputs, so the simple mode is used (SYN = 1, AC0 = 0). The hardware is configured as shown in Figure 12-6. OLMC 19 is configured as a dedicated output [AC1(19) = 0]. Note the matrix connections for generating the desired SOP expression. The input rows to all of the unused AND gates would actually all be programmed as connected to all columns. This assures that the AND gate output is 0 since inputs are ANDed with their complements. The connection symbols (**X**) were omitted from this diagram for clarity.

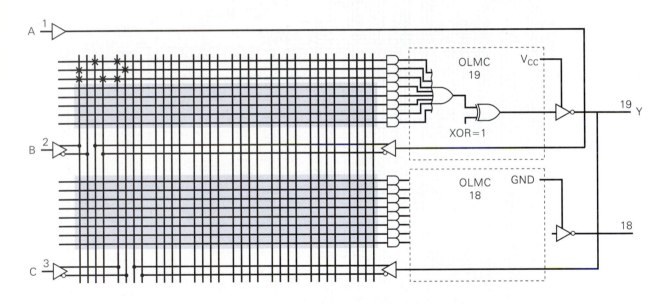

All columns connected to rows

FIGURE 12-6 Simple combinational logic implementation.

Why is it important to know so many details if the software will take care of all of the programming? The designer must decide which pins will be connected (and programmed) as inputs and outputs. If the designer assigns pin 15 as an input and also specifies eight different product terms in a single SOP expression, the software will generate an error message. This is because the simple mode is required for eight product terms, but pin 15 cannot be used as an input in the simple mode. However, if pin 15 were used as an output and pin 14 served as the input, the software would program the device in the simple mode.

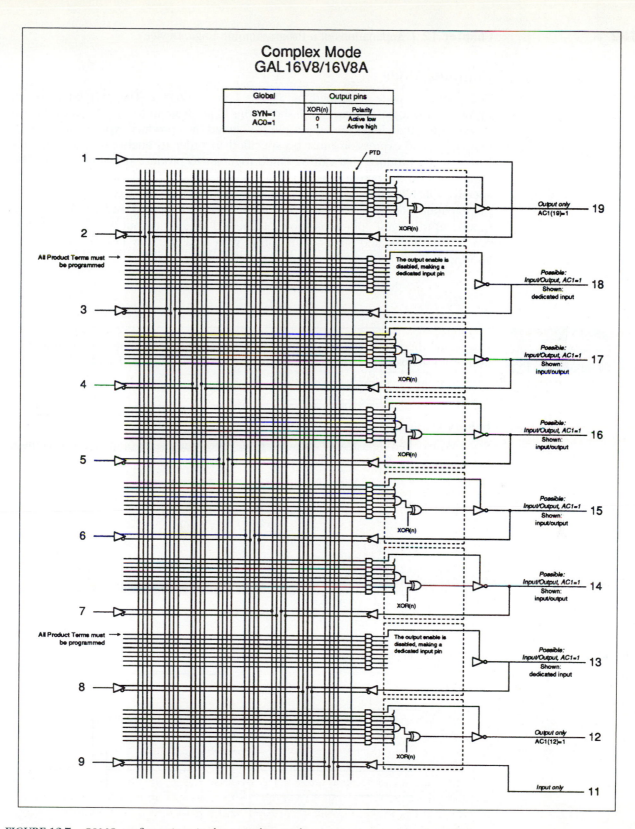

FIGURE 12-7   OLMC configurations in the complex mode.

Complex Mode

The complex mode is defined by SYN = 1 and AC0 = 1. The AC1 bit for each OLMC is also logic 1. Figure 12-7 shows the logic diagram for the 16V8A. The tristate inverter that drives the output pin is enabled by a product expression. In other words, a logic expression must be specified in order to enable the output. This leaves seven products that can be ORed together to produce the SOP output. The logic states on the output pins of OLMCs 13–18 are also fed back through their respective OLMC to the input matrix. OLMCs 12 and 19 do not have feedback or input capability since the feedback path is used to allow pins 11 and 1 to be used as inputs. In this figure, pin 19 is shown to be a dedicated output with no feedback, pin 18 is an input, and pin 17 is an output with feedback. Pin 17 can also serve as an input when the tristate inverter is disabled.

**EXAMPLE
12-2**

Determine the mode, write the logic equations, and draw the hardware configuration of a transparent *D* latch with tristate outputs enabled by *CS*1 and *CS*2, as shown in Figure 12-8(a).

Solution

Since no clocked (registered) outputs are needed, but tristate outputs are specified, the complex mode is used. The equations are:

$$\text{output enable} = CS1 \cdot \overline{CS2}$$
$$Q = D \cdot EN + Q \cdot \overline{EN}$$

The GAL 16V8A configuration is shown in Figure 12-8(b) with OLMC 17 used to generate *Q*. Note the matrix connections for implementing the equations.

FIGURE 12-8 (a) Transparent latch with tristate outputs.

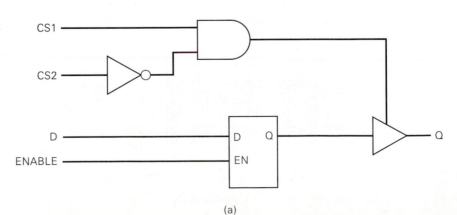

(a)

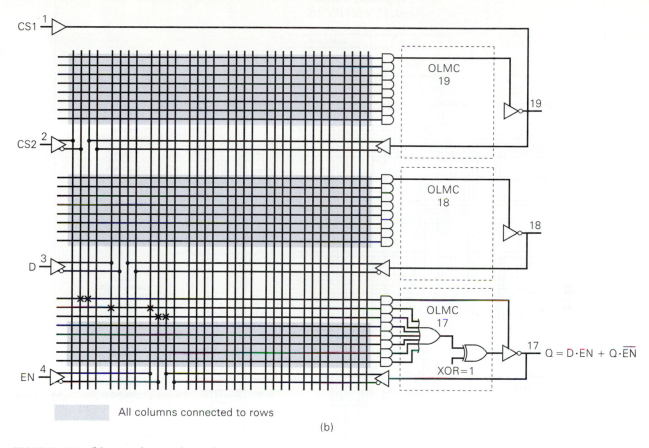

All columns connected to rows

(b)

FIGURE 12-8 (b) Complex mode implementation of the latch.

Registered Mode

The registered mode is characterized by SYN = 0 and AC0 = 1. There are two possible configurations for each OLMC in this mode:

1. *Registered configuration* (when AC1 = 0)
2. *Combinational configuration* (when AC1 = 1)

The operation of the combinational configuration (Figure 12-9, OLMCs 12 and 18) is similar to OLMC operation in the complex mode. The output enable is controlled by a product expression from the input matrix. This can provide the ability to use bidirectional I/O in bus applications. The output signal is also fed back into the input matrix through the corresponding OLMC.

   The registered configuration (OLMCs 13–17, 19) uses a D flip-flop in each OLMC to synchronize all registered output data to a common clock edge. Pin 1 is the dedicated input pin for the clock signal. All of the tristate inverters for the OLMCs that are configured as registered output are controlled by pin 11 ($\overline{OE}$). The registered outputs have up to eight product terms for the SOP logic that drives the *D* input to the flip-flop.

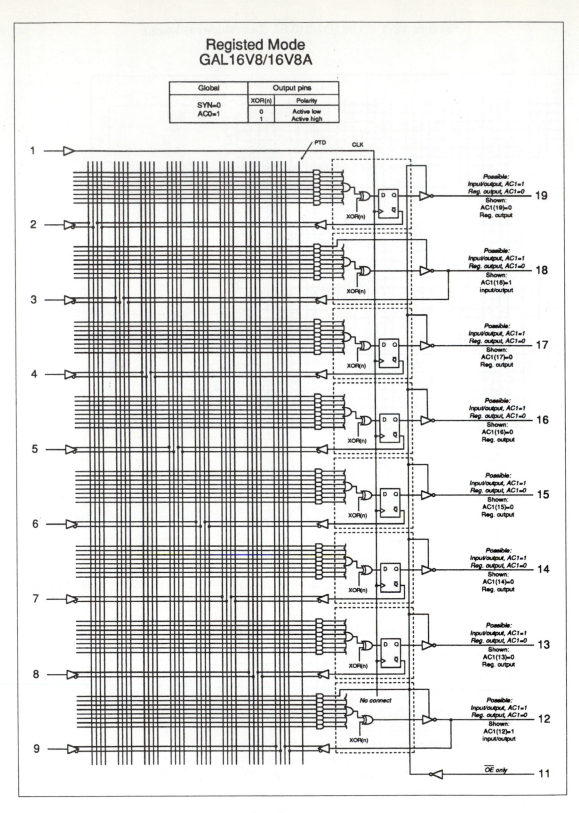

FIGURE 12-9 OLMC configurations in the registered mode.

Determine the GAL 16V8A mode, write the logic equations, and draw the hardware configuration of a two-bit, MOD-4 up counter with a decoded output for the *QB, QA* = 1, 1 state, as shown in Figure 12-10(a).

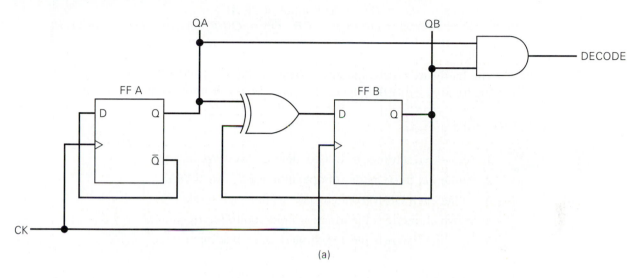

(a)

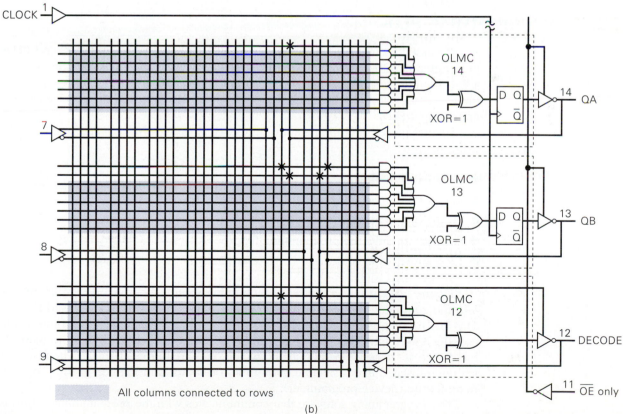

All columns connected to rows

(b)

FIGURE 12-10 (a) A MOD-4 binary counter with decoded output; (b) registered mode implementation of the counter.

Solution

The MOD-4 counter requires registered mode. The equations for the flip-flop D inputs and the decoder output are

$$D_A = \overline{QA} \quad \text{(the } D \text{ input of FF } A)$$
$$D_B = \overline{QB} \cdot QA + QB \cdot \overline{QA} = QB \oplus QA \quad \text{(the } D \text{ input of FF } B)$$
$$\text{DECODE} = QB \cdot QA$$

The hardware configuration is shown in Figure 12-10(b). You should trace through the logic to verify that the expressions above are implemented correctly.

Review Questions

1. Name two advantages of GAL devices over PAL devices.

2. Name the three modes of operation for a GAL 16V8A.

3. Name each OLMC configuration within each mode.

4. In which mode is the tristate output controlled by pin 11?

5. In which mode is pin 1 dedicated as a clock input?

12-2 PROGRAMMING PLDs

We discussed the concept of programming PROMs, EPROMs, EEPROMs, and PLDs in Chapter 11. Obviously, there must be a better way to specify a configuration for a PLD than drawing **X**'s and **O**'s on a matrix diagram. To understand and appreciate the role of development software, let's examine some details in the process of programming a PLD.

Several pieces of equipment are necessary in order to design and build circuits using PLDs:

■ Personal computer (PC)

■ PLD development software

■ Programming fixture

■ Software to drive the programming fixture

■ Programmable logic device

Figure 12-11 shows a typical programming setup. The initial design is entered into the computer in one of several possible ways which will be discussed shortly. The PC, running the development software, translates the input design into a file called a "fuse plot." This file is like a map that shows which fuses in a programmable device are to be zapped open and which ones are to remain intact. The fuse plot is then translated into a suitable output file format for transmission to the programming fixture (device programmer).

The programming software that communicates with the programming fixture is then invoked on the PC. This allows the user to inform the programming fixture of the type of device that is to be programmed. The output file is then sent over a ca-

FIGURE 12-11   A PLD development system.

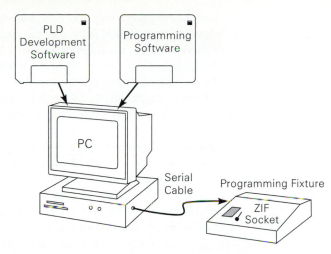

ble to the programming fixture. This process is called **downloading.** Finally, the PLD is inserted into the programming fixture socket, and the command is sent from the PC to program the part. Programming fixtures normally have a special socket that allows you to drop the chip in and then clamp the contacts to the pins. This is called a **zero-insertion force (ZIF) socket.** Universal programming fixtures that can program almost any type of device, including PROMs, EPROMs, single-chip microcomputers, and a host of PLDs, are available from numerous manufacturers.

Fortunately, as programmable parts began to proliferate, manufacturers saw the need to standardize pin assignments and programming methods. As a result, the Joint Electronic Device Engineering Council **(JEDEC)** was formed. One of the results was JEDEC standard 3, a standard format for transferring programming data for PLDs, independent of the PLD manufacturer or programming software. Pin assignments for various IC packages were also standardized, making universal programmers less complicated. Consequently, programming fixtures are able to program numerous types of PLDs. The software that allows the designer to specify a configuration for a PLD simply needs to produce an output file that conforms to the JEDEC standard. Then this JEDEC file can be loaded into any JEDEC-compatible PLD programmer that is capable of programming the desired type of PLD.

Review Questions

1. Name the two software packages that are used to implement PLD circuits.
2. Define the following.
   (a) *fuse plot*   (b) *output file*
3. What is a JEDEC file?

12-3   DEVELOPMENT SOFTWARE

The process of generating a JEDEC file to transfer a design to the PLD programming fixture would be extremely tedious if done by hand. Over the past 20 years, many software packages have been developed to allow users to enter their design in some convenient way and then automatically create the JEDEC file for the specified device. The original software, developed by Monolithic Memories, Inc. (MMI), was called PALASM, an abbreviation for PAL *assembler*. Versions of this software can still be found in the public domain for low-level PLD development. However, the market has since produced software for PLD development that is much more powerful. These tools are referred to as logic **compilers.** Assemblers and compilers are computer programs that run on a personal computer. The user provides an input file in a format that the program can interpret. The primary difference between an assembler and a compiler lies in the method used to define the relationship between the inputs and the outputs. An assembler requires an input file that very concisely defines the operation of the device in terms very closely associated with the programmable device's hardware, such as Boolean logic equations. A compiler can accept a more abstract representation of the same design and translate it into the hardware details necessary to program the device.

All assemblers and compilers allow the user to enter his or her design in the form of Boolean equations that define the output function in terms of the available inputs. In this case the input file is an ASCII text file, created on any generic editor for your PC. In this file the programmable device type is specified, along with other assorted information, such as designer name, date, revision, and so on. The pin assignments must also be specified and labeled with input and output signal names. Next, a set of Boolean logic equations are listed which specify the logical operation of the device. Most of these development tools are able to simplify the equations that are in the input file using reduction algorithms similar to those you have learned in previous chapters. This feature helps the designer by allowing the logic to be specified in the most straightforward form without trying to minimize the equations. If the minimized form of the logic equation requires more gates than the specified programmable device has, an error message is generated.

The high-level compilers have several other options for specifying the circuit operation. One of these options is called *schematic capture*. This mode of entry allows the operation to be specified simply by drawing a logic circuit schematic diagram using a CAD (computer-aided design) software package. This graphic file is then translated into some form of net list which specifies the types of components and how they are connected. Several different programs may be necessary to "massage" the various types of CAD drawings into the form acceptable to the compiler. This method may be quite helpful in retrofitting an existing circuit to use PLDs.

As you have learned from previous chapters, logic circuits are designed by starting with things like truth tables and state tables. These tables are used to simplify the problem and produce logic relationships that are used to implement an actual circuit. You also know that this process is often very long and tedious. The logic compilers allow you to enter your design in the form of truth tables or state tables. Some compilers can even accept a timing diagram as the input. The logic compiler software goes through all of the tedious steps of reduction, generation of logic relationships, and production of the proper type of output file for programming the PLD you had in mind.

These methods of design entry have served the needs of industry very well during the period of transition from discrete logic chips to the use of programmable devices. During the past decade, digital systems have become more and more complex. In the early 1980s, the U.S. Department of Defense was working on its Very High-Speed Integrated Circuit (VHSIC) program. In the process it developed a "hardware description language" to specify these very complex systems. This language has evolved into an IEEE standard method of describing logic circuits for design and documentation purposes. It is referred to as VHDL which stands for VHSIC Hardware Description Language (you can tell that this is a very high-level tool because the acronym has an acronym within it). VHDL and other hardware description languages appear to be the direction in which industry is moving for design entry in PLD development, especially for more complex systems using CPLDs and FPGAs.

Review Questions

1. Describe the difference between an assembler and a compiler.
2. Name four ways of entering a design into a compiler.
3. What does *VHDL* stand for?

12-4 UNIVERSAL COMPILER FOR PROGRAMMABLE LOGIC (CUPL)

Many different software tools are available for developing PLDs. They all have shared similarities as well as distinguishing differences. To provide real examples of simple PLD development, we utilize one of the most popular logic compilers available today. It is called CUPL and is available from Logical Devices. CUPL is capable of producing programming files for a large variety of programmable devices. It also allows many of the convenient entry modes described previously.

The input file contains standard header information that is used by the software to produce the output file and provide documentation of the design. Figure 12-12 shows a typical input file template for the CUPL compiler, including the header information at the top. Normally, a standard input file template like this is created and saved using a text editor. Each time a new design is entered, the template file is simply edited to fill in the blanks. Notice that the /* and */ are used to enclose any comments that might make the input file more understandable. Also notice that each statement must end with a semicolon (;).

CUPL allows the pin assignments to be entered one by one or by means of a shorthand set notation system. Active-LOW inputs and outputs can be specified in the pin definition section by using an exclamation mark (!) in front of the pin name. This is an optional feature that allows the equations to be written in terms of when they are "active" or "asserted" without worrying about whether the active state is represented by a HIGH or a LOW. Some examples of individual pin assignments are given in Table 12-1 as well as the shorthand version.

TABLE 12-1   Methods to specify pin assignments.

Individual Assignments	Shorthand Notation
PIN 1 = CLK;	PIN 1 = CLK;
PIN 2 = !CLR;	PIN [2,3] = ![CLR,SET];
PIN 3 = !SET;	PIN [4..7] = [Q0..3];
PIN 4 = Q0;	
PIN 5 = Q1;	
PIN 6 = Q2;	
PIN 7 = Q3;	

```
Name            XXXXX;
Partno          XXXXX;
Date
Revision
Designer
Company
Assembly
Location
/******************************************************************************/
/*                                                                          */
/*                                                                          */
/*                                                                          */
/******************************************************************************/
/*          Target Device                                                   */
/******************************************************************************/
/*     Inputs   */
pin 1   =                    ;     /*                                       */
pin 1   =                    ;     /*                                       */
pin 1   =                    ;     /*                                       */
pin 1   =                    ;     /*                                       */
pin 1   =                    ;     /*                                       */
pin 1   =                    ;     /*                                       */
pin 1   =                    ;     /*                                       */
pin 1   =                    ;     /*                                       */
pin 1   =                    ;     /*                                       */
pin 1   =                    ;     /*                                       */
/*     Outputs  */
pin 1   =                    ;     /*                                       */
pin 1   =                    ;     /*                                       */
pin 1   =                    ;     /*                                       */
pin 1   =                    ;     /*                                       */
pin 1   =                    ;     /*                                       */
pin 1   =                    ;     /*                                       */
pin 1   =                    ;     /*                                       */
pin 1   =                    ;     /*                                       */
/******************************************************************************/
/*              Equations                                                   */
/******************************************************************************/
```

FIGURE 12-12   An input file "template" for the CUPL compiler.

After all of the inputs and outputs are defined, the logic equations that define the operation of the circuit may be entered. The format of all equations is:

variable = *logical expression*

The left side of the equation (variable) may be any defined output name or any other intermediate variable name or control signal that is defined in the design. The right side of the equation (logical expression) is any logical combination (AND, OR, NOT, EX-OR) of the variables defined in the design. The proper syntax for these logical operators is given in Table 12-2.

In some cases an equation must be written to define the operation of an internal point (node) in the PLD. For example, the GAL 16V8A has a tristate buffer associated with each output. In this device's complex and registered modes this tristate enable is controlled by a product term from the input matrix. Consequently, an equation must be written to define the logic to enable the tristate output. CUPL, and

TABLE 12-2   CUPL syntax for logic operations.

Function	Operator	CUPL Format	Conventional Format
AND	&	A & B	$A \cdot B$
OR	#	A # B	$A + B$
NOT	!	!A	$\overline{A}$
EX-OR	$	A $ B	$A \oplus B$

many of the other development systems, provide this capability by allowing extensions of an output variable name. For example, assume that an output pin is named DECODE as shown in Figure 12-13. The logic equation with DECODE as the variable drives the output to logic 1 only when A is high and B is low. The logic equation for DECODE.OE defines the conditions for enabling the tristate output. In the case shown, the output is in the high-impedance state whenever input C is high and enabled when C is low. If we wanted to unconditionally enable the output, we would write the equation

$$DECODE.OE = \text{'b'}1$$

This specifies that the enable input to the tristate buffer is at a constant logic 1. The "b" notation is used to tell CUPL that the value specified is "binary" and not decimal or hexadecimal.

Another example of the use of extensions can be seen in implementing clocked, sequential circuits. You will recall from Chapter 7 that state machines were

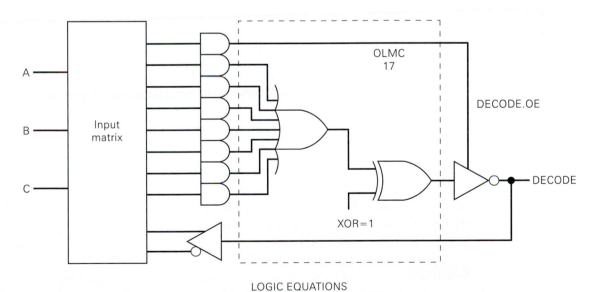

LOGIC EQUATIONS
DECODE = A & !B;   {DECODE = A·$\overline{B}$}
DECODE.OE = !C;   {OUTPUT ENABLE = $\overline{C}$}

FIGURE 12-13   Using extensions to specify the output enable control.

designed by writing equations for the *inputs* to a flip-flop. In the registered mode of the GAL 16V8A, equations must be written for the *D* input of each flip-flop which will determine the flip-flop output after the next clocking edge. This is accomplished by using the .D extension on the output pin name. For example, the equation for the Q_0 output of the D flip-flop that is connected to toggle would be:

$$Q0.D \ = \ !Q0$$

This expression is stated in words as follows: the *D* input of the Q_0 flip-flop (i.e., Q0.D) is connected to the complement of the Q_0 output. PLDs other than the GAL 16V8A may have need for other extensions that CUPL supports.

Development Cycle

The first step in any design is to thoroughly define the problem and its scope. The labeling of all inputs and outputs results from this step. The relationship between all inputs and outputs is also defined and may be expressed in a number of different ways, such as truth tables, state tables, logic equations, or even logic diagrams. The second step is to create the input or "source" file in the format required by the compiler. Next, the compiler is invoked and is given the name of the input file. The compiling process produces a number of different output files. The documentation file (.DOC for CUPL) contains any error messages that were generated by the compiler. The fuse plot file shows the actual fuse pattern that will be burned into the programmable device. This file is also converted into the JEDEC file to be used by the programmer (i.e., programming fixture).

If the compiler generates any error messages, the cause must be determined and corrected using the text editor to alter the input file. This process is repeated until there are no more errors or warnings. At this point the design may be tested using a **simulator.** A simulator is a computer program that calculates the correct output logic states based on a description of the logic circuit and the current inputs. A set of hypothetical inputs that will prove that the device works as expected are developed. These are called **test vectors.** If the test vectors are thorough enough, the design can be proven before the first device is programmed. When the designer is satisfied that the design will work, the JEDEC file is generated and the programming software is invoked. The JEDEC file serves as the input file to the programmer, and the PLD is placed in the programming fixture. Many programming fixtures and the software that comes with them have the capability not only to program the part but also to run the test vectors on the input while monitoring the output. This verifies that the PLD is fully functional. The PLD is then placed in a circuit and is tested functionally with all peripheral components. The flowchart of Figure 12-14 demonstrates the complete development process.

Examples

A simple example using CUPL development software will serve to illustrate the process. Refer to the truth table of Table 12-3, which represents the result of the problem statement and scope specification of a design. If we were using SSI logic chips, the next step would be simplification using K maps. It is usually unnecessary

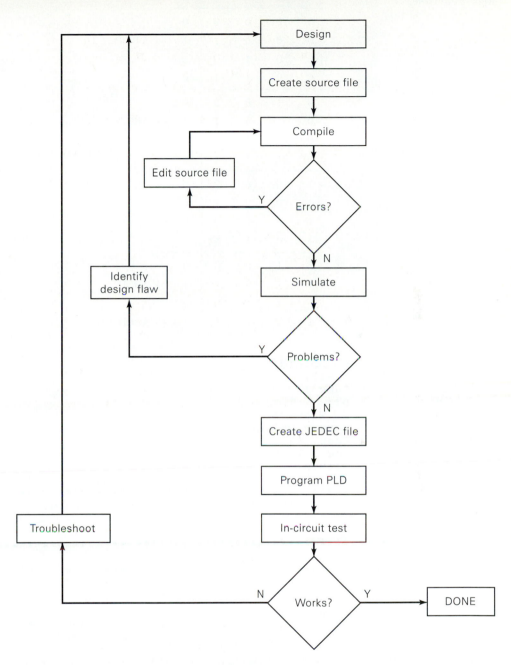

FIGURE 12-14   PLD development cycle flowchart.

to simplify the design when using PLDs, since the compiler will perform the simplification for you. However, the SOP equations must be written from the truth table.

The next step is to create a source (input) file using the text editor. The source file header information is first filled in to provide complete documentation as shown in Figure 12-15. The first major decision that must be made is selection of the input and output pins. This requires some understanding of the architecture of the device

TABLE 12-3 A combinational
logic truth table.

A	B	C	D	X	
0	0	0	0	0	
0	0	0	1	1	→ $\overline{A}\,\overline{B}\,\overline{C}D$
0	0	1	0	0	
0	0	1	1	0	
0	1	0	0	0	
0	1	0	1	1	→ $\overline{A}B\overline{C}D$
0	1	1	0	0	
0	1	1	1	0	
1	0	0	0	0	
1	0	0	1	0	
1	0	1	0	0	
1	0	1	1	0	
1	1	0	0	0	
1	1	0	1	1	→ $AB\overline{C}D$
1	1	1	0	0	
1	1	1	1	1	→ $ABCD$

$$\left\{ \begin{array}{l} X = \overline{A}\,\overline{B}\,\overline{C}D + \overline{A}B\overline{C}D \\ \quad + AB\overline{C}D + ABCD \end{array} \right\}$$

```
Name            combo.pld;
Partno          12-17;
Date            June 1;
Revision        01;
Designer        N. Widmer;
Company         Purdue University;
Assembly        Chap. 12;
Location        Tocci text;
Device          G16V8A;
Format          j;                              /*  JEDEC        */
/******************************************************************/
/*  This is a combinational logic example with 4 inputs and one output  */
/*                                                                */
/*                                                                */
/******************************************************************/
/*            Target Device Gal 16V8A                             */
/******************************************************************/

/*        Inputs   */

pin 1    = A                     ;         /* Notice use of PIN 1 as input.*/
pin 2    = B                     ;         /* B, C, AND D are normal inputs*/
pin 3    = C                     ;         /*                              */
pin 4    = D                     ;         /*                              */

/*        Outputs  */

pin 19   = X                     ;         /* Pin 12 is the output         */

/******************************************************************/
/*              Equations                                         */
/******************************************************************/

X = !A&!B&!C&D # !A&B&!C&D # A&B&!C&D # A&B&C&D;
```

FIGURE 12-15 The source file for the combinational circuit.

that is being programmed. In this simple design using the GAL 16V8A, almost any pins other than V_{CC} and ground could have been used as inputs. The output pin must be chosen from among pins 12–19. Finally, a single expression is written in unreduced SOP form to specify the operation of the output pin. Note the symbols used for the logic operations.

The source file shown in Figure 12-15 is in a very straightforward form and is compatible with most software tools with only slight modification. The compiler actually reduces the logic equation and then produces a documentation file that shows the reduced equations and the actual fuse plot for programming the device. Portions of the documentation file for this design are shown in Figure 12-16. Notice that the reduced expression is the same as the result that would be obtained using K mapping. The fuse plot shows the connections in the input matrix, identifying each programmable bit by an address. Each position designated by an "x" indicates a row/column connection (fuse not blown). Each position designated by a "–" indicates a blown fuse and no connection between the row and a column. Figure 12-17 shows the first two rows of the fuse plot superimposed over the architectural diagram of the GAL 16V8A for this design. The mode select bits (SYN = 1, AC0 = 0) are set for the simple mode, and AC1 = 0 for OLMC 19 to produce the combinational output configuration.

```
*********************************************************************************
                                  combo.pld
*********************************************************************************
================================================================================
                            Expanded Product Terms
================================================================================


X =>
     !A & !C & D
   # A & B & D


================================================================================
                                  Fuse Plot
================================================================================

Syn    02192 -  Ac0     02193 x

Pin #19  02048  Pol -   02120  Ac1 x
  00000 ---x-x--x----------------------
  00032 x-x-----x----------------------
  00064 xxxxxxxxxxxxxxxxxxxxxxxxxxxxxxxx
  00096 xxxxxxxxxxxxxxxxxxxxxxxxxxxxxxxx
  00128 xxxxxxxxxxxxxxxxxxxxxxxxxxxxxxxx
  00160 xxxxxxxxxxxxxxxxxxxxxxxxxxxxxxxx
  00192 xxxxxxxxxxxxxxxxxxxxxxxxxxxxxxxx
  00224 xxxxxxxxxxxxxxxxxxxxxxxxxxxxxxxx
```

FIGURE 12-16　The documentation file with fuse plot.

The previous example is quite trivial and serves only to demonstrate the details of PLD development. This circuit could be implemented using similar board space, power requirements, and speed, and at lower cost, using conventional logic gates. The real power of a PLD is seen when implementing circuits that have no conven-

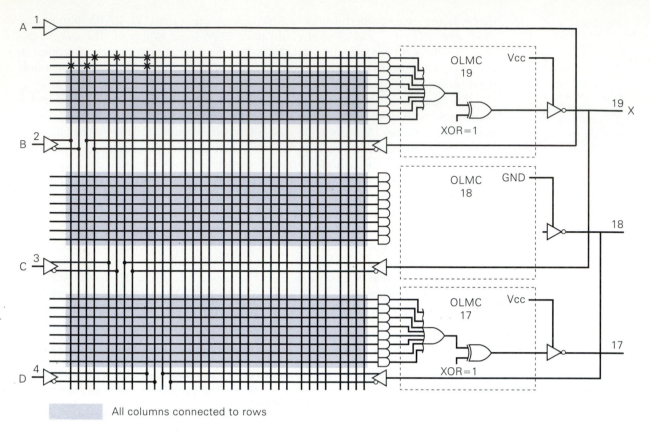

All columns connected to rows

FIGURE 12-17 The PLD implementation of the circuit.

tional alternative or that would require numerous conventional chips. The next example shows a combinational circuit design that requires a monstrous combination of conventional TTL gates to implement. Yet this very functional circuit can be implemented on a single GAL 16V8A at a very reasonable cost.

EXAMPLE 12-4

Design a digital system that will indicate which contestant in a quiz or trivia-type game answers a question first. The system must have a *momentary* contact pushbutton input for each of six contestants and six LEDs to indicate which contestant hit the button first. A reset pushbutton must be provided for the host/moderator to clear all lights.

Solution

The requirements of this problem have elements of combinational logic as well as sequential logic. Consider the conditions under which any given contestant's light should be on. Light N should be on IF either of the following occurs:

1. Contestant N is pushing the button
   AND no other contestant has his/her light on
   AND the host is not trying to reset the lights.

```
Name            GAME.PLD;
Partno          12-20;
Date            June 1;
Revision        01;
Designer        N. Widmer;
Company         Purdue;
Assembly        CHAP. 12;
Location        Tocci text;
Device          G16V8A;
Format          j;              /*       JEDEC   */
/******************************************************************/
/*   THIS DEVICE IS A "TIE BREAKER" FOR USE WITH TRIVIA QUIZ TYPE GAMES  */
/*                                                                */
/*                                                                */
/******************************************************************/
/*              Target Device GAL 16V8A                         */
/******************************************************************/
/*       Inputs  */

pin [2..7]   = [S1..6]      /* These six inputs (S1-S6)   */
                            /* are for the six players.   */
                            /* They would be connected    */
                            /* to normally low, momentary */
                            /* contact, push buttons.     */
                            /*                            */

pin 9    = RESET  ;         /* This push button switch is
                               used by the host to clear
                               the lights.                */

/*       Outputs */

pin 12   = !L1                 ;     /* These outputs go to lights  */
pin 13   = !L2                 ;     /* that indicate which player  */
pin 14   = !L3                 ;     /* answered first.             */


pin 17   = !L4                 ;     /* Notice that they are made   */
pin 18   = !L5                 ;     /* active LOW by using ! in     */
pin 19   = !L6                 ;     /* the output definition.       */
/******************************************************************/
/*              Equations                                        */
/******************************************************************/

L1 = !RESET & S1 &        !L2 & !L3 & !L4 & !L5 & !L6   #   !RESET & L1;

L2 = !RESET & S2 & !L1 &        !L3 & !L4 & !L5 & !L6   #   !RESET & L2;

L3 = !RESET & S3 & !L1 & !L2 &        !L4 & !L5 & !L6   #   !RESET & L3;

L4 = !RESET & S4 & !L1 & !L2 & !L3 &        !L5 & !L6   #   !RESET & L4;

L5 = !RESET & S5 & !L1 & !L2 & !L3 & !L4 &        !L6   #   !RESET & L5;

L6 = !RESET & S6 & !L1 & !L2 & !L3 & !L4 & !L5         #   !RESET & L6;
```

FIGURE 12-18   The "tie-breaker" source file.

OR
2. Contestant N's light is already on
   AND the host is not trying to reset the lights.

The first condition specifies a combination of inputs to turn on the light. The second condition creates the latching action (sequential) to keep the light on after all buttons are released.

The first step in implementing the PLD solution is to name all of the inputs and outputs and specify the active logic levels needed. Switches 1–6, labeled S1–S6, are active-HIGH. The RESET input is also active-HIGH. Each of the outputs labeled L1–L6 should be active-LOW to light the LEDs since the outputs can sink more current than they can source (refer to Chapter 8). Using these labels, the logic statement above can be written as the following expression for output L1:

$$L1 = \underbrace{S1 \cdot \overline{L2} \cdot \overline{L3} \cdot \overline{L4} \cdot \overline{L5} \cdot \overline{L6} \cdot \overline{RESET}}_{\text{Condition 1}} + \underbrace{L1 \cdot \overline{RESET}}_{\text{Condition 2}}$$

The CUPL source file is shown in Figure 12-18. The inputs are designated using CUPL's set notation. Any of the input pins (1–9, or 11) could be selected for the switch inputs. The output pins are selected as shown because this design is implemented in the simple mode. In the simple mode pins 15 and 16 do not have feedback capability, so these two outputs are avoided. Note that to designate an output as active-LOW, the complement operator (!) is used before the pin label definition. This tells the compiler to make the output go LOW when it is active while the logic equation expresses the positive logic required to make it active. CUPL automatically takes care of complementing the outputs and any feedback terms as needed.

Imagine trying to build this circuit using TTL logic! It can be implemented completely using a single GAL 16V8A.

Circuits with registered outputs can also be implemented using the GAL 16V8A. In Chapter 7 we explored synchronous counter design using J-K flip-flops. All possible present states were listed in a table, along with their correct "next states." Then we determined the necessary inputs to cause the present state to change to its desired next state, resulting in logic equations for each J and K input.

The same concept is used when designing synchronous circuits with a PLD. However, the GAL 16V8A has D flip-flops in the OLMCs instead of J-K flip-flops. This actually makes the process much simpler since you have only one equation to write for each D input. The equation for each D input is simply the sum of all present states (product terms) that should make that particular flip-flop go HIGH for the next state.

EXAMPLE 12-5

To illustrate the process, we implement the synchronous counter from Section 7-14 (Figure 7-33) using PLDs. The first step is still to create a present state/next state table as shown in the synchronous design procedure (step 3) of Section 7-14.

Think of this as a set of three truth tables, specifying the next state of each flip-flop based on the present state of all of the inputs. From this table the unreduced SOP expressions for the next state of each output are:

$$\text{Next state of C} = \overline{C} \cdot B \cdot A$$
$$\text{Next state of B} = \overline{C} \cdot \overline{B} \cdot A + \overline{C} \cdot B \cdot \overline{A}$$
$$\text{Next state of A} = \overline{C} \cdot \overline{B} \cdot \overline{A} + \overline{C} \cdot B \cdot \overline{A}$$

Since the next state of a D flip-flop is determined by the present state of the D input, these are also the equations needed to drive the D inputs. The resulting source file then is as shown in Figure 12-19. Remember, C.D is the CUPL notation for the D input of FF C; similarly for B.D and A.D.

```
Name            Counter.PLD;
Partno          12-21;
Date            June 1;
Revision        01;
Designer        N. Widmer;
Company         Purdue University;
Assembly        Chap. 12;
Location        Tocci Text;
Device          G16V8A;
Format          j;
/****************************************************************/
/*   This device will function as a MOD 5 counter.            */
/*   0 > 1 > 2 > 3 > 4 > 0     All other states go to 0.      */
/****************************************************************/
/*           Target Device GAL 16V8A                          */
/****************************************************************/
/*       Inputs  */

PIN 1 = CK;              /* clock input (must be pin 1) */

/*      There are no combinational inputs to this MOD 5 counter     */

/*       Outputs */

pin 19  = C                 ;      /*  Most significant output    */
pin 18  = B                 ;      /*                             */
pin 17  = A                 ;      /*  Least significant output   */

/****************************************************************/
/*                 Equations                                  */
/****************************************************************/

C.D = !C & B & A;

B.D = !C & !B & A  #  !C & B & !A;

A.D = !C & !B & !A #  !C & B & !A;
```

FIGURE 12-19   A MOD-5 counter source file.

Review Questions

1. What are the /* */ characters used for in the input file?
2. What is the purpose of using .OE on an output name?
3. Describe what QA.D represents.
4. Define *source file*.
5. Which output file identifies compiling errors?
6. In which file do you correct compiling errors?

12-5 FINAL COMMENTS

In this chapter we have provided a detailed description of one particular programmable logic device, the GAL 16V8A. Although this description is adequate to get us started using PLDs, it does not provide exhaustive coverage of either the CUPL software or the GAL 16V8A. A more complete understanding can best be obtained by using the tools while experimenting with PLDs. The software provided with this book can be used to do exactly that.

The CUPL compiler is very versatile, and although the parts library that is supplied with this book is very limited, nearly any programmable device can be handled by the complete industrial software package from Logical Devices. The syntax that we have learned in this chapter will apply to many other types of devices programmed through CUPL.

As we come to appreciate the advantages of this particular PLD over SSI and MSI ICs, keep in mind that this device (the GAL 16V8A) represents only the simplest of programmable logic devices. Much larger and more powerful programmable devices are available. A very common part that is used widely today is the 22V10. Several manufacturers offer this part, and it is available in one-time-programmable as well as erasable versions. It offers more inputs and more OLMCs. However, its architecture is very similar to that of the GAL 16V8A.

A new line of parts has been developed by Lattice that are "in-system programmable." The ISPGAL22V10 is the simplest device in this line. The advantage of ISP parts is that they do not require a programming fixture, just a cable from a personal computer printer port to the ISP device. The only drawback is that they come only in PLCC packages. For technical education this would require modifications to conventional laboratory breadboarding practices. However, the prospect of being able to reprogram a device after it is in the system opens up a whole new approach to digital system design that involves reconfigurable hardware. As an example, a microprocessor-based system would be able to determine which options are currently installed in the system and then reconfigure its interface logic accordingly. There are also other lines of parts within the GAL family with special characteristics such as high current outputs.

The field of programmable logic devices is destined to continue to grow. These devices may completely displace the conventional SSI and MSI logic circuits that have served technology so well for over 25 years. This chapter has provided a foundation to build upon in this exciting and progressive field. Table 12-4 lists some vendors of the building materials you will need.

TABLE 12-4   Sources of PLD development tools.

Software and Programming Fixtures	Software	Programming Fixtures
CUPL® Logical Devices, Inc. 130 Capital Dr. Suite A Golden, CO 80401 1-800-331-7766 http://logicaldevices.com	Minc, Inc. 6755 Earl Dr. Colorado Springs, CO 80918 1-719-590-1155 http://www.minc.com	EMP-20 Needham's Electronics 1-916-924-8037 Available through Digi-Key 1-800-344-4539 http://www.digikey.com
ABEL®/Synario 1-888-796-2746 Data I/O® Corp. 1-800-332-8246 10525 Willows Rd. NE Redmond, WA 98052 http://data-io.com	ORCAD Systems, Inc. 9300 SW Nimbus Ave. Beaverton, OR 97008 1-503-671-9500 http://www.orcad.com	

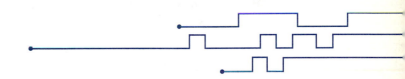

SUMMARY

1. Programmable logic devices (PLDs) appear to be a key technology in the future of digital systems.

2. PLDs can reduce parts inventory, simplify prototype circuitry, shorten the development cycle, reduce the size and power requirements of the product, and allow the hardware of a circuit to be easily upgraded.

3. The GAL 16V8A is one of the simplest PLDs available but is still widely used and demonstrates the basic principles behind all PLDs.

4. The GAL 16V8A has a matrix of programmable connections that are used to select the input terms for a group of AND gates. The outputs of these AND gates are ORed together in an output logic macro cell (OLMC).

5. The OLMC can also be programmed to complement the resulting bit value, store the bit in a D flip-flop, make use of a tristate output buffer, or feed the bit back into the input term matrix. The desired combination of these features is selected by programming the part in one of three modes and choosing one of two configurations for that mode.

6. The simple mode can sum eight product terms for each OLMC. None of the outputs have tristate capability, and the flip-flops are not used to latch the output. All but two OLMC pins (15, 16) have input/feedback capability.

7. The complex mode can sum seven product terms for each OLMC. The tristate outputs are enabled by a separate logic equation. All but two OLMC pins (12, 19) have input/feedback capability.

8. The registered mode can sum eight product terms for each registered output cell. The resulting bit is stored in a D flip-flop. The clock and the output enable for these cells are on pins 1 and 11, respectively. The cells that are configured as combinational behave just like the complex mode.

9. To use PLDs you need a development system consisting of a computer, PLD development software, and a programming fixture with associated software.

10. Logic equations are typed into a file in a format dictated by the development software. The software translates these logic equations into a standard JEDEC file that can be used by the programming fixture. The JEDEC file is sent to the programming fixture, and the device is programmed.

11. PLDs are easy to learn, are fun to use, and are available with capabilities that greatly exceed those of the GAL 16V8A.

IMPORTANT TERMS

input term matrix	zero-insertion force (ZIF)	compiler
output logic macro cell (OLMC)	socket	simulator
downloading	JEDEC	test vector

PROBLEMS

SECTION 12-1

12-1. Make up a table listing each mode and configuration for a GAL OLMC along with its control bit settings (SYN, AC0, AC1). Identify which OLMCs can be used in each configuration.

12-2. Identify all of the modes that could be used to implement the following.
(a) A *D* latch with tristate outputs
(b) A D flip-flop
(c) A synchronous counter circuit
(d) A decoder circuit

12-3. For each mode and configuration, what is the maximum number of product terms in the SOP expression?

12-4. Identify the source of the feedback signal (*FMUX*) for each mode and configuration.

12-5. Identify the source of the tristate enable (*TSMUX*) for each mode and configuration.

12-6. Verify that by programming the XOR bit HIGH, the actual output pin will be the same as the OR gate output in the OLMC for Examples 12-1, 12-2, and 12-3.

SECTION 12-2

12-7. List the equipment needed to develop circuits using PLDs.

SECTION 12-4

12-8. Write out a source file that would program a GAL 16V8A to function as a 74LS138 3-line-to-8-line decoder.

12-9. Draw the complete logic diagram for the "tiebreaker" (Example 12-4) if it were implemented using conventional TTL chips.

12-10. Write out a CUPL source file that would program a GAL 16V8A to function as a MOD-8 binary counter.

12-11. A stepper motor can be made to rotate by energizing its four phase windings in the following sequence:

$$1\ 0\ 1\ 0$$
$$1\ 0\ 0\ 1$$
$$0\ 1\ 0\ 1$$
$$0\ 1\ 1\ 0$$

Write the equations in a CUPL format that will create a counter that can drive the stepper motor.

C 12-12. By sequencing through the states in Problem 12-11 in the opposite direction, a stepper motor will rotate in the opposite direction. Write the equations that will take an external input (dir) and will advance the stepper clockwise when dir = 0 and counterclockwise when dir = 1 (the step occurs on the clock edge). Write out the source file to program a GAL 16V8A.

C 12-13. Design a sequential combinational lock circuit. The circuit must have a three-bit combination entry input and an enter button. If the correct sequence of three-bit values is entered (101 ⟨enter⟩, 100 ⟨enter⟩, 111 ⟨enter⟩), an output bit will go high, unlocking a door.

ANSWERS TO SECTION REVIEW QUESTIONS

SECTION 12-1

1. Erasable and reprogrammable   2. Simple, complex, registered output   3. See text.
4. Registered output/registered configuration
5. Registered output

SECTION 12-2

1. Development software; programming software.
2. **(a)** A file produced by the development software showing which fuses are to be zapped   **(b)** The same information translated into a suitable format for transmission to the programming fixture   3. An output file (fuse plot) conforming to the JEDEC standard

SECTION 12-3

1. Compiler has more options for entering circuit design information into computer.   2. ASCII file; schematic capture; truth tables; state tables; timing diagrams
3. VHSIC hardware description language

SECTION 12-4

1. To enclose comments   2. To indicate that it is the signal that drives the output enable   3. The *D* input of FF Q_A 4. The input file that specifies the relationships between inputs and outputs
5. Documentation file   6. Source (input file)

CHAPTER 13

Introduction to the Microprocessor and the Microcomputer

■ OUTLINE

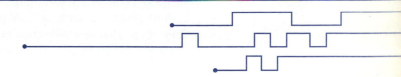

■ OBJECTIVES

Upon completion of this chapter, you will be able to:

■ Describe the function and operation of each one of the five basic elements of any computer organization.

■ Understand that a computer continually repeats a sequence of fetch and execute operations.

■ Understand the difference between a microprocessor and a microcomputer.

■ Analyze the fetch and execute cycles during the execution of a machine-language program.

■ Understand the operational role of the different types of buses and their signals in a microcomputer.

■ Cite the major functions performed by the microprocessor.

■ Describe the different types of computer words.

■ Upgrade your knowledge by learning more details and advanced concepts of microprocessor-based systems.

■ INTRODUCTION

It is no exaggeration to say that the microprocessor and the microcomputer have revolutionized the electronics industry and have had a remarkable impact on many aspects of our lives. The development of extremely high-density ICs has so sharply reduced the size and cost of microcomputers that designers routinely consider using their power and versatility in a wide variety of products and applications.

In this chapter we study the basic principles of microcomputer operation. Even though we focus on the microcomputer, most of the concepts and ideas will apply to computers of all sizes. To illustrate the various aspects of microcomputer operation in a meaningful way, we use a specific microprocessor, the Intel 8051.

The 8051 family represents a branch of the microprocessor family tree. As microprocessor and microcomputer technology grew from its four-bit origins (Intel

4004) in the early 1970s to eight-bit processors (8008, 8080, 8085, 6800, 6502, Z80, etc.) of the late 1970s, its application branched into two distinct directions. One of these branches was the infancy of personal computers. These microprocessor-based computers were intended to be versatile tools that could load and run various programs such as word processors, spreadsheets, databases, and games. They could also be easily custom-programmed by the user to do whatever the programmer imagined. The 16-bit and 32-bit descendants (8086, 80x86 series 680x0 series) have simply improved on this theme. The basic architecture of the microprocessor has not changed substantially from the earliest systems, although the speed and the amount of addressable memory have improved greatly.

The second branch that developed in the 1970s was the use of a microprocessor-based computer as a control unit embedded in a marketable product. This form of microcomputer is made up of the same elements as the personal computer, but it is programmed once by the manufacturer. Then it spends its life performing its intended tasks, such as waiting for buttons to be pressed and turning on and off devices such as lights, motors, beepers, and so on. The 8051 family falls into this general category known as *embedded* microcontrollers. This family of devices was first developed in the early 1980s along with the 68HC11, but the applications of these eight-bit control-oriented devices has become so widespread that they are still in popular demand today. Many different versions of the original 8051 have been developed with special features, but they still use the same basic instruction set and core architecture as the original. Several more powerful and more complex microcontrollers have also been developed for applications that go beyond an eight-bit computer's capability.

The 8051 family was chosen because it is widely used today and demonstrates how all computers work in an uncomplicated way that will be comfortable for the beginning student. Once you have a basic understanding of one of the earlier microprocessors, such as the 8051, it is an easier task to step up to the more advanced chips.

It would take a complete textbook to cover all of the important details on microprocessors and computer operation. The material in this chapter is meant only to provide a foundation for further study.

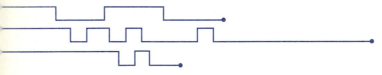

13-1 WHAT IS A DIGITAL COMPUTER?

A digital computer is a combination of digital devices and circuits that can perform a *programmed* sequence of operations with a minimum of human intervention. The sequence of operations is called a **program.** The program is a set of coded instructions that is stored in the computer's internal memory along with all of the data that the program requires. When the computer is commanded to execute the program, it performs the instructions in the order that they are stored in memory until the program is completed. It does this at extremely high speeds.

13-2 HOW DO COMPUTERS THINK?

Computers do not think! The computer **programmer** provides a *program* of instructions and data that specifies every detail of what to do, what to do it to, and when to do it. The computer is simply a high-speed machine that can manipulate data, solve problems, and make decisions, all under the control of the program. If the programmer makes a mistake in the program or puts in the wrong data, the computer will produce wrong results. A popular saying in the computer field is "garbage in/garbage out."

Perhaps a better question to ask at this point is, How does a computer go about executing a program of instructions? Typically, this question is answered by showing a diagram of a computer's architecture (arrangement of its various elements) and then going through the step-by-step process that the computer follows in executing the program. We will do this—but not yet. First, we will look at a somewhat far-fetched analogy that contains many of the concepts involved in computer operation.

13-3 SECRET AGENT 89

Secret Agent 89 is trying to find out how many days before a certain world leader is to be assassinated. His contact tells him that this information is located in a series of post office boxes. To ensure that no one else gets the information, it is spread through 10 different boxes. His contact gives him 10 keys along with the following instructions:

1. The information in each box is written in code.
2. Open box 1 first and execute the instruction located there.
3. Continue through the rest of the boxes in sequence unless instructed to do otherwise.
4. One of the boxes is wired to explode upon opening.

Agent 89 takes the 10 keys and proceeds to the post office, code book in hand.

Figure 13-1 shows the contents of the 10 post office boxes after having been decoded. Assume that you are Agent 89; begin at box 1 and go through the sequence of operations to find the number of days before the assassination attempt. Of course, it should not be as much work for you as it was for Agent 89 because you don't have to decode the messages. The answer is given in the next paragraph.

If you have proceeded correctly, you should have ended up at box 6 with an answer of 17. If you made a mistake, you might have opened box 7, in which case you are no longer with us. As you went through the sequence of operations, you essentially duplicated the types of operations and encountered many of the concepts that are part of a computer. We will now discuss these operations and concepts in the context of the secret-agent analogy and see how they are related to actual computers.

In case you have not already guessed, the post office boxes are like the **memory** in a computer, where **instructions** and **data** are stored. Post office boxes 1 to 6 contain instructions to be executed by the secret agent, and boxes 8, 9, and 10 contain the data called for by the instructions. (The contents of box 7, to our knowl-

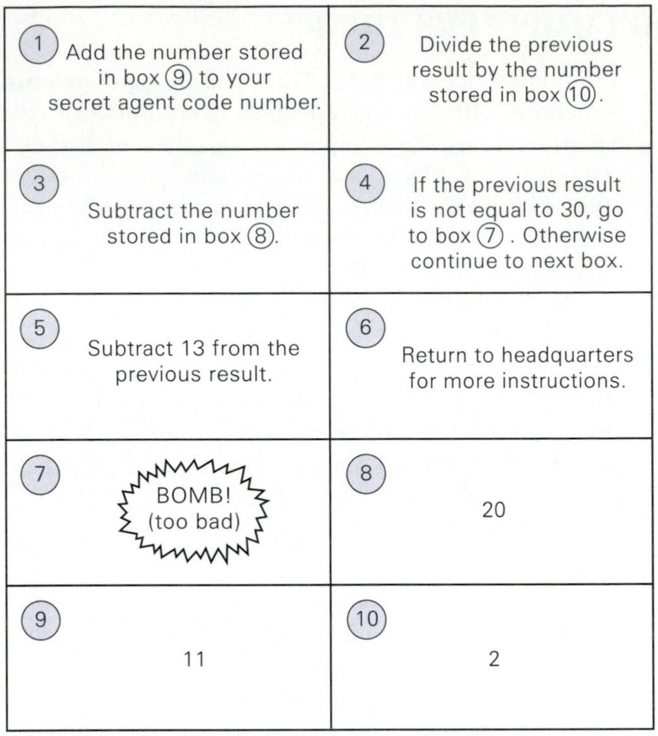

FIGURE 13-1 Ten post office boxes with coded message for Agent 89.

① Add the number stored in box ⑨ to your secret agent code number.	② Divide the previous result by the number stored in box ⑩.
③ Subtract the number stored in box ⑧.	④ If the previous result is not equal to 30, go to box ⑦ . Otherwise continue to next box.
⑤ Subtract 13 from the previous result.	⑥ Return to headquarters for more instructions.
⑦ BOMB! (too bad)	⑧ 20
⑨ 11	⑩ 2

edge, have no counterpart in computers.) The numbers on each box are like the **addresses** of the locations in memory.

Three different classes of instructions are present in boxes 1 to 6. Boxes 1, 2, 3, and 5 are instructions that call for *arithmetic operations*. Box 4 contains a *decision-making* instruction called a *conditional jump* or *conditional branch*. This instruction calls for the agent (or computer) to decide whether to jump to address 7 or to continue to address 5, depending on the result of the previous arithmetic operation. Box 6 contains a simple control instruction that requires no data and refers to no other address (box number). This *return* instruction tells the agent that the procedure is finished (the program is completed) and to go no further. As you study microprocessors in greater depth, you will find out how it knows where to return to.

Each of the arithmetic and conditional jump instructions consists of two parts—an **operation** and an **address.** For example, the first part of the first instruction specifies the operation of addition. The second part gives the address (box 9) of the data to be used in the addition. These data are usually called the **operand,** and their address the **operand address.** The instruction in box 5 is a special case in which no operand address is specified. Instead, the operand (data) to be used in the subtraction operation is included as part of the instruction.

A computer, like the secret agent, decodes and then executes the instructions stored in memory *sequentially,* beginning with the first location. The instructions are executed in order unless some type of *branch* instruction (such as box 4) causes the operation to branch or jump to a new address location to obtain the next instruction. Once the branching occurs, instructions are executed sequentially beginning at the new address.

This is about as much information as we can extract from the secret-agent analogy. Each of the concepts we encountered will be encountered again in subsequent material. Hopefully, the analogy has furnished insights that should prove useful as you begin a more technical study of computers.

13-4 BASIC COMPUTER SYSTEM ORGANIZATION

Every computer contains five essential elements or units: the **arithmetic/logic unit (ALU)**, the **memory unit**, the **control unit**, the **input unit**, and the **output unit**. The basic interconnection of these units is shown in Figure 13-2. The arrows in this diagram indicate the direction in which data, information, or control signals are flowing. Two different-size arrows are used; the larger arrows represent data or information that actually consists of a relatively large number of parallel lines, and the smaller arrows represent control signals that are normally only one or a few lines. The various arrows are also numbered to allow easy reference to them in the following descriptions.

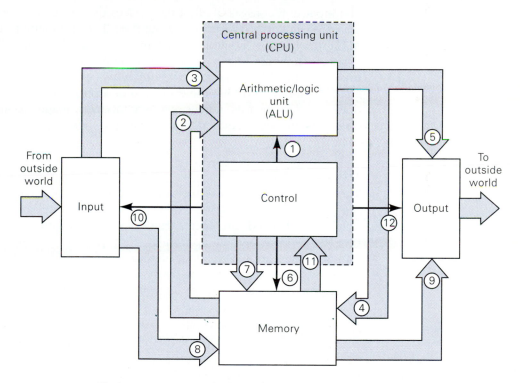

FIGURE 13-2   Basic computer organization.

Arithmetic/Logic Unit

The ALU is the area of the computer in which arithmetic and logic operations are performed on data. The type of operation that is to be performed is determined by signals from the control unit (arrow 1). The data that are to be operated on by the ALU can come from either the memory unit (arrow 2) or the input unit (arrow 3).

Results of operations performed in the ALU can be transferred to either the memory unit for storage (arrow 4) or the output unit (arrow 5).

Memory Unit

The memory stores groups of binary digits (words) that can represent instructions (program) that the computer is to perform and the data that are to be operated on by the program. The memory also serves as storage for intermediate and final results of arithmetic operations (arrow 4). Operation of the memory is controlled by the control unit (arrow 6), which signals for either a read or a write operation. A given location in memory is accessed by the control unit that provides the appropriate address code (arrow 7). Information can be written into the memory from the ALU or the input unit (arrow 8), again under control of the control unit. Information can be read from memory into the ALU (arrow 2) or into the output unit (arrow 9).

Input Unit

The input unit consists of all of the devices used to take information and data that are external to the computer and put them into the memory unit (arrow 8) or the ALU (arrow 3). The control unit determines where the input information is sent (arrow 10). The input unit is used to enter the program and data into the memory unit prior to starting the computer. This unit is also used to enter data into the ALU from an external device during the execution of a program. Some of the common input devices are keyboards, toggle switches, modems, magnetic-strip readers, magnetic disk units, magnetic tape units, and analog-to-digital converters (ADCs).

Output Unit

The output unit consists of the devices used to transfer data and information from the computer to the "outside world." The output devices are directed by the control unit (arrow 12) and can receive data from memory (arrow 9) or the ALU (arrow 5); the data are then put into appropriate form for external use. Examples of common output devices are LED readouts, indicator lights, printers, disk or tape units, video monitors, and digital-to-analog converters (DACs).

As the computer executes its program, it usually has results or control signals that it must present to the external world. For example, a computer system might have a line printer as an output device. Here, the computer sends out signals to print out the results on paper. A small microcomputer might display its results on indicator lights or on LED displays.

Interfacing

The devices that make up the input and output units are called **peripherals** because they are external to the rest of the computer. The most important aspect of peripherals involves interfacing. Computer **interfacing** is specifically defined as transmitting digital information between a computer and its peripherals in a compatible and synchronized way.

Many input/output devices are not directly compatible with the computer because of differences in such characteristics as operating speed, data format (e.g.,

BCD, ASCII, binary), data transmission mode (e.g., serial, parallel), and logic signal level. Such I/O devices require special interface circuits which allow them to communicate with the control, memory, and ALU portions of the computer system. A common example is the video display terminal (VDT), which can operate as both an input and an output device. The VDT transmits and receives data serially (one bit at a time) while most computers handle data in parallel form. Thus, a VDT requires interface circuitry in order to send data to or receive data from a computer.

Control Unit

The function of the control unit should now be obvious. It directs the operation of all of the other units by providing timing and control signals. In a sense, the control unit is like the conductor of an orchestra, who is responsible for keeping each of the orchestra members in proper synchronization. This unit contains logic and timing circuits that generate the proper signals necessary to execute each instruction in a program.

The control unit **fetches** an instruction from memory by sending an address (arrow 7) and a read command (arrow 6) to the memory unit. The instruction word stored at the memory location is then transferred to the control unit (arrow 11). This instruction word, which is in some form of binary code, is then decoded by logic circuitry in the control unit to determine which instruction is being called for. The control unit uses this information to send the proper signals to the rest of the units in order to **execute** the specified operation.

This sequence of fetching an instruction code and then executing the indicated operation is repeated over and over by the control unit (see Figure 13-3). This repetitive fetch/execute sequence continues until the computer is turned off or until RESET is activated. RESET always causes the computer to fetch its first instruction in the program, usually from address 0000.

FIGURE 13-3 A computer continually fetches and executes instructions.

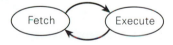

As we see, then, a computer actually keeps doing the same basic operations over and over: fetch, execute, fetch, execute, fetch, execute, and on and on. Of course, the various execute cycles will be different for each type of instruction as the control unit sends different signals to the other units to execute the particular instruction.

Central Processing Unit (CPU)

In Figure 13-2, the ALU and the control unit are shown combined into one unit called the **central processing unit (CPU).** This is commonly done to separate the actual "brains" of the computer from the other units. In a microcomputer the CPU is usually implemented on a single chip, the microprocessor. The CPU also contains a set of registers that perform special functions. These registers can also provide short-term storage of data inside the CPU without needing to access the external memory.

Review Questions

1. Name the five basic units of a computer, and describe the major functions of each.
2. What is the CPU?
3. What is meant by *interfacing* in a computer system?
4. What basic operations occur repeatedly in a computer?

13-5 BASIC μC ELEMENTS

It is important to understand the difference between the microcomputer (μC) and the microprocessor (μP). A microcomputer contains several elements, the most important of which is the microprocessor. The microprocessor is usually a single IC that contains all of the circuitry of the control and arithmetic/logic units—in other words, the CPU. It is common to refer to the microprocessor as the **MPU (microprocessor unit),** since it is the CPU (central processing unit) of the microcomputer. This is illustrated in Figure 13-4, where the basic elements of a microcomputer are shown.

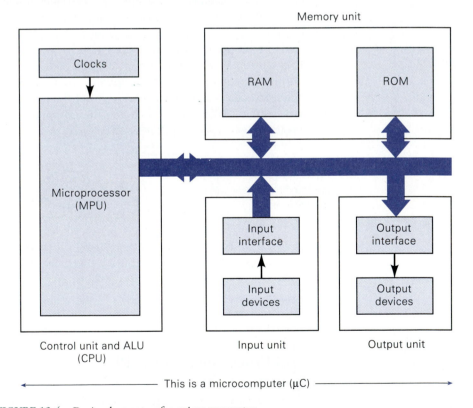

FIGURE 13-4 Basic elements of a microcomputer.

The memory unit shows both RAM and ROM devices. The RAM section consists of one or more LSI chips arranged to provide the designed memory capacity. This section of memory is used to store programs and data, which will change often during the course of operation. It is also used as storage for intermediate and final results of operations performed during execution of a program.

The ROM section contains one or more ROM chips to store instructions and data that do not change and must not be lost when power is shut off. For example, it stores the bootstrap program that the μC executes on power-up, or it might store a table of ASCII codes needed for outputting information to a VDT or a printer.

The input and output sections contain the interface circuits needed to allow the peripherals to properly communicate with the rest of the computer. In some cases these interface circuits are LSI chips designed by the MPU manufacturer to interface the MPU to a variety of I/O devices. In other cases the interface circuits may be as simple as a buffer register. In many embedded control applications, all of the basic elements of a microcomputer are integrated into a single IC: the single-chip microcomputer.

The Microprocessor (MPU)

The MPU is the heart of every microcomputer. It performs a number of functions, including:

1. Providing timing and control signals for all elements of the μC
2. Fetching instructions and data from memory
3. Transferring data to and from memory and I/O devices
4. Decoding instructions
5. Performing arithmetic and logic operations called for by instructions
6. Responding to I/O-generated control signals such as RESET and INTERRUPT

The MPU contains all of the logic circuitry for performing these functions, but its internal logic is generally not externally accessible. Instead, we can control what happens inside the MPU by the *program of instructions* that we put in memory for the MPU to execute. This is what makes the MPU so versatile and flexible—when we want to change its operation, we simply change the programs stored in RAM (software) or ROM (firmware) rather than rewire the electronics (hardware).

The MPU's internal logic is extremely complex, but it can be thought of as consisting of three basic sections: the *control and timing* section, the *register* section, and the *ALU* (see Figure 13-5). Although there are definite interactions among these three sections, each has specific functions.

FIGURE 13-5 Major functional areas of a μP chip.

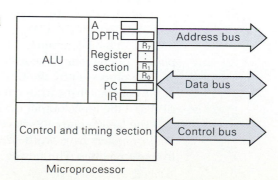

Microprocessor

The main function of the timing and control section is to fetch and decode (interpret) instruction codes from program memory, and then to generate the necessary control signals required by the other MPU sections in order to carry out the execution of the instructions. This section also generates timing and control signals (e.g., *R/W,* clock) that are needed by external RAM, ROM, and I/O devices.

The register section contains various registers (inside the MPU), each of which performs a special function. The most important one is the **program counter (PC),** which keeps track of the addresses of the instruction codes as they are fetched from memory. We will use the PC in our subsequent description of program execution. Other MPU registers are used to perform functions such as: storing instruction codes as they are being decoded (instruction register, IR in Figure 13-5), holding data being operated on by the ALU (A), storing addresses of data to be fetched from memory (data pointer, DPTR), and many general-purpose storage and counting functions (R0–R7). All microprocessors have one particular register that is heavily used called the **accumulator** or A register. It stores one operand for any math or logic instructions, and the result is stored in the accumulator after the instruction is executed. It is sometimes abbreviated Acc.

The ALU performs a variety of arithmetic and logic operations on data. These operations always include addition and subtraction, AND, OR, EX-OR, shifting, incrementing, and decrementing. The more advanced MPUs have ALUs that can do multiplication and division. During a microcomputer's operation, the operations that an ALU is to perform are under the control of the timing and control section, which, of course, does what it is told by the instruction codes that it fetches from memory.

Review Questions

1. Explain the difference between a microprocessor and a microcomputer.
2. Name the basic elements of a microcomputer.
3. Name the three major sections of an MPU.
4. What is the function of the PC?

13-6   COMPUTER WORDS

The smallest unit of information in a computer is the bit. A single isolated bit, however, carries very little information. For this reason, the principal unit of information in a computer is a group of bits referred to as a **word.** The number of bits that make up a word is called the computer's **word size.** Word size is a common way of describing a computer. Computers are often described in terms of their word size, such as an 8-bit computer, a 16-bit computer, and so on. For example, a 16-bit computer is one in which the instructions and data are stored in memory as 16-bit units and are processed by the CPU in 16-bit units. The word size also indicates the size of the data bus that carries data between the CPU and the memory and between the CPU and the input/output devices.

The larger computers have word sizes that are usually in the 32- to 64-bit range. Minicomputers have word sizes from 8 to 32 bits. Microcomputers have word sizes from 4 to 32 bits. The newer microcomputers use word sizes of 16 and 32 bits. In general, a computer with a larger word size can execute programs of instructions at a faster rate because more data and more instruction information are stuffed into one word. The larger word sizes, however, mean more lines making up the data bus, and therefore more interconnections between the CPU and memory and input/output devices.

As we know, a group of 8 bits is called a *byte*. Because 8-bit microcomputers have been widely used for a long time, and because ASCII codes fit neatly into 1 byte, the byte continues to be used as a unit to describe word size and memory capacity even in computers with larger word sizes. An 8-bit computer can be said to have a word size of 1 byte. A 16-bit computer has a word size of 2 bytes, and so on. A memory that stores 128K 16-bit words can also have its capacity described as 256K bytes.

Types of Computer Words

A word stored in a computer's memory can contain either of two kinds of information—**instructions** or **data.** Data can be numerical or character information that is to be processed by a program that the CPU is executing. The data can be in many forms including unsigned or signed binary, BCD, floating-point (something like engineering notation), or ASCII codes for characters, among others. Here is an example of how the numerical value $+86_{10}$ will be stored in an 8-bit word:

$$01010110$$

Here is how the ASCII code for the character "V" would be stored in an 8-bit word:

$$01010110$$

Notice that the two words are the same. The computer doesn't know the difference between the two. It is up to the programmer to know what type of data is being stored and to ensure that the program interprets and processes the data properly.

Here is another example where a 16-bit word is used to store two ASCII-coded characters:

$$\underbrace{0101011}_{V}\underbrace{001010111}_{W}$$

This same 16-bit word could be the representation for $+22103_{10}$. Clearly, larger word sizes can store more character data and larger numbers.

Instruction words are more complex than data words. We will discuss them in detail in the following section.

Review Questions

1. What two types of information are stored in computer words?
2. What is the advantage of a larger-word-size computer?

13-7 INSTRUCTION WORDS

The format used for **data** words varies only slightly among different computers, especially those with the same word size. This is not true, however, of the format for **instruction** words. These words contain the information necessary for a computer to execute its various operations, and the format and codes for these can vary widely from computer to computer. Depending on the computer, the information contained in an instruction word can be different. But, for most computers, the instruction words carry two basic units of information: the *operation* to be performed and the *address* of the *operand* (data) to be operated upon.

Figure 13-6 shows an example of a *single-address instruction word* for the 8051. The eight bits of the instruction word are divided into two parts. The first part of the word (bits 7 through 3) contains the five-bit **operation code** (**op code,** for short). The op code represents the operation that the computer is being instructed to perform, such as addition, subtraction, or moving data. The second part (bits 2 through 0) is the **operand address,** which represents the location in memory where the operand is stored.

FIGURE 13-6 Typical single-address instruction word.

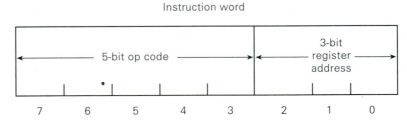

If all of the instructions of the 8051 were of this same form as shown in Figure 13-6 (five bits of op code, three bits of address), the total number of possible instructions (op codes) would be $2^5 = 32$. The total number of registers or memory locations that could store the operand would be $2^3 = 8$. This would severely limit the capability of the microprocessor. As we will see in the next section, there are ways to increase the number of possible instructions without increasing the word size.

The important point to understand from this form of an instruction is that the first five bits tell the micro (microprocessor) what to do. The last three bits tell the micro where to get the data. As an example, the 8051 instruction to "MOVE to the accumulator the data in register 3" is encoded as follows:

11101   011
op code   register address

The op code means move a byte of data into A (the accumulator) from a register. The last three bits specify that the byte of data is to be moved from register 3 (011_2). This binary instruction code then represents a unique operation. Rather than referring to it in binary, this instruction would often be expressed in hexadecimal as EB. This instruction code would be stored in the memory of the microcomputer along with a number of other instructions that make up a program. At the appropriate time, it is fetched from memory and decoded. The result of its execution is:

The eight-bit data word contained in R3 is moved (actually copied) into the accumulator. The original contents of the accumulator are lost.

We will examine this and other instructions more thoroughly later.

Multibyte Instructions

We have seen an instruction-word format that contains op code and operand address information in a *single* word. In other words, a complete instruction such as that in Figure 13-6 is stored in a *single* memory location. If all instructions were to be encoded this way, we would need a larger word size to contain all of the possible instructions and the operand addresses. Computers with larger word sizes make use of this format whenever possible. The 8051 is limited to an eight-bit word size. In order to provide more instructions and more flexibility in accessing data, most computers with small word sizes use more than one word to describe each instruction. Typically there are three basic instruction formats: single-byte, two-byte, and three-byte. These are illustrated in Figure 13-7.

FIGURE 13-7   Instruction formats used in eight-bit microcomputers.

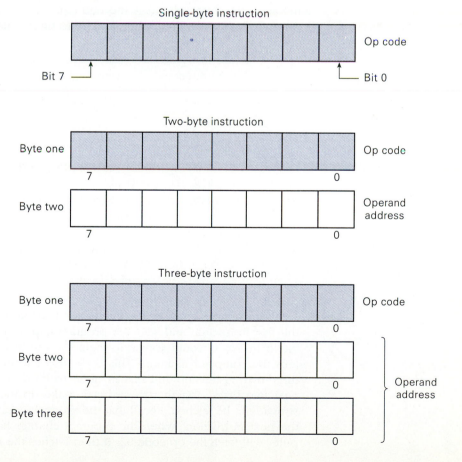

The instruction of Figure 13-6 is a single-byte instruction. Other single-byte instructions have no need of an operand. An example is an instruction to clear the accumulator register to 0 (CLR A), which instructs the computer to clear all of the FFs in the accumulator. For this instruction, all eight bits are considered to be part of the op code since there is no instruction to clear other registers than *A*.

In a two-byte instruction, the first byte always contains the op code. The purpose of the second byte (operand) is to specify the data value that is to be used in the operation. There are various methods of specifying this data. These methods are called **addressing modes.** We will discuss only two popular addressing modes in this text. The first is similar to the method described previously, in which the operand represents an address that directs the computer to the place where the data value is stored. This is called **direct addressing.** The other addressing mode includes the actual data value as part of the instruction. In this mode the operand is the data value itself instead of the address of the data value. Since the data value immediately follows the op code in the program memory, this is called the **immediate addressing** mode.

The three-byte instruction is necessary when the operand must be a 16-bit number. For these multibyte instructions, the two or three bytes making up the complete instruction must be stored in successive memory locations. This is illustrated in Table 13-1 for a 3-byte instruction. The left-hand column lists the address locations in memory where each byte (word) is stored. These addresses are given in hexadecimal code. The second column gives the binary word as it is actually stored in memory; the third column is the hex equivalent of this word. Examine this table carefully before reading further, and try to figure out what it represents.

TABLE 13-1 Program instructions stored in memory.

Memory Address	Binary	Hex	Description
2050	XXXXXXXX	XX	First instruction in a program
2051			
2052			
.			
.			
2377	00000010	02	Op code for Jump (LJMP)
2378	00100000	20	High byte of where to jump
2379	01010000	50	Low byte of where to jump
237A			
.			
.			

For example, consider the instruction that causes the computer to jump back to the first instruction and start the program over again. This instruction is shown in Table 13-1 as it would appear in memory. The first byte is the op code (02) which tells the computer to jump. This code also informs the control unit that this is a three-byte instruction and that in order to know where to jump, it must fetch the next two bytes. Together these bytes make up the 16-bit address of the next instruction to be fetched. Recall that the program counter always holds the address of the next instruction. When the program counter has advanced to 2377, the computer will fetch the op code 02. It then fetches the next two bytes (20 and 50) and loads them back into the program counter. The new address in the program counter means that the next instruction will be fetched from 2050 instead of 237A.

1. What is an op code?
2. What is an operand address?
3. What information is contained in the first byte of a multibyte instruction?

13-8 EXECUTING A MACHINE-LANGUAGE PROGRAM

The instruction words that we have been describing are called **machine-language** instructions because they are represented by 1s and 0s, the only language that the machine (computer) understands. Many other languages can be used to program a computer, and you may be familiar with some of them, such as BASIC or C. These **high-level languages** are designed to make it easy to write a program. It is important to understand that these high-level programs must be converted to machine-language instructions and placed in the computer's internal memory before the computer can execute them. In a typical microcomputer, the conversion from C to machine language is accomplished through a program called a **compiler.** The compiler program typically runs on a personal computer. To use a compiler, the programmer creates a text file by typing instructions in a programming language such as C. The compiler program then translates these high-level instructions into a set of binary instructions (machine language) that can be loaded into the microcomputer's memory.

In order to illustrate how a microcomputer executes a machine-language program, we will use the instructions described in Table 13-2. These instructions are part of the 8051 μP instruction set, but they are typical of the kinds of instructions that most microprocessors can execute. Each instruction is accompanied by a **mnemonic** or abbreviation that is easier to remember than the op code. The complete set of mnemonics for a computer's instruction set is called its **assembly language.** Read the description of each instruction carefully, and keep in mind that only the op codes are shown and not the operands.

We will use some of the 8051 instructions from Table 13-2 to write a machine-language program that starts at address 0000H and does the following:

1. Jumps to the correct address to start the program.
2. Decides if there is a 0 in the accumulator.
3. If $A \neq 0$, displays the accumulator value by outputting it to port 1.
4. Waits 1 second.
5. Decreases the accumulator value by 1.
6. Repeats from step 3 until the value in the accumulator is 0.

Table 13-3 shows a program as it would be entered into the computer's memory. Actually, the first two columns are the machine-language program; the other information is included for descriptive purposes. The first column lists the hex address

TABLE 13-2 Some 8051 instructions.

Mnemonic	Op Code Binary	Op Code Hex	Description of Operation
LJMP address	0000 0010	02	Long Jump. Jump from the current memory location in the program to the address specified in the two-byte operand.
MOV A, direct	1110 0101	E5	Move from an address to Acc. The data value contained in the direct address is moved to Acc.
MOV direct, A	1111 0101	F5	Move from Acc to an address. The data value in Acc is moved to the direct memory address specified in the instruction.
DEC A	0001 0100	14	Decrement the Accumulator. Subtract 1 from the value in Acc.
JNZ address	0111 0000	70	Jump if Acc is Not Zero. If Acc ≠ 0, the next instruction is to be fetched from the operand address. Otherwise, the next instruction in sequence is fetched.
JZ address	0110 0000	60	Jump if Acc is Zero. If Acc = 0, the next instruction is to be fetched from the operand address. Otherwise, the next instruction in sequence is fetched.
LCALL address	0001 0010	12	Long Call to subroutine. Causes a short program called a *subroutine* to execute. When it is done, the program returns to the instruction following LCALL.
RET	0010 0010	22	Return from subroutine. Sends the computer back to wherever it was called from.

TABLE 13-3 Sample machine-language program.

Memory Address (Hex)	Memory Contents (Hex)	Assembly Language	Description
0000	02	LJMP 0100H	;JUMP to start of program
0001	01		
0002	00		
0100	60	JZ 010AH	;Should we cook the food?
0101	08		
0102	F5	MOV P1, A	;Display cook time on port 1
0103	90		
0104	12	LCALL 1__SEC__DELAY	;Waste one sec
0105	28		
0106	55		
0107	14	DEC A	;Subtract one sec from time
0108	70	JNZ 0102H	;Is the food done?
0109	F8		
010A		*********This is where the rest of the program continues.********	

of each memory location being used by the program. The second column gives the hex equivalent of the word stored in each memory location. Remember, these hex values represent the actual binary addresses and instruction codes that the computer understands.

The third column gives the assembly-language mnemonic and the operand address (if any) associated with each instruction. The last column describes the operation performed by each instruction. For example, the first instruction in the program is a three-byte instruction. The first byte stored in memory address 0000 is the op code 02. The second and third bytes stored in addresses 0001 and 0002 represent the operand address 0100. The mnemonic for this instruction is LJMP 0100H. The LJMP is the abbreviation for the long jump operation, and the 0100 is the operand address. The H is often used to indicate that the address is represented in hex.

A very typical application of an embedded microprocessor is a microwave oven control system. A block diagram of such a system is shown in Figure 13-8. If we were to try to analyze all of the machine-language instructions needed to program an actual microwave oven, you would find it overwhelming. Our goal here is to understand how a simple part of a program works and give you a glimpse of what the program does to control the system. In the example of Table 13-3, only a portion of a program is shown in a simplified form that you will find easy to understand. Its purpose is to determine if a nonzero value has been placed in the accumulator. The value in the accumulator represents the number of seconds that the microwave should cook the food. If a nonzero value is in A, it displays the number of seconds on an output port and counts down in 1-second intervals until it reaches 0. It then continues with the rest of the program. The program starts executing at address 0000 when power is first applied which resets the system. The instruction that is generally stored at the reset address is a jump instruction that sends the micro to the main program. The main program in this case starts at 0100 where it makes a decision either to jump immediately to the rest of the program at 010A or to execute the instructions from 0102–0109. In either case, it eventually executes the rest of the program from 010A until it is told to jump back to 0100 and do it all over again. Spend some time now examining the program in Table 13-3 until you understand it.

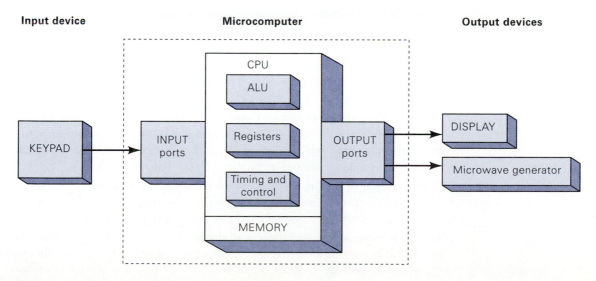

FIGURE 13-8   Block diagram of a microwave oven.

Program Execution

We will now proceed through the complete execution of this program and describe what the computer does at each step. Our intent here is to outline only the main operations without getting bogged down in the details of all of the activity taking place inside the computer. In particular, we will see that the computer is always in one of two kinds of operating cycles: (1) a **fetch cycle** during which the control unit fetches the instruction codes (op code and operand address) from memory and (2) an **execute cycle** during which the control unit performs the operation called for by the op code.

The operation starts when the operator activates the RESET pin by applying power. This will initialize a program counter (PC) to a starting count of 0000. As mentioned earlier, the PC is a counter within the control unit that keeps track of the program addresses as the computer sequences through them.

1. The control unit fetches the first byte from address 0000 as determined by the program counter (PC). This byte is 02H which is the op code for the first instruction. Circuitry within the control unit determines that this op code calls for the program to jump (LJMP), and the next two bytes are operands that tell it where to jump. The control unit then fetches the high half of the destination and then the low half of the destination address.

2. To execute the instruction, the 16-bit destination address (0100H) is loaded into the program counter. The next instruction that will be fetched will be at address 0100H.

3. The op code 60H is fetched from 0100H and is decoded as a conditional jump (JZ). The control unit also knows that this is a two-byte instruction, and it fetches the operand (08H). This tells the control unit how far to jump if the conditions are met. The jump will occur only if the accumulator is 0. The control section examines the accumulator, and if Acc = 0, it advances the program counter to the address 010AH. If Acc ≠ 0, the control unit will fetch the next op code that it finds in memory, in this case from 0102H. How do the nonzero numbers get into the accumulator? Another part of the program would be responsible for inputting a time value from the key pad to the accumulator. We have left this to your imagination to keep the example simple. Assume for now that the microprocessor has been through the program loop several times and that a value has been placed in A.

4. The execution of the JZ instruction simply advances the program counter to address 0102H since Acc ≠ 0.

5. The op code is fetched from address 0102H. The F5 instruction tells the control section to transfer the value in the accumulator. In order to know where to transfer it, the next byte in memory must be fetched. In this case the address (90H) means that we should write the value to output port #1.

6. The execution of this instruction copies the contents of the accumulator to the output port register. This value is written to the output port, which would be connected to circuitry to visually display the number for the user to see.

7. The PC is incremented to 0104H, and the next op code is fetched. This instruction (12H) is a subroutine call. This means that the micro must leave this part of the program and go execute some instructions that are stored elsewhere in

memory. The next two bytes (28H, 55H) tell the CPU where the subroutine is located.

8. To execute the call instruction, the CPU remembers the place in the program to which it must return after this subroutine (address 0107H), and then it loads the PC with address 2855H. At this address it finds the first instruction of a 1-second time-delay program. The last instruction in the subroutine would be RET which returns the PC to address 0107H 1 second later.

9. The op code at address 0107H is fetched and decoded as a decrement accumulator command. It is a single-byte instruction, so no operand is needed. The execution takes place inside the CPU, and the number stored in A is decreased by 1. The PC is automatically advanced to the next instruction at address 0108H.

10. At address 0108H the next instruction's op code (70H) is fetched. It recognizes the op code as a JNZ (jump if not zero), and it knows that it must make a decision based on the current contents of the accumulator.

11. If the value in the accumulator has reached 00H, then the food is done, and the CPU should continue on with the rest of the program by fetching the instruction at address 010AH.

12. If the value in A is still greater than 00H, we want to repeat the loop and count down the seconds until we reach 00H. This means that it must jump backward to address 0102H. In order to know how far to jump back, it must fetch the operand that is stored at address 0109H. This value is combined with the current PC contents to modify the PC to hold address 0102H.

This simple program illustrates many of the kinds of things that take place as a computer executes a machine-language program, but it does not even begin to show the capabilities and versatility of a computer. It is important to understand that the program execution is performed in a step-by-step, sequential manner starting at the first address in the program (0000 in our example). Of course, even though the computer performs one step at a time, each instruction occurs very quickly. For example, each instruction in this program would take approximately 1 to 2 microseconds on a typical microcontroller.

Review Questions

1. What is the difference between a machine-language program and a high-level-language program?
2. What is an instruction mnemonic?
3. What generally takes place during a fetch cycle? During an execute cycle?
4. What is the function of the program counter?

13-9 TYPICAL μC STRUCTURE

We are now prepared to take a more detailed look at μC organization. The many possible μC structures are essentially the same in principle, although they vary as to the size of the data and address buses and the types of control signals they use. In order to provide the clearest means for learning the principles of μC operation, it is necessary to choose a single type of μC structure and study it in detail. Once a solid understanding of this typical μC is obtained, it will be relatively easy to learn about any other type. The μC structure we have chosen to present is shown in Figure 13-9. It is based on the 8051 microprocessor but has essentially the same structure as microcomputers based on most other eight-bit μPs. The CPU shown actually consists of the 8051 μP chip connected to several support chips to produce the desired bus structures. We will not be concerned here with the details of these connections. Our focus is on the various buses that connect the CPU to the other elements of the μC and on how these buses are used during μC operation.

The Bus System

The μC has three buses that carry all of the information and signals involved in the system operation. These buses connect the microprocessor (CPU) to each of the memory and I/O elements so that data and information can flow between the CPU and any of these other elements. In other words, the CPU is continually involved in sending information to or receiving it from a location in memory, an input device, or an output device.

In the μC, all information transfers are referenced to the CPU. When the CPU is sending data to another computer element, it is called a *write* operation, and the CPU is writing into the selected element. When the CPU is receiving data from another element, it is called a *read* operation, and the CPU is reading from the selected element. It is very important to realize that the terms "read" and "write" always refer to operations performed by the CPU.

The buses involved in all of the data transfers have functions that are described as follows:

- **Address Bus** This is a *unidirectional* bus, because information flows over it in only one direction, from the CPU to the memory or I/O elements. The CPU alone can place logic levels on the lines of the address bus, thereby generating $2^{16} =$ 65,536 different possible addresses. Each of these addresses corresponds to one memory location or one I/O element. For example, address $20A0_{16}$ might be a location in RAM or ROM where an eight-bit word is stored, or it might be an eight-bit buffer register that is part of the interface circuitry for a liquid-crystal display (LCD) module or a D/A converter.

  When the CPU wants to communicate with (read from or write to) a certain memory location or I/O device, it places the appropriate 16-bit address code on its 16 address pin outputs, A_0 through A_{15}, and onto the address bus. These address bits are then *decoded* to select the desired memory location or I/O device. This decoding process usually requires decoder circuitry not shown on this diagram.

- **Data Bus** This is a *bidirectional* bus, because data can flow to or from the CPU. The CPU's eight data pins, D_0 through D_7, can be either inputs or outputs, depending on whether the CPU is performing a read or a write operation. During a read operation they act as inputs and receive data that have been placed on the data bus by the memory or I/O element selected by the address code on the address bus. During a write operation the CPU's data pins act as outputs and place data on the data bus, which are then sent to the selected memory or I/O element.

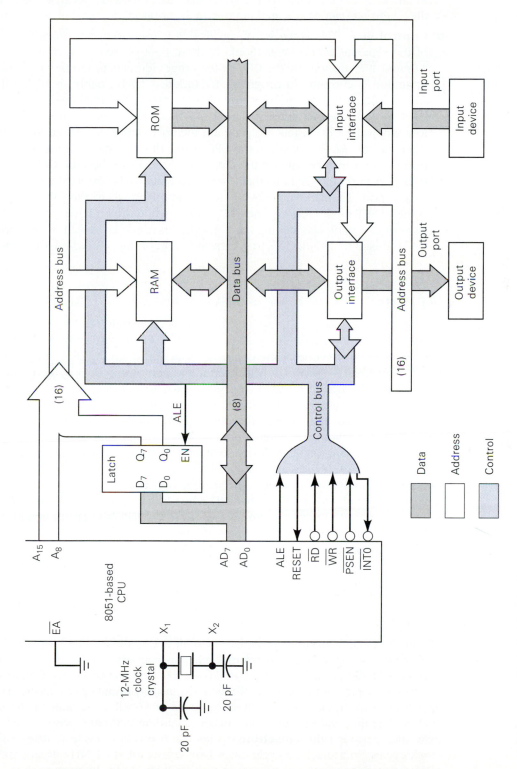

FIGURE 13-9 Typical eight-bit μC structure.

In all cases, the transmitted data words are eight bits wide because the CPU handles eight-bit data words, making this an eight-bit μC.

- **Control Bus** This is the set of signals that is used to synchronize the activities of the separate μC elements. Some of these control signals, such as *ALE, $\overline{PSEN}$, $\overline{RD}$*, and *$\overline{WR}$*, are sent by the CPU to the other elements to tell them what type of operation is currently in progress. *ALE* (address latch enable) is high while the CPU is putting the low address byte on AD_0–AD_7. This signal enables the address latch to grab the low address during this time. *$\overline{PSEN}$* (program store enable) is low when the CPU wants the program memory (store) to put an instruction on the data bus. *$\overline{RD}$* is low when the CPU wants the external data memory or input port to put a byte of data on the data bus. *$\overline{WR}$* is low when the CPU is putting a byte of data on the data bus that it wants to write to the external data memory or output port. The I/O elements can send control signals to the CPU. An example is the RESET input (*RST*) of the CPU, which, when driven HIGH, causes the CPU to reset to a particular starting state. Another example is the CPU's interrupt input (INT0), used by I/O devices to get the attention of the CPU when it is performing other tasks.

I/O Ports

During the execution of a program, the CPU is constantly reading from or writing into memory. The program may also call on the CPU to read from one of the input devices or write into one of the output devices. Although the diagram of the eight-bit μC in Figure 13-9 shows only one input and one output device, there can be any number of each tied to the μC bus system. Each I/O device is normally connected to the μC bus system through some type of interface circuit. The function of the interface is to make the μC and the device compatible so that data can be easily passed between them. The interface is needed whenever the I/O device uses signal levels, signal timing, or signal format that are different from those of the μC.

Although I/O devices are treated like memory locations, they are significantly different from memory in some respects. One big difference is that I/O devices can have the capability to *interrupt* the CPU while it is executing a program. What this means is that an I/O device can send a signal to the CPU's interrupt input (INT0) to tell the CPU that it wishes to communicate with it. The CPU will then suspend execution of the program that it is currently working on and will perform the appropriate operation with the interrupting I/O device. RAM and ROM do not normally have interrupting capability.

Timing

The 8051 contains an on-chip oscillator circuit that generates the basic clock signal to time all of its operations. An external crystal is connected to X_1 and X_2 to produce a precise, stable clock frequency (see Figure 13-9). If we know this frequency, we can precisely predict the amount of time each instruction takes to execute. For 8051 applications the crystal is typically close to 12 MHz. All operations of the system, such as fetching and executing instructions, reading data, and writing data, fit exactly into periods called **machine cycles.** Each machine cycle is made up of 12 clock cycles, so a machine cycle takes 1 microsecond at 12 MHz. Nearly all of the 8051 instructions require either one or two machine cycles to execute.

As we discussed earlier, the microprocessor is constantly fetching and executing instructions. The execution of most instructions involves things internal to the CPU, such as moving data between registers, adding numbers, and so on. However, three distinct types of **bus cycles** can be observed on the external bus system as shown in Table 13-4.

TABLE 13-4 8051 bus cycles.

Bus Cycle	Control Signal	Data Transferred
Fetch	$\overline{PSEN}$	CPU ← Program memory
Data read	$\overline{RD}$	CPU ← I/O or data memory
Data write	$\overline{WR}$	CPU → I/O or data memory

During one machine cycle (12 clocks) there is enough time to perform two fetches or to execute one data-read or one data-write bus cycle. Each bus cycle is a predictable sequence of events:

1. The CPU outputs a stable address on the address bus (*ALE* is HIGH).
2. The CPU asserts the proper control signal to transfer data ($\overline{PSEN}$, $\overline{RD}$, or $\overline{WR}$ is LOW).

Just as you can observe the traffic lights at an intersection and know who has the right of way, you can look at these four timing and control signals and know what type of bus cycle is going on, what the information on the bus means, and where the information came from. The timing diagram of Figure 13-10 shows two instruc-

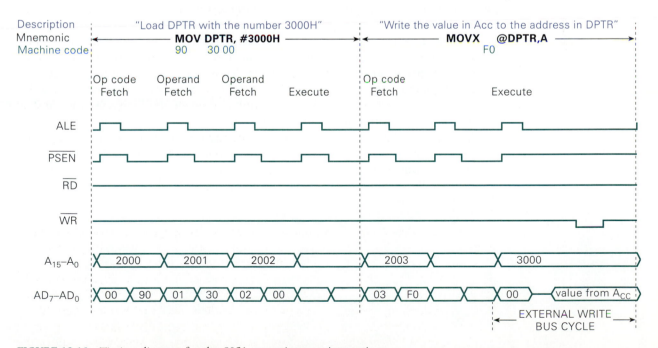

FIGURE 13-10 Timing diagram for the 8051 executing two instructions.

tions being fetched and executed. The first instruction loads the number 3000H into the DPTR register. The second instruction writes the contents of the accumulator to the external memory address specified by the DPTR. Whenever the control signal ALE is HIGH, there is an address on the data bus (AD_0–AD_7). Whenever $\overline{PSEN}$ is LOW, there is an instruction byte on the AD_0–AD_7 lines. Whenever $\overline{WR}$ is LOW, there is a data value that the CPU placed on AD_0–AD_7 in order to write it to data memory. In this example nothing is being read from external data memory, so the $\overline{RD}$ line never goes LOW.

Review Questions

1. Describe the functions of the three buses that are part of a typical microcomputer system.
2. Which bus is unidirectional?
3. What should be on the data bus when
   (a) ALE is HIGH?
   (b) $\overline{PSEN}$ is LOW?
   (c) $\overline{RD}$ is LOW?
   (d) $\overline{WR}$ is LOW?
4. How many external data memory locations can an 8051 access?

13-10 FINAL COMMENTS

Our discussion has been, by necessity, only a brief introduction to the basic principles, terminology, and operations common to most microprocessors and microcomputers. We have not even begun to gain an insight into the capabilities and applications of these devices. Almost all areas of technology have started taking advantage of the inexpensive computer control that microprocessors can provide. Some typical applications include microwave ovens, VCRs, CD players, traffic controllers, home computers, electronic measuring instruments, industrial process control, electronic games, automobile emission control, automatic braking systems, and a rapidly growing number of new products.

With the revolutionary impact that microprocessors have had on the electronics industry, it is not unreasonable to expect that everyone working in electronics and related areas will have to become knowledgeable in the operation of microprocessors. Hopefully, our introduction will serve as a firm foundation for further study in this important area.

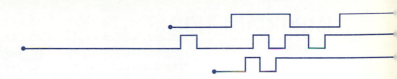

SUMMARY

1. A microprocessor is a sophisticated, sequential, digital circuit that is designed to follow a sequence of instructions called a *program*.

2. The program is stored in memory devices that are connected to the microprocessor.

3. In order to run a program, the microprocessor fetches an instruction from memory, then executes it, then fetches the next instruction, executes it, and so on.

4. The execution of some instructions involves reading in data values from input devices such as keypads, toggle switches, A/D converters, and so on. Other instructions cause the microcomputer to write data values to output devices such as LCD displays, indicator lights, motor control circuits, D/A converters, and so on.

5. Data values can also be stored in and retrieved from memory devices that are connected to the microprocessor.

6. The microprocessor is connected to memory and I/O devices by a group of wires called the *data bus*.

7. An address bus is also connected from the microprocessor to the memory and I/O devices. The address bus carries a number that specifies the location in memory of the instruction or data that the microprocessor is trying to access.

8. A set of control signals form the timing and control bus. They coordinate data transfer and indicate what type of data should currently be on the data bus.

9. A microprocessor along with a memory system and I/O devices makes up a microcomputer.

10. By understanding the timing of the bus activity, we can add peripheral devices to a microcomputer system and customize the hardware to our needs.

11. By understanding the programming language of a microprocessor, we can program it to perform many different types of tasks.

12. Microcomputers can be modular, versatile, easily programmable systems such as personal computers that are intended to be used for many different purposes.

13. Microcomputers can be made up of a single chip that is embedded in a product such as a microwave oven or a VCR for the purpose of controlling the operation of the device.

IMPORTANT TERMS

program	output unit	direct addressing
programmer	peripheral	immediate addressing
memory	interfacing	machine language
instructions	fetch	high-level language
data	execute	compiler
address	central processing unit	mnemonic
operation	(CPU)	assembly language
address	microprocessor unit (MPU)	fetch cycle
operand	program counter (PC)	execute cycle
operand address	accumulator	address bus
arithmetic/logic unit (ALU)	word	data bus
memory unit	word size	control bus
control unit	operation code (op code)	machine cycle
input unit	addressing mode	bus cycle

ANSWERS TO SECTION REVIEW QUESTIONS

SECTION 13-4

1. Input, output, arithmetic/logic, control, memory. See text for functions.   2. Control and arithmetic/logic units combined   3. The synchronization of digital information transmission between the computer and external I/O devices   4. Fetch and execute

SECTION 13-5

1. The microprocessor (MPU) is the CPU portion of the microcomputer.   2. MPU, RAM, ROM, input, output   3. Timing and control, register, ALU   4. Keeps track of instruction addresses

SECTION 13-6

1. Data and instructions   2. Executes programs at a faster rate

SECTION 13-7

1. A binary code that represents the operation to be performed by the CPU   2. The address of the data to be operated on as the CPU executes the instruction called for by the op code   3. Op code

SECTION 13-8

1. A machine-language program consists of the binary instruction codes stored in the computer's memory. A high-level-language program is written in a conversational language that must be converted to machine language before the computer can execute it.
2. A short abbreviation for the operation   3. During a fetch cycle, the CPU fetches the op code and the operand address from memory. During the execute cycle, the CPU executes the operation called for by the op code.   4. The PC keeps track of the addresses of the instructions in memory.

SECTION 13-9

1. Data bus: carries data between CPU and memory and I/O devices. Address bus: carries address code from CPU to memory and I/O devices. Control bus: carries timing and synchronization signals   2. Address bus
3. (a) low byte of address,   (b) instruction byte,
(c) data byte,   (d) data byte   4. 65,536

Manufacturer's IC Data Sheets

These data sheets are presented through the courtesy of Texas Instruments Incorporated.

74LS00	**74LS14**	**7432**	**74ALS86**	**74LS193**
74HCT02	**74ALS20**	**74S32**	**74AS86**	**74ALS193**
74LS04	**74AS20**	**74LS37**	**74LS112**	**74293**
7406	**74LS20**	**7486**	**74S112**	**4001B**
7407	**74HC20**	**74LS86**	**74121**	

SN54LS00, SN74LS00
QUADRUPLE 2-INPUT POSITIVE-NAND GATES

recommended operating conditions

		SN54LS00			SN74LS00			UNIT
		MIN	NOM	MAX	MIN	NOM	MAX	
V_{CC}	Supply voltage	4.5	5	5.5	4.75	5	5.25	V
V_{IH}	High-level input voltage	2			2			V
V_{IL}	Low-level input voltage			0.7			0.8	V
I_{OH}	High-level output current			− 0.4			− 0.4	mA
I_{OL}	Low-level output current			4			8	mA
T_A	Operating free-air temperature	− 55		125	0		70	°C

electrical characteristics over recommended operating free-air temperature range (unless otherwise noted)

PARAMETER	TEST CONDITIONS †			SN54LS00			SN74LS00			UNIT
				MIN	TYP‡	MAX	MIN	TYP‡	MAX	
V_{IK}	V_{CC} = MIN,	I_I = − 18 mA				− 1.5			− 1.5	V
V_{OH}	V_{CC} = MIN,	V_{IL} = MAX,	I_{OH} = − 0.4 mA	2.5	3.4		2.7	3.4		V
V_{OL}	V_{CC} = MIN,	V_{IH} = 2 V,	I_{OL} = 4 mA		0.25	0.4		0.25	0.4	V
	V_{CC} = MIN,	V_{IH} = 2 V,	I_{OL} = 8 mA					0.35	0.5	
I_I	V_{CC} = MAX,	V_I = 7 V				0.1			0.1	mA
I_{IH}	V_{CC} = MAX,	V_I = 2.7 V				20			20	µA
I_{IL}	V_{CC} = MAX,	V_I = 0.4 V				− 0.4			− 0.4	mA
I_{OS} §	V_{CC} = MAX			− 20		− 100	− 20		− 100	mA
I_{CCH}	V_{CC} = MAX,	V_I = 0 V			0.8	1.6		0.8	1.6	mA
I_{CCL}	V_{CC} = MAX,	V_I = 4.5 V			2.4	4.4		2.4	4.4	mA

† For conditions shown as MIN or MAX, use the appropriate value specified under recommended operating conditions.
‡ All typical values are at V_{CC} = 5 V, T_A = 25°C
§ Not more than one output should be shorted at a time, and the duration of the short-circuit should not exceed one second.

switching characteristics, V_{CC} = 5 V, T_A = 25°C (see note 2)

PARAMETER	FROM (INPUT)	TO (OUTPUT)	TEST CONDITIONS		MIN	TYP	MAX	UNIT
t_{PLH}	A or B	Y	R_L = 2 kΩ,	C_L = 15 pF		9	15	ns
t_{PHL}						10	15	ns

NOTE 2: Load circuits and voltage waveforms are shown in Section 1.

TEXAS
INSTRUMENTS
POST OFFICE BOX 655012 • DALLAS, TEXAS 75265

SN54HCT02, SN74HCT02
QUADRUPLE 2-INPUT POSITIVE-NOR GATES

SCLS065A – NOVEMBER 1988 – REVISED JANUARY 1996

recommended operating conditions

			SN54HCT02			SN74HCT02			UNIT
			MIN	NOM	MAX	MIN	NOM	MAX	
V_{CC}	Supply voltage		4.5	5	5.5	4.5	5	5.5	V
V_{IH}	High-level input voltage	V_{CC} = 4.5 V to 5.5 V	2			2			V
V_{IL}	Low-level input voltage	V_{CC} = 4.5 V to 5.5 V	0		0.8	0		0.8	V
V_I	Input voltage		0		V_{CC}	0		V_{CC}	V
V_O	Output voltage		0		V_{CC}	0		V_{CC}	V
t_t	Input transition (rise and fall) time		0		500	0		500	ns
T_A	Operating free-air temperature		–55		125	–40		85	°C

electrical characteristics over recommended operating free-air temperature range (unless otherwise noted)

PARAMETER	TEST CONDITIONS		V_{CC}	T_A = 25°C			SN54HCT02		SN74HCT02		UNIT
				MIN	TYP	MAX	MIN	MAX	MIN	MAX	
V_{OH}	V_I = V_{IH} or V_{IL}	I_{OH} = –20 μA	4.5 V	4.4	4.499		4.4		4.4		V
		I_{OH} = –4 mA		3.98	4.3		3.7		3.84		
V_{OL}	V_I = V_{IH} or V_{IL}	I_{OL} = 20 μA	4.5 V		0.001	0.1		0.1		0.1	V
		I_{OL} = 4 mA			0.17	0.26		0.4		0.33	
I_I	V_I = V_{CC} or 0		5.5 V		±0.1	±100		±1000		±1000	nA
I_{CC}	V_I = V_{CC} or 0,	I_O = 0	5.5 V			2		40		20	μA
ΔI_{CC}‡	One input at 0.5 V or 2.4 V, Other inputs at 0 or V_{CC}		5.5 V		1.4	2.4		3		2.9	mA
C_i			4.5 V to 5.5 V		3	10		10		10	pF

‡ This is the increase in supply current for each input that is at one of the specified TTL voltage levels rather than 0 V or V_{CC}.

switching characteristics over recommended operating free-air temperature range, C_L = 50 pF (unless otherwise noted) (see Figure 1)

PARAMETER	FROM (INPUT)	TO (OUTPUT)	V_{CC}	T_A = 25°C			SN54HCT02		SN74HCT02		UNIT
				MIN	TYP	MAX	MIN	MAX	MIN	MAX	
t_{pd}	A or B	Y	4.5 V		11	20		30		25	ns
			5.5 V		10	18		27		22	
t_t		Y	4.5 V		9	15		22		19	ns
			5.5 V		8	14		20		17	

operating characteristics, T_A = 25°C

PARAMETER		TEST CONDITIONS	TYP	UNIT
C_{pd}	Power dissipation capacitance per gate	No load	20	pF

TEXAS INSTRUMENTS

POST OFFICE BOX 655303 ● DALLAS, TEXAS 75265

SN54LS04, SN74LS04
HEX INVERTERS

recommended operating conditions

		SN54LS04			SN74LS04			UNIT
		MIN	NOM	MAX	MIN	NOM	MAX	
V_{CC}	Supply voltage	4.5	5	5.5	4.75	5	5.25	V
V_{IH}	High-level input voltage	2			2			V
V_{IL}	Low-level input voltage			0.7			0.8	V
I_{OH}	High-level output current			−0.4			−0.4	mA
I_{OL}	Low-level output current			4			8	mA
T_A	Operating free-air temperature	−55		125	0		70	°C

electrical characteristics over recommended operating free-air temperature range (unless otherwise noted)

PARAMETER	TEST CONDITIONS †			SN54LS04			SN74LS04			UNIT
			MIN	TYP‡	MAX	MIN	TYP‡	MAX		
V_{IK}	V_{CC} = MIN,	I_I = −18 mA			−1.5			−1.5		V
V_{OH}	V_{CC} = MIN,	V_{IL} = MAX, I_{OH} = −0.4 mA	2.5	3.4		2.7	3.4			V
V_{OL}	V_{CC} = MIN,	V_{IH} = 2 V, I_{OL} = 4 mA		0.25	0.4			0.4		V
	V_{CC} = MIN,	V_{IH} = 2 V, I_{OL} = 8 mA					0.25	0.5		
I_I	V_{CC} = MAX,	V_I = 7 V			0.1			0.1		mA
I_{IH}	V_{CC} = MAX,	V_I = 2.7 V			20			20		μA
I_{IL}	V_{CC} = MAX,	V_I = 0.4 V			−0.4			−0.4		mA
I_{OS} §	V_{CC} = MAX		−20		−100	−20		−100		mA
I_{CCH}	V_{CC} = MAX,	V_I = 0 V		1.2	2.4		1.2	2.4		mA
I_{CCL}	V_{CC} = MAX,	V_I = 4.5 V		3.6	6.6		3.6	6.6		mA

† For conditions shown as MIN or MAX, use the appropriate value specified under recommended operating conditions.
‡ All typical values are at V_{CC} = 5 V, T_A = 25°C.
§ Not more than one output should be shorted at a time, and the duration of the short-circuit should not exceed one second.

switching characteristics, V_{CC} = 5 V, T_A = 25°C (see note 2)

PARAMETER	FROM (INPUT)	TO (OUTPUT)	TEST CONDITIONS		MIN	TYP	MAX	UNIT
t_{PLH}	A	Y	R_L = 2 kΩ,	C_L = 15 pF		9	15	ns
t_{PHL}						10	15	ns

NOTE 2: Load circuits and voltage waveforms are shown in Section 1.

Texas Instruments
POST OFFICE BOX 655012 • DALLAS, TEXAS 75265

SN5406, SN5416, SN7406, SN7416
HEX INVERTER BUFFERS/DRIVERS WITH
OPEN-COLLECTOR HIGH-VOLTAGE OUTPUTS
DECEMBER 1983 – REVISED MARCH 1988

- Converts TTL Voltage Levels to MOS Levels

- High Sink-Current Capability

- Input Clamping Diodes Simplify System Design

- Open-Collector Driver for Indicator Lamps and Relays

- Inputs Fully Compatible with Most TTL Circuits

SN5406, SN5416 . . . J OR W PACKAGE
SN7406, SN7416 . . . N PACKAGE
(TOP VIEW)

```
        ┌───┬─┬───┐
 1A  [ 1    U    14 ]  VCC
 1Y  [ 2         13 ]  6A
 2A  [ 3         12 ]  6Y
 2Y  [ 4         11 ]  5A
 3A  [ 5         10 ]  5Y
 3Y  [ 6          9 ]  4A
 GND [ 7          8 ]  4Y
        └─────────┘
```

description

These monolithic TTL hex inverter buffers/drivers feature high-voltage open-collector outputs for interfacing with high-level circuits (such as MOS), or for driving high-current loads (such as lamps or relays), and are also characterized for use as inverter buffers for driving TTL inputs. The SN5406 and SN7406 have minimum breakdown voltages of 30 volts and the SN5416 and SN7416 have minimum breakdown voltages of 15 volts. The maximum sink current is 30 milliamperes for the SN5406 and SN5416, and 40 milliamperes for the SN7406 and SN7416.

logic symbol[†]

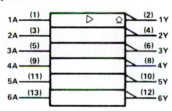

```
 1A ─(1)──┐          ┌──(2)── 1Y
          │  ▷    ◇  │
 2A ─(3)──┤          ├──(4)── 2Y
 3A ─(5)──┤          ├──(6)── 3Y
 4A ─(9)──┤          ├──(8)── 4Y
 5A ─(11)─┤          ├──(10)─ 5Y
 6A ─(13)─┘          └──(12)─ 6Y
```

[†] This symbol is in accordance with ANSI/IEEE Std 91-1984 and IEC Publication 617-12.

logic diagram (positive logic)

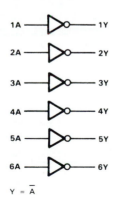

```
 1A ──▷o── 1Y
 2A ──▷o── 2Y
 3A ──▷o── 3Y
 4A ──▷o── 4Y
 5A ──▷o── 5Y
 6A ──▷o── 6Y
```

$Y = \overline{A}$

schematic

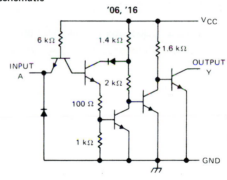

'06, '16

6 kΩ   1.4 kΩ   1.6 kΩ
INPUT A   2 kΩ   OUTPUT Y
100 Ω
1 kΩ
VCC
GND

Resistor values shown are nominal.

TEXAS INSTRUMENTS
POST OFFICE BOX 655012 • DALLAS, TEXAS 75265

2-37

SN5406, SN5416, SN7406, SN7416
HEX INVERTER BUFFERS/DRIVERS WITH
OPEN-COLLECTOR HIGH-VOLTAGE OUTPUTS

absolute maximum ratings over operating free-air temperature range (unless otherwise noted)

Supply voltage, V_{CC} (see Note 1) .... 7 V
Input voltage (see Note 1) .... 5.5 V
Output voltage (see Notes 1 and 2): SN5406, SN7406 Circuits .... 30 V
　　　　　　　　　　　　　　　　　　SN5416, SN7416 Circuits .... 15 V
Operating free-air temperature range: SN5406, SN5416 Circuits .... −55°C to 125°C
　　　　　　　　　　　　　　　　　　　SN7406, SN7416 Circuits .... 0°C to 70°C
Storage temperature range .... −65°C to 150°C

NOTES: 1. Voltage values are with respect to network ground terminal.
　　　　 2. This is the maximum voltage which should be applied to any output when it is in the off state.

recommended operating conditions

			SN5406 SN5416			SN7406 SN7416			UNIT
			MIN	NOM	MAX	MIN	NOM	MAX	
V_{CC}	Supply voltage		4.5	5	5.5	4.75	5	5.25	V
V_{IH}	High-level input voltage		2			2			V
V_{IL}	Low-level input voltage				0.8			0.8	V
V_{OH}	High-level output voltage	'06			30			30	V
		'16			15			15	
I_{OL}	Low-level output current				30			40	mA
T_A	Operating free-air temperature		−55		125	0		70	C

electrical characteristics over recommended operating free-air temperature range (unless otherwise noted)

PARAMETER	TEST CONDITIONS†			SN5406 SN5416			SN7406 SN7416			UNIT
				MIN	TYP‡	MAX	MIN	TYP‡	MAX	
V_{IK}	V_{CC} = MIN,	I_I = −12 mA				−1.5			−1.5	V
I_{OH}	V_{CC} = MIN,	V_{IL} = 0.8 V,	V_{OH} = §			0.25			0.25	mA
V_{OL}	V_{CC} = MIN,	V_{IH} = 2 V	I_{OL} = 16 mA			0.4			0.4	V
			I_{OL} = ¶			0.7			0.7	
I_I	V_{CC} = MAX,	V_I = 5.5 V				1			1	mA
I_{IH}	V_{CC} = MAX,	V_{IH} = 2.4 V				40			40	µA
I_{IL}	V_{CC} = MAX,	V_{IL} = 0.4 V				−1.6			−1.6	mA
I_{CCH}	V_{CC} = MAX			30	48		30	48		mA
I_{CCL}	V_{CC} = MAX			32	51		32	51		mA

† For conditions shown as MIN or MAX, use the appropriate value specified under recommended operating conditions.
‡ All typical values are at V_{CC} = 5 V, T_A = 25°C.
§ V_{OH} = 30 V for '06 and 15 V for '16.
¶ I_{OL} = 30 mA for SN54' and 40 mA for SN74'.

switching characteristics, V_{CC} = 5 V, T_A = 25°C (see note 3)

PARAMETER	FROM (INPUT)	TO (OUTPUT)	TEST CONDITIONS		MIN	TYP	MAX	UNIT
t_{PLH}	A	Y	R_L = 110 Ω	C_L = 15 pF		10	15	ns
t_{PHL}						15	23	ns

NOTE 3: Load circuits and voltage waveforms are shown in Section 1.

TEXAS INSTRUMENTS
POST OFFICE BOX 655012 • DALLAS, TEXAS 75265

SN5407, SN5417, SN7407, SN7417
HEX BUFFERS/DRIVERS WITH
OPEN-COLLECTOR HIGH-VOLTAGE OUTPUTS
DECEMBER 1983–REVISED MARCH 1988

- **Converts TTL Voltage Levels to MOS Levels**
- **High Sink-Current Capability**
- **Input Clamping Diodes Simplify System Design**
- **Open-Collector Driver for Indicator Lamps and Relays**
- **Inputs Fully Compatible with Most TTL Circuits**

SN5407, SN5417 . . . J OR W PACKAGE
SN7407, SN7417 . . . N PACKAGE
(TOP VIEW)

```
        ┌──┬─∪─┬──┐
  1A ──┤1      14├── VCC
  1Y ──┤2      13├── 6A
  2A ──┤3      12├── 6Y
  2Y ──┤4      11├── 5A
  3A ──┤5      10├── 5Y
  3Y ──┤6       9├── 4A
 GND ──┤7       8├── 4Y
        └────────┘
```

description

These monolithic TTL hex buffers/drivers feature high-voltage open-collector outputs for interfacing with high-level circuits (such as MOS), or for driving high-current loads (such as lamps or relays), and are also characterized for use as buffers for driving TTL inputs. The SN5407 and SN7407 have minimum breakdown voltages of 30 volts and the SN5417 and SN7417 have minimum breakdown voltages of 15 volts. The maximum sink current is 30 milliamperes for the SN5407 and SN5417, and 40 milliamperes for the SN7407 and SN7417.

These circuits are completely compatible with most TTL families. Inputs are diode-clamped to minimize transmission-line effects which simplifies design. Typical power dissipation is 145 milliwatts and average propagation delay time is 14 nanoseconds. The SN5407 and SN5417 are characterized for operation over the full military temperature range of −55 C to 125 C; the SN7407 and SN7417 are characterized for operation from 0 C to 70 C.

logic symbol†

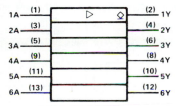

† This symbol is in accordance with ANSI/IEEE Std 91-1984 and IEC Publication 617-12.

logic diagram (positive logic)

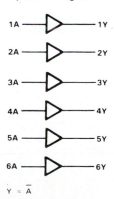

$$Y = \overline{A}$$

schematic

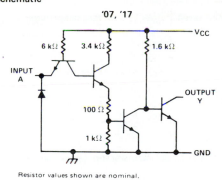

'07, '17

Resistor values shown are nominal.

TEXAS INSTRUMENTS
POST OFFICE BOX 655012 • DALLAS, TEXAS 75265

2-39

SN5407, SN5417, SN7407, SN7417
HEX BUFFERS/DRIVERS WITH
OPEN-COLLECTOR HIGH-VOLTAGE OUTPUTS

absolute maximum ratings over operating free-air temperature range (unless otherwise noted)

Supply voltage V_{CC} (see Note 1) . . . . 7 V
Input voltage (see Note 1) . . . . 5.5 V
Output voltage (see Notes 1 and 2): SN5407, SN7407 Circuits . . . . 30 V
                                                          SN5417, SN7417 Circuits . . . . 15 V
Operating free-air temperature range: SN5407, SN5417 Circuits . . . . − 55°C to 125°C
                                                           SN7407, SN7417 Circuits . . . . 0°C to 70°C
Storage temperature range . . . . − 65°C to 150°C

NOTES: 1. Voltage values are with respect to network ground terminal.
        2. This is the maximum voltage which should be applied to any output when it is in the off state.

recommended operating conditions

		SN5407 SN5417			SN7407 SN7417			UNIT
		MIN	NOM	MAX	MIN	NOM	MAX	
V_{CC}	Supply voltage	4.5	5	5.5	4.75	5	5.25	V
V_{IH}	High-level input voltage	2			2			V
V_{IL}	Low-level input voltage			0.8			0.8	V
V_{OH}	High-level output voltage '07			30			30	V
	'17			15			15	
I_{OL}	Low-level output current			30			40	mA
T_A	Operating free-air temperature	− 55		125	0		70	°C

electrical characteristics over recommended operating free-air temperature range (unless otherwise noted)

PARAMETER	TEST CONDITIONS[†]		SN5407 SN5417			SN7407 SN7417			UNIT
			MIN	TYP[‡]	MAX	MIN	TYP[‡]	MAX	
V_{IK}	V_{CC} = MIN,	I_I = − 12 mA			− 1.5			− 1.5	V
I_{OH}	V_{CC} = MIN,	V_{IL} = 0.8 V, V_{OH} = §			0.25			0.25	mA
V_{OL}	V_{CC} = MIN,	V_{IH} = 2 V, I_{OL} = 16 mA			0.4			0.4	V
		I_{OL} = ¶			0.7			0.7	
I_I	V_{CC} = MAX,	V_I = 5.5 V			1			1	mA
I_{IH}	V_{CC} = MAX,	V_{IH} = 2.4 V			40			40	µA
I_{IL}	V_{CC} = MAX,	V_{IL} = 0.4 V			− 1.6			− 1.6	mA
I_{CCH}	V_{CC} = MAX			29	41		29	41	mA
I_{CCL}	V_{CC} = MAX			21	30		21	30	mA

† For conditions shown as MIN or MAX, use the appropriate value specified under recommended operating conditions.
‡ All typical values are at V_{CC} = 5 V, T_A = 25°C.
§ V_{OH} = 30 V for '07 and 15 V for '17.
¶ I_{OL} = 30 mA for SN54' and 40 mA for SN74'.

switching characteristics, V_{CC} = 5 V, T_A = 25°C (see Note 3)

PARAMETER	FROM (INPUT)	TO (OUTPUT)	TEST CONDITIONS	MIN	TYP	MAX	UNIT
t_{PLH}	A	Y	R_L = 110 Ω, C_L = 15 pF		6	15	ns
t_{PHL}					20	26	
t_{PLH}	A	Y	R_L = 150 Ω, C_L = 50 pF			15	ns
t_{PHL}						26	

NOTE 3: Load circuits and voltage waveforms are shown in Section 1.

TEXAS INSTRUMENTS

POST OFFICE BOX 655012 • DALLAS, TEXAS 75265

SN54LS14, SN74LS14
HEX SCHMITT-TRIGGER INVERTERS

recommended operating conditions

		SN54LS14			SN74LS14			UNIT
		MIN	NOM	MAX	MIN	NOM	MAX	
V_{CC}	Supply voltage	4.5	5	5.5	4.75	5	5.25	V
I_{OH}	High-level output current			−0.4			−0.4	mA
I_{OL}	Low-level output current			4			8	mA
T_A	Operating free-air temperature	−55		125	0		70	C

electrical characteristics over recommended operating free-air temperature range (unless otherwise noted)

PARAMETER	TEST CONDITIONS†			SN54LS14			SN74LS14			UNIT
				MIN	TYP‡	MAX	MIN	TYP‡	MAX	
V_{T+}	$V_{CC} = 5$ V			1.4	1.6	1.9	1.4	1.6	1.9	V
V_{T-}	$V_{CC} = 5$ V			0.5	0.8	1	0.5	0.8	1	V
Hysteresis $(V_{T+} - V_{T-})$	$V_{CC} = 5$ V			0.4	0.8		0.4	0.8		V
V_{IK}	$V_{CC} = $ MIN,	$I_I = -18$ mA				−1.5			−1.5	V
V_{OH}	$V_{CC} = $ MIN,	$V_I = 0.5$ V,	$I_{OH} = -0.4$ mA	2.5	3.4		2.7	3.4		V
V_{OL}	$V_{CC} = $ MIN,	$V_I = 1.9$ V	$I_{OL} = 4$ mA		0.25	0.4		0.25	0.4	V
			$I_{OL} = 8$ mA					0.35	0.5	
I_{T+}	$V_{CC} = 5$ V,	$V_I = V_{T+}$			−0.14			−0.14		mA
I_{T-}	$V_{CC} = 5$ V,	$V_I = V_{T-}$			−0.18			−0.18		mA
I_I	$V_{CC} = $ MAX,	$V_I = 7$ V				0.1			0.1	mA
I_{IH}	$V_{CC} = $ MAX,	$V_{IH} = 2.7$ V				20			20	μA
I_{IL}	$V_{CC} = $ MAX,	$V_{IL} = 0.4$ V				−0.4			−0.4	mA
I_{OS} §	$V_{CC} = $ MAX			−20		−100	−20		−100	mA
I_{CCH}	$V_{CC} = $ MAX				8.6	16		8.6	16	mA
I_{CCL}	$V_{CC} = $ MAX				12	21		12	21	mA

† For conditions shown as MIN or MAX, use the appropriate value specified under recommended operating conditions.
‡ All typical values are at $V_{CC} = 5$ V, $T_A = 25$ C.
§ Not more than one output should be shorted at a time, and duration of the short-circuit should not exceed one second.

switching characteristics, $V_{CC} = 5$ V, $T_A = 25°C$

PARAMETER	FROM (INPUT)	TO (OUTPUT)	TEST CONDITIONS		MIN	TYP	MAX	UNIT
t_{PLH}	A	Y	$R_L = 2$ kΩ,	$C_L = 15$ pF		15	22	ns
t_{PHL}						15	22	ns

TEXAS
INSTRUMENTS

POST OFFICE BOX 655012 ● DALLAS, TEXAS 75265

SN54ALS20A, SN54AS20, SN74ALS20A, SN74AS20
DUAL 4-INPUT POSITIVE-NAND GATES

D2661, APRIL 1982—REVISED MAY 1986

● Package Options Include Plastic "Small Outline" Packages, Ceramic Chip Carriers, and Standard Plastic and Ceramic 300-mil DIPs

● Dependable Texas Instruments Quality and Reliability

description

These devices contain two independent 4-input NAND gates. They perform the Boolean functions $Y = \overline{A \cdot B \cdot C \cdot D}$ or $Y = \overline{A} + \overline{B} + \overline{C} + \overline{D}$ in positive logic.

The SN54ALS20A and SN54AS20 are characterized for operation over the full military temperature range of $-55°C$ to $125°C$. The SN74ALS20A and SN74AS20 are characterized for operation from $0°C$ to $70°C$.

SN54ALS20A, SN54AS20 . . . J PACKAGE
SN74ALS20A, SN74AS20 . . . D OR N PACKAGE
(TOP VIEW)

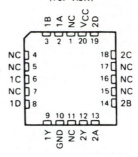

1A	1	14	V_CC
1B	2	13	2D
NC	3	12	2C
1C	4	11	NC
1D	5	10	2B
1Y	6	9	2A
GND	7	8	2Y

SN54ALS20A, SN54AS20 . . . FK PACKAGE
(TOP VIEW)

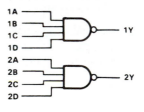

NC—No internal connection

FUNCTION TABLE (each gate)

INPUTS				OUTPUT
A	**B**	**C**	**D**	**Y**
H	H	H	H	L
L	X	X	X	H
X	L	X	X	H
X	X	L	X	H
X	X	X	L	H

logic symbol[†]

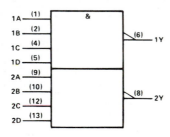

1A —(1)	&	
1B —(2)		(6) 1Y
1C —(4)		
1D —(5)		
2A —(9)		
2B —(10)		(8) 2Y
2C —(12)		
2D —(13)		

[†] This symbol is in accordance with ANSI/IEEE Std 91-1984 and IEC Publication 617-12.
Pin numbers shown are for D, J, and N packages.

logic diagram (positive logic)

1A
1B
1C
1D — 1Y

2A
2B
2C
2D — 2Y

TEXAS INSTRUMENTS
POST OFFICE BOX 655012 • DALLAS, TEXAS 75265

SN54ALS20A, SN74ALS20A
DUAL 4-INPUT POSITIVE-NAND GATES

absolute maximum ratings over operating free-air temperature range (unless otherwise noted)

Supply voltage, V_{CC} . . . . 7 V
Input voltage . . . . 7 V
Operating free-air temperature range: SN54ALS20A . . . . −55°C to 125°C
SN74ALS20A . . . . 0°C to 70°C
Storage temperature range . . . . −65°C to 150°C

recommended operating conditions

		SN54ALS20A			SN74ALS20A			UNIT
		MIN	NOM	MAX	MIN	NOM	MAX	
V_{CC}	Supply voltage	4.5	5	5.5	4.5	5	5.5	V
V_{IH}	High-level input voltage	2			2			V
V_{IL}	Low-level input voltage			0.7			0.8	V
I_{OH}	High-level output current			−0.4			−0.4	mA
I_{OL}	Low-level output current			4			8	mA
T_A	Operating free-air temperature	−55		125	0		70	°C

electrical characteristics over recommended operating-free-air temperature range (unless otherwise noted)

PARAMETER	TEST CONDITIONS		SN54ALS20A			SN74ALS20A			UNIT
			MIN	TYP†	MAX	MIN	TYP†	MAX	
V_{IK}	$V_{CC} = 4.5$ V,	$I_I = -18$ mA			−1.5			−1.5	V
V_{OH}	$V_{CC} = 4.5$ V to 5.5 V,	$I_{OH} = -0.4$ mA	$V_{CC}-2$			$V_{CC}-2$			V
V_{OL}	$V_{CC} = 4.5$ V,	$I_{OL} = 4$ mA		0.25	0.4		0.25	0.4	V
	$V_{CC} = 4.5$ V,	$I_{OL} = 8$ mA					0.35	0.5	
I_I	$V_{CC} = 5.5$ V,	$V_I = 7$ V			0.1			0.1	mA
I_{IH}	$V_{CC} = 5.5$ V,	$V_I = 2.7$ V			20			20	µA
I_{IL}	$V_{CC} = 5.5$ V,	$V_I = 0.4$ V			−0.1			−0.1	mA
I_O‡	$V_{CC} = 5.5$ V,	$V_O = 2.25$ V	−30		−112	−30		−112	mA
I_{CCH}	$V_{CC} = 5.5$ V,	$V_I = 0$ V		0.22	0.4		0.22	0.4	mA
I_{CCL}	$V_{CC} = 5.5$ V,	$V_I = 4.5$ V		0.81	1.5		0.81	1.5	mA

† All typical values are at $V_{CC} = 5$ V, $T_A = 25$°C.
‡ The output conditions have been chosen to produce a current that closely approximates one half of the true short-circuit output current, I_{OS}.

switching characteristics (see Note 1)

PARAMETER	FROM (INPUT)	TO (OUTPUT)	$V_{CC} = 5$ V, $C_L = 50$ pF, $R_L = 500$ Ω, $T_A = 25$°C	$V_{CC} = 4.5$ V to 5.5 V, $C_L = 50$ pF, $R_L = 500$ Ω, $T_A = $ MIN to MAX				UNIT
			'ALS20A	SN54ALS20A		SN74ALS20A		
			TYP	MIN	MAX	MIN	MAX	
t_{PLH}	Any	Y	7	1	18	3	11	ns
t_{PHL}	Any	Y	6	1	15	3	10	

NOTE 1: Load circuit and voltage waveforms are shown in Section 1.

TEXAS
INSTRUMENTS
POST OFFICE BOX 655012 • DALLAS, TEXAS 75265

SN54AS20, SN74AS20
DUAL 4-INPUT POSITIVE-NAND GATES

absolute maximum ratings over operating free-air temperature range (unless otherwise noted)

Supply voltage, V_{CC} . . . . 7 V
Input voltage . . . . 7 V
Operating free-air temperature range: SN54AS20 . . . . −55 °C to 125 °C
                            SN74AS20 . . . . 0 °C to 70 °C
Storage temperature range . . . . −65 °C to 150 °C

recommended operating conditions

		SN54AS20			SN74AS20			UNIT
		MIN	NOM	MAX	MIN	NOM	MAX	
V_{CC}	Supply voltage	4.5	5	5.5	4.5	5	5.5	V
V_{IH}	High-level input voltage	2			2			V
V_{IL}	Low-level input voltage			0.8			0.8	V
I_{OH}	High-level output current			−2			−2	mA
I_{OL}	Low-level output current			20			20	mA
T_A	Operating free-air temperature	−55		125	0		70	°C

electrical characteristics over recommended operating-free-air temperature range (unless otherwise noted)

PARAMETER	TEST CONDITIONS		SN54AS20			SN74AS20			UNIT
			MIN	TYP[†]	MAX	MIN	TYP[†]	MAX	
V_{IK}	V_{CC} = 4.5 V,	I_I = −18 mA			−1.2			−1.2	V
V_{OH}	V_{CC} = 4.5 V to 5.5 V,	I_{OH} = −2 mA	V_{CC}−2			V_{CC}−2			V
V_{OL}	V_{CC} = 4.5 V,	I_{OL} = 20 mA		0.35	0.5		0.35	0.5	V
I_I	V_{CC} = 5.5 V,	V_I = 7 V			0.1			0.1	mA
I_{IH}	V_{CC} = 5.5 V,	V_I = 2.7 V			20			20	μA
I_{IL}	V_{CC} = 5.5 V,	V_I = 0.4 V			−0.5			−0.5	mA
I_O[‡]	V_{CC} = 5.5 V,	V_O = 2.25 V	−30		−112	−30		−112	mA
I_{CCH}	V_{CC} = 5.5 V,	V_I = 0 V		1	1.6		1	1.6	mA
I_{CCL}	V_{CC} = 5.5 V,	V_I = 4.5 V		5.4	8.7		5.4	8.7	mA

[†] All typical values are at V_{CC} = 5 V, T_A = 25 °C.
[‡] The output conditions have been chosen to produce a current that closely approximates one half of the true short-circuit output current, I_{OS}.

switching characteristics (see Note 1)

PARAMETER	FROM (INPUT)	TO (OUTPUT)	V_{CC} = 4.5 V to 5.5 V, C_L = 50 pF, R_L = 500 Ω, T_A = MIN to MAX				UNIT
			SN54AS20		SN74AS20		
			MIN	MAX	MIN	MAX	
t_{PLH}	Any	Y	1	5.5	1	5	ns
t_{PHL}	Any	Y	1	5	1	4.5	

NOTE 1: Load circuit and voltage waveforms are shown in Section 1.

TYPES SN54LS20, SN74LS20
DUAL 4-INPUT POSITIVE-NAND GATES

recommended operating conditions

		SN54LS20			SN74LS20			UNIT
		MIN	NOM	MAX	MIN	NOM	MAX	
V_{CC}	Supply voltage	4.5	5	5.5	4.75	5	5.25	V
V_{IH}	High-level input voltage	2			2			V
V_{IL}	Low-level input voltage			0.7			0.8	V
I_{OH}	High-level output current			−0.4			−0.4	mA
I_{OL}	Low-level output current			4			8	mA
T_A	Operating free-air temperature	−55		125	0		70	°C

electrical characteristics over recommended operating free-air temperature range (unless otherwise noted)

PARAMETER	TEST CONDITIONS †			SN54LS20			SN74LS20			UNIT
			MIN	TYP‡	MAX	MIN	TYP‡	MAX		
V_{IK}	V_{CC} = MIN,	I_I = −18 mA			−1.5			−1.5		V
V_{OH}	V_{CC} = MIN,	V_{IL} = MAX, I_{OH} = −0.4 mA	2.5	3.4		2.7	3.4			V
V_{OL}	V_{CC} = MIN,	V_{IH} = 2 V, I_{OL} = 4 mA		0.25	0.4			0.4		V
	V_{CC} = MIN,	V_{IH} = 2 V, I_{OL} = 8 mA					0.25	0.5		
I_I	V_{CC} = MAX,	V_I = 7 V			0.1			0.1		mA
I_{IH}	V_{CC} = MAX,	V_I = 2.7 V			20			20		μA
I_{IL}	V_{CC} = MAX,	V_I = 0.4 V			−0.4			−0.4		mA
I_{OS} §	V_{CC} = MAX		−20		−100	−20		−100		mA
I_{CCH}	V_{CC} = MAX,	V_I = 0 V		0.4	0.8		0.4	0.8		mA
I_{CCL}	V_{CC} = MAX,	V_I = 4.5 V		1.2	2.2		1.2	2.2		mA

† For conditions shown as MIN or MAX, use the appropriate value specified under recommended operating conditions.
‡ All typical values are at V_{CC} = 5 V, T_A = 25°C.
§ Not more than one output should be shorted at a time, and the duration of the short-circuit should not exceed one second.

switching characteristics, V_{CC} = 5 V, T_A = 25°C (see note 2)

PARAMETER	FROM (INPUT)	TO (OUTPUT)	TEST CONDITIONS		MIN	TYP	MAX	UNIT
t_{PLH}	Any	Y	R_L = 2 kΩ,	C_L = 15 pF		9	15	ns
t_{PHL}						10	15	ns

NOTE 2: See General Information Section for load circuits and voltage waveforms.

**HIGH-SPEED
CMOS LOGIC**

**TABLE I
SPECIFICATIONS FOR HC SSI CIRCUITS**

D2804, DECEMBER 1982 – REVISED MARCH 1984

absolute maximum ratings over operating free-air temperature range[†]

Supply voltage range, V_{CC} . . . . −0.5 V to 7 V
Input diode current, $I_{IK}(V_I < 0$ or $V_I > V_{CC})$ . . . . ±20 mA
Output diode current, $I_{OK}(V_O < 0$ or $V_O > V_{CC})$ . . . . ±20 mA
Continuous output current, I_O $(V_O = 0$ to $V_{CC})$ . . . . ±25 mA
Continuous current through V_{CC} or GND pins . . . . ±50 mA
Lead temperature 1,6 mm (1/16 inch) from case for 60 seconds: FH, FK, or J package . . . . 300°C
Lead temperature 1,6 mm (1/16 inch) from case for 10 seconds: FN or N package . . . . 260°C
Storage temperature range . . . . −65°C to 150°C

[†] Stresses beyond those listed under "absolute maximum ratings" may cause permanent damage to the device. These are stress ratings only and functional operation of the device at these or any other conditions beyond those indicated under "recommended operating conditions" is not implied. Exposure to absolute-maximum-rated conditions for extended periods may affect device reliability.

recommended operating conditions

			SN54HC'			SN74HC'			UNIT
			MIN	NOM	MAX	MIN	NOM	MAX	
V_{CC}	Supply voltage		2	5	6	2	5	6	V
V_{IH}	High-level input voltage	V_{CC} = 2 V	1.5			1.5			V
		V_{CC} = 4.5 V	3.15			3.15			
		V_{CC} = 6 V	4.2			4.2			
V_{IL}	Low-level input voltage	V_{CC} = 2 V	0		0.3	0		0.3	V
		V_{CC} = 4.5 V	0		0.9	0		0.9	
		V_{CC} = 6 V	0		1.2	0		1.2	
V_I	Input voltage		0		V_{CC}	0		V_{CC}	V
V_O	Output voltage		0		V_{CC}	0		V_{CC}	V
t_t	Input transition (rise and fall) times (except Schmitt-trigger inputs)	V_{CC} = 2 V	0		1000	0		1000	ns
		V_{CC} = 4.5 V	0		500	0		500	
		V_{CC} = 6 V	0		400	0		400	
T_A	Operating free-air temperature		−55		125	−40		85	°C

electrical characteristics over recommended operating free-air temperature range (unless otherwise noted)

PARAMETER	TEST CONDITIONS	V_{CC}	T_A = 25°C			SN54HC'		SN74HC'		UNIT
			MIN	TYP	MAX	MIN	MAX	MIN	MAX	
V_{OH} (Totem-pole outputs)	$V_I = V_{IH}$ or V_{IL}, $I_{OH} = -20 \mu A$	2 V	1.9	1.998		1.9		1.9		V
		4.5 V	4.4	4.499		4.4		4.4		
		6 V	5.9	5.999		5.9		5.9		
	$V_I = V_{IH}$ or V_{IL}, $I_{OH} = -4$ mA	4.5 V	3.98	4.30		3.7		3.84		
	$V_I = V_{IH}$ or V_{IL}, $I_{OH} = -5.2$ mA	6 V	5.48	5.80		5.2		5.34		
I_{OH} (Open-drain outputs)	$V_I = V_{IH}$ or V_{IL}, $V_O = V_{CC}$	6 V		0.01	0.5		10		5	μA
V_{OL}	$V_I = V_{IH}$ or V_{IL}, $I_{OL} = 20 \mu A$	2 V		0.002	0.1		0.1		0.1	V
		4.5 V		0.001	0.1		0.1		0.1	
		6 V		0.001	0.1		0.1		0.1	
	$V_I = V_{IH}$ or V_{IL}, $I_{OL} = 4$ mA	4.5 V		0.17	0.26		0.4		0.33	
	$V_I = V_{IH}$ or V_{IL}, $I_{OL} = 5.2$ mA	6 V		0.15	0.26		0.4		0.33	
V_{T+} [†]		2 V	0.8	1.2	1.5					V
		4.5 V	2	2.5	3.15					
		6 V	2.5	3.3	4.2					
V_{T-} [†]		2 V	0.3	0.6	0.8					V
		4.5 V	0.9	1.6	2					
		6 V	1.2	2	2.5					
$V_{T+} - V_{T-}$ [†]		2 V	0.2	0.6	1					V
		4.5 V	0.4	0.9	1.4					
		6 V	0.5	1.3	1.7					
I_I	$V_I = 0$ to V_{CC}	6 V		±0.1	±100		±1000		±1000	nA
I_{CC}	$V_I = V_{CC}$ or 0, $I_O = 0$	6 V			2		40		20	μA
C_I		2 to 6 V		3	10		10		10	pF

[†]This parameter applies only for Schmitt-trigger inputs.

**HIGH-SPEED
CMOS LOGIC**

**TYPES SN54HC20, SN74HC20
DUAL 4-INPUT POSITIVE-NAND GATES**

D2684, DECEMBER 1982–REVISED MARCH 1984

● **Package Options Include Both Plastic and
Ceramic Chip Carriers in Addition to Plastic
and Ceramic DIPs**

● **Dependable Texas Instruments Quality
and Reliability**

description

These devices contain two independent 4-input NAND
gates. They perform the Boolean functions
$Y = \overline{A \cdot B \cdot C \cdot D}$ or $Y = \overline{A} + \overline{B} + \overline{C} + \overline{D}$ in positive logic.

The SN54HC20 is characterized for operation over the
full military temperature range of −55 °C to 125 °C.
The SN74HC20 is characterized for operation from
−40 °C to 85 °C.

logic symbol

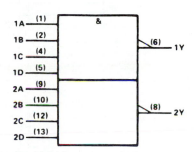

Pin numbers shown are for J and N packages.

SN54HC20 . . . J PACKAGE
SN74HC20 . . . J OR N PACKAGE
(TOP VIEW)

```
       ___ ___
 1A [ 1    14 ] VCC
 1B [ 2    13 ] 2D
 NC [ 3    12 ] 2C
 1C [ 4    11 ] NC
 1D [ 5    10 ] 2B
 1Y [ 6     9 ] 2A
GND [ 7     8 ] 2Y
```

SN54HC20 . . . FH OR FK PACKAGE
SN74HC20 . . . FH OR FN PACKAGE
(TOP VIEW)

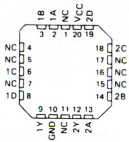

NC — No internal connection

FUNCTION TABLE (each gate)

INPUTS				OUTPUT
A	B	C	D	Y
H	H	H	H	L
L	X	X	X	H
X	L	X	X	H
X	X	L	X	H
X	X	X	L	H

maximum ratings, recommended operating conditions, and electrical characteristics

See Table I, page 2-4.

switching characteristics over recommended operating free-air temperature range (unless otherwise noted), $C_L = 50$ pF (see Note 1)

PARAMETER	FROM (INPUT)	TO (OUTPUT)	V_{CC}	T_A = 25°C			SN54HC20		SN74HC20		UNIT
				MIN	TYP	MAX	MIN	MAX	MIN	MAX	
t_{pd}	A, B, C, or D	Y	2 V		45	110		165		140	ns
			4.5 V		14	22		33		28	
			6 V		11	19		28		24	
t_t		Y	2 V		27	75		110		95	ns
			4.5 V		9	15		22		19	
			6 V		7	13		19		16	

C_{pd}	Power dissipation capacitance per gate	No load, T_A = 25°C	25 pF typ

NOTE 1: For load circuit and voltage waveforms, see page 1-14.

Copyright ©1982 by Texas Instruments Incorporated

POST OFFICE BOX 225012 ● DALLAS, TEXAS 75265

SN5432, SN7432
QUADRUPLE 2-INPUT POSITIVE-OR GATES

recommended operating conditions

		SN5432 MIN	NOM	MAX	SN7432 MIN	NOM	MAX	UNIT
V_{CC}	Supply voltage	4.5	5	5.5	4.75	5	5.25	V
V_{IH}	Hgh-level input voltage	2			2			V
V_{IL}	Low-level imput voltage			0.8			0.8	V
I_{OH}	High-level output current			−0.8			−0.8	mA
I_{OL}	Low-level output current			16			16	mA
T_A	Operating free-air temperature	−55		125	0		70	°C

electrical characteristics over recommended operating free-air temperature range (unless otherwise noted)

PARAMETER	TEST CONDITIONS†			SN5432 MIN	TYP‡	MAX	SN7432 MIN	TYP‡	MAX	UNIT
V_{IK}	V_{CC} = MIN,	I_I = −12 mA				−1.5			−1.5	V
V_{OH}	V_{CC} = MIN,	V_{IH} = 2 V,	I_{OH} = −0.8 mA	2.4	3.4		2.4	3.4		V
V_{OL}	V_{CC} = MIN,	V_{IL} = 0.8 V,	I_{OL} = 16 mA		0.2	0.4		0.2	0.4	V
I_I	V_{CC} = MAX,	V_I = 5.5 V				1			1	mA
I_{IH}	V_{CC} = MAX,	V_I = 2.4 V				40			40	µA
I_{IL}	V_{CC} = MAX,	V_I = 0.4 V				−1.6			−1.6	mA
I_{OS}§	V_{CC} = MAX			−20		−55	−18		−55	mA
I_{CCH}	V_{CC} = MAX,	See Note 2			15	22		15	22	mA
I_{CCL}	V_{CC} = MAX,	V_I = 0 V			23	38		23	38	mA

† For conditions shown as MIN or MAX, use the appropriate value specified under recommended operating conditions.
‡ All typical values are at V_{CC} = 5 V, T_A = 25°C.
§ Not more than one output should be shorted at a time.
NOTE 2: One input at 4.5 V, all others at GND.

switching characteristics, V_{CC} = 5 V, T_A = 25°C (see note 3)

PARAMETER	FROM (INPUT)	TO (OUTPUT)	TEST CONDITIONS		MIN	TYP	MAX	UNIT
t_{PLH}	A or B	Y	R_L = 400 Ω,	C_L = 15 pF		10	15	ns
t_{PHL}						14	22	ns

NOTE 3: Load circuits and voltage waveforms are shown in Section 1.

TEXAS INSTRUMENTS
POST OFFICE BOX 655012 • DALLAS, TEXAS 75265

SN54S32, SN74S32
QUADRUPLE 2-INPUT POSITIVE-OR GATES

recommended operating conditions

		SN54S32			SN74S32			UNIT
		MIN	NOM	MAX	MIN	NOM	MAX	
V_{CC}	Supply voltage	4.5	5	5.5	4.75	5	5.25	V
V_{IH}	High-level input voltage	2			2			V
V_{IL}	Low-level input voltage			0.8			0.8	V
I_{OH}	High-level output current			-1			-1	mA
I_{OL}	Low-level output current			20			20	mA
T_A	Operating free-air temperature	-55		125	0		70	°C

electrical characteristics over recommended operating free-air temperature range (unless otherwise noted)

PARAMETER	TEST CONDITIONS †			SN54S32			SN74S32			UNIT
				MIN	TYP‡	MAX	MIN	TYP‡	MAX	
V_{IK}	V_{CC} = MIN,	$I_I = -18$ mA				-1.2			-1.2	V
V_{OH}	V_{CC} = MIN,	V_{IH} = 2 V,	$I_{OH} = -1$ mA	2.5	3.4		2.7	3.4		V
V_{OL}	V_{CC} = MIN,	V_{IL} = 0.8 V,	I_{OL} = 20 mA			0.5			0.5	V
I_I	V_{CC} = MAX,	V_I = 5.5 V				1			1	mA
I_{IH}	V_{CC} = MAX,	V_I = 2.7 V				50			50	μA
I_{IL}	V_{CC} = MAX,	V_I = 0.5 V				-2			-2	mA
I_{OS} §	V_{CC} = MAX			-40		-100	-40		-100	mA
I_{CCH}	V_{CC} = MAX,	See Note 2			18	32		18	32	mA
I_{CCL}	V_{CC} = MAX,	V_I = 0 V			38	68		38	68	mA

† For conditions shown as MIN or MAX, use the appropriate value specified under recommended operating conditions.
‡ All typical values are at V_{CC} = 5 V, T_A = 25°C.
§ Not more than one output should be shorted at a time and the duration of the short-circuit should not exceed one second.
NOTE 2: One input at 4.5 V, all others at GND.

switching characteristics, V_{CC} = 5 V, T_A = 25°C (see note 3)

PARAMETER	FROM (INPUT)	TO (OUTPUT)	TEST CONDITIONS		MIN	TYP	MAX	UNIT
t_{PLH}	A or B	Y	R_L = 280 Ω,	C_L = 15 pF		4	7	ns
t_{PHL}						4	7	ns
t_{PLH}	A or B	Y	R_L = 280 Ω,	C_L = 50 pF		5		ns
t_{PHL}						5		ns

NOTE 3: Load circuits and voltage waveforms are shown in Section 1.

TEXAS
INSTRUMENTS
POST OFFICE BOX 655012 ● DALLAS, TEXAS 75265

SN54LS37, SN74LS37
QUADRUPLE 2-INPUT POSITIVE-NAND BUFFERS

recommended operating conditions

		SN54LS37			SN74LS37			UNIT
		MIN	NOM	MAX	MIN	NOM	MAX	
V_{CC}	Supply voltage	4.5	5	5.5	4.75	5	5.25	V
V_{IH}	High-level input voltage	2			2			V
V_{IL}	Low-level input voltage			0.7			0.8	V
I_{OH}	High-level output current			−1.2			−1.2	mA
I_{OL}	Low-level output current			12			24	mA
T_A	Operating free-air temperature	−55		125	0		70	°C

electrical characteristics over recommended operating free-air temperature range (unless otherwise noted)

PARAMETER	TEST CONDITIONS †			SN54LS37			SN74LS37			UNIT
			MIN	TYP‡	MAX	MIN	TYP‡	MAX	
V_{IK}	V_{CC} = MIN,	I_I = −18 mA			−1.5			−1.5	V
V_{OH}	V_{CC} = MIN,	V_{IL} = MAX,	I_{OH} = −1.2 mA	2.5	3.4		2.7	3.4		V
V_{OL}	V_{CC} = MIN,	V_{IH} = 2 V,	I_{OL} = 12 mA		0.25	0.4		0.25	0.4	V
	V_{CC} = MIN,	V_{IH} = 2 V,	I_{OL} = 24 mA					0.35	0.5	
I_I	V_{CC} = MAX,	V_I = 7 V				0.1			0.1	mA
I_{IH}	V_{CC} = MAX,	V_I = 2.7 V				20			20	µA
I_{IL}	V_{CC} = MAX,	V_I = 0.4 V				−0.4			−0.4	mA
I_{OS} §	V_{CC} = MAX			−30		−130	−30		−130	mA
I_{CCH}	V_{CC} = MAX,	V_I = 0 V			0.9	2		0.9	2	mA
I_{CCL}	V_{CC} = MAX,	V_I = 4.5 V			6	12		6	12	mA

† For conditions shown as MIN or MAX, use the appropriate value specified under recommended operating conditions.
‡ All typical values are at V_{CC} = 5 V, T_A = 25°C.
§ Not more than one output should be shorted at a time, and the duration of the short circuit should not exceed one second.

switching characteristics, V_{CC} = 5 V, T_A = 25°C (see note 2)

PARAMETER	FROM (INPUT)	TO (OUTPUT)	TEST CONDITIONS		MIN	TYP	MAX	UNIT
t_{PLH}	A or B	Y	R_L = 667 Ω,	C_L = 45 pF		12	24	ns
t_{PHL}						12	24	ns

NOTE 2: Load circuits and voltage waveforms are shown in Section 1.

TEXAS INSTRUMENTS
POST OFFICE BOX 655012 ● DALLAS, TEXAS 75265

SN5486, SN7486
QUADRUPLE 2-INPUT EXCLUSIVE-OR GATES

absolute maximum ratings over operating free-air temperature range (unless otherwise noted)

Supply voltage, V_{CC} (see Note 1) . . . . 7 V
Input voltage . . . . 5.5 V
Operating free-air temperature range: SN5486 . . . . $-55°C$ to $125°C$
  SN7486 . . . . $0°C$ to $70°C$
Storage temperature range . . . . $-65°C$ to $150°C$

NOTE 1: Voltage values are with respect to network ground terminal.

recommended operating conditions

	SN5486			SN7486			UNIT
	MIN	NOM	MAX	MIN	NOM	MAX	
Supply voltage, V_{CC}	4.5	5	5.5	4.75	5	5.25	V
High-level output current, I_{OH}			-800			-800	μA
Low-level output current, I_{OL}			16			16	mA
Operating free-air temperature, T_A	-55		125	0		70	°C

electrical characteristics over recommended operating free-air temperature range (unless otherwise noted)

PARAMETER		TEST CONDITIONS[†]	SN5486			SN7486			UNIT
			MIN	TYP[‡]	MAX	MIN	TYP[‡]	MAX	
V_{IH}	High-level input voltage		2			2			V
V_{IL}	Low-level input voltage				0.8			0.8	V
V_{IK}	Input clamp voltage	V_{CC} = MIN, I_I = -8 mA			-1.5			-1.5	V
V_{OH}	High-level output voltage	V_{CC} = MIN, V_{IH} = 2 V, V_{IL} = 0.8 V, I_{OH} = $-800 \mu A$	2.4	3.4		2.4	3.4		V
V_{OL}	Low-level output voltage	V_{CC} = MIN, V_{IH} = 2 V V_{IL} = 0.8 V, I_{OL} = 16 mA		0.2	0.4		0.2	0.4	V
I_I	Input current at maximum input voltage	V_{CC} = MAX, V_I = 5.5 V			1			1	mA
I_{IH}	High-level input current	V_{CC} = MAX, V_I = 2.4 V			40			40	μA
I_{IL}	Low-level input current	V_{CC} = MAX, V_I = 0.4 V			-1.6			-1.6	mA
I_{OS}	Short-circuit output current[§]	V_{CC} = MAX	-20		-55	-18		-55	mA
I_{CC}	Supply current	V_{CC} = MAX, See Note 2		30	43		30	50	mA

[†]For conditions shown as MIN or MAX, use the appropriate value specified under recommended operating conditions for the applicable type.
[‡]All typical values are at V_{CC} = 5 V, T_A = 25 C.
[§]Not more than one output should be shorted at a time.
NOTE 2: I_{CC} is measured with the inputs grounded and the outputs open.

switching characteristics, V_{CC} = 5 V, T_A = 25°C

PARAMETER[¶]	FROM (INPUT)	TEST CONDITIONS		MIN	TYP	MAX	UNIT
t_{PLH}	A or B	Other input low	C_L = 15 pF, R_L = 400 Ω, See Note 3		15	23	ns
t_{PHL}					11	17	
t_{PLH}	A or B	Other input high			18	30	ns
t_{PHL}					13	22	

[¶]t_{PLH} = propagation delay time, low-to-high-level output
t_{PHL} = propagation delay time, high-to-low-level output
NOTE 3: Load circuits and voltage waveforms are shown in Section 1.

TEXAS
INSTRUMENTS
POST OFFICE BOX 655012 • DALLAS, TEXAS 75265

SN54LS86A, SN74LS86A
QUADRUPLE 2-INPUT EXCLUSIVE-OR GATES

absolute maximum ratings over operating free-air temperature range (unless otherwise noted)

Supply voltage, V_{CC} (see Note 1) . . . . 7 V
Input voltage . . . . 7 V
Operating free-air temperature range: SN54LS86A . . . . −55°C to 125°C
 SN74LS86A . . . . 0°C to 70°C
Storage temperature range . . . . −65°C to 150°C

NOTE 1: Voltage values are with respect to network ground terminal.

recommended operating conditions

	SN54LS86A			SN74LS86A			UNIT
	MIN	NOM	MAX	MIN	NOM	MAX	
Supply voltage, V_{CC}	4.5	5	5.5	4.75	5	5.25	V
High-level output current, I_{OH}			−400			−400	μA
Low-level output current, I_{OL}			4			8	mA
Operating free-air temperature, T_A	−55		125	0		70	°C

electrical characteristics over recommended operating free-air temperature range (unless otherwise noted)

PARAMETER	TEST CONDITIONS[†]		SN54LS86A			SN74LS86A			UNIT
			MIN	TYP[‡]	MAX	MIN	TYP[‡]	MAX	
V_{IH} High-level input voltage			2			2			V
V_{IL} Low-level input voltage					0.7			0.8	V
V_{IK} Input clamp voltage	V_{CC} = MIN,	I_I = −18 mA			−1.5			−1.5	V
V_{OH} High-level output voltage	V_{CC} = MIN, V_{IH} = 2 V, V_{IL} = V_{IL} max, I_{OH} = −400 μA		2.5	3.4		2.7	3.4		V
V_{OL} Low-level output voltage	V_{CC} = MIN, V_{IH} = 2 V, V_{IL} = V_{IL}max	I_{OL} = 4 mA		0.25	0.4		0.25	0.4	V
		I_{OL} = 8 mA					0.35	0.5	
I_I Input current at maximum input voltage	V_{CC} = MAX,	V_I = 7 V			0.2			0.2	mA
I_{IH} High-level input current	V_{CC} = MAX,	V_I = 2.7 V			40			40	μA
I_{IL} Low-level input current	V_{CC} = MAX,	V_I = 0.4 V			−0.8			−0.8	mA
I_{OS} Short-circuit output current[§]	V_{CC} = MAX		−20		−100	−20		−100	mA
I_{CC} Supply current	V_{CC} = MAX,	See Note 2		6.1	10		6.1	10	mA

[†]For conditions shown as MIN or MAX, use the appropriate value specified under recommended operating conditions for the applicable type.
[‡]All typical values are at V_{CC} = 5 V, T_A = 25 C.
[§]Not more than one output should be shorted at a time.
NOTE 2: I_{CC} is measured with the inputs grounded and the outputs open.

switching characteristics, V_{CC} = 5 V, T_A = 25°C

PARAMETER[¶]	FROM (INPUT)	TEST CONDITIONS		MIN	TYP	MAX	UNIT
t_{PLH}	A or B	Other input low	C_L = 15 pF, R_L = 2 kΩ, See Note 3		12	23	ns
t_{PHL}					10	17	
t_{PLH}	A or B	Other input high			20	30	ns
t_{PHL}					13	22	

[¶]t_{PLH} = propagation delay time, low-to-high-level output
 t_{PHL} = propagation delay time, high-to-low-level output
NOTE 3: Load circuits and voltage waveforms are shown in Section 1.

TEXAS INSTRUMENTS
POST OFFICE BOX 655012 ● DALLAS, TEXAS 75265

SN54ALS86, SN54AS86A, SN74ALS86, SN74AS86A
QUADRUPLE 2-INPUT EXCLUSIVE-OR GATES

SDAS006B – APRIL 1982 – REVISED DECEMBER 1994

absolute maximum ratings over operating free-air temperature range (unless otherwise noted)†

Supply voltage, V_{CC}	7 V
Input voltage, V_I	7 V
Operating free-air temperature range, T_A: SN54ALS86	−55°C to 125°C
SN74ALS86	0°C to 70°C
Storage temperature range	−65°C to 150°C

† Stresses beyond those listed under "absolute maximum ratings" may cause permanent damage to the device. These are stress ratings only, and functional operation of the device at these or any other conditions beyond those indicated under "recommended operating conditions" is not implied. Exposure to absolute-maximum-rated conditions for extended periods may affect device reliability.

recommended operating conditions

		SN54ALS86			SN74ALS86			UNIT
		MIN	NOM	MAX	MIN	NOM	MAX	
V_{CC}	Supply voltage	4.5	5	5.5	4.5	5	5.5	V
V_{IH}	High-level input voltage	2			2			V
V_{IL}	Low-level input voltage			0.7			0.8	V
I_{OH}	High-level output current			−0.4			−0.4	mA
I_{OL}	Low-level output current			4			8	mA
T_A	Operating free-air temperature	−55		125	0		70	°C

electrical characteristics over recommended operating free-air temperature range (unless otherwise noted)

PARAMETER	TEST CONDITIONS		SN54ALS86			SN74ALS86			UNIT
			MIN	TYP‡	MAX	MIN	TYP‡	MAX	
V_{IK}	V_{CC} = 4.5 V,	I_I = −18 mA			−1.5			−1.5	V
V_{OH}	V_{CC} = 4.5 V to 5.5 V,	I_{OH} = −0.4 mA	V_{CC}−2			V_{CC}−2			V
V_{OL}	V_{CC} = 4.5 V	I_{OL} = 4 mA		0.25	0.4		0.25	0.4	V
		I_{OL} = 8 mA					0.35	0.5	
I_I	V_{CC} = 5.5 V,	V_I = 7 V			0.1			0.1	mA
I_{IH}	V_{CC} = 5.5 V,	V_I = 2.7 V			20			20	μA
I_{IL}	V_{CC} = 5.5 V,	V_I = 0.4 V			−0.1			−0.1	mA
I_O§	V_{CC} = 5.5 V,	V_O = 2.25 V	−20		−112	−30		−112	mA
I_{CC}	V_{CC} = 5.5 V,	All inputs at 4.5 V		3.9	5.9		3.9	5.9	mA

‡ All typical values are at V_{CC} = 5 V, T_A = 25°C.
§ The output conditions have been chosen to produce a current that closely approximates one half of the true short-circuit output current, I_{OS}.

switching characteristics (see Figure 1)

PARAMETER	FROM (INPUT)	TO (OUTPUT)	V_{CC} = 4.5 V to 5.5 V, C_L = 50 pF, R_L = 500 Ω, T_A = MIN to MAX¶				UNIT
			SN54ALS86		SN74ALS86		
			MIN	MAX	MIN	MAX	
t_{PLH}	A or B	Y	3	22	3	17	ns
t_{PHL}	(other input low)		2	14	2	12	
t_{PLH}	A or B	Y	3	22	3	17	ns
t_{PHL}	(other input high)		2	12	2	10	

¶ For conditions shown as MIN or MAX, use the appropriate value specified under recommended operating conditions.

TEXAS INSTRUMENTS
POST OFFICE BOX 655303 ● DALLAS, TEXAS 75265

SN54ALS86, SN54AS86A, SN74ALS86, SN74AS86A
QUADRUPLE 2-INPUT EXCLUSIVE-OR GATES

SDAS006B – APRIL 1982 – REVISED DECEMBER 1994

absolute maximum ratings over operating free-air temperature range (unless otherwise noted)†

Supply voltage, V_{CC} .... 7 V
Input voltage, V_I .... 7 V
Operating free-air temperature range, T_A: SN54AS86A .... −55°C to 125°C
SN74AS86A .... 0°C to 70°C
Storage temperature range .... −65°C to 150°C

† Stresses beyond those listed under "absolute maximum ratings" may cause permanent damage to the device. These are stress ratings only, and functional operation of the device at these or any other conditions beyond those indicated under "recommended operating conditions" is not implied. Exposure to absolute-maximum-rated conditions for extended periods may affect device reliability.

recommended operating conditions

		SN54AS86A			SN74AS86A			UNIT
		MIN	NOM	MAX	MIN	NOM	MAX	
V_{CC}	Supply voltage	4.5	5	5.5	4.5	5	5.5	V
V_{IH}	High-level input voltage	2			2			V
V_{IL}	Low-level input voltage			0.8			0.8	V
I_{OH}	High-level output current			−2			−2	mA
I_{OL}	Low-level output current			20			20	mA
T_A	Operating free-air temperature	−55		125	0		70	°C

electrical characteristics over recommended operating free-air temperature range (unless otherwise noted)

PARAMETER	TEST CONDITIONS		SN54AS86A			SN74AS86A			UNIT
			MIN	TYP‡	MAX	MIN	TYP‡	MAX	
V_{IK}	V_{CC} = 4.5 V,	I_I = −18 mA			−1.2			−1.2	V
V_{OH}	V_{CC} = 4.5 V to 5.5 V,	I_{OH} = −2 mA	V_{CC}−2			V_{CC}−2			V
V_{OL}	V_{CC} = 4.5 V,	I_{OL} = 20 mA		0.35	0.5		0.35	0.5	V
I_I	V_{CC} = 5.5 V,	V_I = 7 V			0.1			0.1	mA
I_{IH}	V_{CC} = 5.5 V,	V_I = 2.7 V			20			20	μA
I_{IL}	V_{CC} = 5.5 V,	V_I = 0.4 V			−0.5			−0.5	mA
I_O§	V_{CC} = 5.5 V,	V_O = 2.25 V	−30		−112	−30		−112	mA
I_{CCH}	V_{CC} = 5.5 V,	$V_{I(A)}$ = 4.5 V, $V_{I(B)}$ = 0		11	18		11	18	mA
I_{CCL}	V_{CC} = 5.5 V,	V_I = 4.5 V		20	38		20	38	mA

‡ All typical values are at V_{CC} = 5 V, T_A = 25°C.
§ The output conditions have been chosen to produce a current that closely approximates one half of the true short-circuit output current, I_{OS}.

switching characteristics (see Figure 1)

PARAMETER	FROM (INPUT)	TO (OUTPUT)	V_{CC} = 4.5 V to 5.5 V, C_L = 50 pF, R_L = 500 Ω, T_A = MIN to MAX¶				UNIT
			SN54AS86A		SN74AS86A		
			MIN	MAX	MIN	MAX	
t_{PLH}	A or B (other input low)	Y	2	8.5	2	7.5	ns
t_{PHL}			2	8	2	6.5	
t_{PLH}	A or B (other input high)	Y	1	8	1	6.5	ns
t_{PHL}			1	9	1	7	

¶ For conditions shown as MIN or MAX, use the appropriate value specified under recommended operating conditions.

TEXAS INSTRUMENTS
POST OFFICE BOX 655303 ● DALLAS, TEXAS 75265

SN54LS112A, SN54S112, SN74LS112A, SN74S112A
DUAL J-K NEGATIVE-EDGE-TRIGGERED
FLIP-FLOPS WITH PRESET AND CLEAR
D2661, APRIL 1982 – REVISED MARCH 1988

- **Fully Buffered to Offer Maximum Isolation from External Disturbance**
- **Package Options Include Plastic ''Small Outline'' Packages, Ceramic Chip Carriers and Flat Packages, and Plastic and Ceramic DIPs**
- **Dependable Texas Instruments Quality and Reliability**

description

These devices contain two independent J-K negative-edge-triggered flip-flops. A low level at the preset and clear inputs sets or resets the outputs regardless of the levels of the other inputs. When preset and clear are inactive (high), data at the J and K inputs meeting the setup time requirements are transferred to the outputs on the negative-going edge of the clock pulse. Clock triggering occurs at a voltage level and is not directly related to the rise time of the clock pulse. Following the hold time interval, data at the J and K inputs may be changed without affecting the levels at the outputs. These versatile flip-flops can perform as toggle flip-flops by tying J and K high.

The SN54LS112A and SN54S112 are characterized for operation over the full military temperature range of $-55\,^\circ$C to $125\,^\circ$C. The SN74LS112A and SN74S112A are characterized for operation from $0\,^\circ$C to $70\,^\circ$C.

SN54LS112A, SN54S112 . . . J OR W PACKAGE
SN74LS112A, SN74S112A . . . D OR N PACKAGE
(TOP VIEW)

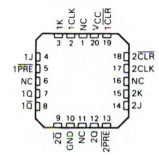

1CLK [1	16] V_{CC}
1K [2	15] 1$\overline{CLR}$
1J [3	14] 2$\overline{CLR}$
1$\overline{PRE}$ [4	13] 2CLK
1Q [5	12] 2K
1$\overline{Q}$ [6	11] 2J
2$\overline{Q}$ [7	10] 2$\overline{PRE}$
GND [8	9] 2Q

SN54LS112A, SN54S112 . . . FK PACKAGE
(TOP VIEW)

NC – No internal connection

logic symbol‡

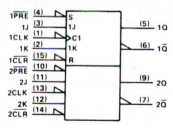

1$\overline{PRE}$	(4)	S	
1J	(3)	1J	(5) 1Q
1CLK	(1)	⊳C1	
1K	(2)	1K	(6) 1$\overline{Q}$
1$\overline{CLR}$	(15)	R	
2$\overline{PRE}$	(10)		
2J	(11)		(9) 2Q
2CLK	(13)		
2K	(12)		(7) 2$\overline{Q}$
2$\overline{CLR}$	(14)		

‡This symbol is in accordance with ANSI/IEEE Std 91-1984 and IEC Publication 617-12.

Pin numbers shown are for D, J, N, and W packages.

FUNCTION TABLE (each flip-flop)

INPUTS					OUTPUTS	
PRE	$\overline{CLR}$	CLK	J	K	Q	$\overline{Q}$
L	H	X	X	X	H	L
H	L	X	X	X	L	H
L	L	X	X	X	H†	H†
H	H	↓	L	L	Q_0	$\overline{Q}_0$
H	H	↓	H	L	H	L
H	H	↓	L	H	L	H
H	H	↓	H	H	TOGGLE	
H	H	H	X	X	Q_0	$\overline{Q}_0$

† The output levels in this configuration are not guaranteed to meet the minimum levels for V_{OH} if the lows at preset and clear are near V_{IL} minimum. Furthermore, this configuration is nonstable; that is, it will not persist when either preset or clear returns to its inactive (high) level.

TEXAS INSTRUMENTS
POST OFFICE BOX 655012 • DALLAS, TEXAS 75265

SN54LS112A, SN74LS112A
DUAL J-K NEGATIVE-EDGE-TRIGGERED
FLIP-FLOPS WITH PRESET AND CLEAR

electrical characteristics over recommended operating free-air temperature range (unless otherwise noted)

PARAMETER		TEST CONDITIONS[†]			SN54LS112A MIN	SN54LS112A TYP[‡]	SN54LS112A MAX	SN74LS112A MIN	SN74LS112A TYP[‡]	SN74LS112A MAX	UNIT
V_{IK}		V_{CC} = MIN,	I_I = -18 mA				-1.5			-1.5	V
V_{OH}		V_{CC} = MIN, V_{IH} = 2 V, V_{IL} = MAX, I_{OH} = -0.4 mA			2.5	3.4		2.7	3.4		V
V_{OL}		V_{CC} = MIN, V_{IL} = MAX, V_{IH} = 2 V, I_{OL} = 4 mA				0.25	0.4		0.25	0.4	V
		V_{CC} = MIN, V_{IL} = MAX, V_{IH} = 2 V, I_{OL} = 8 mA							0.35	0.5	
I_I	J or K	V_{CC} = MAX, V_I = 7 V					0.1			0.1	mA
	$\overline{CLR}$ or $\overline{PRE}$						0.3			0.3	
	CLK						0.4			0.4	
I_{IH}	J or K	V_{CC} = MAX, V_I = 2.7 V					20			20	μA
	$\overline{CLR}$ or $\overline{PRE}$						60			60	
	CLK						80			80	
I_{IL}	J or K	V_{CC} = MAX, V_I = 0.4 V					-0.4			-0.4	mA
	All other						-0.8			-0.8	
I_{OS}[§]		V_{CC} = MAX,	see Note 2		-20		-100	-20		-100	mA
I_{CC} (Total)		V_{CC} = MAX,	see Note 3			4	6		4	6	mA

[†] For conditions shown as MIN or MAX, use the appropriate value specified under recommended operating conditions.
[‡] All typical values are at V_{CC} = 5 V, T_A = 25 °C.
[§] Not more than one output should be shorted at a time, and the duration of the short-circuit should not exceed one second.
NOTES: 2. For certain devices where state commutation can be caused by shorting an output to ground, an equivalent test may be performed with V_O = 2.25 V and 2.125 V for the '54 family and the '74 family, respectively, with the minimum and maximum limits reduced to one half of their stated values.
3. With all outputs open, I_{CC} is measured with the Q and $\overline{Q}$ outputs high in turn. At the time of measurement, the clock input is grounded.

switching characteristics, V_{CC} = 5 V, T_A = 25 °C (see Note 4)

PARAMETER	FROM (INPUT)	TO (OUTPUT)	TEST CONDITIONS		MIN	TYP	MAX	UNIT
f_{max}			R_L = 2 kΩ,	C_L = 15 pF	30	45		MHz
t_{PLH}	$\overline{CLR}$, $\overline{PRE}$ or CLK	Q or $\overline{Q}$				15	20	ns
t_{PHL}						15	20	ns

NOTE 4: Load circuits and voltage waveforms are shown in Section 1.

recommended operating conditions

			SN54LS112A MIN	SN54LS112A NOM	SN54LS112A MAX	SN74LS112A MIN	SN74LS112A NOM	SN74LS112A MAX	UNIT
V_{CC}	Supply voltage		4.5	5	5.5	4.75	5	5.25	V
V_{IH}	High-level input voltage		2			2			V
V_{IL}	Low-level input voltage				0.7			0.8	V
I_{OH}	High-level output current				-0.4			-0.4	mA
I_{OL}	Low-level output current				4			8	mA
f_{clock}	Clock frequency		0		30	0		30	MHz
t_w	Pulse duration	CLK high	20			20			ns
		$\overline{PRE}$ or $\overline{CLR}$ low	25			25			
t_{su}	Set up time-before CLK↓	Data high or low	20			20			ns
		$\overline{CLR}$ inactive	25			25			
		$\overline{PRE}$ inactive	20			20			
t_h	Hold time-data after CLK↓		0			0			ns
T_A	Operating free-air temperature		-55		125	0		70	°C

SN54S112, SN74S112A
DUAL J-K NEGATIVE-EDGE-TRIGGERED
FLIP-FLOPS WITH PRESET AND CLEAR

electrical characteristics over recommended operating free-air temperature range (unless otherwise noted)

PARAMETER		TEST CONDITIONS[†]			SN54S112 MIN	SN54S112 TYP[‡]	SN54S112 MAX	SN74S112A MIN	SN74S112A TYP[‡]	SN74S112A MAX	UNIT
V_{IK}		V_{CC} = MIN,	I_I = −18 mA				−1.2			−1.2	V
V_{OH}		V_{CC} = MIN, I_{OH} = −1 mA	V_{IH} = 2 V,	V_{IL} = MAX,	2.5	3.4		2.7	3.4		V
V_{OL}		V_{CC} = MIN, I_{OL} = 20 mA	V_{IH} = 2 V,	V_{IL} = 0.8 V,			0.5			0.5	V
I_I		V_{CC} = MAX,	V_I = 5.5 V				1			1	mA
I_{IH}	J or K	V_{CC} = MAX,	V_I = 2.7 V				50			50	μA
	All other						100			100	
I_{IL}	J or K						−1.6			−1.6	
	$\overline{CLR}$[§]	V_{CC} = MAX,	V_I = 0.5 V				−7			−7	mA
	$\overline{PRE}$[§]						−7			−7	
	CLK						−4			−4	
I_{OS}[¶]		V_{CC} = MAX			−40		−100	−40		−100	mA
I_{CC}[#]		V_{CC} = MAX,	see Note 3			15	25		15	25	mA

[†] For conditions shown as MIN or MAX, use the appropriate value specified under recommended operating conditions.

[‡] All typical values are at V_{CC} = 5 V, T_A = 25°C.

[§] Clear is tested with preset high and preset is tested with clear high.

[¶] Not more than one output should be shorted at a time, and the duration of the short-circuit should not exceed one second.

[#] Values are average per flip-flop.

NOTE 3: With all outputs open, I_{CC} is measured with the Q and $\overline{Q}$ outputs high in turn. At the time of measurement, the clock input is grounded.

switching characteristics, V_{CC} = 5 V, T_A = 25°C (see Note 4)

PARAMETER	FROM (INPUT)	TO (OUTPUT)	TEST CONDITIONS	MIN	TYP	MAX	UNIT
f_{max}				80	125		MHz
t_{PLH}	$\overline{PRE}$ or $\overline{CLR}$	Q or $\overline{Q}$			4	7	ns
t_{PHL}	$\overline{PRE}$ or $\overline{CLR}$ (CLK high)	$\overline{Q}$ or Q	R_L = 280 Ω, C_L = 15 pF		5	7	ns
	$\overline{PRE}$ or $\overline{CLR}$ (CLK low)				5	7	
t_{PLH}	CLK	Q or $\overline{Q}$			4	7	ns
t_{PHL}					5	7	ns

NOTE 4: Load circuits and voltage waveforms are shown in Section 1.

TEXAS
INSTRUMENTS
POST OFFICE BOX 655012 ● DALLAS. TEXAS 75265

SN54121, SN74121
MONOSTABLE MULTIVIBRATORS
WITH SCHMITT-TRIGGER INPUTS
MAY 1983 – REVISED MARCH 1988

- Programmable Output Pulse Width
  With R_{int} . . . 35 ns Typ
  With R_{ext}/C_{ext} . . . 40 ns to 28 Seconds

- Internal Compensation for Virtual
  Temperature Independence

- Jitter-Free Operation up to 90%
  Duty Cycle

- Inhibit Capability

SN54121 . . . J OR W PACKAGE
SN74121 . . . N PACKAGE
(TOP VIEW)

$\overline{Q}$	1		14	V_{CC}
NC	2		13	NC
A1	3		12	NC
A2	4		11	R_{ext}/C_{ext}
B	5		10	C_{ext}
Q	6		9	R_{int}
GND	7		8	NC

NC - No internal connection.

logic symbol‡

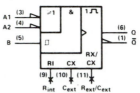

‡This symbol is in accordance with ANSI/IEEE Std 91-1984 and
IEC Publication 617-12.

FUNCTION TABLE

INPUTS			OUTPUTS	
A1	A2	B	Q	$\overline{Q}$
L	X	H	L	H
X	L	H	L↑	H↑
X	X	L	L↑	H↑
H	H	X	L↑	H↑
H	.	H	⊓	⊔
.	H	H	⊓	⊔
.	↓	H	⊓	⊔
L	X	↑	⊓	⊔
X	L	↑	⊓	⊔

For explanation of function table symbols, see page
† These lines of the function table assume that the indicated steady state conditions at the A and B inputs have been setup long enough
to complete any pulse started before the setup.

description

These multivibrators feature dual negative-transition-triggered inputs and a single positive-transition-triggered input
which can be used as an inhibit input. Complementary output pulses are provided.

Pulse triggering occurs at a particular voltage level and is not directly related to the transition time of the input pulse.
Schmitt-trigger input circuitry (TTL hysteresis) for the B input allows jitter-free triggering from inputs with transition
rates as slow as 1 volt/second, providing the circuit with an excellent noise immunity of typically 1.2 volts. A high
immunity to V_{CC} noise of typically 1.5 volts is also provided by internal latching circuitry.

Once fired, the outputs are independent of further transitions of the inputs and are a function only of the timing
components. Input pulses may be of any duration relative to the output pulse. Output pulse length may be varied from
40 nanoseconds to 28 seconds by choosing appropriate timing components. With no external timing components
(i.e., R_{int} connected to V_{CC}, C_{ext} and R_{ext}/C_{ext} open), an output pulse of typically 30 or 35 nanoseconds is achieved
which may be used as a d-c triggered reset signal. Output rise and fall times are TTL compatible and independent of
pulse length.

Pulse width stability is achieved through internal compensation and is virtually independent of V_{CC} and temperature. In
most applications, pulse stability will only be limited by the accuracy of external timing components.

Jitter-free operation is maintained over the full temperature and V_{CC} ranges for more than six decades of timing
capacitance (10 pF to 10 μF) and more than one decade of timing resistance (2 kΩ to 30 kΩ for the SN54121 and
2 kΩ to 40 kΩ for the SN74121). Throughout these ranges, pulse width is defined by the relationship $t_{w(out)} =
C_{ext}R_T\ln2 \approx 0.7\,C_{ext}R_T$. In circuits where pulse cutoff is not critical, timing capacitance up to 1000 μF and timing
resistance as low as 1.4 kΩ may be used. Also, the range of jitter-free output pulse widths is extended if V_{CC} is held
to 5 volts and free-air temperature is 25°C. Duty cycles as high as 90% are achieved when using maximum
recommended R_T. Higher duty cycles are available if a certain amount of pulse-width jitter is allowed.

**TEXAS
INSTRUMENTS**

POST OFFICE BOX 655012 • DALLAS, TEXAS 75265

SN54121, SN74121
MONOSTABLE MULTIVIBRATORS
WITH SCHMITT-TRIGGER INPUTS

electrical characteristics over recommended operating free-air temperature range (unless otherwise noted)

PARAMETER		TEST CONDITONS[†]		MIN	TYP[‡]	MAX	UNIT
V_{IH}	High-level input voltage at B input	V_{CC} = MIN		2			V
V_{IL}	Low-level input voltage at A input	V_{CC} = MIN				0.8	V
V_{T+}	Positive-going threshold voltage at B input	V_{CC} = MIN			1.55	2	V
V_{T-}	Negative-going threshold voltage at B input	V_{CC} = MIN		0.8	1.35		V
V_{IK}	Input clamp voltage	V_{CC} = MIN,	I_I = −12 mA			−1.5	V
I_{OH}	High-level output voltage	V_{CC} = MIN,	I_{OH} = MAX	2.4	3.4		V
V_{OL}	Low-level output voltage	V_{CC} = MIN,	I_{OL} = MAX		0.2	0.4	V
I_I	Input current at maximum input voltage	V_{CC} = MAX,	V_I = 5.5 V			1	mA
I_{IH}	High-level input current	V_{CC} = MAX, V_I = 2.4 V	A1 or A2			40	μA
			B			80	
I_{IL}	Low-level input current	V_{CC} = MAX, V_I = 0.4 V	A1 or A2			−1.6	mA
			B			−3.2	
I_{OS}	Short-circuit output current[§]	V_{CC} = MAX	54 Family	−20		−55	mA
			74 Family	−18		−55	
I_{CC}	Supply current	V_{CC} = MAX	Quiescent		13	25	mA
			Triggered		23	40	

[†]For conditions shown as MIN or MAX, use the appropriate value specified under recommended operating conditions.
[‡]All typical values are at V_{CC} = 5 V, T_A = 25°C.
[†]Not more than one output should be shorted at a time.

switching characteristics, V_{CC} = 5 V, T_A = 25°C

PARAMETER		TEST CONDITIONS		MIN	TYP	MAX	UNIT
t_{PLH}	Propagation delay time, low-to-high-level Q output from either A input	C_L = 15 pF, R_L = 400 Ω, See Note 4	C_{ext} = 80 pF, R_{int} to V_{CC}		45	70	ns
t_{PLH}	Propagation delay time, low-to-high-level Q output from B input				35	55	ns
t_{PHL}	Propagation delay time, high-to-low level $\overline{Q}$ output from either A input				50	80	ns
t_{PHL}	Propagation delay time, high-to-low level $\overline{Q}$ output from B input				40	65	ns
$t_{w(out)}$	Pulse width obtained using internal timing resistor		C_{ext} = 80 pF, R_{int} to V_{CC}	70	110	150	ns
$t_{w(out)}$	Pulse width obtained with zero timing capacitance		C_{ext} = 0, R_{int} to V_{CC}		30	50	ns
$t_{w(out)}$	Pulse width obtained using external timing resistor		C_{ext} = 100 pF, R_T = 10 kΩ	600	700	800	ns
			C_{ext} = 1 μF, R_T = 10 kΩ	6	7	8	ms

NOTE 4: Load circuits and voltage waveforms are shown in Section 1.

TEXAS
INSTRUMENTS
POST OFFICE BOX 655012 • DALLAS, TEXAS 75265

SN54LS192, SN54LS193, SN74LS192, SN74LS193
SYNCHRONOUS 4-BIT UP/DOWN COUNTERS (DUAL CLOCK WITH CLEAR)

recommended operating conditions

		SN54LS192 SN54LS193			SN74LS192 SN74LS193			UNIT
		MIN	NOM	MAX	MIN	NOM	MAX	
V_{CC}	Supply voltage	4.5	5	5.5	4.75	5	5.25	V
I_{OH}	High-level output current			−400			−400	μA
I_{OL}	Low-level output current			4			8	mA
f_{clock}	Clock frequency	0		25	0		25	MHz
t_w	Width of any input pulse	20			20			ns
t_{su}	Clear inactive-state setup time	15			15			ns
	Load inactive-state setup time	15			15			ns
	Data setup time (see Figure 1)	20			20			ns
t_h	Data hold time	5			5			ns
T_A	Operating free-air temperature range	−55		125	0		70	°C

electrical characteristics over recommended operating free-air temperature range (unless otherwise noted)

PARAMETER		TEST CONDITIONS[†]		SN54LS192 SN54LS193			SN74LS192 SN74LS193			UNIT
				MIN	TYP[‡]	MAX	MIN	TYP[‡]	MAX	
V_{IH}	High-level input voltage			2			2			V
V_{IL}	Low-level input voltage					0.7			0.8	V
V_{IK}	Input clamp voltage	V_{CC} = MIN, I_I = −18 mA				−1.5			−1.5	V
V_{OH}	High-level output voltage	V_{CC} = MIN, V_{IH} = 2 V, $V_{IL} = V_{IL}$ max, I_{OH} = −400 μA		2.5	3.4		2.7	3.4		V
V_{OL}	Low-level output voltage	V_{CC} = MIN, V_{IH} = 2 V, $V_{IL} = V_{IL}$ max	I_{OL} = 4 mA		0.25	0.4		0.15	0.4	V
			I_{OL} = 8 mA					0.35	0.5	
I_I	Input current at maximum input voltage	V_{CC} = MAX, V_I = 7 V				0.1			0.1	mA
I_{IH}	High-level input current	V_{CC} = MAX, V_I = 2.7 V				20			20	μA
I_{IL}	Low-level input current	V_{CC} = MAX, V_I = 0.4 V				−0.4			−0.4	mA
I_{OS}	Short-circuit output current[§]	V_{CC} = MAX		−20		−100	−20		−100	mA
I_{CC}	Supply current	V_{CC} = MAX, See Note 2			19	34		19	34	mA

[†] For conditions shown as MIN or MAX, use the appropriate value specified under recommended operating conditions for the applicable type.
[‡] All typical values are at V_{CC} = 5 V, T_A = 25°C.
[§] Not more than one output should be shorted at a time, and duration of the short-circuit should not exceed one second.
NOTE 2: I_{CC} is measured with all outputs open, clear and load inputs grounded, and all other inputs at 4.5 V.

switching characteristics, V_{CC} = 5 V, T_A = 25°C

PARAMETER	FROM INPUT	TO OUTPUT	TEST CONDITIONS	MIN	TYP	MAX	UNIT
f_{max}				25	32		MHz
t_{PLH}	UP	$\overline{CO}$			17	26	ns
t_{PHL}					18	24	
t_{PLH}	DOWN	$\overline{BO}$	C_L = 15 pF, R_L = 2 kΩ, See Figures 1 and 2		16	24	ns
t_{PHL}					15	24	
t_{PLH}	UP OR DOWN	Q			27	38	ns
t_{PHL}					30	47	
t_{PLH}	$\overline{LOAD}$	Q			24	40	ns
t_{PHL}					25	40	
t_{PHL}	CLR	Q			23	35	ns

TEXAS
INSTRUMENTS
POST OFFICE BOX 655012 • DALLAS, TEXAS 75265

SN54ALS193, SN74ALS193A
SYNCHRONOUS 4-BIT UP/DOWN BINARY COUNTERS
WITH DUAL CLOCK AND CLEAR
SDAS211B – DECEMBER 1982 – REVISED DECEMBER 1994

absolute maximum ratings over operating free-air temperature range (unless otherwise noted)†

Supply voltage, V_{CC} .... 7 V
Input voltage, V_I .... 7 V
Operating free-air temperature range, T_A: SN54ALS193 .... −55°C to 125°C
                                       SN74ALS193A .... 0°C to 70°C
Storage temperature range .... −65°C to 150°C

† Stresses beyond those listed under "absolute maximum ratings" may cause permanent damage to the device. These are stress ratings only, and functional operation of the device at these or any other conditions beyond those indicated under "recommended operating conditions" is not implied. Exposure to absolute-maximum-rated conditions for extended periods may affect device reliability.

recommended operating conditions

		SN54ALS193 MIN	NOM	MAX	SN74ALS193A MIN	NOM	MAX	UNIT
V_{CC}	Supply voltage	4.5	5	5.5	4.5	5	5.5	V
V_{IH}	High-level input voltage	2			2			V
V_{IL}	Low-level input voltage			0.7			0.8	V
I_{OH}	High-level output current			−0.4			−0.4	mA
I_{OL}	Low-level output current			4			8	mA
f_{clock}	Clock frequency	0		20	0		30	MHz
t_w	Pulse duration	CLR high	10			10			ns
		LOAD low	25			20			
		UP or DOWN high or low	30			16.5			
t_{su}	Setup time	Data before LOAD↑	25			20			ns
		CLR inactive before UP or DOWN	20			20			
		LOAD inactive before UP or DOWN	20			20			
t_h	Hold time	Data after LOAD↑	5			5			ns
		UP high after DOWN↑	0			0			
		DOWN high after UP↑	0			0			
T_A	Operating free-air temperature		−55		125	0		70	°C

electrical characteristics over recommended operating free-air temperature range (unless otherwise noted)

PARAMETER		TEST CONDITIONS		SN54ALS193 MIN	TYP‡	MAX	SN74ALS193A MIN	TYP‡	MAX	UNIT
V_{IK}		V_{CC} = 4.5 V,	I_I = −18 mA			−1.5			−1.5	V
V_{OH}		V_{CC} = 4.5 V to 5.5 V,	I_{OH} = −0.4 mA	V_{CC}−2			V_{CC}−2			V
V_{OL}		V_{CC} = 4.5 V	I_{OL} = 4 mA		0.25	0.4		0.25	0.4	V
			I_{OL} = 8 mA					0.35	0.5	
I_I		V_{CC} = 5.5 V,	V_I = 7 V			0.1		0.35	0.1	mA
I_{IH}		V_{CC} = 5.5 V,	V_I = 2.7 V			20			20	µA
I_{IL}	UP or DOWN	V_{CC} = 5.5 V,	V_I = 0.4 V			−0.2			−0.2	mA
	All others					−0.1			−0.1	
I_O§		V_{CC} = 5.5 V,	V_O = 2.25 V	−20		−112	−30		−112	mA
I_{CC}		V_{CC} = 5.5 V,	See Note 1		12	22		12	22	mA

‡ All typical values are at V_{CC} = 5 V, T_A = 25°C.
§ The output conditions have been chosen to produce a current that closely approximates one half of the true short-circuit output current, I_{OS}.
NOTE 1: I_{CC} is measured with the clear and load inputs grounded and all other inputs at 4.5 V.

TEXAS INSTRUMENTS
POST OFFICE BOX 655303 ● DALLAS, TEXAS 75265

**SN54290, SN54293, SN54LS290, SN54LS293,
SN74290, SN74293, SN74LS290, SN74LS293
DECADE AND 4-BIT BINARY COUNTERS**
MARCH 1974 — REVISED MARCH 1988

'290, 'LS290 . . . DECADE COUNTERS
'293, 'LS293 . . . 4-BIT BINARY COUNTERS

● GND and V_{CC} on Corner Pins
(Pins 7 and 14 Respectively)

description

The SN54290/SN74290, SN54LS290/SN74LS290, SN54293/SN74293, and SN54LS293/SN74LS293 counters are electrically and functionally identical to the SN5490A/SN7490A, SN54LS90/SN74LS90, SN5493A/SN7493A, and SN54LS93/SN74LS93, respectively. Only the arrangement of the terminals has been changed for the '290, 'LS290, '293, and 'LS293.

Each of these monolithic counters contains four master-slave flip-flops and additional gating to provide a divide-by-two counter and a three-stage binary counter for which the count cycle length is divide-by-five for the '290 and 'LS290 and divide-by-eight for the '293 and 'LS293.

All of these counters have a gated zero reset and the '290 and 'LS290 also have gated set-to-nine inputs for use in BCD nine's complement applications.

To use the maximum count length (decade or four-bit binary) of these counters, the B input is connected to the Q_A output. The input count pulses are applied to input A and the outputs are as described in the appropriate function table. A symmetrical divide-by-ten count can be obtained from the '290 and 'LS290 counters by connecting the Q_D output to the A input and applying the input count to the B input which gives a divide-by-ten square wave at output Q_A.

SN54290, SN54LS290, SN54293,
SN54LS293 . . . J OR W PACKAGE
SN74290, SN74293 . . . N PACKAGE
SN74LS290, SN74LS293 . . . D OR N PACKAGE
(TOP VIEW)

'290

R9(1)	1	14	V_{CC}
NC	2	13	R0(2)
R9(2)	3	12	R0(1)
Q_C	4	11	CKB
Q_B	5	10	CKA
NC	6	9	Q_A
GND	7	8	Q_D

'293

NC	1	14	V_{CC}
NC	2	13	R0(2)
NC	3	12	R0(1)
Q_C	4	11	CKB
Q_B	5	10	CKA
NC	6	9	Q_A
GND	7	8	Q_D

SN54LS290, SN54LS293 . . . FK PACKAGE
(TOP VIEW)

'LS290

```
         NC R9(1) NC VCC R0(2)
          3   2   1  20  19
R9(2)  4                    18  R0(1)
  NC   5                    17  NC
  QC   6                    16  CKB
  NC   7                    15  NC
  QB   8                    14  CKA
          9  10  11 12  13
         NC GND NC QD  QA
```

'LS293

```
         NC  NC  NC VCC R0(2)
          3   2   1  20  19
  NC   4                    18  R0(1)
  NC   5                    17  NC
  QC   6                    16  CKB
  NC   7                    15  NC
  QB   8                    14  CKA
          9  10  11 12  13
         NC GND NC QD  QA
```

NC - No internal connection

**TEXAS
INSTRUMENTS**
POST OFFICE BOX 655012 • DALLAS, TEXAS 75265

SN54290, SN54293, SN54LS290, SN54LS293, SN74290, SN74293, SN74LS290, SN74LS293
DECADE AND 4-BIT BINARY COUNTERS

'290, 'LS290
BCD COUNT SEQUENCE
(See Note A)

COUNT	OUTPUT			
	Q_D	Q_C	Q_B	Q_A
0	L	L	L	L
1	L	L	L	H
2	L	L	H	L
3	L	L	H	H
4	L	H	L	L
5	L	H	L	H
6	L	H	H	L
7	L	H	H	H
8	H	L	L	L
9	H	L	L	H

'290, 'LS290
BI-QUINARY (5-2)
(See Note B)

COUNT	OUTPUT			
	Q_A	Q_D	Q_C	Q_B
0	L	L	L	L
1	L	L	L	H
2	L	L	H	L
3	L	L	H	H
4	L	H	L	L
5	H	L	L	L
6	H	L	L	H
7	H	L	H	L
8	H	L	H	H
9	H	H	L	L

'290, 'LS290
RESET/COUNT FUNCTION TABLE

RESET INPUTS				OUTPUT			
$R_{0(1)}$	$R_{0(2)}$	$R_{9(1)}$	$R_{9(2)}$	Q_D	Q_C	Q_B	Q_A
H	H	L	X	L	L	L	L
H	H	X	L	L	L	L	L
X	X	H	H	H	L	L	H
X	L	X	L	COUNT			
L	X	L	X	COUNT			
L	X	X	L	COUNT			
X	L	L	X	COUNT			

'293, 'LS293
RESET/COUNT FUNCTION TABLE

RESET INPUTS		OUTPUT			
$R_{0(1)}$	$R_{0(2)}$	Q_D	Q_C	Q_B	Q_A
H	H	L	L	L	L
L	X	COUNT			
X	L	COUNT			

'293, 'LS293
COUNT SEQUENCE
(See Note C)

COUNT	OUTPUT			
	Q_D	Q_C	Q_B	Q_A
0	L	L	L	L
1	L	L	L	H
2	L	L	H	L
3	L	L	H	H
4	L	H	L	L
5	L	H	L	H
6	L	H	H	L
7	L	H	H	H
8	H	L	L	L
9	H	L	L	H
10	H	L	H	L
11	H	L	H	H
12	H	H	L	L
13	H	H	L	H
14	H	H	H	L
15	H	H	H	H

NOTES: A. Output Q_A is connected to input B for BCD count.
B. Output Q_D is connected to input A for bi-quinary count.
C. Output Q_A is connected to input B.
D. H = high level, L = low level, X = irrelevant

logic diagrams (positive logic)

'290, 'LS290

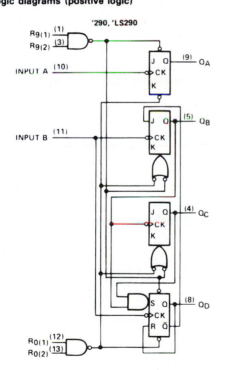

'293, 'LS293

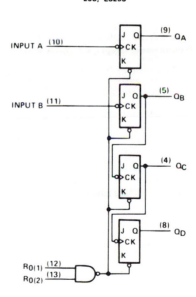

Pin numbers shown are for D, J, N, and W packages.
The J and K inputs shown without connection are for reference only and are functionally at a high level.

TEXAS INSTRUMENTS
POST OFFICE BOX 655012 ● DALLAS, TEXAS 75265

4001B   4002B
QUAD 2-INPUT NOR GATE ● DUAL 4-INPUT NOR GATE

DESCRIPTION — These CMOS logic elements provide the positive input NOR function. The outputs are fully buffered for highest noise immunity and pattern insensitivity of output impedance.

4001B
LOGIC AND CONNECTION DIAGRAM
DIP (TOP VIEW)

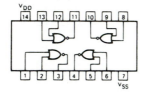

4002B
LOGIC AND CONNECTION DIAGRAM
DIP (TOP VIEW)

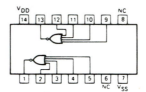

NOTE:
The Flatpak versions have the same pinouts (Connection Diagram) as the Dual In-line Package.

DC CHARACTERISTICS: V_{DD} as shown, V_{SS} = 0 V

SYMBOL	PARAMETER		V_{DD} = 5 V			V_{DD} = 10 V			V_{DD} = 15 V			UNITS	TEMP	TEST CONDITIONS See Note 1
			MIN	TYP	MAX	MIN	TYP	MAX	MIN	TYP	MAX			
I_{DD}	Quiescent Power Supply Current	XC			1			2			4	μA	MIN, 25°C	All inputs at 0 V or V_{DD}
					7.5			15			30		MAX	
		XM			0.25			0.5			1	μA	MIN, 25°C	
					7.5			15			30		MAX	

AC CHARACTERISTICS: V_{DD} as shown, V_{SS} = 0 V, T_A = 25°C, 4001B only (See Note 2)

SYMBOL	PARAMETER		V_{DD} = 5 V			V_{DD} = 10 V			V_{DD} = 15V		UNITS	TEST CONDITIONS See Note 2
		MIN	TYP	MAX	MIN	TYP	MAX	MIN	TYP	MAX		
t_{PLH}	Propagation Delay		60	110		25	60		20	48	ns	C_L = 50 pF, R_L = 200 kΩ Input Transition Times ≤ 20 ns
t_{PHL}			60	110		25	60		20	48	ns	
t_{TLH}	Output Transition Time		60	135		30	70		20	45	ns	
t_{THL}			60	135		30	70		20	45	ns	

AC CHARACTERISTICS: V_{DD} as shown, V_{SS} = 0 V, T_A = 25°C, 4002B only

SYMBOL	PARAMETER		V_{DD} = 5 V			V_{DD} = 10 V			V_{DD} = 15V		UNITS	TEST CONDITIONS See Note 2
		MIN	TYP	MAX	MIN	TYP	MAX	MIN	TYP	MAX		
t_{PLH}	Propagation Delay		65	110		30	60		20	48	ns	C_L = 50 pF, R_L = 200 kΩ Input Transition Times ≤ 20 ns
t_{PHL}			70	110		30	60		23	48	ns	
t_{TLH}	Output Transition Time		75	135		40	70		30	45	ns	
t_{THL}			60	135		23	70		15	45	ns	

NOTES:
1. Additional DC Characteristics are listed in this section under 4000B Series CMOS Family Characteristics.
2. Propagation Delays and Output Transition Times are graphically described in this section under 4000B Series CMOS Family Characteristics.

4001B   FAIRCHILD 4000B SERIES CMOS FAMILY CHARACTERISTICS

DC CHARACTERISTICS FOR THE 4000B SERIES CMOS FAMILY – Parametric Limits listed below are guaranteed for the entire Fairchild CMOS Family unless otherwise specified on the individual data sheets.

DC CHARACTERISTICS: $V_{DD} = 5$ V, $V_{SS} = 0$ V

SYMBOL	PARAMETER			LIMITS		UNITS	TEMP	TEST CONDITIONS
			MIN	TYP	MAX			
V_{IH}	Input HIGH Voltage		3.5			V	All	Guaranteed Input HIGH Voltage
V_{IL}	Input LOW Voltage				1.5	V	All	Guaranteed Input Low Voltage
V_{OH}	Output HIGH Voltage		4.95			V	Min, 25°C	$I_{OH} < 1$ μA, Inputs at 0 or 5 V per
			4.95				MAX	the Logic Function or Truth Table
			4.5			V	All	$I_{OH} < 1$ μA, Inputs at 1.5 or 3.5 V
V_{OL}	Output LOW Voltage				0.05	V	MIN, 25°C	$I_{OL} < 1$ μA, Inputs at 0 or 5 V per
					0.05		MAX	the Logic Function or Truth Table
					0.5	V	All	$I_{OL} < 1$ μA, Inputs at 1.5 or 3.5 V
I_{OH}	Output HIGH Current		-0.63			mA	MIN, 25°C	$V_{OUT} =$ 4.6 V
			-0.36				MAX	Inputs at 0 or 5 V per
I_{OL}	Output LOW Current		1			mA	MIN, 25°C	the Logic Function or Truth Table
			0.8					$V_{OUT} =$ 0.4 V
			0.4				MAX	
C_{IN}	Input Capacitance Per Unit Load				7.5	pF	25°C	Any Input
I_{DD}	Quiescent Power Supply Current	Gates	XC			1	μA	MIN, 25°C	
						7.5		MAX	
			XM			0.25	μA	MIN, 25°C	
						7.5		MAX	
		Buffers and Flip-Flops	XC			4	μA	MIN, 25°C	All Inputs at 0 V or V_{DD} for all Valid Input Combinations
						30		MAX	
			XM			1	μA	MIN, 25°C	
						30		MAX	
		MSI	XC			20	μA	MIN, 25°C	
						150		MAX	
			XM			5	μA	MIN, 25°C	
						150		MAX	

Glossary

Access Time Time between the memory's receiving a new input address and the output data's becoming available in a read operation.

Accumulator Principal register of an arithmetic/logic unit (ALU).

Acquisition Time Time required for a sample-and-hold circuit to capture the analog value that is present on its input.

Active-HIGH (LOW) Decoder Decoder that produces a logic HIGH (LOW) at the output when detection occurs.

Active Logic Level Logic level at which a circuit is considered active. If the symbol for the circuit includes a bubble, the circuit is active-LOW. On the other hand, if it doesn't have a bubble, then the circuit is active-HIGH.

Actuator Electrically controlled device that controls a physical variable.

Addend Number to be added to another.

Address Number that uniquely identifies the location of a word in memory.

Address Bus Unidirectional lines that carry the address code from the CPU to memory and I/O devices.

Addressing Mode Method that a machine-language instruction uses to tell the microprocessor the address of the data.

Address Multiplexing Multiplexing used in dynamic RAMs to save IC pins. It involves latching the two halves of a complete address into the IC in separate steps.

Alphanumeric Codes Codes that represent numbers, letters, punctuation marks, and special characters.

Alternate Logic Symbols A logically equivalent symbol that indicates the active level of the inputs and outputs.

Analog Representation Representation of a quantity that varies over a continuous range of values.

Analog System Combination of devices designed to manipulate physical quantities that are represented in analog form.

Analog-to-Digital Converter (ADC) Circuit that converts an analog input to a corresponding digital output.

Analog Voltage Comparator Circuit that compares two analog input voltages and produces an output that indicates which input is greater.

& When used inside an IEEE/ANSI symbol, an indication of an AND gate or AND function.

AND Gate Digital circuit that implements the AND operation. The output of this circuit is HIGH (logic level 1) only if all of its inputs are HIGH.

AND Operation Boolean algebra operation in which the symbol · is used to indicate the ANDing of two or more logic variables. The result of the AND operation will be HIGH (logic level 1) only if all variables are HIGH.

Application-Specific Integrated Circuit (ASIC) User-defined IC that may contain analog as well as digital circuitry and that is generally manufactured as a fully custom device.

Arithmetic/Logic Unit (ALU) Digital circuit used in computers to perform various arithmetic and logic operations.

ASCII Code (American Standard Code for Information Interchange) Seven-bit alphanumeric code used by most computer manufacturers.

Assembly Language Set of mnemonic terms that correspond to the binary machine-language instructions.

Asserted Term used to describe the state of a logic signal; synonymous with "active."

Astable Multivibrator Digital circuit that oscillates between two unstable output states.

Asynchronous Counter Type of counter in which each flip-flop output serves as the clock input signal for the next flip-flop in the chain.

Asynchronous Inputs Flip-flop inputs that can affect the operation of the flip-flop independent of the synchronous and clock inputs.

Asynchronous Transfer Data transfer performed without the aid of the clock.

Augend Number to which an addend is added.

864

Auxiliary Memory The part of a computer's memory that is separate from the computer's main working memory. Generally has high density and high capacity, such as magnetic disk.

Backplane Electrical connection common to all segments of an LCD.

BCD Adder Special adder containing two four-bit parallel adders and a correction detector circuit. Whenever the addition of two BCD code groups is greater than 1001_2 (9_{10}), the correction detector circuit senses it, adds to the result the correction factor 0110_2 (6_{10}), and generates a carry to the next decimal position.

BCD Counter Binary counter that counts from 0000_2 to 1001_2 before it recycles.

BCD-to-Decimal Decoder Decoder that converts a BCD input into a single decimal output equivalence.

BCD-to-7-Segment Decoder/Driver Digital circuit that takes a four-bit BCD input and activates the required outputs to display the equivalent decimal digit on a 7-segment display.

Bidirectional Data Line Term used when a data line functions as either an input or an output line depending on the states of the enable inputs.

Bilateral Switch CMOS circuit that acts like a single-pole, single-throw switch (SPST) controlled by an input logic level.

Binary-Coded-Decimal Code (BCD Code) Four-bit code used to represent each digit of a decimal number by its four-bit binary equivalent.

Binary Counter Group of flip-flops connected in a special arrangement in which the states of the flip-flops represent the binary number equivalent to the number of pulses that have occurred at the input of the counter.

Binary Digit Bit.

Binary Point Mark that separates the integer from the fractional portion of a binary quantity.

Binary System Number system in which there are only two possible digit values, 0 and 1.

Bipolar DAC Digital-to-analog converter that accepts signed binary numbers as input and produces the corresponding positive or negative analog output value.

Bipolar ICs Integrated digital circuits in which NPN and PNP transistors are the main circuit elements.

Bit Digit in the binary system.

Boolean Algebra Algebraic process used as a tool in the design and analysis of digital systems. In Boolean algebra only two values are possible, 0 and 1.

Boolean Theorems Rules that can be applied to Boolean algebra to simplify logic expressions.

Bootstrap Program Program, stored in ROM, that a computer executes on power-up.

Bubbles Small circles on the input or output lines of logic-circuit symbols which represent inversion of a particular signal. If a bubble is present, the input or output is said to be active-LOW.

Buffer/Driver Circuit designed to have a greater output current and/or voltage capability than an ordinary logic circuit.

Buffer Register Register that holds digital data temporarily.

Bus Group of wires that carry related bits of information.

Bus Contention Situation in which the outputs of two or more active devices are placed on the same bus line at the same time.

Bus Cycle Sequence of events that occur whenever a microprocessor is transferring information over the data bus.

Bus Drivers Circuits that buffer the outputs of devices connected to a common bus; used when a large number of devices share a common bus.

Byte Group of eight bits.

C When used as an input label inside an IEEE/ANSI symbol, an indication that the input controls the entry of data into a storage element.

Capacity Amount of storage space in a memory expressed as number of bits or number of words.

Carry Digit or bit that is generated when two numbers are added and the result is greater than the base for the number system being used.

Carry Propagation Intrinsic circuit delay of some parallel adders that prevents the carry bit (C_{OUT}) and the result of the addition from appearing at the output simultaneously.

Carry Ripple *See* Carry Propagation.

CAS (Column Address Strobe) Signal used to latch the column address into a DRAM.

CAS-before-RAS Method for refreshing DRAMs that have built-in refresh counters. When the *CAS* input is driven LOW and held there as *RAS* is pulsed LOW, an internal refresh operation is performed at the row address given by the on-chip refresh counter.

Cascading Connecting logic circuits in a serial fashion with the output of one circuit driving the input of the next, and so on.

Central Processing Unit (CPU) Part of a computer which is composed of the arithmetic/logic unit (ALU) and the control unit.

Checksum Special data word stored in the last ROM location. It is derived from the addition of all other data words in the ROM, and it is used for error-checking purposes.

Chip Select   Input to a digital device that controls whether or not the device will perform its function. Also called *chip enable.*

Circuit Excitation Table   Table showing a circuit's possible PRESENT-to-NEXT state transitions and the required J and K levels at each flip-flop.

Circulating Shift Register   Shift register in which one of the outputs of the last flip-flop is connected to the input of the first flip-flop.

CLEAR   An input to a latch or FF used to make $Q = 0$.

CLEAR State   The $Q = 0$ state of a flip-flop.

Clock   Digital signal in the form of a rectangular pulse train or a square wave.

Clock Skew   Arrival of a clock signal at the clock inputs of different flip-flops at different times as a result of propagation delays.

Clock Transition Times   Minimum rise and fall times for the clock signal transitions used by a particular IC, specified by the IC manufacturer.

Clocked D Flip-Flop   Type of flip-flop in which the D (data) input is the synchronous input.

Clocked Flip-Flops   Flip-flops that have a clock input.

Clocked J-K FLip-Flop   Type of flip-flop in which inputs J and K are the synchronous inputs.

Clocked S-C Flip-Flop   Type of flip-flop in which the inputs SET and CLEAR are the synchronous inputs.

CMOS (Complementary Metal-Oxide-Semiconductor)   Integrated-circuit technology that uses MOSFETs as the principal circuit element. This logic family belongs to the category of unipolar digital ICs.

Combinational Logic Circuits   Circuits made up of combinations of logic gates, with no feedback from outputs to inputs.

Common Anode   LED display that has the anodes of all of the segment LEDs tied together.

Common Cathode   LED display that has the cathodes of all of the segment LEDs tied together.

Common-Control Block   Symbol used by the IEEE/ANSI standard to describe when one or more inputs are common to more than one of the circuits in an IC.

Compliler   Program that translates a text file written in a high-level language into a machine-language program that can be loaded into a computer's memory.

Complement   *See* Invert.

Complex PLD (CPLD)   Class of PLDs that contain an array of PAL-type blocks that can be interconnected.

Computer Word   Group of binary bits which is the primary unit of information in a computer.

Contact Bounce   The characteristic of all mechanical switches to vibrate when forced to a new position. The vibrations cause the circuit to repeatedly make contact and break contact until the vibrations settle out.

Control Bus   Set of signal lines that are used to synchronize the activities of the CPU and the separate μC elements.

Control Inputs   Input signals synchronized with the active clock transition that determine the output state of a flip-flop.

Control Unit   Part of a computer that provides decoding of program instructions and the necessary timing and control signals for the execution of such instructions.

Crystal-Controlled Clock Generator   Circuit that uses a quartz crystal to generate a clock signal at a precise frequency.

Current-Sinking Logic   Logic family in which the output of a logic circuit sinks current from the input of the logic circuit that it is driving.

Current-Sinking Transistor   Name given to the output transistor (Q_4) of a TTL circuit. This transistor is turned on when the output logic level is LOW.

Current-Sourcing Logic   Logic family in which the output of a logic circuit sources, or supplies, current to the input of the logic circuit that it is driving.

Current-Sourcing Transistor   Name given to the output transistor (Q_3) of most TTL circuits. This transistor is conducting when the output logic level is HIGH.

Current Tracer   Testing tool that detects a changing current in a wire or PC-board trace.

Current Transients   Current spikes generated by the totem-pole output structure of a TTL circuit and caused when both transistors are simultaneously turned on.

D Flip-Flop   *See* Clocked D flip-flop.

D Latch   Circuit that contains a NAND gate latch and two steering NAND gates.

Data   Binary representations of numerical values or non-numerical information in a digital system. Data are used and often modified by a computer program.

Data Acquisition   Process by which a computer acquires digitized analog data.

Data Bus   Bidirectional lines that carry data between the CPU and the memory, or between the CPU and the I/O devices.

Data Distributors   *See* Demultiplexer.

Data-Rate Buffer   Application of FIFOs in which sequential data are written into the FIFO at one rate and read out at a different rate.

Data Selectors   *See* Multiplexer.

Data Transfer   *See* Parallel data transfer *or* Serial data transfer

Decade Counter   Any counter that is capable of going through 10 different logic states.

Decimal System   Number system that uses 10 different digits or symbols to represent a quantity.

Decoder   Digital circuit that converts an input binary code into a corresponding single numeric output.

Decoding   Act of identifying a particular binary combination (code) in order to display its value or recognize its presence.

DeMorgan's Theorems   (1) Theorem stating that the complement of a sum (OR operation) equals the product (AND operation) of the complements, and (2) theorem stating that the complement of a product (AND operation) equals the sum (OR operation) of the complements.

Demultiplexer (DEMUX)   Logic circuit that, depending on the status of its select inputs, will channel its data input to one of several data outputs.

Density   A relative measure of capacity to store bits in a given amount of space.

Dependency Notation   Method used to symbolically represent the relationship between inputs and outputs of logic circuits. This method employs the use of qualifying symbols embedded near the top center or geometric center of a symbol element.

Differential Inputs   Method of connecting an analog signal to an analog circuit's + and − inputs, neither of which is ground, such that the analog circuit acts upon the voltage difference between the two inputs.

Digital Computer   System of hardware that performs arithmetic and logic operations, manipulates data, and makes decisions.

Digital Integrated Circuits   Self-contained digital circuits made by using one of several integrated-circuit fabrication technologies.

Digital-Ramp ADC   Type of analog-to-digital converter in which an internal staircase waveform is generated and utilized for the purpose of accomplishing the conversion. The conversion time for this type of analog-to-digital converter varies depending on the value of the input analog signal.

Digital Representation   Representation of a quantity that varies in discrete steps over a range of values.

Digital Signal Processing (DSP)   Method of performing repetitive calculations on an incoming stream of digital data words to accomplish some form of signal conditioning. The data are typically digitized samples of an analog signal.

Digital Storage Oscilloscope   Instrument that samples, digitizes, stores, and displays analog voltage waveforms.

Digital System   Combination of devices designed to manipulate physical quantities that are represented in digital form.

Digital-to-Analog Converter (DAC)   Circuit that converts a digital input to a corresponding analog output.

Digitization   Process by which an analog signal is converted to digital data.

Direct Addressing   Addressing mode in which the part of the instruction following the op code is the address of the operand.

Disable   Action in which a circuit is prevented from performing its normal function, such as passing an input signal through to its output.

Divide-and-Conquer   Troubleshooting technique whereby tests are performed that will eliminate half of all possible remaining causes of the malfunction.

"Don't Care"   Situation when a circuit's output level for a given set of input conditions can be assigned as either a 1 or a 0.

Down Counter   Counter that counts from a maximum count downward to 0.

Downloading   Process of transferring output files to a programming fixture.

DRAM Controller   IC used to handle refresh and address multiplexing operations needed by DRAM systems.

Driver   Technical term sometimes added to an IC's description to indicate that the IC's outputs can operate at higher current and/or voltage limits than a normal standard IC.

Dual-in-Line Package (DIP)   A very common IC package with two parallel rows of pins intended to be inserted into a socket or through holes drilled in a printed circuit board.

Dual-Slope Analog-to-Digital Converter   Type of analog-to-digital converter that linearly charges a capacitor from a current proportional to V_A for a fixed time interval and then increments a counter as the capacitor is linearly discharged to 0.

Dynamic RAM (DRAM)   Type of semiconductor memory that stores data as capacitor charges that need to be refreshed periodically.

ECL   Emitter-coupled logic; also referred to as *current-mode logic*.

Edge-Detector Circuit   Circuit that produces a narrow positive spike that occurs coincident with the active transition of a clock input pulse.

Edge-Triggered   Manner in which a flip-flop is activated by a signal transition. A flip-flop may be either a positive- or a negative-edge-triggered flip-flop.

Electrically Compatible   When two ICs from different logic series can be connected directly without any special measures taken to ensure proper operation.

Electrically Erasable Programmable ROM (EEPROM)   ROM that can be electrically programmed, erased, and reprogrammed.

Electrostatic Discharge (ESD) The often detrimental act of the transfer of static electricity (i.e., an electrostatic charge) from one surface to another. This impulse of current can destroy electronic devices.

Enable Action in which a circuit is allowed to perform its normal function, such as passing an input signal through to its output.

Embedded Microcontroller Microcontroller that is embedded in a marketable product such as a VCR or an appliance.

Emitter-Coupled Logic *See* ECL.

Encoder Digital circuit that produces an output code depending on which of its inputs is activated.

Encoding Use of a group of symbols to represent numbers, letters, or words.

Erasable Programmable ROM (EPROM) ROM that can be electrically programmed by the user. It can be erased (usually with ultraviolet light) and reprogrammed as often as desired.

Exclusive-NOR (EX-NOR) Circuit Two-input logic circuit that produces a HIGH output only when the inputs are equal.

Exclusive-OR (EX-OR) Circuit Two-input logic circuit that produces a HIGH output only when the inputs are different.

Execute Cycle Period during which a computer's control unit performs the operation specified by the fetched op code.

Fan-Out Maximum number of standard logic inputs that the output of a digital circuit can reliably drive.

Fetch Cycle Period during which a computer's control unit obtains instruction codes from memory.

Field Programmable Gate Array (FPGA) Class of PLDs that contain an array of more complex logic cells that can be very flexibly interconnected to implement high-level logic circuits.

Firmware Computer programs stored in ROM.

First-In, First-Out Memory (FIFO) Semiconductor sequential-access memory in which data words are read out in the same order in which they were written in.

555 Timer TTL-compatible IC that can be wired to operate in several different modes, such as a one-shot and an astable multivibrator.

Flash ADC Type of analog-to-digital converter that has the highest operating speed available.

Flash Memory Nonvolatile memory IC that has the high-speed access and in-circuit erasability of EEPROMs but with higher densities and lower cost.

Flip-Flop Memory device capable of storing a logic level.

Floating Bus When all outputs connected to a data bus are in the Hi-*Z* state.

Floating Input Input signal that is left disconnected in a logic circuit.

Floppy Disk Flexible magnetic disk used for mass storage.

4-to-10 Decoder *See* BCD-to-Decimal Decoder.

Frequency Counter Circuit that can measure and display a signal's frequency.

Frequency Division The use of flip-flop circuits to produce an output waveform whose frequency is equal to the input clock frequency divided by some integer value.

Full Adder Logic circuit with three inputs and two outputs. The inputs are a carry bit (C_{IN}) from a previous stage, a bit from the augend, and a bit from the addend, respectively. The outputs are the sum bit and the carry-out bit (C_{OUT}) produced by the addition of the bit from the addend with the bit from the augend and C_{IN}.

Full-Scale Error Term used by some digital-to-analog converter manufacturers to specify the accuracy of a digital-to-analog converter. It is defined as the maximum deviation of a digital-to-analog converter's output from its expected ideal value.

Full-Scale Output Maximum possible output value of a digital-to-analog converter.

Function Generator Circuit that produces a variety of waveforms. It can be constructed using a ROM, a DAC, and a counter.

Functionally Equivalent When the logic functions performed by two different ICs are exactly the same.

Fusible Link Conducting material that can be made non-conducting (i.e., open) by passing too much current through it.

Gas Discharge Displays Type of display in which the segments or pixels are electrodes that glow when activated by application of a relatively high voltage to a reference electrode.

Glitch Momentary, narrow, spurious, and sharply defined change in voltage.

GSI Giga-scale integration (1,000,000 gates or more).

Half Adder Logic circuit with two inputs and two outputs. The inputs are a bit from the augend and a bit from the addend. The outputs are the sum bit produced by the addition of the bit from the addend with the bit from the augend and the resulting carry (C_{OUT}) bit, which will be added to the next stage.

Hard Disk Rigid metal magnetic disk used for mass storage.

Hexadecimal Number System   Number system that has a base of 16. Digits 0 through 9 plus letters A through F are used to express a hexadecimal number.

High-Level Language   Computer programming language that utilizes the English language in order to facilitate the writing of a computer program.

Hold Time (t_H)   Time interval immediately following the active transition of the clock signal during which the control input must be maintained at the proper level.

Hybrid System   System that employs both analog and digital techniques.

IEEE/ANSI   Institute of Electrical and Electronics Engineers/American National Standards Institute.

Immediate Addressing   Addressing mode in which the part of the instruction following the op code is the actual operand.

Indeterminate   Of a logic voltage level, outside the required range of voltages for either logic 0 or logic 1.

Inhibit Circuits   Logic circuits that control the passage of an input signal through to the output.

Input Term Matrix   Part of a programmable logic device that allows inputs to be selectively connected to or disconnected from internal logic circuitry.

Input Unit   Part of a computer that facilitates the feeding of information into the computer's memory unit or ALU.

Instructions   Binary codes that tell a computer what operation to perform. A program is made up of an orderly sequence of instructions.

Interfacing   Joining of dissimilar devices in such a way that they are able to function in a compatible and coordinated manner; connection of the output of a system to the input of a different system with different electrical characteristics.

Invert   Cause a logic level to go to the opposite state.

INVERTER   Also referred to as the NOT circuit; logic circuit that implements the NOT operation. An INVERTER has only one input, and its output logic level is always the opposite of this input's logic level.

Jam Transfer   *See* Asynchronous Transfer.

JEDEC   Joint Electronic Device Engineering Council.

J-K Excitation Table   Table showing the required J and K input conditions for each possible state transition for a single J-K flip-flop.

Johnson Counter   Shift register in which the inverted output of the last flip-flop is connected to the input of the first flip-flop.

Karnaugh Map (K map)   Two-dimensional form of a truth table used to simplify a sum-of-products expression.

Latch   Type of flip-flop; also, the action by which a logic circuit output captures and holds the value of an input.

Latch-Up   Condition of dangerously high current in a CMOS IC caused by high-voltage spikes or ringing at device input and output pins.

LCD   Liquid-crystal display.

Lead Pitch   The distance between the centers of adjacent pins on an IC.

Least Significant Bit (LSB)   Rightmost bit (smallest weight) of a binary expressed quantity.

Least Significant Digit (LSD)   Digit that carries the least weight in a particular number.

LED   Light-emitting diode.

Linearity Error   Term used by some digital-to-analog converter manufacturers to specify the device's accuracy. It is defined as the maximum deviation in step size from the ideal step size.

Load Operation   Transfer of data into a flip-flop, a register, a counter, or a memory location.

Loading Factor   *See* Fan-Out.

Logic Circuit   Any circuit that behaves according to a set of logic rules.

Logic Function Generation   Implementation of a logic function directly from a truth table by means of a digital IC such as a multiplexer.

Logic Level   State of a voltage variable. The states 1 (HIGH) and 0 (LOW) correspond to the two usable voltage ranges of a digital device.

Logic Probe   Digital troubleshooting tool that senses and indicates the logic level at a particular point in a circuit.

Logic Pulser   Testing tool that generates a short-duration pulse when manually actuated.

Look-Ahead Carry   Ability of some parallel adders to predict, without having to wait for the carry to propagate through the full adders, whether or not a carry bit (C_{OUT}) will be generated as a result of the addition, thus reducing the overall propagation delays.

Looping   Combining of adjacent squares in a Karnaugh map containing 1s for purpose of simplification of a sum-of-products expression.

Low-Power Schottky TTL (LS-TTL)   TTL subfamily that uses the identical Schottky TTL circuit but with larger resistor values.

Low-Power TTL (L-TTL)   TTL subfamily that uses the basic TTL standard circuit except that all resistor values are increased.

Low-Voltage Technology   New line of logic devices that operate from a nominal supply voltage of 3.3 V.

LSI   Large-scale integration (100 to 9999 gates).

Machine Cycle   Different states that a microprocessor goes through in fetching and executing instructions.

Machine Language   Computer programming language in which groups of 1s and 0s are used to represent instructions. Machine language is also the only language that a computer actually understands.

Magnetic Disk Memory   Mass storage memory that stores data as magnetized spots on a rotating, flat disk surface.

Magnetic Tape Memory   Mass storage memory that stores data as magnetized spots on a magnetically coated plastic tape.

Magnitude Comparator   Digital circuit that compares two input binary quantities and generates outputs to indicate whether the inputs are equal or, if not, which is greater.

Main Memory   High-speed portion of a computer's memory that holds the program and data the computer is currently working on. Also called *working memory*.

Mask-Programmed ROM (MROM)   ROM that is programmed by the manufacturer according to the customer's specifications. It cannot be erased or reprogrammed.

Mass Storage   Storage of large amounts of data; not part of a computer's internal memory.

Master/Slave Flip-Flops   Obsolete flip-flops that have as their internal structure two flip-flops—a master and a slave.

Maximum Clocking Frequency (f_{MAX})   Highest frequency that may be applied to the clock input of a flip-flop and still have it trigger reliably.

Memory   Ability of a circuit's output to remain at one state even after the input condition that caused that state is removed.

Memory Cell   Device that stores a single bit.

Memory Foldback   Redundant enabling of a memory device at more than one address range as a result of incomplete address decoding.

Memory Map   Diagram of a memory system that shows the address range of all existing memory devices as well as available memory space for expansion.

Memory Unit   Part of a computer that stores instructions and data received from the input unit, as well as results from the arithmetic/logic unit.

Memory Word   Group of bits in memory that represents instructions or data of some type.

Microcomputer   Newest member of the computer family, consisting of microprocessor chip, memory chips, and I/O interface chips. In some cases all of the aforementioned are in one single IC.

Microcontroller   Small microcomputer used as a dedicated controller for a machine, a piece of equipment, or a process.

Microprocessor (MPU)   LSI chip that contains the central processing unit (CPU).

Minuend   Number from which the subtrahend is to be subtracted.

Mnemonic   Abbreviation that represents the operation that a computer will perform.

MOD Number   Number of different states that a counter can sequence through; the counter's frequency division ratio.

Monostable Multivibrator   *See* One-Shot.

Monotonicity   Property whereby the output of a digital-to-analog converter increases as the binary input is increased.

MOSFET   Metal-oxide-semiconductor field-effect transistor.

Most Significant Bit (MSB)   Leftmost binary bit (largest weight) of a binary expressed quantity.

Most Significant Digit (MSD)   Digit that carries the most weight in a particular number.

MSI   Medium-scale integration (12 to 99 gates).

Multibyte Instruction   Computer instruction that is represented by more than one byte.

Multiple-Address Instruction   Computer instruction word that contains more than one address.

Multiplexer (MUX)   Logic circuit that, depending on the status of its select inputs, will channel one of several data inputs to its output.

Multiplexing   Process of selecting one of several input data sources and transmitting the selected data to a single output channel.

Multistage Counter   Counter in which several counter stages are connected so that the output of one stage serves as the clock input of the next stage to achieve greater counting range or frequency division.

NAND Gate   Logic circuit that operates like an AND gate followed by an INVERTER. The output of a NAND gate is LOW (logic level 0) only if all inputs are HIGH (logic level 1).

NAND Gate Latch   Flip-flop constructed from two cross-coupled NAND gates.

Negation   Operation of converting a positive number to its negative equivalent, or vice versa. A signed binary number is negated by the 2's-complement operation.

Negative-Going Transition   When a clock goes from 1 to 0.

N-MOS (N-Channel Metal-Oxide-Semiconductor)   Integrated-circuit technology that uses N-channel MOSFETs as the principal circuit element.

Noise   Spurious voltage fluctuations that may be present in the environment and cause digital circuits to malfunction.

Noise Immunity   Circuit's ability to tolerate noise voltages on its inputs.

Noise Margin   Quantitative measure of noise immunity.

Nonretriggerable One-Shot Type of one-shot that will not respond to a trigger input signal while in its quasi-stable state.

Nonvolatile Memory Memory that will keep storing its information without the need for electrical power.

Nonvolatile RAM Combination of a RAM array and an EEPROM or flash on the same IC. The EEPROM serves as a nonvolatile backup to the RAM.

NOR Gate Logic circuit that operates like an OR gate followed by an INVERTER. The output of a NOR gate is LOW (logic level 0) when any or all inputs are HIGH (logic level 1).

NOR Gate Latch Flip-flop constructed from two cross-coupled NOR gates.

NOT Circuit *See* INVERTER.

NOT Operation Boolean algebra operation in which the overbar ($\overline{}$) or the prime ($'$) symbol is used to indicate the inversion of one or more logic variables.

Observation/Analysis Process used to troubleshoot circuits or systems in order to predict the possible faults before ever picking up a troubleshooting instrument. When this process is used, the troubleshooter must understand the circuit operation, observe the symptoms of the failure, and then reason through the operation.

Octal Number System Number system that has a base of 8; digits from 0 to 7 are used to express an octal number.

Octets Groups of eight 1s that are adjacent to each other within a Karnaugh map.

Offset Error Deviation from the ideal 0 V at the output of a digital-to-analog converter when the input is all 0s. In reality, there is a very small output voltage for this situation.

1-of-10 Decoder *See* BCD-to-Decimal Decoder.

1's-Complement Form Result obtained when each bit of a binary number is complemented.

One-Shot Circuit that belongs to the flip-flop family but that has only one stable state (normally $Q = 0$).

Op Code Part of a computer instruction that defines what type of operation the computer is to execute on specified data.

Open-Collector Output Type of output structure of some TTL circuits in which only one transistor with a floating collector is used.

Operand Data that are operated on by the computer as it executes a program.

Operand Address Address in memory where the operand is currently stored or is to be stored.

Optical Disk Memory Class of mass memory devices that uses a laser beam to write onto and read from a specially coated disk.

OR Gate Digital circuit that implements the OR operation. The output of this circuit is HIGH (logic level 1) if any or all of its inputs are HIGH.

OR Operation Boolean algebra operation in which the symbol + is used to indicate the ORing of two or more logic variables. The result of the OR operation will be HIGH (logic level 1) if one or more variables are HIGH.

Output Logic Macro Cell (OLMC) A group of logic elements (gates, multiplexers, flip flops, buffers) in a PLD, which can be configured in various ways.

Output Unit Part of a computer that receives data from the memory unit or ALU and presents it to the outside world.

Overflow When in the process of adding signed binary numbers a carry of 1 is generated from the MSB position of the number into the sign bit position.

Override Inputs Synonymous with "asynchronous inputs."

Parallel Adder Digital circuit made from full adders and used to add all of the bits from the addend and the augend together simultaneously.

Parallel Counter *See* Synchronous Counter.

Parallel Data Transfer Operation by which several bits of data are transferred simultaneously into a counter or a register.

Parallel In/Parallel Out Register Type of register that can be loaded with parallel data and has parallel outputs available.

Parallel In/Serial Out Register Type of register that can be loaded with parallel data and has only one serial output.

Parallel Load *See* Parallel Data Transfer.

Parallel-to-Serial Conversion Process by which all data bits are presented simultaneously to a circuit's input and then transmitted one bit at a time to its output.

Parallel Transmission Simultaneous transfer of all bits of a binary number from one place to another.

Parity Bit Additional bit that is attached to each code group so that the total number of 1s being transmitted is always even (or always odd).

Parity Checker Circuit that takes a set of data bits (including the parity bit) and checks to see if it has the correct parity.

Parity Generator Circuit that takes a set of data bits and produces the correct parity bit for the data.

Parity Method Scheme used for error detection during the transmission of data.

Percentage Resolution Ratio of the step size to the full-scale value of a digital-to-analog converter. Percentage resolution can also be defined as the reciprocal of the maximum number of steps of a digital-to-analog converter.

Peripherals Computer input and output devices.

Pin-Compatible When the corresponding pins on two different ICs have the same functions.

Pixel Small dots of light that make up a graphical image on a display.

PLD Development Software Software that takes a logic design entered by the user and translates it into a "fuse plot" output file to be transferred to the programming fixture, which then programs the PLD by zapping the appropriate fuses. The CUPL software used in Chapter 12 is an example of high-level development software.

P-MOS (P-channel Metal Oxide Semiconductor) Integrated-circuit technology that uses P-channel MOSFETs as the principal circuit element.

Positional-Value System System in which the value of a digit is dependent on its relative position.

Positive-Going Transition (PGT) When a clock signal changes from a logic 0 to a logic 1.

Power-Down Operating mode in which a chip is disabled and draws much less power than when it is fully enabled.

Power-Supply Decoupling Connection of a small RF capacitor between ground and V_{CC} near each TTL integrated circuit on a circuit board.

Power-Up Self-Test Program stored in ROM and executed by the CPU on power-up to test RAM and/or ROM portions of the computer circuitry.

PRESET Asynchronous input used to immediately set $Q = 1$.

Presettable Counter Counter that can be preset to any starting count either synchronously or asynchronously.

Priority Encoder Special type of encoder that senses when two or more inputs are activated simultaneously and then generates a code corresponding to the highest-numbered input.

Product-of-Sums Form Logic expression consisting of two or more OR terms (sums) that are ANDed together.

Program Sequence of binary-coded instructions designed to accomplish a particular task by a computer; also, the act of entering information into a programmable device (e.g., EPROM, PLD).

Program Counter (PC) CPU register that stores the address of the next instruction to be fetched.

Programmable Array Logic (PAL) Class of programmable logic devices. Its AND array is programmable, whereas its OR array is hard-wired.

Programmable Logic Array (PLA) Class of programmable logic devices. Both its AND and its OR arrays are programmable. Also called a *field programmable logic array (FPLA)*.

Programmable Logic Device (PLD) IC that contains a large number of interconnected logic functions. The user can program the IC for a specific function by selectively breaking the appropriate interconnections.

Programmable Output Polarity Feature of many PLDs whereby an EX-OR gate with a polarity fuse gives the designer the option of inverting or not inverting a device output.

Programmable ROM (PROM) ROM that can be electrically programmed by the user. It cannot be erased and reprogrammed.

Programmer Person who writes a program for a computer to execute; also, a fixture used to apply the proper voltages to a chip in order to program it.

Propagation Delays (t_{PLH}/t_{PHL}) Delay from the time a signal is applied to the time when the output makes its change.

Pull-Down Transistor *See* Current-Sinking Transistor.

Pull-Up Transistor *See* Current-Sourcing Transistor.

Pulse-Steering Circuit A logic circuit that can be used to select the destination of an input pulse, depending on the logic levels present at the circuit's inputs.

Quantization Error Error caused by the nonzero resolution of an analog-to-digital converter. It is an inherent error of the device.

Quasi-Stable State State to which a one-shot is temporarily triggered (normally $Q = 1$) before returning to its stable state (normally $Q = 0$).

R/2R Ladder DAC Type of digital-to-analog converter whose internal resistance values span a range of only 2 to 1.

Random-Access Memory (RAM) Memory in which the access time is the same for any location.

RAS (Row Address Strobe) Signal used to latch the row address into a DRAM chip.

RAS-Only Refresh Method for refreshing DRAM in which only row addresses are strobed into the DRAM using the *RAS* input.

Read Term used to describe the condition when the CPU is receiving data from another element.

Read-Only Memory (ROM) Memory device designed for applications where the ratio of read operations to write operations is very high.

Read Operation Operation in which a word in a specific memory location is sensed and possibly transferred to another device.

Read/Write Memory (RWM) Any memory that can be read from and written into with equal ease.

Refresh Counter Counter that keeps track of row addresses during a DRAM refresh operation.

Refreshing   Process of recharging the cells of a dynamic memory.

Register   Group of flip-flops capable of storing data.

RESET   Term synonymous with "CLEAR."

RESET State   The $Q = 0$ state of a flip-flop.

Resolution   In a digital-to-analog converter, smallest change that can occur in the output for a change in digital input; also called *step size*. In an analog-to-digital converter, smallest amount by which the analog input must change to produce a change in the digital output.

Retriggerable One-Shot   Type of one-shot that will respond to a trigger input signal while in its quasi-stable state.

Ring Counter   Shift register in which the output of the last flip-flop is connected to the input of the first flip-flop.

Ripple Counter   *See* Asynchronous Counter.

Sample-and-Hold Circuit   Type of circuit that utilizes a unity-gain buffer amplifier in conjunction with a capacitor to keep the input stable during an analog-to-digital conversion process.

Sampling Interval   Time window during which a frequency counter samples and thereby determines the unknown frequency of a signal.

SBD   Schottky barrier diode used in all Schottky TTL series.

Schmitt Trigger   Digital circuit that accepts a slow-changing input signal and produces a rapid, oscillation-free transition at the output.

Schottky TTL   TTL subfamily that uses the basic TTL standard circuit except that it uses a Schottky barrier diode (SBD) connected between the base and the collector of each transistor for faster switching.

Sequential-Access Memory (SAM)   Memory in which the access time will vary depending on the storage location of the data.

Sequential Logic System   Logic system in which the logic output states and the sequence of operations depend on both the present and the past input conditions.

Serial Data Transfer   Transfer of data from one place to another one bit at a time.

Serial In/Parallel Out   Type of register that can be loaded with data serially and has parallel outputs available.

Serial In/Serial Out   Type of register that can be loaded with data serially and has only one serial output.

Serial Transmission   Transfer of binary information from one place to another a bit at a time.

SET   An input to a latch or FF used to make $Q = 1$.

SET State   The $Q = 1$ state of a flip-flop.

Settling Time   Amount of time that it takes the output of a digital-to-analog converter to go from 0 to within one-half step size of its full-scale value as the input is changed from all 0s to all 1s.

Setup Time (t_S)   Time interval immediately preceding the active transition of the clock signal during which the control input must be maintained at the proper level.

Shift Register   Digital circuit that accepts binary data from some input source and then shifts these data through a chain of flip-flops one bit at a time.

Sigma Σ   Greek letter that represents addition and is often used to label the sum output bits of a parallel adder.

Sigma/Delta Modulation   Method of sampling an analog signal and converting its data points into a bit stream of serial data.

Sign Bit   Binary bit that is added to the leftmost position of a binary number to indicate whether that number represents a positive or a negative quantity

Sign-Magnitude System   A system for representing signed binary numbers where the most significant bit represents the sign of the number and the remaining bits represent the true binary value (magnitude).

Simulator   Computer program that calculates the correct output states of a logic circuit based on a description of the logic circuit and on the current inputs.

Speed–Power Product   Numerical value (in joules) often used to compare different logic families. It is obtained by multiplying the propagation delay by the power dissipation of a logic circuit.

Spike   *See* Glitch.

SSI   Small-scale integration (fewer than 12 gates).

Staircase Test   Process by which a digital-to-analog converter's digital input is incremented and its output monitored to determine whether or not it exhibits a staircase format.

Staircase Waveform   Type of waveform generated at the output of a digital-to-analog converter as its digital input signal is incrementally changed.

State Table   A table whose entries represent the sequence of individual FF states (i.e., 0 or 1) for a sequential binary circuit.

State Transition Diagram   A graphic representation of the operation of a sequential binary circuit, showing the sequence of individual FF states and conditions needed for transitions from one state to the next.

Static Accuracy Test   Test in which a fixed binary value is applied to the input of a digital-to-analog converter and the analog output is accurately measured. The measured result should fall within the expected range specified by the digital-to-analog converter's manufacturer.

Static RAM (SRAM)   Semiconductor RAM that stores information in flip-flop cells that do not have to be periodically refreshed.

Step Size   *See* Resolution.

Straight Binary Coding   Representation of a decimal number by its equivalent binary number.

Strobe Another name for an enable input usually used to latch a value into a register.

Strobing Technique often used to eliminate decoding spikes.

Substrate Piece of semiconductor material that is part of the building block of any digital IC.

Subtrahend Number that is to be subtracted from a minuend.

Successive-Approximation ADC Type of analog-to-digital converter in which an internal parallel register and complex control logic are used to perform the conversion. The conversion time for this type of analog-to-digital converter is always the same regardless of the value of the input analog signal.

Sum-of-Products Form Logic expression consisting of two or more AND terms (products) that are ORed together.

Supercomputers Computers with greatest speed and computational power.

Surface Mount A method of manufacturing circuit boards whereby ICs are soldered to conductive pads on the surface of the board.

Synchronous Control Inputs *See* Control Inputs.

Synchronous Counter Counter in which all of the flip-flops are clocked simultaneously.

Synchronous Systems Systems in which the circuit outputs can change states only on the transitions of a clock.

Synchronous Transfer Data transfer performed by using the synchronous and clock inputs of a flip-flop.

Test Vector Sets of inputs that are used to test a PLD design before the PLD is programmed.

Timing Diagram Depiction of logic levels as related to time.

Toggle Mode Mode in which a flip-flop changes states for each clock pulse.

Toggling Process of changing from one binary state to the other.

Totem-Pole Output Term used to describe the way in which two bipolar transistors are arranged at the output of most TTL circuits.

Transducer Device that converts a physical variable to an electrical variable (for example, a photocell or a thermocouple).

Transmission Gate *See* Bilateral Switch.

Transparent Of a D latch, operating so that the Q output follows the D input.

Trigger Input signal to a flip-flop or one-shot which causes the output to change states depending on the conditions of the control signals.

Tristate Type of output structure that allows three types of output states: HIGH, LOW, and high-impedance (Hi-Z).

Truth Table Logic table that depicts a circuit's output response to the various combinations of the logic levels at its inputs.

TTL (Transistor/Transistor Logic) Integrated-circuit technology that uses the bipolar transistor as the principal circuit element.

2's-Complement Form Result obtained when a 1 is added to the least significant bit position of a binary number in the 1's-complement form.

ULSI Ultra-large-scale integration (100,000 or more gates).

Unasserted Term used to describe the state of a logic signal, synonymous with "inactive."

Unipolar ICs Integrated digital circuits in which unipolar field-effect transistors (MOSFETs) are the main circuit elements.

Up Counter Counter that counts upward from 0 to a maximum count.

Up/Down Counter Counter that can count up or down depending on how its inputs are activated.

Up/Down Digital-Ramp ADC Type of analog-to-digital converter that uses an up/down counter to step up or step down the voltage from a digital-to-analog converter until it intersects the analog input.

VLSI Very large-scale integration (10,000 to 99,999 gates).

Volatile Memory Memory requiring electrical power to keep information stored.

Voltage-Controlled Oscillator (VCO) Circuit that produces an output signal with a frequency proportional to the voltage applied to its input.

Voltage-Level Translator Circuit that takes one set of input voltage levels and translates it to a different set of output levels.

Voltage-to-Frequency ADC Type of analog-to-digital converter that converts the analog voltage to a pulse frequency that is then counted to produce a digital output.

Wired-AND Term used to describe the logic function created when open-collector outputs are tied together.

Word Group of bits that represent a certain unit of information.

Word Size Number of bits in the binary words that a computer system operates on.

WRITE Term used to describe the condition when the CPU is sending data to another element.

Write Operation Operation in which a new word is placed into a specific memory location.

ZIF Zero-insertion-force IC socket.

Answers to Selected Problems

CHAPTER 1

1-2. (a) 25 (b) 9.5625 (c) 1241.6875
1-4. 1023
1-5. nine bits
1-6.

4.4 V ⌐ 2 ms ⌐ 4 ms ⌐ 2 ms ⌐
0.2 V

1-7. (a) $2^N - 1 = 15$ and $N = 4$; therefore, four lines are required for parallel transmission. (b) Only one line is required for serial transmission.

CHAPTER 2

2-1. (a) 22 (b) 141 (c) 2313 (d) 983 (e) 191
2-2. (a) 100101 (b) 1110 (c) 10111101
(d) 11001101 (e) 100100001001 (f) 111111111
2-3. 255; 65,535
2-4. (a) 483 (b) 30 (c) 2047 (d) 175 (e) 644
2-5. (a) 73_8 (b) 564_8 (c) 1627_8 (d) 200000_8
(e) 377_8
2-6. (a) 111100011 (b) 011110 (c) 011111111111
(d) 010101111 (e) 001010000100
2-7. (a) 26_8 (b) 215_8 (c) 4411_8 (d) 1727_8 (e) 277_8
2-8. 165, 166, 167, 170, 171, 172, 173, 174, 175, 176, 177, 200
2-9. $100100001001_2 = 4411_8$
2-10. Five
2-11. (a) 146 (b) 422 (c) 14,333 (d) 704 (e) 2047
2-12. (a) 4B (b) 13A (c) 800 (d) 6413 (e) FFF
2-13. (a) 16 (b) 8D (c) 909 (d) 3D7 (e) BF
2-14. (a) 10010010 (b) 000110100110
(c) 0011011111111101 (d) 001011000000
(e) 011111111111
2-15. 280, 281, 282, 283, 284, 285, 286, 287, 288, 289, 28A, 28B, 28C, 28D, 28E, 28F, 290, 291, 292, 293, 294, 295, 296, 297, 298, 299, 29A, 29B, 29C, 29D, 29E, 29F, 2A0

2-16. Five
2-17. (a) 01000111 (b) 100101100010
(c) 000110000111
(d) 01000010011010001001011000100111
2-18. 10 bits for binary, 12 bits for BCD
2-19. (a) 9752 (b) 184 (c) 7775 (d) 492
2-20. (a) 64 (b) FFFFFFFF (c) 999,999
2-21. 01011000 (X); 00111101 (=); 00110010 (2); 10110101 (5); 00101111 (/); 11011001 (Y)
2-22. D8, BD, B2, 35, AF, 59
2-23. BEN SMITH
2-24. (a) 101110100 (parity bit on the left)
(b) 000111000 (c) 0000101100101
(d) 11001001000000001
2-25. (a) no single-bit error (b) single-bit error
(c) double error (d) no single-bit error
2-27. (a) 10110001001 (b) 11111111 (c) 209
(d) 59,943 (e) 4701 (f) 777 (g) 157 (h) 2254
(i) 1961 (j) 15,900 (k) 640 (l) 952B
(m) 100001100101 (n) 947 (o) 135_{16} (p) 5464_8
(q) 1001010 (r) 01011000 (BCD)
2-28. (a) 100101 (b) 00110111 (c) 25
(d) 0110011 0110111 (e) 45
2-29. (a) octal (b) 16 (c) digit (d) Gray
(e) Parity; single-bit errors (f) ASCII (g) octal; hex
(h) byte
2-30. (a) 1000 (b) 010001 (c) 1111
2-31. (a) 0110 (b) 001111 (c) 1101
2-32. (a) 10000 (b) 7778 (c) 2001 (d) 2001
(e) A00 (f) 1001
2-33. (a) 7776 (b) 7776 (c) 1777 (d) 1FFF
(e) 9FE (f) 0FFF
2-34. (a) 1,048,576 (b) five (c) 000FF
2-35. (a) 64; 256; 1024 (b) 440,000 (c) 11,363
2-36. eight

CHAPTER 3

3-1.

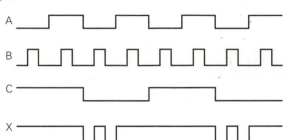

3-2.

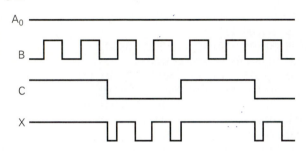

3-3. x will be a constant HIGH.

3-5. 31

3-6. (a) x is HIGH only when A, B, and C are all HIGH. (b) x is a constant LOW. (c) x is HIGH only when B and C are simultaneously HIGH.

3-7. Change the OR gate to an AND gate.

3-8. OUT is always LOW.

3-12. (a) $x = (\overline{A + B})BC$ (b) $x = \overline{A}B\overline{C} + A\overline{B}\overline{C} + \overline{A}\overline{B}D$

3-14. $x = D \cdot (\overline{AB + C}) + E$

3-16. (a)

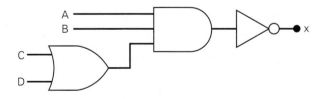

3-17.–3-18.

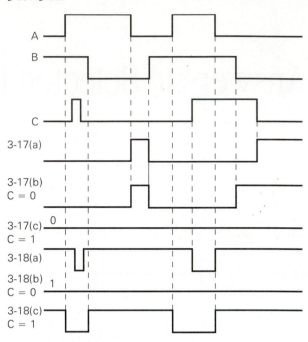

3-19. $x = \overline{(\overline{A + B}) \cdot (\overline{BC})}$

$x = 0$ only when $A = B = 0$, $C = 1$.

3-21. (c)

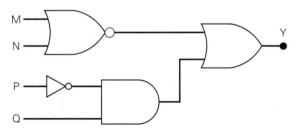

3-22. (a) 1 (b) A (c) 0 (d) C (e) 0 (f) D (g) D (h) 1 (i) G (j) y

3-24. (a) $MP\overline{N} + \overline{M}\overline{P}N$ (b) $B\overline{C}$

3-26. (a) $A + \overline{B} + C$ (b) $A \cdot (B + \overline{C})$ (c) $\overline{A} + \overline{B} + CD$ (d) $\overline{A} + B + \overline{C} + D$ (e) $\overline{M}N + M\overline{N}$ (f) $(\overline{A} + \overline{B})C + \overline{D}$

3-27. $A + B + \overline{C}$

3-34. (a) NOR (b) AND (c) NAND

3-35. (a)

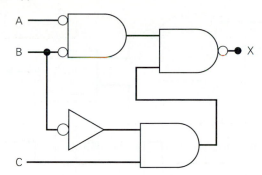

3-36. (a) Z goes HIGH only when $A = B = 0$ and $C = D = 1$.   **(b)** Z goes LOW when A or B is HIGH or when C or D is LOW.

3-38. X will go HIGH when $E = 1$, or $D = 0$, or $B = C = 0$, or when $B = 1$ and $A = 0$.

3-39. X is LOW for $EDCBA = 01011, 01100, 01101,$ and 01111.

3-40. (a) HIGH   **(b)** LOW

3-41. $\overline{\text{LIGHT}} = 0$ when $A = B = 0$ or $A = B = 1$.

3-42. (a)

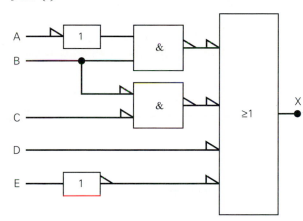

3-43. $Z = \overline{\overline{(\overline{AB} + \overline{C})F + \overline{C}} + (D + E)}$

3-46. Put INVERTERs on the A_7, A_5, A_4, A_2 inputs to the 74HC30.

CHAPTER 4

4-1. (a) $C\overline{A} + CB$ **(b)** $\overline{Q}R + Q\overline{R}$ **(c)** $C + \overline{A}$
(d) $\overline{R}\,\overline{S}\,\overline{T}$ **(e)** $BC + \overline{B}(\overline{C} + A)$ **(f)** $BC + \overline{B}(\overline{C} + A)$
or $BC + \overline{B}\,\overline{C} + \overline{A}\,\overline{C}$ **(g)** $\overline{D} + AB\overline{C} + \overline{A}\overline{B}C$

4-2. $Q(M + N)$

4-3. $MN + Q$

4-4. One solution: $\overline{x} = \overline{B}C + AB\overline{C}$. Another: $x = \overline{A}B + \overline{B}\,\overline{C} + BC$. Another: $BC + \overline{B}\,\overline{C} + \overline{A}\,\overline{C}$

4-5. $x = \overline{A}B + \overline{A}\,\overline{C} + \overline{B}\,\overline{C}$

4-6. $x = AB\overline{C}\overline{D} + \overline{A}BCD$

4-7. $x = \overline{A}_3(A_2 + A_1A_0)$

4-8. alarm $= ID + \overline{I}L$

4-9.

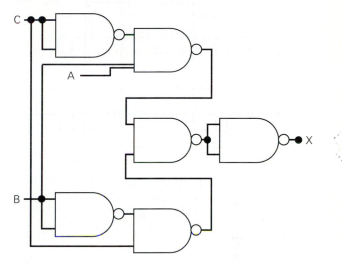

4-11.

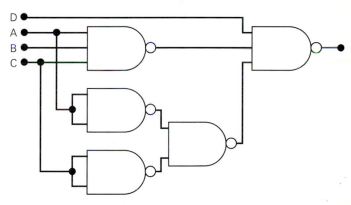

4-12. $x = BC + \overline{B}\,\overline{C} + AC;$ or $x = BC + \overline{B}\,\overline{C} + A\overline{B}$

4-13. $y = \overline{D} + \overline{A}BC + A\overline{B}\,\overline{C}$

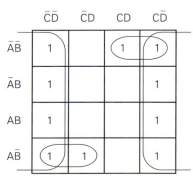

4-14. $x = \overline{A}_3A_2 + \overline{A}_3A_1A_0$

4-15. (a) $x = \overline{A}\overline{C} + \overline{B}C + AC\overline{D}$

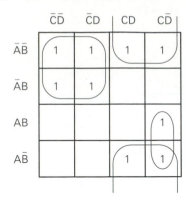

(b) $x = \overline{A}\overline{D} + \overline{B}C + \overline{B}\overline{D}$ (c) $y = \overline{B} + A\overline{C}$

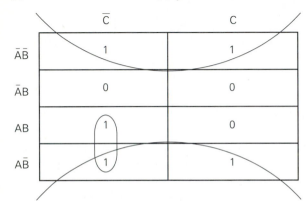

4-16. Best solution: $x = B\overline{C} + AD$

4-17. $x = \overline{S}_1\overline{S}_2 + \overline{S}_1\overline{S}_3 + \overline{S}_3\overline{S}_4 + \overline{S}_2\overline{S}_3 + \overline{S}_2\overline{S}_4$

4-18. (a)

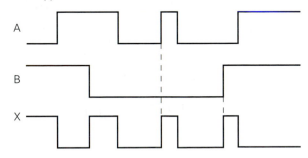

(b) $x = A$ (c) $x = \overline{A}$

4-19. $A = 0$, $B = C = 1$

4-20. One possibility is shown below.

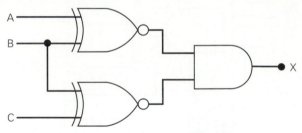

4-22. four outputs where z_3 is the MSB

$z_3 = y_1 y_0 x_1 x_0$
$z_2 = y_1 x_1 (\overline{y}_0 + \overline{x}_0)$
$z_1 = y_0 x_1 (\overline{y}_1 + \overline{x}_0) + y_1 x_0 (\overline{y}_0 + \overline{x}_1)$
$z_0 = y_0 x_0$

4-23. $x = A_3 A_2 + A_3 A_1$

4-24. $x = AB(C \oplus D)$

4-25. $(A + B)(C + D)$

4-26. N–S $= \overline{C}\overline{D}(A + B) + AB(\overline{C} + \overline{D})$; E–W $= \overline{\text{N–S}}$

4-27. Change last EX-OR to EX-NOR.

4-29. $x = A\overline{B}C$

4-30. $x = A + BCD$

4-31. $x = A + (B \oplus C)$

4-32. $z = A_0\overline{S} + A_1 S$

4-33. $z = x_1 x_0 y_1 y_0 + x_1 \overline{x}_0 y_1 \overline{y}_0 + \overline{x}_1 x_0 \overline{y}_1 y_0 + \overline{x}_1 \overline{x}_0 \overline{y}_1 \overline{y}_0$ No pairs, quads, or octets

4-35. (a) indeterminate   (b) 1.4–1.8 V   (c) See below.

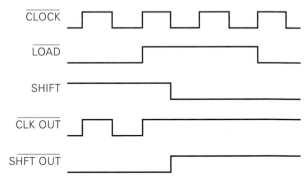

4-38. Possible faults: faulty V_{CC} or ground on Z2; Z2-1 or Z2-2 open internally or externally; Z2-3 internally open

4-39. Yes: (c), (e), (f). No: (a), (b), (d), (g).

4-41. Z2-6 and Z2-11 shorted together

4-43. Most likely faults:
faulty ground or V_{CC} on Z1
Z1 plugged in backwards
Z1 internally damaged

4-44. Possible faults:
Z2-13 shorted to V_{CC}
Z2-8 shorted to V_{CC}
broken connection to Z2-13
Z2-3, Z2-6, Z2-9, or Z2-10 shorted to ground

4-45. (a)

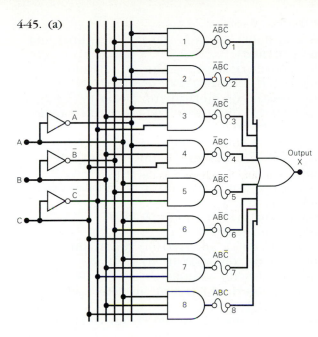

(b) Open links 1, 2, 3, and 5.

4-47. (a) 00_{16} to EF_{16} (b) F0 (c) F1 to FF

CHAPTER 5

5-1.

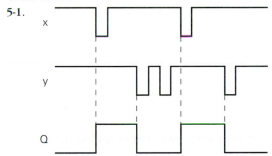

5-2. same as 5-1

5-3.

5-6. Z1-4 stuck HIGH

5-7. 20 ns

5-8.

5-9. Q is a 500-Hz square wave.

5-10.

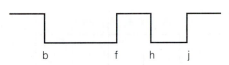

5-11. (a) 5-kHz square wave (b) 2.5 kHz

5-13.

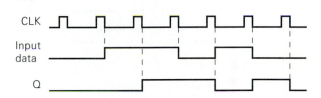

5-14. 500-Hz square wave

5-15. Q stays LOW.

5-18.

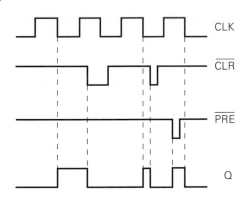

5-19.

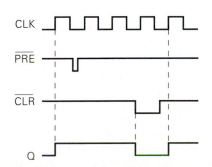

5-21. (a) 200 ns (b) 7474; 74C74 (c) 30 ns

5-22. 48 ns

5-23. Connect A to J, $\overline{A}$ to K.

5-24. (a) A, B, C

5-25. (a) Connect X to J, $\overline{X}$ to K. (b) Use arrangement of Figure 5-43.

5-26. 1011, 1101, 1110, 0111, 1011, 1101, 1110, 0111, 1011

5-27. Connect X_0 to D input of X_3.

5-31. (a) 10 (b) 1953 Hz (c) 1024 (d) 12

5-32. (a) 128 (b) 0 to 127

5-34. Put INVERTERs on A_8, A_{11}, and A_{14}.

5-37.

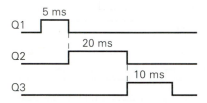

5-38. (a) $\overline{Q}$ will stay LOW. (b) PGT at $\overline{Q}$ will set $X = 1$. (c) Make $t_p = 20\ \mu s$.

5-39. (a) A_1 or A_2 must be LOW when a PGT occurs at B. (b) B and A_2 must be HIGH when a NGT occurs at A_1.

5-41. After 14 pulses, all circuit outputs stop changing with $A = W = X = Y = Z = 0$ and $B = C = 1$.

5-42. One possibility is $R = 1\ k\Omega$ and $C = 80\ nF$.

5-43. One possibility is $R_A = 1\ k\Omega$, $R_B = 10\ k\Omega$, $C = 1800\ pF$.

5-45. (a)

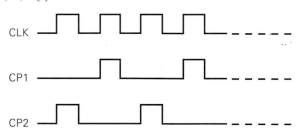

5-46. (a) no (b) yes (c) no (d) no

5-47. Flip-flop X_0 has an open D input.

5-48. (a) yes (b) no

5-49. Two cascaded INVERTERs between Q_1 and Q_2 add enough delay to increase the effective t_{PLH} of Q_1 so that by the time Q_2 gets clocked, the Q_1 signal hasn't reached D_2.

5-51. (a) no (b) no (c) yes (d) no

5-52. First combination: 101. Second combination: 010.

5-53. (a) no (b) no (c) yes

5-54. (a) NAND and NOR latch (b) J-K (c) D latch (d) D flip-flop (e) D flip-flop and D latch (f) all FFs (g) clocked S-C, J-K, D (h) J-K

CHAPTER 6

6-1. (a) 10101 (b) 10010 (c) 1111.0101 (d) 1.1010 (e) 100111000

6-2. (a) 00100000 (incl. sign bit) (b) 11110010 (c) 00111111 (d) 10011000 (e) 01111111 (f) 10000001 (g) 01011001 (h) 11001001 (I) 11111111 (j) 10000000 (k) can't be done in eight bits (l) 00000000

6-3. (a) +13 (b) −3 (c) +123 (d) −103 (e) +127 (f) −64 (g) −1 (h) −127 (i) +99 (j) −39

6-4. (a) −2048 to +2047 (b) 16 bits including sign bit

6-5. -16_{10} to 15_{10}

6-6. (a) 00111; 11001 (b) 10100; 01100

6-7. 0 to 1023; −512 to +511

6-9. (a) 00001111 (b) 11111101 (c) 11111011 (d) 10000000 (e) 00000001 (f) 11011110 (g) 00000000 (h) 00010101

6-11. (a) 100011 (b) 1111001 (c) 100011.00101 (d) .10001111

6-12. (a) 11 (b) 111 (c) 101.11 (d) 1111.0011

6-13. (a) 10010111 (BCD) (b) 10010101 (BCD) (c) 010100100111 (BCD) (e) 0001000000000001 (BCD)

6-14. (a) 6E24 (b) 100D (c) 18AB (d) 3000 (e) 10FE (f) 17C36

6-15. (a) 0EFE (b) 229 (c) 02A6 (d) 01FD (e) 0001 (f) EF00

6-16. 16,849 locations

6-17. (a) 119 (b) +119 (c) 229; −27

6-19. SUM $= A \oplus B$; CARRY $= AB$

6-21. $[A] = 0000$

6-22. 200 ns

6-23. overflow $= A_3 \overline{B_3} S_3 + \overline{A_3} B_3 \overline{S_3}$

6-25. $C_3 = A_2 B_2 + (A_2 + B_2)\{A_1 B_1 + (A_1 + B_1)[A_0 B_0 + A_0 C_0 + B_0 C_0]\}$

6-27. (a) SUM $= 0111$ (b) SUM $= 1010$ (c) 1100

6-29.

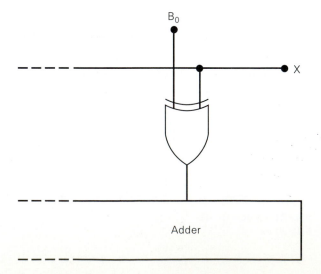

6-30. $[S] = 01110$; $x = 1$; $[\Sigma] = 0100$

6-31. yes

6-32. $[\Sigma] = 100001000101$

6-33.

	[F]	C_{N+4}	OVR
(a)	1001	0	1
(b)	1101	0	0
(c)	0011	1	0

6-34. $[S] = 100$; $[B] = 1111$

6-35. (a) 00001100 (b) 11011100

6-37. (a) 0001 (b) 1010 (c) 0010 (d) 1011
(e) 1000

6-39. (a) yes (b) no (c) yes (d) no

6-41. Use D flip-flops. Connect $(\overline{S_3 + S_2 + S_1 + S_0})$ to the D input of the 0 FF; C_4 to the D input of the carry FF; and S_3 to the D input of the sign FF.

6-42. 0000000001001001; 1111111110101110

CHAPTER 7

7-1. 250 kHz, 50 percent

7-2. Same as 7-1

7-3. 10000_2

7-4. Five FFs are required: Q_0–Q_4 with Q_4 as the MSB. Connect Q_3 and Q_4 outputs to a NAND gate whose output is connected to all CLRs.

7-5.

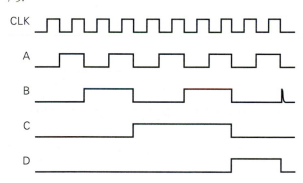

7-6. Glitch at B output on 14th NGT of the clock

7-7. Connect Q_5, Q_4, and Q_1 for MOD-50. A MOD-100 cannot be constructed without more logic.

7-8. (b) 000, 001, 010, 100, 101, 110, and repeats

7-9.

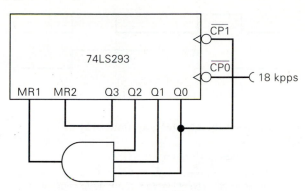

7-10. a MOD-15 (from Problem 7-9) driving a MOD-4

7-11. 60 Hz

7-13. (c) 0001

7-14. 100, 011, 010, 001, 000, and repeats

7-15. 1000 and 0000 states never occur.

7-16. (a) 12.5 MHz (b) 8.33 MHz

7-17. (a) Add two FFs (E and F) to Figure 7-60. Connect AND gates below to appropriate FF inputs.
(b) 33 MHz

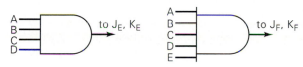

7-18. 0000, 0001, 0010, 0011, 0100, 0101, 0110, 0111, 1000, 1001, and repeats

7-21. Connect 01100100 to parallel data inputs.

7-22. (d) Z will not be cleared and timer cannot be restarted.

7-23. Change the parallel data input to 1010.

7-24. nine

7-26. (a) ten (b) clears counter to 0000 (c) sets counter to 1001 (d) up (e) Connect Q_0 to CP_1 and clock signal to CP_0; ground MR_1, MR_2, MS_1, and MS_2. (f) Connect clock signal to CP_1; connect Q_3 to CP_0; ground all MR and MS inputs.

7-27.

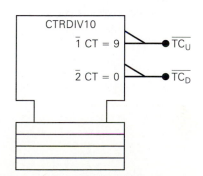

7-30.

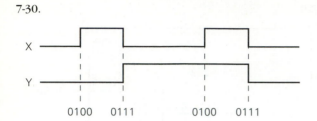

0100   0111   0100   0111

7-32. **(a)** when the counter goes from 0111 to 1000

7-33. 12 FFs

7-34. four; sixteen; thirteen

7-35. **(a)** $J_A = B\overline{C}, K_A = 1, J_B = CA + \overline{C}\,\overline{A}, K_B = 1, J_C = \overline{AB}, K_C = B + \overline{A}$ **(b)** $J_A = B\overline{C}, K_A = 1, J_B = K_B = 1, J_C = K_C = B$

7-36. $J_A = K_A = 1, J_B = K_B = \overline{A}, J_C = K_C = \overline{AB}, J_D = K_D = \overline{A}\,\overline{B}\,\overline{C}$

7-39. See figure in next column.

7-40. Counting sequence is: 00000, 10000, 11000, 11100, 11110, 11111, 01111, 00111, 00011, 00001, and repeat.

7-41. Frequency at z is 5 Hz.

7-42. **(a)** Each light will be ON for 0.5 second of every 4-second interval. **(b)** Each light will be ON for 2 seconds and OFF for 2 seconds.

7-43. **(b)** 257 **(c)** 323

7-44. **(a)** 22 **(b)** 450 **(c)** 0 or 1

7-45. Connect Q_3 of the 74290 to $\overline{CP}_1$ of the 74293.

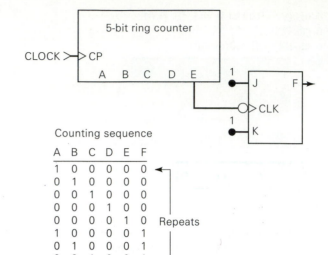

Counting sequence

A	B	C	D	E	F	
1	0	0	0	0	0	←
0	1	0	0	0	0	
0	0	1	0	0	0	
0	0	0	1	0	0	
0	0	0	0	1	0	Repeats
1	0	0	0	0	1	
0	1	0	0	0	1	
0	0	1	0	0	1	
0	0	0	1	0	1	
0	0	0	0	1	1	

7-47. Add a second J-K flip-flop.

7-49. Connect Q_3 of one to D_S of the other.

7-50. The 74178 is loaded with 1101 on the NGT of the sixth clock pulse.

7-52. t_{310}

7-54. **(b)** $Q_0 \cdot \overline{Q}_1 + Q_0 \cdot Q_7$ **(c)** $Q_3 \cdot \overline{Q}_6$

7-55. See figure below.

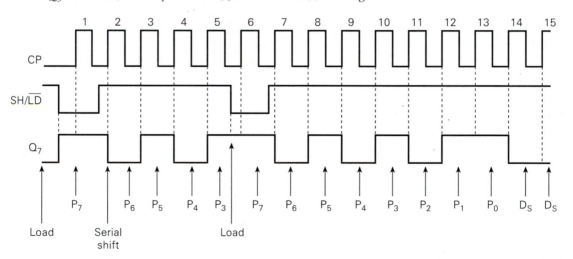

7-56. (a) *CLR* input is asynchronous.   (b) True
(c)

Q_a	Q_b	Q_c	Q_d	
1	0	1	1	
0	1	1	1	After 1 clock pulse
1	1	1	1	After 2 clock pulses
1	1	1	1	After 3 clock pulses
1	1	1	1	After 4 clock pulses

(d)

Q_a	Q_b	Q_c	Q_d	
1	0	1	1	
0	1	0	1	After 1 clock pulse
0	0	1	0	After 2 clock pulses
0	0	0	1	After 3 clock pulses
0	0	0	0	After 4 clock pulses

(e)

Q_a	Q_b	Q_c	Q_d	
0	1	1	0	After 1 clock pulse
0	1	1	0	After 2 clock pulses
0	1	1	0	After 3 clock pulses
0	1	1	0	After 4 clock pulses

(f) Same as (e)
(g)

Q_a	Q_b	Q_c	Q_d	
1	0	1	1	
0	1	1	1	After 1 clock pulse
1	1	1	0	After 2 clock pulses
1	1	0	1	After 3 clock pulses
1	0	1	1	After 4 clock pulses

7-57. MR_1 to Q_1 is open, or Q_3 or MR_2 is shorted to ground.
7-58. *CLR* of flip-flop *X* is open or stuck HIGH or not responding.
7-59. MSB of MOD-6 is stuck LOW.
7-60. (a) display = 001   (b) display = 000
7-61. Counters are not being cleared before each SAMPLE interval.
7-62. (a) Flip-flop *C* will toggle on every NGT of the input.   (b) Will not count up properly; *B* and *C* will not toggle.
7-63. P_1 open or S3 faulty
7-65. (a) parallel   (b) binary   (c) down counter
(d) MOD-10   (e) asynchronous   (f) ring   (g) Johnson

(h) all   (i) presettable   (j) up/down   (k) asynchronous   (l) BCD   (m) synchronous/parallel

CHAPTER 8

8-1. (a) *A; B*   (b) *A*   (c) *A*
8-2. (a) 728.3 pJ   (b) 459.3 pJ   (c) 59.06 pJ
(d) 27.41 pJ   (e) 67.26 pJ
8-3. (a) 0.9 V   (b) 1.4 V
8-4. (a) I_{IH} (b) I_{CCL} (c) t_{PHL} (d) speed–power product   (e) V_{NH} (f) surface-mount   (g) current sinking
(h) fan-out   (i) totem-pole   (j) sinking transistor
(k) 4.75 to 5.25 V   (l) 2.4 V; 2.0 V   (m) 0.8 V; 0.4 V
(n) sourcing
8-5. (a) 0.7 V; 0.3 V   (b) 0.5 V; 0.4 V   (c) 0.5 V; 0.3 V
8-6. (b) AND, NAND   (c) unconnected inputs
8-7. (a) 20 μA/0.4 mA   (c) Five
8-8. (a) 30/15   (b) 24 mA
8-10. Fan-out is not exceeded in either case.
8-11. 10 ns
8-12. 43 ns; 38 ns
8-13. (a) 2 kΩ   (b) 8 kΩ
8-14. (b) 4.7-kΩ resistor is too large.
8-15. (a) amplitude too low   (b) t_p too small
(c) $t_W(L)$ too low
8-18. six AND gates
8-19. $AB + CD + FG$
8-20. choice (a)
8-21. (a) 5 V   (b) $R_S = 110 \Omega$ for LED current of 20 mA
8-22. (a) 12 V   (b) 40 mA
8-24. (a)

x	y	Data on Bus
0	0	*C*
0	1	*B*
1	0	*B*
1	1	*A*

(b) Bus contention due to E_A and E_C simultaneously active when $X = Y = 1$.
8-25. AND
8-27. *a, c, d, e, g, h*
8-28. *a, c, e, f, g, h*
8-29. *b*
8-30. 12.5 mW
8-31. 2.9 V
8-33. Using values at $V_{CC} = 6$ V, the speed–power product is 1.44 pJ per gate.
8-34. 0 V, 1.22 V

8-35.

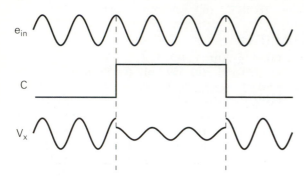

8-36. −1 and −2
8-37. (a) 74HCT   (b) converts logic voltages
(c) CMOS cannot sink TTL current   (d) false
8-38. The choice in (c) is a possible reason.
8-39. (a) none   (b) two
8-42. Fan-out of 74HC00 is exceeded; disconnect pin 3
of 7402 and tie it to ground.
8-44. $R_2 = 1.5$ kΩ, $R_1 = 18$ kΩ
8-47. (b) is a possible fault.
8-48. NAND CMOS gate input is shorted to +5 V.
8-49. 0 V to −11.25 V and back up to −6 V

CHAPTER 9
9-1. (a) all HIGH   (b) $\overline{O}_0 =$ LOW·   (c) $\overline{O}_7 =$ LOW
(d) all HIGH
9-2. 6 inputs, 64 outputs
9-3. $[A] = 110$, $E_3 = 1$, $\overline{E}_1 = \overline{E}_2 = 0$
9-4.

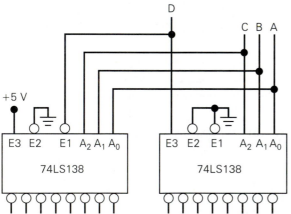

9-5.

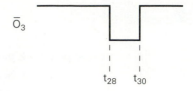

9-6. Connect $\overline{E}_2$ to ground and take output from $\overline{O}_2$.
9-7. enabled when $D = 0$
9-8.

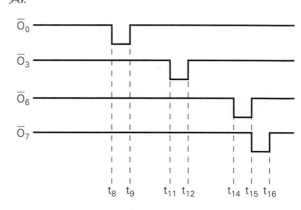

9-10. Resistors are 250 Ω.
9-12.

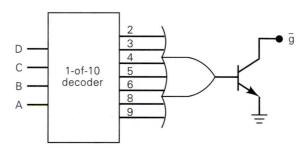

9-13. (a), (b) encoder   (c), (d), (e) decoder
9-14. 0111
9-17. The fourth key actuation would be entered into
the MSD register.
9-18. choice (b)
9-19. choice (a) or (d)
9-20. (a) yes   (b) no   (c) no
9-21. A_2 bus line is open between Z2 and Z3.
9-22. E_2 of Z4 is stuck LOW.
9-23. g segment or decoder output transistor would
burn out.
9-24. Decoder D and C inputs are reversed.
9-25. Decoder outputs: a and b are shorted together.
9-27. A 4-to-1 MUX
9-28. Use nine 74151s.

9-29.

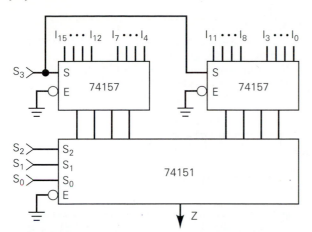

9-30. (b) The total number of connections in the circuit using MUXes is 63, not including V_{CC} and GND, and not including the connections to counter clock inputs. The total number for the circuit using separate decoder/drivers is 66.

9-31.

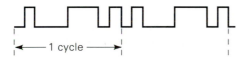

9-32.

9-33.

A	B	C	
0	0	0	$0 \rightarrow I_0$
0	0	1	$0 \rightarrow I_1$
0	1	0	$0 \rightarrow I_2$
0	1	1	$1 \rightarrow I_3$
1	0	0	$0 \rightarrow I_4$
1	0	1	$1 \rightarrow I_5$
1	1	0	$1 \rightarrow I_6$
1	1	1	$1 \rightarrow I_7$

9-34. Connect $I_1, I_5, I_8, I_{11}, I_{14}, I_{15}$ to V_{CC}. All other inputs connect to ground.
9-35. $Z =$ HIGH for $DCBA = 0010, 0100, 1001, 1010$.
9-36. (b) $Z = \overline{A}B\overline{C} + A\overline{B}\overline{C} + \overline{A}\overline{B}C + A\overline{B}C + \overline{A}\overline{B}\,\overline{C}\,\overline{D} + ABCD$

9-37. (a) encoder, MUX **(b)** MUX, DEMUX **(c)** MUX **(d)** encoder **(e)** decoder, DEMUX **(f)** DEMUX **(g)** MUX
9-38.

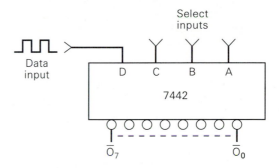

9-39. Each DEMUX output goes LOW, one at a time in sequence.
9-40. (a) All LEDs are off. **(b)** Each LED will flash.
(c) LEDs 2 and 6 will flash.
9-41. five lines
9-43. (a) Sequencing stops after actuator 3 is activated.
(b) Same as (a)
9-44. Probable fault is short to ground at MSB of tens MUX.
9-45. Q_0 and Q_1 are probably reversed.
9-46. Inputs 6 and 7 of MUX are probably shorted together.
9-47. S_1 stuck LOW
9-48. (a) no **(b)** yes
9-51. Final binary output is 1000101.
9-52. A_0 and B_0 probably reversed
9-54. $\overline{OE}_C = 0$, $\overline{IE}_C = 1$; $\overline{OE}_B = \overline{OE}_A = 1$; $\overline{IE}_B = \overline{IE}_A = 0$; apply a clock pulse
9-55. (a) At t_4, each register will have contents of 1011.
9-56.

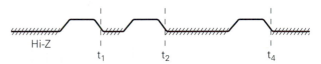

9-57. (b) ON, ON, ON, OFF (left to right)
9-58. (a) At t_3, each register holds 1001.
9-60. (a) 57FA **(b)** 5000 to 57FF **(c)** 9000 to 97FF
(d) no

CHAPTER 10

10-1. (f), (g) false
10-2. 3.58 V
10-3. LSB = 20 mV
10-4. 20 mV; approx. 0.4 percent
10-5. approx. 5 mV
10-6. eight

10-7. 14.3 percent, 0.286 V

10-9. 250.06 rpm

10-10. 10 mV, 0.1 percent, 6.95 V

10-11.

Binary	BCD
3.88 mV	10 mV
0.392%	1.01%

10-13. 800 Ω; no

10-14. (a) −0.3125 V, −4.6875 V (b) 4.27 kΩ
(c) −0.0267

10-15. uses fewer different R values

10-16. 20 μA; yes

10-17. (a) seven

10-19. 242.5 mV is not within specifications.

10-20. offset out of spec

10-21. Bit 1 of DAC is open or stuck HIGH.

10-22. bits 0 and 1 reversed

10-24. (a) 10010111 (b) 10010111 (c) 102 μs, 51 μs

10-27. (a) 1.2 mV (b) 2.7 mV

10-28. (a) 0111110110 (b) 0111110111

10-29. 2.834 to 2.844 V

10-31. Reconstructed waveform frequency is 3.33 kHz.

10-32. Digital ramp: a, d, e, f, h. SAC: b, c, d, e, g, h.

10-35. 80 μs

10-36. 100101

10-37. 2.276 V

10-38. 2.869 V

10-39. (a) 00000000 (b) 500 mV (c) 510 mV
(d) 255 mV (e) 01101110 (f) 0.2°F; 2 mV

10-44. 386 steps

10-45. The MSB of the MSD is not affecting V_{AX}.

10-47. Switch is stuck closed; switch is stuck open, or capacitor is shorted.

10-49. (a) Address is EAxx.

CHAPTER 11

11-1. 16,384; 32; 524,288

11-2. 16,384

11-3. 64K × 4

11-4. 16; 16; 13; 16,384

11-6. (a) data, address, control (b) address (c) data
(d) CPU

11-7. (a) Hi-Z (b) 11101101

11-8. (a) register 11 (b) 0100

11-9. (a) 16,384 (b) four (c) two 1-of-128 decoders

11-11. 120 ns

11-12. 180 ns

11-14. Q_{13}, Q_{14}, Q_{15}

11-15. The following transistors will have open source connections: Q_0, Q_2, Q_5, Q_6, Q_7, Q_9, Q_{15}.

11-17. (a) Erases all memory locations to hold FF$_{16}$.
(b) Writes 3C$_{16}$ into address 2300$_{16}$.

11-18. The waveform at D_0 is shown below.

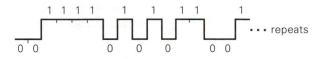

11-19. hex data: 5E, BA, 05, 2F, 99, FB, 00, ED, 3C, FF, B8, C7, 27, EA, 52, 5B

11-20.

A_5	A_4	A_3	A_2	A_1	A_0	D_2	D_1	D_0	C_3	C_2	C_1	C_0
1	0	0	1	0	1	0	1	1	0	1	1	1
0	0	1	1	1	0	0	0	1	0	1	0	0
1	1	1	1	1	0	1	1	0	0	0	1	0
0	1	1	1	0	0	0	1	0	1	0	0	0
1	1	0	1	0	1	1	0	1	0	0	1	1
0	0	0	1	1	0	0	0	0	0	1	1	0
0	1	0	0	1	1	0	0	1	1	0	0	1
1	1	0	0	0	0	1	0	0	1	0	0	0

11-21. (a) 25.6 kHz (b) Adjust V_{ref}.

11-24. (a) 100 ns (b) 30 ns (c) 10 million (d) 20 ns
(e) 30 ns (f) 40 ns (g) 10 million

11-25. eight

11-26.

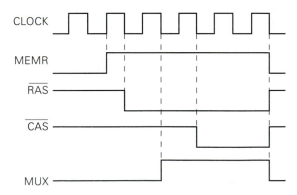

11-27.

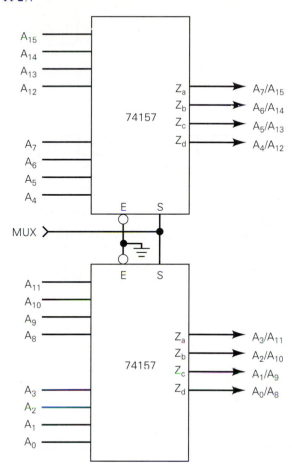

11-30. every 7.8 μs

11-31. (a) 4096 columns, 1024 rows   (b) 2048   (c) It would double.

11-34. Add four more PROMs (PROM-4 through PROM-7) to the circuit. Connect their data outputs and address inputs to data and address bus, respectively. Connect

AB_{13} to C input of decoder, and connect decoder outputs 4 through 7 to CS inputs of PROMs 4 through 7, respectively.

11-35. Connect AB_{13}, AB_{14}, and AB_{15} to a three-input OR gate, and connect the OR gate output to C input of the decoder.

11-38. F000–F3FF; F400–F7FF; F800–FBFF; FC00–FFFF.

11-40. B input of decoder is open or stuck HIGH.

11-41. The OR gate output/C input node is stuck LOW.

11-42. Only RAM modules 1 and 3 are getting tested.

11-43. The RAM chip with data outputs 4 through 7 in module 2 is not functioning properly.

11-44. RAM module 3 output 7 is open or stuck HIGH.

11-46. checksum = 11101010.

CHAPTER 12

12-2. (a) simple, complex, registered   (b) registered   (c) registered   (d) simple, complex, registered

12-3. In registered mode there are eight product terms in registered configuration and seven product terms in combinational configuration.

12-5.

Mode	Configuration	Source of Enable
Simple	Input Output	Ground V_{CC}
Complex		8th product term from input matrix
Registered	Registered Combinational	Pin 11 ($\overline{OE}$) 8th product term

12-8. !Y0 = G1 & !G2A & !G2B & !C & !B & !A

12-10. $D_A = \overline{QA}$
$D_B = \overline{QB} \cdot QA + QB \cdot \overline{QA}$
$D_C = \overline{QC} \cdot QB \cdot QA + QC \cdot \overline{QB} + QC \cdot \overline{QA}$

12-11. $D_B = \overline{QA}; D_A = QB$

12-12. Add an input variable (DIR) to control the direction (DIR = 0 = ccw, DIR = 1 = cw).

Index of ICs

Index